D0046205

Masterpieces of World Literature

IN DIGEST FORM

Masterpieces of World Literature

IN DIGEST FORM

EDITED BY

Frank N. Magill

WITH THE ASSISTANCE OF

DAYTON KOHLER AND STAFF

INTRODUCTION BY CLIFTON FADIMAN

Harper & Brothers – Publishers – New York

MASTERPIECES OF WORLD LITERATURE in Digest Form

M-B

An earlier version of this book originally appeared under the title of MASTERPLOTS.

PRINTED IN THE UNITED STATES OF AMERICA BY
KINGSPORT PRESS, INC., KINGSPORT, TENNESSEE

Library of Congress catalog card number: 51-12454

PREFACE

The array of literature represented in this book is drawn from the vast reservoir of literary achievements which has been accumulating since the legendary beginnings of Western civilizations. All the great literature is not here; perhaps all that is here is not great. But these stories are representative of the places and the times from which they sprang and they have helped to tint the fabric which makes up the composite imprint of our culture. Romance and adventure, laughter and illusion, dreams and desperate hopes, fear and angry resentment—these things have prodded men's minds as they walked toward our century. Their insight is our heritage.

Along with this heritage, our generation has fallen heir to a Busy Age. Never in history has there been so much competition for the attention of the average individual. But though ours is a Busy Age, it is also an age in which—thanks to technological advancements—the chances for enlightenment and cultural development, at all levels, have never before been approached even remotely. Out of this increased "exposure" must surely come a more intellectually alert society. From such a society we may reasonably expect an acceleration of our cultural development. It is in the light of all these circumstances that a book such as *Masterpieces of World Literature in Digest Form* can have a place and a purpose.

From its inception in 1946, this book has been prepared with an eye toward the Busy Age. Each digest is preceded by carefully checked, concisely stated reference data which furnish at a glance the authorship, type of plot, time of plot, locale, and publication date. Following this will be found a list of the principal characters and their relationships, often a highly useful feature. Next is the "Critique," a short, incisive critical analysis of the original book. Finally there is the plot-summary, given as a well-rounded story, newly written and devoid of quotations from the original work. Editorial comments having been confined to the "Critique," the reader is afforded an uninterrupted opportunity to study the action, characterizations, and development of the theme as the plot-story progresses. Perhaps this sequence-by-sequence treatment of the original plot, instead of a mere description of the book, is the most valuable single feature of *Masterpieces of World Literature in Digest Form.*

Of primary importance from the beginning was the selection of titles intended for inclusion in this book. Standard book lists, library lists, various anthologies were consulted as the list was built. Tentative lists were submitted to more than fifty teachers of English at leading colleges and universities. The helpful responses of these men and women who earn their living in teaching had considerable influence on the list as it took shape. It may be interesting to note that in almost every case living authors were consulted about their own books which had been selected. In some instances they recommended substitutions. For example, Mr. Sinclair Lewis suggested *Cass Timberlane* for *Dodsworth*, Mr. Evelyn Waugh *Brideshead Revisited* in place of *Vile Bodies*. Because the relative merit of contemporary writing is likely to be a subject of some controversy, the assistance of authors themselves concerning their own works was valuable. During the preparation of this book, the list was never static, remaining open and subject to additions and deletions as seemed desirable. In the end, about one hundred manuscripts, representing thousands of hours of work, were set aside in favor of new additions to the list which it was hoped would result in a more balanced, interesting, and helpful book.

Actual preparation of this book required an enormous amount of active assistance from a carefully selected staff of twenty-five English Faculty associates, chosen after more than one hundred personal interviews, at the University of Cincinnati, University of Illinois, Indiana University, Miami University, University of North Carolina, North Carolina State College, Ohio State University, Purdue University, Virginia Polytechnic Institute, University of Virginia, and a number of other colleges and universities. Each original book represented in *Masterpieces of World Literature in Digest Form* had to be carefully and completely read at least once and sometimes two or three times by one or more staff members prior to preparation of the summary manuscript. Manuscripts covering the works of certain current authors were submitted to the author concerned for comments and approval. Much of the work of balancing, condensing, or expanding the digest manuscripts was performed, with an unusually high degree of skill, by Dayton Kohler, an associate professor of English at Virginia Polytechnic Institute. As an added precaution against errors in reference data, names, and dates, finished manuscripts were subjected to one more check against a copy of the original book.

The resulting collection offers, in about twelve hundred words each, the basic "cores" around which more than five hundred world-famous literary works have been woven. Some will find in these plot-stories a pleasant renewal of an old acquaintance, a chance meeting with an almost forgotten friend. Others may wish to fill in sketches encountered here for the first time. This impulse should lead one to get the original, to read it, to own it, because a book which has stood the test of time can usually be reread periodically with increased pleasure and perception.

The preparation of this book has been a formidable task. Without unusual assistance and coöperation from many sources it would not have come into existence. I should like first to thank the staff who aided in the preparation of the manuscripts. This expression is intended as an individual "thank you" to the men and women who helped so actively in this phase of the work. I should like also to acknowledge the courtesy and assistance rendered by those in charge of certain facilities of the Library of Congress in Washington. The use of a study room at the library was most helpful; and I am especially indebted to supervisory personnel in the copyright search section for valuable and cheerful aid. As my work progressed, the co-operation of many authors, publishers, agents, and literary trustees was solicited, and I wish to express my appreciation for the generous assistance received from these sources.

It is my hope that this collection will serve a useful purpose for busy people, and that it may find its way into the hands of some who will be stimulated to probe the originals for facets and substance which in this book can be only suggested.

Frank N. Magill

INTRODUCTION

by

CLIFTON FADIMAN

For over two centuries—to be arbitrary, since 1721, the birth date of Bailey's *Universal Etymological English Dictionary*—the dictionary of English words has been our useful, if verbose, chairside companion.

The dictionary of quotations does not go back quite so far: it was in 1855 that Bartlett first published his collection of those echoes the world will not willingly let die.

As I write, a new kind of dictionary, we are told, is shortly to appear—a sort of super-index to the great abstract ideas that have moved Western civilization.

And here under your hand lies still another sort of dictionary—a dictionary of famous plots.

Palpable tools are extensions of the hand. The impalpable tools called works of reference are extensions of the mind and memory. In this sense *Masterpieces of World Literature in Digest Form* is a master tool. It should make its way at once to the shelf of the writer, publisher, editor, teacher, lecturer, after-dinner speaker, literary agent, bookseller, librarian, radio and television director or editor or producer, motion-picture ditto, and of many students and general readers. In its field it seems to me the most useful work of its kind I have encountered.

Its utility arises in part from its properly limited scope. Half a thousand plots are just manageable. To tell the stories of many more would have entailed superficiality. To handle a much smaller number would have resulted in poverty of reference. There happen to be 510 summaries here. Fifty more might have been added, or fifty subtracted—but the number seems about right and serviceable.

Here, then, are *full* summaries (sometimes running to 3,000 words) of a great many of the Western world's best-known novels, plays, and poems, plus a few biographies, autobiographies, and books of travel. These summaries are careful and objective, not casual or tinctured with whim. They are extraordinarily clear—in some cases clear even beyond the author's intention. (For example, one is lost in admiration before the editors' lucid abstract of that masterpiece of calculated confusion, *Tristram Shandy.*)

It should be added that these digests are true summaries, not to be confounded with those other "digests" that pretend to give the reader the entire substance, in abbreviated form, of a story. Our editors do not claim to render anything but the book's basic narrative or content. However, each summary is preceded by a listing of essential facts and by a terse, sensible critique which aims, not at originality, but at a clear reflection of what is generally considered informed judgment.

One finds, as is natural, titles the grounds for whose inclusion appear incomprehensible; but the overwhelming majority of items are here for sufficient reasons. A given book may be included because it is good; or because, whether good or not, it is of historical importance; or because, again whether good or not, it has been or is now generally popular; or for all of these reasons or any pair of them.

Thus Rex Beach lies down with Aristophanes and Dickens with Lloyd Douglas. Grandiose trumpery (*Ben Hur, Quo Vadis*) is here; and so is *The Magic Mountain.* Nobody (well, hardly anybody) today reads poor old Godwin's *Caleb Williams.* Yet it occupies an honored place in the history of the English novel, is constantly referred to, and so, very properly, is here summarized. Rider Haggard's *She* will never occupy an honored place in the history of the English novel, but millions are familiar with it, and so, with equal propriety, it finds a place in *Masterpieces of World Literature.* Best sellers of the past are well represented, if they are still current coin; best sellers of only yesterday are given less space, for they have yet to demonstrate their power to endure, in whatever medium, or merely as a vivid memory.

An immortal, homespun folk-possession such as *The Man Without a Country* is here; but so are highbrow masterpieces like *Ulysses* and *Remembrance of Things Past,* both of which difficult works are forced to yield a remarkably transparent synopsis of what is, of course, least important in them, their "action." Homer is here; and so are a dozen modern novelists who are currently popular but for whom most thoughtful critics would not predict a long life. The editors have not tried to limit their titles to the "best," whatever that may be. The aim is not to elevate taste, nor even to instruct (though much instruction may be found in these pages), but simply to furnish the interested reader with a useful reference tool.

On the whole, they have succeeded in doing what they set out to do: to tell, clearly and fully, the bare stories of many of those works of the imagination that seem, for a variety of reasons, still to be alive and kicking in the consciousness of the Western reader.

The best way to test this reference tool is to sit down and make a list of the first twenty-five really well-known books of fiction that pop into your head. Then check your list in *Masterpieces*. I've tried this game, finding *Masterpieces'* batting average to work out at a little over .600. When you reflect on the difficulties of selection that the editors had to contend with, plus the simple fact that they had to produce a work light enough to be at least liftable, I think you'll agree that this is good enough.

So—if the plot of Dostoevski's *The Idiot* has always baffled you; if you're not sure in which of Jane Austen's novels Lady Catherine de Burgh appears; if you remember reading *Under Two Flags* but have forgotten completely what it's about; if you'd like to check on whether William Faulkner's plots make any sense at all, denuded of the costumery of his syntax; if you want to tell the children the story of *Robinson Crusoe,* but don't want to reread the darned thing; if all your life you've heard references to a book called Hakluyt's *Voyages* and feel it's time to learn something about it; if you want to compare the original story of *Quo Vadis* with the movie version—in all of these cases, and in ten thousand more, *Masterpieces* is ready and waiting to serve you.

The best [illegible] to use this reference tool is to sit down and make a list of [illegible] really [illegible] books of [illegible] that [illegible] [illegible] your [illegible] masterpieces. [illegible] this [illegible] [illegible] to work on at a little over [illegible]. [illegible] that the editors had to [illegible] [illegible] light enough to be at least [illegible] that this is good enough.

[illegible] of Dostoevsky. [illegible] [illegible] of Jane Austen's novels. [illegible] [illegible] [illegible] [illegible] to check on whether [illegible] [illegible] of the [illegible] [illegible] the story of [illegible] [illegible] all your life [illegible] [illegible] [illegible] time to learn [illegible] [illegible] the original story of [illegible] [illegible] and [illegible] thousand more [illegible] [illegible] is ready and waiting to serve you.

COMPLETE LIST OF TITLES

COMPLETE LIST OF TITLES

COMPLETE LIST OF TITLES

COMPLETE LIST OF TITLES

COMPLETE LIST OF TITLES

COMPLETE LIST OF TITLES

COMPLETE LIST OF TITLES

COMPLETE LIST OF TITLES

COMPLETE LIST OF TITLES

COMPLETE LIST OF TITLES

Masterpieces of World Literature

IN DIGEST FORM

THE ABBÉ CONSTANTIN

Type of work: Novel
Author: Ludovic Halévy (1834-1908)
Type of plot: Sentimental romance
Time of plot: 1881
Locale: France
First published: 1882

Principal characters:
ABBÉ CONSTANTIN, a French priest
JEAN REYNAUD, his godson
MRS. SCOTT, an American
MISS PERCIVAL, her sister

Critique:

This tale has long been a favorite book for use in French classes. The story is full of pleasant places and pleasant people. There is little if any conflict; the one character who might possibly be considered the villain is too polite to offer much resistance to the plans of the hero and heroine. The novel was crowned by the French Academy.

The Story:

The kindly old curé, Abbé Constantin, stopped before the chateau of Longueval to look at posters which proclaimed that the chateau and its surroundings were to be sold at auction either in four pieces, or as a unit. The abbé, like the rest of the neighborhood, smiled at the idea that anyone might be able to buy the entire estate; more than two million francs was too large a sum for anyone to have. As he walked along by the old estate, he thought of all the delightful days he had spent with the old marchioness and her family. He dreaded the thought of a new owner who might not ask him to dinner twice a week, who might not contribute generously to the poor, who might not attend all the services of his little church. The abbé was too old to desire a change.

He walked on to the little house where Madame de Lavardens lived with her son Paul. Paul had not turned out well. His mother gave him a generous allowance to spend every year. After spending his money within three months in Paris, he stayed the rest of the year with his mother in the country. At the de Lavardens home, the abbé learned that Madame de Lavardens was hoping that her agent had secured at least one part of the estate for her. She was awaiting news of the auction, and she invited the abbé to wait with her and her son to hear what had happened.

When the agent arrived, he informed them that Mrs. Scott, a wealthy American, had bought the whole estate. The abbé's heart sank. An American! She would be a Protestant—no doubt a heretic. His hopes for his little church grew weak. No longer would the hothouses of the estate keep his altar full of flowers; no longer would the poor be relieved by the charity of the chateau. With a gloomy heart he went home to supper.

Jean Reynaud, the abbé's godson, was his guest at supper that night. Jean's father had been an officer in the same regiment in which the abbé had been chaplain, and the two had been the best of friends. When Jean's father had been killed, the abbé had taken care of Jean as if he were his own son. The boy had insisted on following his father in a military career. Jean's kindness was well-known in the area. He gave a yearly income to the destitute families of two men who had been killed on the same day as his father, and he was always doing charitable deeds for the abbé's poor.

On his arrival Jean set about cutting garden greens for the salad. He was startled when he looked up and saw two beautifully but simply dressed young women who asked to see the abbé. They introduced themselves as Mrs. Scott and Miss Percival, her sister. In a flurry of excitement the old abbé came out to meet his unexpected guests, and to his great pleasure they announced that they were Catholics of French-Canadian blood. When each of the women gave the abbé a thousand francs to give to the poor, the happy man almost burst into tears. The inhabitants of the chateau were still to be a blessing for the town.

Jean, overcome by the beauty of the two women, could not decide who was the more handsome. Miss Percival was the younger and more vivacious, but the serene charm of Mrs. Scott was equally attractive. The women told the abbé the story of their lives; of their poverty as children, of the lawsuit which their dying father had made them promise never to give up, and of the final success of the suit and the millions that became theirs because of it. Mrs. Scott said that she and her husband intended to spend much time in France at their new home. When the ladies left, the abbé and Jean were profuse in their praise.

This meeting was the first of many. The ladies had grown tired of social gaiety during their stay in Paris, and Miss Percival had become disgusted with the great number of men, thirty-four in all, who had proposed marriage to her, for she knew that it was her money, not herself, they were after. The women hoped to spend a quiet few weeks in the chateau, with the abbé and Jean as their only visitors. During the visits Jean fell in love with Miss Percival. He was upset when Paul de Lavardens insisted on being introduced.

Miss Percival knew at once that Paul's proposal would be number thirty-five. He was polite and made conversation easily, but he did not have the qualities she had come to admire in Jean. The more she saw of Jean the more she liked him, and it was not long before she realized that she was in love with the young officer.

At the first ball held at the chateau, Jean's manner showed Miss Percival that he loved her. But he said nothing, for he believed that army life would not be a happy one for her. As he had neither social graces nor the wealth which could be substituted for them, he did not dare to dance with her at the ball for fear he would blurt out his love. When she approached him to ask for a dance, he left abruptly.

Jean's regiment went away for twenty days. When he returned, he realized that he loved Miss Percival more than ever. Finally he decided that his only course was to be transferred to a regiment stationed in another area. On the night he was to leave he sent his excuses to the chateau and went to explain his actions to the abbé, who listened to his story with deep interest. Suddenly there was a knock on the door and Miss Percival walked in. She apologized for her intrusion, but said that she had come to confess to the abbé. She asked Jean not to leave, but to stay and hear her.

She announced that she loved Jean and felt sure that he loved her. Jean had to admit that it was true. She said she knew he had not dared to ask her to marry him because of her wealth. Consequently she was forced to ask him to marry her. The abbé commending her action, they became engaged.

When the marriage ceremony for the happy couple was performed in the little church, a fine new organ played the music for the service. It was Miss Percival's marriage gift to the church. The abbé was happy; the sale of the old chateau had brought more good to the town than it had known before.

ABE LINCOLN IN ILLINOIS

Type of work: Drama
Author: Robert E. Sherwood (1896-)
Type of plot: Historical chronicle
Time of plot: 1831-1861
Locale: New Salem and Springfield, Illinois
First presented: 1938

Principal characters:
MENTOR GRAHAM, a schoolmaster
ABE LINCOLN
ANN RUTLEDGE, Abe's early love
JUDGE BOWLING GREEN, Justice of the Peace
NINIAN EDWARDS, a politician
JOSHUA SPEED, a merchant
WILLIAM HERNDON, Abe's law clerk
MARY TODD, Abe's wife
STEPHEN A. DOUGLAS, Abe's political opponent
SETH GALE, Abe's friend
JIMMIE GALE, Seth's young son

Critique:

Robert Sherwood saw in the struggles of Abe Lincoln a symbol of democracy in action. The playwright was able to stick fairly close to the facts of Lincoln's life in working out his allegory of the growth of the democratic spirit, but in several scenes he was forced to invent fictitious characters or incidents to make his point. Whether the play be viewed as history or allegory, it remains as authentically American as its leading character.

The Story:

In the summer of 1831, when Abe Lincoln was twenty-two years old, he arrived in New Salem, Illinois, at that time a frontier village of fifteen log cabins. Shortly afterward the lanky young man opened a general store in partnership with a friend named Berry. Their stock included whiskey. Berry continued to tap the keg until he drank up all their liquid assets, and the store went bankrupt. Abe voluntarily assumed all the obligations for the partnership and went into debt for about fifteen hundred dollars.

At that time Abe boarded with Mentor Graham, the neighborhood schoolmaster, who began the task of teaching the young backwoodsman the rudiments of grammar. He awakened in Abe an interest in great oratory as well as a love for poetry. Graham sensed his pupil's extreme melancholy and preoccupation with death as well as his marked disinclination to do anything which required much effort. He advised Abe to go into politics, declaring wryly that there were only two professions open to a man who had failed at everything else—schoolteaching and politics.

Abe's opportunity came a year later

while he held the job of local postmaster. A young politician, Ninian Edwards, a vigorous opponent of President Jackson, appeared at the Rutledge tavern in New Salem. He was looking for a possible candidate for the State Assembly. Edwards so much admired Abe's deft handling of several quarrelsome Jackson supporters that he offered Abe the candidacy.

In making his offer he was supported by Abe's two loyal and influential friends in Salem, Joshua Speed, a merchant, and Judge Bowling Green, the justice of the peace. But Abe, who had been considering going farther west, refused. Then several circumstances arose to change his mind. Seth Gale, the friend with whom Abe had planned to make the trip, received news that his father was sick and he had to return to his native state of Maryland at once. And Ann Rutledge, daughter of the local tavernkeeper, with whom Abe had been secretly in love, received a letter from New York State to the effect that a young man named McNeil, with whom Ann had been in love, would not be able to return to New Salem. When Abe declared his devotion, Ann, disillusioned with her former lover, encouraged him. As a consequence, Abe sent word by his friend Judge Bowling Green that he would be a candidate for the State Assembly.

Fate brought about another, more disastrous, turn in Abe's fortunes. Ann Rutledge fell suddenly ill of a fever, and nothing that the doctor or Abe did could save her. After Ann's death, Abe became completely obsessed by a feeling of melancholia from which none of his friends could rouse him. He opened a Springfield law office with his friend, Judge Stuart, but he refused to take much interest in politics, in spite of the urgings of his clerk, William Herndon, who was a firebrand Abolitionist. Although Abe disliked slavery, he failed to see that the Abolitionists were helping their cause by threatening to split the country.

Knowing that something must be done to pull Abe out of his lethargy, his old political mentor, Ninian Edwards, introduced him to his ambitious sister-in-law, Mary Todd. Mary saw immediately that Lincoln was a man she could inspire to great things. Her aristocratic sister, Elizabeth, could not understand what Mary saw in this raw-boned frontiersman, but Mary saw in him the satisfaction of her own frustrated yearnings. They became engaged.

But Abe had not forgotten Ann Rutledge. On the day of his wedding to Mary Todd, he pleaded with his friend, Joshua Speed, to deliver to Mary a letter he had written to tell her that he did not love her. Speed insisted that Abe go to Mary himself and explain that he was afraid of her, of the demands she would make upon him. After he had humiliated Mary Todd with his explanation, Abe drifted back to the prairie frontier once more.

One day he encountered his old friend, Seth Gale, with whom he had once planned to go west. Seth had set out from Maryland with his wife and child, and was headed for Oregon. But his child, Jimmie, was ill, and Seth felt that if his son died neither he nor his wife would have the courage to continue the journey. In a flash of insight, Abe saw in his friend's predicament a symbol of the plight of the country as a whole. The Dred Scott Decision had made it possible to extend slavery in the West, a circumstance that would be fatal to those who, like Seth Gale, were trying to build a new country there. That vision crystallized Abe's purpose in life; and when he offered up a prayer to the Almighty for the life of little Jimmie, he was thinking of the country as a whole. Filled with a new purpose, he pocketed his pride and went back to Mary Todd. Still believing in him, she accepted Abe without a moment's hesitation.

From that day on his career followed one straight line, culminating in his nomination for the presidency. There were his debates with Stephen A. Douglas, who was to be his opponent in the election that followed. Within his own party there were political considerations which Lincoln handled with dignity and tact. But most important of all, there was his own life with Mary Todd. In the years since their marriage she had borne him four sons, one of whom had died, and through those years she had grown more tense and irritable, until the home life of the Lincolns became almost intolerable. Abe patiently endured her tirades in their own home, but when Mary began criticizing him in public, he resisted. On the night of his election she had one of her tantrums, and Abe was forced to send her home on the very eve of her triumph.

With his election to the highest office in the land, Lincoln's troubles increased. The old melancholia returned, the old preoccupation with death. On an eventful day in 1861, standing on the rear platform of the train which was to take him from Springfield to Washington, he tried to express to his old neighbors and friends his ideals for the future of America. As the presidential train pulled out he could hear his well-wishers singing the last strains of "John Brown's Body"—"His soul goes marching on!"

ABSALOM, ABSALOM!

Type of work: Novel
Author: William Faulkner (1897-)
Type of plot: Psychological realism
Time of plot: Nineteenth century
Locale: Mississippi
First published: 1936

Principal characters:
THOMAS SUTPEN, owner of Sutpen's Hundred
ELLEN COLDFIELD SUTPEN, his wife
HENRY, and
JUDITH, their children
ROSA COLDFIELD, Ellen's younger sister
GOODHUE COLDFIELD, Ellen's and Rosa's father
CHARLES BON, Thomas Sutpen's son by his first marriage
QUENTIN COMPSON, Rosa Coldfield's young friend
SHREVE MCCANNON, Quentin's roommate at Harvard

Critique:

This novel is the most involved of William Faulkner's works, for the narrative is revealed by recollections years after the events described have taken place. Experience is related at its fullest expression; its initial import is recollected and its significance years thereafter is faithfully recorded. The conventional method of story-telling has been discarded. Through his special method Faulkner is able to re-create human action and human emotion in its own setting. Sensory impressions gained at the moment, family traditions as powerful stimuli, the tragic impulses—these focus truly in the reader's mind so that a tremendous picture of the nineteenth-century South, vivid down to the most minute detail, grows slowly in the reader's imagination. *Absalom, Absalom!* is a novel of tremendous and tragic import.

The Story:

In the summer of 1910, when Quentin Compson was preparing to go to Harvard, old Rosa Coldfield insisted upon telling him the whole infamous story of Thomas Sutpen, whom she called a demon. According to Miss Rosa, he had brought terror and tragedy to all who had dealings with him.

In 1833 Thomas Sutpen had come to Jefferson, Mississippi, with a fine horse and two pistols and no known past. He had lived mysteriously for a while among people at the hotel, and after a short time he disappeared. Town gossip was that he had bought one hundred square miles of uncleared land from the Chickasaws and was planning to turn it into a plantation.

When he returned with a wagon load of wild-looking Negroes, a French architect, and a few tools and wagons, he was as uncommunicative as ever. At once he set about clearing land and building a mansion. For two years he labored and during all that time he hardly ever saw or visited his acquaintances in Jefferson. People wondered about the source of his money. Some claimed that he had stolen it somewhere in his mysterious comings and goings. Then for three years his house remained unfinished, without windowpanes or furnishings, while Thomas Sutpen busied himself with his crops. Occasionally he invited Jefferson men to his plantation to hunt, entertaining them with liquor, cards, and savage combats between his giant slaves—combats in which he himself sometimes joined for the sport.

At last he disappeared once more, and when he returned he had furniture and furnishings elaborate and fine enough to make his great house a splendid showplace. Because of his mysterious actions, sentiment in the village turned against him. But this hostility subsided somewhat when Sutpen married Ellen Coldfield, daughter of the highly respected Goodhue Coldfield.

Miss Rosa and Quentin's father shared some of Sutpen's revelations. Because Quentin was away in college many of the things he knew about Sutpen's Hundred had come to him in letters from home. Other details he had learned during talks with his father.

He learned of Ellen Sutpen's life as mistress of the strange mansion in the wilderness. He learned how she discovered her husband fighting savagely with one of his slaves. Young Henry Sutpen fainted, but Judith, the daughter, watched from the haymow with interest and delight. Ellen thereafter refused to reveal her true feelings and ignored the village gossip about Sutpen's Hundred.

The children grew up. Young Henry, so unlike his father, attended the university at Oxford, Mississippi, and there he met Charles Bon, a rich planter's grandson. Unknown to Henry, Charles was his half-brother, Sutpen's son by his first marriage. Unknown to all of Jefferson, Sutpen had got his money as the dowry of his earlier marriage to Charles Bon's West Indian mother, a wife he discarded when he learned she was partly of Negro blood.

Charles Bon became engaged to Judith Sutpen but the engagement was suddenly broken off for a probation period of four years. In the meantime the Civil War began. Charles and Henry served together. Thomas Sutpen became a colonel.

Goodhue Coldfield took a disdainful stand against the war. He barricaded himself in his attic and his daughter, Rosa, was forced to put his food in a basket let down by a long rope. His store was looted by Confederate soldiers. One night, alone in his attic, he died.

Judith, in the meanwhile, had waited patiently for her lover. She carried his letter, written at the end of the four-year period, to Quentin's grandmother. About a week later Wash Jones, the handyman on the Sutpen plantation, came to Miss Rosa's door with the crude announcement that Charles Bon was dead, killed at the gate of the plantation by his half-brother and former friend. Henry fled. Judith buried her lover in the Sutpen family plot on the plantation. Rosa, whose mother had died when she was born, went to Sutpen's Hundred to live with her niece. Ellen was already dead. It was Rosa's conviction that she could help Judith.

Colonel Thomas Sutpen returned. His slaves had been taken away, and he was burdened with new taxes on his overrun land and ruined buildings. He planned to marry Rosa Coldfield, more than ever desiring an heir now that Judith had vowed spinsterhood and Henry had become a fugitive. His son, Charles Bon, whom he might, in desperation, have permitted to marry his daughter, was dead.

Rosa, insulted when she understood the true nature of his proposal, returned to her father's ruined house in the village. She was to spend the rest of her miserable life pondering the fearful intensity of Thomas Sutpen, whose nature, in her outraged belief, seemed to partake of the devil himself.

Quentin, during his last vacation, had learned more of the Sutpen tragedy. He now revealed much of the story to Shreve McCannon, his roommate, who listened with all of a Northerner's misunderstanding and indifference.

Quentin and his father had visited the Sutpen graveyard, where they saw a little path and a hole leading into Ellen Sutpen's grave. Generations of opossums lived there. Over her tomb and that of her husband stood a marble monument from Italy. Sutpen himself had died in 1869. In 1867 he had taken young Milly Jones, Wash Jones' granddaughter. When she bore a child, a girl, Wash Jones had killed Thomas Sutpen.

Judith and Charles Bon's son, his child by an octoroon woman who had brought her child to Sutpen's Hundred when he was eleven years old, died in 1884 of smallpox. Before he died the boy had married a Negro woman and they had had an idiot son, Charles Bon. Rosa Coldfield had placed headstones on their graves and on Judith's she had caused to be inscribed a fearful message.

In that summer of 1910 Rosa Coldfield confided to Quentin that she felt there was still someone living at Sutpen's Hundred. Together the two had gone out there at night, and had discovered Clytie, the aged daughter of Thomas Sutpen and a Negro slave. More important, they discovered Henry Sutpen himself hiding in the ruined old house. He had returned, he told them, four years before; he had come back to die. The idiot, Charles Bon, watched Rosa and Quentin as they departed. Rosa returned to her home and Quentin went back to college.

Quentin's father wrote to tell him the tragic ending of the Sutpen story. Months later, Rosa sent an ambulance out to the ruined plantation house, for she had finally determined to bring her nephew Henry into the village to live with her, so that he could get decent care. Clytie, seeing the ambulance, was afraid that Henry was to be arrested for the murder of Charles Bon many years before. In desperation she set fire to the old house, burning herself and Henry Sutpen to death. Only the idiot, Charles Bon, the last surviving descendant of Thomas Sutpen, escaped. No one knew where he went, for he was never seen again. Miss Rosa took to her bed and there died soon afterward, in the winter of 1910.

Quentin told the story to his roommate because it seemed to him, somehow, to be the story of the whole South, a tale of deep passions, tragedy, ruin, and decay.

ADAM BEDE

Type of work: Novel
Author: George Eliot (Mary Ann Evans, 1819-1880)
Type of plot: Domestic romance
Time of plot: 1799
Locale: England
First published: 1859

Principal characters:
ADAM BEDE, a carpenter
SETH BEDE, his brother
MARTIN POYSER, proprietor of Hall Farm
MRS. POYSER, his wife
DINAH MORRIS, her niece, a Methodist preacher
HETTY SORREL, another niece
CAPTAIN ARTHUR DONNITHORNE, the young squire

Critique:

This novel of English pastoral life probably shows George Eliot's quality as a novelist better than any other of her works, with the possible exception of *Middlemarch*. When George Eliot was writing of the peasants, the artisans, the yeomen, the clergy, and the squires of Warwickshire, she was writing out of memories of her own childhood, and her characters come to life as people she had known. Moreover, she superimposes upon them an awareness of fate, not majestic as in Hardy, but growing out of her convictions that there is a cause and effect relationship in human behavior as there is in the rest of nature.

The Story:

In the village of Hayslope at the close of the eighteenth century, there lived a young carpenter named Adam Bede. Tall and muscular, Adam was respected by everyone as a good workman and an honest and upright man. Even the young squire, Captain Arthur Donnithorne, knew Adam and liked him, and Adam in turn regarded the squire as his best friend.

Adam was, in fact, so good a workman that his employer, Mr. Jonathan Burge, the builder, would have welcomed him as his son-in-law and partner. But Adam had no eyes for Mary Burge; his only thoughts were of distractingly pretty Hetty Sorrell, niece of Mrs. Poyser, whose husband, Martin, ran the Hall Farm. Hetty, however, cared nothing for Adam. She was interested only in Captain Donnithorne, whom she had met one day in her aunt's dairy.

No one in Hayslope thought Hetty would make Adam a good wife, least of all Adam's mother, Lisbeth, who would have disapproved of any girl who threatened to take her favorite son from her. Her feelings of dependence upon Adam were intensified after her husband, Matthias Bede, drowned in Willow Brook while on his way home from the village inn.

In the meantime, Adam's brother Seth had fallen in love with the young Methodist preacher, Dinah Morris. Dinah was another niece of Mrs. Poyser, as unlike her cousin Hetty as Adam was unlike Seth. Hetty resembled nothing so much as a soft, helpless kitten, but Dinah was firm and serious in all things. One evening while she and Seth were walking home together from the village green, he had proposed marriage. Dinah sadly declined, saying she had dedicated her life to preaching the gospel.

When funeral services for Matthias Bede were held in Hayslope Church on the following Sunday, the thoughts of the congregation were on many things other than the solemn occasion they were attending. Adam's thoughts of Hetty blended with memories of his father.

Hetty's thoughts were all of Captain Donnithorne, who had promised to make his appearance. She was disappointed, however, for Donnithorne had already departed with his regiment. When he returned on leave, the young squire celebrated his twenty-first birthday with a great feast to which nearly all of Hayslope was invited. Adam was singled out as a special guest to sit at Donnithorne's table. Adam's mother was both proud and jealous lest her son be getting more and more out of her reach.

One August night, exactly three weeks after the Donnithorne party, Adam was returning home from his work on the Donnithorne estate when he saw two figures in close embrace. They were Donnithorne and Hetty Sorrel. When Adam's dog barked, Hetty hurried away. Donnithorne, embarrassed, tried to explain that he had met the girl by chance and had stolen a kiss. Adam called his friend a scoundrel and a coward. They came to blows, and Donnithorne was knocked senseless. Adam, frightened that he might have killed the young squire in his rage, revived him and helped him to a nearby summerhouse. There he demanded that Donnithorne write a letter to Hetty telling her that he would not see her again.

The next day Donnithorne sent the letter to Hetty in Adam's care, thus placing the responsibility for its possible effect upon Adam himself. Adam gave her the letter while they were walking the following Sunday. When, in the privacy of her bedchamber, she read the letter, Hetty was in despair. Her dreams shattered, she thought only of finding some way out of her misery. Then in November Adam was offered a partnership in Mr. Burge's business, and he proposed to Hetty. Mr. and Mrs. Poyser were delighted to find that their niece was to marry the man they so much admired.

But the wedding had to be delayed until two new rooms could be added to the Bede house. In February, Hetty told her aunt she was going to visit Dinah Morris at Snowfield. Actually, however, she was determined to find Donnithorne. When she arrived at Windsor, where he was supposed to be stationed, she found that his regiment had been transferred to Ireland. Now in complete despair Hetty roamed about until in a strange village, and in the house of a widow named Sarah Stone, her child by Donnithorne was born. Frightened, Hetty wandered on, leaving her baby to die in a wood. Later, tortured by her conscience, she returned to find the child gone.

When his grandfather died, Donnithorne returned to Hayslope to discover that Hetty was in prison, charged with the murder of her child. He did everything in his power to free her, and Dinah Morris came to her prison cell and prayed with her to open up her heart and tell the truth. Finally poor Hetty broke down and confessed everything that had happened since she left Hayslope. She had not intended to kill her baby; in fact, she had not actually killed the child. She had considered taking her own life. Two days later, Donnithorne, filled with shame and remorse, brought a reprieve. Hetty's sentence was committed to deportation. A few years later she died on her way home. Donnithorne went to Spain.

Dinah Morris stayed with the Poysers often now, and gradually she and Adam were drawn to each other. But Dinah's heart was still set on her preaching. She left Hall Farm and went back to Snowfield. Adam Bede found his only satisfaction toiling at his workbench. Then one day his mother spoke again of Dinah and her gentle ways. Adam could wait no longer. He went to find her.

THE ADMIRABLE CRICHTON

Type of work: Drama
Author: James M. Barrie (1860-1937)
Type of plot: Humorous satire
Time of plot: Early twentieth century
Locale: Loam House, Mayfair; a desert island
First presented: 1903

Principal characters:
THE EARL OF LOAM
LADY MARY,
LADY CATHERINE, and
LADY AGATHA, his daughters
THE HON. ERNEST WOOLLEY, his nephew
WILLIAM CRICHTON, his butler

Critique:

One of the best of Barrie's comedies, *The Admirable Crichton* contains a more definite theme than Barrie generally put into his plays. His satirical portrait of an English aristocrat with liberal ideas is the most skillful that has been done on the subject. Lord Loam, like many liberals, is a kind of social Jekyll and Hyde, accepting the doctrine of the rights of man in theory, but holding tightly to his vested interests in practice.

The Story:

Once every month, the philanthropic Earl of Loam gave expression to his views on human equality by forcing his servants to have tea with him and his family in the great hall of Loam House in Mayfair. It was a disagreeable experience for everyone concerned, especially for his butler, Crichton, who did not share his master's liberal views. Lord Loam alone enjoyed the occasion, for he was the only one who remained completely himself. He ordered his daughters and his nephew about and treated them exactly as he treated his servants on the remaining days of the month.

Lady Mary, his oldest daughter, was a spirited young woman who resented her father's high-handed methods with his family. Her indignation reached a climax one day when Lord Loam announced that his three daughters were to have but one maid among them on a yachting trip on which the family was about to embark. Lady Mary was furious, but she assumed that her maid, Fisher, would go along. When Fisher learned that she was expected to look after the two younger sisters in addition to Lady Mary, she promptly resigned, and the two maids attending Catherine and Agatha followed suit. Lord Loam was left without any servants for his projected cruise, for his valet also resigned. Although it hurt his pride deeply, Crichton finally agreed, out of loyalty to his master, to act as his valet on the trip. Moreover, he persuaded Tweeny, the housemaid upon whom he had cast a favorable eye, to go along as maid to Lord Loam's daughters.

The cruise ended unhappily when the yacht was pounded to pieces during a violent storm in the Pacific, and the party was cast away on a tropical island. All reached shore except Lord Loam. The other survivors had watched him throw away his life in a frantic but vain attempt to get into the lifeboat first.

On the island all tried to preserve as much as possible the class distinction which had prevailed in England. But the attempt was unsuccessful. Crichton alone knew exactly what he was doing, and it was upon him that the others had to depend. So Crichton, the servant, became on the island the natural leader, and he ruled his former superiors with a gentle but a firm hand. For example, he found the epigrams of the Hon. Ernest, which had seemed so brilliant in England, a bit trying; as a consequence, Crichton adopted the policy of submitting Ernest to a severe ducking whenever he came forth with an epigram. The aristocrats worried over the rising authority of their former butler and the decline in their own prestige. When Lord Loam finally appeared, after washing ashore with some wreckage, they urged him to take a stand of authority. Lord Loam's only recourse was to remove his little party to another section of the island apart from Crichton. But hunger, which the aristocrats by their own efforts could not assuage, brought them meekly back. Crichton became the acknowledged leader of them all.

Crichton took full advantage of his newly acquired authority. Having none of the earl's ideas about equality, he found no necessity for pretending that on the island his former betters were his equals in any sense. Each was kept in his place and required to do his own work according to the needs of the camp.

Under Crichton's rule the aristocrats were happy for perhaps the first time in their lives. The hard physical labor made something approaching a man out of Ernest, and the task of helping to prepare Crichton's food and waiting on him at the table turned Lord Loam's snobbish daughters into attractive and useful women. Lord Loam, dressed in animal skins, was merely a harmless and rather genial old man with no particular talents, whom everyone called Daddy. But the greatest change occurred in Lady Mary. She alone realized that in any environment Crichton was superior to them all, and that only the conventions of so-called civilized society had obscured that fact. Consequently she fell in love with the butler and did everything in her power to make herself his favorite. Crichton, attracted to the beautiful Lady Mary, considered making her his consort on the island. He indulged in the fancy that in some past existence he had been a king and she a Christian slave. But when a ship appeared on the horizon, Crichton realized that his dreams were romantic nonsense. On their return to England he again would be a butler, and she would be Lady Mary.

It was as Crichton had expected. After the rescue Lord Loam and his family returned to their old habits of thought and behavior. Crichton was again the butler. The Hon. Ernest wrote a book about their experiences on the island and made himself the hero of their exploits. Crichton was barely mentioned. Lady Mary reluctantly renewed her engagement to the rather asinine Lord Brocklehurst, whose mother was greatly worried over what had happened on the island and not sure that a daughter of Lord Loam was a fit wife for her son.

But Lady Mary still recognized Crichton's superiority, and told him so frankly. Crichton was shocked. Her views might have been acceptable on the island, he said, but not in England. When she expressed the radical view that something might be wrong with England, Crichton told her that not even from her would he listen to a word of criticism against England or English ways.

THE AENEID

Type of work: Poem
Author: Publius Vergilius Maro (70-19 B.C.)
Type of plot: Heroic epic
Time of plot: The period immediately following the Trojan War

Locale: The Mediterranean region
First transcribed: Augustan manuscript

Principal characters:

AENEAS, Trojan hero destined to found the Roman race
DIDO, Queen of Carthage, in love with Aeneas
ANNA, her sister
ASCANIUS, son of Aeneas
ANCHISES, father of Aeneas
VENUS, goddess of love and beauty, mother of Aeneas
JUNO, queen of the gods and enemy of the Trojans
CUMAEAN SIBYL, prophetess who leads Aeneas to Hades
LATINUS, king of the Latins, whom Aeneas defeats in battle
LAVINIA, his daughter
TURNUS, Latin hero ambitious for the Latin throne and hand of Lavinia
EVANDER, Arcadian king, ally of Aeneas
PALLAS, his son

Critique:

This poem is the distinguished Latin epic which celebrates the glory of Rome in great poetry. It records the traditional story of the establishment of the Roman race and thus traces the lineage of the Romans back to Aeneas and Troy. It has already stood the test of time and will go down in history as one of the world's great epics.

The Story:

Aeneas, driven by storm to the shores of Libya, was welcomed gladly by the people of Carthage. Because Carthage was the favorite city of Juno, divine enemy of Aeneas, Venus had Cupid take the form of Ascanius, son of Aeneas, so that the young god of love might warm the heart of proud Dido and Aeneas come to no harm in her land. At the close of a welcoming feast Aeneas was prevailed upon to recount his adventures.

He described the fall of his native Troy at the hands of the Greeks after a ten-year siege, telling how the armed Greeks had entered the city in the belly of a great wooden horse and how the Trojans had fled from their burning city, among them Aeneas with his father Anchises and young Ascanius. Not long afterward, Anchises had advised setting sail for distant lands. Blown by varying winds, the Trojans had at length reached Buthrotum, where had been foretold a long and arduous journey before Aeneas would reach Italy. Having set sail once more, they had reached Sicily. There Anchises, who had been his son's sage counselor, had died and had been buried. Forced to leave Sicily, Aeneas had been blown by stormy winds to the coast of Libya. Here he ended his tale, and Dido, influenced by Cupid disguised as Ascanius, felt pity and admiration for the Trojan hero.

The next day Dido continued her entertainment for Aeneas. During a royal hunt a great storm drove Dido and Aeneas to the same cave for refuge. There they succumbed to the passion of love. Aeneas spent the winter in Carthage and enjoyed the devotion of the queen. But in the spring he felt the need to continue his destined course. When he set sail, the sorrowing Dido killed herself. The light of her funeral pyre was seen far out at sea.

Again on the shores of Sicily, Aeneas bade his men refresh themselves with food, drink, and games. First of all there was a boat race in which Cloanthus was the victor. The second event was a foot race, won by Euryalus. Entellus engaged Dares in a boxing match, which Aeneas stopped before the obviously superior Entellus achieved a knock-out. The final contest was with bow and arrow. Eurytion and Acestes made spectacular showings and to each was awarded a handsome prize. Following the contests, Ascanius and the other young boys rode out to engage in war games. Meanwhile, the women were grieving the lost guidance of Anchises, and at the instigation of Juno set fire to the ships. Aeneas, sustained by the gods, bade his people repair the damage. Once more the Trojans set sail.

Finally, they reached the shores of Italy, at Cumae, famous for its sibyl. The sibyl granted Aeneas the privilege of visiting his father in the underworld. After due sacrifice, the two of them began their descent into Hades. At length they reached the river Styx and persuaded the boatman Charon to row them across. Aeneas saw the spirits of many people he had known in life, including the ill-fated Dido. Then they came to the beginning of a forked road. One path led to the regions of the damned; the other led to the land of the blessed. Following this latter road, they came at last to Anchises, who showed Aeneas in marvelous fashion all the future history of Rome, and commanded him to found his kingdom at the place where he would eat his tables. On his return to the upper regions Aeneas revisited his men and proceeded to his own abode.

Again the Trojans set sail up the coast of Italy, to the ancient state of Latium, ruled over by Latinus. On the shore they prepared a meal, laying bread under their meat. As they were eating, Ascanius jokingly observed that in eating their bread they were eating their tables. This remark told Aeneas that here was the place Anchises had foretold. Next day the Trojans came to the city of King Latinus on the Tiber. Latinus had been warned by an oracle not to give his daughter Lavinia in marriage to any native man, but to wait for an alien, who would come to establish a great people. He welcomed Aeneas as that man of destiny.

A Latin hero, Turnus, became jealous of the favor Latinus showed Aeneas, and stirred up revolt among the people. Juno, hating Aeneas, aided Turnus. One day Ascanius killed a stag, not knowing that it was the tame favorite of a native family. There grew from the incident such a feud that Latinus shut himself up in his house and ceased to control his subjects. Meanwhile Aeneas made preparations for battle with the Latins under Turnus.

In a dream he was advised to seek the help of Evander, whose kingdom on the Seven Hills would become the site of mighty Rome. Evander agreed to join forces with Aeneas against the armies of Turnus and to enlist troops from nearby territories as well. Now Venus presented Aeneas with a fabulous shield made by Vulcan, for she feared for the safety of her son.

When Turnus learned that Aeneas was with Evander, he and his troops besieged the Trojan camp. One night Nisus and Euryalus, two Trojan youths, entered the camp of the sleeping Latins and slaughtered a great many of them before they were discovered and put to death. The enraged Latins advanced on the Trojans with fire and sword and forced them into open battle. When the Trojans seemed about to beat back their attackers, Turnus entered the fray and put them to flight. But the thought of Aeneas inspired the Trojans to such bravery that they drove Turnus into the river.

Aeneas, warned in a dream of this battle, returned and landed with his allies on the shore near the battlefield, where he encountered Turnus and his armies. Evander's troops were being routed when Pallas, Evander's beloved son, began to urge them on and himself rushed into the fight, killing many of the enemy before he was slain in combat with Turnus. Aeneas sought to take the life of Turnus, who escaped through the intervention of Juno.

Aeneas decreed that the body of Pallas should be sent back to his father with appropriate pomp during a twelve-day truce. The gods had watched the conflict from afar; now Juno relented at

Jupiter's command, but insisted that the Trojans must take the Latin speech and garb before their city could rule the world.

Turnus led his band of followers against Aeneas in spite of a treaty made by Latinus. An arrow from an unknown source wounded Aeneas, but his wound was miraculously healed. The Trojan hero reëntered the battle, was again wounded, but was able to engage Turnus in personal combat and strike him down. Aeneas killed his enemy in the name of Pallas and sacrificed his body to the shade of his dead ally. No longer opposed by Turnus, Aeneas was now free to marry Lavinia and establish his long-promised new nation. This was Rome, the mistress of the ancient world.

THE AGE OF INNOCENCE

Type of work: Novel
Author: Edith Wharton (1862-1937)
Type of plot: Social criticism
Time of plot: Late nineteenth century
Locale: New York City
First published: 1920

Principal characters:
NEWLAND ARCHER, a young attorney
MAY WELLAND, his fiancée
COUNTESS ELLEN OLENSKA, her cousin

Critique:

This novel is an incisive but oblique attack on the intricate and tyrannous tribal customs of a highly stratified New York society with which the author herself was familiar. Her psychological probing of the meaning and motivation behind the apparent façade of her characters' social behavior shows her to be a true disciple of Henry James. The method is indeed that of James, but Edith Wharton's style is clearer and less involved. Here is a well-made novel, the work of a craftsman for whom form and method are perfectly welded, and the action results inevitably from the natures of the characters themselves.

The Story:

Newland Archer, a handsome and eligible young attorney engaged to lovely May Welland, learned that the engagement would be announced at a party to welcome his fiancée's cousin, Countess Ellen Olenska. This reception for Ellen constituted a heroic sacrifice on the part of the many Welland connections, for her marriage to a ne'er-do-well Polish count had not improved her position so far as rigorous and straight-laced New York society was concerned. The fact that she contemplated a divorce action also made her suspect, and, to cap it all, her rather bohemian way of living did not conform to what her family expected of a woman who had made an unsuccessful marriage.

Newland Archer's engagement to May was announced. At the same party Archer was greatly attracted to Ellen. Before long, with the excuse that he was making the cousin of his betrothed feel at home, he began to send her flowers and call on her. To him she seemed a woman who offered sensitivity, beauty, the promise of a life quite different from that he could expect after his marriage to May.

He found himself defending Ellen when the rest of society was attacking her contemplated divorce action. He did not, however, consider breaking his engagement to May, but constantly sought reasons for justifying what was to the rest of his group an excellent union. With Ellen often in his thoughts, May Welland's cool beauty and correct but unexciting personality began to suffer in Archer's estimation.

Although the clan defended her against all outsiders, Ellen was often treated as a pariah. Her family kept check on her, trying to prevent her from indulging in too many bohemianisms, such as her strange desire to rent a house in a socially unacceptable part of town. The women of the clan also recognized her as a dangerous rival, and ruthless Julius Beaufort, whose secret dissipations were known by all, including his wife, paid her marked attention. Archer found himself hating Julius Beaufort very much.

Convincing himself that he was seeing too much of Ellen, Archer went to St. Augustine to visit May, who was vacationing there with her mother and her hypochondriac father. In spite of her cool and conventional welcome and her gentle rebuffs to his wooing, her beauty reawakened in him a kind of affection, and he pleaded with her to advance the date of their wedding. May and her parents refused because their elaborate preparations could not be completed in time.

Archer returned to New York. There, with the aid of the family matriarch, Mrs. Manson Mingott, he achieved his purpose, and the wedding date was advanced. This news came to him in a telegram sent by May to Ellen, which Ellen read to him just as he was attempting to advance the intimacy of their relationship. Archer left Ellen's house and found a similar telegram from May to himself. Telling his sister Janey that the wedding would take place within a month, he suddenly realized that he was now protected against Ellen and himself.

The ornate wedding, the conventional European honeymoon which followed, and May's assumption of the role of the proper wife, soon disillusioned Archer. He realized that he was trapped, that the mores of his society, helped by his own lack of courage, had prepared him, like a smooth ritual, for a rigid and codified life. There was enough intelligence and insight in Archer, however, to make him resent the trap.

On his return to New York, he continued to see Ellen. The uselessness of his work as junior attorney in an ancient law firm, the stale regimen of his social life, and the passive sweetness of May did not satisfy that part of Archer which set him apart from the rest of his clan.

He proposed to Ellen that they go away together, but Ellen, wise and kind, showed him that such an escape would not be a pleasant one, and she indicated that they could love each other only as long as he did not press for a consummation. Archer agreed. He further capitulated when, urged by her family, he advised Ellen, as her attorney and as a relative, not to get a divorce from Count Olenski. She agreed, and Archer again blamed his own cowardice for his action.

The family faced another crisis when Julius Beaufort's firm, built upon a framework of shady financial transactions, failed, ruining him and his duped customers. The blow caused elderly Mrs. Mingott to have a stroke, and the family rallied around her. She summoned Ellen, a favorite of hers, to her side, and Ellen, who had been living in Washington, D. C., returned to the Mingott house to stay. Archer, who had not met Ellen since he advised her against a divorce, began seeing her again, and certain remarks by Archer's male acquaintances along with a strained and martyrlike attitude which May had adopted, indicated to him that his intimacy with Ellen was known among his family and friends. The affair came to an end, however, when Ellen left for Paris, after learning that May was to have a baby. It was obvious to all that May had triumphed, and Archer was treated by his family as a prodigal returned. The rebel was conquered. Archer made his peace with society.

Years passed. Archer dabbled in liberal politics, interested himself in civic reforms. His children, Mary and Dallas, were properly reared. May died when Archer was in his fifties. He lamented her passing with genuine grief. He watched society changing, and saw the old conservative order give way, accepting and rationalizing innovations of a younger, more liberal generation.

One day his son Dallas, about to be married, phoned him and proposed a European tour, their last trip together. In Paris, Dallas revealed to his father that he knew all about Ellen Olenska and had arranged a visit to her apartment. But when they arrived, Archer sent his son ahead, to pay his respects, while he remained on a park bench outside. A romantic to the end, incapable of acting in any situation which made demands on his emotional resources, he sat and watched the lights in Ellen's apartment until a servant appeared on the balcony and closed the shutters. Then he walked slowly back to his hotel. The past was the past; the present was secure.

ALCESTIS

Type of work: Drama
Author: Euripides (480-406 B.C.)
Type of plot: Classical tragedy
Time of plot: Remote antiquity
Locale: Pherae, in ancient Greece
First presented: 438 B.C.

Principal characters:
APOLLO, god of the sun
ADMETUS, King of Pherae
ALCESTIS, his wife
THANATOS, Death
HERCULES, son of Zeus and friend to Admetus

Critique:

Composed by Euripides as the fourth play of a tragic tetrology performed at the Feast of Dionysius in 438 B.C., *Alcestis* has characteristics of both the tragedy and the satyr play. Although this was a rare but not unique form among Attic playwrights, *Alcestis* is the only surviving example. Consistent with Euripidean technique, the conclusion of the drama results from the intervention of a heavenly power that resolves the conflict, in this case the character of Hercules.

The Story:

Phoebus Apollo had a son, Asclepius, who in time became a god of medicine and healing. Asclepius transgressed divine law by raising a mortal, Hippolytus, from the dead, and Zeus, in anger, killed Apollo's son with a thunderbolt forged by the Cyclops. Apollo then slew the Cyclops, a deed for which he was condemned by Zeus to leave Olympus and to serve for one year as herdsman to Admetus, King of Pherae in Thessaly.

Some time after Apollo had completed his term of service, Admetus married Alcestis, daughter of Pelias, King of Iolcus. But on his wedding day he offended the goddess Artemis and so was doomed to die. Apollo, grateful for the kindness Admetus had shown him in the past, prevailed upon the Fates to spare the king on the condition that when his hour of death should come, they should accept in ransom the life of whoever would consent to die in his place.

None of Admetus' kin, however, cared to offer themselves in his place. Then Alcestis, in wifely devotion, pledged herself to die for her husband. Finally the day arrived when she must give up her life.

Concerned for the wife of his mortal friend, Apollo appealed to Thanatos, who had come to take Alcestis to the underworld. But Thanatos rejected his pleas, warning the god not to transgress against eternal judgment or the will of the Fates. Apollo declared that there was one powerful enough to defy the Fates who was even then on his way to the palace of Admetus. Meanwhile Alcestis prepared for her approaching death. On the day she was to die she dressed herself in her rich funeral robes and prayed before the hearth fire to Vesta, goddess of the hearth, asking her to be a mother to the two children she was leaving behind, to find a helpmate for the boy, a gentle lord for the girl, and not to let them follow their mother's example and die before their time. After her prayers, she placed garlands of myrtle on each altar of the house and at each shrine prayed tearlessly, knowing that death was coming. Then in her own chamber she wept as she remembered the happy years she and Admetus had lived together. There her children found her, and she said her farewells to them. The house was filled also with the sound of weeping servants, grieving for the mistress they loved. Admetus also wept bitterly, begging Alcestis not to leave him. But the condition imposed by the Fates had to be met. While he watched, her breath grew fainter, and her cold hand fell languidly. Before she died, she asked him to promise that he would always care tenderly for their children and that he would never marry again.

At that moment Hercules arrived at the palace of Admetus, on his way to slay the wild horses of Diomedes in Thrace as the eighth of his twelve labors. Admetus concealed from Hercules the news of Alcestis' death so that he might keep the son of Zeus as a guest and carry out the proper rites of hospitality. Hercules, ignorant of what had taken place before his arrival in Pherae, spent the night carousing, drinking wine, and singing, only to awaken in the morning and discover that Alcestis had died hours before he came and that his host had purposely deluded him in order to make his stay in Pherae as comfortable as possible. In gratitude for Admetus' thoughtfulness and in remorse for having reveled while the home of his friend was deep in sorrow, he determined to ambush Thanatos and bring Alcestis back from the dead.

Since no labor was too arduous for the hero, he set out after Thanatos and Alcestis. Overtaking them, he wrestled with Thanatos and forced him to give up his victim. Then he brought Alcestis, heavily veiled, into the presence of sorrowing Admetus, and asked the king to protect her until Hercules returned from Thrace. When Admetus refused, Hercules insisted that the king at least peer beneath the woman's veil. Great was the joy of Admetus and his household when they learned that the woman was Alcestis, miraculously returned from the grave. Pleased with his efforts, doughty Hercules set out once more to face the perilous eighth labor which awaited him in Thrace, firm in the knowledge that with him went the undying gratitude of Admetus and the gentle Alcestis.

ALECK MAURY, SPORTSMAN

Type of work: Novel
Author: Caroline Gordon (1895-)
Type of plot: Fictional biography
Time of plot: Late nineteenth, early twentieth centuries
Locale: Virginia, Tennessee, Mississippi, Missouri
First published: 1934

Principal characters:
Aleck Maury, a Southern sportsman

JAMES MORRIS, his uncle
VICTORIA, his aunt
JULIAN, his cousin
MR. FAYERLEE, owner of Merry Point
MRS. FAYERLEE, his wife
MOLLY FAYERLEE, their daughter, Aleck's wife
RICHARD, and
SARAH (SALLY), Aleck's and Molly's children
STEVE, Sarah's husband

Critique:

This novel tells of Aleck Maury, who devoted his life to his twin enthusiasms for gun and rod. To him, hunting and fishing were the very breath of life; everything else was secondary, including his career as a teacher of Latin and Greek. The book is a series of incidents which, when put together, describe Aleck Maury and make him seem real.

The Story:

Aleck Maury's love for hunting and fishing began in childhood. At the age of eight, Rafe, a Negro handyman at the Maury household, took Aleck coon hunting. Not long after, a mill owner named Jones took the boy fishing and encouraged his lifelong love for that sport. Aleck was always happiest when he was out in the fields. One of five children, he was reared by his oldest sister after his mother died. Until he was ten years old, he was educated at home by his father, who put great stress upon the classics and taught his children nothing else.

At the age of ten, Aleck went to live at Grassdale with his Uncle James and Aunt Victoria Morris and their son, Julian. There his education was to be broadened under the tutelage of Aunt Victoria, who was a learned woman. Aleck's life at Grassdale was pleasant, centering chiefly about sport.

When Aleck was graduated from the University of Virginia, he had a classical education but no plans for making a living. He tried several jobs. He cleared out a dogwood thicket for a set sum of money, worked on a construction project on the Missouri River, in the city engineer's office in Seattle, and as a day laborer on a ranch in California. While working at the ranch, he contracted typhoid fever and was sent back east as far as Kansas City, to stay with some relatives there. At last through the efforts of his family Aleck became a tutor at Merry Point, the home of Mr. Fayerlee, near Gloversville, Tennessee.

Aleck, living with the Fayerlees, became the local schoolmaster for the children of most of the landowners in the area. Aleck's first interest, however, was not in the school or the students he taught, but in the possibilities for fishing and hunting.

During his stay with the Fayerlees, Aleck fell in love with Molly Fayerlee, and in 1890 they were married. They continued to live on with the Fayerlees and Aleck continued to teach school. During his first year of marriage Aleck acquired the pup Gyges, a small but thoroughbred bird dog. He trained Gy from a pup and became greatly attached to him. The next fall Aleck's son Richard was born. Two years later a daughter Sarah, nicknamed Sally, was born. They all continued to live at Merry Point.

When Richard was seven, Aleck was offered the presidency of a small seminary in Mississippi, and over the protestations of the Fayerlee family the Maurys left Merry Point. On the way, while spending the night in Cairo, Aleck lost Gy. The dog was never heard of again. They continued their journey to Oakland and the seminary. When Aleck arrived, he found that the school was running smoothly under the able direction of Harry Morrow, his young assistant, who was interested in administration rather than teaching. A few months after arriving at Oakland, Aleck acquired an untrained two-year-old pointer named Trecho from his friend, William Mason. Once again Aleck started the slow, arduous training of a good hunting dog.

When Richard was fifteen, Aleck tried to interest him in the joys of his own life, hunting and fishing, but his son, although he was a splendid swimmer and wrestler, had little interest in his father's fondness for field and stream. That summer Richard, while swimming in the river with a group of his companions, was drowned. The boy had been Molly's favorite and his loss was almost more than she could bear. Aleck thought it would be best for all concerned to leave for different surroundings.

He decided after some correspondence with friends that he would start a school in Gloversville, and the family moved back there. Settled in the small Tennessee town, Aleck found much time for fishing and hunting. He met Colonel Wyndham and from him learned a great deal about casting, flies, and the techniques to be used for catching various fish. Finally he began to grow tired of the same pools and the same river, and it was with pleasure that he accepted Harry Morrow's offer of a job on the faculty of Rodman College at Poplar Bluff, Missouri, of which Morrow had just been made president.

Aleck's main reason for accepting the position was the possibility it offered for fishing in the Black River. Thus once again, after ten years in Gloversville, the Maury family was on the move to newer fishing grounds. Sally, however, did not accompany them, but went to a girls' school in Nashville. The faithful Trecho was also left behind, for he had been destroyed at the age of twelve because of his rheumatism.

At Rodman Aleck had only morning classes, a schedule which left him free to fish every afternoon. This pleasant life—teaching in the morning, fishing in the afternoon—continued for seven years. Then Molly died after an emergency operation. Mrs. Fayerlee and Sally arrived too late to see her alive. The three of them took her back to be buried in the family plot at Merry Point.

Aleck returned to Poplar Bluff and continued teaching there for a few years, but at last he resigned his position and went to live at Jim Buford's, near Gloversville, where he spent the next two years restocking Jim's lakes with bream and bass. Later he decided to go to Lake Harris in Florida to try the fishing; but he found it disappointing because of the eel grass which kept the fish from putting up a fight. About that time he received a letter from Sally, who had married and gone touring abroad with her husband. The letter informed him that she and her husband were soon to return home and that they hoped to find a quiet place in the country on some good fishing water, where Aleck would go to live with them. Aleck wrote and suggested that they start their search for a house near Elk River.

Four weeks later he meet Sally and Steve at Tullahoma, only to learn that Steve and Sally, who had arrived the day before, had already discovered the place they would like to have. They told him it was the old Potter house, close to the river. When Aleck saw the big, clapboard house, however, all his dreams about a white cottage disappeared, and when he looked at the river he decided that it would probably be muddy about half the year. Seeing his disappointment, Steve and Sally promised to continue their attempt to find a more ideal house, but at the end of the day's search they decided that they still liked the old Potter house the best. That night Aleck boarded a bus bound for Caney Fork, the place where he really wanted to live, and he went to stay at a small inn located there. The fishing was always good at Caney Fork.

ALICE ADAMS

Type of work: Novel
Author: Booth Tarkington (1869-1946)
Type of plot: Social criticism
Time of plot: Early twentieth century
Locale: A small Midwestern town
First published: 1921

Principal characters:
ALICE ADAMS, a small-town girl
VIRGIL ADAMS, her father
MRS. ADAMS, his wife
WALTER ADAMS, his son
MILDRED PALMER, Alice's friend
ARTHUR RUSSELL, the Palmers' relative
MR. LAMB, of Lamb and Company

Critique:

Alice Adams is a rather simply told story containing one plot and concerning itself with one central character. The novel is the vehicle through which Tarkington expounds his philosophy of life and his gentle satire on small town manners and morals.

The Story:

Alice Adams had been reared in a town in which each person's business was everybody's business, sooner or later. Her father, Virgil Adams, worked for Lamb and Company, a wholesale drug factory in the town, where he also obtained a job for his son Walter. Alice had been one of the town's young smart set while she was in high school, but when the others of the group had gone to college Alice had remained behind because of economic reasons. As time passed she felt increasingly out of things. To compensate for a lack of attention, Alice often attracted notice to herself by affected mannerisms.

Alice had been invited to a dance given by Mildred Palmer, who, according to Alice, was her best friend. Walter had also been invited so as to provide her with an escort. Getting Walter to go out with Alice, however, was a process which took all the coaxing and cajoling that Mrs. Adams could muster. On the night of the dance Alice departed in a made-over formal, carrying a homemade bouquet of wild violets, and with an unwilling escort who was driving a borrowed flivver. The party itself turned out no better than its inauspicious beginning. Alice was very much a wallflower except for the attentions of Frank Dowling, a fat, unpopular boy. Toward the end of the evening Mildred Palmer introduced Alice to a new young man, Arthur Russell, a distant relative of the Palmers. It was rumored that Mildred and Arthur would become engaged in the near future. Alice asked Arthur to find her brother, whom she had not seen since the second dance. When Arthur found Walter shooting dice with the Negro waiters in the cloakroom, Alice was mortified.

A week later Alice accidently met Arthur Russell and he walked home with her. During their walk Alice learned that Arthur had asked for an introduction to her at the dance. Flattered, Alice built up for herself a background which did not exist. Arthur asked for permission to call on her.

But Arthur failed to appear the next evening. Several nights later, after Alice had helped with the dishes, she was sitting on the front porch when Arthur finally came to call. To hold his in-

ALICE ADAMS by Booth Tarkington. By permission of Brandt & Brandt and the publishers, Doubleday & Co., Inc.

terest, Alice asked him to promise not to listen to any gossip about her. As time went on, she repeated her fear that someone would talk about her. Her protestations were something Arthur could not understand.

For many years Mrs. Adams had been trying to convince her husband to leave his job at Lamb and Company and go into business for himself. Her idea was that he could start a factory to manufacture glue from a formula he and another young man at Lamb and Company had discovered years before. Meanwhile the other man had died and the only people who knew the formula were Mr. Lamb and Mr. Adams. Mr. Lamb had lost interest in the formula. Mr. Adams felt that his wife's scheme was dishonest, and in spite of her nagging he refused to do as she wished. But after Mr. Lamb's granddaughter failed to invite Alice to a dinner party she was giving, Mrs. Adams convinced her husband that the true reason was their own poor economic status. In that way she finally won his grudging agreement to her plan.

Without delay, Mr. Adams began to organize his new business. Walter refused to join him because Mr. Adams would not give him three hundred dollars immediately. But Mr. Adams needed all his money for his new project. He sent Mr. Lamb a letter of resignation, telling of his intention to start a glue factory. He expected some sort of action or at least an outburst on Mr. Lamb's part when he read the letter, but nothing was forthcoming. He went ahead with his arrangements and began to manufacture his glue.

Alice's mother decided the time had come to invite Arthur to dinner, and Alice agreed with great reluctance. An elaborate meal was prepared; a maid was hired to serve, and Mr. Adams was forced into his dress suit. But the dinner was a dismal failure, and everyone, including Arthur, was extremely uncomfortable. Arthur had more reason than the rest for being so, for he had heard Mr. Adam's venture discussed in the most unfavorable light. He had also heard some uncomplimentary remarks about Alice. Before dinner was over, a friend named Charley Lohr came to speak to Mr. Adams. When both her mother and father failed to return to the table, Alice and Arthur went out to the porch. She soon dismissed him, knowing that something had come between them. When she went into the house, Charley Lohr informed her that her brother had been caught short in his accounts and had skipped town.

Mr. Adams decided to get a loan from the bank the first thing in the morning in order to pay back what Walter had taken. However, when he went to his factory in the morning, he discovered that the building which had been erected across the street from his was in reality another glue factory, one started by Mr. Lamb. His hopes of obtaining money on his factory were shattered. Then Mr. Lamb rode up to gloat over his retaliation. Mr. Adams angrily accused Mr. Lamb of waiting until Walter got into trouble before announcing his new factory and thereby making Mr. Adams' property practically worthless. He worked himself into such a state that he had a stroke.

Mr. Lamb, feeling sorry for Mr. Adams, offered to buy him out, and Mr. Adams was forced to agree. Now there was no income in the family. Mrs. Adams decided to take in boarders, and Alice finally made up her mind to enroll in Frincke's Business College. She had lost more than Arthur Russell; she had lost her daydreams as well.

ALICE IN WONDERLAND

Type of work: Imaginative tale
Author: Lewis Carroll (Charles Lutwidge Dodgson, 1832-1898)
Type of plot: Fantasy

Time of plot: Victorian England
Locale: The dream world of an imaginative child
First published: 1865

Principal characters:
ALICE
THE WHITE RABBIT
THE DUCHESS
THE QUEEN OF HEARTS

Critique:

Adults will view this book as a gentle satire on education, politics, literature, and Victorian life in general, seen through the eyes of Alice, a child who is the product of a confusing environment. The book is written with charming simplicity. There are poetic parodies on Wordsworth and Southey which are amusing to the point of hilarity, as well as ingenuous observations on the status of powerful female rulers. Through all her puzzling adventures in the dream world, Alice remains the very essence of little girlhood. Children read this book with delight, finding in Alice a heroine who aptly represents their own thoughts and feelings about growing up.

The Story:

Alice was quietly reading over her sister's shoulder when she saw a White Rabbit dash across the lawn and disappear into its hole. She jumped up to rush after him and found herself falling down the rabbit hole. At the bottom she saw the White Rabbit hurrying along a corridor ahead of her and murmuring that he would be late. He disappeared around a corner, leaving Alice standing in front of several locked doors.

On a glass table she found a tiny golden key which unlocked a little door hidden behind a curtain. The door opened upon a lovely miniature garden, but she could not get through the doorway because it was too small. She sadly replaced the key on the table. A little bottle mysteriously appeared. Alice drank the contents and immediately began to grow smaller, so much so that she could no longer reach the key on the table. Next, she ate a piece of cake she found nearby and soon she began to grow to such enormous size that she could only squint through the door. In despair, she began to weep tears as big as raindrops. As she sat there crying, the White Rabbit appeared, bewailing the fact that the Duchess would be angry if he kept her waiting.

The White Rabbit dropped his fan and gloves. Alice picked them up and as she did so she began to grow smaller. Again she rushed to the garden door, but she found it shut and the golden key once more on the table out of reach.

Then she fell into a pool of her own tears! Splashing along, she encountered a mouse who had stumbled into the pool. Alice tactlessly began a conversation about her cat Dinah, and the mouse became speechless with terror. Soon the pool of tears was filled with living creatures, birds and animals of all kinds. An old Dodo suggested that they run a Caucus Race to get dry. Having asked what a Caucus Race was, Alice was told that the best way to explain it was to do it. Whereupon the animals ran themselves quite breathless and finally became dry.

Afterwards, the mouse told a "Tail" to match its own appendage. Alice was asked to tell something, but the only thing she could think of was her cat Dinah. Frightened, the other creatures went away, and Alice was left alone.

The White Rabbit appeared once more, this time hunting for his gloves and fan. Catching sight of Alice, he sent her to his home to get him a fresh pair of gloves and another fan. In the Rabbit's house she found the fan and gloves and also took a drink from a bottle. Instantly she grew to a giant size, and was forced to put her leg up the chimney and her elbow out of the window in order to keep from being squeezed to death.

She managed to eat a little cake and shrink herself again. As soon as she was small enough to get through the door, she ran into a nearby wood where she found a caterpillar sitting on a mushroom. The caterpillar was very rude to Alice and he scornfully asked her to prove her worth by reciting "You Are Old, Father William." Alice did so, but the words sounded very strange. Disgusted, he left her after giving her some valuable information about increasing or decreasing her size. She broke off pieces of the mushroom and found to her delight that by eating from the piece in her left hand she could become taller, and from the piece in her right hand, smaller.

She came to a little house among the trees. There a footman, who looked very much like a fish, presented to another footman, who closely remembled a frog, an invitation for the Duchess to play croquet with the Queen. The two amphibians bowed to each other with great formality, tangling their wigs together. Alice opened the door and found herself in the chaotic house of the Duchess. The cook was stirring a large pot of soup and pouring plenty of pepper into the mixture. Everyone was sneezing except the cook and a Cheshire cat which sat on the hearth grinning. The Duchess herself held a sneezing, squalling baby, and sang to it a blaring lullaby. Alice, in sympathy with the poor child, picked it up and carried it out into the fresh air, whereupon the baby turned slowly into a pig, squirmed out of her arms, and waddled into the forest.

Standing in bewilderment, Alice saw the grinning Cheshire cat sitting in a tree. He was able to appear and disappear at will, and after exercising his talents, he advised Alice to go to a tea party given by the Mad Hatter. The cat vanished, all but the grin. Finally that, too, disappeared, and Alice left for the party.

There Alice found she had to deal with the strangest people she had ever seen—a March Hare, a Mad Hatter, and a sleepy Dormouse. All were too lazy to set the table properly; dirty dishes were everywhere. The Dormouse fell asleep in its teacup; the Mad Hatter told Alice her hair needed cutting; the March Hare offered her wine and then told her there was none. They asked her foolish riddles that had no answers. Then, worse, they ignored her completely and carried on a ridiculous conversation among themselves. She escaped after the Dormouse fell asleep in the middle of a story he was telling.

Next she found herself in a garden of talking flowers. Just as the conversation was beginning, some gardeners appeared with paint brushes and began to splash red paint on a rose bush. Alice learned that the Queen had ordered a red bush to be placed in that spot, and the gardeners had made a mistake and planted a white one. Now they were busily and fearfully trying to cover their error before the Queen arrived. But the poor gardeners were not swift enough. The Queen caught them in the act, and the wretched gardeners were led off to be decapitated. Alice saved them by shoving them down into a large flower pot, out of sight of the dreadful Queen.

A croquet game began. The mallets were live flamingoes, and the balls were hedgehogs which thought nothing of uncurling themselves and running rapidly over the field. The Duchess cornered Alice and led her away to the seaside to introduce her to the Mock Turtle and the Gryphon.

While engaged in a Lobster Quadrille, they heard the news of a trial. A thief had stolen some tarts. Rushing to the courtroom where a trial by jury was already in session, Alice was called upon to act as a witness before the King and Queen of Hearts. But the excited child upset the jury box and spilled out all its occupants. After replacing all the animals in the box, Alice said she knew nothing of the matter. Her speech infuriated the Queen, who ordered that Alice's head be cut off. The whole court rushed at her, and Alice defiantly called them nothing but a pack of cards. She awoke from her dream as her sister brushed away some dead leaves blowing over her face.

AMELIA

Type of work: Novel
Author: Henry Fielding (1707-1754)
Type of plot: Domestic realism
Time of plot: 1740's
Locale: England
First published: 1751

Principal characters:
CAPTAIN BOOTH, a soldier
AMELIA, his wife
ELIZABETH HARRIS, her sister
SERGEANT ATKINSON, her foster brother
DR. HARRISON, Booth's benefactor
MISS MATTHEWS, a woman of the town
COLONEL JAMES, Booth's former officer

Critique:

As Fielding declared in his introduction to *The History of Amelia,* he satirized nobody in the novel. Amelia, the long-suffering wife of every generation, is charming and attractive. The foibles of her husband still ring true. Dr. Harrison is a man each reader would like to know. Some of the interest of the novel lies in Fielding's accurate presentation of prison life and the courts. Having been a magistrate for many years, he was able to present these scenes in a most modern and realistic way, for aside from presenting the virtuous character of Amelia, Fielding wanted his novel to interest people in prison and legal reform. Although the novel lacks the extravagant humor of his earlier novels, the plot presents many amusing characters and complex situations.

The Story:

One night the watchmen of Westminster arrested Captain William Booth, seizing him during his attempt to rescue a stranger who was being attacked by two ruffians. The footpads secured their own liberty by bribing the constables, but Booth, in spite of his protests, was hailed before an unjust magistrate. The story he told was a straightforward one, but because he was penniless and shabbily dressed the judge dismissed his tale and sentenced him to prison. Booth was desperate, for there was no one he knew in London to whom he could turn for aid. His plight was made worse by his reception at the prison. His fellow prisoners stripped him of his coat, and a pickpocket made off with his snuffbox.

While he was smarting from these indignities, a fashionably dressed young woman was brought through the gates. Flourishing a bag of gold in the face of her keepers, she demanded a private room in the prison. Her appearance and manner reminded Booth of an old friend of questionable background, a Miss Matthews whom he had not seen for several years. But when the woman passed him without a sign of recognition, he believed himself mistaken.

Shortly afterward a guard brought him a guinea in a small parcel, and with the money Booth was able to redeem his coat and snuffbox. The rest of the windfall he lost in a card game. Booth was penniless once more when a keeper came to conduct him to Miss Matthews, for the woman was indeed she. Seeing his wretched condition as he stood by the prison gate, she had sent him the mysterious guinea.

Reunited under these distressing circumstances, they proceeded to relate the stories of their experiences. Miss Matthews told how she had been committed to await sentence for a penknife attack on a soldier who had seduced her under false promises of marriage.

Booth, in turn, told this story. He had met a Miss Amelia Harris, a beautiful girl whose mother at first opposed her daughter's marriage to a penniless soldier. The young couple eloped but were later, through the efforts of Dr. Harrison, a wise and kindly curate, reconciled with Amelia's mother. Booth's regiment was ordered to Gibraltar, shortly before a child was to be born to Amelia. He left reluctantly, leaving Amelia in the care of her mother and her older sister, Elizabeth. At Gibraltar Booth earned the good opinion of his officers by his bravery. Wounded in one of the battles of the campaign, he was very ill, and Amelia, learning of his condition, left her child with her mother and sister and went to Gibraltar to nurse her sick husband. Then Amelia, in her turn, fell sick. Wishing to take her to a milder climate, Booth wrote to Mrs. Harris for money, but in reply received only a rude note from Elizabeth. He hoped to get the money from his army friend, Major James, but that gentleman was away at the time. Finally he borrowed the money from Sergeant Atkinson, his friend and Amelia's foster brother, and went with his wife to Montpelier. There the couple made friends with an amusing English officer named Colonel Bath and his sister.

Joy at the birth of a second child, a girl, was dampened by a letter from Dr. Harrison, who wrote to tell them that old Mrs. Harris was dead, and that she had left her property to Amelia's sister. The Booths returned home, to be greeted so rudely by Elizabeth that they withdrew from the house. But for the help of Dr. Harrison, they would have been destitute. Harrison set Booth up as a gentleman farmer and tried to help him make the best of his half-pay from the Army. But because of several small mistakes, Booth made enemies among the surrounding farmers. Dr. Harrison was traveling on the continent at the time and in his absence Booth was reduced almost to bankruptcy. He came to London to try his fortunes anew. He preceded Amelia, found modest lodgings, and wrote her where they were. It was at this point that another misfortune landed him in prison. At the end of Booth's story, Miss Matthews sympathized with his unfortunate situation, congratulated him on his wife and children, and paid the jailer to let Booth spend the next few nights with her in her cell.

Booth and Miss Matthews were shortly released from prison. The soldier wounded by Miss Matthews having completely recovered, charges against her were dropped. Miss Matthews also secured the release of Booth, and the two were preparing to leave prison when Amelia arrived. She had come up from the country to save him, and his release was a welcome surprise for the distressed wife. The Booths set themselves up in London. Shortly afterward, Booth met his former officer, now Colonel James, who in the meanwhile had married Miss Bath and grown quickly tired of her. Mrs. James and Amelia resumed their old friendship. Booth, afraid that Miss Matthews would inform Amelia of their affair in prison, told Colonel James of his difficulties and fears. The colonel gave him a loan and told him not to worry. Colonel James was himself interested in Miss Matthews, but he was unable to help Booth by his intercession. Miss Matthews continued to send Booth reproachful and revealing letters which might at any time have been intercepted by Amelia.

While walking in the park one day,

the Booths met Sergeant Atkinson. He joined their household to help care for the children, and soon he started a half flirtation with a Mrs. Ellison, Booth's landlady.

Mrs. Ellison proved useful to the Booths, for a lord who came also to visit her advanced money to pay some of Booth's debts. Meanwhile Miss Matthews had spitefully turned Colonel James against Booth. Colonel Bath, hearing his brother-in-law's poor opinion of Booth, decided that Booth was neither an officer nor a gentleman, and challenged him to a duel. Colonel Bath believed in nothing so much as a code of honor, and when, in the duel, Booth had run him through, without serious injury, the colonel was so much impressed by Booth's gallantry that he forgave him and brought about a reconciliation between James and Booth.

During this time Mrs. Ellison had been trying to arrange an assignation between Amelia and the nobleman who had given Booth money to pay his gambling debts. Amelia was innocently misled by her false friends. But the nobleman's plan to meet Amelia secretly at a masquerade was thwarted by another neighbor, Mrs. Bennet. This woman, who had been a boarder in Mrs. Ellison's house, had also met the noble lord, had encountered him at a masquerade, and had drunk the drugged wine he provided. To prevent Amelia's ruin in the same manner, Mrs. Bennet came to warn her friend. Then she informed Amelia that she had recently married Sergeant Atkinson, whom Amelia had thought in love with Mrs. Ellison. But Amelia's joy at learning of both the plot, which she now planned to escape, and of the marriage, was marred by the news that Booth had again been put into prison for debt, this time on a warrant of their old friend Dr. Harrison.

Amelia soon discovered that Dr. Harrison had been misled by false rumors of Booth's extravagance, and had put him in jail in order to stop his rash spending of money. Learning the truth, Dr. Harrison had Booth released from prison.

On the night of the masquerade Amelia remained at home but sent Mrs. Atkinson dressed in her costume. At the dance Mrs. Atkinson was able to fool not only the lord but also Colonel James. The complications of the affair were many, almost every relationship being misunderstood. Booth fell in with an old friend and lost a large sum of money to him. Again he became worried about being put in jail. Then he became involved in a duel with Colonel James over Miss Matthews, whom Booth had visited only at her insistence. Before the duel could take place, Booth was again imprisoned for debt, and Dr. Harrison was forced to clear his name with Colonel James. Finally James forgave Booth, and Miss Matthews promised never to bother him again.

Called by chance into a strange house to hear the deathbed confession of a man named Robinson, Dr. Harrison learned that Robinson had at one time been a clerk to a lawyer named Murphy who had made Mrs. Harris' will. He learned also that the will which had left Amelia penniless was a false one prepared by Elizabeth and Murphy. Dr. Harrison had Robinson write a confession so that Amelia could get the money that was rightfully hers. The lawyer Murphy was quickly brought to trial and convicted of forgery.

Booth's troubles were now almost at an end. With Dr. Harrison he and Amelia returned home to confront Elizabeth with their knowledge of her scheme. Elizabeth fled to France, where Amelia, relenting, sent her an annual allowance. Booth's adventures had finally taught him not to gamble, and with his faithful Amelia he settled down to a quiet and prosperous life blessed with many children and the invaluable friendship of Dr. Harrison and the Atkinsons.

THE AMERICAN

Type of work: Novel
Author: Henry James (1843-1916)
Type of plot: Psychological realism
Time of plot: Mid-nineteenth century
Locale: Paris, France
First published: 1877

Principal characters:

CHRISTOPHER NEWMAN, an American
MR. TRISTRAM, a friend
MRS. TRISTRAM, his wife
M. NIOCHE, a shopkeeper
MLLE. NIOCHE, his daughter
MADAME DE BELLEGARDE, a French aristocrat
CLAIRE DE CINTRÉ, Madame de Bellegarde's daughter
MARQUIS DE BELLEGARDE, Madame de Bellegarde's older son
VALENTIN DE BELLEGARDE, Madame de Bellegarde's younger son
MRS. BREAD, Madame de Bellegarde's servant

Critique:

In this novel Henry James shows the interreaction of two cultures, the American and the French. His primary interest is not in the action; his aim is to analyze the various psychological situations created by the events of the plot. The author scrutinizes the inner lives of his characters and writes about them in an urbane and polished style uniquely his own.

The Story:

In 1868 Christopher Newman, a young American millionaire, withdrew from business and sailed for Paris. He wanted to loaf, to develop his aesthetic sense, and to find a wife for himself. One day, as he wandered in the Louvre, he made the acquaintance of Mlle. Nioche, a young copyist. She introduced him to her father, an unsuccessful shopkeeper. Newman bought a picture from Mlle. Nioche and contracted to take French lessons from her father.

Later, through the French wife of an American friend named Tristram, he met Claire de Cintré, a young widow, daughter of an English mother and a French father. As a young girl, Claire had been married to Monsieur de Cintré, an evil old man. He had soon died, leaving Claire with a distaste for marriage. In spite of her attitude, Newman saw in her the woman he wished for his wife. But an American businessman was not the person to associate with French aristocracy. On his first call, Newman was kept from entering Claire's house by her elder brother, the Marquis de Bellegarde.

True to his promise, M. Nioche appeared one morning to give Newman his first lesson in French. Newman enjoyed talking to the old man. He learned that Mlle. Nioche dominated her father and that he lived in fear that she would leave him and become the mistress of some rich man. M. Nioche assured Newman that he would shoot her if she did. Newman took pity on the old man and promised him enough money for Mlle. Nioche's dowry if she would paint some more copies for him.

Newman left Paris and traveled through Europe during the summer. When he returned to Paris in the autumn he learned that the Tristrams had been helpful; the Bellegardes were willing to receive him. One evening Claire's younger brother, Valentin, called on Newman and the two men found their opposite points of view a basis for friendship. Valentin envied Newman's liberty to do as he pleased; Newman wished himself acceptable to the society in which the Bellegardes moved. After they had become good friends, Newman told Valentin that he wished to marry his sister and asked Valentin to plead his cause. Warning Newman that his social position was against him, Valentin promised to help the American as much as he could.

Newman confessed his wish to Claire, and asked Madame de Bellegarde, Claire's mother, and the marquis for permission to be her suitor. The permission was given, grudgingly. The Bellegardes needed money in the family.

Newman went to the Louvre to see how Mlle. Nioche was progressing with her copying. There he met Valentin and introduced him to the young lady.

Mrs. Bread, an old English servant of the Bellegardes, assured Newman that he was making progress with his suit. He asked Claire to marry him and she accepted. Meanwhile, Valentin had challenged another man to a duel in a quarrel over Mlle. Nioche. Valentin left for Switzerland with his seconds. The next morning Newman went to see Claire. Mrs. Bread met him at the door and said that Claire was leaving town. Newman demanded an explanation. He was told that the Bellegardes could not allow a commercial person in the family. When he arrived home, he found a telegram from Valentin stating that he had been badly wounded and asking Newman to come at once to Switzerland.

With this double burden of sorrow, Newman arrived in Switzerland and found Valentin near death. Valentin guessed what his family had done and told Newman that Mrs. Bread knew a family secret. If he could get the secret from her, he could make them return Claire to him. Valentin died the next morning.

Newman attended the funeral. Three days later he again called on Claire, who told him that she intended to enter a convent. Newman begged her not to take this step. Desperate, he called on the Bellegardes again and told them that he would uncover their secret. Newman arranged to see Mrs. Bread that night. She told him that Madame de Bellegarde had killed her invalid husband because he had opposed Claire's marriage to M. de Cintré. The death had been judged natural, but Mrs. Bread had in her possession a document which proved that Madame de Bellegarde had murdered her husband. She gave this paper to Newman.

Mrs. Bread left the employ of the Bellegardes and came to keep house for Newman. She told him that Claire had gone to the convent and refused to see anyone, even her own family. The next Sunday Newman went to mass at the convent. After the service he met the Bellegardes walking in the park and showed them a copy of the paper Mrs. Bread had given him.

The next day the marquis called on Newman and offered to pay for the document. Newman refused to sell. He offered, however, to accept Claire in exchange for it. The marquis refused.

Newman found he could not bring himself to reveal the Bellegardes' secret. On the advice of the Tristrams he traveled through the English countryside and in a melancholy mood went to some of the places he had planned to visit on his honeymoon. Then he went to America. Restless, he returned to Paris and learned from Mrs. Tristram that Claire had become a nun.

The next time he went to see Mrs. Tristram, he dropped the secret document on the glowing logs in her fireplace and told her that to expose the Bellegardes now seemed a useless and empty gesture. He intended to leave Paris forever. Mrs. Tristram told him that he probably had not frightened the Bellegardes with his threat, because they knew that they could count on his good nature never to reveal their secret. Newman instinctively looked toward the fireplace. The paper had burned to ashes.

AN AMERICAN TRAGEDY

Type of work: Novel
Author: Theodore Dreiser (1871-1945)
Type of plot: Social criticism
Time of plot: Early twentieth century
Locale: Kansas City, Chicago, and Lycurgus, New York
First published: 1925

Principal characters:
CLYDE GRIFFITHS
ROBERTA ALDEN, his mistress
SAMUEL GRIFFITHS, Clyde's wealthy uncle
SONDRA FINCHLEY, society girl whom Clyde loves

Critique:

An American Tragedy is probably Dreiser's best novel. The title itself is, of course, significant. Dreiser believed that Clyde's downfall was due to the American economic system and he presents a strong indictment against that system. If Clyde had had the privileges of wealth and social position, he would never have been tempted to a moral decision and his consequent ruin. The novel is a powerful document on the theme of social inequality and lack of privilege.

The Story:

When Clyde Griffiths was still a child, his religious-minded parents took him and his brothers and sisters around the streets of various cities, where they prayed and sang in public. The family was always very poor, but the fundamentalist faith of the Griffiths was their hope and mainstay throughout the storms and troubles of life.

Young Clyde was never religious, however, and he always felt ashamed of the existence his parents were living. As soon as he was old enough to make decisions for himself, he decided to go his own way. At sixteen he got a job as a bellboy in a Kansas City hotel. There the salary and the tips he received astonished him. For the first time in his life he had money in his pocket, and he could dress well and enjoy himself. Then a tragedy overwhelmed the family. Clyde's sister ran away, supposedly to be married. Her elopement was a great blow to the parents, but Clyde himself did not brood over the matter. Life was too pleasant for him; more and more he enjoyed the luxuries which his job provided. He made friends with the other bellhops and joined them in parties that centered around liquor and women. Clyde soon became familiar with drink and brothels.

One day he discovered that his sister was back in town. The man with whom she had run away had deserted her, and she was penniless and pregnant. Knowing his sister needed money, Clyde gave his mother a few dollars for her. He promised to give her more; instead he bought an expensive coat for a girl in the hope that she would yield herself to him. One night he and his friends went on a party in a car that did not belong to them. Coming back from their outing, they ran over a little girl. In their attempt to escape, they wrecked the car. Clyde fled to Chicago.

In Chicago he got work at the Union League Club, where he eventually met his wealthy uncle, Samuel Griffiths. The uncle, who owned a factory in Lycurgus, New York, took a fancy to Clyde and offered him work in the factory. Clyde went to Lycurgus. There his cousin, Gilbert, resented this cousin from the Middle West. The whole family, with the exception of his uncle, considered

Clyde beneath them socially, and would not accept him into their circle. Clyde was given a job at the very bottom of the business, but his uncle soon made him a supervisor.

In the meantime Sondra Finchley, who disliked Gilbert, began to invite Clyde to parties she and her friends often gave. Her main purpose was to annoy Gilbert. Clyde's growing popularity forced the Griffiths to receive him socially, much to Gilbert's disgust.

In the course of his work at the factory Clyde met Roberta Alden, with whom he soon fell in love. Since it was forbidden for a supervisor to mix socially with an employee, they had to meet secretly. Clyde attempted to persuade Roberta to give herself to him, but the girl refused. At last, rather than lose him, she consented and became his mistress.

At the same time Clyde was becoming fascinated by Sondra. He came to love her and hoped to marry her, and thus acquire the wealth and social position for which he yearned. Gradually he began breaking dates with Roberta in order to be with Sondra every moment that she could spare him. Roberta began to be suspicious and eventually found out the truth.

By that time she was pregnant. Clyde went to drug stores for medicine that did not work. He attempted to find a doctor of questionable reputation. Roberta went to see one physician who refused to perform an operation. Clyde and Roberta were both becoming desperate, and Clyde saw his possible marriage to the girl as a dismal ending to all his hopes for a bright future. He told himself that he did not love Roberta, that it was Sondra whom he wished to marry. Roberta asked him to marry her for the sake of her child, saying she would go away afterward, if he wished, so that he could be free of her. Clyde would not agree to her proposal and grew more irritable and worried.

One day he read in the newspaper an item about the accidental drowning of a couple who had gone boating. Slowly a plan began to form in his mind. He told Roberta he would marry her and persuaded her to accompany him to an isolated lake resort. There, as though accidentally, he lunged toward her. She was hit by his camera and fell into the water. Clyde escaped, confident that her drowning would look like an accident, even though he had planned it all carefully.

But he had been clumsy. Letters that he and Roberta had written were found, and when her condition became known he was arrested. His uncle obtained an attorney for him. At his trial, the defense built up an elaborate case in his favor. But in spite of his lawyer's efforts, he was found guilty and sentenced to be electrocuted. His mother came to see him and urged him to save his soul. A clergyman finally succeeded in getting Clyde to write a statement—a declaration that he repented of his sins. It is doubtful whether he did. He died in the electric chair, a young man tempted by his desire for luxury and wealth.

AND QUIET FLOWS THE DON

Type of work: Novel
Author: Mikhail Sholokhov (1905-)
Type of plot: Historical chronicle
Time of plot: 1913-1918
Locale: Tartask, Russia
First published: 1928

Principal characters:
GREGOR MELEKHOV, a Cossack
PIOTRA, Gregor's brother

Natalia, Gregor's wife
Aksinia Astakhova, Gregor's mistress
Bunchuk, a revolutionary leader

Critique:

Inasmuch as this novel has been so frequently mentioned by the Russians as proof that great art can be produced under their form of government, the book deserves careful consideration. The Russians are quite right in being proud of Sholokhov. *And Quiet Flows the Don* is a good book, free of any propaganda and standing on its own merit as a novel. The book is doubly successful, both as historical narrative and as an interesting story of people living during a difficult period in history.

The Story:

The Melekhov family lived in the small village of Tartask, in the Don basin of Tsarist Russia. Gregor, the oldest son, had a love affair with Aksinia, wife of his neighbor, Stepan Astakhova. Stepan was away serving a term in the army. In an effort to make his son settle down, Gregor's father arranged a marriage with Natalia Korshunov. Because Gregor never loved Natalia, their relationship was a cold one. Soon Gregor went openly to Aksinia and the affair became the village scandal.

When he heard the gossip, Gregor's father whipped him. Humiliated and angry, Gregor left home. With Aksinia he became the servant of the Listnitsky family, well-to-do landowners who lived outside the village of Tartask. When Aksinia bore him a daughter, Gregor's father relented enough to pay a visit before Gregor left for the army.

In the meantime, Gregor's wife, Natalia, tried to commit suicide because Gregor did not return her love. She went back to her own home, but the Melekhovs asked her to come to them. She was glad to do so. When Gregor returned to Aksinia, on his first leave from the army, he discovered that she had been unfaithful to him with Eugene Listnitsky, the young officer-son of his employer. Aksinia's daughter had died, and Gregor felt nothing but anger at his mistress. He fought with Eugene and whipped Aksinia as well. Then he returned to his own home, and there he and Natalia became reconciled. During the time he served in the army, Natalia bore him twins, a boy and a girl.

In the war against the Central Powers, Gregor distinguished himself. Wounded, he was awarded the Cross of St. George and so he became the first Chevalier in the village. While in the army, he met his brother, Piotra, and his enemy, Stepan Astakhova, who had sworn to kill him. Nevertheless, on one occasion he saved Stepan's life during an attack.

Discontent was growing among the soldiers. Bolshevik agitators began to talk against the government and against a continuance of the war. In Eugene Listnitsky's company an officer named Bunchuk was the chief agitator. He deserted before Listnitsky could hand him over to the authorities.

Then the provisional government of Kerensky was overthrown and a Soviet Socialist Republic was established. Civil war broke out. The Cossacks, proud of their free heritage, were strongly nationalistic and wanted an autonomous government for the Don region. Many of them joined the counter-revolutionists, under such men as Kornilov. Many returned to their homes in the Don basin. Gregor, joining the revolutionary forces, was made an officer of the Red Army.

Meanwhile the revolutionary troops in Rostov were under attack. Bunchuk, the machine gunner, was prominent in the battle and in the administration of the local revolutionary government. He fell in love with a woman machine gunner,

Anna Poodko, who was killed during an attack. The counter-revolutionary troops were successful, and the Red Army troops had to retreat.

Gregor returned to the village and resumed the ordinary life he had led before the war. Soon news came that revolutionary troops were advancing on the village. When his neighbors prepared to flee, Gregor refused to do so. Stories of burning, looting, and rape spread through the countryside. A counter-revolutionary officer attempted to organize the villagers against the approaching enemy troops. He named Gregor as commander, but the nomination was turned down in anger because all the village knew that Gregor sympathized with the Reds, had fought with them. Instead, Gregor's brother Piotra was named commander.

The village forces marched out, Gregor going with them. When they arrived at their destination, they found that the revolutionary troops had already been defeated and that the leaders had been captured. Gregor asked what would happen to them. He was told they would be shot. Then Gregor came face to face with Podtielkov, his old revolutionary leader. When the latter accused him of being a traitor and opportunist, all of Gregor's suppressed feelings of disgust and nationalism burst forth. He reminded Podtielkov that he and other Red leaders had ordered plenty of executions, and he charged that Podtielkov had sold out the Don Cossacks. The revolutionists died prophesying that the revolution would live. Gregor went back to his Cossack village.

ANNA KARÉNINA

Type of work: Novel
Author: Count Leo Tolstoy (1828-1910)
Type of plot: Social criticism
Time of plot: Nineteenth century
Locale: Russia
First published: 1875-1877

Principal characters:
Anna Karénina
Alexei Karénin, her husband
Count Vronsky, her lover
Stepan Oblonsky, her brother
Kitty Shtcherbatsky, Stepan's sister-in-law
Konstantine Levin, in love with Kitty

Critique:

Anna Karénina, one of Tolstoy's masterpieces, is distinguished by its realism. The novel contains two plots: the tragedy of Madame Karénina, in love with a man who is not her husband, and the story of Konstantine Levin, a sensitive man whose personal philosophy is Tolstoy's reason for writing about him. The story of Anna is an absorbing one and true; the person of Levin reflects Tolstoy's own ideas about the Russian society in which he lived. Thus the book is a closely knit plot of a woman bound in the fetters of the Russian social system and a philosophy of life which attempts to untangle the maze of incongruities present in this society.

The Story:

Anna Karénina, the sister of Stepan Oblonsky, came to Moscow in an attempt to patch up a quarrel between her brother and his wife, Dolly. There she met the handsome young Count Vronsky, who was rumored to be in love with Dolly's younger sister, Kitty.

But Konstantine Levin, of an old Muscovite family, was also in love with

Kitty, and his visit to Moscow coincided with Anna's. Kitty refused Levin, but to her chagrin she received no proposal from the count. Indeed, Vronsky had no intention of proposing to Kitty. His heart went out to Anna the first time he laid eyes on her, and when Anna returned to her home in St. Petersburg, he followed her.

Soon they began to be seen together at soirees and at the theater, apparently unaware of gossip which circulated about them. Karénin, Anna's husband, became concerned. A coldly ambitious and dispassionate man, he felt that his social position was at stake. One night he discussed these rumors with Anna and pointed out the danger of her flirtation, as he called it. He forbade her to entertain Vronsky at home, and cautioned her to be more careful. He was not jealous of his wife, only worried over the social consequences of her behavior. He reminded her of her duty to her young son, Seryozha. Anna said she would obey him, and there the matter rested.

But Anna was unable to conceal her true feelings when Vronsky was injured in a race-track accident. Karénin upbraided her for her indiscreet behavior in public. He considered a duel, separation, divorce, but rejected all of these courses. When he finally decided to keep Anna under his roof, he reflected that he was acting in accordance with the laws of religion. Anna continued to meet Vronsky in secret.

Levin had returned to his country estate after Kitty had refused him, and there he busied himself in problems of agriculture and peasant labor. One day he went into the fields and worked with a scythe along with the serfs. He felt that he was beginning to understand the old primitive philosophy of their lives. He planned new developments, among them a cooperative enterprise system. When he heard that Kitty was not married after all, and that she had been ill but was soon returning to Moscow, he resolved to seek her hand once more. Secretly, he knew she loved him. His pride, as well as hers, had kept them apart.

Accordingly, Levin made the journey to Moscow with new hope that soon Kitty would be his wife.

Against her husband's orders, Anna Karénina sent for Vronsky and told him that she was with child. Aware of his responsibilities to Anna, he begged her to petition Karénin for a divorce so that she would be free to marry him. Karénin informed her coldly that he would consider the child his and accept it so that the world should never know his wife's disgrace, but he refused to think of going through shameful divorce proceedings. Karénin reduced Anna to submission by warning her that he would take Seryozha away if she persisted in making a fool of herself.

The strained family relationship continued unbroken. One night Karénin had planned to go out, and Anna persuaded Vronsky to come to the house. As he was leaving, Karénin met Vronsky on the front steps. Enraged, Karénin told Anna that he had decided to get a divorce and that he would keep Seryozha in his custody. But divorce proceedings were so intricate, the scandal so great, the whole aspect of the step so disgusting to Karénin that he could not bring himself to go through with the process. As Anna's confinement drew near, he was still undecided. After winning an important political seat, he became even more unwilling to risk his public reputation.

At the birth of her child, Anna became deathly ill. Vronsky, overcome with guilt, attempted suicide, but failed. Karénin was reduced to a state of such confusion that he determined to grant his wife any request, since he thought her to be on her deathbed. The sight of Vronsky seemed to be the only thing that restored her. After many months of illness, she went with her lover and baby daughter to Italy, where they lived under strained circumstances. Meanwhile, Levin proposed once more to Kitty, and after a flurry of preparations they were married.

Anna Karénina and Vronsky returned to Russia and went to live on his estate. It was now impossible for Anna to return home. Although Karénin had not gone through with divorce proceedings, he considered himself separated from Anna and was everywhere thought to be a man of fine loyalty and unswerving honor, unjustly imposed upon by an unfaithful wife. Sometimes Anna stole into town to see Seryozha but her fear of being discovered there by her husband cut these visits short. After each visit she returned bitter and sad. She became more and more demanding toward Vronsky, with the result that he spent less time with her. She took little interest in her child. Before long she convinced herself that Vronsky was in love with another woman. One day she could not stay alone in the house. She found herself at the railway station. She bought a ticket. As she stood on the platform gazing at the tracks below, the thunder of an approaching train roared in her ears. Suddenly she remembered a man run over in the Moscow railroad station on the day she and Vronsky met. Carefully measuring the distance, she threw herself in front of the approaching train.

After her death, Vronsky joined the army. He had changed from a handsome, cheerful man to one who welcomed death; his only reason for living had been Anna.

For Levin and Kitty life became an increasing round of daily work and everyday routine, which they shared with each other. Levin knew at last the responsibility wealth imposed upon him in his dealings with the peasants. Kitty helped him to share his responsibility. Although there were many questions he could never answer satisfactorily to himself, he was nevertheless aware of the satisfying beauty of life, its toil, leisure, pain, and happiness.

ANTHONY ADVERSE

Type of work: Novel
Author: Hervey Allen (1889-1949)
Type of plot: Picaresque romance
Time of plot: Late eighteenth and early nineteenth centuries
Locale: Western Europe, Africa, North America
First published: 1933

Principal characters:

Anthony Adverse
Don Luis, Marquis da Vincitata, husband of Anthony's mother
Maria, Anthony's mother
Mr. Bonnyfeather, Anthony's grandfather
Faith Paleologus, Mr. Bonnyfeather's housekeeper
Angela Guiseppe, Anthony's mistress
Florence Udney, Anthony's first wife
Dolores de la Fuente, Anthony's second wife
Vincent Nolte, Anthony's friend, a banker

Critique:

Anthony Adverse is the story of a soldier of fortune whose ramblings carry him over a large part of Europe, to Africa, and to North America. The book contains a wealth of incident, as well as mention of historical personages. The characters, however, are subordinate to the plot. The novel is also interesting because its various sections represent different types of romantic fiction.

The Story:

The pretty young Marquise Maria da Vincitata, daughter of a Scottish merchant of Leghorn, fell in love with young Denis Moore within a year of her marriage and met with him secretly in France while her husband was taking a cure for his gout. Don Luis, the arrogant Marquis da Vincitata, discovering the intrigue, spirited his wife away and killed her gallant, luckless lover when he started out in pursuit. Maria's baby was born high up in the Alps. After his wife had died in childbirth, Don Luis took the child to Leghorn, where he stealthily deposited the infant at the Convent of Jesus the Child. The only tokens of its parentage were a cape and a statue of the Madonna which had belonged to Maria.

The boy, christened Anthony by the nuns, lived at the convent until he was ten. Then he was delivered to a prominent merchant of the town, Mr. Bonnyfeather, to become his apprentice.

Bonnyfeather and his housekeeper had no trouble recognizing the cape and the doll as possessions of the merchant's daughter, Maria. Although Anthony was given the surname Adverse and was not told of his relationship to his benefactor, he was carefully educated with the tacit understanding that he would one day inherit the flourishing Bonnyfeather business.

Anthony matured early. Seduced by the housekeeper, Faith Paleologus, he also had a brief affair with the cook's daughter, Angela. He was attracted, too, by the English consul's daughter, Florence Udney, but was not encouraged by her mother, who was unaware that Anthony had any expectations.

Anticipating the eventual arrival of Napoleon's army in Leghorn, Mr. Bonnyfeather quietly liquidated his business, sent his money abroad, and made plans to retire. He arranged passage for his grandson on the American ship *Wampanoag,* under Captain Jorham. Anthony was to sail to Cuba to collect some money on a long-overdue account.

The *Wampanoag* stopped first at Genoa. There Anthony visited Father Xavier, a Jesuit, who had been his guardian at the convent. Mr. Bonnyfeather had given the priest the right to decide whether the time had come to tell Anthony he was the merchant's heir. It was from the priest's lips that Anthony learned of his origin and prospects.

When the *Wampanoag* reached Havana Anthony discovered that his creditor, Gallego, was in Africa as a slave trader. With the aid of the captain-general, Don Luis de la Casas, a plan was devised whereby Anthony would sail to Africa as a government agent. There he would impound a cargo of Gallego's slaves, bring them to Cuba for sale, and split the proceeds with the captain-general, thus satisfying the Bonnyfeather debt. Strongly attracted by Don Luis' young relation, Dolores de la Fuente, the young man finally agreed to stay in Africa and to ship several additional cargoes of slaves, for the enrichment of the captain-general and the increase of his own hopes that he might one day marry Dolores.

The trip aboard the *Ariostatica* was a trying one. Father François, a monk who was being shipped to Africa because he had tried to give aid and comfort to the slaves, fell ill of yellow fever and nearly died. Anthony, forced to rule the crew and its captain with an iron hand, was able to put down a mutiny as the ship sailed up the Rio Pongo to the Gallego establishment. There he learned that Gallego had died a few months before, leaving his factor, Ferdinando, in charge.

Anthony took over the trade station and for three years shipped cargoes of human freight to Cuba to be sold there. To the sorrow of Father François, he took the half-breed Neleta, Ferdinando's sister, as his mistress. But he was not able completely to reconcile himself to trading in human bodies.

While Anthony was absent from the trading station, Father François was captured by a native witch doctor, Mnombibi, and crucified. Upon his return, Anthony found the priest pinioned to his own cross. With the knowledge that Mr. Bonnyfeather was dead, and that Captain Bittern of the *Unicorn* was waiting in the Rio Pongo to bear him back to Leghorn, Anthony decided to leave the trading station. He left Neleta behind.

Don Luis, Marquis da Vincitata, arrived in Leghorn at the same time. They were both there on business, the marquis to close up the Casa Bonnyfeather, of which he was landlord, and Anthony to receive the merchant's will from Vincent Nolte, a banker with whom he had been friendly in his youth. Vincent suggested that Anthony take advantage of an offer made by M. Ouvrard, a French financier who was planning to supply the bankrupt Spanish government with French food and money, in return for silver from Mexican mines. Anthony was to take charge of the shipments, which would arrive at New Orleans from Vera Cruz, and to reinvest profitably as much of the money as he could. The rest was to be shipped to Florence Udney's husband, David Parish, in Philadelphia, and from there on to Europe.

Traveling to Paris to make arrangements, Vincent and Anthony were waylaid in the Alps by Don Luis, who tried to force their coach over a cliff. His plans were thwarted, however, and his own carriage and coachman plunged into the deep gorge. At the time Don Luis was traveling with Faith Paleologus, whom he had made his mistress. The two had dismounted to watch the destruction of Anthony and his friend. After their plot failed, they were left to descend the mountain on foot.

In Paris Anthony met Angela for the first time in many years. She had borne him a son, and had become a famous singer and the mistress of Napoleon. She refused to marry Anthony and follow him to America, but she did give him his son. At her entreaty, Anthony left the child with Vincent's childless cousin, Anna.

Anthony's affairs prospered in New Orleans. He was able to invest the silver profitably, to form a bank, and to build a handsome plantation for himself. When David Parish died of heart failure, Anthony married Florence. Their daughter, Maria, was three, when the plantation house caught fire one night while Anthony was away. His wife and daughter were burned to death.

Burdened by his sorrow, Anthony started west. Captured by a tribe of Indians, he escaped, only to fall into the hands of soldiers from Santa Fé. There he was brought before the governor, Don Luis, and sentenced to go to Mexico City in a prison train. That same day Don Luis had a stroke and died. Faith, his wife by that time, prepared to return to Spain.

Anthony spent two years in the Hospital of St. Lazaro before Dolores, widow of a wealthy landowner, found him and arranged for his freedom. Later they were married and went to live in the village of San Luz. Dolores bore him two children. All went well until an ax slipped one day and caught Anthony in the groin while he was felling a tree. He bled to death before he was found.

Many years later, long after the village had been deserted by Dolores and her people, a group of migrants on their way to Santa Fé came to its site. The little Madonna, which Anthony had carried with him through life, still stood in a chapel in the ruins of San Luz. Mary Jorham, the young niece of a Captain Jorham, found the image, but she was not allowed to keep it because her parents thought it a heathen idol. Instead, it served as a fine target for a shooting match. It was splintered into a thousand pieces.

ANTIGONE

Type of work: Drama
Author: Sophocles (495?-406 B.C.)
Type of plot: Classical tragedy
Time of plot: Ancient Greece
Locale: The city of Thebes
First presented: 440 B.C.

Principal characters:
CREON, tyrant of Thebes
ANTIGONE, daughter of Oedipus
ISMENE, her sister
HAEMON, son of Creon
TIRESIAS, a prophet

Critique:

Although the main problem of this play would be unimportant today, the discussions of the responsibilities of a ruler are as pertinent now as in ancient Greece. The characters of the play move to their tragic ends with highly dramatic speeches, while the moral and philosophical problems of the plot are displayed through the chorus and soliloquies. When first presented, the play was so successful with Athenian audiences that Sophocles was made a general in the war against Samos. Recent presentations of the play have been well received by both audience and critic.

The Story:

Polynices and Eteocles, sons of the cursed family of King Oedipus, led two armies against each other before the gates of Thebes, and both brothers were killed in single combat with each other. Creon, their uncle, and now the tyrant ruler of the city, ordered that Eteocles be given full funeral rites, but that Polynices, who had attacked the city, be left unburied and unmourned. Anyone who broke this decree would be punished with death.

Antigone and Ismene, the sisters of Polynices and Eteocles, discussed this order, and with grief for the unburied brother tearing at her heart, Antigone asked Ismene to aid her in giving him burial. When Ismene refused to help in so dangerous a task, Antigone went defiantly to bury Polynices.

Shortly afterward, Creon learned from a sentry that the body had been buried. Angrily he ordered the sentry to find the perpetrator of the deed. The sentry returned to the grave and uncovered the body. During a dust storm Antigone came to look at the grave and, finding it open, filled the air with lamentation. Her cries attracted the attention of the guard, who captured her and took her to Creon.

Questioned by Creon, she said that to bury a man was to obey the laws of the gods, even if it were against the laws of a man. Her reply angered Creon. Antigone must die. Ismene tried to soften Creon's heart toward her sister by reminding him that Antigone was engaged to his son, Haemon. But Creon remained firm.

Haemon incurred his father's anger by arguments that Creon should soften his cruel decree because of popular sympathy for Antigone. Creon said that he cared nothing for the ideas of the town, and Haemon called his answer foolish. As a punishment, Creon ordered that Antigone be killed before Haemon's eyes. Haemon fled with threats of revenge. Creon ordered that Antigone be walled up in a cave outside Thebes and left there to die for her crime against his law.

When Antigone was led out of the city, the people of Thebes followed her, lamenting her fate. She was thrust into the cave. All this while, Polynices' body lay unburied outside the walls. The prophet Tiresias warned Creon that the gods had not been pleased with his action, and that the body should be buried. He foretold that before long Haemon would die if his father did not bury Polynices and rescue Antigone from the cave.

Creon, realizing that Tiresias' prophesies had never proved false, hurried to avert the fate the prophet had foretold. Quickly he ordered a tomb prepared for Polynices, and he himself set off to release Antigone. But the will of the gods could not be changed so easily. When he reached the cave, he heard his son's voice within, crying out in grief. Creon entered and saw that Antigone had hanged herself with a rope made from her own dress. Haemon, sword in hand, rushed at his father as if to attack him, but instead he spat on the old man. He then fell on his sword and killed himself in sorrow over Antigone's death. The news of these events quickly traveled back to the city, and Creon's wife, hearing of so many misfortunes, died by her own hand.

On returning to Thebes with the body of his son, Creon learned of his wife's death. Seeing that his life could no longer have meaning, he had himself led out of the city into exile. He was, himself, the final victim of his harsh tyranny.

THE APOSTLE

Type of work: Novel
Author: Sholem Asch (1880-)
Type of plot: Religious chronicle
Time of plot: Shortly after the Crucifixion
Locale: The Roman Empire
First published: 1943

Principal characters:
SAUL OF TARSHISH, afterwards known as Paul
JOSEPH BAR NABA OF CYPRUS, Saul's friend, an early convert
REB ISTEPHAN, a famous Jewish preacher
SIMON BAR JONAH, called Peter
REB JACOB, Joseph's son

Critique:

The Apostle is a faithful attempt to chronicle the life of the two great apostles, Peter and Paul. Adhering carefully to the history of the period, the author has presented a sympathetic portrait of the struggles of the early Christians. His knowledge of contemporary events gives the reader a vivid picture of the life of the period shortly after the Crucifixion.

The Story:

It was seven weeks after the crucifixion of Yeshua of Nazareth by Pontius Pilate. All the poor of Jerusalem, who had found in Jeshua their Messiah, had gone into hiding; but the word was spreading. Little by little the story was told, of Yeshua who had come back after his death, of the Messiah who had appeared to his disciples. The matter was hotly argued on all sides. The pious Jews could not believe in a Messiah who had been killed; the Messianists devoutly affirmed their faith.

Saul of Tarshish and Joseph bar Naba came upon a street preacher, a rustic Galilean, who told with great conviction of Yeshua's return after he had been entombed. Cries of belief and of repugnance interrupted his talk. Saul himself spoke with great bitterness against this Messiah, for he had no patience with the gentle Yeshua who was hanged.

The agitation rapidly spread. One of the most vigorous upholders of Yeshua was Reb Istephan. He had a gift for moving men's souls, and more and more Jews became persuaded. Joseph bar Naba himself had known Yeshua in his lifetime, and when Joseph heard Reb Istephan he was convinced. Joseph became a Messianist. This conversion disgusted Saul, and in sorrow and bitterness he turned away from his friend Joseph.

Then a dramatic incident took place. Simon, the first of Yeshua's disciples, healed Nehemiah the cripple in the name of the Nazarene. Many were much impressed by the cure, but others resented Simon's use of the Messiah's name. As a result his enemies had their way, and Simon was imprisoned by the High Priest to await trial. Then another miracle happened! Simon and his follower Jochanan had been securely locked in a dungeon, but in the morning they were walking the streets again. It was said that they had passed directly through the stone walls — with the help of Yeshua.

The resentment against the wild Galileans grew among the rulers, while the humble folk followed Simon with trust. The High Priest again brought Simon to trial; but Simon spoke so well in defense of his doctrine that he was freed. And now the tumult increased. The ignorant folk, seeing Simon released, concluded that there was official sanction for the new cult; hence more joined the followers of Yeshua.

Saul was greatly incensed. He believed that the Messiah was yet to come, that the disciples were corrupting Jerusalem. He went to the High Priest and secured appointment as official spy. In his new job Saul tracked down the humble Messianists and sentenced them to the lash. Growing in power, Saul the Zealot finally took Reb Istephan prisoner for preaching the new faith. With grim pleasure Saul led the way to the stoning pit and watched Istephan sink beneath the flung rocks. As he died, the preacher murmured a prayer for the forgiveness of his tormentors. Saul was vaguely troubled.

Then the Messianists were much heartened. Reb Jacob ben Joseph, Yeshua's younger brother, came to Jerusalem to head the humble cult, and Saul could do little against this pious and strict Jew. By chance the High Priest heard of more Messianists in Damascus. Saul volunteered to investigate and hurried to his new field. But on the way a vision appeared to him and said, "Saul, Saul, why dost thou persecute me?" Saul then recognized Yeshua for his Lord and as he was commanded he went on to Damascus, although he was still blinded by the heavenly apparition. A follower of the new religion baptized him and restored his sight. The penitent Saul hurried away from the haunts of man. In all he waited seven years for his mission.

Finally as he prayed in his mother's house, the call came. Joseph bar Naba asked Saul to go with him to Antioch to strengthen the congregation there. At last Saul was on the way to bring the word of the Messiah to others. He left for Antioch with Joseph and the Greek Titus, Saul's first convert.

Now Simon had founded the church at Antioch among the Greeks. The perplexing question was, could a devout Jew even eat with the gentiles, let alone accept them into the church? In Jerusalem Jacob held firmly to the law of the Torah: salvation was only for the circumcised. Simon vacillated. In Jerusalem he followed Jacob; among the Greeks he accepted gentiles fully. Joseph had been sent by the elders of Jerusalem to Antioch to apply the stricter rule to the growing Messianic church.

Saul at first met with much suspicion. The Messianists remembered too well Saul the Zealot who had persecuted them. But little by little the apostle won them over. Yeshua appeared to Saul several times, and he was much strengthened in the faith. At last Saul found his true mission in the conviction that he was divinely appointed to bring the word of Yeshua to the gentiles. He worked wonders at Antioch and built a strong church there, but his acceptance of gentiles cost him Joseph's friendship. As a symbol of his new mission Saul became Paul and began his years of missionary work.

To Corinth, to Ephesus, to Cyprus—to all the gentiles went Paul. Everywhere he founded a church, sometimes small but always zealous. With him much of the time went Lukas, the Greek physician. Lukas was an able minister and a scholar who was writing the life of Yeshua.

The devout Jews in Jerusalem were greatly troubled by this strange preacher who accepted the gentiles. Finally they brought him up for trial. Paul escaped only by standing on his rights as a Roman citizen. As such he could demand a trial before Caesar himself. Paul went to Rome as a captive, but he rejoiced, for he knew the real test of Christianity would be in Rome. Already Simon was there, preaching to the orthodox Jews.

The evil Nero made Paul wait in prison for two years without a hearing, and even then only the intervention of Seneca freed the apostle. For a short time Simon and Paul worked together, one among the Jews and the other among the gentiles. They converted many, and the lowly fervently embraced the promise of salvation.

To give himself an outlet for his fancied talents as an architect, Nero burned Rome and planned to rebuild a beautiful city. But the crime was too much even for the Romans. To divert suspicion from himself, Nero blamed the Christians. He arrested thousands of them, and on the appointed day opened the royal carnage. Jews and Christians hour after hour were gored by oxen, torn by tigers, chewed by crocodiles. At the end of the third day many Romans could no longer bear the sight, but still Nero sat on. It was so strange: the Christians died well, and with their last breath they forgave their persecutors.

Simon, only a Jew, was crucified afterward; Paul, born a Roman citizen, was beheaded. With them to the execution went Gabelus the gladiator, who had accepted Christianity. But the deaths of Simon and Paul were in reality the beginning. The martyrdom of the early Christians was the foundation stone of the Christian church.

THE APPLE OF THE EYE

Type of work: Novel
Author: Glenway Wescott (1901-)
Type of plot: Regional romance
Time of plot: Twentieth century
Locale: Rural Wisconsin
First published: 1924

Principal characters:
Hannah Madoc, a primitive
Jule Bier, Hannah's lover
Selma, Jule's wife
Rosalia, Jule's and Selma's daughter
Mike, Rosalia's lover
Dan Strane, Rosalia's cousin

Critique:

This novel tells of the background and youth of Dan Strane in rural Wisconsin, and the story of Hannah Madoc reveals the set of values against which the author measures his characters. Jule himself believed in Hannah's goodness, but he was too weak to break away from his own social ties to marry the girl he really loved. The emphasis upon sex in the story is typical of a young boy's wonder at the difference between religious doctrines and the natural functions of man's true personality.

The Story:

When her drunken father came home one night and swung at her with a broom handle, patient, hard-working Hannah Madoc pushed him off the porch in self-defense. He died a few days later, leaving his daughter orphaned and penniless, and Hannah went to work in Mrs. Boyle's store. There she waited on customers during the day and served the men liquor in the evening.

One night Jule Bier saw her behind the store counter. Ever since the death of his wife and the piling up of debts, old Mr. Bier had struggled to make enough money from his farm to give Jule a chance in life. Cold and calculating, the elder Bier had sent Jule to work as a hired hand on the neighborhood farms. Jule began to court Hannah during long walks at night; he took her to neighborhood dances, and they went for rides in his buggy. Hannah soon tired of the attentions of other men. When Mr. Boyle attempted to make love to her, she quit her job to go to work on a farm near Jule's home.

Old Mr. Bier sent Jule to court Selma Duncan, the oldest daughter of a wealthy farmer. Blindly obeying his father, Jule proposed to the girl and was accepted. Then he realized what he had done. Facing Hannah, he was bewildered by her grief, only half aware of his own.

Leaving the neighborhood of Sheboygan, Hannah went to Fond du Lac, where she became a prostitute and lost in a few years her beauty and vitality. At last Jule went to Fond du Lac to bring his former sweetheart back to her home. Hannah ended her years in bitter sterility, answering a call for help from a neighbor, nursing a sick calf, or taking care of someone's children when their mother became ill. She died, prematurely aged and broken, as the result of a fall.

Jule and Selma had one daughter, Rosalia. Selma's sister, Mrs. Strane, had a son, Dan, who was a boy of fourteen when Rosalia was in her early twenties. Mike, a young man with a keen zest for life, worked on Jule's farm. Because his mother was so tight-lipped and because she tried to instill in him a chastity of ignorance and abstinence, Dan had developed an adolescent feeling of frustration and curiosity. He longed to know what sex was, how it affected people, but at the same time he was overcome by an inbred feeling of shame. It was Mike who cleared the way for Dan after they became friends. Mike, who believed that life should be full of experience both physical and mental, made life's processes a wonderful thing, not obscene and dirty, as Dan's mother had led the boy to believe. Breaking away from the mother who had been his idol, Dan replaced her with his new friend, Mike. Mike, in love with Rosalia, shared his deeper feelings with his young friend. Dan had grown up.

Mike loved Rosalia and he desired her, but at first Rosalia resisted his love-making. One afternoon he seduced her. Rosalia's subsequent tears frightened him, but soon she learned to hide her terror of love. She told Mike that they ought to get married to redeem their sin, but Mike's suggestion that Selma might not approve quieted the frightened girl. Mike was not certain that he wanted to marry Rosalia. When Jule quietly told Mike that he had noticed Rosalia's and Mike's love and that he would not object to the marriage if Mike wanted it, Mike felt trapped. He quit his job with Jule and left the Bier farm.

Dan was inconsolable. Having looked upon his cousin and Mike as perfect lovers, he could not understand why Mike should leave. Rosalia brooded, her sense of guilt increasing after Mike's departure. Although she hid her feelings from her parents, Dan knew enough of her affair with Mike to be curious about Rosalia's feelings. But he could learn nothing from her. Rosalia herself was not as calm as she appeared to be. The punishment for love was a child. She felt a surge of emotion within her, and it seemed permanently a part of her. She concluded that she must be with child. It was inevitable; she had sinned and this was to be her harvest. Deserted by her lover-husband, she could not bear to think of her shame. She told some neighbors that she was going to run off to meet Mike, and one night during a snowstorm she left her home.

No one had heard from Rosalia or Mike. Dan and Selma waited through the winter. Once, when Dan went to visit his aunt in Milwaukee, he looked for Mike, but he did not find him. In the spring a neighbor brought the news to Jule that Rosalia's body had been found in the swamp. Fearing that the news would kill the already ailing Selma, Jule made the neighbor and Dan promised to tell no one about Rosalia's body. They buried the girl in the swamp.

All summer Dan worked on his father's farm. He had begun to hate the memory of Mike ever since he had helped Jule bury the body of Rosalia. A hundred times over Dan killed Mike in effigy. In the fall Selma died, and Dan went to live with Jule. The kindly, patient man, who had seen so much of life, won Dan's affections.

Jule wanted Dan to tell him all he knew about Rosalia and Mike. The wonderful understanding of the old man impressed his nephew. Mike had done the best he knew how, Jule maintained. In turn, he told Dan about Hannah Madoc. If Hannah had been Rosalia's mother instead of Selma, Jule said, Rosalia would not have been destroyed through fear. Hannah knew how to handle life. Religious people were always trying to make life better than it was, but life should be accepted at its simple, natural values. Dan accepted his uncle's views.

Dan's father had never understood his son. Having completed his high school education, Dan was becoming restless. His father, realizing that Dan was not cut out for farm work, suggested that he go to college. With high hopes that he would find more answers to his questioning of life, Dan prepared to enter the state university.

ARNE

Type of work: Novel
Author: Björnstjerne Björnson (1832-1910)
Type of plot: Pastoral romance
Time of plot: Early nineteenth century
Locale: Norway
First published: 1858

Principal characters:
NILS, a tailor
MARGIT, his wife
ARNE, their son
BAARD BÖEN, Nils' enemy
ELI, Baard's daughter

Critique:

Arne is best described as a pastoral story, but the discerning reader will find it also an allegory of the life of Norse peasants. He will read of their devotion to personal honor, their ability to translate memory into action of word or deed. He will read of a man as wicked as Nils and feel that Nils was in a sense a martyr to evil spirits. He will leave the story of Arne with a sense of completion, for the restless and tragic searching of Nils' life is in a sense fulfilled when the daughter of his enemy marries his son.

The Story:

Arne was born on the hillside farm of Kampen. He was the son of Margit, betrayed one night when she attended a dance. The man said to be the child's father was Nils, the tailor, who in his free time fiddled for country dances. Arne's grandmother was a frugal widow who saved what she earned so that her daughter and her grandson might not want for lack of a man to look after them. In the meantime the fiddler-tailor, Nils, drank more and tailored less so that his business fell off.

By the time Arne was six he knew a local song written about the wild behavior of his father. His grandmother insisted that Arne be taught his origin. Not long afterward Nils suffered a broken back in a barn fight with Baard Böen. About the same time the old grandmother, who felt that her days were numbered, warned her daughter against wasting the money saved for her use.

When the grandmother died, Arne's mother brought Nils home to be nursed. The next spring Margit and Nils were married and Nils recovered enough to help with some of the farm work. At first Nils was gloomy and morose because he was no longer able to join the fiddlers and the dancers at weddings, and he drank heavily. As his strength returned he began to fiddle once more. Arne went along to merry-makings to carry his fiddle case. By this companionship Nils weaned Arne away from Margit by degrees. Occasionally the boy was remorseful, but his father's hold grew stronger as time passed.

Finally, during a scene of drunken violence, Nils died. Arne and his mother took the blame for his death partly upon themselves. Arne became aloof from the villagers; he tended his cattle and wrote a few songs.

He became more and more shy. At a wedding, interpreting one of the folk tales as referring to him, he told a wild story, part truth, part fancy, about his father's death. Then he rushed from the house. He had had too much brandy, and while he lay in the barn recovering, his mother told him she had once found Nils there in the same condition—on the occasion of Arne's christening.

Arne began to take a new interest in old legends and ballads. As he listened to stories told by an old man of the village, he found himself making up tales of his own. Sometimes he wandered alone in the forest and sang songs as they came into his head.

From a distance he observed Eli Böen and her good friend, the pastor's daughter. He began to sing love songs. Arne did some carpentering and his work took him into the village more often. That winter Böen sent for Arne to do some carpentering. Arne's mother was disturbed because it had been Böen who had caused Nils to break his back years before. At first Böen's wife refused to speak to Arne. Eli Böen, who was attentive to him in the beginning, later ignored him. One day Arne brought word that the pastor's daughter was leaving the village. Eli fainted when she heard the news, for the two girls had been close friends.

Baard Böen tried to explain to Arne what had happened years before between Nils and himself. But he did not manage to make himself clear, and after many years he himself was not sure of the cause of their long-standing quarrel.

Eli's mother became friendly with Arne at last and she asked him to sing for Eli, who seemed to be recovering from her illness. While he sang, he and Eli felt a deep intimacy spring up between them. The next day, his work completed, Arne took his tools and left. From that time on he thought more and more about Baard Böen's daughter.

Arne had a friend, Kristian, who had gone to America. Now Kristian began to write urging Arne to join him, but Margit hid the letters as they came. Finally she went to the pastor for advice. He felt that Arne must be allowed to live his own life as he saw fit.

The farm was beautiful when spring came. On one of his rambles Arne came upon Eli and thought her more beautiful than he had ever seen her before. Margit took heart from his fondness for the girl. One midsummer evening she discovered Eli in the village and asked her to go for a walk. She took the girl to her homestead and showed her about, from the stables to the chest in which Arne kept the many gifts that were to belong to his bride, among them a hymn book with a silver clasp. On the clasp Eli saw her own name engraved.

Presently Arne appeared and later he walked with Eli back to her own home. They realized now that they were completely in love.

Shortly afterward they were married. Children stood by the church bearing bits of cake. Baard Böen, remembering his long-ago feud with Arne's father, marveled at this wedding of his daughter and the son of his old enemy.

ARROWSMITH

Type of work: Novel
Author: Sinclair Lewis (1885-1951)
Type of plot: Social criticism
Time of plot: Early twentieth century
Locale: United States and West Indies
First published: 1924

Principal characters:

MARTIN ARROWSMITH, a medical scientist
LEORA, his wife
DR. MAX GOTTLIEB, a scientist
GUSTAVE SONDELIUS, a scientist
TERRY WICKETT, Martin's friend
JOYCE LANYON, a young widow
DR. ALMUS PICKERBAUGH, a public health reformer

Critique:

Arrowsmith is one of the novels in which Sinclair Lewis has attempted to point out the insufficiencies and complacencies of American life. What *Babbitt* did for the American businessman, *Arrowsmith* was intended to do for the American doctor. The thesis of *Arrowsmith* would appear to be that the only decent way for a physician to serve mankind is by research. Using Martin Arrowsmith as his example, Lewis has tried to show that the progressive doctor is not appreciated in private practice; that the field of public health is politically corrupt; that the fashionable clinic is often a commercial enterprise; that even the best institutes of research are interested chiefly in publicity.

The Story:

Martin Arrowsmith was the descendant of pioneers in the Ohio wilderness. He grew up in the raw red-brick town of Elk Mills, in the state of Winnemac, a restless, lonely boy who spent his odd hours in old Doc Vickerson's office. The village practitioner was a widower, with no family of his own, and he encouraged Martin's interest in medicine.

At twenty-one Martin was a junior preparing for medical school at the University of Winnemac. Continuing on at the medical school, he was most interested in bacteriology and research and the courses of Professor Max Gottlieb, a noted German scientist. After joining a medical fraternity, he made many lifelong friends. He also fell in love with Madeline Fox, a shallow, pseudo-intellectual who was taking graduate work in English. To the young man from the prairie, Madeline represented culture. They became engaged.

Martin spent many nights in research at the laboratory, and he became the favorite of Professor Gottlieb. One day Gottlieb sent him to the Zenith City Hospital on an errand. There Martin met an attractive nurse named Leora Tozer. He soon became so interested in Leora that he became engaged to her as well. Thus young Martin Arrowsmith found himself engaged to two girls at the same time. Unable to choose between them, he asked both Leora and Madeline to lunch with him. When he explained his predicament, Madeline stalked angrily from the dining-room and out of his life. Leora, amused, remained. Martin felt that his life had really begun.

Through his friendship with Gottlieb, Martin became a student instructor in bacteriology. Leora was called home to North Dakota. Because of Leora's absence, trouble with the dean, and too much whiskey, Martin left school during the Christmas holidays. Traveling like a tramp, he arrived at Wheatsylvania, the town where Leora lived. In spite of the warnings of the dull Tozer family, Martin and Leora were married. Martin went back to Winnemac alone. A married man now, he gave up his work in bacteriology and turned his attention to general study. Later Leora joined him in Mohalis.

Upon completion of his internship, Martin set up an office in Wheatsylvania with money supplied by his wife's family. In the small prairie town Martin made friends of the wrong sort, according to the Tozers, but he was fairly successful as a physician. He also made a number of enemies. Meanwhile Martin and Leora moved from the Tozer house to their own home. When Leora's first child was born dead, they knew that they could never have another child.

Martin had again become interested in research. When he heard that the Swedish scientist, Gustave Sondelius, was to lecture in Minneapolis, Martin went to hear his lecture. In that way Martin became interested in public health as a means of controlling disease. Back in Wheatsylvania, still under the influence of Sondelius, he became acting head of the Department of Public Health. Because Martin, in his official capacity, found a highly respected seamstress to be a chronic carrier of typhoid and sent her to the county home for isolation, he became generally unpopular. He welcomed the opportunity to join Dr. Almus Pickerbaugh of Nautilus, Iowa, as the Assistant Director of Public Health, at a considerable increase in salary.

In Nautilus he found Dr. Pickerbaugh to be a public-spirited evangelist with little knowledge of medicine or interest in scientific control of disease. The director spent his time writing health slogans in doubtful poetic meter, lecturing to clubs, and campaigning for health by means of Better Babies Week, Banish the Booze Week, and Tougher Teeth Week. Martin was gradually drawn under the influence of the flashy, artificial methods used by his superior. Although he tried to devote some time to research, the young doctor found that his job took up all his time. While Dr. Pickerbaugh was campaigning for election to Congress, Martin investigated the most sanitary and efficient dairy of the town. He found that the dairy was spreading disease through a streptococcus infection in the udders of the cows. Against the advice of Dr. Pickerbaugh, Martin closed the dairy and made many enemies for himself. Despite his act, however, he was made Acting Director of Public Health when Dr. Pickerbaugh was elected to Congress.

In his new capacity, Martin hired a competent assistant in order to have more time for research in bacteriology. Largely because he fired a block of tenements infested with tuberculosis, Martin was asked to resign. For the next year he worked as staff pathologist of the fashionable Rouncefield Clinic in Chicago. Then publication of a scientific paper brought him again to the attention of his old friend and professor, Max Gottlieb, now located at the McGurk Institute in New York. Dr. Arrowsmith was glad to accept the position Gottlieb offered him.

At the McGurk Institute Martin devoted his whole time to research, with Gottlieb as his constant friend and adviser. He worked on staphylococcus germs, producing first a toxin, then an antitoxin. Under the influence of Gottlieb and Terry Wickett, his colleague at McGurk, Martin discovered the X Principle, a bacterial infection which might prove to be a cure for disease. Although Martin wanted to postpone publication of his discovery until he was absolutely certain of its value, the directors of the institute insisted that he make his results public at once. Before his paper was finished, however, it was learned that the same principle had already been discovered at the Pasteur Institute, where it was called a bacteriophage. After that disappointment, Martin began work on the possibility of preventing and curing bubonic plague with the phage, as the new antitoxin was called.

Meanwhile Gustave Sondelius had come to the McGurk Institute. He became so interested in Martin's work that he spent most of his time helping his young friend. When a plague broke out on St. Hubert, an island in the West Indies, Martin and Sondelius were asked to go there to help in the fight against the epidemic. Accompanied by Leora they sailed for the island of St. Hubert. Before leaving, Martin had promised Gottlieb that he would conduct his experiment deliberately by refusing to treat some of the plague cases with phage, so that the effects of the treatment could be tabulated.

The plague spread daily on the tropical island. Sondelius was stricken and he died. Martin was often away from his laboratory as he traveled between villages. During one of his trips Leora lighted a half-smoked cigarette she found on a table in his laboratory. The tobacco had been saturated with germs from an overturned test tube. Leora died of the plague before Martin's return.

Martin forgot to be the pure scientist. He gave the phage to all who asked for it. Although his assistant continued to take notes to carry on the research, Martin was no longer interested in the results. When the plague began to abate, he went back to New York. There, lonely and unhappy, he married Joyce Lanyon, a wealthy young widow whom he had met on St. Hubert. But the marriage was not a success. Joyce demanded more of his time than he was willing to take from research; he felt ill at ease among her rich and fashionable friends. When he was offered the assistant directorship of McGurk Institute, he refused the position. In spite of Joyce's protests, he went off to join his old friend, Terry Wickett, at a rural laboratory in Vermont, where they intended to experiment on a cure for pneumonia. At last, he believed, his work—his life—was really beginning.

AS YOU LIKE IT

Type of work: Drama
Author: William Shakespeare (1564-1616)
Type of plot: Pastoral romance
Time of plot: The Middle Ages

Locale: The Forest of Arden in medieval France
First presented: c. 1600

Principal characters:

THE BANISHED DUKE
FREDERICK, his brother and usurper of his dominions
OLIVER, older son of Sir Rowland de Boys
ORLANDO, younger son of Sir Rowland de Boys
ADAM, a servant to Oliver
TOUCHSTONE, a clown
ROSALIND, daughter of the banished duke
CELIA, daughter of Frederick

Critique:

Shakespeare took most of the plot of this play from a popular novel of the period, *Rosalynde,* by Thomas Lodge. What he added was dramatic characterization and wit. *As You Like It* is a comedy compounded of many elements, but the whole is set to some of Shakespeare's loveliest poetry. Kindliness, good fellowship, good-will—these are the elements of *As You Like It,* and Shakespeare shows how much they are worth.

The Story:

A long time ago the elder and lawful ruler of a French province had been deposed by his younger brother, Frederick. The old duke, driven from his dominions, fled with several faithful followers to the Forest of Arden. There he lived a happy life, free from the cares of the court and able to devote himself at last to learning the lessons nature had to teach. His daughter Rosalind, however, remained at court as a companion to her cousin Celia, the usurping Duke Frederick's daughter. The two girls were inseparable, and nothing her father said or did could make Celia part from her dearest friend.

One day Duke Frederick commanded the two girls to attend a wrestling match between the duke's champion, Charles, and a young man named Orlando, the special object of Duke Frederick's hatred. Orlando was the son of Sir Rowland de Boys, who in his lifetime had been one of the banished duke's most loyal supporters. When Sir Rowland died, he had charged his oldest son, Oliver, with the task of looking after his younger brother's education, but Oliver had neglected his father's charge. The moment Rosalind laid eyes on Orlando she fell in love with him, and he with her. She tried to dissuade him from an unequal contest with a champion so much more powerful than he, but the more she pleaded the more determined Orlando was to distinguish himself in his lady's eyes. In the end he completely conquered his antagonist, and was rewarded for his prowess by a chain from Rosalind's own neck.

When Duke Frederick discovered his niece's interest in Sir Rowland's son, he banished Rosalind immediately from the court. His daughter Celia announced her intention of following her cousin. As a consequence, Rosalind disguised herself as a boy and set out for the Forest of Arden, and Celia and the faithful Touchstone, the false duke's jester, went with her. In the meantime, Orlando also found it necessary to flee because of his brother's harsh treatment. He was accompanied by his faithful servant, Adam, an old man who willingly turned over his life savings of five hundred crowns for the privilege of following his young master.

Orlando and Adam also set out for the Forest of Arden, but before they had traveled very far they were both weary and hungry. While Adam rested in the shade of some trees, Orlando wandered into that part of the forest where the old duke was, and came upon the outlaws at their meal. Desperate from hunger, Orlando rushed upon the duke with a drawn sword and demanded food. The duke immediately offered to share the hospitality of his table, and Orlando blushed with shame over his rude manner. Moreover, he would not touch a mouthful until Adam had been fed. When the old duke found that Orlando was the son of his friend, Sir Rowland de Boys, he took Orlando and Adam under his protection and made them members of his band of foresters.

In the meantime, Rosalind and Celia also arrived in the Forest of Arden, where they bought a flock of sheep and proceeded to live the life of shepherds. Rosalind passed as Ganymede, Celia, as a sister, Aliena. In this adventure they encountered some real Arcadians—Silvius, a shepherd, and Phebe, a dainty shepherdess with whom Silvius was in love. But the moment Phebe laid eyes on the disguised Rosalind she fell in love with the supposed young shepherd and would have nothing further to do with Silvius. As Ganymede, Rosalind also met Orlando in the forest, and twitted him on his practice of writing verses in praise of Rosalind and hanging them on the trees. Touchstone, in the forest, displayed the same willfulness and whimsicality he showed at court, even to his love for Audrey, a country wench whose sole appeal was her unloveliness.

One morning, as Orlando was on his way to visit Ganymede, he saw a man lying asleep under an oak tree. A snake was coiled about the sleeper's neck, and a hungry lioness crouched nearby ready to spring. He recognized the man as his own brother, Oliver, and for a moment Orlando was tempted to leave him to his fate. But he drew his sword and killed the snake and the lioness. In the encounter he himself was wounded by the lioness. Because Orlando had saved his life, Oliver was duly repentant, and the two brothers were joyfully reunited.

His wound having bled profusely, Orlando was too weak to visit Ganymede, and he sent Oliver instead with a bloody handkerchief as proof of his wounded condition. When Ganymede saw the handkerchief the supposed shepherd promptly fainted. The disguised Celia was so impressed by Oliver's concern for his brother that she fell in love with him, and they made plans to be married on the following day. Orlando was so overwhelmed by this news that he was a little envious. But when Ganymede came to call upon Orlando, the young shepherd promised to produce the lady Rosalind the next day. Meanwhile Phebe came to renew her ardent declaration of love for Ganymede, who promised on the morrow to unravel the love tangle of everyone.

In the meantime, Duke Frederick, enraged at the flight of his daughter, Celia, had set out at the head of an expedition to capture his elder brother and put him and all his followers to death. But on the outskirts of the Forest of Arden he met an old hermit who turned Frederick's head from his evil design. On the day following, as Ganymede had promised, with the banished duke and his followers as guests, Rosalind appeared as herself and explained how she and Celia had posed as the shepherd Ganymede and his sister Aliena. Four marriages took place with great rejoicing that day—Orlando to Rosalind, Oliver to Celia, Silvius to Phebe, and Touchstone to Audrey. Moreover, Frederick was so completely converted by the hermit that he resolved to take religious orders, and he straightway dispatched a messenger to the Forest of Arden to restore his brother's lands and those of all his followers.

AUCASSIN AND NICOLETTE

Type of work: Tale
Author: Unknown
Type of plot: Chivalric romance

Time of plot: Twelfth century
Locale: Provence, in France
First transcribed: Fourteenth-century manuscript

Principal characters:

COUNT GARIN DE BEAUCAIRE
AUCASSIN, his son
NICOLETTE, a slave girl

Critique:

Aucassin and Nicolette is considered by many scholars to be the masterpiece of the romances of chivalry. It is written in what is called the *chante-fable,* or song-story style—a prose tale containing verse passages which are sung by a minstrel. In it are found certain Oriental elements and much folklore.

The Story:

Count Bougars de Valence and Count Garin de Beaucaire were at war. Count Garin had one son, Aucassin, who was so smitten by love that he would neither accept the duties of knighthood nor participate in his father's quarrel, unless his father consented to his love for Nicolette. She was a slave girl, bought by a captain of the town from the Saracens and reared as his own daughter. Count Garin agreed to the marriage of Aucassin to any daughter of a king or count, but not to Nicolette. He went to see the captain and told him to send Nicolette away. The captain said that he would keep Nicolette out of sight, and so she was imprisoned in the high chamber of a palace with an old woman to keep her company.

Rumors sped through the countryside: Nicolette was lost; Nicolette had fled the country; Nicolette was slain by order of Count Garin.

Meanwhile the war between the two counts grew more fierce, but Aucassin still refused to fight. Father and son then made a covenant; Aucassin would go into the battle, and if God willed that he should survive, the count must agree to allow him two or three words and one kiss from Nicolette. Aucassin rode into the fray, but thoughts of Nicolette so distracted him that he was captured. Then Aucassin reflected that if he were slain, he would have no chance at all to see Nicolette. Therefore he laid his hand on his sword and began fighting with all his strength. He killed ten knights and wounded seven and took Count Bougars prisoner. But when Count Garin refused to keep the covenant, Aucassin released Count Bougars. Aucassin was cast into a dungeon.

Nicolette, knowing her companion to be asleep, escaped from her prison by a rope made of bed linen and went to the castle where Aucassin lay. While they exchanged lovers' vows, the guards came searching for Nicolette, as her escape had been discovered. But a friendly sentinel warned Nicolette of their coming. She leaped into the moat and, bruised and bleeding, climbed the outer wall.

Nicolette fell asleep in a thicket near the castle. Next day she saw some shepherds eating their lunch at a fountain nearby. She asked them to take a message to Aucassin, saying there was a beast in the forest and that he should have this beast and not part with one of its limbs for any price. Nicolette built herself a lodge within the forest and waited to prove her lover's faith.

Aucassin was taken from his prison and allowed to attend a great feast, but he had no joy in it. A friendly knight offered his horse to Aucassin and suggested that he ride into the forest. Aucassin was only too happy for a chance to get away. He met the shepherds by the fountain and heard what Nicolette had told them. Aucassin prayed God that he would find his quarry.

He rode in all haste through the thorny forest. Toward evening he began to weep because his search had been fruitless. He met a huge, ugly fellow, leaning on a terrible cudgel. Aucassin told him that he mourned for a white hound he had lost. The burly fellow scornfully replied that he had lost his best ox and had searched fruitlessly for three days without meat or drink. Aucassin gave the man twenty sols to pay for the beast. They parted and went their separate ways.

Aucassin found the lodge built by Nicolette and rested there that night. Nicolette heard Aucassin singing and came to him. The next day they mounted Aucassin's horse and journeyed until they came to the seas. Aucassin and Nicolette embarked upon a ship. A terrible storm carried them to Torelore. First Aucassin fought with the king of that strange land and then freed the king of his enemies. He and Nicolette lived happily in Torelore until Saracens besieged the castle and captured all within it. Aucassin was put in one ship and Nicolette in another. A storm scattered the ships, and that in which Aucassin was a prisoner drifted ashore at Beaucaire. He was now the Count of Beaucaire, his parents having died.

Nicolette was in the ship bearing the King of Carthage, who was her true father. They did not recognize each other because Nicolette had been but a child when she was stolen. But when she saw the walls of Carthage memory came back to her, and she revealed her identity in a song. The king gave her great honor and desired to marry her to a king of the Saracens, but Nicolette remained steadfast in her love for Aucassin. She disguised herself as a minstrel and took ship for Provence, where she traveled from castle to castle until she came to Beaucaire.

In the great hall Nicolette sang of her adventures. When Aucassin heard her song, he took her aside and inquired concerning Nicolette. He asked her to return to the land where Nicolette lived and bring her to him. Nicolette returned to the captain's house and there she clothed herself in rich robes and sent for Aucassin. And so at last they were wedded and lived long years with great joy.

BABBITT

Type of work: Novel
Author: Sinclair Lewis (1885-1951)
Type of plot: Social satire
Time of plot: The 1920's
Locale: Zenith, fictional Midwestern town
First published: 1922

Principal characters:
George F. Babbitt, a middle-aged real estate broker
Myra, his wife
Ted, their son
Verona, their daughter
Paul Reisling, Babbitt's friend
Zilla, Paul's shrewish wife

Critique:

Babbitt is a pungent satire about a man who typifies complacent mediocrity. George F. Babbitt, as standardized as his electric cigar lighter, revels in his own popularity, his ability to make money, his fine automobile, and his penny-pinching generosity. Babbitt worships gadgets. He praises prohibition and drinks bootleg whiskey, bullies his wife, ogles his manicurist. Though he is constantly discontented with the life he leads, he is thoroughly satisfied with

George F. Babbitt. Because his character is grounded in realism, Babbitt is one of the most convincing characters in American literature.

The Story:

George F. Babbitt was proud of his house in Floral Heights, one of the most respectable residential districts in Zenith. Its architecture was standardized; its interior decorations were standardized; its atmosphere was standardized. Therein lay its appeal for Babbitt.

He bustled about in a tile and chromium bathroom in his morning ritual of getting ready for another day. When he went down to breakfast, he was as grumpy as usual. It was expected of him. He read the dull real estate page of the newspaper to his patient wife, Myra. Then he commented on the weather, grumbled at his son and daughter, gulped his breakfast and started for his office.

Babbitt was a real estate broker who knew how to handle business with zip and zowie. Having closed a deal whereby he forced a poor businessman to buy a piece of property at twice its value, he pocketed part of the money and paid the rest to the man who had suggested the enterprise. Proud of his acumen, he picked up the telephone and called his best friend, Paul Reisling, to ask him to lunch.

Paul Reisling should have been a violinist, but he had gone into the tar-roofing business in order to support his shrewish wife, Zilla. Lately she had made it her practice to infuriate doormen, theater ushers, or taxicab drivers, and then ask Paul to come to her rescue and fight them like a man. Cringing with embarrassment, Paul would pretend he had not noticed the incident. Later, at home, Zilla would accuse him of being a coward and a weakling.

So sad did Paul's affairs seem to Babbitt that he suggested a vacation to Maine together—away from their wives. Paul was skeptical, but with magnificent assurance Babbitt promised to arrange the trip. Paul was humbly grateful.

Back in his office Babbitt fired a salesman who was too honest. When he got home, he and his wife decided to give a dinner party, with the arrangements taken bodily from the contents of a woman's magazine, and everything edible disguised to look like something else.

The party was a great success. Babbitt's friends were exactly like Babbitt. They all became drunk on prohibition-period gin, were disappointed when the cocktails ran out, stuffed themselves with food, and went home to nurse headaches.

The next day Babbitt and Myra paid a call on the Reislings. Zilla, trying to enlist their sympathy, berated her husband until he was goaded to fury. Babbitt finally told Zilla that she was a nagging, jealous, sour, and unwholesome wife, and he demanded that she allow Paul to go with him to Maine. Weeping in self-pity, Zilla consented. Myra sat calmly during the scene, but later she criticized Babbitt for bullying Paul's wife. Babbitt told her sharply to mind her own business.

On the train, Babbitt and Paul met numerous businessmen who loudly agreed with each other that what this country needed was a sound business administration. They deplored the price of motor cars, textiles, wheat, and oil; they swore that they had not an ounce of race-prejudice; they blamed Communism and socialism for labor unions which got out of hand. Paul soon tired of the discussion and went to bed. Babbitt stayed up late, smoking countless cigars, and telling countless stories.

Maine had a soothing effect upon Babbitt. He and Paul fished and hiked in the quiet of the north woods, and Babbitt began to realize that his life in Zenith was not all it should be. He promised himself a new outlook on life, a more simple, less hurried way of living.

Back in Zenith, Babbitt was asked to make a speech at a convention of real estate men which was to be held in Monarch, a nearby city. For days he tried to write a speech about the good life, as he now thought of it. But at the convention he scrapped his speech, declaimed loudly that real estate was a great profession, that Zenith was God's own country—the best little spot on earth—and to prove his statements quoted countless statistics on waterways, textile production, and lumber manufacture. The speech was such a success that Babbitt instantly won recognition as an orator.

Babbitt was made a precinct leader in the coming election. His duty was to speak to small labor groups about the inadvisability of voting for Seneca Doane, a liberal, in favor of a man named Prout, a solid businessman who represented the conservative element. Babbitt's speeches helped to defeat Doane. He was very proud of himself for having Vision and Ideals.

On a business trip to Chicago, Babbitt spied Paul Reisling sitting at dinner with a middle-aged but pretty woman. Later, in his hotel room, Babbitt indignantly demanded an explanation for Paul's lack of morality. Paul told Babbitt that he could no longer stand living with Zilla. Babbitt, feeling sorry for his friend, swore that he would keep her husband's secret from Zilla. Privately, Babbitt envied Paul's independence.

Babbitt was made vice-president of the Booster's Club. He was so proud of himself that he bragged loudly when his wife called him at the office. It was a long time before he understood what she was trying to tell him; Paul had shot his wife.

Babbitt's world collapsed about him. Though Zilla was still alive, Paul was in prison. Babbitt began to question his ideas about the power of the dollar. Paul was perhaps the only person Babbitt had ever loved. Myra had long since become a habit. The children were too full of new ideas to be close to their father. Babbitt felt suddenly alone. He began to criticize the minister's sermons. He no longer visited the Athletic Club, rarely ate lunch with any of his business acquaintances.

One day a pretty widow Mrs. Judique, came to his office. She became his mistress, and Babbitt joined her circle of Bohemian friends. He drank more than he had ever drunk in his life. He spent money wildly. Two of the most powerful men in town requested that he join the Good Citizen's League—or else. Babbitt refused to be bullied. For the first time in his life he was a human being. He actually made friends with his arch-enemy, Seneca Doane, and discovered that he liked his liberal ideas. He praised Doane publicly. Babbitt's new outlook on life appealed to his children, who at once began to respect him as they never had before. But Babbitt became unpopular among his business-boosting friends. When he again refused to join the Good Citizen's League, he was snubbed in the streets. Gradually Babbitt found that he had no real resources within himself. He was miserable.

When Myra became ill, Babbitt suddenly realized that he loved his colorless wife. He broke with Mrs. Judique. He joined the Good Citizen's League. By the time Myra was well again, there was no more active leader in the town of Zenith than George F. Babbitt. Once more he announced his distrust of Seneca Doane. He became the best Booster the club ever had. His last gesture of revolt was private approval of his son's elopement. Outwardly he conformed!

BAMBI

Type of work: Novel
Author: Felix Salten (1869-1945)
Type of plot: Pastoral allegory
Time of plot: Indefinite

Locale: The woods
First published: 1929

Principal characters:

BAMBI, a deer
THE OLD PRINCE, a stag who befriends Bambi
BAMBI'S MOTHER
FALINE, Bambi's cousin
GOBO, her brother

Critique:

Bambi is one of the few successful attempts to humanize animals in fiction. A fairy tale for children, but an allegory for adults, the book tells the story of a deer who learns that he must travel alone if he is to be strong and wise.

The Story:

Bambi was born in a thicket in the woods. While he was still an awkward young fawn, his mother taught him that he was a deer. He learned that deer did not kill other animals, nor did they fight over food as jaybirds did. He learned, too, that deer should venture from their hiding places to go to the meadow only in the early morning and late in the evening and that they must rely on the rustle of last year's dead leaves to give them warning of approaching danger. On his first visit to the meadow Bambi had a conversation with a grasshopper and a close look at a butterfly.

One evening Bambi and his mother went to the meadow again. On his second visit he was introduced to the hare, an animal with big, soft eyes and flopping ears. Bambi was not impressed. The little deer was considerably happier to meet his cousins, Gobo and Faline, and their mother, Ena. The two families were about to separate when two stags with spreading antlers on their heads came crashing out of the forest. Bambi's mother explained that the larger, statelier stag was Bambi's father.

As he grew older, Bambi learned the sounds and smells of the forest. Sometimes his mother went off by herself. Missing her one day, Bambi started out to look for her and came upon his cousins in the meadow. Faline suggested that both their mothers might have gone to visit their fathers. Bambi decided to continue his search by himself. As he stood at the edge of a clearing, he saw a creature he had never seen before. The creature raised what looked like a stick to its face. Terrified, Bambi ran back into the woods as fast as he could go. His mother appeared suddenly, and they both ran home to their glade. When they were safe again, Bambi learned that he had seen a Man.

On another day he began to call for his mother. Suddenly a great stag stood before him. Coldly he asked Bambi why he was crying, and told him that he ought to be ashamed of himself. Then he was gone. The little deer did not tell his mother of his experience, nor did he call her any more. Later he learned that he had met the Old Prince, the biggest and wisest stag in the forest. One morning Bambi was nibbling in the meadow with his mother when one of the stags came out of the forest. Suddenly there was a crash. The stag leaped into the air and then fell dead. Bambi raced away after his mother. All he wanted was to go deeper and deeper into the forest until he could feel free of that new danger. He met the Old Prince again. When Bambi asked him who Man was, the stag only replied that he would find out for himself. Then he disappeared.

The forest gradually changed as summer passed into fall and then into winter. Snow fell, and grass was not easy to find. All of the deer became more friendly during the cold months. They would gather to talk and sometimes even one of the stags would join them. Bambi grew to admire the stags. He was especially interested in Ronno, the stag who had escaped after a hunter had wounded him in the foot. The constant topic of conversation was Man, for none of the deer could understand the black stick he carried. They were all afraid of it.

As the winter dragged on, the slaughter of the weaker animals in the forest began. A crow killed one of the hare's children. A squirrel raced around with a neck wound a ferret had given him. A fox murdered a pheasant. A party of hunters came into the woods with their noise-making sticks and killed many of the animals. Bambi's mother and his cousin Gobo were not seen again.

That spring Bambi grew his first pair of antlers. With his mother gone, he had to spend most of his time alone. The other stags drove him away when he tried to approach them, and Faline was shy with him. Deciding one day that he was not afraid of any of the stags, Bambi charged at what he thought was one of his tormentors in a thicket. The stag stepped aside, and Bambi charged past him. It was the Old Prince. Embarrassed, the young deer began to tremble when his friend came close to him. With an admonishment to act bravely, the older deer disappeared into the woods.

A year later Bambi met Faline again, and once more they played as they had when they were very young. Then an older stag named Karus appeared and tried to block Bambi's way. When Bambi attacked him, Karus fled, as did the stag named Ronno, who had been pursuing Faline.

Faline and Bambi ventured into the meadow one day and there saw a stranger nibbling the grass. They were surprised when he came skipping up to them and asked if they did not know him. It was Gobo. Hunters had caught him and kept him until he was full-grown. Then he had been sent back to join his family in the forest. His mother was delighted to see him once more.

Gobo explained his absence to an admiring audience, and praised Man for his kindness. While he was talking, the Old Prince appeared and asked Gobo about the strip of horsehair around his neck. Gobo answered that it was a halter. The Old Prince remarked pitingly that he was a poor thing, and vanished.

Gobo would not live as the other deer in the forest did. He insisted on going about during the day and sleeping at night. He had no fear about eating in the meadow, completely exposed. One day, when a hunter was in the woods, Gobo declared that he would go talk to him. He walked out into the meadow. Suddenly there was a loud report, Gobo leaped into the air and then dashed into the thicket, where he fell mortally wounded.

Bambi was alone when he met the Old Prince for the first time since Gobo's death. They were walking together when they found a hare caught in a noose. Carefully the Old Prince managed to loosen the snare with his antlers. Then he showed Bambi how to test tree branches for a trap. Bambi realized for the first time that there was no time when Man was not in the woods.

One misty morning, as Bambi stood at the edge of the clearing, a hunter wounded him. He raced madly for the forest, and in its protection lay down to rest. Soon he heard a voice beside him, urging him to get up. It was the Old Prince. For an hour the veteran led Bambi through the woods, crossing and recrossing the place where he had lain down, showing him the herbs which would stop his bleeding and clear his head. He stayed with Bambi until the wound had healed.

Before he went off to die, the old stag showed Bambi a poacher who had been killed. He explained that man, like animals, must die. Bambi understood then that there is someone even more powerful than Man.

Walking through the forest one day, Bambi spied a brother and sister fawn crying for their mother. As the Old Prince had spoken to him so many years before, he asked them if they could not stay by themselves. Then, as his friend had done, he vanished into the forest.

BARCHESTER TOWERS

Type of work: Novel
Author: Anthony Trollope (1815-1882)
Type of plot: Social satire
Time of plot: Mid-nineteenth century
Locale: "Barchester," an English cathedral town
First published: 1857

Principal characters:

Bishop Proudie, Bishop of Barchester
Mrs. Proudie, his wife
The Reverend Obadiah Slope, his chaplain
The Reverend Septimus Harding, member of the cathedral chapter
Mrs. Eleanor Bold, his daughter
Dr. Grantly, Archdeacon of Barchester
Charlotte Stanhope, Mrs. Bold's friend
La Signora Madeline Vesey Neroni, née Stanhope, Charlotte's sister
Ethelbert Stanhope (Bertie), Charlotte's brother
Mr. Quiverful, Mrs. Proudie's candidate for warden of Hiram's Hospital
The Reverend Francis Arabin, dean of the cathedral

Critique:

This novel is the most famous of Trollope's Barchester chronicles. Its fine ironic tone and pleasantly complex situations make for interesting reading. No problems of social significance are given serious treatment, for the chief purpose is entertainment. The portraits of cathedral town characters are full and varied.

The Story:

At the death of Bishop Grantly of Barchester, there was much conjecture as to his successor. Bishop Grantly's son, the archdeacon, was ambitious for the position, but his hopes were deflated when Dr. Proudie was appointed to the diocese. Bishop Proudie's wife was of Low Church propensities. She was also a woman of extremely aggressive nature, who kept the bishop's chaplain, Obadiah Slope, in constant tow.

On the first Sunday of the new bishop's regime, Mr. Slope was the preacher in the cathedral. His sermon was concerned with the importance of simplicity in the church service and the consequent omission of chanting, intoning, and formal ritual. The cathedral chapter was aghast. For generations the services in the cathedral had been chanted; the chapter could see no reason for discontinuing the practice. In counsel it was decreed that Mr. Slope never be permitted to preach from the cathedral pulpit again.

The Reverend Septimus Harding, who had resigned because of conscientious scruples from his position as warden of Hiram's Hospital, now had several reasons to believe that he would be returned to his post, although at a smaller salary than that he had drawn before. But when Mr. Slope, actually Mrs. Proudie's mouthpiece, told him that he would be expected to conduct several services a week and also manage some Sunday Schools in connection with the asylum, Mr. Harding was perturbed. Such duties would make arduous a preferment heretofore very pleasant and leisurely.

Another change of policy was effected in the diocese when the bishop announced, through Mr. Slope, that absentee clergymen should return and help in the administration of the diocese. Dr. Vesey Stanhope had for years left his duties to his curates while he remained in Italy. Now he was forced to return, bringing with him an ailing wife and three grown children, spinster Charlotte, exotic Signora Madeline Vesey Stanhope Neroni, and ne'er-do-well Ethelbert. Signora Neroni, separated from her husband, was an invalid who passed her days lying on a couch. Bertie had studied art and had been at times a Christian, a Mohammedan, and a Jew. He had amassed some sizable debts.

The Proudies held a reception in the bishop's palace soon after their arrival. Signora Neroni, carried in with great ceremony, quite stole the show. She had a fascinating way with men and succeeded in almost devastating Mr. Slope. Mrs. Proudie disapproved and did her best to keep Mr. Slope and others away from the invalid.

When the living of St. Ewold's became vacant, Dr. Grantly made a trip to Oxford and saw to it that the Reverend Francis Arabin, a High Churchman, received the appointment. With Mrs. Proudie and Mr. Slope advocating Low Church practices, it was necessary to build up the strength of the High Church forces. Mr. Arabin was a bachelor of about forty. The question arose as to what he would do with the parsonage at St. Ewold's.

Mr. Harding's widowed daughter, Mrs. Eleanor Bold, had a good income and was the mother of a baby boy. Mr. Slope had his eye on her and attempted to interest Mrs. Bold in the work of the Sunday Schools. At the same time he asked Mr. Quiverful, of Puddingdale, to take over the duties of the hospital. Mr. Quiverful's fourteen children were reasons enough for his being grateful for the opportunity. But Mrs. Bold learned how her father felt over the extra duties imposed upon him, and she grew cold toward Mr. Slope. In the end, Mr. Harding decided that he simply could not, at his age, undertake the new duties. So Mr. Quiverful, a Low Churchman, was granted the preferment, much to Mrs. Proudie's satisfaction.

Mr. Slope was not the only man interested in Mrs. Bold. The Stanhope sisters, realizing that Bertie could never make a living for himself, decided that he should ask Mrs. Bold to be his wife.

Meanwhile Mr. Slope was losing favor with Mrs. Proudie. That he should throw himself at the feet of Signora Neroni was repulsive to Mrs. Proudie. That he should be interested in the daughter of Mr. Harding, who refused to comply with her wishes, was disgraceful.

The Thornes of Ullathorne were an old and affluent family. One day they gave a great party. Mrs. Bold, driving to Ullathorne with the Stanhopes, found herself in the same carriage with Mr. Slope, whom by this time she greatly disliked. Later that day, as she was walking with Mr. Slope, he suddenly put his arm around her and declared his love. She rushed away and told Charlotte Stanhope, who suggested that Bertie should speak to Mr. Slope about his irregularity. But the occasion for his speaking to Mr. Slope never arose. Bertie himself told Mrs. Bold that his sister Charlotte had urged him to marry Mrs. Bold for her money. Naturally insulted, Mrs. Bold was angered at the entire Stanhope family. That evening, when Dr. Stanhope learned what had happened, he insisted that Bertie go away and earn his own living or starve. Bertie left several days later.

The Dean of Barchester was beyond recovery after a stroke of apoplexy. It was understood that Dr. Grantly would not accept the deanship. Mr. Slope wanted the position but Mrs. Proudie would not consider him as a candidate.

When the dean died, speculation ran high. Mr. Slope felt encouraged by the newspapers, which said that younger men should be admitted to places of influence in the church.

After Bertie had gone, Signora Neroni wrote a note asking Mrs. Bold to come to see her. When Mrs. Bold entered the Stanhope drawing-room, Signora Neroni told her that she should marry Mr. Arabin. With calculating generosity she had decided that he would make a good husband for Mrs. Bold.

Meanwhile, Mr. Slope had been sent off to another diocese, for Mrs. Proudie could no longer bear having him in Barchester. And Mr. Arabin, through Oxford influences, was appointed to the deanship—a victory for the High Churchmen. With Mr. Slope gone, the Stanhopes felt safe in returning to Italy.

Miss Thorne asked Mrs. Bold to spend some time at Ullathorne. She also contrived to have Mr. Arabin there. It was inevitable that Mr. Arabin should ask Mrs. Bold to be his wife. Dr. Grantly was satisfied. He had threatened to forbid the hospitality of Plumstead Episcopi to Mrs. Bold if she had become the wife of a Low Churchman. In fact, Dr. Grantly was moved to such generosity that he furnished the deanery and gave wonderful gifts to the entire family, including a cello to his father-in-law, Mr. Harding.

BARREN GROUND

Type of work: Novel
Author: Ellen Glasgow (1874-1945)
Type of plot: Social criticism
Time of plot: Late nineteenth and early twentieth centuries
Locale: Rural Virginia
First published: 1925

Principal characters:
DORINDA OAKLEY, daughter of a poor white Virginia farmer
JOSIAH, and
RUFUS, her brothers
JASON GREYLOCK, last member of an old Virginia family
GENEVA ELLGOOD, later Jason's wife
NATHAN PEDLAR, a country farmer and merchant

Critique:

Barren Ground is an honest, realistic novel of the South, in which Ellen Glasgow pictured the struggle of a class to maintain high living standards in the face of humiliating and depressing circumstances. Through her heroine she presented the problems of people who are by blood related to both the established aristocracy and the poor white tenant class. The story of Dorinda's vitality stands in sharp contrast to the weakness of her lover, Jason Greylock. In their frustrated union tragedy results for both, a tragedy out of their own blood rather than one of willful creation.

The Story:

Late one cold winter day Dorinda Oakley started to walk the four miles between Pedlar's Mill and her home at Old Farm. The land was bleak and desolate under a gray sky, and a few flakes of snow were falling. For almost a year she had worked in Nathan Pedlar's store, taking the place of his consumptive wife. Her brisk walk carried her swiftly over the rutted roads toward her father's unproductive farm and the dilapidated Oakley house. On the way she passed Green Acres, the fertile farm of James Ellgood, and the run-down farm of Five Oaks, owned by dissolute old Doctor

Greylock, whose son, Jason, had given up his medical studies to take over his father's practice and to care for his drunken father.

As she walked, Dorinda thought of young Jason Greylock. Before she reached Old Farm, Jason overtook her in his buggy. During the ride to her home she remembered the comment of old Matthew Fairlamb, who had told her that she ought to marry Jason. The young doctor was handsome. He represented something different from the drab, struggling life Dorinda had always known. Her father and mother and her two brothers were all unresponsive and bitter people. Mrs. Oakley suffered from headaches and tried to forget them in a ceaseless activity of work. At Old Farm, supper was followed by prayers and prayers by sleep.

Dorinda continued to see Jason. Taking the money she had been saving to buy a cow, she ordered a pretty dress and a new hat to wear to church on Easter Sunday. But her Easter finery brought her no happiness. Jason sat in church with the Ellgoods and their daughter, Geneva, and afterward he went home with them to dinner. Dorinda sat in her bedroom that afternoon and meditated on her unhappiness.

Later, Jason proposed unexpectedly, confessing that he too was lonely and unhappy. He spoke of his attachment to his father which had brought him back to Pedlar's Mill, and he cursed the tenant system which he said was ruining the South. He and Dorinda planned to be married in the fall. When they met during the hot, dark nights that summer, he kissed her with half-angry, half-hungry violence.

Meanwhile Geneva Ellgood told her friends that she herself was engaged to Jason Greylock. Late in September Jason left for the city to buy surgical instruments. When he was overlong in returning, Dorinda began to worry. At last she visited Aunt Mehitable Green, an old Negro conjure woman, in the hope Aunt Mehitable would have heard from the Greylock servants some gossip concerning Jason. There Dorinda became ill and learned that she was to have a child. Distressed, she went to Five Oaks and confronted drunken old Dr. Greylock, who told her, as he cackled with sly mirth, that Jason had married Geneva Ellgood in the city. The old man intimated that Jason was white-livered and had been forced into the marriage by the Ellgoods. He added, leering, that Jason and his bride were expected home that night.

On the way home Dorinda saw, herself unseen, the carriage which brought Jason and Geneva to Five Oaks. Late that night she went to the Greylock house and attempted to shoot Jason. Frightened, Jason begged for pity and understanding. Despising him for his weakness and falseness, she blundered home through the darkness. Two days later she packed her suitcase and left home. By accident she took the north-bound train rather than the one to Richmond, and so she changed the course of her later life.

Dorinda arrived in New York in October, frightened, friendless, with no prospects of work. Two weeks later she fortunately met a kindly middle-aged woman who took her in and gave her the address of a dressmaker who might hire her. But on the way to the shop Dorinda was knocked down by a cab. She awoke in a hospital. Dr. Faraday, a surgeon who had seen the accident, saved her life, but she lost her baby. Dr. Faraday hired her to look after his office and children.

Dorinda lived in New York with the Faradays for two years. Then her father had a stroke and she returned home. Her brother Josiah was married; Mrs. Pedlar was dead. Dorinda had become a woman of self-confidence and poise. She saw Geneva Greylock, who already looked middle-aged, and had only pity for the woman who had married Jason. Her brother Rufus said Jason was drinking heavily and losing all his patients. Five Oaks farm looked more run-down than ever. Determined to make the Oakley land productive once more, Dorinda borrowed enough money to buy seven cows. She found Nathan Pedlar helpful in many ways, for he knew good farming methods and gave her advice. When she saw Jason again, she wondered how she could ever have yielded herself to the husk of a man that Jason was.

After her father's death, Josiah and his wife Elvira went to live on their own land. Rufus, who hated the farm, planned to go to the city. Before he left the farm, however, Rufus was accused of murdering a neighboring farmer. Dorinda was sure that he had committed the murder, but Mrs. Oakley swore under oath that her son had been at home with her at the time of the shooting. Her lie saved Rufus. Mrs. Oakley's conscience began to torment her because of the lie she had told, and she took to her bed. Her mind broken, she lived in dreams of her youth. When she died in her sleep, Dorinda wept. To her it seemed that her parents' lives had been futile and wasted.

During the next ten years Dorinda worked hard. She borrowed more money to improve the farm and she saved and scrimped, but she was happy. Geneva Greylock was losing her mind. One day she told Dorinda that she had borne a child but that Jason had killed it and buried it in the garden. Geneva drowned herself the same day that Nathan Pedlar asked Dorinda to marry him.

Together Dorinda and Nathan prospered. She was now thirty-eight and still felt young. John Abner Pedlar, Nathan's crippled son, looked to her for help and she gave it willingly. Nathan's other children meant less to her, and she was glad when they married and moved away. When Five Oaks was offered for sale, Dorinda and Nathan bought it for six thousand dollars. As Jason signed over the papers to her, Dorinda noticed that he was his dirty, drunken old father all over again.

The next few years Dorinda devoted to restoring Five Oaks. John Abner was still her friend and helper. There were reports that Jason was living in an old house in the pine woods and drinking heavily. Dorinda, busy with her house and dairy farm, had little time for neighborhood gossip.

One day Nathan took the train to the city to have a tooth pulled and to attend a lawsuit. The train was wrecked, and Nathan was killed while trying to save the lives of the other passengers. He was given a hero's funeral.

The years following Nathan's death were Dorinda's happiest, for as time passed she realized that she had regained, through her struggle with the land, her own integrity and self-respect.

One day some hunters found Jason sick and starving in the woods, and her neighbors assumed Dorinda would take him in. Unwillingly, she allowed him to be brought to Old Farm, where she engaged a nurse to look after him. In a few months Jason died. Many of the people at the funeral came only out of curiosity, and a pompous minister said meaningless things about Jason, whom he had never known. Dorinda felt nothing as she stood beside the grave, for her memories of Jason had outlived her emotions. She sensed that for good or ill the fervor and fever of her life were ended.

THE BEGGAR'S OPERA

Type of work: Comic opera
Author: John Gay (1685-1732)
Type of plot: Social satire
Time of plot: Early eighteenth century

Locale: London
First presented: 1728

Principal characters:

CAPTAIN MACHEATH, leader of a band of robbers
POLLY PEACHUM, a young woman who believes she is Macheath's wife
MR. PEACHUM, Polly's father, a fence for stolen goods and an informer
LUCY LOCKIT, a young woman who also believes she is Macheath's wife
MR. LOCKIT, Lucy's father, a jailer
MRS. PEACHUM, Polly's mother

Critique:

The Beggar's Opera follows in the satiric tradition of Swift and Pope. Gay's purpose was to ridicule the corrupt politics of his day and the follies of polite society. Highwaymen and thieves stand for the great lords and powerful public officials of Georgian England. Depiction and intimation of crime and vice in all strata of society and shrewd, humorous characterization give the play its universality.

The Story:

Mr. Peachum, as he sat reckoning up his accounts, declared that his was an honest employment. Like a lawyer, he acted both for and against thieves. That he should protect them was only fitting, since they afforded him a living. In a businesslike manner he was deciding who among arrested rogues should escape punishment through bribes and who had been unproductive enough to deserve deportation or the gallows. Though Mrs. Peachum found a favorite of hers on his list, she made no effort to influence her husband's decision as to his fate, for she knew that the weakness of her sex was to allow her emotions to dominate her practical nature.

She did say, however, that Captain Macheath, a highwayman, stood high in her regard, as well as in that—so she hinted to Mr. Peachum—of their daughter Polly. The news upset her spouse. If the girl married, her husband might learn family secrets and thus gain power over them. Peachum ordered his wife to warn the girl that marriage and a husband's domination would mean her ruin. Consequently they were dismayed when Polly announced her marriage to Macheath. They predicted grimly that she would not be able to keep Macheath in funds for gambling and philandering, that there would not even be enough money to cause quarrels, that she might as well have married a lord.

The Peachums' greatest fear was that Macheath would have them hanged and so gain control of the fortune which would be left to Polly. Before he could do that, they decided, he would have to be disposed of, and they suggested to Polly that she inform on him. Widowhood, they declared, was a very comfortable state. But the girl stubbornly asserted that she loved the dashing highwayman. Overhearing the plan of her parents to have her husband arrested, Polly warned Macheath. They decided that he should go into hiding for a few weeks until, as Polly hoped, her parents should relent.

Parting from his love, Macheath met his gang at a tavern near Newgate to tell them their rendezvous would have to be confined to gatherings at their private hideout for about a week, so that Peachum would be led to believe the highwayman had deserted his companions. After his men had left to go about their business, some street women and female pickpockets joined Macheath. Two of them covered Macheath with his own pistols as Peachum, accompanied by constables, rushed in to arrest him. When Macheath had been carried off to spend the night in Newgate, some of the women expressed their indignation at not having been chosen to spring the trap and share in the reward Peachum had offered for the highwayman's capture.

Though Captain Macheath had funds to bribe his jailer to confine him with only a light pair of fetters, it was another matter to deal with Lucy Lockit, the jailer's daughter. As Macheath freely admitted, she was his wife except for the ceremony. But Lucy, who had heard of his gallantry toward Polly Peachum, could be convinced of his sincerity only by his consent to an immediate marriage.

Meanwhile Peachum and Lockit agreed that they would split the reward for Macheath. As he went over his accounts, however, Peachum found cause to question his partner's honesty. One of his men had been convicted, although he had bribed Lockit to have the man go free. Also, Peachum's informer, Mrs. Coaxer, had been defrauded of information money. The quarrel was short-lived, however, as each was well aware that if they fell out each had the power to hang the other. After his talk with Peachum, Lockit warned his daughter that Macheath's fate had been sealed. He advised her to buy herself widow's weeds and be cheerful; since she could not have the highwayman and his money too, she might as well make use of the time that was left to extract what riches she could from him.

There was no clergyman to be found that day, but Lucy had so far softened toward her philandering lover as to agree to see if her father could not be bought off. She had just consented to help him when Polly appeared in search of her husband. Macheath managed to convince Lucy of his faithfulness by disowning Polly, who was carried off by the angry Peachum.

After they had gone, Lucy agreed to steal her father's keys so that her lover might escape. Macheath, free once more, went to join two of his men at a gambling house. There he made arrangements to meet them again that evening at another den, where he would point out a likely victim for them to rob.

Peachum and Lockit were discussing the disposal of some assorted loot when they were joined by Mrs. Trapes, a procuress who innocently told them that Macheath was at that moment with one of her girls. While Peachum and Lockit went off to recapture him, Polly paid a visit to Lucy Lockit. Together they bewailed their common fate—Macheath's neglect. Lucy tried to give Polly a poisoned drink. When the suspicious girl refused to accept it, Lucy decided that perhaps Polly was too miserable to deserve to die.

When Macheath was brought back to prison once more by Peachum and Lockit, both girls fell on their knees before their fathers and begged that his life be spared. Neither parent would be moved. Lockit announced that the highwayman would die that day. As he prepared to go to the Old Bailey, Macheath said that he was resigned to his fate, for his death would settle all disputes and please all his wives.

While Macheath in his cell reflected ironically that rich men may escape the gallows while the poor must hang, he was visited by two of his men. He asked them to make sure that Lockit and Peachum were hanged before they themselves were finally strung up. The thieves were followed by the distraught Polly and Lucy, come to bid Macheath farewell. When the jailer announced that four more of his wives, each accompanied by a child, had appeared to say goodbye, Macheath declared that he was ready to meet his fate.

But the rabble, feeling that the poor should have their vices as well as the rich, raised so much clamor for Macheath's reprieve that charges were dropped and he was released in triumph. In the merrymaking that followed, he himself chose Polly as his partner, because, he gallantly announced, she was really his wife. From that time on he intended to give up the vices—if not the follies—of the rich.

BEL-AMI

Type of work: Novel
Author: Guy de Maupassant (1850-1893)
Type of plot: Naturalism
Time of plot: About 1885
Locale: Paris and Cannes
First published: 1885

Principal characters:
GEORGES DUROY, later Georges du Roy de Cantel, a newspaper man
MADELEINE FORESTIER, wife of Duroy's benefactor and later Duroy's wife
CLOTILDE DE MARELLE, Duroy's mistress
CHARLES FORESTIER, Duroy's former brother officer and the editor who befriends him
M. WALTER, owner of the newspaper for which Duroy works
BASILE WALTER, M. Walter's wife
SUZANNE WALTER, M. Walter's daughter

Critique:

The subtitle of *Bel-Ami, or The History of a Scoundrel,* is not inappropriate for the story of an intriguer who climbs to a position of wealth and power by publishing the story of his first wife's disgrace and later cheating her of part of her fortune. The unscrupulous parvenu and the women he dupes are among the masterpieces of characterization produced by the French realistic school to which de Maupassant belonged.

The Story:

Georges Duroy, a former soldier, had only three francs in his pocket when he met his former brother officer, Charles Forestier, in Paris one evening. Forestier, an editor of the daily newspaper, *La Vie Francaise,* unhesitatingly lent Duroy money to buy suitable clothes and invited him to come to dinner the following evening to meet the owner of the paper. The Forestiers' party was a success for Duroy. M. Walter hired him as a reporter to write a series of articles on his experiences in Algeria.

It was not easy for Duroy to adapt himself to his new job. His first article was due the day following the dinner party. Unable to write it in proper form, he was forced to hurry to the Forestier home early in the morning to seek stylistic advice. Forestier, just leaving, referred Duroy to Mme. Forestier for help. Together they turned out a successful piece. With her help Duroy slowly built a reputation as a clever reporter, but his salary remained small.

Two months after the Forestiers' dinner party Duroy called on Mme. de Marelle, who had been among the guests that evening. Duroy's friendship with Mme. de Marelle quickly developed into an affair. De Marelle was often away from home, so that his wife had ample time to see her lover, at his lodgings at first and then at an apartment which she rented for their rendezvous. Duroy objected mildly to having Mme. de Marelle bear this expense, but it was not long before he found himself regularly accepting small sums of money from her. It was Mme. de Marelle's daughter Laurine who first called him "Bel-Ami," a nickname gradually adopted by most of his friends.

M. Forestier suffered from a bronchial ailment. As his health grew worse, his disposition became unbearable at the office. Duroy determined to avenge himself by attempting to seduce Mme. Forestier. She gently rebuffed him, but agreed that they could be friends. Duroy was brash enough to propose that she become his wife if she were ever widowed.

At Mme. Forestier's suggestion Duroy began to cultivate Mme. Walter. The week following his first visit to her he was appointed editor of the "Echoes," an important column. He had barely assumed this position when the editor of a rival newspaper, *La Plume,* accused him falsely of receiving bribes and suppressing news. For the honor of *La Vie Francaise* Duroy was forced to challenge his disparager to a duel. Though neither he nor his opponent was injured, M. Walter was pleased with Duroy's spirit.

Duroy moved into the apartment Mme. de Marelle had rented for their meetings after he had promised that he would never bring anyone else there. Shortly afterward Forestier became seriously ill, and Duroy received a telegram asking him to join the Forestiers in Cannes, where they had gone for the invalid's health. After Forestier's death, as he and Mme. Forestier kept a vigil over the corpse, Duroy proposed once more. The widow made no promises but stated the next day that she might consider an alliance, though she warned her swain that she would have to be treated as an equal and her conduct left unquestioned.

Mme. Forestier returned to Paris. A year later she and Duroy were married. Georges du Roy de Cantel, as he now called himself at his wife's suggestion, and his bride had agreed to spend their honeymoon with his parents in Normandy. However, Mme. de Cantel spent only one day with his simple, ignorant peasant family in their tiny home.

The newspaper man found in his wife a valuable ally who not only aided him in writing his articles but also, as the friend of influential men, helped him to find a place in political circles. Unfortunately, friction soon developed between them. After he had moved into his wife's home, de Cantel found that its comforts had been designed to please its old master, and he soon found himself pushed gently into the niche his friend had occupied. Even the meals were prepared according to Forestier's taste. To pique his wife de Cantel began to call Forestier "poor Charles," always using an accent of infinite pity when he spoke the name.

Not long after his marriage de Cantel resumed his relationship with Mme. de Marelle and at the same time began an affair with Mme. Walter. He had briefly bemoaned the fact that he had not married wealthy young Suzanne Walter, but he soon became intrigued with the idea of seducing her mother, a pillar of dignity. His conquest was not a difficult one. Mme. Walter began to meet her lover at his rooms and to shower affection and attentions upon him so heavily that he quickly became bored.

Among Mme. de Cantel's political acquaintances was the foreign minister, Laroche-Mathieu, who supplied news of government activities to *La Vie Francaise.* Because the minister was also a close friend of M. Walter, it was not difficult for de Cantel's new paramour to learn the state secret that France would soon guarantee the Moroccan debt. Mme. Walter planned to buy some shares of the loan with the understanding that de Cantel would receive part of the profit. While Mme. Walter was carrying on her speculations, the de Cantels received a windfall in the form of a bequest from the late Count de Vaudrec, an old family friend of Mme. de Cantel. De Cantel objected to the count's bequest of one million francs, however, on the grounds that appearances would compromise her. He allowed her to accept the money only after she had agreed to divide it equally with him, so that it would seem to outsiders as if they had both received a share.

De Cantel profited handsomely when France assumed the Moroccan debt, but his gains were small compared to those of Laroche-Mathieu and M. Walter, who had become millionaires as a result of the intrigue. One evening he and his wife were invited to view a painting in the Walters' magnificent new mansion. There de Cantel began a flirtation with Suzanne Walter; his own wife and Laroche-Mathieu had become intimates without attempting to conceal their friendship. That evening de Cantel persuaded Suzanne to agree never to accept a proposal without first asking his advice. At home after the reception he received with indifference the cross of the Legion of Honor which the foreign minister had given him. He felt that he was entitled to a larger reward for concealing news of the Moroccan affair from his readers. That spring he surprised his wife and Laroche-Mathieu at a rendezvous. Three months later he obtained a divorce, causing the minister's downfall by naming him corespondent.

A free man again, de Cantel was able to court Suzanne Walter. It was simple for him to persuade the girl to tell her parents she wished to marry him, to have her go away with him until they gave their consent to the match.

Mme. Walter was the only one at the magnificent church wedding to show any signs of sadness. She hated the daughter who had taken her lover, but at the same time she was powerless to prevent the marriage without compromising herself. M. Walter had managed to resign himself to having a conniving son-in-law, had, in fact, recognized his shrewdness by making him chief editor of the newspaper. Suzanne was innocently happy as she walked down the aisle with her father. Her new husband was also content. Greeting their well-wishers in the sacristy after the ceremony, he took advantage of the occasion to reaffirm, with his eyes, his feelings for Mme. de Marelle. As he and his wife left the church, it seemed to him that it was only a stone's throw from that edifice to the chamber of deputies.

A BELL FOR ADANO

Type of work: Novel
Author: John Hersey (1914-)
Type of plot: Social criticism
Time of plot: 1943
Locale: Adano, Italy
First published: 1944

Principal characters:

MAJOR VICTOR JOPPOLO, American Military Governor of Adano
SERGEANT BORTH, Major Joppolo's subordinate
CAPTAIN PURVIS, head of the Military Police
GENERAL MARVIN, Commander-in-Chief of the American invasion troops and Major Joppolo's superior

Critique:

A Bell for Adano is one of the outstanding works of fiction to come out of World War II. John Hersey has told his story in simple but effective language. There is nothing of the artificial, the contrived, or the melodramatic. The portrayal of character is perhaps the author's greatest achievement. Only a good observer, only a person with a deep love for human beings, could have written so realistically and so sympathetically of the American invasion troops, and of an Italian town and its people who had lived under Fascist rule for more than twenty years.

The Story:

When the American army invaded Sicily, Major Victor Joppolo was placed in command of Adano. He set up his office in the city hall, re-hired the janitor, and investigated the records left by the Fascist mayor, who had fled to the hills.

Soon after his arrival Major Joppolo summoned the leading citizens of the

A BELL FOR ADANO by John Hersey. By permission of the author and the publishers, Alfred A. Knopf, Inc.

town and asked them, through Giuseppe, his interpreter, what they considered the most important thing to be done. Some answered that the shortage of food was the most pressing problem. Others insisted that what the town needed most was its bell, which had been removed by the Fascists. The bell, it seemed, had a soothing tone. It also regulated the lives of Adano's residents.

The major promised every effort to recover the bell. Meanwhile the problem was to obtain food and to have produce brought into the town. In order that his directives would be understood and carried out, the major issued proclamations which the town crier, after being silent for so long, hastened to shout in the village.

On Sunday morning the major attended mass at one of the churches. There he noticed a blonde girl sitting in front of him. When he later asked Giuseppe about her, the interpreter assumed that the American's interest had nothing to do with official business. Major Joppolo's primary interest, however, was the girl's father, Tomasino, owner of a fishing fleet. He had Giuseppe ask Tomasino if he would come to see him. But Tomasino, distrustful of authority, would not come to headquarters. The major decided to go to Tomasino. He went, followed by practically all the townspeople. The old Italian was defiant, sure that the major had come to arrest him. Finally the Italian was convinced that the major meant neither to arrest him nor to ask for a cut in the proceeds from the sale of the fish. He agreed to go out with his fishing fleet, despite the danger of mines.

By that time the major and his policies had become the subject of much discussion among the people. The Fascist mayor provided them with a great deal of amusement. He had come out of hiding and had been paroled into Sergeant Borth's custody. Every morning the mayor went to Sergeant Borth and publicly confessed a Fascist sin. Giuseppe was astonished to discover that when the major told him to report for work at seven in the mornings, he meant it. Gargano, the ex-Fascist policeman, learned that he could no longer force the others to make way for him when they stood in line at the bakery.

While driving through Adano one day, General Marvin found the road blocked by a mule cart. The driver, having had his daily quota of wine, was sleeping peacefully.

When the mule refused to budge, the general ordered the vehicle thrown into the ditch. Reluctantly, the soldiers dumped the cart, mule, and sleeping driver. Swearing furiously, the general drove up to the city hall, confronted Major Joppolo, and ordered that the major forbid the entrance of all carts into Adano.

The next day a group of townspeople besieged the major. The carts, they explained, were essential, for they brought food and water into the town. Major Joppolo countermanded the general's order and telephoned Captain Purvis that he would accept full responsibility. Captain Purvis, anxious to keep out of trouble, ordered Lieutenant Trapani to make a memorandum and to send it to General Marvin. But the lieutenant, out of regard for Major Joppolo, put the memorandum among Purvis' papers in the hope that the captain, who rarely looked through his files, would never find it.

Major Joppolo's efforts to restore the bell were not successful, for it had been melted down by the Fascists. However, a young Naval officer, in charge of a nearby station, promised to obtain a ship's bell for him.

In the meantime Captain Purvis had gone through the papers on his desk and had found the memorandum for General Marvin. He ordered it forwarded at once. Lieutenant Trapani mailed it, but addressed it to the wrong person at headquarters in Algiers. From there it was forwarded to the general's aide, Colonel Middleton. Every day the colonel met with General Marvin and went over important communications. Accordingly, he was half-way through Purvis' letter before he realized what it was. He tried to go on to the next letter, but it was too late. The general had heard Major Joppolo's name and that of Adano, and remembered both.

The bell arrived in Adano. It was touched, prodded, sounded by the experts, and admired by everybody. When it pealed forth, the townspeople declared that its tone was even better than that of the old bell. The major was a hero. To show their appreciation and affection, the townspeople had him taken to a photographer. From the resulting picture, a local artist painted his portrait.

At the celebration that night, Sergeant Borth was very, very drunk. He refused to take orders from Major Joppolo, saying that the major was no longer in any position to give orders. Captain Purvis, said the sergeant, almost sobbing, had a letter from General Marvin. It ordered Major Joppolo back to Algiers. Next morning the major said goodbye to Borth, who apologized for his conduct of the previous night. The major asked him to help his successor make the people happy. As he drove away from the town, he heard in the distance the tolling of a bell, the new bell for Adano.

BEN HUR; A TALE OF THE CHRIST

Type of work: Novel
Author: Lewis (Lew) Wallace (1827-1905)
Type of plot: Historical romance
Time of plot: At the time of Christ
Locale: Antioch and Jerusalem
First published: 1880

Principal characters:
BEN HUR, a Roman-educated Jew
BALTHASAR, an Egyptian
SIMONIDES, a Jewish merchant and friend of Ben Hur
ESTHER, daughter of Simonides
IRAS, daughter of Balthasar
MESSALA, a Roman and an enemy of Ben Hur

Critique:

Ben Hur is an amazing book, a mixture of melodramatic adventure and scholarly research. The author shows great familiarity with the customs and traditions of the society that he is describing, and it is this detailed knowledge of Roman and Jewish history that accounts for the value and importance of *Ben Hur*. It is unfortunate that the characters never seem quite real, and that the modern reader cannot feel much sympathy for them.

The Story:

In the Roman year 747 three travelers met in the desert, where the Athenian, the Hindu, and the Egyptian had been led by a new bright star shining in the sky. After telling their stories to one another, they journeyed on, seeking the new-born child who was King of the Jews. In Jerusalem their inquiries aroused the curiosity of King Herod, who asked that they be brought before him. Herod then asked them to let him know if they found the child, for he, too, wished to adore the infant whose birth had been foretold. Arriving at last in Bethlehem, the three men found the new-born child in a stable. But having been warned in a dream of Herod's evil intentions, they did not return to tell the king of the child's whereabouts.

At that time there lived in Jerusalem

three members of an old and eminent Jewish family named Hur. The father, who had been dead for some time, had distinguished himself in service to the Roman Empire and had, consequently, received many honors. The son, Ben Hur, was handsome, and the daughter, Tirzah, was likewise beautiful. Their mother was a fervent nationalist who had implanted in their minds a strong sense of pride in their race and national culture.

When Ben Hur was still a young man, his friend Messala returned from his studies in Rome. Messala had become arrogant, spiteful, cruel. As Ben left Messala's home after their meeting, he was hurt, for he realized that Messala had so changed that their friendship must end.

A few days later, while watching a procession below him in the streets, Ben Hur accidentally dislodged a piece of tile which fell on the Roman procurator. The Roman believed that the accident was an attempt on his life. Led by Messala, who had pointed out his former friend, the Romans arrested the Hur family and confiscated their property.

Ben Hur was sent to be a galleyslave. While he was being led away in chains, a young man took pity on him and gave him a drink. One day, while he was rowing at his usual place in the galley, Ben Hur attracted the attention of Quintus Arrius, a Roman official. Later, during a sea battle, Ben Hur saved the life of Quintus, who adopted the young Jew as his son. Educated as a Roman citizen, Ben Hur inherited his foster father's wealth when Quintus died.

Ben Hur went to Antioch, where he learned that his father's old servant, Simonides, was now a prosperous merchant. In effect, the wealth of Simonides was really the property of the Hur family, for he had been acting as agent for his dead master. Simonides assured himself that Ben Hur was really the son of his old master, and begged that he be allowed to serve the son as well. Ben Hur was attracted to Simonides' daughter, Esther.

In company with a servant of Simonides, Ben Hur went to see a famous well on the outskirts of Antioch. There an aged Egyptian was watering his camel, on which sat the most beautiful woman Ben Hur had ever seen. While he looked, a chariot came charging through the people near the well. Ben Hur seized the lead horse by the bridle and swerved the chariot aside. The driver was his false friend, Messala. The old Egyptian was Balthasar, one of the wise men who had traveled to Bethlehem. The beautiful girl was his daughter, Iras.

Learning that the arrogant Messala was to race his chariot in the games at Antioch, Ben Hur wished to defeat and humiliate his old playfellow. He had Simonides and his friends place large wagers on the race, until Messala had staked his whole fortune. The day of the race came. At the turn Messala suddenly struck with his whip at the horses of the chariot Ben Hur was driving. Ben Hur managed to keep his team under control, and then in the last lap around the arena he drove his chariot so close to Messala's vehicle that the wheels locked. Messala was thrown under his horses and crippled for life. Because Messala had attempted foul play earlier in the race, the judges allowed Ben Hur to be proclaimed the winner. Messala was ruined.

From Balthasar, Ben Hur learned that the King of the Jews to whom the Egyptian and his companions had paid homage some years before was not to be the king of a political realm, but of a spiritual one. But Simonides convinced Ben Hur that the promised king would be a real deliverer who would lead the Jews to victory over the Romans.

From Antioch Ben Hur went to Jerusalem to search for his mother and sister. There he learned the part Messala had played in the ruin of his family. After his own arrest, his mother and sister had been thrown into prison, and Messala and the procurator had divided the confiscated property between them. But

Messala knew nothing of the fate of the two women after the procurator had ordered them confined to an underground cell. There they had contracted leprosy. When Pilate, the new procurator, arrived, he had ordered all political prisoners freed and so the two women had been set at liberty. But there was no place for them to go except to the caves outside the city where the lepers were sent to die. A faithful old servant found them and carried food to them daily, under sacred oath never to reveal their names. When Ben Hur met the old servant, she allowed him to believe that his mother and sister were dead.

Meanwhile Simonides had bought the home of his old master, and he, Esther, Balthasar, and Iras took possession of it. Ben Hur himself could visit it only at night and in disguise. He was plotting to overthrow the Roman rule and was recruiting an army to follow the future King of the Jews. He went one day near the place where the lepers usually gathered on the hill beyond the city gates. On the way, he met a young man whom he recognized as the one who had given him a drink of water years before when he was being led away to slavery. The young man was the Nazarene. That day the old servant had persuaded Tirzah and her mother to show themselves to the Nazarene as he passed. Both were cured, and Ben Hur saw the two lepers transformed into his mother and sister.

Ben Hur's attitude toward the King of the Jews was slowly changing. When he witnessed the crucifixion in company with Simonides and old Balthasar, any doubts that he might have had were removed. He was convinced then that Christ's kingdom was a spiritual one. From that day on, he and his family were Christians.

Some years later, in the beautiful villa at Misenum, Ben Hur's wife, Esther, received a strange visit from Iras, the daughter of Balthasar. Iras told Esther that she had killed Messala for the misery he had brought her. When he learned of the visit, Ben Hur was sure that on the day of the crucifixion, the day that Balthasar himself had died, Iras had deserted her father for Messala.

Ben Hur was happy with Esther and their two children. He and Simonides devoted their fortunes to the Christian cause. When Nero began the persecution of the Christians in Rome it was Ben Hur who went there to build the catacombs under the city itself, so that those who believed in the Nazarene could worship in safety and peace.

BEOWULF

Type of work: Poem
Source: Folk tradition
Type of plot: Heroic epic
Time of plot: c. Sixth century
Locale: Denmark, southern Sweden (land of the Geats)
First transcribed: c. 1000

Principal characters:
BEOWULF, a Geat hero
HROTHGAR, King of the Danes
UNFERTH, a Danish warrior
WIGLAF, loyal noble of Beowulf's court

Critique:

This poem is the great masterpiece of Anglo-Saxon literature. Its scribes were writing down a story transmitted orally for generations by Northern peoples. The poem is a valuable record of the customs of the time, a pagan story overlaid with a veneer of Christian theology, and a narrative of high artistic worth.

The Story:

Once long ago in Hrothgar's kingdom a monster named Grendel roamed the countryside at night. Rising from his marshy home, Grendel would stalk to the hall of the king, where he would seize fifteen of Hrothgar's sleeping warriors and devour them. Departing, he would gather fifteen more into his huge arms and carry them back to his watery lair. For twelve years this slaughter continued.

Word of the terror spread. In the land of the Geats, ruled over by Hygelac, lived Beowulf, a man of great strength and bravery. When he heard the tale of Hrothgar's distress, he set sail for Denmark to rid the land of its fear. With a company of fourteen men he came ashore and asked a coast watcher to lead him to Hrothgar's high hall. There he was feasted in great honor while the mead cup went around. Unferth reminded Beowulf of a swimming contest which Beowulf was said to have lost. Beowulf answered that not only had he won the contest, but he had also killed many deadly monsters in the sea. At the close of the feast Hrothgar and his warriors went to their rest, leaving Beowulf and his band in the hall. Then came the awful Grendel and seized one of the sleeping warriors. But he was fated to kill no more that night, for Beowulf without shield or spear seized the dread monster and wrenched off his mighty right arm. Thus maimed, Grendel fled back to his marshland home. His bloody arm was hung in Hrothgar's hall.

The next night Grendel's mother came to avenge her son. Bursting into the great hall, she seized one of the warriors, Aeschere, Hrothgar's chief counselor, and fled with him into the night. She took with her also the prized arm of Grendel. Beowulf was asleep in a house removed from the hall, and not until morning did he learn of the monster's visit. Then, with Hrothgar leading the way, a mournful procession approached the dire marsh. At its edge they sighted the head of the ill-fated Aeschere and saw the stain of blood on the water. Beowulf prepared for descent to the home of the foe. Unferth offered Beowulf the finest sword in the kingdom, and thus forfeited his own chance of brave deeds.

As Beowulf sank beneath the waters of the marsh, he was beset on every hand by prodigious monsters. After a long swim he came to the lair of Grendel's mother. Failing to wound her with Unferth's sword, he seized the monster by the shoulder and threw her to the ground. During a grim hand-to-hand battle, in which Beowulf was being worsted, he sighted a famous old sword of the giants, which he seized and thrust at Grendel's mother, who fell in helpless death throes. Then Beowulf turned and saw Grendel himself lying weak and maimed on the floor of the lair. Quickly he swung the sword and severed Grendel's head from his body. As he began to swim back up to the surface of the marsh, the sword with which he had killed his enemies melted until only the head and hilt were left. On his return, the Danes rejoiced and fêted him with another high feast. He presented the sword hilt to Hrothgar and returned Unferth's sword without telling that it had failed him.

The time came for Beowulf's return to his homeland. He left Denmark in great glory and sailed toward the land of the Geats. Once more at the court of his lord Hygelac, he was held in high esteem and was rewarded with riches and position. After many years Beowulf himself became king among the Geats. One of the Geats by accident discovered an ancient hoard, and, while its guardian dragon slept, carried away a golden goblet which he presented to Beowulf. The discovery of the loss caused the dragon to rise in fury and to devastate the land. Old man that he was, Beowulf was determined to rid his kingdom of the dragon's scourge. Daring the flames of the dragon's nostrils, he smote his foe with his sword, but without effect. Once more Beowulf was forced to rely on the grip of his mighty hands. Of his warriors only Wiglaf stood by his king; the others fled. The dragon rushed at Beowulf and sank its teeth deeply into his neck. But Wiglaf smote the dragon with his sword, and Beowulf with his war-knife gave the dragon its death blow.

Weak from loss of blood, the old hero was dying. His last act was to give Wiglaf a king's collar of gold. The other warriors now came out of hiding and burned with pagan rites the body of their dead king. From the dragon's lair they took the treasure hoard and buried it in the great mound they built over Beowulf's ashes. Then with due ceremony they mourned the passing of the great and dauntless Beowulf.

THE BIG SKY

Type of work: Novel
Author: A. B. Guthrie, Jr. (1901-)
Type of plot: Adventure romance
Time of plot: 1830-1843
Locale: Western United States
First published: 1947

Principal characters:
BOONE CAUDILL, a mountain man
TEAL EYE, his Indian wife
JIM DEAKINS, his friend
DICK SUMMERS, an old hunter
JOURDONNAIS, a keelboat captain
POORDEVIL, a half-witted Blackfoot
ELISHA PEABODY, a Yankee speculator

Critique:

For constant and varied action this story is outstanding. Between episodes much of the philosophy of the Western hunter and trapper is set forth. Also, there are passages of vivid description in which the author communicates the feel of the open spaces and the elemental emotions of the men who roamed them. Throughout the book realism is added by putting the words and thoughts of the characters into frontier dialect. *The Big Sky* is a notable contribution to regional and historical fiction.

The Story:

In 1830 Boone Caudill set out alone for St. Louis and the West after a fight with his father. Taking his father's rifle with him, he headed for Louisville to get out of the state before his father could catch him. On the road he met Jim Deakins, an easy-going redhead, and the two decided to go West together. At Louisville, where the sheriff and Boone's father were waiting for the runaway, he and Jim were separated. Boone escaped by swimming the Ohio River to the Indiana shore.

When Boone was falsely accused of attempted theft and jailed, Jim, who had followed him after their separation, stole the sheriff's keys and released him. Together the boys continued west.

In St. Louis they signed up on the crew of the keelboat *Mandan*. Most of the crew were French, as was the leader, Jourdonnais. The boat was headed for the country of the Blackfeet with a store of whiskey and other goods to trade for furs. Jourdonnais also had aboard Teal Eye, young daughter of a Blackfoot chief. She had been separated from her tribe for some time; Jourdonnais hoped to gain the friendship of the Indians by returning the girl to them.

The keelboat moved slowly upstream

by means of poles, tow rope, and oars. Boone and Jim found a friend in Dick Summers, the hunter for the *Mandan,* whose job was to scout for Indians and keep the crew supplied with meat. He made Boone and Jim his assistants. Jourdonnais was worried about making Blackfoot country before winter, and he worked the crew hard. At last they passed into the upper river beyond the mouth of the Platte. All the greenhorns, including Boone and Jim, were initiated by being dunked in the river and having their hair shaved off.

At last they were in buffalo country. Summers took Boone with him to get some fresh meat. Attacked by a hunting party of Sioux, the white men escaped unharmed; but Summers expected trouble from the hostiles farther along the line. A few days later the *Mandan* was ambushed by a large Indian war party. Only the swivel gun on the deck of the boat saved the white men from death.

Just before the *Mandan* arrived at Fort Union, two men tried to sabotage the cargo. At Fort Union, Jourdonnais accused the American Fur Company trader, McKenzie, of trying to stop him. McKenzie denied the charge, but he tried to argue Jourdonnais out of continuing upriver and offered to pay double value for the *Mandan's* cargo. Jourdonnais refused. At Fort Union, Boone met his Uncle Zeb, an old-time mountain man. He predicted that the days of hunting and trapping in open country were nearly over, but Boone and Jim did not believe him.

When the *Mandan* arrived in Blackfoot country, Teal Eye escaped. The crew began to build a fort and trading post. One day Indians attacked and killed all but the three hunters, Boone, Jim, and Summers.

For seven years these three hunted together, and Summers made real mountain men out of the others. In the spring of 1837 the three headed for a rendezvous on the Seeds-Kee-Dee River, where they could sell their furs and gamble, drink, and fight with other mountain men. They took with them a half-witted Blackfoot named Poordevil.

At the rendezvous Boone killed a man who said that he was going to take Poordevil's scalp. Then, after they had had their fill of women and liquor, the three friends left the camp. But Summers did not go hunting with them. No longer able to keep up the pace of the mountain men, he went back to settle in Missouri. Boone, Jim, and Poordevil headed up the Yellowstone toward Blackfoot country.

The journey was Boone's idea. He knew that Teal Eye was now a grown woman. Her beauty had remained in his memory all those years; now he wanted her for his squaw. On the way to the Three Forks, Boone stole a Crow horse and took a Crow scalp, two coups that would help him to make friends with the Blackfoot Indians.

They came upon a Blackfoot village ravaged by smallpox, but Boone refused to stop until he was certain that Teal Eye was dead. At last he located her. She was with a small band led by Red Horn, her brother, who sold her to Boone as his squaw.

Life was good to Boone. For five years he lived happily among the Blackfoot Indians with Teal Eye as his wife. Jim lived in the Blackfoot camp also, but he often left for months at a time to go back down the Missouri. He craved companionship, while Boone enjoyed living away from crowds. On one of his trips Jim met Elisha Peabody, a shrewd Yankee speculating upon the future prosperity of the Oregon Territory, who wanted someone to show him a pass where wagons could cross the mountains. Jim and Boone contracted to show him a suitable pass. Before Boone left, Teal Eye told him that he would have a son when he returned.

The expedition had bad luck. Indians stole all the horses and wounded Jim badly. Then snow fell, destroying all chances to get food. Finally, Boone was able to shoot some mountain goats. Jim recovered from his wound, and the party went ahead on foot. Boone and Jim showed Peabody the way across the mountains and into the Columbia Valley. It was spring when Boone returned to Teal Eye and his son.

The child, born blind, had a tinge of red in his hair. The baby's blindness brought a savage melancholy to Boone. Then some of the old Indians hinted that the red hair showed the child was Jim's baby. Boone laid a trap to catch Jim with Teal Eye. Jim, suspecting nothing, found Teal Eye alone in her lodge; he tried to comfort her about her child's blindness and the ugly mood of her husband. Boone mistook the intent of Jim's conversation. Entering the lodge, he shot Jim in the chest, killing him. He cursed Teal Eye and left the Blackfoot camp. Then he headed back to Kentucky to see his mother before she died.

In Kentucky he found his brother married and taking care of the farm. Boone grew restless. Slowly it came to him that he had been wrong about Jim and Teal Eye, for he noticed that one of his brother's children had a tinge of red hair. His mother said that there had been red hair in the family. When a neighbor girl insisted that he marry her because he had made love to her, Boone started back to the West. He longed for freedom and for Teal Eye.

In Missouri he visited Summers, who now had a wife and a farm. Over their whiskey, Boone revealed to Summers that he had killed Jim. He knew now that he had made a mistake. Everything was spoiled for him—Teal Eye, and all the West. The day of the mountain man was nearly over; farmers were going to Oregon. Without saying goodbye, he stumbled out into the night. Summers could see him weaving along the road for a short distance. Then the darkness swallowed him, and he was gone.

THE BLACK ARROW

Type of work: Novel
Author: Robert Louis Stevenson (1850-1894)
Type of plot: Historical romance
Time of plot: Fifteenth century
Locale: England
First published: 1888

Principal characters:

Sir Daniel Brackley, a political turncoat
Richard Shelton (Dick), his ward
Joanna Sedley, Lord Foxham's ward
Sir Oliver Oates, Sir Daniel's clerk
Ellis Duckworth, an outlaw
Lawless, another outlaw, Dick's friend
Richard, Duke of Gloucester

Critique:

The Black Arrow: A Tale of the Two Roses is a historical romance intended primarily for younger readers. Set in the fifteenth century, the historical background of the plot deals with a minor battle of the Wars of the Roses and the appearance of the infamous Richard, Duke of Gloucester, as a young soldier. More interesting are the swiftpaced adventures of Dick Shelton in his attempts to outwit his scheming guardian, Sir Daniel Brackley. Children have been fortunate that one of the gifted writers of the last century lent his talents to their pleasure.

The Story:

One afternoon in the late springtime,

the Moat House bell began to ring. A messenger had arrived with a message from Sir Daniel Brackley for Sir Oliver Oates, his clerk. When the peasants gathered at the summons of the bell, they were told that as many armed men as could be spared from the defense of Moat House were to join Sir Daniel at Kettley, where a battle was to be fought between the armies of Lancaster and York.

There was some grumbling at this order, for Sir Daniel was a faithless man who fought first on one side and then on the other. He had added to his own lands by securing the wardships of children left orphans in those troubled times, and it was whispered that he had murdered good Sir Harry Shelton to make himself the guardian of young Dick Shelton and the lord of the Moat House estates.

Planning to marry Dick Shelton to the orphaned heiress of Kettley, Joanna Sedley, Sir Daniel had ridden there to take charge of the girl. Dick, knowing nothing of his guardian's plans, remained behind as one of the garrison of the manor. Old Nick Appleyard, a veteran of Agincourt, grumbled at the weakness of the defense in a country overrun by stragglers from warring armies and insisted that Moat House lay open to attack. His prophecy came true. While he stood talking to Dick and Bennet Hatch, Sir Daniel's bailiff, a black arrow whirred out of the woods and struck Nick between the shoulder blades. A message on the shaft indicated that John Amend-All, a mysterious outlaw, had killed old Nick.

Sir Oliver Oates trembled when he read the message on the arrow. Shortly afterward, he was further disturbed by a message, pinned on the church door, announcing that John Amend-All would kill Sir Daniel, Sir Oliver, and Bennet Hatch. From it Dick learned that the outlaw accused Sir Oliver of killing Sir Harry Shelton, his father. But Sir Oliver swore that he had had no part in that knight's death. Dick decided to remain quiet until he learned more about the matter and in the meantime to act in all fairness to Sir Daniel.

It was decided that Hatch should remain to guard Moat House while the outlaws were in the neighborhood. Dick rode off with ten men-at-arms to find Sir Daniel. He carried a letter from Sir Oliver telling of John Amend-All's threats.

At Kettley Sir Daniel was awaiting the outcome of a battle already in progress, for he intended to join the winning side at the last minute. Sir Daniel was also upset by the outlaw's threats, and he ordered Dick to return to Moat House with a letter for Sir Oliver. He and his men left to join the fighting; but not before he roundly cursed his luck because Joanna Sedley, whom he held hostage, had escaped in boy's clothing. He ordered a party of men-at-arms to search for the girl and then to proceed to Moat House and strengthen the defenses there.

On his return journey Dick met Joanna, still dressed as a boy, who told him that her name was John Matcham. Dick, unaware that she was Sir Daniel's prisoner, promised to help her reach the abbey at Holywood. As they hurried on, they came upon a camp of the outlaws led by Ellis Duckworth, another man ruined by Sir Daniel. Running from the outlaws, they saw the party of Sir Daniel's retainers shot down one by one. The cannonading Dick heard in the distance convinced him that the soldiers of Lancaster were faring badly in the day's battle. Not knowing on which side Sir Daniel had declared himself, he wondered whether his guardian were among the victors or the vanquished.

Dick and his companion slept in the forest that night. The next morning a detachment of Sir Daniel's men swept by in disorderly rout. Soon afterward they saw a hooded leper in the woods. The man was Sir Daniel, attempting to make his way back to Moat House in disguise. He was dismayed when he heard that the outlaws had killed a party of his men-at-arms.

When the three arrived at Moat House, Sir Daniel accused Dick of distrust. He claimed innocence in the death of Dick's father and forced Sir Oliver to do the same. Another black arrow was shot through a window into a room in which the three were talking. Sir Daniel gave orders to defend Moat House against attack. Dick was placed under close watch in a room over the chapel, and he was not allowed to see his friend, John Matcham.

That night, when John Matcham came secretly to the room over the chapel, Dick learned that the companion of his adventures in the forest was really Joanna Sedley, the girl to whom Sir Daniel had betrothed him. Warned that he was now in danger of his life, Dick escaped into the forest. There he found Ellis Duckworth, who promised him that Sir Daniel would be destroyed.

Meanwhile the war went in favor of Lancaster, and Sir Daniel's fortunes rose with those of the house he followed. The town of Shoreby was full of Lancastrians all of that summer and fall, and there Sir Daniel had his own house for his family and followers. Joanna Sedley was not with him; she was kept in a lonely house by the sea, under the care of the wife of Bennet Hatch. Dick and an outlaw companion, Lawless, went to the town, and while reconnoitering Joanna's hiding place Dick encountered Lord Foxham, enemy of Sir Daniel and Joanna's legal guardian. Lord Foxham promised that if Joanna could be rescued she would become Dick's bride. The two men attempted a rescue by sea in a stolen boat, but a storm almost sank their boat and Lord Foxham was injured when the party attempted to land.

That winter Dick and his faithful companion, Lawless, returned to Shoreby. Disguised as priests, they entered Sir Daniel's house and were there protected by Alicia Risingham, Joanna's friend and the niece of a powerful Lancastrian lord. When Dick and Joanna met, she told him that the following day she was to marry Lord Shoreby against her will. An alarm was given when Dick was forced to kill one of Lord Shoreby's spies. Still in the disguise of a priest, he was taken to Sir Oliver Oates, who promised not to betray Dick if he would remain quietly in the church until after the wedding of Joanna and Lord Shoreby. During the night Lawless found Dick and gave him the message that Ellis Duckworth had returned and would prevent the marriage.

As the wedding procession entered the church, three archers discharged their black arrows from a gallery. Lord Shoreby fell, two of the arrows in his body. Sir Daniel was wounded in the arm. Sir Oliver Oates denounced Dick and Lawless and they were taken before the Earl of Risingham. But Dick argued his cause with such vigor, aided by Joanna and Alicia, that the earl agreed to protect him from Sir Daniel's anger. Later, learning from Dick that Sir Daniel was secretly plotting with the Yorkist leaders, the earl set him and Lawless free.

Dick made his escape from Sir Daniel's men only to be captured by the old seaman whose skiff he had stolen on the night he and Lord Foxham had attempted to rescue Joanna from Sir Daniel. It took him half the night to elude the angry seaman and his friends. In the morning he was in time to meet, at Lord Foxham's request, young Richard of York, Duke of Gloucester. On his arrival at the meeting place he found the duke attacked by bandits. He saved Richard's life and later fought with the duke in the battle of Shoreby, where the army of Lancaster was defeated. For his bravery in the fight he was knighted. Afterward, when Richard was giving out honors, Dick claimed as his portion only the freedom of the old seaman whose boat he had stolen.

Pursuing Sir Daniel, Dick rescued Joanna and took her to Holywood. The next morning he encountered Sir Daniel in the forest near the abbey. Dick was willing to let his enemy escape, but Ellis Duckworth, lurking nearby, killed the faithless knight. Dick asked the outlaw to spare the life of Sir Oliver Oates.

Dick and Joanna were married with great honor. They lived quietly at Moat House, withdrawn from the bloody disputes of the houses of Lancaster and York. Both the old seaman and Lawless were cared for in their old age, and Lawless finally took orders and died a friar.

BLACK LAMB AND GREY FALCON

Type of work: Record of travel
Author: Rebecca West (Cecily Fairfield Andrews, 1892-)
Type of plot: Travel sketches
Time of plot: 1937
Locale: Yugoslavia
First published: 1941

Principal characters:
REBECCA WEST, a journalist
HENRY ANDREWS, her husband
CONSTANTINE, a Yugoslavian poet
GERDA, Constantine's German wife

Critique:

Miss West's book is more than a narrative of her journey through Yugoslavia. She spent several years working on the book, building up a study of Yugoslavia and its people around the impressions she had gained while traveling in the country. The result is that for every page of travel description there are several pages of material about the country gleaned from study and reading. The work is full of digressions on anthropology, architecture, cultural history, literature, politics, philosophy, and Yugoslavian psychology.

The Story:

Rebecca West had not seen Yugoslavia until 1936, when she made a lecture tour in that country; but it impressed her so greatly that she decided to travel throughout the country as a tourist in 1937. She also felt that it was important to know something of the country because of the effect it might have upon world politics after the death of its king, Alexander, in 1937. It had been of great importance twenty-three years before, when the assassination of Franz Ferdinand in Sarajevo had precipitated a world conflict.

The author and her husband entered Yugoslavia by railroad on the line which ran from Munich, Germany, to Zagreb, Yugoslavia. Their journey was not a very interesting one, except for the antics of four fat German tourists who shared their compartment and told of the advantages of Germany over the barbaric country they were entering. Zagreb was interesting because it was inhabited mainly by Croats, one branch of the south Slavic racial group.

In Zagreb they met Constantine, a Yugoslavian poet who had become a friend of the author on her previous trip to his country. Constantine showed them about the city, introduced them to various interesting people, and promised to travel with them during part of their journey. In Zagreb the tourists were surprised at the depth of feeling and the frequent arguments between the various Yugoslavian groups. There were Serbs, Slovenes, and Croats, all under the government at Belgrade, and all disagreeing heartily on government policies. The country was also divided internally by religious beliefs. There were three main religious groups, the Roman Catholics, the Orthodox Catholics, and the Moslems. The latter were either Turks who had remained in the country when the Turkish regime had been driven out over a century before, or Yugoslavs who had accepted the religion of the Moslems during the five centuries of Turkish occupation of that part of Europe. Miss West noted that in Zagreb the people lived in physical comfort, if not in political comfort. She thought that the city had a warm and comfortable appearance, but that the Austrian influence had deprived it of much of its originality and naïveté.

From Zagreb the travelers went to visit a castle which had been turned into a sanatorium. They found the place spotlessly clean for such an old castle. The sanatorium was one of the few places in Yugoslavia in which there was little political speculation or argument. The doctors were too busy for politics. Patients were forbidden to discuss such matters.

Returning to Zagreb, the author and her husband went next to Sushak on the Dalmatian coast. Their first impression of the coast was one of bare, treeless hillsides and shouting, angry men. It was poor country. While at Sushak, they crossed the river to Fiume, which seemed to be the kind of city one would find in a bad dream. What struck the travelers as being the worst aspect of this town was the number of officials throughout the city who demanded to see their passports.

After visiting Fiume they traveled by steamer to Senj, a city which interested them because it had played a decisive part in keeping the Turks from overrunning Western Europe in the sixteenth and seventeenth centuries. The town had financed pirate vessels which terrorized the Turks and had kept them from using the western part of the Mediterranean and the Adriatic.

Farther south on the Dalmatian coast they visited Split, and found it to have an almost Neapolitan air. The town was also famed for the palace Diocletian had built there. Miss West learned that from Diocletian's palace eighteenth-century British architects had borrowed the Georgian style so popular in England and in some parts of the American colonies.

This information came to her from a young Englishman she met at Split. The young man was making a living in the city by teaching English. For him the Dalmatian coast was the closest thing to a terrestrial heaven. Miss West was surprised at the number of old buildings still in use. Diocletian's mausoleum, for example, had been turned into a Christian cathedral. At Split Miss West disclosed that she had little respect for the Romans and thought far more highly of the Croats and Slavs. She hoped that school children were not being impressed with the idea that the Romans had been a great and glorious influence on the Yugoslavian territory and people, for she saw that their poverty and their reputation as barbarians were the result of the Roman attitude toward their forebears, an attitude maintained by Central Europeans in the twentieth century.

The last stop on the Dalmatian coast was Dubrovnik, a disappointment to the travelers. There they wired their friend Constantine to meet them at Sarajevo, to which they were going by automobile from Dubrovnik. On the way to Sarajevo they passed a valley which Miss West could describe only as something out of Baron Munchausen's tales. This valley was a lake in the wintertime, but in the spring the water went out of the valley through some unknown outlet to the sea, leaving fertile fields in which peasants planted crops during the summer months.

At Sarajevo they met Constantine and his German wife, Gerda. The German woman made the air about the party a bit tense because of the deprecating attitude which she, like most Germans, took toward Yugoslavians. While at Sarajevo they wandered all over the town and were able to visit the family of the man who had killed Franz Ferdinand in 1914.

The next phase of their journey was a rail trip to the capital city of Belgrade, where they were impressed by the large supply of good food available and the provincial air of the capital and its people.

That part of the journey by rail from Belgrade to Skoplje was almost as uninteresting as the trip from Munich to Zagreb. More enjoyable was a stay at Lake Naum, on the southern edge of Yugoslavia near Greece and Albania. It was a wild and beautiful part of the country, despite the poverty of the land and its people.

From the Lake Naum area they went back part of the way to Belgrade on the railroad, and then motored to Kotor on the Dalmatian coast. There Constantine and his German wife bade them goodbye. The author and her husband took a ship at Kotor and traveled up the coast, and then returned by rail to Zagreb. They visited the Plivitse Lakes on the way. The last leg of the journey was by rail from Zagreb to Budapest, Hungary.

The sadness of the plight of the Yugoslavs was impressed on Miss West one last time in Budapest. There she met a university student who wanted to write a paper about Miss West's work. The girl tried to prevent Miss West from discovering that her family had come from the Balkans, for the girl wanted to be a part of the Central European culture rather than of the one she had inherited.

BLEAK HOUSE

Type of work: Novel
Author: Charles Dickens (1812-1870)
Type of plot: Social criticism
Time of plot: Mid-nineteenth century
Locale: London, Lincolnshire, and Hertfordshire, England
First published: 1852-1853

Principal characters:
JOHN JARNDYCE, owner of Bleak House
RICHARD CARSTONE, his cousin
ADA CLARE, also his cousin
ESTHER SUMMERSON, his ward and companion to Ada
ALLAN WOODCOURT, a young physician
LADY DEDLOCK, Sir Leicester Dedlock's wife
TULKINGHORN, a solicitor
WILLIAM GUPPY, Tulkinghorn's clerk

Critique:

A satire on the methods of an English equity court, *Bleak House* is a great novel based upon an actual case in Chancery. The story of lives sacrificed on the rack of a meaningless judicial system is an arresting one. Several of the minor characters are caricatures of well-known literary figures of the day. The complicated Lady Dedlock plot which gave *Bleak House* its contemporary popularity is rather thin, but the novel as a whole stands up remarkably well.

The Story:

The suit of Jarndyce vs. Jarndyce was a standing joke in the Court of Chancery. Beginning with a dispute as to how the trusts under a Jarndyce will were to be administered, the suit had dragged on, year after year, generation after generation, without settlement. The heirs, or would-be heirs, spent their lives waiting. Some, like Tom Jarndyce, blew out their brains. Others, like tiny Miss Flite, visited the Court in daily expectation of some judgment which would settle the disputed estate and bring her the wealth of which she dreamed.

Among those involved in the suit were John Jarndyce, great-nephew of the Tom Jarndyce who had shot himself in a coffee house, and his two cousins, Richard Carstone and Ada Clare. Jarndyce was the owner of Bleak House in Hertfordshire, a country place which was not as dreary as its name. His two young cousins lived with him. He had provided a companion for Ada in the person of Esther Summerson. Esther had suffered an unhappy childhood under the care of Miss Barbary, her stern godmother, and a servant, Mrs. Rachel. The two had told the girl that her mother was a wicked woman who had deserted her. Miss Barbary was now dead, and Mr. Jarndyce had become Esther's benefactor.

Two others who took a strange interest in the Jarndyce estate were Sir Leicester and Lady Dedlock of Chesney Wold, in Lincolnshire. Lord Dedlock had a solicitor named Tulkinghorn, who, like every other reputable lawyer in London, was involved in the Jarndyce suit. One day when the Dedlocks were in Tulkinghorn's office, the lawyer presented Lady Dedlock with a document. At the sight of the handwriting on the paper she swooned. Immediately suspicious, Tulkinghorn resolved to trace the handwriting to its source. His search led him to Mr. Snagsby, a stationer, but the best that Snagsby could tell him was that the paper had been copied by a man named Nemo, a lodger in the house of Mr. Krook, a junk dealer. Mr. Tulkinghorn went to the house with Snagsby, only to find Nemo dead of an overdose of opium. Convinced that Nemo was not the dead man's real name, the lawyer could learn nothing of the man's identity or connections.

Esther Summerson soon found an ardent friend and admirer in William Guppy, a clerk in the office of Kenge and Carboy, Jarndyce's solicitors. It was Guppy who first noticed Esther's resemblance to Lady Dedlock. Allan Woodcourt, a young surgeon who had been called to administer to the dead Nemo, requested an inquest. One of the witnesses called was Jo, a crossing sweeper whom Nemo had often befriended. A little later Jo was found with two half-crowns on his person. He explained that they had been given him by a lady he had guided to the gate of the churchyard where Nemo was buried. Jo was arrested, and in the cross-examination which followed, Mr. Guppy questioned the wife of an oily preacher named Chadband and found that the firm of Kenge and Carboy had once had charge of a young lady with whose aunt Mrs. Chadband had lived. Mrs. Chadband was, of course, the Mrs. Rachel of Esther Summerson's childhood. She revealed that Esther's real name was not Summerson, but Hawdon.

The mystery surrounding Esther Summerson began to clear. A French maid who had left Lady Dedlock's service identified her late mistress as the lady who had given two half-crowns to the crossing sweeper. The dead Nemo was promptly proved to have been Captain Hawdon. Years before he and the present Lady Dedlock had fallen in love; Esther was their child. But Miss Barbary, angry at her sister's disgrace, had taken the child and moved to another part of the country. The mother later married Lord Dedlock. She was now overjoyed that the child her unforgiving sister had led her to believe dead was still alive, and she resolved to reveal herself to her.

Mr. Guppy informed Lady Dedlock that a packet of Captain Hawdon's letters was in the possession of the junk dealer, Krook. Fearing that the revelation of these letters would ruin her position, Lady Dedlock asked Guppy to bring them to her, and the wily law clerk agreed. But on the night the letters were to be obtained the drunken Krook exploded of spontaneous combustion, and presumably the letters burned with him.

In the meantime, Richard Carstone, completely obsessed by the Jarndyce case, had abandoned all efforts to establish a career for himself. He lived in a false hope that the Chancery suit would soon be settled, spending the little money he had on an unscrupulous lawyer named Vholes. When Jarndyce remonstrated, Richard thought his cousin's advice prompted by selfish interests. Ada Clare also worried over Richard's behavior, and secretly married him so that her own small fortune might stand between Richard and his folly.

Esther Summerson fell desperately ill of a fever, and when Lady Dedlock heard of the girl's illness she went to her at once and revealed herself. So mother and daughter were finally reunited. As a result of her illness, Esther's beauty was completely destroyed. John Jarndyce, feeling free for the first time to declare his love for a woman so much younger than himself, asked her to marry him, and she accepted.

Lady Dedlock, meanwhile, was threatened by Tulkinghorn with exposure. Desperate, she wandered away from Chesney Wold. On the night of her disappearance Tulkinghorn was murdered by the French maid through whom he had learned of Lady Dedlock's connection with the crossing sweeper. She had attempted to blackmail the lawyer, and when he threatened her with imprisonment she killed him. Inspector Bucket, who solved the mystery of the murder, also informed Lord Dedlock of his wife's past. The baronet told the detective to employ every means to bring about her return. It was Esther Summerson, however, who found her mother dead at the gate of the churchyard where Captain Hawdon was buried.

Among Krook's effects was a Jarndyce will made at a later date than the one which had been disputed in Chancery for so many years. It settled the question of the Jarndyce inheritance forever. Richard and Ada were declared the heirs, but unfortunately the entire fortune had been eaten up in court costs and the two young people were left to face a life of genteel poverty. Richard did not long survive this final blow. He died, leaving his wife and infant son in the care of John Jarndyce.

Esther became the mistress of her own Bleak House. John Jarndyce, discovering that her true love was young Doctor Woodcourt, released her from her promise to marry him and in his generosity brought the two lovers together. Before her wedding to Doctor Woodcourt, Jarndyce took her to see a country house he had bought at Yorkshire. He had named it Bleak House, and it was his wedding present to the bride and groom. There Esther lived, happy in the love of her husband and her two daughters and in the lasting affection of John Jarndyce, proprietor of that other Bleak House which would always be her second home.

BRAVE NEW WORLD

Type of work: Novel
Author: Aldous Huxley (1894-)
Type of plot: Social satire
Time of plot: 632 years After Ford
Locale: London and New Mexico
First published: 1932

Principal characters:
BERNARD MARX, a citizen of the future
LENINA CROWNE, an Alpha worker
JOHN, the Savage
MUSTAPHA MOND, a World Controller

Critique:
Aldous Huxley satirizes our current Western civilization by describing in *Brave New World* the condition in which

it might find itself some six hundred years from our time. Contemporary trends in culture are carried to shocking, amusing, and fantastic extremes in the book. *Brave New World,* because of obvious limitations of space, contains features which beg further elucidation. Within definite limits, however, the author has succeeded in indicting twentieth-century Western culture with delightful acerbity and urbane wit.

The Story:

One day in the year 632 After Ford, as time was reckoned in the brave new world, the Director of the Central London Hatchery and Conditioning Center took a group of new students on a tour of the plant where human beings were turned out by mass production. The entire process, from the fertilization of the egg to the birth of the baby, was carried out by trained workers and machines. Each fertilized egg was placed in solution in a large bottle for scientific development into whatever class in society the human was intended. The students were told that scientists of the period had developed a Bokanovsky Process by means of which a fertilized egg was arrested in its growth. The egg responded by budding, and instead of one human being resulting, there would be from eight to ninety-six humans, all identical.

These Bokanovsky Groups were employed wherever large numbers of people were needed to perform identical tasks. Individuality was a thing of the past; the new society bent every effort to make completely true its motto, Community, Identity, Stability. After birth the babies were further conditioned during their childhood for their predestined class in society. Alpha Plus Intellectuals and Epsilon Minus Morons were the two extremes of the scientific utopia.

Mustapha Mond, one of the World Controllers, joined the inspection party and lectured to the new students on the horrors and disgusting features of old-fashioned family life. To the great embarrassment of the students, he, in his position of authority, dared use the forbidden words *mother* and *father;* he reminded the students that in 632 A. F. everyone belonged to everyone else.

Lenina Crowne, one of the Alpha workers in the Hatchery, took an interest in Bernard Marx. Bernard was different —too much alcohol had been put into his blood surrogate during his period in the prenatal bottle and he had sensibilities similar to those possessed by people in the time of Henry Ford.

Lenina and Bernard went by rocket ship to New Mexico and visited the Savage Reservation, a wild tract where primitive forms of human life had been preserved for scientific study. At the pueblo of Malpais the couple saw an Indian ceremonial dance in which a young man was whipped to propitiate the gods. Lenina was shocked and disgusted by the filth of the place and by the primitive aspects of all she saw.

The pair met a white youth named John. The young man disclosed to them that his mother, Linda, had come to the reservation many years before on vacation with a man called Thomakin. The vacationers had separated and Thomakin had returned alone to the brave new world. Linda, marooned in New Mexico, gave birth to a son and was slowly assimilated into the primitive society of the reservation. The boy educated himself with an old copy of Shakespeare's plays which he had found. Bernard was convinced that the boy was the son of the Director of Hatcheries, who in his youth had taken a companion to New Mexico on vacation and had returned without her. Bernard had enough human curiosity to wonder how this young savage would react to the scientific world. He invited John and his mother to return to London with him. John, attracted to Lenina and anxious to see the outside world, went eagerly.

Upon Bernard's return, the Director of Hatcheries publicly proposed to dismiss him from the Hatchery because of his unorthodoxy. Bernard produced Linda and John, the director's son. At the family reunion, during which such words as *mother* and *father* were used more than once, the director was shamed out of the plant. He later resigned his position.

Linda went on a *soma* holiday, *soma* being a drug which induced forgetfulness. John became the curiosity of London. He was appalled by all he saw—by the utter lack of any humanistic culture and by the scientific mass production of everything, including humans. Lenina tried to seduce him but he was held back by his primitive morality.

John was called to attend the death of Linda, who had taken too much *soma* drug. Maddened by the callousness of people conditioned toward death, he instigated a mutiny of workers as they were being given their *soma* ration. Arrested, he was taken by the police to Mustapha Mond, with whom he had a long talk on the new civilization. Mond explained that beauty caused unhappiness and thus instability; therefore humanistic endeavor was checked. Science was dominant. Art was stifled completely; science, even, was stifled at a certain point. And religion was restrained so that it could not cause instability. Mond explained, with a genial sort of cynicism, the reasons underlying all of the features of the brave new world. Despite Mond's persuasiveness, the Savage continued to champion tears, inconvenience, God, and poetry.

John moved into the country outside London to take up his old way of life. Sightseers came by the thousands to see him; he was pestered by reporters and television men. At the thought of Lenina, whom he still desired, John mortified his flesh by whipping himself. Lenina visited him and was whipped to death by him in a frenzy of passion produced by his dual nature. When he realized what he had done, he hanged himself. Bernard's experiment had failed. Human emotions could end only in tragedy in the brave new world.

BREAD AND WINE

Type of work: Novel
Author: Ignazio Silone (1900-)
Type of plot: Social criticism
Time of plot: 1930's
Locale: Italy
First published: 1937

Principal characters:
Don Benedetto, a liberal priest
Pietro Spina, his former pupil and a political agitator
Bianchina Girasole, a peasant girl befriended by Spina
Cristina Colamartini, Bianchina's schoolmate

Critique:

This novel, which has been dramatized and produced on Broadway, is the study of a character who, despite tremendous intellectual disappointments and physical hardships, remained faithful to his concept of justice. Silone vividly presents the widespread compromising of ideals which took place on all levels of Italian society under the corporate state of Mussolini. By showing the efforts of several generations of honest, courageous Italians in their struggle for justice and social reform, Silone appears to present the thesis that good men, if not triumphant, will continue the fight as long as man exists.

The Story:

In the Italian village of Rocca dei Marsi, Don Benedetto, a former Catholic teacher, and his faithful sister, Marta, prepared to observe the don's seventy-fifth birthday. It was April, and war with the Abyssinians was in the making. Benedetto had invited several of his old students to observe his anniversary with him. Three appeared and the group talked of old acquaintances. Most of Benedetto's students had compromised the moral precepts that the high-minded old scholar had taught them. Benedetto asked about Pietro Spina, his favorite pupil, and learned from his guests that the independent-minded Spina had become a political agitator, a man without a country. It was rumored that Spina had returned to Italy to carry on his work among the peasants.

One day Doctor Nunzio Sacca, one of those who had been at the party, was summoned by a peasant to come to the aid of a sick man. Sacca, upon finding the man to be Spina, was filled with fear, but the sincerity and fervor of Spina made him ashamed. Spina, only in his thirties, had, with iodine, transformed his features to those of an old man. Sacca administered to Spina and arranged for the agitator's convalescence in a near-by mountain village. Later he furnished Spina with clerical clothes. Disguised as a priest and calling himself Don Paolo Spada, Spina went to the Hotel Girasole in Fossa, where he brought comfort to a young girl who was believed dying as the result of an abortion.

In the mountains, at Pietrasecca, Paolo—as Spina now called himself—stayed at the inn of Matelena Ricotta. In his retreat, Paolo began to have doubts concerning the value of the life he was leading, but always the animal existence of the peasants of Pietrasecca spurred him on in his desire to free the oppressed.

Bianchina Girasole, the girl whom Paolo had comforted at Fossa, appeared, well and healthy. Attributing her survival to Paolo, she said that the man was surely a saint. Bianchina, disowned by her family, went to Cristina Colamartini, a school friend who lived in Pietrasecca. The two girls, discussing school days and old friends, concluded that most of their schoolmates had taken to ways of evil in one way or another. When Bianchina seduced Cristina's brother, Alberto, the Colamartinis were scandalized. Paolo lost his respect for Cristina, who showed only too plainly that her devotion to God excluded all reason and any humanity; she avowed that a Colamartini could never marry a Girasole because of difference in caste.

Paolo began to visit more and more among the peasants. Soon he had a reputation as a wise and friendly priest. In his association with those simple people he learned that no reformer could ever hope to be successful with them by use of abstractions; the peasants accepted only facts, either good or bad. He left the valley. At Fossa he again sought out potential revolutionary elements. He spoke of revolution to Alberto and Bianchina, who had moved to Fossa, and to Pompeo, son of the local chemist. The youths were delighted. Paolo enlisted Pompeo in the movement.

Paolo next went to Rome. There, in the church of Scala Santa, he discarded his clerical dress to become Spina once again. In Rome he found an air of futility and despair. Romeo, his chief contact, told him that peasant agitators did not have a chance for success. Spina explained that propaganda by words was not enough; success could be achieved only by living the truth to encourage the oppressed. Spina saw student demonstrations in favor of the leader and of the projected war. He talked to Uliva, who had become completely disillusioned. Then he looked for Murica, a youth from his own district who, perhaps, could direct him to dependable peasants. But Murica had returned to his home. Before Spina left Rome he heard that an explosion had killed Uliva in his apartment. The police learned that Uliva had been preparing to blow up a church at a time when many high government officials were to be in it.

Back at the Hotel Girasole in Fossa, Spina, again disguised as Don Paolo, was sickened by the enthusiasm of the peasants for the success of the Abyssinian war. He sent Bianchina to Rocca to seek out Murica, and during the pro-war demonstrations he went about the village writing anti-war and anti-government slogans on walls. Pompeo, who had gone to Rome, returned during the excitement and revealed that he had been won over by the glory of the new war; he had enlisted for service in Africa. Paolo's charcoaled slogans soon had the village in an uproar. Pompeo, who suspected Paolo, announced publicly that he would disclose the culprit's identity, but Bianchina persuaded the youth not to expose her beloved Paolo.

Paolo went to visit his old schoolmaster, Don Benedetto, at Rocca. He appeared before the venerable old priest as himself, not as Paolo, and the two men, although of different generations, agreed that theirs was a common problem. They asked each other what had become of God in the affairs of men. Neither could offer any solution for the problem, but they both agreed that any compromise to one's belief was fatal, not only to the individual but also to society.

Paolo gave Bianchina money and letters and sent her to Rome; he himself went to Pietrasecca. There a young peasant brought him a letter from Don Benedetto; the messenger was Murica, the man he had been seeking. When Spina revealed his true identity to Murica, the two men swore to work together. News of Murica's work with Paolo circulated in Pietrasecca and Paolo found himself playing the part of confessor to Pietraseccans. What they disclosed to him from their secret hearts disgusted him, but at the same time convinced him more than ever that the peasants must be raised from their squalor. He renewed his acquaintance with Cristina, who had been asked by Don Benedetto to give Paolo help whenever he should need it.

Don Benedetto had been threatened because of his candid opinions. Called to officiate at a mass, he was poisoned when he drank the sacramental wine. At the same time Paolo, having received word that Romeo had been arrested in Rome, went to the Holy City, where he found that Bianchina had become a prostitute. She confessed her undying love for the priest. Paolo, now Spina, found the underground movement in Rome in utter chaos after Romeo's arrest. Despairing, he returned to his home district, where he learned that Murica had been arrested and killed by government authorities. He fled to Pietrasecca to destroy papers which he had left in the inn where he had stayed during his convalescence. Learning that he was sought throughout the district, he fled into the snow-covered mountains. Cristina followed his trail in an attempt to take him food and warm clothing. Mists and deep snow hindered her progress. Night fell. Alone and exhausted, she made the sign of the cross as hungry wolves closed in upon her.

BRIDESHEAD REVISITED

Type of work: Novel
Author: Evelyn Waugh (1903-)
Type of plot: Social criticism
Time of plot: Twentieth century

Locale: England
First published: 1945

Principal characters:
CHARLES RYDER, an architectural painter and the narrator
LORD MARCHMAIN, owner of Brideshead
LADY MARCHMAIN, his wife
BRIDESHEAD (BRIDEY),
SEBASTIAN,
JULIA, and
CORDELIA, their children
CELIA, Charles Ryder's wife
ANTHONY BLANCHE, and
BOY MULCASTER, Oxford friends of Charles and Sebastian
REX MOTTRAM, Julia's husband
CARA, Lord Marchmain's mistress

Critique:

Most of Evelyn Waugh's books are satires on some phase or precept of human life. *Brideshead Revisited* is no exception, but beneath the surface buffoonery and satire is a serious dedication of faith. Members of the Marchmain family attempt, each in a different way, to escape the promptings of their faith, but each is drawn back, sooner or later, into the enduring values of the Church. Even the droll, mocking hero is converted. In Waugh's mordantly comic world, man can no longer find his way without faith. The witty yet serious theme of the novel is suggested in its subtitle, "The Sacred and Profane Memories of Captain Charles Ryder."

The Story:

Captain Charles Ryder of the British Army and his company were moved to a new billet in the neighborhood of Brideshead, an old estate he had often visited during his student days at Oxford. Brideshead was the home of the Marchmains, an old Catholic family. Following the first World War, the Marquis of Marchmain went to live in Italy. There he met Cara, who became his mistress for life. Lady Marchmain, an ardent Catholic, and her four children, Brideshead, Sebastian, Julia, and Cordelia, remained in England. They lived either at Brideshead or at Marchmain House in London.

When Charles Ryder met Sebastian at Oxford, they soon became close friends. Among Sebastian's circle of friends were Boy Mulcaster and Anthony Blanche. With Charles' entrance into that group, his tastes became more expensive so that he ended his year with an overdrawn account of five hundred and fifty pounds.

Just after returning home from school for vacation, Charles received a telegram announcing that Sebastian had been injured. He rushed off to Brideshead, where he found Sebastian with a cracked bone in his ankle. While at Brideshead, Charles met some of Sebastian's family. Julia had met him at the station and later Bridey, the eldest of the Marchmains, and Cordelia, the youngest, arrived. After a month, his ankle having healed, Sebastian took Charles to Venice. There they spent the rest of their vacation with Lord Marchmain and Cara.

Early in the following school year Charles met Lady Marchmain when she visited Sebastian at Oxford. Her famous charm immediately won Charles, and he promised to spend his Christmas vacation at Brideshead. During the first term, Sebastian, Charles, and Boy Mulcaster were invited to a London charity

---

ball by Rex Mottram, a friend of Julia's. Bored, they left early and were later arrested for drunkenness and disorderly conduct. Rex obtained their release.

As a consequence of the escapade, Charles, Sebastian, and Boy were sent back to Oxford, and Mr. Samgrass, who was doing some literary work for Lady Marchmain, kept close watch on them for the rest of the term. Christmas at Brideshead was spoiled for almost everyone by the presence of Samgrass. Back at Oxford, Charles began to realize that Sebastian drank to escape and that he was trying to escape his family. At Brideshead, during the Easter vacation, Sebastian became quite drunk. Later Lady Marchmain went to Oxford to see Sebastian. During her visit he again became hopelessly drunk. Shortly afterward he left Oxford. After a visit with his father in Venice, he was induced to travel in Europe under the guidance of Samgrass.

The next Christmas Charles was invited to Brideshead to see Sebastian, who had returned from his tour. Sebastian told Charles that during their travels Samgrass had had complete control of all their expense money in order that Sebastian might not get any for drink. However, just before coming down to Brideshead, Sebastian had managed to evade Samgrass by pawning his own valuables, and by borrowing. He had enjoyed what he called a happy Christmas; he remembered practically nothing of it. Lady Marchmain tried to stop his drinking by having all liquor locked up, but her efforts proved useless. Instead of going on a scheduled hunt, Sebastian borrowed two pounds from Charles and got drunk. Charles left Brideshead in disgrace and went to Paris. Samgrass was also dismissed when the whole story of the tour was revealed. Rex Mottram was given permission to take Sebastian to a doctor in Zurich, but Sebastian gave him the slip in Paris.

Rex Mottram, a wealthy man with a big name in political and financial circles, wanted Julia not only for herself but also for the prestige and social position of the Marchmains. Julia became engaged to him despite her mother's protests but agreed to keep the engagement secret for a year. Lord Marchmain gave his complete approval. Rex, wanting a big church wedding, agreed to become a Catholic. Shortly before the wedding, however, Bridey informed Julia that Rex had been married once before and had been divorced for six years. They were married by a Protestant ceremony.

When Charles returned to England several years later, Julia told him that Lady Marchmain was dying. At her request Charles traveled to Fez to find Sebastian. When he arrived, Kurt, Sebastian's roommate, told him that Sebastian was in a hospital. Charles stayed in Fez until Sebastian had recovered. Meanwhile word had arrived that Lady Marchmain had died. Charles returned to London. There Bridey gave Charles his first commission; he was to paint the Marchmain town house before it was torn down.

Charles spent the next ten years developing his art. He married Celia, Boy Mulcaster's sister, and they had two children, Johnjohn and Caroline, the daughter born while Charles was exploring Central American ruins. After two years of trekking about in the jungles, he went to New York, where his wife met him. On their way back to London they met Julia Mottram, and she and Charles fell in love. In London and at Brideshead they continued the affair they had begun on shipboard.

Two years later Bridey announced that he planned to marry Beryl Muspratt, a widow with three children. When Julia suggested inviting Beryl down to meet the family, Bridey informed her that Beryl would not come because Charles and Julia were living there in sin. Julia became hysterical. She told Charles that she wanted to marry him, and they both made arrangements to obtain divorces.

Cordelia, who had been working with an ambulance corps in Spain, returned at the end of the fighting there and told them of her visit with Sebastian. Kurt had been seized by the Germans and taken back to Germany, where Sebastian followed him. After Kurt had hanged himself in a concentration camp, Sebastian returned to Morocco and gradually drifted along the coast until he arrived at Carthage. There he tried to enter a monastery, but was refused. Following one of his drinking bouts, the monks found him lying unconscious outside the gate and took him in. He planned to stay there as an under-porter for the rest of his life.

While Bridey was making arrangements to settle at Brideshead after his marriage, Lord Marchmain announced that he was returning to the estate to spend his remaining days. He did not arrive until after he had seen Bridey and Beryl, honeymooning in Rome. Having taken a dislike to Beryl, Lord Marchmain decided that he would leave Brideshead to Julia and Charles. Before long Lord Marchmain's health began to fail. His children and Cara, thinking that he should be taken back into the Church, brought Father Mackay to visit him, but he would not see the priest. When he was dying Julia again brought Father Mackay to his bedside and Lord Marchmain made the sign of the cross.

That day Julia told Charles what he had known all along, that she could not marry him because to do so would be living in sin and without God.

These were some of Captain Charles Ryder's memories when he saw Brideshead again after many years.

THE BRIDGE OF SAN LUIS REY

Type of work: Novel
Author: Thornton Wilder (1897-)
Type of plot: Philosophical romance
Time of plot: Early eighteenth century
Locale: Peru
First published: 1927

Principal characters:
Brother Juniper, a Spanish friar
The Marquesa de Montemayor, a lonely old woman
Pepita, her maid
The Abbess Madre María del Pilar, directress of the Convent of Santa María Rosa de las Rosas
Uncle Pio, an actor-manager
La Périchole, an actress
Manuel, a foundling
Esteban, his brother

Critique:

The Bridge of San Luis Rey tells a story of Peru in the golden days when it was a Spanish colony. The novel is full of life, of interesting sidelights on an interesting period, and, above all, of excellent character sketches. The marquesa is an unforgettable person, tragic and comic at the same time. Wilder has brought together a group of unusual people and made them fit into a narrative pattern in which their individual contrasts stand out more clearly. A Pulitzer prize novel of its day, the story is still popular and widely read.

The Story:

On Friday, July the twentieth, 1714, the bridge of San Luis Rey, the most famous bridge in Peru, collapsed, hurling five travelers into the deep gorge below. Present at the time of the tragedy was Brother Juniper, who saw in the event a chance to prove, scientifically and accurately, the wisdom of that act of God. He spent all his time investigating the lives of the five who had died, and he published a book showing that God had had a reason to send each one of them to his death at exactly that moment. The book was condemned by the Church authorities, and Brother Juniper was burned at the stake. He had gone too far in explaining God's ways to man. Through a strange quirk of fate, one copy of the book was left undestroyed, and it fell into the hands of the author. From it, and from his own knowledge, he reconstructed the lives of the five persons.

The Marquesa de Montemayor had been an ugly child, and was still homely when she grew up. Because of the wealth of her family, she was fortunately able to marry a noble husband, by whom she had a lovely daughter, Doña Clara. As she grew into a beautiful young woman, the marquesa's daughter became more and more disgusted with her crude and unattractive mother, whose possessive and over-expressive love left Doña Clara cold and uncomfortable. The daughter finally married a man who took her to Spain. Separated from her one joy in life, the marquesa became more eccentric than before, and spent her time writing long letters to her daughter in Spain.

In order to free herself of some of her household cares, the marquesa went to the Abbess Madre María del Pilar and asked for a girl from the abbess' school to come and live with her. So Pepita, unhappy that her beloved teacher was sending her away from the school, went to live with the marquesa.

When the marquesa learned by letter that Doña Clara was to have a child, she was filled with concern. She wore charms, bought candles for the saints, said prayers, and wrote all the advice she could discover to her daughter. As a last gesture, she took Pepita with her to pay a visit to a famous shrine from which she hoped her prayers would surely be heard. On the way the marquesa happened to read one of Pepita's letters to her old mistress, the abbess. From the letter the marquesa learned just how heartless she had been in her treatment of the girl, how thoughtless and egotistic. She realized that she had been guilty of the worst kind of love toward her daughter, love that was sterile, self-seeking, and false. Aglow with her new understanding, she wrote a final letter to her daughter, telling her of the change in her heart, asking forgiveness, and showing in wonderful language the change that had come over her. She resolved to change her life, to be kind to Pepita, to her household, to everyone. The next day she and Pepita, while crossing the bridge of San Luis Rey, fell to their deaths.

Uncle Pio had lived a strange life before he came to Peru. There he had found a young girl singing in a tavern. After years of his coaching and training, she became the most popular actress of the Spanish world. She was called La Périchole, and Uncle Pio's greatest pleasure was to tease her and anger her into giving consistently better performances. All went well until the viceroy took an interest in the vivacious and beautiful young actress. When she became his mistress, she began to feel that the stage was too low for her. After living as a lady and becoming prouder and prouder as time went on, she contracted smallpox. Her beauty was ruined, and she retired to a small farm out of town, there to live a life of misery over her lost loveliness.

Uncle Pio had a true affection for his former protégée and tried time and again to see her. One night, by a ruse, he got her to talk to him. She refused to let him help her, but she allowed him to take Jaime, her illegitimate son, so that he could be educated as a gentleman. The old man and the young boy set off for Lima. On the way they came to the bridge, and died in the fall when it collapsed.

Esteban and Manuel were twin brothers who had been left as children on the doorstep of the abbess' school. She had brought them up as well as she could, but the strange relation between them was such that she could never make them talk much. When the boys were old enough, they left the school and took many kinds of jobs. At last they settled down as scribes, writing letters for the uncultured people of Lima. One day Manuel, called in to write some letters for La Périchole, fell in love with the charming actress. Never before had anything come between the brothers, for they had always been sufficient in themselves. For his brother's sake Manuel pretended that he cared little for the actress. Shortly afterward he cut his leg on a piece of metal and became very sick. In his delirium he let Esteban know that he really was in love with La Périchole. The infection grew worse and Manuel died.

Esteban was unable to do anything for weeks after his brother's death. He could not face life without him. The abbess finally arranged for him to go on a trip with a sea captain who was about to sail around the world. The captain had lost his only daughter and the abbess felt he would understand Esteban's problem and try to help him. Esteban left to go aboard ship, but on the way he fell with the others when the bridge broke.

At the cathedral in Lima a great service was held for the victims. Everyone considered the incident an example of a true act of God, and many reasons were offered for the various deaths. Some months after the funeral, the abbess was visited by Doña Clara, the marquesa's daughter. Doña Clara had finally learned what a wonderful woman her mother had really been. The last letter had taught the cynical daughter all that her mother had so painfully learned. The daughter, too, had learned to see life in a new way. La Périchole also came to see the abbess. She had given up bemoaning her own lost beauty, and she began a lasting friendship with the abbess. Nothing could positively be said about the reason for the deaths of those five people on the bridge. Too many events were changed by them; one could not number them all. But the old abbess believed that the true meaning of the disaster was the lesson of love for those who survived.

THE BROTHERS KARAMAZOV

Type of work: Novel
Author: Fyodor Mikhailovich Dostoevski (1821-1881)
Type of plot: Impressionistic realism
Time of plot: Nineteenth century
Locale: Russia
First published: 1880

Principal characters:
FYODOR KARAMAZOV, a profligate businessman
DMITRI, his sensuous oldest son
IVAN, his atheistic, intellectual son
ALEXEY, his youngest son, called Alyosha
GRUSHENKA, a young woman loved by Fyodor and Dmitri
SMERDYAKOV, an epileptic servant of Fyodor
ZOSSIMA, an aged priest
KATERINA, betrothed to Dmitri

Critique:

The anguish caused by the dual nature of man recurs in great chords throughout this powerful novel. Psychologist-novelist Dostoevski chose as the theme for this story of a father and his three sons the effect of sensuality and inherited sensuality on a family and on all with whom the family came in contact. The earthy barbarism of tsarist Russia can be seen beneath the veneer of Western culture which covers Dostoevski's society. Several poorly connected and lengthy sub-plots in the novel detract from the unity of the work; their inclusion suggests that Dostoevski had planned a longer work which, because of the installment form in which the novel first appeared, could not be completed.

The Story:

In the middle of the nineteenth century in Skotoprigonyevski, a town in the Russian provinces, Fyodor Karamazov fathered three sons, the eldest, Dmitri, by his first wife, and the other two, Ivan and Alexey, by his second. Fyodor, a good businessman but a scoundrel by nature, abandoned the children after their mothers died. A family servant, Grigory, saw that they were placed in the care of relatives.

Dmitri grew up believing he would receive a legacy from his mother's estate. He served in the army where he developed wild ways. Becoming a wastrel, he went to his father and asked for money which he believed was due him. Ivan, morose but not timid, went from a gymnasium to a college in Moscow. Poverty forced him to teach and to contribute articles to periodicals, and he achieved modest fame when he published an article on the position of the ecclesiastical courts. Alexey, or Alyosha, the youngest son, a boy of a dreamy, retiring nature, entered a local monastery, where he became the pupil of a famous Orthodox Church elder, Zossima. When Alyosha asked his father's permission to become a monk, Fyodor, to whom nothing was sacred, scoffed but gave his sanction.

When the brothers had all reached manhood, their paths met in the town of their birth. Dmitri returned to collect his legacy. Ivan, a professed atheist, returned home for financial reasons.

At a meeting of the father and sons at the monastery, Fyodor shamed his sons by behaving like a fool in the presence of the revered Zossima. Dmitri, who arrived late, was accused by Fyodor of wanting the legacy money in order to entertain a local adventuress to whom he himself was attracted. Dmitri, who was betrothed at this time to Katerina, a colonel's daughter whom he had rescued from shame, raged at his father, saying that the old man was a great sinner and had no room to talk. Zossima fell down before Dmitri, tapping his head on the floor, and his fall was believed to be a portent of an evil that would befall the oldest son. Realizing that the Karamazovs were sensualists, Zossima advised Alyosha to leave the monastery and go into the world at Zossima's death. There was further dissension among the Karamazovs because of Ivan's love for Katerina, the betrothed of Dmitri.

Marfa, the wife of Grigory, Fyodor's faithful servant, had given birth to a deformed child. The night that Marfa's deformed baby died, Lizaveta, an idiot girl of the town, also died after giving birth to a son. The child, later to be called Smerdyakov, was taken in by Grigory and Marfa and was accepted as a servant in the household of Fyodor, whom everyone in the district believed the child's true father.

Dmitri confessed his wild ways to Alyosha. He opened his heart to his brother, and told how he had spent three thousand roubles of Katerina's money in an orgy with Grushenka, a local woman of questionable character with whom he had fallen passionately in love. Desperate for the money to repay Katerina, Dmitri asked Alyosha to secure it for him from Fyodor.

Alyosha found Fyodor and Ivan at the table, attended by the servant, Smerdyakov, who was an epileptic. Entering suddenly in search of Grushenka, Dmitri attacked his father. Alyosha went to Katerina's house, where he found Katerina trying to bribe Grushenka into abandoning her interest in Dmitri. But Grushenka was not to be bargained with. Upon his return to the monastery, Alyosha found Zossima dying. He returned to Fyodor, to discover his father afraid of both Dmitri and Ivan. Ivan wanted Dmitri to marry Grushenka so that he himself could marry Katerina. Fyodor wanted to marry Grushenka. The father refused to give Alyosha any money for Dmitri.

Katerina, spurned by Dmitri, dedicated her life to watching over him, although she felt a true love for Ivan. Ivan, seeing that Katerina was pledged to torture herself for life, nobly approved of her decision.

Later, in an inn, Ivan disclosed to Alyosha that he believed in God, but that he could not accept God's world. The young men discussed the dual nature of man. Ivan disclosed that he hated Smerdyakov, who was caught between the wild passions of Dmitri and Fyodor and who, out of fear, worked for the interests of each against the other.

The dying Zossima revived long enough to converse once more with his devoted disciples. When he died, a miracle was expected. In the place of a miracle, however, his body rapidly decomposed, delighting certain of the monks who were anxious that the institution of the elders in the Orthodox Church be discredited. They argued that the decomposition of his body proved his teachings had been false.

In his disappointment at the turn of events at the monastery, Alyosha was persuaded to visit Grushenka, who wished to seduce him. He found Grushenka prepared to escape the madness of the Karamazovs by running off with a former lover. The saintly Alyosha saw good in Grushenka; she, for her part, found him an understanding soul.

Dmitri, eager to pay his debt to Katerina, made various fruitless attempts to borrow the money. Mad with jealousy when he learned that Grushenka was not at her home, he went to Fyodor's house to see whether she were there. He found no Grushenka, but he seriously injured old Grigory with a pestle with which he had intended to kill his father. Discovering that Grushenka had fled to another man, he armed himself and went in pursuit. He found Grushenka with two Poles in an inn at another village. The young woman welcomed Dmitri and professed undying love for him alone. During a drunken orgy of the lovers the police appeared and charged Dmitri with the murder of his father, who had been found robbed and dead in his house. Blood on Dmitri's clothing, his possession of a large sum of money and passionate statements he had made against Fyodor were all evidence against him. Dmitri repeatedly protested his innocence, claiming that the money he had spent on his latest orgy was half of Katerina's roubles. He had saved the money to insure his future in the event that Grushenka accepted him. But the testimony of witnesses made his case seem hopeless. He was taken into custody and placed in the town jail to await trial.

Grushenka fell sick after the arrest of Dmitri, and she and Dmitri were plagued with jealousy of each other. Dmitri, as the result of a strange dream, began to look upon himself as an innocent man destined to suffer for the crimes of humanity. Ivan and Katerina, in the meantime, worked on a scheme whereby Dmitri might escape to America.

Before the trial Ivan interviewed the servant Smerdyakov three times. The servant had once told Ivan that he was able to feign an epileptic fit; such a fit had been Smerdyakov's alibi in the search for the murderer of Fyodor. The third interview ended when Smerdyakov confessed to the murder, insisting, however, that he had been the instrument of Ivan, who by certain words and actions had led the servant to believe that the death of Fyodor would be a blessing for everyone in his household. Smerdyakov, depending on a guilt complex in the soul of Ivan, had murdered his master at a time when all the evidence would point directly to Dmitri. He had felt that Ivan would protect him and provide him with a comfortable living. At the end of the third interview, he gave the stolen money to Ivan, who returned to his rooms and fell ill with fever and delirium, during which he was haunted by a realistic specter of the devil which resided in his soul. That same night Smerdyakov hanged himself.

The Karamazov case having attracted widespread attention throughout Russia, many notables attended the trial. Prosecution built up what seemed to be a strong case against Dmitri, but the defense, a city lawyer, refuted the evidence piece by piece. Doctors declared Dmitri to be abnormal, but in the end they could not agree. Katerina had her woman's revenge by revealing to the court a letter Dmitri had written her, in which he declared his intention of killing his father to get the money he owed her. Ivan, still in a fever, testified that Smerdyakov had confessed to the murder. Ivan gave the money to the court, but he negated his testimony when he lost control of himself and told the court of the visits of his private devil.

In spite of the defense counsel's eloquent plea in Dmitri's behalf, the jury returned a verdict of guilty amid a tremendous hubbub in the courtroom.

Katerina, haunted by guilt because she had revealed Dmitri's letter, felt that she was responsible for the jealousy of the two brothers. She left Ivan's bedside and went to the hospital where Dmitri, also ill of a fever, had been taken. Alyosha and Grushenka were present at their interview, when Katerina begged Dmitri for his forgiveness.

Later Alyosha left Dmitri in the care of Grushenka and went to the funeral of a schoolboy friend. Filled with pity and compassion for the sorrow of death and the misery of life, Alyosha gently admonished the mourners, most of them schoolmates of the dead boy, to live for goodness and to love the world of man. He himself was preparing to go with Dmitri to Siberia, for he was ready to sacrifice his own life for innocence and truth.

BUDDENBROOKS

Type of work: Novel
Author: Thomas Mann (1875-   )
Type of plot: Social chronicle
Time of plot: Nineteenth century
Locale: Germany
First published: 1902

Principal characters:
JEAN BUDDENBROOK, head of a German business house
FRAU BUDDENBROOK, Jean's wife
ANTONIE (TONY), Jean's daughter
CHRISTIAN, Jean's son
TOM, Jean's son
HERR GRÜNLICH, Tony's first husband
ERICA, daughter of Tony and Grünlich
GERDA, Tom's wife
HANNO, son of Tom and Gerda
HERR PERMANEDER, Tony's second husband

Critique:

The decadence of a materialistic society is clearly exposed in this novel, which had been compared with Galsworthy's *Forsyte Saga*. Objective in manner, the story nevertheless carries with it a condemnation of its people. The Buddenbrooks were by nature honest and good; they were imbued with family love and loyalty to their own class, but they allowed themselves no room for new blood. Their development, or rather their decay, lay in a kind of intermarriage; not intermarriage of blood relations, but of class. Their only mainstay was wealth. Losing that, they were destroyed.

The Story:

In the year 1875 the Buddenbrook family was at its peak. Johann had maintained intact the business and wealth he had inherited from his father, and the Buddenbrook name was held in high esteem. Johann's oldest son, Jean, inherited the business when old Johann died. Antonie, Jean's first child was born in the family home on Mengstrasse. Tony was an aristocrat by nature and temperament. The next child was Tom, followed by Christian, who seemed peculiar in his manners from birth. Tom displayed an early interest in the Buddenbrook business, but Christian seemed indifferent to all family responsibilities.

Tony grew into a beautiful woman. One day Herr Grünlich came to call on the family. Because of his obvious interest in Tony, Jean investigated Grünlich's financial status. But the headstrong girl despised Grünlich and his obsequious manner. Having gone to the seashore to avoid meeting Grünlich when he called again, she fell in love with a young medical student named Morten Schartzkopf. Learning of Tony's interest in the student, Jean and Frau Buddenbrook hurried their daughter home, and Tony was too much bred with a sense of her family duties to ignore their arguments in favor of Grünlich when he asked for her hand. Her wedding date set, Grünlich received a promise of a dowry of eighty thousand marks.

Grünlich, after taking his twenty-year-old bride to the country, would not allow her to call on any of her city friends. Although she complained in her letters to her parents, Tony resigned herself to obeying her husband's wishes.

Tom held an important position in the business which was still amassing money for the Buddenbrooks. Christian's early distaste for business and his ill health had given him the privilege of going to South America.

When Grünlich found his establishment floundering, his creditors urged him to send to his father-in-law for help. Jean Buddenbrook learned then of Grünlich's motive in marrying Tony; the Buddenbrook reputation had placed Grünlich's already failing credit upon a sounder basis. Actually Grünlich was a poor man who was depending upon Jean's concern for Tony to keep his son-in-law from financial failure. Tony herself assured her father that she hated Grünlich but that she did not wish to endure the hardships that bankruptcy would entail.

Jean brought Tony and his granddaughter, Erica Grünlich, back to the Buddenbrook home. The divorce, based on Grünlich's fraudulent handling of Tony's dowry, was easily arranged.

Jean Buddenbrook, loving his family dearly, firmly believed in the greatness of the Buddenbrook heritage. Tony was once again happy in her father's home, although she bore her sorrows like a cross for everyone to notice and reverence. Tom had grown quite close to his sister, who took pride in his development and in the progress of the Buddenbrook firm.

Christian, having failed in his enterprises in South America, had returned home. His father gave him a job and an office which Christian hated and avoided. His manners were still peculiar and his health poor. Serious Tom handled the business as well as Jean, and he remained fixed in his attachment to family customs. When Jean died and left the business to Tom, Tony felt that the family had lost its strongest tie. Tom, too, was greatly affected by his father's death, but the responsibility of his financial burdens immediately became of foremost importance.

Because Christian could not adjust himself to Buddenbrook interests, the ever-patient Tom sent him to Munich for his health. Reports from Munich that he was seen often in the company of a notoriously loose actress distressed his family. Then Tom made a satisfactory marriage with the daughter of a wealthy businessman. Gerda, whose dowry added to the Buddenbrook fortune, was an attractive woman who loved music. Parties were once more held at the Buddenbrook mansion on Mengstrasse.

Tony returned from a trip with hopes that a man whom she had met while traveling would come to call. Soon Herr Permaneder did call. He was a successful beer merchant in Munich. Tom and Frau Buddenbrook thought that Permaneder, in spite of his crude manners and strange dialect, would make a satisfactory husband for Tony. Fortified with her second, smaller dowry, Tony went to Munich as Frau Permaneder. She sent Erica off to boarding-school.

Once again Tony wrote passionate appeals to her family complaining of her married life. Finally she came home, weeping because Permaneder had betrayed her by making love to a servant. Tom protested against a second divorce, but Tony insisted. Prevailing upon Tom to write to Permaneder, Tony was surprised to learn that her husband would not fight the proceedings, that he felt the marriage had been a mistake, and that he would return to Tony her dowry which he did not need.

Tom and Gerda had produced a son to carry on the family name. Little Johann, or Hanno, as he was called, inherited his mother's love for music, but he was pale and sickly from birth. Tom tried to instill in his son a love for the family business, but Hanno was too shy to respond to his father.

The death of Frau Buddenbrook brought Christian, Tony, and Tom together to haggle over the inheritance. Christian demanded his money, but Tom, as administrator, refused. Infuriated, Christian quarreled bitterly with Tom, all the pent-up feeling of the past years giving vent to a torrent of abuse against the cold, mercenary actions of Tom Buddenbrook.

Tom was not mercenary. He worked hard and faithfully, but in spite of his efforts the business had declined much in the past few years because of economic changes. In poor health, he felt that sickly Christian would outlive him.

Although Tony found a fine husband for her daughter, even the marriage of Erica and Herr Weinschenk was destined to end in disaster. Herr Weinschenk was caught indulging in some foul business practices and went to jail for three years. Accustomed to public scandal, Tony bore that new hardship with forbearance. Erica, too, adopted her mother's attitude.

Suddenly Tom died. He had fallen in the snow, to be brought to his bed and die, a few hours later, babbling incoherently. His loss was greater to Tony than to any of the others. Christian, arriving from Munich for the funeral, had grown too concerned over his own suffering to show grief over the death of his brother. Gerda felt her own sorrow deeply, for her marriage with Tom had been a true love match.

After the will had been read, Christian returned to Munich to marry the mistress whom Tom's control had kept him from marrying. Soon afterward Christian's wife wrote to Tony that his illness had poisoned his mind. She had placed Christian in an institution.

Life at the Buddenbrook home went on. Little Hanno, growing up in a household of women, never gained much strength. Thin and sickly at fifteen, he died during a typhoid epidemic.

So passed the last of the Buddenbrooks. From the days of the first Johann, whose elegance and power had produced a fine business and a healthy, vigorous lineage, to the last pitiably small generation which died with Hanno, the Buddenbrooks had decayed into nothing.

THE CABALA

Type of work: Novel
Author: Thornton Wilder (1897-)
Type of plot: Fantasy
Time of plot: About 1920
Locale: Rome
First published: 1926

Principal characters:
SAMUELE, a young American student and writer
JAMES BLAIR, his friend
THE DUCHESS D'AQUILANERA, a Cabalist
MARCANTONIO, her son
CARDINAL VAINI, a former Chinese missionary
ASTRÉE-LUCE DE MORFONTAINE, a religious fanatic
ALIX D'ESPOLI, in love with James Blair

Critique:

Practically all of Thornton Wilder's work is unusual in one degree or another. *The Cabala*—really a series of sketches held together by locale and a group of people who have something in common—is no exception. The novel is a fantastic story of the pagan gods grown old and weak. Christianity and modern society have doomed them to despair, madness, and death. A young American of Puritan background records their overthrow, an ironic ending to their pagan power and pride.

The Story:

When Samuele went to Rome with his friend, James Blair, he learned of the existence there of a certain group known as the Cabala, talented and wealthy aristocrats, clever esoterics who had mysterious influence in affairs of Church and State. Blair, a bookish person, was familiar with some of its members, and he introduced his friend into that strange circle of Roman society. Samuele soon became a favorite of the Cabalists.

One of them, the Duchess d'Aquilanera, had a great problem on her mind. Her son Marcantonio, who was sixteen, had had five or six love affairs with various women, and she was disturbed by his unsettled habits. She had arranged a marriage for him, but the wedding would not take place unless Marcantonio changed his ways. She pleaded with Samuele to spend a weekend at her villa and to talk to the boy in an effort to show him the errors of the life he was leading. Samuele refused, thinking the whole matter ridiculous. Then he had a talk with Cardinal Vaini, a friend of the duchess, who said that Marcantonio had begun his wild career by imitating his older friends. Later his vicious morality had become a habit, and finally a mania. Samuele was so shocked by the cardinal's description of the boy's character that he finally agreed to go to the villa, as the duchess had requested.

Marcantonio liked to drive automobiles as fast as possible. He also told Samuele that he wished to train for the Olympics. Samuele, in a passionate outburst, denounced the boy's loose loves. The next day Marcantonio jumped from a balcony and killed himself.

Samuele was shocked and grieved. But he was soon to become involved in the strange conduct of another Cabalist, the Princess Alix d'Espoli. Alix always had the habit of falling in love with men who could not possibly be attracted to her. She had beauty and charm, but little intelligence. To make up for her lack, she cultivated a way of speaking that was interesting and appealing. Although people enjoyed having her at dinner, she accepted few invitations.

One day she went to visit Samuele and found James Blair in his apartment. Though Blair was rude, she fell in love with him and proceeded to lay siege to his affections. At last she was convinced that she had scored a triumph, for Blair gave her a book that had once been mentioned in casual conversation. She began going to his rooms uninvited. When Blair became upset, Samuele suggested that the only way out was for him to leave Rome. After Blair left on a trip to Spain, Alix proceeded to lose herself in the life of the city. She accepted all sorts of invitations, even asking to be introduced to various people. She seemed happy in a round of pleasure. Samuele hoped that she had forgotten Blair.

A month later Blair wrote to Samuele, saying that he was returning to Rome. Samuele warned him to stay away, but Blair insisted that his researches into ancient secret societies made his return necessary. One night both of them went to visit a famous seer who was holding a seance in an old Roman palace. While they were there, a heavily veiled woman came in, rushed to the seer, and implored his help in some matter. Recognizing Alix, Samuel and Blair attempted to leave, but the woman saw them before they could get out of the room. Abruptly, angrily, she went away. Later Samuele heard that she had become interested in the fine arts, that she was studying music. She started on a trip to Greece, but returned suddenly without an explanation. Some said that she continued to search for a lover. More and more she was spoken of in a derogatory manner.

One day in her presence a Danish archeologist said that he had met Blair. Upon hearing his name, Alix fainted.

Samuele also spent much of his time with Astrée-Luce de Morfontaine, a deeply religious woman. She saw some spiritual meaning in the initials of an American teacher named Irene H. Spencer, and on one occasion she was deeply offended when someone spoke slightingly of the pelican, because to her the bird was a holy symbol. She had great faith in prayer. One day the cardinal spoke derisively of prayer, and she broke down. The cardinal said that she had never suffered, that she did not know the meaning of suffering. The woman's faith was badly shaken. She invited the cardinal to her house for a party. During the evening she accused him of being the devil, took out a pistol, and shot at him. He was not hurt. But a later reconciliation was impossible. The cardinal decided to go back to his mission in China. En route, he caught a fever, died, and was buried at sea.

Before Samuele left Rome, he called on Miss Elizabeth Grier, an American member of the Cabala. From her he learned at last who the men and women of the Cabala really were. They were the pagan gods of Europe grown old, deities whose brooding ancient wisdom could not save them from the sufferings and follies of ordinary humanity. Miss Grier confused Samuele by stating her belief that he was the new god Mercury, an idea vaguely upsetting to a young American of New England ancestry.

CADMUS

Type of work: Classical legend
Source: Folk tradition
Type of plot: Heroic adventure
Time of plot: Remote antiquity
Locale: Ancient Greece
First transcribed: Unknown

Principal characters:
CADMUS, founder of Thebes
JUPITER, king of the gods
MINERVA, daughter of Jupiter
MARS, god of war
HARMONIA, wife of Cadmus

Critique:

The story of Cadmus is not one of the best known myths, but it is an important one, for it is a basis upon which many other stories have been built. Cadmus, like the other great classical heroes, lived at least thirty centuries ago, and the tales of his great deeds have been told over and over, changing a little with each telling. In reading of Cadmus, we meet the gods and goddesses, the serpents and monsters, and the other great figures who supposedly roamed the world when it was the playground of the gods. All things were possible in those heroic days.

The Story:

Jupiter, in the form of a bull, carried away Europa, who was the daughter of Agenor, king of Phenicia. When her handmaidens told her father of the kidnaping, he commanded his son Cadmus to look for Europa and not to return until he had found her. Cadmus searched for his sister for many years and in strange lands. But though he searched diligently, killing many monsters and endangering himself many times in his quest he could not find her. Afraid to return to his father, he consulted the oracle of Apollo at Delphi and asked where he should settle. The oracle told him that he would find a cow in a field, and if he were to follow her, she would lead him to a good land. Where the cow stopped, Cadmus was to build a great city and call it Thebes.

Cadmus soon saw a cow walking ahead of him, and he followed her. Finally the cow stopped on the plain of Panope. Cadmus prepared to give thanks to the gods, and he sent his slaves to find pure water for the sacrifice he would make. In a dense grove they found a wonderful clear spring. But the spring was guarded by a terrible dragon sacred to Mars, his scales shining like gold and his body filled with a poisonous venom. He had a triple tongue and three rows of huge, ragged teeth. The servants, thinking only to please their master, dipped their pitchers in the water, whereupon all were instantly destroyed by the monster.

Having waited many hours for the return of his servants, Cadmus went to the grove and found the mangled bodies of his faithful slaves and close by the terrible monster of the spring. First Cadmus threw a huge stone at the dragon. The stone did not dent his shining scales. Then he drew back his javelin and heaved it at the serpent. It went through the scales and into the entrails. The monster, trying to draw out the weapon with his mouth, broke the blade and left the point burning his flesh. He swelled with rage as he advanced toward the hero, and Cadmus retreated before him. Cadmus then threw his spear at the monster, the weapon pinning him against a tree until he died.

As Cadmus stood gazing at the terrible creature he heard the voice of the goddess Minerva telling him to sow the dragon's teeth in a field. Hardly had he done so when a warrier in armor sprang up from each tooth. Cadmus started toward the warriors, thinking he must slay them all or lose his own life, but again Minerva spoke to him and told him not to strike. The warriors began to do battle among themselves and all were slain but five, who then presented themselves to Cadmus and said that they would serve him. These six heroes built the city of Thebes.

Jupiter gave Cadmus Harmonia, the daughter of Mars and Venus, goddess of beauty, to be his wife, and the gods came down from Olympus to do honor to the couple. Vulcan forged a brilliant necklace with his own hands and gave it to the bride. Four children were born, and for a time Cadmus and Harmonia lived in harmony with their children. But doom hung over Cadmus and his family for the killing of the serpent, and Mars revenged himself by causing all of Cadmus' children to perish.

In despair, Cadmus and Harmonia left Thebes and went to the country of the Enchelians, who made Cadmus their king. But Cadmus could find no peace because of Mars' curse on him. One day he told Harmonia that if a serpent were so dear to the gods he himself wished to become a serpent. No sooner had he spoken the words than he began to grow scales and to change his form. When Harmonia beheld her husband turned into a serpent, she prayed to the gods for a like fate. Both became serpents, but they continued to love their fellow men and never did injury to any.

CAESAR OR NOTHING

Type of work: Novel
Author: Pío Baroja (1872-)
Type of plot: Political satire
Time of plot: Early twentieth century
Locale: Spain, Italy, France
First published: 1919

Principal characters:
LAURA, Marchesa of Vaccarone, formerly Laura Moncada
CAESAR MONCADA, Laura's brother
AMPARO, Caesar's wife
IGNACIO ALZUGARAY, Caesar's friend

Critique:

Caesar or Nothing is a political novel of satire directed against those elements of Spanish life which Baroja considered opposed to the improved social status of the common man. These elements were the aristocracy and the Church. The novel is interesting in the light of what has happened in Spain since this novel was published thirty years ago.

The Story:

Juan Guillén was a highwayman of Villanueva. When Vicenta, his youngest daughter, was ruined, she went away to Valencia, where she married Antonio Fort, a grocer. Francisco, Juan's eldest son, became a priest and changed his name to Fray José de Calasanz de Villanueva. Juan Fort, son of Vicenta, became a priest and was called Father Vicente de Valencia. He later became Cardinal Fort. Isabel, Vicenta's daughter, married a soldier, Carlos Moncada. Isabel and Carlos became the parents of Caesar Moncada and of Laura, later the Marchesa of Vaccarone.

Defying family tradition, Caesar rebelled at the idea of becoming a cleric. He attended various schools but cared little for the subjects taught there. Convinced that he had a definite mission in life, he set about preparing himself for it. Academic subjects did not enter into his plans. At school in Madrid he met Ignacio Alzugaray, who became his lifelong and intimate friend. He also met Carlos Yarza, a Spanish author employed in a bank in Paris, and through him Caesar became interested in financial speculation. Caesar developed a system, which he could explain only vaguely, to use in playing the stock market, but he had no money at the time with which to try it out.

Caesar and his sister Laura went to Rome, where Laura became popular in fashionable society. Caesar, however, cared little for social functions, art, and the historical relics of ancient Rome. After a time he did meet some important personages, among them Countess Brenda, with whom he had an affair.

Cardinal Fort, their kinsman, sent the Abbé Preciozi to act as a guide for Caesar and Laura. Caesar disliked his uncle, the cardinal, and cared little if the abbé carried back to the cardinal his nephew's frank opinions of his eminence. Through the abbé, Caesar tried to find people who would help him become a financial dictator, and he was directed to sound out Father Herreros and Father Miró. The cardinal, however, learned of Caesar's scheming and put a stop to it.

Archibald Marchmont fell in love with Laura. Both were unhappily married. Susanna Marchmont, Archibald's wife, was in turn attracted to Caesar, and she and Caesar took a trip together as man and wife. While in Rome, Caesar also met an Englishman named Kennedy through whom he learned much about the history of Rome and the history of the Borgias. Caesar Borgia's motto, "Caesar or Nothing," struck a responsive note in the latent ambition of Caesar Moncada. Without quite knowing why, he began to make notes about people in Rome who were members of the Black Party and who had connections in Spain.

Coming from the Sistine Chapel one day, Caesar and Kennedy met a Spanish painter who introduced them to Don Calixto, a senator and the political leader of the province of Zamora in Spain. Caesar accepted Don Calixto's invitation to dine with him and agreed to act as his guide about Rome. The don was appreciative, and when Caesar jokingly asked whether the don would consider making him a deputy, Don Calixto agreed to put Caesar's name on the ballot as a candidate for the district of Castro Duro whenever Caesar returned to Spain.

When Caesar returned to Spain, he reminded Don Calixto of his promise. Deciding to run on the Conservative ticket, Caesar drove about the country to meet the voters and to determine the most important political personages of the district. Don Platón Peribáñez and Antonio San Román were, he discovered, quite influential. Father Martín Lafuerza, the prior of a monastery, had a great deal of political influence in and about Castro Duro. Caesar's friend, Ignacio Alzugaray, came to Castro Duro and made himself useful to Caesar in many ways. At the house of Don Calixto Caesar met Amparo, the don's niece, but at first Caesar and Amparo could not get along. Later, however, they fell in love and planned to be married.

In the election Caesar defeated his two opponents, Garcia Padilla and San Román, and left Castro Duro to go to Madrid as deputy. In Madrid he became quite influential behind the political scene. When the Minister of Finance faced a crisis in his career, he sent Caesar to Paris to meet a financial expert who had a plan to save the government. Caesar, suspecting the minister, planned an airtight speculation which would make his own fortune and remove the minister from office.

With the money he had gained through his speculations, Caesar began to devise and carry into execution many improvements in Castro Duro. He designed a better water system and also a library for the Workmen's Club which he had previously established. In addition, he turned his back on the Conservative party and became a Liberal. Meanwhile the reactionary element in the district was not idle. It formed institutions and organizations to compete with the Workmen's Club, and used every possible means to wreck the political organization of the workers, until there was a state of undeclared war between Caesar's group and the others. During those disturbances Caesar and Amparo were married.

Father Martín's followers had hired a man nicknamed the "Driveller" to threaten and browbeat the more timid members of Caesar's group. The "Driveller" picked a fight with "Lengthy," the son of "The Cub-Slut," and a man known as "Gaffer." When "Lengthy" was killed in the fight, the workmen clamored for blood because they believed that the "Driveller" had done the deed at the request of the reactionaries of Father Martín. Caesar was requested by "The Cub-Slut" and the "Driveller's" mother to spare the "Driveller's" life, but for different reasons. "The Cub-Slut" wanted to revenge herself upon him, whereas the mother wanted to save her son. Caesar was in a quandary, and so he and Amparo went to Italy to visit Laura. It was believed that his act indicated a desire to retire from politics.

At home the political situation grew worse. When Caesar received a letter written by his liberal friends, Dr. Ortigosa, Antonio San Román, and José Camacho, he decided that he would not retire. He returned to Castro Duro and joined his friends in the struggle once more.

The battle continued right up to the next election. One day "The Cub-Slut" sent a note to Caesar, a message which he put distractedly into his pocket. Setting out to tour the district, he was wounded by an assassin when his car came to a crossroads. If he had read "The Cub-Slut's" letter, he might not have been shot. After the attempted assassination of Caesar, the Liberal party began to lose ground, the opposition using every possible method to defeat Caesar. Ballot boxes were stuffed. Messengers carrying ballot boxes were robbed and false ballots substituted. Voting places were hidden and made known only to the reactionary voters. As a result, Padilla won the election. Caesar Moncada retired from politics and, ironically, devoted his time to the collection of antiques and to studying primitive Castilian paintings. The improvements he had planned for Castro Duro were forgotten, for the reactionary elements in the district had gained the upper hand and they kept it. Caesar had not become Caesar. He became nothing.

CAKES AND ALE

Type of work: Novel
Author: W. Somerset Maugham (1874-)
Type of plot: Literary satire
Time of plot: Early twentieth century
Locale: London and Kent
First published: 1930

Principal characters:
Ashenden, a writer
Alroy Kear, a popular novelist
Edward Driffield, a great Victorian
Rosie, Driffield's first wife
Amy Driffield, Driffield's second wife
George Kemp, Rosie's lover

Critique:

This novel is written with a lightness of touch that defies description. By contrasting Alroy Kear's opinion of Driffield with the real Driffield as Ashenden knew him, the author shows up the sham of the literary world and deepens the insight into the character of Driffield. Now and then the author interrupts the story to insert pungent comments on literary matters. For one interested in authors and the world of letters, *Cakes and Ale* is especially good reading.

The Story:

Alroy Kear, the most popular novelist of the day, arranged to lunch with his friend Ashenden, another writer. Ashenden was fond of Kear, but he suspected that his invitation had been extended for a purpose. He was right. Kear wanted to talk about the late Edward Driffield, a famous English author of the past century. Kear had nothing but praise for the old man's books, but Ashenden said that he had never thought Driffield exceptional. Kear enthusiastically told how well he had known Driffield in his last years, and said that he was still a friend of Driffield's widow, his second wife. Luncheon ended without a request for a favor. Ashenden was puzzled.

Returning to his rooms, Ashenden fell into a reverie. He recalled his first meeting with Driffield. Ashenden was then a boy, home for the holidays at Blackstable, a Kentish seacoast town, where he lived with his uncle, the local vicar. Ashenden met Driffield in the company of his uncle's curate; but the boy thought the writer a rather common person. He learned from his uncle that Driffield had married a local barmaid after spending a wild youth away from home.

Two or three days after Ashenden had lunched with Kear, he received a note from Driffield's widow. She wished him to visit her in Blackstable. Puzzled, Ashenden telephoned to Kear, who said that he would come to see him and explain the invitation.

Ashenden had seen Mrs. Driffield only once. He had gone to her house with some other literary people several years before, while Driffield was still alive. Driffield had married his second wife late in life, and she had been his nurse. In the course of the visit Ashenden had been surprised to see old Driffield wink at him several times, as if there were some joke between them.

After that visit Ashenden recalled how Driffield had taught him to bicycle many years before. Driffield and his wife, Rosie, had taught him to ride and had taken him with them on many excursions. He liked the Driffields, but he was shocked to find how outspoken they were with those below and above them in social station.

One evening Ashenden found Rosie visiting his uncle's cook, her childhood friend. After Rosie left, he saw her meet George Kemp, a local contractor. The couple walked out of town toward the open fields. Ashenden could not imagine how Rosie could be unfaithful to her husband.

Ashenden went back to school. During the Christmas holiday he took tea often with the Driffields. Kemp was always there, but he and Rosie did not act like lovers. Driffield sang drinking songs, played the piano, and seldom talked about literature. When Ashenden returned to Blackstable the next summer, he heard that the Driffields had bolted, leaving behind many unpaid bills. He was ashamed that he had ever been friendly with them.

Kear arrived at Ashenden's rooms and explained that he was planning to write Driffield's official biography. He wanted Ashenden to contribute what he knew about the author's younger days. What Ashenden told him was not satisfactory, for the biography should contain nothing to embarrass the widow. Kear insisted that Ashenden write down what he remembered of Driffield and go to Blackstable to visit Mrs. Driffield. Ashenden agreed.

Ashenden remembered how he had met the Driffields again in London when he was a young medical student. By chance he saw Rosie on the street; he was surprised that she was not ashamed to meet someone from Blackstable. But he promised to come to one of the Driffields' Saturday afternoon gatherings. Soon he became a regular visitor in their rooms. Since Driffield worked at night, Rosie often went out with her friends. Ashenden began to take her to shows. She was pleasant company, and he began to see that she was beautiful. One evening he invited her to his rooms. She offered herself to him and remained for the night; after that night Rosie visited his rooms regularly.

One day Mrs. Barton Trafford, a literary woman who had taken Driffield under her care, invited Ashenden to tea. From her he learned that Rosie had run away with Kemp, her old lover from Blackstable. Ashenden was chagrined to learn that Rosie cared for another man more than she did for him.

After that Ashenden lost touch with Driffield. He learned that the author had divorced Rosie, who had gone to New York with Kemp. Mrs. Barton Trafford continued to care for Driffield as his fame grew. Then he caught pneumonia. He went to the country to convalesce and there married his nurse, the present Mrs. Driffield, whom Mrs. Trafford had hired to look after him.

Ashenden went down to Blackstable with Kear. They and Mrs. Driffield talked of Driffield's early life. She and Kear described Rosie as promiscuous. Ashenden said that she was nothing of the sort. Good and generous, she could not deny love to anyone; that was all. Ashenden knew this to be the truth, now that he could look down the perspective of years at his own past experience. The others disagreed and dismissed the subject by saying that, after all, she was dead.

But Rosie was not dead. When Ashenden had last been to New York, she had written him and asked him to call on her. He found her now a wealthy widow; Kemp had died several years before. She was an old woman who retained her love for living. They talked of old times, and Ashenden discovered that Driffield, too, had understood her—even when she was being unfaithful to him.

Rosie said that she was too old to marry again; she had had her fling at life. Ashenden asked her if Kemp had not been the only man she really cared for. She said that it was true. Then Ashenden's eyes strayed to a photograph of Kemp on the wall. It showed him dressed in flashy clothes, with a waxed mustache; he carried a cane and flourished a cigar in one hand. Ashenden turned to Rosie and asked her why she had preferred Kemp to her other lovers. Her reply was simple. He had always been the perfect gentleman.

CALEB WILLIAMS

Type of work: Novel
Author: William Godwin (1756-1836)
Type of plot: Mystery romance
Time of plot: Eighteenth century
Locale: England
First published: 1794

Principal characters:
Caleb Williams
Ferdinando Falkland, Caleb's employer
Collins, Falkland's servant

BARNABAS TYRREL, Falkland's enemy
GINES, Caleb's enemy
EMILY MELVILE, Tyrrel's cousin

Critique:

Godwin titled his novel, *Things As They Are, or the Adventures of Caleb Williams;* it survives under the name of its hero. It is a novel of divided interests, as it was written both to criticize society and to tell an adventure story. All of the elements which contribute to Caleb's misery are the result of weaknesses in eighteenth-century English laws, which permitted the wealthy landowners to hold power over poorer citizens.

The Story:

Caleb Williams was engaged as secretary by Mr. Ferdinando Falkland, the wealthiest and most respected squire in the country. Falkland, although a considerate employer, was subject to fits of distemper which bewildered Caleb. Because these black moods were so contrary to his employer's usual gentle nature, Caleb soon questioned Collins, a trusted servant of the household, and learned from him the story of Falkland's early life.

Studious and romantic in his youth, Falkland lived many years abroad before he returned to England to live on his ancestral estate. One of his neighbors was Barnabas Tyrrel, a man of proud, combative nature. When Falkland returned to his family estate, Tyrrel was the leading gentleman in the neighborhood. Soon Falkland, because of his graceful manners and warm intelligence, began to win the admiration of his neighbors. Tyrrel, jealous, showed his feelings by speech and actions. Falkland tried to make peace, but the ill-tempered Tyrrel refused his proffered friendship.

Miss Emily Melvile, Tyrrel's cousin, occupied somewhat the position of a servant in his household. One night she was trapped in a burning building, and Falkland saved her from burning. Afterward Emily could do nothing but praise her benefactor. Her gratitude annoyed her cousin, who planned to revenge himself on Emily for her admiration of Falkland. He found one of his tenants, Grimes, a clumsy ill-bred lout, who consented to marry Emily. When Emily refused to marry a man whom she could never love, Tyrrel confined her to her room. As part of the plot Grimes helped Emily to escape and then attempted to seduce her. She was rescued from her plight by Falkland, who for the second time proved to be her savior. Further cruelties inflicted on her by Tyrrel finally killed her, and Tyrrel became an object of disgrace in the community.

One evening Tyrrel attacked Falkland in a public meeting and Falkland was deeply humiliated. That night Tyrrel was found dead in the streets. Since the quarrel had been witnessed by so many people just before the murder of Tyrrel, Falkland was called before a jury to explain his whereabouts during that fatal night. No one really believed Falkland guilty, but he was hurt by what he considered the disgrace of his inquisition. Although an ex-tenant was afterward arrested and hanged for the crime, Falkland never recovered his injured pride. He retired to his estate where he became a recluse, moody and disconsolate.

For a long time after learning these details Caleb pondered over the apparent unhappiness of his employer. Attempting to understand his morose personality, he began to wonder whether Falkland suffered from the unearned infamy that accompanied suspicion of murder or from a guilty conscience. Determined to solve the mystery, Caleb proceeded to talk to his master in an insinuating tone, to draw him out in matters concerning murder and justice. Caleb also began to look for evidence which would prove Falkland guilty or innocent. Finally the morose man became aware of his secretary's intent. Swearing Caleb to secrecy, Falkland confessed to the murder of Barnabas Tyrrel and threatened Caleb with irreparable harm if he should ever betray his employer.

Falkland's mansion became a prison for Caleb, and he resolved to run away no matter what the consequences might be. When he had escaped to an inn, he received a letter ordering him to return to defend himself against a charge of theft. When Falkland produced from Caleb's baggage some missing jewels and bank notes, Caleb was sent to prison in disgrace. His only chance to prove his innocence was to disclose Falkland's motive, a thing no one would believe.

Caleb spent many months in jail, confined in a dreary, filthy dungeon and bound with chains. Thomas, a servant of Falkland and a former neighbor of Caleb's father, visited Caleb in his cell. Perceiving Caleb in his miserable condition, Thomas could only wonder at English law which kept a man so imprisoned while he waited many months for trial. Compassion forced Thomas to bring Caleb tools with which he could escape from his dungeon. At liberty once more, Caleb found himself in a hostile world with no resources.

At first he became an associate of thieves, but he left the gang after he had made an enemy of a man named Gines. When he went to London, hoping to hide there, Gines followed him and soon Caleb was again caught and arrested. Falkland visited him and explained that he knew every move Caleb had made since he had escaped from prison. Falkland told Caleb that although he would no longer prosecute him for theft, he would continue to make Caleb's life intolerable. Wherever Caleb went, Gines followed and exposed Caleb's story to the community. Caleb tried to escape to Holland, but as he was to land in that free country, Gines appeared and stopped him.

Caleb returned to England and charged Falkland with murder, asking the magistrate to call Falkland before the court. At first the magistrate refused to summon Falkland to reply to this charge. But Caleb insisted upon his rights and Falkland appeared. The squire had now grown terrible to behold; his haggard and ghostlike appearance showed that he had not long to live.

Caleb pressed his charges, in an attempt to save himself from a life of persecution and misery. So well did Caleb describe his miserable state and his desperate situation that the dying man was deeply touched. Demonstrating the kindness of character and the honesty for which Caleb had first admired him, Falkland admitted his wrong doings and cleared Caleb's reputation.

In a few days the sick man died, leaving Caleb remorseful but determined to make a fresh start in life.

THE CALL OF THE WILD

Type of work: Novel
Author: Jack London (1876-1916)
Type of plot: Adventure romance
Time of plot: 1897
Locale: Alaska
First published: 1903

Principal characters:
Buck, a dog
A Spitz, his enemy
John Thornton, his friend

Critique:

The most popular of all Jack London's books is *The Call of the Wild*. The great dog Buck seems not an animal but a human being. London obviously had a great love for animals and the country he wrote about, and he transferred that love into tales which are read as widely now as they were when first published. For those who like adventure and excitement, *The Call of the Wild* is an excellent evening's entertainment.

The Story:

Buck was the undisputed leader of all the dogs on Judge Miller's estate in California. A crossbreed of St. Bernard and Scottish shepherd, he had inherited the size of the first and the intelligence of the other. Buck could not know that the lust for gold had hit the human beings of the country and that dogs of his breed were much in demand as sled dogs in the frozen North. Consequently he was not suspicious when one of the workmen on the estate took him for a walk one night. The man took Buck to the railroad station, where the dog heard the exchange of money. Then a rope was placed around his neck. When he struggled to get loose, the rope was drawn so tight that it shut off his breath and he lost consciousness.

He recovered in a baggage car. When the train reached Seattle, Buck tried to break out of his cage while he was being unloaded. A man in a red shirt hit him with a club until he was senseless. After that, Buck knew that he could never win a fight against a club. He retained that knowledge for future use.

Buck was put in a pen with other dogs of his type. Each day some of the dogs went away with strange men who came with money. One day Buck was sold. Two French-Canadians bought him and some other dogs and took them on board a ship sailing for Alaska. The men were fair, though harsh, masters, and Buck respected them. Life on the ship was not particularly enjoyable, but it was a paradise compared to that which awaited Buck when the ship reached Alaska. There he found men and dogs to be little more than savages, with no law but the law of force. The dogs fought like wolves, and when one was downed the pack moved in for the kill. Buck watched one of his shipmates being torn to pieces after he lost a fight, and he never forgot the way one dog in particular, a Spitz, watched sly-eyed as the loser was slashed to ribbons. The Spitz was Buck's enemy from that time on.

Buck and the other dogs were harnessed to sleds on which the two French-Canadians carried mail to prospectors in remote regions. It was a new kind of life to Buck, but not an unpleasant one. The men treated the dogs well, and Buck was intelligent enough to learn quickly those things which made him a good sled dog. He learned to dig under the snow for a warm place to sleep and to keep the traces clear and thus make pulling easier. When he was hungry, he stole food. The instincts of his ancestors came to life in him as the sled went farther and farther north. In some vague manner he sensed the great cunning of the wolves who had been his ancestors in the wilderness.

Buck's muscles grew firm and taut, his strength greater than ever. But his feet became sore and he had to have moccasins. Occasionally one of the dogs died or was killed in a fight, and one female went mad. The dogs no longer worked as a team, and the two men had to be on guard constantly to prevent fights. One day Buck saw his chance. He attacked the Spitz, the lead dog on the sled, and killed him. After that Buck refused to be harnessed until he was given the lead position. He proved his worth by whipping the rebellious dogs into shape, and he became the best lead dog the men had ever seen. The sled made record runs, and Buck was soon famous.

When they reached Skaguay, the two French-Canadians had official orders to turn the team over to a Scottish half-

---

breed. The sled was heavier and the weather bad on the long haul back to Dawson. At night Buck lay by the fire and dreamed of his wild ancestors. He seemed to hear a far-away call which was like a wolf's cry.

After two days' rest in Dawson, the team started back over the long trail to Skaguay. The dogs were almost exhausted. Some died and had to be replaced. When the team arrived again in Skaguay, the dogs expected to rest, but three days later they were sold to two men and a woman who knew nothing about dogs or sledding conditions in the northern wilderness. Buck and the other dogs started out again, so weary that it was an effort to move. Again and again the gallant dogs stumbled and fell and lay still until the sting of a whip brought them to their feet for a few miles. At last even Buck gave up. The sled had stopped at the cabin of John Thornton, and when the men and the woman were ready to leave Buck refused to get up. One of the men beat Buck with a club and would have killed him had not Thornton intervened, knocking the man down and ordering him and his companions to leave. They left Buck with Thornton.

As Thornton nursed Buck back to health, a feeling of love and respect grew between them. When Thornton's partners returned to the cabin, they understood this affection and did not attempt to use Buck for any of their heavy work.

Twice Buck saved Thornton's life and was glad that he could repay his friend. In Dawson Buck won more than a thousand dollars for Thornton on a wager, when the dog broke loose from the ice a sled carrying a thousand-pound load. With the money won on the wager, Thornton and his partners went on a gold-hunting expedition. They traveled far into eastern Alaska, where they found a stream yellow with gold.

In his primitive mind Buck began to see a hairy man who hunted with a club. He heard the howling of the wolves. Sometimes he wandered off for three or four days at a time, but he always went back to Thornton. At one time he made friends with a wolf that seemed like a brother to Buck.

Once Buck chased and killed a great bull moose. On his way back to the camp, he sensed that something was wrong. He found several dogs lying dead along the trail. When he reached the camp, he saw Indians dancing around the bodies of the dogs and Thornton's two partners. He followed Thornton's trail to the river, where he found the body of his friend full of arrows. Buck was filled with such a rage that he attacked the band of Indians, killing some and scattering the others.

His last tie with man broken, he joined his brothers in the wild wolf packs. The Indians thought him a ghost dog, for they seldom saw more than his shadow, so quickly did he move. But had the Indians watched carefully, they could have seen him closely. Once each year Buck returned to the river that held Thornton's body. There the dog stood on the bank and howled, one long, piercing cry that was the tribute of a savage beast to his human friend.

CAMILLE

Type of work: Drama
Author: Alexandre Dumas, son (1824-1895)
Type of plot: Sentimental romance
Time of plot: Nineteenth century
Locale: France
First presented: 1852

Principal characters:
CAMILLE GAUTIER, a woman of Paris

NANINE, her maid
COUNT DE VARVILLE, who desired Camille
ARMAND DUVAL, who loved her
M. DUVAL, Armand's father
MADAME PRUDENCE, Camille's friend

Critique:

Although *Camille* was published as a novel in 1848, the story is better known in the dramatic version first presented in 1852. *Camille,* which introduced to the French stage a new treatment of social and moral problems, was received with critical acclaim. To the modern audience the story of Camille and her love affairs seems somewhat exaggerated, for the characters in the play are sentimental and unreal. But the moral problem presented is one that is present in any society, whether it be modern or a thousand years old.

The Story:

Camille Gautier was a woman of poor reputation in the city of Paris. The symbol of her character was the camellia, pale and cold. She had once been a needleworker who, while taking a rest cure in Bagneres, had been befriended by a wealthy duke whose daughter she resembled. After the death of his daughter, the duke had taken Camille back to Paris and introduced her into society. But in some way the story of Camille's past life had been rumored on the boulevards, and society frowned upon her. She was respected only by a few friends who knew that she longed for a true love and wished to leave the gay life of Paris. She was heavily in debt for her losses at cards and had no money of her own to pay her creditors.

The Count de Varville, her latest admirer, offered to pay all her debts if she would become his mistress. Before she gave her consent, however, she met Armand Duval. Armand had nothing to offer her but his love. He was presented to Camille by her milliner, Madame Prudence, who pretended to be her friend but who was loyal to her only because Camille was generous with her money.

At first Camille scorned Armand's love, for although she longed for a simple life she thought she could never actually live in poverty. But Armand was persistent, and at last Camille loved him and told him she would forsake her present friends and go away with him. Because she had a racking cough, Armand wanted Camille to leave Paris and go to a quiet spot where she could rest and have fresh air.

Camille, Armand, and Nanine, her maid, moved to a cottage in the country. For many weeks Armand was suspicious of Camille and feared she missed her former companions. Convinced at last of her true love, Armand lost his uneasiness and they were happy together. The garden flowers he grew replaced the camellias she had always worn in Paris.

Their happiness was brief. Armand's father called on Camille and begged her to renounce his son. He knew her past reputation, and he felt that his son had placed himself and his family in a disgraceful position. Camille would not listen to him, for she knew that Armand loved her and would not be happy without her. Then Armand's father told her that his daughter was betrothed to a man who threatened to break the engagement if Armand and Camille insisted on remaining together. Moved by sympathy for the young girl, Camille promised Armand's father that she would send his son away. She knew that he would never leave her unless she betrayed him, and she planned to tell him that she no longer loved him but was going to return to her former life. Armand's father knew then that she truly loved his son and he promised that after her death, which she felt would be soon, he would tell Armand she had renounced him only for the sake of his family.

Camille, knowing that she could never tell Armand that lie, wrote a note declaring her dislike for the simple life he had provided for her and her intention to return to de Varville in Paris. When Armand read the letter, he swooned in his father's arms.

He left the cottage and then Paris, and did not return for many weeks. Meanwhile Camille had resumed her old life and spent all her time at the opera or playing cards with her former associates, always wearing a camellia in public. Count de Varville was her constant companion, but her heart was still with Armand. Her cough was much worse. Knowing she would soon die, she longed to see Armand once more.

When Camille and Armand met at last, Armand insulted her honor and that of the Count de Varville. He threw gold pieces on Camille, asserting they were the bait to catch and hold her kind, and he announced to the company present that the Count de Varville was a man of gold but not of honor. Challenged by de Varville, Armand wounded the count in a duel and left Paris. He returned only after his father, realizing the sacrifice Camille had made, wrote, telling him the true story of Camille's deception, and explaining that she had left him only for the sake of his sister's honor and happiness.

By the time Armand could reach Paris, Camille was dying. Only Nanine and a few faithful friends remained with her. Madame Prudence remained because Camille, even in her poverty, shared what she had. Camille and Nanine had moved to a small and shabby flat, and there Armand found them. He arrived to find Camille on her deathbed but wearing again the simple flowers he had once given her. He threw himself down beside her, declaring his undying love and begging for her forgiveness. Thus, the once beautiful Camille, now as wasted as the flowers she wore on her breast, died in the arms of her true love.

CANDIDE

Type of work: Novel
Author: François Marie Arouet de Voltaire (1694-1778)
Type of plot: Social satire
Time of plot: Eighteenth century
Locale: Europe and South America
First published: 1759

Principal characters:

Candide, Baroness Thunder-ten-tronckh's illegitimate son
Mlle. Cunegonde, Baron Thunder-ten-tronckh's daughter
Pangloss, Candide's friend and tutor
Cacambo, Candide's servant

Critique:

Candide, the most popular of Voltaire's works, is a masterful satire on the follies and vices of men. Everything which permeates and controls the lives of men is taken to task—romance, science, philosophy, religion, and government. The mistakes of men in this story are exactly the same that men make today. *Candide* is a commentary which is timeless because it is as contemporary as today's newspaper.

The Story:

Candide was born in Westphalia, the illegitimate son of Baron Thunder-ten-tronckh's sister. Dr. Pangloss, his tutor, and a devout follower of Liebnitz, taught him metaphysico-theologo-cosmolonigology and assured his pupil that this is the best of all possible worlds. Cunegonde, the daughter of the baron, kissed Candide one day behind a screen. Candide was expelled from the noble baron's household.

Impressed into the army of the King of Bulgaria, Candide deserted during a battle between the King of Bulgaria and the King of Abares. Later he was befriended by James the Anabaptist. He also met his old friend, Dr. Pangloss, now a beggar. James, Pangloss, and Candide started for Lisbon. Their ship was wrecked in a storm off the coast of Portugal. James was drowned, but Candide and Pangloss swam to shore just as an earthquake shook the city. The rulers of Lisbon, both secular and religious, decided to punish those people whose wickedness had brought about the earthquake, and Candide and Pangloss were among the accused. Pangloss was hanged, Candide thoroughly whipped.

While he was smarting from his wounds, an old woman accosted Candide and told him to have courage and to follow her. She led him to a house where he was fed and clothed. Then Cunegonde appeared. Candide was amazed because Pangloss had told him that Cunegonde was dead. Cunegonde related the story of her life from the time that she last saw Candide to their happy meeting. She was being kept by a Jew and an Inquisitor, but she held both men at a distance. Candide killed the Jew and the Inquisitor when they came to see her.

With the old woman, Cunegonde and Candide fled to Cadiz, where they were robbed. In despair, they sailed for Paraguay, where Candide hoped to enlist in the Spanish army which was fighting the rebellious Jesuits. During the voyage the old woman told her story. They learned that she was the daughter of Pope Urban X and the Princess of Palestrina.

The governor of Buenos Aires developed a great affection for Cunegonde, and through his scheming Candide was accused of having committed robbery while still in Spain. Candide fled with his servant, Cacambo; Cunegonde and the old woman remained behind. When Candide decided to fight for the Jesuits, he learned that the commandant was in reality Cunegonde's brother. But the brother would not hear of his sister's marriage to Candide. They quarreled, and Candide, fearing that he had killed the brother, took to the road with Cacambo once more. Shortly afterward they were captured by the Oreillons, a tribe of savage Indians, but when Cacambo proved they were not Jesuits, the two were allowed to go free. They traveled on to Eldorado. There life was simple and perfect, but Candide was not happy because he missed Cunegonde.

At last he decided to take some of the useless jeweled pebbles and golden mud of Eldorado and return to Buenos Aires to search for Cunegonde. He and Cacambo started out with a hundred sheep laden with riches, but they lost all but two sheep and the wealth these animals carried.

Candide approached a Dutch merchant and tried to arrange passage to Buenos Aires. The merchant sailed away with Candide's money and treasures, leaving Candide behind. Cacambo then went to Buenos Aires to find Cunegonde and take her to Venice to meet Candide. After many adventures, including a sea fight and the miraculous recovery of one of his lost sheep from a sinking ship, Candide arrived at Bordeaux. His intention was to go to Venice by way of Paris. Police arrested him in Paris, however, and Candide was forced to buy his freedom with diamonds. Later he sailed on a Dutch ship to Portsmouth, England, where he witnessed the execution of an English admiral. From Portsmouth he went to Venice. There he found no Cacambo and no Cunegonde. He did, however, meet Paquette, Cunegonde's waiting maid. Shortly afterward Candide encountered Cacambo, who was now a slave, and who informed him that Cunegonde was in Constantinople. In the Venetian galley which carried them to Constantinople, Candide found Pangloss and Cunegonde's brother among the galleyslaves. Pangloss related that he had miraculously escaped from his hanging in Lisbon because the bungling hangman had not been able to tie a proper knot. Cunegonde's brother told how he survived the wound which Candide had thought fatal. Candide bought both men from the Venetians and gave them their freedom.

When the group arrived at Constantinople, Candide bought the old woman and Cunegonde from their masters and also purchased a little farm to which they all retired. There each had his own particular work to do. Candide decided that the best thing in the world was to cultivate one's garden.

CAPTAIN HORATIO HORNBLOWER

Type of work: Novel
Author: C. S. Forester (1899-)
Type of plot: Historical romance
Time of plot: Early nineteenth century
Locale: The Pacific Ocean, South America, the Mediterranean, Spain, France, England, and the Atlantic Ocean
First published: 1937, 1938, 1939
Principal characters:
Captain Horatio Hornblower, captain of H. M. S. *Lydia* and H. M. S. *Sutherland*
Bush, first lieutenant
Brown, captain's coxswain
Don Julian Alvarado (El Supremo), a rich plantation owner of Central America
Maria, Hornblower's wife
Lady Barbara Wellesley, the Duke of Wellington's sister
Admiral Leighton, Hornblower's immediate commander and Lady Barbara's husband

Critique:

C. S. Forester has created in Captain Hornblower a personality of wide general appeal, and the writer's technical knowledge of war at sea is woven into the story with such skill that one learns unconsciously the language of the seamen, the parts of a fighting ship, and something of naval gunnery. The Hornblower novels—*Beat to Quarters, Flying Colours,* and *A Ship of the Line*—have been read with interest and enthusiasm by readers of all classes and all ages.

The Story:

Captain Horatio Hornblower, commander of H. M. S. *Lydia,* a thirty-six-gun frigate, was sailing under sealed orders from England around the Horn to the Gulf of Fonseca on the western shores of Spanish America. He had been ordered to form an alliance with Don Julian Alvarado, a large landowner, to assist in raising a rebellion against Spain. The *Lydia* carried the necessary munitions with which to start the revolution. In addition, Hornblower had fifty thousand guineas in gold which he was to give for the support of the rebellion only if the revolt threatened to fail without English gold to back it. To do otherwise would result in court-martial. His orders also casually mentioned the presence in Pacific waters of a fifty-gun Spanish ship called the *Natividad.* It was his duty to take, sink, burn, or destroy this ship at the first opportunity.

After the ship had been anchored in the Gulf of Fonseca a small boat appeared containing emissaries from Don Alvarado, who now called himself El Supremo. They told Hornblower that El Supremo required the captain's attendance.

Hornblower was not pleased with evidences of El Supremo's tyranny. What he observed made him only the more cautious. He refused to hand over to El Supremo the arms and ammunition which he had until his ship had taken on food and water. The ship was loaded with stores as rapidly as possible, and the operation was going forward when a lookout on the mountain announced the approach of the *Natividad.*

Deciding to try to capture her in the bay, Hornblower hid the *Lydia* behind an island as the *Natividad* approached. At the moment which gave him the greatest advantage, Hornblower ordered the *Lydia* to sail alongside the *Natividad* and rake her decks with grapeshot. The British sailors lashed the two ships together and boarded the *Natividad.* El Supremo demanded the captured ship as his own. Hornblower hesitated to turn over his prize to El Supremo, but he dared not antagonize the dictator if he were to fulfill the requirements of his orders.

Hornblower sailed away and shortly afterward learned that England was now an ally of Spain because of Napoleon's deposition of King Ferdinand. He also received further orders, one from his admiral and one from an English lady in Panama. The Englishwoman was Lady Barbara Wellesley, sister of the Duke of Wellington, who requested transportation to England. During this period the *Lydia* met and defeated the *Natividad,* now under El Supremo. A long period of association between Lady Barbara and Hornblower ended in deep mutual love. But Hornblower could not bring himself to make love to her because of his wife Maria at home and because of his own chivalry. Lady Barbara was carried safely to England.

Captain Horatio Hornblower was next ordered to command H. M. S. *Sutherland,* a seventy-four-gun battleship. He sailed with the *Pluto* and the *Caligula* to protect a convoy of merchant ships as far as the latitude of North Africa. They met French privateers and beat them off. Before parting company with the merchantmen, Hornblower impressed sailors from the convoy.

Sailing along the coast, he captured the *Amelie,* attacked the battery at Llanza, burned and destroyed supply vessels, and shelled two divisions of cavalry on a highway passing near the seashore.

Admiral Leighton—now Lady Barbara's husband—ordered Hornblower to join and take charge of Spanish forces at the siege of French-held Rosas, but the operation failed because the Spaniards did not coöperate. After his retreat Hornblower met the *Cassandra,* a British frigate, and learned that four French ships were bearing down upon them. Hornblower decided to fight, even though the odds were four to one, and sent the *Cassandra* to seek the *Pluto* and the *Caligula.* The *Cassandra* came back and relayed a message to Hornblower to engage the enemy. That order indicated the presence of the admiral's flagship. Hornblower engaged the French ships one at a time. The fourth French ship, however, came upon him as he was fighting a two-decker and forced him to surrender.

After his surrender Hornblower and Bush were imprisoned at Rosas. Admiral Leighton sailed into the bay with the *Pluto* and the *Caligula* and completed the destruction of the French squadron. Hornblower watched the battle from the walls and saw the *Sutherland,* which had been beached, take fire as a raiding party of British seamen burned her to prevent her use by the French. He learned from a seaman that Admiral Leighton had been injured by a flying splinter.

Colonel Calliard, Napoleon's aide, came to Rosas to take Hornblower and the wounded Bush to Paris. Bush was seriously ill as a result of losing a foot in the battle, therefore Hornblower requested a servant to attend Bush on the long journey. He selected Brown, the coxswain, because of his strength, his common sense, and his ability to adapt himself to every situation. In France their stagecoach was halted by a snowstorm near Nevers. Hornblower had noticed a small boat moored to the bank of a river and, as he and Brown assisted the French in trying to move the coach, he laid his plans for escape. He himself attacked Colonel Calliard and Brown tied up the Frenchman and threw him into the bottom of the coach. They lifted Bush out of the coach and carried him to the boat. The whole operation required only six minutes.

The fugitives made their way down the river in the dead of night with Hornblower rowing while Brown bailed the icy water from the boat. When the boat crashed against a rock, Hornblower, thinking he had lost Bush and Brown, swam ashore in the darkness. Brown, however, brought Bush safely to shore. Shivering with cold, the three men made their way to a farmhouse nearby, where they announced themselves as prisoners of war and were admitted.

Throughout the winter they remained as guests of its owner, Comte de Graçay, and his daughter-in-law. Brown made an artificial foot for Bush and, when Bush was able to get around well, he and Brown built a boat in which to travel down the Loire.

In early summer Hornblower disguised himself as a Dutch customs inspector. To complete his disguise the comte gave him the ribbon of the Legion of Honor which had been his son's. That decoration aided Hornblower in his escape.

When Hornblower and his two men arrived in the harbor at Nantes, Hornblower cleverly took possession of the *Witch of Endor*, taking with him a group of prisoners to man the ship. They made their way to England. Upon his arrival, Hornblower was praised for his exploits, knighted, and whitewashed at a court-martial. His sickly wife had died during his absence and Lady Barbara had become guardian of his young son. Hornblower went to the home of Lady Barbara to see his son—and Barbara. She was now a widow, Admiral Leighton having died of wounds at Gibraltar, and Hornblower realized from the quiet warmth of her welcome that she was already his. He felt that life had given him fame and fortune—in Barbara, good fortune indeed.

CAPTAINS COURAGEOUS

Type of work: Novel
Author: Rudyard Kipling (1865-1936)
Type of plot: Adventure romance
Time of plot: 1890's
Locale: Grand Banks of Newfoundland
First published: 1897

Principal characters:
HARVEY CHEYNE, a spoiled young rich boy
DISKO TROOP, owner and captain of the *We're Here*
DAN TROOP, his son
MR. CHEYNE, Harvey's father

Critique:

Captains Courageous is one of the great favorites among lovers of sea stories, for it captures the spirit of the men who risked their lives to catch fish on the Grand Banks in the days before commercial fishing with steam-powered trawlers. One of the aspects of the novel, frequently overlooked, however, is the attention paid by Kipling to the American millionaire in the story. He, also, is one of the "Captains Courageous." As a respecter of power and force, Kipling esteemed the capitalist as well as the captain of the fishing vessel.

The Story:

Harvey Cheyne was a rich, spoiled boy of fifteen years, bound for Europe aboard a swift ocean liner. He was a seasick young man, as well, so seasick that he hardly realized what was happening to him when a huge wave washed him over the rail of the ship into the sea. Luckily, he was picked up by a fisherman in a dory, and put aboard the fishing schooner *We're Here*. The owner and captain of the boat, Disko Troop, was not pleased to have the boy aboard, but told him that he would pay him ten dollars a month and board until the schooner docked in Gloucester the following September. It was then the middle of May. But Harvey insisted upon being taken to New York immediately, asserting that his father would gladly pay for the trip. The captain, doubting that Harvey's father was a millionaire, refused to change his plans and hazard the profits of the fishing season. Harvey became insulting. Disko Troop promptly punched him in the nose to teach him manners.

The captain's son, Dan, soon became the friend of the castaway. He was glad to have someone his own age aboard the fishing boat, and Harvey's stories about mansions, private cars, and dinner parties fascinated him. Being a boy, he recognized the sincerity of the rich lad and knew that he could not possibly have made up all the details of a wealthy man's life.

As Harvey began to fit into the life aboard the schooner, the fishermen all took an interest in his nautical education. Long Jack, one of the crew, escorted him about the boat to teach him the names of the ropes and the various pieces of equipment. Harvey learned quickly, for two reasons. First, he was a bright young lad, and, secondly, the sailor whipped him roughly with the end of a rope when he gave the wrong answers. He also learned how to swing the dories aboard when they were brought alongside with the day's catch, to help clean the cod and salt them away below the decks, and to stand watch at the wheel of the schooner as they went from one fishing ground to another on the Grand Banks. Even Disko Troop began to admit that the boy would be a good hand before they reached Gloucester in the fall.

Gradually Harvey became used to the sea. There were times of pleasure as well as work. He enjoyed listening while the other eight members of the crew talked and told sea yarns in the evenings or on the days when it was too rough to lower the dories and go after cod. He discovered that the crew came from all over the world. Disko Troop and his son were from Gloucester, Long Jack was from Ireland, Manuel was a Portuguese, Salters was a farmer, Pennsylvania was a former preacher who had lost his family in the Johnstown flood, and the cook was a Negro who had been brought up in Nova Scotia and swore in Gaelic. All these men fascinated Harvey, for they were different from anyone he had ever known. What pleased the boy most was that they accepted him on his own merits as a workman and a member of the crew, and not as an heir to millions. Of all the crew, only Dan and the Negro cook believed Harvey's story.

One day a French brig hailed the *We're Here*. Both vessels shortened sail while Harvey and Long Jack were sent from the schooner to the brig to buy tobacco. Much to Harvey's chagrin, he discovered that the sailors on the French boat could hardly understand his schoolboy French but that they understood Long Jack's sign language perfectly.

The French brig figured in another of Harvey's adventures. He and Dan went aboard the ship at a later time to buy a knife that had belonged to a deceased sailor. Dan bought the knife and gave it to Harvey, thinking it had added value because the Frenchman had killed a man with it. While fishing from a dory several days later, Harvey felt a weight on his line and pulled in the Frenchman's corpse. The boys cut the line and threw the knife into the sea, for it seemed to them that the Frenchman had returned to claim his knife.

Although they were the same age, Harvey was not nearly as handy on the schooner or in the dory as was Dan, who had grown up around fishing boats and fishermen. But Harvey surpassed Dan in the use of a sextant. His acquaintance with mathematics and his ability to use his knowledge seemed enormous to the simple sailors. So impressed was Disko Troop that he began to teach Harvey what he knew about navigation.

Early in September the *We're Here* joined the rest of the fishing fleet at a submerged rock where the cod fishing was at its best, and the fishermen worked around the clock to finish loading the holds with cod and halibut. The vessel which first filled its holds was not only honored by the rest of the fleet, but it also got the highest price for the first cargo into port. For the past four years the *We're Here* had finished first, and it won honors again the year Harvey was aboard. All canvas was set, the flag was hoisted, and the schooner made the triumphant round of the fleet picking up letters to be taken home. The homeward-bound men were the envy of all the other fishermen.

As soon as the *We're Here* had docked at Gloucester, Harvey sent a telegram to his father informing him that he had not been drowned, but was well and healthy. Mr. Cheyne wired back that he would take his private car and travel to Gloucester as quickly as he could leave California. Great was the surprise of Disko Troop and the rest of the crew, except Dan and the Negro cook, when they discovered that Harvey's claims were true.

Mr. Cheyne and Harvey's mother were overjoyed to see their son, and their happiness was increased many times when they observed how much good the work aboard the fishing schooner had done him. It had changed him from a snobbish adolescent into a self-reliant young man who knew how to make a living with his hands and who valued people for what they were rather than for the money they had. Mr. Cheyne, who had built up a fortune after a childhood of poverty, was particularly glad to see the change in his son.

Disko Troop and the crew of the *We're Here* refused to accept any reward for themselves. Dan was given the chance to become an officer on a fleet of fast freighters Mr. Cheyne owned. The Negro cook left the sea to become a bodyguard for Harvey. In later years, when Harvey had control of the Cheyne interests, the Negro got a great deal of satisfaction out of reminding Dan, who was by then a mate on one of Harvey's ships, that he had told the two boys years before that some day Harvey would be Dan's master.

THE CAPTAIN'S DAUGHTER

Type of work: Novel
Author: Alexander Pushkin (1799-1837)
Type of plot: Historical romance
Time of plot: About 1774
Locale: Russia
First published: 1836

Principal characters:
PETER ANDREITCH GRINEFF, a young Russian officer
MARIA IVANOVNA, his sweetheart
ALEXEY IVANITCH SHVABRIN, Peter's fellow officer
SAVELITCH, Peter's servant
EMELYAN POUGATCHEFF, a rebel Cossack leader

Critique:

One of the first pure examples of Russian realism, *The Captain's Daughter, or The Generosity of the Russian*

Usurper, Pougatcheff, is a narrative concisely and excitingly told. Using the touch of a master, Pushkin delineated a gallery of characters ranging from the simple Maria to the cruel rebel, Pougatcheff. The novel was written as the result of Pushkin's appointment to the office of crown historian, a position which gave him access to the state archives and the private papers of the Empress Catherine II.

The Story:

Although Peter Andreitch Grineff was registered as a sergeant in the Semenovsky regiment when he was very young, he was given leave to stay at home until he had completed his studies. When he was nearly seventeen, his father decided that the time had arrived to begin his military career. With his parents' blessing, Peter set out for distant Orenburg, in the company of his faithful servant, Savelitch.

The trip was not without incident. One night the travelers put up at Simbirsk. There, while his man went to see about some purchases, Peter was lured into playing billiards with a fellow soldier, Zourin, and quickly lost one hundred roubles. Toward evening of the following day the young man and Savelitch found themselves on the snowy plain with a storm coming up. As darkness fell the snow grew thicker, until finally the horses could not find their way and the driver confessed that he was lost. They were rescued by another traveler, a man with such sensitive nostrils that he was able to scent smoke from a village some distance away and to lead them to it. The three men and their guide spent the night in the village. The next morning Peter presented his hareskin jacket to his poorly-dressed rescuer. Savelitch warned Peter that the coat would probably be pawned for drink.

Late that day the young man reached Orenburg and presented himself to the general in command. It was decided that he should join the Bailogorsk fortress garrison under Captain Mironoff, for his superior felt that the dull life at Orenburg might lead the young man into a career of dissipation.

The Bailogorsk fortress, on the edge of the Kirghis steppes, was nothing more than a village surrounded by a log fence. Its real commandant was not Captain Mironoff but his lady, Vassilissa Egorovna, a lively, firm woman who saw to the discipline of her husband's underlings as well as the running of her own household.

Peter quickly made friends with a fellow officer, Shvabrin, who had been exiled to the steppes for fighting a duel. He spent much time with his captain's family and grew deeply attached to the couple and to their daughter, Maria Ivanovna. After he had received his commission, he found military discipline so relaxed that he was able to indulge his literary tastes.

The quiet routine of Peter's life was interrupted by an unexpected quarrel with Shvabrin. One day he showed his friend a love poem he had written to Maria. Shvabrin criticized the work severely and went on to make derogatory remarks about Maria until they quarreled and Peter found himself challenged to a duel for having called the man a liar.

The next morning the two soldiers met in a field to fight but they were stopped by some of the garrison, for Vassilissa Egorovna had learned of the duel. Peter and his enemy, although apparently reconciled, intended to carry out their plan at the earliest opportunity. Discussing the quarrel with Maria, Peter learned that Shvabrin's actions could be explained by the fact that he was her rejected suitor.

Assuring themselves that they were not watched, Shvabrin and Peter fought their duel the following day. Peter, wounded in the breast, lay unconscious for five days after the fight. When he began to recover, he asked Maria to marry him. Shvabrin had been jailed. Then

Peter's father wrote that he disapproved of a match with Captain Mironoff's daughter, and that he intended to have his son transferred from the fortress so that he might forget his foolish ideas. As Savelitch denied having written a letter home, Peter could only conclude that Shvabrin had been the informer.

Life would have become unbearable for the young man after his father's letter arrived if the unexpected had not happened. One evening Captain Mironoff informed his officers that the Yaikian Cossacks, led by Emelyan Pougatcheff, who claimed to be the dead Emperor Peter III, had risen and were sacking fortresses and committing outrages everywhere. The captain ordered his men to keep on the alert and to ready the cannon.

The news of Pougatcheff's uprising quickly spread through the garrison. Many of the Cossacks of the town sided with the rebel, so that Captain Mironoff did not know whom he could trust or who might betray him. It was not long before the captain received from the Cossack leader a manifesto ordering him to surrender.

It was decided that Maria should be sent back to Orenburg, but the attack came early the next morning before she could leave. Captain Mironoff and his officers made a valiant effort to defend the town, but with the aid of Cossack traitors inside the walls Pougatcheff was soon master of the fortress.

Captain Mironoff and his aides were hanged. Shvabrin deserted to the rebels. Peter, at the intercession of old Savelitch, was spared by Pougatcheff. The townspeople and the garrison soldiers had no scruples about pledging allegiance to the rebel leader. Vassilissa Egorovna was slain when she cried out against her husband's murderer.

When Pougatcheff and his followers rode off to inspect the fortress, Peter began his search for Maria. To his great relief, he found that she had been hidden by the wife of the village priest, and that Shvabrin, who knew her whereabouts, had not revealed her identity. From Savelitch he learned that the servant had recognized Pougatcheff as the man to whom he had given his hareskin coat months before. Later the rebel leader sent for Peter and acknowledged his identity.

The rebel tried to persuade Peter to join the Cossacks, but respected his wish to rejoin his own forces at Orenburg. The next day Peter and his servant were given safe conduct, and Pougatcheff gave Peter a horse and a sheepskin coat for the journey.

Several days later the Cossacks attacked Orenburg. During a sally against them Peter received a disturbing message from one of the Bailogorsk Cossacks; Shvabrin was forcing Maria to marry him. Peter went at once to the general and tried to persuade him to raise the siege and go to the rescue of the village. When the general refused, Peter and Savelitch started out once more for the Bailogorsk fortress. Intercepted and taken before Pougatcheff, Peter persuaded the rebel to give Maria safe conduct to Orenburg.

On the way they met a detachment of soldiers led by Captain Zourin, who persuaded Peter to send Maria, under Savelitch's protection to his family, while he himself remained with the troops in Orenburg.

The siege of Orenburg was finally lifted, and the army began its task of tracking down rebel units. Some months later Peter found himself near his own village and set off alone to visit his parents' estate. Reaching his home, he found the serfs in rebellion and his family and Maria captives. That day Shvabrin swooped down upon them with his troops. He was about to have them all hanged, except Maria, when they were rescued by Zourin's men. The renegade was shot during the encounter and taken prisoner.

Peter's parents had changed their attitude toward the captain's daughter, and

Peter was able to rejoin Captain Zourin with the expectation that he and Maria would be wed in a month. Then an order came for his arrest. He was accused of having been in the pay of Pougatcheff, of spying for the rebel, and of having taken presents from him. The author of the accusations was the captive, Shvabrin. Though Peter could easily have cleared himself by summoning Maria as a witness, he decided not to drag her into the matter. He was sentenced to spend the rest of his life in exile in Siberia.

Maria, however, was not one to let matters stand at that. Leaving Peter's parents, she traveled to St. Petersburg and went to Tsarskoe Selo, where the court was. Walking in the garden there one day, she met a woman who declared that she went to court on occasion and would be pleased to present her petition to the empress. Maria was summoned to the royal presence the same day and discovered that it was the empress herself to whom she had spoken. Peter received his pardon and soon afterward married the captain's daughter.

CARMEN

Type of work: Novelette
Author: Prosper Mérimée (1803-1870)
Type of plot: Picaresque romance
Time of plot: Early nineteenth century
Locale: Spain
First published: 1847

Principal characters:
Don José, a soldier
Carmen, a cigarette worker
Garcia, Carmen's husband
Lucas, a toreador

Critique:

The importance of this short novel should not be underestimated. First of all, it is a romantic and satisfying work, displaying all the gifts that have earned Mérimée an honored place in world literature. Secondly, it was on this story that Bizet based his opera. Bizet's version changes a few details of plot and characterization, but it is safe to say that without the original story there would have been no opera. Thus we owe Mérimée a twofold debt, for a good story and one of the world's most popular operas.

The Story:

Don José was a young, handsome cavalryman from Navarre. The son of a good Basque family, he had excellent chances of being quickly promoted and making his name as a soldier. But a short time after arriving at his post in Seville, he happened to meet a beautiful and clever young gipsy. Her name was Carmen. Don José fell in love with her at once, and allowed her to go free after she had attacked with a knife another worker in a cigarette factory.

One night she persuaded him to desert his post and go with her. He was punished by being ordered to stand guard. She went to him again and urged him to go with her once more. When he refused, they argued for more than an hour, until Don José was exhausted by his struggle between anger and love. After he became her lover, she caressed him and ridiculed him by turn. Carmen was independent, rebellious, and tormenting. The more fickle she was, the more madly Don José loved her.

One night, having agreed to a rendezvous with Carmen, he went to her apartment. While they were together, a lieutenant, who was Carmen's lover, entered. There was an argument and swords flashed. In the struggle that followed Don José killed the lieutenant. He himself suffered a head wound from the officer's sword. Carmen had remained in the room throughout the struggle, and when the lieutenant fell to the floor she accused Don José of being stupid. Then she left him, only to return a few minutes later with a cloak. She told him to put it on and flee because he would be a hunted man. All of Don José's hopes for a brilliant career were shattered. His love had led him to murder, and he was doomed to live the life of an outlaw with a woman who was a pickpocket and a thief.

Carmen had many friends and acquaintances who were outlaws. Because Don José had no choice in the matter, he agreed to go with her and join a small band of smugglers and bandits for whom Carmen was a spy. In the meantime a reward was posted for Don José's capture. The two set out together. Eventually they found the smugglers. For a long time Don José lived with them, throwing himself into his new, lawless life with such vigor and enthusiasm that he became known as a desperate and ruthless bandit. But all the time his life was unhappy. By nature he was kind and had nothing of the desperado in him. His wild life was not the type of existence he had envisioned. Further, he knew that Carmen was not faithful to him, that she had other lovers, and he grew silent and sullen.

His anger and jealousy increased when he discovered that Garcia, the one-eyed leader of the gang, was Carmen's husband. The band had already been reduced in numbers by that time. One day, while Carmen was absent because of a quarrel with Don José, the latter killed Garcia. A fellow outlaw told Don José that he had been very stupid, that Garcia would have given Carmen to him for a few dollars. When Carmen returned, he informed her that she was a widow. Also, the death of Garcia meant that there were only two of the band left, on the eve of a dangerous raid which they had planned.

Don José and a smuggler named Dancaire organized a new band. Carmen continued to be useful to them. She went to Granada and there she met a toreador named Lucas. Jealous of his rival, Don José asked her to live with him always, to abandon the life they were leading and to go off with him to America. Carmen refused, telling him that nobody had ever successfully ordered her to do anything, that she was a gipsy, and that she had read in coffee grounds that she and Don José would end their lives together. Her words half convinced Don José that there was no reason for him to worry.

A short time later Carmen defied him again and went to Cordova, where Lucas was appearing in a bullfight. Don José followed her, but he caught only a glimpse of her in the arena. Lucas was injured by a bull. Outside the arena, Don José met Carmen. Once more he implored her to be his forever, to go with him to America. She laughed at him and jeered at his request.

Don José went to a monk and asked him to say a mass for a person who was in danger of death. He returned to Carmen. When he asked her to follow him, she said that she would go with him, even to her death. She knew that he was about to kill her, but she was resigned to her fate. No longer did she love him, she insisted; and even if Lucas did not love her, she could not love Don José any more; their affair was ended. In desperate rage, Don José took out his knife and killed her. With the same knife he dug her grave and buried her in a grove of trees. Then he went to the nearest constabulary post and surrendered. The monk said the mass for the repose of Carmen's soul.

THE CASE OF SERGEANT GRISCHA

Type of work: Novel
Author: Arnold Zweig (1887-)
Type of plot: Social criticism
Time of plot: 1917
Locale: Russia
First published: 1927

Principal characters:
GRISCHA, a Russian soldier
BABKA, his mistress
VON LYCHOW, a divisional general
SCHIEFFENZAHN, an administrative general
WINFRIED, a German lieutenant

Critique:

The plot of this novel, an absorbing account of the last months of World War I, appeared first as a play in 1921. Its great and deserved popularity led Zweig to recast his characters in the larger framework of a novel. Sergeant Grischa, a Russian prisoner, is only a pawn in the struggle between the Prussian caste system and middle-class opportunism. The reader senses at the outset that Grischa has little chance to escape in this clash of two German philosophies.

The Story:

In the year 1917 the Russians were nearly beaten, and the Germans contented themselves with consolidating their hold on Russian territory from Riga south through Poland. With the end of the bitter fighting a comradeship grew up between the German soldiers and their Russian prisoners. Even so, Sergeant Grischa Iljitsch Paprotkin was determined to get away. His work was not hard and his cheerful strength had made him foreman of the labor gang and a general favorite with his German captors. But Grischa, thinking of his wife and son far to the east, made his plans as he loaded lumber into freight cars on the railroad siding. He made a tunnel in the car, a wooden tunnel about the size of a coffin. That night he succeeded in concealing himself in his hideout. Before daybreak the train pulled out.

Grischa did not know it, but his train went far to the south. After four days the train came to a stop. With his stolen pliers Grischa opened the door and walked cautiously away from the railroad tracks. Guided only by his small compass, he set his path toward the east.

The thick underbrush made traveling difficult. Somewhere along the route Grischa picked up an old umbrella. By binding several ribs together with a string and using a long thong, he had a serviceable bow. Another rib made an arrow. With patient waiting he could shoot rabbits in the snow and he seldom went hungry. One day he came to the blasted area of a battlefield, where he built a fire in a ruined dugout and heated snow water for a bath. Taking off his upper clothes, Grischa stretched out and began to wash himself.

A curious pair, attracted by his fire, surprised him in his retreat. One was a Russian soldier, a deserter, and the other was Babka, a small, dirty woman whose gray hair justified her name, "Grandmother." Both were armed. After they became acquainted, Grischa knew he was in luck, for they were the leaders of a band of refugees camped comfortably nearby in a wooden house made from old German dugouts.

Grischa stayed with the refugees the rest of the winter. He cut wood energetically and traded in the villages of friendly peasants. More important, he slept with Babka, who was young and vital under her misshapen clothes. Three years of war had turned her hair gray. Under the shrewd leadership of Babka by day, and warmed in her bed at night, Grischa became a man again.

The band of refugees scattered in the spring. Grischa and two companions were the first to leave. Grischa felt reasonably safe. Babka had given him the identification tag of a dead Russian soldier and he called himself by a new name. He was no longer Grischa Paprotkin, an escaped prisoner, but Sergeant Pavlovitsch Bjuscheff, a deserter from the Russian army who was trying to get back to the Russian lines.

In Mervinsk the Germans had established military headquarters. With little fighting to be done, the rivalry between field troops and the military police grew more bitter. The fighting men under old General von Lychow were technically in charge of the town, but the military police under General Schieffenzahn had been stationed in Mervinsk so long that Schieffenzahn had consolidated his hold on the whole district. Von Lychow was a Prussian, a stern man but just and human; Schieffenzahn was an upstart more concerned with power.

Outside the city stood several rows of small wooden villas. Many of them now housed German officers. Grischa, gaunt and dirty, came upon these villas one day and hid in an empty one. A few days later alert military police discovered him there.

The man called Bjuscheff was not really afraid at his trial. Even when they said he must be a spy because he had spent so many months behind the German line, he was easy in his mind. They would merely hold him prisoner a little while in the town of Mervinsk. Surely the war would end soon. But the court declared that a Russian deserter who, according to his own story, had wandered about in German territory for nearly two years was by definition a spy. Sergeant Bjuscheff was condemned to die.

Scarcely understanding what he was told, Grischa was led back to his cell. When the truth dawned on him, he called out so violently that an officer came to quiet the disturbance and to him Grischa told his whole story. He was not Bjuscheff the deserter, but Grischa the escaped prisoner.

Ponsanski, a famous Jewish lawyer and aide to General von Lychow, questioned the prisoner. Impressed by the story of changed identity, but interested only from a legal point of view, Ponsanski collected all the evidence he could and went to von Lychow. With the general's permission, two guards who had known Grischa in his former prison camp went all the way to Mervinsk and identified him. With legal logic Ponsanski claimed that the court-martial decision should be set aside. All the evidence, depositions, and signatures were put in a neat packet and forwarded to Schieffenzahn with a request that the Komandatur indicate which military court now had jurisdiction over the case of Sergeant Grischa.

In some way Babka learned where Grischa was imprisoned. Walking barefoot, she went to Mervinsk in the disguise of a peddler woman. She was now carrying Grischa's child. Her plan was simple. She would bring berries and fruit to the post to sell to the Germans. She would get in to see Grischa. Then, after she had become a familiar visitor, she would poison the guards' schnapps. With the Germans dead, Grischa could walk out a free man once more.

But Grischa would not agree to her plan. He knew that all his papers had been sent away for final judgment. Anyway, the war would soon be over.

When Grischa's papers went to the Komandatur, they came before Wilhelmi, his aide. Knowing the temper of Schieffenzahn, Wilhelmi recommended that

Grischa be executed. When that advice was known in Mervinsk, von Lychow was indignant. A new request was forwarded to Schieffenzahn.

Schieffenzahn grew a little tired of the affair. Hearing that von Lychow was coming to see him, he sent a telegram ordering Grischa's execution within twenty-four hours. Von Lychow protested. Because the old Prussian had influence at court, Schieffenzahn telegraphed a reprieve.

That telegram was never delivered in Mervinsk because of a snowstorm. Grischa knew at last that he would be shot. When Babka brought in the poisoned schnapps, he poured the drink down the drain. He was shot according to Schieffenzahn's orders, and he died like a soldier after digging his own grave. Babka's child and his was born just after his death.

In Berlin von Lychow smarted. He drew up the full particulars of the case and presented his report to the emperor. The kaiser promised to demote Schieffenzahn, but his mind was distracted by a present of a jeweled casket. Because of the kaiser's joy in a new toy, Schieffenzahn got off with a light reprimand. The case of Sergeant Grischa was closed.

CASS TIMBERLANE

Type of work: Novel
Author: Sinclair Lewis (1885-1951)
Type of plot: Social criticism
Time of plot: 1940's
Locale: Grand Republic, Minnesota
First published: 1945

Principal characters:

CASS TIMBERLANE, a district judge
JINNY MARSHLAND TIMBERLANE, his wife
BRADD CRILEY, Jinny's lover

Critique:

In *Cass Timberlane,* Sinclair Lewis has once again attacked his favorite enemy, the smugness and cruelty of small-town life. With his usual double-edged pen he has drawn portraits of the newly rich, who consider anyone with an income of less than ten thousand dollars to be a revolutionist; of the "good" families, who are but one generation removed from bartenders or hod carriers; of the virtuous gossips who attack the morals of the lower classes but who are more generous in their attitudes toward the affairs of their social equals. The story of Cass Timberlane continues the examination of American manners and morals Lewis began in *Main Street* and *Babbitt.*

The Story:

After his divorce from his wife, Blanche, Judge Cass Timberlane continued to meet his old friends socially and to hold court in his usual honest and effective manner, but it was not until Jinny Marshland appeared in his court as witness in a routine case that Cass once more began to find his life interesting. Because Cass was forty-one and Jinny in her early twenties, he told himself that he was foolish to think of her in a romantic manner. But in spite of his logical reasoning, Cass thought more and more about Jinny; and within a few days of their first meeting he had arranged to see her again. Dignified Judge Cass Timberlane was falling in love.

He had no smooth romance. His friends thought him stupid to become involved with a young girl of the working class. It seemed strange to Cass that his friends would dare to criticize anyone. For example, there was Dr. Roy Drover, who openly made love to any and every cheap girl he met without bothering to conceal his infidelities from his wife. In the same class were Boone and Queenie Havock, both loud, brassy and very vulgar; Jay Laverick, rich, lustful, and a drunkard; Bradd Criley, notorious for his affairs with the wives of his best friends. Cass Timberlane's friends were not the only ones opposed to the affair. Jinny's young radical friends thought Cass a stuffy conservative. The only two people who were sympathetic with Cass were Chris Grau, who also wanted to marry him, and Mrs. Higbee, his housekeeper.

What his friends thought of Jinny did not matter; it was what Jinny would think of them that worried Cass at the time of their marriage. After the honeymoon they lived in his old family home, although Jinny would have preferred a new house in the country club section. They went out seldom, for they were happy enough to stay at home together. It was the first year of the war, and Jinny found work to do in various civic activities. Cass hoped that the work would keep her stimulated. When he noticed that she was beginning to be bored by civic duties, he encouraged her to accept a part in a little theater production. Later he was sorry that he had encouraged her, for the town began to talk about Jinny and various male members of the cast, particularly Jay Laverick. When Cass spoke to her about the gossip, Jinny accused him of being unreasonably jealous and then apologized. Cass loved her more than ever.

Cass sold some property at an unexpectedly high price and bought the new house in the country club district. While waiting for it to be finished, they took a trip to New York. At first Jinny was enchanted with the size and brightness of the city, but soon she was bored by the unfriendliness of everyone she met until Bradd Criley arrived in New York and took them under his wing. Then Jinny enjoyed herself. Cass was not so happy.

Shortly after they returned home, they learned that Jinny was pregnant. But their happiness was marred by the knowledge that Jinny had diabetes. Roy Drover, her doctor, assured Cass there was no cause for worry if Jinny followed her diet and got plenty of rest. Because Bradd Criley seemed to amuse her, Cass often invited him to the house.

Jinny went through her delivery safely, but the baby died. For many weeks afterward she would see no one but Cass. Then she suddenly, for no apparent reason, wanted to have a party almost every night. Cass tried to be patient with her, for he knew that she was still reacting from the death of the baby and also that the restrictions placed on her by her illness were irritating. When his friends once again warned him about allowing Jinny to see so much of Bradd, his patience wore thin; he almost ordered Jinny to stop seeing Bradd, and he told Bradd to stay away from Jinny. Later Bradd apologized to Cass and the three were friends once more. After Bradd moved to New York, all tension between Jinny and Cass seemed to disappear for a time. Then Jinny grew restless again and began to talk of moving to a larger city. Although Cass prized his judgeship and hated to give it up, he was still willing to do anything for his wife. They took another trip to New York, where Cass hoped to find a partnership in an established law firm. They met Bradd during their visit. Although he trusted his wife, Cass was relieved when Jinny told him that she knew she would not really like living in New York and that she wanted to go home. They left hurriedly, without seeing Bradd again before their departure.

On their first night at home Jinny told

Cass that she loved Bradd, that he had become her lover while she was in New York. When Cass refused to give her a divorce until she had had ample time to consider her own wishes carefully, she went back to New York, to stay with Bradd's sister until Cass would free her. For Cass, the town, the house, his friends, and his work were now meaningless. He could think only of Jinny. Then he had a telegram from her. Failing to follow her diet, she was desperately ill and she wanted Cass. He flew to New York that night. He found Jinny in a coma, but she awakened long enough to ask him to take her home.

After Jinny could be moved, Cass took her to a seashore hotel and then home. He had forgiven her completely, but he warned her that she would have to work hard to win back their friends. They still had to make their own private adjustment. It was not until Bradd returned to Grand Republic that Jinny was able to see him as the charming philanderer that he really was. That night she went to Cass' room. He received her as if she had never been away.

THE CASTLE

Type of work: Novel
Author: Franz Kafka (1883-1924)
Type of plot: Philosophical and religious allegory
Time of plot: Any time
Locale: Indefinite
First published: 1926

Principal characters:
K., a seeker
FRIEDA, a barmaid
BARNABAS, a young man
OLGA, and
AMALIA, his sisters
ARTHUR, and
JEREMIAH, K.'s assistants

Critique:

This unfinished novel has been called a modern *Pilgrim's Progress.* K. tries to find the grace of God so that he can fulfill his life, but his path is beset with the confusion of the modern world. K.'s straightforward attack on the confusion that surrounds the castle and his unrelenting desire to solve his problems are finally rewarded, but only at the time of his death. The unique thing about Kafka's allegory is the humor which runs through it. The story itself is emotionally and intellectually appealing.

The Story:

It was late in the evening when K. arrived in the town which lay before the castle of Count West-west. After his long walk through deep snow K. wanted to do nothing so much as go to sleep. He went to an inn and fell asleep by the fire, only to be awakened by a man wanting to see his permit to stay in the town. K. explained that he had just arrived and that he had come at the count's request to be the new land surveyor. A telephone call to the castle established the fact that a land surveyor was expected. K. was allowed to rest in peace.

The next morning, although his assistants had not yet arrived, K. decided to go to the castle to report for duty. He set off through the snowy streets towards the castle, which as he walked seemed farther and farther away. After a while he became tired, and he stopped in a house for refreshment and directions. As he left the house he saw two men coming from the castle. He tried to speak to them, but they refused to stop. As evening came on K. got a ride back to the inn in a sledge.

At the inn he met the two men he had seen coming from the castle. They introduced themselves as Arthur and Jeremiah, and said that they were his old assistants. They were not, but K. accepted them, because he knew that they had come from the castle, and therefore must have been sent to help him. Because he could not tell the two men apart, so alike were they, he called them both Arthur. He ordered them to have a sledge to take him to the castle in the morning. When they refused, K. telephoned the castle. A voice told him that he could never come to the castle. Shortly afterward a messenger named Barnabas arrived with a letter from Klamm, a chief at the castle. K. was ordered to report to the superintendent of the town.

K. arranged for a room in the inn. He asked Barnabas to let him go for a walk with him. Barnabas, a kind young man, agreed. He took K. to his home to meet his two sisters, Olga and Amalia, and his sickly old mother and father. But K. was ill at ease; it was Barnabas, not he, who had come home. When Olga left to get some beer from a nearby inn, K. went with her. At the inn it was made clear that he would be welcome only in the bar. The other rooms were reserved for the gentlemen from the castle.

In the bar K. quickly made friends with the barmaid, Frieda, who seemed to wish to save him from Olga and her family. She hid K. underneath the counter. K. did not understand what was happening. He learned that Frieda had been Klamm's mistress.

Frieda was determined to stay with K. from then on, if K. were willing. K. thought he might as well marry her. Determined to get through to the castle, he thought his chances would improve if he married a girl who had been a chief's mistress. Arthur and Jeremiah came into the room and watched them. K. sent the men away. Frieda decided to go to the inn where K. was staying.

K. went to call on the village superintendent, whom he found sick in bed with gout. From him K. learned that a land surveyor had been needed several years before, but that nobody knew why K. had now come to fill the unnecessary post. When K. showed him Klamm's letter, the superintendent said that it was of no importance. The superintendent convinced him that his arrival in the town was a result of confusion. K. decided to remain and find work so that he could become an accepted citizen of the town.

By the time K. returned to the inn Frieda had made his room comfortable. The schoolmaster came to offer K. the job of janitor at the school. At Frieda's insistence, K. accepted. That night K., Frieda, and the two assistants went to the school to live. The next morning the assistants tricked K. into so many arguments with the teachers that K. dismissed both of them. After he had done his day's work, he slipped away from Frieda and went to Barnabas' house, to see if he had received a message from the castle.

Barnabas was not at home. Olga explained that her family was an outcast group because of Amalia's refusal to become the mistress of one of the gentlemen of the castle. He had written her a very crude and obscene letter, which Amalia tore up. Afterward the whole town had turned against them. K. was so interested in this story that he did not realize how late he had stayed. When he finally got ready to go, he saw that Jeremiah was outside spying on him.

K. slipped out the back way, but came back down the street and asked Jeremiah why he was there. The man sullenly answered that Frieda had sent him. She had gone back to her old job at the tavern and never wanted to see K. again. Barnabas came up with the news that one of the most important men from the castle was waiting at the tavern to see K.

At the tavern he learned that the gentleman had gone to sleep. As he stood in the hall, he saw Frieda going down another corridor. He ran after her to explain why he had stayed away so long with Olga, and he asked her to come back to him. Just as she seemed to relent, Jeremiah came from one of the rooms and persuaded Frieda to go with him. Frieda left K. forever.

(At this point the novel in its published form ends, and for the rest of the story we have only the few statements made by Kafka to his friends in conversation. K. was to continue his fight to live and work in the town and eventually to reach the castle. On his deathbed he was to receive a call from the castle, a message granting him the right to live in the town in peace.)

THE CASTLE OF OTRANTO

Type of work: Novel
Author: Horace Walpole (1717-1797)
Type of plot: Gothic romance
Time of plot: Twelfth century
Locale: Italy
First published: 1764

Principal characters:
MANFRED, Prince of Otranto
MATILDA, Manfred's daughter
CONRAD, Manfred's son
ISABELLA, Conrad's fiancée
FATHER JEROME, a priest
THEODORE, a young peasant, true heir to Otranto

Critique:

This book is one of the earliest and most famous of the Gothic novels, a literary type characterized by supernatural occurrences and a mysterious or sinister atmosphere. These supernatural occurrences do not excite much horror and dread in the modern reader, for they are patently tricks of the author to create interest. *The Castle of Otranto* is of particular interest to the student of literature for its technique and style.

The Story:

Manfred, the prince of Otranto, planned to marry his fifteen-year-old son, Conrad, to Isabella, daughter of the Marquis of Vicenza. But on the day of the wedding a strange thing happened. A servant ran into the hall and informed the assembled company that a huge helmet had appeared mysteriously in the courtyard of the castle.

When Count Manfred and his guests rushed into the courtyard, they found Conrad crushed to death beneath a gigantic helmet adorned with waving black plumes. Theodore, a young peasant, declared the helmet was like that on a statue of Prince Alfonso the Good which stood in the chapel. Another spectator shouted that the helmet was missing from the statue. Prince Manfred imprisoned the young peasant as a magician and charged him with the murder of the heir to Otranto.

That evening Manfred sent for Isabella. He informed her that he intended to divorce his wife so that he himself might marry Isabella and have another male heir. Frightened, Isabella ran away and lost herself in the passages beneath the castle. There she encountered Theodore, who helped her to escape through an underground passage into a nearby church. Manfred, seaching for the girl, accused the young man of aiding her. As he was threatening Theodore, servants rushed up to tell the prince of a giant sleeping in the great hall of the castle. When Manfred returned to the hall, the giant had disappeared.

The following morning Father Jerome came to inform Manfred and his wife that Isabella had taken sanctuary at the altar of his church. Sending his wife away, Manfred called upon the priest to aid him in divorcing his wife and marrying Isabella. Father Jerome refused, warning Manfred that heaven would have revenge on him for harboring such thoughts. The priest unthinkingly suggested Isabella might be in love with the handsome young peasant who had aided in her escape.

Manfred, enraged at the possibility, confronted Theodore. Although the young man did not deny having aided the princess, he claimed never to have seen her before. The frustrated Manfred ordered him to the courtyard to be executed, and Father Jerome was called to give absolution to the condemned man. But when the collar of the lad was loosened, the priest discovered a birthmark which proved the young peasant was Father Jerome's son, born before the priest had entered the Church. Manfred offered to stay the execution if the priest would deliver Isabella to him. At that moment a trumpet sounded at the gates of the castle.

The trumpet signaled the arrival of a herald from the Knight of the Gigantic Sabre, champion of Isabella's father, the rightful heir to Otranto. Greeting Manfred as a usurper, the herald demanded the immediate release of Isabella and the abdication of Manfred, or else the satisfaction of mortal combat. Manfred invited the Knight of the Gigantic Sabre to the castle, hoping through him to get permission to marry Isabella and keep the throne. The knight entered the castle with five hundred men at arms and a hundred more carrying one gigantic sword.

After a feast, during which the strange knight kept silence and raised his visor only to pass food into his mouth, Manfred broached the question of marrying Isabella, telling the knight he wished to marry again to insure himself an heir. Before he had finished, Father Jerome arrived with the news of Isabella's disappearance from the church. After everyone had gone to find Isabella, Matilda assisted Theodore to escape from the castle.

In the forest Theodore met Isabella and promised to protect her. Shortly thereafter they met the Knight of the Gigantic Sabre. Fearing the knight meant harm to Isabella, the young man overcame him in combat. Thinking himself about to die, the knight revealed to Isabella that he was her father in disguise.

They all returned to the castle. There Isabella's father confided to her that he had discovered the gigantic sword in the Holy Land. It was a miraculous weapon, for on the blade it was written that only the blood of Manfred could atone for the wrongs committed on the family of the true ruler of Otranto. Manfred returned to the castle, where he found Theodore dressed in armor. It seemed to Manfred that the young man resembled the prince whose throne Manfred had usurped.

Manfred still hoped to wed Isabella, and he craftily won her father's consent by betrothing that nobleman to Matilda. At that point a nearby statue dripped blood from its nose, an omen that disaster would follow those proposed marriages.

Manfred saw only two courses open to him. One was to surrender all claims to Otranto; the other was to go ahead with his plan to marry Isabella. In either case it appeared that fate was against his success. Nor did a second appearance of the giant in the castle ease the anxiety he felt. When news of the giant came to Isabella's father, he decided not to court disaster for himself by marrying Matilda or by permitting Manfred to marry his daughter. His resolution was increased when a skeleton in the rags of a hermit called upon him to renounce Matilda.

Hours later Manfred was told that Theodore was in the chapel with a woman. Jealous, he went to the chapel and stabbed the woman, who was his own daughter Matilda. Over the body of Matilda, Theodore announced that he was the true ruler of Otranto. Suddenly there appeared the giant form of the dead Prince Alfonso, who proclaimed Theodore to be the true heir. Then he ascended to heaven where he was received by St. Nicholas.

The truth was now made known. Theodore was the son of Father Jerome, then prince of Falconara, and Alfonso's daughter. Manfred confessed his usurpation and he and his wife entered neighboring convents. Theodore married Isabella and ruled as the new prince of Otranto.

CASTLE RACKRENT

Type of work: Novel
Author: Maria Edgeworth (1767-1849)
Type of plot: Social criticism
Time of plot: Eighteenth century
Locale: Ireland
First published: 1800

Principal characters:
HONEST THADY QUIRK, the narrator
SIR KIT RACKRENT, owner of Castle Rackrent
SIR CONDY RACKRENT, Sir Kit's heir
ISABELLA, Condy's wife
JUDY MCQUIRK, Thady's niece
JASON, Thady's son

Critique:

Partly imaginative and partly critical, the story of *Castle Rackrent* is related with all the native candor of an Irish family servant, Thady Quirk. The story is bare of any stylistic embellishments and comes out as a straightforward narrative of events, colored only by the authentic Irish wit and language of the narrator. A footnoted copy would enable a modern reader to enjoy some of the hidden references in Thady's language.

The Story:

After the death of his fine and generous master, Sir Patrick O'Shaughlin, Honest Thady Quirk found himself working at Castle Rackrent for the heir, Sir Murtagh, a penny-pinching owner with a vicious temper. Lady Murtagh, too, was more interested in money than in the happiness of her tenants, and after Sir Murtagh died in a fit of temper she stripped Castle Rackrent of its treasures and went to live in London. The estate passed to her husband's younger brother, Sir Kit Rackrent, a wild, carefree man. Finding the estate in debt and heavily mortgaged, Sir Kit went to England to marry a rich wife who would repair the estate and bring a dowry for his support.

At last he came back with the wealthy wife, a Jewess he had married while staying in Bath. To Honest Thady it was soon apparent that there was no love between the honeymooners. One serious difficulty arose over the presence of pig meat on the dinner table. Lady Kit had insisted that no such meat be served, but Sir Kit defied her orders. When the meat appeared on the table, Lady Kit retired to her room and her husband locked her in. She remained a prisoner for seven years. When she became very ill and seemed to be dying, Sir Kit tried to influence her to leave her jewels to him, but she refused. It was assumed she would die shortly, and all eligible ladies in the neighborhood were endeavoring to become the next wife of Kit Rackrent. So much controversy arose over his possible choice that Sir Kit was finally challenged and killed in a duel. Miraculously recovering from her illness Lady Kit went to London. The next heir was Sir Condy Rackrent, a distant cousin of Sir Kit.

Sir Condy Rackrent was a spendthrift, but a good-natured master. Although the estate was more deeply in debt than ever, the new master made no attempt to relieve the impoverished condition of his holdings. On the neighboring estate lived a family with whom Sir Condy soon began a steadfast friendship. The youngest daughter, Isabella, took a fancy to Sir Condy, but her father would not hear of a match between his family and the owner of Castle Rackrent. Sir Condy really loved Judy, the grandniece of Honest Thady. One day in Thady's presence Sir Condy tossed a coin to determine which girl he would marry. Judy lost, and in a short while Sir Condy eloped with Isabella.

It had been expected that Isabella could bring some money to the estate, but when she married Sir Condy she was disinherited by her father. While the newlyweds lived in careless luxury, the house and grounds fell into neglect, and the servants and the tenants wrung their hands in distress. At last Sir Condy, learning of a vacancy in the coming elections, decided to stand for Parliament. He won the election, but too late to save himself from his creditors.

Honest Thady's son, Jason, a legal administrator, helped a neighbor to buy up all of Sir Condy's debts. With so much power in his hands Jason even scorned his own father. When Lady Condy learned that her husband's debtors were closing in on him, she complied with the demands of her family and returned to her father's house. True to his good-natured generosity, Sir Condy wrote a will for his wife in which he willed her his land and five hundred pounds a year after his death. When Jason demanded payment for the Rackrent debts, Sir Condy said he had no way of paying, explaining that he had given an income of five hundred a year to Lady Condy. Jason insisted Sir Condy sell Castle Rackrent and all the estates to satisfy his creditors. With no other recourse, Sir Condy agreed. The five hundred a year was still guaranteed for Isabella. Thady was grief-stricken that his son had maneuvered this piece of villainy against Sir Condy. Jason now would have nothing to do with Honest Thady.

On her way back to her father's house, Lady Condy's carriage was upset and she was nearly killed. Assuming she would surely die, Jason hurried to Sir Condy with a proposal that Sir Condy sell him Lady Condy's yearly income. Sir Condy, needing the cash, complied with Jason's proposal.

Judy McQuirk had been married and her husband had died. She paid a call on Sir Condy, who was staying at Thady's lodge. The old servant felt certain that now Judy would become Lady Rackrent, but Judy told her uncle that there was no point to being a lady without a castle to accompany the title. She hinted she might do better to marry Jason, who at least held the lands. Thady tried to dissuade her from such a thought, but Judy was bent on fortune hunting.

Sir Condy had been indulging in such excesses of food and drink that he suffered from gout. One night at a drinking party he drank a large draught too quickly and died a few days later. After Sir Condy's death Jason and Lady Condy, who had now recovered, went to court over the title of the estate. Some said Jason would get the land and others said Lady Condy would win. Thady could only guess how the suit would come out.

CASUALS OF THE SEA

Type of work: Novel
Author: William McFee (1881-)
Type of plot: Domestic realism
Time of plot: Early twentieth century
Locale: England
First published: 1916

Principal characters:
BERT GOODERICH, a machinist
MARY, his wife
YOUNG BERT, his son
HANNIBAL, another son
MINNIE, Mary's daughter
BRISCOE, a ship's captain
NELLIE, Hannibal's wife

Critique:

Casuals of the Sea is a family study, the story of three children who did what they wanted to do. William McFee is especially well qualified to write of the the sea, and those portions of the novel which take place aboard the *Caryatid* are particularly vivid.

The Story:

Mary fell in love with the baker's boy. When he deserted her, she went home, with country-bred fortitude, to bear her child. After Minnie was born, Mary received a proposal from Bert Gooderich, a stolid machinist. Bert offered nothing in the way of romance, but Mary accepted him thankfully. They settled in suburban London. In time Bert Junior was born, and later Hannibal.

Young Bert early showed a talent for fighting. He was big and strong and led the graders against the boarder pupils and the parochial boys. Noting his carefully-planned skirmishes, the school inspector, an old army man, resolved to keep the boy in mind. His resolution was strengthened when Bert blurted out in school that he hoped to be a soldier. A few years later the inspector encouraged the boy to enlist. But young Bert's career in the army was short. He was killed at Pretoria.

Minnie was difficult. She was thin and reserved, and her mother, feeling powerless to mold her, finally let her go her own way. Minnie became engaged to a coal clerk, but broke the engagement publicly when her fiancé asked her if she smoked.

Minnie worked at a shop where she retouched photographs. One day an American firm took over the place and introduced machines. Let out for a time, she refused to go back on the usual terms. Mary begged her to take back the coal clerk, but Minnie was adamant.

Next to the Gooderich family lived an American woman, Mrs. Gaynor, and her small son Hiram. Mrs. Gaynor wrote an odd letter of reference for Minnie which stated that the girl was proud, stubborn, and conceited. She sent the girl with the letter to Mrs. Wilfley, who was having a party when Minnie arrived at the door. Despite her assurance, the girl was afraid to go in, but middle-aged Anthony Gilfillan helped her to overcome her shyness. Minnie attended the party, listened to Spanish music, and ate cucumber sandwiches. She kept close to Anthony.

After the company had left, Mrs. Wilfley engaged Minnie as her secretary. When Bert Gooderich fell off a bridge one night and was drowned, Mrs. Wilfley promptly arranged a benefit for the family, a musicale which grossed seventy-four pounds. Mrs. Wilfley's fee was sixty-seven pounds; the bereaved family got seven. Minnie was bitter on the subject.

One day Anthony Gilfillan sent a telegram to Minnie and asked her to meet him at his office. He offered her a way to escape from the life she hated. They went away to the continent.

Five years later Minnie, now known as Mabel, was staying in a little hotel in Rouen. The mistress of Captain Briscoe, she was respected and even envied by the world of occasional light ladies in Rouen. But Minnie was apprehensive; the ship captain had been gone three weeks, and he had promised to be back in one. When Captain Briscoe finally did return, he came only to say goodbye, explaining that he no longer dared to keep her because his first mate was from his home town. They parted without a scene. Minnie went into dressmaking in London. Soon, however, her smitten captain sought her out and offered to marry her. A little amused at the idea, she consented.

Hannibal had grown into a big lout of eighteen, troublesome to his mother, who often had to get him out of foolish scrapes. He had lost his factory job. One day Mrs. Gaynor and Hiram came to call, Hiram in his merchant marine uniform. Hannibal, inarticulate and bungling, was attracted by the idea of going to sea and even went so far as to visit Hiram's ship. Later he heard that the S. S. *Caryatid* needed a mess boy, and so he signed on.

On shore, meanwhile, Minnie had asked her mother to come and live with her during Captain Briscoe's long absences. Satisfied with this arrangement, Briscoe joined his ship at Swansea, the S. S. *Caryatid*.

In port Hannibal was spreading his wings. Quite by chance he met Nellie, a plump, merry girl who had come to town to work for her uncle, a tavern keeper. Never understanding quite how it happened, Hannibal became an engaged man before his ship sailed. He adapted himself easily to life at sea. In time he grew tired of his job in the mess room, and at Panama he became a trimmer. Wheeling coal was hard work, but after a while Hannibal felt proud of his physical prowess.

In Japan he met Hiram, and they went ashore together. Soon after the ship pulled out on the long trip home, Hannibal was stricken with fever.

Captain Briscoe wanted to look after his young brother-in-law but he had other matters to worry him. He had picked up an English paper in port and had learned that Minnie was in jail, arrested for taking part in a suffragette demonstration. To add to his confusion, Minnie's letters were short and disappointing. Then near the Dutch East Indies the ship piled up on a coral reef and was refloated only after long delay. The ship barely reached England in time for Christmas.

Captain Briscoe met Hannibal on the dock and persuaded him to go to the hotel where Minnie was waiting. Reluctant to go because of Nellie, Hannibal found both his mother and Minnie at the hotel. During her husband's absence Minnie had earned fat fees by writing advertisements for a cough syrup. She and her mother urged Hannibal to stay with them, but he refused.

At Swansea he learned that Nellie, now the licensee of the tavern, still wished to marry him. So Hannibal settled down in the pub, secure and well-loved by a capable wife.

His cough kept bothering him. Finally, after trying a patent cough syrup to no avail, Nellie called the doctor. Hannibal had lobar pneumonia. The coal dust had settled in his lungs and the cough syrup, which Nellie had bought after seeing an ad written by Minnie, had nearly killed him. Hannibal rallied a little, but he died within a few days. Death seemed as casual as life had always been.

CAWDOR

Type of work: Poem
Author: Robinson Jeffers (1887-)
Type of plot: Psychological realism
Time of plot: 1900
Locale: Carmel Coast Range, California
First published: 1928

Principal characters:
CAWDOR, a farmer
HOOD CAWDOR, his son
GEORGE CAWDOR, another son
MICHAL CAWDOR, a daughter
MARTIAL, a neighbor
FERA, Martial's daughter
CONCHA ROSAS, Cawdor's Indian servant

Critique:

The tragedy of *Cawdor* is that all the characters lived inwardly for themselves, not outwardly or creatively. Out of this picture of violence and self-inflicted suffering, Jeffers shows us Cawdor arriving at a greater understanding of the mystery of life and death. Man must look to himself for the strength to exist and for forbearance until death brings release. This poem is in keeping with the violent writing of its author, a further demonstration of his pessimistic philosophy of life.

The Story:

In 1899 a terrible fire devastated many of the farms along the Carmel coast, but Cawdor's farm was untouched. Early one morning he saw two figures approaching his house, a young girl leading a blind old man. They were the Martials, who held the land bordering his, and with whom Cawdor had an old feud. Martial had been blinded by the fire, his farm destroyed. His daughter Fera had only Cawdor to turn to for relief.

Cawdor took them in and sent his servant, Concha Rosas, to live in a hut. When the old man was well enough to walk around, Cawdor spoke of sending the two away unless Fera would marry him. She agreed.

Hood Cawdor had left home after a fight with his father. On the night of the wedding he dreamed that the old man had died, and he decided to return to the farm to see if all were well. When he reached a hill overlooking the farm, he camped and lit a fire. His sister Michal saw him and went to tell him of their father's marriage. Cawdor received his son in a friendly manner. For a wedding present, Hood gave Fera a lion skin.

Fera found in Hood the same quality of hardness which had drawn her at first to Cawdor. She openly confessed to Hood that although she had loved his father when she married him, she no longer cared for him. She was jealous, too, of Concha Rosas, who had been Cawdor's mistress before he married Fera, and whom he again seemed to prefer to his wife. Disturbed by Fera's advances, Hood resolved to leave. But after a prowling lion killed one of the farm dogs, he decided to stay until he had killed the animal. A terrible storm arose which prevented his hunting for several days.

Fera's father was dying. On the pretext that Martial wished to talk to Hood, Fera called him into the sick room. Openly, before her unconscious father, she confessed her passion. That night Fera asked Concha to watch with her by the old man's bedside. Toward morning Martial died.

But instead of summoning her husband, Fera went to Hood's room, where Cawdor found them. Fera tried to lull his suspicions by declaring that she had tried to awaken him but could not, and so she had gone to rouse Hood.

The next morning the men dug a grave for the old man. Fera who had been watching them, called Hood into the wood to help her pick laurels for the grave. Again she begged for his love. Suddenly he drew his knife and stabbed himself deep in the thigh. Once more he had been able to resist her. The funeral service for her father was short but painful. Afterward Fera found her way home alone.

Desperate now, she covered herself with the lion skin Hood had given her and hid in the bushes. Hood shot at her, his bullet entering her shoulder. He carried Fera to her room, where Cawdor attempted to set the bones which had been fractured. Fera begged him to stop torturing her. Then, as if it were wrenched out of her because of the pain, she said that Hood had seduced her by force. Her lie was a last resort to prevent Hood's leaving. But Hood had already left the farm and was camped once more on the top of the hill. There the infuriated father found him. In the fight that followed Hood was pushed off the cliff, his body falling upon the rocks below. Cawdor met Michal on his way down the cliff and told her that Hood had fled. Meanwhile Fera sent Concha from the room to get some water. Quickly she unfastened the strap around her arm, and slung it over the head of the bed and around her own neck. When Concha returned, Fera was almost dead. For many days she lay in bed, slowly recovering. Neither George nor Michal would visit her. They hated her for what they knew must have been false charges against Hood.

Cawdor was haunted by his secret sin. Fera tried to destroy him with her own death wish. She told him the truth about Hood; how, rather than betray his father, he had stabbed himself with his knife. Cawdor's grief was uncontrollable. When Fera taunted him, demanding that he kill her, his fingers fastened around her throat. But when she began to struggle, he released her and ran into Hood's old room. There he thought he saw Hood lying on the bed, and for a moment he imagined all that had passed had been a dream.

He was aroused when Fera came to tell him that every one knew he had killed Hood, that soon the authorities were bound to hear of his crime. Again she urged him to seek the peace that death would bring. They were walking near her father's grave, with George and Michal nearby. Cawdor suddenly declared to them that their suspicions were correct, that he had killed Hood, and that they were to send for the authorities. Then he reached down and picked up a flint. Without warning, he thrust it into his eyes. Then, patiently, he asked them to lead him back to the house, to wait for whatever fate his deed would merit. Fera followed him weeping. Once again she felt that she had failed. She had tried to get Cawdor to kill her and then himself; instead, he had shown the courage to face his crime and pay for it as humanity saw fit.

THE CENCI

Type of work: Dramatic poem
Author: Percy Bysshe Shelley (1792-1822)
Type of plot: Romantic tragedy
Time of plot: 1599
Locale: Rome and the Apennines
First published: 1819

Principal characters:

COUNT CENCI, a Roman nobleman
BEATRICE, his daughter
BERNARDO, his son
GIACOMO, his son
LUCRETIA, his wife and stepmother to his children
COUNT ORSINO, a priest once loved by Beatrice
OLIMPIO and MARZIO, assassins of Cenci
SAVELLA, a papal legate who discovers the murder of Cenci

Critique:

This play, in spite of eloquent and moving passages, has not been successful on the stage. It is at best a play for reading, as the author's purpose was to present dramatically the events of a typical late Renaissance tragedy.

The Story:

Count Cenci was a cruel and brutal man whose greatest delight was to make people suffer. He had sent two of his sons to Salamanca in hopes that they would starve. His daughter, Beatrice, had been in love with Count Orsino, who had entered the priesthood. She was wretched because she did not know where to turn for solace. Her father was worse than cruel to her and her lover had become a priest. Orsino promised to present to the Pope a petition in which Beatrice begged relief from the constant punishment she and the rest of her family were suffering from her father. Beatrice told Orsino of a banquet her father was giving that night in celebration of some news from Salamanca and said that she would give him the petition at that time. When she left him, Orsino contemplated his own problem and resolved not to show the Pope her petition, lest she be married by the Pope's order and Orsino be left without a chance of winning her outside wedlock. He resolved also not to ask for special permission to marry lest he lose his own large income from the Church.

At the banquet that night, Cenci announced the purpose of his celebration; his two sons had been killed by accident in Salamanca. Since they had been given to disobedience and rebellion, Cenci felt that this punishment was well deserved. At first the guests could not believe their ears. Beatrice boldly begged that the guests protect her, her stepmother, and her remaining two brothers from further cruelties at the hands of her father. Cenci, telling them she was insane, asked the guests to leave. Then he turned on his daughter, threatened her with a new cruelty, and ordered her and his wife to accompany him to his castle in the Apennines on the following Monday.

At the Cenci palace, Beatrice disclosed to her stepmother that Cenci had committed a crime against her which she dared not name. Orsino came to the women and proposed a plan for the assassination of Cenci. At the bridge on the way to the Apennines he would station two desperate killers who would be glad to murder Cenci. As the women left the apartment, Giacomo entered to announce that he had lent his father his wife's dowry and had never been able to recover it. In fact, Cenci had accused him of spending the money in a riotous night, and had suggested to Giacomo's wife that her husband was a secret wastrel. Orsino assured Giacomo that the money would never be restored and explained to him that the murder of Cenci had been planned.

Later Orsino came to report to Giacomo that his father had escaped from the plot and was safe within his castle in the Apennines. Giacomo now resolved to kill his father by his own hand, but Orsino, restraining him, said that he knew two men whom Cenci had wronged and who would be willing to rid the earth of their persecutor. At the

Apennine castle, Cenci raged against the insolence of his daughter and confessed to Lucretia that he had tried to corrupt the soul of Beatrice. While he was sleeping, the two murderers, Olimpio and Marzio, appeared. Lucretia said she had put a sleeping potion in Cenci's drink so that he would be sure to sleep soundly. But the two men were hesitant. Olimpio reported that he could not kill an old man in his sleep. Marzio thought he heard the ghost of his own dead father speaking through the lips of the sleeping Cenci. Beatrice snatched a dagger from them and cried out that she herself would kill the fiend. Shamed into action, the assassins strangled Cenci and threw his body over the balustrade into the garden.

The Papal Legate, Savella, arrived with a warrant for the immediate execution of Cenci for his crimes. When Savella and his followers discovered that Cenci was already dead, they began an investigation. The guards seized Marzio on whose person they found Orsino's note introducing the two murderers. Lucretia and Beatrice denied knowledge of the handwriting, but Savella arrested them and said that they must appear before the court in Rome. Giacomo, tricked by Orsino, fell into the hands of the Roman police. Orsino escaped in disguise.

Conflicting testimony at the trial turned against the Cenci family. Beatrice appealed to Marzio to save the innocent prisoners from death, but the assassin died on the rack without changing his testimony. Consigned to cells to await the Pope's final decision, the Cenci family lived on in misery. Beatrice tried to comfort her stepmother in vain. The Pope decreed that the prisoners must die. Beatrice at first was delirious with despair. Then the young and innocent Bernardo went to beg clemency from the Pope, but later returned filled with grief that his petition had been useless. When the guards came to take them away, Beatrice and her stepmother went out to their execution with noble resignation.

CHARLES O'MALLEY

Type of work: Novel
Author: Charles Lever (1806-1872)
Type of plot: Picaresque romance
Time of plot: 1808-1812
Locale: Ireland and Europe
First published: 1841

Principal characters:
CHARLES O'MALLEY, an Irish dragoon
GODFREY O'MALLEY, his uncle
WILLIAM CONSIDINE, a family friend
CAPTAIN HAMMERSLEY, O'Malley's rival
GENERAL DASHWOOD
LUCY DASHWOOD, his daughter

Critique:

Charles O'Malley, the Irish Dragoon is a light novel in the Irish romantic style. It has little plot and slight structure. The value of the book lies in its great fund of stories and anecdotes of Irish prowess and cunning and in a highly romanticized picture of the Napoleonic wars. To the Irish dragoon, war is a gay and adventurous affair much like a combination fox hunt and banquet. The novel ranks high among works written simply to delight the reader.

The Story:

At seventeen Charles O'Malley was tall and broad-shouldered, deadly with a gun and sure in the saddle. He possessed in abundance the qualities of generosity and honor expected of Godfrey O'Malley's nephew. Godfrey, of O'Malley Castle, Galway, was still a good man on a horse and quick to pass the bottle. In his ruined old castle hard by the river Shannon, he held the staunch affections of his tenants.

Old Godfrey was standing for election to the Irish Parliament. Unable to leave home during the election campaign, he sent Charles to the home of a distant cousin named Blake to ask his support in the coming election. But Blake belonged to the opposition, and although Charles did his best to win help for his uncle, he hardly knew how to handle the situation.

Part of the trouble was Lucy Dashwood. She and her father were visiting Blake while the general tried to buy some good Galway property. Charles was jealous of the general's aide, Captain Hammersley, who was attentive to Lucy. At a fox hunt Charles led the way at first, but Hammersley kept up with him. Charles' horse fell backward in jumping a wall. With cool daring Charles kept on and took a ditch bordered by a stone rampart. Hammersley, not to be outdone, took the ditch too, but fell heavily. Charles was first at the kill, but both he and Hammersley had to spend several days in bed.

One night at dinner one of the guests spoke insultingly of Godfrey O'Malley, and Charles threw a wine glass in his face. Billy Considine, who had been in more duels than any other Irishman in Galway, arranged the affair as Charles' second. Charles left his man for dead on the field. Luckily the man recovered, and Charles escaped serious consequences for his rashness.

Charles went to Dublin to study law. There chance led him to share rooms with Frank Webber. College life became for Charles a series of dinners, brawls and escapades, all under the leadership of Frank.

While in Dublin, Charles saw Lucy again, but she was distant to him. Hammersley was now a favored suitor. Charles became increasingly attracted to military life, the more so since he seemed unfitted for study. Perhaps Lucy would approve his suit if he became a dashing dragoon. Godfrey arranged for a commission through General Dashwood, and Charles became an ensign.

His first duty was in Portugal. Napoleon had invaded the peninsula, and England was sending aid to her Portuguese and Spanish allies. In Lisbon Charles' superb horsemanship saved Donna Inez from injury. His friendship with Donna Inez was progressing satisfactorily when he learned that Inez was an intimate of Lucy Dashwood.

At his own request Charles was sent to the front. There he soon distinguished himself by bravery in battle and was promoted to a lieutenancy.

Lucy had given him letters for Hammersley. When Charles delivered them, Hammersley turned pale and insulted him. Only the good offices of Captain Powers prevented a duel.

Charles saw action at Talavera and Ciudad Roderigo. In one engagement he sneaked under cover of darkness to the French trenches, and by moving the engineers' measuring tape he caused the French to dig their trenches right under the British guns. Wherever Charles went, his man Michael Free looked out for his master, polished his buttons, stole food for him, and made love to all the girls.

After Charles received his captaincy, news came from home that the O'Malley estates were in a bad way. The rents were falling off, mortgages were coming due, and Godfrey's gout had crippled him. Charles went home on leave, arriving in Galway shortly after his uncle's death. There was little money for the many debts, and the estate would require close management. Because a last letter from his uncle had asked him to stay in Galway, Charles decided to sell his commission and retire to civil life.

Billy Considine, who acted as his adviser, told him a distressing story. General Dashwood had sent an agent to Galway to buy property. Thinking of Dashwood as an English interloper, Godfrey had written him a harsh letter of warning to stay out of Ireland. In spite of his gout, Godfrey had offered to go to England to do battle with the general. Billy himself had sent a direct challenge to Dashwood. The general had answered in mild tone, and the two hot-headed Irishmen felt their honor had been vindicated. But Charles heard the story with a heavy heart. Lucy seemed lost to him forever. For two years Charles led a secluded life, scarcely quitting his farm.

Charles and Michael, his servant, were in Dublin on the day news came of Napoleon's return from Elba, and Charles decided to go back into the army. He and Michael went to London. There he was appointed to his old rank on the general staff.

Charles arrived in Brussels just before Waterloo. The Belgian city was crowded. General Dashwood and Lucy were there, as were Donna Inez and her father. Charles was safe in one quarter, however, for Captain Powers and Inez were to be married. One day in a park Lucy sat down alone to await her father. Hammersley came to her and asked hoarsely if he could ever hope for her hand. Although not meaning to eavesdrop, Charles heard Lucy dismiss Hammersley. Charles saw Lucy again at the ball, but she seemed as distant and cool as ever.

Charles became a special courier, and in the discharge of his duties he was captured by the French and thrown into prison. To his amazement his cellmate was General Dashwood, condemned to die for having used spies against the French. St. Croix, a French officer whom Charles had befriended in Spain, offered to help him escape. Unselfishly Charles let General Dashwood go in his place. Napoleon himself summoned Charles to an audience, and throughout the battle of Waterloo he saw the action from the French lines. He was watching his chances, however, and when the French troops were scattered he made his way back to the English lines.

After Charles' heroic action in saving her father from execution, Lucy could not longer refuse him. Charles and Lucy went back to Galway to stay, and the Irish tenantry bared their heads in welcome to the new mistress of O'Malley Castle.

THE CHARTERHOUSE OF PARMA

Type of work: Novel
Author: Stendhal (Marie-Henri Beyle, 1783-1842)
Type of plot: Historical romance
Time of plot: Early nineteenth century
Locale: Italy
First published: 1839

Principal characters:
FABRIZIO DEL DONGO, a young adventurer
GINA PIETRANERA, his aunt
COUNT MOSCA, Gina's lover
MARIETTA, an actress
CLELIA CONTI, Fabrizio's mistress

Critique:

The Charterhouse of Parma is one of the earlier examples of French romantic prose. The scene is the principality of Parma in Italy, and the long, involved plot takes the reader through many adventures, light-hearted and tragic, from Waterloo to Bologna. The story, a historical romance, contains also the elements of social comedy and more serious reflections on the futility of life. The novel has a sustained dramatic interest which contributes much to its recognition as a classic of French romanticism.

The Story:

Early in the nineteenth century Fabrizio, son of the Marchese del Dongo, grew up at his father's magnificent villa at Grianta on Lake Como. His father was a miserly fanatic who hated Napoleon and the French, his mother a long-suffering creature cowed by her domineering husband. In his boyhood Fabrizio was happiest when he could leave Grianta and go to visit his mother's widowed sister, Gina Pietranera, at her home in Milan. Gina looked upon her handsome nephew very much as a son.

When he was nearly seventeen, Fabrizio determined to join Napoleon. Both his aunt and his mother were shocked but the boy stood firm. Fabrizio's father was too stingy to allow his womenfolk to give Fabrizio any money for his journey, but Gina sewed some small diamonds in his coat. Under a false passport Fabrizio made his way to Paris as a seller of astrological instruments.

Following one of Napoleon's battalions out of Paris, Fabrizio was arrested and thrown into jail as a spy. His enthusiastic admiration for the emperor and his bad French were against him. Released from jail by the kind-hearted wife of the turnkey, Fabrizio pressed on, anxious to get into the fighting. Mounted on a horse he bought from a good-natured camp follower, he rode by accident into a group of hussars around Marshall Ney at the battle of Waterloo. When a general's horse was shot, the hussars lifted Fabrizio from the saddle and the general commandeered his mount. Afoot, Fabrizio fell in with a band of French infantrymen and in the retreat from Waterloo killed a Prussian officer. Happy at being a real soldier, he threw down his gun and ran away.

Meanwhile, at home, Gina had succumbed to the pleadings of Count Mosca, prime minister of Parma. They made a happy arrangement. Old Duke Sanseverina wanted a diplomatic post very badly. In return for Mosca's favor in giving him the post, he agreed to marry Gina and set her up as the Duchess of Sanseverina. Then the duke left the country for good, and Mosca became Gina's accepted lover. It was a good thing for Fabrizio that his aunt had some influence. When he returned to Grianta, the gendarmes came to arrest him on a false passport charge. He was taken to Milan in his aunt's carriage. On the way the party passed an older man and his younger daughter, also arrested but condemned to walk. Graciously Gina and Fabrizio took General Conti and his daughter Clelia into the carriage with them. At Milan Fabrizio's difficulties were easily settled.

Gina was growing very fond of Fabrizio, who was a handsome youth, and she took him with her to Parma to advance his fortune. There, upon the advice of Mosca, it was decided to send the young man to Naples to study for three years at the theological seminary. When he came back, he would be given an appointment at court.

At the end of his studies Fabrizio was a suave, worldly young monsignor, not yet committed to a life of piety in spite of his appointment as alternate for the archbishop. At the theater one night the young cleric saw a graceful young actress named Marietta Valsera. His attention soon aroused the anger of a rascal called Giletti, Marietta's protector.

Fearing the consequences of this indiscretion, Mosca sent Fabrizio to the country for a while to supervise some archeological diggings. While looking over the spot, Fabrizio borrowed a shotgun and walked down the road to look for rabbits. At that moment a carriage drove by, with Marietta and Giletti inside. Thinking that Fabrizio intended to take Marietta, Giletti leaped from the carriage and rushed at Fabrizio with his dagger. In the fight, Fabrizio killed Giletti. The alarmed Marietta took Fabrizio with her to Bologna. There his aunt's emissaries supplied him with ample funds, and Fabrizio settled down to enjoy his lovely Marietta.

News of the affair reached Parma. Political opponents of Mosca found an opportunity to strike at him through Gina, and they influenced the prince to try the fugitive for murder. Fabrizio was tried in his absence and condemned to death or imprisonment as a galleyslave.

Fabrizio soon tired of his Marietta. Attracted by a young singer named Fausta, he followed her to Parma. There he was recognized and imprisoned. In spite of his influence, Mosca could do little for Gina's nephew. But Fabrizio was happy in jail, for Clelia, the daughter of his jailer, was the girl to whom Fabrizio had offered a ride years before. By means of alphabet cards the two were soon holding long conversations.

Outside Gina laid her plans for Fabrizio's escape. With the help of a poet named Ferrante, she arranged to have ropes smuggled to her nephew. Clelia herself was to carry them in. Fabrizio escaped from the tower and fled to Piedmont. At Parma, according to Gina's instructions, Ferrante poisoned the prince who had condemned Fabrizio to imprisonment. In the resulting confusion Gina and Fabrizio returned to Parma, now governed by the new prince. Pardoned, he was named coadjutor by the archbishop. Later he became archbishop and attracted great crowds with his preaching. In the meantime Clelia had married a rich marchese. One day, moved by curiosity, she came to hear Fabrizio preach. Her love finally led her to take him for a lover. Every night he came to her house. After their child was born, Fabrizio took the baby to his own house and Clelia visited her small son there. But Fabrizio was to be happy only a short time. The infant died and Clelia did not long survive her child. Saddened by her death, Fabrizio gave up his office and retired to the Charterhouse of Parma, a monastery on the river Po, where quiet meditation filled his days.

CHILDREN OF GOD

Type of work: Novel
Author: Vardis Fisher (1895-)
Type of plot: Historical chronicle
Time of plot: 1820-1890
Locale: New York, Illinois, Utah
First published: 1939

Principal characters:
JOSEPH SMITH, the founder of the Church of Latter day Saints
BRIGHAM YOUNG, the leader of the Church after Smith's death
JOHN TAYLOR, a later leader of the Mormon Church

Critique:

Vardis Fisher calls his book an American epic. Certainly the material dealt with is of an epic character, for no one can doubt the bravery and the sincerity of the Mormons after reading this account of the great migration from New York to Illinois and Missouri and, finally, to Utah. Taking the bare bones of fact, Fisher rounded out the personalities and events of Mormonism in such manner that the facts seemed to take on flesh and come to life. The result is a novel in which history and fiction are one.

The Story:

In the early 1820's a young man in Palmyra, New York, had visions which led him to believe himself a prophet of the Lord. The young man was Joseph Smith and his visions were the basis upon which he built the Church of the Latter-day Saints, more commonly known as the Mormon Church. In those days his followers were few, being only his family and a handful of friends.

In March of 1830 the Book of Mormon was published. Shortly after it appeared, Joseph Smith ordained his brothers and the men of the Whitmer family as Latter-day Saints. After Joseph was reported to have cast out the personal devil of a man called Newel Knight, word of the miracle spread about the country near Palmyra and many were converted.

But with success came trouble. On one occasion a mob of men almost lynched the new prophet. On another, he was taken to court for trial. He realized that his life was no longer safe in the state of New York.

Joseph's three hundred followers left New York State for Ohio. Meanwhile Joseph sent two men, one of them Oliver Cowdery, his first convert, to travel beyond the Mississippi River for the purpose of converting the Indians and locating the place where the Saints were to build their Zion. In Ohio, Joseph Smith was again persecuted. One winter night a mob abducted him from his house and tarred and feathered him. Shortly afterward Joseph decided to take his flock to Missouri, and he went with a few of his followers to survey the country.

More trouble awaited him when he returned to Ohio. Several of his converts had set themselves up as prophets during his absence. Reports reached him that the people he had left in Missouri were being mobbed. Then one day two men came to offer their services to Joseph Smith. One was Brigham Young, the other Heber Kimball. Brigham Young was a great help to the Saints' community because he could make men do what he wished, something that Joseph Smith, the mystic, was never able to learn.

While the Saints in Ohio were facing internal strife, the people of the new faith in Missouri were being horsewhipped, murdered, and driven from their homes by mobs. Eventually Brigham Young was authorized to organize an army to march upon Missouri and rescue the Mormons there. At the last minute Joseph Smith went with it as leader. The expedition was doomed to failure. Cholera and Indians took their toll among the men. They never fought the Missouri mobs.

For the next few years the Saints prospered in Ohio. Joseph Smith and Brigham Young opened a Mormon-operated bank, which failed, along with many others, in the panic of 1837. The loss of their money turned the Saints against their leaders as nothing else had done, and Brigham Young and Joseph Smith fled to Missouri for their lives. They were soon joined by three hundred families from Ohio who remained true to Joseph's religion and prophetic power.

In Missouri mobs again harassed their settlements. The desperate Saints organized a retaliating secret society called the Danites or Destroying Angels. Finally the governor of Missouri ordered all the Mormons to leave the state or be killed. Again Joseph Smith and his leaders were tried for treason. Through a friendly guard they escaped execution.

The Saints settled next at Nauvoo, in Illinois, where Joseph Smith began the practice of plural marriages in an effort to keep the women in the church, who outnumbered the men, from becoming charity cases or harlots. Joseph himself soon had twenty wives. His first wife, Emma, made him send away all but two.

Joseph Smith never left Illinois. He was killed by a mob when he gave himself up to stand trial for treason a third time. Brigham Young then took over the leadership of the Mormons, not as a prophet, but as a leader. He decided that the only way for the Mormons to find peace was to leave the United States, to seek a place in the far West.

Trudging westward through the snow, three thousand Mormons started out under Brigham's leadership. Those left behind felt lost without their leader and soon there were fifteen thousand more people following Brigham westward.

In the spring of 1847 Brigham Young set out from his winter camp for the Rocky Mountains with a hundred and fifty picked men. The others were to follow later. Brigham had determined to settle south of the salt lake in Utah. By the winter of 1847 seventeen hundred Mormons were already in Utah. When Brigham learned that the Utah territory had been ceded to the United States by Mexico, he felt that the Mormons would never have a land of their own. The next winter five thousand of the Mormons lived through a year of intense cold and starvation rations. The third year in Utah brought a new problem to Brigham Young. California gold attracted thousands of rascals and adventurers, many of whom passed through the settlement of the Mormons on their way to the coast. Those scoundrels stole from the scanty stores of the settlers and made trouble among the women.

As the years passed, the Saints flourished. Brigham Young was elected governor of Utah Territory. In 1852 he took a bold step when he announced publicly what many people had long known or at least suspected, the practice of polygamy by the leaders of the Mormon Church. The hue and cry against the practice amazed and embittered Brigham, for he could say truthfully that it had maintained morality in the Mormon settlements.

In 1855 locusts demolished their crops. Many of the Saints turned against the practice of polygamy, for in times of famine a man could not secure enough food for his over-expanded family.

Two years later the Mormons heard that the Federal government had sent an army to deal with them. From their previous experiences, the Mormons knew they could expect little mercy. The territorial governor sent by the president was vigorously defied and the Mormons threatened to burn Salt Lake City and leave the country a desert as they had found it. Finally the president sent a pardon to the Mormons.

With General Grant in the White House, the Mormon problem again became a pressing one. Federal prosecutors invoked the anti-bigamy law and began to imprison Mormon leaders. Then the prosecutors attempted to indict the leaders, including Brigham Young, for murder. Young was never tried, however, for he died of natural causes.

After Young's death, the authorities secured more indictments in the hope that the Mormons would repudiate polygamy. They also moved against the coöperative stores and industries which had been founded, and attempted to deprive the Mormon Church of all assets in excess of fifty thousand dollars. The sum of those strains was too great. The president of the Mormon Council denounced plural marriages. No longer could the Mormon community hold itself apart in order to continue its existence. The Saints and the settlers from the East would live side by side in the new state of Utah.

A CHRISTMAS CAROL

Type of work: Novelette
Author: Charles Dickens (1812-1870)
Type of plot: Sentimental romance
Time of plot: Nineteenth century
Locale: London, England
First published: 1843

Principal characters:
Ebenezer Scrooge, a miser
Jacob Marley's Ghost

Bob Cratchit, Scrooge's clerk
Tiny Tim, Cratchit's son
Scrooge's Nephew

Critique:

This story has become as much a part of the tradition of Christmas as holly wreaths, mistletoe, and Christmas carols. Dickens' skill with humor and character analysis are particularly evident. At the beginning of the story, we are made to dislike Scrooge for his miserly ways, but we are in sympathy with him as he is subjected to the tortures of his ghostly journeys. Dickens provides a psychological explanation for Scrooge's bitterness and desire to live apart from the rest of the world. At the same time he paves the way for Scrooge's reform, so that it comes as no surprise. It is entirely right that Scrooge should become an example of the meaning of Christmas among men.

The Story:

Ebenezer Scrooge was a miser. Owner of a successful counting-house, he would have in his bleak office only the smallest fire in the most bitter weather. For his clerk, Bob Cratchit, he allowed an even smaller fire. The weather seldom mattered to Scrooge, who was always cold within, never warm—even on Christmas Eve.

As the time approached for closing the office on Christmas Eve, Scrooge's nephew stopped in to wish him a Merry Christmas. Scrooge only sneered, for he abhorred sentiment and thought only of one thing—money. To him Christmas was a time when people spent more money than they should, and found themselves a year older and no richer.

Grudgingly Scrooge allowed his clerk, Bob Cratchit, to have Christmas Day off; that was the one concession to the holiday that he made. But he warned Cratchit to be at work earlier the day after Christmas. Scrooge left his office and went home to his rooms in a building in which he was the only tenant. They had been the rooms of Scrooge's partner, Jacob Marley, dead for seven years. As he approached his door, he saw in the knocker Marley's face. It was a horrible sight. Marley was looking at Scrooge with his eyes motionless, his ghostly spectacles on his ghostly forehead. As Scrooge watched, the knocker resumed its usual form. Shaken by this vision, Scrooge entered the hall and lighted a candle; then he looked behind the door, half expecting to see Marley's pigtail sticking out into the hall. Satisfied, he double-locked the door. He prepared for bed and sat for a time before the dying fire. Suddenly an unused bell hanging in the room began to ring, as did every bell in the house.

Then from below came the sound of heavy chains clanking. The cellar door flew open, and someone mounted the stairs. Marley's ghost walked through Scrooge's door—Marley, dressed as always, but with a heavy chain of cash boxes, keys, padlocks, ledgers, deeds, and heavy purses around his middle.

Marley's ghost sat down to talk to the frightened and bewildered Scrooge. Forcing Scrooge to admit that he believed in him, Marley explained that in life he had never done any good for mankind and so in death he was condemned to constant traveling with no rest and no relief from the torture of remorse. The ghost said that Scrooge still had a chance to save himself from Marley's fate. Scrooge would be visited by three spirits who would show him the way to change. The first spirit would appear the next day at the stroke of one. The next would arrive on the second night, and the last on the third. Dragging his chain, the ghost disappeared.

After Marley's ghost had vanished, Scrooge went to bed and in spite of his nervousness fell asleep instantly. When he awoke, it was still dark. The clock struck twelve. He waited for the stroke of one. As the sound of the bell died away, his bed curtains were pulled apart, and there stood a figure with a childlike face, but with long, white hair and a strong, well-formed body. The ghost introduced itself as the Ghost of Christmas Past, Scrooge's past. When the ghost invited Scrooge to go on a journey with him, Scrooge was unable to refuse.

They traveled like the wind and stopped first at Scrooge's birthplace. There Scrooge saw himself as a boy, neglected by his friends and left alone to find adventure in books. Next he saw himself at school, where his sister had come to take him home for Christmas. Scrooge recalled his love for his sister, who had died young. The ghost reminded him that she had had a son whom Scrooge neglected. Their next stop was the scene of Scrooge's apprenticeship, where everyone made merry on Christmas Eve. Traveling on, they saw a young girl weeping as she told young Scrooge that she realized he loved money more than he loved her. The ghost showed him the same girl, grown older but happy with her husband and children. Then the ghost returned Scrooge to his room, where he promptly fell asleep again.

When the Ghost of Christmas Present appeared, he led Scrooge through the city streets on Christmas morning. Their first stop was at the Cratchit home, where Bob Cratchit appeared with frail, crippled Tiny Tim on his shoulder. In the Cratchit home a skimpy meal became a banquet. After dinner Bob proposed a toast to Mr. Scrooge, even though it put a temporary damper on the holiday gaiety. Then the ghost and Scrooge crossed swiftly through the city where everyone paused to wish one another a Merry Christmas. As they looked in on the home of Scrooge's nephew, gaiety prevailed and Scrooge was tempted to join in the games. There, too, a toast was proposed to Scrooge's health. As the clock began to strike twelve, Scrooge found himself in his room, and the ghost of Christmas Present faded away.

With the last stroke of twelve, Scrooge saw a black-shrouded phantom approaching him, the Ghost of Christmas Future. The phantom extended his hand and forced Scrooge to follow him until they came to a group of scavengers selling the belongings of the dead. One woman had entered a dead man's room, had taken his bed curtains, bedding, and even the shirt in which he was to have been buried. Scrooge saw a dead man with his face covered, but he refused to lift the covering. Revisiting the Cratchits, he learned that Tiny Tim had died.

After seeing his empty counting-house and his own neglected grave, Scrooge realized that it was he who had lain on the bed in the cold, stripped room with no one to mourn his death. Scrooge begged the spirit that it should not be so, vowing that he would change, that he would forever honor Christmas in his heart. He made a desperate grasp for the phantom's hand and realized that the ghost had shriveled away and dwindled into a bedpost. Scrooge bounded out of bed and thanked Jacob Marley's ghost for his chance to make amends. Dashing into the street, he realized that it was Christmas Day. His first act was to order the largest turkey available to be sent anonymously to the Cratchits. He stopped a man whom the day before he had ordered from his counting-house for asking for a contribution, and to him Scrooge gave a large sum of money for the poor. Then he astounded his nephew by arriving at his house for Christmas dinner and making himself the life of the party.

Scrooge never reverted to his old ways. He raised Bob Cratchit's salary, improved conditions in his office, contributed generously to all charities, and became a second father to Tiny Tim. It was said of him thereafter that he truly knew how to keep Christmas well.

THE CID

Type of work: Drama
Author: Pierre Corneille (1606-1684)
Type of plot: Romantic tragedy
Time of plot: Eleventh century
Locale: Seville
First presented: 1636

Principal characters:

Don Fernand, King of Castile
Doña Urraque, Infanta, daughter of Fernand
Don Diègue, father of Rodrigue
Don Gomès, father of Chimène
Don Rodrigue, accepted suitor of Chimène
Don Sanche, in love with Chimène
Chimène, daughter of Don Gomès

Critique:

In France, "Good as *The Cid*" became a proverb used to bestow high praise. *The Cid,* a tragedy in the neo-classical tradition, is generally ranked as the best of Corneille's works. The subject of the drama is man himself, and the hero determines his own fate in this tragedy of renunciation.

The Story:

Because she was the princess royal, the Infanta felt she could not openly love Rodrigue, a nobleman of lower rank. She encouraged, therefore, the growing attachment between Chimène and Rodrigue. Chimène asked her father, Don Gomès, to choose for his son-in-law either Rodrigue or Sanche. She awaited the choice anxiously; her father was on his way to court and she would soon hear his decision. Don Gomès chose Rodrigue without hesitation, chiefly because of the fame of Don Diègue, Rodrigue's father.

A complication soon arose at court. The king had chosen Don Diègue as preceptor for his son, the heir apparent. Don Gomès felt that the choice was unjust. Don Diègue had been the greatest warrior in Castile, but he was now old. Don Gomès considered himself the doughtiest knight in the kingdom. In a bitter quarrel Don Gomès unjustly accused Don Diègue of gaining the king's favor through flattery and deceit. He felt the prince needed a preceptor who would be a living example, not a teacher who would dwell in the past. In the quarrel, Don Gomès slapped his older rival. Don Diègue, too feeble to draw his sword against Don Gomès, upbraided himself bitterly for having to accept the insult. His only recourse was to call on his young son to uphold the family honor.

Torn between love and duty, Rodrigue challenged Don Gomès to a duel. After some hesitation because of Rodrigue's youth and unproved valor, Don Gomès accepted the challenge of his daughter's suitor. To the surprise of the court, Rodrigue, the untried novice, killed the mightiest man in Castile, piercing with his sword the man whom he respected as his future father-in-law.

Chimène now felt herself in a desperate plight because her love for Rodrigue was mixed with hatred for the murderer of her father. She finally decided to avenge her father by seeking justice from the king. Since she had the right to petition the king, Don Fernand was forced to hear her pleas. In the scene at court, Don Diègue made a strong counter-plea for his son, reminding the king that Rodrigue had done only what honor forced him to do—uphold the family name.

The king was saved from the vexing decision when fierce Moors assaulted the walls of Seville. Chimène awaited the outcome of the battle with mixed emotions. The army of Castile returned in triumph, bringing as captives two Moorish kings. And the man who had inspired and led the Castilians by his audacity was Rodrigue. The grateful king gave the hero a new title, The Cid, a Moorish name meaning "lord." The Infanta was wretched. Although her high position would not allow her to love Rodrigue, she could love The Cid, a high noble and the hero of Castile. She showed her nobility by yielding to Chimène's prior right.

Chimène was still bound to seek redress. The king resolved to test her true feelings. When she entered the throne room, he told her gravely that Rodrigue had died from battle wounds. Chimène fainted. The king advised her to follow the promptings of her heart and cease her quest for vengeance.

Still holding duty above love, however, Chimène insisted on her feudal right of a champion. Sanche, hoping to win the favor of Chimène, offered to meet Rodrigue in mortal combat and avenge the death of Don Gomès. Chimène accepted him as her champion. The king decreed that Chimène must marry the victor.

In private, Rodrigue came to Chimène. Indignant at first, Chimène soon softened when she learned that Rodrigue had resolved to let himself be killed because she wished it. Again wavering between love and duty, Chimène begged him to defend himself as best he could.

Sanche went bravely to meet Rodrigue who easily disarmed his opponent and showed his magnanimity by refusing to kill Chimène's champion. He sent his sword to Chimène in token of defeat. As soon as Chimène saw her champion approach with Rodrigue's sword in his hand, she immediately thought that Rodrigue was dead. She ran in haste to the king and begged him to change his edict because she could not bear to wed the slayer of her lover. When the king told her the truth, that Rodrigue had won, Don Diègue praised her for at last avowing openly her love. Still Chimène hesitated to take Rodrigue as her husband. The king understood her plight. He ordered The Cid to lead an expedition against the Moors. He knew that time would heal the breach between the lovers. The king was wise.

CLARISSA HARLOWE

Type of work: Novel
Author: Samuel Richardson (1689-1761)
Type of plot: Sentimental romance
Time of plot: Early eighteenth century
Locale: England
First published: 1747-1748

Principal characters:

- Clarissa Harlowe, a young woman of family and fortune
- Robert Lovelace, her seducer
- John Belford, Lovelace's friend
- William Morden, Clarissa's cousin
- Arabella, Clarissa's older sister
- James, Clarissa's older brother

Critique:

This novel is unusual for the modern reader because of its style. It is an epistolary novel, made up entirely of letters written by the various characters to each other, in which characterization and plot are revealed to the reader. The drawbacks to this form of novel are its tediousness and its superfluities. One wonders how the characters found the time during their adventures to pen such long, involved, and painstaking letters. It is also difficult for a twentieth-century reader to follow Clarissa's logic. Her decision to die, rather than marry the man who had seduced her, is not of a pattern to be quickly assimilated by a mind conditioned to the pragmatism of the modern world. The book is, in spite of sentimental theme and physical bulk, Richardson's best novel.

The Story:

Robert Lovelace, a young Englishman of a noble family, was introduced into the Harlowe household by Clarissa's uncle, who wished Lovelace to marry Clarissa's older sister, Arabella. The young man, finding nothing admirable in the older girl, fell deeply in love with Clarissa, but he quickly learned that his suit was balked by Clarissa's brother and sister. James Harlowe had disliked Lovelace since they had been together at Oxford, and Arabella was offended because he had spurned her in favor of Clarissa. Both were jealous of Clarissa because she had been left a fortune by their grandfather and they had not.

James Harlowe, having convinced his mother and father that Lovelace was a profligate, proposed that Clarissa be married to Mr. Solmes, a rich, elderly man of little taste and no sensibility. When Solmes found no favor in the eyes of Clarissa, her family assumed she was in love with Lovelace, despite her protestations to the contrary.

Clarissa refused to allow Solmes to visit with her in her parlor or to sit next to her when the family was together. Her father, outraged by her conduct, ordered her to be more civil to the man he had chosen as her husband. When she refused, saying she would never marry a man against her will, not even Lovelace, her father confined her to her room.

Lovelace, smitten with the girl's beauty and character, resolved to seduce her away from her family, partly out of love for her and partly in vengeance for the insults heaped upon him by the Harlowe family.

He was greatly aided in his scheme by the domineering personalities of Mr. Harlowe and his son. They took away Clarissa's trusted maid and replaced her with a girl who was impertinent and insolent to the young woman. They refused to let her see any member of the family, even her mother. Clarissa's only adviser whom she could trust was Miss Howe, a friend and correspondent who advised her to escape the house if she could, even if it meant accepting Lovelace's aid and his proposal of marriage.

One evening Lovelace slipped into the garden where Clarissa was walking and entreated her to elope with him. Thinking only to escape her domineering father, she went with him after some protest. Lovelace told her she would be taken to the home of Lord M—, a kinsman of Lovelace, who would protect her until her cousin, Colonel Morden, could return to England and arrange for a reconciliation between Clarissa and her family. Lovelace was not as good as his word, however, for he took her to a house of ill repute, where he introduced her to a woman he called Mrs. Sinclair. Inventing reasons why he could not take her to Lord M—'s house, he persuaded the bewildered girl to pass as his wife, for the time being, and he told Mrs. Sinclair that Clarissa was his wife with whom he could not live until certain marriage settlements had been arranged. Clarissa permitted him to tell the lie, in the belief that it would prevent her father and her brother from discovering her whereabouts.

In Mrs. Sinclair's house she was almost as much a prisoner as she had been in her father's home. Meanwhile her family had disowned her and refused to send her either money or clothes. Indeed, her father declared she was no longer his daughter and he hoped she would have a miserable existence in both this world and the next.

This state of affairs was distressing to Clarissa, who was now dependent upon Lovelace for her very existence. He took advantage of the circumstances to press his love upon her without mentioning his earlier promises of marriage. Clarissa tried to escape and got as far as Hampstead before Lovelace overtook her. There he had two women impersonate his cousins to convince Clarissa that she should return to her lodgings with them. Upon her return to Mrs. Sinclair's house, they filled her with drugs and later Lovelace raped her. A few days later Clarissa received from Miss Howe a letter in which she learned that she was in a house in which no woman of her station would be seen. Again Clarissa tried to escape, this time by calling for aid from a window. Lovelace finally promised to leave her unmolested until she could get aid from her cousin or from Miss Howe.

Lovelace left London for a few days to visit Lord M—, who was ill. While he was gone, Clarissa contrived to steal the clothes of a serving-girl and escape from the house, but within a day or two Mrs. Sinclair discovered Clarissa's whereabouts and had her arrested and imprisoned for debt. When John Belford, a friend of Lovelace, heard of the girl's plight, he rescued her by proving the debt a fraud. He found shelter for Clarissa with a kindly glove-maker and his wife. Tired of her miserable existence, Clarissa began to go into physical decline, in spite of all that the apothecary and doctor secured by John Belford could do for her.

She spent her time writing letters in an effort to secure a reconciliation with her family and to acquaint her friends with the true story of her plight. She refused to have anything to do with Lovelace, who was by that time convinced that he loved her dearly. He wished to marry her, to make amends for the treatment she had suffered at his hands, but she refused his offer with gentle firmness.

As she declined in health, Clarissa's friends did what they could to have her family forgive her. When her father and brother refused to receive her, she went to an undertaking establishment and bought a coffin which she had fitted as she wished, including a plaque which gave the date of her death as the day on which she left her father's house.

On his return to England Colonel Morden tried to raise her spirits, but his efforts failed because he, too, was unable to effect any change in the attitude of the Harlowe family. He also had an interview with Lovelace and Lord M—. The nobleman and Lovelace assured him that their family thought very highly of Clarissa and wished her to marry Lovelace and that Lovelace wanted to marry her. But even her cousin was unable to persuade Clarissa to accept Lovelace as a husband.

Everyone, including the Harlowe family, saw that Clarissa was determined to die. Her father and brother lifted their ban upon her ever entering the Harlowe house; her sister was sorry she had been cruel to Clarissa; and the mother was convinced that she had failed in her duty toward her daughter. They all wrote to Clarissa, begging the girl's forgiveness and expressing their hope she would recover quickly and be reunited with her family. Their letters, however, arrived too late, for Clarissa had breathed her last.

Clarissa was returned to her father's house for her funeral. She was interred in the family vault at the feet of the grandfather whose fortune had been one of the sources of her troubles. Lovelace, who was quite broken up at her death, was persuaded by Lord M— to go to the continent.

There Clarissa was avenged. Lovelace met Colonel Morden in France, and early one winter morning Clarissa's cousin fought a duel with her betrayer. Lovelace was mortally wounded by a thrust through his body. As he lay dying, he expressed the hope that his death would expiate his crimes.

CLAUDIUS THE GOD

Type of work: Novel
Author: Robert Graves (1895-)
Type of plot: Historical chronicle
Time of plot: A.D. 41-54
Locale: Rome, Britain, the Near East
First published: 1934

Principal characters:
TIBERIUS CLAUDIUS DRUSUS NERO GERMANICUS, Emperor of Rome
MESSALINA, his third wife
CALPURNIA, his mistress
AGRIPPINILLA, his fourth wife
LUCIUS DOMITIUS, later called Nero, Agrippinilla's son and Claudius' grandnephew
HEROD AGRIPPA, Tetrarch of Bashan

Critique:

Claudius the God and His Wife Messalina is characterized by meticulous care of detail and scrupulous handling of incident and character. Graves' technique is such that he is able to re-create a strikingly vivid picture of the life and the times about which he writes. A sequel to *I, Claudius,* this novel is, nevertheless, an entity in itself.

The Story:

When the Emperor Claudius was the neglected scholar of the Claudian family, before his accession to the throne, one of his friends and well-wishers was Herod Agrippa. The Emperor Tiberius had imprisoned Herod for treasonous sentiments, but when Caligula came to the throne he made Herod Tetrarch of Bashan. When Caligula was murdered and Claudius proclaimed emperor by the palace guards, Herod was back in Rome on official business.

Claudius' position was a difficult one at first, especially so as the result of popular opinion that he was a cripple, a stammerer, and an idiot. The Roman Senate did not expect much of such a man and certainly not a capable handling of public affairs after Caligula's four years of misrule. But Claudius immediately began a program of reforms, among them a reorganization of the Senate, a stabilization of the state's finances, and the abolition of many of Caligula's cruel decrees. To carry out his widespread program Claudius appointed many new ministers of state. To his wife, Messalina, he entrusted the office of the Director of Public Morals, as she had been most helpful in reorganizing the Senate list. To his loyal friend, Herod, Claudius gave the lands of Judea, Samaria, and Edom. Then in the open market place before an immense crowd Claudius and Herod made a solemn pact of friendship and loyalty.

Soon after Claudius' ascent to the throne his son Brittanicus was born, followed approximately eleven months later by a daughter named Octavia. After the birth of his second child, Messalina came to Claudius and requested his permission to move into an apartment in the new palace and thus live apart from him. Claudius ruefully agreed to her plan. Messalina's real desire to move to the new palace was greater freedom than she could enjoy under the eyes of Claudius, and her removal to her new quarters began a life of debauchery, licentiousness, political intrigue, bribery, cheating, and murder. Claudius was so busy with matters of state that seven years passed before he heard rumors of Messalina's depravities.

After beginning a public works program, sending an expedition into Germany to recover the eagle standard lost by Varus' army, and putting down a minor revolt at home, Claudius turned his attention to the conquest of Britain. The war was hastened by the detention of Roman trading ships by Togodumnus, who was joint ruler with his brother Caractacus, and also by the rapid spread of the Druid cult through Britain and France. Claudius sent Aulus Plautius to Britain with a large invasion force and the promise of additional legions if Roman losses exceeded a certain figure. Aulus managed to cross the Thames and capture London. Then he camped just outside London to await the arrival of Claudius and reinforcements. A decisive battle took place at Brentwood Hill, a ridge between London and Colchester. The Romans won it by means of Claudius' armchair strategy. At the age of fifty-three Claudius fought his first battle, won it, and never fought again. In Britain he was deified as a god and upon his return to Rome he received a full triumph.

He now had to turn his attentions to the East, where for some time he had been receiving disquieting reports regarding Herod Agrippa and his plot to establish a united Jewish empire. Herod had been making secret alliances with neighboring princes and potentates, and he hoped to obtain the support of the Jews by declaring himself the long-awaited Messiah. Claudius realized that affairs had progressed to the stage where there was little he could do to forestall Herod's plans. Herod, at the great festival at which he proposed to proclaim himself the Messiah, permitted neighboring rulers to address him as God without bothering to correct their error. At that moment an owl flew into the arena. Herod remembered a prophecy that when next he saw an owl his death would be near and the number of days left to him would be the same as the number of hoots. The owl hooted five times; five days later Herod was dead. His plot to set up a Jewish kingdom collapsed.

About eight years after they were married, Messalina came to Claudius with a strange tale. Barbillus the astrologer had predicted that her husband would die within thirty days, not later than the Ides of September. She proposed that Claudius' death might be averted if he permitted her to divorce him in order to remarry Silius, her former husband. Claudius finally gave in to her pleading. But the whole story was a ruse to rid herself of Claudius so that she might marry Silius; the two were plotting Claudius' murder and their own accession to the throne. Her marriage to Silius was announced for September tenth, but on the fifth of September, while Claudius was out of the city, she married Silius. Calpurnia, a former mistress of Claudius, finally told him the whole truth regarding Messalina and her behavior throughout their marriage. Claudius tried and executed over one hundred people, most of them the men with whom Messalina had committed adultery. Messalina herself was killed by an officer of the palace guards.

Claudius married again, this time his niece, Agrippinilla, the mother of Lucius Domitius, later the emperor Nero. He no longer took any interest in life but allowed the affairs of state to be handled by Agrippinilla and his ministers. Claudius adopted Lucius and made him joint heir with Brittanicus. Lucius became of age first, and Agrippinilla, who wished to see her son sole ruler of Rome, poisoned Claudius. His death was concealed from the people until the empire had been secured for Nero. Thus Claudius, Emperor of Rome and a Roman god, ended his troubled reign.

THE CLAYHANGER TRILOGY

Type of work: Novel
Author: Arnold Bennett (1867-1931)
Type of plot: Domestic realism
Time of plot: 1870-1895
Locale: England
First published: 1910, 1911, 1915

Principal characters:
EDWIN CLAYHANGER, a businessman
HILDA LESSWAYS, his wife
MAGGIE CLAYHANGER, Edwin's sister
MR. INGPEN, Edwin Clayhanger's friend
GEORGE CANNON, Hilda's first husband
DARIUS CLAYHANGER, Edwin's father

Critique:

In *The Clayhanger Trilogy (Clayhanger, Hilda Lessways, These Twain)* Bennett depicted the middle class of late nineteenth-century England with sympathy and understanding. He, unlike the naturalistic novelists, was not after ugliness for its own sake. Though the region he drew was one of the least picturesque in England's industrial Midlands, he did not see its ugliness alone; in it he perceived a homely beauty. Certainly, if the events of the work do not linger brilliantly in the mind, the characters will be remembered clearly and long.

The Story:

In 1872 sixteen-year-old Edwin Clayhanger left school to aid his father in the Clayhanger printing shop. His father had disregarded Edwin's request that he be allowed to go to school and study to be an architect. Old Darius Clayhanger was a self-made man who had risen from a boyhood experience in the workhouse to the position of affluence he held in the Midland community, and it was his desire that his work be carried on by his only son. Since he was a complete tyrant in the home, no one dared to cross him.

Several years later Darius Clayhanger built a new house in a more pretentious part of town. Edwin became friendly with the Orgreave family, who lived next door. The elder Orgreave was an architect, with whom Edwin spent many hours discussing his own interest in that profession. Unknown to Edwin, the oldest Orgreave daughter, Janet, fell in love with him.

Edwin met Hilda Lessways at the Orgreave home. She was an orphan living in Brighton with the sister of a former employer, George Cannon, who wished to marry her. Although she was attracted to Edwin, she returned to Brighton and soon married Cannon. At the time of her marriage she gave Cannon her small patrimony to invest for her.

A year later Hilda returned to visit the Orgreaves. During that year she had learned that her husband had been married earlier and that her marriage to him was void. On this second visit she fell in love with Edwin and promised to marry him, for no one knew of her marriage at Brighton. Then, learning that she was to have a baby, she returned to Brighton. She wrote to Janet Orgreave, saying that she was married and asking Janet to inform Edwin. He, deeply hurt, turned himself entirely to his father's business, for his father had become mentally ill.

Hilda, meanwhile, had had her child

and had named him George Edwin, after its father and Edwin Clayhanger. She managed a rooming-house owned by her husband's sister. Cannon, discovered by his first wife, was sentenced to serve a two-year prison term for bigamy. After his release he was again imprisoned for ten years for passing a forged check. The money he had imprudently invested for Hilda was lost when the hotel corporation, whose shares he had bought, collapsed. Hilda was no longer financially independent.

After his father's death, Edwin and his sister Maggie continued to live alone in the Clayhanger house. Both of them became old-maidish in their habits, although many young women, including Janet Orgreave, would have gladly married Edwin, whose printing business continued to prosper and grow.

Edwin became quite fond of Hilda's son, who was living temporarily with the Orgreaves. When George Edwin became ill with influenza, it was Edwin who sent for the doctor and notified Hilda.

Although neither spoke openly of their feelings, Hilda and Edwin renewed their affection for one another when they met at the sick child's bed. When he was well again, George Edwin and his mother went back to Brighton. Nine years had passed since Edwin and Hilda first had met. Hilda was still struggling along with the failing boarding-house at Brighton.

Months later Edwin went to see Hilda and found her penniless and about to be evicted. Edwin paid her bills, and Hilda told him all that had happened to her, explaining that her marriage was void and her child illegitimate. Edwin returned home but at last he resolved to marry Hilda quietly. He met her in London, where they were married. They then moved into the Clayhanger house and Maggie went to live with a maiden aunt. Edwin also adopted Hilda's son and gave him his name.

Edwin, long having had his own way, was accustomed to a certain routine in his home and to making his own decisions. But Hilda was a person of equally strong personality, and Edwin felt that she was trying to make him conform too much to her own domestic views and habits. Worst of all, she attempted to influence Edwin in business affairs, a realm which he thought was solely his own.

A few months after the marriage, the aunt with whom Maggie Clayhanger was living became seriously ill. During her last days, Mr. Ingpen, Edwin's business friend was injured in a factory accident. At Ingpen's request, Edwin went to his rooms to destroy some letters and pictures, so they would not be found if Ingpen died in the hospital. There Edwin found a woman asleep. She was Ingpen's mistress, a woman whose husband was incurably insane. Edwin was disturbed for his friend, but Ingpen laughed and said that the situation was best as it was because he did not want to be trapped in a marriage.

When Edwin's aunt died, her estate was left to the children of Edwin's younger sister, Clara. Edwin and Maggie were pleased, but Hilda thought that she and Edwin should have received part of the estate. Her selfishness irked Edwin. He felt that he was rich enough and that his nieces and nephews deserved the money. Seriously thinking that a divorce was the answer to his present situation, he recalled with nostalgia his bachelor days. The only bright ray in his life seemed to be George Edwin, his stepson, who was studying the elements of architecture with the aid of John Orgreaves. Edwin hoped that his son might now have the chance to become an architect.

On a visit to a nearby city, Hilda and Edwin were taken to inspect a prison. There they saw George Cannon. He was released soon afterward when he was found to be innocent of the forgery charge. Cannon then went to Edwin, unknown to Hilda, and Edwin gave him money to go to America. Edwin never expected to see the money again, but he wanted to get the man out of the country. He was also bothered by the fact that Hilda had been in correspondence with Cannon's other wife.

The climax of Edwin's unhappiness with Hilda came on Christmas day, when she took him to see a house in the country. She tried to force him into buying it by diplomatic moves and conversations with their friends and family, so that Edwin would appear foolish if he did not buy the house.

After a violent argument with his wife, whom he accused of being grasping, underhanded, and dishonest, Edwin left the house in a rage. But after a long walk in the cold winter night he realized that his marriage and his wife meant a great deal to him. He saw in his mind that he had to make concessions for his wife and for the fact that they had been married so late in life that they had already fixed their habits. Finally he saw, in his mind, his friend Ingpen, who was unable to marry the woman he loved.

He went back to the house to reconcile himself with Hilda. His faith in human nature was completely reëstablished when he found in the mail a check from America for the money he had lent to George Cannon.

THE CLOISTER AND THE HEARTH

Type of work: Novel
Author: Charles Reade (1814-1884)
Type of plot: Historical romance
Time of plot: Fifteenth century
Locale: Holland, Germany, France and Italy
First published: 1861

Principal characters:
Gerard Eliason, a young artist
Margaret Brandt, his betrothed
Denys, a Burgundian bowman
Margaret Van Eyck, sister of Jan Van Eyck
Ghysbrecht Van Swieten, a burgomaster

Critique:

The two outstanding features of this novel are its photographic details of fifteenth century European life, and the vivid character portrayal of Denys, the Burgundian crossbowman. Reade did tremendous research in order to achieve his accurate descriptions of fifteenth century European life. His Denys is one of the most delightful characters in English literature. Among the variety of literary types found in *The Cloister and The Hearth* are the long letter, poetry, dramatic dialogue, the tale within the tale, and picaresque romance. The description of the Catholic Church and clergy in the late Middle Ages is illuminating.

The Story:

Gerard, the son of Elias, a Dutch cloth and leather merchant, and Katherine, his wife, developed at an early age his talent for penmanship and illuminating. At first he was aided by the monks of the local convent for which he was destined. When the monks could teach the young artist no more, he became the pupil of Margaret Van Eyck, sister of the famous painter, Jan Van Eyck. She and her servant, Reicht Heynes, encouraged the lad to enter a prize art competition sponsored by Philip the Good, Duke of Burgundy and Earl of Holland.

On his way to Rotterdam to an exhibit of the entries, Gerard met an old man, Peter Brandt, and his daughter, Margaret, who sat exhausted by the wayside. He went with them into the town. There he took to the Princess Marie, daughter of Prince Philip, a letter of introduction from Dame Van Eyck. Impressed by the lad's talent, the princess promised him a benefice near his village of Tergou as soon as he had taken holy orders. He won a prize in the contest and returned to Tergou wondering whether he would ever again see Margaret Brandt, with whom he had fallen in love.

Gerard, learning accidentally from Ghysbrecht Van Swieten, Tergou's burgomaster, that the old man and his daughter lived in Sevenbergen, a nearby village, began to frequent their cottage. Ghysbrecht disclosed to Katherine, Gerard's mother, that the young man was interested in Margaret Brandt. A quarrel ensued in the family, Elias threatening to have Gerard imprisoned to prevent his marrying. Margaret Van Eyck gave Gerard money and valuable advice on art and recommended that he and the girl go to Italy, where Gerard's talents were sure to be appreciated. Gerard and Margaret Brandt became betrothed, but before they could be married the burgomaster had Gerard seized and put in jail. He was rescued at night from the prison by Margaret, his sweetheart, Giles, his dwarf brother, and Kate, his crippled sister. In the rescue, Giles removed from a chest in the cell some parchments which the villainous Ghysbrecht had hidden there. At Sevenbergen, Gerard buried all of the parchments except a deed which concerned Margaret's father.

After an exciting pursuit, Gerard and Margaret escaped the vicinity of Tergou. They separated, Margaret to return to Sevenbergen, Gerard to proceed to Rome. On the way, he was befriended by a Burgundian soldier named Denys, and the pair traveled toward the Rhine. They went through a variety of adventures together.

In Sevenbergen, meanwhile, Margaret Brandt fell sick and was befriended by Margaret Van Eyck. Martin, an old soldier friend of the young lovers, went to Rotterdam where he procured a pardon for Gerard from Prince Philip. Dame Van Eyck gave a letter to Hans Memling to deliver to Gerard in Italy, but Memling was waylaid by agents of the burgomaster and the letter was taken from him.

Gerard and Denys came upon a company of Burgundian soldiers on their way to the wars and Denys was ordered to ride with them to Flanders. Gerard was left to make his solitary way to Rome. Later Denys, released because of wounds received in the duke's service, set out for Holland, where he hoped to find Gerard. Elias and Katherine welcomed him in Tergou when he told them that he had been Gerard's comrade. Meanwhile old Brandt and Margaret disappeared from Sevenbergen, and Denys searched all Holland for the girl. They had gone to Rotterdam, but only the burgomaster knew their whereabouts. When Margaret practiced medicine illegally, she was arrested and sentenced to pay a large fine. In order to stay alive, she took in laundry. Denys discovered Margaret in Rotterdam and the pair returned to Tergou, where Gerard's family had become reconciled to Gerard's attachment to the girl.

Gerard made his dangerous way through France and Germany to Venice. From there he took a coastal vessel and continued to Rome. When the ship was wrecked in a storm, Gerard displayed bravery in saving the lives of a Roman matron and her child. He went on to Rome and took lodgings, but he found work all but impossible to obtain. He and another young artist, Pietro, decorated playing cards for a living. Finally through the good graces of the woman whose life he had saved in the shipwreck, Gerard was hired to decorate manuscripts for Fra Colonna, a leading classical scholar.

Hans Memling brought to Rome a letter, sent by Ghysbrecht, which gave Gerard the false news that Margaret had died. Gerard forsook the Church and in despair threw himself into the Tiber. But he was saved and carried to a monastery, where he recovered and eventually took monastic vows. He became Brother Clement of the Dominican Order. After a period of training he was sent to teach at the University of Basle, in Switzerland. Meanwhile, in Holland, Margaret gave birth to Gerard's son.

Brother Clement received orders to proceed to England. Preaching as he went, he began the journey down the Rhine.

In Rotterdam, Luke Peterson became Margaret's suitor. She told him he could prove his love for her by seeking out Gerard, but Luke's and Brother Clement's paths were fated not to cross. The priest went to Sevenbergen, where he was unable to find the grave of Margaret. He proceeded to Rotterdam, and there Margaret heard him preach without recognizing him as Gerard. He next went to Tergou to see Ghysbrecht. The burgomaster was dying; he confessed to Brother Clement that he had defrauded Margaret of wealth rightfully hers. On his deathbed Ghysbrecht made full restitution.

When Brother Clement left the burgomaster, he returned to Rotterdam and took refuge in a hermit's cave outside the city. There he mortified himself out of hatred for mankind.

Margaret, having learned his whereabouts through court gossip, went to him, but he repulsed her in the belief that she was a spirit sent by Satan. Margaret took her son to the cave in an attempt to win back his reason. Brother Clement's acquaintance with his son, also named Gerard, brought him to his senses. Margaret by shrewd argument persuaded him to come with her to Gouda, where he would be parson by arrangement with church authorities. They lived in Gouda, but apart, Gerard tending his flock and Margaret assisting him in his many charitable works.

After ten years at Gouda, Margaret died of the plague. Gerard, no longer anxious to live after her death, died two weeks later. Their son, Gerard, grew up to be Erasmus, the world-famous sixteenth-century Biblical scholar and man of letters.

THE CLOUDS

Type of work: Drama
Author: Aristophanes (c. 448-385 B.C.)
Type of plot: Social satire
Time of plot: Fifth century B.C.
Locale: Athens
First presented: 423 B.C.

Principal characters:
STREPIADES, an Athenian gentleman
PHIDIPPIDES, his son
SOCRATES, a Sophist philosopher

Critique:

The Clouds is one of the best known of Aristophanes' many comedies. This Greek master, recognized as a leading playwright in his day and still acknowledged as the foremost of comedy writers, colors this play with an air of buffoonery and raillery, sometimes savage and biting. The attacks on the Sophists, the logic lessons that Socrates administers to Strepiades, and the lesson that Phidippides gives his father, gave the Athenian audience moments of high entertainment. Aristophanes rejected the school of Sophists, whom he considered irreverent and artificial, and he satirized their teachings in *The Clouds.*

The Story:

Strepiades, a rich gentleman of Athens, was plunged into poverty and debt by his profligate son, Phidippides. Hounded by his son's creditors, Strepiades pondered ways and means to prevent complete ruin. Hearing reports that the Sophists taught a new logic which could be used to confuse one's creditors and so get one out of debt, Strepiades saw in the Sophist teachings a possible solution to his problem. He pleaded with Phidippides to enter the school of the Sophists and learn the new doctrines. When Phidippides, more interested in horse-racing than in learning, refused to become a pupil, Strepiades denounced his son as a wastrel and decided to enroll himself.

He went to the Thoughtery or Thinking-School, which was the term used for the classroom of the Sophists, and asked to see Socrates, the philosopher. After Strepiadies had explained his purpose, Socrates proceeded to demonstrate several logical conclusions of the new school. More certain than ever that the new logic would save him from ruin and disgrace, Strepiades pleaded until Socrates admitted him to the Thoughtery.

Unfortunately, Strepiades proved too old to master the Sophist technique in the classroom. Socrates then decided that Strepiades could learn to do his thinking outdoors. But when Socrates put questions concerning poetry to Strepiades, his answers showed such complete ignorance that Socrates finally admitted defeat and returned to the Thoughtery. Strepiades, disgusted with his own efforts, decided that he would either make Phidippides go to the Sophist school or turn him out of the house.

Approached a second time by his father, Phidippides again protested against enrolling in the school but finally yielded to his father's demands. Strepiades felt that all now would be well.

Some time afterward Strepiades went to learn what progress his son had made. Socrates assured him that Phidippides had done well. At this news, Strepiades felt sure that his plan had been a good one and that the new logic, as learned by his son, would soon deliver him from his creditors. He asked Socrates to call Phidippides from the classroom. When Phidippides emerged, Strepiades greeted him between tears and laughter, and said it was fitting that he should be saved by the son who had plunged him into debt.

He asked Phidippides to demonstrate his new learning, and Strepiades was amazed by the cunning of the new logic. At that moment one of Strepiades' creditors appeared to demand money that was owed him for a horse. Strepiades, confident that the Sophist-taught Phidippides could turn the tables on any creditor in the law court, refused to pay, ignoring threats of court action. He treated a second creditor in the same way and went home convinced that the new logic, as argued by Phidippides, would save him in the pending law suits.

It became a different matter, however, when Phidippides proceeded to demonstrate the Sophist teaching at home. Arguing that Strepiades had beaten him often for his own good, Phidippides buffeted his father during a family argument and declared that he was beating Strepiades for his own good. The old man protested, but with the new logic Phidippides silenced his protests and threatened to beat his mother on the same principle.

Strepiades realized that the Sophists could justify all manner of evil with their tricky logic. Thinking the teachings dangerous to the youth of Athens, he took a torch and set fire to the Thoughtery. As Socrates and the Sophist disciples screamed their objection, the Thoughtery went up in flames. Strepiades watched it burn, certain that he had eliminated an evil.

A CONNECTICUT YANKEE AT KING ARTHUR'S COURT

Type of work: Novel
Author: Mark Twain (Samuel L. Clemens, 1835-1910)
Type of plot: Social satire
Time of plot: Sixth century
Locale: England
First published: 1889

Principal characters:
THE CONNECTICUT YANKEE, the Boss
CLARENCE, a page
KING ARTHUR
SANDY, wife of the Boss
MERLIN, a magician

Critique:

Buried beneath a layer of wit is the serious social satire of Mark Twain's imaginative chronicle. The glorified days of knight errantry are exposed as a form of childish barbarism. The Connecticut Yankee finds instead of the legendary gallantry a cruel system of feudalism where the common people are abused and impoverished. Examining the Yankee's ideas about democracy, one can discern Mark Twain's own principles. He demonstrates that a government is good only insofar as the bulk of the people benefit by it.

The Story:

Struck on the head during a quarrel in a New England arms factory, a skilled mechanic awoke to find himself being prodded by the spear of an armored knight on horseback. The knight was Sir Kay of King Arthur's Round Table and the time was June, A.D. 528 in Merrie England, as a foppish young page named Clarence informed the incredulous Yankee, when his captor took him back to white-towered Camelot. The Yankee remembered that there had been a total eclipse of the sun on June 21, 528. If the eclipse took place, he was indeed a lost traveler in time turned backward to the days of chivalry.

At Camelot the Yankee listened to King Arthur's knights as they bragged of their mighty exploits. The magician, Merlin, told again of Arthur's coming. Finally Sir Kay told of his encounter with the Yankee, and Merlin advised that the prisoner be thrown into a dungeon to await burning at the stake on the twenty-first of June.

In prison the Yankee thought about the coming eclipse. Merlin, he told Clarence, was a humbug, and he sent the boy to the court with a message that on the day of his death the sun would darken and the kingdom would be destroyed. The eclipse came, and at the right time, for the Yankee was about to be burned when the sky began to dim. Awed, the king ordered the prisoner released. The people shouted that he was a greater magician than Merlin.

The court demanded another display of his powers. With the help of Clarence, the Yankee mined Merlin's tower with some crude explosives he had made and then told everyone he would cause the tower to crumble and fall. When the explosion took place, the Yankee was assured of his place as the new court magician. Merlin was thrown into prison.

The lack of mechanical devices in King Arthur's castle bothered the ingenious New Englander, and the illiteracy of the people hurt his American pride in education. He decided to make the commoners more than slaves to the nobility. He had a title of his own by this time, for the people called him the Boss.

A CONNECTICUT YANKEE AT KING ARTHUR'S COURT by Mark Twain. Published by Harper & Brothers.

As the Boss, he intended to modernize the kingdom.

His first act was to set up schools in small communities throughout the country. He had to work in secret, for he feared the interference of the Church. He trained workmen in mechanical arts. Believing that a nation needed a free press, he instructed Clarence in the art of journalism. He had telephone wires stretched between hamlets, haphazardly, however, because there were no maps by which to be guided.

When Sir Sagramor challenged the Boss to a duel, the court decided that he should go upon some knightly quest to prepare himself for the encounter. His mission was to help a young girl named Alisande, whose story he could not get straight. With many misgivings he put on a burdensome coat of mail and on his heavy charger started off with Sandy, as he called her. Sandy was a talkative companion who told endless tall tales as they traveled through the land. Along the way the Boss marveled at the pitiable state of the people under the feudal system. Whenever he found a man of unusual spirit he sent him back to Clarence in Camelot, to be taught reading, writing, and a useful trade. He visited the dungeons of the castles at which he stayed and released prisoners unjustly held by their grim masters.

In the Valley of Holiness he found another opportunity to prove his magic skill. There a sacred well had gone dry because someone, according to legend, had bathed in it. When he arrived, Merlin, now released from prison, was attempting magic to make the spring flow. With a great deal of pomp and flourish, the Boss repaired a leak in the masonry at the bottom of the well. As the well filled, Merlin went home in shame.

By chance the Boss came upon one of his telephone installations in a cave nearby. He talked to Clarence, who told him that King Arthur was on his way to the Valley of Holiness to see the flowing spring. He returned to the spring to find a fake magician assuring the gaping pilgrims that he could tell what anyone was doing at that moment. The Boss asked him about King Arthur. The magician said that he was asleep in his bed at Camelot. The Boss grandly predicted that the king was on his way to the Valley of Holiness. When the king did arrive, the people were again awed by the Boss's magic.

Anxious that King Arthur be convinced of the sufferings of his people, the Boss suggested that he and the king disguise themselves as commoners and travel as pilgrims through the country. The Boss knew that Arthur was not to blame for his own social doctrines; he was a victim of his place in society. On their journey the king proved to be courageous and kind.

Misfortune soon overtook them. They were seized by an earl and sold as slaves, because they were unable to prove themselves free men. The slaves were taken to London, where the Boss picked the lock that held him and escaped. The rest of the slaves were ordered to be hanged after his escape. But the Boss located one of his telephones and called Clarence in Camelot, ordering him to send Sir Lancelot and an army of knights to London to save their king from hanging.

The Boss came back to Camelot in glory, but not for long. He still had to fight a duel with Sir Sagramor—in reality a battle between Merlin and the Boss. Merlin professed to cover Sir Sagramor with an invisible shield, but the credulous knight was invisible to no one but himself. The Boss wore no armor, and so on the field of the tournament he was able to dodge the charging knight until Sir Sagramor grew tired. Then the Boss lassoed him and pulled him from his horse. When Sir Sagramor returned once again to the field, Merlin stole the Boss's lasso. There was no alternative; the Boss shot Sir Sagramor with his gun. Then he challenged all the knights of the Round Table. He had only twelve shots in his two revolvers, but fortunately, when he had killed eleven of the charging knights, the line wavered and gave up.

Three years passed. By this time the Boss had married Sandy and they had a little girl. He and Clarence were planning to declare a republic after the death of Arthur, for the sixth-century kingdom was now a nineteenth-century land with schools, trains, factories, newspapers, the telephone and the telegraph. Although the code of chivalry had been abolished, the knights still insisted on wearing their armor. Then little Hello-Central, the Boss' daughter, became ill, and he and Sandy took the child to the seashore for recuperation. On their return, the Boss found Camelot in a shambles. Only Clarence remained to tell him the story. There had been a battle between King Arthur and Sir Lancelot over Queen Guinevere. The king was dead, and by interdict the Church had destroyed the work of the Boss. Clarence and the Boss built a fortress surrounded by an electrically charged barrier. In a battle with the surviving chivalry of England the Boss was stabbed. When an old woman came to the fortress from the enemy lines and offered to nurse him, no one recognized her as Merlin. The magician cast a spell on the Boss and declared that he would sleep for thirteen hundred years. And, indeed, the Yankee did awake once more in the nineteenth century.

CONSUELO

Type of work: Novel
Author: George Sand (Mme. Aurore Dudevant, 1804-1876)
Type of plot: Historical romance
Time of plot: Eighteenth century
Locale: Venice, Bohemia, Vienna
First published: 1842

Principal characters:

CONSUELO, a singer
ANZOLETO, her betrothed
PORPORA, her music master and godfather
COUNT RUDOLSTADT, a Bohemian nobleman
ALBERT, his son
CORILLA, Consuelo's rival
JOSEPH HAYDN, a composer

Critique:

Although George Sand was one of the most popular novelists of the nineteenth century, her style seems somewhat tedious to present-day readers. The plot of *Consuelo,* interesting as it is, suffers at times from the excessive detail with which the thoughts and movements of the main characters are depicted. The author's many literary skills are exhibited, however, in this novel. Her descriptive passages are beautiful and moving, and her intimate knowledge of music and musicians enabled her to write convincing characterizations of many of the people whom Consuelo met in her travels. All told, *Consuelo* is well worth the effort spent reading it, for its virtues at least balance, if not outweigh, its defects.

The Story:

At the church of the Mendicanti in Venice, Consuelo was the most gifted of all the pupils of the famous teacher, Porpora. Consuelo was a poor orphan child, and Porpora had made her his goddaughter. Before the death of her mother, Consuelo had promised that she would one day become betrothed to Anzoleto, another poor musician of Venice.

Through the efforts of Anzoleto, Consuelo was engaged as the prima donna at the theater of Count Zustiniani, replacing Corilla, who had also been Porpora's student. Consuelo was a great success, but Anzoleto, who had also been engaged in the theater at the insistence of Consuelo, was not much of a musician and was not well received. Anzoleto, afraid that he would be discharged, pretended to be in love with Corilla, thinking that he would be safe if both singers were in love with him.

Porpora had never liked Anzoleto, and at last he contrived to have Consuelo visit Corilla's home. When they found Anzoleto there, Consuelo was so hurt that she left Venice at once, vowing that she would never set foot on the stage again, and renouncing the false Anzoleto forever.

From Venice Consuelo went to Bohemia, where she was engaged by Count Rudolstadt as a companion for his niece, Amelia. This young noblewoman had been betrothed to young Count Albert Rudolstadt, but she feared him because he seemed to be insane. Albert often had visions in which he saw scenes of the past and often imagined himself to be the reincarnated body of some person long dead.

When Albert first heard Consuelo sing, he called her by her name, even though she had taken another name to hide her unhappy life in Venice. Albert told Consuelo and the whole family that she was his salvation—that she had been sent to remove the curse from him. Consuelo was bewildered.

Albert often disappeared for many days at a time, no one knew where. Consuelo followed him, but could never find his hiding place until the night she descended into a deep well and found steps leading to a grotto where Albert and an idiot called Zdenko spent many days together. Zdenko loved Albert more than his own life; when he saw Consuelo coming into the well, he thought she wanted to harm Albert and almost killed her. Consuelo escaped from Zdenko and found Albert, and after she spoke soothingly to him he ceased his mad talk and seemed to regain normal behavior. She persuaded him to return to his family and not to go back to the grotto without her. Albert told Consuelo that he loved her and needed her; but although she no longer loved Anzoleto, she could not forget how she had once loved him, and she asked Albert to wait a while for her answer.

Albert's father and the rest of the family were grateful to Consuelo for helping restore Albert to his senses. The father, Count Rudolstadt, even told Consuelo that he would give his consent to a marriage between his son and her, for the old gentleman believed that only Consuelo could keep his son sane. While Consuelo was debating whether she loved Albert and could accept the honor, Anzoleto, having deserted Corilla, came to the castle in search of her. Consuelo slipped away from the castle, leaving a note for Albert. She went to Vienna to rejoin Porpora.

Without funds, Consuelo had great difficulty in reaching Vienna, and had to walk most of the way. In her travels, she met Joseph Haydn, a young composer who had been on his way to the castle to find her; he had hoped he could persuade her to take him to Porpora, under whom he wished to study. Dressed as a peasant boy, Consuelo accompanied Haydn to Vienna. One night they took refuge in the home of a canon of the Church. While they were there, Corilla came to the door, seeking a safe place to give birth to her child. Consuelo had pity on her former enemy and took Corilla to an inn, where she helped to deliver the child. From a maid, Consuelo learned that Anzoleto was the father. Corilla did not recognize Consuelo, who continued to wear the disguise of a boy.

When Joseph and Consuelo finally reached Vienna, the girl found Porpora overjoyed to see her again. Haydn became Porpora's pupil, and Consuelo sang for the Empress. Then Corilla, who had also come to Vienna and learned that it was Consuelo who befriended her during the birth of her child, arranged for Consuelo to sing in the theater there. Corilla hoped to seal the lips of Consuelo, who knew of the illegitimate child and knew also that Corilla had abandoned the baby in the home of the canon who had given Consuelo and Joseph shelter. Anzoleto was never heard from again.

Consuelo wrote to Albert, telling him that she was almost ready to return to him, but Porpora intercepted the letter and tore it up. Consuelo waited in vain for a reply from Albert. At last, Porpora told her that he had received a letter from the count, saying that he did not wish his son to marry an actress, and that Albert had concurred in the decision. Consuelo so trusted her godfather that she believed him, not realizing how ambitious Porpora was for her musical career.

Porpora went with Consuelo to accept a theater engagement in Berlin. On the way they met the brother of Count Rudolstadt. Albert had asked his father to have someone at a certain place on the road on a specific day and at a specific hour, saying that the messenger was to bring the travelers he would meet there to the castle at once. Albert was very ill, and Consuelo persuaded Porpora to allow her to go to Albert. When she arrived at the castle, she learned that his father had received a letter from Porpora saying that he would never consent to a marriage between Consuelo and Albert and that Consuelo herself had renounced Albert. It had been the deathblow. Albert grew very weak and begged Consuelo to marry him before he died so that his soul could find peace; he still believed that only through Consuelo could he find salvation. So the marriage vows were repeated, and Albert, crying that he was now saved, died in Consuelo's arms.

Consuelo stayed with her husband all night, leaving him only when he was carried to his bier. She then bade Albert's family goodbye, refusing to accept any of the fortune which was now hers. Then she left the castle and went to join Porpora in Berlin, where Frederick the Great himself worshipped both her beauty and her art.

THE COUNT OF MONTE-CRISTO

Type of work: Novel
Author: Alexandre Dumas, father (1802-1870)
Type of plot: Historical romance
Time of plot: Nineteenth century
Locale: France
First published: 1844

Principal characters:

Edmond Dantès, a young sailor
Mercédès, his sweetheart
Ferdinand Mondego, a rival
M. Danglars, an ambitious shipmate
M. Villefort, a deputy
Valentine, his daughter
Abbé Faria, a prisoner at Chateau D'If
Caderousse, an innkeeper
M. Morrel, a shipping master
Maximilian, his son
Albert, Mondego's son
Haidée, An Albanian

Critique:

The Count of Monte-Cristo is a good story, and that seems to be its chief merit. The characters are flat; they remain courageous, avaricious, kind, loyal, selfish or treacherous, in the conventional mold the author has set for them. But in spite of many defects the novel remains a great work in literature, for the story of the Count of Monte-Cristo is still a breath-taking experience for all who read his adventure, a dramatic tale filled with mystery and intrigue.

The Story:

When Edmond Dantès sailed into Marseilles harbor that day in 1815, he was surrounded by enemies. His shipmate, Danglars, coveted his appointment as captain of the *Pharaon*. Ferdinand Mondego wished to wed Mercédès, who was betrothed to Edmond.

Danglars and Ferdinand wrote a note accusing Edmond of carrying a letter from Elba to the Bonapartist committee in Paris. Caderousse, a neighbor, learned of the plot but kept silent. On his wedding day Edmond was arrested and taken before a deputy named Villefort, a political turncoat, who, to protect himself, had Edmond secretly imprisoned in the dungeons of the Château D'If. There Dantès' incarceration was secured by the plotting of his enemies outside the prison, notably Villefort, who wished to cover up his own father's connections with the Bonapartists.

Napoleon came from Elba, but Edmond lay forgotten in his cell. The cannonading at Waterloo died away. Years passed. Then one night Edmond heard the sound of digging from an adjoining cell. Four days later a section of the flooring fell in and Edmond saw an old man in the narrow tunnel below. He was the Abbé Faria, whose attempt to dig his way to freedom had led him only to Edmond's cell. Thereafter the two met daily, and the old man taught Edmond history, mathematics, and languages. In Edmond's fourteenth year of imprisonment Faria, mortally ill, told Edmond where to find a tremendous fortune should he escape after the old man's death. When death did come, the abbé's body was placed in a sack, and Edmond conceived the idea of changing places with the dead man, whom he dragged through the tunnel into his own bed. Jailers threw the sack into the sea. Edmond ripped the cloth and swam through the darkness to an islet in the bay.

At daybreak he was picked up by a gang of smugglers with whom he worked until a stroke of luck brought him to the island of Monte-Cristo, where Faria's fortune awaited him. He landed on the island with the crew of the ship, and, feigning injury in a fall, persuaded the crew to leave him behind until they could return for him. Thus he was able to explore the island and to find his treasure hidden in an underground cavern. He returned to the mainland and there sold some small jewels to provide himself with money enough to carry out his plans to bring his treasure from Monte-Cristo. There he learned that his father had died and Mercédès, despairing of Edmond's return, had married Ferdinand.

Disguised as an abbé, he visited M. Caderousse to seek information of those who had caused his imprisonment. M. Villefort had gained fortune and station in life. Danglars was a rich banker. Ferdinand had won wealth and a title in the Greek war. For this information Edmond gave Caderousse a diamond worth fifty thousand francs.

He learned also that his old shipping master, M. Morrel, was on the verge of bankruptcy. In gratitude, because Morrel had given the older Dantès money to keep him from starvation, Edmond saved Morrel's shipping business.

Edmond took the name of his treasure island. As the Count of Monte-Cristo he dazzled all Paris with his fabulous wealth and his social graces. He and his mysterious protégée, a beautiful girl named Haidée whom he had bought during his travels in Greece, became the talk of the boulevards.

Meanwhile he was slowly plotting the ruin of the four men who had caused him to be sent to the Château D'If. Caderousse was the first to be destroyed. Monte-Cristo had awakened his greed with the gift of a diamond. Later, urged by his wife, Caderousse had committed robbery and murder. Now, released from prison, he attempted to rob Monte-Cristo but was mortally wounded by an escaping accomplice. As the man lay dying, Monte-Cristo revealed his true name—Edmond Dantès.

In Paris, Monte-Cristo had succeeded in ingratiating himself with the banker, Danglars, and was secretly ruining him. Ferdinand was the next victim on his list. Ferdinand had gained his wealth by betraying Pasha Ali in the Greek revolution of 1823. Monte-Cristo persuaded Danglars to send to Greece for confirmation of Ferdinand's operations there. Ferdinand was exposed and Haidée, daughter of the Pasha Ali, appeared to confront him with the story of her father's betrayal. Albert, the son of Mercédès and Ferdinand, challenged Monte-Cristo to a duel to avenge his father's disgrace. Monte-Cristo intended to make his revenge complete by killing the young man, but Mercédès came to him and begged for her son's life. Aware of Monte-Cristo's true identity, she interceded with her son as well, and at the scene of the duel the young man publicly declared his father's ruin had been justified. Mother and son left Paris. Ferdinand shot himself.

Monte-Cristo had also become intimate with Madame Villefort and encouraged her desire to possess the wealth of her stepdaughter, Valentine, whom Maximilian Morrel, son of the shipping master, loved. The count had slyly directed Madame Villefort in the use of poisons, and the depraved woman murdered three people. When Valentine herself succumbed to poison, Maximilian went to Monte-Cristo for help. Upon learning that his friend Maximilian loved Valentine, Monte-Cristo vowed to save the young girl. But Valentine had apparently died. Still Monte-Cristo promised future happiness to Maximilian.

Meanwhile Danglars' daughter, Eugénie, ran off to seek her fortune independently, and Danglars found himself bankrupt. He deserted his wife and fled the country. Villefort having discovered his wife's treachery and crimes, confronted her with a threat of exposure. She then poisoned herself and her son Edward, for whose sake she had poisoned the others. Monte-Cristo revealed his true name to Villefort, who subsequently went mad.

But Monte-Cristo had not deceived Maximilian. He had rescued Valentine while she lay in a drugged coma in the tomb. Now he reunited the two lovers on his island of Monte-Cristo. They were given the count's wealth, and Monte-Cristo sailed away with Haidée never to be seen again.

THE COUNTERFEITERS

Type of work: Novel
Author: André Gide (1869-1951)
Type of plot: Psychological realism
Time of plot: Early 1920's
Locale: Paris
First published: 1925

Principal characters:
EDOUARD, a writer
OLIVIER MOLINIER, his nephew
GEORGE MOLINIER, Olivier's younger brother
VINCENT MOLINIER, Olivier's older brother
BERNARD PROFITENDIEU, Olivier's friend and Edouard's secretary

LAURA DOUVIERS, Edouard's friend
COMTE DE PASSAVANT, a libertine
ARMAND VEDEL, Laura's brother and Olivier's friend

Critique:

The Counterfeiters traces the behavior pattern of a group of youths, each stimulated by intimate contact with an older individual. It is generally considered Gide's finest novel and one of the noteworthy novels in contemporary fiction. The author's ability to create real characters, to understand them and present them for our understanding, is remarkable. His intention is to show that man must follow the dictates of his own heart and ignore convention, if he wishes to find full expression and happiness.

The Story:

When seventeen-year-old Bernard Profitendieu discovered an old love letter of his mother's and realized that he was an illegitimate son, he left a scathing letter for the man whom he had considered his real father and ran away from home. He spent that night with his friend, Olivier Molinier. Olivier told him of his Uncle Edouard, a writer, who would be arriving from England the following day, and also of a woman with whom his older brother Vincent was involved.

The next morning Bernard left before Olivier had awakened. For a time he wondered what to do. He idly decided to go to the station and watch Olivier meet his uncle.

That same morning Vincent visited his friend, the notorious homosexual, Comte de Passavant. He was disturbed over his affair with Laura Douviers, a married woman whom he had met while both were patients in a sanatorium. Upon her release she had followed Vincent to Paris.

Edouard was returning to Paris because of a promise to Laura. He had known her before her marriage, and had told her to call upon him whenever necessary. He was also looking forward to seeing his nephew Olivier, of whom he was very fond. So excited was he, in fact, that, after checking his bag, he threw away his checkroom ticket. But the meeting with his nephew was unsatisfactory.

Bernard, unobserved, had watched the meeting between the two. He picked up the checkroom ticket Edouard had dropped and claimed the bag. In it he discovered a large sum of money, which he quickly pocketed; Edouard's journal, which he read without scruple; and Laura's supplicating letter.

With no definite plan in mind, he called on Laura. Laura was disturbed by the young man who knew so much about her affairs, but his actions became understandable when Edouard arrived and Bernard admitted the theft of the bag. Bernard said that he had stolen it as a means of getting in touch with Edouard. Edouard was very much taken with the young man's impudent charm. When Bernard suggested that he might fill the role of a secretary, Edouard agreed.

A few days later, with Bernard as his secretary, Edouard took Laura to Switzerland. Bernard wrote to Olivier in glowing terms about his new position. Olivier was jealous of Bernard, who, he felt, had taken his place in Edouard's affections. He decided to take an editorial assignment offered him by Comte de Passavant.

In the meantime Bernard fell in love with Laura. When he confessed his love, Laura showed him a letter from her husband, begging her to come back to him with her child and Vincent's. She had decided to return to him. Bernard and Edouard returned to Paris.

A letter arrived from Olivier to Bernard. He was in Italy with de Passavant, and he wrote complacently about the wonderful journal they intended to publish. Bernard showed the letter to Edouard, who failed to realize that the letter disguised the boy's real feelings of jealousy and hurt.

Bernard, although still acting as Edouard's secretary, had enrolled in the Vedel School and was living in the Vedel household. The Vedels were Laura's parents and Edouard's close friends. Edouard was particularly fond of Rachel, Laura's older sister, and it distressed him to see that she was devoting all her time and energy to managing the school.

Bernard told Edouard about some children, including George Molinier, Olivier's younger brother, who were engaged in some underhanded activities. The boys, as Bernard was soon to learn, were passing counterfeit coins.

Olivier returned to Paris to get in touch with Bernard. The meeting between the two was strained. As they parted, Olivier invited Edouard and Bernard to a party which de Passavant was giving that evening. Olivier then went to call on another old friend, Armand Vedel, Laura's younger brother. Armand refused the invitation to the party, but suggested that Olivier ask his sister Sarah to go in his place. Bernard, who was living at the school, was to serve as her escort.

The party was an orgy. Olivier became drunk and quarrelsome. Edouard led him from the room, and Olivier, ashamed, begged his uncle to take him away.

Bernard escorted Sarah home. Her room was beyond Armand's, and her brother handed Bernard the candle to light the way. As soon as Bernard had gone into her bedroom, Armand bolted the door. Bernard spent the night with Sarah.

The next morning he found Edouard attempting to revive Olivier. The boy, after spending the night with his uncle, had risen early in the morning on the pretext that he wanted to rest on the sofa. Getting up later, Edouard had discovered his nephew lying on the bathroom floor unconscious, the gas jets turned on. Edouard nursed Olivier until the boy recovered. When Olivier's mother went to see her son, she expressed to Edouard her concern for George and his wayward habits. Edouard promised to speak to George. He also learned that Vincent had gone away with Lady Griffith, a friend of de Passavant.

A few days later Edouard received a call from M. Profitendieu, Bernard's foster father. Ostensibly he had called in his office as magistrate to ask Edouard to speak to his nephew George, who was suspected of passing counterfeit coins. But it soon became evident that the real object of his visit was to inquire about Bernard. Since the boy had left home, Profitendieu had worried about him. He wanted very much to have him home once more.

Meanwhile Bernard's affair with Sarah had attracted Rachel's attention, and she asked him to leave the school. Bernard went to Edouard, who told him of the interview with Profitendieu. For some time Bernard had regretted the harsh letter he had written, and the hatred he had felt for his foster father had changed to sympathy and fondness. It was evident that Bernard was no longer needed as Edouard's secretary. He decided to return home.

Armand had succeeded Olivier as editor of de Passavant's journal. He went to see Olivier and showed him a letter from an older brother in Egypt. The writer told of a man with whom he was living who was almost out of his mind. From what he could gather from the fellow's ravings, the man had been responsible for his woman companion's death. Neither Armand nor Olivier guessed that the man was Olivier's brother Vincent.

George and his friends caused a tragedy at their school. Boris, the young grandson of an old friend of Edouard, had been invited to join a secret society if he would perform the act of initiation

—stand up before the class and shoot himself through the temple. It was understood that the cartridge would be a blank. One of the boys, however, substituted a real bullet for the dummy, and when Boris, pale but resolute, walked to the front of the class and shot himself, the joke became a tragedy. The experience was terrible enough to bring George to his senses.

Olivier having completely recovered, Edouard settled down again to writing his book, with a great sense of peace and happiness.

THE COUNTRY OF THE POINTED FIRS

Type of work: Novel
Author: Sarah Orne Jewett (1849-1909)
Type of plot: Regional romance
Time of plot: Late nineteenth century
Locale: Maine seacoast
First published: 1896

Principal characters:

MRS. TODD, a New England herbalist
MRS. BLACKETT, her mother
WILLIAM, her brother
THE BOARDER, a writer
ESTHER, William's sweetheart
MRS. HIGHT, Esther's mother

Critique:

In this book there are few episodes that could be called exciting. Instead, the interest lies in character portrayal and nature description. Each chapter can stand alone as a local-color sketch, a self-contained unit. For one who wishes to explore the deep springs of New England character, however, this book is pleasant and leisurely reading.

The Story:

A woman writer came one summer to Dunnet Landing, a Maine seacoast town, to find seclusion for her work. She boarded with Mrs. Almira Todd, a friendly widow and the local herb doctor. Besides having a garden full of herbs, Mrs. Todd often roamed far afield for rarer specimens. The boarder sometimes took care of Mrs. Todd's sales of herbs and birch beer when Mrs. Todd was away.

At last the boarder realized that she must get to work on her book and give up the society of Mrs. Todd in the daytime. The boarder found the village schoolhouse a quiet place for her writing, and she spent most of her days there. One morning she was surprised to have a visit from old Captain Littlepage, a retired seaman who seldom left his house. For a time he spoke seriously of the great English poets. When he saw that the boarder did not laugh at him, he launched upon a long narrative. It seemed that he had been shipwrecked upon a small island and had met there another sailor who had been to the North Pole. He told Captain Littlepage of a town of ghosts he had discovered. It was Captain Littlepage's theory that in this town souls awaited their passage into the next world. The old man's narrative stopped suddenly as his mind returned to the present. The boarder helped him home and told no one about his strange story.

On another day Mrs. Todd took her boarder out to Green Island, where Mrs. Todd's mother lived. Mrs. Blackett was over eighty, her daughter past sixty. Mrs. Blackett still did her own work and kept house for her son William, who was past fifty. William was a bashful man, but he found a friend to his liking in the boarder. Mrs. Todd and the boarder gathered some herbs before they left the island, and Mrs. Todd showed her the spot offshore where her husband had gone down in his boat.

Mrs. Fosdick came to visit Mrs. Todd. The two old ladies and the boarder often spent their evenings together. One night Mrs. Todd told of her husband's Cousin Joanna, who had lived on Shell-heap Island. Disappointed in love, Joanna went to live alone on the tiny island. Passing fishermen often left presents on the shore for her, but no one ever visited her. Finally Mrs. Todd and the minister went to see her, for the minister was worried about the state of Joanna's soul. They found Joanna living comfortably but simply. Satisfied with her lonely life, she could not be induced to return to the mainland. Joanna lived out her life on the island and was buried there.

Late in August Mrs. Todd took her boarder and Mrs. Blackett to the Bowden family reunion. They hired a carriage and drove far inland to the family seat. All the Bowdens for miles around came to the reunion, and Mrs. Blackett was one of the privileged guests because of her age. For once Mrs. Todd forgot her herbs and spent the entire day in the enjoyment of the society of her friends. William had not come to the gathering because of his bashfulness. Mrs. Blackett treasured every moment of the day, for she knew it was one of the last reunions she would attend.

One day the boarder stood on the shore below Dunnet Landing. There she met Mr. Tilley, one of the oldest fishermen in the village. Mr. Tilley was reserved toward strangers, but he had at last accepted the boarder as a friend and he invited her to visit him that afternoon. When the boarder arrived, he was knitting some socks. The two friends sat in the kitchen while Mr. Tilley told the boarder about his wife. She had died eight years before, but her husband had never got over his sorrow. He kept the house just as she had left it. Proudly he showed the boarder the seldom-used parlor and Mrs. Tilley's set of china. She left the cottage feeling the loneliness that surrounded the old fisherman.

When the clear, cool autumn came, it was time for the boarder to leave. Mrs. Todd helped her pack and get her belongings down on the wharf for the steamer. Mrs. Todd took her leave of the boarder before she left the house. From the deck of the steamer the boarder watched Dunnet Landing fade into the distance. She recalled a day of the past summer when William had come to the mainland. He was going trout fishing in an inland stream. Self-consciously he asked the boarder to go with him. They caught no fish, but William took her afterward to see Mrs. Hight and her daughter Esther. The boarder stayed to talk to Mrs. Hight, while William went out to speak to Esther, who supported her aged and crippled mother by tending sheep. As William and the boarder left, she realized that William and Esther were lovers.

When the boarder returned to Dunnet Landing in the spring, Mrs. Todd told her that Mrs. Hight had recently died and that Esther and William were to be married immediately. He was to come to the mainland the next day if the weather proved good.

Early in the morning Mrs. Todd was up to watch for a sail from Green Island. Finally she saw it approaching. Then neighbors began to drop in to inquire why William was coming to the mainland. After the ceremony William and Esther stopped for a moment at Mrs. Todd's house before returning to the island. Mrs. Todd and the boarder accompanied the pair to the landing to see them off. The older woman expressed no emotion at the leavetaking; but as she and the boarder returned to the house, they walked holding hands all the way.

THE COURTSHIP OF MILES STANDISH

Type of work: Poem
Author: Henry Wadsworth Longfellow (1807-1882)
Type of plot: Sentimental romance
Time of plot: 1621
Locale: Massachusetts
First published: 1858

Prinicpal characters:
MILES STANDISH, a soldier
JOHN ALDEN, Miles Standish's friend
PRISCILLA, a girl loved by Standish and Alden

Critique:

The ironic situation which results when Miles Standish sent John Alden to plead his lover's case before Priscilla is tempered by the genial, placid tone of this poem. Simply and gracefully written, it has long been a favorite among American romantic poems.

The Story:

In the Pilgrim colony Miles Standish and John Alden shared a cabin. The latter was a young scholar; the former was a gruff captain of the soldiers, whose wife had died after the landing of the Mayflower the previous fall.

One night Standish dropped his copy of *Caesar's Commentaries* and turned to John, who was writing a letter filled with praise for Priscilla, one of the young girls of the colony. Standish spoke of the loneliness and weariness of his own life, and of the fact that Priscilla, too, was living alone, her parents having died during the winter. Since he himself was no scholar but only a blunt soldier, he asked John to take to Priscilla his proposal of marriage.

Taken aback by the request, John could only stammer that it would be wiser for Standish to plead his own case. When the captain asked the favor in the name of friendship, the youth could not refuse.

Priscilla was singing the Hundredth Psalm as John approached her cabin, and as he opened the door he saw her industriously spinning. Filled with woe at what he must do, he nevertheless stepped resolutely inside. Seizing what seemed the opportune moment, John blurted out the captain's proposal. Priscilla flatly refused, for she felt that Standish himself should have come if she were worth the wooing. And she further confused the young man by asking him why he did not speak for himself.

Caught between his own love for Priscilla and his respect for Standish, John decided to go back to England when the Mayflower sailed next day.

Miles Standish was enraged when he heard the outcome of John's wooing, but the captain's tirade was interrupted by news of Indians on the warpath. He strode into the colony's council room and there saw a snakeskin full of arrows, the challenge to battle. Pulling out the arrows, he filled the skin with bullets and powder, and defiantly handed it back to the Indian. The savage quickly disappeared into the forest. Captain Standish, his eight men and their Indian guide left the village next morning before anyone else was awake.

Alden did not sail that day. Among the people on the beach he saw Priscilla, who looked so dejected and appealing that he decided to stay and protect her. They walked back to the village together, and John described the reaction of Miles Standish to Priscilla's question. He also confided that he had planned to leave the colony, but had remained in order to look after her.

Miles Standish, marching northward along the coast, brooded over his defeat, but finally concluded that he should confine himself to soldiering and forget wooing. When he returned to the village from his attack on the Indian camp, he brought with him the head of one of the savages and hung it on the roof of the fort. Priscilla was glad then that she had not accepted Miles Standish.

That autumn the village was at peace with the Indians. Captain Standish was out scouring the countryside. John Alden had built his own house, and often walked through the forest to see Priscilla. One afternoon he sat holding a skein of thread as she wound it. As they sat talking, a messenger burst in with the news that Miles Standish had been killed by a poisoned arrow and his men cut off in ambush.

At last John felt free to make his own declaration. He and Priscilla were married in the village church, before all the congregation. The magistrate had read the service and the elder had finished the blessing when an unexpected guest appeared at the door. It was Miles Standish—recovered from his wound—and he came striding in like a ghost from the grave.

Before everyone, the gruff soldier and the bridegroom made up their differences. Then, tenderly, Standish wished John and Priscilla joy, and merrily the wedding procession set off through the forest to Priscilla's new home.

COUSIN BETTE

Type of work: Novel
Author: Honoré de Balzac (1799-1850)
Type of plot: Social criticism
Time of plot: Early nineteenth century
Locale: Paris, France
First published: 1847-1848

Principal characters:
BARON HULOT
ADELINE, his wife
HORTENSE, their daughter
VICTORIN, their son
LISBETH, Adeline's Cousin Bette
M. CREVEL, Baron Hulot's enemy
CÉLESTINE, Victorin's wife and daughter of M. Crevel
COLONEL HULOT, the baron's older brother
MADAME MARNEFFE, Baron Hulot's mistress
M. MARNEFFE, Madame Marneffe's husband
COUNT STEINBOCK, Hortense's husband
BARON MONTÈS, Mme. Marneffe's lover

Critique:

The plot of this book is involved; many of the incidents seem contrived, like the death of the newly-wed Crevels and the rescue of Baron Hulot from the slums. Yet the forces at work upon the characters give the book a unity. The characters, more than anything else, make the story what it is. Balzac is a master at depicting human nature; he knows what motive force lies behind good and evil actions. Cousin Bette, the author's attempt to present a person consumed by hate, will remain in the reader's mind long after he has forgotten the rest of the book.

The Story:

One day in the summer of 1838, M. Crevel called upon Adeline, the Baroness Hulot, with an offer to make her his mistress, but she refused his offer. M. Crevel swore that he would be revenged upon Baron Hulot, who had stolen his former mistress. Her price had been the baron's fortune. Now he was unable to give his daughter Hortense a satisfactory dowry. Hortense was able to forget her sorrow over her own marriage prospects by teasing Lisbeth, Adeline's cousin, about her lover. Lisbeth—Cousin Bette—was the old maid of the family; her lover was Count Steinbock, a sculptor and a Polish refugee. The attachment was that of mother and son, but Cousin Bette was insanely jealous.

That evening the baron's older brother, Colonel Hulot, and his son and daughter-in-law, Victorin and Célestine, came for dinner. Célestine, the daughter of M. Crevel, did not share her father's dislike of Baron Hulot. After dinner Baron Hulot escorted Cousin Bette home and then went to see his mistress. He found that she had deserted him for a rich duke.

The next morning Baron Hulot laid plans to seduce Madame Marneffe, the wife of a clerk who worked for him. In the meantime, Hortense had managed to speak to Count Steinbock by buying one of his pieces of sculpture. He called shortly afterward. The Hulots felt that the penniless young nobleman might be a good match for Hortense, but the plan was kept secret from Cousin Bette.

Baron Hulot arranged to meet Madame Marneffe in Cousin Bette's rooms. Later he moved the Marneffes into a more lavish establishment in the Rue Varennes, and Cousin Bette went there to live. Through her new friend, Cousin Bette learned of the coming marriage between Hortense and Count Steinbock, for Baron Hulot had no secrets from Madame Marneffe. Cousin Bette had always been treated in the family as the eccentric old maid and the ugly duckling; this stealing of her lover was the final humiliation. She swore vengeance upon the whole Hulot family, and Madame Marneffe agreed to aid her.

As her first step, Cousin Bette introduced M. Crevel to Madame Marneffe. As her second step, she had Count Steinbock imprisoned for debt. Then she told Hortense that he had returned to Poland. When he obtained his release through some friends, the wedding plans went ahead. No one suspected that Cousin Bette had put him in prison. Meanwhile, Baron Hulot managed to raise a dowry for Hortense and planned to keep himself solvent by sending Adeline's uncle to Algiers. There Baron Hulot had arranged to steal money from the government through dealings with the Army commissary; the uncle was to be an innocent dupe.

As soon as Hortense was married, Baron Hulot moved Adeline to a more modest house so that he could spend more money upon Madame Marneffe. She and the baron conducted their affair quietly so as to attract little notice. At the same time she was also intimate with M. Crevel. M. Marneffe gave little trouble to either of these gentlemen as long as they kept him supplied with money and a good position at the war office.

The appearance one evening of Baron Montès, an old lover of Madame Marneffe, worried Baron Hulot and M. Crevel. That same night Madame Marneffe denied Baron Hulot access to her apartment. M. Crevel revealed to Baron Hulot how he also had been the lover of Madame Marneffe. Reconciled, the two old rivals went next day to Madame Marneffe's house. She agreed to consider M. Crevel's offer to marry her after her husband died, but she told Baron Hulot that he need not hope to be her lover again. After the two old men had left, she asked Cousin Bette to try to get Count Steinbock to come to her. She had always wanted to make a conquest of him; his downfall would also be Cousin Bette's revenge upon Hortense.

Count Steinbock was in need of money, and Cousin Bette slyly suggested borrowing from Madame Marneffe. The count went to see her secretly. Madame Marneffe's conquest was complete.

When Madame Marneffe found herself pregnant, she told each lover separately that he was the father. Hortense believed that Count Steinbock was the father and deserted him to return to her mother. Baron Hulot found it necessary to visit Adeline in order to see Hortense and ask her to return to her husband. Hortense refused and made a violent scene. Cousin Bette arrived to take the side of Hortense. She said that she could no longer stay with Madame Marneffe; she would keep house for old Colonel Hulot. It was her plan to marry the old man and gain control of the only money left in the family.

The baron's affairs were growing desperate. Adeline's uncle in Algiers wrote that the plot to steal from the government was discovered; money was needed to stop an investigation. Madame Marneffe was insisting upon money for her child and a better position for her husband. One night M. Marneffe brought the police to the lovers' room and said that he would prosecute unless he were promoted at the war office. Madame Marneffe had led Baron Hulot into a trap; her husband got his appointment.

At last, the Algerian scandal broke and the uncle killed himself. When Colonel Hulot learned of his brother's deed, he was crushed by this blow to the family honor. He paid the necessary money from his own savings and died only a few days later from wounded pride. Cousin Bette had her revenge. Baron Hulot was a ruined man.

In disgrace, he sought shelter with the mistress who had deserted him for the duke. She provided him with some capital and a pretty seamstress to keep him company. He lived in the slums under an assumed name. Through the efforts of Victorin, now a successful lawyer, the family slowly regained its wealth. Meanwhile Madame Marneffe's child was stillborn, and her husband died. Victorin was determined to keep his father-in-law from throwing himself away on the wretched woman. He hired an underworld character to inform Baron Montès that Madame Marneffe was having an affair with Count Steinbock and was to marry M. Crevel. Baron Montès took his revenge upon Madame Marneffe and M. Crevel by infecting them with a fatal tropical disease; they both died soon after their marriage.

Adeline began to do charity work in the slums. On one of her visits she discovered her husband and brought him back to live with his family. Cousin Bette meanwhile had taken to her bed with consumption; she died soon after Baron Hulot's return.

Baron Hulot became the model husband. Then one day his wife hired Agathe, a peasant girl, as a cook. A few evenings later Adeline discovered her husband in the servants' quarters. Three days later Adeline died. Shortly after his wife's funeral Baron Hulot left Paris, and as soon as possible he and Agathe were married. This impropriety caused Victorin to remark that parents can hinder the marriages of their children; but children can do nothing about the actions of their parents in their second childhood.

THE CREAM OF THE JEST

Type of work: Novel
Author: James Branch Cabell (1879-)
Type of plot: Satiric fantasy
Time of plot: Twentieth century
Locale: Virginia
First published: 1917

Principal characters:
Felix Kennaston, an author
Kathleen Kennaston, his wife
Richard Harrowby, his neighbor
Ettarre, a woman in his novel and his dreams

Critique:

The Cream of the Jest is fiction compounded of philosophic speculation, a fragile plot, and much literary allusion, often somewhat obscure. The novel is typical of that period of Cabell's career when his books maintained a skeptical tone and presented over and over again the values of chivalric love. The story represents Cabell's effort to escape the realities of naturalism through the speculations of romanticism.

The Story:

Felix Kennaston told his neighbor, Richard Harrowby, about his dreams. In writing his novels, Kennaston had created a world much different from the ordinary world of the Virginia countryside, and his dreams contained similar elements of the romantic and the marvelous. To Harrowby the whole thing seemed indecent, for Harrowby was a conventional, unimaginative gentleman farmer, who had made his money in soaps and beauty aids.

Kennaston was writing a novel called *The Audit at Storisende,* and in his dreams he identified himself with a character named Horvendile, who was looking for the elusive and highly improbable creature, the ideal woman. In Ettarre, his heroine, Kennaston felt he had found her. Much of his plot centered about a broken round medallion bearing mysterious symbols, a medallion he called the sigil of Scoteia.

One afternoon Kennaston, walking in his garden, stooped to pick up a little piece of shining metal, apparently a broken half of a small disc, and casually dropped it into his pocket. Later, while looking over some books in his library, he thought of the little piece of metal in his pocket. He brought it out and laid it where the light of the lamp fell upon it. At once he seemed to be talking with Ettarre, who explained that he had picked up half the broken sigil of Scoteia and that it had brought him back to her imagined world of romance and dream. As he reached out to touch her, she disappeared, and Kennaston found himself sitting again in his library.

Kennaston's novel was published as *The Men Who Loved Alison,* a title which his publisher assured him would bring better sales. When several readers, shocked by what they called indecency in the novel, wrote indignant letters to the newspapers, the book became a best seller. Mrs. Kennaston, who made it a point never to read her husband's books, enjoyed his success. She treated Kennaston with polite boredom.

Strange things happened to Kennaston. One day at a luncheon a famous man took him aside and asked him whether he bred white pigeons. This question puzzled Kennaston, as did the little mirror the man held in his hand. At another time he saw an ugly old woman who told him that there was no price of admission to her world but that one paid on leaving. Several times he talked to Ettarre in his dreams.

One day Kennaston received an invitation to call on a prelate who had come to Linchfield to attend the bishop's funeral. The prelate praised Kennaston's book. He spoke of pigeons, too, and mentioned how useful he found his little mirror. Kennaston was frankly puzzled. He returned to his dreamland, where, as Horvendile, he experienced almost every passion and emotion known to man. And always, as he reached out to touch Ettarre, the dream would come to an end.

Kennaston read widely in philosophy and the classics, and he began to question the reason for his own existence. He came to the conclusion that the present moment was all that was real—that the past and future had no part in the reality of today. As a man of letters, he became interested in the artistry of creation and decided that God must have been happy

---

over his creation of the character of Christ. Probably because of his interest in God as an artist, Kennaston was confirmed in the country church nearby. This act on his part increased his stature among the people of the neighborhood. They even elected him to the vestry.

One day Kennaston went to the station to meet his wife's train. While he was waiting, a woman with whom he had once been in love came up to him and started to talk. She was about to go back to her home in St. Louis. They recalled the past and, as she left him to get on her train, he had a moment in which he identified her with Ettarre. But his remark to his wife about her was that she was not keeping her good looks as she grew older. What haunted him, however, was that the woman had drawn from her purse a medallion resembling the sigil of Scoteia.

Kennaston—as Horvendile—dreamed of being in many parts of the world in many eras; and one of the mysteries was that he was always a young man of about twenty-five. He was at Queen Elizabeth's court; he was at Whitehall with Cromwell; he was at the French court of Louis Quartorze; he was among the aristocrats about to be beheaded during the French Revolution. And always beside him was Ettarre, whose contact would bring his dreams to an end.

One afternoon he found, quite by accident, the missing piece of the sigil of Scoteia in his wife's bathroom. After securing the other piece, he put them together on his wife's dressing table and began speculating about the relation of his wife to Ettarre. He hoped that her discovery of the entire sigil would express to her what he had never been able to convey. But she paid no attention to it and their life continued its banal rounds. Eleven months later Mrs. Kennaston died in her sleep without ever having discussed the sigil or its significance with her husband. After her death he showed Harrowby the two halves of the sigil, by which he had almost made his dreams come true. Far from being a magic emblem, the pieces proved to be merely the broken top of a cold cream jar. It was the final disillusionment for Kennaston, compelled at last to give up romantic youthful dreaming for the realities of middle age.

CRIME AND PUNISHMENT

Type of work: Novel
Author: Fyodor Mikhailovich Dostoevski (1821-1881)
Type of plot: Psychological realism
Time of plot: Mid-nineteenth century
Locale: Russia
First published: 1866

Principal characters:
RASKOLNIKOV, a Russian student
DOUNIA, his sister
SONIA, a prostitute
PORFIRY, inspector of police
RAZUMIHIN, Raskolnikov's friend

Critique:

The theme of this novel is that man pays by suffering for his crimes against men. Dostoevski's Raskolnikov is a tremendous study of a sensitive intellectual driven by poverty to believe that he was exempt from moral law. Other features of *Crime and Punishment* are the use of psychology in police investigation, the author's sympathy for the downtrodden as expressed in the person of Sonia, a young prostitute, and realistic descriptions of slum life in a large Russian city of the nineteenth century.

The Story:

Rodion Raskolnikov, an impoverished student in St. Petersburg, dreamed of committing the perfect crime. With an ax he murdered an old widowed pawnbroker and her stepsister, and stole some jewelry from their flat.

Back in his room, Raskolnikov received a summons from the police. Weak from hunger and illness, he prepared to make a full confession. But the police had called merely to ask him to pay a debt his landlady had reported to them. When he discovered what they wanted, he collapsed from relief. Upon being revived, he was questioned; his answers provoked suspicion.

Raskolnikov hid the jewelry under a rock in a courtyard. He returned to his room, where he remained for four days in a high fever. When he recovered, he learned that the authorities had visited him while he was delirious and that he had said things during his fever which tended to cast further suspicion on him.

Luzhin, betrothed to Raskolnikov's sister Dounia, came to St. Petersburg from the provinces to prepare for the wedding. Raskolnikov resented Luzhin because he knew his sister was marrying to provide money for her destitute brother. Luzhin visited the convalescent and left in a rage when the young man made no attempt to hide his dislike for him.

A sudden calm came upon the young murderer; he went out and read the accounts of the murders in the papers. While he was reading, a detective joined him. The student, in a high pitch of excitement caused by his crime and by his sickness, talked too much, revealing to the detective that he might well be the murderer. However, no evidence could be found that would throw direct suspicion on him.

Later, witnessing a suicide attempt in the slums of St. Petersburg, Raskolnikov decided to turn himself over to the police; but he was deterred when his friend, an ex-clerk named Marmeladov, was struck by a carriage and killed. Raskolnikov gave the widow a small amount of money he had received from his mother. Later he attended a party given by some of his friends and discovered that they, too, suspected him of complicity in the murder of the two women.

Back in his room, Raskolnikov found his mother and his sister, who were awaiting his return. Unnerved at their appearance and not wanting them to be near him, he placed them in the care of his friend, Razumihin, who, upon meeting Dounia, was immediately attracted to her.

In an interview with Porfiry, the chief of the murder investigation, Raskolnikov was mentally tortured by questions and ironic statements until he was ready to believe that he had been all but apprehended for the double crime. Partly in his own defense, he expounded his theory that any means justified the ends of a man of genius, and that sometimes he believed himself a man of genius.

Raskolnikov proved to his mother and Dounia that Luzhin was a pompous fool, and the angry suitor was dismissed. Razumihin had by that time replaced Luzhin in the girl's affections.

Meanwhile Svidrigailov, who had caused Dounia great suffering while she had been in his employ as a governess, arrived in St. Petersburg. His wife had died and he had followed Dounia, as he explained, to atone for his sins against her by settling upon her a large amount of money.

Razumihin received money from a rich uncle and went into the publishing business with Dounia. They asked Raskolnikov to join them in the venture, but the student, whose mind and heart were full of turmoil, declined; he said goodbye to his friend and to his mother and sister and asked them not to try to see him again.

He went to Sonia, the prostitute daughter of the dead Marmeladov. They read Sonia's Bible together, Raskolnikov deeply impressed by the wretched girl's faith. He felt a great sympathy for Sonia and promised to tell her who had committed the murders of the old pawnbroker and stepsister. Svidrigailov, who rented the room next to Sonia's, overheard the conversation; he anticipated Raskolnikov's disclosure with interest.

Tortured in his own mind, Raskolnikov went to the police station, where Porfiry played another game of cat-and-mouse with him. His conscience and his imagined insecurity had resulted in immense suffering and torment of mind for Raskolnikov.

At a banquet given by Marmeladov's widow for the friends of her late husband, Luzhin accused Sonia of stealing money from his room. He had observed Raskolnikov's interest in Sonia and he wished to hurt the student for having spoken against him to Dounia. The girl was saved by the report of a neighbor who had seen Luzhin slipping money into Sonia's pocket. Later, in Sonia's room, Raskolnikov confessed his crime and admitted that in killing the two women he had actually destroyed himself.

Svidrigailov, having overheard the confession, disclosed his knowledge to Raskolnikov. Believing that Porfiry suspected him of the murder and realizing that Svidrigailov knew the truth, Raskolnikov found life unbearable. Then Porfiry told Raskolnikov outright that he was the murderer, at the same time promising Raskolnikov that a plea of temporary insanity would be placed in his behalf and his sentence would be mitigated if he confessed. Raskolnikov delayed his confession.

Svidrigailov, having informed Dounia of the truth concerning her brother, offered to save the student if Dounia would consent to be his wife. He made this offer to her in his room, which he had locked after tricking her into the meeting. He released her when she attempted unsuccessfully to shoot him with a pistol she had brought with her. Convinced at last that Dounia would have none of him, Svidrigailov gave her a large sum of money and ended his life with a pistol.

Raskolnikov, after being reassured by his mother and his sister of their love for him, and by Sonia of her undying devotion, turned himself over to the police. He was tried and sentenced to serve eight years in Siberia. Dounia and Razumihin, now successful publishers, were married. Sonia followed Raskolnikov to Siberia, where she stayed in a village near the prison camp. In her goodness to Raskolnikov and to the other prisoners, she came to be known as Little Mother Sonia. With her help, Raskolnikov began his regeneration.

THE CRISIS

Type of work: Novel
Author: Winston Churchill (1871-1947)
Type of plot: Historical romance
Time of plot: Civil War period
Locale: Missouri and Virginia
First published: 1901

Principal characters:
STEPHEN BRICE, a young lawyer from Boston
VIRGINIA CARVEL, his sweetheart
CLARENCE COLFAX, Brice's rival for Virginia Carvel
JUDGE WHIPPLE, Brice's employer and friend
COLONEL CARVEL, Virginia's father
ABRAHAM LINCOLN

Critique:

The American-born Winston Churchill had several reasons for choosing St. Louis as the setting for this novel. First, it was his aim to show the remarkable contrasts in the lives of Sherman, Grant, and Lincoln, all of whom came from St. Louis and the neighboring state of Illinois. Secondly, two streams of emigration, from the North and from the South, met at St. Louis, with the result that Northern and Southern culture could be brought into focus and examined in detail. *The Crisis* remains one of the best novels of its type. The author brought in the historical characters, including the almost legendary Lincoln, in a natural way not found in many later efforts.

The Story:

In 1858 Stephen Brice emigrated from Boston to St. Louis with his widowed mother. He went to accept the offer of Judge Whipple, his father's friend, who had promised Stephen an opportunity to enter his law firm. Being a personable young man, Stephen Brice found favor among the people of St. Louis, including Colonel Carvel, and the colonel's daughter, Virginia. Stephen promptly fell in love with Virginia Carvel. He was not encouraged by the girl at first because he was a New Englander.

One day Judge Whipple sent Stephen to Springfield, Illinois, with a message for the man who was running for senator against Stephen A. Douglas. When Stephen Brice finally found his man, Abraham Lincoln, he was in time to hear the famous Freeport debate between Lincoln and Douglas. Lincoln made a deep impression on Stephen, who went back to St. Louis a confirmed Republican, as Judge Whipple had hoped. Feeling that Stephen would some day be a great politician, the judge had sent him to Lincoln to catch some of Lincoln's idealism and practical politics.

Convinced by Lincoln that no country could exist half-slave and half-free, Stephen Brice became active in Missouri politics on behalf of the Republicans; a dangerous course to take in St. Louis because of the many Southerners living in the city. His anti-slavery views soon alienated Stephen from the girl he wanted to marry, who then promised to marry Stephen's rival, her cousin and fellow Southerner, Clarence Colfax.

Lincoln lost the election for the senate, but in doing so won for himself the presidency of the United States in 1860. During both campaigns, Stephen Brice worked for the Republican party. An able orator, he became known as a rising young lawyer of exceptional abilities.

The guns at Fort Sumter reverberated loudly in St. Louis in 1861. The city was divided into two factions, pro-slavery Southerners and anti-slavery Northerners. Friends of long standing no longer spoke to each other and members of the same family found themselves at odds over the question of which side Missouri should favor, the Union or the Confederacy. It was a trying time for Stephen Brice. Because of his widowed mother and his political activities, he was unable to join the army. Judge Whipple convinced him that, for the time being, he could do more for his country as a civilian. It was hard for the young man to believe the judge when all of Stephen's friends and acquaintances were going about the city in uniform.

When war was declared, Missouri had a little campaign of its own, for the state militia under the direction of the governor attempted to seize the state. This action was defeated by the prompt action of Federal forces in capturing the militia training camp without firing a shot. A spectator at that minor engagement, Stephen made the acquaintance of an ex-army officer named Sherman and of another shambling man who claimed he should be given a regiment. The young officers laughed at him; his name was Ulysses S. Grant.

Among those captured when Federal troops overcame the Missouri militia was Clarence Colfax, Stephen's rival. Clarence refused to give his oath and go on parole, and he soon escaped from prison and disappeared into the South. Virginia Carvel thought him more of a hero than ever.

Because communications with the South and the Southwest had been cut by the Union armies, Colonel Carvel went bankrupt. He and his daughter aided Southern sympathizers attempting to join the Confederate Army. At last the colonel himself felt that it was his duty to leave St. Louis and take an active part in the hostilities.

The war continued, putting the lie to those optimists who had prophesied that hostilities would end in a few months. By the time of the battle at Vicksburg, Stephen had become a lieutenant in the Union Army. He distinguished himself in that battle and came once more to the attention of Sherman. When the city fell, Stephen found Clarence Colfax, now a lieutenant-colonel in the Confederate Army. The Southerner had received a severe wound. To save Clarence's life, Stephen arranged for him to be sent to St. Louis on a hospital ship. Stephen knew that he was probably sending his rival back to marry Virginia Carvel. Young Colfax realized what Stephen had done, and told Virginia as much while he was convalescing in St. Louis. The girl vowed that she would never marry a Yankee, even if Colfax were killed.

Judge Whipple had fallen ill, and he was nursed by Virginia and by Stephen's mother. While the judge was sinking fast, Colonel Carvel appeared. At the risk of his life, he had come through the lines in civilian clothes to see his daughter and his old friend. There was a strange meeting at Judge Whipple's deathbed. Clarence Colfax, Colonel Carvel, and Stephen Brice were all there. They all risked their lives, for the Confederates could have been arrested as spies, and Stephen, because he was with them, could have been convicted of treason. That night Virginia realized that she was in love with Stephen.

After the judge's death Stephen returned to the army. Ordered to General Sherman's staff, he accompanied the general on the march through Georgia. At the battle of Bentonville, Stephen again met Clarence Colfax, who had been captured by Union soldiers while in civilian clothes and brought to Sherman's headquarters as a spy. Once again Stephen interceded with Sherman and saved the Southerner's life. Soon afterward Stephen, promoted to the rank of major, was sent by Sherman with some dispatches to General Grant at City Point, in Virginia. Stephen recognized Grant as the man he had seen at the engagement of the militia camp back in St. Louis.

During the conference with the general an officer appeared to summon Stephen to meet another old acquaintance, Abraham Lincoln. The president, like Grant, wished to hear Stephen's first-hand account of the march through Georgia to the sea. When Stephen asked for a pardon for Clarence Colfax, Lincoln said he would consider the matter. Stephen went with Lincoln to Richmond for an inspection of that city after it had fallen to Grant's armies.

Virginia Carvel, not knowing of Stephen's intercession on behalf of Clarence Colfax, traveled to Washington to ask Lincoln for a pardon. She gained an audience with the president, during which she met Stephen once again. Lincoln granted them the pardon, saying that with the war soon to end the time to show clemency had come. He left Virginia and Stephen alone when he hurried to keep another appointment. The young people had realized during their talk with Lincoln that there was much to be forgiven and forgotten by both sides in the struggle which was drawing to a close. The emotion of the moment overcame their reticence at last, and they declared their love for each other. They were married the following day.

After the wedding they went to visit

Virginia's ancestral home in Annapolis. A few days later word came to them that Lincoln had died from an assassin's bullet.

THE CROCK OF GOLD

Type of work: Novel
Author: James Stephens (1882-1950)
Type of plot: Fantasy
Time of plot: Any time
Locale: Irish countryside
First published: 1912

Principal characters:
THE PHILOSOPHER
THE THIN WOMAN, his wife
SEUMAS AND BRIGID, two children
ANGUS OG, an early Irish god
CAITILIN, his mortal wife

Critique:

This tale of adventure and philosophical discussions is a modern classic in its field. Stephens is most successful in his attempt to bring old Irish legends to life in the pages of a delightful book. The philosophic discussions abound with a delightful humor, and the seriousness of some of the observations in no way lessens the magic quality of the story. The tale is a wandering one, containing many elements and telling many stories. All of them are entertaining to read, and most of them are perfect in execution.

The Story:

In the center of a very dark pine wood lived the two old Philosophers and their wives, the Grey Woman of Dun Gortin and the Thin Woman of Inis Magrath. One couple had a little boy named Seumas, the other a little girl named Brigid. Both were born on the same day.

When the children were ten years old, one of the old Philosophers decided that he had now learned all he was capable of learning. This conclusion depressed him so much that he decided to die. It was unfortunate, as he pointed out, that at the time he was in the best of health. However, if the time had come for him to die, then die he must. He took off his shoes and spun around in the center of the room for fifteen minutes until he fell over dead. So grieved was the Grey Woman that she, too, killed herself, but as she was much tougher than her husband she spun for forty-five minutes before she died. The Thin Woman calmly buried the two bodies under the hearthstone.

The people who lived on the edge of the pine wood often came to see the Thin Woman's husband when they needed advice. One day Meehawl MacMurrachu came to the Philosopher to learn who had stolen his wife's scrubbing board. The Philosopher, after much questioning, finally decided that the fairies had taken it. He advised Meehawl to go to a certain spot and steal the Crock of Gold that the Leprecauns of Gort na Gloca Mora had buried there. For years the Leprecauns had been filling their Crock of Gold by clipping the edges of gold coins that they found in men's houses at night. They needed the gold to ransom any of the little people caught by human beings.

Losing their gold to Meehawl made the Leprecauns angry, and they tried to make Meehawl bring it back by giving him and his wife all kinds of aches and pains. Next they came stealthily and lured Brigid and Seumas down into a little house in the roots of a tree, but fear of the Thin Woman was on them and they set the children free. Then they sent the Great God Pan, the god of the beast which is in every man, to lure away Caitilin, Meehawl's daughter, with the music of his pipes.

When Meehawl came with his tale of sorrow, the Philosopher sent Brigid and Seumas to tell Pan to let the girl go. But Pan refused to answer their questions. When they told the Philosopher, he became so angry that he ordered his wife to bake him some cakes to eat on the way, and he started off by himself to visit Pan. But none of the Philosopher's arguments could persuade Pan to free Caitilin, and the Philosopher went off to get the help of Angus Og of the old gods.

Angus Og himself went to see Pan and the girl in their cave and forced the girl to choose between them. Caitilin, who had learned the true meaning of hunger and pain with Pan, did not know how to choose. Angus Og explained to her that he was Divine Inspiration, and that if she would come and live with him and be his wife, he would show her peace and happiness. By several signs he proved that he was the favorite of the gods of the earth and had more power than Pan. Caitilin sensed that true happiness, which she had never known, would be found with Angus Og, and that only hunger could be found with Pan. So she chose to leave Pan and go with Angus Og. Thus she was saved from the beast in man.

The Philosopher, on his way back home, delivered several messages from the god. One message he gave to a young boy, a promise from Angus Og that in time the old gods would return, and that before they did the boy would write a beautiful poem in their praise. Cheered by the news that the gods would soon come back, the Philosopher finally arrived home, where he greeted his wife with such affection that she decided always to be kind to him and never again to say a cross word.

Unknown to them, the Leprecauns had informed the police in the village that there were two bodies buried under the hearthstone in the Philosopher's house. One day the police broke into the house, found the bodies, and accused the Philosopher of murder. Meanwhile Brigid and Seumas were playing in the woods, and quite by chance they happened to dig a hole and find the Crock of Gold where Meehawl had buried it. They gave it back to the Leprecauns, but the return of the gold was not enough to set matters right. The police kept the Philosopher in jail. Then the Thin Woman baked some cakes and set out to find Angus Og, dragging the children behind her and saying the worst curses there were against the police. The first gods she met were the Three Absolutes, the Most Beautiful Man, the Strongest Man, and the Ugliest Man. By her wisdom the Thin Woman was able to answer their questions and save herself and the children from their frightful powers. When they had passed these gods, they found the house of Angus Og. He was waiting for someone to come and ask him to aid the Philosopher, for it is impossible for the gods to help anyone unasked.

Calling all the old gods together, Angus Og and his wife led a great dance across the fields, and then they went down into the town with all the gods following. In the town their merry laughter brought happiness to all who saw them except the most evil of men. The charges against the Philosopher were forgotten and he was free to go back to his house in the pine woods and dispense wisdom once more. Then the gods returned singing to their own country to await the birth of Caitilin's and Angus Og's child and the day when the old Irish gods could again leave their hidden caves and hollows and rule over the land with laughter and song.

CROME YELLOW

Type of work: Novel
Author: Aldous Huxley (1894-)
Type of plot: Social satire
Time of plot: 1920's
Locale: England
First published: 1922

Principal characters:
HENRY WIMBUSH, owner of Crome
ANNE WIMBUSH, his niece
DENIS STONE, a young poet
MR. SCROGAN, a man of reason
GOMBAULD, an artist
MARY BRACEGIRDLE, a victim of repressions
JENNY MULLION, a keen-eyed observer

Critique:

Aldous Huxley has written an amusing satire on the ill-fated love affair of a sensitive young poet. Using the plot as an excuse for bringing together all sorts of interesting and unusual facts and stories, he holds the reader's interest by an almost continual shift of emphasis. We learn of each of the guests at the house party, their faults, interests, and virtues. As in all of Huxley's novels, there is much philosophical discussion. No particular ideas are set forth as correct, but a precise picture of the early twenties as Huxley saw them is presented to the reader with wit and dexterity.

The Story:

Denis Stone, a shy young poet, went to a house party at Crome, the country home of Henry Wimbush and his wife. He went because he was in love with Wimbush's niece, Anne. Anne looked down on Denis because he was four years younger than she, and treated him with scorn when he attempted to speak of love.

Mr. Wimbush was interested in little except Crome and the histories of the people who had lived in the old house. Mrs. Wimbush was a woman with red hair, probably false, and an interest in astrology, especially since she had recently won a bet on a horse with her star-given information. Other guests at the party included Gombauld, an artist who had been invited to paint Anne's picture; the diabolically reasonable Mr. Scrogan; deaf Jenny Mullion; and Mary Bracegirdle, who was worried about her Freudian dreams. Denis and Anne quarreled, this time over their philosophies of life. Denis tried to carry all the cares of the world on his back, but Anne thought that things should be taken for granted as they came. The quarrel cost Denis his first opportunity to tell Anne that he loved her.

Mary Bracegirdle discussed with Anne her dreams and repressions. Having decided to secure either Gombauld or Denis for a husband, she chose the wrong times to talk with both men. Gombauld was busy painting when Mary came up to him. Denis was smarting with jealousy over the time Anne and Gombauld spent together.

Ivor Lombard arrived for the party. Ivor, a painter of ghosts and spirits, turned his attentions toward repressed Mary, and secretly visited her one night in the tower. He went away without seeing her again.

From time to time Mr. Wimbush called the party together while he read stories of the early history of Crome. These stories were from a history at which Mr. Wimbush had worked for thirty years. Denis often wondered if he would ever get a chance to tell Anne that he loved her. Walking in the garden after a talk with Mr. Scrogan, whose cold-blooded ideas about a rationalized world annoyed him, he found a red notebook in which Jenny had been writing for the past week. In it he found a collection of sharply satirical cartoons of all the people at the house party. Jenny had drawn him in seven attitudes which showed up his absurd jealousy, incompetence, and shyness. The cartoons deeply wounded his vanity and shattered his conception of himself.

He was further discouraged by the fact that there was nothing for him to do at a charity fair held in the park outside Crome a few days later. Mr. Scrogan made a terrifying and successful fortune-teller; Jenny played the drums; Mr. Wimbush ran the various races; and Denis was left to walk aimlessly through the fair as an official with nothing to do. Gombauld made sketches of the people in the crowd, and Anne stayed by his side.

The night after the fair Denis overheard part of a conversation between Gombauld and Anne. Without knowing that Anne had repulsed Gombauld, for she had made up her mind to accept Denis if he ever got around to asking her, Denis spent hours of torture thinking of the uselessness of his life. At last he decided to commit suicide by jumping from the tower. There he found Mary grieving because she had received only a brisk postcard from Ivor. She convinced Denis that both their lives were ruined, and advised him to flee from Anne. Convinced, Denis arranged a fake telegram calling him back to London on urgent business. When it arrived, Denis realized with dismay that Anne was miserable to see him go. The telegram was the one decisive action of his life. Ironically, it separated him from Anne.

THE CRUISE OF THE CACHALOT

Type of work: Pseudo-factual account
Author: Frank T. Bullen (1857-1915)
Type of plot: Adventure romance
Time of plot: Late nineteenth century
Locale: At sea
First published: 1898

Principal characters:
FRANK T. BULLEN, the narrator
MR. JONES, fourth mate
ABNER CUSHING, a sailor
MR. COUNT, first mate
CAPTAIN SLOCUM, of the *Cachalot*

Critique:

The Cruise of the Cachalot was for some years a favorite with boys, because of its dramatic picture of life aboard an American whaler during the last century. There is no plot and almost no character analysis; indeed the author made no pretense at writing a literary work. The chief value of the book lies in its full descriptions of whale hunting. As natural history the book must seem inexact to a modern reader; and the author's unquestioning acquiescence in the many needless hardships of the common sailor is indicative of an uncritical approach.

The Story:

By a strange combination of circumstances, Frank Bullen found himself in

New Bedford, Massachusetts, looking for a ship. He was only eighteen at the time, but already he had spent six years at sea.

He was strolling down a street in New Bedford, intent on a possible berth aboard any ship, for his pockets were empty, when he was hailed by a scraggy Yankee with the inevitable tobacco juice dribbling down his whiskers. Asked if he wanted to ship out, he accepted eagerly without knowing the type of craft or any of the conditions of employment. He accompanied the sharp-featured Yankee to a small, dirty hall where he joined a group of men all bound for the same ship. When he saw the motley crowd of greenhorns, he felt doubts about joining the ship, but there was little chance to back out. After hastily signing the ship's articles, he went with his mates to the docks.

All of the crew were carefully kept together until they were safe in the small boat. On the trip out into the harbor Bullen saw with many misgivings the *Cachalot,* which would be his home for three years. He deeply regretted signing on, for the *Cachalot* was a whaler and whalers were notoriously the worst ships afloat. The *Cachalot* did not compare favorably with the trim English whalers with which he was more familiar. She was small, a three hundred and fifty tonner, dirty and unpainted, and quite dumpy-looking because she had no raised bow or poop.

Once on board, Bullen's worst fears were realized. The officers were hard and mean; they carried lashes with them and a clumsy or slow sailor often felt the sting of a lash on his back. The men needed a great deal of discipline, however, to do a halfway decent job. Of the twelve white crew members, Bullen was the only one who had been to sea before. The hands were beaten and cursed, and they were not even allowed to rest while they were seasick.

Along with the white greenhorns, there were a score of Portuguese, all experienced whaling men. There were also four mates and Captain Slocum. The captain was a hard driver and a foul talker. The first mate, Mr. Count, was an older man, the only decent officer aboard. The fourth mate, Mr. Jones, was a giant Negro.

Because of his past experience, Bullen escaped most of the abuse meted out to his fellows. After the ship had been scrubbed and polished, and the men had been licked into shape, he became almost fond of the ship. That feeling was heightened when he learned the *Cachalot* was, in spite of her lines, seaworthy.

The ship was heading toward the Azores, to the delight of the Portuguese. At last the first whale was sighted. Bullen was put into the boat of the first mate and told to mind the sail. The boat came up almost on top of the whale before Louis, the harpooner, threw his great hook. When the whale sounded, the hands paid out over two hundred fathoms of line. Then the whale began to rush away at full speed, towing the boat in his wake. When he slowed down, the boat was brought close enough for the harpooner to use his lance. After a final flurry, the whale died and was towed alongside.

After some months at sea, Bullen had an unpleasant picture of ship's discipline. Abner Cushing, a Yankee sailor, tried to make some beer in the forecastle. Needing some potatoes for his brew, he stole a few from the officers' galley. One of the Portuguese reported the theft to the captain and, as punishment, Abner was strung up by the thumbs and lashed vigorously by one of the harpooners until he fainted. When his punishment was over, he was not allowed to go below, but was forced to turn to immediately.

The cruise was an ill-fated one for Abner. He was in a small boat when a whale unexpectedly turned and bore down on the frail craft. The line was hurriedly pulled in. Then the whale sounded, and as the line was paid out Abner's neck caught in a loop. The weight of the descending whale severed his head neatly.

Mr. Jones, after the *Cachalot* had been at sea over a year, became greatly depressed. He recalled a fortune-teller's prediction that he would die in a fight with a white man and finally decided that Captain Slocum was destined to cause his death. Deranged, he went on the bridge, wrapped his huge arms around the captain, and jumped with him into the sea. When Mr. Count assumed command, he promoted Bullen to Mr. Jones' vacant post.

Once Bullen nearly met his end when a harpooned cachalot suddenly turned sidewise and with his mighty tail smashed a boat to bits. His foot tangled in the wreckage, Bullen went under. When he came up, nearly exhausted, he caught blindly at a rope and hauled himself along until he came to the inert whale. He clambered aboard and clung to the harpoon in the side of the dead whale. But the whale suddenly came to life. When the other boats came alongside after the whale had finally died, Bullen had a dislocated thigh and severe rope burns on each arm.

At last, after three years, the *Cachalot's* barrels were full, and the ship headed home around Cape Horn. In good time the lookout sighted Cape Navesink. With every flag flying, she came into New Bedford. The cruise of the *Cachalot* was ended.

CUPID AND PSYCHE

Type of work: Classical myth
Source: Folk tradition
Type of plot: Allegory of love
Time of plot: The Golden Age
Locale: Ancient Greece
First transcribed: Unknown

Principal characters:
Psyche, daughter of a Greek king
Cupid, the god of love
Venus, the goddess of beauty

Critique:

Cupid and Psyche is the simple but moving story of the union of a mortal, Psyche, and the god Cupid. In this ancient mythological tale a beautiful maiden achieved immortality because her love and faith triumphed over mistrust.

The Story:

Psyche, daughter of a Greek king, was as beautiful as Venus and sought after by many princes. Her father, seeking to know what fate the gods might have in store for her, sent some of his men to Apollo's oracle to learn the answer.

To the king's horror, the oracle replied that Psyche was to become the mate of a hideous monster, and the king was ordered to leave his daughter to her fate upon a mountaintop, to prevent the destruction of his people. Psyche was led, clad in bridal dress, to a rocky summit and left there alone. The weary girl soon fell into a swoon.

Venus, jealous of Psyche's beauty, called her son Cupid and ordered him to use his arrows to turn Psyche's heart toward a creature so hideous that mortals would be filled with loathing at the sight of Psyche's mate. But when Cupid saw his victim asleep he fell in love with her and decided that she should be his forever. While Psyche slept, Zephyrus came at Cupid's bidding and carried her to the valley in which Love's house stood. There she awoke in a grove of trees in which stood a magnificent golden palace. She entered the building and wandered through the sumptuously furnished rooms.

At noon Psyche found a table lavishly

spread. A voice invited her to eat, assured her that the house was hers, and told her that the being who was to be her lover would come that night.

As she lay in bed that night a voice close beside her told her not to be afraid. The voice spoke so tenderly that the girl welcomed her unseen suitor and held out her arms to him. When Psyche awoke the next morning, her lover had gone, but he had left behind a gold ring and had placed a circlet on her head.

For a time Psyche lived happily in the golden palace, visited each night by the lover whose face she had not seen. But at last she became homesick for her two sisters and her father. One night she asked her lover to permit her sisters to visit her the next day. He gave his consent, but he warned that she was not to tell them about him.

Zephyrus carried the sisters to the valley. Overjoyed to see them, Psyche showed them the beauties of the palace and loaded them with gifts. Jealous of her good fortune, they tried to make her suspicious of her unseen lover. They suggested that her lover was a serpent who changed into the form of a youth at night, a monster who would at last devour her. To save herself, they advised her to hide a lamp and a knife by her bed so that she might see him and slay him as he slept.

Psyche did as they had suggested. That night, as her love lay asleep, she lit the lamp and brought it close so that she might look at him. When she saw the handsome young man by her side, she was powerless to use her knife. As she turned, sobbing, to extinguish the flame, a drop of burning oil fell on Cupid's shoulder. Awaking with a cry, he looked at her reproachfully. With the warning that love cannot live with suspicion, he left the palace. Psyche tried to follow, but fell in a swoon at the threshold.

When she awoke, the palace had vanished. Determined to seek her lover, she wandered alone across the countryside and through cities hunting the god. Meanwhile Cupid took his vengeance on her sisters. To each he sent a dream that she would become his bride if she were to throw herself from the mountaintop. Both sisters, obeying the summons, found only the arms of Death to welcome them.

No god would give the wandering Psyche shelter or comfort, or protect her from the wrath of Venus. At the temples of Ceres and Juno she was turned away. At last she came to the court of Venus herself. Warned by her heart to flee, she was nevertheless drawn before the throne of the goddess. Venus decided that Psyche should be kept as a slave. She was to be given a new task to do each day and was to live until she once more began to hope.

Psyche's first task was to sort a huge pile of mixed seeds and grain into separate heaps, with the warning that if there were so much as one seed in the wrong pile she would be punished. But by dusk she had separated only small heaps of grain. Cupid so pitied her that he commanded myriads of ants to complete the task for her.

Next day Psyche was ordered to gather the golden fleece of Venus' sheep. Obeying the advice of a reed at the edge of the river, she waited until the animals had lain down to sleep and then collected the wool which had been left clinging to the bushes.

Psyche's third task was to fill a jug with the black water which flowed down a steep mountain into the rivers Styx and Cocytus. This task she was able to complete with the aid of a bird who carried the jug to the stream, collected the water, and brought it back to her.

On the fourth day Psyche was given her most difficult task; she was to go to the land of the dead and there collect some of the beauty of the goddess Proserpine in a golden box. If she succeeded, Venus promised, she would treat Psyche kindly thereafter. But to visit Proserpine and to return was an almost impossible achievement. In despair, Psyche determined to cast herself from a tower, but as she was about to kill herself a voice called to her and told her how she might fulfill her mission.

Following instructions, Psyche traveled to Proserpine's realm. There she might have stayed on forever if she had not thought suddenly of her love. On her way back, she had almost reached the daylight when envy seized her. She opened the box, thinking she would have whatevei it contained for herself, but no sooner had she lifted the lid than she fell into a deep sleep filled with nightmares.

She might have lain that way forever if Cupid, going in search of her, had not found her. He awoke her with one of his arrows and sent her on to his mother with the box. Then he flew off and presented himself before Jove with his petition that Psyche be made immortal. Jove, after hearing his pleas, sent Mercury to conduct Psyche into the presence of the gods. There she drank from the golden cup of ambrosia Jove handed her and became immortal. So she and Cupid were at last united for all time.

DAISY MILLER

Type of work: Novelette
Author: Henry James (1843-1916)
Type of plot: Psychological realism
Time of plot: Mid-nineteenth century
Locale: Vevey, Switzerland, and Rome
First published: 1878

Principal characters:
Daisy Miller, an American tourist
Winterbourne, an American expatriate
Giovanelli, Daisy's Italian suitor

Critique:

As in most of James' work, there is practically no plot in *Daisy Miller*. Rather, James is interested in a conflict between European and American customs and ideals. The crudities and touching innocence of Daisy Miller are revealed against a background of European manners and morals, and both are shown from the point of view of an expatriate American who has lived abroad too long. The special point of view makes *Daisy Miller* an ironic study of contrasts.

The Story:

Winterbourne was a young American who had lived in Europe for quite a while. He spent a great deal of time at Vevey, which was a favorite spot of his aunt, Mrs. Costello. One day, while he was loitering outside the hotel, he was attracted by a young woman who appeared to be related to Randolph Miller, a young American boy with whom he had been talking. After a while the young woman exchanged a few words with him. Her name was Daisy Miller. The boy was her brother, and they were in Vevey with their mother. They came from Schenectady, Winterbourne learned, and they intended to go next to Italy. Randolph insisted that he wanted to go back home. Winterbourne learned that Daisy hoped to visit the Castle of Chillon. He promised to take her there, for he was quite familiar with the old castle.

Winterbourne asked his aunt, Mrs. Costello, to meet Daisy. Mrs. Costello, however, would not agree because she thought the Millers were common. That evening Daisy and Winterbourne planned to go out on the lake, much to the horror of Eugenio, the Millers' traveling companion, who was more like a member of the family than a courier. At the last moment Daisy changed her mind about the night excursion. A few days later Winterbourne and Daisy visited the Castle of Chillon. The outing confirmed Mrs. Costello's opinion that Daisy was uncultured and unsophisticated.

Winterbourne made plans to go to Italy. When he arrived, he went directly to the home of Mrs. Walker, an American whom he had met in Geneva. There he met Daisy and Randolph. Daisy reproved him for not having called to see her. Winterbourne replied that she was unkind, as he had just arrived on the train. Daisy asked Mrs. Walker's permission to bring an Italian friend, Mr. Giovanelli, to a party Mrs. Walker was about to give. Mrs. Walker agreed. Then Daisy said that she and the Italian were going for a walk. Mrs. Walker was shocked, as young unmarried women did not walk the streets of Rome with Italians. Daisy suggested that there would be no objection if Winterbourne would go with her to the spot where she was to meet the Italian and then walk with them.

Winterbourne and Daisy set out and eventually found Giovanelli. They walked together for a while. Then Mrs. Walker's carriage drew alongside the strollers. She beckoned to Winterbourne and implored him to persuade Daisy to enter her carriage. She told him that Daisy had been ruining her reputation by such behavior; she had become familiar with Italians and was quite heedless of the scandal she was causing. Mrs. Walker said she would never speak to Winterbourne again if he did not ask Daisy to get into the carriage at once. But Daisy, refusing the requests of Mrs. Walker and Winterbourne, continued her walk with the Italian.

Mrs. Walker determined to snub Daisy at the party. When Winterbourne arrived, Daisy had not made her appearance. Mrs. Miller arrived more than an hour before Daisy appeared with Giovanelli. Mrs. Walker had a moment of weakness and greeted them politely. But as Daisy came to say goodnight, Mrs. Walker turned her back upon her. From that time on Daisy and Giovanelli found all doors shut to them. Winterbourne saw her occasionally, but she was always with the Italian. Everyone thought they were carrying on an intrigue. When Winterbourne asked her if she were engaged, Daisy said that she was not.

One night, despite the danger from malarial fever, Giovanelli took Daisy to the Colosseum. Winterbourne, encountering them in the ancient arena, reproached the Italian for his thoughtlessness. Giovanelli said that Daisy had insisted upon viewing the ruins by moonlight. Within a few days Daisy was dangerously ill. During her illness she sent word to Winterbourne that she had never been engaged to Giovanelli. A week later she was dead.

As they stood beside Daisy's grave in the Protestant cemetery in Rome, Giovanelli told Winterbourne that Daisy would never have married her Italian suitor, even if she had lived. Then Winterbourne realized that he himself had loved Daisy without knowing his own feelings, that he could have married her had he acted differently. He reasoned, too late, that he had lived in Europe too long, that he had forgotten the freedom of American manners and the complexity of the American character.

DAPHNIS AND CHLOË

Type of work: Tale
Author: Attributed to Longus (third century)
Type of plot: Pastoral romance

Time of plot: Indefinite
Locale: Island of Lesbos
First transcribed: Third century manuscript

Principal characters:
DAPHNIS, a young shepherd
CHLOË, a shepherdess

Critique:

A product of decadent Greek literature, *Daphnis and Chloë* is one of the most popular of the early predecessors of the modern novel. Highly romantic in both characterization and incident, it centers about the innocent though passionate love of two children of nature amid idyllic scenes of natural beauty. We forgive the many extravagant improbabilities of the story because of the charming portrayal of the refreshing, often amusing, naïveté of two children unspoiled by contact with city manners.

The Story:

On the Greek island of Lesbos a goatherd named Lamo one day found a richly dressed infant boy being suckled by one of his goats. Lamo and his wife, Myrtale, hid the purple cloak and ivory dagger the boy had worn and pretended he was their own son. They named him Daphnis. Two years later a shepherd named Dryas discovered in a cave of the Nymphs an infant girl being nursed by one of his sheep. This child also was richly dressed. Dryas and his wife Nape kept the girl as their own, giving her the name Chloë.

When the two children were fifteen and thirteen respectively, they were given flocks to tend. Daphnis and Chloë played happily together, amusing themselves in many ways. One day, while chasing a goat, Daphnis fell into a wolf-pit, from which he was rescued unharmed by Chloë and a herdsman she had summoned to help her. Daphnis began to experience delightful but disturbing feelings about Chloë. Dorco, a herdsman, asked permission to marry Chloë but was refused by Dryas. Disguising himself in a wolfskin, Dorco shortly afterward attempted to seize Chloë. Attacked by the flock dogs, he was rescued by Daphnis and Chloë, who innocently thought he had merely been playing a prank. Love, little understood by either, grew between Daphnis and Chloë.

In the autumn some Tyrian pirates wounded Dorco, stole some of his oxen and cows, and took Daphnis away with them. Chloë, who heard Daphnis calling to her from the pirate ship, ran to aid the mortally wounded Dorco. Dorco gave her his herdsman's pipe, telling her to blow upon it. When she blew, the cattle jumped into the sea and overturned the ship. The pirates drowned, but Daphnis, catching on to the horns of two swimming cows, came safely to shore.

After the celebration of the autumn vintage Daphnis and Chloë returned to their flocks. They attempted in their innocence to practice the art of love, but they were not successful. Some young men of Methymne came to the fields of Mitylene to hunt. When a goat gnawed in two a withe used as a cable to hold their small ship, the Methymneans blamed Daphnis and set upon him. In a trial over the affair Daphnis was judged innocent. The angry Methymneans later carried away Chloë. The god Pan warned the Methymnean captain in a dream that he should bring back Chloë, and she was returned. Daphnis and Chloë joyfully celebrated holidays in honor of Pan.

The two lovers were sad at being parted by winter weather, which kept the flocks in their folds. In the spring the lovers happily drove their flocks again to the fields. When a woman named Lycaenium became enamored of the boy, Daphnis finally learned how to ease the pains he had felt for Chloë; but Lycaenium warned him that Chloë would be hurt the first time she experienced the ecstasy of love. Through fear of doing physical harm to his sweetheart the tender Daphnis would not deflower his Chloë. Meanwhile many suitors, Lampis among them, asked for the hand of Chloë, and Dryas came near consenting. Daphnis bewailed his inability to compete successfully with the suitors because of his poverty. Then with the aid of the Nymphs he found a purse of silver, which he gave Dryas in order to become contracted to Chloë. In return Dryas asked Lamo to consent to the marriage of his son, but Lamo answered that first he must consult his master, Dionysophanes.

Lamo, Daphnis, and Chloë prepared to entertain Dionysophanes; but Lampis ravaged the garden they had prepared because he had been denied Chloë's hand. Fearing the wrath of his master, Lamo lamented his ill fortune. Eudromus, a page, helped to explain the trouble to Lamo's young master Astylus, who promised to intercede with his father and blame the wanton destruction on some horses in the neighborhood. Astylus' parasite, Gnatho, fell in love with Daphnis but was repulsed. Finally the depraved Gnatho received Astylus' permission to take Daphnis with him to the city. Just in time Lamo revealed the story of the finding of Daphnis, who was discovered to be Dionysophanes' son. Meanwhile Lampis stole Chloë, who was later rescued by Gnatho. After Dryas told how Chloë had been found as a child, it was learned that she was the daughter of Megacles of Mitylene. Thus the supposed son and daughter of Lamo and Dryas were revealed as the children of wealthy parents who were happy to consent to their marriage. The wedding was celebrated amid the rural scenes dear to both bride and groom. Daphnis became Philopoemen and Chloë was named Agéle. On her wedding night Chloë at last learned from Daphnis how might be obtained the delights of love.

DARK LAUGHTER

Type of work: Novel
Author: Sherwood Anderson (1876-1941)
Type of plot: Psychological realism
Time of plot: 1920's
Locale: Old Harbor, Indiana
First published: 1925

Principal characters:

BRUCE DUDLEY, formerly John Stockton, a Chicago reporter
SPONGE MARTIN, a workman close to the grass roots
FRED GREY, owner of an automobile wheel factory
ALINE, his wife

Critique:

Dark Laughter, Sherwood Anderson's most popular novel, is a book of moods rather than of plot. Its simple story is that of two individuals in revolt against the restrictions of modern life and seeking happiness together. Anderson seems to say that Bruce Dudley and Aline Grey were unhappy because they were repressed; they gave themselves over to the secret desires within them and therefore they became happy. One may question whether Bruce and Aline were not merely restless and somewhat adolescent emotionally, rather than strong and brave in their attempt to live by amoral standards.

The Story:

Bruce Dudley's name was not Bruce Dudley at all. It was John Stockton. But he had grown tired of being John Stockton, reporter on a Chicago paper, married to Bernice who worked on the same paper and who wrote magazine stories on the side. She thought him flighty and he admitted it. He wanted adventure. He wanted to go down the Mississippi as Huckleberry Finn had done. He wanted to go back to Old Harbor, the river town in Indiana where he had spent his childhood. And so, with less than three hundred dollars, he left Chicago, Bernice, and his job on the paper. He picked up the name Bruce Dudley from two store signs in an Illinois town. After his trip to New Orleans he went to Old Harbor and got a job varnishing automobile wheels in the Grey Wheel Company.

Sponge Martin worked in the same room with Bruce. Sponge, a wiry old fellow with a black mustache, lived a simple, elemental life. That was the reason, perhaps, why Bruce liked him so much. Sometimes when the nights were fair and the fish were biting, Sponge and his wife took sandwiches and some moonshine whiskey and went down to the river. They fished for a while and got drunk, and then Sponge's wife made him feel like a young man again. Bruce wished he could be as happy and carefree as Sponge.

When Bruce was making his way down the Mississippi and when he stayed for five months in an old house in New Orleans—that was before he came to Old Harbor—he watched the Negroes and listened to their songs and laughter. It seemed to him that they lived as simply as children and were happy, laughing their dark laughter.

Aline, the wife of Fred Grey, who owned the Grey Wheel Company, saw Bruce Dudley walking out the factory door one evening as she sat in her car waiting for Fred. Who he was she did not know, but she remembered another man to whom she had felt attracted in the same way. It happened in Paris after the war. She had seen the man at Rose Frank's apartment and she had wanted him. Then she had married Fred, who was recovering from the shock of the war. He was not what she wished for, but, somehow, she had married him.

One evening Bruce Dudley passed by the Grey home as Aline stood in the yard. He stopped and looked first at the house and then at Aline. Neither spoke but something passed between them. They had found each other.

Aline, who had advertised for a gardener, hired Bruce after turning down several applicants. Bruce had quit his job at the factory shortly before he saw her advertisement. When Bruce began to work for her, the two maintained some reserve, but each was determined to have the other. Bruce and Aline carried on many imaginary conversations. Fred apparently resented Bruce's presence about the grounds, but he said nothing to the man. When he questioned his wife, he learned that she knew nothing of Bruce except that he was a good worker.

As Aline watched her husband leave for the factory each morning she wondered how much he knew. She thought a great deal about her own life and about life in general. Her husband was no lover. Few women nowadays had true lovers. Modern civilization told one what he could not have. One belittled what he could not possess. Because one did not have love, one made fun of it, was skeptical of it, and besmirched it. The little play of the two men and the woman went on silently. Two Negro women who worked in Aline's house watched the proceedings. From time to time they laughed, and their dark laughter seemed mocking. White folks were queer. They made life so involved. Negroes took what they wanted—simply, openly, happily.

One day in June, after Fred had gone

to march in a veterans' parade and the Negro servants had gone to watch the parade, Aline and Bruce were left alone. She sat and watched him working in the garden. Finally he looked at her, and he followed her into the house through a door she purposely left open. Before Fred returned, Bruce had left the house. He disappeared from Old Harbor. Two months later Aline told Fred she was going to have a child.

As Fred came home one evening in the early fall, he saw his wife and Bruce together in the garden. Aline calmly called to him and announced that the child she was expecting was not his. She and Bruce had waited, she went on, so that she might let him know they were leaving. Fred pleaded with her to stay, knowing she was hurting herself, but they walked away, Bruce carrying two heavy bags.

Fred told himself, as he stood with his revolver in his hand a few minutes later, that he could not dispassionately let another man walk away with his wife. His mind was filled with confused anger. For a moment he thought of killing himself. Then he followed the pair along the river road. He was determined to kill Bruce. But he lost them in the darkness. In a blind fury he shot at the river. On the way back to his house he stopped to sit on a log. The revolver fell to the ground and he sat crying like a child for a long time.

After Fred had returned to his home and gone to bed, he tried to laugh at what had happened. He could not. But outside in the road he heard a sudden burst of laughter. It was the younger of the two Negresses who worked in the Grey home. She cried out loudly that she had known it all the time, and again there came a burst of laughter—dark laughter.

DARKNESS AT NOON

Type of work: Novel
Author: Arthur Koestler (1905-   )
Type of plot: Social criticism
Time of plot: 1930's
Locale: Russia
First published: 1941

Principal characters:
NICHOLAS RUBASHOV, a political prisoner
IVANOV, a prison official
GLETKIN, another official
MICHAEL BOGRAV, another prisoner
KIEFFER (HARE-LIP), an informer

Critique:

This remarkable modern novel by Arthur Koestler is a highly analytical piece of writing which transports the reader into a Russian prison and into the very consciousness of a political prisoner, accused of crimes he never committed. *Darkness at Noon* represents an ironic and scathing criticism of the Moscow trials. At the same time, it presents a careful analysis of the Soviet principles. Reference to Russia is made only in the foreword, however, and the party leader is known only as No. 1 in this powerful but highly restrained social document.

The Story:

Nicholas Rubashov, ex-Commissar of the People and once a power in the party, was in prison. Arrested at his lodgings in the middle of the night, he had been taken secretly to cell 404, which bore his name on a card just above the spy-hole. He knew that he was located in an isolation cell for condemned political suspects.

At seven o'clock in the morning Rubashov was awakened by a bugle, but he did not get up. Soon he heard sounds in the corridor. He imagined that someone was to be tortured, and he dreaded hearing the first screams of pain from the victim. When the footsteps reached his own section, he saw through the judas-eye that guards were serving breakfast. Rubashov did not receive any breakfast because he had reported himself ill. He began to pace up and down the cell, six and a half steps to the window, six and a half steps back.

Soon he heard a quiet knocking from the wall of adjoining cell 402. In communicating with each other prisoners used the "quadratic alphabet," a square of twenty-five letters, five horizontal rows of five letters each. The first series of taps represented the number of the row; the second series the number of the letter in the row. From the tappings Rubashov pictured his neighbor as a military man, one not in sympathy with the methods of the great leader or with the views of Rubashov himself. From his window he saw prisoners walking in the courtyard for exercise. One of these, a man with a hare-lip, looked repeatedly up at Rubashov's window. From his neighbor in cell 402, Rubashov learned that Hare-lip was a political prisoner who had been tortured by a steam bath the day before. A little later Hare-lip, in cell 400, sent Rubashov his greetings, through the inmate of 402, but he would not give his name.

Three days later Rubashov was brought up for his first examination. The examiner was Ivanov, Rubashov's old college friend and former battalion commander. During the interview the prisoner learned that he was accused of belonging to the opposition to the party and that he was suspected of an attempt on the party leader's life. Ivanov promised a twenty-year prison term instead of the death penalty if Rubashov confessed. The prisoner was given a fortnight to arrive at a decision.

After the hearing Rubashov was allowed to have paper, pencil, soap, towels, and tobacco. He started writing in his journal and recasting his ideas about the party and the movement. He recalled a young man named Richard arrested in Germany while Rubashov was at the head of the party Intelligence and Control Department. He could not forget an incident which had happened in Belgium two years later. There Rubashov had been tortured and beaten. In Belgium he expelled from the party a hunchbacked, eager worker who later hanged himself in his room. Rubashov also thought constantly of Arlova who had been his mistress and who had met her death because of him.

The night before the time set by Ivanov had expired, Rubashov felt a tenseness in the atmosphere. His friend in 402 communicated to him that one of the prisoners was to be shot. This prisoner was Michael Bograv, who had always been Rubashov's close friend. As the condemned man was brought through the corridors, the prisoners tapped his progress from one cell to another and drummed on the doors of their cells as he passed. The beaten, whimpering figure of Bograv came by Rubashov's cell. Rubashov believed that his friend shouted to him as he was dragged down the stairs.

Rubashov's second hearing took place late at night. Ivanov came to Rubashov's cell with a bottle of brandy and convinced him that to keep faith with the living was better than betrayal of the dead. Accordingly, Rubashov wrote a letter to the Public Prosecutor renouncing his own oppositional attitude and acknowledging his errors. The third night after delivering the letter to the warder, Rubashov was awakened and taken to the office of Gletkin, another official of the prison. Under blinding lights in Gletkin's office, he was questioned day and night for an interminable period of time. Ivanov, he learned, had been liquidated for conducting Rubashov's case negligently. Gletkin called in Hare-lip as a witness against Rubashov. It was only with great difficulty that Rubashov recognized in that broken, cringing man the son of his former friend and associate, Keiffer. The bright spotlight, the lack of sleep, the constant questionings—these factors combined to make Rubashov sign a trumped-up charge that he had plotted to take the life of the party leader.

Rubashov had committed none of these crimes. He was merely the victim of a change in party policy. One night he heard the sound of drumming along the corridor. The guards were taking Hare-lip to be executed. When the drumming started again, Rubashov knew that his time had come. He was led into the cellar. An officer struck him twice on the head with a revolver. Another party incident was closed.

DAVID COPPERFIELD

Type of work: Novel
Author: Charles Dickens (1812-1870)
Type of plot: Sentimental romance
Time of plot: Early nineteenth century
Locale: England
First published: 1849-1850

Principal characters:

DAVID COPPERFIELD, the narrator
CLARA COPPERFIELD, his mother
MISS BETSY TROTWOOD, David's great-aunt
PEGGOTTY, a nurse
MR. PEGGOTTY, her brother
LITTLE EM'LY, his orphan niece
HAM, his orphan nephew
MR. MURDSTONE, David's stepfather
MISS JANE MURDSTONE, his sister
MR. CREAKLE, master of Salem House
JAMES STEERFORTH, David's schoolmate
TOMMY TRADDLES, a student at Salem House
MR. WILKINS MICAWBER, a man of pecuniary difficulties
MR. WICKFIELD, Miss Trotwood's solicitor
AGNES WICKFIELD, his daughter
URIAH HEEP, a clerk
MR. SPENLOW, under whom David studied law
DORA SPENLOW, his daughter, later David's wife
MR. DICK, Miss Betsy's protégé

Critique:

One of the many qualities that distinguish *David Copperfield* from more modern and more sophisticated novels is its eternal freshness. It is, in short, a work of art which can be read and re-read, chiefly for the gallery of characters Dickens has immortalized. The novel has its flaws. These faults seem insignificant, however, when the virtues of the novel as a whole are considered. The first-person point of view adds much to realistic effects and sympathetic treatment of character and helps to explain, in part, why *David Copperfield* is the most loved piece of fiction in the English language.

The Story:

David Copperfield was born at Blunderstone, in Suffolk, six months after his father's death. Miss Betsy Trotwood, an eccentric great-aunt was present on the night of his birth, but she left the house abruptly and indignantly when she learned that the child was a boy who could never bear her name. David spent his early years with his pretty young mother, Clara Copperfield, and a devoted servant named Peggotty. Peggotty was plain and plump; when she bustled about the house her buttons popped off her dress.

The youthful widow was soon courted by Mr. Murdstone, who proved, after marriage, to be stingy and cruel. When his mother married a second time, David was packed off with Peggotty to visit her relatives at Yarmouth. There her brother had converted an old boat into a seaside cottage, where he lived with his niece, Little Em'ly, and his sturdy young nephew, Ham. Little Em'ly and Ham were David's first real playmates, and his visit to Yarmouth remained a happy memory of his lonely and unhappy childhood. After Miss Jane Murdstone arrived to take charge of her brother's household, David and his mother were never to feel free again from the dark atmosphere of suspicion and gloom the Murdstones brought with them.

One day in a fit of childish terror David bit his stepfather on the hand. He was immediately sent off to Salem House, a wretched school near London. There his life was more miserable than ever under a brutal headmaster named Creakle. But in spite of the harsh system of the school and the bullyings of Mr. Creakle, his life was endurable because of his friendship with two boys whom he was to meet again under much different circumstances in later life—lovable Tommy Traddles and handsome, lordly James Steerforth.

His school days ended suddenly with the death of his mother and her infant child. When he returned home, he discovered that Mr. Murdstone had dismissed Peggotty. Barkis, the stage driver, whose courtship had been meager but earnest, had taken Peggotty away to become Mrs. Barkis and David was left friendless in the home of his cruel stepfather.

David was put to work in an export warehouse in which Murdstone had an interest. As a ten-year-old worker in the dilapidated establishment of Murdstone and Grinby, wine merchants, David was overworked and half-starved. He loathed his job and associates such as young Mick Walker and Mealy Potatoes. The youngster, however, met still another person with whom he was to associate in later life. That was Wilkins Micawber, a pompous ne'er-do-well in whose house David lodged. The impecunious Mr. Micawber found himself in debtor's prison shortly afterward. On his release he decided to move with his brood to Plymouth. Having lost these good friends, David decided to run away from the environment he detested.

When David decided to leave Murdstone and Grinby, he knew he could not return to his stepfather. The only other relative he could think of was his father's aunt, Miss Betsy Trotwood, who had flounced indignantly out of the house on the night of David's birth. Hopefully he set out for Dover, where Miss Betsy lived, but not before he had been robbed of all his possessions. Consequently, he arrived at Miss Betsy's home physically and mentally wretched.

David's reception was at first not cordial. Miss Betsy had never forgotten the injustice done her when David was born instead of a girl. However, upon the advice of Mr. Dick, a feeble-minded distant kinsman who was staying with her, she decided to take David in, at least until he had been washed thoroughly. While she was deliberating further about what to do with her bedraggled nephew, she wrote to Mr. Murdstone, who came with his sister to Dover to claim his stepson. Miss Betsy decided she disliked both Murdstones intensely. Mr. Dick solved her problem by suggesting that she keep David.

Much to David's joy and satisfaction, Miss Betsy planned to let the boy continue his education, and almost immediately sent him to a school in Canterbury, run by a Mr. Strong, a headmaster quite different from Mr. Creakle. During his stay at school David lodged with Miss Betsy's lawyer, Mr. Wickfield, who had a daughter, Agnes. David became very fond of her. At Wickfield's he also met Uriah Heep, Mr. Wickfield's cringing clerk, whose hypocritical humility and clammy handclasp filled David with disgust.

David finished school when he was seventeen. Miss Betsy suggested he travel for a time before deciding on a profession. On his way to visit his old nurse, Peggotty, David met James Steerforth and went home with his former schoolmate. There he met Steerforth's mother and Rosa Dartle, a girl passionately in love with Steerforth. Years before, the quick-tempered Steerforth had struck Rosa, who carried a scar as a reminder of Steerforth's brutality.

After a brief visit, David persuaded Steerforth to go with him to see Peggotty and her family. At Yarmouth, Steerforth met Little Em'ly. In spite of the fact that she was engaged to Ham, she and Steerforth were immediately attracted to each other.

At length David told his aunt he wished to study law. Accordingly, he was articled to the law firm of Spenlow and Jorkins. At this time David saw Agnes Wickfield, who told him she feared Steerforth and asked David to stay away from him. Agnes also expressed a fear of Uriah Heep, who was on the point of entering into partnership with her senile father. Shortly after these revelations by Agnes, David encountered Uriah himself, who confessed he wanted to marry Agnes. David was properly disgusted.

On a visit to the Spenlow home, David met Dora Spenlow, his employer's pretty but childish daughter, with whom he fell instantly in love. Soon they became secretly engaged. Before this happy event, however, David heard some startling news—Steerforth had run away with Little Em'ly.

Nor was this elopement the only blow to David's happiness. Shortly after his engagement to Dora, David learned from his aunt that she had lost all her money, and from Agnes that Uriah Heep had become Mr. Wickfield's partner. David tried unsuccessfully to be released from his contract with Spenlow and Jorkins. Determined to show his aunt he could repay her, even in a small way, for her past sacrifices, he took a part-time job as secretary to Mr. Strong, his former headmaster.

But the job with Mr. Strong paid very little; therefore David undertook to study for a position as a reporter of parliamentary debates. Even poor simple Mr. Dick came to Miss Betsy's rescue, for Traddles, now a lawyer, gave him a job as a clerk.

The sudden death of Mr. Spenlow dissolved the partnership of Spenlow and Jorkins, and David learned to his dismay that his former employer had died almost penniless. With much study on his part, David became a reporter. At twenty-one he married Dora, who, however, never seemed capable of growing up. During these events, David had kept in touch with Mr. Micawber, now Uriah Heep's confidential secretary. Though something had finally turned up for Mr. Micawber, his relations with David, and even with his own family, were mysteriously strange, as though he were hiding something.

David soon learned what the trouble was, for Mr. Micawber's conscience got the better of him. At a meeting arranged by him at Mr. Wickfield's, he revealed in Uriah's presence and to an assembled company, including Agnes, Miss Betsy, David, and Traddles, the criminal perfidy of Uriah Heep, who for years had robbed and cheated Mr. Wickfield. Miss Betsy discovered that Uriah was also responsible for her own financial losses. With the exposure of the villainous Uriah, partial restitution both for her and for Mr. Wickfield was not long in coming.

His conscience cleared by his exposure of Uriah Heep's villainy, Mr. Micawber proposed to take his family to Australia. There, he was sure something would again turn up. To Australia, too, went Mr. Peggotty and Little Em'ly; she had turned to her uncle in sorrow and shame after Steerforth had deserted her. David watched as their ship put out to sea. It seemed to him the sunset was a bright promise for them as they sailed away to a new life in the new land. The darkness fell about him as he watched.

The great cloud now in David's life was his wife's delicate health. Day after day she failed, and in spite of his tenderest care he was forced to see her grow more feeble and wan. Agnes Wickfield, like the true friend she had always been, was with him on the night of Dora's death. As in his earlier troubles, he turned to Agnes in the days that followed and found comfort in her sympathy and understanding.

Upon her advice he decided to go abroad for a while. But first he went to Yarmouth to put into Ham's hands a last letter from Little Em'ly. There he witnessed the final act of her betrayal. During a storm the heavy seas battered a ship in distress off the coast. Ham went to his death in a stout-hearted attempt to rescue a survivor clinging to a broken mast. The bodies washed ashore by the rolling waves were those of loyal Ham and the false Steerforth.

David lived in Europe for three years. On his return he discovered again his need for Agnes Wickfield's quiet friendship. One day Miss Betsy Trotwood slyly suggested that Agnes might soon be married. Heavy in heart, David went off to offer her his good wishes. When she burst into tears, he realized that what he had hoped was true—her heart was already his. They were married, to matchmaking Miss Betsy's great delight, and David settled down to begin his career as a successful novelist.

DAVID HARUM

Type of work: Novel
Author: Edward Noyes Westcott (1846-1898)
Type of plot: Regional romance
Time of plot: Late nineteenth century
Locale: Upstate New York
First published: 1898

Principal characters:
DAVID HARUM, a banker and horse trader
JOHN LENOX, Harum's assistant
MARY BLAKE, John's sweetheart
POLLY BIXBEE, Harum's widowed sister

Critique:

Westcott, who himself had been a banker in upper New York State, wrote *David Harum* to give the country at large a picture of his region and its people. The greatness of the book lies in the characterization of David Harum, that original and delightfully humorous horse trader who has fascinated two generations of readers. Harum was a dry, quaint, semi-literate countryman with a shrewd knowledge of human nature. Unfortunately, the horse-trading banker does not dominate the story completely. The novel is threaded together by a love story involving Harum's banking assistant and a young heiress. The best chapters, by far, are those in which David Harum tells stories in dialect, swaps horses, or indulges in reminiscences of other days.

The Story:

John Lenox was the son of a well-to-do businessman in New York. After college he lived for several years in Europe at his father's expense. He was twenty-six years old when he returned to America, without having done anything which fitted him to earn a living.

John returned to find that his father's business was failing rapidly and that he would soon have to make a living for himself. His father found a place for him with a New York law firm, but reading law proved uncongenial. When his father died, John left the firm. Then, through an old friend of his father's, John became assistant to the owner of a small bank in Homeville, New York.

David Harum, the owner of the bank, was a crusty old man who enjoyed his reputation as a skinflint. What most of the townspeople did not know was that he was quite a philanthropist in his own way, but preferred to cover up his charity and good deeds with gruff words. Harum's one vice was horse trading. His sister, who kept house for him, firmly believed that he would rather trade horses than eat or sleep. Moreover, he usually came out ahead in any swapping deal.

David Harum was well pleased with the appearance of his new assistant, John Lenox. And when John took hold of his duties better than any other clerk in the bank had ever done, David Harum began to think seriously of looking after the young man's future. Harum felt that John should have an opportunity to better himself, but he wanted first to be certain that he was not mistaken in judging the young man's character. He set out to discover what he wanted to know in a peculiar way. He let John live uncomfortably in a broken-down hotel for several months to ascertain his fortitude. He also gave John several chances to be dishonest by practices which a sharp trader like Harum might be expected to approve. John's straightforward dealings won Harum's respect and approval. He casually gave John five ten-dollar gold pieces and asked him to move into a room in Harum's own large house with him and his sister, Polly.

John had begun to discover that Harum was not the selfish and crusty old man he appeared. He knew that Harum had called in a widow whose mortgage was overdue and had torn up the paper because the woman's husband had at one time taken Harum to the circus when the banker was a little boy without a cent to his name. Even Harum's horse trading was different when one came to know him. As John Lenox discovered, Harum only let people cheat themselves. If someone professed to know all about horses, Harum used the trade to teach him a lesson, but if a tyro professed his ignorance of the animals Harum was sure to give him a fair exchange. He was a living example of the proverb which propounds shrewdly that it is impossible to cheat an honest man, and the corollary, that it is almost impossible not to cheat a dishonest one.

John Lenox's life in Homeville was restricted, and he was thrown much on his own resources. He secured a piano for himself and played in the evenings or read from a small collection of books which he had saved from his father's library. His only real friends were David Harum and Harum's sister, Polly, both old enough to be John's parents. He spent many pleasant hours in Harum's company. They would often take Harum's horses out for a drive, during which the loquacious banker would regale the young man with stories of horse trading, of the foibles of the people in the community, or of Harum's early life when he had run away from home to work along the Erie Canal. On one of these rides Harum learned that John was in love with an heiress he had met in Europe. John felt that he could not ask her to marry him until he had proved himself a success.

Soon afterward Harum gave John an opportunity to make a large amount of money. Harum had a tip on a corner in pork on the Chicago market. Harum and John bought several thousand barrels of pork and sold them at a considerable profit. This deal was the first step Harum took to make John financially independent.

John's second year in Homeville was more eventful. By that time he had been accepted as a member of the community and had made friends both in the town and among the wealthy people who came to Homeville during the summer months. Meanwhile Harum revealed to his sister his plan to retire from active work in the bank and to make John his partner. He also revealed to her that John had a tract of land in Pennsylvania which everyone had considered worthless, but which was likely to produce oil. Harum, in his younger days, had spent some time in the Pennsylvania oil fields, and like most small-town bankers of the time, he knew something about a great many financial activities. What he did not reveal to his sister was that he also planned to leave his estate to John, for, excepting Polly, he had no relatives.

By the end of his third year in Harum's bank, John had made enough money through market operations to make himself independent, and he could have left the bank and the town for New York City if he had cared to do so. When the banker broached the subject to him, John admitted that two years before the prospect of returning to the city would have been welcome. Now he had come to like Homeville and had no desire to leave the home of David Harum and his sister. That was exactly what Harum wanted to hear. He told John that he was to become a partner in the bank. Harum also told him that a company wanted to lease his Pennsylvania land for the purpose of drilling for oil.

Then John fell ill, and his doctor sent him on a Mediterranean cruise. While aboard ship, John met Mary Blake, the young heiress with whom he had fallen in love several years before. At first John thought, because of an error in the ship's passenger list, that Mary Blake was already married. One moonlight night, on a mountain overlooking the bay at Naples, Mary informed John of his mistake and promised to marry him, and a few days later Harum was overjoyed to receive a cable announcing John's marriage. Harum wired back the good news that drilling had begun on the property in Pennsylvania.

When John and Mary Lenox returned to the United States several months later, they settled in Homeville and John took over the bank. Then David Harum was free to spend the rest of his days driving about the countryside and swapping horses.

DEAD SOULS

Type of work: Novel
Author: Nikolai V. Gogol (1809-1852)
Type of plot: Social satire
Time of plot: Early nineteenth century
Locale: Russia
First published: 1842

Principal characters:
Pavel Ivanovitch Tchitchikoff, an adventurer
Maniloff, from whom he bought souls
Tentetnikoff, whom he tried to marry off
Platon Platonoff, with whom he later traveled
Klobueff, whose estate he bought
Kostanzhoglo, who lent him money
Alexei Ivanovitch Lyenitzen, who threw him into jail

Critique:

This novel is written in high good humor. Its portraits of various Russian types—peasant, landholder, prince—are delightful. The plot itself is not complex. The length of the novel is accounted for by the author's numerous digressions, which add up to a rich picture of provincial Russian life in the early nineteenth century. The satire ranks with the best the world has produced.

The Story:

Pavel Ivanovitch Tchitchikoff had arrived in the town accompanied by his coachman, Selifan, and his valet, Petrushka. He had been entertained gloriously and had met many interesting people, who insisted on his visiting them in their own homes. Nothing could have suited Tchitchikoff better. After several days of celebration in the town, he took his coachman and began a round of visits to the various estates in the surrounding country.

His first host was Maniloff, a genial man who wined him and dined him in a manner fit for a prince. When the time was ripe, Tchitchikoff began to question his host about his estate and learned, to his satisfaction, that many of Maniloff's souls, as the serfs were called, had died since the last census and that Maniloff was still paying taxes on them and would continue to do so until the next census. Tchitchikoff offered to buy these dead souls from Maniloff and so relieve him of his extra tax burden. The contract signed, Tchitchikoff set out for the next estate.

Selifan got lost and in the middle of the night drew up to a house which belonged to Madame Korobotchkina, from whom Tchitchikoff also bought dead souls. When he left his hostess, he found his way to an inn in the neighborhood. There he met Nozdreff, a notorious gambler and liar. Nozdreff had recently lost a great deal of money at gambling, and Tchitchikoff thought he would be a likely seller of dead souls. But when he broached the subject, Nozdreff asked him the reason for his interest in dead souls. For every reason Tchitchikoff gave, Nozdreff called him a liar. Then Nozdreff wanted to play at cards for the souls, but Tchitchikoff refused. They were arguing when a police captain came in and arrested Nozdreff for assault on a man while drunk. Tchitchikoff thought himself well rid of the annoying Nozdreff.

His next host was Sobakevitch, who at first demanded the unreasonable sum of one hundred roubles for each name of a dead soul. Tchitchikoff finally argued him into accepting two and a half roubles apiece, a higher price than he had planned to pay.

Pliushkin, with whom he negotiated next, was a miser. He bought one hundred and twenty dead souls and seventy-eight fugitives after considerable haggling. Pliushkin gave him a letter to Ivan Grigorievitch, the town president.

Back in town, Tchitchikoff persuaded the town president to make his recent purchases legal. Since the law required that souls when purchased be transferred to another estate, Tchitchikoff told the officials that he had land in the Kherson province. He had no trouble in making himself sound plausible. Some bribes to minor officials helped.

Tchitchikoff proved to be such a delightful guest that the people of the town insisted that he stay on and on. He was the center of attraction at many social functions, including a ball at which he was especially interested in the governor's daughter. Soon, however, rumors spread that Tchitchikoff was using the dead souls as a screen, that he was really planning to elope with the governor's daughter. The men, in consultation at the police master's house, speculated variously. Some said he was a forger; others thought he might be an officer in the governor-general's office; one man put forth the fantastic suggestion that he was really the legendary Captain

Kopeykin in disguise. They questioned Nozdreff, who had been the first to report the story of the purchase of dead souls. At their interrogation Nozdreff confirmed their opinions that Tchitchikoff was a spy and a forger who was trying to elope with the governor's daughter.

Meanwhile Tchitchikoff had caught a cold and was confined to his bed. When at last he had recovered sufficiently to go out, he found himself no longer welcome at the houses of his former friends. He was, in fact, turned away by servants at the door. Tchitchikoff realized it would be best for him to leave town.

The truth of the matter was that Tchitchikoff had begun his career as a humble clerk. His father had died leaving no legacy for his son, who served in various capacities, passing from customs officer to smuggler to pauper to legal agent. When he learned that the Trustee Committee would mortgage souls, he hit upon the scheme of acquiring funds by mortgaging dead souls that were still on the census lists. It was this purpose which had sent him on his current tour.

He turned up next on the estate of Andrei Ivanovitch Tentetnikoff, a thirty-three-year-old bachelor who had retired from public life to vegetate in the country. Learning that Tentetnikoff was in love with the daughter of his neighbor, General Betrishtcheff, Tchitchikoff went to see the general and won his consent to Tentetnikoff's suit. He brought the conversation around to a point where he could offer to buy dead souls from the general. He gave as his reason the story that his old uncle would not leave him an estate unless he himself already owned some property. The scheme so delighted the general that he gladly made the transaction.

Tchitchikoff's next stop was with Pyetukh, a generous glutton whose table Tchitchikoff enjoyed. There he met a young man named Platonoff, whom Tchitchikoff persuaded to travel with him and see Russia. The two stopped to see Platonoff's sister and brother-in-law, Konstantin Kostanzhoglo, a prosperous landholder. Tchitchikoff so impressed his host that Kostanzhoglo agreed to lend him ten thousand roubles to buy the estate of a neighboring spendthrift named Klobueff. Klobueff said he had a rich old aunt who would give great gifts to churches and monasteries but would not help her destitute relatives. Tchitchikoff proceeded to the town where the old woman resided and forged a will to his own advantage. But he forgot to insert a clause canceling all previous wills. On her death he went to interview His Excellency, Alexei Ivanovitch Lyenitzen, who told him that two wills had been discovered, each contradicting the other. Tchitchikoff was accused of forging the second will and was thrown into prison. In the interpretation of this mix-up, Tchitchikoff learned a valuable lesson in deception from the crafty lawyer he consulted. The lawyer managed to confuse the affair with every public and private scandal in the province, so that the officials were soon willing to drop the whole matter if Tchitchikoff would leave town immediately. The ruined adventurer was only too glad to comply.

DEAR BRUTUS

Type of work: Drama
Author: James M. Barrie (1860-1937)
Type of plot: Romantic fantasy
Time of plot: Midsummer Eve
Locale: England
First presented: 1917

Principal characters:
LOB, the ancient Puck
MATEY, his butler
GUESTS AT LOB'S HOUSE PARTY

Critique:

Barrie's thesis—that the exigencies of human life are the fault of the individual, not of so-called Fate—is fancifully developed in *Dear Brutus* by means of a folk superstition concerning Midsummer Eve. The play is fantastic and realistic at the same time, fantastic in that its characters are transported into the realm of the unreal, realistic in the perfectly candid way in which the various relationships among the characters are set forth.

The Story:

Dinner was over, and the ladies of Lob's house party returned to the drawing-room after leaving the gentlemen to their cigars and wine. Matey, the butler, had stolen jewelry from one of the guests. The women called him in to tell him they knew he was the thief. When Matey returned the jewelry, the women stated that they would not report him if he told them why they were guests at the house. Matey either could not or would not give them a direct answer. In the course of the conversation it was learned that their host was mysteriously ageless and that Lob was another name for the legendary Puck. Matey admitted that Lob always asked a different party of guests to his house for Midsummer Week. He warned the women not to venture outside the garden on this Midsummer Eve. When he left them with the warning not to go into the wood, the women were puzzled because there was no wood within miles of the house.

Host Lob entered thoughtfully. He was followed by old Mr. Coade, who was collecting notes for a projected work on the Feudal System, and Mr. Purdie, an intellectual young barrister. Coade and Purdie suggested that the group take a walk to discover a mysterious wood. Lob said slyly that the villagers believed that a wood appeared in a different part of the neighborhood each Midsummer Eve. He pretended skepticism to sharpen the curiosity of his guests, who went to prepare for the adventure.

Among Lob's guests was Lady Caroline Laney, unmarried and of disdainful poise, and Joanna Trout, single and in love with love. Joanna and Mr. Purdie were caught kissing in the living room by Mabel Purdie, who saw them from the garden. She came in. Joanna, surprised, asked Mabel what she was doing in the garden. Mabel answered that she was looking for her lost love. Her calm candor caught Jack Purdie and Joanna completely off guard. Jack admitted his love for Joanna. Mabel left the lovers grieving that fate had not brought them together earlier. Alice Dearth entered. Cattishly, Joanna revealed that Mrs. Dearth had at one time been an artist's model. Dearth, an artist now broken by drink, entered. Alice Dearth had grown to despise him for his sottishness. Dearth regretted not having a child; Alice Dearth regretted not having married a former suitor.

When the party reassembled, Lob revealed that to go into the forest gave one another chance, something nearly everyone in the group was seeking. Dearth drew aside the curtain to reveal a forest in the place of the garden. He entered the wood and disappeared. Mabel Purdie followed him. Next went Jack Purdie and Joanna, followed by Alice Dearth, Lady Caroline, and old Mr. Coade. Lob enticed Matey to the edge of the wood and pushed him into it.

In the moonlight of Midsummer Eve, in the fanciful realm of the second chance, Matey and Lady Caroline discovered that they were vulgar husband and wife. Joanna was in search of her husband. When Mr. Coade, now a woodlander, appeared dancing and blowing a whistle, Joanna said that she was Mrs. Purdie; she suspected her husband of being in the forest with another woman. They saw Purdie in the company of Mabel, whom he chased among the trees. In the forest, Mabel and Joanna had changed places. Purdie and Mabel mourned that they had met too late.

In another part of the forest, Will Dearth and his young daughter Margaret raced to the spot where the artist's easel was set up, for Dearth was painting a moonlit landscape. Margaret was worried over her excess of happiness; she expressed her fear that her father would be taken from her. The pair agreed that artists, especially, needed daughters and that fame was not everything.

Alice, a vagrant searching for scraps to eat, passed the happy pair. She told them that she was the Honorable Mrs. Finch-Fallowe, the wife of the suitor that she had recalled in Lob's house, and that she had seen good times. Dearth approached a nearby house to get food for the vagrant woman. Margaret, somehow afraid, tried to restrain him.

Back in the house, Lob was waiting for the return of his guests. There was a tapping on the window and Jack Purdie and Mabel, still charmed, entered. They noticed but did not recognize the sleeping Lob. Still under the influence of Midsummer magic, Purdie spoke words of love to Mabel. He was interrupted by the entrance of Joanna, his Midsummer Eve wife. Lob seemed to leer in his sleep. Suddenly the enchantment disappeared; the trio recognized the room and Lob. After the complete return to reality, Purdie realized that fate was not to blame for human destiny. Ashamed but honest, he admitted that he was a philanderer and asked Mabel to forgive him.

Matey returned, still the vulgarian in speech and dress. He stated, to the surprise of those present, that his wife was with him and he introduced Lady Caroline Matey. The charm was broken, to the horror of the fastidious Caroline Laney and to the embarrassment of Matey.

Still piping on his whistle, Mr. Coade returned. Although he did not recognize Mrs. Coade, he expressed his admiration for her lovable face. The old man returned to reality after making his wife proud that he had chosen her again in the world of the second chance.

Alice Dearth, hungry, entered and looked ravenously at the refreshments. Between mouthfuls of cake she bragged of her former affluence as Mrs. Finch-Fallowe; she mystified the other guests with talk of a painter and his daughter in the forest. Dearth, the happy painter of the forest, came in. In their disenchantment, Alice knew that she would have been unhappy with the former suitor, and that Will Dearth would have been happier without her. Dearth was momentarily crushed by the loss of Margaret, but he recovered to thank Lob for providing that night's experience.

Lob, who had been curled up in a chair in a trance-like sleep during the adventures, and who had leered and smiled in his sleep as his guests came back to the actual world, returned to the care of his beloved flowers. Midsummer Eve was past; the world of might-have-been had ended.

DEATH COMES FOR THE ARCHBISHOP

Type of work: Novel
Author: Willa Cather (1876-1947)
Type of plot: Historical chronicle
Time of plot: Last half of the nineteenth century
Locale: New Mexico and Arizona
First published: 1927

Principal characters:
FATHER JEAN MARIE LATOUR, Vicar Apostalic of New Mexico
FATHER JOSEPH VAILLANT, his friend, a missionary priest
KIT CARSON, frontier scout
JACINTO, an Indian guide

Critique:

Death Comes for the Archbishop is a novel reaffirming the greatness of the American past. This chronicle of the Catholic Southwest is a story, beautifully told, which re-creates in the lives of Bishop Latour and Father Vaillant, his vicar, the historical careers of Bishop Lamy and Father Macheboeuf, two devout and noble missionary priests in the Vicarate of New Mexico during the second half of the nineteenth century. Bishop Latour is scholarly and urbane; Father Vaillant, energetic and passionately the man of feeling. A novel of these dedicated lives, the book presents also a picture of a region and a culture. There are many strands of interest here —the bleak desert country of sand and gaunt red mountains, colorful adobe towns and Mexican customs, conflicts with a stubborn and sometimes corrupt native clergy, missionary journeys in all weathers, the rituals and legends of the Indian pueblos, frontier heroes like Kit Carson and desperadoes like Buck Scales, relics of the conquistadores who brought the sword and the Cross into the New World. The novel lives in its bright glimpses of the past, stories that cut backward into time so that the action is not always upon the same level. Tales and legends that go beyond the period of American occupation into three centuries of Spanish colonial history and back to the primitive tribal life of the Hopi, the Navajo, and the vanished cliff-dwellers break this chronicle at many points and give the effect of density and variety to a work which recaptures so completely the spirit and movement of the pioneer West.

The Story:

In 1851 Father Jean Marie Latour reached Santa Fé, where he was to become Vicar Apostolic of New Mexico. His journey from the shores of Lake Ontario had been long and arduous. He had lost his belongings in a shipwreck at Galveston and had suffered painful injury in a wagon accident at San Antonio.

Upon Father Latour's arrival, in company with his good friend, Father Joseph Vaillant, the Mexican priests refused to recognize his authority. He had no choice but to ride three thousand miles into Mexico to secure the necessary papers from the Bishop of Durango.

On the road he lost his way in an arid landscape of red hills and gaunt junipers. His thirst became a vertigo of mind and senses, and he could blot out his own agony only by repeating the cry of the Saviour on the Cross. As he was about to give up all hope, he saw a tree growing in the shape of a cross. A short time later he arrived in the Mexican settlement called *Agua Secreta,* Hidden Water. Stopping at the home of Benito, Bishop Latour first performed the marriage ceremonies and then baptized all the children.

At Durango he received the necessary documents and started the long trip back to Santa Fé. Meanwhile Father Vaillant had won over the inhabitants from enmity to amity and had set up the Episcopal residence in an old adobe house. On the first morning after his return to Santa Fé the bishop heard the unexpected sound of a bell ringing the Angelus. Father Vaillant told him that he had found the bell, bearing the date 1356, in the basement of old San Miguel Church.

On a missionary journey to Albuquerque in March, Father Vaillant acquired as a gift a handsome cream-colored mule and another just like it for his bishop. These mules, Contento and Angelica, served the men in good stead for many years.

On another such trip the two priests were riding together on their mules. Caught in a sleet storm, they stopped at the rude shack of an American, Buck Scales. His Mexican wife warned the travelers by gestures that their lives were in danger, and they rode on to Mora without spending the night. The next morning the Mexican woman appeared in town. She told them that her husband had already murdered and robbed four travelers, and that he had killed her four babies. The result was that Scales was brought to justice, and his wife, Magdalena, was sent to the home of Kit Carson, the famous frontier scout. From that time on Kit Carson was a valuable friend of the bishop and his vicar. Magdalena later became the housekeeper and manager for the kitchens of the Sisters of Loretto.

During his first year at Santa Fé, the bishop was called to a meeting of the Plenary Council at Baltimore. On the return journey he brought back with him five nuns sent to establish the school of Our Lady of Light. Next, Bishop Latour, attended by the Indian Jacinto as his guide, spent some time visiting his own vicarate. Padre Gallegos, whom he visited at Albuquerque, acted more like a professional gambler than a priest, but because he was very popular with the natives Bishop Latour did not remove him at that time. At last he arrived at his destination, the top of the mesa at Ácoma, the end of his long journey. On that trip he heard the legend of Fray Baltazar, killed during an uprising of the Ácoma Indians.

A month after the bishop's visit, he suspended Padre Gallegos and put Father Vaillant in charge of the parish at Albuquerque. On a trip to the Pecos Mountains the vicar fell ill with an attack of the black measles. The bishop, hearing of his illness, set out to nurse his friend. Jacinto again served as guide on the cold, snowy trip. When Bishop Latour reached his friend's bedside, he found that Kit Carson had arrived before him. As soon as the sick man could sit in the saddle, Carson and the bishop took him back to Santa Fé.

Bishop Latour decided to investigate the parish of Taos, where the powerful old priest, Antonio José Martinez, was the ruler of both spiritual and temporal matters. The following year the bishop was called to Rome. When he returned, he brought with him four young priests from the Seminary of Montferrand and a Spanish priest to replace Padre Martinez at Taos.

Bishop Latour had one great ambition; he wanted to build a cathedral in Santa Fé. In that project he was assisted by the rich Mexican *rancheros,* but to the greatest extent by his good friend, Don Antonio Olivares. When Don Antonio died, his will stated that his estate was left to his wife and daughter during their lives, and after their decease to the Church. Don Antonio's brothers contested the will on the grounds that the daughter, Señorita Inez, was too old to be Doña Isabella's daughter, and the bishop and his vicar had to persuade the vain, coquettish widow to swear to her true age of fifty-three, rather than the forty-two years she claimed. Thus the money was saved for Don Antonio's family and, eventually, the Church.

Father Vaillant was sent to Tucson, but after several years Bishop Latour decided to recall him to Santa Fé. When he arrived, the bishop showed him the stone for building the cathedral. About that time Bishop Latour received a letter from the Bishop of Leavenworth. Because of the discovery of gold near Pike's Peak, he asked to have a priest sent there from Father Latour's diocese. Father Vaillant was the obvious choice.

Father Vaillant spent the rest of his life doing good works in Colorado, though he did return to Santa Fé with the Papal Emissary when Bishop Latour was made an archbishop. Father Vaillant became the first Bishop of Colorado. He died there after years of service, and Archbishop Latour attended his impressive funeral services.

After the death of his friend, Father Latour retired to a modest country estate near Santa Fé. He had dreamed during all his missionary years of the time when he could retire to his own fertile green Auvergne in France, but in the end he decided that he could not leave the land of his labors for his faith. Memories of the journeys he and Father Vaillant had made over thousands of miles of desert country became the meaning of his later years. Bernard Ducrot, a young Seminarian from France, became like a son to him.

When Father Latour knew that his time had come to die, he asked to be taken into town to spend his last days near the cathedral. On the last day of his life the church was filled with people who came to pray for him, as word that he was dying spread through the town. He died in the still twilight, and the cathedral bell, tolling in the early darkness, carried to the waiting countryside the news that at last death had come for Father Latour.

THE DEATH OF THE GODS

Type of work: Novel
Author: Dmitri Merejkowski (1865-1941)
Type of plot: Historical romance
Time of plot: Fourth century
Locale: Ancient Rome
First published: 1896

Principal characters:

CAESAR CONSTANTIUS, the Roman Emperor
JULIAN FLAVIUS, Caesar's cousin
GALLUS FLAVIUS, Julian's brother
ARSINOË, Julian's beloved

Critique:

Merejkowski, one of the most successful of modern Russian novelists of the old régime, saw European civilization as a result of the meeting of Hellenism and Christianity. In this novel he attempted to show how that meeting was carried on in the reign of Julian the Apostate, a Roman emperor of the fourth century. The novelist's success in re-creating what is distant, both in point of time and place, is almost unparalleled in any national literature. Little street urchins of Constantinople, common soldiers in the Roman legions, innkeepers of Asia Minor, and fawning courtiers of Caesar's court, all take on flesh and life as they pass through the story, all of them reflecting in greater or lesser degree the struggle between the two great philosophies, paganism and Christianity.

The Story:

The Roman Emperor Constantius had risen to power by a series of assassinations. Two of his cousins, Julian and Gallus, were still alive, prisoners in Cappadocia. No one knew why they were permitted to live, for they were the last people who could challenge the right of the emperor to his position. Julian was the greater of the two, a young man steeped in the teachings of the philosophers. His brother was younger and more girlish in his habits. Both knew that they could expect death momentarily.

When Julian was twenty years old, Constantius gave him permission to travel in Asia Minor, where the lad affected the dress of a monk and passed as a Christian. His younger brother, Gallus, was given high honors as co-regent with Constantius and named Caesar. The affection which Constantius seemed to bestow on Gallus was shortlived, however, for soon the young man was recalled to Milan and on his journey homeward he was beheaded by order of the emperor. When word of his brother's death reached Julian, he wondered how much longer he himself had to live.

While Julian wandered about Asia Minor, he met many philosophers, and was initiated into the mysteries of Mithra, the sun god. Julian felt more power in the religion of the pagans than he did in the Christ which his grandfather had declared the official religion of the Roman Empire. Knowing the danger of his beliefs, Julian kept them secret.

One day, Publius Porphyrius took Julian to an ancient wrestling arena where they watched a young woman playing at the ancient Grecian games. She was Arsinoë, who, like Julian, found more joy in paganism than in Christianity. One night she told him that he must believe in himself rather than in any gods, and he replied to her that such was his aim.

Before long Julian had an opportunity to strike at Constantius. Raised to a position of honor at court and given the purple robe of a Caesar, he was trained as a warrior and sent to Gaul to tame the barbarians. Contrary to Constantius' hopes that the young man would be killed, he was highly successful in Gaul. When Constantius sent an emissary to recall several of Julian's legions, the soldiers revolted and hailed Julian as the emperor and made him accept the crown. Meanwhile Julian's anger against all Christians had risen; his wife refused to share his bed because she had decided to become a nun. He felt no pity when she fell ill and died. He thought her actions had disgraced him.

With his loyal legions Julian began a march of conquest through the empire. While he was crossing Macedonia, he received word that Constantius had died in Constantinople.

As soon as word spread among Julian's legions that he was now the rightful emperor, he gathered his men together for a ceremony at which he denied Christianity and affixed the statue of Apollo in place of the Cross on his standards. That act was only the beginning of changes in the empire. On his arrival in Constantinople he reinstated the pagan gods and returned to their temples the treasure which had been taken from them by the Christian monks.

The Christians were outraged at his practices, and his popularity waned. Few visited the reopened pagan temples. Soon Julian began to wonder if he would be successful in restoring a golden age of Hellenism to his empire. He discovered that even his beloved Arsinoë had become a Christian nun in his absence. When he went to visit her, she agreed to see him; but she refused to marry him and become the empress. Julian began to wonder to what end he was headed.

At the end of the first year of his reign as emperor of the Eastern Roman Empire, Julian found that he had become the laughing-stock of his people, despite his power as a ruler. His appearance and his scholarly activities earned him the disrespect of all his subjects, who were accustomed to a Caesar of martial power. When the Christians began to ridicule him and openly defy his edicts, Julian decided to adopt a different course. He hit upon the idea of a campaign against Persia. He hoped that after he had conquered that country and returned as a victor, his people would respect both him and his anti-Christian views.

Julian's army assembled at Antioch, but before it was ready to march Julian had a demonstration of the feeling he had evoked by championing the Olympian deities against Christianity. When he ordered a Christian chapel removed from the temple of Apollo at Antioch, the Christians burned the temple and destroyed the idol in the presence of the emperor and his legions.

In the spring Julian and his armies left Antioch and started toward the Persian frontier. They marched along the Euphrates until they came to the canal which the Persians had built to connect that river with the Tigris. The Persians had flooded the area to halt the invaders, and Julian's army marched in water up to their knees until they were far down the Tigris. After days of marching under a burning sun, they reached Perizibar, a Persian fortress. The fort was gallantly defended, but the Romans finally battered down the walls.

After resting his army for two days, Julian pushed on to Maogamalki. By brilliant strategy and some luck, he carried the second of the Persian defense posts and then pushed onward to Ctesiphon, the Persian capital.

Arriving at a point across the river from the city, Julian consulted his pagan priests. When they failed to foretell a successful attack on the city, Julian became as enraged at Apollo and the other pagan gods as he had been at Christianity. In a frenzy he overturned the altars, said that he trusted no god but himself, and added that he meant to attack the city immediately.

By a ruse, Julian and his army crossed the Tigris in boats at night. The next morning a single Persian came to their camp and persuaded Julian to burn his boats so that his men would not lose heart and retreat from the assault. He promised also to lead the Romans into the city by a secret way. Too late, his boats destroyed, Julian realized he had been tricked. Unable to take the city, he ordered a retreat. After the Romans had been weakened by forced marches under burning desert suns, the Persians attacked.

In the battle, the Romans won a victory against heavy odds; but it was a victory for the Romans, not for their emperor. In the battle Julian, dressed in his purple robes, refused to wear any armor. He was mortally wounded by a javelin while giving chase to a band of Persians. When he was carried to his tent, Arsinoë, who was still a nun, came to him and attempted to make him see that Christ was a god of beauty and mercy. Julian would not listen to her. As he died, he lifted himself up and cried out to his attendants that the Galilean had defeated him.

THE DEERSLAYER

Type of work: Novel
Author: James Fenimore Cooper (1789-1851)
Type of plot: Historical romance
Time of plot: 1740
Locale: Northern New York State
First published: 1841

Principal characters:

NATTY BUMPPO, called Deerslayer by the Delawares

HURRY HARRY, a frontier scout
CHINGACHGOOK, Deerslayer's Indian friend
THOMAS HUTTER, owner of the lake
JUDITH HUTTER, a girl Thomas Hutter claims as his daughter
HETTY HUTTER, Judith's sister
WAH-TA!-WAH, Chingachgook's beloved

Critique:

There is no question that the savages and the woodsman, Natty Bumppo, come off best in this first of the Leatherstocking Tales. Deerslayer and the Indians, good and bad, are depicted as having codes of honor and morality. Tom Hutter and Hurry Harry are motivated by greed and viciousness in their efforts to obtain Iroquois scalps and in their murder of an innocent Indian girl. The simple-minded Hetty Hutter and Judith, her vain sister, are but two-dimensioned characters, however, in this novel of atmosphere and exciting action.

The Story:

Natty Bumppo, a young woodsman known as Deerslayer, and Hurry Harry traveled to the shores of Lake Glimmerglass together. It was a dangerous journey, for the French and their Iroquois allies were on the warpath. Deerslayer was planning to meet his friend Chingachgook, the young Delaware chief, so that they might go against the Iroquois. Hurry Harry was on his way to the lake to warn Thomas Hutter and his daughters that hostile Indians were raiding along the frontier. Harry was accustomed to hunt and trap with Hutter during the summer, and he was an admirer of Hutter's elder daughter, the spirited Judith.

Hutter and his daughters lived in a cabin built on piles in the middle of the lake. Hutter had also built a great, scow-like vessel, known among frontiersmen as the ark, on which he traveled from one shore of the lake to the other on his hunting and trapping expeditions. On their arrival at the lake the two found a hidden canoe. Having paddled out to the cabin and found it deserted, they proceeded down the lake and came upon the ark anchored in a secluded outlet. Hutter had already learned of the Indian raiders. The party decided to take refuge in the cabin, where they could be attacked only over the water. The men managed to maneuver the ark out of the narrow outlet and sail it to the cabin. They had one narrow escape. As the ark was clearing the outlet, six Indians tried to board the boat by dropping from the overhanging limbs of a tree. Each missed and fell into the water.

Under cover of darkness, Hutter, Deerslayer, and Hurry Harry took the canoe and paddled to shore to get Hutter's two remaining canoes hidden there. They found the canoes and, on their way back to the ark, sighted a party of Indians camped under some trees. While Deerslayer waited in a canoe offshore, the other two men attacked the Iroquois camp in an attempt to obtain scalps, for which they could obtain bounties. They were captured. Deerslayer, knowing that he was powerless to help them, lay down to sleep in the canoe until morning.

When Deerslayer awoke, he saw that one of the canoes had drifted close to shore. To rescue it, he was forced to shoot an Indian, the first man he had ever killed.

Returning to the fort with his prizes, Deerslayer told the girls of their father's fate. It was agreed that they should delay any attempt at rescue until the arrival of Chingachgook, whom Deerslayer was to meet that night.

Under cover of darkness, the party went in the ark and met Chingachgook at the spot where the river joined the lake. Back in the cabin, Deerslayer explained that the Delaware had come to the lake to rescue his sweetheart, Wah-ta!-Wah, who had been stolen by the Iroquois. Suddenly they discovered that

Hetty Hutter had disappeared. The girl, who was somewhat feeble-minded, had cast off in one of the canoes with the intention of going to the Indian camp to rescue her father and Hurry Harry.

The next morning Wah-ta!-Wah came upon Hetty wandering in the forest. She took the white girl to the Iroquois camp. Because the Indians believed deranged persons were protected by the Great Spirit, she suffered no harm.

It was Deerslayer's idea to ransom the prisoners with some rich brocades and carved ivory he and Judith found in Tom Hutter's chest. Its contents had been known only to Hutter and the simple-minded Hetty, but in this emergency, Judith did not hesitate to open the coffer. Meanwhile a young Iroquois had rowed Hetty back to the cabin on a raft. Deerslayer told him that the party in the cabin would give two ivory chessmen for the release of the captives. He was unable to drive quite the bargain he had planned. In the end, four chessmen were exchanged for the men, who were returned that night.

Hetty brought a message from Wah-ta!-Wah. Chingachgook was to meet the Indian girl at a particular place on the shore when the evening star rose above the hemlocks that night. Hurry Harry and Tom Hutter were still determined to obtain scalps, and when night closed in they and Chingachgook reconnoitered the camp. To their disappointment, they found it deserted and the Indians camped on the beach, at the spot where Wah-ta!-Wah was to wait for Chingachgook.

While Hutter and Harry slept, the Delaware and Deerslayer attempted to keep the rendezvous. Unfortunately, the girl was under such close watch that it was impossible for her to leave the camp. The two men entered the camp and boldly rescued her from her captors. Deerslayer, who remained at their rear to cover their escape, was taken prisoner.

When Judith heard from Chingachgook of Deerslayer's capture, she rowed Hetty ashore to learn what had become of the woodsman. Once more Hetty walked unharmed among the superstitious savages. Deerslayer assured her there was nothing she could do to help, that he must await the Iroquois' pleasure. She left to return to Judith.

As the girls paddled about, trying to find the ark in the darkness, they heard the report of a gun. Torches on shore showed them that an Indian girl had been mortally wounded by a shot from the ark. Soon the lights went out. Paddling to the center of the lake, they tried to get what rest they might before morning came.

When daylight returned, Hutter headed the ark toward the cabin once more. Missing his daughters, he had concluded the cabin would be the most likely meeting place. Hutter and Harry were the first to leave the ark to go into the cabin. There the Iroquois, who had come aboard in rafts under cover of darkness, were waiting in ambush. Harry managed to escape into the water, where he was saved by Chingachgook. Judith and Hetty came to the ark in their canoe. After the savages had gone ashore, those on the ark went to the cabin. They found Hutter lying dead. That evening he was buried in the lake. Hurry Harry took advantage of the occasion to propose to Judith, but she refused him.

Shortly afterward they were surprised to see Deerslayer paddling toward the ark. He had been given temporary liberty in order to bargain with the fugitives. The Iroquois sent word that Chingachgook would be allowed to return to his own people if Wah-ta!-Wah and Judith became brides of Iroquois warriers. Hetty, they promised, would go unharmed because of her mental condition. Although Deerslayer's life was to be the penalty for refusal, these terms were declined.

Deerslayer did not have to return to his captors until the next day, and that evening he and Judith examined carefully the contents of her father's chest. To the girl's wonder, she found letters indicating that Hutter had not been her real father, but a former buccaneer whom her mother had married when her first husband deserted her. Saddened by this knowledge, Judith no longer wished to live at the lake. She intimated slyly to Deerslayer that she loved him, only to find he considered her above him in education and intelligence.

When Deerslayer returned to the Iroquois the next day, he was put to torture with hatchets. Hetty, Judith, and Wah-ta!-Wah came to the camp and attempted to intercede for him, but to no avail. Suddenly Chingachgook bounded in, and cut his friend's bonds. Deerslayer's release was the signal for the regiment from the nearest fort to attack, for Hurry Harry had gone to summon help during the night.

The Iroquois were routed. Hetty was mortally wounded during the battle. The next day she was buried in the lake beside her parents. Judith joined the soldiers returning to the fort. Deerslayer departed for the Delaware camp with Chingachgook and his bride.

Fifteen years later, Deerslayer, Chingachgook, and the latter's young son, Uncas, revisited the lake. Wah-ta!-Wah was long since dead, and, though the hunter inquired at the fort about Judith Hutter, he could find no one who knew her. Rumor was that a former member of the garrison, then living in England on his paternal estates, was influenced by a woman of rare beauty who was not his wife. The ark and the cabin in the lake were falling into decay.

DIANA OF THE CROSSWAYS

Type of work: Novel
Author: George Meredith (1828-1909)
Type of plot: Psychological realism
Time of plot: Nineteenth century
Locale: England
First published: 1885

Principal characters:
Diana Merion Warwick, a woman of beauty and charm
Augustus Warwick, her husband
Lady Emma Dunstane, Diana's friend
Thomas Redworth, Diana's friend and admirer
Lord Dannisburgh, another friend
Sir Percy Dacier, a young politician in love with Diana

Critique:

Any novel by George Meredith requires attention not only to the book in question but also to the wider aspects of the technique of fiction, for Meredith, always an original, was a writer of deep concentration and mature force. His Diana is a character head and shoulders above most heroines in nineteenth-century English novels. She offers the charm of femininity, perplexed by convention and yet aware of its force. Her predicament is at once an error in judgment and a glory to her. Her career compels our belief that a life which will not let go its harvest of errors until they are thoroughly winnowed is a human drama of deepest interest, for that life extracts the wisdom experience can offer. Diana, beautiful, witty, skeptical of social convention and moral expediency, is the embodiment of Meredith's philosophy and art.

The Story:

All of fashionable London was amazed and shocked when Diana Warwick suddenly left her husband's house. Society should not have been surprised at her action, however; the marriage had been ill-fated from the start. For Augustus Warwick, a calculating, ambitious politician, his marriage to the beautiful and charming Diana Merion had been largely one of convenience. Diana, in her turn, accepted his proposal as a refuge from unwelcome attentions to which her own position as an orphan had exposed her.

Diana Merion had first appeared in society at a state ball in Dublin, where her unspoiled charm and beauty attracted many admirers. Lady Emma Dunstane introduced Diana to Thomas Redworth, a friend of her husband, Sir Lukin Dunstane, and Redworth's attentions so enraged Mr. Sullivan Smith, a hot-tempered Irishman, that he attempted to provoke the Englishman to a duel. Redworth pacified the Irishman, however, to avoid compromising Diana by a duel fought on her account.

Later, while visiting Lady Emma at Copsley, the Dunstane country home in England, Diana was forced to rebuff Sir Lukin when he attempted to make love to her. Leaving Copsley, she went to visit the Warwicks. Meanwhile, Thomas Redworth announced to Lady Emma that he loved Diana. His announcement came too late. Diana was already engaged to Augustus Warwick.

In London the Warwicks took a large house and entertained lavishly. Among their intimates was Lord Dannisburgh, an elderly peer who became Diana's friend and adviser. While Warwick was away on a government mission, the two were often seen together, and Diana was so indiscreet as to let Lord Dannisburgh accompany her when she went to visit Lady Emma. Gossip began to circulate. On his return Warwick, who was incapable of understanding his wife's innocence and charm, served Diana with a process in suit. Accusing her of infidelity, he named Lord Dannisburgh as corespondent. Diana disappeared from Warwick's house and from London. In a letter to Lady Emma she had said that she intended to leave England. Her friend, realizing that flight would be tantamount to confession, felt sure that Diana would go to Crossways, her father's old home, before she left the country. Determined that Diana should remain and boldly defend the suit, Lady Emma sent Redworth to Crossways with instructions to detain Diana and persuade her to go to stay with the Dunstanes at Copsley.

Lady Emma had guessed correctly; Diana was at Crossways with her maid. At first Diana was unwilling to see Lady Emma's point of view, for she thought of her flight as a disdainful stepping aside from Warwick's sordid accusations; but at last she gave in to Redworth's arguments and returned with him to Copsley.

Although the court returned a verdict of not guilty to the charge Warwick had brought against her, Diana felt that her honor had been ruined and that in the eyes of the world she was still guilty. For a time she was able to forget her own distress by nursing her friend, Lady Emma, who was seriously ill. Later she left England to go on a Mediterranean cruise. Before her departure she had written a book, *The Princess Egeria.*

In Egypt she met Redworth, now a brilliant member of Parliament. He was accompanied by Sir Percy Dacier, Lord Dannisburgh's nephew and a rising young politician. Falling in love with Diana, Sir Percy followed her to the continent. He was recalled to London by the illness of his uncle. Diana followed him a short time later, to learn on her arrival in London that Redworth had been active in making her book a literary triumph. He had stirred up interest among the critics because he knew that Diana was in need of money.

Lord Dannisburgh died, with Diana at his bedside during his last illness. He had been her friend, and she paid him that last tribute of friendship and respect regardless of the storm of criticism it created. When Lord Dannisburgh's will was read, it was learned that he had left a sum of money to Diana.

In the meantime Diana had made an enemy of the socially ambitious Mrs. Wathin, who thought it her social duty to tear Diana's reputation to shreds. Part of her dislike was motivated by jealousy that Diana should be accepted by people who would not tolerate Mrs. Wathin. Some of her actions were inspired by Warwick, Mrs. Wathin's friend, who, having lost his suit against Diana, was trying to force his wife to return to him.

Sir Percy's attentions were also distressing to Diana. Half in love with him, she was not free to marry again. She faced a crisis in her affairs when Mrs. Wathin called to announce that Warwick, now ill, wanted Diana to return and to act as his nurse. Diana refused. Warwick then threatened to exercise his legal rights as her husband. Sir Percy, who informed her of Warwick's intention, asked her to elope with him to Paris. She agreed. She was saved from that folly by the appearance of Redworth, who arrived to tell her that Lady Emma was ill and about to undergo a serious operation at Copsley. Diana went with him to be at her friend's side.

Lady Emma nearly died, and the gravity of her condition restored Diana's own sense of responsibility. She ordered Sir Percy to forget her, but in spite of her protests he continued to follow her about. One day he confided a tremendous political secret to her—the prime minister was about to call upon Parliament to pass some revolutionary reform measures. Having told her his secret, he attempted to resume his former courtship. Diana refused to listen to his pleadings. After he had gone, she felt broken and cheated. If she would not have Sir Percy as a lover, she felt, she could not keep him as a friend. Diana was desperately in need of money. She had been forced to sell Crossways to pay her debts and her later novels had been failures. Feeling herself a complete adventuress, she went to the editor of a paper which opposed the government party and sold him the information Sir Percy had given her.

When the paper appeared with a full disclosure of the prime minister's plan, Sir Percy accused her of betraying him and broke with her. A short time later he proposed to a young lady of fortune. About the same time Warwick was struck down by a cab in the street and killed. Diana had her freedom at last, but she was downcast in spirit. She knew that she was in public disgrace. Although she had burned the check in payment for the information she had disclosed, it was common knowledge that she had betrayed Sir Percy and that he had retaliated by his marriage to Constance Asper, an heiress. When Sullivan Smith proposed for her hand, Diana refused him and sought refuge in the company of her old friend, Lady Emma. Her stay at Copsley freed her of her memories of Sir Percy, so much so that on her return to London she was able to greet him and his bride with dignity and charm. Her wit was as sharp as ever, and she took pleasure in revenging herself upon those who had attempted to destroy her reputation with their gossip and slander.

On another visit to Copsley she again encountered Redworth, now a railroad promoter and still a distinguished member of Parliament. When he invited her and Lady Emma to visit Crossways, Diana learned that it was Redworth who had bought her old home and furnished it with her own London possessions, which she had been forced to sell in order to pay her debts. He bluntly told Diana that he had bought the house and furnished it for her because he expected her to become his wife. Not wishing to involve him in the scandals which had circulated about her, she at first pretended indifference to his abrupt wooing. Lady Emma, on the other hand, urged her to marry Redworth, who had loved her for many years, so that he could protect her from social malice. At last, knowing that she brought no real disgrace to Redworth's name, she consented to become his wife.

THE DISCIPLE

Type of work: Novel
Author: Paul Bourget (1852-1935)
Type of plot: Psychological realism
Time of plot: Late nineteenth century
Locale: Paris and Riom
First published: 1889

Principal characters:
ADRIEN SIXTE, a philosopher
ROBERT GRESLOU, his disciple
M. DE JUSSAT, a hypochondriac nobleman
CHARLOTTE, his daughter
LUCIEN, her younger brother
ANDRÉ, her older brother

Critique:

Bourget represents in some ways the transition in French letters from naturalistic materialism to the more traditional religious and moral disciplines, and *The Disciple* is the mid-point in the work of this distinguished critic, novelist, and academician. This novel is a psychological study of the moral bases in abstract learning. Bourget has written an impeccable novel which combines solid psychological analysis with a sensational murder story.

The Story:

Adrien Sixte grew up in a peculiar way. His hardworking father wanted him to study for one of the professions, but despite the boy's early promise in school he never went to a university. His indulgent parents allowed him to spend ten lonely years in study. In 1868, at the age of twenty-nine, Adrien Sixte published a five-hundred-page study of *The Psychology of God*. By the outbreak of the Franco-Prussian War, Adrien had become the most discussed philosopher in the country. He followed his first study with two books even more provocative, *The Anatomy of the Will* and *The Theory of the Passions*.

Soon after the death of his parents, Adrien settled down to a well-regulated life in Paris. So regular was he that the inhabitants of the quarter could set their watches by his comings and goings. He spent eight hours of the twenty-four in work, took two walks each day, received callers, chiefly students, one afternoon a week, and on another afternoon made calls on other scholars. By patient labor and brilliant insight he developed to his complete satisfaction his deterministic theory that each effect comes from a cause, and that if all causes are known, results can be predicted accurately. He applied his theory to all forms of human activity, to vices as well as virtues.

One day the neighbors were startled to see Adrien leave his apartment hurriedly at an unusual hour. He had received, to his great consternation, a notice to appear before a magistrate in the affair of Robert Greslou, one of his students, and he had also a letter from Robert's mother saying that she would visit him that very day at four on an urgent matter.

The sophisticated judge was incredulous when he learned that Adrien never read the papers. The celebrated savant had not heard of Greslou's imprisonment after being charged with the murder of Charlotte de Jussat. Adrien soon learned that the suspect had been arrested on purely circumstantial evidence, that the proof of his guilt or innocence might well be only psychological. Hence Adrien, the master, must testify as to his

THE DISCIPLE by Paul Bourget. By permission of the publishers, Charles Scribner's Sons.

disciple's ideas on multiplied psychological experience. Adrien explained that if a chemist can analyze water into hydrogen and oxygen, he can synthesize hydrogen and oxygen into water. Similarly, if a psychological result can be analyzed into its causes, the result can be reproduced by those same causes; that is, by scientific method one can predict human behavior. The judge was much interested and inquired if his theory applied to vices. Adrien said that it did, for psychologically vices are forms of behavior as interesting and valid as social virtues.

When he returned home, Adrien found Robert's mother waiting for him. She protested her son's innocence and begged Adrien to save her boy. Adrien remembered Robert as a precocious student of philosophy, but he really knew little of him as a person. The mother begged Adrien to help and gave him a manuscript written by Robert while in jail. On the outside of the manuscript was a note. If Adrien read the document, he must agree not to try to save Robert; if the condition were unacceptable, he must burn the manuscript immediately. With many misgivings Adrien took the document and read it. It was a minute and detailed account of Robert's upbringing, his studies, and his experiences in the de Jussat home.

Robert was always brilliant. He did outstanding work in school and early in his studies showed a pronounced talent in psychology. Most of his time was devoted to study, but a developing sensuality showed itself sporadically. Since he grew up at Clermont, he lacked some of the polish imparted at Paris; in consequence he failed an examination. While waiting another opportunity to enter the university, Robert accepted a year's appointment as tutor to Lucien de Jussat. At the de Jussat country home Robert found an interesting household. Lucien, his pupil, was a fat, simple boy of thirteen. André, the older brother, was an army officer fond of hunting and riding. The father was a hypochondriac and a boor. But Charlotte, the daughter of the family, was a beautiful girl of nineteen.

Robert soon began the studied seduction of Charlotte. He had three reasons for such a step. First, he wanted to have some sort of revenge against the wealthy family. In the second place, his developed sexuality made the project attractive. Also, and probably more important, he wanted to test his theory that if he could determine the causes leading to love and sexual desire, he could produce desire by providing the causes. Robert kept careful notes on procedures and results.

He knew that pity is close to love. Consequently he aroused the pity of Charlotte by mysterious allusions to his painful past. Then, by carefully selecting a list of novels for her to read, he set about inflaming her desire for passionate, romantic love. But Robert was too hasty. He made an impassioned avowal to Charlotte and frightened her into leaving for Paris. Just as Robert began to despair of ever accomplishing his purpose, the illness of Lucien recalled Charlotte. Robert wrote her a note telling her he would commit suicide if she did not come to his room by midnight. He prepared two vials of strychnine and waited. When Charlotte came, he showed her the poison and proposed a suicide pact. Charlotte accepted, provided she could be the first to die. They spent the night together. Robert had triumphed.

Robert repudiated the pact, prompted in part by a real love for Charlotte. The next day she threatened to call her brother if Robert attempted to stop her own attempt at suicide, for she had read Robert's notes and knew she was simply the object of an experiment. After writing to her brother André a letter telling him of her intended suicide, she drank the strychnine. Robert was arrested soon afterward on suspicion of murder.

When Adrien Sixte came to the end of the manuscript, he began to feel a moral responsibility for his disciple's act. Disregarding the pledge implicit in his reading, he sent a note to André asking him if he intended to let Robert be convicted of murder by concealing Charlotte's letter. André resolved to tell the truth, and in a painful courtroom scene Robert was acquitted.

Immediately after the trial, André went to look for Robert. Scarcely able to resist, since he had been ready to die with Charlotte's secret safe, Robert went with André willingly. On the street, André pulled out a gun and shot Robert in the head. Robert's mother and Adrien mourned beside the coffin, Adrien because he accepted moral responsibility for the teachings that had prompted his disciple's deed.

THE DIVINE COMEDY

Type of work: Poem
Author: Dante Alighieri (1265-1321)
Type of plot: Christian allegory
Time of plot: The Friday before Easter, 1300
Locale: Hell, Purgatory, Paradise
First transcribed: c. 1307

Principal characters:
DANTE
VIRGIL, his guide
BEATRICE, the soul of Dante's beloved

Critique:

No words can describe the greatness of this work, a greatness both of theme and poetry. As a poet, Dante takes his place in the ranks of the foremost artists the world has ever known. The theme which he treats is universal; it involves the greatest concepts which man has ever attained. Only a master could find the loftiness of tone and the splendor and variety of images and scenes which are presented in *The Divine Comedy.*

The Story:

Dante found himself lost in a dark and frightening wood, and as he was trying to regain his path, he came to a mountain which he decided to climb in order to get his bearings. Strange beasts blocked his way, however, and he was forced back to the plain. As he was bemoaning his fate, the poet Virgil approached Dante and offered to conduct him through Hell, Purgatory, and blissful Paradise.

When they arrived at the gates of Hell, Virgil explained that here were confined those who had lived their lives without regard for good or evil. At the River Acheron, where they found Charon, the ferryman, Dante was seized with terror and fell into a trance. Aroused by a loud clap of thunder, he followed his guide through Limbo, the first circle of Hell. The spirits confined there, he learned, were those who, although they had lived a virtuous life, had not been baptized.

At the entrance to the second circle of Hell, Dante met Mino, the Infernal Judge, who warned him to take heed how he entered the lower regions. Dante was overcome by pity as he witnessed the terrible punishment which the spirits were undergoing. They had been guilty of carnal sin, and for punishment they were whirled around without cessation in the air. The third circle housed those who had been guilty of the sin of gluttony. They were forced to lie deep in the mud, under a constant fall of snow and hail and stagnant water. Above them stood Cerberus, a cruel monster, barking at the helpless creatures and tearing at their flesh. In the next circle, Dante witnessed the punishment of the prodigal and the avaricious, and realized the vanity of fortune.

He and Virgil continued on their journey until they reached the Stygian

Lake, in which the wrathful and gloomy were suffering. At Virgil's signal, a ferryman transported them across the lake to the city of Dis. They were denied admittance, however, and the gates were closed against them by a multitude of horrible demons. Dante and Virgil gained admittance into the city only after an angel had interceded for them. There Dante discovered that tombs burning with a blistering heat housed the souls of heretics. Dante spoke to two of these tormented spirits and learned that although they had the power to predict the future, they had no way of knowing what was occurring in the present.

The entrance to the seventh circle was guarded by the Minotaur, and only after Virgil had pacified him could the two travelers pass down the steep crags to the base of the mountain. There they discerned a river of blood in which those who had committed violence in their lifetimes were confined. On the other side of the river they learned that those who had committed suicide were doomed to inhabit the trunks of trees. Beyond the river they came to a desert in which were confined those who had sinned against God, or Art, or Nature. A stream flowed near the desert and the two poets followed it until the water plunged into an abyss. In order that they might descend to the eighth circle, Virgil summoned Geryon, a frightful monster, who conducted them below. There they saw the tortured souls of seducers, flatterers, diviners, and barterers. Continuing along their way, they witnessed the punishment accorded hypocrites and robbers. In the ninth gulf were confined scandalmongers and spreaders of false doctrine. Among the writhing figures they saw Mahomet. Still farther along, the two discovered the horrible disease-ridden bodies of forgerers, counterfeiters, alchemists, and all those who deceived under false pretenses.

They were summoned to the next circle by the sound of a trumpet. In it were confined all traitors. A ring of giants surrounded the circle, one of whom lifted both Dante and Virgil and deposited them in the bottom of the circle. There Dante conversed with many of the spirits and learned the nature of their particular crimes.

After this visit to the lowest depths of Hell, Dante and Virgil emerged from the foul air to the pure atmosphere which surrounded the island of Purgatory. In a little while, they saw a boat conducted by an angel, in which were souls being brought to Purgatory. Dante recognized that of a friend among them. The two poets reached the foot of a mountain, where passing spirits showed them the easiest path to climb its slope. On their way up the path they encountered many spirits who explained that they were confined to Purgatory because they had delayed their repentance too long. They pleaded with Dante to ask their families to pray for their souls when he once again returned to earth. Soon Dante and Virgil came to the gate of Purgatory, which was guarded by an angel. The two poets ascended a winding path and saw men, bent under the weight of heavy stones, who were expiating the sin of pride. They examined the heavily carved cornices which they passed, and found them covered with inscriptions urging humility and righteousness. At the second cornice were the souls of those who had been guilty of envy. They wore sackcloth and their eyelids were sewed with iron thread. Around them were the voices of angels singing of great examples of humility and the futility of envy. An angel invited the poets to visit the third cornice, where those who had been guilty of anger underwent repentance. Dante was astonished at the examples of patience which he witnessed there. At the fourth cornice he witnessed the purging of the sin of indifference or gloominess. He discussed with Virgil the nature of love. The Latin poet stated that there were two kinds of love, natural love, which was always right, and love of the soul, which might be misdirected. At the fifth cornice, avarice was purged. On their way to the next cornice, the two were overtaken by Statius, whose spirit had been cleansed and who was on his way to Paradise. He accompanied them to the next place of purging, where the sin of gluttony was repented, while voices sang of the glory of temperance. The last cornice was the place for purging by fire of the sin of incontinence. Here the sinners were heard to recite innumerable examples of praiseworthy chastity.

An angel now directed the two poets and Statius to a path which would lead them to Paradise. Virgil told Dante that he might wander through Paradise at his will until he found his love, Beatrice. As he was strolling through a forest, Dante came to a stream, on the other side of which stood a beautiful woman. She explained to him that the stream was called Lethe, and helped him to cross it. Then Beatrice descended from heaven and reproached him for his unfaithfulness to her during her life, but the virgins in the heavenly fields interceded with her on his behalf. Convinced of his sincere repentance and remorse, she agreed to accompany him through the heavens.

On the moon Dante found those who had made vows of chastity and determined to follow the religious life, but who were forced to break their vows. Beatrice led him to the planet Mercury, the second heaven, and from there to Venus, the third heaven, where Dante conversed with many spirits and learned of their virtues. On the sun, the fourth heaven, they were surrounded by a group of spirits, among them Thomas Aquinas. He named each of the spirits in turn and discussed their individual virtues. A second circle of blessed spirits surrounded the first, and Dante learned from each how he had achieved blessedness.

Then Beatrice and Dante came to Mars, the fifth heaven, where were cherished the souls of those who had been martyred. Dante recognized many renowned warriors and crusaders among them.

On Jupiter, the sixth heaven, Dante saw the souls of those who had administered justice faithfully in the world. The seventh heaven was on Saturn, where Dante found the souls of those who had spent their lives in meditation and religious retirement. From there Beatrice and her lover passed to the eighth heaven, the region of the fixed stars. Dante looked back over all the distance which extended between the earth and this apex of Paradise and was dazzled and awed by what he saw. As they stood there, they saw the triumphal hosts approaching, with Christ leading, followed by Mary.

Dante was questioned by the saints. Saint Peter examined his opinions concerning faith; Saint James, concerning hope, and Saint John, concerning charity. Adam then approached and told the poet of the first man's creation, of his life in Paradise, and of his fall and what had caused it. Saint Peter bitterly lamented the avarice which his apostolic successors displayed, and all the sainted host agreed with him.

Beatrice then conducted Dante to the ninth heaven, where he was permitted to view the divine essence and to listen to the chorus of angels. She then led him to the Empyrean, from the heights of which, and with the aid of her vision, he was able to witness the triumphs of the angels and of the souls of the blessed. So dazzled and overcome was he by this vision that it was some time before he realized Beatrice had left him. At his side stood an old man whom he recognized as Saint Bernard, who told him Beatrice had returned to her throne. He then told Dante that if he wished to discover still more of the heavenly vision, he must join with him in a prayer to Mary. Dante received the grace to contemplate the glory of God, and to glimpse, for a moment, the greatest of mysteries, the Trinity and man's union with the divine.

DR. JEKYLL AND MR. HYDE

Type of work: Novelette
Author: Robert Louis Stevenson (1850-1894)
Type of plot: Fantasy
Time of plot: Nineteenth century
Locale: London
First published: 1886

Principal characters:
DR. HENRY JEKYLL, a London physician
MR. UTTERSON, counselor for Dr. Jekyll
POOLE, Dr. Jekyll's manservant
DR. HASTIE LANYON, Dr. Jekyll's close friend

Critique:

The Strange Case of Dr. Jekyll and Mr. Hyde has steadily maintained the popularity which it had originally. The story is basically one of romantic adventure and fantasy, of the type currently found in paper pulps. Yet by merit of Stevenson's understanding of human nature and his mastery of English prose, the story holds subtle values as an illustration of man's dual nature. It is not necessary to believe the story in order to understand and believe the symbolism.

The Story:

Mr. Richard Enfield, and his cousin, Mr. Utterson, a lawyer, were strolling according to their usual Sunday custom when they came upon an empty building on a familiar street. Mr. Enfield told that some time previously he had seen an ill-tempered man trample down a small child at the doorway of the deserted building. He and other indignant bystanders had forced the stranger, who gave his name as Hyde, to pay over a sum of money for the child's welfare. Enfield remembered the man Hyde with deep loathing.

Utterson had reasons to be interested in Hyde. When he returned to his apartment he reread the strange will of Dr. Henry Jekyll. The will stipulated that in the event of Dr. Jekyll's death all of his wealth should go to a man named Edward Hyde.

Utterson sought out Hyde, the man whom Enfield had described, to discover if he were the same who had been named heir to Dr. Jekyll's fortune. Suspicious of Utterson's interest, Hyde became enraged and ran into his house. Questioned, Dr. Jekyll refused to discuss the matter, but insisted that in the event of his death the lawyer should see to it that Mr. Hyde was not cheated out of his fortune. The lawyer believed that Hyde was an extortioner who was getting possession of Dr. Jekyll's money and who would eventually murder the doctor.

About a year later Hyde was wanted for the wanton murder of a kindly old man, Sir Danvers Carew, but he escaped before he could be arrested. Dr. Jekyll presented the lawyer and the police with a letter signed by Hyde, in which the murderer declared his intention of making good his escape forever. He begged Dr. Jekyll's pardon for having ill-used his friendship.

About this time Dr. Lanyon, who had been for years a great friend of Dr. Jekyll, became ill and died. Among his papers was a letter addressed to Utterson. Opening it, Utterson discovered an inner envelope also sealed and bearing the notice that it was not to be opened until after Dr. Jekyll's death. Utterson felt that it was somehow associated with the evil Hyde, but he could in no way fathom the mystery.

One Sunday Enfield and Utterson were walking again in the street where Enfield had seen Hyde mistreating the child. They now realized that the strange deserted building was a side entrance to the house of Dr. Jekyll, an additional wing used as a laboratory.

Looking up at the window, they saw Dr. Jekyll sitting there. He looked disconsolate. Then his expression seemed to change, so that his face took on a grimace of horror or pain. Suddenly he closed the window. Utterson and Enfield walked on, too overcome by what they had seen to talk further.

Not long afterward Utterson was sitting by his fireside when Poole, Dr. Jekyll's manservant, sought entrance. He related that for a week something strange had been going on in Dr. Jekyll's laboratory. The doctor himself had not appeared. Instead, he had ordered his meals to be sent in and had written curious notes demanding that Poole go to all the chemical houses in London in search of a mysterious drug. Poole was convinced that his master had been slain and that the murderer, masquerading as Dr. Jekyll, was still hiding in the laboratory.

Utterson and Poole returned to Dr. Jekyll's house and broke into his laboratory with an ax. Entering, they discovered that the man in the laboratory had killed himself by draining a vial of poison just as they broke the lock. The man was Edward Hyde.

They searched in vain for the doctor's body, certain it was somewhere about after they discovered a note of that date addressed to Utterson. In the note Dr. Jekyll said he was planning to disappear, and he urged Utterson to read the note which Dr. Lanyon had left at the time of his death. An enclosure contained the confession of Henry Jekyll.

Utterson returned to his office to read the letters. The letter of Dr. Lanyon described how Dr. Jekyll had sent Poole to Dr. Lanyon with a request that Dr. Lanyon search for some drugs in Dr. Jekyll's laboratory. Hyde had appeared to claim the drugs. Then, in Dr. Lanyon's presence, Hyde had taken the drugs and had been transformed into Dr. Jekyll. The shock of this transformation had caused Dr. Lanyon's death.

Dr. Jekyll's own account of the horrible affair was more detailed. He had begun early in life to live a double life. Publicly he had been genteel and circumspect, but privately he had practiced strange vices without restraint. Becoming obsessed with the idea that people had two personalities, he reasoned that men were capable of having two physical beings as well. Finally, he had compounded a mixture which transformed his body into the physical representation of his evil self. He became Hyde. In his disguise he was free to haunt the lonely, narrow corners of London and to do the darkest acts without fear of recognition.

He tried in every way to protect Hyde. He cautioned his servants to let him in at any hour; he took an apartment for him, and he made out his will in Hyde's favor. His life proceeded safely enough until he awoke one morning in the shape of Edward Hyde and realized that his evil nature had gained the upper hand. Frightened, he determined to cast off the nature of Hyde. He sought out better companions and tried to occupy his mind with other things. However, he was not strong enough to change his true nature. He finally permitted himself to assume the shape of Hyde again, and on that occasion Hyde, full of an overpowering lust to do evil, murdered Sir Danvers Carew.

Dr. Jekyll renewed his effort to abandon the nature of Hyde. Walking in the park one day, he suddenly changed into Hyde. On that occasion he had sought out his friend Dr. Lanyon to go to his laboratory to obtain the drugs which would change him back to the personality of the doctor. Dr. Lanyon had watched the transformation with horror. Thereafter the nature of Hyde seemed to assert itself constantly. When his supply of chemicals had been exhausted and could not be replenished, Dr. Jekyll, as Hyde, shut himself up in his laboratory while he experimented with one drug after another. Finally, in despair, as Utterson now realized, he killed himself.

A DOLL'S HOUSE

Type of work: Drama
Author: Henrik Ibsen (1828-1906)
Type of plot: Social criticism
Time of plot: Nineteenth century
Locale: Norway
First presented: 1879

Principal characters:
TORVALD HELMER, a bank manager
NORA HELMER, his wife
MRS. LINDE, Nora's old school friend
KROGSTAD, a bank clerk
DR. RANK, a friend of the Helmers

Critique:

A Doll's House is the best known and one of the most popular of Ibsen's works. A classic expression of the theme of woman's rights, the play shocked Ibsen's contemporaries, because in the end Nora leaves her husband and children. In the character of Dr. Rank there is a foreshadowing of the heredity theme later to be developed by Ibsen in *Ghosts*.

The Story:

On the day before Christmas, Nora Helmer was busying herself with last minute shopping, for this was the first Christmas since her marriage that she had not had to economize. Her husband, Torvald, had just been made manager of a bank and after the New Year their money troubles would be over. She bought a tree and plenty of toys for the children, and she even indulged herself in some macaroons, her favorite confection, but of which Torvald did not entirely approve. He loved his wife dearly, but he regarded her very much as her own father had seen her, as an amusing doll—a plaything.

It was true that she did behave like a child sometimes in her relations with her husband. She pouted, wheedled, and chattered because Torvald expected these things; he would not have loved his doll-wife without them. Actually, Nora was not a doll but a woman with a woman's loves, hopes, and fears. This was shown seven years before, just after her first child was born, when Torvald had been ill, and the doctor said that unless he went abroad immediately he would die. Nora was desperate. She could not seek Torvald's advice because she knew he would rather die than borrow money. She could not go to her father, for he himself was a dying man. She did the only thing possible under the circumstances. She borrowed the requisite two hundred and fifty pounds from Krogstad, a money-lender, forging her father's name to the note, so that Torvald could have his holiday in Italy.

Krogstad was exacting, and she had to think up ways and means to meet the regular payments. When Torvald gave her money for new dresses and such things, she never spent more than half of it, and she found other ways to earn money. One winter she did copying, but she kept this work a secret from Torvald, for he believed that the money for their trip had come from her father.

Then Krogstad, who was in the employ of the bank of which Torvald was now manager, determined to use Torvald to advance his own fortunes. But Torvald hated Krogstad, and was just as determined to be rid of him. The opportunity came when Christina Linde, Nora's old school friend, applied to Torvald for a position in the bank. Torvald resolved to dismiss Krogstad and hire Mrs. Linde in his place.

When Krogstad discovered that he was to be fired, he called on Nora and informed her that if he were dismissed he would ruin her and her husband. He reminded her that the note supposedly signed by her father was dated three days after his death. Frightened at the turn matters had taken, Nora pleaded unsuccessfully with Torvald to reinstate Krogstad in the bank. Krogstad, receiving from Torvald an official notice of his dismissal, wrote in return a letter in which he revealed the full details of the forgery. He dropped the letter in the mailbox outside the Helmer home.

Torvald was in a holiday mood. The following evening they were to attend a fancy dress ball, and Nora was to go as a Neapolitan fisher girl and dance the tarantella. To divert her husband's attention from the mailbox outside, Nora practiced her dance before Torvald and Dr. Rank, an old friend. Nora was desperate, not knowing quite which way to turn. She had thought of Mrs. Linde, with whom Krogstad had at one time been in love. Mrs. Linde promised to do what she could to turn Krogstad from his avowed purpose. Nora thought also of Dr. Rank, but when she began to confide in him he made it so obvious that he was in love with her that she could not tell her secret. However, Torvald had promised her not to go near the mailbox until after the ball.

What bothered Nora was not her own fate, but Torvald's. She pictured herself as already dead, drowned in icy black water. She pictured the grief-stricken Torvald taking upon himself all the blame for what she had done and being disgraced for her sake. But the reality did not quite correspond with Nora's picture. Mrs. Linde, by promising to marry Krogstad and look after his children, succeeded in persuading him to withdraw all accusations against the Helmers, but she realized that Nora's affairs had come to a crisis and that sooner or later Nora and Torvald would have to come to an understanding.

This crisis came when Torvald read Krogstad's letter after their return from the ball. He accused Nora of being a hypocrite, a liar, and a criminal, of having no religion, no morality, no sense of duty. He declared that she was unfit to bring up her children. He informed her that she might remain in his household but she would no longer be a part of it.

Then another letter arrived from Krogstad, declaring that he intended to take no action against the Helmers. Torvald's whole attitude changed, and with a sigh of relief he boasted that he was saved. For the first time Nora saw her husband for what he was—a selfish, pretentious hypocrite with no regard for her position in the matter. She reminded him that no marriage could be built on inequality, and announced her intention of leaving his house forever. Torvald could not believe his ears and pleaded with her to remain. But she declared she was going to try to become a reasonable human being, to understand the world—in short, to become a woman, not a doll to flatter Torvald's selfish vanity. She went out and with irrevocable finality, slammed the door of her doll house behind her.

DON JUAN

Type of work: Poem
Author: George Gordon, Lord Byron (1788-1824)
Type of plot: Social satire
Time of plot: Late eighteenth century
Locale: Spain, Turkey, Russia, England
First published: By Cantos, 1819-1824

Principal characters:
Don Juan, a young Spaniard
Donna Inez, his mother
Donna Julia, his first mistress

HAIDÉE, his second love
THE SULTANA, who coveted Juan
CATHERINE, Empress of Russia
LADY ADELINE AMUNDEVILLE, Juan's adviser
DUCHESS OF FITZ-FULKE, who pursued Juan
AURORA RABY, pursued by Juan

Critique:

Although Byron said that *Don Juan* was to be an epic, his story does not follow epic tradition but becomes a vehicle for digression on any and every subject and person that entered his mind as he wrote. The plot itself is almost a minor part of the poem, for much more interesting are Byron's bitter tirades on England, wealth, power, society, chastity, poets, and diplomats. For that reason, Juan's adventures being largely incidental, the poem holds a high place among literary satires, even though unfinished at Byron's death.

The Story:

When Don Juan was a small boy, his father died, leaving the boy in the care of his mother, Donna Inez. Donna Inez was a righteous woman who had made her husband's life miserable. She had her son tutored in the arts of fencing, riding, and shooting, and she herself attempted to rear him in a moral manner. But even though young Don Juan read widely in the sermons and lives of the saints, he did not seem to absorb from his studies the qualities his mother thought essential.

At sixteen, he was a handsome lad much admired by his mother's friends. Donna Julia, in particular, often looked pensively at the youth. Donna Julia was just twenty-three and married to a man of fifty. Although she loved her husband, or so she told herself, she thought often of young Don Juan. One day, finding herself alone with him, she gave herself to the young man.

The young lovers spent long hours together during the summer, and it was not until November that Don Alfonso, her husband, discovered their intrigue. When Don Alfonso found Don Juan in his wife's bedroom, he tried to throttle him. But Don Juan overcame Don Alfonso and fled, first to his mother's home for clothes and money. Then Donna Inez sent him to Cadiz, there to begin a tour of Europe. The good lady prayed that the trip would mend his morals.

Before his ship reached Leghorn a storm broke it apart. Don Juan spent many days in a lifeboat without food or water. At last the boat was washed ashore, and Don Juan fell exhausted on the beach and slept. When he awoke, he saw bending over him a beautiful girl who told him that she was called Haidée and that she was the daughter of the ruler of the island, one of the Cyclades. Her father, Lambro, was a pirate, dealing in jewels and slaves. Because she knew her father would sell Don Juan to the first trader who came by, Haidée hid Don Juan in a cave and sent her maids to wait on him.

When Lambro left on another expedition, Haidée took Don Juan from the cave and they roamed together over the island. Haidée heaped jewels and fine foods and wines on Don Juan, for he was the first man she had ever known except her father and her servants. Although Don Juan still tried to think of Donna Julia, he could not resist Haidée. A child of nature and passion, she gave herself to him with complete freedom. Again Don Juan lived an idyllic existence, until Haidée's father returned unexpectedly. Don Juan again fought gallantly, but at last he was overcome by the old man's servants and put aboard a slave ship bound for a distant market. He never saw Haidée again, and he never knew that she died giving birth to his child.

The slave ship took Don Juan to a Turkish market, where he and another prisoner were purchased by a Negro eunuch and taken to the palace of a sultan. There Don Juan was made to dress as a dancing maiden and present himself to the sultana, the fourth and favorite wife of the sultan. She had passed by the slave market and had seen Don Juan and wanted him for a lover. In order to conceal his sex from the sultan, she forced the disguise on Don Juan. But even at the threat of death, Don Juan would not become her lover, for he still yearned for Haidée. Perhaps his constancy might have wavered, if the sultana had not been an infidel, for she was young and beautiful.

Eventually Don Juan escaped from the palace and joined the army of Catherine of Russia. The Russians were at war with the sultan from whose palace Don Juan had fled. Don Juan was such a valiant soldier that he was sent to St. Petersburg, to carry the news of a Russian victory to Empress Catherine. Catherine also cast longing eyes on the handsome stranger, and her approval soon made Don Juan the toast of her capital.

In the midst of his luxury and good fortune, Don Juan grew ill. Hoping that a change of climate would help her favorite, Catherine resolved to send him on a mission to England. When he reached London he was well received, for he was a polished young man, well versed in fashionable etiquette. His mornings were spent in business, but his afternoons and evenings were devoted to lavish entertainment. He conducted himself with such decorum, however, that he was much sought after by proper young ladies and much advised by older ones. Lady Adeline Amundeville, made him her protégé, and advised him freely on affairs of the heart. Another, the Duchess of Fitz-Fulke, advised him too, but her suggestions were of a more personal nature and seemed to demand a secluded spot where there was no danger from intruders. Because of the Duchess of Fitz-Fulke's attentions to Don Juan, Lady Adeline began to talk to him about selecting a bride from the chaste and suitable young ladies attentive to him.

Don Juan thought of marriage, but his interest was stirred by a girl not on Lady Adeline's list. Aurora Raby was a plain young lady, prim, dull, and seemingly unaware of Don Juan's presence. Her lack of interest served to spur him on to greater efforts, but a smile was his only reward from the cold maiden.

His attention was diverted from Aurora Raby by the appearance of the ghost of the Black Friar, who had once lived in the house of Lady Adeline, where Don Juan was a guest. The ghost was a legendary figure reported to appear before births, deaths, or marriages. To Don Juan, the ghost was an evil omen, and he could not laugh off the tightness about his heart. Lady Adeline and her husband seemed to consider the ghost a great joke. Aurora Raby appeared to be a little sympathetic with Don Juan, but the Duchess of Fitz-Fulke merely laughed at his discomfiture.

The second time the ghost appeared, Don Juan followed it out of the house and into the garden. It seemed to float before him, always just out of his reach. Once he thought he had grasped it, but his fingers touched only a cold wall. Then he seized it firmly and found that the ghost had a sweet breath and full, red lips. When the monk's cowl fell back, the Duchess of Fitz-Fulke was revealed.

On the morning after, Don Juan appeared at breakfast, wan and tired. Whether he had overcome more than the ghost, no one will ever know. The duchess, too, came down, seeming to have the air of one who had been rebuked. . . .

DON QUIXOTE DE LA MANCHA

Type of work: Novel
Author: Miguel de Cervantes Saavedra (1547-1616)
Type of plot: Picaresque romance
Time of plot: Spanish Renaissance
Locale: Spain
First published: Part I, 1605; Part II, 1615

Principal characters:
DON QUIXOTE DE LA MANCHA, a knight-errant
SANCHO PANZA, his squire
DULCINEA DEL TOBOSO, a village wench
PEDRO PEREZ, a village curate
MASTER NICHOLAS, a barber
SAMSON CARRASCO, a young bachelor of arts

Critique:

Macauley said that *Don Quixote* is "the best novel in the world, beyond comparison." This belief was, is, and certainly will be shared by lovers of literary excellence everywhere. Cervantes' avowed purpose was to ridicule the books of chivalry which enjoyed popularity even in his day. But he soared beyond this satirical purpose in his wealth of fancy and in his irrepressible high spirit as he pokes fun at social and literary conventions of his day. The novel provides a cross-section of Spanish life, thought, and feeling at the end of the chivalric age.

The Story:

A retired and impoverished gentleman named Alonzo Quixano lived in the Spanish province of La Mancha. He had read so many romances of chivalry that his mind became stuffed with fantastic accounts of tournaments, knightly quests, damsels in distress, and strange enchantments, and he decided one day to imitate the heroes of the books he read and to revive the ancient custom of knight-errantry. Changing his name to Don Quixote de la Mancha, he had himself dubbed a knight by a rascally publican whose miserable inn he mistook for a turreted castle.

For armor he donned an old suit of mail which had belonged to his great-grandfather. Then upon a bony old nag he called Rosinante, he set out upon his first adventure. Not far from his village he fell into the company of some traveling merchants who thought the old man mad and beat him severely when he challenged them to a passage at arms.

Back home recovering from his cuts and bruises, he was closely watched by his good neighbor, Pedro Perez, the village priest, and Master Nicholas, the barber. Hoping to cure him of his fancies, the curate and the barber burned his library of chivalric romances. Don Quixote, however, believed that his books had been carried off by a wizard. Undaunted by his misfortunes, he determined to set out on the road again, with an uncouth rustic named Sancho Panza as his squire. As the mistress to whom he would dedicate his deeds of valor he chose a buxom peasant wench famous for her skill in salting pork. He called her Dulcinea del Toboso.

The knight and his squire had to sneak out of the village under cover of darkness, but in their own minds they presented a brave appearance: the lean old man on his bony horse and his squat, black-browed servant on a small ass, Dapple. The don carried his sword and lance, Sancho Panza a canvas wallet and a leather bottle. Sancho went with the don because in his shallow-brained way he hoped to become governor of an isle.

The don's first encounter was with a score of windmills on the plains of Montiel. Mistaking them for monstrous giants, he couched his lance, set spurs to Rosinante's thin flanks, and charged full tilt against them. One of the whirling vanes lifted him from his saddle and threw him into the air. When Sancho Panza ran to pick him up, he explained that sorcerers had changed the giants into windmills.

Shortly afterward he encountered two monks riding in company with a lady in a coach escorted by men on horseback. Don Quixote imagined that the lady was a captive princess. Haughtily demanding her release, he unhorsed one of the friars in an attempted rescue. Sancho was beaten by the lady's lackeys. Don Quixote bested her Biscayan squire in a sword fight, sparing the man's life on condition that he go to Toboso and yield himself to the peerless Dulcinea. Sancho, having little taste for violence, wanted to get on to his isle as quickly as possible.

At an inn Quixote became involved in an assignation between a carrier and a servant girl. He was trounced by the carrier. The don, insulted by the innkeeper's demand for payment, rode away without paying. Sancho, to his terror, was tossed in a blanket as payment for his master's debt.

The pair came upon dust clouds stirred up by two large flocks of sheep. Don Quixote, sure that they were two medieval armies closing in combat, intervened, only to be pummeled with rocks by the indignant shepherds, whose sheep he had scattered.

At night the don thought a funeral procession was a parade of monsters. He attacked and routed the mourners and was called the Knight of the Sorry Aspect by Sancho. The two came upon a roaring noise in the night. Quixote, believing it to be made by giants, wanted to attack immediately, but Sancho judiciously hobbled Rosinante so he could not move. The next day they discovered the noise came from the pounding of a mill.

Quixote attacked an itinerant barber and seized the poor barber's bowl, which he declared to be the famous golden helmet of Mambrino, and his packsaddle, which he believed to be a richly-jeweled caparison.

Next, the pair came upon a chaingang being taken to the galleys. The don interviewed various prisoners and decided to succor the afflicted. He freed them, only to be insulted by their remarks concerning his lady, the fair Dulcinea. Sancho, afraid of what would ensue from their releasing of the galleyslaves, led Quixote into the mountains for safety. There they came upon a hermit, a nobleman, who told them a long story of unrequited love. Quixote and the hermit fought over the virtues of their inamoratas. Deciding to do penance and to fast for the love of Dulcinea, Quixote gave a letter to Sancho to deliver to the maiden. When Sancho returned to the village Don Quixote's friends learned from Sancho the old man's whereabouts. They returned with Sancho to the mountains, in hopes that they could trick Don Quixote into returning with them. The priest devised a scheme whereby a young peasant woman would pose as a distressed princess. Don Quixote, all but dead from hunger and exposure, was easily deceived, and the party started homeward.

They camc to the inn where Sancho had been tossed in the blanket. The priest explained the don's vagaries to the alarmed innkeeper, who admitted that he, too, was addicted to the reading of romances of chivalry. At the inn Don Quixote fought in his sleep with ogres and ran his sword through two of the innkeeper's precious wine-skins. The itinerant barber stopped by and demanded the return of his basin and packsaddle. After the party had sport at the expense of the befuddled barber, restitution was made. An officer appeared with a warrant for the arrest of the don and Sancho for releasing the galleyslaves. The priest explained his friend's mental condition and the officer departed.

Seeing no other means of getting Don Quixote quietly home, his friends disguised themselves and placed the don in a cage mounted on an oxcart. He was later released under oath not to attempt to escape. A canon, joining the party, sought to bring Quixote to his senses by logical argument against books of knight-errantry. The don refuted the canon with a charming and brilliant argument and went on to narrate a typical romance of derring-do. Before the group reached home, they came upon a goatherd who told them a story and by whom Quixote was beaten through a misunderstanding.

Sometime later the priest and the barber visited the convalescing Don Quixote to give him news of Spain and of the world. When they told him there was danger of an attack on Spain by the Turks, the don suggested that the king assemble all of Spain's knights-errant to repulse the enemy. At this time, Sancho entered despite efforts to bar him. He brought word that a book telling of their adventures had appeared. The sight of Sancho inspired the don to sally forth again. His excuse was a great tournament to be held at Saragossa.

Failing to dissuade Don Quixote from going forth again, his friends were reassured when a village student promised he would waylay the flighty old gentleman.

Don Quixote's first destination was the home of Dulcinea in nearby El Toboso. While the don awaited in a forest, Sancho saw three peasant girls riding out of the village. He rode to his master and told him that Dulcinea with two handmaidens approached. Frightened by the don's fantastic speech, the girls fled. Don Quixote swore that Dulcinea had been enchanted.

Benighted in a forest, the knight and his squire were awakened by the arrival of another knight and squire. The other knight boasted that he had defeated in combat all Spanish knights. The don, believing the knight to be mistaken, challenged him. They fought by daylight and, miraculously, Don Quixote unhorsed the Knight of the Wood, who was Carrasco, the village student, in disguise. His squire was an old acquaintance of Sancho. The don declared the resemblances were the work of magicians and continued on his way. Upset by his failure, Carrasco swore vengeance on Don Quixote.

Sancho filled Quixote's helmet with curds which he procured from shepherds. When the don suddenly clapped on his helmet at the approach of another adventure, he thought his brains were melting. This new adventure took the form of a wagon bearing two caged lions. Quixote, ever intrepid, commanded the keeper to open one cage—he would engage a lion in combat. Unhappily, the keeper obeyed. Quixote stood ready, but the lion yawned and refused to come out.

The don and Sancho joined a wedding party and subsequently attended a wedding festival at which the rejected lover tricked the bride into marrying him instead of the rich man she had chosen.

Next, the pair were taken to the Caves of Montesinos, where Quixote was lowered underground. He was brought up an hour later asleep, and, upon awakening, he told a story of having spent three days in a land of palaces and magic forests where he had seen his enchanted Dulcinea.

At an inn Quixote met a puppeteer who had a divining ape. By trickery, the rascal identified the don and Sancho with the help of the ape. He presented a melodramatic puppet show which Don Quixote, carried away by the make-believe story, demolished with his sword. The don paid for the damage done and struck out for the nearby River Ebro. He and Sancho took a boat and were carried by the current toward some churning mill wheels, which the don thought were a beleaguered city awaiting deliverance. They were rescued by millers after the boat had been wrecked and the pair thoroughly soaked.

Later, in a forest, the pair met a huntress who claimed knowledge of the famous knight and his squire. They went with the lady to her castle and were welcomed by a duke and his duchess who had read of their previous adventures and who were ready to have great fun at the pair's expense. The hosts arranged an elaborate night ceremony to disenchant Dulcinea, who was represented by a disguised page. Sancho was told, to his great discomfort, that he would receive five hundred lashes as his part of the disenchantment. Part of the jest was a ride through space on a magic wooden horse. Blindfolded, the pair mounted their steed and servants blew air in their faces from bellows and thrust torches near their faces.

Sancho departed to govern his isle, a village in the domains of the duke and duchess, while the female part of the household turned to the project of compromising Quixote in his worship of Dulcinea. Sancho governed for a week. He made good laws and delivered wise judgments, but at the end of a week he yearned for the freedom of the road. Together he and his master proceeded toward Saragossa. Don Quixote changed their destination to Barcelona, however, when he heard that a citizen of that city had written a spurious account of his adventures.

In Barcelona they marveled at the city, the ships, and the sea. Don Quixote and Sancho were the guests of Moreno, who took them to inspect the royal galleys. The galley which they visited suddenly put out to sea in pursuit of pirates and a fight followed. Sancho was terrified.

There came to Barcelona a Knight of the White Moon, who challenged Don Quixote to combat. After the old man had been overcome, the strange knight, in reality the student Carrasco, sentenced him to return home. Don Quixote went back, determined next to follow a pastoral shepherd life. At home, the tired old man quickly declined. Before he died, he renounced as nonsense all to do with knight-errantry, not realizing that in his high-minded, noble-hearted nature he himself had been a great chivalric gentleman.

THE DOWNFALL

Type of work: Novel
Author: Émile Zola (1840-1902)
Type of plot: Social criticism
Time of plot: 1870-1871
Locale: France
First published: 1892

Principal characters:
MAURICE LEVASSEUR, a private in the French Army
JEAN MACQUART, his corporal
DELAHERCHE, a textile manufacturer
WEISS, his secretary
HENRIETTE, twin sister of Maurice and wife of Weiss
FOUCHARD, a shrewd farmer
HONORÉ, his son
SILVINE, Fouchard's servant

Critique:

Zola's theme in this highly contrived novel would seem to be that France paid in full measure for the indulgences of seventy years in her wretched defeat at the hands of Bismarck and Von Moltke in 1870-71. Each character is a symbol of an economic or social group. Zola's account of Sedan, of the events leading up to Sedan, and of the insurrection in Paris, command admiration for his research. The plot makes even more dramatic the historical facts.

The Story:

Corporal Jean Macquart, a sturdy French peasant, led the squad of infantry of which Private Maurice Levasseur was a member. The squad was a part of the 106th Regiment of the Seventh Corps of the French Army. A state of war existed between France and Prussia; the year was 1870. At the outset it had been felt in France that the war would be nothing more than a quick promenade to Berlin, but shortages of equipment, the rivalry of the French commanders, and quick Prussian success made the outcome of the conflict doubtful.

Maurice, a scapegrace who had enlisted to get away from financial troubles in Paris, believed in the evolutionary necessity of war. As a member of the middle class, he loathed Jean, whose peasant common sense was unendurable to him.

Misinformation and lack of information led the leader of the Seventh Corps to order his divisions to fall back from their positions around Mulhausen, in Alsace. Defeat was in the air. Civilians, having heard that the Prussians were sweeping all before them, were fleeing westward. Demoralized, the troops threw away their packs and rifles. At Belfort the corps entrained for Rheims, where the retreating and disorganized French forces were regrouping.

Prussian victories cost Emperor Napoleon III his command of the French armies. But Napoleon, with his official entourage, remained with the troops. Maurice, in Rheims, learned from battle veterans that the Prussians were young, healthy, well-organized, and well-equipped. He lost all hope for France when he caught sight of the sickly emperor in Rheims.

The army was ordered to march to Verdun. Mendacious ministers and journalists lulled the French forces into a false sense of security. When the troops reached the Ardennes, there were marches and counter-marches, for the positions of the Prussian armies were not known by the French commanders. Regiments became mobs as the French approached Sedan. By that time Maurice had become reconciled to his fate, and had even grown to admire Jean, whose steadiness had kept the squad together.

Near Sedan, Maurice, Jean, and Honoré, an artilleryman, rescued Honoré's father, old Fouchard, from pillaging soldiers. There Honoré also promised to marry Silvine, Fouchard's servant, who had had a baby by Fouchard's hired hand, Goliath. The hired man was suspected of being a Prussian spy, for at the beginning of hostilities he had disappeared from the Fouchard farm.

Sedan was a place of confusion, where men were separated from their units because there was no discipline and no organization. In the confusion, Jean and Maurice met at the house of Delaherche, a Sedan textile manufacturer, whose secretary, Weiss, was the husband of Maurice's twin sister, Henriette. After a rest Jean and Maurice rejoined their regiment. Napoleon III accompanied the troops to Sedan.

As the French poured into Sedan, it became evident that the Prussians were drawing a ring around the fortified town. Weiss and Delaherche went to Bazeilles, a village near Sedan, to check the safety of property which they owned there. Weiss, caught in a battle which took place in the village, joined the French forces against the Prussians. Delaherche hastened back to Sedan. Maurice, in the meantime, experienced his first artillery barrage.

At Bazeilles the Prussians closed in on inferior French forces. Weiss, in his house, was joined by a small group of French soldiers and one civilian to make a last ditch stand. Captured, Weiss was put up against a wall to be shot. Henriette appeared, and despite her plea to be shot with her husband, she was pushed aside while the Prussians shot Weiss. Henriette, nearly out of her mind with grief, wandered about the field where the battle was still going on.

The 106th Regiment was decimated in a futile attempt to retake a strategic hill. When Jean was wounded, Maurice carried him to safety. Honoré Fouchard was killed at his gun. Napoleon had a white flag raised over a city roof, but it was torn down. Delaherche's factory was converted into a hospital, soon filled to overflowing with French wounded. Napoleon sent General Reille to the Prussians with a letter of capitulation.

Maurice, Jean, and several survivors of the 106th made their way into Sedan, where Maurice met Henriette and learned of Weiss' gallant death. They were engaged in a fight with Prussian Guards commanded by an officer whom Maurice recognized to be his cousin Gunther. Henriette kept Maurice from shooting Gunther.

By nightfall all had become silent except for the turmoil created by the movement of thousands of French troops into Sedan. The French were forced to accept the demands of Bismarck and Von Moltke.

The next day Silvine went out to the battlefield and recovered the body of Honoré. Henriette learned that Weiss' body had been consumed in fires started by the Prussians at Bazeilles.

The surrendered French soldiers were herded together to await deportation to Germany. A few French officers who promised never to take up arms again were released. In the camp men were murdered for filthy scraps of bread and spoiled horseflesh. Maurice, who no longer believed in anything, nearly lost control of himself. Jean, a cool veteran of previous campaigns, placed himself and Maurice among soldiers of a regiment leaving for Germany. At a stop along the way, Jean procured civilian clothes from a sympathetic French girl who was selling bread. The pair changed quickly inside a tent and escaped into a forest. When they came to a Prussian outpost, Jean was wounded by rifle fire, but they managed to escape and make their way back to old Fouchard's farm, where they found Henriette. Maurice went on to aid in the defense of Paris; Jean remained with Fouchard to be nursed back to health by Henriette.

The proclamation of the Second Republic was followed by the capitulation of Marshal Bazaine at Metz. Paris was invested by the Prussians while frantic attempts were made to organize new French armies in other parts of France.

Goliath, employed by the Prussians as a spy around Sedan, came to Silvine seeking her good graces. Upon her refusal, he threatened to expose Fouchard's connection with French partisans. When Goliath returned for his answer, two of the partisans, assisted by Silvine, killed him.

In Sedan Delaherche became friendly with Prussian Captain Von Gartlauben, who was billeted in the Delaherche house; he found the captain's friendship to be most advantageous in the matter of reëstablishing his textile works.

Jean, well again, joined the Army of the North. Maurice, meanwhile, took part in the defense of Paris. Sick of the Republic, he deserted after the capitulation of Paris and took a room near the boulevards. When the Commune took command in Paris and civil war broke out, Maurice joined the forces of the Commune to fight against the Republican forces, of which Jean's regiment was a part. The insurrectionists fired the city as they were pushed back. Maurice was bayoneted by Jean during night fighting in the streets. Jean disguised Maurice as a Republican soldier and took him to Maurice's lodgings, where Henriette, who had come to Paris to seek Maurice, was waiting. There Maurice passed the crisis safely, but a later hemorrhage killed him. Jean, broken-hearted at having been the cause of his friend's death, told Henriette goodbye, with the feeling that here was a pin-point of the desolation all France must know.

DRAGON SEED

Type of work: Novel
Author: Pearl S. Buck (1892-)
Type of plot: Social chronicle
Time of plot: World War II
Locale: China
First published: 1942

Principal characters:
LING TAN, a Chinese farmer
LING SAO, his wife
LAO TA,
LAO ER,
LAO SAN, and
PANSIAO, their children
ORCHID, Lao Ta's wife
JADE, Lao Er's wife
WU LIEN, Ling Tan's son-in-law
MAYLI, a mission teacher

Critique:

The plot of this novel as a social chronicle is swiftly paced and convincing until the appearance of Mayli; then the emphasis shifts to the rather improbable love affair of Mayli and Lao San. Background and character remain superior to plot. As a result, the reader absorbs an excellent impression of these people of an alien culture, through colorful details woven into the pattern of the narrative. *Dragon Seed* also tells what World War II meant to the Chinese peasantry.

The Story:

Ling Tan's family all lived together in his ancestral home. Besides Ling Tan and his wife, Ling Sao, there were three sons, Lao Ta, Lao Er, and Lao San, and a daughter, Pansiao. Lao Ta and his wife Orchid had two children. Lao Er and his wife Jade as yet had none.

Jade was a strange woman who cared little for the old rules and customs governing Chinese wives. Her free manners and frank tongue were an embarrassment to Lao Er, for the men chided him about it. Then, too, he felt as if he did not really understand his wife. One evening, after they had both heard how the Japanese had begun war in the north, they unburdened their hearts to each other, and Lao Er accepted the fact that he was married to a woman who was not like the others. He promised to go to the city and buy her a book so that she could learn what was happening in the world.

While Lao Er was in the city, he visited Wu Lien, a merchant who had married his older sister. Some Chinese students destroyed the Japanese merchandise that Wu Lien had for sale and branded him as a traitor. When Ling Sao heard this bad news, she too went to the city. Wu Lien was sick with worry over what had happened to him; he had also heard that the Japanese had landed on the coast nearby and were pushing inland. Ling Sao comforted him as well as she could and returned home.

The next morning Ling Tan was working in his fields when he saw Japanese aircraft approaching to bomb the city. He and the other farmers watched the planes, curious and unafraid. That night Wu Lien came to his father-in-law's house seeking refuge, for his shop had been hit by a bomb. Only then did Ling Tan's family learn the meaning of what had happened that day.

The next day Ling Tan and Lao San went to the city, where they were caught in the second air raid. Gravely, Ling Tan asked his family how they were going to resist this enemy. Lao Er and Jade said that they must go westward into the hills, for Jade was now with child. The rest of the family decided to stay and hold the ancestral land at all costs.

Streams of refugees passed along the road toward the west, and Lao Er and Jade joined a group of students who were moving their school inland. Lao Er promised to send word when the baby was born. Other students passed through the village and stopped to tell of the atrocities of the Japanese, but the simple farmers could not believe the stories they heard. After a month or so Ling Tan and his family could hear the roar of the Japanese guns as they approached the city. Chinese soldiers deserted to the hills, leaving the inhabitants at the mercy of the enemy. For a few days after the city was taken all was peaceful. Then some Japanese marched to the village and demanded wine and women. Ling Tan hid his family in the fields. The soldiers discovered Wu Lien's mother, who was too old and fat to flee. When they found no other women, they attacked her and killed her. Then they wrecked the house and left.

Since he knew now that no woman was safe from the Japanese, Ling Tan put all of the women of his family with the white missionary lady in the city. The men remained at the farm, except for Wu Lien. He returned to his shop in the city and advertised for Japanese business.

Meanwhile the soldiers came again to Ling Tan's house in search of women. When they found none, they attacked Lao San, the youngest son. Humiliated and filled with hatred, the boy left to join the hill people who were fighting the Japanese.

Wu Lien ingratiated himself with the conquerors and was appointed to a job in the new city government. He took his family from the mission and moved into spacious quarters provided by the Japanese.

Orchid grew bored in the mission. She thought that the city was quiet now and nothing could happen to her. One day she went for a walk. Five soldiers captured her and killed her while they satisfied their lust. When her body was returned to the mission, Ling Sao sent for Ling Tan and Lao Ta. She could no longer stay in the city. She returned to the farm with Ling Tan, Lao Ta, and the two children of Orchid and Lao Ta. Pansiao was sent westward to a mission school in the hills, where she would be safe.

A message from Lao Er announced that Jade had a son. Ling Tan sent for Lao Er and his family to come and help with the farm. Lao Er obeyed the summons, for he could be useful as a messenger between the village and the guerilla warriors in the hills. He and Jade made a secret cavern under the house where they could store arms for the villagers. Meanwhile the children of Lao Ta died of flux and fever. Despondent, he left for the hills to join Lao San. Ling Tan worked his farm as best he could and held back from the enemy as much grain as he dared.

Lao San and Lao Ta returned from the hills with rifles to hide in the secret cavern. Whenever there were no witnesses, the farmers killed Japanese soldiers and secretly buried them. Jade succeeded in poisoning many Japanese leaders at a great feast in the city. A cousin of Ling Tan went to the city and stole a radio from Wu Lien. Afterwards he was able to report to the people the progress of the war. The people took heart from the knowledge that there were others fighting the Japanese.

Lao San had become a ruthless killer and Ling Tan thought that he needed a spirited wife to tame him. Jade wrote to Pansiao, asking her to find a wife for Lao San among the girls at the mission. Pansiao told one of her teachers, the daughter of a Chinese ambassador, about her brother. This girl, Mayli, traveled to see Lao San for herself. The young people fell in love at first sight, but Mayli returned to the hills to wait for Lao San to come after her. Lao Ta also returned home with a new wife. Ling Tan's house was full again, for Jade gave birth to twin boys.

The hardships continued. Losing all hope of conquering the Japanese, Ling Tan began to brood. Then one day Lao Er took the old man to the city to hear the news from the hidden radio. They heard that England and the United States were now fighting on their side. Ling Tan wept for joy. Perhaps some day there would be an end to the war. Once again there was hope.

DRUMS

Type of work: Novel
Author: James Boyd (1888-1944)
Type of plot: Historical romance
Time of plot: American Revolution
Locale: North Carolina and London
First published: 1925

Principal characters:

SQUIRE FRASER, a North Carolina planter
MRS. FRASER, his wife
JOHN FRASER, their son
SIR NAT DUKINFIELD, a sportsman
CAPTAIN TENNANT, Collector of the Port at Edenton
EVE TENNANT, his daughter
WYLIE JONES, a plantation owner
PAUL JONES, a sailor
SALLY MERRILLEE, a neighbor of the Frasers

Critique:

In *Drums* the author attempted to reproduce the feelings and actions of all classes of Americans during the Revolution, and he accomplished his purpose admirably, sometimes, however, at the expense of the movement of the plot. The episodes at the race track and on the sea stand out in vividness above the rest of the action. The book is a pleasing mixture of history and adventure, with little emphasis upon character.

The Story:

John Fraser lived with his mother and father in the backwoods of North Carolina. Squire Fraser, a strict but kind Scotsman, was determined that his son should have a gentleman's education, and so he sent John to the coastal town of Edenton to be tutored by Dr. Clapton, an English clergyman.

There John made many friends. Sir Nat Dukinfield, a young rake, asked John to go riding with him one afternoon. They parted close friends. Through Dr. Clapton, John met Captain Tennant, the Collector of the Port at Edenton. Captain Tennant took John home with him and introduced him to Eve, his daughter, who overwhelmed John and embarrassed him with her coquettish manners. Captain Flood, a river boat skipper, was another of his friends. The old man taught him some sea lore and on his trips up and down the river acted as a messenger between John and his parents.

John went often to visit Captain Tennant and Eve. One evening two other gentlemen arrived at their house, Mr. Hewes, a shipbuilder, and Mr. Battle, a young lawyer. A bitter argument began among the gentlemen over the new tax on tea. Autumn came, and Squire Fraser sent for John to come home for a short vacation. Captain Flood took John up the river to Halifax. There he stayed overnight at the plantation of Wylie Jones, a rich young landowner.

After three years of schooling from Dr. Clapton, John became a young provincial gentleman. The only cloud on his horizon was the report of troubles with the British in Boston. Many people were angry; some predicted violence. But John thrust dark thoughts aside, for tomorrow was the day of the races. Sir Nat was to match his horse against a thoroughbred from Virginia. Everyone seemed to be excited over the holiday except Mr. Hewes, Mr. Battle, and Wylie Jones. The three sat apart at a table in the tavern and talked seriously among themselves while the rest of the company sang songs. At last Wylie Jones rose and announced that the ministers in Parliament had requested the king to declare the American Colonies in a state of rebellion.

The next day John rode to the races with Sir Nat; Eve was going with fat Master Hal Cherry, a repulsive boy, but rich. Sir Nat's horse was in perfect condition; his jockey, who had been drunk the night before, was not. He lost the first heat to the horse from Virginia. Then Sir Nat turned to John and asked him to ride. John rode the next two heats and won both of them. His friends celebrated the victory he had won for North Carolina.

Spring came. Sir Nat, putting no stock in rumors of war with the Colonies, volunteered for the English cavalry; he wanted to fight the French. The day after Sir Nat left for England, John learned of the battle fought at Lexington.

Squire Fraser sent a letter to his son with instructions to come home at once if British authority were overthrown at Edenton. John went to say goodbye to Captain Tennant and Eve, and then, following his father's instructions, he took leave of Dr. Clapton and went up the river with Wylie Jones. At Wylie's plantation he met Paul Jones, an adventurous seaman who had taken Wylie's last name. Mr. Battle, Paul Jones, and Wylie discussed a naval war against the British. They urged John to decide soon on which side he would be. He rode sadly home from Wylie's, but he brightened when he met Sally Merrillee, an old playmate. He suddenly decided that he liked her backwoods manners, so different from those of Eve Tennant. Later a company of militia camped on the Merrillee property, and the officers were billeted in Sally's house. John became angry at Sally's attentions to the militia officers and ceased courting her. Finally, Squire Fraser sent John to England to put the family money in a safe bank. John was happy at a chance for an honorable escape from his problem. But when he went to say goodbye to Sally, she had only contempt for him. Her brother had gone with the militia.

In London, John became the clerk of an importing firm and again met Eve and Captain Tennant. He received a letter from Wylie Jones, who asked him to deliver some money to Paul Jones' mother in Scotland. John was staying at an inn on the Scottish coast the night American sailors made a shore raid. Suddenly homesick for America, he went back with them to their ship. The captain was Paul Jones. Grateful for the favor John had done for him in Scotland, he signed John on as a crew member.

After a naval engagement, the ship anchored in the French harbor of Brest. Then came long months of waiting while Paul Jones tried to get a larger ship from the French. Sir Nat arrived from England to visit John. One evening the two became involved in a tavern brawl, and Sir Nat was killed. At last Paul Jones obtained another ship, the *Bonhomme Richard*.

The ship put to sea with a motley crew and captured several British merchant vessels. Then, in a running fight with the Baltic Fleet, John was wounded in the left elbow. No longer fit for active duty and still feverish from his wound, he sailed home to North Carolina on a Dutch ship. As soon as his arm had healed, he volunteered in the militia, but they wanted no stiff-armed men. He helped out Sally's mother on her farm. Sally had gone north to nurse her brother, who had smallpox. Mr. Merrillee had been killed in the war.

When Sally returned, John went to call on her. But when he tried to tell her that he loved her, she wept. Thinking she was rejecting his love, he left disconsolately. He volunteered again for the militia and was accepted. In a skirmish with British troops he was wounded a second time.

His arm now useless, John spent his days sitting on the front porch. One day Sally's mother came to call on him and scolded him for neglecting her daughter. Sally was in love with him; he had mistaken her reason for crying. John suddenly felt much better. He felt better still when his father heard that the British were retreating. As he sat on the porch, General Greene's victorious army passed along the road. John stumbled down to the fence and raised his stiff arm in an Indian salute as the last man of the rear guard came to the crest of a hill. The distant soldier, silhouetted against the sunset, raised his rifle over his head in answer. The war was over. In a few days he would be strong enough to visit Sally.

DRUMS ALONG THE MOHAWK

Type of work: Novel
Author: Walter D. Edmonds (1903-)
Type of plot: Historical chronicle
Time of plot: 1775-1783
Locale: The Mohawk Valley
First published: 1936

Principal characters:
GILBERT MARTIN, a young pioneer
MAGDELANA BORST MARTIN (LANA), his wife
MARK DEMOOTH, a captain of the militia
JOHN WOLFF, a Tory
BLUE BLACK, a friendly Oneida Indian
MRS. MCKLENNAR, Captain Barnabas McKlennar's widow
JOSEPH BRANT, an Indian chief
GENERAL BENEDICT ARNOLD
NANCY SCHUYLER, Mrs. Demooth's maid
JURRY MCLONIS, a Tory
HON YOST, Nancy's brother

Critique:

Drums Along the Mohawk depicts with great clarity the history of those stirring years from 1775 to 1783. Edmonds does not attempt a sweeping picture of the Revolutionary War. Instead, he shows how the times affected the farmers and residents of the Mohawk Valley in upstate New York. Realistically told, the novel gains added authenticity because its people, with some exceptions, actually lived during that period of American history. Edmonds lists his fictitious characters in an Author's Note.

The Story:

Magdelana Borst, the oldest of five daughters, married Gilbert Martin and together they started off from her home at Fox's Mill to settle farther west in their home at Deerfield. The time was July,

1776, and the spirit of the revolution was reaching into the Mohawk Valley, where settlers who sided with the rebels had already formed a company of militia commanded by Mark Demooth. Soon after he came to his new home Gil had to report for muster day. Some Indians had been seen in the vicinity. Also, the militia had decided to investigate the home of John Wolff, suspected of being a king's man. Finding evidence that a spy had been hidden on the Wolff farm, they arrested John Wolff, convicted him of aiding the British, and sent him to the Newgate Prison at Simsbury Mines.

A few months after their arrival at Deerfield, Gil decided to have a log-rolling to clear his land for farming. The Weavers, the Realls, and Clem Coppernol all came to help with the work. When they were about half finished, Blue Black, a friendly Oneida Indian, came to warn them that a raiding party of Seneca Indians and whites was in the valley. The settlers immediately scattered for home to collect the few movable belongings which they might save, and then drove to Fort Schuyler. Lana, who was pregnant, lost her baby as a result of the wild ride to the fort. The enemy destroyed the Deerfield settlement. All the houses and fields were burned; Gil's cow was killed, and Mrs. Wolff, who had refused to take refuge with the people who had sent her husband to prison, was reported missing. Gil and Lana rented a one-room cabin in which to live through the winter. With spring coming on and needing a job to support himself and Lana, Gil became the hired man of Mrs. McKlennar, a widow. The pay was forty-five dollars a year plus the use of a two-room house and their food.

General Herkimer tried to obtain a pledge of neutrality from the Indian chief, Joseph Brant, but was unsuccessful. At the end of the summer, word came that the combined forces of British and Indians, commanded by General St. Leger, were moving down from Canada to attack the valley. The militia was called up and set out westward to encounter this army. But the attack by the militia was badly timed and the party was ambushed. Of nearly six hundred and fifty men, only two hundred and fifty survived. The survivors returned in scattered groups. Gil received a bullet wound in the arm. General Herkimer, seriously injured in the leg, died of his wounds.

After the death of General Herkimer, General Benedict Arnold was sent out to reorganize the army and lead it in another attack—this time against General St. Leger's camp.

When Nancy Schuyler, Mrs. Demooth's maid, heard that her brother, Hon Yost, was in the neighborhood with a group of Tories, she decided to sneak out to see him. On the way she met another Tory, Jurry McLonis, who seduced her. Before she was able to see Hon, the American militia broke up the band. Hon was arrested but was later released when he agreed to go back to the British camp and spread false reports of the American strength. As a result of her meeting with Jurry McLonis, Nancy became pregnant. About that same time John Wolff escaped from the prison at Simsbury Mines and made his way to Canada to join Butler and to look for his wife.

The following spring brought with it General Butler's destructives, raiding parties that would swoop down to burn and pillage small settlements or farms. Mrs. Demooth tormented Nancy constantly because of her condition and one night frightened the girl so completely that Nancy, in terror, packed a few of her belongings in a shawl and ran away. Her only idea was to try to get to Niagara and find her brother Hon, but she had not gone far before labor pains overtook her and she bore her child beside a stream. An Indian found her there and took her with him as his wife. Lana had her child in May. The destruction by the raiding parties continued all through that summer, and the harvest was small. Mrs.

McKlennar's stone house was not burned, but there was barely enough food for her household that winter. In the spring Colonel Van Schaick came to the settlement with an army, and the militia headed west once again, this time to strike against the Onondaga towns.

Lana had her second child the following August. Because of the lack of food during the winter, she was still weak from nursing her first boy, Gilly, and after the birth of her second boy it took her a long while to recover. The next winter they all had enough to eat but the cold was severe. During that winter Mrs. McKlennar aged greatly and kept mostly to her bed. The destructives continued their raids through the next spring and summer. The men never went out to their fields alone; they worked in groups with armed guards. One day, after all the men had gone to the fort, Lana took the two boys for a walk and then sat down at the edge of a clearing and fell asleep. When she awoke, Gilly was gone. Two Indians were near the house. She put the baby, Joey, into a hiding place and then searched for Gilly. She found him at last and the two of them crawled into the hiding place also. Meanwhile the two Indians had entered the house and set it on fire. Overwhelmed by Mrs. McKlennar's righteous indignation, they carried out her bed for her. They fled when men, seeing the smoke, came hurrying from the fort. Gil and the two scouts, Adam Helmer and Joe Boleo, built a cabin to house them all during the coming winter.

With the spring thaws, a flood inundated the valley. As the waters receded, Marinus Willett came into the Mohawk Valley with his army, with orders to track down and destroy the British forces under General Butler. Butler's army already was having a difficult time, for British food supplies were running out and tracking wolves killed all stragglers. The militia finally caught up with Butler, harassed his army for several miles, killed Butler, and scattered the routed army in the wilderness. The Mohawk Valley was saved.

Three years later, the war over, Gil and Lana went back to their farm at Deerfield. They now had a baby girl and Lana and Gil felt content with their hard-won security, their home, their children, and each other.

THE DUCHESS OF MALFI

Type of work: Drama
Author: John Webster (1580-1638)
Type of plot: Romantic tragedy
Time of plot: Sixteenth century
Locale: Amalfi and Milan, Italy
First presented: c. 1613

Principal characters:
GIOVANNA, Duchess of Amalfi
ANTONIO, her second husband
FERDINAND, Duke of Calabria, jealous brother of the duchess
THE CARDINAL, another brother of the duchess
BOSOLA, the brothers' spy and executioner

Critique:

Webster's play is a blood-tragedy typical of the so-called decadent drama of the reign of James I of England. The melodrama of its scenes, however, is not enough to detract from the general dignity and tragedy of the play. A peculiarity of this play is that a year elapses between the first and second acts and another two years between the second and third acts, the passage of time made apparent to the audience by the birth of children to the duchess. As in most of the bloody tragedies, the setting is a Latin country.

The Story:

The Duchess of Malfi was a young widow whose two brothers, one a Cardinal and the other Ferdinand, the Duke of Calabria, were desperately jealous lest she marry again, for they planned to inherit her title and estates. Their spy in her household was Bosola, her master of horse.

In spite of the warnings of her brothers, the duchess fell in love with Antonio, her steward, and married him. Later, unknown to any person in the court except Antonio and Cariola, a servant girl, she had a child, a boy. Unfortunately, the happy father wrote out the child's horoscope according to the rules of astrology and then lost the paper. Bosola found the document and so learned about the duchess' child. He dispatched a letter immediately to Rome to inform the brothers. The duke swore that only her blood could quench his anger and threatened that once he knew for certain the duchess' lover, he would be content only with her complete ruin.

The years passed and the duchess bore Antonio two more children, a second son and a daughter. Antonio told his friend Delio that he was worried because Duke Ferdinand was too quiet about the matter and because the people of Malfi, not aware of their duchess' marriage, were calling her a common strumpet.

Duke Ferdinand had come to the court to propose Count Malateste as a second husband for the duchess. She refused. Meanwhile Bosola had not been able to discover the father of the duchess' children. Impatient with his informer, the duke decided on a bolder course of action. He determined to gain entrance to the duchess' private chamber, and there to wring a confession from her. That night, using a key Bosola had given him, the duke went to her bedroom. Under threats she confessed to her second marriage, but she refused to reveal Antonio's name. After the duke left, she called Antonio and Cariola to her chamber. They planned Antonio's escape from Malfi before his secret became known to the duchess' brothers.

The duchess called Bosola and told him that Antonio had falsified some accounts. As soon as Bosola left, she recalled Antonio and told him of the feigned crime of which she had accused him to shield both their honors, and then bade him flee to the town of Ancona, where they would meet later. In the presence of Bosola and the officers of her guard she again accused Antonio of stealing money, and banished him from Malfi. Antonio replied that such was the treatment of stewards of thankless masters, and then left for Ancona. The duped Bosola upheld Antonio in an argument with the duchess. She then felt that she could trust Bosola with the secret of her marriage, and she asked him to take jewels and money to her husband at Ancona. Bosola, in return, advised her to make her own departure from the court more seemly by going to Ancona by way of the shrine of Loretto, so that the flight might seem a religious pilgrimage.

Bosola immediately traveled from Malfi to Rome, where he betrayed the plans of Antonio and the duchess to Duke Ferdinand and the Cardinal. They had the lovers banished from Ancona.

Bosola met the duchess and Antonio near Loretto with a letter from Duke Ferdinand bidding Antonio report to him, since now he knew Antonio as his sister's husband. Antonio refused and fled with his oldest son toward Milan. After Antonio's departure, Bosola took the duchess back to her palace at Malfi, a prisoner by Duke Ferdinand's command. At Malfi the duke again visited her in her chamber. He presented her with a dead man's hand, implying that it was from Antonio's corpse. Finally Bosola came to the duchess and strangled her. Cariola and the children were also strangled, though not with the quiet dignity with which the duchess was murdered. When Bosola asked Duke Ferdinand for his reward, the hypocritical duke laughed and replied that the only reward for such a crime was its pardon.

In Milan, meanwhile, Antonio planned to visit the Cardinal's chamber during the night to seek a reconciliation with the duchess' brothers. He intended to approach the Cardinal because Duke Ferdinand had lost his mind after causing his sister's murder. The Cardinal ordered Bosola that same evening to seek out Antonio, who was known to be in Milan, and murder him. But when so ordered, Bosola accused the Cardinal of having plotted the duchess' murder and requested his reward. When a reward was again refused, Bosola swore to himself to join forces with Antonio to avenge the duchess' death.

That night all plans miscarried. In the dark Bosola accidentally murdered Antonio, the man he hoped to make an ally in his revenge on Duke Ferdinand and the Cardinal. A few minutes later, Bosola stabbed the Cardinal and was in turn stabbed by the mad Duke Ferdinand, who had rushed into the room. Bosola, with his last strength, stabbed the duke and they both died. Alarmed, the guards broke into the apartments to discover the bodies. Into the welter of blood a courtier led the young son of the Duchess of Malfi and Antonio, whom Antonio had taken to Milan. He was proclaimed ruler of the lands held by his mother and uncles.

THE DYNASTS

Type of work: Dramatic poem
Author: Thomas Hardy (1840-1928)
Type of plot: Historical epic
Time of plot: 1806-1815
Locale: Europe
First published: 1903-1908

Principal characters:
- NAPOLEON I
- JOSEPHINE, his first wife
- MARIE LOUISE, his second wife
- KING GEORGE III OF ENGLAND
- TSAR ALEXANDER OF RUSSIA
- EMPEROR FRANCIS OF AUSTRIA
- SIR WILLIAM PITT, Prime Minister of England
- SPIRIT OF YEARS,
- SHADE OF EARTH,
- SPIRIT OF PITIES,
- SPIRIT SINISTER, and
- SPIRIT IRONIC, allegorical figures

Critique:

Written in various types of verse and in poetic prose, *The Dynasts,* a vast epic-drama of the tragedy of Napoleon, marks Hardy's greatest effort to portray Man as completely subject to a disinterested Destiny. Among his manifold points of view, shifting from a point somewhere above the earth to the courts of emperors or the cottager's fireside, that of the rural folk of southern England is the most effective. Long prose stage directions fill out the historical perspective of this sweeping panoramic treatment of the constant turmoil in Europe from 1805 to 1815. The array of allegorical spectators who comment on the events of the drama as they occur, and Hardy's device of switching the point of view, tend to make strikingly trivial the alarums and excursions of earth-bound humanity.

The Story:

The Spirit of Years, Shade of Earth, Spirit Sinister, Spirit Ironic, Spirit of Pities, and their accompanying choruses, forgathered somewhere above the earth to watch the larger movements of men in western Europe in 1805. The design of the Immanent Will manifested itself at the time in Napoleon's preparations for the invasion of England.

Sir William Pitt, in England, contended with isolationist members of Parliament in order to secure proper defense against the invasion. Meanwhile Napoleon went to Milan to be crowned King of Italy. The spirits made light of the chicanery and pomp that attended the coronation. The Spirit of Pities descended to earth and disturbed Napoleon by reminding him of his original intention of championing liberty.

At sea, a Pyrrhic victory of the French and Spanish over the English prevented the support required for the planned invasion. On the south coast of England the Phantoms of Rumor caused great disturbance. A fleet of fishing craft was mistaken for the invasion fleet, and civilians fled from the coastal towns as signal fires flared upon the cliffs and hills.

When Napoleon learned that his admiral, Villeneuve, had returned to Cadiz, he discarded his invasion plan and moved eastward against Austria and Russia, countries which Pitt had enlisted in the English cause. The Spirit of Years remarked that the ensuing campaign would be a model in tactics for all time.

At Ulm, Napoleon defeated the Austrians, who had hoped in vain that the English fleet would hold the French forces in northern France. In London, Pitt, unsuccessful in gaining permission from the king to form a coalition government, visibly declined in health under his terrible burden.

Villeneuve was ordered out of Cadiz. The British under Nelson met the French and Spanish off Trafalgar and defeated them. Nelson was killed in the engagement; Villeneuve subsequently ended his own life in an inn at Rennes.

Napoleon defeated the Austrians and Russians at Austerlitz. Then, hearing of the English victory at Trafalgar, he declared his intention of closing all continental ports to English ships. He dictated peace terms to Emperor Francis of Austria while attendant Austrian officers stood by in disgust at the sight of a nobody dictating to true royalty. In Paris the Spirit of Rumor commented on the way Napoleon was uprooting old dynasties and founding new ones.

Pitt having died and King George III being mentally ill, England, in the person of Charles James Fox, negotiated with Napoleon for peace; but the emperor used the negotiations as a screen for his real plans. He marched on Prussia and defeated the Germans at the Battle of Jena. In Berlin he decreed that all British ships were barred from continental ports. Next, Napoleon and Tsar Alexander of Russia met at the River Niemen, where the two drew up a Franco-Russian alliance. During this meeting Napoleon expressed the desire to cement his various alliances with blood ties. The Spirit of Years remarked ironically that Napoleon was one of the few men who could see the working of the Immanent Will.

Napoleon invaded Spain as a friend to help the Spanish gain Portugal. The Spanish Bourbons abdicated and Napoleon's brother, Joseph, was proclaimed king. When Bourbon partisans enlisted English aid, an English invasion fleet sailed for Portugal.

Back in Paris, Napoleon told his wife, Josephine, that he wished a divorce. Josephine had borne the emperor no children and he was anxious to perpetuate the dynasty he had founded. The British invasion of the Iberian Peninsula drew the emperor to Spain to direct the campaign there. Preparation for war in Austria caused Napoleon next to invade that country and to defeat its forces at Wagram. The British, under the Duke of Wellington, held their own against the French in Spain. At that point the Spirit Sinister reminded the Spirit Ironic not to sneer for fear Immanent Will would cut short the comedy that was taking place.

A British force was sent to the Scheldt, but the expedition ended disastrously when the army was decimated by miasmal fever. Napoleon, fearful of assassination and still anxious to perpetuate his line, negotiated with the Russians for the hand of a Russian princess, and with the Austrians for the hand of Princess Marie Louise. The tsar accepted the offer, but Napoleon had already arranged, through Metternich, for a marriage with the Austrian princess, Marie Louise. The marriage was performed in the conspicuous absence of many high clergy, and the Russians, incensed, prepared for war. In the meantime the British in Spain under the Duke of Wellington gained a decisive victory at Albuera.

In due time Marie Louise gave birth to Napoleon's heir. The insane King of England died after hearing of British successes in Spain. On the continent war became imminent between France and Russia.

Again on the banks of the Niemen, Napoleon received an evil portent when he was thrown from his horse. The Spirit of Pities foresaw misery for the French Grand Army in the Russian campaign. Wellington in Spain defeated the French at Salamanca. Napoleon gained a costly victory over the Russians at Borodino, and the French entered Moscow to find the city deserted and in flames. There followed a general retreat by the French across snow-covered Russian steppes to Lithuania. Thousands perished from the cold or were killed by harassing Russian cavalry. Napoleon deserted his army and raced back to Paris in order to arrive there before the news of his failure in Russia. His chief task now was to hold his empire together.

As the British continued their successes in Spain, Austria joined the allies. Napoleon met defeat at the hands of the Austrians and Prussians at Leipzig. The allies invaded France. Napoleon, forced to abdicate, was exiled to Elba, an island in the Mediterranean. Marie Louise and the infant King of Italy went to Austria to stay. The Bourbons reassumed the throne of France and a congress to deliberate on general peace in Europe met in Vienna.

Napoleon escaped from Elba and returned to Paris at the head of an army he had picked up on his way. The allies outlawed Napoleon and prepared to overthrow him again.

A private ball in Brussels was broken up by the news that the French army was nearing the Belgian frontier. Almost overnight, Napoleon had organized and put into the field a large army. But he failed to separate the British and Prussians in Belgium, and he was brought to utter defeat on the fields south of Waterloo. The Hundred Days were ended.

The Spirit of Years pointed out to the Spirits assembled that the human beings below them behaved as though they were in a dream, as though they were puppets being drawn by strings manipulated by Immanent Will. The Spirit of Years pointed to Napoleon in defeat and compared him to a tiny insect on an obscure leaf in the chart of the Ages. When the Spirit of Pities asked for what purpose the events below had taken place, the Spirit of Irony answered that there was no purpose, for only a dumb thing turned the crank which motivated and directed human behavior.

EDMUND CAMPION

Type of work: Novelized biography
Author: Evelyn Waugh (1903-)
Type of plot: Historical chronicle
Time of plot: Sixteenth century
Locale: Oxford, London, Douai, Rome, Prague
First published: 1935

Principal characters:
EDMUND CAMPION, an English martyr
DR. WILLIAM ALLEN, head of the English College at Douai
ROBERT PERSONS, Campion's classmate at Oxford
GEORGE ELIOT, a priest-hunter

Critique:

This book is an intelligent, sober, and admirably written biography of a man dear to the hearts of Anglo-Saxon Catholics. Evelyn Waugh has written a fine impressionistic portrait of the English martyr after whom Campion Hall at Oxford was named. Waugh warns that intolerance is a growing evil in our modern world, and martyrs may again be forced to die for their faith.

The Story:

Edmund Campion, born in 1540, was one of the most promising young men at Oxford. When Elizabeth visited the university in 1566, she was so impressed by him that she assured him of her patronage. Although there was a strong Protestant group in the university, Oxford then had a population of students who were mostly Catholic in religion, for laws against Catholics were not rigidly enforced. Campion, who as proctor held a responsible position, was suspected of Catholicism, however, and was asked to make a public declaration of his principles by delivering a sermon in a suitable church. He refused, and when his term was over he left for Dublin, where he was warmly received by the Stanihurst family. A university was to be built in Dublin, and he was waiting to accept a post on its faculty. Then rebellion threatened, and all Catholics were ordered arrested. Campion managed to escape and make his way to Douai and the English College there.

The mild restrictions against Catholics turned into persecution when the Pope issued a Bull of Excommunication against Queen Elizabeth. Because of the fear of a French-Spanish alliance against England, the Bull caused grave anxiety in England and led to reprisals against Catholics. It became illegal to hear mass, to harbor a priest, or openly to profess Catholicism.

With the Catholic bishops imprisoned, thereby preventing the ordination of priests, and with all Catholic schools closed, the faith began to die out in England. The college at Douai sent young English priests into England to preserve the faith of the English Catholics.

Campion went to Douai and became a priest. Then he announced his intention of going to Rome and entering the Society of Jesus. Although Dr. Allen, the venerable head of the college, did not like to lose him to the Jesuits, he made no objection to Campion's plans. Admitted into the Society, Campion was sent to Bohemia, where he held important posts at the University of Prague.

Dr. Allen wrote Campion a letter informing him that he was to go to England. He and a few others, including Robert Persons, who had been an undergraduate at Oxford during the time of Campion's proctorship, were to be smuggled into England, there to carry on the work of the Church. They all realized that capture meant certain death. Campion demanded that Persons be made his superior before the group departed. Though the English government had learned of the group's intentions and had all the ports guarded, the priests succeeded in getting into England.

In disguise, Campion visited the homes of various Catholics, where he said mass and brought the sacraments to the faithful who had been long without them. He wrote his famous *Campion's Brag,* a defense of himself and his Church, which the best minds of the Anglican Church were called upon to answer. Persons wrote his own *Censure* of the Anglican reply. Later Campion wrote his equally famous *Ten Reasons.*

Persecution grew more intense, with Campion the prize the government most hoped to capture. During one of his tours Campion was persuaded to stop at Lyford Grange, the home of Mr. Yate, a well-known Catholic. He stayed there briefly, warning everyone not to tell the neighbors of his presence. After his departure some neighbors heard of his visit and were distressed that they had missed the visit of Father Campion. Father Ford was sent after him and reluctantly Campion returned.

A certain George Eliot, a professional priest-hunter, stopped at Lyford Grange. He was informed by a servant, who presumed Eliot to be Catholic, that Father Campion was there. He was shown into the room where Campion was saying mass. After receiving communion from Campion, Eliot went to notify the authorities. They came at once, but all evidence of the mass had been destroyed and the priests had been hidden behind a secret panel. The guards found nothing and were preparing to go when one of the searchers happened to tap a hollow-sounding portion of the wall. The priests were discovered in a secret room.

Months of imprisonment followed. Four conferences were held at which Campion and the Anglican clergy disputed points of doctrine. Campion was tortured and finally brought to trial with some other prisoners who were charged with having plotted to murder Queen Elizabeth and with conspiring with foreign powers. But Campion insisted that their only crime was their faith. They were tried by a court that was absolutely biased. Found guilty, they were sentenced to die by hanging, and their bodies to be drawn and quartered. Father Campion and the others went to the scaffold and died the death of martyrs on December first, 1581.

THE EDUCATION OF HENRY ADAMS

Type of work: Novelized autobiography
Author: Henry Adams (1838-1918)
Type of plot: Intellectual and social history
Time of plot: 1838-1905
Locale: America, England, France
First published: 1907

Principal characters:
HENRY ADAMS, an American
CHARLES FRANCIS ADAMS, his father
JOHN HAY, his friend
CLARENCE KING, whom he admired

Critique:

The theme of *The Education of Henry Adams* is the process of multiplication and acceleration of mechanical forces which, during his own lifetime, led to the breakdown of moral relationships between men and the degeneration of their pursuits into money-seeking or complete lassitude. The book is, too, an excellent autobiography, tracing Adams' thought processes intimately, and on an intellectual plane not generally achieved by most writers. Both for style and content this book ranks with the finest of American autobiographies.

The Story:

Henry Brooks Adams was born of the union of two illustrious Massachusetts families, the Brookses and the Adamses, and he was, in addition, the grandson and the great-grandson of presidents. His wealth and social position should have put him among the leaders of his generation.

Although the period of mechanical invention had begun in 1838, Henry Adams was raised in a colonial atmosphere. He remembered that his first serious encounter with his grandfather, John Quincy Adams, occurred when he refused to go to school, and that gentleman led him there by the hand. For Henry Adams, the death of the former president marked the end of his eighteenth-century environment.

Charles Francis Adams, Henry's father, was instrumental in forming the Free-Soil party in 1848, and he ran on its ticket with Martin Van Buren. Henry considered that his own education was chiefly a heritage from his father, an inheritance of Puritan morality and interest in politics and literary matters. In later life, looking back on his formal education, he concluded that it had been a failure. Mathematics, French, German, and Spanish were needed in the world in which he found himself an adult, not Latin and Greek. He had opportunity to observe the use of force in the violence with which the people of Boston treated the anti-slavery Wendell Phillips, and he had seen Negro slaves restored to the South.

Prompted by his teacher, James Russell Lowell, he spent nearly two years abroad after his graduation from college. He enrolled to study civil law in Germany, but finding the lecture system atrocious he devoted most of his stay to enjoying the paintings, the opera, the theater in Dresden.

When he returned to Boston in 1860, Henry Adams settled down briefly to read Blackstone. In the elections that year, however, his father became a Congressman, and Henry accompanied him to the capitol as his secretary. There he met John Hay, who was to become his best friend.

In 1861 President Lincoln named Charles Francis Adams Minister to England. Henry went with his father to Europe. The Adams party had barely disembarked when they were met by bad news. England had recognized the belligerency of the Confederacy. The North was her undeclared enemy. The battle of Bull Run proved so crushing a blow to American prestige that Charles Francis Adams felt he was in England on a day-to-day sufferance. The Trent Affair and the second battle of Bull Run were equally disastrous abroad. Finally, in 1863, the tide began to turn. Secretary Seward sent Thurlow Weed and William Evarts to woo the English, and they were followed by announcements of victories at Vicksburg and Gettysburg. Charles Francis Adams remained in England until 1868, for Andrew Johnson had too many troubles at home to make many diplomatic changes abroad.

At the end of the war Henry Adams had no means of earning a livelihood. He had, however, developed some taste as a dilletante in art, and several of his articles had been published in the *North American Review*. On his return to America, Henry Adams was impressed by the fact that his fellow-countrymen, because of the mechanical energy they had harnessed, were all traveling in the same direction. Europeans, he had felt, were trying to go in several directions at one time. Handicapped by his education and by his long absence from home, he had difficulty in adapting himself to the new industrial America. He achieved some recognition with his articles on legal tender and his essays in the *Edinburgh Review,* and he hoped that he might be offered a government position if Grant were elected president. But Grant, a man of action, was not interested in reformers or intellectuals like Henry Adams.

In 1869 Adams went back to Quincy to begin his investigation of the scandals of the Grant administration, among them Jay Gould's attempts to obtain a corner on gold, Senator Charles Sumner's efforts to provoke war with England by compelling her cession of Canada to the United States, and the rivalries of Congressmen and Cabinet members.

He decided it would be best to have his article on Gould published in England, to avoid censorship by the powerful financier. Gould's influence was not confined to the United States, however, and Adams was refused by two publications. His essay on Gould was finally published by the *Westminster Review.*

Adams became assistant professor of Medieval History at Harvard and taught at Cambridge for seven years. During that time he tried to abandon the lecture system by replacing it with individual research. He found his students apt and quick to respond, but he felt that he needed a stone against which to sharpen his wits. He gave up his position in 1871 and went west to Estes Park with a Government Geological Survey. There he met Clarence King, a member of the party, with whom he could not help contrasting himself. King had a systematic, scientific education and could have his choice of scientific, political, or literary prizes. Adams felt his own limitations.

After his flight from Harvard he made his permanent home in Washington, where he wrote a series of books on American history. In 1893 he visited the Chicago Exhibition. From his observations of the steamship, the locomotive, and the newly-invented dynamo, he concluded that force was the one unifying factor in American thought. Back in Washington, he saw the gold standard adopted, and concluded that the capitalistic system and American intervention in Cuba offered some signs of the direction in which the country was heading. During another visit to the Exhibition in 1900 Adams formulated an important theory. In observing the dynamo, he decided that history is not merely a series of causes and effects, of men acting upon men, but the record of forces acting upon men. For him, the dynamo became the symbol of force acting upon his own time as the Virgin had been the symbol of force in the twelfth century.

During the next five years Henry Adams saw his friends drop away. Clarence King was the first to go. He lost his fortune in the panic of 1893 and died of tuberculosis in 1901. John Hay, under McKinley, became American Minister to England, and then Secretary of State. He was not well when he accepted the President's appointments, and the enormous task of bringing England, France, and Germany into accord with the United States, and of attempting to keep peace, unsuccessfully, between Russia and Japan, caused his death in 1905.

Adams considered that his education was continuous during his lifetime. He had found the tools which he had been given as a youth utterly useless and he had to spend all of his days forging new ones. As he grew older, he found the moral standards of his father's and grandfather's times disintegrating, so that corruption and greed existed on the highest political levels. According to his calculations, the rate of change, due to mechanical force, was accelerating, and the generation of 1900 could rely only on impersonal forces to teach the generation of 2000. He himself could see no end to the multiplicity of forces which were so rapidly dwarfing mankind into insignificance.

THE EGOIST

Type of work: Novel
Author: George Meredith (1828-1909)
Type of plot: Social satire
Time of plot: Nineteenth century
Locale: England
First published: 1879

Principal characters:
SIR WILLOUGHBY PATTERNE, the egoist
VERNON WHITFORD, his cousin
COLONEL DE CRAYE, his relative
LAETITIA DALE, a neighbor
CLARA MIDDLETON, Sir Willoughby's betrothed
DOCTOR MIDDLETON, her father
CROSSJAY PATTERNE, Sir Willoughby's distant kinsman

Critique:

The Egoist creates a fantastic world where, in scenes of subtle comedy, the characters are treated realistically. The effect is one of drollery. Each character is a symbol of some virtue or vice rather than a living individual. All the characters speak alike, and they speak the language of Meredith. This novel stands apart from Meredith's other novels, distinguished as it is by its originality of technique and purpose. It is, to use Meredith's own term, "a comedy in narrative."

The Story:

On the day of his majority Sir Willoughby Patterne announced his engagement to Miss Constantia Durham. Laetitia Dale, who lived with her old father in a cottage on Willoughby's estate, bore her love for him—she thought—secretly, but everyone, including Willoughby himself, knew about it. Ten days before the wedding day Constantia astonished her betrothed by eloping with Harry Oxford, a military man. For a few weeks after that, the proud Willoughby courted Laetitia while the neighborhood gossiped about the poor girl's chances to become his wife. There was great disappointment when he suddenly decided to go abroad for three years. On his return to his estate he brought with him his cousin, Vernon Whitford, as an adviser in the management of his properties, and a young distant kinsman named Crossjay Patterne.

At first Laetitia, the faithful, was overjoyed at Willoughby's return, but soon she saw that again she was to lose him, for he became engaged to Clara Middleton, the daughter of a learned doctor. Middleton and his daughter came to Willoughby's estate to visit for a few weeks. It might have been the controversy over Crossjay or even the existence of Laetitia that caused Clara to see Willoughby for what he really was. In spite of Willoughby's objections, Vernon wanted Crossjay to enter the Marines and the young man was sent to Laetitia to be tutored for his examination. Vernon, a literary man, wanted to go to London, but Willoughby overruled him. Noting Willoughby's self centered attitude toward Crossjay, his complete and selfish concern with matters affecting himself and his attempt to dominate her own mind, Clara began to feel trapped by her betrothal. She reflected that Constantia had escaped by finding a gallant Harry Oxford to take her away, but she sorrowfully realized that she had no one to rescue her.

When Clara attempted to break her engagement, she found Willoughby intractable and her father too engrossed in his studies to be disturbed. Meanwhile, Willoughby had picked Laetitia Dale as Vernon's wife. This was Willoughby's plan to keep near him both his cousin and the woman who fed his ego with her devotion. Vernon could retire to one of the cottages on the estate and write and study. Asked by Willoughby to aid him in his plan, Clara took the opportunity to ask Vernon's advice on her own problem. He assured her that she must move subtly and slowly.

In desperation, she persuaded Doctor Middleton to agree to take a trip to France with her for a few weeks. From such a trip she hoped never to return to Willoughby. But this wary lover introduced Dr. Middleton to his favorite brand of claret. Two bottles of the wine put the doctor in such an amiable mood that when Clara asked him if he were ready to go to London with her, he told her that the thought was preposterous. Willoughby had won the first round.

Colonel De Craye arrived to be best man at the wedding. Little by little he sensed that Clara was not happy at the prospect of her approaching marriage. In desperation Clara resorted to other means of escape. She wrote to her friend Lucy Darleton in town and received from that young lady an invitation to visit her in London.

Clara gave Crossjay the privilege of accompanying her to the train station. A hue and cry was raised at her absence from the estate, and Vernon, accidentally discovering her destination, followed her to the station and urged her to come back. Only because she believed that her behavior might cause an injury to Crossjay's future did Clara return to her prison. If she were to leave now, Willoughby would have full control of the young boy, for Vernon was soon to go to London to follow his writing career.

Complications resulted from Clara's attempted escape. At the station Vernon had had her drink some brandy to overcome the effects of the rainy weather. The neighborhood began to gossip. Willoughby confronted Crossjay, who told him the truth about Clara's escape. Clara hoped that Willoughby would release her because of the gossip, but he refused. Doctor Middleton seemed ignorant of what was happening. He was determined that his daughter should fulfill her pledge to marry Sir Willoughby. Furthermore, he liked Willoughby's vintage wines and Willoughby's estate.

By this time the Egoist knew that his marriage to Clara would not take place. He decided upon the one move that would soothe his wounded vanity—he asked Laetitia to become his wife. She refused, declaring she no longer loved him.

Colonel De Craye shrewdly surmised what had happened. He told Clara the hopeful news. Clara felt that her only remaining obstacle was her father's insistence that she must not break her promise to Willoughby. Now she could show that Willoughby had broken his promise first by proposing to Laetitia while he was still pledged to Clara.

Willoughby's world blew up in his face. Dr. Middleton announced firmly that Clara need not marry Willoughby. He had decided that he admired Vernon's scholarship more than he liked Willoughby's wines. But the twice-jilted lover had other plans for his own protection. He must even the score. If he could get Clara to consent to marry Vernon, he felt there would be some measure of recompense for himself, for such a marriage would have the ironic touch to satisfy Willoughby. But Clara told him it was already her intention to wed Vernon as soon as her engagement to Willoughby could be broken. The Egoist's selfishness and arrogance had brought them together.

The Egoist was defeated. He went straight to Laetitia, offering her his hand without love. He was willing for her to marry him only for money. Laetitia accepted on the condition that Crossjay be permitted to enter the Marines. Clara and the doctor planned to leave for Europe. Vernon arranged to meet them in the Swiss Alps, where he and Clara would marry.

ELECTRA

Type of work: Drama
Author: Euripides (480-406 B.C.)
Type of plot: Classical tragedy
Time of plot: After the fall of Troy
Locale: Argos
First presented: c. 413 B.C.

Principal characters:
ELECTRA, daughter of Agamemnon
ORESTES, her brother
CLYTEMNESTRA, her mother
AEGISTHUS, lover of Clytemnestra

Critique:

The *Electra* of Euripides is a psychological study of a woman's all-consuming hatred for her mother and stepfather on the one hand, and love for her murdered father and exiled brother on the other. The character of Electra clearly dominates the action, for it is she who spurs her brother on to kill those whom she hates. In Electra, her brother, and her mother, Euripides created three characters who are as alive today as they were on the Athenian stage.

The Story:

After Agamemnon, King of Argos, had returned home from the Trojan War, his wife, Clytemnestra, and her lover, Aegisthus, murdered him in cold blood during the home-coming banquet. Afterward Aegisthus and Clytemnestra were married, and Aegisthus became king. Orestes, young son of Agamemnon, was sent by a relative to Phocis before Aegisthus could destroy him. Electra, the daughter, remained, but was given in marriage to an old peasant, lest she marry a warrior powerful enough to avenge her father's death.

One day, after Electra and the peasant had gone out to do the day's work, Orestes came in disguise with his best friend, Pylades, to the farm to seek Electra. They heard her singing a lament for her lot and for the death of her father. A messenger interrupted her lament with word that a festival would be held in honor of the Goddess Hera and that all Argive maidens were to attend. Electra said she preferred to remain on the farm away from the pitying eyes of the people of Argos. The messenger advised her to pay honor to the gods and to ask their help.

Electra mistook Orestes and Pylades for friends of her brother and told them the story of her grief. She urged that Orestes avenge the death of Agamemnon and the ill treatment of himself and Electra. Aegisthus, meanwhile, had offered a reward for the death of Orestes.

The peasant returned from his work and asked Orestes and Pylades to remain as his guests. Electra sent her husband to bring the relative who had taken Orestes away from Argos. On his way to the peasant's cottage, the old foster father noticed that a sacrifice had been made at the tomb of Agamemnon and that there were some red hairs on the grave. He suggested to Electra that Orestes might be in the vicinity, but Electra answered that there was no chance of his being in Argos. When Orestes came out of the cottage, the old man recognized a scar on his forehead; thus brother and sister were made known to each other.

At the advice of the old peasant, Orestes planned to attend a sacrificial feast over which Aegisthus would preside. Electra sent her husband to tell Clytemnestra that she had given birth to a baby. Electra and Orestes invoked the aid of the gods in their venture to avenge the death of their father.

Orestes and Pylades were hailed by

Aegisthus as they passed him in his garden. The pair told Aegisthus that they were from Thessaly and were on their way to sacrifice to Zeus. Aegisthus informed them that he was preparing to sacrifice to the nymphs and invited them to tarry. At the sacrifice of a calf, Orestes plunged a cleaver into Aegisthus' back while Aegisthus was examining the entrails of the beast. Orestes then revealed his identity to the servants, who cheered the son of their former master. Orestes carried the corpse of Aegisthus back to the cottage where it was hidden after Electra had reviled it.

At the sight of Clytemnestra approaching the peasant's hut, Orestes had misgivings about the plan to murder her. He felt that matricide would bring the wrath of the gods upon his head. But Electra, determined to complete the revenge, reminded Orestes that an oracle had told him to destroy Aegisthus and Clytemnestra.

Clytemnestra defended herself before Electra with the argument that Agamemnon had sacrificed Iphegenia, their child, as an offering before the Trojan venture and that he had returned to Argos with Cassandra, princess of Troy, as his concubine. Electra indicted her mother on several counts and said that it was only just that she and Orestes murder Clytemnestra. The queen entered the hut to prepare a sacrifice for Electra's supposed first-born; within, she was killed by Orestes, who moaned in distress at the violence and bloodshed and matricide in which the gods had involved him.

The Dioscuri, twin sons of Zeus and brothers of the half-divine Clytemnestra, appeared to the brother and sister, who were overcome with mixed feelings of hate and love and pride and shame at what they had done. The twin gods questioned the wisdom of Apollo, whose oracle had advised this violent action; they decreed that Orestes should give Electra to Pylades in marriage and that Orestes himself should be pursued by the Furies until he could face a trial in Athens, from which trial he would emerge a free man.

THE EMIGRANTS

Type of work: Novel
Author: Johan Bojer (1872-)
Type of plot: Regional romance
Time of plot: Late nineteenth century
Locale: Norway and the American West
First published: 1925

Principal characters:
Erik Foss, an emigrant leader
Ola Vatne, a laborer
Else, his wife
Morten Kvidal, a joiner
Kal Skaret, a crofter
Karen, his wife
Per Föll, a young workman
Anne, his wife
Bergitta, Morten's wife; Anne's sister

Critique:

The Emigrants is a saga of the Norwegians who settled the wheat lands of the Dakotas. Bojer is well qualified for his subject. A Norwegian, he knows the stock from which our prairie pioneers came, and his visits to America have made him familiar with the American scene. The result is a lasting novel, an

American story written in Norwegian. It is a vital part of our cultural heritage.

The Story:

Erik Foss came back to Norway after some time spent working in America, and to the cramped, class-conscious farmers and laborers of his Norwegian countryside he held out hope for a more free and generous life in the new country. Many resolved to join his party of emigrants to America.

There was Ola, the colonel's hired boy. Ola had a way with people, especially with girls, and Else, the colonel's daughter, looked on him with eager eyes. But Ola was poor and the stories about him did not please the colonel. After his dismissal from the farm, Ola set fire to the barn. He spent a year in prison and came out in time to join the emigrants. Else came too, as Ola's wife. There was Per Föll, a big, hulking man and his new wife, Anne, the most attractive girl in the parish, already carrying a baby who was to be born too soon after her marriage. There were Kal Skaret and Karen, a kindly and slow-moving couple. The tax collector took their only cow when they could not pay even the previous year's taxes. There was Morten Kvidal, a skilled joiner.

When the steamer left, the little band sorrowed to leave Norway. But Erik was strong and he knew the way and he had enough money to help them.

That first summer the emigrants reached Wisconsin. They stayed there during the bleak winter, the men working in the sawmills to add to their meager funds. Early the next spring, they started out across the prairie. Erik had been to the Red River Valley before; he had tested the soil and knew it was good. The settlers had wagons and oxen, now, and all their supplies.

Erik said they had arrived when they came to a vast level land covered with a six-foot stand of grass.

Kal took the quarter farthest to the west. There he swung his scythe in sweeping strokes. The children and Karen piled the fodder, enough to feed a cow all winter! Now he would plow. Morten took no heed of the buffalo grass; he set his great breaking plow and turned it under. They built their homes from the grass, too, piling squares of turf for their sod houses.

That summer there was drought and the wheat crop was poor. Ola went into town with one of the loads, and gambled and drank up all his money. Without the help of the others, Ola and Else would never have survived the winter. During a blizzard Erik's feet were frostbitten while he hunted his strayed stock. When gangrene set in, Morten made the long trip to town on skis; but he returned too late with medicine for the sick man.

After Erik's death, the leadership of the small band fell to Morten. Good times and bad followed.

Per thought long and bitterly about Anne, for he could never forget that his first-born boy had come into the world too soon after his marriage. When Morten's young brother visited his house too frequently, Per began to roam the prairie. They had to tie him finally and take him to the madhouse, leaving Anne with her children and a sense of sin.

Although well established, Morten felt compelled to go back to Norway. When he returned to Dakota, he brought with him a wife, Bergitta, Anne's sister. He became an agent for the new railroad. He said that the people should have their own bank and grain elevators so that they would not be at the mercy of speculators. The Norwegians became Americans. At a party they put up an American flag beside the Norwegian banner.

Kal and Karen built outbuildings of wood, and each son took up another quarter. Before long Kal's fields stretched to the horizon, and he had to ride from one wheat planting to the other. When the steam thresher came, an army of laborers piled up the mounds of grain;

it poured too fast to cart away. In his machine shed, in a tiny strong room, Kal stored wheat, so that his family would never be hungry. Under his bed, in his emigrant chest, he kept his money. He and Karen were proud on the day their son came back from school in St. Louis and preached in their own church.

Morten grew old. He still acted for the railroad; he ran the bank; he was elder of the church; he put up buildings for the growing town. Bergitta died. A lamp exploded in Morten's face, blinding him. Now his grandson read to him. The old man thought of Norway often. He went back, blind and old, to his home. His people were dead; only the old land remained. It must be like that, he realized. The old settlers are a part Norwegian always, but their children belong to the new world.

EMMA

Type of work: Novel
Author: Jane Austen (1775-1817)
Type of plot: Social comedy
Time of plot: Early nineteenth century
Locale: Surrey, England
First published: 1816

Principal characters:

EMMA WOODHOUSE, heiress of Hartfield
MR. WOODHOUSE, her father
HARRIET SMITH, Emma's protégée
MISS BATES, the village gossip
JANE FAIRFAX, Miss Bates' niece
MR. GEORGE KNIGHTLEY, Emma's brother-in-law
MRS. WESTON, Emma's former governess
FRANK CHURCHILL, stepson of Emma's former governess
MR. ELTON, a rector
ROBERT MARTIN, a yeoman

Critique:

The major problem in the world of Jane Austen's novels is that of getting the characters properly married, and *Emma* is no exception. Its plot is concerned with the complications taking place before the couples are paired off correctly, and with Emma's sometimes unwise attempts to help things along. She is perhaps a less generally appealing heroine than Elizabeth Bennet in *Pride and Prejudice,* but she is excellently done, as are her father and the rest of the Highbury circle. Miss Bates and Mrs. Elton remain unsurpassed in English satire.

The Story:

Emma Woodhouse, rich, clever, beautiful, and no more spoiled and self-satisfied than one would expect under such circumstances, had just seen her friend, companion, and ex-governess, Miss Taylor, married to a neighboring widower, Mr. Weston. While the match was suitable in every way, Emma could not help sighing over her loss, for now only she and her father were left at Hartfield and Mr. Woodhouse was too old and too fond of worrying about trivialities to be a companion for his daughter.

The Woodhouses were the great family in the village of Highbury. In their small circle of friends there were enough middle-aged ladies to make up card tables for Mr. Woodhouse but no young lady to be friend and confidante to Emma. Lonely for her beloved Miss Taylor, now Mrs. Weston, Emma took under her wing Harriet Smith, the parlor boarder at a nearby boarding-school. Harriet was an extremely pretty girl of seventeen, not in the least brilliant, but with pleasing, unassuming manners, and a gratifying habit of looking up to Emma as a paragon.

Harriet was the natural daughter of some mysterious person, and Emma, believing that the girl might be of noble family, persuaded her that the society in which she had moved was not good enough for her. She encouraged her to give up her acquaintance with the Martin family, respectable farmers of some substance though of no fashion. Instead of thinking of Robert Martin as a husband for Harriet, Emma influenced the girl to aspire to Mr. Elton, the young rector.

Emma believed from Mr. Elton's manner that he was beginning to fall in love with Harriet, and she flattered herself upon her matchmaking schemes. Mr. Knightley, brother of a London lawyer married to Emma's older sister and one of the few people who could see Emma's faults, was concerned about her intimacy with Harriet. He warned her that no good could come of it for either Harriet or herself, and he was particularly upset when he learned that Emma had influenced Harriet to turn down Robert Martin's proposal of marriage. Emma herself suffered from no such qualms, for she was certain that Mr. Elton was as much in love with Harriet as Harriet—through Emma's instigation—was with him.

Emma suffered a rude awakening when Mr. Elton, finding her alone, asked her to marry him. She suddenly realized that what she had taken for gallantries to Harriet had been meant for herself, and what she had intended as encouragement to his suit of her friend, he had taken as encouragement to aspire for Emma's hand. His presumption was bad enough, but the task of breaking the news to Harriet was much worse.

Another disappointment now occurred in Emma's circle. Frank Churchill, who had promised for months to come to see his father and new stepmother, again put off his visit. Churchill, Mr. Weston's son by a first marriage, had taken the name of his mother's family. Mr. Knightley believed that the young man now felt himself above his father. Emma argued with Mr. Knightley, but she found herself secretly agreeing with him.

Although the Hartfield circle was denied Churchill's company, it did acquire an addition in the person of Jane Fairfax, niece of the garrulous Miss Bates. Jane rivaled Emma in beauty and accomplishment, one reason why, as Mr. Knightley hinted, Emma had never been friendly with Jane. Emma herself blamed Jane's reserve for their somewhat cool relationship.

Soon after Jane's arrival, the Westons received a letter from Churchill setting another date for his visit. This time he actually appeared, and Emma found him a handsome, well-bred young man. He called frequently upon the Woodhouses, and also upon the Bates family, because of prior acquaintance with Jane Fairfax. Emma rather than Jane was the recipient of his gallantries, however, and Emma could see that Mr. and Mrs. Weston were hoping that the romance would prosper.

About this time Jane Fairfax received the handsome gift of a pianoforte, anonymously given. It was presumed to have come from some rich friends with whom Jane, an orphan, had lived, but Jane herself seemed embarrassed with the present and refused to discuss it. Emma wondered if it had come from Mr. Knightley, after Mrs. Weston pointed out to her his seeming preference and concern for Jane. Emma could not bear to think of Mr. Knightley's marrying Jane Fairfax, and after observing them together, she concluded to her own satisfaction that he was motivated by friendship, not love.

It was now time for Frank Churchill to end his visit, and he departed with seeming reluctance. During his last call at Hartfield, he appeared desirous of telling Emma something of a serious nature; but she, believing him to be on the verge of a declaration of love, did not encourage him because in her daydreams she always saw herself refusing him and their love ending in quiet friendship.

Mr. Elton returned to the village with a hastily wooed and wedded bride, a lady of small fortune, extremely bad manners, and great pretensions to elegance. Harriet, who had been talked into love by Emma, could not be so easily talked out of it; but what Emma had failed to accomplish, Mr. Elton's marriage had, and Harriet at last began to recover. Her recovery was aided by Mr. Elton's rudeness to her at a ball. When he refused to dance with her, Mr. Knightley, who rarely danced, offered himself as a partner, and Harriet, without Emma's knowledge, began to think of him instead of Mr. Elton.

Emma herself began to think of Churchill as a husband for Harriet, but she resolved to do nothing to promote the match. Through a series of misinterpretations, Emma thought Harriet was praising Churchill when she was really referring to Mr. Knightley.

The matrimonial entanglement was further complicated because Mrs. Weston continued to believe that Mr. Knightley was becoming attached to Jane Fairfax. Mr. Knightley, in his turn, saw signs of some secret agreement between Jane Fairfax and Frank Churchill. His suspicions were finally justified when Churchill confessed to Mr. and Mrs. Weston that he and Jane had been secretly engaged since October. The Westons' first thought was for Emma, for they feared that Churchill's attentions to her might have had their effect. Emma assured Mrs. Weston that she had at one time felt some slight attachment to Churchill, but that that time was now safely past. Her chief concerns now were that she had said things about Jane to Churchill which she would not have said had she known of their engagement, and also that she had, as she believed, encouraged Harriet in another fruitless attachment.

When she went to break the news gently to Harriet, however, Emma found her quite unperturbed by it, and after a few minutes of talking at cross purposes Emma learned that it was not Churchill but Mr. Knightley upon whom Harriet had now bestowed her affections. When she told Emma that she had reasons to believe that Mr. Knightley returned her sentiments, Emma suddenly realized the state of her own heart; she herself loved Mr. Knightley. She now wished she had never seen Harriet Smith. Aside from the fact that she wanted to marry Mr. Knightley herself, she knew a match between him and Harriet would be an unequal one, hardly likely to bring happiness.

Emma's worry over this state of affairs was soon ended when Mr. Knightley asked her to marry him. Her complete happiness was marred only by the fact that she knew her marriage would upset her father, who disliked change of any kind, and that she had unknowingly prepared Harriet for another disappointment. The first problem was solved when Emma and Mr. Knightley decided to reside at Hartfield with Mr. Woodhouse as long as he lived. As for Harriet, when Mr. Knightley was paying attention to her, he was really trying to determine the real state of her affections for his young farm tenant. Consequently Mr. Knightley was able to announce one morning that Robert Martin had again offered himself to Harriet and had been accepted. Emma was overjoyed that Harriet's future was now assured. She could always reflect that all parties concerned had married according to their stations, a prerequisite for their true happiness.

ENOCH ARDEN

Type of work: Poem
Author: Alfred, Lord Tennyson (1809-1892)
Type of plot: Sentimental romance
Time of plot: Late eighteenth century
Locale: England
First published: 1864

Principal characters:
ENOCH ARDEN, a shipwrecked sailor
ANNIE LEE, his wife
PHILIP RAY, his friend
MIRIAM LANE, a tavern keeper

Critique:

To some modern readers the language of *Enoch Arden* may seem stilted and the story of his unselfish love mawkishly romantic, but we must remember that it was written during a period when unrequited love and unselfish devotion to one's family were favorite subjects of the reading public of England and America. Tennyson has one virtue not shared by all of his contemporaries; his poems are easily read and understood. He expressed better than any other poet of his time the essential character of the English people of the nineteenth century.

The Story:

Annie Lee, Philip Ray, and Enoch Arden played together as children. Sometimes Philip was the husband, sometimes Enoch, but Annie was always the mistress. If the boys quarreled over her, Annie would weep and beg them not to quarrel and say she would be a wife to both of them.

As they grew older and ceased their childish games, Enoch and Philip grew to love Annie. Enoch told her of his love, but Philip kept silent. Philip was the miller's son and a rich boy; Enoch was a poor orphan. He bought a small boat and became a fisherman. He sailed aboard a merchant ship for a full year before he had enough money to make a home for Annie. When he reached his twenty-first year he asked her to be his wife. While the two lovers talked together, Philip looked down on them as they sat at the edge of the wood. He went away quietly, locking his love for Annie deep in his heart.

For seven years Enoch and Annie lived in health and prosperity. They had two children, a girl and a boy. Then misfortune came. Enoch slipped and fell and lay months recovering. While he was ill, a sickly child was born, his favorite. There was no money and the children were hungry, and Enoch's heart almost broke to see his family in want.

The chance came for him to sail again on a merchantman bound for China. He sold his fishing boat that he might get a small store of goods and set Annie up as a trader while he was gone, so that she and the children might not be in want before his return. Annie begged him for their children's sake not to take this dangerous voyage. But Enoch laughed at her fears and told her to give all her cares to God, for the sea was His as well as the land, and He would take care of Enoch and bring him safely home. Annie cut a lock of hair from the sickly child and gave it to Enoch when he sailed.

For many months Annie waited for word from Enoch. Her business did not prosper; she did not know how to bargain. In the third year the sickly child died and Annie was crushed by grief.

After the funeral Philip broke his silence. He begged to send the children to school and care for them for the sake of his friendship with her and Enoch. Enoch had been gone for ten long years before Philip asked Annie to be his wife. He had not spoken before because he knew that she still waited for Enoch's return. Annie asked him to wait one year more. Six months beyond the year passed before she and Philip were wed. But still she feared to enter her own house and thought that one day she would see Enoch waiting for her. It was not until after she bore Philip a child that she was at peace with herself.

Enoch had been shipwrecked and cast upon a desert island. Although he did not lack for food and shelter, his heart was heavy with loneliness and worry about his wife and children. One day a ship came to the island and took him aboard. When he returned to England he was old and stooped and no one knew him. Finding his old house empty, he took lodging in a tavern kept by a widow, Miriam Lane. Not knowing who he was, Mrs. Lane told him of Annie and Philip and their new baby. Enoch could only murmur that he was lost. Watching from a high wall behind Philip's house, he saw Annie and the children in their happiness. He knew he could never shatter that new life.

He lived quietly and did what work he could and told no one his name or from where he came. At last, sick and dying, he called Mrs. Lane to his bedside and told her his story. He asked her to tell Annie and Philip and the children that he died blessing them, and he sent the lock of hair to Annie so she would know he spoke the truth. His was a great unselfish love until the end.

THE ENORMOUS ROOM

Type of work: Novel
Author: E. E. Cummings (1894-)
Type of plot: Autobiographical fiction
Time of plot: 1917
Locale: France
First published: 1922

Principal characters:
E. E. Cummings, an American ambulance driver
W. S. B., his American friend
Apollyon, head of the French prison
Rockyfeller,
The Wanderer,
Zoo-Loo,
Surplice, and
Jean Le Nègre, fellow prisoners

Critique:

The Enormous Room tells of more than three uncomfortable months in prison; it tells of the outrage and terror and hope and fear of men caught in the mesh of wartime government. E. E. Cummings did not want the book to stand merely as an indictment of the French government; he wanted it to tell of the strange and amazing things he had learned about people while in prison. In reading the book, one gets to know not only the author and his friend B., but all the inmates of the enormous room. Each is a study of some human quality. Abounding with sharply drawn scenes and portraits, the novel is compelling in its vivid detail. The book is not so much a study of the stupidity and brutality of war as it is a quietly passionate vindiction of the animal Man.

The Story:

E. E. Cummings and his friend, B., were unhappy as members of the Norton-

Harjes Ambulance Service, a unit sent by Americans to aid the French during World War I. One day they were arrested by French military police. From hints dropped during an investigation Cummings gathered that B. had written some letters suspected by the censor. Because they were good friends, both men were held for questioning. Exactly what they were suspected of doing they never found out. On one occasion Cummings was asked whether he hated the Germans. He replied that he did not, that he simply loved the French very much. The investigating official could not understand how one could love the French and not hate Germans. Finally Cummings and B. were separated and sent to different prisons. As time went by, Cummings was questioned again and again and moved from one spot to another, always under strict guard.

Late one night he was taken to a prison in the little provincial town of Macé. There he was thrown into a huge darkened room, given a straw mattress, and told to go to sleep. In the darkness he counted at least thirty voices speaking eleven different languages. Early the next morning he was told that B., his friend, was in the same room. The two men were happy to see each other again. B. told him that the prisoners in the room were all suspected of being spies, some only because they spoke no French.

That morning he learned the routine of the prison. The enormous room was lined with mattresses down each side, with a few windows to let in light at one end. It smelled of stale tobacco and sweat. Some of the men in the room were mad; most of them were afraid they might become so. To all of them life consisted of following dull prison routine. At five-thirty in the morning someone went down to the kitchen under guard and brought back a bucket of sour, cold coffee. After coffee, the prisoners drew lots to see who would clear the room, sweep the floors, and collect the trash. At seven-thirty they were allowed to walk for two hours in a small, walled-in courtyard. Then came the first meal of the day, followed by another walk in the garden. At four they had supper. At eight they were locked in the enormous room for the night.

There was little entertainment except fighting and conversation. Some of the men spent their time trying to catch sight of women kept in another part of the prison. Cummings began to accustom himself to the enormous room and to make friends among the various inmates. One of the first of these was Count Bragard, a Belgian painter who specialized in portraits of horses. The count was a perfect gentleman, even in prison, and always looked neat and suave. He and Cummings discussed painting and the arts as if they were at some polite party. Before Cummings left, the count began to act strangely. He withdrew from his old friends. He was losing his mind.

One day Cummings was taken to see the head of the prison, a gross man he called Apollyon, after the devil in *Pilgrim's Progress.* Apollyon had no interest in the prisoners as long as they made as little trouble as possible for him. He questioned Cummings for a considerable time in an effort to learn why the American was there, a circumstance over which the American himself often wondered.

When new inmates arrived in the room, everyone looked them over hopefully, some to find a man with money he would lend, some to find a fellow-countryman, and some to find a friend. One day a very fat, rosy-cheeked man joined the group. He had been a successful manager of a disreputable house. Because he had a large sum of money with him, he was nicknamed Rockyfeller. He hired a strong man to act as his bodyguard. Nobody liked him, for he bought special privileges from the guards.

During his stay in the room, Cummings met three men, very different from each other, whose personal qualities were such that they made life seem meaningful to him. He called them the Delectable Mountains, after the mountains Christian found in *Pilgrim's Progress.* The first was the Wanderer, whose wife and three little children were in the women's ward of the prison. He was a strong man, simple in his emotions and feelings. Cummings liked to talk with him about his problems. One of the Wanderer's children, a little boy, sometimes came to the enormous room to visit his father. His pranks and games both bothered and amused the men. The Wanderer treated his son with love and the deepest kind of understanding. Until he was sent away he remained Cummings' best friend.

The second Delectable Mountain was called Zoo-loo, a Polish farmer who could speak neither French nor English, but who could communicate by signs. In a short time he and Cummings knew all about each other. Zoo-loo had a knack for hiding money, and despite the fact that the head of the prison had him searched from head to toe, and all his belongings searched, he seemed always able to produce a twenty franc note from his left ear or the back of his neck. His kindnesses to Cummings and B. were innumerable.

The third Delectable Mountain was an amazing little man named Surplice. Everything astonished him. When Cummings had some candy or cheese, Surplice was sure to come over to his cot and ask questions about it in a shy manner. His curiosity and friendly conversation made everything seem more important and interesting than it really was.

One morning Jean le Nègre was brought to the enormous room, a gigantic, simple-minded Negro whom Cummings was to remember as the finest of his fellow prisoners. Jean was given to practical jokes and tall tales; he had been arrested for impersonating an English officer and had been sent to the prison for psychopathic observation. Because of his powerful body, the women prisoners called their approval and admiration when he walked in the courtyard. His favorite was Lulu, who smuggled money and a lace handkerchief to him. When she was sent to another prison, Jean was disconsolate. When one of the prisoners pulled at Lulu's handkerchief, Jean handled him roughly. A scuffle followed. The guards came and Jean was taken away for punishment. Calls from the women prisoners aroused him so that he attacked the guards and sent them flying until he was quieted and bound by a fellow prisoner whom he trusted. After that experience Jean grew quiet and shy.

Just before Cummings himself was released, B. was sent away. Jean le Nègre tried to cheer Cummings with his funny stories and exaggerated lies, but without much success. Cummings was afraid B. might never get free from the prisons of France, a groundless fear as he learned later. He himself left the enormous room knowing that in it he had learned the degradation and nobility and endurance of human nature.

EREWHON

Type of work: Novel
Author: Samuel Butler (1835-1902)
Type of plot: Utopian satire
Time of plot: 1870's
Locale: Erewhon and England
First published: 1872

Principal characters:
Strong, a traveler in Erewhon
Chowbok, a native

NOSNIBOR, a citizen of Erewhon
AROWHENA, his daughter

Critique:

Erewhon is an anagram of nowhere, but the institutions satirized in this story of an imaginary land are unmistakably British. Beginning as an adventure story, the book becomes an elaborate allegory. Some of Butler's satire grows out of the ideas of Darwin and Huxley. In the main the book is original and often prophetic, The "straighteners" of Erewhon are the psychologists of today, and the treatment of Erewhonian criminals is somewhat like that advocated by our own liberal thinkers. The novel is humorous, but it is also serious.

The Story:

Strong, a young man of twenty-two, worked on a sheep farm. From the plains he looked often at the seemingly impassable mountain range that formed the edge of the sheep country and wondered about the land beyond those towering peaks. From one old native named Chowbok he learned that the country was forbidden. Chowbok assumed a strange pose when questioned further and uttered unearthly cries. Curious, Strong persuaded Chowbok to go on a trip with him into the mountains.

They were unable to find a pass through the mountains. One day Strong came upon a small valley and went up it alone. He found that it led through the mountains. When he went back to get Chowbok, he saw the old native fleeing toward the plains. He went on alone. After climbing down treacherous cliffs and crossing a river on a reed raft, he finally came to beautiful rolling plains. He passed by some strange manlike statues which made terrifying noises as the wind circled about them. He recognized in them the reason for Chowbok's performance.

Strong awoke next morning to see a flock of goats about him, two girls herding them. When the girls saw him they ran and brought some men to look at him. All of them were physically handsome. Convinced at last that Strong was a human being, they took him to a small town close by. There his clothing was searched and a watch he had with him was confiscated. The men seemed to be especially interested in his health, and he was allowed to leave only after a strict medical examination. He wondered why there had been such confusion over his watch until he was shown a museum in which was kept old pieces of machinery. Finally he was put in jail.

In jail he learned the language and something of the strange customs of the country, which was called Erewhon. The oddest custom was to consider disease a crime; anyone who was sick was tried and put in jail. On the other hand, people who committed robbery or murder were treated sympathetically and given hospital care. Shortly afterward the jailor informed Strong that he had been summoned to appear before the king and queen, and that he was to be the guest of a man named Nosnibor. Nosnibor had embezzled a large sum of money from a poor widow, but he was now recovering from his illness. The widow, Strong learned, would be tried and sentenced for allowing herself to be imposed upon.

In the capital Strong stayed with Nosnibor and his family and paid several visits to the court. He was well received because he had blond hair, a rarity among the Erewhonians. He learned a great deal about the past history of the country. Twenty-five hundred years before a prophet had preached that it was unlawful to eat meat, as man should not kill his fellow creatures. For several hundred years the Erewhonians were vegetarians. Then another sage showed that animals were no more the fellow creatures of man than plants were, and that if man could not kill and eat animals he should not kill and eat plants. The logic of his arguments overthrew the old philosophy. Two hundred years before a great scientist had presented the idea that machines had minds and feelings and that if man were not careful the machine would finally become the ruling creature on earth. Consequently all machines had been scrapped.

The economy of the country was unusual. There were two monetary systems, one worthless except for spiritual meaning, one used in trade. The more respected system was the valueless one, and its work was carried on in Musical Banks where people exchanged coins for music. The state religion was a worship of various qualities of godhead, such as love, fear, and wisdom, and the main goddess, Ydgrun, was at the same time an abstract concept and a silly, cruel woman. Strong learned much of the religion from Arowhena, one of Nosnibor's daughters. She was a beautiful girl, and the two fell in love.

Because Nosnibor insisted that his older daughter, Zulora, be married first, Strong and his host had an argument, and Strong found lodgings elsewhere. Arowhena met him often at the Musical Banks. Strong visited the University of Unreason, where the young Erewhonian boys were taught to do anything except that which was practical. They studied obsolete languages and hypothetical sciences. He saw a relationship between these schools and the mass-mind which the educational system in England was producing. Strong also learned that money was considered a symbol of duty, and that the more money a man had the better man he was.

Nosnibor learned that Strong was meeting Arowhena secretly. Then the king began to worry over the fact that Strong had entered the country with a watch, and he feared that Strong might try to bring machinery back into use. Planning an escape, Strong proposed to the queen that he make a balloon trip to talk with the god of the air. The queen was delighted with the idea. The king hoped that Strong would fall and kill himself.

Strong smuggled Arowhena aboard the balloon with him. The couple soon found themselves high in the air and moving over the mountain range. When the balloon settled on the sea, Strong and Arowhena were picked up by a passing ship. In England, where they were married, Strong tried to get up an expedition to go back to Erewhon. Only the missionaries listened to his story. Then Chowbok, Strong's faithless native friend, showed up in England teaching religion, and his appearance convinced people that Erewhon actually did exist. Strong hoped to return to the country soon to teach it Christianity.

ESTHER WATERS

Type of work: Novel
Author: George Moore (1852-1933)
Type of plot: Naturalism
Time of plot: Late nineteenth century
Locale: England
First published: 1894

Principal characters:
ESTHER WATERS, a servant girl
WILLIAM LATCH, her betrayer
MRS. BARFIELD, her mistress
SARAH TUCKER, her enemy
JACKIE, her son
FRED PARSONS, her betrothed
MISS RICE, her employer

Critique:

Esther Waters is a landmark in the development of realism in English fiction. The story of Esther and her struggle against almost insurmountable odds shows the influence of Balzac and Zola. Between Richardson's *Pamela* and Moore's *Esther Waters* there is a dividing line of a completely new theory of art as well as a division of time in the history of the novel.

The Story:

The first person Esther Waters met when she arrived at Woodview was William Latch, the son of the cook under whose direction Esther was to work. William was the bane of his mother's life, for he was like his dead father, a gambler. Mrs. Latch had hoped that William would become a delivery boy and leave Woodview, but William was determined to go into service for Mr. and Mrs. Barfield, the owners of Woodview, in order to observe their racing stable.

The position as kitchenmaid at Woodview was a godsend to Esther, for her stepfather, claiming that he had too many mouths to feed, had forced her to leave home. The workhouse might have been her only refuge if she had not secured a position with the Barfields. But in spite of her efforts to do her work well, it was hard for her to get along with the other servants. Mrs. Latch seemed to go out of her way to make life unpleasant for Esther, and the maids teased her because she was religious. Among the servants, William was at first her only champion, and she was grateful to him. Then Esther found an unexpected friend in her mistress, Mrs. Barfield. She, too, was deeply religious, and she invited Esther to join the services she held in her room each Sunday morning. Learning that Esther could not read, Mrs. Barfield tried to teach her. To Esther, Mrs. Barfield seemed a friend as well as an employer.

Mrs. Barfield's interest made Esther's life easier for a time. William continued to pay her special attention, to the anguish of Sarah Tucker, another of the maids. After a servant's ball in celebration of the victory of one of the Woodview horses, William took Esther out to some wheat stacks and seduced her after telling her that they would be married as soon as he had enough money. By the following morning Esther had convinced herself that she had been betrayed, and she refused to speak to William. He tried to reason with her, telling her that he loved her and they would be married soon, but she would not listen. Tiring at last of her sulking, he turned to Miss Peggy Barfield, a cousin of his master, and after a few weeks eloped with her.

Three months later Esther realized that she was pregnant. Strangely, the servant girls who had been her former tormentors became kind and sympathetic, and their kindness made her feel even more ashamed of her wickedness. In spite of her sympathy, Mrs. Barfield had to send Esther away, for she had become a bad example for the other girls.

There was no place for her to go but to her home. There she found her mother also pregnant and her stepfather more cruel than ever. But he tolerated her as long as she paid her rent and gave him money to buy beer. At last Esther knew that she would have to leave before all her savings were used up and there would be nothing left for her baby.

She took lodgings close to the hospital where she was to be confined. After her son, Jackie, was born, she was filled with a happiness she had never known before, but her joy was lessened when she learned that her mother had died in childbirth, just a few days after Esther's baby was born. Soon afterward Esther's stepfather and the other children went to Australia; with their going Esther felt that she was really alone in the world.

For Esther the next few years were terrible ones. Sometimes she worked seventeen and eighteen hours a day. Once she had to go to the workhouse. Her greatest grief was the need to leave her child in someone's care while she worked, for Jackie was her whole life. When he was six years old, Esther found work with Miss Rice, a writer whose home was a haven to Esther. Miss Rice knew Esther's story and tried to make the girl's life easier for her.

One day Esther met Fred Parsons, a colorless man, but honest, dependable, and religious. When Esther told him her story, he readily forgave her. She took Fred to see Jackie, and the man and the boy were fast friends from the first meeting. Esther and Fred planned to be married as soon as Miss Rice could get another servant, for Esther would not leave her mistress uncared-for. One evening, while on an errand for Miss Rice, Esther unexpectedly met William Latch, who told her that Peggy had left him. When he learned that Esther had borne his child, he pleaded to come back to her, and hinted that it was her Christian duty to Jackie to give the boy his rightful father. Esther knew that she would be better off with Fred, as would Jackie, for William had become a tavern keeper and a bookie. But Jackie met his father and loved him instantly. For his sake Esther and William were married.

At first William made money. Jackie was put in a good school, and Esther had two servants to wait on her. But there were days of anxious waiting to hear the results of a race. Often William had thousands of pounds to cover if the favorite won. After a time he began to lose heavily. It was against the law to accept bets at the tavern, and William was in constant danger of being reported to the police. Fred Parsons came to warn Esther to leave William, to tell her that the tavern was to be raided, but Esther refused to desert her husband. Then Sarah Tucker came to the tavern to ask for help after she had stolen a silver plate from her employer. The police found her there. Later, when the tavern was raided, William's fine was heavy. Business began to dwindle, and Esther and William had lean times.

After William became tubercular, the dampness and fog of the race tracks only made him cough more, and at last he had to go to the hospital. There the doctors told him that he must go to Egypt for his health. He and Esther gambled all their money on a single race, and lost. Esther tried to be cheerful for William's sake, but when he died a few days later she wished that she had died with him. She had no money and no place to go. Her only blessing was that Jackie was big enough to take care of himself.

Esther went back to Woodview. Only Mrs. Barfield was left, and she was poor. Most of the land had gone to pay racing debts. But Esther would have stayed with Mrs. Barfield without wages, for she had never forgotten her old friend's kindness. Jackie enlisted in the army and went to Woodview to tell his mother goodbye. With pride she introduced him to Mrs. Barfield. She knew that her sin had been redeemed and that she would never have to be ashamed again. She had given her country a fine soldier. Few women could do more.

ETHAN FROME

Type of work: Novel
Author: Edith Wharton (1862-1937)
Type of plot: Domestic tragedy
Time of plot: Late nineteenth century
Locale: Starkfield, Massachusetts
First published: 1911

Principal characters:

ETHAN FROME, a New England farmer
ZENOBIA FROME (ZEENA), his wife
MATTIE SILVER, Zeena's cousin

Critique:

Although not considered representative of Edith Wharton's works, *Ethan Frome* is probably the best and most popular of her novels. Told in less than two hundred pages, it is a tragic story of three peoples' wasted lives: Ethan Frome; Zeena, his wife; and young Mattie Silver, Zeena's cousin. Through the flash-back technique, Edith Wharton permits us to glimpse the fate of Ethan Frome at the beginning, but we must wait until the end of the book to see how that fate is brought about. Although we know that the story is to have an unhappy ending, the author's crushing use of irony makes the conclusion come as a surprise.

The Story:

Ethan Frome was twenty-eight years old when he married Zenobia Pierce, a distant cousin who nursed his sick mother during her last illness. It was a wedding without love. Zenobia, called Zeena, had no home of her own, and Ethan was lonely. So they were married. But Zeena's talkativeness, which had been pleasing to Ethan during his mother's illness, quickly subsided, and within a year of their marriage Zeena developed the sickliness which was to plague her husband all her life. Ethan became increasingly dissatisfied with his life. He was an intelligent and ambitious young man who had hoped to become an engineer or a chemist. But he soon found himself chained to a wife he detested and a farm he could not sell.

The arrival of Mattie Silver brightened the gloomy house considerably. Mattie, Zeena's cousin, had come to Starkfield partly because she had no other place to go and partly because Zeena felt in need of a companion around the house. Ethan saw in Mattie's goodness and beauty every fine quality that Zeena lacked.

When Zeena suggested that Ethan help Mattie find a husband, he began to realize how much he himself was attracted to the girl. When he went to a church social to bring Mattie home and saw her dancing with the son of a rich Irish grocer, he realized that he was jealous of his rival and in love with Mattie. On his way home with her, Ethan felt his love for Mattie more than ever, for on that occasion as on others, she flattered him by asking him questions on astronomy. His dreams of happiness were short-lived however, for when he reached home Zeena was her nagging, sour self. The contrast between Zeena and Mattie impressed him more and more.

One day Ethan returned from his morning's work to find Zeena dressed in her traveling clothes. She was going to visit a new doctor in nearby Bettsbridge. Ordinarily Ethan would have objected to the journey because of the expensive remedies which Zeena was in the habit of buying on her trips to town. But on that occasion he was overjoyed at the news of Zeena's proposed departure, for he realized that he and Mattie would have the house to themselves overnight.

With Zeena out of the way, Ethan again became a changed man. Later in the evening, before supper, Ethan and Mattie sat quietly before the fire, just as Ethan imagined happily married couples would do. During supper the cat broke Zeena's favorite pickle dish, which Mattie had used to brighten up the table. In spite of the accident, they spent the rest of the evening happily. They talked about going sledding together, and Ethan told shyly—and perhaps wistfully—that

---

he had seen Ruth Varnum and Ned Hale, a young engaged couple, stealing a kiss earlier in the evening.

In the morning Ethan was happy, but not because of anything out of the ordinary the night before. In fact, when he went to bed, he remembered sadly that he had not so much as touched Mattie's fingertips or looked into her eyes. He was happy because he could imagine what a wonderful life he could have if he were married to Mattie. He got glue to mend the pickle dish, but Zeena's unexpected return prevented him from repairing it. His spirits were further dampened when Zeena told him that the Bettsbridge doctor considered her quite sick. He had advised her to get a girl to relieve her of all household duties, a stronger girl than Mattie. She had already engaged the new girl. Ethan was dumbfounded by this development. In her insistence that Mattie be sent away Zeena gave the first real hint that she may have been aware of gossip about her husband and Mattie.

When Ethan told Mattie of Zeena's decision, the girl was as crestfallen as Ethan. Zeena interrupted their lamentations, however, by coming downstairs for something to eat. After supper she required stomach powders to relieve a case of heartburn. In getting the powders, which she had hidden in a spot supposedly unknown to Mattie, Zeena discovered the broken pickle dish, which had been carefully reassembled in order to give the appearance of being unbroken. Having detected the deception and learned that Mattie was responsible for the broken dish, Zeena called Mattie insulting names and showed plainly that the girl would be sent away at the earliest possible moment.

Faced with the certainty of Mattie's departure, Ethan thought of running away with her. But his poverty, as well as his sense of responsibility to Zeena, offered no solution to his problem, only greater despair. On the morning Mattie was to leave Starkfield, Ethan, against the wishes of his wife, insisted on driving Mattie to the station. The thought of parting was unbearable to both. They decided to take the sleigh ride that Ethan had promised Mattie the night before. Down the hill they went, narrowly missing a large elm tree at the bottom. Mattie, who had told Ethan that she would rather die than leave him, begged until Ethan agreed to take her down the hill a second time and run the sled into the elm at the bottom of the slope. But they failed to hit the tree with force sufficient to kill them. The death they sought became a living death, for in the accident Mattie suffered a permanent spine injury and Ethan an incurable lameness. The person who received Mattie into her home, who waited on her, and who cooked for Ethan was—Zeena.

EUGÉNIE GRANDET

Type of work: Novel
Author: Honoré de Balzac (1799-1850)
Type of plot: Naturalism
Time of plot: Early nineteenth century
Locale: Saumur, France
First published: 1833

Principal characters:
MONSIEUR GRANDET, a miser
EUGÉNIE, his daughter
CHARLES GRANDET, his nephew
MONSIEUR DE GRASSINS, a banker
MONSIEUR CRUCHOT, a notary

Critique:

Eugénie Grandet is one of the best of Balzac's novels. His use of realistic detail, so cumbersome and boring in many of his works, is restricted here to what is actually needed. Primarily the book is a character sketch of a loathsome miser whose greed has warped his own life and made the lives of his wife and daughter miserable. The story is told simply and concisely. Its tragedy lies in the fact that Eugénie is doomed to a lonely and loveless life. In any event, she and Grandet are two of Balzac's most successful creations.

The Story:

In the French town of Saumur, old Grandet was a prominent personality, and the story of his rise to fortune was known throughout the district. He was a master cooper who had married the daughter of a prosperous wood merchant. When the new French Republic offered for sale the church property in Saumur, Grandet used his savings and his wife's dowry to buy an old abbey, a fine vineyard, and several farms. Under the Consulate he became mayor and grew still more wealthy. In 1806 he inherited three fortunes from his wife's mother, her grandfather, and her grandmother. By this time he owned the abbey, a hundred acres of vineyard, thirteen farms, and the house in which he lived. In 1811 he bought the nearby estate of an impoverished nobleman.

He was known for his miserliness, but he was respected for the same reason. His manners were simple, his table was meager, but his speech and gestures were the law of the countryside. His household consisted of his wife, his daughter, Eugénie, and a servant, Nanon. Old Grandet had reduced his wife almost to slavery, using her as a screen for his devious financial dealings. Nanon, who did all of the housework, was gaunt and ugly but of great strength. She was devoted to her master because he had taken her in after everyone else had refused to hire her because of her appearance. On each birthday Eugénie received a gold piece from her father and a winter and a summer dress from her mother. Each New Year's Day Grandet would ask to see the coins and would gloat over their yellow brightness.

He begrudged his family everything except the bare necessities of life. Every day he would carefully measure and dole out the food for the household—a few lumps of sugar, several pieces of butter, a loaf of bread. He forbade the lighting of fires in the rooms before the middle of November. His family, like his tenants, lived under the austere circumstances he imposed upon them.

The townspeople wondered whom Eugénie would marry. There were two rivals for her hand. One of them, M. Cruchot, was the son of the local notary. The other, M. de Grassins, was the son of the local banker. On Eugénie's birthday, in the year 1819, both called at the Grandet home. During the evening there was an unexpected knock at the door, and in came Charles Grandet, the miser's nephew. Charles' father had amassed a fortune in Paris, and Charles himself, dressed in the most fashionable Parisian manner, was an example of Parisian customs and habits for these awkward, gawking provincials whom he tried to impress with his superior airs.

Eugénie outdid herself in an effort to make the visitor welcome, even defying her father in the matter of heat, candlelight, and other luxuries for Charles. Grandet was polite enough to his nephew that evening, as he read a letter Charles had brought from his father. In it Grandet's brother announced he had lost his fortune, that he was about to commit suicide, and that he entrusted Charles to his brother's care. The young man was quite unaware of what his father had written, and when informed next day of his father's failure and suicide, he burst into tears and remained in his room for several days. Finally he wrote to a friend in Paris and asked him to dispose of his property and pay his debts. To Eugénie, her mother, and Nanon, he gave little trinkets. Grandet looked at them greedily and said he would have them appraised. He informed his wife and daughter that he intended to turn the young man out as soon as his father's affairs were settled.

Charles felt there was a stain on his honor. Grandet felt so too, especially since he and his late brother had the same family name. In consultation with the local banker, M. de Grassins, he arranged a plan whereby he could save the family reputation without, at the same time, spending a penny. M. de Grassins went to Paris to act for Grandet. He did not return, but lived a life of pleasure in the capital.

In the meantime, Eugénie fell in love with Charles. Sympathizing with his penniless state, she decided to give him her hoard of coins so that he could go to the Indies and make his fortune. The two young people pledged everlasting love to each other, and Charles left Saumur.

On the following New Year's Day, Grandet asked to see Eugénie's money. Her mother, who knew her daughter's secret, kept silent. In spite of Eugénie's denials, Grandet guessed what she had done with the gold. He ordered her to keep to her room, and he would have nothing to do with either her or her mother. Rumors began to arise in the town. The notary, M. Cruchot, told Grandet that if his wife died, there would have to be a division of the property—if Eugénie insisted on it. The village whispered that Mme. Grandet was dying of a broken heart and the maltreatment of her husband. Realizing that he might lose a part of his fortune, Grandet relented and forgave them both. When his wife died, he tricked Eugénie into signing over to him her share of the property.

Five years passed, with no word from Charles to brighten Eugénie's drab existence. In 1827, when Grandet was eighty-two years old, he was stricken with paralysis. He died urging Eugénie to take care of his money.

Eugénie lived with old Nanon, still waiting for Charles to return. One day a letter came. Charles no longer wished to marry her. Instead, he hoped to marry the daughter of a titled nobleman and secure by royal ordinance his father-in-law's title and coat of arms. Eugénie released Charles, but M. de Grassins hurried to Charles and told him that his father's creditors had not been satisfied. Until they were, his fiancée's family would not allow a marriage. Learning of his predicament, Eugénie herself paid the debt, and Charles was married.

Eugénie continued to live alone. The routine of the house was exactly what it had been while Grandet lived. Suitors came again. Young de Grassins was now in disgrace because of the loose life his father was living in Paris, but M. Cruchot, who had risen to a high post in the provincial government, continued to press his suit. At last Eugénie agreed to marry him, providing he did not demand the prerogatives of marriage, for she would be his wife in name only. They were married only a short time before M. Cruchot died. To her own property Eugénie added his. Nanon herself had married and she and her husband stayed with Eugénie. Convinced that Nanon was her only friend, the young widow resigned herself to a lonely life. She lived as she had always lived in the bare old house. She had great wealth, but, lacking everything else in life, she was indifferent to it.

EVANGELINE

Type of work: Poem
Author: Henry Wadsworth Longfellow (1807-1882)
Type of plot: Pastoral romance
Time of plot: Mid-eighteenth century
Locale: French Canada and the United States
First published: 1847

Principal characters:
EVANGELINE BELLEFONTAINE
GABRIEL LAJEUNESSE, her betrothed
BASIL LAJEUNESSE, Gabriel's father
BENEDICT BELLEFONTAINE, Evangeline's father

Critique:

The note of gentleness on which *Evangeline, A Tale of Acadie* begins never falters throughout the poem. The description of a kindly, contented people, who accept their exile as God's will, is followed by an account of Evangeline's wanderings and her patience through a lifetime of disappointment. Force and drama exist only in distilled forms, but the freshness, music, and poetic imagery of *Evangeline* give it wide popularity.

The Story:

In the Acadian province, in the village of Grand-Pré, lived a peaceful farming people who were undisturbed by the wars between the French and British. In a land where there was enough for all, there was no covetousness and no envy, and every man lived at peace with his neighbor. Benedict Bellefontaine had his farm somewhat apart from the village. His daughter, Evangeline, directed her father's household. Although she had many suitors, she favored only one, Gabriel Lajeunesse, the son of Basil, the village blacksmith. Their fathers were friends, and the children had grown up together.

One fall day, while Benedict rested by the fire and Evangeline sat at her spinning wheel, Basil brought word that the men of the village were to meet at the church the next day. They were to be told the plans of the English, whose ships were riding at anchor in the harbor.

That night Benedict and Basil signed the wedding contract which would unite their children. Then, while their fathers played draughts, Evangeline and Gabriel whispered in the darkening room until it was time to say goodnight.

The next morning everyone, including the folk from the outlying districts, came to the village to hear the announcement the English commander was to make. Everybody wore holiday dress, as if the occasion were one for celebration. At the Bellefontaine farm there was especial joy, for with a feast and dancing the family and its guests were celebrating the betrothal of Gabriel and Evangeline. In the afternoon the church bell rang, summoning the men to the church. When they filed in, they were followed by the guard from the ship. Outside the women stood, waiting.

The news the English commander had for the little community was a crushing blow. By order of the king, their land, houses, and cattle were forfeited to the crown, and the entire population of Grand-Pré was to be transported. The men were to consider themselves his prisoners.

The tragic news spread quickly through the village, and to the farm where Evangeline was awaiting Benedict's return. At sunset she started toward the church, on her way comforting the downcast women she met. Outside she called Gabriel's name, but there was no answer from the church where the men were imprisoned.

The men were held prisoners for five days. On the fifth, the women brought their household goods to the shore to be loaded in boats, and late that afternoon the men were led out of the church by their guards. Evangeline, standing at the side of the road, watched them coming toward her. She was able to comfort Gabriel with the assurance that their love would keep them from harm, but for her father she could do nothing. In the five days he had aged greatly.

Basil and his son were put on separate ships. Evangeline remained on the beach with Benedict. That night the villagers of Grand-Pré watched their homes go up in flames, and listened to their animals bellowing as the barns burned. Turning from the sight, Evangeline saw that her father had fallen dead. She dropped in a swoon upon his breast and lay there until morning; then with the aid of Father Felician, the village priest, the Acadians buried Benedict Bellefontaine by the shore. That day Evangeline sailed with the other exiles.

The scattered exiles from Grand-Pré wandered far over the face of North America in search of their friends and families. Sometimes Evangeline lingered for a while in a town, but always she was driven on by her longing for Gabriel. Looking at unmarked graves, she imagined they might contain her lover. Sometimes she heard rumors of his whereabouts; sometimes she spoke with people who had actually seen and known him, but always long ago. The notary's son, Baptiste Leblanc, followed her faithfully and loyally through her years of searching, but she would have no one but Gabriel for a husband.

Finally a band of exiles rowed down the Mississippi, bound for Louisiana, where they hoped to find some of their kinsmen. Evangeline and Father Felician were among them, Evangeline heartened because she felt she was nearing Gabriel at last. Then in the heat of the noonday, the voyagers pulled their craft to shore and lay down to sleep behind some bushes. While they slumbered, Gabriel, in the company of hunters and trappers, passed the spot on his way to the West

That evening, when the exiles went ashore, the prosperous herdsman who welcomed them proved to be Basil. Evangeline learned that Gabriel had left home that day, too troubled by thoughts of his love to endure the quiet life in his father's house.

For a time Basil helped Evangeline carry on her search. Leaving his peaceful home in the South, the herdsman traveled with the girl to the base of the Ozark Mountains. They were guided by rumors of Gabriel's whereabouts, and sometimes, from the distance, they saw, or thought they saw, his campfire. But when they reached the spot, he had already gone ahead.

One evening a Shawnee Indian woman came into the camp, on her way back to her own people after her husband's murder by Comanches. In the night, after the others were asleep, she and Evangeline exchanged stories. When Evangeline had finished hers, the woman told the tale of Mowis, the bridegroom made of snow, and of the Indian girl who married and followed him, only to see him dissolve and fade with the sunshine. She told of Lilinau, who had followed her phantom lover into the woods until she disappeared forever. Evangeline felt that she, too, was following a phantom.

The next day the party traveled to the Jesuit Mission on the western side of the mountains, where they hoped to hear some word of Gabriel. A priest told them Gabriel had gone to the north to hunt six days before. Because it seemed certain he would pass that way on his journey home in the fall, Evangeline decided to wait at the mission. Basil and his companions returned to their homes.

Autumn and winter passed and spring came, with no news of Gabriel. Finally Evangeline heard that he was camping in the forests of Michigan on the Saginaw River. When she reached his camp, it was deserted and in ruins.

For many years she wandered over the country in search of her lover, but always she met with disappointment. At last, grown gray, her beauty gone, she became a Sister of Mercy in Philadelphia, where she went because the soft-spoken Quakers reminded her of her own people. When pestilence struck the town, she visited the almshouse to nurse the destitute. One Sunday morning, she saw on the pallet before her a dying old man. It was Gabriel. In his last moments he dreamed of Evangeline and Grand-Pré. Trying to utter her name, he died. Evangeline murmured a prayer of thanks as she pressed her lover to her.

The lovers lie side by side in nameless graves in Philadelphia, far from their old home in the north. But a few peasants who wandered back from exile still keep their story alive.

THE EVE OF ST. AGNES

Type of work: Poem
Author: John Keats (1795-1821)
Type of plot: Chivalric romance
Time of plot: Middle Ages
Locale: A castle
First published: 1820

Principal characters:
MADELINE, a young girl
PORPHYRO, her lover
ANGELA, an old nurse

Critique:

The Eve of St. Agnes is doubtless Keats' most beautiful and compelling composition. Musical in its matchless verse, vivid in colors, sights, and sounds, the poem is generally thought of as a highly idealized picture of the world as imagined by two young, ecstatic lovers. The story itself is built around the ancient superstition that a maiden who retires to her bed after practising a certain ritual on St. Agnes' Eve will be awakened in a dream by her lover. The use of medieval legend and setting add to the romantic effects of the poem.

The Story:

A cold St. Agnes' Eve it was—so cold that the owl with all its feathers shivered, so cold that the old Beadsman's fingers were numb as he told his rosary and said his prayers. Passing by the sculptured figures of the dead, he felt sorry for them in their icy graves. As he walked through the chapel door, he could hear the sound of music coming from the castle hall. He sadly turned again to his prayers.

The great hall of the castle was a scene of feasting and revelry, but one among the merry throng was scarcely aware of her surroundings. The lovely Madeline's thoughts were on the legend of St. Agnes' Eve, which told that a maiden, if she followed the ceremonies carefully and went supperless to bed, might there meet her lover in a dream.

Meanwhile, across the moonlit moors came Porphyro. He entered the castle and hid behind a pillar, aware that his presence meant danger, because his family was an enemy of Madeline's house. Soon the aged crone, Angela, came by and offered to hide him, lest his enemies find him there and kill him.

He followed her along dark arched passageways, out of sight of the revelers. When they stopped, Porphyro begged Angela to let him have one glimpse of Madeline. He promised on oath that if he so much as disturbed a lock of her hair, he would give himself up to the foes who waited below. He seemed in such sorrow that the poor woman gave in to him. She took Porphyro to the maiden's chamber and there hid him in a closet where was stored a variety of sweet meats and confections brought from the feast downstairs. Angela then hobbled away, and soon the breathless Madeline appeared.

She came in with her candle, which blew out, and kneeling before her high arched casement window, she began to pray. Watching her kneel there, her head a halo of moonlight, Porphyro grew faint at the sight of her beauty. Soon she disrobed and crept into bed, where she lay entranced until sleep came over her.

Porphyro stole from the closet and gazed at her in awe as she slept. For an instant a door opened far away, and the noises of another world, boisterous and festive, broke in; but soon the sounds faded away again. In the silence he brought dainty foods from the closet—quinces, plums, jellies, candies, syrups and spices that perfumed the chilly room. Madeline slept on, and Porphyro began to play a soft melody on a lute. Madeline opened her eyes and thought her lover a vision of St. Agnes' Eve. Porphyro, not daring to speak, sank upon his knees until she spoke, begging him never to leave her or she would die.

St. Agnes' moon went down. Outside the casements, sleet and ice began to dash against the windowpanes. Porphyro told her that they must flee before the house awakened. Madeline, afraid and trembling, followed her lover down the cold, gloomy corridors, through the wide deserted hall, and past the porter, asleep on his watch. So they fled—into the wintry dawn.

THE FAERIE QUEENE

Type of work: Poem
Author: Edmund Spenser (1552?-1599)
Type of plot: Allegorical epic
Time of plot: Middle Ages
Locale: England
First published: 1590-1595

Principal characters:

GLORIANA, the Fairy Queen, representing Queen Elizabeth
THE RED CROSS KNIGHT, representing Holiness
UNA, representing Religion
ARCHIMAGO, a magician
DUESSA, representing Roman Catholicism
BRITOMART, representing Chastity
GUYON, representing Temperance
ARTEGALL, representing Justice
PRINCE ARTHUR, legendary English king

Critique:

The Faerie Queen was the first sustained poetic creation after Chaucer, and its beauty and poetic power made for it a secure place in our literature as soon as it was given to the world. At present it is generally accorded a high place in the history of English literary art. The Spenserian stanza—nine lines, eight of five feet and one of six, riming ababbcbcc—is a genuine artistic innovation. Combined with his poetic power, Spenser was animated by a high moral purpose. Only six books of the twelve planned by Spenser were completed. The fragmentary seventh book was published in 1609, ten years after his death.

The Story:

Gloriana, the Fairy Queen, was holding her annual twelve-day feast. As was the custom, any one in trouble could appear before the court and ask for a champion. The fair lady Una came riding on a white ass, accompanied by a dwarf. She complained that her father and mother had been shut up in a castle by a dragon. The Red Cross Knight offered to help her, and the party set out to rescue Una's parents.

In a cave the Red Cross Knight encountered a horrible creature, half serpent, half woman. Although the foul stench nearly overpowered him, the knight slew the monster. After the battle, the Red Cross Knight and Una lost their way. A friendly stranger who offered them shelter was really Archimago, the wicked magician. By making the Red Cross Knight dream that Una was a harlot, Archimago separated Una from her champion.

Una went on her way alone. Archimago quickly assumed the form of the Red Cross Knight and followed her to do her harm. Meanwhile the Red Cross Knight fell into the company of Duessa, an evil enchantress. They met the great giant Orgoglio, who overcame the Red Cross Knight and made Duessa his mistress. Prince Arthur, touched by Una's misfortunes, rescued the Red Cross Knight from Orgoglio and led him to Una. Once again Una and her champion rode on their mission.

At last they came to Una's kingdom, and the dragon who had imprisoned her parents came out to do battle. After two days of fighting, the Red Cross Knight overthrew the dragon. After the parents had been freed, the Red Cross Knight and Una were betrothed.

Still hoping to harm the Red Cross Knight, Archimago told Sir Guyon that the Red Cross Knight had despoiled a virgin of her honor. Shocked, Guyon set out to right the wrong. The cunning Archimago disguised Duessa as a young girl and placed her on the road, where she told a piteous tale of wrong done by the Red Cross Knight and urged Guyon to avenge her. When Guyon and the Red Cross Knight met, they lowered their lances and began to fight. Fortunately the signs of the Virgin Mary on the armor of each recalled them to their senses, and Guyon was ashamed that he had been tricked by the magician.

In his travels Guyon fell in with Prince Arthur, and the two visited the Castle of Alma, the stronghold of Temperance. The most powerful enemy of Temperance was the demon Maleger. In a savage battle Prince Arthur vanquished Maleger. Guyon went on to the Bower of Bliss, where his arch enemy Acrasy was living. With stout heart Guyon overthrew Acrasy and destroyed the last enemy of Temperance.

After sending Acrasy back to the fairy court under guard, Guyon and Prince Arthur went on their way until on an open plain they saw a knight arming for battle. With Prince Arthur's permission, Guyon rode against the strange knight, and in the meeting Guyon was unhorsed by the strong lance of his opponent. Ashamed of his fall, Guyon snatched his sword and would have continued the fight on foot.

The palmer, attending Guyon, saw that the champion could not prevail against the stranger, for the strange knight was enchanted. When he stopped the fight, the truth was revealed; the strange knight was really the lovely Britomart, a chaste and pure damsel, who had seen the image of her lover, Artegall, in Venus' looking-glass and had set out in search of him. With the situation explained, Britomart joined Guyon, Prince Arthur, and Arthurs' squire, Timias; and the four continued their quest.

In a strange wood they traveled for days, seeing no one, but everywhere they met bears, lions, and bulls. Suddenly a beautiful lady on a white palfrey galloped out of the brush. She was Florimell, pursued by a lustful forester who spurred his steed cruelly in an attempt to catch her. The three men joined the chase, but out of modesty Britomart stayed behind. She waited a long time; then, despairing of ever finding her companions again, she went on alone.

As she approached Castle Joyous she saw six knights attacking one. She rode into the fight and demanded to know why they were fighting in such cowardly fashion. She learned that any knight passing had to love the lady of Castle Joyous or fight six knights. Britomart denounced the rule and with her magic lance unhorsed four of the knights. She entered Castle Joyous as a conqueror.

After meeting the Red Cross Knight in the castle, Britomart resolved to go on as a knight errant. She heard from Merlin, whom she visited, that she and Artegall were destined to have illustrious descendants.

Meanwhile Timias had been wounded while pursuing the lustful forester. Belphoebe, the wondrous beauty of the Garden of Adonis, rescued him and healed his wounds. Timias fell in love with Belphoebe.

Amoret, the fair one, was held prisoner by a young knight who attempted to defile her. For months she resisted his advances. Then Britomart, hearing of her sad plight, overcame the two knights who guarded Amoret's prison and freed her. Greatly attracted to her brave rescuer, Amoret set out with Britomart.

At a strange castle a knight claimed Amoret as his love. Britomart jousted with him to save Amoret, and after winning the tourney Britomart was forced to take off her helmet. With her identity revealed, Britomart and Amoret set off together in search of their true loves.

Artegall, in search of adventure, joined Scudamour, knight errant. They met Amoret and Britomart, who was still disguised as a knight. Britomart and Artegall fought an indecisive battle during which Artegall was surprised to discover that his opponent was his lost love, Britomart. The two lovers were reunited at last, but in the confusion Amoret was abducted by Lust. With the help of Prince Arthur, Scudamour rescued Amoret from her loathsome captor. He wooed Amoret in the Temple of Love, where they found shelter.

Artegall, champion of true justice, was brought up and well-trained by Astraea. When Artegall was of age, Astraea gave him a trusty groom, and the new knight set out on his adventures. Talus, the groom, was an iron man who carried an iron flail to thresh out falsehood. Irene, who asked at the fairy court for a champion against the wicked Grantorto, set out with Artegall and Talus to regain her heritage. With dispatch Artegall and Talus overcame Grantorto and restored Irene to her throne.

Later Artegall entered the lists against a strange knight who was really the disguised Amazon, Radigund. Artegall wounded Radigund, but when he saw that his prostrate foe was a comely woman, he threw away his weapons. The wounded Amazon then rushed on the defenseless Artegall and took him prisoner. Artegall was kept in shameful confinement until at last Talus informed Britomart of his fate. Britomart went to her lover's rescue and slew Radigund.

Continuing his quest, Artegall met two hags, Envy and Detraction, who defamed his character and set the Blatant Beast barking at his heels. But Artegall forbade Talus to beat the hags and returned to the fairy court.

The Blatant Beast, defamer of knightly character and the last remaining enemy of the fairy court, finally met his match. The courteous Calidore, the gentlest of all the knights, conquered the beast and led him, tamed, back to the court of the Fairy Queen.

FAR FROM THE MADDING CROWD

Type of work: Novel
Author: Thomas Hardy (1840-1928)
Type of plot: Psychological realism
Time of plot: 1869-1873
Locale: "Wessex," England
First published: 1874

Principal characters:
GABRIEL OAK, a shepherd
BATHSHEBA EVERDENE, mistress of Weatherbury Farm
SERGEANT TROY, her first husband
FARMER BOLDWOOD, her suitor
FANNY ROBIN, betrayed by Troy

Critique:

This early novel by Thomas Hardy is less marked by the cold fate-ridden philosophy characteristic of his later work. The clarity and realism of the characters hold the reader's interest throughout, and Hardy's poetic style and constant citation of Biblical phrase and incident give the novel a unique quality of language and atmosphere. Although the end of the story has been considered contrived by some, the general structure of the plot leads logically to Hardy's conclusion.

The Story:

Gabriel Oak was a farmer on a small scale, but his honesty, integrity, and ability had won him the respect of all his neighbors. When he heard that a young girl named Bathsheba Everdene had moved into the neighborhood, he went out of his way to see her and fell immediately in love. Gabriel was the kind of man who had to look only once to know that he had found the right woman for him. After seeing her only a few times, he went to her aunt, for whom Bathsheba worked, and asked for the girl's hand in marriage. Although he was refused, he felt that it was the relative, not Bathsheba, who had denied him.

A short time later Gabriel's sheep dog became excited and chased his flock of sheep over a cliff, killing them all. Ruined, Gabriel had to give up his farm and go elsewhere to find work. On his way across the country he happened to pass a burning barn and ran to aid the men fighting the flames. After the fire had been put out, the owner of Weatherbury Farm arrived, and it was suggested that Gabriel be hired as shepherd in return for the fine work he had done. To his surprise, the owner of the farm was Bathsheba Everdene, who had recently inherited the place from her uncle. Gabriel became her shepherd. He was struck by the change in their positions in such a short while. Now Bathsheba was landowner, Gabriel the servant.

On his way to his new quarters Gabriel met a girl standing in the woods. She spoke to him and asked him not to say that he had seen her, and he promised to keep silent. The next morning, while working at his new job, he heard that Fanny Robin, one of Bathsheba's maids, had disappeared, and he rightly guessed that Fanny was the girl he had met. It was suspected that she had gone off to meet a soldier who had been stationed in the area a short time before. This suspicion was correct. Fanny had gone to find Sergeant Troy at his new station, for he had promised to marry her if she came to him. A date was set for the wedding, but Fanny went to the wrong church. When she finally found Troy he refused to make arrangements for a marriage a second time.

Weatherbury Farm prospered, for Bathsheba was a good manager. But, being a woman, she had her caprices. One of these was to send an anonymous valentine to Farmer Boldwood, a conservative, serious man who was her neighbor. Boldwood was upset by the valentine, especially after he learned that Gabriel had recognized Bathsheba's handwriting. The more Boldwood saw of Bathsheba, however, the more deeply he fell in love with her. One day during the sheep-washing he asked her to marry him, but she refused his proposal. Nevertheless, Gabriel and the rest of the workers felt sure that she would eventually marry Boldwood.

About that time Sergeant Troy re

turned to the neighborhood. Bathsheba was attracted to him at once. Gabriel knew enough of Troy's character to know that he was not the man for Bathsheba and he told her so. Not knowing the story of Fanny Robin, Bathsheba was furious. She and Troy were married soon afterward and the former sergeant became the master of Weatherbury Farm.

With Troy running the farm, things did not go very well. Gabriel was forced to do most of the work of overseeing, and often he was compelled to correct the mistakes Troy made. Troy gambled and drank and caused Bathsheba much unhappiness. Gabriel and Bathsheba were alternately friendly and unfriendly. One day Troy and Bathsheba, riding in a horse cart, passed a young girl walking down the road. Troy stopped the cart and went to talk to her. The woman was Fanny Robin, who was feeble and ill. Troy told her to go on to the next town and there wait for him to come and give her money. As soon as they arrived home, Troy asked Bathsheba for some money. She gave it to him after a quarrel.

Fanny went on to Casterbridge, but she was so weak and ill when she arrived there that she died shortly afterward. When news of her death reached Weatherbury Farm, Bathsheba, not knowing that Troy had been the girl's lover, sent a cart to bring the body to the farm for burial. When the body arrived, Gabriel saw scrawled on the coffin lid a message that both Fanny and a child were inside. He erased the last words in his fear that the real relationship of Fanny and Troy might reach Bathsheba's ears. But Bathsheba, suspecting that the coffin concealed some secret, opened the casket late that night. At the same moment Troy entered the room and learned of Fanny's death and the death of his child. Torn with grief, he told Bathsheba that she meant nothing to him, that Fanny had been the only woman he had ever loved. He had married Bathsheba only for her looks and her money. Bathsheba shut herself up in an attic room.

Troy had a beautiful tombstone put up over Fanny's grave, which he covered with roses and lilies. During the night there was a heavy storm and water, pouring from the church roof through the mouth of a gargoyle, splashed on the grave and ruined all his work. Troy disappeared from Casterbridge. News came shortly afterward that he had been caught in a dangerous current while swimming in the ocean and had been drowned.

Bathsheba did not believe that Troy was really dead. But Farmer Boldwood, convinced of Troy's death, did his best to get Bathsheba to promise to marry him if Troy did not reappear within seven years, at the end of which time he would be legally declared dead. One night, at a party Boldwood gave for her, Bathsheba yielded to his protestations of love and said that after the time had passed she would marry him. As she was leaving the party, Troy entered. He had been rescued at sea and had wandered slowly back to Casterbridge in the character of a strolling player.

At his entrance Bathsheba fell to the floor in a faint. Everyone was so concerned for her and surprised by Troy's appearance that they did not see Boldwood when he took down a gun from the wall. Boldwood aimed at Troy and shot him in the chest. Troy died immediately.

Boldwood was tried for the murder, but because his mind had given way he was committed to an institution. Gabriel, who had made every effort to save Boldwood from hanging, had become a leader in the neighborhood. As Bathsheba's bailiff, he managed her farm and that of Boldwood as well. Of her three lovers, he was the only one left.

One day Gabriel went to Bathsheba and told her that he was planning to leave her service. Bathsheba listened quietly and agreed with all he had to say. Later that night, however, she went to his cottage and there told him, by gesture more than by word, that he was the only person left to her now and that she needed both his help and his love. The farmers of the district were all delighted when Bathsheba became Mrs. Oak, and Gabriel became the master of Weatherbury Farm.

A FAREWELL TO ARMS

Type of work: Novel
Author: Ernest Hemingway (1898-)
Type of plot: Impressionistic realism
Time of plot: World War I
Locale: Northern Italy and Switzerland
First published: 1929

Principal characters:
FREDERIC HENRY, an American serving with an Italian ambulance unit
CATHERINE BARKLEY, an English nurse

Critique:

Hemingway combines austere realism and poetic language to present a powerful argument against war and to tell a touching love story at the same time. Possessed of the most remarkable time sense of the period between wars, his disillusioned temperament and technical skill have influenced a whole generation of writers. In spite of its hard-boiled realism of detail and its tragic ending, *A Farewell to Arms* is nevertheless an idealistic book. The novel was dramatized by Laurence Stallings and was made into a motion picture.

The Story:

Lieutenant Frederic Henry was a young American attached to an Italian ambulance unit on the Italian front. An offensive was soon to begin, and when Henry returned to the front from leave he learned from his friend, Lieutenant Rinaldi, that a group of British nurses had arrived in his absence to set up a British hospital unit. Rinaldi introduced him to nurse Catherine Barkley.

Between ambulance trips to evacuation posts at the front, Henry called on Miss Barkley. He liked the frank young English girl in a casual sort of way, but he was not in love with her. Before he left for the front to stand by for an attack, she give him a St. Anthony medal.

At the front, as Henry and some Italian ambulance drivers were eating in a dugout, an Austrian projectile exploded over them. Henry, badly wounded in the legs, was taken to a field hospital. Later he was moved to a hospital in Milan.

Before the doctor was able to see Henry in Milan, the nurses prohibited his drinking wine, but he bribed a porter to bring him a supply which he kept hidden behind his bed. Catherine Barkley came to the hospital and Henry knew that he was in love with her. The doctors told Henry that he would have to lie in bed six months before they could operate on his knee. Henry insisted on seeing another doctor, who said that the operation could be performed the next day. Meanwhile, Catherine managed to be with Henry constantly.

After his operation, Henry convalesced in Milan with Catherine Barkley as his attendant. Together they dined in out of the way restaurants, and together they rode about the countryside in a carriage. Henry was restless and lonely at nights and Catherine often came to his hospital room.

Summer passed into autumn. Henry's wound had healed and he was due to take convalescent leave in October. He and Catherine planned to spend the leave together, but he came down with jaundice before he could leave the hospital. The head nurse accused him of bringing on the jaundice by drink, in order to avoid being sent back to the front. Before he left for the front, Henry and Catherine stayed together in a hotel room; already she had disclosed to him that she was pregnant.

Henry returned to the front with orders to load his three ambulances with hospital equipment and go south into the Po valley. Morale was at low ebb. Rinaldi admired the job which had been done on the knee and observed that Henry acted like a married man. War weariness was all-pervasive. At the front, the Italians, having learned that German divisions had reinforced the Austrians, began their terrible retreat from Caporetto. Henry drove one of the ambulances loaded with hospital supplies. During the retreat south, the ambulance was held up several times by wagons, guns, and trucks which extended in stalled lines for miles. Henry picked up two straggling Italian sergeants. During the night the retreat was halted in the rain for hours.

At daybreak Henry cut out of the long line and drove across country in an attempt to reach Udine by side roads. The ambulance got stuck in a muddy side road. The sergeants decided to leave, but Henry asked them to help dislodge the car from the mud. They refused and ran. Henry shot and wounded one; the other escaped across the fields. An Italian ambulance corpsman with Henry shot the wounded sergeant through the back of the head. Henry and his three comrades struck out on foot for Udine. On a bridge, Henry saw a German staff car and German bicycle troops crossing another bridge over the same stream. Within sight of Udine, one of Henry's group was killed by an Italian sniper. The others hid in a barn until it seemed safe to circle around Udine and join the main stream of the retreat toward the Tagliamento River.

By that time the Italian army was nothing but a frantic mob. Soldiers were throwing down their arms and officers were cutting insignia of rank from their sleeves. At the end of a long wooden bridge across the Tagliamento military carabiniere were seizing all officers, giving them drumhead trials, and executing them by the river bank. Henry was detained, but in the dark of night he broke free, plunged into the river, and escaped on a log. He crossed the Venetian plain on foot, then jumped aboard a freight train and rode to Milan, where he went to the hospital in which he had been a patient. There he learned that the English nurses had gone to Stresa.

During the retreat from Caporetto Henry had made his farewell to arms. He borrowed civilian clothes from an American friend in Milan and went by train to Stresa, where he met Catherine, who was on leave. The bartender of the hotel in which Henry was staying warned Henry that authorities were planning to arrest him for desertion the next morning; he offered his boat by means of which Henry and Catherine could escape to Switzerland. Henry rowed all night. By morning his hands were so raw that he could barely stand to touch the oars. Over his protests, Catherine took a turn at the rowing. They reached Switzerland safely and were arrested. Henry told the police that he was a sportsman who enjoyed rowing and that he had come to Switzerland for the winter sports. The valid passports and the ample funds that Henry and Catherine possessed saved them from serious trouble with the authorities.

During the rest of the fall and the winter the couple stayed at an inn outside Montreux. They discussed marriage, but Catherine would not be married while she was with child. They hiked, read, and talked about what they would do together after the war.

When the time for Catherine's confinement approached, she and Henry went to Lausanne to be near a hospital. They planned to return to Montreux in the spring. At the hospital Catherine's pains caused the doctor to use an anaesthetic on her. After hours of suffering she was delivered of a dead baby. The nurse sent Henry out to get something to eat. When he went back to the hospital, he learned that Catherine had had a hemorrhage. He went into the room and stayed with her until she died. There was nothing he could do, no one he could talk to, no place he could go. Catherine was dead. He left the hospital and walked back to his hotel in the dark. It was raining.

FATHER GORIOT

Type of work: Novel
Author: Honoré de Balzac (1799-1850)
Type of plot: Naturalism
Time of plot: About 1830
Locale: Paris
First published: 1835

Principal characters:
FATHER GORIOT, a boarder at the Maison Vauquer
EUGÈNE DE RASTIGNAC, a young law student
COUNTESS ANASTASIE DE RESTAUD, Goriot's daughter
BARONESS DELPHINE DE NUCINGEN, another daughter
MADAME DE BEAUSÉANT, Rastignac's cousin
MONSIEUR VAUTRIN, Rastignac's fellow boarder
VICTORINE TAILLEFER, another boarder

Critique:

This account of the subtle transformation of Eugène de Rastignac from a naïve provincial to a Parisian gentleman is among the most credible stories in fiction. The story of the ruin of a successful merchant, Goriot, because of his love for two ungrateful daughters is effective but less realistic. These are but a few of the fascinating gallery of characters Balzac assembled at Mme. Vauquer's boarding-house.

The Story:

There were many conjectures at Madame Vauquer's boarding-house about the mysterious Monsieur Goriot. He had taken the choice rooms on the first floor when he first retired from his vermicelli business, and for a time his landlady had eyed him as a prospective husband. When, at the end of his second year at the Maison Vauquer, he had asked to move to a cheap room on the second floor, he was credited with being an unsuccessful speculator, a miser, a money-lender. The mysterious young women who flitted up to his rooms from time to time were said to be his mistresses, although he protested that they were only his two daughters. The other boarders called him Father Goriot.

At the end of the third year, Goriot moved to a still cheaper room on the third floor. By that time he was the common butt of jokes at the boarding-house table, and his daughters visited him only rarely.

One evening the impoverished law student, Eugène de Rastignac, came home late from the ball his wealthy cousin, Madame de Beauséant, had given. Peeking through the mysterious Goriot's keyhole, he saw him molding some silver plate into ingots. The next day he heard his fellow boarder, Monsieur Vautrin, say that early in the morning he had seen Father Goriot selling a piece of silver to an old money-lender. What Vautrin did not know was that the money thus obtained was intended for Goriot's daughter, Countess Anastasie de Restaud, whom Eugène had met at the dance the night before.

That afternoon Eugène paid his respects to the countess. Father Goriot was leaving the drawing-room when he arrived. The countess, her lover, and her husband received Eugène graciously because of his connections with Madame de Beauséant. But when he mentioned they had the acquaintance of Father Goriot in common, he was quickly shown to the door, the count leaving word with his servant that he was not to be at home if Monsieur de Rastignac called again.

After his rebuff, Eugène went to call on Madame de Beauséant, to ask her aid in unraveling the mystery. She quickly understood what had happened, and explained that de Restaud's house would be barred to him because both of Goriot's daughters, having been given sizable dowries, were gradually severing all connection with their father and therefore would not tolerate anyone who had knowledge of Goriot's shabby circumstances. She suggested that Eugène send word through Goriot to his other daughter, Delphine de Nucingen, that Madame de Beauséant would receive her. Delphine, she knew, would welcome the invitation, and would be grateful to Eugène and become his sponsor.

Vautrin had another suggestion for the young man. Under Madame Vauquer's roof lived Victorine Taillefer, who had been disinherited by her wealthy father in favor of her brother. Eugène had already found favor in her eyes, and Vautrin suggested that for a two hundred thousand francs he would have the brother murdered, so that Eugène might marry the heiress. He was to have two weeks in which to consider the offer.

Eugène escorted Madame de Beauséant to the theater next evening. There he was presented to Delphine de Nucingen, who received him graciously. The next day he received an invitation to dine with the de Nucingens and to go to the theater. Before dinner he and Delphine drove to a gambling house where, at her request, he gambled and won six thousand francs. She explained that her husband would give her no money, and she needed it to pay a debt she owed to an old lover.

Before long Eugène learned that it cost money to keep the company of his new friends. Unable to press his own family for funds, he would not stoop to impose on Delphine. Finally, as Vautrin had forseen, he was forced to take his fellow boarder's offer. The tempter had just finished explaining the duel between Victorine's brother and his confederate which was to take place the following morning when Father Goriot came in with the news that he and Delphine had taken an apartment for Eugène.

Eugène wavered once more at the thought of the crime which was about to be committed in his name. He attempted to send a warning to the victim through Father Goriot, but Vautrin, suspicious of his accomplice, thwarted the plan. Vautrin managed to drug their wine at supper so that both slept soundly that night.

At breakfast Eugène's fears were realized. A messenger burst in with the news that Victorine's brother had been fatally wounded in a duel. After the girl hurried off to see him, another singular event occurred. Vautrin, after drinking his coffee, fell to the ground as if he had suffered a stroke. When he was carried to his room and undressed, it was ascertained by marks on his back that he was the famous criminal, Trompe-la-Mort. One of the boarders, an old maid, had been acting as an agent for the police; she had drugged Vautrin's coffee so that his criminal brand could be exposed. Shortly afterward the police appeared to claim their victim.

Eugène and Father Goriot were preparing to move to their new quarters, for Goriot was to have a room over the young man's apartment. Delphine arrived to interrupt Goriot's packing. She was in distress. Father Goriot had arranged with his lawyer to force de Nucingen to make a settlement so that Delphine would have an independent income on which to draw, and she brought the news that her money had been so tied up by investments it would be impossible for her husband to withdraw any of it without bringing about his own ruin.

Hardly had Delphine told her father of her predicament when Anastasie de Restaud drove up. She had sold the de Restaud diamonds to help her lover pay off his debts, and had been discovered by her husband. De Restaud had bought them back, but as punishment he demanded control of her dowry.

Eugène could not help overhearing the conversation through the thin partition between the rooms, and when Anastasie said she still needed twelve thousand francs for her lover he forged one of Vautrin's drafts for that amount and took it to Father Goriot's room. Anastasie's reaction was to berate him for eavesdropping.

The financial difficulties of his daughters and the hatred and jealousy they had shown proved too much for Father Goriot. At the dinner table he looked as if he were about to have a stroke of apoplexy, and when Eugène returned from an afternoon spent with his mistress, Delphine, the old man was in bed, too ill to be moved to his new home. He had gone out that morning to sell his last few possessions, so that Anastasie might pay her dressmaker for an evening gown.

In spite of their father's serious condition, both daughters attended Madame de Beauséant's ball that evening, and Eugène was too much under his mistress' influence to refuse to accompany her. The next day Goriot was worse. Eugène tried to summon his daughters. Delphine was still abed and refused to be hurried over her morning toilet. Anastasie arrived at his bedside only after Father Goriot had lapsed into a coma and no longer knew her.

Father Goriot was buried in a pauper's grave the next day. Eugène tried to borrow burial money at each daughter's house, but they sent word they were in deep grief over their loss and could not be seen. He and a poor medical student from the boarding-house were the only mourners at the funeral. Anastasie and Delphine sent their empty carriages to follow the coffin. It was their final tribute to an indulgent father.

FATHERS AND SONS

Type of work: Novel
Author: Ivan Turgenev (1818-1883)
Type of plot: Social criticism
Time of plot: 1859
Locale: Russia
First published: 1862

Principal characters:
KIRSANOFF, a Russian gentleman
PAVEL, his older brother
ARKADY, his son
FENICHKA, Kirsanoff's mistress
BAZAROFF, Arkady's friend
VASILY, Bazaroff's father
MADAME ODINTZOFF, a widow
KATYA, her younger sister

Critique:

Fathers and Sons is important in the political history of Russia. Turgenev was here the first to use the word nihilist to describe a believer in political anarchy at a time when nihilism was the main current of liberal thought. There are excellent studies of the unsettled Russian peasants just before their emancipation.

Beyond this historical importance, *Fathers and Sons* is a novel which dramatizes the conflict and differences between generations. The novel is relatively straightforward in plot and the characters are simply drawn. These characteristics are not common in nineteenth-century Russian novels; the clarity of *Fathers and Sons* is probably a big factor in its popularity.

The Story:

At a provincial posting station Kirsanoff waited impatiently for his son, Arkady, who had completed his education at the university in St. Petersburg. Kirsanoff reflected that Arkady had probably changed, but he hoped his son had not grown away from him entirely. Arkady's mother was dead, and the widower was strongly attached to his son.

At last the coach appeared, rolling along the dusty road. Arkady jumped out. But he was not alone. Lounging superciliously behind was a stranger whom Arkady introduced as Bazaroff, a fellow student. Something in Arkady's manner told Kirsanoff that here was a special attachment. In a low aside Arkady begged his father to be gracious to his guest.

Feeling some qualms about his unexpected guest, Kirsanoff was troubled during the trip home. He was hesitant about his own news, but finally told Arkady that he had taken a mistress, Fenichka, and installed her in his house. To his great relief, Arkady took the news calmly and even congratulated his father on the step. Later Arkady was pleased to learn that he even had a little half-brother.

Very soon Kirsanoff found he had good reason to distrust Bazaroff, who was a doctor and a clever biologist. Arkady seemed too much under his influence. Worse, Bazaroff was a nihilist. At the university the liberal thinkers had consciously decided to defy or ignore all authority—state, church, home, pan-Russianism. Bazaroff was irritating to talk to, Kirsanoff decided, because he knew so much and had such a sarcastic tongue.

Pavel, Kirsanoff's older brother, was especially irritated by Bazaroff. Pavel was a real aristocrat, bound by tradition, who had come to live in retirement with his younger brother after a disappointing career as an army officer and the lover of a famous beauty, the Princess R—. With his background and stiff notions of propriety, Pavel often disagreed with Bazaroff.

Luckily, Bazaroff kept busy most of the time. He collected frogs and infusoria and was always dissecting and peering into a microscope. He would have been an ideal guest, except for his calmly superior air of belonging to a generation far surpassing Pavel's. Kirsanoff, loving his son so much, did his best to keep peace, but all the while he regretted the nihilism which had so affected Arkady.

Kirsanoff was harassed by other troubles. Soon, by law, the serfs would be freed. Kirsanoff strongly approved this change and had anticipated the new order by dividing his farm into smaller plots which the peasants rented on a sharecropping basis. But with their new independence the peasants cheated him more than ever and were slow in paying their rent.

Arkady and Bazaroff, growing bored with quiet farm life, went to visit in the provincial capital, where they had introductions to the governor. In town they ran into Sitnikoff, a kind of polished jackal who felt important because he was one of the nihilist circle. Sitnikoff introduced them into provincial society.

At a ball the two friends met and were greatly taken by a young widow, Madame Odintzoff. Arkady did not dance, but he sat out a mazurka with her. They became friends at once, especially when she found that Arkady's mother had been an intimate friend of her own mother. After the ball Madame Odintzoff invited the two men to visit her estate.

Arkady and Bazaroff accepted the invitation promptly, and in a few days they settled down to the easy routine of favored guests in a wealthy household. Katya, Madame Odintzoff's young sister, was especially attracted to Arkady. Bazaroff, older and more worldly, became the good friend of the widow.

Although Bazaroff, as a good nihilist, despised home and family life, he made a real effort to overcome his scruples. But when he finally began to talk of love and marriage to Madame Odintzoff, he was politely refused. Chagrined at his rejection, he induced Arkady to leave with him at once. The two friends then went on to Bazaroff's home.

Vasily, Bazaroff's father, was glad to see his son, whom he both feared and admired. He and his wife did all they could to make the young men comfortable. At length Arkady and Bazaroff quarreled, chiefly because they were so bored. Abruptly they left, and impulsively called again on Madame Odintzoff. She received them coolly. Feeling that they were unwelcome, they went back to the Kirsanoff estate.

Because Bazaroff was convinced that Arkady was also in love with Madame Odintzoff, his friendship with Arkady became greatly strained. Arkady, thinking all the time of Katya, returned by himself to the Odintzoff estate to press his suit of the younger sister.

At the Kirsanoff home Bazaroff became friendly with Fenichka. He prescribed for her sick baby and even for her. Fenichka, out of friendship, spent much of her time with Bazaroff. One morning, as they sat in a garden, Bazaroff kissed her unexpectedly, to her distress and confusion. Pavel witnessed the scene by accident and became incensed all the more at the strange nihilist.

Although Pavel did not consider Bazaroff a gentleman, he challenged him to a duel with pistols. In the encounter Pavel was wounded in the leg, and Bazaroff left the house in haste, never to return. Pavel recovered from his wound, but he felt a never-ending shame at being wounded by a low nihilist. He urged Kirsanoff to marry Fenichka, and returned to his old life. He spent the rest of his days as an aging dandy in Dresden.

Bazaroff stopped briefly at the Odintzoff home. Still convinced that Arkady was in love with Madame Odintzoff, he attempted to help his friend in his suit. Madame Odintzoff ridiculed him, however, when Arkady made his request for the hand of Katya. With a sense of futility, Bazaroff took his leave and rejoined his own family.

Vasily was the local doctor, and he eagerly welcomed his son as a colleague. For a time Bazaroff led a successful life, helping to cure the ailments of the peasants and pursuing his research at the same time. When one of his patients came down with typhus, he accidentally scratched himself with a scalpel he had used. Although Vasily cauterized the wound as well as he could, Bazaroff became ill with a fever. Sure that he would die, he summoned Madame Odintzoff to his side. She came gladly and helped to ease him before his death.

Madame Odintzoff eventually made a good marriage with a lawyer. Arkady was happy managing his father's farm and playing with the son born to him and Katya. Kirsanoff became a magistrate and spent most of his life settling disputes brought about by the liberation of the serfs. Fenichka, at last a respected wife and mother, found great happiness in her daughter-in-law, Katya.

FAUST

Type of work: Dramatic poem
Author: Johann Wolfgang von Goethe (1749-1832)
Type of plot: Philosophical allegory
Time of plot: Timeless
Locale: The world
First published: 1790-1831

Principal characters:
FAUST, a student of all knowledge
GRETCHEN, a maiden
MEPHISTOPHELES, the devil
WAGNER, Faust's servant
HELEN OF TROY
HOMUNCULUS, a spirit

Critique:

The philosophical problem of human damnation through desire for knowledge is here presented. Goethe, echoing the eighteenth-century Age of Reason, asserted that man's rationality was the supreme truth in life. This poem contains some of the most beautiful and aspiring passages in all literature. Faust's lofty, anguished cry for one moment in life which would cause him to desire its continuance is echoed throughout the ages in the emotions of all men of all times. The universal problem presented by the play renders it impossible to place the locale of the action or the time of the action, for Faust exists forever and everywhere.

The Story:

While three archangels were singing the praise of God's lofty works, Mephistopheles, the devil, appeared and said that he found conditions on earth to be bad. The Lord tacitly agreed that man had his weaknesses, but He slyly pointed out that His servant Faust could not be swayed from the path of righteousness. Mephistopheles made a wager with the Lord that Faust could be tempted from his faithful service. The Lord knew that He could rely on the righteous integrity of Faust, but that Mephistopheles could lead Faust downward if he were able to lay hold of Faust's soul. Mephistopheles considered Faust a likely victim, for Faust was trying to obtain the unobtainable.

Faust was not satisfied with all the knowledge he had acquired. He realized man's limits, and he saw his own insignificance in the great macrocosm. In this mood, he went for a walk with his servant, Wagner, among people who were not troubled by thoughts of a philosophical nature. In such a refreshing atmosphere, Faust was able to feel free and to think clearly. Faust told Wagner of his two souls, one which clung to earthly things, and another which strove toward supersensual things that could never be attained as long as his soul resided within his fleshly body. Feeling so limited in his daily life and desiring to learn the meaning of existence, Faust was ready to accept anything which would take him to a new kind of life.

Mephistopheles recognized that Faust was ready for his attack. In the form of a dog, Mephistopheles followed Faust to his home when the scholar returned to his contemplation of the meaning of life. After studying the Bible, he concluded that man's power should be used to produce something useful. Witnessing Faust's struggle with his ideas, the dog stepped forth in his true identity. But Faust remained unmoved by the arguments of Mephistopheles.

The next time Mephistopheles came,

FAUST by Johann Wolfgang von Goethe. Published by Alfred A. Knopf, Inc.

he found Faust much more receptive to his plot. Faust had decided that, although his struggles were divine, he had produced nothing to show for them. Faust was interested in life on this earth. At Mephistopheles' suggestion that he could peacefully enjoy a sensual existence, Faust declared that if ever he could lay himself in sloth and be at peace with himself, or if ever Mephistopheles could so rule him with flattery that he became self-satisfied, then let that be the end of Faust. But Faust had also renounced all things that made life worthwhile to most men. So he further contracted with Mephistopheles that if ever he found experience so profound that he would wish it to endure, then Faust would cease to be. This would be a wager, not the selling of a soul.

After two trials Mephistopheles had failed to tempt Faust with cheap debauchery. The next offering he presented was love for a woman. First Faust was brought to the Witch's Kitchen, where his youth was restored. Then a pure maiden, Gretchen, was presented to Faust, but when he saw her in her own innocent home, he vowed he could not harm her. Mephistopheles wooed the girl with caskets of jewels which she thought came from Faust, and Faust was so tempted that he returned to Gretchen. She surrendered herself to him as a fulfillment of her pure love.

Gretchen's brother convinced her that her act was a shameful one in the eyes of society. Troubled by Gretchen's grief, Faust finally killed her brother. Gretchen at last felt the full burden of her sin. Mephistopheles showed Faust more scenes of debauchery, but Faust's spirit was elevated by the thought of Gretchen and he was able to overcome the evil influence of the devil. Mephistopheles had hoped that Faust would desire the moment of his fulfillment of love to endure. However, Faust knew that enduring human love could not satisfy his craving. He regretted Gretchen's state of misery, and he returned to her; but she had killed her child and would not let her lover save her from the death to which she had been condemned.

Mephistopheles brought Faust to the emperor, who asked Faust to show him the most beautiful male and female who had ever existed—Paris, and Helen of Troy. Faust produced the images of these mythological characters, and at the sight of Helen, his desire to possess her was so strong that he fainted, and Mephistopheles brought him back in a swoon to his own laboratory. Mephistopheles was unable to comprehend Faust's desire for the ideal beauty that Helen represented.

With the help of Wagner, Mephistopheles created a formless spirit of learning, Homunculus, who could see what was going on in Faust's mind. Homunculus, Mephistopheles, and Faust went to Greece, where Mephistopheles borrowed from the fantastic images of classical mythology one of their grotesque forms. With Mephistopheles' intervention, a living Helen was brought to Faust. It seemed now, with the attainment of this supreme joy of beauty in Helen, that Faust would cry for such a moment to linger forever, but he soon realized that the enjoyment of transitory beauty was no more enduring than his other experiences.

With a new knowledge of himself, Faust returned to his native land. Achievement was now his goal, as he reaffirmed his earlier pledge that his power should be used to produce something useful to man. The mystical and magical powers which Faust had once held were banished so that he could stand before nature alone. He obtained a large strip of swamp land and restored it to productivity.

Many years passed. Now old and blind, Faust realized he had created a vast territory of land occupied by people who would always be active in making something useful for themselves. Having participated in this achievement, Faust beheld himself as a man standing among free and active people as one of them. At the moment when he realized what he had created, he cried out for this moment, so fair to him, to linger on. Faust had emerged from a self-centered egoist into a man who saw his actions as a part of a creative society.

He realized that life could be worth living, but in that moment of perception he lost his wager to Mephistopheles. The devil now claimed Faust's soul, but in reality he too had lost the wager. The Almighty was right. Although Faust had made mistakes in his life, he had always remained aware of goodness and truth.

Seeing his own defeat, Mephistopheles attempted to prevent the ascension of Faust's soul to God. Angels appeared to help Faust, however, and he was carried to a place in Heaven where all was active creation—exactly the kind of after-life that Faust would have chosen.

FILE NO. 113

Type of work: Novel
Author: Émile Gaboriau (1835-1873)
Type of plot: Mystery romance
Time of plot: 1866
Locale: Paris
First published: 1867

Principal characters:

M. André Fauvel, a Parisian banker
Valentine, his wife
Madeleine, his niece
Prosper Bertomy, his cashier
Raoul de Lagors, Valentine's nephew
Louis de Clameran, an adventurer
Gypsy, Prosper's mistress
M. Lecoq, a detective
Fanferlot, another detective

Critique:

Gaboriau's mystery stories have always been popular among readers of this type of fiction, and during the latter part of the nineteenth century he had a large following both in France and abroad. Many of our common conceptions of the French Sureté and French detectives come from his work. In Gaboriau's novels the detective is a brilliant individualist who always gets his man by reasoning, theatrics, and agility. M. Lecoq, for instance, is always disguised; not even his fellows at the police department have ever seen his true appearance. Usually he is even disguised from the reader. Gaboriau makes full use of melodrama, extravagant emotions, and improbable motives.

The Story:

Prosper Bertomy, a trusted cashier, came into the bank rather late one morning. Louis de Clameran was impatiently waiting, for the bank had agreed to have his three hundred and fifty thousand francs ready for him that day. Prosper hurried to the safe to get the money, but when he opened the door he discovered that the money was gone.

In great agitation he called for M. Fauvel. When a search failed to reveal the missing money, M. Fauvel called the police. During a preliminary questioning, it was learned that only Prosper and his employer, M. Fauvel, had keys to the safe. Only they knew the word to use on the alphabetical combination. Either M. Fauvel or Prosper had taken the money.

It was unthinkable that dignified, upright M. Fauvel would steal from himself. Prosper, on the other hand, had lost heavily at the gaming tables and he was the intimate of Raoul de Lagors, the dissolute nephew of Mme. Valentine Fauvel. Prosper's richly furnished apartment was presided over by the beautiful but notorious woman known as Gypsy. In the light of these facts, M. Fauvel raised no objection when the police took Prosper off to jail.

As Prosper left the bank, he contrived to throw a folded note to Cavaillon, a young friend. Following the directions, Cavaillon set off to deliver the message. Fanferlot, a detective, followed Cavaillon until the youth turned into an apartment building. There the detective easily cowed Cavaillon and took away the note, which warned Gypsy to flee immediately. Fanferlot, posing as Prosper's friend, delivered the note and induced the frightened girl to move into lodgings at the Archangel, a hotel run by Mme. Alexandre, secretly Fanferlot's wife. Well pleased with himself, Fanferlot went back to headquarters to report.

The examining judge, convinced of Prosper's guilt, pried into the cashier's financial affairs with detailed knowledge of that unhappy man's speculations. He even knew that Gypsy's real name was Chocareille and that she had once been in prison. The judge brought out the fact that Prosper had also been the favored suitor of Madeleine, the niece of the Fauvels, but that the intimacy had been broken off suddenly. Throughout the investigation Prosper stoutly maintained his innocence. Unable to shake his story, the judge sent Prosper back to his cell.

At the Archangel, Fanferlot kept a close watch on Gypsy. One day she received a note asking her to meet an unknown man at a public rendezvous. Fanferlot trailed her to the meeting and saw her talking to a fat man with red whiskers. When they left in a cab, Fanferlot jumped on the springs behind them. As soon as the horses pulled up, he withdrew into an areaway to watch. But no one got out. Gypsy and her escort had given him the slip by getting in one door of the cab and out the other. Dejected at his failure, Fanferlot went to report to Lecoq, his chief.

To his amazement the fat man with red whiskers was in Lecoq's apartment. Lecoq himself, with his great talent for disguise, had been Gypsy's mysterious companion. Then Lecoq showed Fanferlot a photograph of the safe and pointed out a scratch on the door. With sure logic he explained that two people had been involved in the robbery. One held the key and started to open the door; the second tried to draw away the hand of the first. In the struggle the door was scratched.

After Lecoq had convinced the judge that there was no strong case against Prosper, the cashier was released in the company of Lecoq, who had become transformed into the clownish M. Verduret. Prosper put himself completely in the hands of his new friend and the two of them began the work of locating the guilty parties.

Suspicion pointed to Raoul de Lagors and Louis de Clameran. They had a great deal of influence in the Fauvel household, and Valentine Fauvel seemed greatly taken with her brilliant, handsome nephew. Suspecting a clandestine love affair, Lecoq went to the south of France to ferret out the backgrounds of Raoul and de Clameran. There he learned that in 1841 the de Clameran family had lived on the banks of the Rhone near Tarascon. The family consisted of the old marquis, his older son Gaston, and his younger son Louis. Across the river lived the Countess de la Verberie and her daughter Valentine. Between the two families there had been a feud for generations.

Gaston, the older brother, fell in love with Valentine and often met her secretly. When their affair became known, Gaston defended her honor in a public brawl in which he killed two men. After the fight he fled to South America. The old marquis died from the shock, and Louis left home to lead a life of depravity. Within a few months Valentine gave birth to Gaston's child in England, and her mother sternly took the baby away and placed him with an English family. Later Valentine married M. Fauvel without telling him about her child.

By chance Louis de Clameran discovered Mme. Fauvel's secret. Her son, he claimed, was the man known as Raoul de Lagors. With de Clameran's help the conscience-stricken woman introduced Raoul to her husband as her nephew and made him one of the Fauvel household. Raoul, at the instigation of de Clameran, extorted large sums of money from her.

At last the time came when she had neither money nor jewels left, and de Clameran threatened to expose her. Madeleine, overhearing his threats, loyally stood by her aunt and promised to marry de Clameran to buy his silence. Raoul, playing on his mother's sympathies, persuaded her to give him the key to the bank safe, and she even went with him to rob her husband. At the last moment Valentine regretted her decision, and in her attempts to take away the key she scratched the door. Raoul, ignoring her pleas, took the money from the safe.

When Lecoq told the whole story to Prosper, the cashier was shocked. He had, in an anonymous letter, told M. Fauvel that Raoul was Valentine's lover.

Angry and grief-stricken after reading the letter, M. Fauvel confronted Raoul and his wife. He was threatening to shoot Raoul when Lecoq appeared, unmasked Raoul as an imposter, and returned the stolen money to M. Fauvel. Valentine's real son had died years ago; Raoul had been coached in the part by de Clameran. M. Fauvel forgave his wife's past and was reunited with her.

With his innocence established, Prosper was free to marry Madeleine. De Clameran went mad in prison. Lecoq at last revealed that he had saved Prosper merely to shame Gypsy, who had deserted Lecoq to become Prosper's mistress.

THE FINANCIER

Type of work: Novel
Author: Theodore Dreiser (1871-1945)
Type of plot: Naturalism
Time of plot: About 1850 to 1874
Locale: Philadelphia
First published: 1912

Principal characters:
FRANK A. COWPERWOOD, the financier
LILLIAN SEMPLE COWPERWOOD, his wife
EDWARD BUTLER, contractor and politician
AILEEN BUTLER, his daughter
HENRY COWPERWOOD, Frank's father

Critique:

In this novel characters are more sharply drawn and more dynamic than they are in other of Dreiser's creations. Cowperwood himself, by contrast with Sister Carrie, Jennie Gerhardt, and Clyde Griffiths, is more than a pawn of destiny, a victim of society. He is an aggressive person who fights and plans, who can adapt himself to circumstances and environment. He is both a realist and a fighter. It is plain that Dreiser thought of him as the typical capitalist, the financier.

The Story:

From his very early years Frank Cowperwood was interested in only one thing —making money. When he was still in his teens he made his first successful business transaction. While passing by an auction sale, he successfully bid for a lot of Java coffee, which he sold to a grocer at a profit of one hundred per cent. His family marveled at Frank's ability and his wealthy uncle, Seneca Davis, encouraged him to go into business as soon as possible.

Through several well-paying positions and shrewd speculation Frank acquired enough money to open his own brokerage house. Within a short time he was immensely successful, one of the most enterprising young financiers in Philadelphia.

One day he met Lillian Semple, the wife of a business associate. About a year later her husband died and Frank married the widow. By that time he had accumulated a large fortune, and he was familiar with local and state politicians, among them Edward Butler, who had risen from being a mere collector of garbage to a leading position in local politics. Through Butler Frank met many other influential people as his business and popularity increased.

Frank and Lillian had several children, but the youngsters did not particularly interest him. Rather, his sole interest was his business. His father, Henry Cowperwood, finally became president of the bank in which he was employed. Both Cowperwoods built expensive houses and furnished them luxuriously. Frank bought fine paintings and other rare objects of art.

His home life was not satisfactory. Lillian was older, more passive than he, and her beauty had almost disappeared. By contrast, Edward Butler's daughter Aileen was tremendously appealing. She was young, beautiful, high-spirited. Frank fell in love with her, and in spite of her strong religious training she became his mistress. He rented a house where they met and furnished it with the paintings and statues he had bought.

Though Frank had become one of the financial powers in Philadelphia, he had to plan and scheme continually in order to thwart more powerful monopolists. He managed to acquire large sums from the state treasury through local politicians. The city treasurer, Stener, proved amenable in many ways, and he and Frank became involved in many shady transactions. Frank bought shares in railroads and local streetcar properties.

After the great Chicago fire, some of Frank's investments were in a perilous state. He went to friends and associates and urged them to stand together in order to avoid losses. But so widespread were the effects of the fire that the manipulations of the city politicians were certain to be discovered on the eve of an election. Something had to be done to satisfy indignant reform groups who would demand action when they discovered what had occurred.

In the meantime someone had sent an anonymous note to Edward Butler, telling him that Frank and Aileen were living together. When Frank went to Butler, the contractor refused to help him, and Frank knew that somehow he had discovered his relationship with Aileen. Butler, who had become his enemy, urged the other politicians to make Frank a scapegoat for their dishonest dealings.

As a result Frank and Stener, the city treasurer, were indicted on charges of embezzlement and grand larceny. Ruined financially, Frank pleaded not guilty, but the jury convicted both him and Stener. He appealed, and posted bail to avoid jail. The appeal was denied, although the judges were not united in their decision. As soon as the appeal had been denied, the sheriff was supposed to take Frank to jail until he should be sentenced. But the sheriff was bribed, and Frank had a few more days of freedom. His property was sold to pay his debts. His father resigned his position at the bank.

Frank and Aileen had given up the house where they formerly met. Their meetings now took place at a house in another part of town. Determined to put an end to the affair, Butler and Pinkerton detectives entered the house and confronted the couple. Butler tried various schemes to make Aileen leave Philadelphia, but all failed after Aileen learned that her father had hired detectives to trail her.

Frank was sentenced to four years and nine months in the penitentiary. Aileen remained faithful to him. When Lillian went to visit him, Frank asked her for a divorce. She refused.

After Edward Butler died, Frank's friends managed to get him a parole. At the end of thirteen months in jail, he was freed in March, 1873. Through Wingate, a friend and business associate, he had succeeded in rebuilding his business. He had a bachelor apartment where Aileen visited him. Though he was ostensibly still living with his wife, all of the town had long ago known of his relationship with Aileen.

In September, 1873, the panic came. Frank, who had bought stocks cheaply, made a fortune. Several months later he went with Aileen to Chicago, where he planned to reëstablish himself. Lillian got a divorce but remained friendly with the Cowperwood family. She lived luxuriously; Frank, to buy his own freedom, had provided handsomely for her and the children.

FOR WHOM THE BELL TOLLS

Type of work: Novel
Author: Ernest Hemingway (1898-)
Type of plot: Impressionistic realism
Time of plot: 1937
Locale: Spain
First published: 1940

Principal characters:

ROBERT JORDAN, an American fighting with the Spanish Loyalists
PABLO, a guerrilla leader
PILAR, his wife
MARIA, loved by Jordan
ANSELMO, another guerrilla

Critique:

In order to understand Ernest Hemingway's motive in writing *For Whom the Bell Tolls,* it is necessary to know the essence of the quotation from John Donne, from which Hemingway took his theme: ". . . any mans death diminishes me, because I am involved in Mankinde; And therefore never send to know for whom the bell tolls; It tolls for thee." Hemingway wanted his readers to feel that what happened to the Loyalists in Spain in 1937 was a part of that crisis of the modern world in which we all share. The novel tells the story of three days in the life of a young American who had concerned himself with the Loyalist cause in Spain. It is a story of courage, of loyalty, of the human will to endure. *For Whom the Bell Tolls* is a tragic novel, but one of great nobility and compassion. Hemingway is one of the great spokesmen of our time.

The Story:

At first nothing was important but the bridge, neither his life nor the imminent danger of his death—just the bridge. Robert Jordan was a young American teacher who was in Spain fighting with the Loyalist guerrillas. His present and most important mission was to blow up a bridge which would be of great strategic importance during a Loyalist offensive three days hence. Jordan was behind the Fascist lines, with orders to make contact with Pablo, the leader of a guerrilla band,

and with his wife Pilar, who was the really strong figure among the partisans. While Pablo was weak and a drunken braggart, Pilar was strong and trustworthy. She was a swarthy, raw-boned woman, vulgar and outspoken, but she was so fiercely devoted to the Loyalist cause that Jordan knew she would carry out her part of the mission regardless of her personal danger.

The plan was for Jordan to study the bridge from all angles and then to make final plans for its destruction at the proper moment. Jordan had blown up many bridges and three trains, but this was the first time that everything must be done on a split-second schedule. Pablo and Pilar were to assist Jordan in any way they could, even to rounding up other bands of guerrillas if Jordan needed them to accomplish his mission.

At the cave hideout of Pablo and Pilar, Jordan met a beautiful young girl named Maria, who had escaped from the Fascists. Maria had been subjected to every possible indignity that a woman could suffer. She had been starved and tortured and raped, and she felt unclean. At the camp Jordan also met Anselmo, a loyal old man who would follow orders regardless of his personal safety. Anselmo hated having to kill but, if he were so ordered, faithful Anselmo would kill.

Jordan loved the brutally shrewd, desperate, loyal guerrillas, for he knew their cruelties against the Fascists stemmed from poverty and ignorance. But the Fascists' cruelty he abhored, for the Fascists came largely from the wealthy, ambitious people of Spain. Maria's story of her suffering at their hands filled him with such hatred that he could have killed a thousand of them, even though he, like Anselmo, hated to kill.

The first night he spent at the guerrilla camp destroyed his cold approach to the mission before him, for he fell deeply in love with Maria. She came to his sleeping bag that night, and although they talked but little he knew after she left that he was no longer ready to die. He told Maria that one day they would be married, but he was afraid of the future. And fear was dangerous for a man on an important mission.

Jordan made many sketches of the bridge and laid his plans carefully. There his work was almost ruined by Pablo's treachery. On the night before the blowing up of the bridge Pablo deserted after stealing and destroying the explosives and the detonators hidden in Jordan's pack. Pablo returned, repentant, on the morning of the mission, but the damage had been done. The loss of the detonators and the explosives meant that Jordan and his helper would have to blow the bridge with hand grenades, a much more dangerous method. Pablo had tried to redeem himself by bringing with him another small guerrilla band and their horses. Although Jordan despised Pablo by that time, he forgave him, as did Pilar.

At the bridge Jordan worked quickly and carefully. Each person had a specific job to do, and each did his work well. First Jordan and Anselmo had to kill the sentries, a job Anselmo hated. Pablo and his guerrillas attacked the Fascist lines approaching the bridge, to prevent their crossing before the bridge was demolished. Jordan had been ordered to blow up the bridge at the beginning of a Loyalist bombing attack over the Fascist lines. When he heard the thudding explosions of the bombs, he pulled the pins and the bridge shot high into the air. Jordan got to cover safely, but Anselmo was killed by a steel fragment from the bridge. As Jordan looked at the old man and realized that he might be alive if Pablo had not stolen the detonators, he wanted to kill Pablo. But he knew that his duty was otherwise, and he ran to the designated meeting place of the fugitive guerrillas.

There he found Pablo, Pilar, Maria, and the two remaining gipsy partisans. Pablo, herding the extra horses, said that all the other guerrillas had been killed. Jordan knew that Pablo had ruthlessly killed the other men so that he could get their horses. When he confronted Pablo with this knowledge, Pablo admitted the slaughter, but shrugged his great shoulders and said that the men had not been of his band.

The problem now was to cross a road which could be swept by Fascist gunfire, the road that led to safety. Jordan knew that the first two people would have the best chance, since probably they could cross before the Fascists were alerted. Because Pablo knew the road to safety, Jordan put him on the first horse. Maria was second, for Jordan was determined that she should be saved before the others. Pilar was to go next, then the two remaining guerrillas, and last of all Jordan. The first four crossed safely, but Jordan's horse, wounded by Fascist bullets, fell on Jordan's leg. The others dragged him across the road and out of the line of fire, but he knew that he could not go on; he was too badly injured to ride a horse. Pablo and Pilar understood, but Maria begged to stay with him. Jordan told Pilar to take Maria away when he gave the signal, and then he talked to the girl he loved so much. He told her that she must go on, that as long as she lived, he lived also. But when the time came, she had to be put on her horse and led away.

Jordan, settling down to wait for the approaching Fascist troops, propped himself against a tree, with his submachine gun across his knees. As he waited, he thought over the events that had brought him to that place. He knew that what he had done was right, but that his side might not win for many years. But he knew, too, that if the common people kept trying, kept dying, someday they would win. He hoped they would be prepared when that day came, that they would no longer want to kill and torture, but would struggle for peace and for good as they were now struggling for freedom. He felt at the end that his own part in the struggle had not been in vain. As he saw the first Fascist officer approaching, Robert Jordan smiled. He was ready.

THE FORSYTE SAGA

Type of work: Novel
Author: John Galsworthy (1867-1933)
Type of plot: Social chronicle
Time of plot: 1886-1920
Locale: England
First published: 1906, 1920, 1921

Principal characters:

SOAMES FORSYTE, a man of property
IRENE, his wife
OLD JOLYON FORSYTE, his uncle
YOUNG JOLYON, Old Jolyon's son
JUNE, Young Jolyon's daughter
PHILIP BOSINNEY, an architect engaged to June
ANNETTE, Soames' second wife
FLEUR, their daughter
JON, Irene's and Young Jolyon's son
WINIFRED DARTIE, Soames' sister; Monty Dartie's wife

Critique:

Galsworthy's trilogy — *The Man of Property, In Chancery, To Let*—concerns an upper middle-class English family and traces, through the story of a group of related characters, the changing aspects of manners and morals from the Victorian age to the period between wars. In his preface John Galsworthy points to the general theme of the series—the disturbance that Beauty creates in the lives of men, as exemplified by the story of Irene. *The Forsyte Saga* achieves a high point of excellence as social history and art.

The Story:

In 1886 all the Forsytes gathered at Old Jolyon Forsyte's house to celebrate the engagement of his granddaughter, June, to Philip Bosinney, a young architect. Young Jolyon Forsyte, June's father, was estranged from his family because he had run away with a governess, whom he had married after June's mother died.

Old Jolyon complained that he saw little of June. Lonely, he called on Young Jolyon, whom he had not seen in many years. He found his son working as an underwriter for Lloyd's and painting water-colors. By his second wife he had two children, Holly and Jolly.

The family knew that Soames had been having trouble with his lovely wife, Irene. She had a profound aversion for Soames, and had recently reminded him of her premarital stipulation that she should have her freedom if the marriage were not a success. In his efforts to please her, Soames planned to build a large country place. Deciding that June's fiancé would be a good choice for an architect, he bought an estate at Robin Hill and hired Bosinney to build the house.

When Soames made suggestions about the plans, Bosinney appeared offended, and in the end the plans were drawn as Bosinney wished. As the work proceeded, Soames and Bosinney argued over costs that exceeded the original estimate.

One day Swithin Forsyte, Soames' uncle, took Irene to see the house. Bosinney met them, and while Swithin dozed the architect talked to Irene alone. That day Irene and Bosinney fell hopelessly in love with one another. Irene's already unbearable life with Soames became impossible. She asked for a separate room.

There were new troubles over the house. Bosinney had agreed to decorate it, but only if he could have a free hand. Soames finally agreed. Irene and Bosinney began to meet secretly. As their affair progressed, June became more unhappy and self-centered. Finally Old Jolyon took June away for a holiday. He wrote to Young Jolyon, asking him to see Bosinney and learn his intentions toward June. Young Jolyon talked to Bosinney, but the report he made to his father was vague.

When the house was completed, Soames sued Bosinney for exceeding his highest estimate and Irene refused to move to Robin Hill. When the lawsuit over the house came to trial, Soames won his case without difficulty. That same night Bosinney, after spending the afternoon with Irene and learning that Soames had forced himself on her, was accidentally run over. Irene left her husband on the day of the trial, but that night she returned to his house because there was now no place else for her to go. June persuaded her grandfather to buy Robin Hill for Jolyon's family.

A short time after Bosinney's death Irene left Soames permanently, settled in a small flat, and gave music lessons to support herself. Several years later she visited Robin Hill secretly and there met Old Jolyon. She won him by her gentleness and charm, and during that summer she made his days happy for him. Late in the summer he died quietly while waiting for her.

After his separation from Irene, Soames devoted himself to making money. Then, still hoping to have an heir, he began to court a French girl, Annette Lamotte. At the same time his sister Winifred was in difficulties. Her husband, Monty Dartie, stole her pearls and ran away to South America with a Spanish dancer. When he decided to marry Annette, Soames went to Irene to see if she would provide grounds for his suit. He found that she had lived a model life. While visiting her, Soames realized that he still loved her and he tried to persuade her to come back to him. When she refused, he hired a detective to get the evidence he needed.

Old Jolyon had willed a legacy to Irene, with Young Jolyon, now a widower, as trustee. When Soames annoyed Irene, she appealed to Young Jolyon for protection. Irene went to Paris to avoid Soames and shortly afterward Young Jolyon joined her. His visit was cut short by Jolly, who announced that he had joined the yeomanry to fight in the Boer War. Holly had in the meantime fallen in love with Val Dartie, her cousin. When Val proposed to Holly, he was overheard by Jolly, who dared Val to join the yeomanry with him. Val accepted. June then decided to become a Red Cross nurse, and Holly went with her. Monty Dartie reappeared unexpectedly. To avoid further scandal, Winifred decided to take him back.

Soames went to Paris in a last effort to persuade Irene. Frightened, Irene returned to Young Jolyon. Before they became lovers in deed, they were presented with papers by Soames' lawyer. They decided to go abroad together. Before their departure Young Jolyon received word that Jolly had died of enteric fever during the African campaign. Later Soames secured his divorce and married Annette. Val married Holly, to the discomfiture of both branches of the family.

Irene presented Jolyon with a son, Jon. When Annette was about to give birth to a child, Soames had to choose between saving the mother or the child. Wishing an heir, Soames chose to save the child. Fortunately, both Annette and the baby lived.

Little Jon grew up under the adoring eyes of his parents. Fleur grew up spoiled by her doting father.

Years passed. Monty Dartie was dead. Val and Holly were training race horses. One day in a picture gallery Soames impulsively invited a young man, Michael Mont, to see his collection of pictures. That same afternoon he saw Irene and her son Jon for the first time in twenty years. By chance Fleur and Jon met. Having decided that he wanted to try farming, Jon went to stay with Val Dartie. Fleur also appeared to spend the week with Holly. Jon and Fleur fell deeply in love.

They had only vague ideas regarding the cause of the feud between their respective branches of the family. Later Fleur learned all the details from Prosper Profond, with whom Annette was having an affair, and from Winifred Dartie. She was still determined to marry Jon. Meanwhile Michael Mont had Soames' permission to court Fleur. When Soames heard of the affair between Annette and Prosper, she did not deny it, but she promised there would be no scandal.

Fleur tried to persuade Jon into a hasty marriage. She failed because Young Jolyon reluctantly gave his son a letter revealing the story of Soames and Irene. Reading it, Jon realized that he could never marry Fleur. His decision became irrevocable when his father died. He left England at once and went to America, where Irene joined him. Fleur, disappointed, married Michael Mont.

When Timothy, the last of the old Forsytes, died, Soames realized that the Forsyte age had passed. Its way of life was like an empty house—to let. He felt lonely and old.

FORTITUDE

Type of work: Novel
Author: Hugh Walpole (1884-1941)
Type of plot: Sentimental romance
Time of plot: Late nineteenth century
Locale: England
First published: 1913

Principal characters:
PETER WESTCOTT, a young writer
STEPHEN BRANT, a friend
CLARE, Peter's wife
BOBBY GALLEON, a student at Dawson's
JERRY CARDILLAC (CARDS), another student
MR. ZANTI, a bookseller
NORA MONOGUE, Peter's friend and adviser

Critique:

Hugh Walpole's novel is likely to attract readers for some time to come because of its sympathetic story. As the title suggests, the author points to the fact that life is not a simple process and that fortitude is the most desirable quality for a young man facing life.

The Story:

Peter Westcott lived with his harsh father and his invalid mother at Scaw House, near the town of Treliss in Cornwall. As he grew up, Peter made friends with Stephen Brant, a farmer who occasionally took the child to the Bending Mule Inn. One Christmas Eve, at the inn, Peter watched Stephen fighting with another man over a girl. That night he arrived home late from the Bending Mule and his father gave him the most severe whipping he had yet received. On another day, Stephen took him to the curiosity shop operated by Zachary Tan. There Peter was introduced to a jovial Mr. Emilio Zanti, from London, who treated the boy with special consideration. At supper that night Peter's father told him that he was to go off to school in Devonshire.

The next phase of Peter's life revolved about Dawson's School, where his best friends were Bobby Galleon and Jerry Cardillac. Bobby was the son of a famous writer. Cardillac, called Cards, was Peter's idol; he was everything which Peter would have liked to have been, and was not. After Cards left at the end of Peter's second year, affairs did not progress so smoothly for Peter. One day he found Jerrard, the best bowler in school, forcing whiskey down the throat of a small boy. Despite the fact that it was the eve of a big game in which Jerrard's services were needed, Peter, in his capacity as a monitor, turned him in to the authorities. Jerrard was expelled, and Dawson's lost the game. On the last day of the term the whole school joined in hissing Peter when he called the roll. Bobby Galleon was the single exception.

He was spared the indignity of returning to Dawson's when the school was closed after the summer holidays because of lack of funds. His father then sent Peter to read law in the office of Mr. Aitchinson in Treliss. Meanwhile Peter became aware of his mother. She had been for many years an invalid who never left her room, and Peter was not encouraged to visit her. One day, when his father was away, Peter went to her room. He found that she was dying as the result of his father's cruel and harsh attitude toward her, and his visit hastened her death. A short time after her funeral Peter again saw Mr. Zanti, who offered the lad a job in his bookshop in London. Peter, finding life at Scaw House intolerable, decided to leave home. On Easter morning he met a little girl who gave her name as Clare Elizabeth Rossiter. According to his plans, Peter left home, but only after fighting with his father.

In London Peter worked in Mr. Zanti's bookshop as an assistant to Gottfried Hanz. Mr. Zanti had found him lodgings with Mrs. Brockett, and there he met Nora Monogue, who encouraged Peter when he began to write. A strange aspect of the bookshop was the great number of people who visited it without buying any books, visitors who passed mysteriously into the back room of the shop. For seven years Peter Westcott worked in Zanti's shop and wrote in his room at Brockett's. In November, 1895, he finished his first novel, *Reuben Hallard,* and began to look for a publisher. One day he again met Clare Rossiter, who had come to call on Nora Monogue. Almost at once Peter found himself falling in love with her. Meanwhile strange things had been happening at the bookstore. When the Prince and Princess of Schloss visited London, one of the visitors to the shop threw a bomb at Queen Victoria as the royal procession passed. Shortly afterward Stephen Brant appeared to take Peter away from the shop. They found lodgings in the slums of Bucket Lane.

Neither of the two was able to find steady employment. When Peter became ill from lack of food, Stephen notified Peter's friend from Dawson's, Bobby Galleon, whom Peter had met in the city. Peter was moved to his friend's house, where Bobby and his wife nursed him back to health. In a short time *Reuben Hallard* was published. It was an immediate success, and Peter Westcott became known in literary circles. Thus he met Mrs. Launce, who was finally instrumental in bringing Peter and Clare together. After they were married, they took a house in Chelsea. There a child was born to Clare, a son named Stephen. But the marriage was not a success. Clare disapproved of Stephen and Mr. Zanti. Peter's second novel brought little money. Back to London came Peter's old school friend, Jerry Cardillac, and Clare became interested in him.

The final blow to Peter's happiness came when little Stephen died. Peter blamed Clare for the child's death. A short time later she left him to join Cardillac in France, after refusing Peter's constant offers to try to make her life as she wanted it. Then Peter's third novel proved a failure. He decided to leave London and return to Scaw House. In Treliss he encountered Nora Monogue; she had been sent to Cornwall because she could live, at the most, only a few weeks. At Scaw House he found his father sodden in drink and sharing the musty house with a slatternly housekeeper. Peter was slipping into the same useless life. But Nora Monogue felt that Peter, now thirty years old, could still be a successful writer, and she used the last of her rapidly failing strength to persuade him to go back to London. As a final resort, Nora admitted that she had always loved him, and her dying request was that he leave his father and return to London to start writing again. So Peter became a man, realizing for the first time that during his whole life his attitude had been childish. He learned fortitude from the dying Nora, and he became the master of his own destiny.

THE FORTRESS

Type of work: Novel
Author: Hugh Walpole (1884-1941)
Type of plot: Historical chronicle
Time of plot: Nineteenth century
Locale: England
First published: 1932

Principal characters:
JUDITH PARIS, Rogue Herries' daughter
WALTER HERRIES, Judith's cousin
JENNIFER HERRIES, another cousin
ADAM PARIS, Judith's son
JOHN, Jennifer's son
ELIZABETH, Walter's daughter
UHLAND, Walter's son
MARGARET, Adam's wife

Critique:

The Fortress is part three of the Herries chronicle, which covers more than two hundred years of English social history. The present work portrays the later life of Judith Paris and her quarrel with Walter. The scope of the chronicle is vast, and *The Fortress* alone covers a space of over fifty years and a host of people. Although at times *The Fortress* stalls among the multitude of characters and their gossip, it has considerable narrative power. Walpole must be considered a competent popular novelist.

The Story:

The quarrel between Walter Herries of Westaways and Jennifer Herries, his kinswoman at Fell House, went back a long way. Christabel, Walter's weak mother, had been insulted by Jennifer over the breaking of a fan at a ball, and Walter never forgot the slight to his proud, snobbish family. He resented also the presence of Judith Paris and her illegitimate son, living brazenly, as he thought, at Fell House, so near his own fine house, Westaways. By one method or another he had determined to drive out the whole household. And he might have succeeded had it not been for Judith.

Judith accused her cousin outright of having incited a riot in which Reuben Sunwood, another kinsman, had been killed. Admitting the charge, Walter Herries said he had had no way of foreseeing Reuben's death. He proposed that Jennifer and Judith should sell him Fell House at a fair price and move away. If they did not, Walter would persecute them until they would be glad to leave. When Judith refused, Walter bought Ireby, a high hill overlooking Fell House. There he planned to build a huge mansion to dwarf Jennifer's modest home and he would be there always to spy on the people of Fell House and hurt them. He also reminded Judith of Francis, Jennifer's husband, who had committed suicide. Walter had exposed Jennifer's lover to him, and the coward had shot himself rather than the man who had defiled his home. But Judith defied Walter's angry boasts of his power and cunning.

At Fell House she took complete charge and Jennifer thankfully let her assume management of the household. Since she was firm and headstrong, they did not give in to Walter even when he poisoned their cows.

Uhland and Elizabeth were Walter's children. The girl was beautiful and kind, but Uhland was his father's pride. The son was lame and pampered. At an early age he shared his father's hatred of Judith and her close kin. One day as he walked in the woods he saw his sister Elizabeth and John, Jennifer's son, together. He ordered his sister to see no more of John. But Elizabeth, who had a mind of her own, refused, knowing that her brother could never bring himself to tell his father. Uhland himself, lame and pale, was much attracted to robust Adam Paris, Judith's son.

As Adam Paris grew up into a strong, rebellious boy, he soon learned that he was illegitimate and that his aunt had taken a lover. The knowledge made him resentful of all restraint and only by the grace of the family name was he allowed to remain at Rugby.

When Walter really began to build on Ireby hill, the countryfolk named his great mansion The Fortress. Walter had carried out his threat to dwarf the house of Judith and to spy on her people. Jennifer was greatly disturbed. Her fear of Walter made her go every day to Ireby and survey the progress made. Finally the strain was too much to bear; Jennifer died quietly from sheer apprehension.

When Walter's family moved into The Fortress they gave a big reception, but even the crowds and the huge fires could not warm the great stone house. Elizabeth, especially, was unhappy in the gloomy, rambling mansion. She and John had agreed not to see each other any more, as marriage seemed an impossibility while their families were enemies. Consequently, when she was invited to visit her Herries cousins in London, she accepted gratefully. But once in fine society, she was troubled. She felt lonely and left out. Mr. Temple, a fat lawyer, pursued her vigorously.

Uhland followed his sister to London. When he saw that Elizabeth could marry the rich and eligible Mr. Temple, he fiercely urged the match. Elizabeth felt more than ever estranged from her family, and when her father wrote and commanded the marriage, Elizabeth promptly and vehemently refused Mr. Temple's awkward proposal. Enlisting the help of a friendly maid, she stole out of the Herries house and took a job as governess with a family named Golightly.

In her new position Elizabeth had little to do. Her employers, however, were common, noisy people and she soon began to detest her place with them. Then her ridiculous employer, old enough to be her father, declared his love for her and his resolution to leave his wife. Terrified, Elizabeth wrote an appeal to John. Forgetting their families' enmity, John and Elizabeth were quietly married.

At the age of twenty-two Adam Paris decided to leave Fell House. He had been threatening to go away for five years, but each time his mother had put him off.

In London Adam found only temporary employment, and in a few weeks he was hungry and penniless. Taken in by chance by the Kraft family, he soon joined the Chartist movement. In that struggle Caesar Kraft became Adam's guide and Kraft's daughter, Margaret, offered Adam sympathy and finally love.

The 1840's were stirring times in England. Widespread unemployment, poverty, and child labor made reform necessary. The Chartists, helped by Adam and many others, planned their big procession to Parliament. Caesar Kraft was a moderate man, and at a Chartist meeting he counseled patience. When the procession was broken up, the hotheads blamed him for their failure, and in the riot that followed Kraft was clubbed to death.

Adam and Margaret were married shortly afterward. Adam's small skill at editing and hack writing kept them going in a tiny apartment. On their visits to Fell House, Margaret was very unhappy. She saw her husband engulfed by his mother's love and herself an outsider. When she broke down one night and wept, Adam began to understand her feelings and desires. From that time on Judith took second place with him, even after they moved to Fell House to stay.

In London John Herries did well, and as a parliamentary secretary his future seemed bright. But Uhland was madly determined to make John pay for having the impertinence to marry his sister. Everywhere John went he knew Uhland was dogging his path. John was not exactly afraid, but contact with Uhland left him powerless before that great hatred.

In a desperate attempt to shake off his incubus, John met Uhland in a deserted country house. There he suddenly lost his terror of his tormentor and jumped up, daring Uhland to follow him any more. In a mad rage Uhland seized his gun and shot John and then killed himself. So Elizabeth was left with Benjie, her small son. Walter's hate had borne its final, bitter fruit.

In The Fortress Walter lived out his drunken old age with a gaudy housekeeper. Steadfastly he refused to answer Elizabeth's letters or to let her call. Finally, when she was over sixty, Elizabeth heard that her father was seriously ill. She stormed The Fortress, sent the blowzy housekeeper packing, and nursed the old drunkard back to health. So successful was she with the chastened old man that on Judith's hundredth birthday Elizabeth brought her father with her as a guest to Fell House.

THE FORTY DAYS OF MUSA DAGH

Type of work: Novel
Author: Franz Werfel (1890-1945)
Type of plot: Historical romance
Time of plot: 1915
Locale: Near Antioch, Syria
First published: 1934

Principal characters:
GABRIEL BAGRADIAN, an Armenian patriot
JULIETTE BAGRADIAN, his wife
STEPHAN BAGRADIAN, their son
TER HAIGASUN, Armenian priest of the village of Yoghonoluk

Critique:

The triumphant defense of the stronghold of Musa Dagh by a small band of Armenians is a moving story in itself. It can only be added that Franz Werfel has, with beautiful restraint, given this narrative of sacrifice and devotion a universal meaning.

The Story:

After twenty-three years spent in Paris, Gabriel Bagradian returned with his wife and child to his ancestral village of Yoghonoluk. He had gone back to Turkey in order to settle the affairs of his dying brother, and after his death Gabriel stayed on in the village to await the end of European hostilities.

One Sunday his son's tutor told him officials had been through the village collecting all passports. To learn what had happened, Bagradian saddled a horse and started for Antioch. There the Kaimakam, or governor, gave only evasive answers about the passport incident. Later, in a Turkish bath, Bagradian heard that the Turkish war minister had ordered all Armenians disarmed and given menial work. From his Mohammedan friend, Agha Rifaat Bereket, Bagradian learned that rich and prominent Armenians would soon be persecuted.

Gabriel was worried. On his return to Yoghonoluk he began to collect data on the number of men of fighting age in the vicinity. Ter Haigasun, the Gregorian priest, told him one day that there had been a mass arrest in Antioch. Bagradian began a survey of Musa Dagh, a mountain which lay between the Armenian villages and the Mediterranean Sea. After having maps drawn of the terrain, Bagradian knew that the plateau with its natural fortifications offered a refuge for his people.

One day a friendly Turkish policeman confided to Bagradian that in three days the village would be ordered to prepare for its trip into exile. Bagradian called a meeting of the people. The Protestant pastor, Nokhudian, and his congregation voted to accept banishment, the rest of the population to defend Musa Dagh. Ter Haigasun was elected leader. The next morning the young men under Bagradian's directions began the construction of trenches and other defenses on Musa Dagh, and at night the people carried provisions up the mountain. Unfortunately there were not enough rifles to go around and very little ammunition, but the men of the village were augmented by army deserters who drifted in from the desert until there were sixty armed men in the community. On the third day the convoy escort arrived. The village pretended to busy itself with preparations for the trip, but that night everyone but Pastor Nokhudian's flock secretly departed for Musa Dagh.

It took five days for the Turks to discover Bagradian's mountain retreat, for the woods were so thick and the trenches dug so cleverly that the encampment was not visible from below. During that time the trenches were completed, posts assigned, and patterns for daily living laid down. Everyone was given a task, and the food of the community was held in common so that all might be treated fairly.

The first sortie ended in a victory for the holders of Musa Dagh. The four hundred regulars and gendarmes who boldly attacked, not even seeking cover, were quickly routed and substantial booty of badly needed ammunition, boots, and uniforms was recovered. The second attack came several days later. Turkish howitzers managed to do considerable damage, wounding six non-combatants in the town enclosure and setting the grain depot on fire. Sarkis Kilikian, commander of the south bastion, rigged up a catapult to hurl stones at the attackers. These in turn caused a landslide which killed or maimed half the Turkish force. Young Stephan Bagradian and his friend, Haik, raided the Turkish gun emplacements. Sixteen of the defenders were killed.

Three days later there were again signs of activity in the valley. The Kaimakam had imported families of Arabs to take over the Armenian houses and farms. On Musa Dagh a Greek-American adventurer, Gonzague Maris, who had fled with the Armenians and who had since seduced Juliette Bagradian, tried to persuade her to flee with him under the protection his passport afforded. She was undecided. Bagradian and his wife had grown apart in those troubled times. He was burdened with military duties, and she seemed indifferent to his fate. Bagradian found his only companionship in Iskuhi, a refugee from Zeitun.

The next attack was carried out by two thousand trained Turkish soldiers. In fierce fighting they captured the first line of trenches below the southern bastion. That night Bagradian had his troops counterattack and the trenches were retaken. The defenders also set a fire which raced down the mountain, driving the Turks into the valley. Musa Dagh was again saved.

Gonzague Maris begged Juliette several times to go away with him, but she did not have the courage to tell her husband she was leaving him. Then Bagradian discovered the lovers together and took his wife off, half-unconscious, to her tent. She was seriously ill with fever. The Greek disappeared of his own accord.

That same night Stephan Bagradian left Musa Dagh, without permission, to accompany his friend Haik, who was being sent to the American consul in Aleppo to ask for intervention on behalf of his people. Haik made his way safely to Aleppo, but Stephan developed a fever and had to start back to the mountain. On the way, the Turks captured and killed him. His body was thrown into the cemetery yard in Yoghonoluk where it was found by some old women who took it to his father. The last of the Bagradians was buried on Musa Dagh.

The next day flocks grazing beyond the fortifications were captured by the Turks. There was now only enough food to last three or four days more.

On the fortieth day on Musa Dagh the people were suffering. It was their third day of famine. Gabriel had planned one last desperate attack for that night, an attempt to reach the valley with his men, capture some high officials as hostages, and return to the mountain. But that afternoon, as Ter Haigasun held a service to petition God for help, Sarkis Kilikian and his deserters broke into the town enclosure to steal ammunition and food. They fled, setting fire to the buildings to cover their escape. The Turks took advantage of their desertion to capture the south bastion. The next day they would capture the plateau.

Kilikian was brought back by deserters who felt it would be better to die with their own people than to be captured by the Turks. He was put to death.

As the Turks prepared to advance at dawn, a French cruiser dropped its first shell into the valley. Its commander had seen the fire in the town enclosure the day before. Approaching to investigate, he had seen the enormous flag the Armenians were using as a distress signal. The Turks retreated into the valley. Bagradian led the weary defenders to the coast and saw them safely aboard a cruiser and a troopship. Then he started back up the mountain for a last view of his son's grave. Exhausted by his ordeal, he fell asleep halfway up the mountainside. When he awoke, the ships were already standing out at sea. He started to signal them but changed his mind. He felt that his life was now complete. Up he climbed until he reached his son's grave. There a bullet from a Turkish scout caught him in the temple. On his son's grave he lay, Stephan's cross on his heart.

FRAMLEY PARSONAGE

Type of work: Novel
Author: Anthony Trollope (1815-1882)
Type of plot: Domestic romance
Time of plot: 1850's
Locale: "Barsetshire" and London
First published: 1861

Principal characters:
MARK ROBARTS, vicar of Framley in Barsetshire
FANNY, his wife
LUCY, his sister
LADY LUFTON, mistress of Framley Court, Mark's benefactress
LORD LUFTON, her son, Mark's close friend
SOWERBY, squire of Chaldicotes, acquaintance of Lord Lufton and Mark
MISS DUNSTABLE, Sowerby's benefactress
DR. THORNE, the man she married

Critique:

This novel is one of the long, leisurely Barchester series. It contains no great moral theme, but it does present some delightful portraits of ecclesiastical characters and other nineteenth-century figures. It is marked by slowly paced development of plot and by conversational interruptions from the author. Without stepping over into sentimentality, but rather maintaining a wise, ironical tone, the novel provides pleasant, heart-warming entertainment.

The Story:

Mark Robarts was the vicar of Framley, an appointment secured through Lady Lufton of Framley, who was very fond of him. He was ambitious, however, and he went to a house party at Chaldicotes, the estate of Mr. Sowerby, of whom Lady Lufton disapproved. Sowerby was notorious for living on other people's money, for he had long since run through his own fortune. While Mark was visiting him, Sowerby played on the vicar's sympathy to such an extent that Mark signed his name to a note for four hundred pounds. From Chaldicotes Mark went to another house party at Gatherum Castle, home of the Duke of Omnium. The Duke of Omnium was also an enemy of Lady Lufton. Mark felt the contacts he would make at these parties would help him in climbing higher in his career.

When Mark returned home, he told Lord Lufton he had signed a note for Sowerby. Young Lufton could hardly believe a man of Mark's position would do such a thing, for Mark could not afford to pay the note and certainly he would never recover the money from

Sowerby. Before Mark told his wife, Fanny, about the debt he had incurred, his father died and his sister Lucy came to live at Framley parsonage. During the next three months Lucy and Lord Lufton became very friendly. Lucy was a small girl without striking beauty, and inclined to be quiet, but when she was with Lord Lufton, she found herself talking with great ease.

When Sowerby's note came due, he asked Mark to sign another for five hundred pounds, a sum which would cover the first note and allow an additional hundred pounds for extras. Mark saw the treachery of Sowerby's scheme, but, unable to pay the note due, he was forced to sign.

Lady Lufton hinted to Fanny that she hoped to find a better match than Lucy for her son, but by this time the two young people had fallen in love with each other. Disturbed also by Mark's attentions to the Chaldicotes set, Lady Lufton sent Mr. Crawley, a strait-laced clergyman from the nearby austere parish of Hogglestock, to remonstrate with Mark. After his visit Mark resolved to act more in accordance with Lady Lufton's wishes.

One day Lord Lufton declared his love for Lucy and asked her to marry him. Lucy, mindful of Lady Lufton's feelings, said she could not love him. Lufton was full of disappointment and grief.

Sowerby informed Mark that the new prime minister had it in his power to appoint the new precentor at Barchester Cathedral. Through Sowerby's influence, Mark received the appointment. He bought a race horse from Sowerby to show his gratitude.

Sowerby, greatly in debt to the Duke of Omnium, was about to lose his estate. Sowerby's sister, Mrs. Harold Smith, was a close friend of Miss Dunstable, a middle-aged spinster whose father had left her a fortune made in patent medicine. Mrs. Smith suggested that Sowerby ask Miss Dunstable to marry him and to say frankly that he wanted her chiefly for her money, since Miss Dunstable herself was a forthright, outspoken woman. Sowerby sent his sister to propose for him. Although Miss Dunstable refused his proposal, she agreed to buy Chaldicotes and let Sowerby live in the house for the remainder of his life. She said she would marry only a man who was not interested in her money.

That man, she thought, was Dr. Thorne, a bachelor physician from Barsetshire. She had informed Dr. Thorne's niece of her admiration for him and the niece had tried to show her uncle how wonderful life would be with Miss Dunstable. He was shocked at the idea of proposing. Though Miss Dunstable talked to him alone at a party she gave in London, Dr. Thorne said nothing at all about marriage. Back home, he decided that Miss Dunstable would, after all, make an admirable wife. He wrote her a letter of proposal and was accepted.

Lord Lufton went to Norway on a fishing trip. While he was away, Mrs. Crawley became ill of typhoid fever at Hogglestock, and Lucy went to nurse her through her sickness. The Crawley children were taken to Framley parsonage against Crawley's will, for he felt they might become accustomed to comforts he could not afford.

Sowerby's second note was coming due. Mark could consider no plan to get him out of his difficulty. If he had to go to jail, he would go. If he had to forfeit the furniture in his house, he would forfeit it. But under no circumstances would he ever put his name to another note.

Lord Lufton returned from Norway and learned from his mother that she thought Lucy insignificant. When he heard Lucy was at Hogglestock, he went there and again asked her to marry him. She replied that she did indeed love him but she would not marry him unless his mother approved. At first Lady Lufton refused to consider the match, but when she saw how determined her son was to have Lucy, she gave in and actually asked

Lucy to become her daughter-in-law.

Meanwhile, the bailiffs had come to Framley parsonage to take inventory of the furniture, which was to be sold to pay Mark's obligations. When Lord Lufton discovered what was going on, he dismissed the bailiffs and persuaded Mark to accept a loan for payment of the note.

Sowerby lived at Chaldicotes for only a short time before he disappeared, and Mark was relieved of worry over his foolish debt. Miss Dunstable married Dr. Thorne and, after the departure of Sowerby, moved into the house at Chaldicotes. Lucy married Lord Lufton and became mistress, at least nominally, of Framley Court. Fate seemed to have for each some fair reward.

FRANKENSTEIN

Type of work: Novel
Author: Mary Godwin Shelley (1797-1851)
Type of plot: Gothic romance
Time of plot: Eighteenth century
Locale: Europe
First published: 1817

Principal characters:
ROBERT WALTON, an explorer
VICTOR FRANKENSTEIN, an inventor
ELIZABETH, his foster sister
WILLIAM, his brother
JUSTINE, the Frankensteins' servant
CLERVAL, Victor's friend
THE MONSTER

Critique:

Frankenstein: or, The Modern Prometheus is a weird tale, a wholly incredible story told with little skill. Although not often read now, it is known very widely by name. The endurance of this Gothic romance depends on perhaps two factors. First, Mary Shelley would be remembered if she had written nothing, for she was the wife of Percy Bysshe Shelley under romantic and scandalous circumstances. Indeed, *Frankenstein* was written as a result of a conversation between Byron and the Shelleys. Second, the idea of creating a monster has wide appeal. *Frankenstein* has become part of the popular imagination.

The Story:

Walton was an English explorer whose ship was held fast in polar ice. As the company looked out over the empty ice field, they were astonished to see a sledge drawn by dogs speeding northward. The sledge driver looked huge and misshapen. That night an ice floe carried to the ship another sledge, one dog, and a man in weakened condition. When the newcomer learned that his was the second sledge sighted from the ship, he became much agitated.

Walton was greatly attracted to the man during his convalescence, and as they continued fast in the ice, the men had leisure to get acquainted. At last, after he had recovered somewhat from exposure and hunger, the man told Walton his story:

Victor Frankenstein was born of good family in Geneva. As a playmate for their son, the parents had adopted a lovely little girl of the same age. Victor and Elizabeth grew up as brother and sister. Much later another son, William, was born to the Frankensteins.

Victor early showed promise in the natural sciences. He devoured the works of Paracelsus and Albertus Magnus, and thought in his ignorance that they were the real masters. When he grew older, his father decided to send Victor to the university at Ingolstadt. There he soon learned all that his masters could teach him in the fields of natural science. Engaged in brilliant and terrible research, he stumbled by chance on the secret of creating life. Once he had that knowledge he could not rest until he had employed it to create a living being. By haunting the butcher shops and dissecting rooms, he soon had the necessary raw materials. With great cunning he fashioned an eight-foot monster and endowed him with life.

But as soon as he had created his monster, he was subject to strange misgivings. During the night the monster came to his bed. At the sight of that horrible face, he shrieked and frightened the monster away. The horror of his act prostrated him with a brain fever. His best friend, Henry Clerval, arrived from Geneva and helped to nurse him through his illness. He was unable to tell Clerval what he had done.

Terrible news came from Geneva. William, Victor's young brother, was dead by the hand of a murderer. He had been found strangled in a park, and a faithful family servant, Justine, had been charged with the crime. Victor hurried to Geneva.

At the trial Justine told a convincing story. She had been looking for William in the countryside and, returning after the city gates had been closed, had spent the night in a deserted hut. But she could not explain how a miniature from William's neck came to be in her pocket. Victor and Elizabeth believed the girl's story, but in spite of all their efforts Justine was convicted and condemned.

Depressed by these tragic events, Victor went hiking over the mountainous countryside. Far ahead on the glacier, he saw a strange, agile figure that filled him with horrible suspicions. Unable to overtake the figure, he sat down to rest. Suddenly the monster appeared before him. The creature demanded that Victor listen to his story.

When he left Victor's chambers in Ingolstadt, everyone he met screamed and ran away. Wandering confusedly, the monster finally found shelter in an abandoned hovel adjoining a cottage. By great stealth he remained there during daylight and at night sought berries for food. Through observation he began to learn the ways of man. Feeling an urge to friendship, he brought wood to the cottage every day. But when he attempted to make friends with the cottagers, he was repulsed with such fear and fury that his heart became bitter toward all men. When he saw William playing in the park, he strangled the boy and took the miniature from his neck. Then during the night he came upon Justine in the hut and put the picture in her pocket.

Presently the monster made a horrible demand. He insisted that Victor fashion a mate for him who would give him love and companionship. The monster threatened to ravage and kill at random if Victor refused the request. But if Victor agreed, the monster promised to take his mate to the wilds of South America where they would never again be seen by man. It was a hard choice but Victor felt that he must accept.

Victor left for England with his friend Clerval. After parting from his friend he went to the distant Orkneys and began his task. He was almost ready to animate the gross mass of flesh when his conscience stopped him. He could not let the two monsters mate and spawn a race of monsters. He destroyed his work.

The monster was watching at a window. Angered to see his mate destroyed, he forced his way into the house and warned Victor that a terrible punishment would fall upon the young man on his wedding night. Then the monster escaped by sea. Later, to torment his maker, he fiendishly killed Clerval.

Victor was suspected of the crime. Released for lack of evidence, he went back to Geneva. There he and Elizabeth were married. Although Victor was armed and alert, the monster got into the nuptial chamber and strangled the bride. Victor shot at him, but he escaped again. Victor vowed eternal chase until the monster could be killed.

That was Victor's story. Weakened by exposure, he died there in the frozen North, with Elizabeth, William, Justine, and Clerval unavenged. Then to the dead man's cabin came the monster, and Walton, stifling his fear, addressed the gigantic, hideous creature. Victor's was the greater crime, the monster said. He had created a man, a man without love or friend or soul. He deserved his punishment. So saying, the monster vanished over the ice field.

THE FROGS

Type of work: Drama
Author: Aristophanes (c. 448-385 B.C.)
Type of plot: Humorous satire
Time of plot: Fifth century B.C.
Locale: Underworld
First presented: 405 B.C.

Principal characters:
BACCHUS, god of wine and revelry
XANTHIAS, his slave
HERCULES, mythological hero
CHARON, ferryman of Hades
EURIPIDES, a famous Greek playwright
AESCHYLUS, another Greek dramatist

Critique:

So vigorous was the mind of Aristophanes that his comedies extant today maintain vitality which is still a sharp and penetrating comment upon human nature. One does not need to be a scholar to understand and love the work of Aristophanes. Satirist for all ages, he wrote to expose the timeless foibles and follies of human nature.

The Story:

Wishing to visit the underworld, Bacchus set out with his slave, Xanthias, to visit Hercules, from whom the god of the vine hoped to get directions for his visit to the lower regions. On the way Xanthias continued to grumble and moan about his many bundles. Xanthias was really riding a donkey, but he complained loudly until Bacchus finally lost patience and suggested that perhaps Xanthias would like to carry the donkey for a while.

Hercules, when consulted, suggested that Bacchus allow himself to be killed and thus arrive in the land of the dead. But Bacchus wanted to go there alive because he was anxious to see and talk to the great playwrights, the critics having told him that all who were good were dead and gone. He was particularly anxious to meet Euripides. Hercules advised him to be content with the playwrights still alive. Bacchus argued that none of them was good enough for him, and so, after getting directions from Hercules, he started out, Xanthias still complaining about his bundles.

They came to the River Acheron and met Charon, who ferried Bacchus across. The grim ferryman insisted, however, that Bacchus row the boat, and he made Xanthias walk around the margin of the stream since Xanthias had dishonored himself by not volunteering for a naval victory. Xanthias tried to excuse himself on the grounds that he had had sore eyes, but Charon refused to listen.

While Bacchus and Xanthias talked to Charon, a chorus of frogs set up a hoarse croaking, imitating the noisy plebeians at the theater with a senseless kind of hooting. Bacchus sprained his back with his rowing and the frogs thought his groans quite amusing.

Safely on the other side, Bacchus paid his fare and joined his slave. The two met a monster which Bacchus took care to avoid until it turned into a beautiful woman. They found their way with difficulty to the doorway of Pluto's realm. Xanthias still grumbled because he had his heavy bundles.

At the entrance to Hades, Bacchus foolishly pretended to be Hercules—a mistake on his part, for Aeacus, the doorman, raised a clamor over the theft of Cerberus, the watchdog. When Aeacus threatened all sorts of punishment, Bacchus revealed himself as he really was. Xanthias accused him of cowardice but Bacchus stoutly denied the charge.

Bacchus and Xanthias decided to change characters. Xanthias pretended to be Hercules and Bacchus took up the bundles his slave had carried. But when servants of Proserpine entered and offered Xanthias a fine entertainment, Bacchus demanded his rightful character once more.

Aeacus returned, eager to punish someone, and Xanthias gave him permission to beat Bacchus. Bacchus said that he was a deity; therefore, they should not beat him. Xanthias countered by saying that since Bacchus was an immortal he need not mind the beating. Aeacus decided they both should be beaten soundly.

Aeacus finally decided to take them both to Pluto and Proserpine, to discover who really was the deity. Aeacus said Bacchus was apparently a gentleman and Xanthias agreed wholeheartedly, saying Bacchus did not do anything except dissipate and carouse.

In Pluto's realm they found two dead dramatists, Aeschylus and Euripides, fighting for favor. The rule in Hades was that the most famous man of any art or craft ate at Pluto's table until some more talented man in his field should die and come to Hades. Aeschylus had held the seat Euripides was now claiming.

Aeacus said that the dramatists intended to measure their plays line for line by rules and compasses to determine the superior craftsman. The quarreling dramatists debated, accusing each of the other's faults. Aeschylus said he was at a disadvantage because Euripides' plays died with him and were present to help him, whereas his own plays still lived on earth.

Bacchus offered to be the judge, and each dramatist then began to defend himself. In the midst of their violent quarrel Pluto appeared. Bacchus ordered each to recite from his own works. Euripides seemed to have the worst of this contest, but Bacchus wisely refused to judge so as not to make either playwright angry with him. Pluto wearily insisted that he pick one winner and take his choice back with him to the upper world in order to stop needless rivalry in Hades.

At last Bacchus voted for Aeschylus. Euripides complained at the choice. He was consoled, however, when Pluto said he might be sure of a good meal in the underworld, while Aeschylus would be burdened forever with the task of earning his living by his attempts to reform folly and evil in the world above.

GARGANTUA AND PANTAGRUEL

Type of work: Mock-heroic chronicle
Author: François Rabelais (1490?-1553)
Type of plot: Burlesque romance
Time of plot: Renaissance
Locale: France
First published: Begun 1533; first complete edition, 1567

Principal characters:
GRANGOSIER, a giant king
GARGAMELLE, his wife

GARGANTUA, their son
PANTAGRUEL, son of Gargantua
PANURGE, a clever rascal
FRIAR JOHN OF THE FUNNELS, a lusty monk

Critique:

The book Rabelais titled *The Lives, Heroic Deeds and Sayings of Gargantua and His Son Pantagruel* is a vast panorama of an amiable dynasty of giants. The characters are prodigious eaters and drinkers, gay and earthy. The five books which contain the adventures of a galaxy of types are loosely held together by the main actors. Discursive and monumental, *Gargantua and Pantagruel* is an astounding achievement. *Rabelaisian* and *gargantuan* as adjectives indicate the opinion of many readers. But Rabelais had a serious purpose. He demonstrated heroically his theme that the real meaning of life is to expand the soul by knowing all the sources of experience.

The Story:

Grangosier and Gargamelle were expecting a child. During the eleventh month of her pregnancy, Gargamelle ate too many tripes and then played tag on the green. That afternoon in a green meadow Gargantua was born from his mother's left ear.

Gargantua was a prodigy, and with his first breath he began to clamor for drink. Seventeen thousand nine hundred and thirteen cows were needed to supply him with milk. For his clothing the tailors used nine hundred ells of linen to make his shirt and eleven hundred and five ells of white broadcloth to make his breeches. Eleven hundred cowhides were used for the soles of his shoes.

At first Gargantua's education was in the hands of two masters of the old school, Holofernes and Joberlin Bridé. Seeing that his son was making no progress, however, Grangosier sent him to Paris to study with Ponocrates. Aside from some mishaps, as when he took the bells from the tower of Notre Dame to tie around his horse's neck, Gargantua did much better with his studies in Paris.

Back home a dispute arose. The bakers of Lerné refused to sell cakes to the shepherds of Grangosier. In the quarrel a shepherd felled a baker, and King Picrochole of Lerné invaded the country. Grangosier baked cartloads of cakes to appease Picrochole, but to no avail, for no one dared oppose Picrochole except doughty Friar John of the Funnels. Finally Grangosier asked Gargantua to come to his aid.

Gargantua fought valiantly. Cannon balls seemed to him as grape seeds, and when he combed his hair cannon balls dropped out. After he had conquered the army of Lerné, he generously let all the prisoners go free.

All his helpers were rewarded well, but for Friar John, Gargantua built the famous Abbey of Thélème, where men and women were together, all could leave when they wished, and marriage and the accumulation of wealth were encouraged.

When he was more than four hundred years old, Gargantua had a son, Pantagruel. Pantagruel was a remarkable baby, hairy as a bear at birth and of such great size that he cost the life of his mother. Gargantua was sorely vexed between weeping for his wife and rejoicing for his son.

Pantagruel required the services of four thousand six hundred cows to nurse him. Once he got an arm out of his swaddling clothes and, grasping the cow nursing him, he ate the cow. Afterwards Pantagruel's arms were bound with anchor ropes. One day the women forgot to clean his face after nursing, and a bear came and licked the drops of milk from the baby's face. By a great effort Pantagruel broke the ropes and ate the bear. In despair, Gargantua bound his son with four great chains, one of which was later used to bind Lucifer when he had the colic. But Pantagruel broke the five-foot beam which constituted the footboard of his cradle and ran around with the cradle on his back.

Pantagruel showed great promise as a scholar. After a period of wandering he settled down in Paris. There he was frequently called on to settle disputes between learned lawyers. One day he met a ragged young beggar. On speaking to him, Pantagruel received answers in twelve known and unknown tongues. Greatly taken by this fluent beggar, Pantagruel and Panurge became great friends. Panurge was a merry fellow who knew sixty-three ways to make money and two hundred fourteen ways to spend it.

Pantagruel learned that the Dipsodes had invaded the land of the Amaurots. Stirred by this danger to Utopia, he set out by ship to do battle. By trickery and courage, Pantagruel overcame the wicked giants. Their king, Anarchus, he married to an old lantern-carrying hag and made the king a crier of green sauce. Now that the land of Dipsody had been conquered, Pantagruel transported there a colony of Utopians numbering 9,876,543,210 men, besides many women and children. All these people were very fertile. Every nine months each married woman bore seven children. In a short time Dipsody was populated by virtuous Utopians.

For his services and friendship Panurge was made Laird of Salmigondin. The revenue from this lairdship amounted to 6,789,106,789 gold royals a year, but Panurge managed to spend his income well in advance. Then, thinking to settle down, Panurge began to reflect seriously on marriage, and he consulted his lord Pantagruel. They came to no conclusion in the matter because they got into an argument about the virtues of borrowing and lending money. But the flea in his ear kept reminding Panurge of his contemplated marriage, and he set off to seek other counsel.

Panurge consulted the Sibyl of Panzoult, the poet Raminagrobis, Herr Tripa, and Friar John. When all the advice he received proved contradictory, Panurge prevailed on Pantagruel and Friar John to set out with him to consult the Oracle of the Holy Bottle. From Saint Malo the party sailed in twelve ships for the Holy Bottle, located in Upper India. The Portuguese sometimes took three years for that voyage, but Pantagruel and Panurge cut that time to one month by sailing across the Frozen Sea north of Canada.

The valiant company had many adventures on the way. On the Island of the Ennasins, they found a race of people with noses shaped like the ace of clubs. The people who lived on the Island of Ruach ate and drank nothing but wind. At the Ringing Islands they found a strange race of Siticines who had long ago turned to birds. On Condemnation Island they fell into the power of Gripe-men-all, Archduke of the Furred Law-cats, and Panurge was forced to solve a riddle before the travelers were given their freedom.

At last they came to the island of the Sacred Bottle. Guided by a Lantern from Lanternland, they came to a large vineyard planted by Bacchus himself. Then they went underground through a plastered vault and came to marble steps. Down they went, a hundred steps or more. Panurge was greatly afraid, but Friar John took him by the collar and heartened him. At the bottom they came to a great mosaic floor on which was shown the history of Bacchus. Finally they were met by the priestess Bacbuc, who was to conduct them to the Bottle. Panurge knelt to kiss the rim of the fountain. Bacbuc threw something into the well and the water began to boil. When Panurge sang the prescribed ritual, the Sacred Bottle pronounced the one word, "trinc." Bacbuc looked up the word in a huge silver book. It meant drink, a word declared to be the most gracious and intelligible she had ever heard from the Sacred Bottle. Panurge took the word as a sanction for his marriage.

GHOSTS

Type of work: Drama
Author: Henrik Ibsen (1828-1906)
Type of plot: Social criticism
Time of plot: Nineteenth century
Locale: Rosenvold, Norway
First presented: 1881

Principal characters:
MRS. HELEN ALVING, a widow
OSWALD ALVING, her son, an artist
MANDERS, pastor of the parish
JACOB ENGSTRAND, a carpenter
REGINA ENGSTRAND, his daughter, in Mrs. Alving's service

Critique:

Ghosts is Ibsen's effort to substitute the modern scientific concept of heredity for the Greek idea of Fate. But there is more to the play than merely a study in degenerative heredity; it is a mordant attack upon society and the standards by which it lives. Ibsen explicitly says that these standards were responsible for the tragedy of Mrs. Alving, and in so doing he tossed a bombshell into the conventional and even the liberal thought of his day. The play can still be read as a study in what has come to be known as the science of semantics—the disruptive effect caused when words or concepts are, in society, divorced from the realities for which they are supposed to stand.

The Story:

Pastor Manders called on Mrs. Helen Alving on the eve of the tenth anniversary of her husband's death, to discuss certain details concerning the opening of an orphanage in memory of her late husband. The pastor found Mrs. Alving in the best of spirits, for her son Oswald, an artist, had returned from Paris to attend the dedication of the memorial to his father. Although he was now twenty-six, Oswald had lived away from his parents since he was seven, and Mrs. Alving was delighted at the prospect of having her son spend the entire winter with her.

Oswald had idealized his father, for in her letters his mother had always pictured Captain Alving as a sort of hero. The boy's own memories of his father were confined to one incident in his childhood when his father had taken him on his knee and encouraged him to smoke a large meerschaum pipe. Oswald remembered this episode, and upon his return home he took a certain pride in lighting up his father's old pipe and parading in front of his mother and Pastor Manders.

Pastor Manders did not approve of smoking; in fact, he did not approve of anything which could even loosely be interpreted as sin. He did not approve of Oswald's bohemian way of life in Paris and blamed Mrs. Alving's neglect for her son's ideas. He reminded Mrs. Alving that hardly a year after her marriage she had come to him willing to leave her husband, and that he had sent her back to her duty. This was an act Manders considered the greatest moral victory of his life.

Mrs. Alving thought it high time that Manders be informed of the truth about her late husband. Years before, when he advised her return to Captain Alving, the minister had been quite aware of her husband's profligacy. What he did not know was that the profligacy continued after his wife's dutiful return. Her entire relationship with her husband consisted largely of helping him into bed after

GHOSTS by Henrik Ibsen. Published by Charles Scribner's Sons.

one of his drinking bouts, and on one occasion she had surprised him making love to her own maidservant. But the most abominable aspect of the situation was the fact that she had discovered, soon after her marriage, that her husband was diseased and her son would have to go through life with his father's curse upon his head. Manders' religious influence and Mrs. Alving's cowardice had conspired to keep silence.

Now it began to look as if the moral consequences would play themselves out. While Mrs. Alving and the minister talked, Oswald was attempting familiarities in the adjoining dining-room with the maid, Regina, his own stepsister. To Mrs. Alving it seemed as if this act were the ghost of her unhappy marriage, for Regina, ostensibly the daughter of a drunken carpenter named Jacob Engstrand, was actually the result of Captain Alving's escapade with the maidservant, the discovery of which had sent Mrs. Alving flying to Pastor Manders for solace and help. Engstrand had been willing to turn Regina over to Mrs. Alving for her education and care. Now, however, he had other ideas for the girl's future. He planned to enlist her aid in the establishment of a seamen's home. But Regina had other plans for herself, and saw no reason why she should throw herself away on worthless and irresponsible sailors when she might have the heir of a wealthy family.

Oswald himself, unaware of any blood relationship, wanted to marry Regina. He confided to his mother that before he left Paris he had gone to a doctor regarding a feeling of malaise which robbed him of his ambition to paint. The doctor had commented on the sins of fathers. Oswald, knowing only the picture of his father that his mother's letters had given him, was furious, and he thought he had brought about his own downfall. He told his mother that he wanted to marry Regina and make what was left of his life happy. Mrs. Alving realized that at last she must tell the two young people the truth. But before she had a chance to do so, news came that the orphanage which was to have been Captain Alving's memorial was afire.

When the orphanage caught fire, Manders and Engstrand were in the carpenter shop nearby. After the fire, Engstrand accused the pastor of dropping a lighted candle wick into some shavings. Though not guilty, Manders was frightened because of his position in the community. When Engstrand offered to take the blame for the fire in return for enough money from the remainder of Captain Alving's fortune to build his sailor's home, the self-righteous Manders agreed to this blackmail and promised to help Engstrand in the transaction.

Mrs. Alving told Oswald and Regina the story of their late father. She tried to explain why Alving had been doomed from the beginning. When it was revealed that she was really Alving's daughter, Regina was angry, feeling that she should have been reared and educated as a lady. She preferred to cast her lot with Engstrand. Alone with his mother, Oswald revealed the final horror; an affliction had already attacked his brain and would result in complete regression to childhood. Mrs. Alving assured her son that she would always be by his side to take care of him. Oswald urged his mother to kill him if the need should arise. Shocked, Mrs. Alving refused when he showed her the morphia tablets he had brought with him. They were still talking at daybreak. Mrs. Alving blew out the light. But while she stood and looked in horror, Oswald sat crying childishly for the sun.

GIANTS IN THE EARTH

Type of work: Novel
Author: O. E. Rölvaag (1876-1931)
Type of plot: Regional romance
Time of plot: Late nineteenth century
Locale: The Dakotas
First published: 1924-1925

Principal characters:
PER HANSA, a Norwegian settler
BERET, his wife
OLE,
ANNA MARIE,
HANS KRISTIAN, and
PEDER VICTORIOUS, their children

Critique:

Giants in the Earth is a tremendous contribution to our understanding of pioneer life. Perhaps some day it will be condensed into a saga, its story sharpened down into the short, keen points of myth and its Per Hansa viewed as an American folk hero. It is important to realize that Rölvaag, writing in the tradition of Western Europe, and writing for a European audience, was able to blend old and new and to create a story which an American audience would accept. The theme of the novel is a great one: man's struggle with the stubborn earth. This theme is of principal importance to Americans. It is the story of man bearing his memory of other lands into a new country, and out of that experience building a new homeplace and a new people.

The Story:

Per Hansa moved all his family and his possessions from Minnesota into the Dakota territory. His family consisted of his wife, Beret, and three children, Ole, Anna Marie, and Hans Kristian. Beret was fearful and sad, for she had been uprooted too often and the prairie country through which they traveled seemed bleak, lonely, savage.

Per Hansa staked out his claim near the family of Hans Olsa at Spring Creek. Then Beret announced that she was carrying another child. Money was scarce. Per Hansa faced overwhelming odds and thoughts of the great risks he was taking kept him awake long after Beret and the children slept. Being something of a poet, Per Hansa thought at times that the land spoke to him, and often he watched and listened and forgot to keep to his work as he cleared his land and built his house. He labored from before dawn until after dark during those long, northern summer days.

When Indians came and drove away the settlers' cows, only Per Hansa had the courage to follow after them. Only he had the sense to doctor a sick Indian. Beret mistrusted his wisdom for foolishness and there were harsh words between them. The grateful Indian gave Per Hansa a pony. Then Per Hansa went on a buying expedition and returned with many needed supplies and, what was more, news of coming settlers.

The next summer Per Hansa discovered claim stakes which bore Irish names. The stakes were on his neighbor's land; the homesteaders had settled where others had already filed claim. Secretly he removed the stakes and burned them, but not before Beret realized what he was doing. She began to worry over her husband's deed. Per Hansa sold some potatoes to people traveling through and awoke the slumbering jealousy of his neighbors.

In midsummer more people arrived, the settlers who had set out the stakes that Per Hansa had burned. They called the Norwegians claim jumpers, but after a fight they took up other land nearby. Per Hansa managed to sell some of his goods to them. That fall more Norwegians came. The little community was thriving. But Beret, depressed by the open spaces and her fear that her husband had done a bad thing, brewed a dark remorse within herself. Day by day she brooded over her lonely life, and she covered her window at night because of her nameless fears. At least Per Hansa on his infrequent trips around to different settlements met other people.

When winter came Per Hansa rested. He could sleep long hours while the winds blew outside, but his wife worried and fretted. He began to quarrel with her. Soon, however, he noticed that his neighbors were suffering hardship and privation. The unmarried young men who had settled near the Hansas were planning to desert the settlement. It required all his ability to convince them to stay and to face the desolate, bitter winter to its end.

The settlers began to talk of a school which would move from house to house so that the parents might learn English along with the children.

During the winter Per Hansa became lost in a blizzard and only his tremendous strength and courage saw him and his oxen safely through the storm to the Trönders' settlement. The following day, forgetting how Beret must be worrying about him, he stayed on and cut a load of wood to take back home with him.

His next expedition was to bargain with the Indians for furs. He suffered greatly from exposure and lost two toes through frostbite.

When spring came, Per Hansa could not wait to get into his fields to plant his wheat. His friends thought he was planting too early. And so it seemed, for snow fell the next day and freezing weather set in. Determined not to lose heart, Per Hansa decided to plant potatoes in place of the wheat. Beret took to her Bible, convinced that evil was working its way into their lives. Then, unexpectedly, their wheat came up.

Another couple arrived. They were exhausted with travel, the wife saddened by the death of her son on the prairie. Per Hansa and Beret took them in. When they moved on, greater despondency seized Beret. She felt some doom was working its way closer and closer to her life.

That summer grasshoppers destroyed much of the grain. Most of Per Hansa's crop was saved, but Beret took his good fortune only as a sign that the underground trolls, or evil spirits, were planning greater ruin for her and her husband.

In the following years the scourge of the grasshoppers returned. Many of the settlers were ruined. Some starved. Some went mad. One summer a traveling Norwegian minister took up residence with them to plan a religious service for the whole community. His coming worked a change in Per Hansa's household. Per Hansa took courage from it and consolation, but deeper and stranger grew the reveries in Beret's mind. Because it was the largest house in the district the minister held a communion service in Per Hansa's cabin. Disconnected parts of the service floated all that week in Beret's head. Her mind was filled with strange fancies. She began to think of Peder Victorious, her youngest child, who was born on the prairie, as a savior who would work their salvation.

As the autumn came on, the great plains seemed hungry for the blood and strength of those who had come to conquer it.

That winter Hans Olsa froze his legs and one hand. In spite of all that Per Hansa and the others did for their neighbor, Hans Olsa grew weaker. Beret stood beside him, predicting that he had not long to live. She put into the sick man's mind the idea to send for the minister. Per Hansa thought that Hans Olsa was weak in calling for a minister and that the way to throw off illness was to get out of bed and go to work. He had never spared himself, nor had he spared his sons. He was the man to go for the minister, but this time he was unwilling to set out on a long winter journey. Hans Olsa was a good man; he did not need a minister to help him die. The weather itself was threatening. However, Per Hansa reconsidered. His sons were digging a tunnel through snow to the pigsty. Inside, his wife was preparing a meal for him. They watched as he took down his skis and prepared to make the journey for the sake of his dying friend. He did not look back at his house or speak farewell to Beret as he started out.

So Per Hansa, on his errand of mercy, walked into the snowstorm. There death overtook him.

GIL BLAS OF SANTILLANE

Type of work: Novel
Author: Alain René Le Sage (1668-1747)
Type of plot: Picaresque romance
Time of plot: Seventeenth century
Locale: Spain
First published: 1715, 1724, 1735

Principal characters:
GIL BLAS, a rogue
SCIPIO, his secretary
DON ALPHONSO, his patron

Critique:

The Adventures of Gil Blas of Santillane is a long novel made up of many disconnected episodes. One of the first works to introduce thieves, vagabonds, and vulgar peasantry into fiction, it is a precursor of the realism of Flaubert and Balzac. The setting is supposedly Spain, but the characters and settings are in reality French, and particularly Breton. The appeal of this book comes from the skilled narration of exciting tales, and from its author's shrewd insight into the minds of his picturesque characters.

The Story:

Blas of Santillane retired from the wars and married a chambermaid no longer young. After the birth of Gil, the parents settled in Oviedo, where the father became a minor squire and the mother went into service.

Happily, Gil Perez, Gil Blas' uncle, was a canon in the town. He was three and a half feet high and enormously fat. Without his aid, Gil Blas would never have received an education. He provided a tutor for his nephew and at the age of seventeen Gil Blas had studied the classics and some logic.

When the time came for him to seek his fortune, the family sent Gil Blas to Salamanca to study. The uncle provided him with forty pistoles and a mule. Shortly after setting out, Gil Blas was foolish enough to join the train of a muleteer who concocted a story that he had been robbed of a hundred pistoles and threatened all his passengers with arrest and torture. His purpose was to frighten the men away so that he could seduce the wife of one of the travelers. Gil Blas had some thought of helping the woman, but he fled upon the arrival of a police patrol.

Gil Blas was found in the woods by a band of ruffians who had an underground hideout nearby. Under Captain Rolando, they made Gil their serving-boy. After an unsuccessful attempt to escape, he set out to ingratiate himself with the captain. At the end of six months he became a member of the gang and embarked on a career of robbery and murder. One day the robbers attacked a coach, killed all the men, and captured a beautiful woman. Since she was well-born and modest, Gil Blas resolved to rescue her. Waiting until the robbers were asleep, he tied up the cook and escaped with the woman, whose name, he learned, was Donna Mencia. She was very grateful for her rescue, and, dressing Gil Blas in fine clothes, she presented him with a bag of money. So he went on his way, comparatively rich and comfortable.

On his travels he met Fabricio, a former schoolmate who had become a barber. Scornful of Gil's intention to study, Fabricio soon prevailed upon him to go into service as a lackey. As it turned out, Gil was well adapted to flattery and intrigue, and he soon became proficient by serving a variety of masters, among them Doctor Sangrado, a physician. The doctor's one remedy for all maladies was forced drinking of water and frequent bleeding. Gil Blas won the doctor's esteem and was permitted to attend poor patients in his master's place. During an epidemic, he made a record as good as that of Sangrado; all of their patients died.

Another master was Don Matthias, a fashionable man about town. By means of a little judicious thievery and daring, Gil Blas found his new life highly satisfying. Each day was spent in eating and polite conversation, every night in carousing. During this service Gil dressed in his master's clothes and tried to get a mistress among the titled ladies of the town. An old lady who arranged these affairs introduced him to a grand lady who was pining for a lover. Gil was disillusioned when he went with Don Matthias to the house of Arsenia, an actress, and found that his grand lady was really a serving-maid.

After Don Matthias was killed in a duel, Gil attended Arsenia for a time. Later he went into service in the household of Aurora, a virtuous young woman who grieved because a student named Lewis paid no attention to her charms. At Gil's suggestion, Aurora disguised herself as a man and took an apartment in the same house with Lewis. Striking up a friendship with him, Aurora skillfully led him on. Then she received him in her own house in her proper person, and soon Lewis and Aurora were married. Gil Blas left their service content with his part in the romance.

On the road again, Gil was able to frustrate a band of robbers who had planned to kill Don Alphonso. Thus Gil and the don began a lasting friendship.

After losing a situation because he learned that the duenna had an ulcer on her back, Gil next took service with an archbishop. His work was to write out the homilies composed by the archbishop. After he had won his master's confidence, the churchman made Gil promise to tell him when his homilies showed signs of degenerating in quality. After a stroke, the archbishop failed mentally, and Gil told him his homilies were not up to the usual standard. In his rage, the archbishop dismissed Gil, who learned in this manner the folly of being too truthful.

Engaged as secretary by the Duke of Lerma, prime minister of Spain, Gil soon became the duke's confidential agent. Now Gil was in a position to sell favors, and his avarice grew apace with his success in court intrigue. During this successful period, he engaged Scipio as his servant. Gil's high position enabled him to secure the governorship of Valencia for Don Alphonso.

Gil became involved in high court scandal. At the request of the prime minister, he acted as pander for the prince of Spain, the heir apparent. About the same time Scipio arranged a wealthy marriage for Gil with the daughter of a rich goldsmith. But one night the king's spies caught Gil conducting the prince to a house of pleasure and Gil was confined to prison. Faithful Scipio shared his imprisonment. After months of sickness, Gil was released and exiled from

Madrid. Fortunately Don Alphonso gave Gil a country estate at Lirias, and there he and Scipio settled to lead the simple lives of country gentlemen. Attracted by Antonia, the daughter of one of his farmers, Gil married, but his happiness was brief. After Antonia and his baby daughter died, Gil became restless for new fields. The prince was now king, and Gil resolved to try court life again. He became an intimate of the new prime minister, Count Olivarez. Once again he was employed to arrange a liaison for the king, a mission that turned out badly. Forced to resign, Gil returned for good to Lirias.

There he made a second marriage with a girl named Dorothea. Now content, Gil Blas hoped for children whose education would provide amusement for his old age.

THE GLASS KEY

Type of work: Novel
Author: Dashiell Hammett (1894-)
Type of plot: Mystery romance
Time of plot: 1930's
Locale: New York area
First published: 1931

Principal characters:
NED BEAUMONT, gambler and amateur detective
PAUL MADVIG, his friend and the city's political boss
SENATOR HENRY, Madvig's candidate for reëlection
JANET HENRY, his daughter
SHAD O'RORY, Madvig's rival
OPAL MADVIG, Madvig's daughter
BERNIE DESPAIN, a gambler owing Ned money

Critique:

In this detective novel Hammett has followed the customary pattern but has varied the circumstances so as to give the story an interesting twist. In addition to tracking down the murderer, the hero also breaks up a bootlegging gang and gives the city officials something about which to worry. The novel has stylistic qualities above the ordinary. It is an excellent example of the modern school of hard-boiled realism.

The Story:

Ned Beaumont reported to his friend, Paul Madvig, the political boss of the city, that he had found the dead body of Taylor Henry in the street. Taylor was the son of Senator Henry, Madvig's candidate for reëlection. When Madvig failed to show much interest, Ned told his story to the police. Next day he went to collect from Bernie Despain the thirty-two hundred and fifty dollars that he had won on a horse race and found that Bernie had vanished, leaving behind twelve hundred dollars worth of Taylor's I.O.U.'s. Ned had himself appointed special investigator in the district attorney's office so that he could work on Taylor Henry's case. What he really wanted to do was to find Bernie and get his money.

His first step was to get the help of Madvig's daughter Opal, who had been meeting Taylor secretly. Ned had found no hat on Taylor the night of the murder. Opal got one for him from the room she and Taylor had rented. Then Ned went to New York to a speakeasy that Bernie frequented. Bernie came in accompanied by a burly bodyguard who, when Ned asked for his money, struck Ned a terrific blow. With the help of Jack Rumsen, a private detective, Ned trailed Bernie from the hotel where he was staying to a brownstone house on Forty-ninth Street. There he told Bernie that he had planted Taylor's hat behind a sofa cushion in Bernie's hotel room and would leave it there for the police to find if Bernie did not pay him the money. Bernie paid off.

Back from New York, Ned went to see Farr, the district attorney. Farr showed Ned an envelope enclosing paper on which were typed three questions implicating Madvig in Taylor's murder. Meanwhile Madvig had decided to have the police close down several speak-easies belonging to Shad O'Rory, gangster and ward boss. O'Rory reopened the Dog House, where Ned went to get information. O'Rory had him tortured for several days. Finally he escaped. He was taken to a hospital.

There he had many callers, including Madvig and Janet Henry, Taylor's sister. Opal Madvig went to tell Ned she was sure her father had killed Taylor. Ned assured her he did not believe Madvig had committed the murder. Partly recovered, he left the hospital against orders.

Shortly afterward Ned and Madvig dined with Senator Henry and his daughter Janet. Ned made Janet admit that she secretly hated Madvig, who was in love with her.

Ned went to see Madvig and told him that even his henchmen were beginning to betray him because they thought he had committed the murder. Madvig admitted Taylor had followed him out of the Henry house that night, that they had quarreled, and that he killed Taylor with a brown, knobby cane which Taylor had been carrying. Madvig claimed that he had then carried the cane away under his coat and burned it. Ned later asked Janet to look for the cane. She said it was with some others in the hall of their home. She also told him of a dream in which she and Ned had found a house with a banquet spread inside; they had to unlock the door and let out a great many snakes before they could go in to enjoy the food.

Ned went next to Farr's office and signed an affidavit telling of Madvig's confession. Then he went to a bar where he found Jeff, O'Rory's bodyguard. In a private room upstairs he accused Jeff of a gangster killing planned by O'Rory. O'Rory walked in on them and in the ensuing quarrel Jeff strangled O'Rory. Ned had a waiter call the police to the scene.

Ned went to the Madvig home, where Madvig's mother said that Madvig was nowhere to be found and that Opal had unsuccessfully attempted to commit suicide. Next morning Ned went to Senator Henry's house and told the senator that Madvig had confessed. It was all Janet and Ned could do to keep the senator from rushing out to kill Madvig. The senator asked Janet to leave him alone with Ned. Ned told him that Janet hated Madvig. The senator insisted he was not going to permit the murderer of his son to go unpunished. Then Ned accused the senator of killing Taylor, of wanting to kill Madvig so that he would not testify against him, of caring more for his own reëlection than for the life of his son. The senator confessed that he had interfered in a street quarrel between Taylor and Madvig and had asked the political boss to leave him with his son. Madvig had done so after giving him the cane Madvig had taken away from Taylor. The senator, angry with his son because of the quarrel he had forced upon Madvig, had angrily struck Taylor with the cane and killed him. He had then carried home the cane. After hearing the old man's confession, Ned refused to leave him alone because he feared the senator would kill himself before the police arrived.

Next day Janet begged Ned to let her go with him to New York. She said the key to the house in her dream had been of glass and had shattered just as they opened the door because they had had to force the lock. When Madvig came in, he learned that he had lost Janet, that she was going away with Ned Beaumont.

THE GOLDEN ASS OF LUCIUS APULEIUS

Type of work: Tale
Author: Lucius Apuleius (125?-?)
Type of plot: Picaresque romance
Time of plot: Early second century
Locale: Greece
First transcribed: Second century manuscript

Principal characters:

LUCIUS, a traveler
CHARITES, a Greek lady
LEPOLEMUS, her husband
THRASILLUS, in love with Charites
MILO, a usurer
PAMPHILE, his wife
FOTIS, her maid

Critique:

The Golden Ass is a rich repository of gusty, fantastic anecdotes. In tone it is bawdy and realistic; in approach it is a mixture of fancy and shrewd observation. An allegory runs through the story, the maturing of man, but the symbolism is dim and inconclusive. Two notable themes distinguish Apuleius' work—the metamorphosis of the hero into an ass, which is a reworking of an earlier Greek tale, and a lengthy retelling of the story of Cupid and Psyche.

The Story:

When Lucius set out on his travels in Thessaly, he happened to fall in with two strangers who were telling unusual stories of the mysterious life of the region. At the urging of Lucius, one of the strangers, a merchant named Aristomenes, told of his strange adventure in Hippata, the chief city of Thessaly.

Aristomenes had gone to the market to buy honey and cheese, but he found that a rival merchant had been there before him and had bought up the supply. As he turned sadly away, he spied his friend Socrates, clad in rags, sitting on the ground. Socrates had fallen among thieves, who beat him and robbed him even of his clothes. Touched by his friend's plight, Aristomenes led him to an inn, bathed and clothed him, and took him to his own chamber to sleep.

Socrates warned of the woman who kept the inn, a carnal woman possessed of magical powers. When she saw a comely man, she wanted him for a lover; if he refused, he was changed into a beast or bird. Aristomenes was a little frightened; he barred the door securely and moved his bed against it for safety. Socrates was already sleeping soundly.

About midnight two hags came to the door, which fell away at their approach. One bore a torch and the other a sponge and sword. While the landlady stood over Socrates and accused him of trying to get away from her, the two hags seized his head, thrust the sword into his throat, and reached in and took out his heart. They caught all his blood in a bladder. Then they put the sponge in the gaping throat wound.

THE GOLDEN ASS OF LUCIUS APULEIUS by Lucius Apuleius. Published by Liveright Publishing Corp.

In the morning Socrates looked like a whole man. The two friends crept away quietly, without arousing the landlady. A few miles out of town, they stopped to eat. Socrates, after eating a whole cheese, leaned over to drink from the stream. As he did so, the wound in his throat opened, the sponge fell out, and Socrates fell dead.

Warned by this story of what he might expect in Thessaly, Lucius presented his letter of introduction to Milo, a rich usurer. He was well received in Milo's house. Attracted by Fotis, a buxom maid, Lucius hung around the kitchen admiring her hair and hips. She agreed quickly to come to his room that night as soon as she had put her mistress, Pamphile, to bed. Fotis was as good as her word, and several nights were passed agreeably enough.

In the city Lucius met a cousin, Byrrhaena, a rich gentlewoman. She invited him to dine and at dinner warned him of the witch Pamphile. Full of wine, Lucius on his way home saw three thugs trying to get into Milo's house. He rushed on them and slew them with his sword. The next day was the Feast of Laughter. As an elaborate hoax, Lucius was arrested and tried for murder in the public place. At the last minute the three "corpses" were revealed to be three bladders, blown up and given temporary life by Pamphile.

One night Fotis let Lucius look through the keyhole of Pamphile's bedroom. To his amazement, Lucius saw the witch smear herself with ointment and turn into an eagle that flew away in majestic flight. Filled with envy, Lucius demanded of Fotis that she smear him with ointment and turn him into an eagle. Fotis consented but with reluctance.

At a propitious time Fotis stole a box of ointment and smeared Lucius, but to his horror he found himself turned into an ass instead of an eagle. He looked around at the mocking Fotis, who professed to have made a mistake and promised to get him some roses in the morning. If he would only eat roses, he would turn into a man again. So Lucius resigned himself to being an ass for the night.

But during the darkness thieves broke into Milo's house, loaded much of Milo's gold on Lucius' back, and drove him out on the road. That morning Lucius saw some roses along the way, but as he was about to eat them he suddenly thought that if he turned into a man in the company of thieves they would surely kill him. He trotted on until they came to the thieves' lair, which was governed by an old woman.

On another night the thieves took captive the gentle Charites, whom they had abducted from her wedding with Lepolemus. Charites wept bitterly. To console her, the old hag told the story of Cupid and Psyche.

There was a merchant who had three daughters. The two older girls, well-favored, were soon married off. The youngest, a true beauty, was admired by all who saw her. No man came to woo her, however, for Venus had become jealous of her beauty and had put a spell upon the girl.

In despair, the parents consulted an oracle, who told them to expose the girl on a rocky cliff, where she would become the bride of a loathsome beast. The sorrowing couple obeyed, and the lovely virgin was exposed one night on a cliff. After she had been left alone, a gentle wind whisked her down into a rich castle.

That night a man with a caressing voice, but whose face she never saw, made her his wife. For a while she was content not to see her husband, but at last her jealous sisters persuaded her to light a lamp in order to see his face. When she did, she learned her husband was Cupid, who had succumbed to her charms when Venus had sent him to make her fall in love with a monster.

Although the girl was pregnant, Venus refused to recognize her son's marriage with a mortal. Then Jupiter took pity on her and brought her to heaven. There he conferred immortality on her and named her Psyche. So Cupid and Psyche became the epitome of faithful love.

Lepolemus, the resourceful bridegroom, rescued Charites by ingratiating himself with the robbers and becoming one of their band. Watching his chance, he made them all drunk and chained them. Setting Charites on the back of Lucius, Lepolemus took his bride home and returned with a band of aroused citizens, who killed all the thieves of the den.

Lucius was given over to a herdsman of Charites, and for a time he lived a hard life as a mill ass. One day news came of the death of Lepolemus, who was killed on a hunting trip with his friend, Thrasillus. In a dream, Lepolemus told Charites that Thrasillus had killed him. When Thrasillus came wooing Charites soon afterward, she pretended to listen to his proposals. He came to her chamber late one night, and there the old nurse of Charites gave him wine. When he was drunk, Charites took a pin and pricked out both his eyes.

These irregularities of their owners made the shepherds uneasy. In a body they left Charites' estate and struck out on their own. Lucius passed through several hands, some good owners, some bad. He bore his lot as best he could, but he could never be a proper ass because he still longed to eat bread and meat. One of his owners discovered this peculiarity and exhibited Lucius as a performing ass.

As a performer Lucius led an easier life. Now that spring was approaching, he hoped to find some roses. In the meantime he enjoyed himself; he even had a rich matron as his mistress for a few nights. But when his master proposed to exhibit him in a cage, making love to a harlot, Lucius decided to rebel.

He escaped and sought the aid of Queen Isis. Taking pity on Lucius, she caused a priest to carry a garland of roses in a parade. The priest offered the flowers to Lucius, who ate them eagerly. Once again Lucius became a man.

THE GOOD COMPANIONS

Type of work: Novel
Author: J. B. Priestley (1894-)
Type of plot: Picaresque romance
Time of plot: The 1920's
Locale: England
First published: 1929

Principal characters:

Miss Trant, a well-to-do British woman
Inigo Jollifant, a teacher at a boys' school
Jess Oakroyd, a workman
Susie Dean, a comedienne
Jerry Jerningham, a dancer

Critique:

J. B. Priestley's novel is a very human portrayal of a group of his contemporary Britishers in the 1920's. In many ways the novel is reminiscent of the work of Charles Dickens, both in characterization and in atmosphere. The descriptions of the English countryside and towns are particularly good. With such descriptions the author effectively sets the locale of the various parts of the novel. The best character of the novel is the Yorkshire workman, Jess Oakroyd. His northern dialect is a source of amusement both to the characters in the novel and to the reader, and he is the English parallel to the almost mythical American Yankee who says little, thinks much, and ends up by proving more astute than the sophisticated people about him.

The Story:

Jess Oakroyd was a stolid, proper sort of Yorkshireman, but his wife's nagging, coupled with the sarcastic remarks of his son, finally forced him to pack a small basket of clothes and set off to travel about England. His adventures began immediately, for he got a ride in a large van loaded with stolen goods. The driver of the van and the driver's helper left Jess at an inn in a small hamlet after having robbed him while he was asleep. Rudely awakened by the innkeeper, Jess had no money to buy his breakfast. Setting off afoot, he came upon another van, in which a man was attempting to repair a battered peddler's stall. In return for Jess' help, the owner gave him breakfast and a ride. Jess stayed for three days with the peddler, who sold fancy balloons.

After leaving the balloon trade, the Yorkshireman set out to walk the roads of England once again. Within the hour he came upon a stalled car and helped the woman driver to start the motor. The woman was Miss Trant, who had inherited several hundred pounds from her father. Since all her previous adventures had been in the realm of historical novels, Miss Trant had also decided to travel over England. At the age of thirty-five she was already an old maid.

While they were getting the car started, rain began to fall, and Jess and Miss Trant headed for a little tearoom nearby. There they met Inigo Jollifant and an odd-looking companion who was carrying a banjo. Inigo had begun his adventures on the previous Monday evening, as had Jess and Miss Trant.

An instructor at a boys' school, Inigo had been unhappy there because of the petty tyranny of the headmaster and his termagant wife. On Monday evening he had been dismissed because he became drunk and played the piano in celebration of his twenty-sixth birthday. Inigo, too drunk to do the prudent thing, had packed a knapsack and set out on his travels immediately. In the railroad station of a small town he had met his banjo-carrying companion, Morton Mitcham, a professional entertainer.

In the tearoom the shrewish woman proprietress was berating a group of customers who were unable to pay their bill. The banjo player recognized them as members of a theatrical troupe stranded, as they explained, when their manager ran away with a young woman and their funds.

On impulse, Miss Trant decided to take over the stranded company. That night they made plans for taking the show on the road once more. The new troupe took the name of The Good Companions. It was made up of an elderly comedian, a young and pretty comedienne named Susie Dean, Morton Mitcham, a dancer named Jerry Jerningham, a girl singer, and an older couple who sang duets. Miss Trant was the manager, Inigo the accompanist, and Jess, at Miss Trant's insistence, the handyman.

Their first appearance was in the little town where Miss Trant had found them. The show was not successful, but their second engagement, at a seaside hotel, met with obvious favor. The most appreciated actors were Jerry Jerningham and Susie Dean, who were aided by the gay songs which were written for their acts by Inigo Jollifant. For several weeks the routine of the company was one of rehearsals and performances, with train rides between two or three-night engagements in each town.

As the weeks passed, Inigo Jollifant fell in love with Susie Dean, who laughed at him, saying she could not fall in love and marry until she had become a musical comedy star and had played in London. Miss Trant was having a delightful experience. All her life had been spent in the sleepy village of Hitherton in southern England, where her father had settled upon his retirement from the army. Her theatrical associates were far more interesting than the small sedate group of her father's village friends.

Next The Good Companions played in an almost deserted mill town in the Midlands. The mills had been shut down for some months and the townspeople had little money or interest in a traveling vaudeville troupe. Since the audiences were small and not sympathetic, the troupe became dispirited and almost broke up. But Jess Oakroyd persuaded the troupe to stick with Miss Trant, since she would lose her money if they did not carry on with their engagements.

At last the fortunes of the troupe had a turn for the better. Inigo Jollifant composed new tunes for the acts which met with great success. His love affair, however, did not fare as well. Susie Dean could not understand why he did not take his music as seriously as he did his writing for literary periodicals. She felt sure that he was making a mistake in trying to be a second-rate essayist when he could be a first-rate song writer.

The Good Companions finally had a long engagement in a series of prosperous manufacturing towns. The large audiences they drew began to recoup the money Miss Trant had invested. They became bold enough to engage a large hall for a stand of several nights. In the meantime Inigo went to London, where a famous producer listened to his new songs. Inigo, determined to help Susie become a top-ranking musical comedy star, refused to let the producer use his songs unless the man went with him to hear Susie Dean.

The first night in the large auditorium was disastrous. The operator of the local motion picture houses hired toughs to start a riot and set fire to the hall during the performance. The producer from London was punched on the nose in the melee and so refused to hear any more about either Inigo's music or Susie Dean. Miss Trant was injured during the riot.

Finally, when the future looked darkest, an elderly woman took a fancy to Jerry Jerningham. She married him and put her money and influence at his disposal. The result was that an even greater producer gave Susie Dean her chance at musical comedy in London and bought Inigo's music.

The troupe disbanded; but at Jerningham's request the other performers found excellent places with the same producer. In the hospital Miss Trant met a doctor with whom she had been in love for many years, and she prepared to marry him as soon as she was well. Jess Oakroyd did a little detective work in connection with the riot. With the help of the balloon peddler, he discovered who had hired the men to start the rioting and set fire to the theater. Held responsible for the disturbance, these men had to take over Miss Trant's debts for the damages.

After solving the mystery of the riot, Jess went back to his home in Yorkshire, for he had had a telegram from his son telling him that Mrs. Oakroyd was seriously ill. She died shortly thereafter and Jess made preparations to continue his traveling. He decided to visit his married daughter in Canada, for he had discovered that even a man as old and settled as he could become addicted to the pleasures of adventuring away from home.

THE GOOD EARTH

Type of work: Novel
Author: Pearl S. Buck (1892-   )
Type of plot: Social chronicle
Time of plot: Early twentieth century
Locale: Northern China
First published: 1931

Principal Characters:
WANG LUNG, a Chinese farmer
O-LAN, his wife
LOTUS BLOSSOM, his concubine
PEAR BLOSSOM, his slave
NUNG EN, Wang Lung's oldest son
NUNG WEN, Wang Lung's second son
THE FOOL, Wang Lung's first daughter

Critique:

In an almost pastoral style, *The Good Earth* describes the cycle of birth, marriage, and death in a Chinese peasant family. The book is written realistically, without any overt attempts to awaken sympathy for any of the characters. It is the absorbing story of Wang Lung's life on the farm, his trip to the city when starvation threatens, and of his life until it is time for him to be claimed by the good earth.

The Story:

His father had chosen a slave girl to be the bride of Wang Lung, a slave from the house of Hwang, a girl who would keep the house clean, prepare the food, and not waste her time thinking about clothes. On the morning he led her out through the gate of the big house, they stopped at a temple and burned incense. That was their marriage.

O-lan was a good wife. She thriftily gathered twigs and wood, so that they would not have to buy fuel. She mended Wang Lung's and his father's winter clothes and scoured the house. She worked in the fields beside her husband, even on the day she bore their first son.

The harvest was a good one that year. Wang Lung had a handful of silver dollars from the sale of his wheat and rice. He and O-lan bought new coats for themselves and new clothes for the baby. Together they went to pay their respects, with their child, at the home in which O-lan had once been a slave. With some of the silver dollars Wang Lung bought a small field of rich land from the Hwangs.

The second child was born a year later. It was again a year of good harvest.

Wang Lung's third baby was a girl. On the day of her birth crows flew about the house, mocking Wang Lung with their cries. The farmer did not rejoice when his little daughter was born, for poor farmers raised their daughters only to serve the rich. The crows had been an evil omen. The child was born feebleminded.

That summer was dry, and for months no rain fell. The harvest was poor. After the little rice and wheat had been eaten and the ox killed for food, there was nothing for the poor peasants to do but die or go south to find work and food in a province of plenty. Wang Lung sold their furniture for a few pieces of silver, and after O-lan had borne their fourth child, dead with bruises on its neck when he saw it for the first time, the family began their journey. Falling in with a crowd of refugees, they were lucky. The refugees led them to a railroad, and with the money Wang Lung had received for his furniture they traveled on a train to their new home.

In the city they constructed a hut of mats against a wall, and, while O-lan and the two older children begged, Wang Lung pulled a ricksha. In that way they spent the winter, each day earning enough to buy rice for the next.

One day an exciting thing happened. There was to be a battle between soldiers in the town and an approaching enemy. When the wealthy people in the town fled, the poor who lived so miserably broke into the houses of the rich. By threatening one fat fellow who had been left behind, Wang Lung obtained enough money to take his family home.

O-lan soon repaired the damage which the weather had done to their house during their absence; then, with jewels which his wife had managed to plunder during the looting in the city, Wang Lung bought more land from the house of Hwang. He allowed O-lan to keep two small pearls which she fancied. Now Wang Lung had more land than one man could handle, and he hired one of his neighbors, Ching, as overseer. Several years later he had six men working for him. O-lan, who had borne him twins, a boy and a girl, after their return from the south, no longer went out into the fields to work, but kept the new house he had built. Wang Lung's two oldest sons were sent to school in the town.

When his land was flooded and work impossible until the water receded, Wang Lung began to go regularly to a tea shop in the town. There he fell in love with Lotus and brought her home to his farm to be his concubine. O-lan would have nothing to do with the girl, and Wang Lung was forced to set up a separate establishment for Lotus in order to keep the peace.

When he found that his oldest son visited Lotus often while he was away, Wang Lung arranged to have the boy marry the daughter of a grain merchant in the town. The wedding took place shortly before O-lan, still in the prime of life, died of a chronic stomach illness. To cement the bond between the farmer and the grain merchant, Wang Lung's second son was apprenticed to Liu, the merchant, and his youngest daughter was betrothed to Liu's young son. Soon after O-lan's death Wang Lung's father followed her. They were buried near one another on a hill on his land.

When he grew wealthy, an uncle, his wife, and his shiftless son came to live with Wang Lung. One year there was a great flood, and although his neighbors' houses were pillaged by robbers during the confusion, Wang Lung was not bothered. Then he learned that his uncle was second to the chief of the robbers. From that time on he had to give way to his uncle's family, for they were his insurance against robbery and perhaps murder.

At last Wang Lung coaxed his uncle and aunt to smoke opium, and so they became too involved in their dreams to bother him. But there was no way he could curb their son. When the boy began to annoy the wife of Wang Lung's oldest son, the farmer rented the deserted house of Hwang and he, with his own family, moved into town. The cousin left to join the soldiers. The uncle and aunt were left in the country with their pipes to console them.

After Wang Lung's overseer died, he did no more farming himself. From that time on he rented his land, hoping that his youngest son would work it after his death. But he was disappointed. When Wang Lung took a slave young enough to be his granddaughter, the boy, who was in love with her, ran away from home and became a soldier.

When he felt that his death was near, Wang Lung went back to live on his land, taking with him only his slave, young Pear Blossom, his foolish-witted first daughter, and some servants. One day as he accompanied his sons across the fields, he overheard them planning what they would do with their inheritance, with the money they would get from selling their father's property. Wang Lung cried out, protesting that they must never sell the land because only from it could they be sure of earning a living. He did not know that they looked at each other over his head and smiled.

GOODBYE, MR. CHIPS

Type of work: Novelette
Author: James Hilton (1900-)
Type of plot: Sentimental romance.
Time of plot: 1870-1933
Locale: An English boys' school
First published: 1933

Principal characters:
MR. CHIPS, an old schoolmaster
MRS. WICKETT, his landlady
BROOKFIELD BOYS

Critique:

This charming story of an old schoolmaster was written when the young journalist, James Hilton, was given an assignment to produce a Christmas story for an English newspaper. The almost instantaneous success of the book determined to a large degree the wide public reputation of its author. The novel consists largely of a series of happy and sad reminiscences of a beloved and almost legendary teacher who, sitting in his little room one gray November day, thinks of the many years he has spent in a boys' school.

The Story:

Chips was old — eighty-five — but of course, he thought, far from ill. Dr. Merivale had told him he should not venture out on this cold November day, but he also added that Chips was fitter than the doctor himself. What Chips did not know was that the doctor had told the landlady, Mrs. Wickett, to look after him; Chips' chest clouded in bad weather.

Chips sank into his armchair by the fire, happy in the peace and warmth. The first thing about his remembered career set him laughing. He had come to teach at Brookfield in 1870, and in a kindly talk old Wetherby, the acting head, advised him to watch his disciplinary measures. Mr. Wetherby had heard that discipline was not one of Chips' strong points. On the first day of class, when one of the boys dropped his desk top rather too loudly, Chips assigned him a hundred lines and had no trouble after that. The boy's name was Colley—Chips seldom forgot a name or a face—and years later, he remembered, he taught Colley's son, and then his grandson, who, he said pleasantly, was the biggest young nitwit of them all. Chips was fond of making little jokes about the boys, who took his jibes well and grew to love him for his honesty and friendliness. Indeed, Chips' jokes were regarded as the funniest anywhere, and the boys had great sport telling of his latest.

Remembering these things, Chips thought growing old was a great joke, though a little sad. And when Mrs. Wickett came in with his tea, she could not tell whether Chips was laughing or crying. Tears were spilling down his withered cheeks.

Brookfield had known periods of grandeur and decay. When Chips arrived there, the school was already a century old and regarded as a place for boys whose lineage was respectable but seldom distinguished. Chips' own background was not distinguished, either, but it had been hard for him to realize that his mind was not the type to assume leadership. He had longed to work his way into the position of headmaster, but after many failures he knew that his role was one of teaching, and he gave up his administrative ambitions. But he grew to love his students. They would often come to chat with him over tea and crumpets. Sometimes they remarked, as they left, what a typical bachelor old Chips was.

It was painful to Chips that no one at Brookfield remembered his wife. He had married Kathy Bridges at forty-eight, and even now he wondered how the miracle had taken place. He had seen a girl waving from the top of a rocky ledge one day when he was out walking, and thinking her in trouble he set out to rescue her. On the way he sprained his ankle, and Kathy had assisted him. It was a remarkable love, for she was years younger than he. But Kathy left an enduring mark upon Chips. He grew more lenient with the boys, more understanding of their problems, and more courageous in his teaching. Ironically, Kathy died on April first, in childbirth, and that day, not realizing the tragedy that had befallen Chips, the boys played April Fool jokes on the stricken teacher.

Chips began to remember the war years. Names of boys whose faces he could still vizualize were read out in chapel from the casualty lists. When the headmaster died and no one could be found to fill his place, Chips was asked to head Brookfield. Standing in his tattered gown, which was often considered disgraceful by newcomers, he read out the names as tears filled his eyes. Even now, sitting in front of the fire, he could recall that roll, and he read it over to himself, remembering the faces that had looked so hopefully at him in the classroom.

One day he was meeting a Latin class while German bombs were crashing nearby. The boys squirmed in their seats as the explosions sounded nearer and nearer, but Chips quietly told them that they should never judge the importance of anything by the noise it made. Then, asking one of the more courageous lads to translate, Chips chose from Caesar a passage which was particularly apt because it dealt with German methods of fighting. Later the boys told how Chips stood steady and calm, and they remarked that even though they might consider Latin a dead language, it was nevertheless valuable at times.

After the war Chips gave up his headmastership and returned to his room at Mrs. Wickett's. Now, fifteen years later, he was always asked to greet visiting dignitaries who came to Brookfield. He was amused to find that many of the barons, Parliament members, and war heroes had been his former pupils, and he remembered their faces, though now, to his chagrin, he often forgot their names. He would make amusing, appropriate remarks, not always complimentary, and the visitors would shake with laughter. Sometimes during those postwar years, he was asked to make little speeches at school banquets, and because of his reputation for funny sayings his audience would laugh uproariously, often before Chips reached the point of his jokes. Chips was privileged now; his eccentricities only made him more loved at Brookfield. Indeed, Chips was Brookfield.

Chips thought of the rich life he had led. There were so many things for laughter and sorrow. Now, as he sat by the fire, he heard a timid knock at the door, and a youngster, much abashed, came in. He had been told that Chips had sent for him. The old man laughed, knowing that this was a prank the old boys often played on a newcomer, and he saved the boy from embarrassment by saying that he had sent for him. After conversation and tea, Chips dismissed the boy in his abrupt but kindly fashion. The boy waved as he went down the walk.

Later that youth thought of Chips sadly and told his comrades that he had been the last to tell him goodbye. For Mr. Chips died quietly in his sleep that cold November night.

GRAND HOTEL

Type of work: Novel
Author: Vicki Baum (1888-)
Type of plot: Social chronicle
Time of plot: 1920's
Locale: Berlin
First published: 1930

Principal characters:
BARON GAIGERN, a gambler and thief
ELISAVETA ALEXANDROVNA GRUSINSKAYA, a ballerina
OTTO KRINGELEIN, a junior clerk of the Saxonia Cotton Company
HERR GENERALDIREKTOR PREYSING, manager of the Saxonia Cotton Company
DR. OTTERNSCHLAG, a retired physician
MISS FLAMM (FLAEMMCHEN), a public stenographer and model

Critique:

In this novel Vicki Baum uses a time-honored device of fiction by bringing together a group of characters in a particular time and place, and showing how they react upon and influence each other. The parallel, concurrent actions of her characters are well synthesized into a picture of European society in the period between wars.

The Story:

Through the revolving doors of the Grand Hotel in Berlin came people from various walks of life. The meetings of these people and their effects upon one another thereafter were as varied as the people themselves. Each one had his own life, his own worries, and his own problems, and each pursued his own selfish ends.

Baron Gaigern was living in luxury at the hotel. He never seemed to lack money and he possessed well-tailored clothes. The baron, however, was a gambler and a thief staying at the hotel for the purpose of stealing Elisaveta Alexandrovna Grusinskaya's famous pearls, which had been given to the ballerina by the Grand Duke Sergei. Gaigern's plan to steal the pearls was based on a timing of Grusinskaya's actions. One night he crawled along the outside of the building to the dancer's room, where she kept her jewels in an unlocked case. That night Grusinskaya returned earlier than usual and found him in her room.

Grusinskaya, the aging ballerina, knew that her youth was slipping away from her. On that particular night, feeble applause after one of her best numbers made her leave the theater before the performance was over and return to her room at the hotel. When she discovered Gaigern in her room, he convinced her that because he loved her he had come to sit there while she was away at the theater. Willing to believe him, she let him stay with her the rest of the night. The next morning, before she awoke, he replaced the pearls in their case. Grusinskaya left Berlin that morning and Gaigern promised to meet her in Vienna three days later.

Still in need of money, Gaigern decided to get it from the wealthy and apparently ailing provincial in room 70. Gaigern did not suspect that the rich provincial, Otto Kringelein by name, was in reality only a junior clerk of the Saxonia Cotton Company of Fredersdorf. Kringelein at forty-six, had learned that he was dying, and he decided that before his death he would see something of life after years of being bullied at the office by his superiors and at home by his wife Anna. With a small legacy left him by his father, his savings in the bank, and a loan on his life insurance policy, he planned to live the life of a rich man for a few weeks before he died. On the morning Grusinskaya left Berlin, Gaigern met Kringelein and took him to be outfitted by his own tailor. In the evening they went to the boxing matches and then to a gambling casino. Kringelein paid for the evening's entertainment, for Gaigern admitted that he was without funds. Gaigern had hoped to win enough money to pay his way to Vienna, but he lost steadily. Kringelein won thirty-four hundred marks. They ended the evening at the Alhambra, a shabby night club, where Kringelein became ill. On the way back to the hotel Gaigern stole Kringelein's pocketbook. Later in Kringelein's room, he returned it at Dr. Otternschlag's insistence.

Dr. Otternschlag, a middle-aged physician badly disfigured in the war, spent one or two months every year at the Grand Hotel. He did nothing, went practically nowhere, and seemed to have no interests whatsoever. He had begun to show a slight interest in Kringelein when Gaigern intruded. It was Otternschlag who gave Kringelein a hypodermic to lessen his pains, but after a polite word of thanks to the doctor Kringelein turned to Gaigern, whom he begged to remain with him. Otternschlag was forgotten.

In the morning Kringelein received a letter from his wife, complaining about the inconveniences of the house in which they lived, a house owned by the Saxonia Cotton Company. Kringelein angrily stamped down to Generaldirektor Preysing's room to air his grievance. Herr Preysing had married the daughter of the owner of the Saxonia Cotton Company years before and had gradually worked himself up to the position of manager. He was in Berlin to bring about an amalgamation between his company and the Chemnitz Manufacturing Company, a merger necessary to forestall huge losses for the Saxonia Company. When Preysing saw that the representatives of the Chemnitz Company were about to reject his offer, he told a lie which he knew would win him their consent. He assured them that a trade agreement existed between the company and Burleigh & Sons, importers, of Manchester, England. The merger was then signed. During his stay in Berlin, Preysing had hired a stenographer, Miss Flamm, a beautiful girl who worked part time as a photographer's model. Preysing became quite enamored of her. When she hinted that she would be willing to travel with him as his secretary, Preysing decided to go to Manchester and confer with the English company. He asked Flaemmchen, as he called her, to accompany him and she agreed, after setting her price at one thousand marks. Preysing immediately engaged an adjoining room for her at the Grand Hotel.

That night Preysing was in Flaemmchen's room when he heard a noise in his own room and went to see what it was. There stood Gaigern in his pajamas. Preysing saw that his billfold was missing from the table where he had placed it, and he demanded its return. Gaigern threatened to shoot. Preysing seized a bronze inkstand and hit Gaigern over the head with it, killing him. Flaemmchen ran to call for help. Kringelein heard her and opened his door, to have her fall unconscious into his arms. He took her in and when she regained consciousness he learned the whole story from her. He then went down to Preysing's room, gathered up Flaemmchen's clothes, and told Preysing to call the police. When they arrived, Preysing was arrested and his plea of self-defense after robbery seemed weak, for Gaigern had had no gun on him. Preysing stayed in jail for three months. During that time his affair with Flaemmchen was exposed, his wife divorced him, and his father-in-law discharged him. Meanwhile Kringelein and Flaemmchen, having become friends, decided to go to England together.

Lives had been changed by chance meetings. Gaigern, the strong, vital man, was now dead. Preysing, the respectable citizen, was in jail accused of murder. Otternschlag, who claimed to have no interest in life, found when he tried to commit suicide that he wanted very much to live. Meek, downtrodden Kringelein began to assume the authority that came with responsibility, responsibility in the form of Flaemmchen. The tired and aging ballerina, Grusinskaya, had left the hotel feeling young and loved once more. And as their rooms were vacated one by one, new visitors entered the hotel where life, mysterious or stupid or cruel, went on.

THE GRANDISSIMES

Type of work: Novel
Author: George W. Cable (1844-1925)
Type of plot: Regional romance
Time of plot: 1804
Locale: New Orleans
First published: 1880

Principal characters:

HONORÉ GRANDISSIME, head of the Grandissimes
THE DARKER HONORÉ GRANDISSIME, his quadroon half-brother
AGRICOLA FUSILIER, Honoré's uncle
AURORA NANCANOU, a young widow
CLOTILDE NANCANOU, her daughter
JOSEPH FROWENFELD, a young American
DR. KEENE, Joseph's physician and friend
PALMYRE, a freed slave

Critique:

George W. Cable knew intimately the Creole society of New Orleans, and this novel re-creates for the reader a segment of American life which has vanished forever. Through the author's attempt at reproducing Creole dialect, the book acquires a unique flavor. The plot presents the tragedy of the Negro in a more effective and more truthful manner than do many modern books on the subject.

The Story:

Honoré Grandissime and Aurora Nancanou, both members of the Creole aristocracy, met at a masked ball and fell in love at first sight. Each was unaware of the other's identity. Honoré was a young merchant, the head of the Grandissime family. Aurora, a young widow, was the daughter of a De Grapion. Honoré's uncle, Agricola Fusilier, had killed Aurora's husband in a duel, after he had accused Agricola of cheating at cards. Agricola won the duel, cleared his honor, and collected the gambling debt, the entire estate of Aurora's husband. Aurora and her daughter Clotilde, were left penniless. Agricola gave Aurora's estate to Honoré and made him a wealthy man.

Shortly afterward Joseph Frowenfeld, a young American immigrant, arrived in New Orleans with his parents and sisters. All were stricken with fever; only Joseph survived. The lonely young man formed a friendship with his physician, Dr. Keene. Joseph and Honoré met by chance one day and found a common interest in their concern over the injustice of slavery and the caste system of New Orleans society. Honoré's life however depended upon these institutions. Joseph wished to have them wiped out at once.

Deciding to earn his living as a druggist, Joseph opened a small shop and soon became friendly with his aristocratic landlord. The landlord was actually Honoré's half-brother and he bore the same name, but he was not acknowledged as a member of the family because he was a quadroon. He was called the darker Honoré.

Joseph found another new friend in old Agricola. He was also struck by the charm of Aurora and Clotilde when they called to make purchases. He learned more about Aurora from Dr. Keene. The physician told him about Palmyre, a freed slave who had once been Aurora's maid. The girl hated Agricola. One night Joseph was awakened by pistol shots nearby. A few minutes later Dr. Keene and several others entered the shop with the wounded Agricola; he had been stabbed, and his companions had fired upon his assailant.

Several days later Aurora called upon her landlord in order to make some arrangements about the rent she could not pay. She knew her landlord's name was Honoré Grandissime, but she did not connect this name with the man she loved. Upon learning that they were half-brothers, Aurora was upset and her family pride caused her to be harsh with Honoré.

When Dr. Keene fell sick, he asked Joseph to attend one of his patients. The patient was Palmyre, who had been wounded as she ran away after stabbing Agricola. Joseph promised Dr. Keene to keep her trouble a secret and went to dress the wound.

Joseph paid his last visit to the wounded Palmyre, now almost recovered. Palmyre begged him to help her make the white Honoré love her. But Palmyre's maid, misunderstanding the conversation, thought that Joseph had wronged her mistress. She struck him over the head, and Joseph reeled groggily into the street. Some passing pedestrians, seeing him emerge bleeding from Palmyre's house, drew a natural inference, and soon everyone knew about Joseph's misfortune. Only Clotilde and Honoré believed him innocent.

Public feeling was running high against the Americans, and Joseph found himself despised by most of the Creoles. Both his liberal views and his trouble at Palmyre's house were against him.

Honoré's conscience bothered him. He felt that he unjustly held Aurora's property, but he also knew he could not return it to her without ruining the finances of his family. But he made his choice. He called upon Aurora and Clotilde and presented them with their property and the income from it. Now he could not declare his love for Aurora; if he did so, his family would think he had returned the property because of love instead of a sense of justice.

On his way home from Aurora's house, Honoré met the darker Honoré with Dr. Keene. The physician had risen from his sickbed because he had heard of Honoré's call at Aurora's house. Dr. Keene, also in love with Aurora, was jealous. His exertion caused a hemorrhage of the lungs, and the two Honorés carried him home and watched over him.

While they attended the sick man, the darker Honoré proposed to his brother that they go into partnership, so that the darker Honoré's money could save the family from ruin. His brother accepted the offer. But this action turned Honoré's family against him. Agricola led an unsuccessful lynching party to find the darker Honoré. Not finding him, the mob broke the windows of Joseph's shop as a gesture against liberal views in general.

Aurora set Joseph up in business again on the ground floor of her house and made Clotilde a partner in the store. Brought together in this manner, the two young people fell in love. At the same time, the darker Honoré lay wasting away for love of Palmyre, who was trying to revenge herself upon Agricola by voodoo spells. When Agricola could no longer sleep at night, his family determined to catch Palmyre in her acts of witchcraft. They caught her accomplice, but Palmyre escaped.

Meanwhile the darker Honoré went to Joseph's store to get some medicine for himself. Meeting Agricola, who insulted him, the darker Honoré stabbed Agricola and escaped. The wounded man was carried upstairs to Aurora's house to die:

there the two families were united again at his deathbed. Agricola revealed that he had once promised to Aurora's father a marriage between Aurora and Honoré.

The darker Honoré and Palmyre escaped together to France. There he committed suicide because she still would not accept his love.

Joseph finally declared his love for Clotilde. But Aurora would not accept Honoré's offer of marriage because she thought he had made it out of obligation to Agricola. Then Honoré made his offer again as a man in love. As a last gesture of family pride Aurora refused him, but at the same time she threw herself into her lover's arms.

THE GRANDMOTHERS

Type of work: Novel
Author: Glenway Wescott (1901-)
Type of plot: Regional chronicle
Time of plot: 1830-1925
Locale: Wisconsin
First published: 1927

Principal characters:
Alwyn Tower, a young boy
Henry Tower, his grandfather
Rose Tower, his grandmother
Jim Tower, his uncle
Evan Tower, another uncle
Flora Tower, his aunt
Ralph Tower, his father
Marianne Tower, his mother

Critique:

The heritage which Alwyn Tower studied as he pored over the family albums is the heritage of most Americans. The struggles of the pioneers of the Tower family were the struggles of all pioneers. Glenway Wescott has told a story of the loves and hates, the madness, the strength, and the weakness found in the histories of all families. The characters are vivid and authentic, the events realistic and moving. The writer must have loved the people about whom he wrote; he portrays them so sympathetically. *The Grandmothers* is a truly American story.

The Story:

During his childhood, Alwyn Tower spent many hours poring over the family albums, for everything any of his ancestors or relatives had done was interesting to the boy. He begged his Grandmother Tower to tell him stories of her childhood and stories about her children and other relatives. Often the old lady could not remember what he wanted to know, and sometimes she seemed reluctant to talk about the past. But piece by piece, from his Grandmother Tower, his parents, his aunts and uncles, and from the albums, Alwyn learned something of what he wanted to know.

Alwyn's Grandfather Tower died when the boy was twelve years old, and so his memories of that old man were rather vague. Grandfather Tower's chief interest during his old age was his garden, where he never allowed his grandchildren to go without his permission. He had failed at farming, but he was the best gardener in that part of Wisconsin.

Grandfather Tower had come to Wisconsin from New York. Like so many others, he had planned to get rich in the new West; like so many others, he had failed. He had been a young boy full of dreams when he first cleared the wilderness for his farm. He fell in love with and married Serena Cannon, and shortly afterward went off to the Civil War. When he returned, Serena was ill with a fever and died soon after, leaving a baby boy. Grandfather Tower could never love another as he had loved Serena. Because the boy needed a mother, however, he married Rose Hamilton, who had been jilted by his brother Leander. Serena's boy died, a week before Rose bore his first child. After that life seemed unimportant to Henry Tower. There were more children, some a small pleasure to him, some a disgrace. But they seemed to be Rose's children, not his. Part of Grandfather Tower had died with Serena, and although he lived to be eighty-two years old, he had never seemed to be completely alive as far as Alwyn was concerned.

Grandmother Tower, too, had come to Wisconsin when she was a child. Growing up in the wilderness, she suffered all the hardships of the pioneers —hunger and cold and fear of Indians. When she was in her early teens she met and fell in love with Leander Tower. When the Civil War came, Leander enlisted, and the girl went to stay with Serena Tower. While Serena lay ill with fever, the young girl cared for her and the baby. Leander returned, but he had changed. Although he could not explain himself clearly, Rose knew that he no longer wanted to marry her. After Serena's husband came home and Serena had died, Leander went to California. Rose married Serena's widower and bore his children, but like him she was only partly alive. She never ceased to love Leander, but she was faithful to Grandfather Tower, even after Leander returned to Wisconsin. To Alwyn, she was a quiet, serene woman, resigned to life, but not unhappy with her lot.

Alwyn learned about many of his more distant relatives as he studied the albums and listened to the stories of his elders. There was his Great-Aunt Nancy Tower, who had been insane for part of her life. There was his Great-Aunt Mary Harris, who had been married three times and had traveled all over the world. Grandmother Tower said that Great-Aunt Mary was a real pioneer. She had seen her first husband killed by Southerners because he sympathized with the Union. Her second husband was a drunken sot who beat her, and often she had to beg for food to stay alive. After her second husband divorced her, she married one of the Tower men, and for the first time she knew happiness and prosperity.

Old Leander Tower seemed to be happy only when he was helping a young boy. His younger brother Hilary had disappeared in the war, and it seemed almost as if Leander were trying to find a substitute for his brother.

Alwyn knew his father's brothers and sisters quite well. His Uncle Jim was a minister who had married a rich woman, and they took Alwyn to live with them in Chicago, giving the boy his only chance for a good education. Uncle Jim's wife persuaded her husband to give up preaching. After her death he continued to live with her mother and sisters and to humor their whims. Alwyn liked his Uncle Jim, but he could not admire him.

Uncle Evan, a deserter in the Spanish-American War, had gone west to live after taking a new name. Once or twice he came home to visit his father, but both men seemed embarrassed during those meetings. Grandfather Tower had always been ashamed of Evan, and during the last visit Evan made the old man refused to enter the house while his son was there.

Aunt Flora was an old maid, although she still thought of herself as a young girl. She had had many chances to marry, but she was afraid of the force of love, afraid that something hidden in her would be roused and not satisfied. It was a mysterious thing she could not understand. She turned to Alwyn, giving him her love and accepting his, for she could love the young boy whole-heartedly, having nothing to fear from him. When she was twenty-nine years old, she fell ill and died. Alwyn thought she looked happy as she took her last breath.

Alwyn's father, Ralph Tower, had always wanted to be a veterinarian, for he had a way with animals. But Uncle Jim had been the one chosen for an education, and after Uncle Evan deserted and went west, Ralph had to take over the farm for his father. He was never bitter; merely resigned. Perhaps he would have envied Jim if it had not been for Alwyn's mother.

His parents had one of the few really happy marriages in the family, Alwyn realized as he watched them together. Alwyn knew something of the girlhood of his mother. Her parents had hated each other fiercely, and had taken pleasure in showing that hatred. Alwyn's mother was a lonely child until she met Ralph Tower. Sometimes it embarrassed Alwyn to see his parents together because they revealed so much of their feeling for each other.

Alwyn realized that the Towers were one of the last pioneer families in America. He knew that in his heritage there was a deep religious feeling, a willingness to accept poverty and hardship as the will of God. His heritage was a disordered one; a deserter, an insane woman, a man and a wife who hated each other, an uncle who lived on the wealth of his wife's mother. But these people were just as much a part of him as were the others. Alwyn knew that his life would be a rearrangement of the characters of the others. He knew that he could understand himself if once he understood his people.

THE GRAPES OF WRATH

Type of work: Novel
Author: John Steinbeck (1902-)
Type of plot: Social criticism
Time of plot: 1930's
Locale: Southwest United States and California
First published: 1939

Principal characters:
Tom Joad, an ex-convict
Pa Joad, an Okie
Ma Joad, his wife
Rose of Sharon, Tom's sister
Jim Casy, a labor agitator

Critique:

In *The Grapes of Wrath* Steinbeck has achieved an interesting contrapuntal effect by breaking the narrative at intervals with short, impressionistic passages recorded as though by a motion picture camera moving quickly from one scene to another and from one focus to another. The novel is a powerful indictment of our capitalistic economy and a sharp criticism of the southwestern farmer for his imprudence in the care of his land. The outstanding feature of *The Grapes of Wrath* is its photographically detailed, if occasionally sentimentalized, description of the American farmers of the Dust Bowl in the mid-thirties of the twentieth century.

The Story:

Tom Joad was released from the Oklahoma state penitentiary where he had served a sentence for killing a man in self-defense. He traveled homeward through a region made barren by drought and dust storms. On the way he met Jim Casy, an ex-preacher; the pair went together to the home of Tom's people. They found the Joad place deserted. While Tom and Casy were wondering what had happened, Muley Graves, a die-hard tenant farmer, came by and disclosed that all of the families in the neighborhood had gone to California or were going. Tom's folks, Muley said, had gone to a relative's place preparatory to going west. Muley was the only sharecropper to stay behind.

All over the southern Midwest states, farmers, no longer able to make a living because of land banks, weather, and machine farming, had sold or were forced out of the farms they had tenanted. Junk dealers and used-car salesmen profiteered on them. Thousands of families took to the roads leading to the promised land, California.

Tom and Casy found the Joads at Uncle John's place, all busy with preparations to leave for California. Assembled for the trip were Pa and Ma Joad; Noah, their mentally backward son; Al, the adolescent younger brother of Tom and Noah; Rose of Sharon, Tom's sister, and her husband, Connie; the Joad children, Ruthie and Winfield; and Granma and Grampa Joad. Al had bought an ancient truck to take them west. The family asked Jim Casy to go with them. The night before they started, they killed the pigs they had left and salted down the meat so that they would have food on the way.

Spurred by handbills which stated that agricultural workers were badly needed in California, the Joads, along with thousands of others, made their torturous way, in a worn-out vehicle, across the plains toward the mountains. Grampa died of a stroke during their first overnight stop. Later there was a long delay when the truck broke down. Small business people along the way treated the migrants as enemies. And, to add to the general misery, returning migrants told the Joads that there was no work to be had in California, that conditions were even worse than they were in Oklahoma. But the dream of a bountiful West Coast urged the Joads onward.

Close to the California line, where the group stopped to bathe in a river, Noah, feeling he was a hindrance to the others, wandered away. It was there that the Joads first heard themselves addressed as *Okies*, another word for tramps.

Granma died during the night trip across the desert. After burying her, the group went into a Hooverville, as the migrants' camps were called. There they learned that work was all but impossible to find. A contractor came to the camp to sign up men to pick fruit in another county. When the Okies asked to see his license, the contractor turned the leaders over to a police deputy who had accompanied him to camp. Tom was involved in the fight which followed. He escaped, and Casy gave himself up in Tom's place. Connie, husband of the pregnant Rose of Sharon, suddenly disappeared from the group. The family was breaking up in the face of its hardships. Ma Joad did everything in her power to keep the group together.

Fearing recrimination after the fight, the Joads left Hooverville and went to a government camp maintained for transient agricultural workers. The camp had sanitary facilities, a local government made up of the transients themselves, and simple organized entertainment. During the Joads' stay at the camp the Okies successfully defeated an attempt of the local citizens to give the camp a bad name and thus to have it closed to the migrants. For the first time since they had arrived in California, the Joads found themselves treated as human beings.

Circumstances eventually forced them to leave the camp, however, for there was no work in the district. They drove to a large farm where work was being offered. There they found agitators attempting to keep the migrants from taking the work because of unfair wages offered. But the Joads, thinking only of food, were escorted by motorcycle police in to the farm. The entire family picked peaches for five cents a box and earned in a day just enough money to buy food for one meal. Tom, remembering the pickets outside the camp, went out at night to investigate. He found Casy, who was the leader of the agitators. While Tom and Casy were talking, deputies, who had been searching for Casy, closed in on them. The pair fled, but were caught. Casy was killed. Tom received a cut on his head, but not before he had felled a deputy with an ax handle. The family concealed Tom in their shack. The rate for a box of peaches dropped, meanwhile, to two-and-a-half cents. Tom's danger and the futility of picking peaches drove the Joads on their way. They hid the injured Tom under the mattresses in the back of the truck and told the suspicious guard at the entrance to the farm that the extra man they had had with them when they came was a hitchhiker who had stayed on to pick.

The family found at last a migrant crowd encamped in abandoned boxcars along a stream. They joined the camp and soon found temporary jobs picking cotton. Tom, meanwhile, hid in a culvert near the camp. Ruthie innocently disclosed Tom's presence to another little girl. Ma, realizing that Tom was no longer safe, sent him away. Tom promised to carry on Casy's work in trying to improve the lot of the downtrodden everywhere.

The autumn rains began. Soon the stream which ran beside the camp overflowed and water entered the boxcars. Under these all but impossible conditions, Rose of Sharon gave birth to a dead baby. When the rising water made their position no longer bearable, the family moved from the camp on foot. The rains had made their old car useless. They came to a barn, which they shared with a boy and his starving father. Rose of Sharon, bereft of her baby, nourished the famished man with the milk from her breasts. So the poor kept each other alive in the depression years.

GREAT EXPECTATIONS

Type of work: Novel
Author: Charles Dickens (1812-1870)
Type of plot: Mystery romance
Time of plot: Nineteenth century
Locale: England
First published: 1860-1861

Principal characters:
Pip, an orphan
Joe Gargery, Pip's brother-in-law
Miss Havisham, an eccentric recluse
Estella, Miss Havisham's ward
Herbert Pocket, Pip's roommate
Mr. Jaggers, a solicitor
Abel Magwitch (Mr. Provis), a convict
Compeyson, a villain

Critique:

Miss Havisham was deserted on her wedding day. Pip gave help to an escaped prisoner hiding in a marsh. From these two events Dickens weaves an amazing story of vindictiveness on one hand and gratitude on the other; and both of these motives affected Pip's life, for Miss Havisham had marked him as one of her victims, and the prisoner had sworn to reward the small boy who had helped him in the marsh. Although an absorbing tale, this is also a gloomy one, not lightened by Dickens' usual capricious characterizations. There are few moments to relieve the reader from the pressure of Pip's problems in life.

The Story:

Little Pip had been left an orphan when he was a small boy, and his sister, much older than he, had grudgingly reared him in her cottage. Pip's brother-in-law, Joe Gargery, on the other hand, was kind and loving to the boy. In the marsh country where he lived with his sister and Joe, Pip wandered alone. One day he was accosted by a wild-looking stranger who demanded that Pip secretly bring him some food, a request which Pip feared to deny. The stranger, an escaped prisoner, asked Pip to bring him a file to cut the iron chain that bound his leg. When Pip returned to the man with a pork pie and file, he saw another mysterious figure in the marsh. After a desperate struggle with the escaped prisoner, the stranger escaped into the fog. The man Pip had aided was later apprehended. He promised Pip he would somehow repay the boy for helping him.

Mrs. Joe sent Pip to the large mansion of the strange Miss Havisham upon that lady's request. Miss Havisham lived in a gloomy, locked house where all clocks had been stopped on the day her bridegroom failed to appear for the wedding ceremony. She often dressed in her bridal robes; a wedding breakfast moldered on the table in an unused room. There Pip went every day to entertain the old lady and a beautiful young girl, named Estella, who delighted in tormenting the shy boy. Miss Havisham enjoyed watching the two children together, and she encouraged Estella in her haughty teasing of Pip.

Living in the grim atmosphere of Joe's blacksmith shop and the uneducated poverty of his sister's home, Pip was eager to learn. One day a London solicitor named Jaggers presented him with the opportunity to go to London and become a gentleman. Both Pip and Joe accepted the proposal. Pip imagined that his kind backer was Miss Havisham herself. Perhaps she wanted to make a gentleman out of him so he would be fit some day to marry Estella.

In London Pip found a small apartment set up for him, and for a living companion he had a young relative of Miss Havisham, Herbert Pocket. When Pip needed money, he was instructed to go to Mr. Jaggers. Although Pip pleaded with the lawyer to disclose the name of his benefactor, Jaggers advised the eager young man not to make inquiries, for when the proper time arrived Pip's benefactor would make himself known.

Soon Pip became one of a small group of London dandies, among them a disagreeable chap named Bentley Drummle. Joe Gargery came to visit Pip, much to Pip's disturbance, for by now he had outgrown his rural background and he was ashamed of Joe's manners. But Herbert Pocket cheerfully helped Pip to entertain the uncomfortable Joe in their apartment. Plainly Joe loved Pip very much, and after he had gone Pip felt ashamed of himself. Joe had brought word that Miss Havisham wanted to see the young man, and Pip returned with his brother-in-law. Miss Havisham and Estella marked the changes in Pip, and when Estella had left Pip alone with the old lady, she told him he must fall in love with the beautiful girl. She also said it was time for Estella to come to London, and she wished Pip to meet her adopted daughter when she arrived. This request made Pip feel more certain he had been sent to London by Miss Havisham to be groomed to marry Estella.

Estella had not been in London long before she had many suitors. Of all the men who courted her, she seemed to favor Bentley Drummle. Pip saw Estella frequently. Although she treated him kindly and with friendship, he knew she did not return his love.

On his twenty-first birthday Pip received a caller, the man whom Pip had helped in the marsh many years before. Ugly and coarse, he told Pip it was he who had been financing Pip ever since he had come to London. At first the boy was horrified to discover he owed so much to this crude ex-criminal, Abel Magwitch. He told Pip that he had been sent to the colonies where he had grown rich. Now he had wanted Pip to enjoy all the privileges he had been denied in life, and he had returned to England to see the boy to whom he had tried to be a second father. He warned Pip that he was in danger should his presence be discovered, for it was death for a prisoner to return to England once he had been sent to a convict colony. Pip detested his plight. Now he realized Miss Havisham had had nothing to do with his great expectations in life, but he was too conscious of his debt to consider abandoning the man whose person he disliked. He determined to do all in his power to please his benefactor. Magwitch was using the name Provis to hide his identity. Provis told Pip furthermore that the man with whom Pip had seen him struggling long ago in the marsh was his enemy, Compeyson, who had vowed to destroy him. Herbert Pocket, who was a distant cousin of Miss Havisham, told Pip that the lover who had betrayed her on the day of her wedding was named Arthur Compeyson.

Pip went to see Miss Havisham to denounce her for having allowed him to believe she was helping him. On his arrival he was informed that Estella was to marry Bentley Drummle. Since Miss Havisham had suffered at the hands of one faithless man, she had reared Estella to inflict as much hurt as possible upon the many men who loved her. Estella reminded Pip that she had warned him not to fall in love with her, for she had no compassion for any human being. Pip returned once more to visit Miss Havisham after Estella had married. An accident started a fire in the old, dust-filled mansion, and although Pip tried to save the old woman she died in the blaze that also badly damaged her gloomy house.

From Provis' story of his association with Compeyson and from other evidence, Pip had learned that Provis was Estella's father; but he did not reveal his discovery to anyone but Jaggers, whose housekeeper, evidently, was Estella's mother. Pip had learned also that Compeyson was in London and plotting to kill Provis. In order to protect the man who had become a foster father to him, Pip with the help of Herbert Pocket arranged to smuggle Provis across the channel to France. There Pip intended to join the old man. Elaborate and secretive as their plans were, Compeyson managed to overtake them as they were putting Provis on the boat. The two enemies fought one last battle in the water, and Provis killed his enemy. He was then taken to jail, where he died before he could be brought to trial.

When Pip fell ill shortly afterward, it was Joe Gargery who came to nurse him. Older and wiser from his many experiences, Pip realized that he need no longer be ashamed of the kind man who had given so much love to him when he was a boy. His sister, Mrs. Joe, had died and Joe had married again, this time very happily. Pip returned to the blacksmith's home to stay awhile, still desolate and unhappy because of his lost Estella. Later Herbert Pocket and Pip set up business together in London.

Eleven years passed before Pip went to see Joe Gargery again. Curiosity led Pip to the site of Miss Havisham's former mansion. There he found Estella, now a widow, wandering over the grounds. During the years she had lost her cool aloofness and had softened a great deal. She told Pip she had thought of him often. Pip was able to foresee that perhaps he and Estella would never have to part again. The childhood friends walked hand in hand from the place which had once played such an enormous part in both their lives.

THE GREAT GATSBY

Type of work: Novel
Author: F. Scott Fitzgerald (1896-1940)
Type of plot: Social criticism
Time of plot: 1922
Locale: New York City and Long Island
First published: 1925

Principal characters:
NICK CARRAWAY, a young bond salesman
DAISY BUCHANAN, his cousin
TOM BUCHANAN, her husband
MYRTLE WILSON, Tom's mistress
JAY GATSBY, a racketeer of the Twenties

Critique:

The short life of F. Scott Fitzgerald was long enough for that brilliant young man to show what the United States meant in terms of the reckless Twenties. Prohibition and speak-easies, new automobiles, victory abroad, popular fads, new wealth—he understood and wrote about all these things. Despite its limitations of style and its imperfections in character development, *The Great Gatsby* belongs to that literature which endeavors honestly to present the American scene during those riotous years from the first World War to the depression. If F. Scott Fitzgerald's view of character was limited, it may be because his over-all comprehension of society was so positive. His acute sensibility was devoted to an understanding of the results of human action, rather than an understanding of the reasons for human action.

The Story:

Young Nick Carraway decided to forsake the hardware business of his family in the Middle West in order to sell bonds in New York City. He took a small house in West Egg on Long Island and there became involved in the lives of his neighbors. At a dinner party at the home of Tom Buchanan he renewed his acquaintance with Tom and Tom's wife, Daisy, a distant cousin, and he met an attractive young woman, Jordan Baker. Almost at once he learned that Tom and Daisy were not happily married. It appeared that Daisy knew her husband was deliberately unfaithful.

Nick soon learned to despise the drive to the city through unkempt slums; particularly, he hated the ash heaps and the huge commercial signs. He was far more interested in the activities of his wealthy neighbors. Near his house lived Jay Gatsby, a mysterious man of great wealth. Gatsby entertained lavishly, but his past was unknown to his neighbors.

One day Tom Buchanan took Nick to call on his mistress, a dowdy, overplump, married woman named Myrtle Wilson, whose husband, George Wilson, operated a second-rate auto repair shop. Myrtle, Tom, and Nick went to the apartment Tom kept, and there the three were joined by Myrtle's sister Catherine and Mr. and Mrs. McKee. The party settled down to an afternoon of drinking, Nick unsuccessfully doing his best to get away.

A few days later Nick attended another party, one given by Gatsby for a large number of people famous in speak-easy society. Food and liquor were dispensed lavishly. Most of the guests had never seen their host before.

At the party Nick met Gatsby for the first time. Gatsby, in his early thirties, looked like a healthy young roughneck.

He was offhand, casual, eager to entertain his guests as extravagantly as possible. Frequently he was called away by long-distance telephone calls. Some of the guests laughed and said that he was trying to impress them with his importance.

That summer Gatsby gave many parties. Nick went to all of them, enjoying each time the society of people from all walks of life who appeared to take advantage of Gatsby's bounty. From time to time Nick met Jordan Baker there, but he began to lose interest in her after he heard that she had cheated in an amateur golf match.

Gatsby took Nick to lunch one day and introduced him to a man named Wolfshiem, who seemed to be Gatsby's business partner. Wolfshiem hinted at some dubious business deals that betrayed Gatsby's racketeering activities and Nick began to identify the sources of some of Gatsby's wealth.

Jordan Baker told Nick the strange story of Daisy's wedding. Before the bridal dinner Daisy, who seldom drank, became wildly intoxicated and announced there would be no wedding, that she had changed her mind and intended to go back to an old flame, Jay Gatsby. Her friends and family, however, had argued with her until she finally married Tom Buchanan. At the time Gatsby was poor and unknown; Tom was rich and influential.

But Gatsby was still in love with Daisy, and he wanted Jordan and Nick to bring Daisy and him together again. It was arranged that Nick should invite Daisy to tea the same day he invited Gatsby. Gatsby awaited the invitation nervously.

On the eventful day it rained. Determined that Nick's house should be presentable, Gatsby sent a man to mow the wet grass; he also sent over flowers for decoration. The tea was a strained affair at first, both Gatsby and Daisy shy and awkward in their reunion. Afterward they went over to Gatsby's mansion, where he showed them his furniture, clothes, swimming pool, and gardens. Daisy promised to attend his next party.

When Daisy disapproved of his guests, Gatsby stopped entertaining. The house was shut up and the bar-crowd turned away.

Gatsby informed Nick of his origin. His true name was Gatz, and he had been born in the Middle West. His parents were poor. But when he was a boy he had become the protégé of a wealthy old gold miner and had accompanied him on his travels until the old man died. Then he changed his name to Gatsby and began to dream of acquiring wealth and position. In the war he had distinguished himself. After the war he had returned penniless to the States, too poor to marry Daisy, whom he had met during the war. Later he became a partner in a drug business. He had been lucky and had accumulated money rapidly. He told Nick that he had acquired the money for his Long Island residence after three years of hard work.

Gatsby gave a quiet party for Jordan, the Buchanans, and Nick. The group drove into the city and took a room in a hotel. The day was hot and the guests uncomfortable. On the way, Tom, driving Gatsby's new yellow car, stopped at Wilson's garage. Wilson complained because Tom had not helped him in a projected car deal. He said he needed money because he was selling out and taking his wife, whom he knew to be unfaithful, away from the city.

At the hotel Tom accused Gatsby of trying to steal his wife and also of being dishonest. He seemed to regard Gatsby's low origin with more disfavor than his interest in Daisy. During the argument, Daisy sided with both men by turns.

On the ride back to the suburbs Gatsby drove his own car, accompanied by Daisy, who temporarily would not speak to her husband.

Following them, Nick and Jordan and Tom stopped to investigate an accident in front of Wilson's garage. They discovered an ambulance picking up the dead body of Myrtle Wilson, struck by a hit-and-run driver in a yellow car. They tried in vain to help Wilson and then went on to Tom's house, convinced that Gatsby had struck Myrtle Wilson.

Nick learned the next day from Gatsby that Daisy had been driving when the woman was hit. However, Gatsby was willing to take the blame if the death should be traced to his car. Gatsby explained that Myrtle, thinking that Tom was in the yellow car, had run out of the house, and Daisy, an inexpert driver, had run her down and then collapsed. Gatsby had driven on.

In the meantime George Wilson, having traced the yellow car to Gatsby, appeared on the Gatsby estate. A few hours later both he and Gatsby were discovered dead. He had shot Gatsby and then killed himself.

Nick tried to make Gatsby's funeral respectable, but no one attended except Gatsby's father, who thought his son had been a great man. None of Gatsby's racketeering associates appeared. His bar-friends had also deserted him.

Shortly afterward Nick learned of Tom's part in Gatsby's death. Tom had visited Wilson and had let Wilson believe that Gatsby had been Myrtle's lover. Nick vowed that his friendship with Tom and Daisy was at an end. He decided to return to his people in the Middle West.

THE GREEN BAY TREE

Type of work: Novel
Author: Louis Bromfield (1896-)
Type of plot: Social chronicle
Time of plot: Early twentieth century
Locale: Middle West
First published: 1924

Principal characters:
JULIA SHANE, a wealthy widow
LILY, and
IRENE SHANE, her daughters
THE GOVERNOR, father of Lily's child
HATTIE TOLLIVER, Julia Shane's niece
ELLEN TOLLIVER, Hattie's daughter
MONSIEUR CYON, Lily's husband

Critique:

This novel has a double theme. The first is that the children of the United States have a problem which their parents did not face, the problem of being pioneers with no frontier left in which to exercise their energy and their talents. The second theme is that all of us have secrets of the soul which cannot be violated. Through the book also runs a deprecation of material progress and the materialistic philosophy of America in the early twentieth century. Bromfield, however, is not carried away by the naturalism or sharp social criticism of his contemporaries in dealing with this aspect of American life.

The Story:

Julia Shane was a wealthy old woman, living with her two daughters in a mansion which had decayed greatly since the mills of the town had encroached upon her grounds. Although the house was now surrounded on three sides by railroad yards and steel mills, Julia Shane refused to move away. Mrs. Shane was worried about her girls. Irene, the younger, was, in her mother's opinion, too pious to live. Lily, who was twenty-four years old, had been in love with the governor, a man twenty years older than she. The real complication was that Lily was going to have a baby and refused to marry the governor despite the urgings of both the man and her mother.

The Shanes were wealthy; it was easy for Lily to leave the town for a trip abroad. Her departure caused no talk or scandal, although Mrs. Harrison, whose son Lily had also refused, was suspicious.

During the four years Lily was in Europe, life was dull in the gloomy old mansion. Irene taught English to the workers in the mills and tried to convince her mother that she wanted to become a nun. Old Julia Shane, the last of a long line of Scottish Presbyterians, would hear none of such nonsense.

Then, unexpectedly, Lily came home. Once again there were parties and dances in the old house. Lily was much impressed by her cousin, Ellen Tolliver, a talented pianist, and offered to help the girl if she would go to Paris. The day after Christmas, Irene and Lily were taken on a tour of the steel mills by Willie Harrison, the mill owner, who once again asked Lily to marry him. She refused, disgusted with the spineless businessman who was ruled by his mother. When news came from Paris that her small son had the measles, Lily was glad to leave the town again. Shortly afterward Ellen Tolliver also escaped from the town by marrying a salesman from New York.

Several years later there was a strike in the steel mills. Only Hattie Tolliver, Julia Shane's niece and Ellen's mother, braved the pickets to enter the mansion. Without her help life at the house would have been extremely difficult. Although Julia Shane was dying and confined to her bed, the merchants of the town refused to risk deliveries to a house so near to the mills where shots were occasionally fired and where mobs of hungry strikers loitered. On one of her errands of mercy Hattie Tolliver learned that her daughter, now a widow, was in Paris studying music.

When she heard that her mother was dying, Lily returned from Europe. She and Hattie Tolliver stayed with Julia Shane until she died a few weeks later. Irene was no help. Hattie Tolliver shrewdly summed up Irene for Lily by noting that the younger girl was selfish in her unselfishness to the poor workers and filled with pride in her lack of ordinary worldly pride.

After her death, Julia Shane's daughters remained in the mansion until the estate was settled. Lily was bored, but excitement came to her through the strikers. Her sister had given them permission to hold meetings in the large park surrounding the house. Lily watched the meetings from a darkened window. She recognized Krylenko, a huge Russian who had been Irene's pupil and who was now a close friend. While Krylenko was speaking, he was shot by a gun fired from one of the mill sheds. Krylenko entered the mansion with a key Irene had given him. Lily bound up his wound. When she almost fainted, Krylenko placed her on the sofa. As he did so, Irene entered and saw them. She berated them both with all the suspicions which her sterile mind evoked. Both she and Lily refused to speak the next day. Lily returned to Paris.

In Paris Lily confined herself to the friends of her chaperon, Mme. Gigon. It was a quiet life, but Lily was happy with her house, her growing son, and her lover, the officer son of an old aristocratic family. Ellen Tolliver, who had taken the professional name of Lily Barr, was now a famous concert pianist on the continent and in England, and lived part of the time with Lily.

In 1913 Lily's lover told her that war with Germany was inevitable. The news increased Lily's moods of depression which had begun to come upon her as she approached middle age. The news that the town wished to buy the old Shane mansion and use the grounds for a railroad station further aroused her antagonism. She did not need the money and also felt that the attempt to buy the place was an intrusion into her private life. Later Lily's lawyer wrote that the Shane mansion had burned down.

One day Lily unexpectedly met Willie Harrison in Paris. He had left the mills and sold most of his holdings. He brought word that Irene had become a Carmelite nun and was in France in a convent at Lisieux.

When France entered the First World War, Lily's lover and her son were sent to the front. Only the son was to return, and he was to come back a cripple. When the Germans invaded France, Lily was at her country house with Mme. Gigon, who was dying. During the night the soldiers were there Lily discovered they were going to blow up the bridge in the vicinity. Armed with a pistol she had stolen from a German officer, she killed several men and an officer and saved the bridge, not for France particularly, but with the hope that it might be of some help to her lover and her son, for she knew that their regiment was in the area.

During the years of the war she became closely acquainted with M. Cyon, a French diplomat whom she married shortly after the Armistice. During the peace meetings at Versailles she saw the governor whom she had refused to marry years before. She was glad she had not married him, for he had become a florid, portly, vulgar politician. She preferred her dignified French diplomat for a husband, despite his white hair and greater number of years.

Shortly after her meeting with the governor, Lily received a letter from the Carmelites telling her that Sister Monica had died. For a few moments Lily did not realize that the person of whom they had written was Irene. Lily had come to think of her sister as dead when she had entered the Church; it was something of a shock to receive word of a more recent death.

Lily's last link with America and the town was broken when she read in a Socialist newspaper that Krylenko, who had become an international labor leader, had died of typhus in Moscow. Now her family and old friends were all gone. Only Lily survived. It was with pleasure that she saw her white-haired husband enter the garden and walk toward her. There, at least, was peace and security, instead of a lonely old age in a drab Midwestern town.

GREEN MANSIONS

Type of work: Novel
Author: W. H. Hudson (1841-1922)
Type of plot: Fantasy
Time of plot: Nineteenth century
Locale: South American jungles
First published: 1904

Principal characters:
MR. ABEL, an old man
RIMA, a creature of the forest
NUFLO, an old hunter

Critique:

The only legend of its kind that has become a modern classic, *Green Mansions* owes its popularity to its mystic, religious feeling and to the beauty of Rima's halting, poetic expressions. Loving nature and the wild life of the countries which he explored, Hudson was able to express his own deep feeling through the character of Rima, the strange birdlike girl who was one with the forest and whose sorrow of loneliness was so great that she would suffer no one to look into the depth of her soul. Perhaps, to Hudson, nature was like that; too lonely and sorrowful to impart complete understanding and knowledge of herself to mankind.

The Story:

No one in Georgetown could remember his full name, and so he was known only as Mr. Abel. He told a strange story one evening as he sat talking to a friend, a tale of his youth.

While he was living among the Indians in the jungle, a nearby savannah caught his fancy. The Indians claimed it was haunted and would not go near it. One day he set out to explore the savannah for himself. For a long while he sat on a log trying to identify the calls of the birds. One particularly engaging sound seemed almost human, and it followed him as he returned to the Indian village. Soon he bribed one of the Indians to enter the haunted savannah. The Indian became frightened, however, and ran away, leaving Abel alone with the weird sound. The Indian had said that the daughter of the spirit Didi inhabited the forest. Abel felt sure that the nearly intelligible language of the birdlike sounds were associated with the one to whom the Indian referred.

Again and again Abel returned to the forest in his search for the source of the warbling sound, but always it eluded him. Then one day he saw a girl playing with a bird. The girl disappeared among the trees, but not before Abel had decided that she must be connected in some way with the warbling sounds he had heard.

The Indians had been encouraging him to continue his quests into the area of mystery. He decided at last that they were hoping he would try to kill the creature who seemed to be haunting their forest. He was stricken with horror at the idea. One day he came face to face with the elusive being. He had been menaced by a small venomous snake, and he was about to kill it with a rock when the girl appeared before him to protest vigorously in her odd birdlike warbling language. She was not like any human he had ever seen. Her coloring was her most striking characteristic; it was luminescent and it changed with her every mood. As he stood looking at her, fascinated by her loveliness, the snake bit him on the leg.

He started back toward the village for help, but a blinding rainstorm overtook him on the way. After falling unconscious while running through the trees, he awakened in a hut with a bearded old man named Nuflo. The man expressed fear and hatred of the Indians who, he said, were afraid of his grandchild, Rima. It was she who had saved Abel from dying of the snake's venom and it was she who had been following him in the forest. Abel could not believe that the listless, colorless girl standing in a corner of the hut was the lovely birdlike creature he had met. On closer examination he could detect a likeness of figure and features, but her luminous radiance was missing. When Rima addressed him in Spanish, he questioned her about the musical language that she emitted in the trees. She gave no explanation and ran away.

In a few days Abel learned that Rima would harm no living creature, not even for her own food. Abel grew to love the strange, beautiful, untamed girl of the green forest. When he questioned her, she spoke willingly, but her speech was strangely poetic and difficult to understand. She expressed deep, spiritual longings and made him understand that in the forest she communed with her mother, who had died long ago.

Rima began to sense that since Abel, the only person she had known except her grandfather, could not understand her language and did not understand her longings, she must be unlike other human beings in the world. In her desire to meet other people and to return to the place of her birth where her mother had died, Rima revealed to Abel the name of her birthplace, a mountain he knew well. Rima demanded that her grandfather guide her to Riolama Mountain. Old Nuflo consented and requested that Abel come also.

Before he took the long journey with Rima and Nuflo, Abel returned to the Indian village. There, greeted with quiet suspicion and awe because of where he had been, Abel was held a prisoner. After six days' absence he returned to Rima's forest. Nuflo and Abel made preparations for their journey. When they started, Rima followed them, only showing herself when they needed directions.

Nuflo began Rima's story. He had been wandering about with a band of outlaws when a heavenly-looking woman appeared among them. After she had fallen and broken her ankle, Nuflo, who thought she must be a saint, nursed her back to health. Observing that she was to have a baby, he took her to a native village. Rima was born soon after. The woman could learn neither Spanish nor the Indian tongue, and the soft melodious sounds which fell from her lips were unintelligible to everyone. Gradually the woman faded. As she lay dying, she made the rough hunter understand that Rima could not live unless she were taken to the dry, cool mountains.

Knowing their search for her mother's people to be in vain, Abel sought to dissuade Rima from the journey. He explained to her that they must have disappeared or have been wiped out by Indians. Rima believed him, but at the thought of her own continued loneliness she fell fainting at his feet. When she had recovered, she spoke of being alone, of never finding anyone who could understand the sweet warbling language which she had learned from her mother. Abel promised to stay with her always in the forest. Rima insisted on making the journey back alone so that she could prepare herself for Abel's return.

The return to the savannah was not easy for Abel and the old man. They were nearly starving when they came to their own forest and saw, to their horror, that the hut was gone. Rima could not be found. As Abel ran through the forest searching for her, he came upon a lurking Indian. Then he realized that she must be gone, for the Indian would not have dared to enter the savannah if the daughter of Didi were still there. He went back to the Indian village for food and learned from them that Rima had returned to her forest. Finding her in a tree, the Indian chief, Runi, had ordered his men to burn the tree in order to destroy the daughter of Didi.

Half mad with sorrow, Abel fled to the village of an enemy tribe. There he made a pact with the savages for the slaughter of the tribe of Runi. He then went to the forest, where he found Nuflo dead. He also found Rima's bones lying among the ashes of the fire-consumed tree. He placed her remains in an urn which he carried with him back to civilization.

Living in Georgetown, Abel at last understood Rima's sorrowful loneliness. Having known and lost her, he was suffering the same longings she had felt when she was searching for her people.

GRETTIR THE STRONG

Type of work: Saga
Author: Unknown
Type of plot: Adventure romance
Time of plot: Eleventh century
Locale: Iceland, Norway, Constantinople
First transcribed: Thirteenth-century manuscript

Principal characters:
GRETTIR THE STRONG, an outlaw
ASMUND LONGHAIR, his father

ILLUGI, his youngest brother
THORBJORN OXMAIN, Grettir's enemy
THORBJORN SLOWCOACH, Oxmain's kinsman, killed by Grettir
THORIR OF GARD, an Icelandic chief
THORBJORN ANGLE, Grettir's slayer
THORSTEINN DROMUND, Grettir's half-brother and avenger

Critique:

One of the most famous of all Norse sagas is the story of Grettir, hero and outlaw of medieval Iceland. Grettir, born about 997, was descended from Vikings who colonized Iceland in the second half of the ninth century, after they had refused to acknowledge Harold Fairhair as their king. Grettir emerges from his mist-shrouded, lawless world as a man so memorable that his story was handed down by word of mouth for more than two hundred years after his death. By the time his story was finally committed to writing, it had absorbed adventures of other folk heroes as well; but in the main the saga is true to the political and social history of the age.

The Story:

Grettir the Strong was descended from Onund, a Viking famed for enemies killed in war and the taking of booty from towns plundered on far sea raids. In a battle at Hafrsfjord Onund lost a leg and was thereafter known as Onund Treefoot. His wife was Aesa, daughter of Ofeig. Thrand, a great hero, was his companion in arms. During a time of great trouble in Norway the two heroes sailed to Iceland to be free of injustice in their homeland, where the unscrupulous could rob without fear of redress. Onund lived in quiet and plenty in the new land and his name became renowned, for he was valiant. At last he died. His sons fought after his death and his lands were divided.

Grettir of the line of Onund was born at Biarg. As a child he showed strange intelligence. He quarreled constantly with Asmund Longhair, his father, and he was very lazy, never doing anything cheerfully or without urging. When he was fourteen years old, grown big in body, he killed Skeggi in a quarrel over a provision bag fallen from his horse, and for that deed his father paid blood money to the kinsmen of Skeggi. Then the Lawman declared that he must leave Iceland for three years. In that way the long outlawry of Grettir began.

Grettir set sail for Norway. The ship was wrecked on rocks off the Norwegian coast, but all got safely ashore on land that belonged to Thorfinn, a wealthy landman of the district. With him Grettir made his home for a time. At Yuletide, Thorfinn with most of his household went to a merrymaking and left Grettir to look after the farm. In Thorfinn's absence a party of berserks, or raiders, led by Thorir and Ogmund, came to rob and lay waste to the district. Grettir tricked them by locking them in a storehouse. When they broke through the wooden walls, Grettir, armed with sword and spear, killed Thorir and Ogmund and put the rest to flight. Some time before this adventure he had entered the tomb of Karr-the-Old, father of Thorfinn, a long-dead chieftain who guarded a hidden treasure. For his brave deed in killing the berserks Thorfinn gave him an ancient sword from the treasure hoard of Karr-the-Old.

Next Grettir killed a great bear which had been carrying off the sheep. In doing so he incurred the wrath of Bjorn, who was jealous of Grettir's strength and bravery. Then Grettir killed Bjorn and was summoned before Jarl Sveinn. Friends of Bjorn plotted to take Grettir's life. After he killed two of his enemies, his friends saved him from the wrath of the jarl, who had wished to banish him. His term of outlawry being ended, Grettir sailed back to Iceland in the spring.

At that time in Iceland young Thorgils Maksson, Asmund's kinsman, was slain in a quarrel over a whale, and Asmund took up the feud against those who had killed him. The murderers were banished.

When Grettir returned, Asmund gave him the welcome that was his due because of his fame as a brave hero. Shortly after his return, Grettir fought with some men after a horse fight. The struggle was halted by a man named Thorbjorn Oxmain. The feud might have been forgotten if Thorbjorn Oxmain's kinsman, Thorbjorn Slowcoach, had not sneered at the hero.

Word came that a fiend had taken possession of the corpse of Glam, a shepherd. At night Glam ravaged the countryside. Because he could find no man with whom he could prove his strength, Grettir went to meet Glam. They struggled in the house of Thorhall and ripped down beams and rafters in their angry might. At last Glam fell exhausted. Defeated, he predicted that Grettir would have no greater strength and less honor in arms from that day on, and that he would grow afraid of the dark. Grettir cut off Glam's head and burned the body to destroy the evil spirit that possessed the dead shepherd.

Grettir decided to return to Norway. Among the passengers on the boat was Thorbjorn Slowcoach; they fought and Grettir killed his foe. The travelers landed on a barren shore where they were without fire to warm themselves and Grettir swam across the cove to get burning brands at an inn where the sons of Thorir of Gard, an Icelandic chieftain, were holding a drunken feast. He had to fight to get the fire he wanted, and in the struggle hot coals set fire to the straw on the inn floor and the house burned. Charged with deliberately setting fire to the inn and burning those within, Grettir went to lay the matter before the king. To prove his innocence of the charge of willful burning, he was sentenced to undergo trial by fire in the church, but the ordeal ended when Grettir became angry and threw a bystander into the air. The king then banished him from Norway, but because no ships could sail to Iceland before the spring Grettir was allowed to remain in the country that winter. He lived some time with a man named Einar, on a lonely farm to which came the berserk Snaekoll, a wild man who pretended great frenzy during his lawless raids. Grettir seized him in his mad fit and killed the robber with his own sword. Grettir fell in love with Einar's beautiful daughter but he knew that Einar would never give his child to a man of Grettir's reputation. Giving up his suit, he went to stay with his half-brother, Thorsteinn Dromund. Because they were men of the same blood, Thorsteinn swore to avenge Grettir if ever he were killed.

Grettir's father, Asmund, died. On his deathbed he said that little good would come of his son. Grettir's time of bad luck in Iceland began. Thorbjorn Oxmain killed Atli, Grettir's brother, in revenge for the slaying of Thorbjorn Slowcoach, and Thorir of Gard, hearing that his sons had been killed in the burning of the inn, charged Grettir with their murder before the court of the Althing. By the time Grettir returned, he had been proclaimed an outlaw throughout Iceland. He had little worry over his outlawry from the inn-burning. Determined to avenge his brother, he went alone to Thorbjorn Oxmain's farm and killed both the man and his son. Grettir's mother was delighted with his deed, but she predicted that Grettir would not live freely to enjoy his victory. Thorir of Gard and Thorodd, Thorbjorn Oxmain's kinsman, each put a price of three silver marks upon his head. Soon afterward Grettir was captured by some farmers but he was released by a wise woman named Thorbjorg.

Avoided by most of his former friends, who would no longer help him, Grettir went far north to find a place to live.

He met in the forest another outlaw named Grim, but a short time later he was forced to kill his companion because Grim intended to kill him for the reward offered for Grettir's head. About that time there was growing upon Grettir a fear of the dark, as Glam had prophesied. Thorir of Gard hired Redbeard, another outlaw, to kill Grettir, but Grettir discovered the outlaw's plans and killed him also. At last Grettir realized that he could not take any forest men into his trust, and yet he was afraid to live alone because of his fear of the dark.

Thorir of Gard attacked Grettir with eighty men, but the outlaw was able to hold them off for a time. Unknown to him, a friend named Hallmund attacked Thorir's men from the rear, and the attempt to capture Grettir failed. But Grettir could no longer stay long in any place, for all men had turned against him. Hallmund was treacherously slain for the aid he had given Grettir; as he died he hoped that the outlaw would avenge his death.

One night a troll-woman attacked a traveler named Gest in the room where he lay sleeping. They struggled all night, but at last Gest was able to cut off the monster's right arm. Then Gest revealed himself as Grettir.

Steinvor of Sandhauger gave birth to a boy whom many called Grettir's son, but he died when he was seventeen and left no saga about himself.

Thorodd then tried to gain favor by killing Grettir, but the outlaw soon overcame him and refused to kill his enemy. Grettir went north once more, but his fear of the dark was growing upon him so that he could no longer live alone even to save his life. At last, with his youngest brother, Illugi, and a servant, he settled on Drangey, an island which had no inlet so that men had to climb to its grassy summit by rope ladders. There Grettir, who had been an outlaw for some sixteen years, was safe for a time, because none could climb the steep cliffs to attack him. For several years he and his companions lived on the sheep which had been put there to graze and on eggs and birds. His enemies tried in vain to lure him from the island. At last an old woman cut magic runes upon a piece of driftwood which floated to the island. When Grettir attempted to chop the log, his ax slipped, gashing his leg. He felt that his end was near, for the wound became swollen and painful.

Thorbjorn Angle, who had paid the old woman to cast a spell upon the firewood, led an attack upon the island while Grettir lay near death. Grettir was already dying when he struck his last blows at his enemies. Illugi and the servant died with him. After Thorbjorn had cut off Grettir's head as proof of the outlaw's death, Steinn the Lawman decreed that the murderer had cut off the head of a man already dead and that he could not collect the reward because he had used witchcraft to overcome Grettir. Outlawed for his deed, Thorbjorn went to Constantinople, where he enlisted in the emperor's guard. There Thorsteinn Dromund followed him and cut off the murderer's head with a sword which Grettir had taken, years before, from the treasure hoard of Karr-the-Old.

GROWTH OF THE SOIL

Type of work: Novel
Author: Knut Hamsun (Knut Pedersen Hamsund, 1859-)
Type of plot: Social chronicle
Time of plot: Late nineteenth century
Locale: Norway
First published: 1917

Principal characters:

ISAK, a Norwegian peasant
INGER, his wife
ELESEUS,
SIVERT,
LEOPOLDINE, and
REBECCA, their children
OLINE, Inger's relative
GEISSLER, Isak's friend
AXEL STRÖM, a neighbor
BARBRO, Axel's wife

Critique:

One of the great modern novels, *Growth of the Soil* won for its author the Nobel prize for literature in 1921. It is the story of the development of a homestead in the wilds of Norway. The simplicity and power of the style are reminiscent of the Bible. Reading the book is like crumbling the earth between one's fingers; it brings nature to life on the printed page. The reader will not soon forget Isak, the silent pioneer to whom the soil is life.

The Story:

Isak left a small Norwegian village and set out into the wilds to claim a homestead. Carrying some food and a few rude implements, he wandered until he found a stretch of grass and woodland, with a stream nearby. There he cleared his farmsite. He had to carry everything out from the village on his own back. He built a sod house, procured some goats, and prepared for winter.

He sent word by some traveling Lapps that he needed a woman to help in the fields. One day Inger appeared with her belongings. She was not beautiful because of her harelip. But she was a good worker, and she shared Isak's bed. She brought more things from her home, including a cow.

That winter Inger bore her first child, Eleseus. He was a fine boy, with no harelip. In the spring Inger's relative Oline came to see the new family. She promised to return in the fall to take care of the farm while Inger and Isak went to be married and to have the child baptized. The farm grew through the summer.

The harvest was not good, but potatoes carried Isak's family through the winter without hunger. Inger bore a second son, Sivert. Then Geissler, the sheriff's officer, came to tell Isak that he would have to pay the government for his land. He promised to make the terms as easy as possible for Isak. But Geissler lost his position. A new officer came to look at the land with his assistant, Brede Olsen. He also promised to do what he could for Isak.

One day Inger sent her husband to town. While he was gone, she bore her third child, a girl with a harelip. Knowing what the deformed child would suffer, Inger strangled the infant and buried the body in the woods. Later she convinced Isak she had not really been pregnant.

But Oline had known of Inger's condition, and when she came again she found the grave in the woods. Inger explained her deed as well as she could to Isak; he was satisfied. Then Lapp beggars told the story of the hidden grave and the sheriff's officer heard of it. There was an investigation. After her trial, Inger was sent away to prison at Bergen for eight years. For lack of anyone else, Isak was forced to hire Oline to come and help with the farm and the children.

Isak got the deed for his land and paid

GROWTH OF THE SOIL by Knut Hamsun. Translated by W. W. Worster. By permission of the publishers, Alfred A. Knopf, Inc.

the first installment. But there was no joy in his farming, now that Inger was gone. He worked only from habit and necessity. Geissler reappeared to tell Isak that he had seen Inger in Bergen. She had borne a girl in prison, a child without a blemish.

The old life was changing. Men came through putting up a telegraph line. Between Isak's place and the village, Brede, the helper of the sheriff's officer, started a farm. Other settlers appeared as the years passed. Oline was unbearable. She stole livestock from Isak and spent his money for trifles. Speculating on copper mining, Geissler bought some of Isak's land. With the help of Geissler, Inger was finally released from prison.

At first Inger, whose harelip had been operated on in Bergen, was happy to return with little Leopoldine. But she had learned city ways, and now farm life seemed rough and lonely. She no longer helped Isak with his work. Eleseus was sent to town, where he got a job in an office. Sivert, who was much like his father, remained at home.

Axel Ström now had a farm near Isak's. Brede's daughter, Barbro, came to stay with Axel and help him with his work.

Inger bore another daughter, Rebecca, and Isak hired a girl to help with the housework. Eleseus returned from town to help on the farm. Geissler sold the copper mine property and Isak also received a large sum for the rights he had retained on the property. He was able to buy the first mowing machine in the district.

Eleseus took an interest in Barbro, but when he discovered she was pregnant, he went back to the city. Axel bought Brede's farm when Brede moved back to town. One day he found Barbro down by the brook with her drowned baby. She said she had fallen and the baby had been born in the water. Axel did not quarrel with her, for fear she would leave him.

That winter Barbro went to Bergen and Axel had to manage the farm himself. One day he was pinned to the ground by a falling tree during a snowstorm. Brede, who was angry with Axel, passed by without offering to help. By chance, Oline heard Axel's cries for help and released him. Afterward she stayed to manage his house for him, and never did she let him forget his debt to her for saving his life. Little by little, she learned the story of Barbro and the baby.

A man named Aronsen built a big store in the new neighborhood. Soon miners moved in to begin work on the land Geissler and Isak had sold. Then the mine played out. Geissler owned the additional land needed to keep the mine working, but he asked more than the mine owners would pay. The mine remained idle.

The trouble about Barbro and the baby at last came to the attention of the authorities, and Axel and Barbro had to appear for trial in the town. Because there was so little evidence, Axel went free. Barbro went to work for the wife of the sheriff's officer, who promised to see that Barbro behaved herself.

There seemed little hope that the mine would reopen, for Geissler would not sell his land. After Aronsen sold his store to Isak, Eleseus was persuaded to return from the city and take over the store property. Isak was now a rich man. Then in the spring Geissler sold his land and work resumed at the mine. But the miners lived on the far side of the property in another district. The village was no better off than before.

Barbro could no longer stand the watchfulness of the wife of the sheriff's officer. When she returned to Axel, he took her in again after he was sure she meant to stay and marry him. Old Oline would not leave Axel's farm. But she soon grew ill and died, leaving the young people by themselves.

Eleseus did not manage the store well. At last, when he saw the failure he had made, he borrowed more money from his father and set out for America. He never returned. Sivert and two other men carried some of the goods from the store to the new mine. But the mine had shut down again. They found Geissler wandering about the deserted mine; he said that he was thinking of buying back the property.

When the three men returned, Isak was sowing corn. The copper mine and the store, good times and bad, had come and gone. But the soil was still there. For Isak and Inger, the first sowers in the wilds, the corn still grew.

GULLIVER'S TRAVELS

Type of work: Simulated record of travel
Author: Jonathan Swift (1667-1745)
Type of plot: Social satire
Time of plot: 1699-1713
Locale: England and various fictional lands
First published: 1726-1727

Principal character:
LEMUEL GULLIVER, surgeon, sea captain, and traveler

Critique:

It has been said that Dean Swift hated Man, but loved individual men. His hatred is brought out in this caustic political and social satire aimed at the English people, representing mankind in general, and at the Whigs in particular. By means of a disarming simplicity of style and of careful attention to detail in order to heighten the effect of the narrative, Swift produced one of the outstanding pieces of satire in world literature. Swift himself attempted to conceal his authorship of the book under its original title—*Travels into Several Remote Nations of the World, by Lemuel Gulliver*.

The Story:

Lemuel Gulliver, a physician, took the post of ship's doctor on the *Antelope,* which set sail from Bristol for the South Seas in May, 1699. When the ship was wrecked in a storm somewhere near Tasmania, Gulliver had to swim for his life. Wind and tide helped to carry him close to a low-lying shore where he fell, exhausted, into a deep sleep. Upon awaking, he found himself held to the ground by hundreds of small ropes. He soon discovered that he was the prisoner of humans six inches tall. Still tied, Gulliver was fed by his captors; then he was placed on a special wagon built for the purpose and drawn by fifteen hundred small horses. Carried in this manner to the capital city of the small humans, he was exhibited as a great curiosity to the people of Lilliput, as the land of the diminutive people was called. He was kept chained to a huge Lilliputian building into which he crawled at night to sleep.

Gulliver soon learned the Lilliputian language, and through his personal charm and natural curiosity he came into good graces at the royal court. At length he was given his freedom, contingent upon his obeying many rules devised by the emperor prescribing his deportment in Lilliput. Now free, Gulliver toured Mildendo, the capital city, and found it to be similar to European cities of the time.

Learning that Lilliput was in danger of an invasion by the forces of the neighboring empire, Blefuscu, he offered his services to the emperor of Lilliput. While the enemy fleet awaited favorable winds to carry their ships the eight hundred yards between Blefuscu and Lilliput, Gulliver took some Lilliputian cable, waded to Blefuscu, and brought back the entire fleet by means of hooks attached to the cables. He was greeted with great acclaim and the emperor made him a nobleman. Soon, however, the emperor and Gulliver fell out over differences concerning the fate of the now helpless Blefuscu. The emperor wanted to reduce the enemy to the status of slaves; Gulliver championed their liberty. The pro-Gulliver forces prevailed in the Lilliputian parliament; the peace settlement was favorable to Blefuscu. But Gulliver was now in disfavor at court.

He visited Blefuscu, where he was received graciously by the emperor and the people. One day, while exploring the empire, he found a ship's boat washed ashore from some wreck. With the help of thousands of Blefuscu artisans, he repaired the boat for his projected voyage back to his own civilization. Taking some little cattle and sheep with him, he sailed away and was eventually picked up by an English vessel.

Back in England, Gulliver spent a short time with his family before he shipped aboard the *Adventure,* bound for India. The ship was blown off course by fierce winds. Somewhere on the coast of Great Tartary a landing party went ashore to forage for supplies. Gulliver, who had wandered away from the party, was left behind when a gigantic human figure pursued the sailors back to the ship. Gulliver was caught in a field by giants threshing grain that grew forty feet high. Becoming the pet of a farmer and his family, he amused them with his human-like behavior. The farmer's nine-year-old daughter, who was not yet over forty feet high, took special charge of Gulliver.

The farmer displayed Gulliver first at a local market town. Then he took his little pet to the metropolis, where Gulliver was put on show to the great detriment of his health. The farmer, seeing that Gulliver was near death, sold him to the queen, who took a great fancy to the little curiosity. The court doctors and philosophers studied Gulliver as a quaint trick of nature. He subsequently had adventures with giant rats the size of lions, with a dwarf thirty feet high, with wasps as large as partridges, with apples the size of Bristol barrels, and with hailstones the size of tennis balls.

He and the king discussed the institutions of their respective countries, the king asking Gulliver many questions about Great Britain that Gulliver found impossible to answer truthfully without embarrassment.

After two years in Brobdingnag, the land of the giants, Gulliver escaped miraculously when a large bird carried his portable quarters out over the sea. The bird dropped the box containing Gulliver and he was rescued by a ship which was on its way to England. Back home, it took Gulliver some time to accustom himself once more to a world of normal size.

Soon afterward Gulliver went to sea again. Pirates from a Chinese port attacked the ship. Set adrift in a small sailboat, Gulliver was cast away upon a rocky island. One day he saw a large floating mass descending from the sky. Taken aboard the flying island of Laputa, he soon found it to be inhabited by intellectuals who thought only in the realm of the abstract and the exceedingly impractical. The people of the island, including the king, were so absent-minded they had to have servants following them to remind them even of their trends of conversation. When the floating island arrived above the continent of Balnibari, Gulliver received permission to visit that realm. There he inspected the Grand Academy, where hundreds of highly impractical projects for the improvement of agriculture and building were under way.

Next Gulliver journeyed by boat to Glubbdubdrib, the island of sorcerers. By means of magic, the governor of the island showed Gulliver such great historical figures as Alexander, Hannibal, Caesar, Pompey, and Sir Thomas More. Gulliver talked to the apparitions and learned from them that history books were inaccurate.

From Glubbdubdrib, Gulliver went to Luggnagg. There he was welcomed by the king, who showed him the Luggnaggian immortals, or stuldbruggs—beings who would never die.

Gulliver traveled on to Japan, where he took a ship back to England. He had been away for more than three years.

Gulliver became restless after a brief stay at his home, and he signed as captain of a ship which sailed from Portsmouth in August, 1710, destined for the South Seas. The crew mutinied, keeping Captain Gulliver prisoner in his cabin for months. At length, he was cast adrift in a long boat off a strange coast. Ashore, he came upon and was nearly overwhelmed by disgusting half-human, half-ape creatures who fled in terror at the approach of a horse. Gulliver soon discovered, to his amazement, that he was in a land where rational horses, the Houyhnhnms, were masters of irrational human creatures, the Yahoos. He stayed in the stable-house of a Houyhnhnm family and learned to subsist on oaten cake and milk. The Houyhnhnms were horrified to learn from Gulliver that horses in England were used by Yahoo-like creatures as beasts of burden. Gulliver described England to his host, much to the candid and straightforward Houyhnhnm's mystification. Such things as wars and courts of law were unknown to this race of intelligent horses. As he did in the other lands he visited, Gulliver attempted to explain the institutions of his native land, but the friendly and benevolent Houyhnhnms were appalled by many of the things Gulliver told them.

Gulliver lived in almost perfect contentment among the horses, until one day his host told him that the Houyhnhnm Grand Assembly had decreed Gulliver either be treated as an ordinary Yahoo or be released to swim back to the land from which he had come. Gulliver built a canoe and sailed away. At length he was picked up by a Portuguese vessel. Remembering the Yahoos, he became a recluse on the ship and began to hate all mankind. Landing at Lisbon, he sailed from there to England. But on his arrival the sight of his own family repulsed him; he fainted when his wife kissed him. His horses became his only friends on earth.

HAJJI BABA OF ISPAHAN

Type of work: Novel
Author: James Morier (1780-1849)
Type of plot: Picaresque romance
Time of plot: Early nineteenth century
Locale: Persia
First published: 1824

Principal characters:
HAJJI BABA, a rogue
OSMAN AGHA, a Turkish merchant
ZEENAB, a slave girl

Critique:

The Adventures of Hajji Baba of Ispahan is a combination of travel book and rogue story, and it does for Persia very much what Le Sage's *Gil Blas* did for Spain. Persia, even in this day of broad travel, has never been widely viewed by Americans. Moreover, the Persia of the time of Napoleon Bonaparte was a Persia that has now disappeared. Customs and manners are as much a part of Morier's entertaining narrative as the picaresque humor of Hajji Baba's adventures and the satire of the rogue's shrewd comments on human nature.

The Story:

Hajji Baba was the son of a successful barber of Ispahan. By the time he was sixteen he had learned the barber's trade, as well as a store of bazaar tales and quotations from the Persian poets. With these he entertained the customers who came to his father's shop, among them a wealthy Turkish merchant named Osman Agha, who was on his way to Meshed to buy goatskins of Bokhara. So taken was this merchant with Hajji Baba that he begged the young man to accompany him on the journey. With his father's blessing and a case of razors, Hajji Baba set out with his new patron.

Before the caravan had been many days on its way it was attacked by a band of Turcoman robbers. Osman Agha had prudently sewed fifty gold ducats in the skullcap under his turban, but when the caravan was captured he was stripped of his finery and the skullcap was tossed in a corner of the robber chief's tent. The robbers spared Hajji Baba's life when they learned he was a skilled barber, and he became a favorite of the wife of the chief. One day he persuaded the foolish woman to let him borrow Osman Agha's cap. He ripped the gold pieces from the lining and hid them, against the time when he might escape from his captors. Osman Agha had been sold to some camel herders.

Hajji Baba traveled with the robbers on their raids throughout the region. One of these raids was on Ispahan itself, from which the robbers carried away a rich booty. But at the division of the spoils, Hajji Baba got only promises and praise.

One day the robbers encountered the armed escort of a Persian prince. When the others fled, Hajji Baba gladly allowed himself to be taken prisoner by the prince's men. They mistook him for a Turcoman, however, and cruelly mistreated him, stripping him of his clothes and his hidden gold. When he complained to the prince, the nobleman sent for the guilty ones, took the money from them, and then kept the gold himself.

Hajji Baba went with the prince and his train to Meshed, where he became a water vendor, carrying a leather bag filled with dirty water which he sold to pilgrims with assurances that it was holy water blessed by the prophet. With money so earned, he bought some tobacco which he blended with dung and then peddled through the streets of the holy city. His best customer, Dervish Sefer, introduced him to other dervishes. They applauded Hajji Baba's shrewdness and enterprise and invited him to become one of their number. But one day a complaint was lodged against him on account of the bad tobacco he sold, and the authorities beat his bare feet until he lost consciousness. Having in the meantime saved a small amount of money, he decided to leave Meshed, which seemed to him an ill-omened city.

He set out on his way to Teheran. On the road a courier overtook him and asked him to read some letters the messenger was carrying. One was a letter from a famous court poet, commending the bearer to officials high at court. Hajji Baba waited until the courier was fast asleep, took the messenger's horse, and rode away to deliver the courier's letters. Through these stolen credentials he was able to obtain a position of confidence with the court physician.

Hajji Baba remained with the physician, even though his post brought him no pay. He soon found favor with Zeenab, the physician's slave, and sought her company whenever he could do so without danger of being caught. Then the shah himself visited the physician's establishment and received Zeenab as a gift. Hajji Baba was disconsolate, but he was soon made happy by a new appointment, this time to the post of sub-lieutenant to the chief executioner of the shah. Again he received no pay, for he was supposed to get his money as other members of the shah's entourage did, by extortion. It was soon discovered that Zeenab was in a condition which could only be regarded as an insult to the shah's personal honor, and Hajji Baba was summoned to execute the girl. Soon afterward suspicion fell on him for his own part in the affair, and he fled to the holy city of Koom.

In Koom he pretended to be a priest.

The shah made a pilgrimage to the city, and during his visit the chief priest presented Hajji Baba's petition to the ruler. Hajji Baba explained that he had acted in all innocence because he had no idea of the high honor to be conferred upon Zeenab. The shah reluctantly pardoned Hajji Baba and allowed him to return to Ispahan.

He arrived to discover that his father had died and that his fortune had disappeared. Hajji Baba sold his father's shop and used the money to set himself up as a learned scribe. Before long he found service with Mollah Nadan, a celebrated priest, who planned to organize an illegal but profitable marriage market. Hajji Baba was supposed to find husbands for women the mollah would provide. When Hajji Baba visited the three women for whom he was supposed to find husbands, he discovered them all to be ugly old hags, one the wife of his former master, the physician, who had recently died. Later, Hajji Baba discovered his first master, Osman Agha, who had finally escaped from the Turcomans and regained some of his fortune. Hajji Baba tricked Agha into marrying one of the three women.

Mollah Nadan undertook to gain favor by punishing some Armenians during a drought, but he incurred the shah's wrath and he and Hajji Baba were driven from the city. Mollah Nadan's property was confiscated. Hajji Baba stole back into the city to see if any of the mollah's property could be saved, but the house had been stripped. He went to visit the baths, and there he discovered Mollah Bashi, who had been taken with a cramp and had drowned. Hajji Baba was afraid that he would be accused of murder, as Mollah Bashi had helped to bring about Mollah Nadan's ruin. But the slave attendant failed to recognize Hajji Baba in the darkness and Hajji Baba escaped, dressed in the mollah's robes. On the horse of the chief executioner he set out to collect money owed to Mollah Bashi. In the clothes of the mollah and riding a fine horse, he cut a dashing figure until he met Mollah Nadan and was persuaded to change robes with him. Mollah Nadan was arrested and charged with the death of Mollah Bashi. Hajji Baba, who had kept the money he had collected, decided to become a merchant.

He encountered the caravan of the widow of Mollah Bashi. She was taking her husband's body to Kerbelai for holy burial. When the leader of the caravan revealed that Hajji Baba was suspected of the murder, he began to fear for his life. But about that time a band of marauders attacked the caravan, and in the confusion Hajji Baba escaped. In Bagdad he reëncountered his old master, Osman Agha, and with him proceeded to invest the money he had available. He bought pipe sticks and planned to sell them at a profit in Constantinople.

There a wealthy widow sought him out and he decided to marry her, first, however, intimating that he was as wealthy as she. He married her and began to live on her income. But his old bazaar friends, jealous of his good luck, betrayed him to his wife's relatives. Thrown out as an imposter, he was obliged to seek the help of the Persian ambassador. The ambassador advised him not to seek revenge upon his former wife's relatives, as they would surely murder him in his bed. Instead, he found use for Hajji Baba in an intrigue developing among representatives of England and France. Hajji Baba was employed as a spy to find out what the foreign emissaries sought in the shah's court.

Here at last Hajji Baba found favor. He discovered that his life among cutthroats and rogues had admirably fitted him for dealing diplomatically with the representatives of foreign countries, and he was finally made the shah's representative in his own city of Ispahan. He returned there with considerable wealth and vast dignity, to lord it over those who had once thought his station in life far below their own.

HAKLUYT'S VOYAGES

Type of work: Travel narratives
Author: Richard Hakluyt (c. 1553-1616)
Type of plot: Adventure and exploration
Time of plot: c. 517 to 1600
Locale: The known world
First published: 1589

Critique:

This work is an anthology of the explorations and travels of British adventurers down to the author's own time. The accounts are bold and vigorous, usually giving only the main events of the journeys, many of them written by the men who made the voyages. Published by Hakluyt in refutation of a French accusation that the English were insular and spiritless, the book is of value in several lights. It gives faithful accounts of many sixteenth-century exploratory journeys; it is an index to the temper of Elizabethan England; and it reflects the enthusiasm for travel literature which was so prevalent at the time of the original publication.

The Stories:

The first group of voyages give thirty-eight accounts of travel and exploration made by Britons up to the end of the sixteenth century. The first stories go back to the medieval ages, for the narrative which begins the work is that of a probably mythical voyage by King Arthur of Britain to Iceland and the most northern parts of Europe in 517.

The first ten narratives deal with voyages made before 1066, the year of the Norman Conquest. They include such journeys as the conquest of the isles of Man and Anglesey by Edwin, King of Northumberland, in 624, the trips of Octher into Norway and Denmark in 890 and 891, the voyage of Wolstan into Danish waters in the tenth century, the voyage of King Edgar, with four thousand ships, about the island of Britain, and the journey of Edmund Ironside from England to Hungary in 1017.

The other voyages described are those taken after the Norman Conquest. The first of these is an account of a marvelous journey made by a company of English noblemen to escort the daughter of King Harold to Russia, to marry the Duke of Russia in 1067. The next account is of the surprising journey of an unknown Englishman who traveled as far into Asia as Tartaria in the first half of the thirteenth century.

One notable voyage describes the adventures of Nicolaus de Linna, a Franciscan friar, to the northern parts of Scandinavia. The twenty-second voyage was that of Anthony Jenkinson who traveled to Russia from England in order to return Osep Napea, the first ambassador from Muscovia to Queen Mary of England, to his own country in 1557.

Surprisingly, almost half of the journeys described in this first collection are those made to Russia by way of the Arctic Ocean, around northern Scandinavia. It is not ordinarily realized that there was any traffic at all between England and Russia at that time, because of the difficulty of both water and land transportation between the two countries.

The final narrative of the first group tells of the greatest event of Elizabethan England, the meeting of the British fleet with the great Armada which Philip II of Spain had sent to subdue England and win for Spain the supremacy of the seas.

The second group of voyages describe trips taken to the region of the Straits of Gibraltar and the countries surrounding the Mediterranean Sea. Eleven of these accounts describe trips made before the Norman Conquest in 1066 and fifty-two describe trips made after that date. The earliest story is that of Helena, the wife of a Roman emperor and a daughter of Coelus, one of the early kings of Britain. Helena, famous as the mother of Constantine the Great, who made Christianity the official religion of Rome, traveled to Jerusalem in 337 because of her interest in the early Christian church. She built several churches there and brought back to Europe a collection of holy relics. One of the relics was a nail reputed to be from the True Cross. It was incorporated some time later into the so-called Iron Crown of Lombardy.

Another voyage which took place before the Norman Conquest was that of a man named Erigena, who was sent by Alfred, King of the West Saxons, to Greece. Alfred was one of the most cultured of British kings in pre-medieval times and very much interested in the classic civilizations. His emissary, Erigena, went as far as Athens in 885, a long voyage for those ancient times.

Several of the post-Conquest voyages were trips made by Englishmen to help in the recovery of Jerusalem from the Saracens during the Crusades. Among the best known are those of Richard the First, often called the Lion-Hearted, and of Prince Edward, son of Henry III, who went to Syria in the last half of the thirteenth century.

Another story is a narrative of the voyage of the English ship, *Susan,* which took William Hareborne to Turkey in 1582. Hareborne was the first ambassador sent by a British monarch to the ruler of Turkey, who was at that time Murad Khan.

Another interesting voyage was that of Ralph Fitch, a London merchant. Between the years 1583 and 1591 he traveled to Syria, to Ormuz, to Goa in the East Indies, to Cambia, to the River Ganges, to Bengala, to Chonderi, to Siam, and thence back to his homeland. It was rare for people to travel, even in the spice trade, as far as did merchant Fitch during the sixteenth century.

A third group of voyages are accounts connected with the exploration and discovery of America. The first account is of a voyage supposedly made to the West Indies in 1170 by Madoc, the son of Owen Guined, a prince of North Wales. It is also recorded that in February of 1488 Columbus offered his services to Henry VII of England and petitioned that monarch to sponsor a voyage to the westward seas for the purpose of discovering a new route to the East Indies. Bartholomew, brother of Columbus, repeated the request a year later, but was refused a second time by the English king.

Several voyages described are those made to America for the purpose of discovering a Northwest Passage to the Orient. The early voyage of Cabot is among them, as well as the voyages of Martin Frobisher and John Davis. Frobisher made three voyages in search of the Northwest Passage, in the three successive years between 1576 and 1578. John Davis also made three fruitless efforts to find the passage in the years from 1585 to 1587. All of these were an important part of the colonial effort in Hakluyt's own time.

Several exploratory trips to Newfoundland and the Gulf of the St. Lawrence River are also related, the earliest the voyage of Sir Humfrey Gilbert to Newfoundland. The ship *Grace* of Bristol, England, also made a trip up the Gulf of St. Lawrence, as far as Assumption Island. There are also accounts of trips made by explorers of other European nations in the New World, such as the journeys made in Canada as far as Hudson's Bay by Jacques Cartier in 1534 and 1535.

There are full accounts of all the voyages made to Virginia in the sixteenth century and the two unsuccessful attempts by Sir Walter Raleigh to found a colony there in 1585 and in 1587.

Another group of stories tell of both English and Spanish explorations of the

Gulf of California. The voyage of Francis Drake is given, particularly that part of his around-the-world trip during which he sailed up the western coast of America to a point forty-three degrees north of the equator and landed to take possession of what he called Nova Albion, in the name of his monarch, Queen Elizabeth, thus giving the British a claim to that part of the New World.

Also described is a voyage taken under orders of the viceroy of New Spain by Francis Gualle. Gualle crossed the Pacific Ocean to the Philippine Islands, where he visited Manila. From there he went to Macao in the East Indies and to Japan, and returned from the Orient to Acapulco, Mexico, in the 1580's.

Another group of stories contain short accounts of trips by Englishmen to various parts of Spanish America. Among these were trips to Mexico City as early as 1555, barely a quarter of a century after it had been conquered by Cortez, as well as to the Antilles Islands in the West Indies, to Guiana, to the coast of Portuguese Brazil, to the delta of the Rio Plata, and to the Straits of Magellan.

Every schoolboy knows the stories of the first two voyages made to the Straits of Magellan and thence around the world, first by Magellan himself and then by Sir Francis Drake. The third man to sail through the Straits and then to proceed around the world is one of the forgotten men of history. Hakluyt gave the credit for this trip to Thomas Cavendish, an Englishman who circled the globe in the years 1586 to 1588.

HAMLET, PRINCE OF DENMARK

Type of work: Drama
Author: William Shakespeare (1564-1616)
Type of plot: Romantic tragedy
Time of plot: c. 1200
Locale: Elsinore, Denmark
First presented: 1602

Principal characters:
HAMLET, Prince of Denmark
THE GHOST, Hamlet's father, former King of Denmark
CLAUDIUS, the present king
GERTRUDE, Hamlet's mother
POLONIUS, a courtier
OPHELIA, his daughter
LAERTES, his son

Critique:

Whether *Hamlet* is considered as literature, as philosophy, or simply as a play, its great merit is generally admitted; but to explain in a few words the reasons for its excellence would be an impossible task. The poetry of the play is superb; its philosophy, although not altogether original with Shakespeare, is expressed with matchless artistry. The universality of its appeal rests in large measure on the character of Hamlet himself. Called upon to avenge his father's murder, he was compelled to face problems of duty, morality, and ethics, which have been the concern of men throughout the ages. In Hamlet himself are mirrored the hopes and fears, the feelings of frustration and despair, of all mankind.

The Story:

Three times the ghost of Denmark's dead king had stalked the battlements of Elsinore Castle. On the fourth night Horatio, Hamlet's friend, brought the young prince to see the specter of his father, two months dead. Since his father's untimely death, Hamlet had been grief-stricken and in an exceedingly melancholy frame of mind. The mysterious circumstances surrounding the death of his father had perplexed him; then too, his mother had married Claudius, the dead king's brother, much too hurriedly to suit Hamlet's sense of decency.

That night Hamlet saw his father's ghost and listened in horror to what it had to say. He learned that his father had not died from the sting of a serpent, as had been supposed, but that he had been murdered by his own brother, Claudius, the present king. The ghost added that Claudius was guilty not only of murder but also of incest and adultery. But the spirit cautioned Hamlet to spare Queen Gertrude, his mother, so that heaven could punish her.

The ghost's disclosures should have left no doubt in Hamlet's mind that Claudius must be killed. But the introspective prince was not quite sure that the ghost was his father's spirit, for he feared it might have been a devil sent to torment him. Debating with himself the problem of whether or not to carry out the spirit's commands, Hamlet swore his friends, including Horatio, to secrecy concerning the appearance of the ghost, and in addition told them not to consider him mad if from then on he were to act queerly.

Meanwhile Claudius was facing not only the possibility of war with Norway, but also, and much worse, his own conscience, which had been much troubled since his hasty marriage to Gertrude. In addition, he did not like the melancholia of the prince, who, he knew, resented the king's hasty marriage. Claudius feared that Hamlet would take his throne away from him. The prince's strange behavior and wild talk made the king think that perhaps Hamlet was mad, but he was not sure. To learn the cause of Hamlet's actions—madness or ambition—Claudius commissioned two of Hamlet's friends, Rosencrantz and Guildenstern, to spy on the prince. But Hamlet saw through their clumsy efforts and confused them with his answers to their questions.

Polonius, the garrulous old chamberlain, believed that Hamlet's behavior resulted from lovesickness for his daughter, Ophelia. Hamlet, meanwhile, had become increasingly melancholy. Rosencrantz and Guildenstern, as well as Polonius, were constantly spying on him. Even Ophelia, he thought, had turned against him. The thought of deliberate murder was revolting to him, and he was constantly plagued by uncertainty as to whether the ghost were good or bad. When a troupe of actors visited Elsinore, Hamlet saw in them a chance to discover whether Claudius were guilty. He planned to have the players enact before the king and the court a scene like that which, according to the ghost, took place the day the old king died. By watching Claudius during the performance, Hamlet hoped to discover for himself signs of Claudius' guilt.

His plan worked. Claudius became so unnerved during the performance that he walked out before the end of the scene. Convinced by the king's actions that the ghost was right, Hamlet had no reason to delay in carrying out the wishes of his dead father. Even so, Hamlet failed to take advantage of his first real chance after the play to kill Claudius. He came upon the king in an attitude of prayer, and could have stabbed him in the back. Hamlet did not strike because he believed that the king would die in grace at his devotions.

The queen summoned Hamlet to her chamber to reprimand him for his insolence to Claudius. Hamlet, remembering what the ghost had told him, spoke to her so violently that she screamed for help. A noise behind a curtain followed her cries, and Hamlet, suspecting that Claudius was eavesdropping, plunged his sword through the curtain, killing old Polonius. Fearing an attack on his own life, the king hastily ordered Hamlet to England in company with Rosencrantz and Guildenstern, who carried a warrant for Hamlet's death. But the prince discovered the orders and altered them so that the bearers should be killed on their arrival in England. Hamlet then returned to Denmark.

Much had happened in that unhappy land during Hamlet's absence. Because Ophelia had been rejected by her former lover, she went mad and later drowned. Laertes, Polonius' hot-tempered son, returned from France and collected a band of malcontents to avenge the death of his father. He thought that Claudius had killed Polonius, but the king told him that Hamlet was the murderer and even persuaded Laertes to take part in a plot to murder the prince.

Claudius arranged for a duel between Hamlet and Laertes. To allay suspicion of foul play, the king placed bets on Hamlet, who was an expert swordsman. At the same time, he had poison placed on the tip of Laertes' weapon and put a cup of poison within Hamlet's reach in the event that the prince became thirsty during the duel. Unfortunately, Gertrude, who knew nothing of the king's treachery, drank from the poisoned cup and died. During the contest, Hamlet was mortally wounded with the poisoned rapier, but the two contestants exchanged foils in a scuffle, and Laertes himself received a fatal wound. Before he died, Laertes was filled with remorse and told Hamlet that Claudius was responsible for the poisoned sword. Hesitating no longer, Hamlet seized his opportunity to act, and fatally stabbed the king. Then the prince himself died. But the ghost was avenged.

A HANDFUL OF DUST

Type of work: Novel
Author: Evelyn Waugh (1903-)
Type of plot: Social satire
Time of plot: Twentieth century
Locale: England
First published: 1934

Principal characters:
Tony Last, owner of Hetton Abbey
Brenda Last, his wife
John, their son
Mrs. Beaver, an interior decorator
John Beaver, her son
Jock Grant-Menzies, Tony's friend
Dr. Messinger, an explorer
Todd, a half-caste trader who loved Dickens

Critique:

This novel, which portrays the decline of the English landed aristocracy, is full of foolish people who find their lives to be no more than "a handful of dust." The contrasts between the Gothic magnificence of Hetton Abbey, the lives of Brenda and Tony, and the aspirations of the successors to Tony's property, are effective instruments for bringing out the meaning of the story. The author writes finished dialogue; the narrative moves smoothly from beginning to end.

The Story:

John Beaver lived in London with his mother, an interior decorator. Beaver was a worthless young man of twenty-five who moved in the social circles of his mother's wealthy customers. He was not well liked, but he was often invited to parties and weekends to fill a space made vacant at the last moment.

One weekend Beaver was invited to Hetton Abbey by its young owner, Tony Last. Tony lived in the old Gothic abbey with his wife, Brenda, and his young son, John. It was Tony's dream that some day he would restore his mansion to its former feudal glory. Brenda was bored with her husband's attachment to the past, however; she found relief in her weekly trips to London.

Beaver's stay at Hetton Abbey was rather dull, but Brenda liked him and did her best to entertain him. On her next trip to London she saw him again and asked him to take her to a party. At first Beaver seemed reluctant; then he agreed to escort her.

Beaver and Brenda left the party early, creating some idle gossip. In a way, the gossipers were correct, for Brenda had definitely decided to have an affair with Beaver. She returned home to the unsuspecting Tony and told him that she was bored with life in the country. She said that she wanted to take some courses in economics at the university in London. Tony, feeling sorry for her, allowed her to rent a one-room flat in a building owned by Mrs. Beaver. Brenda moved to London and returned to Hetton Abbey only on weekends.

One day, when Tony went to London on impulse, he found that his wife already had engagements. He was forced to spend the evening getting drunk with his bachelor friend, Jock Grant-Menzies.

Tony's escapade bothered his conscience so much that when Brenda returned for the weekend she was able to persuade him to let Mrs. Beaver redecorate in modern style one of the rooms of the old house.

Brenda's conscience bothered her also. She tried to interest Tony in a girl she brought down for a weekend, but it was no use. He only wanted to have his wife back home. However, he still trusted her and suspected nothing of her intrigue in London.

Things might have gone on that way indefinitely if young John Last had not been killed by a horse while he was fox hunting. Tony sent Jock up to London to break the news to Brenda. At first Brenda thought that Jock was speaking of John Beaver's death, for he was out of town. When she learned the truth, she was relieved, realizing for the first time how much she cared for Beaver.

With young John dead, she felt that nothing held her to Tony any longer. She wrote, telling him everything, and asked for a divorce. Stunned, Tony could not believe that Brenda had been false to him. At last he consented to spend a weekend at Brighton with another woman to give her grounds for divorce.

Brenda's family was against the divorce and attempted to prevent it. Then, when they saw that the divorce would go through, they tried to force Tony to give Brenda more alimony than he had planned. He refused, for he could raise more money only by selling Hetton Abbey. The proposal angered him so much that he changed his mind about the divorce. He would not set Brenda free.

Tony, wishing to get away from familiar faces, accompanied an explorer, Dr. Messinger, on an expedition to find a lost city in the South American jungles. During the voyage across the Atlantic Tony had a short affair with a young French girl from Trinidad. But when she learned that he was married she would have nothing more to do with him.

Once the explorers had left civilization behind them, Tony found himself thinking of what was going on in London. He did not enjoy jungle life at all; insect bites, vermin, and vampire bats made sleep almost impossible.

When Negro boatmen had taken Tony and Dr. Messinger far up the Demarara River, they left the explorers in the hands of Indian guides. Then the expedition struck out into unmapped territory.

Meanwhile, back in London, Brenda no longer found Beaver an ardent lover. He had counted strongly on getting a considerable amount of money when he married Brenda; now Brenda could get neither the money nor a divorce.

Brenda began to grow desperate for money. She asked Mrs. Beaver for a job, but Mrs. Beaver thought that it would not look well for her to employ Brenda. A short time later Beaver decided to accompany his mother on a trip to California.

At last Tony and Dr. Messinger came to a river they believed must flow into the Amazon, and they ordered the Indians to build canoes. The Indians obeyed, but they refused to venture down the river. There was nothing for the white men to do but to continue the journey without guides. Soon after they set out Tony came down with fever. Dr. Messinger left him on shore and went on alone to find help, but the explorer drowned when his boat capsized. Tony in his delirium struggled through the jungle and came by chance to the hut of a trader named Todd, who nursed him back to health but kept him a prisoner. Tony was forced to read the novels of Dickens aloud to his captor. When some Englishmen came in search of Tony, the trader made them believe his captive had died of fever. Tony faced lifelong captivity to be spent reading over and over Dickens' novels to the illiterate half-caste, for no white man could travel in the jungle without native help.

Beaver left for California. Brenda knew that their affair was over. No news came from Tony in South America. Without his permission, Brenda could not draw upon the family funds.

Then Tony was officially declared dead, and Hetton Abbey became the property of another branch of the Last family. The new owner of Hetton Abbey bred silver fox. Although he had even fewer servants than his predecessor and had shut off most of the house, he still dreamed that some day Hetton Abbey would again be as glorious as it was in the days of Cousin Tony.

He erected a memorial to Tony at Hetton Abbey, but Brenda was unable to attend its dedication. She was engaged elsewhere with her new husband, Jock Grant-Menzies.

HANDLEY CROSS

Type of work: Novel
Author: Robert Smith Surtees (1803-1864)
Type of plot: Humorous satire
Time of plot: Nineteenth century
Locale: England
First published: 1843; enlarged 1854

Principal characters:

John Jorrocks, a wealthy grocer
Mrs. Jorrocks, his wife
Belinda, his niece
Pigg, his huntsman
Captain Doleful, a master of ceremonies

Critique:

Handley Cross is a fairly typical example of nineteenth-century English sporting tales. The novel contains little plot and little attempt at dramatic motivation, but to an enthusiastic fox hunter *Handley Cross* is fascinating because of its gusty hunting tales and the single-minded devotion of its characters to the sport. Jorrocks, appearing in a number of Surtees' works, is dear to devotees of the hard-riding, hard-drinking sporting set.

The Story:

For years Michael Hardy had been the leader of the hunt in Sheepwash

Vale. While he did not pay quite all the expenses of the sport, his personality and vigor kept fox hunting popular in the district. Michael was one of the old school; his hounds were unkenneled and boarded here and there, and the horses were mostly pickups. At his death it seemed that fox hunting could no longer be accounted an attraction in the county.

There were some other difficulties. The village of Handley Cross was rapidly growing. Having discovered by chance the curative values of the local spring, a reprobate physician named Swizzle had set up as a spa doctor, and in a few years Handley Cross became a fashionable watering place. Swizzle was a perfect doctor for many people. He invariably prescribed game pie and rare beef for his patients, and advised two quarts of port wine at dinner. He became a familiar sight in the village, as he buttonholed his patients on the street and inspected their coated tongues and gouty joints. With this new fame as a health resort hotels and souvenir stands sprang up to bring life to the sleepy village.

But there is no good proposition without competition. Another shady practitioner, a sanctimonious doctor named Mello, moved in. He bought land with a small spring on it, poured epsom salts in the water every night, and set up a rival establishment. In no time the town was divided into Melloites and Swizzleites. The important change, however, was in the social life of Handley Cross.

Captain Doleful, a lean, hypocritical half-pay captain, appointed himself master of ceremonies for the town. With the help of august Mrs. Barnington, the social arbiter of the fashionable set, balls and teas soon became popular and social eminence became the goal of the visiting gentry.

In a resort so fashionable it was unthinkable not to have a hunt club. Captain Doleful and some other worthies attempted to carry on after Michael Hardy died, but their efforts were unsuccessful. For one thing, the leaders of the hunt rode in gigs, conveyances unthinkable in Hardy's day. In addition, the townspeople were too poor or too parsimonious to hire a whipper-in and a huntsman. Worst of all, subscribers to the hunt were often slow in paying; soon there were not enough funds to pay for damage done to crops and fences.

The fashionables decided that the only solution was a real master of the hunt, one not too elegant for a small spa but rich enough to pay the difference between subscriptions and expenses. A committee headed by Captain Doleful and the secretary Fleeceall decided to invite John Jorrocks, whose fame had spread far, to become master of the hunt. Accordingly a letter was sent, and the negotiations were soon brought to a conclusion, for Jorrocks was an easy victim.

After a life devoted to selling tea and other groceries, Jorrocks was a wealthy man. He had turned to hunting as a hobby, and in spite of his Cockney accent and ample girth, he was soon accepted in the field. Although he had the bad habit of selling cases of groceries to his fellow huntsmen, in Surrey Jorrocks soon became a fixture among the sporting set. Now, he was to be master in his own right. Captain Doleful secured a lodge for him, and the date was set for his arrival in Handley Cross.

On the appointed day, the four-piece band turned out and the whole town assembled at the station. Several of the villagers carried banners bearing the legend "Jorrocks Forever." When the train pulled in, Captain Doleful looked through the first-class section but found no Jorrocks. The second-class carriages produced no Jorrocks. Finally, on a flat car at the end of the train, he found Jorrocks and his family snugly sitting in their own coach with the horses already hitched. Loud were the cheers as the new hunt master drove through the streets of Handley Cross.

Jorrocks was soon installed in his new lodging with Mrs. Jorrocks and Belinda, his pretty niece. Belinda added greatly to Jorrock's popularity.

The new hunt master looked over his kennels and the few broken-down hacks in the stable. Besides building up both the pack and the stud, he had to have a real huntsman. He finally hired Pigg, chiefly because his skinny shanks and avowed delicate appetite outweighed his speech of such broad Scots that few could understand what he said. Jorrocks was quickly disillusioned about his new huntsman. When Pigg ate his first meal in the kitchen, there was a great uproar. Hurrying in, Jorrocks found Pigg greedily eating the whole supper joint and holding the other servants at bay. And Pigg could drink more ale and brandy than Jorrocks himself.

Many were the fine hunts that winter. Because Pigg was skillful and Jorrocks persistent, the collection of brushes grew fast. One night Jorrocks was far from home, separated from his trusty Pigg and the pack, and caught in a downpour of rain. He turned into the first gate he saw and knocked. An efficient groom took his horse and two flunkies politely conducted the dripping Jorrocks to his room. On the bed were dry clothes, in the small tub was hot water, and on the table was a bottle of brandy. Jorrocks peeled off his clothes and settled into the tub. He had just started on his third glass of brandy when some one knocked. Jorrocks ignored the noise for a while but the knocker was insistent.

At last a determined voice from the hall demanded his clothes. Jorrocks quickly got out of the tub, put on the clothes which did not fit, and took a firm, possessive grip on the brandy bottle. Then he shouted forcefully that he would keep the clothes.

When Jorrocks came down to dinner, he was surprised to be told that he was in Ongar Castle. His unwilling host was the Earl of Bramber, whose servants had mistaken Jorrocks for an invited guest and by mistake had put him in the room of a captain. Jorrocks looked at the angry captain, who was wearing an outfit of his host. Only Jorrocks' Cockney impudence could have brazened out such a situation.

At last the company sat down to dinner. As usual, Jorrocks drank too much, and while giving a rousing toast to fox hunting he fell fast asleep on the floor. He awoke immersed in water. Calling lustily for help, he struck out for the shore. When a flunky brought a candle, he saw that he had been put to bed in the bathhouse and that while walking in his sleep he had fallen into the small pool. But Jorrocks was irrepressible; in the morning he parted from the earl on good terms.

After a hard-riding winter, spring finally spoiled the hunting and the Jorrocks family left for London. Pigg stayed in Handley Cross to dispose of the dogs and horses. Captain Doleful bought Jorrocks' own mount for twenty-five pounds. When the horse became sick and died soon afterward, parsimonious Doleful sued Jorrocks for the purchase price. The court decided in favor of Jorrocks, holding that no one can warrant a horse to stay sound in wind and limb.

Jorrocks' business associates looked on his hunting capers as a tinge of madness. That fall Jorrocks was heard to exclaim in delight at the sight of a frostbitten dahlia; it would soon be fox hunting time. But at last Jorrocks was committed by a lunacy commission for falling victim to the fox hunting madness. In vain Jorrocks sputtered and protested; his vehemence only added to the charge against him. Poor, fat Jorrocks spent some time in an asylum before an understanding chancellor freed him. Luckily he regained his freedom before the hunting season was too far gone.

THE HEART OF MIDLOTHIAN

Type of work: Novel
Author: Sir Walter Scott (1771-1832)
Type of plot: Historical romance
Time of plot: Early eighteenth century
Locale: Scotland
First published: 1818

Principal characters:
DAVID DEANS, a dairyman
JEANIE DEANS, his daughter
EFFIE DEANS, another daughter
REUBEN BUTLER, Jeanie's betrothed
GEORDIE ROBERTSON, Effie's betrayer, in reality George Staunton
MEG MURDOCKSON, an evil woman
THE DUKE OF ARGYLE, Jeanie's benefactor

Critique:

The story of Jeanie Deans and her great effort to save her sister's life is supposedly based on fact. Fact or fiction, it is an exciting story, told as only Sir Walter Scott could tell it. *The Heart of Midlothian* is filled with suspense, mystery, and romance, and there is a happy ending. Many consider this Scott's greatest novel.

The Story:

The first knowledge Jeanie Deans had that her sister Effie was in trouble came just a few moments before officers of justice arrived at the cottage to arrest Effie for child murder. They told Jeanie and her father, David Deans, that Effie had borne a male child illegitimately and had killed him or caused him to be killed soon after he was born. Effie admitted the birth of the child but refused to name her seducer. She denied that she had killed her baby, saying that she had fallen into a stupor and had recovered to find that the midwife who attended her had disposed of the child in some fashion unknown to Effie. In the face of the evidence, however, she was convicted of child murder and sentenced to be hanged. Jeanie might have saved her sister, for it was the law that if a prospective mother had told anyone of her condition she would not be responsible for her baby's death. But Jeanie would not lie, even to save her sister's life. Since there was no one to whom Effie had told her terrible secret, there was no defense for her, and she was placed in the Tolbooth prison to await execution.

Another prisoner in the Tolbooth was Captain John Porteous, who was awaiting execution for firing into the crowd attending the hanging of Andrew Wilson, a smuggler. Wilson's accomplice, Geordie Robertson, had escaped, and the officers feared that Robertson might try to rescue Wilson. For that reason, Porteous and a company of soldiers had been sent to the scene of the execution to guard against a possible rescue. Because Porteous had fired into the crowd without provocation, killing several people, he was to be hanged. But when his execution was stayed for a few weeks, a mob headed by Robertson, disguised as a woman, broke into the prison, seized Porteous, and hanged him. For that deed Robertson became a hunted man.

Meanwhile Jeanie Deans, who had refused to lie to save her sister, had not forsaken Effie. When she visited Effie in prison, she learned that Robertson was the father of her child. He had left her in the care of old Meg Murdockson, considered by many to be a witch, and it must have been Meg who had killed or sold the baby. Meg's daughter Madge had long before been seduced by Robertson and had lost her mind for love of him, and Meg had sworn revenge on any other woman Robertson might love. But proving the old woman's guilt or Effie's innocence was not possible, for Robertson had disappeared, and Meg swore that she had seen Effie coming back from the river after drowning the baby.

Jeanie, determined to save her sister, decided to walk to London to seek a pardon from the king and queen. She told her plans to Reuben Butler, a minister to whom she had long been betrothed. Reuben had not been able to marry her, for he had no position other than that of an assistant schoolmaster and his salary was too small to support a wife. Although he objected to Jeanie's plan, he was able to aid her when he saw that she could not be swayed from her purpose. Reuben's grandfather had once aided an ancestor of the present Duke of Argyle, and Reuben gave Jeanie a letter asking the duke's help in presenting Jeanie to the king and queen.

The journey to London was a long and dangerous one. Once Jeanie was captured by Meg Murdockson, who tried to kill her so that she could not save Effie. But Jeanie escaped from the old woman and sought refuge in the home of the Rev. Mr. Staunton. There she met the minister's son, George Staunton, and learned from him that he was Geordie Robertson, the betrayer of her sister. He admitted his responsibility to Effie, telling Jeanie that he had planned and executed the Porteous incident in order to rescue Effie from the prison. But she had refused to leave with him. He had tried many other schemes to save her, including an attempt to force from Meg the confession that she had taken the baby, but everything had failed. He told Jeanie that he had been on his way to give himself up in exchange for Effie's release when he fell from his horse and was injured. He told Jeanie to bargain with the Duke of Argyle, and as a last resort to offer to lead the authorities to Robertson in exchange for Effie's pardon. George promised not to leave his father's house until Effie was free.

Jeanie at last reached London and presented herself to the Duke of Argyle with Reuben's letter. The duke, impressed with Jeanie's sincerity and simplicity, arranged for an audience with the queen. She too believed Jeanie's story of Effie's misfortune, and through her efforts the king pardoned Effie, with the stipulation that she leave Scotland for fourteen years. Jeanie secured the pardon without revealing George Staunton's secret.

The duke was so impressed with Jeanie's goodness and honesty that he made her father the master of an experimental farm on one of his estates in Scotland, and he made Reuben the minister of the church. Jeanie's heart was overflowing with joy until she learned that Effie had eloped with her lover just three nights after her release from prison. No one knew where they were, as the outlaw's life was in constant danger because of his part in the Porteous hanging.

Reuben and Jeanie were married and were blessed with three fine children. They prospered in their new life, and Jeanie's only sorrow was her sister's marriage to George Staunton. She kept Effie's secret, however, telling no one that George was actually Robertson. After several years, George and Effie returned to London, George having inherited a title from his uncle, and as Sir George and Lady Staunton they were received in court society. Effie wrote secretly to Jeanie and sent her large sums of money which Jeanie put away without telling her husband about them. Even to him she could not reveal Effie's secret.

By chance Jeanie found a paper containing the last confession of Meg Murdockson, who had been hanged as a witch. In it Meg confessed that she had stolen Effie's baby and had given him to an outlaw. Jeanie sent this information to Effie, in London, and before long Effie, as Lady Staunton, paid Jeanie a visit. Effie had used a pretext of ill health to go to Scotland while her husband, acting on the information in Meg's letter, tried to trace the whereabouts of their son. Although it was dangerous for George to be in Scotland, where he might be recognized as Geordie Robertson, he followed every clue given in Meg's confession. In Edinburgh he met Reuben Butler, who was there on business, and secured an invitation to accompany Reuben back to the manse. Reuben, not knowing George's real identity, was happy to receive the Duke of Argyle's friend. Reuben, at that time, did not know that Effie was also a guest in his home.

As Reuben and George walked toward the manse, they passed through a thicket where they were attacked by outlaws. One, a young fellow, ran his sword through George and killed him. It was not until Reuben had heard the whole story of the Stauntons from Jeanie that he searched George's pockets and found there information which proved beyond doubt that the young outlaw who had killed George was his own son, stolen many years before. Because Effie was grief-stricken by George's death, Jeanie and Reuben thought it useless to add to her sorrow by revealing the identity of his assailant. Reuben later traced the boy to America, where the young man continued his life of crime until he was captured and probably killed by Indians.

Effie stayed with Reuben and Jeanie for more than a year. Then she went back to London and the brilliant society she had known there. No one but Jeanie and Reuben ever knew the secret of Effie and George. After ten years, Effie retired to a convent on the continent, where she spent her remaining years grieving for her husband and the son she had never known.

Reuben and Jeanie Butler, who had been so unavoidably involved in sordidness and crime, lived out their lives happily and carried their secret with them to the grave.

HEAVEN'S MY DESTINATION

Type of work: Novel
Author: Thornton Wilder (1897-)
Type of plot: Social satire
Time of plot: 1930-1931
Locale: Middle West
First published: 1935

Principal characters:
George Marvin Brush, a traveling salesman
Roberta, a farmer's daughter
George Burkin, a peeping Tom
Herb, a newspaper reporter
Elizabeth, his daughter

Critique:

In George Marvin Brush, Thornton Wilder would seem to have synthesized the American character with its many tragic inconsistencies. One admires George Brush one moment and detests him as a prig the next. The irony and the deceptive simplicity of *Heaven's My Destination* are terrifying. Although George Brush is not the picaresque hero-type, the novel, with its many colorful and unprincipled characters and its episodic form, resembles the picaresque genre.

The Story:

George Marvin Brush, a straight-laced, clean-living non-smoker and non-drinker of twenty-three, was a salesman for the Caulkins Educational Press; his territory was the Middle West. He was the amusement and the despair of all the traveling salesmen in the same territory who knew him. One day Doremus Blodgett, a hosiery salesman, caught George in the act of penning a Bible text on a hotel blotter and invited George up to his room to chaff him. The righteousness of George infuriated Blodgett, but the hosiery man was almost reconciled when George admitted to him that he had once wronged a farmer's daughter.

At another time George withdrew all his savings from the bank. In his attempt to explain to the bank president his plan of voluntary poverty, he insulted that executive by saying that banks owed their existence only to man's fear of insecurity. Being thought mad, George was jailed, but his ingenuousness confounded even his jailers. One of them, after hearing George propound his theories, withdrew his own savings from the bank.

In Oklahoma City George again saw Blodgett and his "cousin," Mrs. Margie McCoy. There he talked of the injustice of his receiving raises in pay, to the utter confusion of Blodgett and Mrs. McCoy. He told them that he had gone through college and had had a religious conversion in order to be of an independent mind. All he wanted, he said, was a perfect girl for his wife, six children, and a real American home. He confessed that he was hindered in his quest for these ideals by his having wronged a Kansas farm girl, one Roberta, whose farm home he had been unable to find since he had left it.

George went from Oklahoma City to the Chautauqua at Camp Morgan, Oklahoma, to see Judge Corey, a state legislator who was interested in textbook contracts. There he was shocked by Jessie, a college girl who believed in evolution; he pestered a distraught businessman who wanted to be left alone; and he turned down Judge Corey's offer of thirty-five thousand dollars and a state job if he would marry the judge's daughter, Mississippi.

From Camp Morgan George went to Kansas City, where he stayed in Queenie's boarding-house with his four wild friends, Herb and Morrie, reporters; Bat, a motion picture mechanic; and Louie, a hospital orderly. Accord lasted between the four and George as long as George did not preach his anti-tobacco and anti-alcohol creeds. They, in turn, restrained their actions and their speech in his presence. Three of them and George, who had a beautiful voice, formed an expert barbershop quartet. In Kansas City George became the victim of an elaborate practical joke arranged by his friends. After they had tricked him into drunkenness, the five went on a rampage. The second step in their plan to lead George to perdition came when Herb tricked George into going to dinner one Sunday at a brothel. Herb represented the house to George as an old mansion, its proprietor, Mrs. Crofut, as a pillar of Kansas City society, and the troop of prostitutes as her daughters. George, completely duped, was impressed by the graciousness of Mrs. Crofut and by the beauty of her daughters. He treated the girls to a neighborhood movie.

Back at Queenie's, George would not believe Herb when his friend told him the truth about Mrs. Crofut's genteel establishment. Irritated by George's priggishness and stupidity, his four friends beat him nearly to death. Later, at the hospital, Louie told George that he ought to live and let live.

Out of the hospital, George continued his book selling. On a train he met an evangelist who said that money did not matter; however, George gave the man money when he learned that the man's family was destitute. In Fort Worth George exasperated a bawdy house proprietor posing as a medium, by telling her that she was a fake.

Having learned that Roberta had taken a job as a waitress in Kansas City, George went there and forced himself upon the girl, who wanted nothing to do with him. He adopted Elizabeth, the daughter of his friend Herb, who died with few illusions about life.

In Ozarkville, Missouri, George angered a father when he talked to the man's young daughter in the street. Then he went to a country store to buy a doll for the girl and became involved in a hold-up. Carrying out one of his strange theories, he assisted the amazed burglar. The storekeeper, Mrs. Efrim, thought that George was out of his mind. Arrested, he was put in jail, where he met George Burkin, a movie director who had been arrested as a peeping Tom. Burkin explained to George that he peeped only to observe unself-conscious human behavior.

George's trial was a sensation in Ozarkville. The little girl and Mrs. Efrim lied in their testimony, and George attempted to explain his theories of life to a confounded court. When he explained what he called ahimsa, or the theory of reacting to every situation in a manner that was the exact opposite from what was expected, the bewildered judge released him, telling him to be cautious, however, because people were afraid of ideas.

After George and Burkin had left Ozarkville in Burkin's car, they picked up a hitchhiker who turned out to be the burglar whom George had tried to help. George attempted to work his radical theory for the treatment of criminals on the burglar, but the man only fled in confused anger. George and Burkin argued about George's theories, Burkin saying that George had never really grown up, and George claiming that Burkin had thought too much and had not lived enough.

Back in Kansas City, George met Roberta and her sister Lottie for the purpose of reaching a decision in his relationship with Roberta. Lottie suggested that the couple marry and get a divorce as soon as possible, so that Roberta could be accepted again by her family. George, however, could not countenance divorce. Being finally persuaded, Roberta married George and the couple moved into a flat over a drug store. But their married life grew more and more trying. George found himself taking notes for topics that he and Roberta could safely discuss. They competed for Elizabeth's affections. At last Roberta decided to leave George and return to the farm.

George, unhappy, continued to sell books. He lost his faith and began to lead what many people would call a normal life. At length he fell sick and was hospitalized. In the hospital he admitted to a Methodist pastor that he had broken all but two of the ten commandments but that he was glad he had broken them. He shocked the pastor by saying that one cannot get better and better. While in the hospital he received a spoon which had been willed to him by a man whom he had never met but whom he had admired reciprocally through a mutual friend. He recovered, left the hospital, and reverted to his old ways. George Brush was incurable.

HEDDA GABLER

Type of work: Drama
Author: Henrik Ibsen (1828-1906)
Type of plot: Social criticism
Time of plot: Late nineteenth century
Locale: Norway
First presented: 1890

Principal characters:
George Tesman, a scholar
Hedda Tesman, his wife
Miss Juliana Tesman, his aunt
Mrs. Elvsted, Hedda's old schoolmate
Judge Brack, a friend of the Tesmans
Eilert Lovberg, Hedda's former suitor

Critique:

Hedda Gabler has in it most of the elements of good theater which Ibsen painstakingly learned from the popular French playwrights of the last half of the nineteenth century. In Hedda, he created a woman with hardly one redeeming virtue. She is spiritually as empty as she assumes her environment to be. Nearly every great actress of the last half-century has played Hedda and audiences have always been attracted to her powerful but ruthless personality.

The Story:

When aristocratic Hedda Gabler, daughter of the late General Gabler, consented to marry Doctor George Tesman, everyone in Hedda's set was surprised and a little shocked. Although George was a rising young scholar soon to be made a professor in the university, he was hardly considered the type of person Hedda would marry. He was dull and prosaic, absorbed almost exclusively in his dusty tomes and manuscripts, while Hedda was the beautiful, spoiled darling of her father and of all the other men who had flocked around her. But Hedda was now twenty-nine, and George was the only one of her admirers who was willing to offer her marriage and a villa which had belonged to the widow of a cabinet minister.

The villa was somewhat beyond George's means, but with the prospect of a professorship and with his Aunt Juliana's help, he managed to secure it because it was what Hedda wanted. He arranged a long wedding tour lasting nearly six months because Hedda wished that also. On their honeymoon George spent most of his time delving into libraries for material on his special field, the history of civilization. Hedda was bored. She returned to the villa hating George. Then it began to look as if George might not get the professorship, in which case Hedda would have to forego her footman and saddlehorse and some of the other luxuries she craved. George's rival for the post was Eilert Lovberg, a brilliant but erratic genius who had written a book, acclaimed a masterpiece, in George's own field. Hedda's boredom and disgust with her situation was complete. She found her only excitement in practicing with the brace of pistols which had belonged to General Gabler, the only legacy her father had left her.

George discovered that Eilert had written another book, more brilliant and important than the last, a book written with the help and inspiration of a Mrs. Elvsted, whose devotion to the erratic genius had reformed him. The manuscript of this book Lovberg brought with him one evening to the Tesman villa. Hedda proceeded to make the most of this situation. In the first place, Thea Elvsted was Hedda's despised schoolmate, and her husband's former sweetheart. The fact that this mouse-like creature had been the inspiration for the success and rehabilitation of Eilert Lovberg was more than Hedda could bear. For Eilert Lovberg had always been in love with Hedda, and she knew it. In the distant past, he had urged her to throw in her lot with him and she had been tempted to do so but had refused because his future had been uncertain. Now Hedda felt a pang of regret mingled with anger that another woman possessed what she had lacked the courage to hold for herself.

Her only impulse was to destroy, and circumstances played into her hands. When Lovberg called at the Tesman villa with his manuscript, George was on the point of leaving with his friend, Judge Brack, for a bachelor party. They invited Lovberg to accompany them, but he refused, preferring to remain at the villa with Mrs. Elvsted and Hedda. But Hedda, determined to destroy the handiwork of her rival, deliberately sent Lovberg off to the party. All night, Hedda

HEDDA GABLER by Henrik Ibsen. Published by Charles Scribner's Sons.

and Mrs. Elvsted awaited the revelers' return. George was the first to appear with the story of the happenings of the night before.

The party had ended in an orgy, and on the way home Lovberg had lost his manuscript, which George recovered and brought home. In despair over the supposed loss of his manuscript, Lovberg had spent the remainder of the evening at Mademoiselle Diana's establishment. When he finally made his appearance at the villa, George had gone. Lovberg told Mrs. Elvsted he had destroyed his manuscript, but later he confessed to Hedda that it was lost and that, as a consequence, he intended to take his own life. Without revealing that the manuscript was at that moment in her possession, Hedda urged him to do the deed beautifully, and she pressed into his hand a memento of their relationship, one of General Gabler's pistols—the very one with which she had once threatened Lovberg.

After his departure, Hedda coldly and deliberately thrust the manuscript into the fire. When George returned and heard from Hedda's own lips the fate of Lovberg's manuscript, he was unspeakably shocked; but half believing that she burned it for his sake, he was also flattered. He resolved to keep silent and devote his life to reconstructing the book from the notes kept by Mrs. Elvsted.

Except for two circumstances, Hedda would have been safe. The first was the manner in which Lovberg met his death. Leaving Hedda, he had returned to Mademoiselle Diana's, where instead of dying beautifully, as Hedda had planned, he became embroiled in a brawl in which he was accidentally killed. The second was the character of Judge Brack, a sophisticated man of the world, as ruthless in his way as Hedda was in hers. He had long admired Hedda's cold, dispassionate beauty, and had wanted to make her his mistress. The peculiar circumstances of Eilert Lovberg's death gave him his opportunity. He had learned that the pistol with which Lovberg met his death was one of a pair belonging to Hedda. If the truth came out, there would be an investigation followed by scandal in which Hedda would be involved. She could not face either a public scandal or the private ignominy of the judge's proposal. So while her husband and Mrs. Elvsted were beginning the long task of reconstructing the dead Lovberg's manuscript, Hedda calmly went to her boudoir and with the remaining pistol she died beautifully—as she had urged Lovberg to do—by putting a bullet through her head.

HENRY ESMOND

Type of work: Novel
Author: William Makepeace Thackeray (1811-1863)
Type of plot: Historical romance
Time of plot: Late seventeenth, early eighteenth centuries
Locale: England and the Low Countries
First published: 1852

Principal characters:
Henry Esmond, a Castlewood ward
Francis Esmond, Viscount Castlewood
Rachel Esmond, his wife
Beatrix, their daughter
Frank, their son
Lord Mohun, a London rake
Father Holt, a Jacobite spy
James Stuart, the exiled pretender

Critique:

Thackeray did not have high regard for the average historian of his day. To present history as he thought it should be presented, he wrote *The History of*

Henry Esmond, a novel which contains a blend of fact and fiction. There is fact in the many historical characters of the book. There is fiction in the love story of Colonel Henry Esmond, who was in love with two women. Today's reader is likely to lose patience with Henry Esmond, whose attempts at winning Beatrix are so ineffectual as to be almost ludicrous; but no reader can escape the witchery of Beatrix's charms. In her, Thackeray has created one of the most delightfully puzzling and fascinating coquettes in all English literature.

The Story:

Henry Esmond grew up at Castlewood. He knew there was some mystery about his birth and he dimly remembered that long ago he had lived with weavers who spoke a foreign tongue. Thomas Esmond, Viscount Castlewood, had brought him to England and turned him over to Father Holt, the chaplain, to be educated. That much he learned as he grew older.

All was not peace and quiet at Castlewood in those years, when his lordship and Father Holt were engaged in a plot for the restoration of the exiled Stuart king, James II. When James attempted to recover Ireland for the Stuarts, Thomas Esmond rode off to his death at the battle of the Boyne. His widow fled to her dower house at Chelsea. Father Holt disappeared. Henry, a large-eyed, grave-faced twelve-year-old boy, was left alone with servants in the gloomy old house.

There his new guardians and distant cousins, Francis and Rachel Esmond, found him when they arrived to take possession of Castlewood. The new Viscount Castlewood, a bluff, loud-voiced man, greeted the boy kindly enough. His wife was like a girl herself—she was only eight years older than Henry—and Henry thought her the loveliest lady he had ever seen. With them were a little daughter, Beatrix, and a son, Frank, a baby in arms.

As Henry grew older he became more and more concerned over the rift he saw coming between Rachel Esmond and her husband, both of whom he loved because they had treated him as one of the immediate family in the household at Castlewood. It was plain that the hard-drinking, hard-gambling nobleman was wearying of his quiet country life. After Rachel's face was disfigured by smallpox, her altered beauty caused her husband to neglect her even more. Young Beatrix also felt that relations between her parents were strained.

When Henry was old enough, he went to Cambridge, sent there on money left Rachel by a deceased relative. Later, when he returned to Castlewood on a vacation, he realized for the first time that Beatrix was exceptionally attractive. Apparently he had never really noticed her before. Rachel, for her part, had great regard for her young kinsman. Before his arrival from Cambridge, according to Beatrix, Rachel went to Henry's room ten times to see that it was ready.

Relations between Rachel and the viscount were all but severed when the notorious Lord Mohun visited Castlewood. Rachel knew her husband had been losing heavily to Mohun at cards, but when she spoke to the viscount about the bad company he was keeping, he flew into a rage. He was by no means calmed when Beatrix innocently blurted out to her father, in the company of Mohun, that that gentleman was interested in Rachel. Jealous of another man's attentions to the wife he himself neglected, the viscount determined to seek satisfaction in a duel.

The two men fought in London, where the viscount had gone on the pretext of seeing a doctor. Henry, who suspected the real reason for the trip, went along, for he hoped to engage Mohun in a fight and thus save the life of his beloved guardian. The viscount, however, was in no mood to be cheated out of an excuse to provoke a quarrel. He was heavily in debt to Mohun and thought a fight was the only honorable way out of his difficulties. Moreover, he knew Mohun had written letters to Rachel, although, as the villain explained, she had never answered them. They fought, and Mohun foully and fatally wounded the viscount. On his deathbed the viscount confessed to his young kinsman that Henry was not an illegitimate child, but the son of Thomas, Lord Castlewood, by an early marriage, and the true heir to the Castlewood title. Henry Esmond generously burned the dying man's confession and resolved never to divulge the secret.

For his part in the duel Henry Esmond was sent to prison. When Rachel visited Henry in prison, she was enraged because he had not stopped the duel and because he had allowed Mohun to go unpunished. She rebuked Henry and forbade him to return to Castlewood. When Henry left prison he decided to join the army. For that purpose he visited the old dowager viscountess, his stepmother, who bought him a commission.

Henry's military ventures were highly successful, and won for him his share of wounds and glory. He fought in the campaign of the Duke of Marlborough against Spain and France in 1702 and in the campaign of Blenheim in 1704. Between the two campaigns he returned to Castlewood, where he was reconciled with Rachel. There he saw Frank, now Lord Castlewood, and Beatrix, who was cordial toward him. Rachel herself cautioned Henry that Beatrix was selfish and temperamental and would make no man happy who loved her.

After the campaign of 1704 Henry returned to his cousins, who were living in London. To Henry, Beatrix was more beautiful than ever and even more the coquette. But he found himself unable to make up his mind whether he loved her or Rachel. Later, during the campaign of 1706, he learned from Frank that the ravishing Beatrix was engaged to an earl. The news put Henry in low spirits because he now felt she would never marry a poor captain like himself.

Henry's affairs of the heart were put temporarily into the background when he came upon Father Holt in Brussels. The priest told Henry that while on an expedition in the Low Countries, Thomas Esmond, his father, had seduced the young woman who was Henry's mother. A few weeks before his child was born Thomas Esmond was injured in a duel. Thinking he would die, he married the woman so that her child would be born with an untainted name. But Thomas Esmond did not die, and when he recovered from his wounds he deserted his wife and married a distant kinswoman, the dowager viscountess, Henry's stepmother.

When Henry returned to Castlewood, Rachel informed him she had learned his secret from the old viscountess and consequently knew that he, not Frank, was the true heir. For the second time Henry refused to accept the title belonging to him.

Beatrix's interest in Henry grew after she became engaged to the Duke of Hamilton and learned that Henry was not illegitimate in birth but the bearer of a title her brother was using. Henry wanted to give Beatrix a diamond necklace for a wedding present, but the duke would not permit his fiancée to receive a gift from one of illegitimate birth. Rachel came to the young man's defense and declared before the duke, her daughter, and Henry the secret of his birth and title. Later the duke was killed in a duel with Lord Mohun, who also met his death at the same time. The killing of Rachel's husband was avenged.

The Duke of Hamilton's death gave Henry one more chance to win Beatrix's heart. He threw himself into a plot to put the young Stuart pretender on the throne when old Queen Anne died. To this end he went to France and helped to smuggle into England the young chevalier whom the Jacobites called James III, the king over the water. The two came secretly to the Castlewood home in London, the prince passing as Frank, the young viscount, and there the royal exile saw and fell in love with Beatrix.

Fearing the results of this infatuation, Lady Castlewood and Henry sent Beatrix against her will to Castlewood. When a report that the queen was dying swept through London, the prince was nowhere to be found. Henry and Frank made a night ride to Castlewood. Finding the pretender there, in the room used by Father Holt in the old days, they renounced him and the Jacobite cause. Henry realized his love for Beatrix was dead at last. He felt no regrets for her or for the prince as he rode back to London and heard the heralds proclaiming George I, the new king.

The prince made his way secretly back to France, where Beatrix joined him in his exile. At last Henry felt free to declare himself to Rachel, who had grown very dear to him. Leaving Frank in possession of the title and the Castlewood estates, Henry and his wife went to America. In Virginia he and Rachel built a new Castlewood, reared a family, and found happiness in their old age.

HENRY THE FIFTH

Type of work: Drama
Author: William Shakespeare (1564-1616)
Type of plot: Historical romance
Time of plot: Early part of the fifteenth century
Locale: England and France
First presented: 1600

Principal characters:
Henry the Fifth, King of England
Charles the Sixth, King of France
Princess Katharine, his daughter
The Dauphin, his son
Montjoy, a French herald

Critique:

In *The Life of Henry the Fifth* Shakespeare skillfully combined poetry, pageantry, and history in his effort to glorify England and Englishmen. King Henry himself represents all that is finest in English royalty; and yet when Henry notes on the eve of the battle of Agincourt that he is also a man like other men, Shakespeare shows us an Englishman who possesses that quality of humility which makes great men even greater. Few can see or read the play without sharing, at least for the moment, Shakespeare's pride in England and in things English, and without sensing the vigor and the idealism that are part of the Anglo-Saxon heritage.

The Story:

Once the toss-pot prince of Falstaff's tavern brawls, Henry V was now king at Westminster, a stern but just monarch concerned with his hereditary claim to the crown of France. Before the arrival of the French ambassadors, the young king asked for legal advice from the Archbishop of Canterbury. The king thought that he was the legal heir to the throne of France through Edward III, whose claim to the French throne was, at best, questionable. The Archbishop assured Henry that he had as much right to the French throne as did the French king; consequently, both the Archbishop and the Bishop of Ely urged Henry to press his demands against the French.

When the ambassadors from France arrived, they came, not from Charles, the king, but from his arrogant eldest son, the Dauphin. According to the ambassadors, the Dauphin considered the English monarch the same hot-headed, irresponsible youth he had been before he ascended the throne. To show that he considered Henry an unfit ruler whose demands were ridiculous, the Dauphin presented Henry with some tennis balls. Enraged by the insult, Henry told the French messengers to warn their master that the tennis balls would be turned into gun-stones for use against the French.

The English prepared for war. The Dauphin remained contemptuous of Henry, but others, including the French Constable and the ambassadors who had seen Henry in his wrath, were not so confident. Henry's army landed to lay siege to Harfleur, and the king threatened to destroy the city, together with its inhabitants, unless it surrendered. The French governor had to capitulate because help promised by the Dauphin never arrived. The French, meanwhile, were—with the exception of King Charles—alarmed by the rapid progress of the English through France. That ruler, however, was so sure of victory that he sent his herald, Montjoy, to Henry to demand that the English king pay a ransom to the French, give himself up, and have his soldiers withdraw from France. Henry was not impressed by this bold gesture, and retorted that if King Charles wanted him, the Frenchman should come to get him.

On the eve of the decisive battle of Agincourt, the English were outnumbered five to one. Henry's troops were on foreign soil and ridden with disease. To encourage them, and also to sound out their morale, the king borrowed a cloak and in this disguise walked out among his troops, from watch to watch and from tent to tent. As he talked with his men, he told them that a king is but a man like other men, and that if he were a king he would not want to be anywhere except where he was, in battle with his soldiers. To himself, Henry mused over the cares and responsibilities of kingship. Again he thought of himself simply as a man who differed from other men only in ceremony, itself an empty thing.

Henry's sober reflections on the eve of a great battle, in which he thought much English blood would be shed, were quite different from those of the French, who were exceedingly confident of their ability to defeat their enemy. Shortly before the conflict began, Montjoy again appeared before Henry to give the English one last chance to surrender. Henry again refused to be intimidated. He was not discouraged by the numerical inferiority of his troops, for, as he reasoned in speaking with one of his officers, the fewer troops the English had, the greater would be the honor to them when they won.

The following day the battle began. Because of Henry's leadership, the English held their own. When French reinforcements arrived at a crucial point in the battle, Henry ordered his men to kill all their prisoners so that the energies of the English might be directed entirely against the enemy in front of them, not behind. Soon the tide turned. A much humbler Montjoy approached Henry to request a truce for burying the French dead. Henry granted the herald's request, and at the same time learned from him that the French had conceded defeat. Ten thousand French had been killed, and only twenty-nine English.

The battle over, nothing remained for Henry to do but to discuss with the French king terms of peace. Katharine, Charles' beautiful daughter, was Henry's chief demand, and while his lieutenants settled the details of surrender with the French, Henry made love to the princess and asked her to marry him. Though Katharine's knowledge of English was slight and Henry's knowledge of French little better, they were both acquainted with the universal language of love. French Katharine consented to become English Kate and Henry's bride.

HERCULES AND HIS TWELVE LABORS

Type of work: Classical myth
Source: Folk tradition
Type of plot: Heroic adventure
Time of plot: Remote antiquity
Locale: Mediterranean region
First transcribed: Unknown

Principal characters:
HERCULES, hero of virtue and strength
EURYSTHEUS, his cousin

Critique:

Hercules is the mighty hero of popular imagination in Western culture. Art galleries feature paintings and sculpture of the splendid body of the hero. The latest engines, the strongest building materials, the most powerful utilities bear his name. Hercules, not born a god, achieved godhood at the time of his death, according to tradition, because he devoted his life to the service of his fellow men. Some authorities link Hercules with legends of the sun, as each labor took him further from his home and one of his tasks carried him around the world and back. His twelve labors have been compared to the signs of the zodiac.

The Story:

Hercules was the son of a mortal, Alcmena, and the god Jupiter. Because Juno was hostile to all children of her husband by mortal mothers, she decided to be revenged upon the child. She sent two snakes to kill Hercules in his crib, but the infant strangled the serpents with ease. Then Juno caused Hercules to be subject to the will of his cousin, Eurystheus.

Hercules as a child was taught by Rhadamanthus, who one day punished the child for misdeeds. Hercules immediately killed his teacher. For this his foster father, Amphitryon, took Hercules away to the mountains, to be brought up by rude shepherds. Early in youth Hercules began to attract attention for his great strength and courage. He killed a lion single-handedly and took heroic part in a war. Juno, jealous of his growing success, called on Eurystheus to use his power over Hercules. Eurystheus then demanded that Hercules carry out twelve labors. The plan was that Hercules would perish in one of them.

The first labor: Juno had sent a lion to eat the people of Nemea. The lion's hide was so protected that no arrow could pierce it. Knowing that he could not kill the animal with his bow, Hercules met the lion and strangled it with his bare hands. Thereafter he wore the lion's skin as a protection when he was fighting, for nothing could penetrate that magic covering.

The second labor: Hercules had to meet the Lernaean hydra. This creature lived in a swamp, and the odor of its body killed all who breathed its fetid fumes. Hercules began the battle but discovered that for every head he severed from the monster two more appeared. Finally he obtained a flaming brand from a friend and burned each head as he severed it. When he came to the ninth and invulnerable head, he cut it off and buried it under a rock. Then he dipped his arrows into the body of the hydra so that he would possess more deadly weapons for use in future conflicts.

The third labor: Hercules captured the Erymanthian boar and brought it back on his shoulders. The sight of the wild beast frightened Eurystheus so much that he hid in a large jar. With a fine sense of humor the hero deposited the captured boar in the same jar. While on this trip Hercules incurred the wrath of the centaurs by drinking wine which they had claimed for their own. In order to escape from them he had had to kill most of the half-horse men.

The fourth labor: Hercules had to capture a stag which had antlers of gold and hoofs of brass. In order to capture this creature Hercules pursued it for a whole year.

The fifth labor: The Stymphalian birds were carnivorous. Hercules alarmed them with a bell, shot many of them with his arrows, and caused the rest to fly away.

The sixth labor: Augeas, king of Elis, had a herd of three thousand oxen whose stables had not been cleansed for thirty years. Commanded to clean the stables, Hercules diverted the rivers Alpheus and Peneus through them and washed them clean in one day. Augeas refused the payment agreed to and as a result Hercules later declared war on him.

The seventh labor: Neptune had given a sacred bull to Minos king of Crete. Minos' wife, Pasiphaë, fell in love with the animal and pursued it around the island. Hercules overcame the bull and took it back to Eurystheus by making it swim the sea while he rode upon its back.

The eighth labor: Like the Stymphalian birds, the mares of Diomedes fed on human flesh. Usually Diomedes found food for them by feeding to them all travelers who landed on his shores. Diomedes tried to prevent Hercules from driving away his herd. He was killed and his body was fed to his own beasts.

The ninth labor: Admeta, daughter of Eurystheus, persuaded her father to send Hercules for the girdle of Hippolyta, queen of the Amazons. The Amazon queen was willing to give up her girdle, but Juno interfered by telling the other Amazons that Hercules planned to kidnap their queen. In the battle that followed Hercules killed Hippolyta and took the girdle from her dead body.

The tenth labor: Geryoneus, a three-bodied, three-headed, six-legged, winged monster possessed a herd of oxen. Ordered to bring the animals to Eurystheus, Hercules traveled beyond the pillars of Hercules, now Gibraltar. He killed a two-headed shepherd dog and a giant herdsman, and finally slew Geryones. He loaded the cattle on a boat and sent them to Eurystheus. He himself returned afoot across the Alps. He had many adventures on the way, including a fight with giants in the Phlegraean fields, near the present site of Naples.

The eleventh labor: His next labor was more difficult, for his task was to obtain the golden apples in the garden of the Hesperides. No one knew where the garden was, and so Hercules set out to roam until he found it. In his travels he killed a giant, a host of pygmies, and burned alive some of his captors in Egypt. In India he set Prometheus free. At last he discovered Atlas holding up the sky. This task Hercules assumed, releasing Atlas to go after the apples. Atlas returned with the apples and reluctantly took up his burden. Hercules brought the apples safely to Eurystheus.

The twelfth labor: This was the most difficult of all his labors. After many adventures he brought the three-headed dog Cerberus from the underworld. He was forced to carry the struggling animal in his arms because he had been forbidden to use weapons of any kind. Afterward he took Cerberus back to the king of the underworld. So ended the labors of this mighty ancient hero.

HEREWARD THE WAKE

Type of work: Novel
Author: Charles Kingsley (1819-1875)
Type of plot: Historical romance
Time of plot: Eleventh century
Locale: England, Scotland, Flanders
First published: 1866

Principal characters:
HEREWARD THE WAKE, a Saxon thane and outlaw
LADY GODIVA, his mother
TORFRIDA, his wife
ALFTRUDA, his second wife
MARTIN LIGHTFOOT, a companion in his wanderings
WILLIAM THE CONQUEROR, Duke of Normandy and King of England

Critique:

Hereward the Wake is one of the very few stories that deal realistically and credibly with the Anglo-Saxon period of English history. Although elements of the chivalric romance, in the more academic sense of that term, are present in this novel, Kingsley has re-created the age and its people in a believable and highly interesting manner. *Hereward the Wake* is both an interesting story and a valuable historical study.

The Story:

Hereward was the son of the powerful Lord of Bourne, a Saxon nobleman of a family close to the throne. A high-spirited, rebellious youth, he was a source of constant worry to his mother, Lady Godiva. Hereward lacked a proper respect for the Church and its priests and lived a boisterous life with boon companions who gave him their unquestioning loyalty.

One day a friar came to Lady Godiva and revealed that Hereward and his friends had attacked him and robbed him of what the priest insisted was money belonging to the Church. Lady Godiva was angry and hurt. When Hereward came in and admitted his crime, she said that there was no alternative. For his own good, she maintained, he should be declared a wake, or outlaw. Upon his promise not to molest her messenger, for Hereward really did not mind being outlawed as he wished to see more of the world, Lady Godiva sent Martin Lightfoot, a servant, to carry the news of Hereward's deed to his father and to the king. Hereward was then declared an outlaw subject to imprisonment or death.

Before he left his father's house, however, he released his friends from their oath of allegiance. Martin Lightfoot begged to be allowed to follow him, not as his servant but as his companion. Then Hereward set out to live among the rude and barbarous Scottish tribes of the north.

His first adventure occurred when he killed a huge bear that threatened the life of Alftruda, ward of a knight named Gilbert of Ghent. For his valorous deed he achieved much renown. But the knights of Gilbert's household, jealous of Hereward's courage and his prowess, tried to kill him. Though he escaped the snares laid for him, he decided that it would be best for him to leave Scotland.

Accordingly, he went to Cornwall, where he was welcomed by the king. There the king's daughter was pledged in marriage to a prince of Waterford. But a giant of the Cornish court had become so powerful that he had forced the king's agreement to give his daughter in marriage to the ogre. Hereward, with the help of the princess and a friar, slew the giant, whose death freed the princess to marry the prince whom she really loved.

After leaving Cornwall, Hereward and his companions were wrecked upon the Flemish coast. There Hereward stayed for a time in the service of Baldwin of Flanders and proved his valor by defeating the French in battle. There, too, Torfrida, a lady wrongly suspected of sorcery, schemed to win his love. They were wed after Hereward had fought in a successful campaign against the Hollanders, and a daughter was born of the marriage.

Meanwhile King Edward had died and Harold reigned in England. A messenger came to Hereward with the news that Duke William of Normandy had defeated the English at the battle of Hastings and that King Harold had been killed. Hereward then decided to return to Bourne, his old home. There, accompanied by Martin Lightfoot, he found the Norman raiders encamped. He found too that his family had been despoiled of all its property and that his mother had been sent away. He and Martin, without revealing their identity, secretly went out and annihilated all the Normans in the area. Hereward swore that he would return with an army that would push the Norman invaders into the sea.

Hereward then went to his mother, who received him happily. Lady Godiva accused herself of having wronged her son and lamented the day she had proclaimed him an outlaw. He took her to a place of refuge in Croyland Abbey. Later he went to the monastery where his aged, infirm uncle, Abbot Brand, was spending his last days on earth. There Hereward was knighted by the monks, after the English fashion. Hereward went secretly to Bourne and there recruited a rebel army to fight against Duke William.

Although there were many men eager to fight the Normans, the English forces were disunited. Another king, an untried young man, had been proclaimed, but because of his youth he did not have the support of all the English factions. Hereward had been promised help from Denmark, but the Danish king sent a poor leader through whose stupidity the Danes were inveigled into positions where they were easily defeated by the Normans at Dover and Norwich. Then, instead of coming to Hereward's aid, the Danes fled. Hereward was forced to confess the failure of his allies to his men, but they renewed their pledge to him and promised to keep on fighting. The situation seemed hopeless when Hereward and his men took refuge on the island of Ely. There, with Torfrida's wise advice, Hereward defeated Duke William's attack upon the beleaguered island. Hereward and his men retreated to another camp of refuge.

Shortly afterward Torfrida learned of Hereward's infidelity with Alftruda, the ward of Gilbert of Ghent. She left Hereward and went to Croyland Abbey, where she proposed to spend the last of her days ministering to the poor and to Hereward's mother. Hereward himself went to Duke William and submitted to him. The conqueror declared that he had selected a husband for Hereward's daughter. In order to free herself from Hereward, Torfrida falsely confessed that she was a sorceress, and her marriage to Hereward was annulled by the Church. Hereward then married Alftruda and became Lord of Bourne under Duke William. His daughter, despite her entreaties, was married to a Norman knight.

But Hereward, the last of the English, had many enemies among the French, who continually intrigued against him for the favor of Duke William. As a result, Hereward was imprisoned. The jailer was a good man who treated his noble prisoner as kindly as he could, although, for his own sake, he was forced to chain Hereward.

One day, while Hereward was being transported from one prison to another, he was rescued by his friends. Freed, he went back to Alftruda at Bourne, but his life was not a happy one. His enemies plotted to kill him. Taking advantage of a day when his retainers were escorting Alftruda on a journey, a group of Norman knights broke into Bourne castle. Though Hereward fought valiantly, he was outnumbered. He was killed and his head was exhibited in victory over the door of his own hall.

When she heard of his death, Torfrida came from Croyland Abbey and demanded Hereward's body. All were so frightened, especially Alftruda, by Torfrida's wild appearance and her reputation as a witch, that Hereward's first wife got her way and the body was delivered to her. She carried it away to Croyland for burial. Thus did Hereward, the last of the English, die, and thus, too, did William of Normandy become William the Conqueror and King of England.

H. M. S. PINAFORE

Type of work: Comic opera
Author: W. S. Gilbert (1836-1911)
Type of plot: Humorous satire
Time of plot: Latter half of the nineteenth century
Locale: Portsmouth harbor, England
First presented: 1878

Principal characters:

JOSEPHINE, the Captain's daughter
RALPH, the lowly sailor who loves Josephine
SIR JOSEPH PORTER, First Lord of the Admiralty, and Josephine's suitor
THE CAPTAIN, Josephine's father
LITTLE BUTTERCUP, who loves the Captain

Critique:

W. S. Gilbert shared the honors of this operetta with his composer-partner, Sir Arthur Sullivan. *H. M. S. Pinafore;* or, *The Lass That Loved A Sailor* was written to be sung and acted on the stage; it was not meant to be published and read by itself. Gilbert and Sullivan obviously were poking fun at the extravagances of grand opera, and at the improbable plots in particular. The plot of *Pinafore,* which effectively disregards the element of time, is a successful vehicle of comedy and satire. Every song, every scene is full of mischievous and clever rhymes, adroit and ingenious dialogue.

The Story:

Lying at anchor in Portsmouth harbor, the *Pinafore* was the scene of hectic activity, for Sir Joseph Porter, K.C.B., First Lord of the Admiralty, had announced his intention to visit the ship. The sailors swabbed the decks and were inspected by the Captain, who was as content with them as they were with him. One member of the crew, however, was far from happy. Ralph, the lowly foremast hand, was sunk in gloom and despair. He loved Josephine, the Captain's daughter, but because of his low rank she repulsed his advances and rejected his love.

Before Sir Joseph's arrival, Little Buttercup came on board, plying her trade as a seller of ribbons and laces, scissors and knives, treacle and toffee. In a conversation with the Captain she hinted that appearances are often deceiving. The Captain noticed that Little Buttercup had physical charms not displeasing to him.

Sir Joseph's barge approached, and the First Lord was soon on board, accompanied by his sisters, his cousins, and his aunts. After inspecting the crew, he gave them instructions for success. His own formula had been simple enough. He had polished door handles, stuck close to his desk, and never gone to sea. Sir Joseph then proceeded to the purpose of his visit. He had come to ask Josephine to marry him.

Josephine had no intention of marrying Sir Joseph, whom she disliked. Not able to give an outright refusal, she informed him that marriage with such a high-ranking officer was impossible because she was only a captain's daughter. Sir Joseph admired her modesty, but brushed the objection aside. Rank, he assured her, was absolutely no barrier, for love leveled all rank. Josephine hastened to agree with him, and everyone immediately assumed that a marriage would soon take place.

Giving up all hope of winning Josephine, Ralph put a pistol to his head and prepared to pull the trigger. At that moment Josephine rushed in, told him not to destroy himself, and proclaimed her undying love for him. At this turn of events there was general rejoicing among Ralph's messmates, with the exception of an unsavory character by the name of Dick Dead-eye.

The couple laid plans to steal ashore the next evening to be married. Once the ceremony was performed, they reasoned, nobody could do anything about it. But Dick Dead-eye went to the Captain and warned him of the plan. Accordingly, just as the lovers and their accomplices were quietly tiptoeing away, the Captain entered, enraged at Ralph's presumption and at the low company in which he found his daughter. Ralph was thrown into the brig.

Attracted by the Captain's swearing, Sir Joseph came rushing up in time to hear what had happened. The sisters, the cousins, and the aunts were horribly shocked. Sir Joseph was equally shocked, so shocked that he administered a very severe rebuke to the Captain. In the midst of the argument, Little Buttercup appeared. To the astonishment of everyone, she announced that many years ago she had been a baby-farmer. Two infants had been put into her care, one of lowly birth, the other of high position. Because she was very fond of one of them she had changed them around. The Captain was really of low birth, and Ralph was the patrician.

This astounding announcement resulted in a very odd situation which was quickly and amicably arranged. The Captain changed places with Ralph, who became captain instead. Sir Joseph announced that he could not marry Josephine since she was only the daughter of a common sailor. Accordingly, Josephine married Ralph; the Captain married Little Buttercup, and Sir Joseph had no one to marry except a well-born cousin.

HONEY IN THE HORN

Type of work: Novel
Author: H. L. Davis (1896-)
Type of plot: Regional romance
Time of plot: 1906-1908
Locale: Oregon
First published: 1935

Principal characters:

CLAY CALVERT, a migrant worker
WADE SHIVELEY, his stepfather
UNCLE PRESS SHIVELEY, Wade's father
LUCE, Clay's woman
THE HORSE TRADER, Luce's father

Critique:

The story told in this novel is less important than the character studies of some people who settled Oregon in the early part of this century. In his introduction the author states that he is neither criticizing any social group nor suggesting reforms; rather, he attempts to give an accurate picture of the migrants who were always seeking new homes in better lands. The story itself is excellent, however—fast-moving and interestingly told. There have been many novels of pioneers and early settlers during the last two decades, but few surpass *Honey in the Horn.*

The Story:

Wade Shiveley had killed his own

brother in a fight over a squaw and had murdered and robbed old man Howell. Now he had been captured. The officers wanted Uncle Press Shiveley, Wade's father, to try to get Wade to say where he had hidden the money. But Uncle Press had threatened to shoot Wade if he ever laid eyes on him again, and so in his place he sent Clay Calvert, the son of one of Wade's wives. Clay did not want to go because he also hated Wade. Uncle Press gave Clay a gun to slip to Wade in the jail. Having loaded the gun with blank cartridges, he hoped Wade would use the worthless gun to attempt an escape and thus be shot down by the officers.

On the way to the jail, Clay met a horse trader and his wife and daughter. When Clay slipped the gun to Wade in the jail, Wade said that he had not killed Howell, that Howell was killed by a bullet that split when it was fired and that such a bullet did not fit his own gun. Wade had always been a liar, but Clay suspected that this time he might be telling the truth.

Clay left town to hide in Wade's abandoned shack until after Wade had been killed and buried. Later Uncle Press sent a half-breed Indian to tell him that Wade had escaped and that the sheriff was now looking for Clay as an accomplice. Clay left the shack with the Indian, taking with him Wade's rifle he had found there, and after traveling awhile they met the horse trader and his women again. Clay learned that the girl was called Luce and that she traveled around with her father and stepmother, trading horses, racing them, and picking hops in season. Since he wanted to get out of the immediate territory and because he was strongly attracted to Luce, Clay decided to travel with the horse trader's family. The Indian stole Wade's rifle from Clay and ran away.

Clay and the horse trader's family worked for a time in the hop fields. The trader was a weak man who lost all he and his family earned by gambling, and Luce took the responsibility for the family on her shoulders. Clay and Luce liked each other very much, but they quarreled frequently, and one day Clay moved away from the wagon. When the sheriff appeared at the field one day, Clay became frightened and left hurriedly, traveling toward the coast.

Luce and her folks found him after awhile, and Luce and Clay decided to stay together. There was no place for them to get married. They spent the winter in a little settlement on the coast, in a cabin apart from the horse trader's. Luce rescued some bags of flour which had floated to shore from a wrecked ship, and with money earned by selling the flour to the Indians she and Clay were able to buy a wagon and start on their own.

Clay and Luce left for eastern Oregon, but Clay refused to let her father and stepmother go with them, for he could not stand the sight of the weak horse trader. They traveled across the mountains and into Looking Glass Valley, where they joined another group of settlers led by Clark Burdon. Burdon described to Clay a stranger who was looking for him, and Clay knew the man was Wade. Clay liked Burdon and told him the story of Wade and his killings and escape. Burdon promised to help him get rid of Wade. That night Clay shot a man he thought was Wade, but the dead prowler turned out to be the son of one of the settlers. When Burdon and Clay declared that Wade had shot the boy, the men formed a posse and captured Wade. After Wade tried to kill Clay, the men believed that the outlaw was trying to keep Clay from testifying against him; and the posse vowed to hang Wade. Clay felt guilty, for he doubted that Wade had killed Howell and he knew that he himself had shot the prowler. But it was his life or Wade's, and so he kept silent. He felt dirty and sick when he saw Wade hanged.

The settlers traveled eastward, Clay

and Luce with them. Luce had a miscarriage. She would not let Clay go for a doctor, for she was terrified that he would leave her and never come back. The rest of the caravan had gone on and they were alone. Clay finally left Luce, promising to return with help as soon as possible. He came back with an Indian midwife, to find that Luce had gone away in the wagon. There were two sets of wagon wheels, and Clay knew instinctively that her father had come by and that Luce had left with him. Angry and hurt by her desertion, Clay decided to go on alone.

He rode his horse into the threshing country and worked with a mowing crew. There he met the half-breed from the Shiveley ranch and told the Indian to be on the lookout for Luce and her father. The Indian did meet the horse trader and made a large wager on a race with him. The horse trader lost the race and the Indian collected the money. Next day the Indian was found with a bullet in the back of his head and no money in his clothing, and the horse trader and Luce had disappeared. Clay helped bury the Indian, but before the burial he shot Wade's rifle, which the Indian had stolen. The bullet did not split. Clay knew then that Wade had been telling the truth about not killing Howell. He suspected that Luce's father had killed and robbed both Howell and the Indian.

Clay joined a party moving on to a railroad construction camp. On their way there was an accident, and one of the horses had to be killed. When Clay saw the horse, he recognized it as one belonging to Luce's father, and he knew that she was in the group. He volunteered to shoot the horse, but first he found Luce and asked for her rifle. With it he killed the animal and later, examining the bullet, he saw that it was split. When he told her that the trader had murdered Howell and the Indian, she claimed she had done the killings. She said that her father, who was now dead, had lost a lot of money to Howell and that her stepmother and Howell had fought. Luce had shot the old man during the fight and had taken the money her father had lost to him. Later she killed the Indian because he had won her father's money in the horse race.

Clay suspected that Luce was trying to protect her dead father. Besides, he still wanted her. He climbed into her wagon and they joined the long line of settlers who were still seeking a place where they could make real homes. Whatever their past, they would always go on together.

THE HOOSIER SCHOOLMASTER

Type of work: Novel
Author: Edward Eggleston (1837-1902)
Type of plot: Regional romance
Time of plot: About 1850
Locale: Indiana
First published: 1871

Principal characters:

RALPH HARTSOOK, a young schoolmaster
BUD MEANS, Ralph's pupil and friend
HANNAH THOMSON, the Means' bound-girl
DR. SMALL, Ralph's enemy
PETE JONES, Dr. Small's partner in crime
WALTER JOHNSON, Ralph's cousin, one of the robbers
MARTHA HAWKINS, Bud Means' sweetheart
SHOCKY, Hannah's brother

Critique:

Eggleston wrote *The Hoosier Schoolmaster* as a regional study. In it he caught the Hoosiers of his day, with their singular twists of phrasing, their rough frontier conduct. His simple plots, stock characters and thinly-disguised morality were all subordinate to his main purpose. If *The Hoosier Schoolmaster* is not a great book, it certainly is not to be overlooked, for its author faithfully recorded the place and time he wished to describe.

The Story:

Ralph Hartsook had not thought schoolteachers were judged by their muscular ability when he applied for the job as schoolmaster of Flat Creek, Indiana. Before long, however, he learned his competence would be judged by his power to keep his pupils from driving him out of the schoolhouse. His first step was to make friends with Bud and Bill Means, sons of the school trustee, in whose house he was to board for a time. He was tired from the ten miles he had trudged to apply for his job, but he walked almost the same distance that evening when he went coon hunting with the boys.

Ralph Hartsook held his own against the pranks and challenges of his pupils until the night of the big spelling-bee. Then before most of the people in Flat Creek he was defeated by the Means' bound-girl, Hannah Thomson.

Finding himself strongly attracted to the girl, he escorted her home after the spelling-bee.

Kept awake by curiosity about Hannah's past, Ralph had trouble sleeping that night. At two in the morning he got up, restless, and strolled down the road toward the schoolhouse. Three horsemen passed him in the darkness, one riding a horse with white markings. A few minutes later Dr. Small rode by, returning, Ralph supposed, from a night call. He went back to Pete Jones' house, where he was staying at the time. The next morning he discovered that the horse with the white markings stood in Pete's stable, and he learned from Shocky Thomson, Hannah's young brother, that there had been a robbery the night before.

He decided not to tell what he knew. He had no proof that Pete Jones was connected with the housebreaking and it would have been awkward to explain his own ramblings at an early hour. To add to his misery that day, Mirandy Means, who had been casting sheep's eyes at him, informed him that her brother Bud was fond of Hannah.

Squire Hawkins invited Ralph to spend the weekend with him. Walking toward the squire's house with Shocky, who took the same direction home from school, he learned from the boy that his father was dead and his blind mother in the poorhouse. When Hannah went to live with the Means, he himself had been taken in by Mr. Pearson, a basket-maker.

That evening Ralph was surprised to see Dr. Small's horse tied in front of Granny Sander's cabin. She had a reputation as a witch among the people of Flat Creek, and she was a malicious gossip. Ralph did not know that the doctor was busy planting the seeds of rumors in Granny Sander's mind, rumors that Ralph had been a philanderer at home, and that he was somehow implicated in the robbery. Small disliked Ralph, though Ralph had never been able to find any reason for it. Rumor had done its ugly work by Sunday morning. At church Ralph's neighbors had little to say to him.

On Christmas Day, which came the following week, the boys did not follow the custom of asking the teacher for a holiday. Instead Bud and others of the older pupils barricaded themselves in the schoolhouse to keep Ralph from entering and had to be forced out by sulphur thrown down the chimney. Later Bud threatened to thrash Ralph because the schoolmaster had taken the squire's niece,

Martha, to church the Sunday before. Bud was jealous. Ralph immediately declared he was really inclined toward Hannah, but had avoided seeing her because of Mirandy's statement. He and Ralph quickly became fast friends. Now, the schoolmaster felt, he had a clear field for courting.

Before Bud and Ralph finished their talk, Shocky burst into the schoolhouse with the news that Mr. Pearson was about to be tarred and feathered by the people of Flat Creek, who had been led by Pete Jones to believe the basket-maker was guilty of the robbery. Pearson, too, had seen three men riding by on the night of the robbery, and Jones had decided the best way to divert suspicion from himself would be to accuse Shocky's benefactor.

Hoping to protect the old man, Bud Means started toward the Pearson home. On the way he met Jones to whom he gave a sound drubbing.

That night Bud helped Pearson to escape to his brother's home in the next county. To thwart Pete Jones' efforts to have Shocky Thomson bound out by declaring the Pearsons paupers, Ralph took the boy to stay with his friend, Miss Nancy Sawyer, in his home town of Lewisburg. His aunt, Mrs. Matilda White, refused to have Shocky's mother in her house because she was a pauper, and so, at Miss Sawyer's own suggestion, Mrs. Thomson was brought to the Sawyer home to spend the weekend with her son. Through Miss Sawyer's efforts, a collection was taken up at church that Sunday afternoon, and with that donation and the money she earned knitting socks, Mrs. Thompson was able to make a home of her own for Shocky.

That same Sunday Bud, intending to ask Martha to marry him, visited Squire Hawkins' house. Suddenly bashful, he told her only of the spelling-bee to take place at the schoolhouse on Tuesday night. Shortly afterward the squire received an anonymous letter, threatening him with the burning of his barn if Martha associated with Bud, the implication being that Bud was incriminated in the robbery. The squire persuaded Martha to ignore Bud. Chagrined by her refusal to let him escort her home from the spelling-bee, Bud began to cultivate Pete Jones and his friends, among them Dr. Small and Walter Johnson, Ralph's cousin.

Bud soon proved he was still Ralph's friend. One day Hannah brought Ralph a letter Bud had sent warning him that he was suspected of the robbery and that there was a plan afoot to tar and feather him that night. Ralph saved himself from the mob by going to a nearby town and giving himself up to the authorities there. His trial was held the next day.

All of Flat Creek was present to see the schoolmaster convicted. Mrs. Means and Pete Jones, particularly, were willing to offer damaging testimony, the former because Ralph had spurned Mirandy's attentions. It was Dr. Small who vindicated Ralph, however, by overshooting the mark in his anxiety to clear himself of Ralph's testimony that the doctor had been out on the night of the robbery.

Small had Walter Johnson called to the stand to testify they had spent the evening together in the physician's office. But Johnson, at a prayer meeting he had attended with Bud, had been deeply impressed by the minister's warning of eternal damnation for sinners. Summoned before the court, he gave way to his guilty conscience and declared that he, Small, Pete Jones, and Pete's brother had committed the robbery, and that Ralph and Mr. Pearson were innocent.

Walter Johnson went free because of his testimony, but Dr. Small, who had been the ringleader of the band, was hanged. Jones and his brother were given prison sentences.

Ralph Hartsook returned to Lewisburg to teach in a new academy there. Shortly afterward he married Hannah. At Ralph's wedding Bud found his courage at last and proposed to Martha.

HORSESHOE ROBINSON

Type of work: Novel
Author: John P. Kennedy (1795-1870)
Type of plot: Historical romance
Time of plot: 1780
Locale: The Carolinas
First published: 1835

Principal characters:
SERGEANT HORSESHOE ROBINSON, a colonial patriot
MAJOR ARTHUR BUTLER, his friend
MR. LINDSAY, a Loyalist
MILDRED, Lindsay's daughter
HENRY, Lindsay's son
WAT ADAIR, a Tory
TYRREL, a British officer
MARY MUSGROVE, a patriot
JOHN RAMSAY, Mary's sweetheart

Critique:

Horseshoe Robinson, A Tale of the Tory Ascendency is a love story and a war story. A good narrative description of the effect of the American Revolution on the people of the Carolinas, the novel is unspoiled by flag-waving sentimentality. Horseshoe Robinson is a hunter and a woodsman with a personality much like that of our common story-book conception of early American pioneers. The love story is important in this novel, but it is trivial compared to the importance of the war itself. From a historical point of view, the book makes a valuable contribution with its portrayal of the confusion caused by divided loyalties between England and the Colonies.

The Story:

In the secluded back country of South Carolina two men in the service of the revolutionary colonial forces were traveling together. They were Major Arthur Butler and his shrewd sergeant, a man known throughout the region as Horseshoe Robinson, because of his former occupation as a blacksmith. Although they passed as chance travelers, they were on a secret mission to trace the movements of the enemy and to enlist aid for the cause of colonial independence.

Before setting out on their dangerous journey, Arthur Butler was moved to stop near Dove-Cote, the residence of Mr. Lindsay, a Loyalist gentleman who had come to this territory to live because he wished to avoid the conflict between the colonists and the British government. He himself was loyal to the crown because of financial interests in England, but his son Henry was sympathetic to the American cause. Mildred, Lindsay's daughter, was in love with Arthur Butler, but because of the major's connections with the colonial army Mr. Lindsay had forbidden her to see Butler. For this reason they met secretly in a grove not far from Dove-Cote. After the meeting she returned unseen to Mr. Lindsay's house, and Butler and Horseshoe Robinson went to the inn of Mistress Dimock, not far away.

That night at the inn Horseshoe encountered a Tory spy named James Curry, a stealthy rascal who was passing as the servant of Mr. Tyrrel, a guest at Dove-Cote. Tyrrel, a disguised British officer, was often at Mr. Lindsay's home, ostensibly to secure that gentleman's aid for the Loyalists, but in reality to court Mildred, who despised him and everything he stood for. Seeing Curry at the inn, Horseshoe knew that Tyrrel was again visiting Dove-Cote. Although he let the fellow escape, he was afraid that Tyrrel and Curry might cause trouble for

Butler and himself on their trip through South Carolina.

Major Butler had been sent by General Gates on a mission to another rebel general in Georgia. With Horseshoe as a companion, the major felt certain that he could complete his undertaking. On their first night in the forest Horseshoe led Butler to the home of Wat Adair, an old friend whom he thought loyal to the rebel cause. However, Wat was not a true friend. Having been bought off by the Tories, he planned that night to direct Butler and Horseshoe to an ambush in the forest. But a relative of Wat, Mary Musgrove, overheard Wat plotting with another Tory, and being loyal to the rebels she whispered to Butler the plans she had learned.

Through her warning Horseshoe and Butler avoided one trap, only to fall into an ambush of some rough Tories, among them Curry. Fearing that the drunken crew planned to murder Butler and himself, Horseshoe escaped, hoping to rescue Butler later.

The family of Mary Musgrove was a rebel family, and Horseshoe proceeded to their home to get help in his plan. In addition, the family of Mary's sweetheart, John Ramsay, was a rebel family. With the Ramsays and the Musgroves, Horseshoe planned to engage the enemy and bring Butler to safety. Mary, pretending to be a vendor of fruit, was to enter the Tory camp where Butler was being held. There she was to communicate with the major and give him word of his rescuers' plans.

James Curry had charged Butler with conspiring to murder Mr. Lindsay, a loyal subject of the king. In order to disprove this charge, Horseshoe returned to Dove-Cote. Mildred's distress at the news of her lover's arrest had caused her father great grief, and he relented his stern stand against Butler and assured Mildred that he would not punish her for her concern over the major. When Horseshoe found Mildred and her brother Henry at Dove-Cote, Mr. Lindsay had gone off with Tyrrel to a meeting of Loyalists in a nearby town. Having heard Horseshoe's account of the charges against Butler, Mildred resolved to go to Cornwallis, the English general, and plead with him for Butler's life. Mildred was confident she could prove that Butler could never have had designs on the father of the girl he loved. Accompanied by Henry Lindsay and Horseshoe Robinson, she set out for Cornwallis' headquarters.

John Ramsay and Mary were able to effect Butler's escape from the camp where he was held prisoner, but John was killed before they reached a place of safety. Grief-stricken by the loss of her sweetheart, Mary attended the funeral services, which were conducted by her father, Allen Musgrove. While the services were going on, they were interrupted by some British troops, and Butler was once again taken prisoner.

When Mildred and her two companions succeeded in getting an interview with Cornwallis, the courtly general gave Mildred his promise that no harm would befall Butler. While the general was speaking with Mildred, he received a message that Butler had escaped. Mildred set out for Dove-Cote with Horseshoe and her brother. On their way they met Mary Musgrove, her family, and the Ramsays, who told them of Butler's second capture by British troops from a nearby camp. Again Mildred resolved to intercede on behalf of her lover, and Henry and Horseshoe agreed to accompany her.

While Mildred awaited an opportunity to seek Butler, the forces of the Loyalists and the rebels were engaging in the battle of King's Mountain. During the fighting Horseshoe rescued Butler and brought him safely back to Mildred. Then the two lovers revealed that they had been married for over a year, in a secret ceremony witnessed by Mistress Dimock and Henry Lindsay.

Wat Adair was captured, and Horseshoe saw to it that he received just punishment for betraying his American friends. Wat told Horseshoe that Tyrrel was really an English general who had bribed Wat to lead Butler and Horseshoe into a trap. Henry, who had participated in the battle, found Tyrrel's body lying among the dead and wounded. James Curry was captured by rebel forces. It seemed certain that the Tory ascendency in South Carolina was at an end.

But the happy reunion of the lovers was clouded by the death of Mr. Lindsay. When he learned that Mildred had gone to see Cornwallis, he set out to find her before the battle began. Following Tyrrel toward the scene of the fighting, Mr. Lindsay was fatally wounded and Tyrrel killed. Mildred and Henry were able to speak with their father before he died, however, and he lived long enough to take the hands of Mildred and Butler and forgive them for having disobeyed him. He died shortly afterward in a delirium brought on by his fever.

Mildred and Butler returned to Dove-Cote to live a long and prosperous life together.

THE HOUSE OF ATREUS

Type of work: Drama
Author: Aeschylus (525-456 B.C.)
Type of plot: Classical tragedy
Time of plot: After the fall of Troy
Locale: Argos
First presented: 458 B.C.

Principal characters:

AGAMEMNON, the king
CLYTEMNESTRA, his queen
CASSANDRA, a Trojan captive
AEGISTHUS, paramour of Clytemnestra
ORESTES, son of Agamemnon
ELECTRA, his sister

Critique:

In the archonship of Philocles, in 458 B.C., Aeschylus won first prize with his dramatic trilogy, *The House of Atreus.* This story of the doomed descendants of the cruel and bloody Atreus is one of the great tales of classic literature. Aeschylus, building his plays upon themes of doom and revenge, was deeply concerned with moral law in the Greek state. For this reason the moral issues of the plays are clear and steadfast, simple and devastating in implication, especially the working of conscience in the character of Orestes. *Agamemnon, The Libation-Bearers,* and *The Furies* are the individual titles which make up the trilogy.

The Story:

The house of Atreus was accursed because in the great palace at Argos the tyrant, Atreus, had killed the children of Thyestes and served their flesh to their father at a royal banquet. Agamemnon and Menelaus were the sons of Atreus. When Helen, wife of Menelaus, was carried off by Paris, Agamemnon was among the Greek heroes who went with his brother to battle the Trojans for her return. But on the way to Troy, while the fleet lay idle at Aulis, Agamemnon was prevailed upon to sacrifice his daughter, Iphigenia, to the gods. Hearing of this deed, Clytemnestra, his wife, vowed revenge. She gave her son, Orestes, into the care of the King of Phocis, and in the darkened palace nursed her consuming hate.

In her desire for vengeance she was joined by Aegisthus, surviving son of Thyestes, who had returned from his long exile. Hate brought the queen and Aegisthus together in a common cause;

they became lovers as well as plotters in crime.

The ship of Menelaus having been delayed by a storm, Agamemnon returned alone from the Trojan wars. A watchman first saw the lights of his ship upon the sea and brought to his queen the news of the king's return. Leaving his men quartered in the town, Agamemnon drove to the palace in his chariot, beside him Cassandra, captive daughter of the king of Troy and an augeress of all misfortunes to come, who had fallen to Agamemnon in the division of the spoils. She had already warned the king that some evil was to befall him.

Agamemnon, however, had no suspicions of his homecoming, as Clytemnestra came to greet him at the palace doorway, her armed retainers about her, magnificent carpets unrolled for the feet of the conqueror of Troy. Agamemnon chided his queen for the lavishness of her reception and entered the palace to refresh himself after his long journey. He asked Clytemnestra to receive Cassandra and to treat his captive kindly.

After Agamemnon had retired, Clytemnestra returned and ordered Cassandra, who had refused to leave the chariot, to enter the palace. When Cassandra persisted in remaining where she was, the queen declared she would not demean herself by bandying words with a common slave and a madwoman. She reentered the palace. Cassandra lifted her face toward the sky and called upon Apollo to tell her why she had been brought to this cursed house. She informed the spectators in front of the palace that Clytemnestra would murder Agamemnon. She lamented the fall of Troy, recalled the butchery of Thyestes' children, and the doom that hung over the sons of Atreus, and foretold again the murder of Agamemnon by his queen. As she entered the palace, those outside heard the death cry of Agamemnon within.

A moment later Clytemnestra appeared in the doorway, the bloody sword of Aegisthus in her hand. Behind her lay the body of the king, entangled in the rich carpets. Clytemnestra defended herself before the citizens, saying she had killed the king for the murder of Iphigenia, and had also killed Cassandra, with whom Agamemnon had shamed her honor. Her deed, she told the citizens defiantly, had ended the bloody lust of the house of Atreus.

Then she presented Aegisthus, son of Thyestes, who asserted that his vengeance was just and that he intended to rule in the palace of Agamemnon. Reproaches were hurled at the guilty pair. There were cries that Orestes would avenge his father's murder. Aegisthus and Clytemnestra, in a fury of guilty horror, roared out their self-justification for the crime and defied the gods themselves to end their seizure of power.

Orestes, grown to manhood, returned from the land of Phocis, to discover that his mother and Aegisthus had murdered his father. He mourned his father's death and asked the king of the gods to give him ability to take vengeance upon the guilty pair. Electra, daughter of Agamemnon, also mourned and cursed the murderers. Encountering her brother, she did not at first recognize him, for he appeared in the disguise of a messenger who brought word of the death of Orestes. They met at their father's tomb, where he made himself known to his sister. There he begged his father's spirit to give him strength in his undertaking. Electra assured him nothing but evil could befall any of the descendants of Atreus and welcomed the quick fulfillment of approaching doom.

Learning that Clytemnestra had once dreamed of suckling a snake which drew blood from her breast, Orestes saw in this dream the image of himself and the deed he intended to commit. He went to the palace in disguise and killed Aegisthus. Then he confronted Clytemnestra, his sword dripping with the blood of his mother's lover, and struck her down.

Orestes displayed the two bodies to

the people and announced to Apollo that he had done the deed required of him. But he realized that he must suffer for his terrible crime. He began to go mad as Furies, sent by his mother's dead spirit, pursued him.

The Furies drove Orestes from land to land. Finally he took refuge in a temple, but the Pythian priestess claimed the temple was profaned by the presence of the horrible Furies, who lay asleep near Orestes. Then Apollo appeared to tell Orestes that he had put the Furies to sleep so the haunted man could get some rest. He advised Orestes to visit the temple of Pallas Athena and there gain full absolution for his crime.

While Orestes listened, the ghost of Clytemnestra spitefully aroused the Furies and commanded them to torture Orestes again. When Apollo ordered the Furies to leave, the creatures accused him of blame for the murder of Clytemnestra and Aegisthus and the punishment of Orestes. The god confessed he had demanded the death of Agamemnon's murderers. He was told that by his demands he had caused an even greater crime, matricide. Apollo said Athena should decide the justice of the case.

In Athens, in the temple of the goddess, Orestes begged Athena to help him. Replying the case was too grave for her to decide alone, she called upon the judges to help her reach a wise decision. There were some who believed the ancient laws would be weakened if evidence were presented, and they claimed Orestes deserved his terrible punishment.

When Orestes asked why Clytemnestra had not been persecuted for the murder of Agamemnon, he was told her crime had not been the murder of a blood relative, as his was. Apollo was another witness at the trial. He claimed the mother was not the true parent, that the father, who planted the seed in the mother's womb, was the real parent, as shown in the tracing of descent through the male line. Therefore, Orestes was not guilty of the murder of a true member of his blood family.

The judges decided in favor of Orestes. There were many, however, who in an angry rage cursed and condemned the land where such a judgment might prevail. They cried woe upon the younger gods and all those who tried to wrest ancient rights from the hands of established tradition. But Athena upheld the judgment of the court and Orestes was freed from the anger of the Furies.

THE HOUSE OF MIRTH

Type of work: Novel
Author: Edith Wharton (1862-1937)
Type of plot: Social criticism
Time of plot: Early twentieth century
Locale: New York
First published: 1905

Principal characters:
Lily Bart, a social schemer
Mr. Selden, her friend
Mr. Rosedale, a financier
Percy Gryce, an eligible young man
Gus Trenor, a wealthy socialite
Judy Trenor, his wife
Bertha Dorset, who hated Lily
George Dorset, Bertha's husband

Critique:

The House of Mirth is still popular among readers who enjoy stories about the social life of the early part of this century. The theme of the book is a criticism of the emptiness and folly of life among the idle rich. Lily Bart sacrificed herself, her principles, her chance for real love, and even her life, in a vain attempt to find a life of ease for herself. The conflict arose when her better nature exerted itself. In that respect she was superior to those who scorned her, for most of them had no redeeming qualities of character. The story is easily read, for it is written with Edith Wharton's usual skill.

The Story:

Selden enjoyed watching Lily Bart put a new plan into operation. She was a very beautiful and clever young lady, and no matter how impromptu any action of hers appeared, Selden knew that she never moved without a definitely worked out plan.

Lily had almost no money of her own; her beauty and her good family background were her only assets. Her father had died soon after a reversal of his financial affairs, and her mother had drilled into her the idea that a wealthy marriage was her only salvation. After her mother's death, Lily was taken in by her aunt, Mrs. Peniston. Mrs. Peniston supplied her with fashionable clothes and a good home, but Lily needed jewels, gowns, and cash to play bridge if she were to move in a social circle filled by wealthy and eligible men.

Mr. Rosedale, a Jewish financier, would gladly have married Lily and provided her with a huge fortune, for he wanted to be accepted into the society in which Lily moved. But Lily thought that she still had other prospects less repulsive to her, the most likely one being Percy Gryce, who lived protected from scheming women by his watchful widowed mother.

Lily used her knowledge of his quiet life to her advantage. Selden, Lily, and Gryce were all house guests at the home of Gus and Judy Trenor, and the opportunity was a perfect one for Lily, who assumed the part of a shy, demure young girl. But when Gryce was ready to propose, she let the chance slip away from her, for Lily really hated the kind of person she had become. In addition, although Selden was poor and offered her no escape from her own poverty, she was attracted to him because only he really understood her.

Gus Trenor offered to invest some of Lily's small income, and over a period of time he returned to her more than eight thousand dollars, which he assured her was profit on the transaction. With that amount she was able to pay most of her creditors and reopen her charge accounts. Gus seemed to think, however, that his wise investment on her account should make them better friends than Lily felt was desirable.

In the meantime, Lily unexpectedly got possession of some letters which Bertha Dorset had written to Selden. Bertha had once loved Selden, but George Dorset's fortune was great and she had left Selden for George. She continued to write to Selden after her marriage.

When Gus Trenor began to get more insistent in his demands for Lily's companionship, she became really worried. She knew that people were talking about her a great deal and that her position in society was precarious. She turned to Selden for advice. He told her that he loved her for what she could be, but that he could give her nothing now. He had no money, and he would not even offer her his love because he could not love her as she was, a scheming, ruthless fortune-hunter.

One night Lily received a message that Judy Trenor wanted her to call. When she arrived at the Trenor home, Lily found Gus there alone. He had sent the message. Gus told her then that the money had not been profit on her investment, but a gift from him. When he intimated that she had always known the money was from him personally, Lily was terrified, but at last she managed to get out of the house. She knew then that there was only one thing for her to do. She must accept Rosedale's offer of marriage. But before she wrote to Rosedale accepting his offer, the Dorsets invited her to take a Mediterranean cruise on their yacht. The moment of decision was postponed for a time.

Selden also left New York. Unknown to her, he had seen Lily leave the Trenor house on the night Gus had tricked her into thinking Judy wanted her to call. Selden had always refused to believe the unsavory stories circulating about Lily, but the evidence of his own eyes, he thought, was too plain to be ignored. When he met Lily abroad, he treated her with courteous disinterest.

Lily returned to New York. Her aunt, Mrs. Peniston, had died, leaving Lily ten thousand dollars. Lily planned to repay Gus Trenor with her inheritance, and she found intolerable the delay in settling her aunt's estate. Meanwhile Bertha Dorset's insinuations about Lily's conduct abroad, coupled with the talk about Lily and Gus Trenor, finished Lily's reputation. She took various positions, until at last she was reduced to working in the factory of a milliner. She had first offered to accept Rosedale's former proposal of marriage, but she was no longer useful to Rosedale since her fall from favor, and he refused to marry her. He knew that Lily had the letters Bertha had written Selden, and he also knew that George Dorset no longer loved his wife and would gladly marry Lily. It seemed to Rosedale that Lily had only two alternatives, either to take George Dorset away from Bertha or to go to Bertha with the letters and force her to receive Lily once more.

At first Lily's feeling for Selden made her shrink from doing anything that would harm him. Then she lost her position. Without money to buy food or to pay for her room in a dingy boarding-house, she reluctantly took the letters and started to the Dorset home. On the way she stopped to see Selden. When he again told her that he loved her, or rather that he would love her if she would only give up her greed for wealth and position, she gave up her plan and, unseen by him, dropped the letters into the fireplace. Then she thanked him for the kindness he, and he alone, had given her, and walked out into the night.

When she returned to her room, she found the check for the ten thousand dollars of her inheritance. She sat down at once and wrote a check to Gus Trenor for the amount she owed him and put it in an envelope. In another envelope she placed the ten thousand dollar check and addressed the envelope to her bank. She put the two envelopes side by side on her desk before she lay down to sleep.

But sleep would not come. At last she took from her bureau a bottle of chloral, which she had bought for those nights when she could not sleep. She poured the contents of the bottle into a glass and drank the whole. Then she lay down again upon her bed.

The next morning, feeling a sudden need to see Lily at once, Selden went early to her rooming-house. There he found a doctor already in attendance and Lily dead from an overdose of chloral. On her desk he saw the two envelopes. The stub of the open checkbook beside them told the whole story of Lily's last effort to get her accounts straight before she died. He knew then that his love for her had been justified, but the words he spoke as he knelt by her bed came too late.

THE HOUSE OF THE SEVEN GABLES

Type of work: Novel
Author: Nathaniel Hawthorne (1804-1864)
Type of plot: Psychological romance
Time of plot: 1850
Locale: Salem, Massachusetts
First published: 1851

Principal characters:
Miss Hepzibah Pyncheon, a spinster
Clifford Pyncheon, her brother
Judge Jaffrey Pyncheon, a kinsman
Phoebe Pyncheon, a distant cousin
Mr. Holgrave, Miss Hepzibah's lodger

Critique:

The theme of Hawthorne's justly famous novel is obviously that the sins of the fathers are passed on to the children in succeeding generations. In the ingenious plot of this novel the reader watches the gradual expiation of old Matthew Maule's curse on the Pyncheon family, as youth in the guise of Phoebe and Holgrave enters the old house. Evident in the finely-written pages of *The House of the Seven Gables* is the author's lively interest in New England history, and his increasing doubts about a moribund New England that looked backward to past times.

The Story:

The House of the Seven Gables was a colonial house built in the English style of half-timber and half-plaster. It stood on Pyncheon Street in quiet Salem. The house had been built by Colonel Pyncheon, who had wrested the desirable site from Matthew Maule, a poor man executed as a wizard. Because Colonel Pyncheon was responsible and because he was taking the doomed man's land, Maule at the moment of his execution declared that God would give the Pyncheons blood to drink. But in spite of this grim prophecy the colonel had his house, and its builder was Thomas Maule, son of the old wizard.

Colonel Pyncheon, dying in his great oak chair just after the house had been completed, choked with blood so that his shirt front was stained scarlet. Although doctors explained the cause of his death as apoplexy, the townsfolk had not forgotten old Maule's prophecy. The time of the colonel's death was inauspicious. It was said he had just completed a treaty by which he had bought huge tracts of land from the Indians, but this deed had not been confirmed by the general court and was never discovered by any of his heirs. Rumor also had it that a man was seen leaving the house about the time Colonel Pyncheon died.

More recently another startling event had occurred at the House of the Seven Gables. Jaffrey Pyncheon, a bachelor, had been found dead in the colonel's great oaken armchair, and his nephew, Clifford Pyncheon, had been sentenced to imprisonment after being found guilty of the murder of his uncle.

These events were in the unhappy past, however, and in 1850, the House of the Seven Gables was the home of Miss Hepzibah Pyncheon, an elderly, single woman, who let one wing of the old house to a young man of radical tendencies, a maker of daguerreotypes, whose name was Mr. Holgrave.

Miss Hepzibah was about to open a shop in one of the rooms of her house. Her brother Clifford was coming home from the state prison after thirty years, and she had to earn money in some way to support him. But on the first day of her venture as a storekeeper Miss Hepzibah proved to be a failure. The situation was saved, however, by the arrival of young Phoebe Pyncheon from the country. Soon she was operating the shop at a profit.

Clifford arrived from the prison a broken man of childish, querulous ways. Once he tried to throw himself from a big arched window which afforded him almost his only contact with the outside world. He was fond of Phoebe, but Miss Hepzibah irritated him with her sullen scowling. For acquaintances Clifford had Uncle Venner, a handy man who did odd jobs for the neighborhood, and the tenant of the house, Mr. Holgrave, the daguerreotypist.

The only other relative living in town was the highly-respected Judge Pyncheon, another nephew of the old Jaffrey Pyncheon, for whose murder Clifford had spent thirty years in prison. He was, in fact, the heir of the murdered man and he had been somehow involved with Clifford's arrest and imprisonment. For these reasons Clifford refused to see him when the judge offered to give Clifford and Hepzibah a home at his countryseat.

Meanwhile, Phoebe had become friendly with Mr. Holgrave. In turn, he thought that she brought light and hope into the gloomy old house, and he missed her greatly when she returned to her home in the country. Her visit was to be a brief one, however, for she had gone only to make some preparations before coming to live permanently with Miss Hepzibah and Clifford.

Before Phoebe returned from the country, Judge Pyncheon visited the House of the Seven Gables and, over Miss Hepzibah's protest, insisted on seeing Clifford, who, he said, knew a family secret which meant great wealth for the judge. When at last she went out of the room to summon her brother, Judge Pyncheon sat down in the old chair by the fireplace, over which hung the portrait of the Colonel Pyncheon who had built the house. As the judge sat in the old chair, his ticking watch in his hand, an unusually strong family likeness could be noted between the stern judge and his Puritan ancestor in the portrait. Unable to find Clifford to deliver the judge's message, Miss Hepzibah returned. As she approached the door, Clifford appeared from within, laughing and pointing to the chair where the judge sat dead of apoplexy under the portrait of the old colonel. His shirt front was stained with blood. The wizard's curse had been fulfilled once more; God had given him blood to drink.

The two helpless old people were so distressed by the sight of the dead man that they crept away from the house without notifying anyone and departed on the train. The dead body of the judge remained seated in the chair.

It was some time before the body was discovered by Holgrave. When Phoebe returned to the house, he admitted her. He had not yet summoned the police because he wished to protect the old couple as long as possible. While he and Phoebe were alone in the house, Holgrave declared his love for her. They were interrupted by the return of Miss Hepzibah and the now calm Clifford. They had decided that to run away would not solve their problem.

The police attributed the judge's death to natural causes, and Clifford, Miss Hepzibah, and Phoebe became the heirs to his great fortune. It now seemed certain that Jaffrey Pyncheon had also died of natural causes, not by Clifford's hand, and that the judge had so arranged the evidence as to make Clifford appear a murderer.

In a short time all the occupants of the House of the Seven Gables were ready to move to the judge's country estate which they had inherited. They gathered for the last time in the old room under the dingy portrait of Colonel Pyncheon. Clifford said he had a vague memory of something mysterious connected with the picture. Holgrave offered to explain the mystery and pressed a secret spring near the picture. When he did so, the portrait fell to the floor, disclosing a recess in the wall. From this niche Holgrave drew out the ancient Indian deed to the lands which the Pyncheons had claimed. Clifford then remembered he had once found the secret spring. It was this secret which Judge Pyncheon had hoped to learn from Clifford.

Phoebe asked how Holgrave happened to know these facts. The young man explained his name was not Holgrave, but Maule. He was, he said, a descendant of the wizard, Matthew Maule, and of Thomas Maule who built the House of the Seven Gables. The knowledge of the hidden Indian deed had been handed down to the descendants of Thomas Maule, who built the compartment behind the portrait and secreted the deed there after the colonel's death. Holgrave was the last of the Maules and Phoebe, the last of the Pyncheons, would bear his name. Matthew Maule's curse had been expiated.

HOW GREEN WAS MY VALLEY

Type of work: Novel
Author: Richard Llewellyn (Richard D. V. Llewellyn Lloyd, 1907-   )
Type of plot: Domestic realism
Time of plot Nineteenth century
Locale: Wales
First published: 1940

Principal characters:
GWILYM MORGAN, a Welsh miner
BETH MORGAN, his wife
HUW MORGAN, their son and the narrator
IVOR,
DAVY,
OWEN,
IANTO, and
GWILYM, other sons
ANGHARAD, their daughter
BRONWEN, Ivor's wife
MARGED, Gwilym's wife
IESTYN EVANS, Angharad's husband

Critique:

How Green Was My Valley is a story of the life of a Welsh boy, seen through the eyes of an old man who has only memory to sustain him. The novel was published during the war years, and perhaps the strife that was everywhere then accounted somewhat for its great popularity. There was trouble in the lives of the people we meet in this story, but the kindness of the main characters was so great that even death seemed gentle and not to be feared. The novel is simply and beautifully told.

The Story:

How beautiful and peaceful the valley looked to Huw Morgan when he was ready to leave it! All the memories of a long lifetime came back to him.

Huw's earliest memories were of his father and brothers when they came home from the mines on Saturday night. There was trouble brewing at the mines. The men talked of unions and organizing, and the owners were angry.

Huw loved his family very much, and when he learned that his brother Ivor was to marry he was sorry to lose his brother. But from the first moment Huw saw Ivor's Bronwen, he loved her, and that love for his sister-in-law stayed with him all of his life.

Another brother, Ianto, married soon afterward. His wife was a girl from the village, where Ianto went to live.

Trouble came at last to the mines. The men in the pits went on strike for twenty-two weeks, but the owners were the stronger because they were not watching their families starve. The men finally went back to work for less money than before. After that first strike, the father would never again join the men trying to form a union, for he could not bring himself to lead men out of work. Davy and the other boys, however, were more bitter than ever. When the father ordered his sons never to attend another meeting, Davey, Owen, and Gwilym left home and took a room in a lodging-house. Their mother cried all night, but the father would not change his mind. It was a miserable time for six-year-old Huw. When his sister Angharad found that the three boys were living in filth, she went to the rooming-house to take care of them. Then the father relented and allowed the boys to come home, but he said that they would be lodgers only, not sons.

After the father became superintendent at the mine, Huw heard some of the miners say that his father and Ivor, who agreed with him, might be beaten or even killed by some of the more violent miners. Frightened, he told his mother what he had heard. One winter night she and Huw went to the mountain where the miners were meeting, and she told the men there that she would kill anyone who harmed her husband. On the way home his mother slipped on the bank of a little river. Huw, standing in the icy water, supported his mother on the bank until help came. After that he knew nothing until he awoke in his bed and his father told him that he had saved his mother's life and the life of his new baby sister. Huw had fever in his legs for almost five years and never left his bed during that time.

During his sickness Bronwen nursed him and his brothers read to him until he was far beyond his years in learning. While he was in bed, he first met the new minister, Mr. Gruffydd, who was to become his best friend.

Huw's brother Owen fell in love with Marged Evans. When Marged's father found Owen kissing Marged, he said terrible things to the boy, so that Owen would have nothing more to do with Marged. Gwilym married her, for he had always loved her.

Ianto's wife died and he came home to live. By this time Huw, well once more, went to the National School, over the mountain. He had many fights before he was accepted by the other boys.

Angharad and Iestyn Evans, the son of the mine owner, began to keep company, but Angharad did not seem to be happy. It was some time before Huw learned that Angharad loved Mr. Gruffydd but that he could not take a wife because he was poor. Huw began to think love caused heartache instead of happiness.

One day he took a basket of food to Gwilym's house, and there he found Marged completely mad. Thinking he was Owen, she told him she could not live without him. Huw ran to find Gwilym. Before he returned with his brother, Marged had thrown herself into the fire and burned to death. Afterward Gwilym and Owen went away together, no one knew where.

Iestyn Evans' father died, and soon after Iestyn and Angharad were married in London. Davy was married before they came home, and for the wedding Huw had his first long trousers. Bronwen told him that he was now a man.

Shortly afterward Huw was put out of school for giving the teacher a beating because he had made a small child wear around her neck a sign announcing that she was Welsh. Huw went to work in the pits with his brothers. Owen and

Gwilym had returned home and all the boys lived again in the valley. But soon Owen had a telegram from London about an engine he was trying to perfect, and he and Gwilym left again. From London they went to America. Soon afterward Davy went to London on mine union business.

Angharad came home from London alone, Iestyn having gone to Cape Town on business. Soon gossip started because Mr. Gruffydd and Angharad often took carriage rides together. Finally Angharad left the valley and went to Cape Town. Mr. Gruffydd also left the valley.

When Ivor was killed in a cave-in at the mine, Huw's mother sent him to live with Bronwen in her loneliness. Discharged from the mines for striking one of the workmen who made a slurring remark about Angharad and Mr. Gruffydd, Huw became a carpenter. Ianto had already left the pits and only his father and Davy were left in the mines. Davy decided to go to New Zealand. Ianto went to Germany, where he thought he could do better in his trade. The family was now scattered.

One day the workers flooded the mines and Huw's father was crushed by a cave-in. Huw crawled to his father and stayed with him until he died. Huw's heart was as empty as his mother's when he told her the terrible news.

Everyone of whom Huw had thought during this reverie was now dead. He walked slowly away from his valley and from his memories.

HUCKLEBERRY FINN

Type of work: Novel
Author: Mark Twain (Samuel L. Clemens, 1835-1910)
Type of plot: Humorous satire
Time of plot: Nineteenth century
Locale: Along the Mississippi River
First published: 1885

Principal characters:
HUCKLEBERRY FINN
TOM SAWYER, his friend
JIM, a Negro slave

Critique:

Not to have read *The Adventures of Huckleberry Finn* is nearly as sad as never having been to a circus or never having played baseball with the neighborhood gang. Huck is every young boy who ever lived, and he is also an individual worth knowing. He swears and smokes, but he has a set of ethics of his own. Reared haphazardly in the South, he believes that slaves belong to their rightful owners, yet in his honest gratitude toward his friend Jim, he helps him escape his slavery. Huck could not bear to cheat the three Wilks girls, but he did not hesitate to steal food when he was hungry. Huck talks with a lowbrow dialect, but he is keen-witted and intelligent. He tells his story with a straight-faced forwardness, but the reader finds laughter and shrewd, sharp comment on human nature in every chapter of his adventures along the Mississippi.

The Story:

Tom Sawyer and Huckleberry Finn had found a box of gold in a robber's cave. After Judge Thatcher had taken the money and invested it for the boys, each had a huge allowance of a dollar a day. The Widow Douglas and her sister, Miss Watson, had taken Huck home with them to try to reform him. At first Huck could not stand living in a tidy house where smoking and swearing were

HUCKLEBERRY FINN by Mark Twain. Published by Harper & Brothers.

forbidden. Worse, he had to go to school and learn how to read. But he managed to drag himself to school almost every day, except for the times when he sneaked off for a smoke in the woods or to go fishing in the Mississippi.

Life was beginning to become bearable to him when one day he noticed some tracks in the snow. Examining them closely, he realized that they belonged to the worthless father whom Huck had not seen for over a year. Knowing that his father would be back hunting him when the old man learned about the six thousand dollars, Huck rushed over to Judge Thatcher and persuaded the judge to take the fortune for himself. The judge was puzzled, but he signed some papers, and Huck was satisfied that he no longer had any money for his father to take from him.

Huck's father finally showed up one night in Huck's room at Widow Douglas' home. Complaining that he had been cheated out of his money, the old drunkard took Huck away with him to a cabin in the woods, where he kept the boy a prisoner, beating him periodically and half starving him. Before long Huck began to wonder why he had ever liked living with the widow. With his father, he could smoke and swear all he wanted, and his life would have been pleasant if it had not been for the beatings. One night Huck sneaked away, leaving a bloody trail from a pig he had killed in the woods. Huck wanted everyone to believe he was dead. He climbed into a boat and went to Jackson's Island to hide until all the excitement had blown over.

After three days of freedom, Huck wandered to another part of the island and there he discovered Jim, Miss Watson's Negro slave. Jim told Huck that he had run off because he had overheard Miss Watson planning to sell him down south for eight hundred dollars. Huck swore he would not report Jim. The two stayed on the island many days, Jim giving Huck an education in primitive superstition. One night, Huck rowed back to the mainland. Disguised as a girl, he called on a home near the shore. There he learned that his father had disappeared shortly after the people of the town had decided that Huck had been murdered. Since Jim's disappearance had occurred just after Huck's alleged death, there was now a three hundred dollar reward posted for Jim's capture, as most people believed that Jim had killed Huck.

Fearing that Jackson's Island would be searched, Huck hurried back to Jim and the two headed down the Mississippi. They planned to leave the raft at Cairo and then go on a steamboat up the Ohio into free territory. Jim told Huck that he would work hard in the North and then buy his wife and children from their masters in the South. Helping a runaway slave bothered Huck's conscience, but he reasoned that it would bother him more if he betrayed such a good friend as Jim. One night as they were drifting down the river on their raft, a large boat loomed before them, and Huck and Jim, knowing that the raft would be smashed under the hull of the ship, jumped into the water. Huck swam safely to shore, but Jim disappeared.

Huck found a home with a friendly family named Grangerford. The Grangerfords were feuding with the Shepherdsons, another family living nearby. The Grangerfords left Huck mostly to himself and gave him a young slave to wait on him. One day the slave asked him to come to the woods to see some snakes. Following the boy, Huck came across Jim, who had been hiding in the woods waiting for an opportunity to send for Huck. Jim had repaired the broken raft. That night one of the Grangerford daughters eloped with a young Shepherdson, and the feud broke out once more. Huck and Jim ran away during the shooting and set off down the river.

Shortly afterward, Jim and Huck met two men who pretended they were royalty and made all sorts of nonsensical demands on Huck and Jim. Huck was not taken in, but he reasoned that it would do no harm to humor the two men to prevent quarreling. The Duke and the King were clever schemers. In one of the small river towns they staged a fake show which lasted long enough to net them a few hundred dollars. Then they ran off before the angered townspeople could catch them.

The Duke and the King overheard some people talking about the death of a Peter Wilks, who had left considerable property and some cash to his three daughters. Wilks' two brothers, whom no one in the town had ever seen, were living in England. The King and the Duke went to the three daughters, Mary Jane, Susan, and Joanna, and presented themselves as the two uncles. They took a few thousand dollars of the inheritance and then put up the property for auction and sold the slaves. This high-handed deed caused great grief to the girls, and Huck could not bear to see them so unhappy. He decided to expose the two frauds, but he wanted to insure Jim's safety first. Jim had been hiding in the woods waiting for his companions to return to him. Employing a series of lies, subterfuges, and maneuverings that were worthy of his ingenious mind, Huck exposed the Duke and King. Huck fled back to Jim, and the two escaped on their raft. Just as Jim and Huck thought they were on their way and well rid of their former companions, the Duke and King came rowing down the river toward them.

The whole party set out again with their royal plots to hoodwink the public. In one town where they landed, Jim was captured, and Huck learned that the Duke had turned him in for the reward. Huck had quite a tussle with his conscience. He knew that he ought to help return a slave to the rightful owner, but, on the other hand, he thought of all the fine times he and Jim had had together and how loyal a friend Jim had been. Finally, Huck decided that he would help Jim to escape.

Learning that Mr. Phelps was holding Jim, he headed for the Phelps farm. There, Mrs. Phelps ran up and hugged him, mistaking him for the nephew whom she had been expecting to come for a visit. Huck wondered how he could keep Mrs. Phelps from learning that he was not her nephew. Then to his relief he learned they had mistaken him for Tom Sawyer. Huck rather liked being Tom for a while, and he was able to tell the Phelps all about Tom's Aunt Polly and Sid and Mary, Tom's brother and sister. Huck was feeling proud of himself for keeping up the deception. When Tom Sawyer really did arrive, he told his aunt that he was Sid.

At the first opportunity Huck told Tom about Jim's capture. To his surprise, Tom offered to help him set Jim free. Huck could not believe that Tom would be a slave stealer, but he kept his feelings to himself. Huck had intended merely to wait until there was a dark night and then break the padlock on the door of the shack where Jim was kept. But Tom said the rescue had to be done according to the books, and he laid out a most complicated plan with all kinds of story-book ramifications. It took fully three weeks of plotting, stealing, and deceit to let Jim out of the shack. Then the scheme failed. A chase began after Jim escaped, and Tom was shot in the leg. After Jim had been recaptured, Tom was brought back to Aunt Sally's house to recover from his wound. Then Tom revealed the fact that Miss Watson had died, giving Jim his freedom in her will. Huck was greatly relieved to learn that Tom was not really a slave stealer after all.

To complicate matters still more, Tom's Aunt Polly arrived. She quickly set straight the identities of the two boys. Jim was given his freedom and Tom gave him forty dollars. Tom told Huck that his money was still safely in the hands of Judge Thatcher, but Huck moaned that his father would likely be back to claim it again. Then Jim told

Huck that his father was dead; Jim had seen him lying in an abandoned boat along the river.

Huck was ready to start out again because Aunt Sally said she thought she might adopt him and try to civilize him. Huck thought that he could not go through such a trial again after he had once tried to be civilized under the care of Widow Douglas.

HUGH WYNNE, FREE QUAKER

Type of work: Novel
Author: Silas Weir Mitchell (1829-1914)
Type of plot: Historical romance
Time of plot: 1753-1783
Locale: Colonial America
First published: 1897

Principal characters:
JOHN WYNNE, a Quaker
MARIE, his wife
HUGH WYNNE, John's son
JACK WARDER, Hugh's friend
ARTHUR WYNNE, Hugh's cousin
DARTHEA PENISTON, who marries Hugh
GAINOR WYNNE, John's sister

Critique:

Hugh Wynne, Free Quaker is one of the best novels of the American Revolution. The veracity of its events in the historical sense can be judged by any student of history, and its faithfulness to the social history of the time can be judged by reading diaries and chronicles of those who lived through the war years. More than historical fiction, however, the novel is a touching revelation of a child-parent relationship and of the consequences of too much doctrinal discipline.

The Story:

The Wynne family had descended from an ancient Welsh line. That part of the family which had remained in Wales now held the family estate of Wyncote. The American branch, being Quaker, had dissociated itself from the more worldly family at Wyncote, and Hugh Wynne grew up under the stern discipline of John Wynne's orthodoxy. John's sister, Gainor Wynne, had not become a Quaker. Because Hugh was his aunt's favorite, early in his life he fell under the influence of those who were outside the ways of the Quakers.

Jack Warder was Hugh's closest friend, the two boys having gone to school together. Aunt Gainor often invited both boys to her home in Philadelphia, where she was surrounded by a worldly group of English officers, men upon whom the Quakers frowned. Hugh enjoyed their society, to the delight of his aunt, who wished her nephew to break his Quaker ties. Jack Warder, however, did not like Gainor Wynne's friends. When he and Hugh were old enough to judge moral values for themselves, their friendship became strained. Hugh's father was never fully aware of the way Hugh spent his time away from home.

One night, while drinking and gambling with his worldly friends, Hugh met a cousin, Arthur Wynne, of the family at Wyncote. He instinctively disliked his relative because of his superior ways and his deceitful manner. During the evening Hugh became very drunk. Suddenly his mother and Jack Warder burst into the room.

This incident marked the beginning of Hugh's break with his father's church and the renewal of his friendship with Jack Warder. Hugh, realizing his folly, was thankful that Jack had seen him on the streets and had led his mother to rescue him from the drunken party. He began to realize the depth of his mother's love and understanding. John Wynne was quite different in his attitude. A few nights later he took Hugh to a Quaker meeting, where public prayers were offered to save Hugh's soul. Hugh's embarrassment caused him to lose all of his love for the Quaker religion and to bear a deep resentment against his father.

At Gainor Wynne's home, Jack and Hugh heard much conversation about disagreement between the Americans and the British. Gainor was a Whig, and under her influence Jack and Hugh gained sympathy for their American compatriots. Arthur Wynne too had become part of the society that gathered at Gainor Wynne's house. Jack and Hugh had never liked Arthur, but now they had a new cause for their dislike. Arthur made no secret of his admiration for Darthea Peniston, a schoolmate of Jack and Hugh, and his bragging about Wyncote seemingly won her interest, thus arousing Hugh's jealousy. When Hugh told Darthea of his love, she insisted that she did not love him.

Meanwhile Hugh's parents went abroad. During their absence he stayed with Gainor Wynne. Claiming that the time was not far off when he would need such a skill, she urged him to take fencing lessons. Jack practiced the sport with his friend, although he knew it to be contrary to the laws of the church. Hugh and Jack both knew that soon they would join the American cause for liberty.

While John Wynne and his wife were abroad, Hugh received a letter telling that his mother had died. On his return John showed no signs of his grief at the loss of his wife. Hugh himself felt her loss deeply.

At Gainor's home, where he spent more time than ever since the death of his mother, Hugh quarreled with an English officer and was challenged to a duel. With Jack as his second, Hugh answered the challenge. As a result the Quakers notified both boys that unless they changed their ways and repented for their sins, they could no longer belong to the Society of Friends. Jack and Hugh announced that they intended to join the American army; fighting had already begun at Lexington.

Jack went to join the troops. After a short time Hugh decided to follow him, in spite of his father's crafty excuses that he needed Hugh to conduct his business affairs for him. When he did join the army, Hugh was captured by the British and sent, wounded and sick, to a filthy prison. In the prison Arthur Wynne, now a Tory captain, saw his cousin, but left Hugh to die. Hugh never forgave him for this cruelty and for his subsequent lie concerning the meeting.

Hugh recovered and escaped from prison to return to Gainor Wynne's house. Arthur Wynne was staying at the home of John Wynne and ingratiating himself in the eyes of the old man. Hugh knew that there was something mysterious in relation to the Welsh estate of Wyncote. Supposedly Arthur's father owned the estate, having bought it from John's father. Gainor Wynne urged Hugh to investigate the title of the estate. John Wynne, it seemed, still possessed the title, and out of sympathy for Arthur's alleged poverty had promised to give it to him. Hugh was unable to change his father's decision, even after he told of Arthur's cruel desertion when Hugh lay near death in prison. His father refused to believe Hugh's story.

Hugh could not tell Darthea about Arthur's behavior, for he felt that she would rush to Arthur's defense if he said anything against his cousin.

Once, while Hugh was at home, his father, thinking Hugh was Arthur, handed him the deed to Wyncote. Knowing that his father's mind had often misled him of late, Hugh tried to convince the old man that he was not Arthur, but John insisted that Hugh take the deed. Hugh took it to Gainor Wynne.

After a rest of a few months, Hugh rejoined the American troops. He was able to perform a courageous service for General Washington, for which he received praise and a captaincy. Jack, too, had become an officer.

When Hugh and Jack returned to Philadelphia on leave, Gainor Wynne managed to expose Arthur to Darthea. Although the young girl had lost her earlier love for the Tory officer, she had been unwilling to break her promise to him. But with proof of Arthur's villainy before her, she felt that she was free at last to break her engagement.

Again Hugh asked her to marry him and she surprised him by accepting. Hugh still did not want the title to Wyncote, and Darthea agreed with him that after he had taken Arthur's betrothed it would not become Hugh to take his inheritance from him as well. Although Gainor Wynne wished to press the legality of the ancient deed, Darthea threw it into the fire, and so destroyed any claim Hugh might have upon the ancestral estate.

John Wynne, who had ceased to live for Hugh when he had lost his mental faculties, died soon after the war ended. Darthea and Hugh were happily married, and they lived long years together to watch their children and their grandchildren grow up unburdened by the rigorous religious control which Hugh had known in his youth.

THE HUMAN COMEDY

Type of work: Novel
Author: William Saroyan (1908-)
Type of plot: Sentimental romance
Time of plot: Twentieth century
Locale: Ithaca, California
First published: 1943

Principal characters:
KATEY MACAULEY, a widow
HOMER,
ULYSSES, and
MARCUS, her sons
BESS, her daughter
MARY ARENA, Marcus' sweetheart
THOMAS SPANGLER, manager of the telegraph office
MR. GROGAN, assistant in the telegraph office
TOBEY GEORGE, Marcus' friend from the army
LIONEL, Ulysses' friend

Critique:

This novel has for its theme the idea that no human can ever die as long as he lives in the hearts of those who loved him. The story deals with the family of a soldier who died in the war. Frankly sentimental, *The Human Comedy* is one of the most touching of Saroyan's works.

The Story:

Mr. Macauley was dead and his wife and children had to take care of themselves. When Marcus went into the army, Homer, the next oldest, obtained a job on the night shift in the telegraph office at Ithaca, California. He worked at night because he was still attending school during the day. Little Ulysses watched his family and wondered what was going on, for his baby's mind could not comprehend all the changes that had taken place in his home.

Every morning Homer arose early and exercised in his room so that he would be physically fit to run the two-twenty low hurdles at high school. After he and Bess had eaten their breakfast, Mary Arena, who was in love with Marcus, came from next door, and she and Bess walked to school together.

In the ancient history class, taught by Miss Hicks, Homer and Hubert Ackley the Third insulted each other, and Miss Hicks kept the boys after school. But Coach Byfield had picked Hubert to run the two-twenty low hurdles that afternoon, and Hubert told Miss Hicks that the principal had asked that he be excused. Indignant at the deceit, Miss Hicks also sent Homer to run the race. Although Hubert was the winner, Homer felt that justice had been done.

Thomas Spangler was in charge of the telegraph office and Mr. Grogan, an old man with a weak heart, was his assistant. Because Mr. Grogan got drunk every night, one of Homer's duties was to see to it that Mr. Grogan stayed awake to perform his duties. A problem which had weighed on Homer's mind ever since he had taken his new job and had grown up overnight was whether the war would change anything for people. Mr. Grogan and Homer often talked about the world, Homer declaring that he did not like things as they were. Seeing everyone in the world mixed up and lonely, Homer said, he felt that he had to say and do things to make people laugh.

Mrs. Macauley was happy that her children were so human. Ever since her husband had died, Katey Macauley had pretended to see him and discuss with him problems that arose concerning the rearing of her family. She felt that the father was not dead if he lived again in the lives of his children. One afternoon she had a premonition of Marcus' death, for she imagined that her husband came to her and told her he was going to bring Marcus with him.

Little Ulysses had a friend, Lionel, who was three years older than Ulysses. The older boys chased Lionel away from their games because they said that he was dumb. When Lionel came to Mrs. Macauley to ask her whether he was stupid, the kind woman assured him that he was as good as everyone else. Lionel took Ulysses to the library with him to look at all the many-colored books on the shelves. Ulysses, who spent his time wandering around and watching everything, was pleased with the new experience.

Marcus wrote to Homer from an army camp somewhere in the South, and Homer took the letter back to the telegraph office with him. The letter told about Marcus' friend, an orphan named Tobey George. Marcus had described his family, Homer, Ulysses, Bess, his mother, and his sweetheart, Mary, to Tobey. Because Tobey had no family of his own, he was grateful to Marcus for bringing to him second-hand the Macauley family. Marcus had told Tobey that after the war he wanted Tobey to go to Ithaca and marry Bess. Tobey was not so certain that Bess would want to marry him, but he felt for the first time in his life that he had a family that was almost his own. Marcus had written to Homer, as the new head of the family, to tell him about Tobey George and to ask him to look after his mother and Bess.

Homer was moved by his brother's letter. When he had finished reading it, he told Mr. Grogan that if Marcus should be killed he would spit at the world. Homer could express his love for Marcus in no other way.

The same events repeated themselves many times in Ithaca. Ulysses continued to watch everything with increasing interest. Mary and Bess sang their songs and went for their evening walks. Telegrams came, and Homer delivered them.

Soldiers began coming home to Ithaca, to their mothers and to their families.

Homer had been working at the telegraph office for six months. One Sunday night, while he was walking downtown with Lionel and Ulysses, he saw through the window of the telegraph office that Mr. Grogan was working alone. He sent the two small boys home and went in to see if Mr. Grogan needed him. The old man had suffered one of his heart attacks, and Homer ran to the drug store to get some medicine for him. Mr. Grogan attempted to type out one more telegram, a message for Katey Macauley telling her that her son Marcus had been killed in action. When Homer returned with the medicine, he found Mr. Grogan slumped over the typed-out message. He was dead. Homer went home with the message that Marcus had been killed.

That night a soldier had got off the train at Ithaca. He was Tobey George. He walked around for a time before he went to see Marcus' family. When he came to the Macauley porch, he stood and listened to Bess and Mary singing inside the house. Bess came outside and sat next to him while he told her that Marcus had sent him to be a member of the family. When Homer came to the porch with the telegram, Tobey called him aside and told him to tear up the message. Tobey assured him that Marcus was not dead; Marcus could never die. Mrs. Macauley came onto the porch, and Ulysses ran to Tobey and took his hand. For a while the mother looked at her two remaining sons. Then she smiled at her new son as the family walked into the house.

HUMPHRY CLINKER

Type of work: Novel
Author: Tobias Smollett (1721-1771)
Type of plot: Social satire
Time of plot: Mid-eighteenth century
Locale: England, Scotland, Wales
First published: 1771

Principal characters:
MATTHEW BRAMBLE, a Welsh squire
MISS TABITHA BRAMBLE, his sister
LYDIA MELFORD, his niece
JERRY MELFORD, his nephew
WINIFRED JENKINS, a maid
HUMPHRY CLINKER, a servant, discovered to be Mr. Bramble's natural son
LIEUTENANT OBADIAH LISMAHAGO, an adventurer and sportsman
MR. DENNISON, a country gentleman
GEORGE DENNISON, his son, the actor known as Wilson

Critique:

This novel, written in the form of letters, is easy to read and continually amusing. The characters of the writers of the letters are shown by the variation of their descriptions of the same events. The picture is one of a realistic if somewhat eccentric family, whose members display the manners and customs of eighteenth-century society. *The Expedition of Humphry Clinker,* to use its full title, has often been called the greatest of the letter-novels, and an outstanding example of English humor.

The Story:

Squire Matthew Bramble was an eccentric and skeptical gentleman with large estates in Wales. With him lived his sister, Miss Tabitha Bramble, a middle-aged maiden of high matrimonial hopes that were greater than her expectations. Painfully afflicted with the gout, the squire set out for Bath to try the waters, but with few hopes of their healing properties. With him went his sister; her servant, Winifred Jenkins; his own manservant, and, at the last minute, his niece and nephew, Lydia and Jerry Melford.

The young Melfords were orphans and Squire Bramble's wards. Lydia had been in boarding-school, where, unfortunately, she had fallen in love with an actor—a circumstance Squire Bramble hoped she would soon forget among the gay and fashionable gatherings at Bath. Her brother, who had just finished his studies at Oxford, had tried to fight a duel with the actor, but an opportunity to defend his sister's honor had not presented itself to his satisfaction.

On the way to Bath a Jewish peddler made his way into Squire Bramble's lodgings on the pretext of selling glasses, and in a whisper made himself known to Lydia as George Wilson, the strolling player. The lovesick girl ordered Winifred Jenkins to follow the actor and talk with him. The maid came back in a great flurry. He had told her that Wilson was not his real name, that he was a gentleman, and that he intended to sue for Lydia's hand in his proper character. But, alas, the excited maid had forgotten Wilson's real name. There was nothing for poor Lydia to do but to conjecture and daydream as the party continued on toward Bath.

Arriving at Bath without further incident, the party entered the gay festivities there with various degrees of pleasure. Tabitha tried to get proposals of marriage out of every eligible man she met, and the squire became disgusted with the supposed curative powers of the waters which were drunk and bathed in by people with almost any infirmity in hopes of regaining their health. Lydia was still languishing over Wilson, and Jerry enjoyed the absurdity of the social gatherings. In an attempt to lighten his niece's spirits, Squire Bramble decided to go on to London.

They had traveled only a short way toward London when the coach accidentally overturned and Miss Tabitha's lapdog, in the excitement, bit the squire's servant. Miss Tabitha made such loud complaint when the servant kicked her dog in return that the squire was forced to discharge the man on the spot. He also needed another postilion, as Miss Tabitha declared herself unwilling to drive another foot behind the clumsy fellow who had overturned the coach. The squire hired a ragged country fellow named Humphry Clinker to take the place of the unfortunate postilion, and the party went on to the next village.

Miss Tabitha was shocked by what she called Humphry's nakedness, for he wore no shirt. The maid added to the chorus of outraged modesty. Yielding to these female clamors, the squire asked about Humphry's circumstances, listened to the story of his life, gruffly read him a lecture on the crimes of poverty and sickness, and gave him a guinea for a new suit of clothes. In gratitude Humphry refused to be parted from his new benefactor and went on with the party to London.

In London they were well entertained by a visit to Vauxhall Gardens as well as by several public and private parties. Squire Bramble was disconcerted by the discovery that Humphry was a preacher by inclination, and had begun giving sermons in the manner of the Methodists. Miss Tabitha and her maid were already among Humphry's followers. The squire attempted to stop what he considered either hypocrisy or madness on Humphry's part. Miss Tabitha, disgusted with her brother's action, begged him to allow Humphry to continue his sermons.

The family was shocked to learn one day that Humphry had been arrested as a highway robber, and was in jail. When the squire arrived to investigate the case, he discovered that Humphry was obviously innocent of the charge against him, which had been placed by an ex-convict who made money by turning in criminals to the government. Humphry had made a fine impression on the jailer and his family and had converted several of his fellow prisoners. The squire found the man who supposedly had been robbed and got him to testify that Humphry was not the man who had committed the robbery. In the meantime Humphry preached so eloquently that he kept the prison taproom empty of customers. When this became evident he was hurriedly released, and Squire Bramble promised to allow him to preach his sermons unmolested.

Continuing their travels north after leaving London, the party stopped in Scarborough, where they went bathing. Squire Bramble undressed in a little cart which could be rolled down into the sea, so that he was able to bath nude with the greatest propriety. When he entered the water, he found it much colder than he had expected and gave several shouts as he swam away. Hearing these calls from the squire, Humphry thought his good master was drowning, and rushed fully clothed into the sea to rescue him. He pulled the squire to shore, almost twisting off his master's ear, and leaving the modest man shamefaced and naked in full view upon the beach. Humphrey was forgiven, however, because he had meant well.

At an inn in Durham, the party made the acquaintance of Lieutenant Lismahago, who seemed somewhat like Don Quixote. The lieutenant, regaling the company with tales of his adventures among the Indians of North America, quite captured the heart of Miss Tabitha. Squire Bramble was also charmed with the crusty conversation of the retired soldier, and made plans to meet him later on in their journey. The group became more and more fond of Humphry as time went on, especially Winifred. After a short and frivolous flirtation with Jerry's part-time valet, she settled down to win Humphry as a husband.

The party continued its trip through Scotland. In Edinburgh Lydia fainted when she saw a man who looked like Wilson, an action which showed her uncle that she had not yet forgotten the affair. After visiting several parts of Scotland and enjoying the most gracious hospitality everywhere, they continued by coach back to England. As they were traveling south, Lieutenant Lismahago rejoined the party and Miss Tabitha renewed her designs on him.

Just outside Dumfries the coach was overturned in the middle of a stream. Jerry and Lismahago succeeded in getting the women out of the water after a struggle, and Humphry staged a heroic rescue of the squire, who had been caught in the bottom of the coach. They found lodgings at a nearby inn until the coach could be repaired. While all were gathered in the parlor of a tavern, Squire Bramble was accosted by an old college friend named Dennison, a successful farmer of the county. Mr. Dennison had known the squire only as Matthew Lloyd, a name he had taken for a while in order to fulfill the terms of a will. When Humphry heard his master called Lloyd, he rushed up in a flutter of excitement and presented the squire with certain papers he had always carried with him. These papers proved that Humphry was the squire's natural son. In a gracious way, Squire Bramble welcomed his offspring, and presented him to the rest of his family. Humphry was overcome with pleasure and shyness. Winifred was afraid that his discovery would spoil her matrimonial plans, but Humphry continued to be the mild religious man he had been before.

The squire was also surprised to learn that the actor who had called himself Wilson was really Dennison's son, a fine proper young man who had run away from school and become an actor only to escape a marriage his father had planned for him long before. He had told his father about his love for Lydia, but Dennison had not realized that the Mr. Bramble who was her uncle was his old friend Matthew Lloyd. Now the two young lovers were brought together for a joyous reunion.

Lieutenant Lismahago was moved to ask for Miss Tabitha's hand in marriage, and both the squire and Miss Tabitha eagerly accepted his offer. The whole party went to stay at Mr. Dennison's house while preparations were being made for the marriage of Lydia and George. The coming marriages prompted Humphry to ask Winifred for her hand, and she also said yes. The three weddings were planned for the same day.

George and Lydia were a most attractive couple. The lieutenant and Tabitha seemed to be more pleasant than ever before. Humphry and Winifred both thanked God for the pleasures He saw fit to give them. The squire planned to return home to the tranquility of Brambleton Hall and the friendship of his invaluable doctor there.

THE HUNCHBACK OF NOTRE DAME

Type of work: Novel
Author: Victor Hugo (1802-1885)
Type of plot: Historical romance
Time of plot: Fifteenth century
Locale: France
First published: 1831

Principal characters:
QUASIMODO, the hunchback of Notre Dame
ESMERELDA, a gipsy dancer
CLAUDE FROLLO, archdeacon of Notre Dame
PHOEBUS DE CHATEAUPERS, Esmerelda's sweetheart
GRINGOIRE, a stupid and poverty-stricken poet

Critique:

Victor Hugo, leader of the French romantic movement, not only could tell a gripping story, but also could endow his essentially romantic characters with a realism so powerful that they have become monumental literary figures. *The Hunchback of Notre Dame* has every quality of a good novel: an exciting story, a magnificent setting, and deep, lasting characterizations. Perhaps the compelling truth of this novel lies in the idea that God has created in man an imperfect image of Himself, an image fettered by society and by man's own body and soul, but one which, in the last analysis, has the freedom to transcend these limitations and achieve spiritual greatness.

The Story:

Louis XI, King of France, was to marry his oldest son to Margaret of Flanders, and in early January, 1482, the king was expecting Flemish ambassadors to his court. The great day arrived, coinciding both with Epiphany and the secular celebration of the Festival of Fools. All day long, raucous Parisians had assembled at the great Palace of Justice to see a morality play and to choose a Prince of Fools. The throng was supposed to await the arrival of the Flemish guests, but when the emissaries were late Gringoire, a penniless and oafish poet, ordered the play to begin. In the middle of the prologue, however, the play came to a standstill as the royal procession passed into the huge palace. After the procession passed the play was forgotten, and the crowd shouted for the Prince of Fools to be chosen.

The Prince of Fools had to be a man of remarkable physical ugliness. One by one the candidates, eager for this one glory of their disreputable lives, showed their faces in front of a glass window, but the crowd shouted and jeered until a face of such extraordinary hideousness appeared that the people acclaimed this candidate at once as the Prince of Fools. It was Quasimodo, the hunchback bell-ringer of Notre Dame. Nowhere on earth was there a more grotesque creature. One of his eyes was buried under an enormous wen. His teeth hung over his protruding lower lip like tusks. His eyebrows were red bristles, and his gigantic nose curved over his upper lip like a snout. His long arms protruded from his shoulders, dangling like an ape's. Though he was deaf from long years of ringing Notre Dame's thunderous bells, his eyesight was acute.

Quasimodo sensed that he had been chosen by popular acclaim, and he was at once proud and suspicious of his honor as he allowed the crowd to dress him in ridiculous robes and hoist him above their heads. From this vantage point he maintained a dignified silence while the parade went through the streets of Paris, stopping only to watch the enchanting dance of a gipsy girl, La Esmerelda, whose grace and charm held her audience spellbound. She had with her a little trained goat that danced to her tambourine. The pair were celebrated throughout Paris, though there were some who thought the girl a witch, so great was her power in captivating her audience.

Late that night the poet Gringoire walked the streets of Paris. He had no shelter, owed money, and was in desperate straits. As the cold night came on, he saw Esmerelda hurrying ahead of him. Then a black-hooded man came out of the shadows and seized the gipsy. At the same time, Gringoire caught sight of the hooded man's partner, Quasimodo, who struck Gringoire a terrible blow. The following moment a horseman came riding from the next street. Catching sight of Esmerelda in the arms of the black-hooded man, the rider demanded that he free the girl or pay with his life. The attackers fled. Esmerelda asked the name of her rescuer. It was Captain Phoebus de Chateaupers. From that moment Esmerelda was hopelessly in love with Phoebus.

Gringoire did not bother to discover the plot behind the frustrated kidnaping, but had he known the truth he might have been more frightened than he was. Quasimodo's hooded companion had been Claude Frollo, archdeacon of Notre Dame, a man who had once been a pillar of righteousness, but who now, because of loneliness and an insatiable thirst for knowledge and experience, had succumbed to the temptations of necromancy and alchemy.

Frollo had befriended Quasimodo when the hunchback had been left at the gates of Notre Dame as an unwanted baby, and to him Quasimodo was slavishly loyal. He acted without question when Frollo asked his aid in kidnaping the beautiful gipsy. Frollo, having admired Esmerelda from a distance, planned to carry her off to his small cell in the cathedral, where he could enjoy her charms at his leisure.

As Quasimodo and Frollo hurried back to the cathedral, Gringoire continued on his way and found himself in a disreputable quarter of Paris. Captured by thugs, he was threatened with death if none of the women in the thieves' den would marry him. When no one wanted the pale, thin poet, a noose was lowered about his neck. Suddenly Esmerelda appeared and volunteered to take him. But Gringoire enjoyed no wedding night. Esmerelda's heart belonged to Phoebus; she had rescued the poet only out of pity.

In those days the courts of Paris often picked innocent people from the streets, tried them, and convicted them with little regard for justice. Quasimodo had been seen in his role as the Prince of Fools and had been watched as he stood before the gipsy girl while she danced. It was rumored that Esmerelda was a witch, and most of Paris suspected that Frollo, Quasimodo's only associate, was a sorcerer. Consequently Quasimodo was brought into a court, accused of keeping questionable company, and sentenced to a severe flogging and exposure on the pillory. Quasimodo endured his disgrace, stoically, but after his misshapen back had been torn by the lash, he was overcome with a terrible thirst. The crowd jeered and threw stones. They hated and feared Quasimodo because of his ugliness.

Presently Esmerelda mounted the scaffold and put her flask to Quasimodo's blackened lips. This act of kindness moved him deeply and he wept. At that same time Frollo had happened upon the scene, caught sight of Quasimodo, and departed quickly. Later Quasimodo was to remember this betrayal.

One day Phoebus was entertaining a lady in a building overlooking the square where Esmerelda was dancing. The gipsy was so smitten with Phoebus that she had taught her goat to spell out his name with alphabet blocks. When she had the animal perform this trick, the lady called her a witch and a sorceress. But Phoebus followed the gipsy and arranged for a rendezvous with her for the following night.

Gringoire, meanwhile, happened to meet Frollo, who was jealous of the poet because he was rumored to be Esmerelda's husband. But Gringoire explained that Esmerelda did not love him; she had eyes and heart only for Phoebus.

Desperate to preserve Esmerelda for himself, Frollo trailed the young gallant and asked him where he was going. Phoebus said that he had a rendezvous with Esmerelda. The priest offered him money in exchange for an opportunity to conceal himself in the room where this rendezvous was to take place, ostensibly to discover whether Esmerelda were really the girl whose name Phoebus had mentioned. It was a poor ruse at best, but Phoebus was not shy at love-making and he agreed to the bargain. When he learned that the girl was really Esmerelda, Frollo leaped from concealment and wounded Phoebus with a dagger. Esmerelda could not see her lover's assailant in the darkness and when she fainted Frollo escaped. A crowd gathered, murmuring that the sorceress had slain Phoebus. They took the gipsy off to prison.

Now tales of Esmerelda's sorcery began to circulate. At her trial she was convicted of witchcraft, sentenced to do penance on the great porch of Notre Dame and from there to be taken to a scaffold in the Place de Greve and publicly hanged.

Captain Phoebus was not dead, but he had kept silence rather than implicate himself in a case of witchcraft. When Esmerelda was on her way to Notre Dame, she caught sight of him riding on his beautiful horse, and called out to him, but he ignored her completely. She then felt that she was doomed.

When she came before Frollo to do penance, he offered to save her if she would be his; but she refused. Quasimodo suddenly appeared on the porch, took the girl in his arms, and carried her to sanctuary within the church. Esmerelda was now safe as long as she remained within the cathedral walls.

Quasimodo hid her in his own cell, where there was a mattress and water, and brought her food. He kept the cell door locked so that if her pursuers did break the sanctuary, they could not reach her. Aware that she would be terrified of him if he stayed with her, he entered her cell only to bring her his own dinner.

Frollo, knowing that the gipsy was near him in the cathedral, secured a key to the chamber and stole in to see Esmerelda one night. She struggled hopelessly, until suddenly Quasimodo entered and dragged the priest from the cell. With smothered rage, he freed the trembling archdeacon and allowed him to run away.

One day a mob gathered and demanded that the sorceress be turned from the cathedral. Frollo was jubilant. Quasimodo, however, barred and bolted the great doors. When the crowd charged the cathedral with a battering ram, Quasimodo threw huge stones from a tower where builders had been working. The mob persisting, he poured melted lead upon the crowd below. Then the mob secured ladders and began to mount the façade, but Quasimodo seized the ladders and pushed them from the wall. Hundreds of dead and wounded lay below him.

The king's guards joined the fray. Quasimodo, looking down, thought that the soldiers had arrived to protect Esmerelda. He went to her cell, but to his amazement he found the door open and Esmerelda gone.

Frollo had given Gringoire the key to her chamber and had led the poet through the cathedral to her cell. Gringoire convinced her that she must fly, since the church was under siege. She followed him trustingly, and he led her to a boat where Frollo was already waiting. Frightened by the violence of the priest, Gringoire fled. Once more, Frollo offered to save Esmerelda if she would be his, but she refused him. Fleeing, she sought refuge in a cell belonging to a madwoman. There the soldiers found her and dragged her away for her execution the next morning at dawn.

Quasimodo, meanwhile, roamed the cathedral searching for Esmerelda. Making his way to the tower which looked down upon the bridge of Notre Dame, Quasimodo came upon Frollo, who stood shaking with laughter as he watched a scene far below. Following the direction of the priest's gaze, Quasimodo saw a gibbet erected in the Place de Greve and on the platform a woman in white. It was Esmerelda. Quasimodo saw the noose lowered over the girl's head and the platform released. The body swayed in the morning breeze. Then Quasimodo picked up Frollo and thrust him over the wall on which he had been leaning. At that moment Quasimodo understood everything that the priest had done to ensure the death of Esmerelda. He looked at the crushed body at the foot of the tower and then at the figure in white upon the gallows. He wept.

After the deaths of Esmerelda and Claude Frollo, Quasimodo was not to be found. Then in the reign of Charles VIII the vault of Montfaucon, in which the bodies of criminals were interred, was opened to locate the remains of a famous prisoner who had been buried there. Among the skeletons were those of a woman who had been clad in white and of a man whose bony arms were wrapped tightly around the woman's body. His spine was crooked, one leg was shorter than the other, and it was evident that he had not been hanged, for his neck was unbroken. When those who discovered these singular remains tried to separate the two bodies, they crumbled into dust.

HUNGER

Type of work: Novel
Author: Knut Hamsun (Knut Pedersen Hamsund, 1859-)
Type of plot: Impressionistic realism
Time of plot: Late nineteenth century
Locale: Norway
First published: 1890

Principal character:
THE NARRATOR, a young writer

Critique:

Hunger was the work that immediately brought Hamsun to the attention of a wide literary audience, and the novel has been reprinted and translated many times. Realistic in subject, its form and treatment are highly impressionistic. Hamsun has given us a striking study of a man's mind under stress, but it is not a clinical study; it is an artistic piece of literature.

The Story:

I awoke at six o'clock and lay awake in my bed until eight. Hungry, I searched in my packet of odds and ends, but there was not even a crumb of bread. I knew that I should have gone out early to look for work, but I had been refused so often I was almost afraid to venture out again.

At last I took some paper and went out, for if the weather permitted I could write in the park. There were several good ideas in my head for newspaper articles. In the street an old cripple with a big bundle was using all his strength to keep ahead of me.

When I caught up with him he turned around and whined for a halfpenny to buy milk. Not having a cent on me, I hurried back to the pawnbroker's dark shop. In the hall I took off my waistcoat and rolled it in a ball. The pawnbroker gave me one and six for it. I found the old cripple again and gave him his halfpenny. He stared at me with his mouth open as I hurried away.

Two women, one of them young, were idly strolling about. When I told the young woman that she would lose her book, she looked frightened and they hurried on. Seeing them standing before a shop window, I went up to them again and told the younger woman that she was losing her book. She looked herself over in a bewildered way; she had no book. I kept following them, but they put me down as a harmless madman.

In the park I could not write a thing. Little flies stuck to my paper. All afternoon I tried to brush them off. Then I wrote an application for a job as bookkeeper. After a day or two I went to see the man in person. He laughed at my desire to become a bookkeeper because I had dated my letter 1848, years before I was born. I went home discouraged.

On my table was a letter. I thought it a notice from my landlady, for I was behind in my rent. But no, my story had been accepted. The editor said it would be printed right away. He had included a half sovereign in payment. I had written a masterpiece and I had a half sovereign.

A few weeks later I went out for an evening walk and sat in a churchyard with a new manuscript. At eight o'clock, when the gates were closed, I meant to go straight home to the vacant tinker's workshop which I had permission to occupy, but I stumbled around hardly knowing where I was. I felt feverish because I had not eaten for several days. At last I sat down and dozed off. I dreamed that a beautiful girl dressed in silk waited for me in a doorway and led me down a hall, she holding my hand. We went into a crimson room where she clasped me tightly and begged me to kiss her.

A policeman woke me up and advised me to go to the police barracks as a homeless man. When I got there, I lied about my name and said that it was too late for me to get back to my lodgings. The officer believed me and gave me a private room. In the morning, thinking I was only a young rake instead of a destitute, the police gave me no breakfast ticket. I drank a lot of water but I could scarcely keep it down.

Faint with hunger, I cut the buttons from my coat and tried to pawn them, but the pawnbroker laughed at me. On the way out I met a friend bringing his watch to pawn. He fed me and gave me five shillings.

I went to see an editor who critically read my sketch on Corregio. He was kind, saying that he would like to publish my work but that he had to keep his subscribers in mind. He asked if I could write something more to the common taste. When I prepared to leave, he also asked me if I needed money. He was sure I could write it out. Although I had not eaten a real meal for some time, I thanked him and left without an advance payment.

A lady in black stood every night on the corner by my tinker's garret. She would look intently at my lodging for a while and then pass on. After several days I spoke to her and accompanied her on her walk. She said she had no special interest in my poor garret or in me. When she lifted her veil, I saw she was the woman I had followed and spoken to about the book. She was merry with me and seemed to enjoy my company.

One night she took me to her home. Once inside, we embraced; then we sat down and began to talk. She confessed that she was attracted to me because she thought I was a madman. She was an adventurous girl, on the lookout for odd experiences. I told her the truth about myself, that I acted queerly because I was so poor. Much of the time I was so hungry that I had a fever. She found my story hard to believe, but I convinced her. She was sympathetic for a moment. I had to leave, for her mother was returning, and I never saw her again.

I awoke sick one morning. All day I shivered in bed. Toward night I went down to the little shop below to buy a candle, for I felt I had to write something. A boy was alone in the store. I gave him a florin for my candle, but he gave me change for a crown. I stared stupidly at the money in my hand for a long time, but I got out without betraying myself.

I took a room in a real hotel and had a chamber to myself and breakfast and supper. About the time my money was gone I started on a medieval play. The landlady trusted me for quite a while, for I explained that I would pay her as soon as my play was finished. One night she brought a sailor up to my room and turned me out, but she let me go down and sleep with the family.

For some time I slept on a sofa in the entryway, and once in a while a servant gave me bread and cheese. In my nervous condition it was hard to be meek and grateful. The break came one evening when the children were amusing themselves by sticking straws into the nose and ears of the paralyzed grandfather who lay on a bed before the fire. I protested against their cruel sport. The landlady flew at me in a rage and ordered me out.

I wandered down to the docks and got a berth on a Russian freighter going to England. I came back to the hotel for my possessions and on the step met the postman. He handed me a letter addressed in a feminine hand. Inside was a half sovereign. I crumpled the envelope and coin together and threw them in the landlady's face.

HYPATIA

Type of work: Novel
Author: Charles Kingsley (1819-1875)
Type of plot: Historical romance
Time of plot: Fifth century
Locale: Egypt and Italy
First published: 1853

Principal characters:

PHILAMMON, a young monk
HYPATIA, a female Greek philosopher and teacher
RAPHAEL ABEN-EZRA, a young Jew, Hypatia's pupil
MIRIAM, an old Jewish crone
AMAL, a young Gothic chief
PELAGIA, Amal's mistress
ORESTES, Roman prefect of Alexandria

Critique:

In Alexandria in the fifth century after Christ's death, there were many forces, Pagan, Christian, and Jewish, all struggling for the souls of men. *Hypatia* is the story of that conflict, which ended with the disintegration of a victorious Christian faction that used violence to gain its ends. The larger background of the novel is the dissolving Roman Empire.

The Story:

Philammon might never have left the little colony of monks three hundred miles above Alexandria if he had not strayed into an ancient temple in search of kindling. There, on the temple walls, he saw paintings of a life undreamed of in his monastic retreat, and he longed to visit the greater outside world. That very day, against the advice of the abbot and Aufugus, a monk whom he highly respected, he started out in a small boat and traveled down the river toward Alexandria.

In that splendid city at the mouth of the Nile lived Hypatia, the beautiful philosopher and teacher, one of the last to champion the ancient Greek gods. As she sat with her books one day, she was visited by the Roman prefect, Orestes, with the news that Pelagia, a beautiful courtesan who was Hypatia's rival for the hearts and souls of men, had left the city. Pelagia had transferred her affections to Amal, a Goth chieftain, and had joined him on a trip up the Nile in search of Asgard, home of the old Gothic gods.

Cyril, the patriarch of Alexandria, had reported to Orestes that the Jews of the city were about to rise and slaughter the Christians, but Orestes chose to ignore the matter and let events take their course. Hypatia, who also had reason to oppose the Christian patriarch, suggested that Cyril make his charges before the Roman tribunal, which would, of course, postpone action against the Jews.

A wealthy young Jew, Raphael Aben-Ezra, whom Orestes met on his way to the palace, suggested that the prefect plead ignorance of any plot in his reply to Cyril. Raphael disclosed to the Roman that Heraclian, a Roman leader, had recently sailed for Italy, where he planned to destroy the Gothic conquerors of Rome and make himself emperor. His news led Orestes to think of the power he might hold south of the Mediterranean if the expedition succeeded.

Sailing down the Nile, Philammon met Pelagia and the party of Goths traveling in the opposite direction. He helped the men kill a hippopotamus. When he warned them that they could never cross the cataracts to the south, the Goths decided to turn back. Philammon was given a place in their boat.

Orestes sent Hypatia a letter delivered by the old Jewish crone, Miriam. It contained Raphael's news and a proposal that Hypatia marry the prefect and share the throne he was planning to create for himself in Egypt. Hypatia's reply was that she would accept the offer if Orestes would renounce his Christian faith and aid her in restoring the Greek gods.

Orestes, having no desire to face excommunication, was disturbed by her answer. At Raphael's suggestion, he decided to wait for a month in the hope that Hypatia's desire to marry a future emperor would overcome her religious zeal.

When they arrived in Alexandria, Philammon left the Goths and went to deliver to the Patriarch Cyril the letters of introduction he carried. While waiting to see the patriarch, Philammon overheard a plot to raid the Jewish quarter the next day.

That night, as he lay in bed in the patriarch's house, Philammon heard cries that the Jews were burning Alexander's Church. Joining a crowd of monks hurrying toward that edifice, he was attacked by a band of Hebrew marauders.

But the report of the conflagration was false; it had been a trick of the Jews to lure the Christians into ambush. During the street fighting the Roman constabulary, which was supposed to keep order, remained aloof.

The next morning Miriam, who took a mysterious interest in Raphael's welfare, hastened to his quarters to warn him to flee. Christians, attacking the Jewish quarter, were pillaging the houses and expelling their inhabitants. To Miriam's exasperation, Raphael showed no interest in the fate of his wealth. Calmly exchanging his rich robes for a Christian's tattered rags, he prepared to leave the city. Miriam was left to save what she could of his possessions.

Philammon was one of the Christians who aided in despoiling the Jews. During the rioting he began to compare the conduct of the monks of Alexandria with the principles of charity and good works he himself had been taught. Hearing of Hypatia and her teachings, he naïvely went to the museum where she lectured, in the hope of converting her to Christianity by his arguments. Nearly put out of the building by her pupils when he rose to dispute with her, he was spared at Hypatia's request. After the lecture she invited him to visit her the following day.

The Alexandrian monks were incensed when they learned that one Philammon had been to listen to the discourse of a pagan. When he visited Hypatia again, they accused him of being a heretic, and the young monk barely escaped being murdered. Philammon, charmed by Hypatia's beauty and purity, begged to become her pupil.

Raphael, who had fled to Italy, found himself in a devastated Rome. Heraclian, after his defeat by the Goths, was preparing to reëmbark for Africa. After Raphael had saved one member of the ill-fated expedition and his daughter, Victoria, from two barbarian soldiers, he sailed with them from Ostia to Berenice, a port on the coast of Africa.

Meanwhile, in Alexandria, Philammon had become Hypatia's favorite pupil. Aufugus, learning that the youth had deserted his Christian brethren, went to the city to find him. One day the two men met in the street. Aufugus, seeing that Philammon was determined to remain with his mentor, declared that the young monk was actually his slave, and he appealed to Orestes, who was passing by, to force Philammon to go with his legal owner. Philammon fled to take temporary refuge with the Goths in Pelagia's house.

After Philammon had returned to his own rooms, he received a summons from Miriam. She confirmed the fact that he was Aufugus' slave, for she had seen Philammon bought in Athens fifteen years before. Although Miriam had received the report of Heraclian's defeat by fast messenger, she wrote a letter which declared that Heraclian had been the victor. She sent Philammon to deliver the letter to Orestes.

The prefect immediately planned a great celebration, in which the beautiful Pelagia should dance as Venus Anadyomene. Philammon hotly objected to the plan, for when Miriam told him he was a slave she had implied also that Pelagia was his sister. Annoyed, Orestes ordered the monk to be thrown into jail. There Philammon was held prisoner until the day of the celebration. Released, he hurried to the arena in time to witness the slaughter of some Libyan slaves by professional gladiators. Orestes, with Hypatia beside him, watched from his box.

When Pelagia was carried into the amphitheater by an elephant and introduced as Venus, Orestes' hirelings tried to raise a cry to proclaim him Emperor of Africa. No one responded. Pelagia danced before her audience until Philammon, overcome by shame, could bear the sight no longer. Running to stop her shameful dance, he was caught up by the elephant's trunk and would have been dashed to death if Pelagia had not persuaded the animal to put him down. Pelagia left the amphitheater. Philammon was hustled away by the guards.

Orestes, however, was determined that his plan should succeed. When the uproar caused by Philammon began to die down, he stepped forward and offered himself as emperor. As had been prearranged, the city authorities began a clamor for him; but hardly had they started their outcry when a monk in the topmost tiers shouted that Heraclian had been defeated. Orestes and Hypatia fled.

Philammon, when he returned home, found Pelagia in his quarters. He begged his sister, as he now called her, to leave the Goth, Amal, and repent her ways, but the courtesan refused. Instead, she entreated him to ask Hypatia to accept her as a pupil, so that Amal, whose affection for her was failing, would love and respect her as the Greek woman was respected. But Hypatia had no pity for her hated rival. Philammon, carrying the news of her refusal to his sister, could not help thinking fondly of his own religion, with its offer of pity to all transgressors.

Hypatia knew the populace would soon be clamoring for her blood and that she would be forced to flee. In one last desperate effort to hold to her creed, she forced herself into a trance that she might have a visitation from the gods. The only face she saw, however, was Pelagia's.

When Miriam visited Hypatia the same day with the promise that she should see Apollo that night if she would visit the house of the Jewess, the distraught philosopher agreed. But the Apollo the crone showed her was Philammon, stupefied by drugged wine. As Miriam had foreseen, Hypatia realized at last that the only gods she would ever see were those that existed in her own mind. Shamed and angry, she went away. The final blow to fall on Hypatia was the news Raphael brought her on his return to Alexandria the next day. Under the persuasion of Augustine, the famous philosopher-monk, he had become a converted Catholic before leaving Berenice, and he had married Victoria. That afternoon, as she started for the museum to give her farewell lecture, Hypatia was torn to pieces by some of Cyril's monks.

Philammon, when he learned of Hypatia's fate, visited Pelagia and pleaded with her to flee with him. By chance he met Amal, and in a struggle that ensued they fell from a tower together, and the Goth was killed. After Amal's death, Pelagia was willing to leave the city. Together they returned to the desert, where Pelagia lived in solitary penitence and Philammon became abbot, eventually, of the community he had left. Brother and sister died at the same time and were buried in a common grave.

Before he departed from Alexandria forever, Raphael learned from Miriam that she was his mother. A Jewess by birth, she had been converted to Christianity and had lived in a convent until it was sacked by the heathen. Afterward she had renounced her faith and had sworn the destruction of everyone not of her own race. Raphael had been given to a rich Jewess, who had represented him to her husband as her own child. After confessing her relationship to her son, Miriam died on his shoulder. She had been mortally wounded by the Goths after the death of their leader.

The victory which the Patriarch Cyril gained by Hypatia's death was only temporary. Though it marked the end of her creed in Egypt, it also signified the decline of the Egyptian Church, for the Christians, splitting into many factions, did not hesitate to use on each other the same violence they had once displayed toward the Greek philosopher.

I, CLAUDIUS

Type of work: Novel
Author: Robert Graves (1895-)
Type of plot: Historical chronicle
Time of plot: 10 B. C.-A. D. 41
Locale: Rome
First published: 1934

Principal characters:
TIBERIUS CLAUDIUS DRUSUS NERO GERMANICUS, Emperor of Rome after Caligula
AUGUSTUS CAESAR, first Emperor of Rome
LIVIA, his wife, Claudius' grandmother
TIBERIUS, Claudius' uncle, successor to Augustus
GERMANICUS, Claudius' brother
CALIGULA, Germanicus' son, successor to Tiberius

Critique:

I, Claudius is a semi-fictional reconstruction of an interesting period in the history of the Roman empire. In it are snatches of history, records of conquest, Roman scenes, and names famous in history books. It is told in an informal manner, Claudius going to great lengths to reveal plot after plot, and the narrative method obscures in part the scholarly research and historical accuracy of the author.

The Story:

Claudius, Emperor of Rome, was held in little esteem because he was a stammerer. He was, moreover, a scholar in a nation which worshipped soldiering. He had compiled state histories but he realized that they were dull, sententious drivel. At last he decided to tell the true story of his own life. As the source of his inspiration he cited the Cumaean sibyl whom he had visited in her inner cavern. She had said that eventually he would speak clearly.

From the beginning, the Claudian family felt ashamed of young Claudius because he was a lame stammerer who seemed unlikely to carry on the family tradition of power. For that reason he developed into a scholarly person interested in the lives of others. His teachers told him stories about famous people and from many sources he picked up stray scraps of knowledge about them as he grew up.

He was greatly interested in his grandmother, the Empress Livia. Bored with her husband, she had secured a divorce, arranged her own marriage with the Emperor Augustus, and poisoned thereafter anyone who interfered with her plans. Power was her sole delight.

Another of the infamous people about him was Tiberius, who was for years the successor-to-be of Augustus. Son of Livia by an early marriage, he married the wanton Julia, daughter of Livia and Augustus. When Tiberius, having offended Augustus, was banished, Livia insisted that Julia be banished too. Tiberius, tired of his banishment, promised that if Livia would secure his return he would agree with her every wish thereafter. About that time the two sons of Julia and Tiberius died mysteriously.

Between Claudius' ninth and sixteenth years he occupied himself with affairs of his older relatives. He was married early to a girl named Urgulanilla, who detested him as much as he detested her. Claudius' first love had been mysteriously poisoned and Claudius suspected Livia, who later forced him to marry Urgulanilla. Claudius' scholarship and stability eventually brought him into the good graces of Augustus and Livia. They made him a priest of Mars and showed by public interest in him that he was an accepted member of the imperial family.

Grain shortage caused rioting accompanied by arson. Augustus distributed grain according to the usual custom, banished such people as did not hold property in Rome, and rationed what food was available. Livia staged a sword fight in the arena to restore the good will of the populace. Because Claudius fainted publicly at the brutal sports, Livia decided that never again might he show his face in public. Soon afterward the last of Augustus' sons was banished for life. Tiberius was proclaimed the adopted son and successor of Augustus.

Tiberius and young Germanicus, brother of Claudius, campaigned against the barbarians, but Tiberius was not popular in spite of his victories with the army. Augustus suffered stomach disorders and died. Claudius knew that about a month before his death he had decided to restore his banished son, Postumus, grant money and honor to Claudius, and replace Tiberius. Claudius suspected Livia of the emperor's death.

Postumus was reported killed by a captain of the guard which had been placed around him. Livia slowly starved Julia to death. Because Germanicus was too honorable to seize the empire from Tiberius, there remained only the proof that Postumus was really dead to make Tiberius safe upon the throne. When Postumus returned, to disprove reports of his death, Tiberius had him tortured and killed.

Germanicus continued his successful campaign against the Germans. Tiberius, jealous, insisted that Germanicus return to Rome for his triumph. In A. D. 17 Germanicus returned. By that time Livia suspected Claudius and Germanicus of plotting against Tiberius. She sent Claudius to Carthage to dedicate a temple to Augustus, who had been deified by the Roman Senate.

Germanicus was next dispatched to the East to command the armies there. But Livia and Tiberius began to fear that Germanicus would win favor in the East as he had already done in the West. Germanicus was finally poisoned. His wife, Agrippina, sought protection from Claudius.

Claudius promised his thirteen-year-old son in marriage to the daughter of Sejanus, the friend of Tiberius. A few days later his son was found dead. Again he suspected Livia. Shortly afterward a divorce was arranged for Claudius by Sejanus, who was anxious to have Claudius marry Aelia, his sister by adoption. Claudius knew better than to oppose the wills of those in power and he accepted his new wife with practically no concern.

Tiberius set Livia aside. She was now growing old and he no longer had great reason to fear her. Bitter at the removal of her power, she began to make plans for his successor. She determined that Caligula, the son of Germanicus, should succeed him. She called in Claudius to declare a truce with him on the condition that he would have her declared a goddess after her death. In return, she told Claudius most of her state secrets; she said that all the murders she had planned were committed solely for the good of the state.

Tiberius, sixty-seven years old, seemed destined to die before long. He was living on Capri with a court of scholars, doctors, confidants, and entertainers, Sejanus having been left in Rome with authority to rule for him. When Livia finally died at the age of eighty-six, Tiberius refused to return to Rome even for her funeral.

Tiberius began a reign of terror against all members of Livia's faction. When Sejanus attempted to rebel against the emperor's cruel decrees, Tiberius ordered his execution. His children were also put to death. Claudius was ordered to divorce Aelia.

At last the mad Tiberius lay dying at

Misenum. Macro, commander of the guards, and Caligula, next in line for the throne, planned to take over the country. Caligula, already infamous among people who knew him, was still popular with the Romans. In too great a hurry they took command of the army. Then, learning that Tiberius was still alive, they smothered him.

In order to establish himself, Caligula pretended sympathy and generosity, but Claudius wrote in his history that Caligula held the record for infamy among princes up to that time. He began by spending the money Tiberius and Livia had hoarded so long. Then he fell ill. When he began to recover, he announced to Claudius that he had been transformed into a god, in fulfillment of the many prophecies that a god was soon to be given to the earth.

Caligula celebrated his godhood by wholesale assassination. Claudius' mother committed suicide because of Caligula's infamies. Soon Macro was forced to kill himself. At last the people began to turn against Caligula because of levies forced from the populace and the indescribable depravities of the palace brothel. Caligula, deciding to become a general, led an expedition into Germany. On his return he forced Claudius to marry his cousin Messalina. Calpurnia, Claudius' only true friend, was banished. The Romans were now plotting, almost openly, the assassination of Caligula. Before long he was murdered, and Claudius, the retiring scholar, was named Emperor of Rome.

I SPEAK FOR THADDEUS STEVENS

Type of work: Biography
Author: Elsie Singmaster (Mrs. E. S. Lewars, 1879-)
Type of plot: Historical chronicle
Time of plot: 1792-1868
Locale: Vermont, Pennsylvania, Washington, D. C.
First published: 1947

Principal characters:
THADDEUS STEVENS, lawyer and statesman
SALLY MORRILL STEVENS, his mother
JOSHUA,
MORRILL, and
ALANSON, his brothers
LYDIA SMITH, his housekeeper
ABRAHAM LINCOLN
ANDREW JOHNSON
MEMBERS OF CONGRESS, the CABINET, and the ARMED FORCES

Critique:

I Speak for Thaddeus Stevens is a biography in the form of a novel, a work making understandable as a man the complex and often contradictory character of the famous partisan statesman of the Civil War period. The author tells the story of his life as a series of dramatic episodes, each under its proper date and each presenting some crisis, either a triumph or a defeat, in his private affairs or public career. Much of the material in the book is based upon Stevens letters and papers previously unused by historians; the result is a carefully detailed portrait of the man against the unsettled age in which he lived. A native of Pennsylvania, Elsie Singmaster has presented faithfully in her novels and short stories the regional patterns of Pennsylvania German life and the history of the state through three decisive periods in our national life—the frontier in French and Indian days, the American Revolution, and the Civil War.

The Story:

In a Vermont cabin, on April 4, 1792, neighbor women had looked pityingly at a sleeping young mother while they wrapped the deformed foot of her newborn child. There was no need, however, to pity Sally Morrill Stevens, whose brave spirit was greater than her frail body. She would care for her second son as tenderly as she had looked after little Joshua, his father's namesake and a cripple at birth. She called the baby Thaddeus, after Thaddeus Kosciusko—a hero's name.

When Joshua Stevens, shiftless cobbler and surveyor, disappeared at last into the wilderness, there were two more children in the cabin. Morrill and Alanson stood up straight and were quick on their feet, but lame Thaddeus was Sally's favorite. Ambitious for her sons, she never complained as she worked and planned for their future.

Thaddeus struggled to excel. One day he limped through deep snow, his legs cut and bleeding on the icy crust, to speak before patrons and students of the grammar school in Peacham. His subject was free and universal education. Sensitive because of his own deformity, he learned to hate suffering and to sympathize with the weak. Swimming and riding gave him an athlete's body. His teachers and books borrowed from John Mattocks, Peacham lawyer, had trained him well by the time he was ready for Dartmouth College. Sally had hoped he would preach. He thought of Webster, already famous, and told her that he wanted to be a lawyer.

Vermont seemed a sparse land to her ambitious sons. Crippled Joshua traveled west with his bride. Thaddeus went to York, Pennsylvania, to teach and read for the law. Too impatient and poor to complete another year's residence before he could practice in York County, he rode south across the state line and became a member of the Maryland bar.

Returning, he settled in Gettysburg. At first no clients found their way to his office and few Gettysburgians wanted to hear his frank opinions on slavery and education, but children flocked around him to hear his stories of the Vermont woods. Blacks watched him on the street and whispered that he was their friend as well.

Defense lawyer in a murder trial, he lost his first case in court, but his townsmen praised him after he made his plea for justice and mercy. As his reputation grew men could measure his success by his fine house in Gettysburg and the great tract of mountain land providing ore and charcoal for Caledonia Forge, of which he was a partner. Sally Stevens now owned a fine farm in Peacham; he gave openhandedly to his brothers—Joshua in Indiana; Morrill, a doctor in Vermont; Alanson, with Sally on the farm. He fought Masons and Jackson Democrats and men cheered all night under his windows when he was elected to the Legislature. He was forty-one. There was still time for Washington, for Congress, perhaps the White House.

In 1837 word came to him in Philadelphia that the free education bill was about to be repealed. By train and stagecoach he hurried to Harrisburg and risked his political future with his proposed amendment to strike out the bill of repeal and to insert after the clause, "Be it enacted," the words "To establish a General System of Education by Common Schools." Speaking on that motion, he saved the free school system of Pennsylvania.

His fame spread. Men respected and hated and feared the blunt, shrewd orator whose voice was heard everywhere. In Philadelphia, during the Buckshot War, a mob attacked an assembly hall and he and his friends escaped through a window. Campaigning for Harrison, he hoped for a Cabinet appointment. But

Harrison died and Tyler forgot campaign promises. Ruined by his partner's failure in 1842, he moved to Lancaster. There he made money and paid his debts. Young men begged the opportunity to read law in his office. He became an ironmaster, owner of a great furnace at Caledonia. Sometimes Washington seemed a long way off. He waited.

Free-Soil Whigs elected him to Congress in 1848. Fighting the compromise measures and the Fugitive Slave Law, he spoke for gentle Sally Stevens, for old John Mattocks, lover of justice, for slaves fleeing northward along the Underground Railroad. He defended the three white men and thirty-eight Negroes accused after the death of a Maryland farmer in the Christiana riot; later he was to recall how Lucretia Mott and other Quakers had dressed the Negroes alike, to the confusion of witnesses and prosecution. Retired from Congress, he traveled to Vermont in 1854. Sally Stevens was dead, Morrill and Alanson before her. The slander of his enemies could never hurt her now. Joshua was soon to die. Thaddeus was sixty-two and failing, but men were mistaken when they said he was too old for public life.

In 1855 he helped to launch the Republican Party in Lancaster. In 1858 he returned to Congress. In Chicago, in 1860, he heard Abraham Lincoln nominated.

He rode the war years like an eagle breasting a whirlwind. Abraham Lincoln was President, but Thaddeus Stevens spoke for the Republican Party. Often impatient with the sad-eyed, brooding man in the White House, he steered through Congress the bills which gave Lincoln men and money to fight the Civil War. Lydia Smith, the decent mulatto at whom men sneered, kept his house on B Street. Sometimes he thought of the Cabinet post or Senate seat he believed his due, but usually more important matters filled his mind. Confederate troops, marching toward Gettysburg, had burned Caledonia Furnace. A nephew died at Chickamauga. Unbowed by personal misfortune, he argued for the Thirteenth Amendment, insisted upon education and suffrage for the Negro. There was little time for the card games he loved; he read more often when he went to bed at night—Shakespeare, Homer, the Bible.

Hating weakness and compromise, he fought Andrew Johnson after Lincoln's death. Congress, he thundered, should be the sovereign power of the nation. Sick and weak, he proposed Article Eleven by which the House hoped to impeach Johnson. Too ill to walk, he was carried into the Senate to hear that decisive roll call. He heard around him whispers of relief, anger, and despair as the telling votes were cast. Friends asked him if he wished to lie down after his ordeal. He answered grimly that he would not.

Although bitter in defeat, he would not let his fellow Republicans punish Vinnie Ream, the little sculptress involved in Johnson's trial, and he angrily insisted that she keep her studio in the Capitol. His detractors claimed he was too mean to die when he refused to take to his bed during that hot Washington summer, but by August the end was near. Devoted son, generous kinsman, loyal friend, harsh enemy, he died at midnight on August 11, 1868. The telegraph clicked the news to the world.

AN ICELAND FISHERMAN

Type of work: Novel
Author: Pierre Loti (Julien Viaud, 1850-1923)
Type of plot: Impressionistic romance
Time of plot: Nineteenth century
Locale: Brittany and at sea
First published: 1886

Principal characters:

SYLVESTER, a young Breton
YVONNE, his grandmother
GAUD, his cousin
YANN, a fisherman

Critique:

The number of translations and editions of *An Iceland Fisherman* are indicative of the warmth created by the reading of this beautiful story. Pierre Loti, of the French Academy, exemplified in this unadorned tale the virtues of French literature: clarity, simplicity, power. The exotic always appealed to Loti, and *An Iceland Fisherman* reflects this appeal in the descriptions of the fishing fleet in Iceland waters. The love interest is well presented and well within bounds. The characters of little Sylvester, big Yann, and serious Gaud are those of real people, whose fortunes are of genuine concern to the reader.

The Story:

In the foc's'l head, a hollow, pointed room like the inside of a gigantic sea gull, five men were sitting around the massive table which filled almost all the space between the bulkheads. They were waiting to take their turn on watch, for it was nearly midnight. They had cracked some biscuit with a hammer and had eaten. Now they were drinking wine and cider.

Around the room little pigeonholes near the ceiling served as bedchambers, for these fishermen were outside so much they seemed to need no air while they slept. A murky lamp swung back and forth with the gentle swell of the sea.

Sylvester, who was only seventeen, was impatient for the appearance of Yann. They were celebrating in honor of their patron, the Virgin Mary, and Yann had to take part in the toasts. Finally Yann opened the little hatch in the deck and came down the narrow ladder. Yann, in his late twenties, and a giant of a man, was a hero to Sylvester. The whole company brightened on his arrival.

It was midnight. The toasts were quickly drunk. Then the watch went on deck for their turn to fish. Outside it was daylight, for in those latitudes it never got dark in summer. It was monotonous and soothing to fish in the daylight.

At the rail Yann and Sylvester baited their hooks and dropped their lines. Behind them William waited with sheath knife and salt. Regularly, in turn, Yann and Sylvester brought up their hooks, passed the plump cod to William, and rebaited. Quickly William slit the fish, cleaned them, and packed them in the salt barrel. The pile of kegs in the hold represented the income of whole Breton families for a year. For his share of the catch Yann would bring home fifteen hundred francs to his mother.

While they were fishing Sylvester talked of marriage. Although still a boy, he was already engaged to Yann's sister. He did his best, as he had done all summer, to talk Yann into the idea of marriage with Gaud. Always Yann shook his head; he was engaged to the sea, he said, and some day he would celebrate that wedding.

Gentle and serious Gaud, Sylvester's cousin, was attracted to Yann. She was, however, a mademoiselle with fine hands and good clothes. Her father was rich. Yann could scarcely help knowing that Gaud liked him, but with Breton stubborness and simplicity he could not think of pretending seriously to a young woman of the upper class.

In September the fishing boat returned to Paimpol in Brittany. The return of the Iceland fleet was the signal for quickened

AN ICELAND FISHERMAN by Pierre Loti. Published by Alfred A. Knopf, Inc.

life among these simple folk. The women and children and the old men spent the whole spring and summer raising small gardens and waiting. Then in the fall, when the men came back, there were weddings and engagements and feasts and pardons. Too often a ship did not return, and several families would wear black that winter.

That fall there was a big wedding with the traditional procession to the seashore and afterward a ball. Yann went to the ball and danced the whole evening with Gaud. Yann told her of his life at sea and of his big family in Pors-Even. Part of the time Yann watched his little sister, who danced with Sylvester. The seriousness of the engaged children amused Yann. Gaud was greatly pleased, for at last Yann had unbent and his talk seemed to her too gentle for casual conversation.

Gaud waited all that winter in her rich home with its fine furniture, but Yann never came to see her. At length, overcoming her modesty, she went on a business errand for her father to Yann's house, in the hope of seeing him. She paid a sum of money to Yann's father and waited longer than she should have, but Yann did not come home. Later, she knew, Yann would come to see her father to conclude the business, and she resolved to talk with him then. But when Yann came to see her father, he prepared to leave without inquiring for her. As he came into the hall, Gaud stopped him. Yann simply told her he could not court her because she was rich and he was poor.

In the spring Yann and Sylvester sailed again with the Iceland fleet. Gaud, during that summer, felt an occasional thrill when she wrote letters to Sylvester for his grandmother, Yvonne. Often the doting old woman would dictate a short message to Yann. So Gaud was not completely out of touch with her simple, stubborn fisherman.

Events were soon to bring Gaud and Yann close together. Sylvester, the next winter, had to leave for his military service. His grandmother, Yvonne, visited him once at the barracks just before he left for French Indo-China. He was to be gone five years, and Yvonne was inconsolable.

Sylvester made a brave sailor in the French navy. On shore in the East he was sent with an armed patrol to reconnoiter. When the small band was surprised and surrounded by a large detachment of Tonkinese, Sylvester led a spirited counter-attack, until he was cut down by a sharpshooter. He was buried far from the rocky Breton coast in a green, strange land. An efficient, soulless government sent back his poor effects to Yvonne. She was now really alone, with only a memory growing dimmer as time passed.

Gaud's father committed one folly after another and lost more money trying to recoup earlier losses. Finally, at his death, he was a ruined man. Gaud, the rich man's daughter, became a seamstress. With quick sympathy she went to live with Yvonne, so that the two bereft women could comfort each other.

Yvonne, infirm of limb and mind, was unmercifully teased by a group of small boys who thought she was drunk. Falling into the mud, she vainly tried to regain her footing. Gaud came along to set the old woman on her feet again and brush the mud from her clothes. Just then Yann happened on the scene and chased the tormentors away. He escorted the two women home.

Yann was slowly changing his mind. Now that Gaud was poor, he felt a barrier between them had been removed. He also felt a great bond of sympathy for Yvonne because of her grandson, and Gaud was part of that sympathy. At the urging of his relatives and Yvonne, he proposed to Gaud. Much of that winter the couple sat by the fire in Yvonne's poor hut while the old woman slept. Six days before the fleet was to leave in March, Gaud and Yann were married.

When the fishermen departed on their

summer cruise, Gaud for the first time was part of the busy, weeping crowd. Yann's ship was towed out into the harbor to wait a favorable wind. During the delay Yann came ashore again for a final three hours. Gaud watched the ship disappear in the twilight.

The summer passed uneventfully enough. Gaud made fair wages from her sewing, enough to refurnish Yvonne's poor cottage. In September the fishing fleet came straggling back. Yann's ship was not among them. At the end of the month Gaud still had hope. Each masculine step along the path sent her scurrying to the window. Yann's father, also worried, called to comfort her. He told her many stories of ships delayed by fog until December. The fall and early winter came and went, and still Gaud waited.

She never saw Yann again. In August his ship had become separated from the others and was blown north. Somewhere off Iceland, Yann had kept a tryst, his wedding with the sea.

THE IDES OF MARCH

Type of work: Novel
Author: Thornton Wilder (1897-)
Type of plot: Historical chronicle
Time of plot: 45 B. C.
Locale: Ancient Rome
First published: 1948

Principal characters:
JULIUS CAESAR
POMPEIA, his second wife
CALPURNIA, his third wife
LADY CLODIA PULCHER, a conspirator
CATULLUS, a famous poet
CLEOPATRA, Queen of Egypt
MARCUS BRUTUS, another conspirator

Critique:

When an author writes a novel whose plot is already well-known, and that novel becomes a best seller, we must assume that his style is superior or that the story is so loved that we want to hear it again and again. In *The Ides of March* we have both factors. Thornton Wilder has retold the events of the last months of Caesar's life with warmth and depth of feeling. From imaginary letters and documents he has reconstructed the plots and intrigues leading to the fatal stabbing of the great Roman.

The Story:

There were so many different groups plotting to assassinate Caesar that it was impossible for him to guard himself from all of them. Each day new leaders rose to incite the people against him. Many of the leaders were friends of Caesar; some were relatives; some were merely ambitious men; and some were citizens who sincerely believed that Rome was suffering under Caesar's rule and wanted to free her. The last group had Caesar's admiration. He knew that he had restricted the freedom of the people, but he knew, too, that the masses of people shrink from accepting responsibility for their actions. They want to be ruled by one who will make all important decisions for them, yet they resent that ruler because he has taken their freedom from them. Caesar knew that he would one day be assassinated, but he hoped that he would see in the face of his murderer a love for Rome.

Among the most persistent of the plotters was the mother of Marcus Brutus. She had long hated Caesar and wanted her son to assume the place of the dictator. Many Romans said that Brutus was the illegitimate son of Caesar, but no one had ever been able to prove the accusation. Brutus was loyal to Caesar until the very end; only his mother's repeated urging led him at last to join the conspirators.

Another important figure among Caesar's enemies was Clodia Pulcher, a woman of high birth, great wealth, and amazing beauty. Because of her ambitions and lusts she had become a creature of poor reputation, so much so that her name was scribbled on public walls, accompanied by obscene verses. She was aided in her plots by her brother and by Catullus, the most famous poet in Rome. Catullus was a young man so much in love with Clodia that he would do anything she asked, and he wrote many poems and tracts against Caesar. Clodia spurned Catullus and his love, but her ridicule of him only strengthened his passion for her.

While all these plots against Caesar were taking shape, he and the rest of Rome were preparing for the visit of Cleopatra, Queen of Egypt. She, too, suffered from a bad reputation, for her many conquests in love were well-known in Rome. Most of the high ladies planned to receive her only because Caesar had so ordered, among them Pompeia, Caesar's wife, who knew of his earlier relations with the queen. But at Caesar's command Cleopatra was accorded the honor due a queen. He visited her many times, always in disguise, and on one of his visits barely missed being killed. He could never be sure whether Cleopatra knew of the plot. Marc Antony had begun to find favor in the eyes of Cleopatra, and as Marc Antony was involved in the attempted assassination, Caesar suspected that she too might be involved.

After Cleopatra's arrival, all Rome began to plan for the mysteries of the Good Goddess. This festival took place each year on December 11, and every Roman woman of high birth and moral virtue took part in the ceremonies. The Vestal Virgins participated in the festival also, and only women whose reputations were above reproach were allowed to attend the mysteries. Clodia's recent actions had given rise to the possibility that she might be rejected. In fact, petitions had been sent to Lady Julia Marcia, Caesar's aunt and a directress of the mysteries, to debar Clodia. Caesar interfered in behalf of Clodia, however, for just as he could understand the reasoning of his enemies, he could understand Clodia. She felt that she was fated to live the life she did and blamed the gods for her actions rather than herself.

But Clodia was vengeful. When she learned a compromise had been reached —she was to be allowed to attend the mysteries only until the Vestal Virgins appeared—she arranged to have her brother dress in the robes of a woman and attend the ceremonies with her. No man had ever been present at that sacred rite, and the profanation was the greatest scandal ever to reach the streets of Rome. The two criminals, for so they were called, were arrested, but Caesar pardoned them, thus adding another reason for public resentment. Once again it was suspected that Cleopatra knew of the plot, for she too had wanted to attend the mysteries and had been told she would have to leave when the Virgins appeared. It was rumored that Pompeia had known of Clodia's plan, and for these rumors Caesar divorced Pompeia, his reason being that regardless of whether the rumors were true Pompeia should have conducted herself so that no rumors could be started about her.

After his divorce Caesar married Calpurnia. Catullus had died in the meantime, and Caesar reflected much on the poet's death. He was not sure about his own beliefs concerning the gods and their influence on the world. Often he felt that there were no gods, that each man was the master of his own destiny. He wished that he were not guided by fear and superstition concerning life and death, but he continued to employ soothsayers and magicians and hoped daily for good omens from the heavens.

There were few good omens for Caesar at that time. His chief soothsayer had warned him of several dangerous days, but as all of them had passed uneventfully Caesar began to be less careful; and he planned to leave for the Parthian battlefront on March 17. He asked Brutus and his wife to care for Calpurnia while he was gone. He knew Brutus had been among his enemies, but he loved the younger man and believed that Brutus was now his friend.

Brutus promised Caesar to care for Calpurnia; but Brutus was to play a different role within a few days. The fateful Ides of March came. Caesar walked to the Senate chambers to make his farewell speech before leaving for the war. Approaching the capitol, he was surrounded by the conspirators. One plunged his dagger into Caesar's throat as the others closed in. Caesar was stabbed twenty-three times. When he saw that he was surrounded, he sat down and wrapped his robe about him. He did not cry out, but there are those who say that when he saw Brutus he said, "You, too, Brutus?" and ceased to struggle. Perhaps he was satisfied with his assassin.

THE IDIOT

Type of work: Novel
Author: Fyodor Mikhailovich Dostoevski (1821-1881)
Type of plot: Psychological realism
Time of plot: Mid-nineteenth century
Locale: St. Petersburg, Russia
First published: 1868-1869

Principal characters:
Prince Lef Nicolaievitch Myshkin
Parfen Rogozhin, friend of the prince
Mme. Epanchin, friend and relative of the prince
Aglaya Epanchin, her daughter
Natasya Filipovna, Aglaya's rival
Ganya Ardalionovitch, secretary to General Epanchin

Critique:

Because this book was written by the author of *Crime and Punishment* and *The Brothers Karamazov,* it will always have a significant place in literature. Like so many characters in Russian fiction, however, the people in this novel exhibit a behavior so foreign to the American temperament that the majority of readers may find the entire story rather incredible. Perhaps the most serious handicap lies in the author's portrayal of Prince Myshkin. It would seem that he is meant to be the foil for the other characters, the person who seems foolish but is, in reality, very wise and good. But the fact that the prince suffers from epilepsy confuses the issue, and one wonders if he really is an idiot. However, as a panorama of Russian morals, manners, and philosophy of the period, *The Idiot* is an interesting and informative novel.

The Story:

After four years spent in Switzerland, where he was treated for epilepsy at a sanitarium, Prince Myshkin returned to

THE IDIOT by Fyodor Mikhailovich Dostoevski. Published by The Modern Library, Inc.

St. Petersburg. On the train the threadbare shabbiness of his clothing attracted the attention of the other passengers. One of these, Parfen Rogozhin, began to question him. By the time they reached St. Petersburg, the prince and Rogozhin were well-informed about one another, and Rogozhin offered to take the prince to his home and to give him money.

Myshkin, however, first wanted to introduce himself to General Epanchin, whose wife was distantly related to him. At the Epanchin home he met the general and his secretary, Ganya, who invited him to become one of his mother's boarders. The prince interested the general, who gave him some money, and he also fascinated the general's wife and three daughters. His lack of sophistication, his naïveté, his frankness, charmed and amused the family. Soon they began to call him "the idiot," half in jest, half in earnest, but he remained on good terms with them.

Ganya, a selfish young man given to all kinds of scheming, wanted to marry the beautiful Aglaya Epanchin, chiefly for her money. At the time he was also involved in an affair with the notorious Natasya, an attractive young woman who lived under the protection of a man she did not love. Extremely emotional and neurotic, Natasya was really innocent of the sins charged against her. Myshkin realized her helplessness and pitied her. At a drinking party one night soon after his arrival, he asked her to marry him, saying that he had received an unexpected inheritance. She refused, declaring that she had no desire to cause his ruin. Instead she went with Rogozhin, who had brought her a hundred thousand roubles.

More than ever, Natasya became the object of spirited controversy among the Epanchins and their circle. Myshkin alone remained unembittered and always kind-hearted. Ganya and Rogozhin poured out their troubles to him, bared the sordidness and shamelessness of their lives, and swore undying friendship for him. Nevertheless, they distrusted Myshkin and plotted against him. When Natasya left Rogozhin, he swore that he would kill "the idiot" because he was sure that Natasya had fled from him because she really loved Myshkin.

Myshkin then became the victim of an extortion attempt. During a violent, repugnant scene, at which the Epanchins were present, he successfully refuted the charge that he had deprived Rogozhin's supposed illegitimate son of his rightful heritage. Having proved that the individual who sought the money was not the illegitimate son, he then, to the disgust of Mme. Epanchin, offered to give money to the extortionist and to become his friend. Mme. Epanchin considered the prince more of an idiot than ever.

Meanwhile, Aglaya Epanchin fell in love with Myshkin, but she continued to treat him scornfully and at first refused to admit that she was in love with him. When her true feelings at last became apparent, Mme. Epanchin gave reluctant consent to their betrothal and planned an evening party to introduce Myshkin to St. Petersburg society. Worried lest he should commit some social blunder, she and her daughter advised him to sit quietly and to say nothing during the evening. But at the party Mme. Epanchin herself drew out the prince, so that he was soon launched on one of his wild and peculiar conversations. The staid, conservative guests were astounded. In the midst of the discussion he knocked over a huge and priceless vase, then stared at the debris like "an idiot." A few minutes later he fell into an epileptic fit and had to be carried to his home. For several days the Epanchins were cold to him, but Mme. Epanchin finally relented and invited him to their home once more.

In the meantime Aglaya had been corresponding with Natasya, and a friendship had strangely developed between them. One evening Aglaya asked Myshkin to go with her to see Natasya.

In Natasya's apartment a hectic and

turbulent argument developed, so that the two women showed their anger and bitterness against each other. For the first time Aglaya revealed fully her love for Myshkin. During the argument Natasya fainted. When Myshkin rushed to her aid, Aglaya considered herself rejected and angrily left the house. The scene between the two women became a scandal, and the Epanchins barred their home to Myshkin. Natasya agreed to marry him and made preparations for the wedding. But on the day of the wedding, while Myshkin waited at the church, Natasya fled with Rogozhin, still haunted by her own helplessness and his terrible possessiveness.

Myshkin received the news calmly. Although there were many who laughed at "the idiot," there were some who were sorry for him when he attempted to discover Natasya's whereabouts. He left the village where the ceremony was to have been performed and went to the city. There he inquired among Natasya's acquaintances, but nobody knew where she was. Finally he went to Rogozhin's apartment and learned from a porter that Rogozhin had slept there the previous night. Myshkin continued his search, convinced that Rogozhin would kill him if he could. But Rogozhin himself stopped him on the street and took him to the apartment, where Myshkin found Natasya lying on the bed. Rogozhin had killed her.

Filled with compassion for the miserable Rogozhin, Myshkin spent that night with the body of Natasya and her murderer. At daybreak Natasya's worried friends and the police broke into the apartment. Rogozhin confessed to the murder. Myshkin was questioned by the police, but he was not implicated in the crime. He was sent back to the sanitarium in Switzerland, where he was visited, from time to time, by the Epanchin family and other friends. There was little hope that he would ever recover from his epilepsy.

THE IDYLLS OF THE KING

Type of work: Poem
Author: Alfred, Lord Tennyson (1809-1892)
Type of plot: Chivalric romance
Time of plot: Fifth century
Locale: England
First published: Separately, 1859-1885

Principal characters:

King Arthur
Queen Guinevere
Sir Lancelot,
Gareth,
Geraint,
Balin,
Balan,
Gawain,
Sir Galahad,
Sir Bors,
Sir Pelleas,
Sir Percivale,
Sir Modred,
Sir Tristram, and
Sir Bedivere, Knights of the Round Table
Merlin, a magician
Lynette, who married Gareth
Enid, who married Geraint

VIVIEN, an enchantress
ELAINE, the lily maid of Astalot
ETTARRE, loved by Pelleas and Gawain
ISOLT, of the white hands, Tristram's wife

Critique:

Divided into twelve sections, each symbolic of one month of the year, these poems present to the reader the span of a man's life, extending from the coming of Arthur to his passing. If one cared to search into the symbolism of this long narrative poem, he would find it filled with mystic and spiritual meanings. Although Tennyson's stories of King Arthur and the Knights of the Round Table lack the realism and vitality of Malory's tales, *The Idylls of the King* have a poetic compactness and allegorical significance lacking in the original.

The Stories:

THE COMING OF ARTHUR

Gorloïs and Ygerne had borne one daughter, Bellicent. King Uther overcame Gorloïs in battle and forced the widow to marry him immediately. Shortly afterward King Uther died. Ygerne's son, Arthur, was born at a time when he could have been the son of Gorloïs or the son of Uther born too soon.

The birth of Arthur was shrouded in great mystery. Merlin the magician reared the prince until it was time for him to take over Uther's kingdom and to receive from the Lady of the Lake the magic sword, Excalibur. After the marriage of Arthur and Guinevere, the king and his loyal members of the Round Table, in twelve battles, drove the enemy out of the kingdom.

GARETH AND LYNETTE

Bellicent, Arthur's sister, allowed her youngest son to join his two brothers in King Arthur's court on the condition that Gareth serve as a kitchen knave under the surly directions of Sir Kay the seneschal. When the young boy presented himself to King Arthur, Gareth made the king promise to give him the first quest which came along without revealing his identity. One day Lynette came to the court asking for Sir Lancelot to save her sister from wicked knights who held her captive. King Arthur sent Gareth questing with Lynette, who grumbled disdainfully at the kitchen knave ordered to serve her.

The first knight Gareth overcame was the Morning Star. Lynette still sneered at the knave. After Gareth had defeated another knight, Lynette began to relent. When he conquered a third strong knight, she allowed him to ride at her side. Next Gareth encountered a terrible knight, Death, who proved to be a mere boy forced by his brothers to assume a fierce appearance. Gareth returned to the Round Table victorious and married Lynette.

THE MARRIAGE OF GERAINT
and GERAINT AND ENID

Geraint, on a quest for Guinevere, came to the impoverished castle of Earl Yniol and his daughter Enid, a girl whose faded brocades spoke of former wealth and family pride. There Geraint learned that the rejected suitor of Enid had caused the ruin of Yniol. The earl gave Geraint Enid for his wife.

Geraint, fearing that the sin of the queen's love for Lancelot would taint Enid's love, went to his own castle and there idled away the hours in company with his wife until neighbors began to gossip that Geraint had lost his courage. Enid feared to tell her lord about the gossip, and Geraint, observing her strange attitude, decided that she had fallen in love with some knight of the Round Table. One morning, bidding Enid to don her faded brocade gown, Geraint set out with his wife after ordering her not to speak to him. Riding ahead of Geraint, Enid encountered men who would attack her husband, and each time she broke his command by warning him of his danger. After a while Enid was able to prove her love to her suspicious husband. They returned to Camelot, where Guinevere warmly welcomed Enid to the court.

BALIN AND BALAN

Balan left the care of Balin, his mad brother, and went on a mission to quell King Pellam, who had refused to pay his yearly tribute to King Arthur. With his brother gone, Balin was left alone in his gloomy moods. He worshipped the purity of Lancelot and the faithfulness of Guinevere until one day he saw his two idols speaking familiarly in the garden. Disillusioned, Balin fled to the woods. There he met Vivien, a wanton woman of the court, who further poisoned his mind against Lancelot and Guinevere. He left hanging on a tree the shield Guinevere had given him years before. Hearing Balin's mad shrieks among the trees, Balan rushed at Balin, whom he did not recognize without the shield of Guinevere. In the struggle Balin killed Balan and then was crushed by his own horse.

VIVIEN

Vain and coquettish Vivien set out to ensnare the most chivalric man in all the kingdom, King Arthur, but her wiles failed to win the attention of a king whose mind could harbor no evil thoughts. Vivien then turned to Merlin, who she knew possessed a magic spell. She tried to charm the magician with her beauty, pretending to love the ancient, bearded man, but he knew that she was not to be trusted. When she asked him to teach her the spell, he refused. But Vivien was not to be denied. At last, tricked by her beauty, Merlin taught her his magic powers. She enchanted him and caused him to disappear forever, a prisoner in a hollow tree.

LANCELOT AND ELAINE

Lancelot in disguise went to Astalot, where he left his shield with Elaine and rode off with her brother Lavaine to the tournaments. Lancelot won the jousts; then, wounded, he fled before anyone could discover who he was. King Arthur sent Gawain to search for the winner of the tournament. Gawain rode to Astalot, where he lingered because he had fallen in love with Elaine. She told him that she loved the knight who had left his shield with her. When Gawain saw the shield, he identified it as that of Lancelot.

Elaine nursed Lancelot back to health in the hope that he would return her love. Recovered, he sadly told her that he could never marry any woman. After he had gone, Elaine became ill and finally died in her grief. Her dying wish was to be put into a boat and sent to Camelot, in her hand a letter to Lancelot.

In Camelot Guinevere coldly rejected Lancelot, for Gawain had told of the affair between Lancelot and Elaine. When the body of Elaine floated to Camelot, King Arthur and Lancelot found the beautiful maiden in her boat, the letter in her hand.

Lancelot authorized a fitting burial for the lily maid. He unhappily lamented his hopeless love for the queen, not knowing that he would die a monk.

THE HOLY GRAIL

One day while Sir Galahad, the youngest and purest of all the knights, sat in Merlin's chair, the Holy Grail descended upon the Round Table in a flash and then was gone. When the knights swore to go on a quest for the Holy Grail, King Arthur gloomily predicted that the search would end in disaster for many of his knights because none was pure enough, save Galahad or Percivale, to see the holy vessel.

To Galahad the Grail appeared in all its splendor. Percivale, who followed him, also saw the holy sign. Sir Bors returned to King Arthur to report that he had viewed the Grail; but Lancelot had seen only a sign of it. Some of the other knights never returned to the Round Table from their perilous quest.

PELLEAS AND ETTARRE

Pelleas had given Ettarre a trophy he

had won in a tournament, but she, scorning the young knight, barred him from her court. Gawain, meeting Pelleas in his despair, offered to help him. After telling the knight to hide in the forest, Gawain went to Ettarre and told her he had killed Pelleas. As the days passed, Pelleas became impatient. One night, stealing into the castle, he found Gawain and Ettarre sleeping together and placed his naked sword across the throats of the sleeping lovers. Then in a mad rage he rode through the forest until he met Percivale, who accidentally revealed to Pelleas the scandal about Lancelot and Guinevere. Disillusioned, the young knight returned to the Round Table, where his rude manner to the queen foreshadowed evil to Lancelot and Guinevere. Sir Modred saw that the ruin of the Round Table was near at hand.

THE LAST TOURNAMENT

To a tournament at Camelot came Tristram, who had left his bride, Isolt of the white hands. Her name was the same as that of his beloved, Isolt, the wife of King Mark of Cornwall. Lancelot, laboring under the guilt of his sinful love for Guinevere, decided to fight with the similarly guilty Tristram, who won the tournament. Tristram then went to Isolt of Cornwall. King Mark was away on a hunting trip. He returned unexpectedly, found the lovers together, and killed Tristram.

In the north a knight rebelled against King Arthur's rule and charged that the Round Table was a thing of falseness and guilt where harlots and adulterers lived disguised as ladies and knights. King Arthur rode to quell the revolt and the guilty man was killed; but King Arthur was heavy in heart when he returned to Camelot.

GUINEVERE

Fearing exposure of her love for Lancelot, Guinevere asked him to leave Camelot. On the night of their farewell Modred trapped the lovers together, and Guinevere, feeling that she was shamed forever, went to Almesbury and took refuge in a nunnery. There she recalled how Lancelot had brought her from her father's home to marry Arthur, how she had thought Arthur cold and had fallen in love with the courtly, gay Lancelot.

King Arthur went to Almesbury. To Guinevere he spoke of his pride in the marvelous truths which the Round Table had upheld, and which Guinevere had inspired. Now all was lost, but he forgave Guinevere before he went off to fight against Modred and his traitor knights.

Filled with remorse, Guinevere asked the nuns to accept her in their order. There she gave her services until they made her abbess. After three years in that rank she died.

THE PASSING OF ARTHUR

In Modred's revolt King Arthur was wounded. As he lay dying he told Sir Bedivere to cast the sword Excalibur into the lake. When Bedivere finally brought to King Arthur the tale that amid flashing and strange sights an arm reached out from the lake to receive the sword, King Arthur knew that Bedivere had truly sent Excalibur back to the Lady of the Lake. Next King Arthur told Bedivere to carry him to the shore. There three maidens came in a barge to take King Arthur away. As Bedivere stood weeping, King Arthur assured him that the old order of the Round Table must pass to give way to something new.

So King Arthur passed, in the manner of his legendary beginning, back across the waters to Avalon, but many men believed that some day he would return to his people in their need. Bedivere watched on the shore until the wintry dawn broke bringing a new year.

IF WINTER COMES

Type of work: Novel
Author: A. S. M. Hutchinson (1880-)
Type of plot: Social criticism
Time of plot: 1912-1919
Locale: Southern England
First published: 1920

Principal characters:
MARK SABRE, an idealist
MABEL SABRE, his wife
LADY NONA TYBAR, a friend
MR. FORTUNE, Mark's employer
MR. TWYNING, a business associate
HAROLD TWYNING, Twyning's son
EFFIE BRIGHT, Sabre's friend

Critique:

The very least that can be said about *If Winter Comes* is that it is a beautiful and heart-warming novel. It is the story of a man who loved all humanity, but who was persecuted and betrayed by those who did not understand him. Although the book makes no pretensions to great literature, it is a perennial favorite among all classes of readers.

The Story:

Most of his friends thought Mark Sabre a queer sort, in spite of the normal life he led. He was married to a girl of his own class and he worked in the very respectable firm of Fortune, East, and Sabre, suppliers for the best churches and schools in England. It was his attitude toward life that seemed queer. He had no definite convictions about anything, and he could always see both sides of any controversy. He hated the restrictions that convention placed on people, but at the same time he believed that conventions were based on sound principles. Mabel Sabre, one of the most conventional women alive, was totally unable to understand anything her husband tried to discuss with her.

The only person who understood him well was Lady Nona Tybar, with whom Sabre had once been in love. Nona's husband, Lord Tybar, was a charming man, but completely without moral principles. When he flaunted other women in Nona's face, she turned to Sabre for comfort in his friendship, but Mabel, Sabre's wife, could not understand their friendship any better than she could understand anything else about her husband. After five years of marriage Mabel and Sabre were living almost as strangers under one roof. Mark Sabre's employer, Mr. Fortune, and his business associate Mr. Twyning, despised him because they did not understand him, and so Sabre felt that he lived only as he bicycled between his home and his office, for then he could know himself as he really was. Sabre felt that there was a mystery to life which he could unlock if he found the right key. And his life was almost dedicated to finding that key.

In addition to Nona, Sabre had three friends with whom he liked to spend his time. They were his neighbors, Mr. Fargus and old Mrs. Perch and her son. When the war came, young Perch wanted to enlist, but he could not leave his invalid mother alone. Sabre knew that Effie Bright, daughter of an employee at his office, wanted a position as a companion, and he arranged to have her stay with Mrs. Perch after her son went to the army. Young Perch was killed, and when his mother received the news she died too. Shortly after the old lady's death, Sabre himself joined the army. Because Mabel did not want to stay alone, she employed Effie to stay with her. However, she treated Effie as a servant.

Lord Tybar was a hero in the war, winning the Victoria Cross before he was killed. Nona went to France after her husband's death and drove an ambulance for the rest of the war years. When Sabre came home on leave, Mabel discharged Effie. She said that the girl was impertinent and unreliable.

Late in 1917, Sabre was wounded and sent home to stay. Mabel took no more interest in him than she had before, until the day she received a letter from Effie. Effie begged to come back to the Sabres. She now had an illegitimate child and no one, including her father, would take her in. Mabel was righteously angry at the proposal, and when Sabre tried to defend the girl she began to suspect that he might have a reason to help Effie. Before they reached a decision Effie, having no other place to go, arrived with her baby. When Sabre insisted that she stay, Mabel left, declaring she would not return until the girl and her baby had gone. Mr. Fortune and Mr. Twyning, who had been made a partner in the firm, would not allow Sabre to return to the firm unless he sent Effie away. They feared scandal would hurt their business. But Sabre would not be forced to do what he felt would be an injustice and a sin. For he had found the key to the puzzle; he knew that the solution to the mystery of the world is simply that God is love. Love for one's fellow men could set the world right again. He loved Effie as he loved all mankind, as he loved even his wife and the others who hated him.

But keeping Effie in the face of criticism brought only disaster to him and to the girl. Mabel sued for divorce on grounds of adultery, naming Effie. Sabre was away from his home when the papers were served, and before he could quite comprehend that his wife could believe such a foul thing he was arrested. Effie had taken poison, first killing her baby. She had learned of Mabel's suit and thought she could help Sabre best by committing suicide. Sabre's enemies were not satisfied. He was taken to court and accused of being responsible for her death. Effie's father, Mabel, and Mr. Twyning all claimed that he was the father of Effie's baby and that he had bought the poison which she drank. It was proved that he could have been the father of the child. Only one voice was raised in his defense. Nona returned from France and appeared at the trial. But there was little she could do.

The verdict made Sabre responsible for Effie's suicide. Sabre went home, but he would not allow Nona to go with him. In his house he found a letter from Effie. In it she told him that she was taking her life and that of her baby because she had caused him so much trouble. She also named the father of her baby; it was Harold Twyning, the son of Sabre's enemy. The boy had been afraid of his father's anger and had not claimed his responsibility.

Enraged, Sabre went to his old office prepared to kill Mr. Twyning. But when he reached the office, he learned that his enemy had just received word of Harold's death in battle. Sabre dropped Effie's letter in the fire and offered his sympathy to the man mainly responsible for ruining him. Then he went into his old office and collapsed from a cerebral hemorrhage. Nona found him there and took him home. For many months he could remember nothing that had happened to him, but gradually he began to piece together the sordid, tragic story. He learned that Mabel had secured her divorce and remarried. He learned to know Nona again, but he asked her to go away because he had accepted disgrace rather than reveal the story of Effie's letter. Nona refused to leave him, and after a year they were married. Sabre knew then that he had really found the key to the mystery of existence in that dark season of life before winter gives way to spring.

THE ILIAD

Type of work: Poem
Author: Homer (c. ninth century B. C.)
Type of plot: Heroic epic
Time of plot: Trojan War
Locale: Troy
First transcribed: Sixth century B. C.

Principal characters:
PRIAM, King of Troy
HECTOR, a Trojan warrior, Priam's son
HELEN OF TROY
PARIS, Hector's brother and Helen's lover
MENELAUS, Helen's husband
AGAMEMNON, Menelaus' brother
ACHILLES, a Greek warrior
PATROCLUS, Achilles' friend

Critique:

Homer has been hailed as the father of all poetry, and the *Iliad* has survived as a masterpiece for all time. The *Iliad,* within a three-day period of the Trojan wars, tells the story of the wrath of Achilles against King Agamemnon. The battle episodes reveal the true characters of the warriors, their strength and their weaknesses. These figures step out of unrecorded history as human beings, not of one era, but of all eras and for all time.

The Story:

The Greeks were camped outside the walls of Troy, in the tenth year of their siege on that city. Agamemnon, king of the Achaians, wanted the maid, Briseis, for his own, but she was possessed by Achilles, the son of Zeus. When Achilles was forced to give up the maid, he withdrew angrily from the battle and returned to his ship. But he won from Zeus the promise that the wrong which he was enduring would be revenged on Agamemnon.

That evening Zeus sent a messenger to the Greek king to convey to him in a dream an order to rise and marshal his Achaian forces against the walls of Troy. When the king awoke, he called all his warriors to him and ordered them to prepare for battle. All night long the men armed themselves in battle array, making ready their horses and their ships. The gods appeared on earth in the disguise of warriors, some siding with the Greeks, some hastening to warn the Trojans. With the army mustered, Agamemnon began the march from the camp to the walls of the city, while all the country around was set on fire. Only Achilles and his men remained behind, determined not to fight on the side of Agamemnon.

The Trojan army came from the gates of the city ready to combat the Greeks. Then Paris, son of King Priam and Helen's lover, stood out from the ranks and suggested that he and Menelaus settle the battle in a fight between them, the winner to take Helen and all her possessions, and friendship to be declared between the warring nations. Menelaus agreed to these words of his rival, and before the warriors of both sides, and under the eyes of Helen, who had been summoned to witness the scene from the walls of Troy, he and Paris began to battle. Menelaus was the mightier warrior. As he was about to pierce his enemy, the goddess Aphrodite, who loved Paris, swooped down from the air and carried him off to his chamber. She summoned Helen there to minister to her wounded lord. Then the victory was declared for Menelaus.

In the heavens the gods who favored the Trojans were much disturbed by this decision. Athena appeared on earth to Trojan Pandarus and told him to seek out Menelaus and kill him. He shot an arrow at the unsuspecting king, but the goddess watching over Menelaus deflected the arrow so that it only wounded him. When Agamemnon saw that treacherous deed, he revoked his vows of peace and exhorted the Greeks once more to battle. Many Trojans and many Greeks lost their lives that day, because of the foolhardiness of Pandarus.

Meanwhile Hector, son of King Priam, had returned to the city to bid farewell to Andromache, his wife, and to his child, for he feared he might not return from that day's battle. He rebuked Paris for remaining in his chambers with Helen when his countrymen were dying because of his misdeeds. While Paris made ready for battle, Hector said goodbye to Andromache, prophesying that Troy would be defeated, himself killed, and Andromache taken captive. Then Paris joined him and they went together into the battle.

When evening came the Greeks and the Trojans retired to their camps. Agamemnon instructed his men to build a huge bulwark around the camp and in front of the ships, for fear the enemy would press their attack too close. Zeus then remembered his promise to Achilles to avenge the wrong done to him by Agamemnon. He summoned all the gods and forbade them to take part in the war. The victory was to go to the Trojans.

The next day Hector and the Trojans swept through the fields slaughtering the Greeks. Hera, the wife of Zeus, and many of the other goddesses could not be content to watch the defeat of their mortal friends. But when they attempted to intervene, Zeus sent down his messengers to warn them to desist.

Fearing his armies would be destroyed before Achilles would relent, Agamemnon sent Odysseus to Achilles and begged the hero to accept gifts and be pacified. But Achilles, still wrathful, threatened to sail for home at the break of day. Agamemnon was troubled by the proud refusal of Achilles. That night he stole to the camp of the wise man, Nestor, to ask his help in a plan to defeat the Trojans. Nestor told him to awaken all the great warriors and summon them to a council. It was decided that two warriors should steal into the Trojan camp to determine its strength and numbers. Diomedes and Odysseus volunteered. As they crept toward the camp, they captured and killed a Trojan spy. Then they themselves stole into the camp of the enemy, spied upon it, and as they left, took with them the horses of one of the kings.

The next day the Trojans pressed hard upon the Greeks with great slaughter. Both Diomedes and Odysseus were wounded and many warriors killed. Achilles watched the battle from his ship but made no move to take part in it. He sent his friend Patroclus to Nestor to learn how many had been wounded. The old man sent back a despairing answer, pleading that Achilles give up his anger and help his fellow Greeks. At last the Trojans broke through the walls of the enemy, and Hector was foremost in an attack upon the ships.

Meanwhile many of the gods plotted to aid the Greeks. Hera lulled Zeus to sleep, and Poseidon urged Agamemnon to resist the onrush of the Trojans. In the battle that day Hector was wounded by Aias, but as the Greeks were about to seize him and bear his body away the bravest of the Trojans surrounded their hero and covered him with their shields until he could be carried to safety.

When Zeus awakened and saw what

had happened, his wrath was terrible, and he ordered Apollo to restore Hector to health. Once again the walls were breached and the Trojans stormed toward the ships, eager to fire them. Zeus inspired the Trojans with courage and weakened the Greeks with fear. But he determined that after the ships were set afire he would no longer aid the Trojans but would allow the Greeks to have the final victory.

Patroclus went to his friend Achilles and again pleaded with him to return to the fight. Achilles, still angry, refused. Then Patroclus begged that he be allowed to wear the armor of Achilles so that the Greeks would believe their hero fought with them, and Achilles consented. Patroclus charged into the fight and fought bravely at the gates of the city. But there Hector mortally wounded Patroclus and stripped from his body the armor of Achilles.

All that day the battle raged over the body of Patroclus. Then a messenger carried to Achilles word of his friend's death. His sorrow was terrible, but he could not go unarmed into the fray to rescue the body of Patroclus.

The next morning his goddess mother, Thetis, brought him a new suit of armor from the forge of Hephaestus. Then Achilles decked himself in the glittering armor which the lame god of fire had prepared for him and strode forth to the beach. There he and Agamemnon were reconciled before the assembly of the Greeks, and he went out to battle with them. The whole plain was filled with men and horses, battling one another. Achilles in his vengeance pushed back the enemy to the banks of the River Xanthus, and so many were the bodies of the Trojans choking the river that at length the god of the river spoke to Achilles, ordering him to cease throwing their bodies into his waters. Proud Achilles mocked him and sprang into the river to fight with the god. Feeling himself overpowered, he struggled out upon the banks, but still the wrathful god pursued him. Achilles then called on his mother to help him, and Thetis, with the aid of Hephaestus, quickly subdued the angry river god.

As Achilles drew near the walls of Troy, Hector girded on his armor. Amid the wailing of all the Trojan women he came from the gates to meet the Greek warrior. Not standing to meet Achilles in combat, he fled three times around the city walls before he turned to face Achilles' fatal spear. Then Achilles bound Hector's body to his chariot and dragged it to the ships, a prey for dogs and vultures.

In the Trojan city there was great grief for the dead hero. The aged King Priam resolved to drive in a chariot to the camp of Achilles and beg that the body of his son Hector be returned to him. The gods, too, asked Achilles to curb his wrath and restore the Trojan warrior to his own people, and so Achilles received King Priam with respect, granted his request, and agreed to a twelve-day truce that both sides might properly bury and mourn their dead. Achilles mourned for Patroclus as the body of his friend was laid upon the blazing funeral pyre. In the city the body of mighty Hector was also burned and his bones were buried beneath a great mound in the stricken city.

INDEPENDENT PEOPLE

Type of work: Novel
Author: Halldór Laxness (1902-)
Type of plot: Social chronicle
Time of plot: Twentieth century
Locale: Iceland
First published: 1934-1935

Principal characters:
BJARTUR, a crofter
ROSA, his first wife
FINNA, his second wife
ASTA SOLLILJA, Rosa's daughter
GVENDUR, Bjartur's son
NONNI, his younger son
INGOLFUR ARNARSON, Asta's father

Critique:

Independent People is one of the few novels to give us a faithful and artistic picture of the essentially unrewarding life in bleak, small Iceland. In addition to the background, Laxness has written in a style and with a scope approaching the epic. We get some of the feeling of the traditions of the Vikings, and we see the old give way to the new. Only the hard, barren life of the crofter is unchanging, for the Icelander in the remoter sections of his country lives on about the plane of the primitive savage.

The Story:

After working for eighteen years for Bailiff Jon, Bjartur was at last able to buy, with a heavy mortgage, the croft called Winterhouses. Proud of his new status as a landowner and fiercely independent, Bjartur promptly renamed the place Summerhouses. It was a poor place, fit only for sheep grazing. The house, which Bjartur rebuilt, consisted of one room over the stable. The walls were of sod, and the roof was made of a few sheets of corrugated iron covered with turf. But it was his own place, and Bjartur was determined to be hired workman for no man and to put his trust in sheep.

For his wife he chose the twenty-six year-old Rosa, a small sturdy girl with a cast in one eye, who had also been in service to the bailiff.

Rosa was disappointed in her house, and Bjartur was disappointed in Rosa. He soon found that she was far from innocent, and worse, she was already pregnant. He suspected, and was sure much later, that the man had been the bailiff's son, Ingolfur.

After a few months of marriage Bjartur left on a cold winter day to look for his sheep. Seeing a buck reindeer in the woods, he jumped on the animal's back and attempted to subdue him. But the reindeer was too strong and took off in mad flight for the river. With Bjartur still holding on, the animal swam downstream and finally landed on the other shore. Bjartur, nearly frozen to death, stayed to recuperate at a nearby croft.

He returned home after several days to find his wife dead from childbirth and a baby daughter still alive. Disregarding the parentage of the girl, he proudly named her Asta Sollilja. The bailiff's wife sent pauper Finna and her mother to look after Bjartur and the baby. Finna was nearly forty but strong and well preserved. To settle the problem of the child's care, Bjartur married her.

Each year Finna had another child, usually stillborn. But after some years there were Helgi, Gvendur, and Nonni, and their sister Asta. The croft was crowded, and the beds were all dirty and filled with vermin, but the land was clear of debt.

A southerner came to the croft one day to ask permission to camp and hunt. The stranger delighted Asta, who was awkward and uncouth but bursting with love. The stranger hardly noticed her, however, and each night he was gone most of the night. The reason for his visit came out later, when the bailiff's daughter left the country in great haste.

After little Helgi was lost on the moor,

---

the tie between Asta and Bjartur became closer. When Finna died from poor diet and rapid childbearing, the father tried his best to make life easier for the girl. He refused to let Asta go to school, but he did teach her much of the old Icelandic poetry.

Bjartur took Asta on his yearly trip to town, where, after doing the shopping, they stayed overnight in a lodging-house for country folk. To save money, father and daughter both slept in the same bed. Asta was unhappy. The town people had laughed at her homely clothes, and the snores of the drunken farmers in the nearby beds were terrifying. She snuggled closer to her father and kissed him. He put his arms around her, but to his horror found that she was kissing him repeatedly. Abruptly Bjartur got up and went out for their horse. Father and daughter left for home in the rainy night.

Then a series of misfortunes, which the Icelanders laid to a witch buried near Summerhouses, greatly reduced Bjartur's flock of sheep, and he went to town to work. Trying to meet his obligations to his children, Bjartur sent a schoolmaster to instruct Asta, Gvendur, and Nonni during the winter. But Bjartur's choice of teacher was unfortunate. After getting drunk one night the schoolmaster took Asta. When Bjartur came home in the spring, Asta was pregnant. In his rage Bjartur cast out his daughter, who went gladly, full of romantic notions of her lover. She walked to his fine town house, which turned out to be a shack. There she learned that he had many children and that his wife was again pregnant.

Nonni, just before the World War, went to America to join his uncle. Only Gvendur and Bjartur were left, in addition to the old mother-in-law. The war boom raised the price of lambs and Bjartur prospered. He now had two cows and three horses. At the same time, a cooperative movement, with Ingolfur at its head, was organized. In the parish only Bjartur held out; he remained loyal to the merchants who had been gouging him for years.

Nonni sent two hundred dollars from America to pay for Gvendur's passage. In spite of his father's objections, Gvendur, who was seventeen and big and strong for his age, decided to emigrate. He put on his best clothes and went to town to take the coastal steamer. There he was admired because he was going to America. During the day and night Gvendur had to wait before his ship sailed, he met the bailiff's granddaughter. She took him riding on the moor, where they spent the night together. Hoping to win her love, Gvendur renounced his emigration and went back to Summerhouses.

In spite of the depression following the war, Bjartur resolved to build his new house. He went deeply into debt to buy great supplies of stone and timber. That year he got the walls and roof completed, but there were no doors and windows. Before he could finish the house, the mortgage was foreclosed and Summerhouses passed into the hands of the bank.

The only place left for the family was the mother-in-law's old croft, long since abandoned. During the moving Bjartur met Asta and was reconciled to her. Asta had a second child by another man, and she was carrying a third. The family was complete again, except for Nonni.

Asta, like Bjartur, was independent. Ingolfur, now rich and a member of Parliament, had revealed to her that he was her father. His offer of support had been soundly rejected.

Bjartur fell in with some strikers who had struck against the government's low wages. For a while he was sympathetic with the men, who were, in a way, Communist led. Gvendur was even more sympathetic. But they both rejected in principle the idea of collective action. They were independent farmers and herders.

So they moved to the wretched hovel

far to the north, with only Blesi, their twenty-five-year-old horse, to do the hauling. By hard work they could continue their old way of life. They would have one room in a turf-covered hut. Their diet would be refuse fish. With luck they would be only a little less comfortable than savages in a jungle.

THE INVISIBLE MAN

Type of work: Novel
Author: H. G. Wells (1866-1946)
Type of plot: Mystery romance
Time of plot: Late nineteenth century
Locale: England
First published: 1897

Principal characters:
GRIFFIN, the Invisible Man
MR. HALL, landlord of the Coach and Horses Inn
MRS. HALL, his wife
DR. KEMP, a Burdock physician
COLONEL AYDE, chief of the Burdock police
MARVEL, a tramp

Critique:

The Invisible Man belongs to that series of pseudo-scientific romances which H. G. Wells wrote early in his literary career. The plot is one of sheer and fantastic invention, but it achieves an air of probability by means of the homely and realistic details with which it is built up. The characters involved in Griffin's strange predicament are also in no way remarkable; their traits, habits, and fears are revealed convincingly. The novel has outlived the time of its publication because of the psychological factors arising from the central situation and the suspense created by the unfolding of an unusual plot.

The Story:

The stranger arrived at Bramblehurst railway station on a cold, snowy day in February. Carrying a valise, he trudged through driving snow to Iping, where he stumbled into the Coach and Horses Inn and asked Mrs. Hall, the hostess, for a room and a fire. The stranger's face was hidden by dark-blue spectacles and bushy side-whiskers.

He had his dinner in his room. When Mrs. Hall took a mustard jar up to him, she saw that the stranger's head was completely bandaged. While she was in his room, he covered his mouth and chin with a napkin.

His baggage arrived the next day—several trunks and boxes of books and a crate of bottles packed in straw. The drayman's dog attacked the stranger, tearing his glove and ripping his trousers. Mr. Hall, landlord of the inn, ran upstairs to see if the stranger had been hurt and entered his room without knocking. He was immediately struck on the chest and pushed from the room. When Mrs. Hall took up the lodger's supper, she saw that he had unpacked his trunks and boxes and set up some strange apparatus. The lodger was not wearing his glasses; his eyes looked sunken and hollow.

In the weeks that followed the villagers made many conjectures as to the stranger's identity. Some thought he suffered from a queer disease that had left his skin black-and-white spotted. Unusual happenings also mystified the village. One night the vicar and his wife were awakened by a noise in the vicar's study and the clinking of money.

Upon investigation, they saw no one, although a candle was burning and they heard a sneeze.

In the meantime Mr. Hall found clothing and bandages scattered about the lodger's room; the stranger had disappeared. The landlord went downstairs to call his wife. They heard the front door open and shut, but no one came into the inn. While they stood wondering what to do, their lodger came down the stairs. Where he had been or how he had returned to his room unnoticed was a mystery he made no attempt to explain.

A short time later, the stranger's bill being overdue, Mrs. Hall refused to serve him. When the stranger became abusive, Mr. Hall swore out a warrant against him. The constable, the landlord, and a curious neighbor went upstairs to arrest the lodger. After a struggle, the man agreed to unmask. The men were horror-stricken; the stranger was invisible to their view. In the confusion the Invisible Man, as the newspapers were soon to call him, fled from the inn.

The next person to encounter the Invisible Man was a tramp named Marvel. The Invisible Man frightened Marvel into accompanying him to the Coach and Horses Inn to get his clothing and three books. They arrived at the inn while the vicar and the village doctor were reading the stranger's diary. They knocked the two men about, snatched up the clothes and books, and left the inn.

Newspapers continued to print stories of unnatural thefts; money had been taken and carried away, the thief invisible but the money in plain view. Marvel always seemed to be well-supplied with funds.

One day Marvel, carrying three books, came running into the Jolly Cricketers Inn. He said that the Invisible Man was after him. A barman, a policeman, and a cabman awaited the Invisible Man's arrival after hiding Marvel. But the Invisible Man found Marvel, dragged him into the inn kitchen, and tried to force him through the door. The three men struggled with the unseen creature while Marvel crawled into the bar-parlor. When the voice of the Invisible Man was heard in the inn yard, a villager fired five shots in the direction of the sound. Searchers found no body in the yard.

Meanwhile, in Burdock, Dr. Kemp worked late in his study. Preparing to retire, he noticed drops of drying blood on the stairs. He found the doorknob of his room smeared with blood and red stains on his bed. While he stared in amazement at a bandage that was apparently wrapping itself about nothing in midair, a voice called him by name. The Invisible Man had taken refuge in Kemp's rooms.

He identified himself as Griffin, a young scientist whom Kemp had met at the university where both had studied. Griffin asked for whiskey and food. He said that except for short naps he had not slept for three days and nights.

That night Kemp sat up to read all the newspaper accounts of the activities of the Invisible Man. At last, after much thought, he wrote a letter to Colonel Adye, chief of the Burdock police.

In the morning Griffin told his story to Kemp. He explained that for three years he had experimented with refractions of light on the theory that a human body would become invisible if the cells could be made transparent. Needing money for his work, he had robbed his father of money belonging to someone else and his father had shot himself. At last his experiments were successful. After setting fire to his room in order to destroy the evidence of his research, he had begun his strange adventures. He had terrorized Oxford Street, where passersby had seen only his footprints. He discovered that in his invisible state he was compelled to fast, for all unassimilated food or drink was grotesquely visible. At last, prowling London streets and made desperate by his plight, he had gone to a shop selling theatrical supplies. There he had stolen the dark glasses, side-whiskers, and clothes he wore on his arrival in Iping.

Griffin planned to use Kemp's house as a headquarters while terrorizing the neighborhood. Kemp believed Griffin mad. When he attempted to restrain Griffin, the Invisible Man escaped, and shortly thereafter a Mr. Wicksteed was found murdered. A manhunt began.

The next morning Kemp received a note which announced that the reign of terror had begun; one person would be executed daily. Kemp himself was to be the first victim. He was to die at noon; nothing could protect him.

Kemp sent at once for Colonel Adye. While they were discussing possible precautions, stones were hurled through the windows. The colonel left to return to the police station for some bloodhounds to set on Griffin's trail, but outside the house Griffin snatched a revolver from Adye's pocket and wounded the police officer. When Griffin began to smash Kemp's kitchen door with an ax, the doctor climbed through a window and ran to a neighbor's house. He was refused admittance. He ran to the inn. The door was barred. Suddenly his invisible assailant seized him. While they struggled, some men came to the doctor's rescue. Kemp got hold of Griffin's arms. A constable seized his legs. Someone struck through the air with a spade. The writhing unseen figure sagged to the ground. Kemp announced that he could not hear Griffin's heartbeats. While the crowd gathered, Griffin's body slowly materialized, naked, dead. A sheet was brought from the inn and the body was carried away. The reign of terror was ended.

IVANHOE

Type of work: Novel
Author: Sir Walter Scott (1771-1832)
Type of plot: Historical romance
Time of plot: 1194
Locale: England
First published: 1820

Principal characters:
CEDRIC THE SAXON, of Rotherwood Grange
WILFRED OF IVANHOE, his disinherited son
THE LADY ROWENA, his ward, loved by Ivanhoe
ISAAC OF YORK, a Jewish money-lender
REBECCA, his daughter
SIR BRIAN DE BOIS-GUILBERT, a Norman Knight Templar
KING RICHARD I, returned from the Third Crusade
ROBIN HOOD, an outlaw

Critique:

For over a hundred years *Ivanhoe* has held its charm in the popular mind as the epitome of chivalric novels. It has among its characters two of the most popular of English heroes, Richard the Lion-Hearted and Robin Hood, and tells a story of chivalric romance. It has sufficient action and color to appeal to a great number of people. Although *Ivanhoe* may not be Scott's greatest novel, it is without doubt his most popular.

The Story:

Night was drawing near when Prior Aymer of Jorvaux and the haughty Templar, Brian de Bois-Guilbert, overtook a swineherd and a fool by the roadside and asked directions to Rotherwood, the dwelling of Cedric the Saxon. The answers of these serfs so confused the Templar and the prior that they would have gone far afield had it not been for a pilgrim from the Holy Land whom they encountered shortly afterward. The pilgrim was also traveling to Rotherwood, and he brought them safely to Cedric's hall, where they claimed lodging for the night. The custom of those rude days afforded hospitality to all benighted travelers, and so Cedric gave a grudging welcome to the Norman lords.

There was a feast at Rotherwood that night. On the dais beside Cedric the Saxon sat his ward, the lovely Lady Rowena, descendant of the ancient Saxon princes. It was the old man's ambition to wed her to Athelstane of Coningsburgh, of the line of King Alfred. Because his son, Wilfred of Ivanhoe, had fallen in love with Rowena, Cedric had banished him, and the young knight had gone with King Richard to Palestine. None in the banquet hall that night suspected that the pilgrim was Ivanhoe himself.

Another traveler who had claimed shelter at Rotherwood that night was an aged Jew, Isaac of York. Hearing some orders the Templar muttered to his servants as the feast ended, Ivanhoe warned the old Jew that Bois-Guilbert had designs on his moneybag or his person. Without taking leave of their host the next morning, the disguised pilgrim and Isaac of York left Rotherwood and continued on their way to the nearby town of Ashby de la Zouche.

Many other travelers were also on their way to the town, for a great tournament was to be held there. Prince John, Regent of England in King Richard's absence, would preside. The winner of the tournament would be allowed to name the Queen of Love and Beauty and receive the prize of the passage of arms from her hands.

Ivanhoe attended the tournament with the word *Disinherited* written upon his shield. Entering the lists, he struck the shield of Bois-Guilbert with the point of his lance and challenged that knight to mortal combat. In the first passage both knights splintered their lances but neither was unhorsed. At the second passage Ivanhoe's lance struck Bois-Guilbert's helmet and upset him. Then one by one Ivanhoe vanquished five knights who had agreed to take on all comers. When the heralds declared the Disinherited Knight victor of the tourney, Ivanhoe named Rowena the Queen of Love and Beauty.

In the tournament on the following day Ivanhoe was pressed hard by three antagonists, but he received unexpected help from a knight in black, whom the spectators had called the Black Sluggard because of his previous inactivity. Ivanhoe, because of his earlier triumphs during the day, was named champion of the tournament once more. In order to receive the gift from Lady Rowena, Ivanhoe had to remove his helmet. When he did so, he was recognized. He received the chaplet, his prize, kissed the hand of Lady Rowena, and then fainted from loss of blood. Isaac of York and his daughter, Rebecca, were sitting nearby, and Rebecca suggested to her father that they nurse Ivanhoe until he was well. Isaac and his daughter started for their home with the wounded knight carried in a horse litter. On the way they joined the train of Cedric the Saxon, who was still ignorant of the Disinherited Knight's identity.

Before the travelers had gone far, however, they were set upon and captured by a party led by three Norman knights, Bois-Guilbert, Maurice de Bracy, and Reginald Front de Boeuf. They were imprisoned in Front de Boeuf's castle of Torquilstone. De Bracy had designs upon Lady Rowena because she was an heiress of royal lineage. The Templar desired to possess Rebecca. Front de Boeuf hoped to extort a large sum of money from the aged Jew. Cedric was held for ransom. The wounded knight was put into the charge of an ancient hag named Ulrica.

Isaac and his daughter were placed in separate rooms. Bois-Guilbert went to Rebecca in her tower prison and asked her to adopt Christianity so that they might be married. But the plot of the Norman nobles with regard to their prisoners was thwarted by an assault on the castle by Richard the Lion-Hearted, The Black Sluggard of the tournament at Ashby, in company with Robin Hood and his outlaws. Ulrica aided the besiegers by starting a fire within the castle walls. Robin Hood and his men took the prisoners to the forest along with the Norman nobles. In the confusion, however, Bois-Guilbert escaped with Rebecca, and Isaac made preparation to ransom her from the Templar. De Bracy was set free and he hurried to inform Prince John that he had seen and talked with Richard. John plotted to make Richard his prisoner.

Isaac went to the establishment of the Knights Templar and begged to see Bois-Guilbert. Lucas de Beaumanoir, the grand master of the Templars, ordered Isaac admitted to his presence. Isaac was frightened when the grand master asked him his business with the Templar. When he told his story, the grand master learned of Bois-Guilbert's seizure of Rebecca. It was suggested that Bois-Guilbert was under a spell cast by Rebecca. Condemned as a witch, she was sentenced to be burned at the stake. In desperation she demanded, as was her right, a champion to defend her against the charge. Lucas de Beaumanoir agreed and named Bois-Guilbert champion of the Temple.

The day arrived for Rebecca's execution. A pile of wood had been laid around the stake. Rebecca, seated in a black chair, awaited the arrival of her defender. Three times the heralds called upon her champion to appear. At the third call a strange knight rode into the lists and announced himself as Rebecca's champion. When Bois-Guilbert realized that the stranger was Ivanhoe, he at first refused combat because Ivanhoe's wounds were not completely healed. But the grand master gave orders for the contest to begin. As everyone expected, the tired horse of Ivanhoe and its exhausted rider went down at the first blow, so that Ivanhoe's lance merely touched the shield of the Templar. Then to the astonishment of all, Bois-Guilbert reeled in his saddle and fell to the ground. Ivanhoe arose from where he had fallen and drew his sword. Placing his foot on the breast of the fallen knight, he called upon Bois-Guilbert to yield himself or die on the spot. There was no answer from Bois-Guilbert, for he was dead, a victim of the violence of his own passions. The grand master declared that Rebecca was acquitted of the charge against her.

At that moment the Black Knight appeared, followed by a band of knights and men-at-arms. It was King Richard, come to arrest Rebecca's accusers on a charge of treason. The grand master saw the flag of the Temple hauled down and the royal standard raised in its place.

King Richard had returned in secret to reclaim his throne. Robin Hood became his true follower. Athelstane relinquished his claims to Lady Rowena's hand so that she and Ivanhoe could be married. Cedric the Saxon, reconciled at last with his son, gave his consent, and Richard himself graced their wedding.

Isaac and Rebecca left England for Granada, hoping to find in that foreign land greater happiness than could ever be theirs in England.

JANE EYRE

Type of work: Novel
Author: Charlotte Brontë (1816-1855)
Type of plot: Psychological romance
Time of plot: 1800
Locale: Northern England
First published: 1847

Principal characters:
Jane Eyre, an orphan
Mrs. Reed, mistress of Gateshead Hall

BESSIE LEAVEN, a nurse
EDWARD ROCHESTER, owner of Thornfield
ST. JOHN RIVERS, a young clergyman
MARY, and
DIANA RIVERS, his sisters

Critique:

Charlotte Brontë published *Jane Eyre* under the pseudonym of Currer Bell, a name chosen, she said, because it was neither obviously feminine nor masculine. But the emotions behind the book are purely feminine. Literary criticism may point to the extravagance, melodrama, and faulty structure of the novel, but lasting popularity is sufficient evidence of its charm and character for generations of readers. Charlotte Brontë wrote wisely when she cast her novel in the form of an autobiography. The poetry and tension of *Jane Eyre* marked a new development in adult romanticism, just as Jane herself brought to English fiction a new type of heroine, a woman of intelligence and passion.

The Story:

Jane Eyre was an orphan. Both her father and mother had died when Jane was a baby, and the little girl passed into the care of Mrs. Reed of Gateshead Hall. Mrs. Reed's husband, now dead, had been the brother of Jane Eyre's mother, and on his deathbed he had directed Mrs. Reed to look after the orphan as she would her own three children. At Gateshead Hall Jane knew ten years of neglect and abuse. One day a cousin knocked her to the floor. When she fought back, Mrs. Reed punished her by sending her to the gloomy room where Mr. Reed had died. There Jane lost consciousness. Furthermore, the experience caused a dangerous illness from which she was nursed slowly back to health by sympathetic Bessie Leaven, the Gateshead Hall nurse.

Feeling that she could no longer keep her unwanted charge in the house, Mrs. Reed made arrangements for Jane's admission to Lowood School. Early one morning, without farewells, Jane left Gateshead Hall and rode fifty miles by stage to Lowood, her humble possessions in a trunk beside her.

At Lowood, Jane was a diligent student, well-liked by her superiors, especially by Miss Temple, the mistress, who refused to accept without proof Mrs. Reed's low estimate of Jane's character. During the period of Jane's schooldays at Lowood an epidemic of fever caused many deaths among the girls. It resulted, too, in an investigation which caused improvements at the institution. At the end of her studies Jane was retained as a teacher. When Jane grew weary of her life at Lowood, she advertised for a position as governess. She was engaged by Mrs. Fairfax, housekeeper at Thornfield, near Millcote.

At Thornfield the new governess had only one pupil, Adele Varens, a ward of Jane's employer, Mr. Edward Rochester. From Mrs. Fairfax, Jane learned that Mr. Rochester traveled much and seldom came to Thornfield. Jane was pleased with the quiet country life, with the beautiful old house and gardens, the book-filled library, and her own comfortable room.

Jane met Mr. Rochester for the first time while she was out walking, going to his aid after his horse had thrown him. She found her employer a somber, moody man, quick to change in his manner toward her, brusque in his speech. He commended her work with Adele, however, and confided that the girl was the daughter of a French dancer who had deceived him and deserted her daughter. Jane felt that this experience alone could not account for Mr. Rochester's moody nature.

Mysterious happenings occurred at Thornfield. One night Jane, alarmed by a strange noise, found Mr. Rochester's door open and his bed on fire. When she attempted to arouse the household, he commanded her to keep quiet about the whole affair. She also learned that Thornfield had a strange tenant, a woman who laughed like a maniac and who stayed in rooms on the third floor of the house. Jane believed that this woman was Grace Poole, a seamstress employed by Mr. Rochester.

Mr. Rochester attended numerous parties at which he was obviously paying court to Blanche Ingram, daughter of Lady Ingram. One day the inhabitants of Thornfield were informed that Mr. Rochester was bringing a party of house guests home with him. In the party was the fashionable Miss Ingram. During the house party Mr. Rochester called Jane to the drawing-room, where the guests treated her with the disdain which they thought her humble position deserved. To herself Jane had already confessed her interest in her employer, but it seemed to her that he was interested only in Blanche Ingram. One evening while Mr. Rochester was away from home the guests played charades. At the conclusion of the game a gipsy fortune-teller appeared to read the palms of the lady guests. Jane, during her interview with the gipsy, discovered that the so-called fortune-teller was Mr. Rochester in disguise.

While the guests were still at Thornfield, a stranger named Mason arrived to see Mr. Rochester on business. That night Mason was mysteriously wounded by the strange inhabitant of the third floor. The injured man was taken away secretly before daylight.

One day Bessie Leaven came from Gateshead to tell Jane that Mrs. Reed, now on her deathbed, had asked to see her former ward. Jane returned to her aunt's home. The dying woman gave Jane a letter, dated three years before, from John Eyre in Madeira, who asked that his niece be sent to him for adoption. Mrs. Reed confessed that she had let him believe that Jane had died in the epidemic at Lowood. The sin of keeping from Jane news which would have meant relatives, adoption, and an inheritance had become a heavy burden on the conscience of the dying woman.

Jane went back to Thornfield, which she now looked upon as her home. One night in the garden Edward Rochester embraced her and proposed marriage. Jane accepted and made plans for a quiet ceremony in the village church. She wrote also to her uncle in Madeira, explaining Mrs. Reed's deception and telling him she was to marry Mr. Rochester.

Shortly before the date set for the wedding Jane had a harrowing experience. She awakened to find a strange, repulsive-looking woman in her room. The intruder tried on Jane's wedding veil and then ripped it to shreds. Mr. Rochester tried to persuade Jane that the whole incident was only her imagination, but in the morning she found the torn veil in her room. At the church, as the vows were being said, a stranger spoke up declaring the existence of an impediment to the marriage. He presented an affirmation, signed by the Mr. Mason who had been wounded during his visit to Thornfield. The document stated that Edward Fairfax Rochester had married Bertha Mason, Mr. Mason's sister, in Spanish Town, Jamaica, fifteen years before. Mr. Rochester admitted this fact; then he conducted the party to the third-story chamber at Thornfield. There they found the attendant Grace Poole and her charge, Bertha Rochester, a raving maniac. Mrs. Rochester was the woman Jane had seen in her room.

Jane felt that she must leave Thornfield at once. She notified Mr. Rochester and left quietly early the next morning, using all her small store of money for the coach fare. Two days later she was set down on the moors of a north midland shire. Starving, she actually begged for food. Finally she was befriended by the Reverend St. John Rivers and his sisters, Mary and Diana, who took Jane in and nursed her back to health. Assuming the name of Jane Elliot, she refused to divulge anything of her history except her connection with the Lowood institution. Reverend Rivers eventually found a place for her as mistress in a girl's school.

Shortly afterward St. John Rivers received from his family solicitor word that John Eyre had died in Madeira, leaving Jane Eyre a fortune of twenty thousand pounds. Because Jane had disappeared under mysterious circumstances, the lawyer was trying to locate her through the next of kin, St. John Rivers. Jane's identity was now revealed through her connection with Lowood School, and she learned, to her surprise, that St. John and his sisters were really her own cousins. She then insisted on sharing her inheritance with them.

When St. John decided to go to India as a missionary, he asked Jane to go with him as his wife—not because he loved her, as he frankly admitted, but because he admired her and wanted her services as his assistant. Jane felt indebted to him for his kindness and aid, but she hesitated to accept his proposal.

One night, while St. John was awaiting her decision, she dreamed that Mr. Rochester was calling her name. The next day she returned to Thornfield by coach. Arriving there, she found the mansion gutted—a burned and blackened ruin. Neighbors told her that the fire had broken out one stormy night, set by the madwoman, who died while Mr. Rochester was trying to rescue her from the roof of the blazing house.

Mr. Rochester, blinded during the fire, was living at Ferndean, a lonely farm some miles away. Jane Eyre went to him at once, and there they were married. For both, their story had an even happier ending. After two years Mr. Rochester regained the sight of one eye, so that he was able to see his first child when it was put in his arms.

JASON AND THE GOLDEN FLEECE

Type of work: Classical legend
Source: Folk tradition
Type of plot: Heroic adventure
Time of plot: Remote antiquity
Locale: Ancient Greece
First transcribed: Unknown

Principal characters:
Jason, Prince of Iolcus
King Pelias, his uncle
Chiron, the Centaur who reared Jason
Æetes, King of Colchis
Medea, his daughter

Critique:

The story of *Jason and the Golden Fleece* has been repeated in story and song for more than thirty centuries. Jason lived when great heroes lived and gods supposedly roamed the earth in human form. The story of the golden ram and his radiant fleece is read and loved by adults as it is by children. The story has been told in many different forms, but its substance remains unchanged.

The Story:

In ancient Greece there lived a prince named Jason, son of a king who had been driven from his throne by a wicked brother named Pelias. To protect the boy from his cruel uncle, Jason's father took him to a remote mountaintop where he was raised by Chiron the Centaur, whom many say was half man and half horse. When Jason had grown to young manhood, Chiron the Centaur told him

Pelias had seized his brother's crown. Jason was instructed to go and win back his father's kingdom.

Pelias had been warned to beware of a stranger who came with one foot sandaled and the other bare. It happened that Jason had lost one sandal in a river he crossed as he came to Iolcus, where Pelias ruled. When Pelias saw the lad he was afraid and plotted to kill him. But he pretended to welcome Jason. At a great feast he told Jason the story of the golden fleece.

In days past a Greek king called Athamas banished his wife and took another, a beautiful but wicked woman who persuaded Athamus to kill his own children. But a golden ram swooped down from the skies and carried the children away. The girl slipped from his back and fell into the sea, but the boy came safely to the country of Colchis. There the boy let the king of Colchis slaughter the ram for its golden fleece. The gods were angered by these happenings and placed a curse on Athamus and all his family until the golden fleece should be returned to Colchis.

As Pelias told Jason the story, he could see that the young prince was stirred, and he was not surprised when Jason vowed that he would bring back the golden fleece. Pelias promised to give Jason his rightful throne when he returned from his quest, and Jason trusted Pelias and agreed to the terms. He gathered about him many great heroes of Greece—Hercules, the strongest and bravest of all heroes; Orpheus, whose music soothed savage beasts; Argus, who with the help of Juno built the beautiful ship *Argo;* Zetes and Calais, sons of the North Wind, and many other brave men.

They encountered great dangers on their journey. One of the heroes was drawn under the sea by a nymph and was never seen again by his comrades. They visited Salmydessa where the blind King Phineus was surrounded by Harpies, loathsome creatures, with the faces of women and the bodies of vultures. Zetes and Calais chased the creatures across the skies, and the heroes left the old king in peace.

Phineus had warned the heroes about the clashing rocks through which they must pass. As they approached the rocks they were filled with fear, but Juno held the rocks back and they sailed past the peril. They rowed along the shore until they came to the land of Colchis.

Æetes, King of Colchis, swore never to give up the treasure, but Jason vowed that he and his comrades would do battle with Æetes. Then Æetes consented to yield the treasure if Jason would yoke to the plow two wild, fire-breathing bulls and sow a field with dragon's teeth. When a giant warrior sprang from each tooth, Jason must slay each one. Jason agreed to the trial.

Æetes had a beautiful daughter Medea, who had fallen in love with the handsome Jason, and she brewed a magic potion which gave Jason godlike strength; thus it was that he was able to tame the wild bulls and slay the warriors. Æetes promised to bring forth the fleece the next day, but Jason saw the wickedness in the king's heart and warned his comrades to have the *Argo* ready to sail.

In the night Medea secured the seven golden keys that unlocked the seven doors to the cave where the golden fleece hung and led Jason to the place. Behind the seven doors he found a hideous dragon guarding the treasure. Medea's magic caused the dragon to fall asleep, and Jason seized the fleece. It was so bright that night seemed like day.

Fearing for her life, Medea sailed away from her father's house with Jason and the other heroes. After many months they reached their homeland, where Jason placed the treasure at the feet of Pelias. But the fleece was no longer golden. Pelias was wrathful and swore not to give up his kingdom. But in the night the false king died. Afterward Jason wore the crown and the enchantress Medea reigned by his side.

JAVA HEAD

Type of work: Novel
Author: Joseph Hergesheimer (1880-)
Type of plot: Period romance
Time of plot: 1840's
Locale: Salem, Massachusetts
First published: 1919

Principal characters:
GERRIT AMMIDON, a Yankee sea captain
TAOU YUEN, Gerrit's Chinese bride
NETTIE VOLLAR, Gerrit's former sweetheart
EDWARD DUNSACK, Nettie's uncle
JEREMY AMMIDON, Gerrit's father

Critique:

Java Head is a novel of colorful detail and romantic incident, its scene laid in a historic port town during the period when the clipper ship was making America the mistress of the seas. In this novel Hergesheimer recaptures the spirit of an era, and by placing the exotic Taou Yuen against a late Puritan background he presents also a contrast of civilizations. One of the interesting features of the book is the fact that each chapter is written from the point of view of a different character.

The Story:

In Salem, Massachusetts, one spring in the early 1840's, there was concern because the ship *Nautilus,* owned by Ammidon, Ammidon, and Saltonstone, was seven months overdue. The captain of the ship was young Gerrit Ammidon, son of Captain Jeremy Ammidon, senior partner of the firm. Nettie Vollar grew more disturbed as the weeks passed. On the day the *Nautilus* left Salem, her grandfather had ordered Gerrit from the house before he reached the point of announcing his love for Nettie and asking her to marry him. The old man's reason for his action had been that Nettie was an illegitimate child and, as such, did not deserve to be married and lead a normal life. His theory was that the girl had been placed on earth only as a punishment for her mother.

Old Jeremy Ammidon also awaited the return of the *Nautilus,* for Gerrit was the favorite of his two sons. The other son, William, was primarily a tradesman interested in making money. Old Jeremy and William clashed regularly over the kind of trade the firm was to take, the liberty to be given its captains in trading, and whether the ships of the firm should be replaced by the swift new clippers that were revolutionizing the Pacific trade. William had never told old Jeremy that the firm had two schooners engaged in carrying opium, a cargo the older man detested. The atmosphere at Java Head, the Ammidon mansion in Salem, was kept more or less in a state of tension because of the disagreements between the father and son. Rhoda Ammidon, William's cheerful and sensible wife, was a quieting influence on both men.

Not many days later the *Nautilus* was sighted. When it cast anchor off the Salem wharves, Gerrit asked that the Ammidon barouche be sent to carry him to Java Head. The reason for his request became clear when the carriage discharged at the door of the mansion not only Gerrit but also his Manchu wife, Taou Yuen. The sight of her resplendent clothes and lacquered face was almost too much for Gerrit's conservative New England family. Only William's wife was able to be civil; the father said nothing, and William declared that the painted foreign woman was an unpleasant surprise.

Gerrit's first difficulty came when he assured his family that the Chinese marriage ceremony which had united him with Taou Yuen was as binding as the Christian service of William and Rhoda. The people of Salem wished to look upon the Chinese noblewoman as a mistress rather than as a wife. Nor did they understand that Taou Yuen was from one of the finest families of China, as far removed from the coolies and trading classes of Chinese ports as the New Englanders themselves.

The first Sunday afternoon after the arrival of the *Nautilus* Edward Dunsack appeared to thank Gerrit Ammidon for bringing a chest from China for him. The sight of Taou Yuen stirred Dunsack, largely because he was homesick for China. When he left Java Head, his mind was filled with a sense of injustice that Gerrit Ammidon should have the Manchu woman as his bride instead of Edward Dunsack and that Gerrit had married the Chinese woman instead of Dunsack's niece, Nettie Vollar.

Back in port, Gerrit saw to the refitting of the *Nautilus*. He did not see Nettie Vollar. Then, on the Fourth of July, the Ammidons met Nettie on the street and took her back to Java Head for the evening, lest she be injured or insulted by rough sailors on the streets. She did not see Taou Yuen, however, for the Chinese woman had remained in her room during the day. When it was time for Nettie to return home, Gerrit escorted her. It was the first time they had been alone together since he had been ordered from her home months before. Gerrit returned to the Ammidon house realizing that he had done Nettie a great wrong when he married Taou Yuen.

The following morning misfortune struck the Ammidons. Old Jeremy accompanied his son William down to the offices of the firm to inspect the specifications for two new clipper ships, and among some papers he discovered a bill of lading for one of the firm's two schooners engaged in the opium trade. His anger was roused to such an extent that his heart could not carry the strain. He collapsed and died in the office.

After the funeral, Gerrit, sick of the life ashore, took the *Nautilus* as his share in the estate, left the company, and prepared to return to sea as an independent trader. Even his wife had become unbearable to him since he had renewed his friendship with Nettie. Nevertheless, he determined to take Taou Yuen back with him and to establish their household in Shanghai, where he would no longer face the complications which arose from residence in Salem.

One day Edward Dunsack appeared at the Ammidon home to ask Gerrit to pay a call on his niece Nettie, who had been severely injured by a carriage. Gerrit left immediately, and Dunsack took the opportunity to attempt the seduction of Taou Yuen. Failing in his design, he poisoned her mind with an account of the love affair between his niece and Gerrit. In the meantime Gerrit, after a regretful interview with Nettie, had gone down to the *Nautilus* to regain his peace of mind.

The next day Taou Yuen was driven in the Ammidon carriage to pick up Rhoda Ammidon at the Dunsack home, where the latter had made a call on Nettie Vollar. Rhoda had already left. On an impulse Taou Yuen went into the house to see her rival. Angered because she thought Nettie commonplace and plain, Taou Yuen began to contemplate suffocating the girl. Suddenly Edward Dunsack, drug-crazed, entered the room and locked the door. Nettie fainted. When Taou Yuen repelled Edward, he threatened to strangle her so as to leave marks on her throat. To escape such disfiguration, forbidden by Confucius, Taou Yuen quickly swallowed some opium pills lying on the table beside the invalid Nettie's bed.

When help came a short time later, Taou Yuen was already unconscious. She died soon afterward. Edward Dunsack had gone mad.

Several days later, after the Christian burial of Taou Yuen, the *Nautilus* sailed from Salem harbor. It carried its young captain and his new wife, Nettie, to what they hoped would be a happier life.

JEAN-CHRISTOPHE

Type of work: Novel
Author: Romain Rolland (1866-1944)
Type of plot: Social chronicle
Time of plot: Late nineteenth and early twentieth centuries
Locale: Germany, France, Switzerland
First published: 1904-1912

Principal characters:
JEAN-CHRISTOPHE KRAFFT, a musician
MELCHIOR, his father
JEAN MICHEL, his grandfather
LOUISA, his mother
ANTOINETTE, a French girl
OLIVIER, her brother
GRAZIA, Jean-Christophe's friend

Critique:

Jean-Christophe is a two-thousand-page novel originally published in ten volumes, the painstaking record of the artistic development of a musical genius. Romain Rolland set out to portray the adventures of the soul of his hero and succeeded magnificently; in addition he broke down the artistic barrier between France and Germany. The experiences of Jean-Christophe are those of every genius who turns from the past to serve the future. In 1915 Rolland was awarded the Nobel Prize for Literature, in great part for *Jean-Christophe.*

The Story:

Melchior Krafft was a virtuoso, his father Jean Michel a famous conductor. It was no wonder that Melchior's son, Christophe, should be a musician.

Louisa, Melchior's wife, was a stolid woman of the lower class. Her father-in-law had been furious at his son for marrying beneath him, but he was soon won over by the patient goodness of Louisa. It was fortunate that there was a strong tie between them, for Melchoir drank and wasted his money. Often the grandfather gave his little pension to Louisa because there was no money for the family.

Melchior by chance one day heard his three-year-old Christophe playing at the piano. In his drunken enthusiasm, Melchior conceived the idea of creating a musical prodigy. So began Christophe's lessons. Over and over he played his scales; over and over he practiced until he was letter perfect. Often he rebelled. Whipping only made him more rebellious, but in the end the piano always pulled him back.

His grandfather noticed that he would often improvise melodies as he played with his toys. Sitting in a different room, he would transcribe those airs and arrange them. Christophe showed real genius in composition.

At the age of seven and a half Christophe was ready for his first concert. Dressed in a ridiculous costume, he was presented at court as a child prodigy of six. He played works of some of the German masters and then performed with great success his own compositions gathered into an expensive privately printed volume, *The Pleasures of Childhood: Aria, Minuetto, Valse, and Marcia, Opus 1,* by *Jean-Christophe Krafft.* The grand duke was delighted and bestowed the favor of the court on the prodigy.

Before reaching his teens, Christophe was firmly installed as official second violinist in the court orchestra, where his father was concert master. Rehearsals, concerts, composition, lessons to give and take—that was his life. He became the mainstay of the family financially, even collecting his father's wages before Melchior could get his hands on them. All the other phases of his life were neglected; no one even bothered to teach him table manners.

When Melchior finally drowned himself, his death was a financial benefit to the Kraffts. But when Jean Michel died, it was a different matter. Christophe's two brothers were seldom home, and only Louisa and her musician son were left. To save money, they moved into a smaller, more wretched flat.

Meanwhile Christophe was going through a series of love affairs which always terminated unhappily because of his unswerving honesty and lack of social graces. In his early twenties he took Ada, a vulgar shop girl, for his mistress. Because of gossip, he found it much harder to get and keep pupils. When he dared to publish a criticism of the older masters, he lost his standing at court. He had almost decided to leave Germany.

At a peasant dance one night he protected Lorchen, a farm girl, from a group of drunken soldiers. In the ensuing brawl, one soldier was killed and two were seriously injured. With a warrant out for his arrest, Christophe escaped to Paris.

Once in France, a country he greatly admired, Christophe found it difficult to acclimate himself. He met a group of wealthy and cynical Jews, Americans, Belgians, and Germans, but he judged their sophistication painful and their affectations boring. His compositions, although appreciated by a few, were not generally well received at first.

After a time, with increasing recognition, he found himself alternately praised and blamed by the critics. But he was noticed, and that was the important thing. Although he was received in wealthy homes and given complimentary tickets for theaters and concerts, he was still desperately poor.

At the home of the Stevens family, where he was kindly received, he instructed Colette, the coquettish daughter, and the younger, gentler Grazia, her cousin. Without falling in love with Colette, he was for a time her teacher and good friend. Grazia, who adored him, was only another pupil.

One night a blushing, stammering young man of letters was introduced to him. It was Olivier, who had long been a faithful admirer of Christophe's music. Christophe was immediately attracted to Olivier, although at first he was not quite sure why. Olivier's face was only hauntingly familiar.

It turned out that Olivier was the younger brother of Antoinette, a girl whose image Christophe cherished. Before he left Germany, a Jewish friend had given Christophe tickets for a box at the theater. Knowing no one to ask to accompany him, he went alone and in the lobby saw a French governess who was being turned away from the box office. Impulsively, Christophe took her in with him. The Grunebaums, the girl's employers, had expected to be invited also, and they were angry at the fancied slight. Antoinette was dismissed from their employ.

As she was returning to France, Christophe caught a glimpse of her on the train. That was all the contact he ever had with Antoinette. Now he learned that she had worn herself out by supporting Olivier until he could enter the École Normale. When he finally passed the entrance examinations, she had already contracted consumption, and she died before Christophe came to Paris.

Finding a real friend in Olivier, Christophe took an apartment with him. The house was only middle-class or less; but in that house and its inhabitants, and with Olivier's guidance, Christophe began to find the real soul of France. Away from the sophisticated glitter of Paris, the ordinary people lived calm and purposeful lives filled with the ideal of personal liberty.

Olivier became a champion of Christophe and helped establish his reputation in the reviews. Then some one, an important person, worked anonymously on Christophe's behalf. In a few years he found himself famous in France and abroad as the foremost composer of the new music.

Olivier's marriage to the shallow Jacqueline separated the two friends. In his eventful life Christophe made many more friends, but none so dear as Olivier. He did, however, discover his anonymous benefactor. It was Grazia, no longer in love with him and married to a secretary of the Austrian legation.

Jacqueline left Olivier, and he and Christophe became interested in the syndicalist movement. They attended a May Day celebration which turned into a riot. Olivier was fatally stabbed. After killing a soldier, Christophe fled the country.

During his exile in Switzerland, Christophe went through an unhappy love affair with Anna, the wife of a friend, and the consequent sense of guilt temporarily stilled his genius. But with the help of the now widowed Grazia, Christophe spent ten fruitful years in Switzerland.

When he returned to France, he was sought after and acclaimed. He was vastly amused to find himself an established master, and even considered out of date by younger artists.

Although Grazia and Christophe never married, they remained steadfast and consoling friends. Grazia died in Egypt, far from her beloved Christophe. He died in Paris. To the end, Christophe was uncompromising, for he was a true artist.

JERUSALEM DELIVERED

Type of work: Poem
Author: Torquato Tasso (1544-1595)
Type of plot: Historical romance
Time of plot: Middle Ages
Locale: The Holy Land
First published: 1580-1581

Principal characters:
GODFREY DE BOUILLON, leader of the Crusaders
CLORINDA, a female warrior
ARGANTES, a pagan knight
ERMINIA, princess of Antioch
ARMIDA, an enchantress
RINALDO, an Italian knight
TANCRED, a Frankish knight

Critique:

Jerusalem Delivered is one of the great poems to come out of the Italian Renaissance, and since that time the work has remained a landmark of heroic literature. The treatment of the Crusades is highly romantic, with both God and Satan freely taking an active part and magicians, angels, and fiends frequently changing the course of events. The descriptions of the fighting are in the typical romantic, chivalric vein. The action is rapid, scene following scene in kaleidoscopic review. In all, we have here an absorbing tale.

The Story:

For six years the Crusaders had remained in the Holy Land, meeting with success. Tripoli, Antioch, and Acre were in their hands, and a large force of Christian knights occupied Palestine. Yet there was a lassitude among the nobles; they were tired and satiated with fighting. They could not generate enough warlike spirit to continue to the real objective of their Crusade, the capture of Jerusalem.

In the spring of the seventh year, God sent the Archangel Gabriel to Godfrey de Bouillon, ordering him to assemble all his knights and encouraging him to begin the march on Jerusalem. Obeying the Lord's command, Godfrey called a council of the great nobles and reminded them stirringly of their vows. When Peter the Hermit added his exhortations, the Crusaders accepted their charge, and all preparations were make to attack the Holy City.

Within the walls of Jerusalem the wicked King Aladine heard of the projected attack. At the urging of Ismeno the sorcerer he sent soldiers to steal the statue of the Virgin Mary, hoping to make the Christian symbol a palladium for Jerusalem. But next morning the statue had disappeared. Enraged when he could not find the culprit who had spirited away the statue, Aladine ordered a general massacre of all his Christian subjects. To save her co-religionists, the beautiful and pure Sophronia confessed to the theft. Aladine had her bound to the stake. As her guards were about to light the fire, Olindo, who had long loved Sophronia in vain, attempted to save her by confessing that he himself had stolen the statue.

Aladine ordered them both burned. While they were at the stake, Sophronia admitted her love for Olindo. They were saved from burning, however, by the arrival of Clorinda, a beautiful woman warrior who knew that both were admitting the theft to save the other Christians from death. Released, Sophronia and Olindo fled from the city.

Clorinda was a great warrior who scorned female dress. On a previous campaign she had met Tancred, a mighty Christian noble, and Tancred had fallen in love with her; but she rejected his love. On the other hand, Erminia of Antioch had become enamored of Tancred when he had taken her city, but Tancred felt only friendship for her.

The Christians came within sight of Jerusalem. A foraging party encountered first a small force under Clorinda. She was so valorous that she defeated them.

The King of Egypt, whose army was advancing to the aid of Jerusalem, sent Argantes to parley with Godfrey. The Crusader chief haughtily rejected the overtures of the Egyptians, and Argantes angrily joined the infidel defenders of the Holy City. Although the Crusaders met with some initial successes, Argantes was always a formidable opponent.

Satan was annoyed at the prospect of the fall of Jerusalem. He induced Armida, an enchantress, to visit the Christian camp and tell a false story of persecution. Many of the knights succumbed to her wiles and eagerly sought permission to redress her wrongs. Godfrey was suspicious of her, but he allowed ten knights chosen by lot to accompany her. In the night forty others slipped away to join her, and she led the fifty to her castle where she changed them into fishes. Their loss was a great blow to Godfrey because the pagans were slaying many of his men.

Rinaldo, one of the Italian knights among the Crusaders, sought the captaincy of a band of Norwegian adventurers. Gernando, who sought the same post, quarreled with him, and in a joust Gernando was killed. For this breach of discipline Rinaldo was banished.

When Argantes challenged to personal combat any champion in the Crusaders' camp, Tancred was chosen to meet him. On the way to the fight, Tancred saw Clorinda and stopped to admire her. Otho, his companion, took advantage of his bemusement and rushed in ahead to the battle. Otho was defeated by Argantes and taken prisoner. Then Tancred, realizing what had happened, advanced to meet the pagan knight. Both men were wounded in the mighty, daylong duel. They retired to recuperate, agreeing to meet again in six days.

When Erminia heard of Tancred's wounds, she put on Clorinda's armor and went to his camp to attend him. He heard of her coming and waited impatiently, thinking his beloved Clorinda was approaching. But Erminia was surprised by the sentries, and in her maidenly timidity she ran away to take refuge with a shepherd.

When the supposed Clorinda did not arrive, Tancred went in search of her and came to the castle of Armida, where he was cast into a dungeon.

Godfrey received word that Sweno, Prince of Denmark, who had been occupying Palestine, had been surprised by pagan knights and killed with all his followers. The messenger announced that he had been divinely appointed to deliver Sweno's sword to Rinaldo. Although Rinaldo was still absent, Godfrey set out to avenge the Palestine garrison.

Godfrey and his army fought valiantly, but Argantes and Clorinda were fighters too powerful for the shaken Christians to overcome. Then Tancred and the fifty knights, who had been freed from Armida's enchantment, arrived to rout the pagans with great losses. Godfrey learned that the missing men had been liberated by Rinaldo. Peter the Hermit was then divinely inspired to foretell the glorious future of Rinaldo.

In preparation for the attack on Jerusalem the Christians celebrated a solemn mass on the Mount of Olives before they began the assault. Wounded by one of Clorinda's arrows, Godfrey retired from the battle while an angel healed his wound. The Christians set up rams and towers to break the defense of the city.

At night Clorinda came out of the city walls and set fire to the great tower by which the Christians were preparing to scale the wall. She was seen, however, by the Crusaders, and Tancred engaged her in combat. After he had run his sword through her breast, he discovered to his sorrow that he had killed his love. He had time to ask her pardon and baptize her before her death.

Godfrey was taken in a vision to heaven where he talked with Hugh, the former commander of the French forces. Hugh bade him recall Rinaldo, and Godfrey sent two knights to find the banished Italian. On the Fortunate Islands the messengers discovered the Palace of Armida where Rinaldo, having fallen in love with the enchantress, was dallying with his lady love. The sight of the two knights quickly reminded him of his duty. Leaving his love, he joined the besieging forces of Godfrey.

With the arrival of Rinaldo, the Christians were greatly heartened. Then the Archangel Michael appeared to Godfrey and showed him the souls of all the Christians who had died in the Crusades. With this inspiration, the Crusaders redoubled their efforts to capture Jerusalem.

The walls of the city were breached. Tancred met Argantes and killed him in single combat. Finally the victorious invaders stormed through the streets and sacked the Holy City. When the Egyptians arrived to help the pagan defenders of Jerusalem, they too were beaten and their king was slain by Godfrey. Armida, all hope gone, surrendered herself to Rinaldo, who had been the most valorous of the conquerors.

After the fighting was over, Godfrey and all his army worshipped at the Holy Sepulchre.

THE JEW OF MALTA

Type of work: Drama
Author: Christopher Marlowe (1564-1593)
Type of plot: Romantic tragedy
Time of plot: Fifteenth century
Locale: Malta
First presented: c. 1589

Principal characters:
BARABAS, a Jewish merchant
ABIGAIL, his daughter
ITHAMORE, a slave
THE GOVERNOR OF MALTA

Critique:

The Machiavellian character of Barabas dominates *The Jew of Malta;* the other characters are merely sketched in. The plot of the play seems to have come wholly from the fertile mind of Marlowe, whose exotic plots and romantic heroes set a pattern which was followed by subsequent Elizabethan playwrights, including Shakespeare. Mechanically, *The Jew of Malta* begins well, but it degenerates into an orgy of blood after the second act.

The Story:

Barabas, a Christian-hating merchant of Malta, received in his counting-house a party of merchants who reported the arrival of several vessels laden with wealth from the East. At the same time three Jews arrived to announce an important meeting at the senate.

The import of the meeting was that the Turkish masters of Malta had demanded tribute long overdue. The Turkish Grand Seignior had purposely let the payment lapse over a period of years so that the Maltese would find it impossible to raise the sum demanded. The Maltese had a choice of payment or surrender. The Christian governor of the island, attempting to collect the tribute within a month, decreed that the Jews would have to give over half of their estates or become Christians. All of the Jewish community except Barabas submitted to the decree of the governor in one way or another. The governor seized all of Barabas' wealth as punishment and had the Jew's house turned into a Christian convent.

Barabas, to avoid complete ruin, purposely failed to report part of his treasure hidden in the foundation of his house. Then he persuaded his daughter, Abigail, to pretend that she had been converted to Christianity so that she might enter the convent and recover the treasure. Abigail dutifully entered the nunnery as a convert and subsequently threw the bags of money out of the window at night to her waiting father.

Martin Del Bosco, vice-admiral of Spain, sailed into the harbor of Malta for the purpose of selling some Turkish slaves he had aboard his ship. The governor was reluctant to allow the sale because of the difficulties he was having with the Grand Seignior. Del Bosco, by promising military aid from Spain, persuaded the governor to defy the Turks and to permit the sale.

Barabas bought one of the slaves, an Arabian named Ithamore. During the sale, Barabas fawned upon Don Lodowick, the governor's son, and Don Mathias. He invited the two young men to his house and ordered Abigail, now returned from the convent, to show favor to both. In his desire for revenge, Barabas arranged with each young man, separately, to marry his daughter. He then sent forged letters to Don Lodowick and Don Mathias, and provoked a duel in which the young men were killed. Meanwhile Barabas trained his slave, Ithamore, to be his creature in his plot against the governor and the Christians of Malta.

Because of her father's evil intentions, Abigail returned to the convent. Barabas, enraged, sent poisoned porridge to the convent as his gesture of thanks on the Eve of St. Jacques, the patron saint of Malta. All in the convent were poisoned, and Abigail, before she died, confessed to Friar Jacomo, disclosing to him all that Barabas had done and all that he planned to do.

When the Turks returned to Malta to collect the tribute, the governor defied them and prepared for a siege of the island.

Meanwhile the friars, in violation of canon law, revealed the information they had gained from Abigail's confession. Barabas, again threatened, pretended a desire to become a convert and promised all of his worldly wealth to the friars who would receive him into the Christian faith. The greediness of the friars caused differences to arise among them; Barabas took advantage of this situation and with the help of Ithamore strangled a friar named Bernardine. He then propped up Bernardine's body in such a way that Friar Jacomo knocked it down. Observed in this act, Friar Jacomo was accused of the murder of one of his clerical brothers.

Ithamore met a strumpet, Bellamira, who, playing upon the slave's pride and viciousness, persuaded him to extort money from his master by threatening to expose Barabas. His master, alarmed by threats of blackmail, disguised himself as a French musician, went to the strumpet's house, and poisoned Bellamira and Ithamore with a bouquet of flowers.

Before their deaths, they managed to communicate all they knew to the governor, who, despite his preoccupation with the fortifications of Malta, threw Barabas into prison. By drinking poppy essence and cold mandrake juice, Barabas appeared to be dead. His body was placed outside the city. Reviving, he joined the Turks and led them into the city. As a reward for his betraying Malta, Barabas was made governor. He now turned to the conquered Maltese, offering to put the Turks into their hands for a substantial price.

Under the direction of Barabas, explosives were set beneath the barracks of the Turkish troops. Then Barabas invited the Turkish leaders to a banquet in the governor's palace, after planning to have them fall through a false floor into cauldrons of boiling liquid beneath. On signal, the Turkish troops were blown sky-high, but the Christian governor, who preferred to seize the Turkish leaders alive, exposed Barabas' scheme. The Jew of Malta perished in the trap he had set for the Turks.

JOHN BROWN'S BODY

Type of work: Poem
Author: Stephen Vincent Benét, (1898-1943)
Type of plot: Historical romance
Time of plot: 1858-1865
Locale: The United States
First published: 1928

Principal characters:
JACK ELLYAT, a soldier from Connecticut
CLAY WINGATE, a soldier from Georgia
LUKE BRECKINRIDGE, a Southern mountaineer
MELORA VILAS, Jack Ellyat's beloved
SALLY DUPRÉ, Clay Wingate's fiancée
LUCY WEATHERBY, Sally's rival
SHIPPY, a Union spy
SOPHY, a Richmond hotel employee

Critique:

John Brown's Body, which won the Pulitzer Prize for 1929, tells, in free and formal verse, the tragic story of the Civil War and its effects upon the nation. Benét achieves an effective counterpoint by weaving several small plots concerned with fictional characters into the main plot which we know as the actual history of the time. He manipulates his characters so that important phases of the war are interfused with his minor plots, and the two are carried forward simultaneously. His re-creation of the atmosphere of a burgeoning, adolescent United States is excellent.

The Story:

Jack Ellyat, a Connecticut youth, had premonitions of trouble as he walked with his dog in the mellow New England Indian summer. He and his family were Abolitionists. The influence of Emerson and Thoreau was felt in Concord, where they talked about an ideal state. But in Boston Minister Higginson and Dr. Howe waited for reports of a project planned for Harper's Ferry. In Georgia young Clay Wingate also received a premonition of impending disaster and great change.

John Brown, rock-hard fanatic, believing he was chosen by God to free the black man in America, led his troop of raiders to seize the United States arsenal at Harper's Ferry, Virginia. The first man killed in the fracas was Shepherd Heyward, a free Negro. The South was alarmed. Federal troops under Robert E. Lee subdued the Brown party in fifteen minutes; all was ended but the slow, smoldering hates and the deaths to come.

At Wingate Hall in Georgia all was peaceful. Sally Dupré and Clay Wingate were expected to marry. When Cudjo, the major-domo of the Wingate plantation, heard of the Harper's Ferry raid and John Brown, he opined that the Negro's business was not the white man's business. In Connecticut Mrs. Ellyat prayed for John Brown.

Brown was tried at Charles Town, Virginia. During the trial he denied the complicity of anyone but himself and his followers in the raid. He insisted that he had done what he thought was right. A legend grew around his name and mushroomed after he was hanged. Songs were sung. John Brown's body rested in its grave, but his spirit haunted the consciences of North and South alike.

Fort Sumter surrendered, and the Confederate States of America elected gaunt, tired Jefferson Davis president. Lank, sad-faced Abraham Lincoln, the frontier wit and small-time politician, was President of the United States. He ordered conscription of fighting men. Clay Wingate, loyal to Dixie, joined the Black Horse Troop and rode away to the war. Jack Ellyat marched off with the Connecticut volunteers.

Raw soldiers of North and South met at Bull Run under the direction of Generals McDowell, Johnston, and Beauregard. Congressmen and their ladies drove out from Washington to watch the Union victory. While they watched, the Union lines broke and retreated in panic. A movement to treat with the Confederacy for peace got under way in the North. Lincoln was alarmed, but he remained steadfast.

Jack Ellyat was mustered out after Bull Run. Later he joined the Illinois volunteers in Chicago and became known as "Bull Run Jack." Near Pittsburg Landing, in Tennessee, he lost his head and ran during a surprise attack. He was captured but escaped again during a night march. Hungry and worn out, Jack arrived at the Vilas farm, where he stayed in hiding and fell in love with Melora Vilas. At last he left the farm to seek the manhood he had lost near

Pittsburg Landing, but not before he had got Melora with child. He was recaptured soon afterward.

Meanwhile Clay Wingate returned to Georgia on leave. At Wingate Hall the war seemed far away, for the successful running of the Union blockade of Southern ports made luxuries still available. Lucy Weatherby, a Virginian whose sweetheart had been killed at Bull Run, attended a dance at Wingate Hall and replaced Sally Dupré in Clay's affections. Spade, a slave on the nearby Zachary plantation, escaped that same night.

New Orleans was captured. Davis and Lincoln began to bow under the burdens of the war. McClellan began his Peninsular campaign. Lee inflicted defeat after defeat on the Army of the Potomac. Jack Ellyat was sent to a prison in the deep South. The fortunes of the Union were at their lowest ebb after the Confederate victory at the Second Manassas, and the spirit of John Brown was generally invoked by editors and preachers. Lincoln issued the Emancipation Proclamation. In the meantime, Spade made his way north and swam across a river to freedom, but when he arrived in the land of the free he was railroaded into a labor gang. McClellan was relieved by Burnside, who, in turn, was relieved by Hooker, as commander of the Army of the Potomac. Jack Ellyat, sick, was returned to the North in an exchange of prisoners of war.

Slowly the Confederacy began to feel the effects of the blockade and the terrible cost of war. Clay Wingate thought of his next leave—and of Lucy Weatherby. Jack Ellyat spent the dark winter of 1862-63 convalescing at his home in the cold Connecticut hills. He had been assigned to the Army of the Potomac as soon as his recovery was complete. In Tennessee, Melora Vilas gave birth to a baby boy.

Grant and Sherman led the Union forces to victory in the West; Vicksburg was surrounded. Hunger and anti-inflation riots broke out in Richmond. America, meanwhile, was expanding. New industries sprang up in the North, and the West was being developed. In Richmond, Shippy, a Union spy posing as a peddler, promised Sophy, a servant at the Pollard Hotel, to bring her some perfume from the North. Sophy knew that Clay Wingate and Lucy Weatherby had stayed together in the hotel. Luke Breckinridge, Sophy's rebel suitor, was a member of a patrol that stopped Shippy to search him. When they found incriminating papers in his boots, Luke gloated, for he was jealous of Shippy.

Stonewall Jackson was killed by his own pickets, and Lee, desperate for provisions, invaded the North. Jack Ellyat was in the Union army that converged on Gettysburg and was wounded during a battle there. After three days of bloody fighting at Gettysburg, Lee fell back to Virginia. Then Vicksburg surrendered. Defeated, the South continued to hang on doggedly. Sheridan marched through the Shenandoah Valley and left it bare and burned. Petersburg was besieged. Luke, along with thousands of other rebel troops, deserted from the Confederate Army, and when he headed back toward his laurel-thicket mountains he took Sophy with him. Melora and her father, John Vilas, traveled from place to place in search of Jack Ellyat; they became a legend in both armies.

General Sherman captured Atlanta and marched on to the sea. During Sherman's march, Wingate Hall caught fire accidentally and burned to the ground. Clay Wingate was wounded in a rear-guard action in Virginia. The war came to an end when Lee surrendered to Grant at Appomattox.

Spade, who had gone from the labor gang into the Union Army and who had been wounded at the Petersburg crater, hired out as a farm laborer in Cumberland County, Pennsylvania. Clay Wingate returned to his ruined home in Georgia, where Sally Dupré was waiting. And in Connecticut Jack Ellyat heard stories of strange gipsy travelers who were going from town to town looking for a soldier who was the father of the child of the woman who drove the creaking cart. One day he was standing beneath the crossroads elms when he saw a cart come slowly up the hill. He waited. The woman driving was Melora.

JOSEPH ANDREWS

Type of work: Novel
Author: Henry Fielding (1707-1754)
Type of plot: Comic epic
Time of plot: Early eighteenth century
Locale: England
First published: 1742

Principal characters:

JOSEPH ANDREWS, a footman to Lady Booby
PAMELA ANDREWS, his sister, wife of Squire Booby
LADY BOOBY, aunt of Squire Booby
FANNY, Joseph's sweetheart
MRS. SLIPSLOP, Lady Booby's maid
PARSON ADAMS, parson of Booby parish and friend of Joseph

Critique:

The History of the Adventures of Joseph Andrews, and of his Friend Mr. Abraham Adams is the full title of the work often called the first realistic novel of English literature. Henry Fielding turned aside from the episodic sentimental writing of the age to give an honest picture of the manners and customs of his time and to satirize the foibles and vanities of human nature. In particular, he ridiculed affectation, whether it stemmed from hypocrisy or vanity. Although the structure of the novel is loose and rambling, the realistic settings and the vivid portrayal of English life in the eighteenth century more than compensate for this one weakness. Joseph is presented as the younger brother of Samuel Richardson's heroine, Pamela.

The Story:

Joseph Andrews was ten or eleven years in the service of Sir Thomas Booby, uncle of the Squire Booby who married the virtuous Pamela, Joseph's sister. When Lord Booby died, Joseph remained in the employ of Lady Booby as her footman. This lady, much older than her twenty-one-year-old servant, and apparently little disturbed by her husband's death, paid entirely too much attention to pleasant-mannered and handsome Joseph. But Joseph was as virtuous as his famous sister, and when Lady Booby's advances became such that even his innocence could no longer deny their true nature, he was as firm in resisting her as Pamela had been in restraining Squire Booby. Insulted, the lady discharged Joseph on the spot, in spite of the protests of Mrs. Slipslop, her maid, who found herself also attracted to the young man.

With very little money and fewer prospects, Joseph set out from London to Somersetshire to see his sweetheart, Fanny, for whose sake he had withstood Lady Booby's advances. The very first night of his journey, Joseph was attacked by robbers, who stole his money, beat him soundly, and left him lying naked and half dead in a ditch. A passing coach stopped when the passengers heard his cries, and he was taken to a nearby inn.

Joseph was well cared for until the innkeeper's wife discovered that he was penniless. He was recognized, however, by another visitor at the inn, his old tutor and preceptor, Parson Adams, who was on his way to London to sell a collection of his sermons. He paid Joseph's bill with his own meager savings; then, discovering that in his absent-mindedness he had forgotten to bring the sermons with him, he decided to accompany Joseph back to Somersetshire.

They started out, alternately on foot and on the parson's horse. Fortunately, Mrs. Slipslop overtook them in a coach on her way to Lady Booby's country place. She accommodated the parson in the coach while Joseph rode the horse. The inn at which they stopped next had an innkeeper who gauged his courtesy according to the appearance of his guests. There Joseph was insulted by the host. In spite of the clerical cassock he was wearing, Parson Adams stepped in to challenge the host, and a fist fight followed, the ranks being swelled by the hostess and Mrs. Slipslop. When the battle finally ended, Parson Adams was the bloodiest looking, since the hostess in the excitement had doused him with a pail of hog's blood.

The journey continued, this time with Joseph in the coach and the parson on foot, for with typical forgetfulness the good man had left his horse behind. However, he walked so rapidly and the coach moved so slowly that he easily outdistanced his friends. While he was resting on his journey, he heard the shrieks of a woman. Running to her rescue, he discovered a young woman being cruelly attacked by a burly fellow, whom the parson belabored with such violence that he laid the attacker at his feet. As some fox hunters rode up, the ruffian rose from the ground and accused Parson Adams and the woman of being conspirators in an attempt to rob him. The parson and the woman were quickly taken prisoners and led off to the sheriff. On the way the parson discovered that the young woman whom he had aided was Fanny. Having heard of Joseph's unhappy dismissal from Lady Booby's service, she had been on her way to London to help him when she had been so cruelly molested.

After some uncomfortable moments before the judge, the parson was recognized by an onlooker, and both he and Fanny were released. They went to the inn where Mrs. Slipslop and Joseph were staying.

Joseph and Fanny were overjoyed to be together once more. Mrs. Slipslop, displeased to see Joseph's display of affection for another woman, drove off in the coach, leaving Parson Adams and the young lovers behind.

None of the three had any money to pay their bill at the inn. Parson Adams, with indomitable optimism, went to visit the clergyman of the parish in order to borrow the money, but with no success. Finally a poor peddler at the inn gave them every penny he had, just enough to cover the bill.

They continued their trip on foot, stopping at another inn where the host was more courteous than any they had met, and more understanding about their financial difficulties. Still farther on their journey, they came across a secluded house at which they were asked to stop and rest. Mr. and Mrs. Wilson were a charming couple who gave their guests a warm welcome. Mr. Wilson entertained the parson with the story of his life. It seemed that in his youth he had been attracted by the vanity of London life, had squandered his money on foppish clothes, gambling, and drinking, and had eventually been imprisoned for debt. From this situation he was rescued by a kindly cousin whom he later married. The two had retired from London to this quiet country home. They had two lovely children and their only sorrow, but that a deep one, was that a third child, a boy with a strawberry mark on his shoulder, had been stolen by gipsies and had never been heard of since.

After a pleasant visit with the kindly family, the travelers set out again. Their adventures were far from ended. Parson Adams suddenly found himself caught in the middle of a hare hunt, with the hounds inclined to mistake him for the hare. Their master goaded on the dogs, but Joseph and the parson were victorious in the battle. They found themselves face to face with an angry squire and his followers. But when the squire caught sight of the lovely Fanny, his anger softened, and he invited the three to dine.

Supper was a trying affair for the parson, who was made the butt of many practical jokes. Finally the three travelers left the house in great anger and went to an inn. In the middle of the night, some of the squire's men arrived, overcame Joseph and the parson, and abducted Fanny. On the way, however, an old acquaintance of Fanny, Peter Pounce, met the party of kidnapers, recognized Fanny, and rescued her.

The rest of the journey was relatively uneventful. When they arrived home however, further difficulties arose. Joseph and Fanny stayed at the parsonage and waited eagerly for the publishing of their wedding banns. Lady Booby had also arrived in the parish, the seat of her summer home. Still in love with Joseph, she exerted every pressure of position and wealth to prevent the marriage. She even had Fanny and Joseph arrested. At this point, however, Squire Booby and his wife Pamela arrived. That gentleman insisted on accepting his wife's relatives as his own, even though they were of a lower station, and Joseph and Fanny were quickly released from custody.

All manner of arguments were presented by Pamela, her husband, and Lady Booby in their attempts to turn Joseph aside from his intention of marrying Fanny. Her lowly birth made a difference to their minds, now that Pamela had made a good match and Joseph had been received by the Boobys.

Further complications arose when a traveling peddler revealed that Fanny, whose parentage until then had been unknown, was the sister of Pamela. Mr. and Mrs. Andrews were summoned at this disclosure, and Mrs. Andrews described how, while Fanny was still a baby, gipsies had stolen the child and left behind them a sickly little boy she had brought up as her own. Now it appeared that Joseph was the foundling. However, a strawberry mark on Joseph's chest soon established his identity. He was the son of the kindly Wilsons.

Both lovers were now secure in their social positions, and nothing further could prevent their marriage, which took place, to the happiness of all concerned, soon afterward.

JOSEPH VANCE

Type of work: Novel
Author: William De Morgan (1839-1917)
Type of plot: Simulated autobiography
Time of plot: Mid-nineteenth century
Locale: England
First published: 1906

Principal characters:
JOSEPH VANCE, who wrote his memoirs
MR. CHRISTOPHER VANCE, his father
DR. RANDALL THORPE, Joseph's foster father
LOSSIE THORPE, Dr. Thorpe's daughter
JOE THORPE (BEPPINO), her brother
VIOLET THORPE, her sister
NOLLY THORPE, another brother
BONY MACALLISTER, Joseph's business partner
GENERAL DESPREZ, Lossie's husband
JANEY SPENCER, Joseph's wife
PHEENER, a maid

Critique:

Joseph Vance is an early example of the now popular type of autobiographical novel. It is the story of the life of Joseph Vance from his earliest recollections until the last years of his life. As the author tells us through the words of his main character, there is much that might have been left out, since there are many threads of the plot which are unimportant to the story. Humor and pathos are successfully mixed; the humor particularly is the quiet kind that makes us chuckle to ourselves. It comes largely from the character of Vance's father, whose firm belief it is that to be a success a person must know absolutely nothing about doing the job he is hired to do. De Morgan gave his novel a subtitle, *An Ill-Written Autobiography,* but few of his readers will agree with him.

The Story:

Joseph Vance's father was more often drunk than sober. But he was a good man, never mean when he was drunk. Having lost several positions because of his drinking, he was in no way depressed. He took Joe with him to visit a pub on the night of his discharge from his last position, and while there he quarreled with a chimney sweep and had the poor end of the fight. Forced to spend some time in the hospital after the affair, he decided to give up his excessive drinking.

After his release from the hospital he set himself up as a builder and drain repairman, by virtue of acquiring a signboard advertising the possessor as such a workman. Mr. Vance knew nothing about the building trade, but he believed that it was his ignorance which would cause him to be a success at the business. He appeared to be right. His first job was for Dr. Randall Thorpe, of Poplar Villa, and Dr. Thorpe was so pleased with the work that he recommended Mr. Vance for more jobs until his reputation was such that he was much in demand. Mr. Vance took Joe with him on his first call at Poplar Villa, and there Joe met Miss Lossie Thorpe, the first real young lady he had ever seen. At this time Joe was nine and Lossie fifteen, but he knew from the first meeting that she was to be his lady for the rest of his life.

When Dr. Thorpe learned that Joe was a bright boy, he sent him to school and made him almost one of the family. Lossie was like a sister to him; in fact, she called him her little brother and encouraged him in his studies. In the Thorpe household were also young Joe Thorpe, called Beppino, a sister Violet, and another brother named Nolly. With these young people Joe Vance grew up, and Dr. Thorpe continued to send him to school, even to Oxford when he was ready. Although Dr. Thorpe had hoped that Joe Vance might excel in the classics, the boy found his interest in engineering. Beppino did grow up to be a poet, but he wrote such drivel that his father was disgusted. Meanwhile a deep friendship had developed between Joe Vance and Lossie, a brother-and-sister love that made each want the other's happiness above all else.

Mr. Vance's business prospered so much that he and his wife took a new house and hired a cook and a maid. After Joe had finished at Oxford, he joined his old school friend, Bony Macallister, and they established an engineering firm. Their offices were in the same building with Mr. Vance. By that time Lossie had married General Desprez, a wealthy army officer, and had moved with him to India. Joe suffered a great deal at the loss of his dear friend, but he knew that General Desprez was a fine man who would care for Lossie and love her tenderly.

Shortly after Lossie sailed for India, Joe's mother died, and his father began

JOSEPH VANCE by William De Morgan. By permission of the publishers, Henry Holt & Co., Inc. Copyright, 1906, by Henry Holt & Co., Inc. Renewed, 1934, by Mary Beatrice De Morgan.

to drink once more. Joe tried to think of some way to help his father. Joe thought that if he married his wife might influence his father, and he asked Janey Spencer, a friend of Lossie, to marry him. She accepted, but when she learned that Joe wanted to marry her only for the sake of his father, she broke the engagement and did not relent until two years later. By that time Joe knew he really loved her, and she married him. In the meantime, Joe's father had married Pheener, his housemaid, and for a time she kept him from the bottle.

After Janey and Joe had been married for five years, they took a trip to Italy. The ship caught on fire and almost all on board were lost. When Janey refused to get into a lifeboat without her husband, they tried to swim to shore. Janey was drowned. Joe's life was empty without her, and only his visits with Dr. Thorpe and his letters from Lossie gave him any comfort.

Joe's business prospered, as did his father's. But one day Mr. Vance, while drunk, caused an explosion and a fire in the building. He was seriously injured, and he seemed to be ruined because he had let his insurance lapse. But before the catastrophe he had given Pheener a tiara worth fifteen thousand pounds, and with the money received from the sale of the jewels he was able to start his business anew.

In the meantime Beppino was grieving his family by an affair with a married woman. For the sake of the Thorpes, Joe took Beppino to Italy. On Joe's return Beppino remained behind. When Beppino returned, he met and married Sibyl Perceval, an heiress, and the family believed he had changed his ways. But Beppino died of typhoid fever shortly after his marriage, and then Joe learned what Beppino had done while in Italy. He had married an Italian girl, using the name of Joe Vance, and she had had a child. The Italian girl had died, too, and her relatives wrote to Joe in the belief that he was the father. Joe told General Desprez of Beppino's duplicity, the General and Lossie having come home for a visit, and the two men agreed that Lossie must never know of her brother's deed. Joe went to Italy and told the girl's relatives that he was a friend of the baby's father. He arranged to send money for the boy's care.

Shortly afterward Joe went to Brazil on an engineering project. While there, he sent for Beppino's boy and adopted him. The next twenty years of his life he spent in Brazil. He heard from Lossie and Dr. Thorpe frequently, but otherwise he had no connection with England. His father died and Pheener remarried. While Joe was in Brazil, Lossie heard rumors from Italy that he was the baby's real father. She was so disappointed in her foster brother that she never wrote again. Joe returned to England. Living near Lossie, he did not see her or let her know he was back in the country. The boy was attending school in America. Lossie's husband died without telling the real story about the child, and Joe would not tell the truth even to save himself in Lossie's eyes. He wrote the story in his memoirs, but left his papers to be burned after his return to Brazil.

But a maid burned the wrong package, and a publisher's note completed Joe's story. Lossie found a letter from Beppino in some of her husband's papers and surmised the truth. She found Joe Vance before he left for Brazil and made him confess that he had acted only to save her feelings. She begged Joe to forgive her. Reunited, the two friends went to Italy and spent their remaining days together.

JOURNEY TO THE END OF THE NIGHT

Type of work: Novel
Author: Louis-Ferdinand Céline (Louis Ferdinand Destouches, 1894-)
Type of plot: Naturalism
Time of plot: World War I and following years
Locale: France
First published: 1932

Principal characters:
FERDINAND, a rogue
LÉON, his friend
MADELON, engaged to Léon

Critique:

In tone *Journey to the End of the Night* is pessimistic, in style abrupt and whittled down, in form experimental. The action is seen through the eyes of a neurotic narrator who reduces all his experience to a cynical level. In a way the approach can be called symbolical; that is, impressions are suggested rather than realistically described. The abrupt, fragmentary recounting of important events lends a tough, terse quality to the work. The philosophy is that of postwar disillusionment.

The Story:

Ferdinand, an indifferent student of medicine in Paris, was violently pacifistic, even anarchistic in his reaction to authority. Just prior to World War I he was expounding his cynical disregard for nationalistic pride in a café. Down the street came a colonel at the head of a military band. Because the music and the uniforms captured Ferdinand's fickle fancy, he rushed off to enlist. During the fighting he was a runner constantly exposed to scenes of savage brutality and to dangerous errands. On one mission he met Léon, who was always to be a kind of incubus to him.

When Ferdinand suffered a slight wound in his arm, he was given convalescent leave in Paris. There he met Lola, an American Red Cross worker who idolized the French. She romanticized his wound, became his temporary mistress, and filled him with stories of the United States. When she finally discovered Ferdinand's cowardice and cynicism, she left him.

The thought of losing Lola was more than Ferdinand could bear. When his mind gave way, he was sent to a variety of mental hospitals, where he quickly learned to ingratiate himself with the psychiatrists by agreeing with everything they said. His tactics at last procured his release as cured but unfit for active duty.

In Paris he led a precarious life for a time, but later he bettered his existence considerably by acting as a go-between for Musyne, a dancer who was greatly sought after by rich Argentine meat dealers. The thought of all that beef to be sold at high prices was too much for Ferdinand after some months with Musyne, and he left for Colonial Africa.

In French West Africa he was assigned to a trading post far in the interior. He made the ten-day trip by canoe into the hot, lush jungle, where his trading post turned out to be a cozy shack anchored by two big rocks. The mysterious trader he had come to relieve was frankly a thief, who told Ferdinand that he had no goods left to trade, very little rubber, and only canned stew for provisions. The rascal gave Ferdinand three hundred francs, saying it was all he had, and left in the direction of a Spanish colony. Only after he had gone did Ferdinand realize that his predecessor had been Léon.

After several weeks of fever and canned stew, Ferdinand left the trading post. The shack having accidentally burned, his only baggage was the three hundred francs and some canned stew. His overland safari was a nightmare. His fever rose dangerously high, and during much of the trip he was delirious. At last his black porters stole his money and left him with a Spanish priest in a seaport. The priest, for a fee, delivered him to a captain of easy scruples. Ferdinand, still sick, was shanghaied on a ship bound for the United States.

When he attempted to jump ship in New York, he was caught by the immigration authorities. Pretending to be an expert on flea classification, he was put to work in a quarantine station catching and sorting fleas for the Port of New York. After gaining the confidence of his chief, he was sent into the city to deliver a report, although technically he was still under detention. In New York he looked up Lola, now older but still attractive, who gave him a hundred dollars to get rid of him. With the money he took a train to Detroit. Soon he was employed by the Ford Motor Company.

In Dearborn he fell in love with Molly, who lived in a brothel. Each day he escorted her to the bordello in the early evening. Then he rode streetcars until she was through for the night. On one of his nightly trips he met Léon again. Léon was unhappy in America because he could not learn enough English to get along. He had to be content with a janitor's job. Ferdinand learned that Léon also wished to return to France.

Although he loved Molly very much, Ferdinand left her and Detroit to go back to Paris. Completing his medical course, he was certified as a doctor, and he settled down to practice in a poor suburb. All his patients were poor and rarely paid him. Mostly he was called in on shady abortion cases.

One day the Henrouilles summoned him to attend the old grandmother who lived in a hut behind their house. They hated to spend the money necessary to feed the old woman and Mme. Henrouille offered Ferdinand a thousand francs if he would certify that the grandmother was insane. Through conscience or fear, Ferdinand refused. Then Léon was called in on the same case. He agreed to set a bomb next to the old woman's hut so that she would kill herself when she opened the door. But clumsy Léon bungled the job; he accidentally detonated the bomb and lost his sight.

With the help of the Abbé Protiste, the family worked out a scheme to get rid of both the old woman and Léon. They proposed to send the two to Toulouse, where there was a display of mummies connected with a church. Léon would be a ticket seller and old Mme. Henrouille would be the guide. For persuading Léon to accept the proposition, Ferdinand received a fee of a thousand francs.

Ferdinand's practice grew smaller. At last he went to the Montmartre section of Paris, where for a time he was well pleased with his job as supernumerary in a music hall. The Abbé Protiste looked him up after some months and offered to pay his expenses to Toulouse, where Ferdinand was to see if Léon were likely to make trouble for the Henrouilles on the score of attempted murder.

In Toulouse Ferdinand learned that Léon was regaining his sight. He had also become engaged to Madelon. The old lady was a vigorous and successful guide. Ferdinand dallied a little with the complaisant Madelon, but decided to leave before their intimacy was discovered. Old Mme. Henrouille fell, or was tripped, on the stairs and was killed in the fall. It was a good time for Ferdinand to leave—hurriedly.

Dr. Baryton ran a genteel madhouse. By great good luck Ferdinand was hired on his staff. He ingratiated himself with his employer by giving him English lessons. Dr. Baryton read Macaulay's *History of England* and became so enamored of things English that he departed for foreign lands and left Ferdinand in charge. Shortly afterward Léon showed up, broke and jobless. He had run away from Madelon. Ferdinand took him in and gave him a job.

Madelon came looking for Léon and haunted the hospital gate. Hoping to appease her, Ferdinand arranged a Sunday party to visit a carnival. In the party were Léon, Madelon, Ferdinand, and Sophie, Ferdinand's favorite nurse. After a hectic day they took a taxi home. On the way Léon declared he no longer loved Madelon. The spurned girl took out her revolver and killed him. Ferdinand knew that the time had arrived for him to move on once more.

JUDE THE OBSCURE

Type of work: Novel
Author: Thomas Hardy (1840-1928)
Type of plot: Philosophical realism
Time of plot: Eighteenth century
Locale: Wessex
First published: 1894

Principal characters:
JUDE FAWLEY, a stonemason
ARABELLA DONN, a vulgar country girl
SUE BRIDEHEAD, Jude's cousin, a neurotic free-thinker
LITTLE FATHER TIME, Jude's son by Arabella
RICHARD PHILLOTSON, a schoolmaster
DRUSILLA FAWLEY, Jude's great-grandaunt

Critique:

Jude the Obscure marks the peak of Hardy's gloom and deterministic philosophy. Sunshine never breaks through the heavy clouds of tragedy that smother this narrative of war between the flesh and the spirit. The gloom becomes steadily heavier as circumstances conspire to keep the hero from realizing any happiness he seeks. The plot is believable; the characters are three-dimensional. The story itself is a vehicle for Hardy's feelings toward contemporary marriage laws and academic snobbery. His sexual frankness, his unconventional treatment of the theme of marriage, and his use of pure horror in scenes like the deaths of Little Father Time and the younger children outraged readers of his generation.

The Story:

In the nineteenth century eleven-year-old Jude Fawley said goodbye to his schoolmaster, Richard Phillotson, who was leaving the small English village of Marygreen for Christminster, to study for a degree. Young Jude, hungry for learning, yearned to go to Christminster too, but he had to help his great-grandaunt, Drusilla Fawley, in her bakery. At Christminster, Phillotson did not forget his former pupil. He sent Jude some classical grammars which the boy studied eagerly.

Anticipating a career as a religious scholar, Jude apprenticed himself, at nineteen, to a stonemason engaged in the restoration of medieval churches in a nearby town. Returning to Marygreen one evening, he met three young girls who were washing pigs' chitterlings by a stream bank. One of the girls, Arabella Donn, caught Jude's fancy and he arranged to meet her later. The young man was swept off his feet and tricked into marriage, but he soon realized that he had married a vulgar country girl with whom he had nothing in common.

Embittered, he tried unsuccessfully to commit suicide; when he began to drink, Arabella left him.

Jude, now free, decided to carry out his original purpose. With this idea in mind, he went to Christminster, where he took work as a stonemason. He had heard that his cousin, Sue Bridehead, lived in Christminster, but he did not seek her out because his aunt had warned him against her and because he was already a married man. Eventually he met her and was charmed. She was an artist employed in an ecclesiastical warehouse. Jude met Phillotson, again a simple schoolteacher. Sue, at Jude's suggestion, became Phillotson's assistant. The teacher soon lost his heart to his bright and intellectually independent young helper. Jude was hurt by evidence of intimacy between the two. Disappointed in love and ambition, he turned to drink and was dismissed by his employer. He went back to Marygreen.

At Marygreen Jude was persuaded by a minister to enter the church as a licentiate. Sue, meanwhile, had won a scholarship to a teacher's college at Melchester; she wrote Jude asking him to come to see her. Jude worked at stonemasonry in Melchester in order to be near Sue, even though she told him she had promised to marry Phillotson after her schooling. Dismissed from the college after an innocent escapade with Jude, Sue influenced him away from the church with her unorthodox beliefs. Shortly afterward she married Phillotson. Jude, despondent, returned to Christminster, where he came upon Arabella working in a bar. Jude heard that Sue's married life was unbearable. He continued his studies for the ministry and thought a great deal about Sue.

Succumbing completely to his passion for Sue, Jude at last forsook the ministry. His Aunt Drusilla died, and at the funeral Jude and Sue realized that they could not remain separated. Phillotson, sympathizing with the lovers, released Sue, who now lived apart from her husband. The lovers went to Aldbrickham, a large city where they would not be recognized. Phillotson gave Sue a divorce and subsequently lost his teaching position. Jude gave Arabella a divorce so that she might marry again.

Sue and Jude now contemplated marriage, but they were unwilling to be joined by a church ceremony because of Sue's dislike for any binding contract. The pair lived together happily, Jude doing simple stonework. One day Arabella appeared and told Jude that her marriage had not materialized. Sue, jealous, promised Jude that she would marry him. Arabella's problem was solved by eventual marriage, but out of fear of her husband she sent her young child by Jude to live with him and Sue, This pathetic boy, nicknamed Little Father Time, joined the unconventional Fawley household.

Jude's business began to decline, and he lost a contract to restore a rural church when the vestry discovered that he and Sue were unmarried. Forced to move on, they traveled from place to place and from job to job. At the end of two and a half years of this itinerant life, the pair had two children of their own and a third on the way. They were five, including Little Father Time. Jude, in failing health, became a baker and Sue sold cakes in the shape of Gothic ornaments at a fair in a village near Christminster. At the fair Sue met Arabella, now a widow. Arabella reported Sue's poverty to Phillotson, who was once more the village teacher in Marygreen.

Jude took his family to Christminster, where the celebration of Remembrance Week was under way. Utterly defeated by failure, Jude still had a love for the atmosphere of learning which pervaded the city.

The family had difficulty finding lodgings and they were forced to separate. Sue's landlady, learning that Sue was an unmarried mother and fearful lest she should have the trouble of childbirth in her rooming-house, told Sue to find other lodgings. Bitter, Sue told Little Father Time that children should not be brought into the world. When she returned from a meal with Jude, she found that the boy had hanged the two babies and himself. She collapsed and gave premature birth to a dead baby.

Her experience brought about a change in Sue's point of view. Believing she had sinned and wishing now to conform, she asked Jude to live apart from her. She also expressed the desire to return to Phillotson, whom she believed, in her misery, to be still her husband. She returned to Phillotson and the two remarried. Jude, utterly lost, began drinking heavily. In a drunken stupor, he was again tricked by Arabella into marriage. His lungs failed; it was evident that his end was near. Arabella would not communicate with Sue, whom Jude desired to see once more, and so Jude traveled in the rain to see her. The lovers had a last meeting. She then made complete atonement for her past mistakes by becoming Phillotson's wife completely. This development was reported to Jude, who died in desperate misery of mind and body. Fate had grown tired of its sport with a luckless man.

JUDITH PARIS

Type of work: Novel
Author: Hugh Walpole (1884-1941)
Type of plot: Historical chronicle
Time of plot: Nineteenth century
Locale: England
First published: 1931

Principal characters:
JUDITH HERRIES, later Judith Paris, daughter of Rogue Herries
DAVID HERRIES, her half-brother
FRANCIS HERRIES, her nephew
JENNIFER, Francis' wife
REUBEN SUNWOOD, Judith's cousin
GEORGES PARIS, Judith's husband
WILLIAM HERRIES, Francis' brother
CHRISTABEL, William's wife
WALTER HERRIES, William's son

Critique:

Judith Paris is the second of four novels dealing with the history of the Herries family. Like the others, it contains many characters and covers about half a century. While *Judith Paris* is an independent novel, it should be read in sequence with the others, or many of the allusions may confuse the reader. Like the preceding *Rogue Herries* and the succeeding *The Fortress* and *Vanessa,* Judith Paris is long and comprehensive in scope, with many references to the political and social background of the period.

The Story:

On the wild winter night Judith Herries was born in the gloomy old house at Herries in Rosthwaite, her aged father and young gipsy mother both died. The country midwife laid out the parents with as much respect as she thought Rogue Herries and his strange wife deserved. The baby she wrapped up warmly, for it was bitterly cold. Then to fortify her own thin blood she sat down with a bottle of strong drink. The wind rose and a loose windowpane blew in. The snow drifted in upon the cradle, but the midwife slept on.

Squire Gauntry, tough and taciturn, came by tired from hunting. He stopped when he heard the child's thin wail above the howling wind. Failing to arouse the stupid countrywoman, he took the baby home to his masculine hall until her half-brother, David Herries, arrived to claim her.

Judith Herries grew up at Fell House, near Uldale, with David Herries and his family. But David was fifty-five years older than Judith and often he clashed with his young sister. She was spanked many times; the most serious punishment came when she danced naked on the roof. Judith frequently visited Stone Ends, Squire Gauntry's place, where there were no restrictions.

One significant visit came in her eleventh year, when she ran away from Fell House after being punished for disobedience. Rough Gauntry welcomed her to a strange gathering. With the gentlemen who were drinking and playing cards, there were two women. One was vast Emma, Gauntry's mistress, who was always to be Judith's friend, and the other was beautiful Madame Paris, the mother of Georges. Georges, only a year or so older than Judith, came up to her and enticed her away on a childish prank. He kissed her soundly and she slapped his face.

That night, when Judith went to bed, she entered the room she usually slept in at Stone Ends. There she saw Georges' beautiful mother standing naked beside the bed. On his knees before her, dressed only in his shirt, knelt a gentleman who was kissing Madame Paris' knees. From that night on Judith thought as a woman.

When she was fourteen, she saw Georges again at a display of fireworks by the lake. Disobeying orders, she went out in a boat with him. His kisses that night were more grown-up.

When she was seventeen, Judith married Georges. It was a bad match in every way, except that Judith really loved her husband. Georges installed her at Watendlath, a remote northern farm. There she lived a lonely life. Georges, a smuggler, spent little time at home.

After some years Georges and Judith went to London, where the smuggler turned gambler and intriguer to recoup their fortunes. During a comparatively harmonious interval, they attended the famous ball given by Will Herries.

Jennifer Cards was the belle of the ball. She was a strikingly beautiful woman of twenty-six, still single by preference. Many of the married Herries men followed her like sheep. Christabel, Will's wife, was much upset and scolded Jennifer for being without a chaperon. Jennifer answered roughly and in her anger she seized Christabel's fan and broke it. That was the occasion for the great Herries quarrel. Ever after Will and then his son Walter were intent on destroying Jennifer.

Their quarrel eventually involved Francis, Judith's well-loved nephew, for Francis, thirty-six years old and a pathetic, futile man of deep sensibility, married Jennifer soon afterward.

Georges at last seemed to be serious in attempting to advance his fortunes. Judith never knew exactly what he was doing, but part of his project meant standing in well with Will Herries, who was a real power in the city. Mysterious men came and went in the Paris' shabby rooms. Stane was the one whom Judith distrusted most, and often she begged Georges to break with him. Her suspicions were verified one day when Georges came home exhausted and in wild despair. All his projects had failed, and Stane had lied his way into Will's favor.

Despondent, Georges and Judith went back to Watendlath, and Georges returned to smuggling. After one of his mysterious trips Georges appeared haggard and upset, to tell her that off Norway he choked Stane to death. Then he had overturned the small boat, to make the death appear an accident, and swam ashore. Although Georges was unsuspected, he needed Judith now. She had him to herself at last.

Then old Stane came, professing to seek shelter with his dead son's friend. When he had satisfied his suspicion of Georges' guilt, the powerful old man threw Georges over the rail and broke his back, killing him.

Now a widow, Judith left Watendlath and at their strong urging went to stay with Francis and Jennifer. The beautiful Jennifer now had two children, John and Dorothy. Since she had never loved Francis, Jennifer felt no compulsion to keep his love. She gave herself to Fernyhirst, a neighbor. Although most of the people in the neighborhood knew of her infidelity, Francis shut his eyes to it.

Then came the news that Will Herries had bought Westaways, only eight miles away from Fell House, where Judith lived in the uneasy home of Jennifer and Francis. They were sure that Will meant to harm them for the slight to his wife years before, and indeed Will hated them savagely. It was Walter, however, who was to be the agent for his father's hate.

Warren Forster brought the news of Will's plans to Fell House. He was a tiny, kindly man who had long admired Judith. The two went riding one day, and out of pity and friendship Judith gave herself to Warren, whose wife had left him years before.

When Judith, who was nearly forty, knew that she was carrying Warren's child, she went to Paris with blowzy Emma, now on the stage. It was just after Waterloo, and Paris was filled with Germans and Englishmen. When Warren finally found them, he was a sick man. In their little apartment, he died with only Judith and Emma to attend him.

One night, while Judith was dining in a café, a vengeful Frenchman shot a Prussian sitting at the next table. The shock unnerved Judith, and there, behind a screen, her son Adam was born.

In England, Walter was determined to harm Jennifer. He knew of her affair with Fernyhirst and he knew also of a journey Francis was taking. After he sent a note of warning to the inn where Francis was staying, Francis returned unexpectedly to Fell House. There he found his wife's lover in her room and fell on him savagely. Later he overtook the fleeing Fernyhirst and fought a duel with him, but Fernyhirst ran away. In futile despair Francis killed himself.

Now Judith had to manage a shaken and crumpled Jennifer and fight a savage Walter. A riot, incited by Walter, caused the death of Reuben Sunwood, Judith's kinsman and staunch friend, and a fire of mysterious origin broke out in the stables. Judith gave up her plan to return to Watendlath. For Jennifer's sake she and Adam went back to Fell House to stay.

THE JUNGLE

Type of work: Novel
Author: Upton Sinclair (1878-)
Type of plot: Social criticism
Time of plot: Early twentieth century
Locale: Chicago
First published: 1906

Principal characters:
JURGIS RUDKUS, a stockyards worker
ANTANAS RUDKUS, his father
ONA, Jurgis' wife
ELZBIETA, Ona's stepmother
JONAS, Elzbieta's brother
MARIJA, Ona's orphan cousin

Critique:

The Jungle is an indignant book, written in anger at the social injustices of the meat-packing industry, and from this anger the novel derives its power. At the time of publication the book served its purpose in arousing public sentiment against unfair practices in the meat industry. It is still an honestly told and gripping story.

The Story:

While he was still a peasant boy in Lithuania, Jurgis Rudkus had fallen in love with a gentle girl named Ona. When Ona's father died, Jurgis, planning to marry her as soon as he had enough money, came to America with her family. Besides the young lovers, the emigrant party was composed of Antanas, Jurgis' father; Elzbieta, Ona's stepmother; Jonas, Elzbieta's brother; Marija, Ona's orphan cousin, and Elzbieta's six children.

By the time the family arrived in Chicago they had very little money. Jonas, Marija, and Jurgis at once got work in the stockyards. Antanas tried to find work, but he was too old. They all decided that it would be cheaper to buy a house on installments than to rent. A crooked agent sold them a ramshackle house which had a fresh coat of paint and told his ignorant customers that it was new.

Jurgis found his job exhausting, but he thought himself lucky to be making forty-five dollars a month. At last Antanas also found work at the plant, but he had to give part of his wages to the foreman in order to keep his job. Jurgis and Ona saved enough money for their wedding feast and were married. Then the family found that they needed more money. Elzbieta lied about the age of her oldest son, Stanislovas, and he too got a job at the plant. Ona had already begun to work in order to help pay for the wedding.

Antanas worked in a moist, cold room where he developed consumption. When he died, the family had scarcely enough money to bury him. Winter came, and everyone suffered in the flimsy house. When Marija lost her job, the family income diminished. Jurgis joined a union and became an active member. He went to night school to learn to read and speak English.

At last summer came with its hordes of flies and oppressive heat. Marija found work as a beef trimmer, but at that job the danger of blood poisoning was very great. Ona had her baby, a fine boy, whom they called Antanas after his grandfather. Winter came again, and Jurgis sprained his ankle at the plant. Compelled to stay at home for months, he became moody. Two more of Elzbieta's children left school to sell papers.

When Jurgis was well enough to look for work again, he could find none, because he was no longer the strong man he had been. Finally he got a job in a fertilizer plant, a last resource, for men lasted only a few years at that work. One of Elzbieta's daughters was now old enough to care for the rest of the children, and Elzbieta also went to work.

Jurgis began to drink. Ona, pregnant again, developed a consumptive cough and was often seized with spells of hysteria. Hoping to save the family with the money she made, she went to a house of prostitution with her boss, Connor. When Jurgis learned what she had done, he attacked Connor and was sentenced to thirty days in jail. Now that he had time to think, Jurgis saw how unjustly he had been treated by society. No longer would he try to be kind, except to his own family. From now on he would recognize society as an enemy rather than a friend.

After he had served his sentence, Jurgis went to look for his family. He found that they had lost the house because they

---

could not meet the payments, and had moved. He found them at last in a rooming-house. Ona was in labor with her second child, and Jurgis frantically searched for a midwife. By the time he found one, Ona and the child had died. Now he had only little Antanas to live for. He tried to find work. Blacklisted in the stockyards for his attack on Connor, he finally found a job in a harvesting machine factory. Shortly afterward he was discharged when his department closed down for a lack of orders.

Next he went to work in the steel mills. In order to save money he moved near the mills and came home only on weekends. One weekend he came home to find that little Antanas had drowned in the street in front of the house. Now that he had no dependents, he hopped a freight train and rode away from Chicago. He became one of the thousands of migratory farm workers; his old strength came back in healthful surroundings.

In the fall Jurgis returned to Chicago. He got a job digging tunnels under the streets. Then a shoulder injury made him spend weeks in a hospital. Discharged with his arm still in a sling, he became a beggar. By luck he obtained a hundred-dollar bill from a lavish drunk. When he went to a saloon to get it changed, however, the barkeeper tried to cheat him out of his money. In a rage Jurgis attacked the man. He was arrested and sent to jail again. There he met a dapper safe-cracker, Jack Duane. After their release, Jurgis joined Duane in several holdups and became acquainted with Chicago's underworld. At last he was making money.

Jurgis became a political worker. About that time the packing plant workers began to demand more rights through their unions. When packing house operators would not listen to union demands, there was a general strike. Jurgis went to work in the plant as a scab. One day he met Connor and attacked him again. Jurgis fled from the district to avoid a penitentiary sentence. On the verge of starvation, he found Marija working as a prostitute. Jurgis was ashamed to think how low he and Marija had fallen since they came to Chicago. She gave him some money so that he might look for a job.

Jurgis was despondent until one night he heard a Socialist speak. Jurgis believed that he had found a remedy for the ills of the world. At last he knew how the workers could find self-respect. He found a job in a hotel where the manager was a Socialist. It was the beginning of a new life for Jurgis, the rebirth of hope and faith.

THE JUNGLE BOOKS

Type of work: Short stories
Author: Rudyard Kipling (1865-1936)
Type of plot: Beast fables
Time of plot: Nineteenth century
Locale: India
First published: 1894, 1895

Principal characters:
MOWGLI, an Indian boy
FATHER WOLF
MOTHER WOLF
SHERE KHAN, the tiger
AKELA, leader of the wolf pack
BAGHEERA, the black panther
BALOO, the bear
KAA, the rock python

THE BANDAR-LOG, the monkey people
HATHI, the elephant
MESSUA, a woman who adopted Mowgli for a time
MESSUA'S HUSBAND
BULDEO, a village hunter
GRAY BROTHER, a young wolf

Critique:

Rudyard Kipling, winner of the Nobel Prize in 1907, wrote these stories for children while living in Brattleboro, Vermont. *The Jungle Book* and *The Second Jungle Book* are children's classics which attempt to teach the lessons of justice, loyalty, and tribal laws. It is evident from reading these books that here is a master writer who loved children and could tell them a good story with an underlying meaning that adults can appreciate as well.

The Stories:

Shere Khan, the tiger, pursued a small Indian boy who had strayed from his native village, but Shere Khan was lame and missed his leap upon the child. When Father Wolf took the boy home with him to show to Mother Wolf, Shere Khan followed and demanded the child as his quarry. Mother Wolf refused. The tiger retired in anger. Mowgli, the frog, for such he was named, was reared by Mother Wolf along with her own cubs.

Father Wolf took Mowgli to the Council Rock to be recognized by the wolves. Bagheera, the panther, and Baloo, the bear, spoke for Mowgli's acceptance into the Seeonee wolf pack. Thus Mowgli became a wolf.

Baloo became Mowgli's teacher and instructed him in the lore of the jungle. Mowgli learned to speak the languages of all the jungle people. Throughout his early life the threat of Shere Khan hung over him, but Mowgli was certain of his place in the pack and of his friends' protection. But some day when Akela, the leader of the wolves, would miss his kill, the pack would turn on him and Mowgli. Bagheera told Mowgli to get the Red Flower, or fire, from the village to protect himself. When Akela missed his quarry one night and was about to be deposed and killed, Mowgli attacked all of their mutual enemies with his fire sticks and threatened to destroy anyone who molested Akela. That night Mowgli realized that the jungle was no place for him, and that some day he would go to live with men. But that time was still far off.

One day Mowgli climbed a tree and made friends with the Bandar-Log, the monkey tribe, who because of their stupidity and vanity were despised by the other jungle people. When the Bandar-Log carried off Mowgli, Bagheera and Baloo went in pursuit, taking along Kaa, the rock python, who loved to eat monkeys. Mowgli was rescued at the old ruined city of the Cold Lairs by the three pursuers, and Kaa feasted royally upon monkey meat.

One year during a severe drought in the jungle, Hathi the elephant proclaimed the water truce; all animals were allowed to drink at the water hole unmolested. Shere Khan announced to the animals gathered there one day that he had killed a Man, not for food but from choice. The other animals were shocked. Hathi allowed the tiger to drink and then told him to be off. Then Hathi told the story of how fear came to the jungle and why the tiger was striped. It was the tiger who first killed Man and earned the human tribe's unrelenting enmity, and for his deed the tiger was condemned to wear stripes. Now for one day a year the tiger was not afraid of Man and could kill him.

This day was called, among jungle people, the Night of the Tiger.

One day Mowgli wandered close to a native village, where he was adopted by Messua, a woman who had lost her son some years before. Mowgli became a watcher of the village herds, and so from time to time he met Gray Wolf, his brother, and heard the news of the jungle. Learning that Shere Khan intended to kill him, he laid plans with Akela and Gray Brother to kill the tiger. They lured Shere Khan into a gully and then stampeded the herd. Shere Khan was trampled to death. Stoned from the village because he was believed to be a sorcerer who spoke to animals, Mowgli returned to the jungle resolved to hunt with the wolves for the rest of his life.

Buldeo, the village hunter, followed the trail of Mowgli, Gray Brother, and Akela. Mowgli overheard Buldeo say that Messua and her husband were imprisoned in their house and would be burned at the stake. Messua's husband had saved some money and he had one of the finest herds of buffaloes in the village. Knowing that the imprisonment of Messua and her husband was a scheme for the villagers to get their property, Mowgli laid plans to help his friends. Entering the village, he led Messua and her husband beyond the gates in the darkness. Then the jungle people began to destroy, little by little, the farms, the orchards, and the cattle, but no villager was harmed because Mowgli did not desire the death of any human. Finally, just before the rains, Hathi and his three sons moved into the village and tore down the houses. The people left and thus the jungle was let into the village.

Kaa took Mowgli to Cold Lairs to meet the guardian of the king's treasure, an old white cobra who had expressed a desire to see Mowgli. The old cobra showed them all the treasure, and when he left Mowgli took a jeweled elephant goad, a king's ankus, with him, even though the cobra had said it brought death to the person who possessed it.

Back in the jungle Mowgli threw the ankus away. Later that day he went with Bagheera to retrieve the ankus and discovered that it was gone. They followed the trail of the man who had picked it up and found that altogether six men who had had possession of the ankus had died. Believing it to be cursed, Mowgli returned the ankus to the treasure room in the Cold Lairs.

Sometimes fierce red dogs called dholes traveled in large packs, destroying everything in their paths. Warned of the approach of the dholes, Mowgli led the marauders, by insults and taunts, toward the lairs of the Little People, the bees. Then he excited the bees to attack the dholes. The destruction of the red dogs that escaped the fury of the bees was completed by the wolves lying in ambush a little farther down the river which flowed under the cliffs where the Little People lived. But it was the last battle of old Akela, the leader of the pack when Mowgli was a little boy. He crawled out slowly from under a pile of carcasses to bid Mowgli goodbye and to sing his death song.

The second year after the death of Akela, Mowgli was about seventeen years old. In the spring of that year Mowgli knew that he was unhappy, but none of his friends could tell him what was wrong. Mowgli left his own jungle to travel to another, and on the way he met Messua. Her husband had died, leaving her with a child. Messua told Mowgli that she believed he was her own son lost in the jungle years before and that her baby must be his brother. Mowgli did not know what to make of the child and the unhappiness he felt. When Gray Brother came to Messua's hut, Mowgli decided to return to the jungle. But on the outskirts of the village he met a girl coming down the path. Mowgli melted into the jungle and watched the girl. He knew at last that the jungle was no longer a place for him and that he had returned to the Man-pack to stay.

JURGEN

Type of work: Novel
Author: James Branch Cabell (1879-)
Type of plot: Fantasy
Time of plot: Middle Ages
Locale: Poictesme, a land of myth
First published: 1919

Principal characters:
JURGEN, a middle-aged pawnbroker
DAME LISA, his wife
DOROTHY LA DÉSIRÉE, his childhood sweetheart
QUEEN GUENEVERE
DAME ANAÏTIS
CHLORIS, a Hamadryad
QUEEN HELEN of Troy
MOTHER SEREDA
KOSHCHEI, the maker of things as they are

Critique:

Jurgen, A Comedy of Justice, is one of a series dealing with the mythical country of Poictesme. Although it was once charged in the courts with being an obscene book, it is by no means merely an erotic tale. This novel can be read on many levels; as a narrative of fantastic love and adventure, as a satire, and as a philosophic view of life. The book is an interesting product of a romantic imagination and a critical mind.

The Story:

Once in the old days a middle-aged pawnbroker named Jurgen said a good word for the Prince of Darkness. In gratitude, the Prince of Darkness removed from the earth Dame Lisa, Jurgen's shrewish wife. Some time later Jurgen heard that his wife had returned to wander on Amneran Heath; consequently the only manly thing for him to do was to look for her.

It was Walburga's Eve when Jurgen met Dame Lisa on the heath. She led him to a cave, but when he followed her inside she disappeared and Jurgen found a Centaur instead. Jurgen inquired for his wife. The Centaur replied that only Koshchei the Deathless, the maker of things as they are, could help Jurgen in his quest. The Centaur gave Jurgen a beautiful new shirt and started off with him to the Garden between Dawn and Sunrise, the first stopping place of Jurgen's journey to find Koshchei.

In the garden Jurgen found Dorothy la Désirée, his first sweetheart, who retained all the beauty he had praised in his youthful poetry. She no longer knew him, for she was in love only with Jurgen as he had been in youth, and he could not make her understand that in the real world she also had become middle-aged and commonplace. So he parted sadly from her and found himself suddenly back in his native country.

His friend the Centaur had now become an ordinary horse. Jurgen mounted and rode through a forest until he came to the house of Mother Sereda, the goddess who controlled Wednesdays and whose job it was to bleach the color out of everything in the world. By flattery Jurgen persuaded her to let him live over a certain Wednesday in his youth with Dorothy la Désirée. But when the magic Wednesday ended, Dorothy la Désirée turned into the old woman she really was, and Jurgen quickly departed.

He wandered again to Amneran Heath and entered the cave to look for Koshchei and Dame Lisa. There he found a beautiful girl who said that she was Guenevere, the daughter of King Gogyrvan. Jurgen offered to conduct her back to her home. When they arrived at the court of King Gogyrvan, Jurgen, pretending to be the Duke of Logreus, asked for the hand of Guenevere as a reward for her safe return. But she had already been promised to King Arthur. Jurgen stayed on at court. He had made the discovery that he still looked like a young man; the only trouble was that his shadow was not his shadow; it was the shadow of Mother Sereda.

King Arthur's envoys, Dame Anaïtis and Merlin, had arrived to take Guenevere to London. Jurgen watched her depart for London without feeling any sorrow because of a magic token Merlin had given him. Then Dame Anaïtis invited Jurgen to visit her palace in Cocaigne, the country where Time stood still. There Jurgen participated with her in a ceremony called the Breaking of the Veil, to learn afterwards that it had been a marriage ceremony and that Dame Anaïtis was now his wife. Dame Anaïtis, a myth woman of lunar legend, instructed Jurgen in every variety of strange pleasures she knew.

Jurgen visited a philologist, who said that Jurgen had also become a legend; consequently he could not remain long in Cocaigne. When the time came for him to leave the country, Jurgen chose to go to Leukê, the kingdom where Queen Helen and Achilles ruled. Jurgen's reason for wishing to go there was that Queen Helen resembled his first sweetheart, Dorothy la Désirée.

In Leukê, Jurgen met Chloris, a Hamadryad, and married her. He was still curious about Queen Helen, however, and one evening he entered her castle and went to her bedchamber. The sleeping queen was Dorothy la Désirée, but he dared not touch her. Her beauty, created from the dreams of his youth, was unattainable. He left the castle and returned to Chloris.

Shortly afterward the Philistines invaded Leukê and condemned all its mythical inhabitants to limbo. Jurgen protested because he was flesh and blood and he offered to prove his claim by mathematics. Queen Dolores of the Philistines agreed with him after he had demonstrated his proof to her by means of a concrete example. However, he was condemned by the great tumble-bug of the Philistines for being a poet.

After Chloris had been condemned to limbo, Jurgen went on to the hell of his fathers. There he visited Satan and learned that Koshchei had created hell to humor the pride of Jurgen's forefathers. Then he remembered that he was supposed to be looking for Dame Lisa. Learning that she was not in hell, he decided to look for her in heaven. Mistaken for a pope by means of the philologist's charm, he managed to gain entrance to heaven. Dame Lisa was not there. St. Peter returned him to Amneran Heath.

On the heath he again met Mother Sereda, who took away his youth and returned him to his middle-aged body. Actually, it was a relief to Jurgen to be old again. Then for the third time he entered the cave in search of Dame Lisa. Inside he found the Prince of Darkness who had taken her away. The Prince was really Koshchei; Jurgen was near the end of his quest. He asked Koshchei to return Dame Lisa to him.

Koshchei showed him Guenevere, Dame Anaïtis, and Dorothy la Désirée again. But Jurgen would not have them. He had had his youth to live over, and he had committed the same follies. He was content now to be Jurgen the pawnbroker.

Koshchei agreed to return Jurgen to his former life, but he asked for the Centaur's shirt in return. Jurgen gladly gave up the shirt. Koshchei walked with him from the heath into town. As they walked, Jurgen noticed that the moon was sinking in the east. Time was turning backward.

It was as if the past year had never been. For now he approached his house and saw through the window that the table was set for supper. Inside, Dame Lisa sat sewing and looking quite as if nothing had ever happened.

JUSTICE

Type of work: Drama
Author: John Galsworthy (1867-1933)
Type of plot: Social criticism
Time of plot: 1910
Locale: London
First presented: 1910

Principal characters:
WILLIAM FALDER, a solicitor's clerk
COKESON, a senior clerk
RUTH HONEYWILL, with whom Falder is in love

Critique:

Since 1910, when this play was written, prison reforms have progressed considerably. The play is a protest against dehumanized institutionalism, with particular attention directed toward the evils of solitary confinement and the strict parole system. The problem of making a convicted man into a useful citizen once more is complex. Galsworthy thought rehabilitation likely only if all who came into contact with the man accepted their share of the responsibility.

The Story:

Cokeson, managing clerk for the firm of James and Walter How, solicitors, was interrupted one July morning by a woman asking to see the junior clerk, Falder. The woman, Ruth Honeywill, seemed in great distress, and though it was against office rules, Cokeson permitted her to see Falder.

Falder and Ruth Honeywill were planning to run away together. Ruth's husband, a drunken brute, had abused her until she would no longer stay with him. Falder arranged to have Ruth and her two children meet him at the railway station that night. Ruth left and Falder went back to work.

Young Walter How came to the office. Cokeson was skeptical of the young man's desire to keep the firm not only on the right side of the law but also on the right side of ethics. James How entered from the partners' room. He and Walter began to check the firm's balance, which they decided was below what they remembered it should have been. Then they discovered that a check written the previous Friday had been altered from nine to ninety pounds.

The check had been cashed on the same day that another junior clerk, Davis, had gone away on some firm business. Cokeson was quickly cleared. When it became certain that the check stub had been altered after Davis had started on his trip, suspicion fell on Falder.

The bank cashier was summoned. He recognized Falder as the man who had cashed the check. James How accused Falder of the felony. Falder asked for mercy, but How, convinced that the felony had been premeditated, sent for the police. Falder was arrested.

When the case came to court, Frome, Falder's counsel, tried to show that Falder had conceived the idea and carried it out within the space of four minutes, and that at the time he had been greatly upset by the difficulties of Ruth Honeywill with her husband. Frome called Cokeson as the first witness, and the managing clerk gave the impression that Falder had not been himself on the day in question. Ruth Honeywill was the most important witness. She indicated that Falder had altered the check for her sake. Cleaver, the counsel for the prosecution, tried his utmost to make her appear an undutiful wife.

In defense of Falder, Frome tried to press the point that Falder had been almost out of his mind. Cleaver questioned Falder until the clerk admitted that he had not known what he was doing. Then Cleaver declared Falder had known enough to keep the money he had stolen and to turn in the sum for which the check originally had been written. The jury found Falder guilty and the judge sentenced him to three years.

At Christmas time Cokeson visited the prison on Falder's behalf. He attempted to have Falder released from solitary confinement and asked for permission to bring Ruth Honeywill to see Falder. Cokeson's visit accomplished nothing. Both the chaplain and the prison governor were indifferent to his appeal.

When Falder was finally released on parole, Ruth Honeywill went to intercede for him at How's office. She intimated that she had kept herself and her children alive by living with another man after she left her husband. Falder went to tell Cokeson that his relatives wanted to give him money to go to Canada. He was depressed and ill at ease; he had seen Ruth only once since his release. James How made it clear that if Falder refused to abide by strict standards of justice there would be no hope that the firm would take him back.

James How, aware that Ruth Honeywill had been living with another man, crudely broke the news to Falder. He did, however, give Falder and Ruth an opportunity to talk over their predicament. While they were talking in a side room, a detective sergeant came looking for Falder. Falder was to be arrested again because he had failed to report to the police according to the parole agreement. Although How and Cokeson refused to disclose Falder's whereabouts, the detective discovered Falder in the side room. As he was rearresting Falder, the clerk suddenly broke loose and killed himself by jumping from the office window.

KATE FENNIGATE

Type of work: Novel
Author: Booth Tarkington (1869-1946)
Type of plot: Domestic realism
Time of plot: Twentieth century
Locale: The Middle West
First published: 1943

Principal characters:
KATE FENNIGATE, a managing woman
AUNT DAISY, her aunt
MARY, Aunt Daisy's daughter
AMES LANNING, Mary's husband
CELIA, their daughter
LAILA CAPPER, Kate's schoolmate
TUKE SPEER, Ames' friend
MR. ROE, owner of Roe Metal Products

Critique:

Twenty years intervene between the publication of *Alice Adams* and *Kate Fennigate*. By comparing the two, one observes the great improvement of the latter over the former. A single protagonist is offered to the reader in each novel; but the technique of *Kate Fennigate* is vastly superior to that of *Alice Adams*. In *Kate Fennigate* the chief characters have more of a third dimension; the background seems more realistic, and, as a whole, the novel is a more unified work.

The Story:

Kate Fennigate was a manager, even as a young child; she influenced her mother, her schoolmates, and, particularly, her father. But because of her good manners Kate was never offensive in her desire to lead. Her father, who had showed great promise as a lawyer when he was young, had permitted both women and liquor to interfere with his career. Mrs. Fennigate had no great interest in life except eating, and Mr. Fennigate had no great interest in her. Kate grew into a pretty, quiet, well-mannered girl with a managing complex. Her only intimate was Laila Capper, a self-centered, unintelligent, but beautiful girl who attended Miss Carroll's day school with Kate. Kate found it flattering to help Laila with her homework, and to get for her invitations to parties to which Laila would not otherwise have been invited.

At a school dance, just before she graduated, Kate first became aware of her love for Ames Lanning, her cousin Mary's husband. Not long after Kate's graduation, her mother died, and she and her father sold the house and went to Europe for two years. Her father, who had been ill even before they left America, died and was buried in Europe.

When Kate returned home, Aunt Daisy, the tyrant of her family, insisted that Kate stay with her. With the excuse of protecting Kate, she made a household drudge of her. Kate was nurse to Mary, Aunt Daisy's daughter, governess to Mary's child, Celia, and maid-of-all-work about the house. In return, she received only her room and board. Kate realized what Aunt Daisy was doing, but she preferred to stay on. She wanted to help Ames make something of his talents as a lawyer and to get him from under his mother-in-law's thumb.

Ames introduced Kate to Tuke Speer, his friend. But Laila also took an interest in Tuke, who fell deeply in love with Kate's friend. Aunt Daisy taunted Kate for losing out to Laila, but since Aunt Daisy did not guess where Kate's true feelings lay, the girl did not mind.

When Mary, a semi-invalid for years, died, Aunt Daisy was inconsolable. Her whole life had been wrapped up in her child, her money, and her house. The first of her interests was gone. Kate convinced Ames that he could now take the position he wanted with Mr. Bortshleff, an established lawyer. The second blow fell on Aunt Daisy not long afterward, when the stock market crashed and she lost everything. Her mind broken, she had a fall from the roof and lay an uncomprehending invalid for years afterwards.

Kate obtained a position at the Roe Metal Products. She and Ames shared the expenses of caring for Aunt Daisy and the house, which no one would buy. Tuke asked Kate to renew her friendship with Laila because Laila would need someone now that her family was moving out of town. Laila became a frequent visitor at the house and soon tried her wiles on Ames. When he asked Laila to marry him, she agreed, but later she changed her mind and eloped with Tuke Speer. Ames, hurt and disillusioned, asked Kate to marry him. She accepted.

Ten years later their life together was running smoothly enough. Officially, Ames was Mr. Roe's chief adviser at the plant. War was threatening, and Roe Metal Products, which had been expanding all during the depression, would soon open its fifth plant. Mr. Roe thought highly of both Ames and Kate, and they planned a party to introduce his twin grandchildren, Marjie and Marvin, to society. Miley Stuart, a new young engineer at the plant, met Celia at the party and the two became good friends. After the party Ames informed Kate that he was tired of her efforts to manage his life. She then and there silently resolved to offer him no more suggestions.

Laila, who in the passing years had lost none of her beauty, had also lost none of her selfishness. She had hounded poor Tuke for more money and a better position, until the good-looking young redhead he had been was no longer visible in the gaunt, hollow-cheeked, graying man. Laila tormented Tuke by once again trying her charms on Ames. Having built up among their friends the idea that she was a martyr to Tuke's drunken moods, she nagged him into an insulting remark while they were calling on the Lannings. Laila turned to Ames for comfort. He took her into the library, where she threw herself, weeping, into his arms. Ames tried to console her and ended up by kissing her. Two interested observers of that scene were Tuke, who was looking in the window from outside, and Celia, who was passing the library door. Celia also saw Tuke's face while he watched Laila and Ames in each other's arms.

Celia, thoroughly frightened, asked Miley Stuart to keep an eye on Tuke for fear he would do something violent. Planning to divorce Tuke, Laila asked Ames to divorce Kate so that he would be free to marry her. When she revealed her intention to Ames in his office, he was aghast, for he regarded her only as a good friend who needed help. Laila was furious when he refused to do as she wished, and she threatened to ruin him with false gossip.

It was necessary for Kate to become a manager once more, to save Ames from disaster. She proposed to Ames and Mr. Roe that Tuke be offered the opportunity of managing the New York office for the firm. Tuke accepted the position, which provided enough money to allow Laila to live in the manner she desired. It also took her far away from Kate and Ames.

KENILWORTH

Type of work: Novel
Author: Sir Walter Scott (1771-1832)
Type of plot: Historical romance
Time of plot: 1575
Locale: England
First published: 1821

Principal characters:

Dudley, Earl of Leicester
Richard Varney, his master of horse
Amy Robsart, wife of Dudley
Edmund Tressilian, a Cornish gentleman, friend of Amy Robsart
Wayland Smith, his servant
The Earl of Sussex
Queen Elizabeth
Sir Walter Raleigh
Michael Lambourne, nephew of Giles Gosling, an innkeeper
Doctor Doboobie, alias Alasco, an astrologer and alchemist
Dickie Sludge, alias Flibbertigibbet, a bright child and friend of Wayland Smith

Critique:

Kenilworth is evidence that Scott spoke the truth when he said that the sight of a ruined castle or similar relic of the medieval period made him wish to reconstruct the life and times of what he saw. Scott spends much time and space in setting the stage for the action. However, this scene setting is not without literary merit, for it offers a detailed historical background for his novel. Although the plot itself is very slight, the characters are well portrayed.

The Story:

Michael Lambourne, who in his early youth had been a ne'er-do-well, had just returned from his travels. While drinking and boasting in Giles Gosling's inn, he wagered that he could gain admittance to Cumnor Place, a large manor where an old friend was now steward. It was rumored in the village that Tony Foster was keeping a beautiful young woman prisoner at the manor. Edmund Tressilian, another guest at the inn, went with Michael to Cumnor Place. As Tressilian had suspected, he found the woman there to be his former sweetheart, Amy Robsart, apparently a willing prisoner. At Cumnor Place he also encountered Richard Varney, her supposed seducer, and a sword fight ensued. The duel was broken up by Michael Lambourne, who had decided to ally himself with his old friend, Tony Foster.

Contrary to Tressilian's idea, Amy was not Varney's paramour but the lawful wife of Varney's master, the Earl of Leicester, Varney being only the go-between and accomplice in Amy's elopement. Leicester, who was a rival of the Earl of Sussex for Queen Elizabeth's favor, feared that the news of his marriage to Amy would displease the queen, and he had convinced Amy that their marriage must be kept secret.

Tressilian returned to Lidcote Hall to obtain Hugh Robsart's permission to bring Varney to justice on a charge of seduction. On his way there he employed as his manservant Wayland Smith, formerly an assistant to Dr. Doboobie, an alchemist and astrologer. Later he visited the Earl of Sussex, through whom he hoped to petition either the queen or the Earl of Leicester in Amy's behalf. While there, Wayland Smith saved Sussex's life after the earl had been poisoned.

When the earl heard Tressilian's story, he presented the petition directly to the queen. Confronted by Elizabeth, Varney swore that Amy was his lawful wife, and Leicester, who was standing by, confirmed the lie. Elizabeth then ordered Varney to present Amy to her when she visited Kenilworth the following week.

Leicester sent a letter to Amy asking her to appear at Kenilworth as Varney's wife. She refused. In order to have an excuse for disobeying Elizabeth's orders regarding Amy's presence at Kenilworth, Varney had Alasco, the former Dr. Doboobie, mix a potion which would make Amy ill but not kill her. This plan was thwarted, however, by Wayland Smith, who had been sent by Tressilian to help her. She escaped from Cumnor Place and with the assistance of Wayland Smith made her way to Kenilworth to see Leicester.

When she arrived at Kenilworth, the place was bustling in preparation for Elizabeth's arrival that afternoon. Wayland Smith took Amy to Tressilian's quarters, where she wrote Leicester a letter telling him of her escape from Cumnor Place and asking his aid. Wayland Smith lost the letter and through a misunderstanding he was ejected from the castle. Amy, disappointed that Leicester did not come to her, left her apartment and went into the garden. There the queen discovered her. Judging Amy to be insane because of her contradictory statements, she returned Amy to the custody of Varney, her supposed husband.

Leicester decided to confess the true story to the queen. But Varney, afraid for his own fortunes if Leicester fell from favor, convinced the earl that Amy had been unfaithful to him, and that Tressilian was her lover. Leicester, acting upon Varney's lies, decided that the death of Amy and her lover would be just punishment. Varney took Amy back to Cumnor Place and plotted her death. Leicester relented and sent Michael Lambourne to tell Varney that Amy must not die, but Varney killed Lambourne in order that he might go through with his murder of Amy. Leicester and Tressilian fought a duel, but before either harmed the other they were interrupted by Dickie Sludge, the child who had stolen Amy's letter. Reading it, Leicester realized that Amy had been faithful to him and that the complications of the affair had been caused by the machinations of Varney.

Leicester immediately went to the queen and told her the whole story. Elizabeth was angry, but she sent Tressilian and Sir Walter Raleigh to bring Amy to Kenilworth. Unfortunately, Tressilian arrived too late to save Amy. She had fallen through a trapdoor so rigged that when she stepped upon it she plunged to her death.

Tressilian and Sir Walter Raleigh seized Varney and carried him off to prison. There Varney committed suicide. Elizabeth permitted grief-stricken Leicester to retire from her court for several years but later recalled him and installed him once more in her favor. Much later in life he remarried. He met his death as a result of poison he intended for someone else.

KIDNAPPED

Type of work: Novel
Author: Robert Louis Stevenson (1850-1894)
Type of plot: Adventure romance
Time of plot: 1751
Locale: Scotland
First published: 1886

Principal characters:
DAVID BALFOUR, who was kidnapped
EBENEZER BALFOUR OF SHAW, his uncle
MR. RANKEILLOR, a lawyer
ALAN BRECK, a Jacobite adventurer

Critique:

For a tale of high adventure, told simply but colorfully, there are few to equal *Kidnapped*. Stevenson was a master story-teller. He wove this tale around the great and the small, the rich and the poor, men of virtue and scoundrels, and each character was truly drawn. A stolen inheritance, a kidnapping, a battle at sea, several murders—these are only a few of the adventures that befell the hero. It is easily understood why *Kidnapped* is a favorite with all who read it.

The Story:

When David Balfour's father died, the only inheritance he left his son was a letter to Ebenezer Balfour of Shaw, who was his brother and David's uncle. Mr. Campbell, the minister of Essendean, delivered the letter to David and told him that if things did not go well between David and his uncle he was to return to Essendean, where his friends would help him. David set off in high spirits. The house of Shaw was a great one in the Lowlands of Scotland, and David was eager to take his rightful place among the gentry. He did not know why his father had been separated from his people.

As he approached the great house, he began to grow apprehensive. Everyone of whom he asked the way had a curse for the name of Shaw and warned him against his uncle. But he had gone too far and was too curious to turn back before he reached the mansion. What he found was not a great house. One wing was unfinished and many windows were without glass. No friendly smoke came from the chimneys, and the closed door was studded with heavy nails.

David found his Uncle Ebenezer even more forbidding than the house, and he began to suspect that his uncle had cheated his father out of his rightful inheritance. When his uncle tried to kill him, he was sure of Ebenezer's villainy. His uncle promised to take David to Mr. Rankeillor, the family lawyer, to get the true story of David's inheritance, and they set out for Queen's Ferry. Before they reached the lawyer's office, David was tricked by Ebenezer and Captain Hoseason into boarding the *Covenant,* and the ship sailed away with David a prisoner, bound for slavery in the American colonies.

At first he lived in filth and starvation in the bottom of the ship. The only person who befriended him was Mr. Riach, the second officer. Later, however, he found many of the roughest seamen to be kind at times. Mr. Riach was kind when he was drunk, but mean when he was sober; while Mr. Shuan, the first officer, was gentle except when he was drinking. It was while he was drunk that Mr. Shuan beat to death Ransome, the cabin boy, because the boy had displeased him. After Ransome's murder, David became the cabin boy, and for a time life on the *Covenant* was a little better.

One night the *Covenant* ran down a small boat and cut her in two. Only one man was saved, Alan Breck, a Highlander of Scotland and a Jacobite with a price on his head. Alan demanded that Captain Hoseason set him ashore among his own people, and the captain agreed. When David overheard the captain and Mr. Riach planning to seize Alan, he warned Alan of the plot. Together the two of them held the ship's crew at bay, killing Mr. Shuan and three others and wounding many more, including Captain Hoseason. Afterwards Alan and David were fast friends and remained so during the rest of their adventures. Alan told David of his part in the rebellion against King George and of the way he was hunted by the king's men, particularly by Colin of Glenure, known as the Red Fox. Alan was the king's enemy while David was loyal to the monarch, yet out of mutual respect they swore to help each other in time of trouble.

It was not long before they had to prove their loyalty. The ship broke apart on a reef, and David and Alan, separated at first, soon found themselves together again, deep in the part of the Highlands controlled by Alan's enemies. When Colin of Glenure was murdered, the blame fell on Alan. To be caught meant they would both hang. So began their attempt to escape to the Lowlands and to find Mr. Rankeillor, their only chance for help. They hid by day and traveled by night. Often they went for several days without food and only a flask of rum for drink. They were in danger not only from the king's soldiers, but also from Alan's own people. There was always the danger that a trusted friend would betray them for the reward offered. But David was to learn what loyalty meant. Many of Alan's clan endangered themselves to help the hunted pair.

When David was too weak to go on and wanted to give up, Alan offered to carry him. They finally reached Queen's Ferry and Mr. Rankeillor. At first Mr. Rankeillor was skeptical when he heard David's story, but it began to check so well with what he had heard from others that he was convinced of the boy's honesty; and he told David the whole story of his father and his Uncle Ebenezer. They had both loved the same woman, and David's father had won her. Because he was a kind man and because Ebenezer had taken to his bed over the loss of the woman, David's father had given up his inheritance as the oldest son in favor of Ebenezer. The story explained to David why his uncle had tried to get rid of him. Ebenezer knew that his dealings with David's father would not stand up in the courts, and he was afraid that David had come for his inheritance.

With the help of Alan and Mr. Rankeillor, David was able to frighten his uncle so much that Ebenezer offered him two-thirds of the yearly income from the land. Because David did not want to submit his family to public scandal in the courts, and because he could better help Alan if the story of their escape were kept quiet, he agreed to the settlement. In this way he was able to help Alan reach safety and pay his debt to his friend.

So ended the adventures of David Balfour of Shaw. He had been kidnapped and sent to sea; he had known danger and untold hardships; he had traveled the length of his native island; but now he had come home to take his rightful place among his people.

KIM

Type of work: Novel
Author: Rudyard Kipling (1865-1936)
Type of plot: Adventure romance
Time of plot: Late nineteenth century
Locale: British India
First published: 1901

Principal characters:
KIMBALL O'HARA (KIM), a street boy
A TIBETAN LAMA, Kim's teacher
MAHBUB ALI, a horse trader
COLONEL CREIGHTON, director of the British Secret Service
HURREE CHUNDER MOOKERJEE, a babu

Critique:

Kim gives a vivid picture of the complexities of India under British rule. It shows the life of the bazaar mystics, of the natives, of the British military. The dialogue, as well as much of the indirect discourse, makes use of Indian phrases, translated by the author, to give the flavor of native speech. There is a great deal of action and movement, for Kipling's vast canvas is painted in full detail. There are touches of irony as well as a display of native shrewdness and cunning.

The Story:

Kim grew up on the streets of Lahore. His Irish mother had died when he was born. His father, a former color-sergeant of an Irish regiment called the Mavericks, died eventually of drugs and drink, and left his son in the care of a half-caste woman. So young Kimball O'Hara became Kim, and under the hot Indian sun his skin grew so dark that one could not tell he was a white boy.

One day a Tibetan lama, in search of the holy River of the Arrow that would wash away all sin, came to Lahore. Struck by the possibility of exciting adventure, Kim attached himself to the lama as his pupil. His adventures began almost at once. That night, at the edge of Lahore, Mahbub Ali, a horse trader, gave Kim a cryptic message to deliver to a British officer in Umballa. Kim did not know that Mahbub was a member of the British Secret Service. He delivered the message as directed, and then lay in the grass and watched and listened until he learned that his message meant that eight thousand men would go to war.

Out on the big road the lama and Kim encountered many people of all sorts. Conversation was easy. One group in particular interested Kim, an old lady traveling in a family bullock cart attended by a retinue of eight men. Kim and the lama attached themselves to her party. Toward evening, they saw a group of soldiers making camp. It was the Maverick regiment. Kim, whose horoscope said that his life would be changed at the sign of a red bull in a field of green, was fascinated by the regimental flag, which was just that, a red bull against a background of bright green.

Caught by a chaplain, the Reverend Arthur Bennett, Kim accidentally jerked loose the amulet which he carried around his neck. Mr. Bennett opened the amulet and discovered three papers folded inside, including Kim's baptismal certificate and a note from his father asking that the boy be taken care of. Father Victor arrived in time to see the papers. When Kim had told his story, he was informed that he would be sent away to school. Kim parted sadly from the lama, sure, however, that he would soon escape. The lama asked that Father Victor's name and address, and the costs of schooling Kim, be written down and given to him. Then he disappeared. Kim, pretending to prophesy, told the priests what he had heard at Umballa. They and the soldiers laughed at him. But the next day his prophecy came true, and eight thousand soldiers were sent to put down an uprising in the north. Kim remained in camp.

One day a letter arrived from the lama. He enclosed enough money for Kim's first year at school and promised to provide the same amount yearly. He requested that the boy be sent to St. Xavier's for his education. Meanwhile the drummer who was keeping an eye on Kim had been cruel to his charge. When Mahbub Ali came upon the two boys, he gave the drummer a beating, and began talking to Kim. While they were thus engaged, Colonel Creighton came up and learned from Mahbub Ali, in an indirect way, that Kim would be, when educated, a valuable member of the secret service.

At last Kim was on his way to St. Xavier's. Near the school he spied the lama, who had been waiting a day and a half to see him. They agreed to see each other often. Kim was an apt pupil, but he disliked being shut up in classrooms and dormitories. When vacation time came, he went to Umballa and persuaded Mahbub Ali to let him return to the road until school reopened.

Traveling with Mahbub Ali, he played the part of a horse boy and saved the trader's life when he overheard two men plotting to kill the horse dealer. At Simla, Kim stayed with Mr. Lurgan, who taught him a great many subtle tricks and games and the art of make-up and disguise. For, as Mahbub Ali had said, he was now learning the great game, as the work of the secret service was called. At the end of the summer Kim returned to St. Xavier's. He studied there for a total of three years.

In conference with Mr. Lurgan and Colonel Creighton, Mahbub Ali advised that Kim be permitted once more to go out on the road with his lama. Kim's skin was stained dark and again he resumed the dress of a street boy. Given the password by Hurree Chunder Mookerjee, a babu who was another member of the secret service, Kim set out with his lama after begging a train ticket to Delhi.

Still seeking his river, the lama moved up and down India with Kim as his disciple. The two of them once more encountered the old woman they had met on the road three years before. A little later Kim was surprised to see the babu, who told him that two of the five kings of the north had been bribed and that the Russians had sent spies down into India through the passes that the kings had agreed to guard. Two men, a Russian and a Frenchman, were to be apprehended, and the babu asked Kim's aid. To the lama Kim suggested a journey into the foothills of the Himalayas, and so he was able to follow the babu on his mission.

During a storm the babu came upon the two foreigners. Discovering that one of their baskets contained valuable letters, including a message from one of the traitorous kings, he offered to be their guide, and in two days he had led them to the spot where Kim and the lama were camped. When the foreigners tore almost in two a holy drawing made by the lama, the babu created a disturbance in which the coolies, according to plan, carried off the men's luggage. The lama conducted Kim to the village of Shamlegh. There Kim examined all of the baggage which the coolies had carried off. Everything except letters and notebooks he threw over an unscalable cliff. The documents he hid on his person.

In a few days Kim and the lama set out again. At last they came to the house of the old woman who had befriended them twice before. When she saw Kim's emaciated condition, she put him to bed, where he slept many days. Before he went to sleep, he asked that a strongbox be brought to him. In it he deposited his papers; then he locked the box and hid it under his bed. When he woke up, he heard that the babu had arrived, and to him Kim delivered the papers. The babu told him that Mahbub Ali was also in the vicinity. They assured Kim that he had played his part well in the great game. The old lama knew nothing of these matters. He was happy because Kim had brought him to his river at last, a brook on the old lady's estate.

KING SOLOMON'S MINES

Type of work: Novel
Author: H. Rider Haggard (1856-1925)
Type of plot: Adventure romance
Time of plot: Nineteenth century
Locale: Africa
First published: 1886

Principal characters:
Allan Quatermain, an English explorer
Sir Henry Curtis, his friend
Captain John Good, Curtis' friend
Umbopa, a Zulu, in reality Ignosi, hereditary chieftain of the Kukuanas
Twala, ruler of the Kukuanas
Gagool, a native sorceress

Critique:

This story of the search for King Solomon's legendary lost treasure, hidden in the land of the Kukuanas, provides absorbing reading for children and adults alike. The slaughter provoked by the cruelty of King Twala and the character of the ancient sorceress, Gagool, make *King Solomon's Mines* a book which is not soon forgotten.

The Story:

Returning to his home in Natal after an unsuccessful elephant hunt, Allan Quatermain met aboard ship Sir Henry Curtis and his friend, retired Captain John Good. Sir Henry inquired whether Quatermain had met a man named Neville in the Transvaal. Learning that he had, Sir Henry explained that Neville was his younger brother, George, with whom he had quarreled. When Sir Henry inherited his parents' estate, George had taken the name Neville and had gone to Africa to seek his fortune. He had not been heard from since.

Quatermain said that Neville was reported to have started for King Solomon's Mines, diamond mines reputed to lie far in the interior. Ten years before he himself had met a Portuguese, José Silvestre, who had tried unsuccessfully to cross the desert to the mines and had dragged himself into his camp to die. Before he expired, José had given him a map showing the location of the treasure. It was written on a piece of a shirt which had belonged to his relative, another José Silvestre, three hundred years before. That Silvestre had seen the mines, but had died in the mountains while trying to return. His servant had brought the map back to his family, and it had been passed down through succeeding generations of the Silvestre family. By the time the ship reached Natal, Quatermain had agreed to help Sir Henry Curtis find his brother.

In Natal, Quatermain got their equipment together, and the trio chose the five men who were to go with them. Besides the driver and the leader for the oxen which were to pull their cart, they hired three servants; a Hottentot named Ventvögel, and two Zulus, Khiva and Umbopa. Umbopa explained that his tribe lived far to the north, in the direction in which they were traveling, and that he was willing to serve for nothing if he might go with the party. Quatermain was suspicious of the native's offer, but Sir Henry agreed to take Umbopa as his servant.

On the journey from Durban they lost Khiva when, trying to save Captain Good from attack by a wounded bull elephant, the native was torn in two by the animal. At Sitandra's Kraal, at the edge of the desert, the men left all the equipment they could not carry on their backs. Quatermain's plan was to travel at night so as to avoid the heat of the sun and to sleep during the day. On the third day out, however, the men could find no shelter from the heat. They decided that trekking was more comfortable than trying to rest. By the fourth day they were out of water, but on the following day Ventvögel discovered a spring. Refreshing themselves, they started off again that night. At the end of the next night they reached the lower slope of a mountain marked on the map as Sheba's left breast. On the other side of the mountain lay King Solomon's road, which was supposed to lead to the diamond mines.

The climb up the mountain was not an easy one. The higher they ascended, the colder it grew. At the top of the ridge they found a cave and climbed into it to spend the night. Ventvögel froze to death before morning.

Ventvögel was not the only dead man in the cave. The next morning, when it grew light, one of the party saw the body of a white man in its rocky recesses. Quatermain decided that it was the body of the first José Silvestre, preserved by the cold.

Leaving the bodies in the cave, the remaining men started down the mountain slope. As the mist cleared they could distinguish fertile lands and woods below them. Reaching King Solomon's road, they followed it into the valley. The road was a magnificent engineering feat which crossed a ravine and even tunneled through a ridge. In the tunnel the walls were decorated with figures driving in chariots. Sir Henry declared the pictures had been painted by ancient Egyptians.

When Quatermain and his party had descended to the valley, they stopped to eat and rest beside a stream. Captain Good undressed to shave and bathe. Suddenly Quatermain realized that they were being observed by a party of natives. As the leader of the band, an old man stepped up to speak to them, Quatermain saw that he greatly resembled Umbopa.

If it had not been for Captain Good's peculiarities, the four men would surely have been killed. Luckily, Captain Good's false teeth, bare legs, half-shaven face and monocle fascinated the savages so that they were willing to believe Quatermain's story that he and his friends had descended from the stars. To make the story more credible, he shot an antelope with what he declared was his magic tube. At Quatermain's insistence, the old man, whose name was Infadoos, agreed to lead the men to Twala, King of the Kukuanas. After a three-day journey Quatermain and his party reached Loo, where Twala was holding his summer festival. The white men were introduced to the hideous one-eyed giant before an assemblage of eight thousand of his soldiers.

Before Twala's annual witch hunt began that evening, the four travelers had a conference with Infadoos. From him they learned that Twala and his son, Scragga, were hated for their cruelty. Umbopa then revealed that he was, in reality, Ignosi, son of the rightful king, whom Twala had murdered. On the death of her husband his mother had fled across the mountains and desert with her child. As proof of his claim, Ignosi displayed a snake which was tattooed around his middle. The snake was the sign of Kukuana kingship.

All the men, including Infadoos, agreed that they would help him overcome Twala and gain the throne. Infadoos declared that he would speak to some of the chiefs after the witch hunt and win them to Ignosi's cause. He was certain that they could have twenty thousand men in their ranks by the next morning.

That night Gagool and her sister sorceresses helped Twala search out over a hundred of his men charged with evil thoughts or plots against their sovereign. When in their wild dances they stopped before any one of the twenty thousand soldiers who were drawn up in review, the victim was immediately stabbed to death. Gagool did not hesitate, in her blood thirst, to stop in front of Ignosi. Quatermain and his friends fired their guns to impress Twala and persuade him that Ignosi's life should be spared.

Infadoos was true to his word. He brought the chiefs he could muster, and Ignosi again exhibited the tattooing around his waist. The men feared he might be an impostor, however, and asked for a further sign. Captain Good, who knew from his almanac that an eclipse of the sun was due, swore that they would darken the sun the following day.

King Twala, continuing his festival, had his maidens dance before him the next afternoon. When they had finished, he asked Quatermain to choose the most beautiful, it being his custom to have the loveliest of the dancers slain each year. The girl Foulata was selected, but before she could be killed the white men interfered on her behalf. As they did so, the sun began to darken. Scragga, mad with fear, threw his spear at Sir Henry, but the Englishman was luckily wearing a mail shirt, a present from Twala. Seizing the weapon, he hurled it back at Scragga and killed him.

Quatermain and his friends, including Infadoos and the girl, took advantage of the eclipse to flee from the town with the chiefs who had rallied to them. On a hill about two miles from Loo approximately twenty thousand men prepared for battle.

Twala's regiments, numbering about thirty thousand soldiers, attacked the next day. They were driven back and then set upon by their enemies who, driving at them from three directions, surrounded and slaughtered many of the Kukuanas. The vanquished Twala was slain in a contest with Sir Henry, who lopped off his head with a battle-ax.

In return for the help which his white friends had given him, the new king, Ignosi, ordered Gagool to lead them to King Solomon's mines, which lay in the mountains at the other end of the great road. Deep into the hills they went, past three enormous figures carved in the rock, images which Quatermain believed might be the three false gods for whom Solomon had gone astray. To reach the treasure room they had to pass through a cave which Gagool called the Place of Death. There, seated around a table, were all the dead kings of the Kukuanas, petrified by siliceous water dripping upon them.

While the men stood dumbfounded by the sight, Gagool, unobserved moved a lever which caused a massive stone to rise. On the other side of it were boxes full of diamonds and stores of ivory.

As the men stood gloating over the treasure, Gagool crept away. After stabbing Foulata fatally, she released a lever to bring the door down again. Before she could pass under it to the other side, however, it dropped and crushed her.

For several hours Quatermain and his friends believed that they were buried alive, for they had no idea where to find the secret of the door. At last, in the dark, they found a lever which disclosed a subterranean passage. Through it they found their way once more to the outside and to Infadoos, who was waiting for them.

A few weeks later some of Ignosi's men guided them out of Kukuanaland, across the mountains, and on the first stage of their trip back across the desert. The only treasure they had with them was a handful of diamonds Quatermain had stuffed into his pockets before they found a way out of the treasure room.

Their guides who knew of a better trail than that by which the travelers had come, led them to an oasis from which they could pass on to other green spots along their way.

On their return trip they found, near the bank of a stream, a small hut and in it Sir Henry's lost brother, George. He had been badly injured by a boulder, two years before, and had not been able to travel since that time. Quatermain and his friends supported George across the desert to Sitandra's Kraal, and then on to Quatermain's home. According to their agreement before setting out on the expedition, the diamonds were divided. He and Captain Good each kept a third, and the rest of the stones they gave to George, Sir Henry's brother.

KING'S ROW

Type of work: Novel
Author: Henry Bellamann (1882-1945)
Type of plot: Social criticism
Time of plot: Late nineteenth century
Locale: The Middle West
First published: 1940

Principal characters:

PARRIS MITCHELL, of King's Row
DRAKE MCHUGH, Parris' friend
RANDY MONAGHAN, who married McHugh
CASSANDRA TOWER (CASSIE), Parris' friend
ELISE SANDOR, newcomer to King's Row, Parris' friend

Critique:

Although Parris Mitchell is the hero of this novel, the story is also that of his home town, King's Row. For the struggle is always between Parris and the town. Life in King's Row is more tragic than happy, and Henry Bellamann has vividly depicted the town and its people. The result is an extremely skillful and moving story.

The Story:

Parris Mitchell lived with his German-born grandmother. Speaking English with a decided accent, he seemed different from the other boys his own age, and he was, consequently, much alone. He had only a few friends. There was Jamie Wakefield, whom Parris liked but who made him feel uncomfortable. There was Renée, with whom he went swimming and experienced his first love affair. Renée suddenly moved away. Later Cassandra Tower gave herself to him. Although he always remembered Renée, he was also in love with Cassie. But his best friend was another orphan like himself, Drake McHugh, a young idler whose life was almost completely concerned with women.

Parris studied with Cassie's father, Dr. Tower, a mysterious figure in King's Row, but a doctor who other physicians admitted was superior to them in knowledge. Parris' grandmother, Madame von Eln, saw to it, too, that he studied the piano with Dr. Perdorff. His grandmother arranged her affairs so that he could go to Vienna for his medical studies.

He knew that his grandmother was dying because Cassie Tower told him so. Shortly after her death, Cassie herself died, shot by Dr. Tower, who later committed suicide, leaving his money and property to Parris. Parris went to stay with Drake McHugh, who lived by himself following the deaths of his aunt and uncle. Drake told Parris not to mention to anyone his connection with the Towers. No one knew why Dr. Tower had killed himself and Cassie. While going through Dr. Tower's papers, Parris discovered that Dr. Tower had been having incestuous relations with his daughter.

While Parris was in Europe, Drake continued his life of pleasure. His romance with Louise Gordon, daughter of a local doctor, was forbidden by her parents. Drake made plans to invest in a real estate development. In the meantime, he became friendly with Randy Monaghan, daughter of a railroad employee. Then Drake's guardian absconded with his money and he was left penniless. For weeks he haunted the saloons and drank heavily. One morning, unkempt and weary, he went to Randy's home. Shortly afterward Randy's father got him a job on the railroad. One day he had an accident. Dr. Gordon was summoned, and he immediately amputated both of Drake's legs.

Meanwhile Parris had known nothing of what had happened to his friend, for Drake asked Randy and Jamie Wakefield not to mention his misfortunes in their letters to Parris. But after the accident Randy wrote to Parris, who answered and gave instructions for taking care of Drake. A short time later, Randy and Drake were married. Parris cabled congratulations and turned over the Tower property to them.

With that money, Drake and Randy went into the real estate business. Then Parris came back to King's Row as a staff physician at the insane asylum. Louise Gordon suddenly accused her father of having been a butcher, of having performed needless operations and amputations. When Mrs. Gordon called in Dr. Mitchell to attend Louise, he was advised by his superior, Dr. Nolan, that Louise would fall in love with him. In fact, local gossip was already linking Dr. Mitchell's name with Louise.

Parris investigated Louise's charges and found them to be true. With that discovery, he realized that Drake's legs had been cut off perhaps needlessly. Parris told Randy that at the bottom of every tragedy in King's Row the hand of Dr. Gordon could probably be found. Drake and Randy made Parris a silent partner in their business. While he was away on another trip to Europe, a local newspaper published a story charging he had profited from the sale of land to the hospital. Following the advice of Dr. Nolan, Parris kept silent and nothing came of the charges.

Parris became friendly with Elise Sandor, whose father had bought his grandmother's house, and soon he was spending much of his time there. Then Drake McHugh became seriously ill, and it seemed clear that his illness resulted from the amputation. Parris knew that his friend had no chance to survive. Drake died several weeks later.

Randy, only thirty-two years old, was

a widow. She decided to sell the business and look after her brother Tod, who was mentally incompetent. Those happenings were all matters of concern to Dr. Parris Mitchell on the night he walked towards the Sandor home where Elise was waiting for him.

THE KNIGHTS

Type of work: Drama
Author: Aristophanes (c. 448-385 B.C.)
Type of plot: Political satire
Time of plot: Fifth century B.C.
Locale: Athens
First presented: 424 B.C.

Principal characters:
DEMUS, a slave master, a personification of the Athenian people
DEMOSTHENES, slave of Demus
NICIAS, another slave
CLEON THE PAPHLAGONIAN, a favorite slave and a personification of the Athenian tyrant
A SAUSAGE-SELLER, later called Agoracritus

Critique:

In 426 B.C., Cleon, tyrant of Athens, accused Aristophanes of fraudulently using the privileges of his citizenship. In this play, presented two years later, the playwright attacked and ridiculed his powerful enemy, whom he presents as a fawning slave to his master but insolent and arrogant to his fellow slaves. As political satire, the play is one of wit and wisdom. Aristophanes' message is that as long as men will not look beyond their noses, they will continue to sell each other short, never realizing that at the same time they are giving themselves the shortest weight.

The Story:

Demus, a selfish and irritable old man, a tyrant to his slaves, had purchased a tanner, who was nicknamed the Paphlagonian. This slave, a fawning, foxy fellow, quickly ingratiated himself with his new master, to the dismay of all the other slaves in Demus' household, Demosthenes and Nicias in particular. Because of the Paphlagonian's lies, Demosthenes and Nicias received many floggings. The two at one time considered running away, but decided against this course because of the terrible punishment they would receive if caught and returned to their owner. They also considered suicide, but in the end they decided to forget their troubles by tippling. Going for the wine, Nicias found the Paphlagonian asleep in a drunken stupor.

While the drunken man slept, Nicias stole the writings of the sacred oracle that the Paphlogonian guarded carefully. In the prophecies of the oracle, Demosthenes and Nicias read that an oakum-seller should first manage the state's affairs; he should be followed by a sheep-seller, and he in turn should be followed by a tanner. At last the tanner would be overthrown by a sausage-seller.

As they were about to set out in search of a sausage-seller, a slave of that butcher's trade came to the house of Demus to sell his wares. Nicias and Demosthenes soon won him over to their cause, flattering him out of all reason and assuring him that his stupidity and ignorance fitted him admirably for public life.

When the Paphlagonian awoke, he loudly demanded the return of the oracle's writings. The Sausage-Seller, however, was able to out-bawl him. Spectators became involved. Some of the citizens protested against the Paphlagonian's unjust accusations of the Sausage-Seller. Others claimed that the state was falling into ruin while this shameless name-calling continued. Others accused the Paphlagonian of deafening all Athens with his din. The Sausage-Seller accused the Paphlagonian of cheating everybody. A few citizens gloated that someone even more arrogant and dishonest than the Paphlagonian had been found in the person of the Sausage-Seller. Others feared that this new demagogue would destroy all hope of defending Athens from her enemies.

While the citizens clamored, the Sausage-Seller and the Paphlagonian continued to out-boast, out-shout, and out-orate each other. The Sausage-Seller said that he would make meatballs out of the Paphlagonian. Demus' pampered slave threatened to twitch the lashes off both the Sausage-Seller's eyes. Demosthenes broke in to suggest that the Sausage-Seller inspect the Paphlagonian as he would a hog before butchering it.

At last both began to clamor for Demus, asking him to come out of his house and decide the merits of their claims. When he answered their calls, both boasted of a greater love to do him service. Convinced by the assurances of the Sausage-Seller, Demus decided to dismiss the Paphlagonian and demanded that his former favorite return his seal of office. Both continued their efforts to bribe Demus for his favor. At last the rivals ran to consult the oracles, to prove to Demus the right of their contentions.

Each brought back a load of prophetic writings and insisted upon reading them aloud to Demus. In their prophecies they continued to insult one another, at the same time flattering Demus. The Sausage-Seller related a dream in which Athena had come down from Olympus to pour ambrosia upon Demus and the sourest of pickles upon the Paphlagonian.

Demus sent them off on another foolish errand, laughing meanwhile because he had duped both of them into serving him. But at last the Sausage-Seller convinced the Paphlagonian that he had the right of stewardship by the word of an ancient oracle in whom both believed. Having won his victory, the Sausage-Seller, now calling himself Agoracritus, began to browbeat his new master and to accuse him of stupidity and avarice. He boasted that he would now grow wealthy on bribes the Paphlagonian had formerly pocketed. To show his power, he ordered Cleon the Paphlagonian to turn sausage-seller and peddle tripe in the streets.

THE KREUTZER SONATA

Type of work: Novel
Author: Count Leo Tolstoy (1828-1910)
Type of plot: Social criticism
Time of plot: Late nineteenth century
Locale: Russia
First published: 1889

Principal characters:
VASYLA POZDNISHEF, a Russian aristocrat
MME. POZDNISHEF, his wife
TRUKHASHEVSKY, lover of Mme. Pozdnishef

Critique:

This book has been much misunderstood as representing Tolstoy's own views on marriage and the relationships of the sexes in Russian society. Actually, the story is the confession of an insane man who had murdered his wife in a fit of jealousy brought on by his insanity. Most important, however, is the Christian aspect of sexual morality which underlies the book. Explaining his novel, Tolstoy said that he wanted to do away with the false conception that sexual relationships were necessary for health, to bring to public attention the fact that sexual immorality was based in part on a wrong attitude toward marriage, and to restore the birth of children to a proper place in the sphere of marriage.

The Story:

One spring night a railway train was speeding across Russia. In one of the cars a sprightly conversation about the place of women, both in public and in the home, was in progress among a group of aristocrats. One of the listeners finally broke into the conversation with the statement that Russians married only for sexual reasons and that marriage was a hell for most of them unless they, like himself, secured release by killing the other party to the marriage. With that remark he left the group and retired to his own seat in the car. Later on he told his story to his seat companion.

His name was Pozdnishef and he was a landed proprietor. As a young man he had learned many vices, but he had always kept his relationships with women on a monetary basis, so that he would have no moral responsibility for the unfortunates with whom he came in contact. His early life had taught him that people of his class did not respect sex. The men looked on women only in terms of pleasure. The women sanctioned such thoughts by openly marrying men who had become libertines; the older people by allowing their daughters to be married to men whose habits were known to be of a shameful nature.

At the age of thirty Pozdnishef fell in love with a beautiful woman of his own class, the daughter of an impoverished landowner in Penza. During his engagement to the girl he was disturbed because they had so little about which to converse when they were left alone. They would say one sentence to each other and then become silent. Not knowing what should come next, they would fall to eating bonbons. The honeymoon was a failure, shameful and tiresome at the beginning, painfully oppressive at the end. Three or four days after the wedding they quarreled, and both realized that in a short time they had grown to hate each other. As the months of marriage passed, their quarrels grew more frequent and violent. Pozdnishef became persuaded in his own mind that love was something low and swinish.

The idea of marriage and sex became an obsession with him. When his wife secured a wet-nurse for their children, he felt that she was shirking a moral duty by not nursing her offspring. Worse, Pozdnishef was jealous of every man who came into his wife's presence, who was received in his home, or who received a smile from his wife. He began to suspect that his wife had taken a lover.

The children born to Pozdnishef and his wife were a great trouble to him in other ways as well. They were continually bothering him with real or fancied illnesses, and they broke up the regular habits of life to which he was accustomed. They were new subjects over which he and his wife could quarrel.

In the fourth year of their marriage, the couple had reached a state of complete disagreement. They ceased to talk over anything to the end. They were almost silent when they were alone, much as they had been during their engagement. Finally the doctors told the woman she could have no more children with safety. Pozdnishef felt that without children to justify their relations, the only reason for their life together was the other children who had been born and who held them like a chain fastening two convicts.

In the next two years the young woman filled out and bloomed in health, after the burden of bearing children was taken from her. She became more attractive in the eyes of other men, and her husband's jealousy sharply increased.

Mme. Pozdnishef had always been interested in music, and she played the piano rather well. Through her musical interest she met a young aristocrat who had turned professional musician when his family fortune had dwindled away. His name was Trukhashevsky. When he appeared on the scene the Pozdnishefs had passed through several crises in their marriage. The husband had at times considered suicide and the wife had tried to poison herself. One evening, after a violent scene in which Pozdnishef had told his wife he would like to see her dead, she had rushed to her room and swallowed an opium compound. Quick action on the part of the husband and a doctor had saved her life, but neither could forget her desperate attempt.

One evening Trukhashevsky came to Pozdnishef's home in Moscow. He and Mme. Pozdnishef played during the evening for a number of guests. The first piece they played together was Beethoven's Kreutzer Sonata. The first movement, a rapid allegro, worked upon the highly-strung emotions of the husband until he began to imagine that there was already an understanding between the musician and his wife. The idea obsessed him so that he could hardly wait until the other man was out of the house. Never in his life had music affected Pozdnishef in that manner. Between it and his jealousy, he was almost violently insane.

Two days later Pozdnishef left Moscow to attend a meeting. He went away fearful of what might happen while he was gone. On the second day of his absence, Pozdnishef received a letter from his wife saying that the musician had called at the house.

Jealousy immediately seized the husband. He rushed back to Moscow as fast as carriage and trains could carry him. He arrived at his home after midnight. Lights were burning in his wife's apartment. Taking off his shoes, he prowled about the house. He soon discovered the musician's overcoat. He went to the nursery and the children's rooms, but found everyone there asleep. Returning to his study, he seized a dagger and made his way to his wife's apartment. There he found his wife and the musician seated at a table, eating. He rushed at the man, who escaped by ducking under the piano and then out the door. Pozdnishef, beside himself with anger and jealousy, seized his wife and stabbed her. When she dropped to the floor, he ran from the room and went to his study. There he fell asleep on a sofa.

A few hours later his sister-in-law awakened him and took him to see his dying wife. Shortly afterward the authorities carried Pozdnishef away to prison. He went under police escort to his wife's funeral. It was only after he had looked at the waxen face of the corpse that he realized he had committed a murder. Then, at his trial, Pozdnishef was found innocent because he had murdered while in the heat of anger at finding his wife unfaithful to him.

Now judged insane, Pozdnishef declared that if he had it to do over, he would never marry. Marriage, he insisted, was not for true Christians with strong sensibilities and weak moral restraints.

KRISTIN LAVRANSDATTER

Type of work: Novel
Author: Sigrid Undset (1882-1949)
Type of Plot: Historical chronicle
Time of plot: Fourteenth century
Locale: Norway
First published: 1920-1922

Principal characters:
KRISTIN LAVRANSDATTER
LAVRANS BJÖRGULFSÖN, Kristin's father, owner of Jörundgaard
RAGNFRID IVARSDATTER, Kristin's mother
ULVHILD, and

RAMBORG, Kristin's sisters
ERLEND NIKULAUSSÖN, owner of Husaby
SIMON ANDRESSÖN, son of a neighboring landowner
LADY AASHILD, Erlend's aunt
NIKULAUS (NAAKVE),
BJÖRGULF,
GAUTE,
SKULE,
IVAR,
LAVRANS
MUNAN, and
ERLEND, sons of Erlend and Kristin

Critique:

Kristin Lavransdatter is a trilogy—*The Bridal Wreath, The Mistress of Husaby,* and *The Cross*—for which Sigrid Undset received the Nobel Prize in Literature. Madame Undset's work is characterized by consummate artistry in her delineation of character, in her selection of detail, and above all in her ability to tell a story. These three novels laid in medieval Norway, a period little known to the general reader, make possible the reader's acquaintance with many characters who lived long ago, but who faced many of the same great problems that the world knows today.

The Story:

Lavrans Björgulfsön and his wife Ragnfrid Ivarsdatter were descended from powerful landowners. Although Kristin had been born at her father's manor Skog, she spent most of her childhood at Jörundgaard, which fell to Lavrans and Ragnfrid upon the death of Ragnfrid's father. Kristin's childhood was exceedingly happy.

A second daughter, Ulvhild, was crippled at the age of three. Lady Aashild, a declared witch-wife, was sent for to help the child. Kristin became well acquainted with Lady Aashild that summer.

When she was fifteen, Kristin's father betrothed her to Simon Andressön of Dyfrin. One evening Kristin slipped away to bid goodbye to a childhood playmate, Arne Gyrdsön, and on her way home Bentein, Sira Eirik's grandson, accosted her. She escaped after a fight with him, physically unharmed but mentally tortured. Later that year Arne was brought home dead after having fought with Bentein over Bentein's sly insinuations regarding Kristin. Kristin persuaded her father to put off the betrothal feast and permit her to spend a year in a convent at Oslo.

Soon after entering the Convent of Nonneseter, Kristin and her bed-partner, Ingebjörg Filippusdatter, went into Oslo to shop, accompanied by an old servant. When they became separated from the old man, they were rescued by a group of men riding through the woods. In that manner Kristin met Erlend Nikulaussön, the nephew of Lady Aashild. In July, Kristin and Erlend met once more at the St. Margaret's Festival and that night vowed to love each other. The following morning Kristin learned from Ingebjörg of Eline Ormsdatter, whom Erlend had stolen from her husband, and by whom Erlend had had two children. Later that summer, while visiting her uncle at Skog, Kristin and Erlend met secretly and Kristin surrendered to Erlend. During the following winter Kristin and Erlend managed to meet frequently. In the spring, Kristin told Simon of her love for Erlend and her desire to end their betrothal. He agreed, much against his will. Lavrans and Ragnfrid unwillingly accepted Kristin's and Simon's decision.

When Erlend's kinsmen brought suit for Kristin's hand in marriage, Lavrans refused. During the winter Erlend and Kristin planned to elope to Sweden. While they were making their plans at Lady Aashild's home, Eline Ormsdatter overtook them. Discovered by Erlend when she was trying to give poison to Kristin, she stabbed herself. Erlend and Sir Björn, Lady Aashild's husband, put her on a sled and took her south to be buried. Kristin returned home.

The following spring Erlend's relatives again made a bid for Kristin's hand, and worn out with suffering—Ulvhild's death and Kristin's unhappiness—Lavrans agreed to the betrothal. During Erlend's visit at Whitsuntide, Kristin became pregnant. On the night of the wedding Lavrans realized that Kristin already belonged to Erlend. He had given to Erlend what Erlend had already possessed.

After her marriage Kristin moved to Erlend's estate at Husaby. She was quick to notice the neglect everywhere evident. In the next fifteen years she bore Erlend seven sons—Nikulaus, Björgulf, Gaute, the twins Ivar and Skule, Lavrans, and Munan. At the same time she struggled to save her sons' inheritance by better management of Husaby. But Erlend, intent on becoming a great man, sold land to pay his expenses and granted tenants free rent in exchange for supplies for his military musters.

Simon Andressön who lived at Formo with his sister Sigrid and his illegitimate daughter, Arngjerd, made suit to Lavrans for Kristin's youngest sister, Ramborg. The following year Lavrans died, followed two years later by Ragnfrid. Kristin's part of the inheritance was Jörundgaard.

There was much unrest in the country at that time. A boy, Magnus VII, had been named king of both Sweden and Norway, and during his childhood Erling Vidkunssön was made regent of Norway. When Magnus reached the age of sixteen, Sir Erling resigned and soon Norway had little law or order. During those years of unrest Erlend conspired to put another claimant on the throne of Norway. Arrested, he was tried for treason by a king's-men's court. Erlend came off with his life, but he had to forfeit all his lands.

Erlend went with Kristin and his sons to Jörundgaard to live; but he cared little for farming or for the people of the dale, and the neighbors avoided Jörundgaard. As the children grew to manhood, Kristin became more fearful for their future. In her desire to further their fortunes, she and Erlend came to harsh words and she told him he was not a fit lord of Jörundgaard. He left her and went to Haugen, the farm where Lady Aashild had spent her last days. Kristin, although she longed to have Erlend back, felt that she had been in the right and struggled along with the help of Ulf, a servant, to make Jörundgaard produce.

The following winter her brother-in-law Simon died as a result of a cut on the arm, sustained while separating two drunken fighters. Before he died, he asked Kristin to go to Erlend and settle their quarrel. Kristin promised to do so. Ramborg gave birth to her son six weeks early, and upon Simon's death named the child Simon Simonssön.

Kristin kept her promise and went to Haugen to ask Erlend to return to Jörundgaard, but he refused. She stayed at Haugen that summer and then returned home to her sons. Finding herself again with child, she sent her sons to tell her husband. When the child was born, Erlend still did not come to her. The child died before it was three months old. Soon thereafter, when Bishop Halvard came to the parish, Jardtrud, Ulf's wife, went to him and charged Ulf with adultery with Kristin. Lavrans, unknown to the rest of the family, rode to Haugen to get his father. Erlend returned immediately with his son, but in a scuffle in the courtyard he was wounded and he died. The same year Munan died of a sickness which went around the parish. Thus Kristin was left with six sons, each of whom must make his way in the world.

Ivar and Skule, the twins, took service with a distant kinsman. Ivar married Signe Gamalsdatter, a wealthy young widow. Nikulaus and Björgulf entered the brotherhood at Tautra. Gaute fell in love with Jofrid Helgesdatter, heiress of a rich landowner. The two young people eloped and were not married until the summer after the birth of their child, Erlend. During that winter they lived at Jörundgaard and after their marriage Kristin relinquished the keys of the manor to Jofrid. Lavrans took service with the Bishop of Skaalholt and sailed to Iceland.

Kristin, who felt out of place in her old home after she was no longer mistress there, decided to go to Nidaros and enter a convent. In the year 1349, after Kristin had been in the cloister for about two years, her son Skule went to see her. From him she received the first news of the Black Plague. The disease soon engulfed the whole city, carried off her two sons in the convent, Nikulaus and Björgulf, and finally caused Kristin's own death.

LADY INTO FOX

Type of work: Novelette
Author: David Garnett (1892-)
Type of plot: Fantasy
Time of plot: 1880
Locale: England
First published: 1923

Principal characters:
Mr. Richard Tebrick
Silvia Fox Tebrick, *his wife*

Critique:

Lady Into Fox is a story in which its author, like Coleridge in *The Rime of the Ancient Mariner,* attempts to make the unreal seem probable. Perhaps many a bridegroom, and as suddenly, has found himself married to a vixen. The book is fantasy, but fantasy written with scrupulous regard for realistic detail. So far as the book's underlying meaning is concerned, the reader may make whatever interpretation he will. It is first of all an entertaining story.

The Story:

Silvia Fox married Richard Tebrick in 1879 and went to live with him at Rylands, near Stokoe, Oxon. The bride was oddly beautiful, a woman with small hands and feet, reddish hair, brownish skin, and freckles. Early in the year 1880, while the two were still very much in love, Silvia accompanied her husband on a walk. Hearing the sounds of a hunt, Mr. Tebrick pulled his bride forward to get a good view of the hounds. Suddenly she snatched her hand away and cried out. Beside him on the ground where his wife had stood Mr. Tebrick saw a small red fox.

Even in her changed form, he could still recognize his wife. When she began to cry, so did he, and to soothe her he kissed her on the muzzle. Waiting until after dark, he buttoned her inside his coat and took her home. First he hid her in the bedroom; then he announced to the maid that Mrs. Tebrick had been called to London. When he carried her tea to the bedroom and found his poor fox trying to cover herself with a dressing gown, he dressed her properly, set her up on some cushions, and served her tea, which she drank daintily from a saucer while he fed her sandwiches.

Because the dogs had all that time been making a clamor, he went out into the yard and shot them. Then he dismissed the servants and retired to bed, sleeping soundly with his vixen in his arms. The next morning their daily routine started. First he would cook breakfast; later he would wash and brush his wife. Next they would eat breakfast together, the same food Silvia had enjoyed before her transformation. Once he started reading to her from *Clarissa Harlowe,* but he found her watching a pet dove in its cage nearby. Soon Mr. Tebrick began to take his vixen outdoors to walk. On such occasions her chief joy was chasing ducks near the pond.

One day after tea she led him to the drawing-room with gestures that showed she wished him to play the piano. But when she continued to watch the bird, he freed the dove from its cage and tore his wife's picture into bits. He also found himself disgusted by the way she ate a chicken wing at the table. One night she refused to share his bed and pranced about the room all night.

The next morning the poor husband tried an experiment. From town he brought her a basket containing a bunch of snowdrops and a dead rabbit. Silvia pretended to admire the flowers; but when her husband left the room purposely, she devoured the rabbit. Later she repented and showed by motions that she wanted him to bring out the stereoscope so that she could admire the views. She refused to sleep with him again that night. Next day she pulled off her clothes and threw them into the pond. From that time on she was a naked vixen, and Richard Tebrick drank frequently to drown his sorrows.

At last Mr. Tebrick decided that to avoid scandal he must move to another location with his vixen, and he chose the cottage of Nanny Cork, Silvia's old nurse, as his place of retreat. He drove over in a dog cart with his wife in a wicker basket on the seat beside him. The best feature of their new home was a walled garden in which the fox could enjoy the air without being seen, but she soon began to dig under the walls in her attempts to escape. Once, thwarted in an attempt to escape, she bit her husband on the hand. Finally he gave his vixen her freedom, and allowed her to run wild in the woods.

Stricken with grief over the loss of his wife, Mr. Tebrick hired a jockey named Askew to follow the hunts and report on the foxes killed. He shot two fox hounds who strayed on his land.

One night Mr. Tebrick heard a fox bark. He heard the barking again in the morning. His vixen had returned to lead him to her earth and proudly display her litter of five tiny cubs. Mr. Tebrick was jealous, but at last he overcame his scruples and went each day to visit the young foxes. Able to identify the cubs by that time, he christened them Sorel, Kaspar, Selwyn, Esther, and Angelica. Of the whole litter, Angelica was his favorite because she reminded him of her mother.

The Reverend Canon Fox arrived to visit Mr. Tebrick. After hearing Mr. Tebrick's story, the clergyman decided that the man was insane. As the cubs grew older, Mr. Tebrick spent most of his time in the woods, hunting with the vixen and her young by day and sleeping outside with them at night. Once he purchased and brought to them a beehive of honey.

One winter day Mr. Tebrick was outside listening to the sounds of a hunting chase that ended at his own gate. Suddenly the vixen leaped into his arms, the dogs so close after her that Mr. Tebrick was badly mauled. Silvia was dead. For a long time Mr. Tebrick's life was despaired of; but he recovered to live to a hale old age, and may be still living.

LADY WINDERMERE'S FAN

Type of work: Drama
Author: Oscar Wilde (1856-1900)
Type of plot: Comedy of manners
Time of plot: Nineteenth century
Locale: London
First presented: 1892

Principal characters:
LADY WINDERMERE, a proper woman
LORD WINDERMERE, her husband
LORD DARLINGTON, a man about town
MRS. ERLYNNE, an adventuress
LORD AUGUSTUS LORTON, Mrs. Erlynne's fiancé

Critique:

This play is noted for one of the wittiest and best constructed first acts in the history of drama. The exposition, terse and interesting, leads inevitably to the scene in which Lady Windermere threatens to strike with a fan her own mother, whose true relationship she does not know. The plot of the drama is dated today, but it still conveys, to an amazing degree, Wilde's central idea that the "good woman" often costs a great deal more than she is worth.

The Story:

On her birthday Lord Windermere presented his wife with a very beautiful and delicately wrought fan with her name, Margaret, engraved upon it. She intended to carry the fan at a ball she was giving that evening, a ball to which everyone of importance in London had been invited.

That afternoon the Duchess of Berwick called on Lady Windermere, to tell her friend of a rumored affair between Lord Windermere and Mrs. Erlynne, a fascinating but notorious woman not received in the best houses. According to the duchess' story, Lord Windermere had for some months been supplying Mrs. Erlynne with funds for her support, and the old dowager's suggestion was that Lady Windermere should take immediate steps to learn the relationship between the two.

Lady Windermere was naturally upset. Determined to find out if there were any truth in the gossip, she opened her husband's desk. In a locked bank book, which she ripped open, she found evidence of her husband's duplicity, a record of checks issued to Mrs. Erlynne over a long period of time.

Angry and hurt at Lord Windermere's apparent failure to appreciate love and virtue, she turned on him the moment he appeared. His main concern was annoyance that his wife had dared tamper with his property behind his back. He informed her that his relations with Mrs. Erlynne were perfectly honorable, that she was a fine but unfortunate woman who wished to win the regard of society once more. Moreover, Lord Windermere explicitly ordered his wife to send Mrs. Erlynne an invitation to the ball. When Lady Windermere refused, her husband wrote an invitation. Angered at his act, Lady Windermere threatened to strike Mrs. Erlynne with the fan if she dared cross the threshold of Windermere House.

But when Mrs. Erlynne appeared at the ball, Lady Windermere lost her resolution and let the fan drop to the floor. The guests, believing that Mrs. Erlynne had been invited by Lady Windermere herself, naturally accepted her. She was lionized by all the men, and the women, curious because of the many stories they had heard, wanted to see at first hand what she was really like. Among her special admirers was Lord Augustus Lorton, the Duchess of Berwick's disreputable brother, to whom she had just become engaged to be married. Mrs. Erlynne was not the only woman greatly admired that evening. Lord Darlington was persistently attentive to Lady Windermere. Mrs. Erlynne's presence at the ball having put Lady Windermere into a reckless mood, Lord Darlington succeeded in persuading his hostess to leave her husband and come to him.

After the guests had gone, Lady Windermere had a violent struggle with herself, the outcome being a letter informing Lord Windermere that she was leaving his house forever. She gave the letter to a servant to deliver and left for Lord Darlington's apartments.

Mrs. Erlynne, who with Lord Augustus had remained behind to talk with Lord Windermere, discovered the letter Lady Windermere had written, and the thought of that lady's rash act brought back old memories. Twenty years before Mrs. Erlynne had written a similar letter to her husband, and had left him and their child for a lover who had deserted her. Her years of social ostracism had made her a stranger to her own daughter. Perhaps, however, she could keep her daughter from making the same mistake. Lady Windermere should never feel the remorse that her mother, Mrs. Erlynne, had known.

Mrs. Erlynne took Lady Windermere's letter and hurried to Lord Darlington's apartments, first persuading Lord Augustus to take Lord Windermere to his club and keep him there for the rest of the night. In Lord Darlington's rooms, without revealing her identity, Mrs. Erlynne managed to persuade Lady Windermere to think of her child and go back to her husband. Out of the depths of her own bitter experience, Mrs. Erlynne insisted that Lady Windermere's first duty was not to her husband but to her child.

As Lady Windermere was leaving, Lord Darlington returned, accompanied by Lord Windermere and Lord Augustus. Mrs. Erlynne, after hurrying her daughter to a waiting carriage, remained to face the gentlemen. It was an ordeal, for in her haste Lady Windermere had forgotten her fan and Lord Windermere, discovering it, became suspicious. Mrs. Erlynne appeared from behind a curtain with the explanation that she had taken the fan in mistake for her own when she left Windermere House. Her explanation saved Lady Windermere at the cost of her own reputation. Lord Windermere was furious, for he felt that he had in good faith befriended and helped a woman who was beneath contempt. Lord Augustus promptly declared that he could have nothing further to do with Mrs. Erlynne.

Lady Windermere alone defended Mrs. Erlynne. She realized at last that by some strange irony the bad woman had accepted public disgrace in order to save the good one. Lord Windermere, knowing nothing of what had happened, resolved to learn the whole truth when Mrs. Erlynne arrived to return the fan. But the mother, not wanting to shatter Lady Windermere's illusions, refused to reveal herself to the daughter. Waiting for Mrs. Erlynne outside the house, however, was Lord Augustus, who had accepted her explanation that his own interests had taken her to Lord Darlington's rooms. Lord Windermere felt that Lord Augustus was marrying a very clever woman. Lady Windermere insisted that he was marrying someone rarer, a good woman.

THE LAST DAYS OF POMPEII

Type of work: Novel
Author: Edward George Earle Bulwer-Lytton (1803-1873)
Type of plot: Historical romance
Time of plot: A.D. 79
Locale: Pompeii
First published: 1834

Principal characters:
GLAUCUS, a wealthy young Greek
ARBACES, Egyptian priest of Isis
IONE, his Greek ward
APAECIDES, her brother
NYDIA, a blind flower girl

Critique:

This novel has found many readers among those who are interested in the classical civilization which ended when barbarians took over the Mediterranean world. Bulwer-Lytton's handling of plot, character, and passion followed a tradition which has not maintained its hold. It is the tradition of nineteenth-century drama, direct, obtuse, fiery. Concerned with indirection today, the reader finds the descriptions of the characters' thoughts unrealistic. Their passions are too apparent, their actions too much explained. Cast in a different mold from novels of today, *The Last Days of Pompeii* offers one of the longest, most sustained views of the world we call classic.

The Story:

Late one afternoon in the ancient city of Pompeii the fashionable rich young men were congregating for the daily rite of the public baths. Among them were Clodius, a foppish Roman, and Glaucus, a popular young Greek. Together the two strolled toward the baths, mingling with slaves bearing bronze buckets, idlers gowned in purple robes. Along the way they saw the beautiful blind flower girl, Nydia. She, too, was from Greece and for that reason Glaucus took an interest in her. It was still too early for the baths, and the two friends walked along the sea front as Glaucus described a Neapolitan girl of Greek birth with whom he had fallen in love. Unfortunately, he had lost contact with the girl and was now morose. While they talked, Arbaces, the evil-looking Egyptian priest of Isis, intercepted them. The two young men were barely able to conceal their dislike for the Egyptian.

Arbaces secretly defied the Romans and the Greeks, and prayed for the day when Egypt would once more be powerful. He revealed to a lesser priest his interest in the brother and sister, Apaecides and Ione, his wards. He hoped to make a priest of Apaecides, and he planned to marry Ione. They had been in Naples, but recently he had brought them to Pompeii, where he could influence them.

Glaucus met Ione at a party. She was the girl he had seen and lost in Naples. At the same time Arbaces developed his hold over Apaecides, who was growing more and more confused after coming in contact with the sophistries of the corrupt priest of Isis. Meanwhile the blind flower girl, Nydia, was falling hopelessly in love with Glaucus.

It happened that Glaucus and Clodius were loitering in the establishment of Burbo, the wine-seller, when the innkeeper and his wife were beating Nydia, whose slave she was. Glaucus, hearing the girl's cries, bought her; he planned to give her to Ione. Nydia realized Glaucus could never love her after he gave her a letter to deliver to Ione. In this letter he accused Arbaces of false imputations. On reading his letter, Ione decided to go at once to Arbaces' palace and to face him with Glaucus' charges.

Knowing the danger to Ione at Arbaces' palace, Nydia warned both Ione's brother and Glaucus. Glaucus hurried to the palace to confront the priest. An earthquake interrupted the quarrel between the two men. When the goddess Isis fell from a pedestal, striking Arbaces, Glaucus and Ione ran from the building to join the throng in the street. Alone, deserted, the blind slave wept bitterly.

The next day, the earthquake having passed with but little damage, the people of Pompeii took up again the threads of their varied lives. Apaecides became a convert to Christianity. Glaucus and Ione remained together.

Julia, daughter of a wealthy freedman named Diomed, was also in love with Glaucus and sought to interfere between him and Ione. She went to the house of Arbaces, where the two plotted together. Arbaces had a drug prepared which was administered to Glaucus. The drug drove him into a demented stupor so that he ran from his house into a cemetery. To this cemetery came Apaecides and Arbaces. They quarreled and Arbaces stabbed Apaecides, killing him. Then, hoping to kill Glaucus indirectly, the priest summoned the crowd and declared that Glaucus in his drunken rage had killed Apaecides. Glaucus and a Christian who attempted to defend him were arrested. They were condemned to be given to wild beasts at the public games.

After the funeral of her brother, Ione resolved to declare her belief in the innocence of Glaucus. But before she could carry out her plan Arbaces had seized her and carried her off to his palace. The only one who knew of Arbaces' guilt was a priest who was also his prisoner. But Arbaces reckoned without Nydia, who as a dancing girl had learned most of the secrets of his palace. Nydia, contacting the priest imprisoned by Arbaces, agreed to carry his story to the authorities. Unfortunately, she too was captured. She persuaded a slave to carry the message to Sallust, a friend of Glaucus. But the message was delivered while Sallust was drunk and he refused to read it.

The last day of Pompeii arrived. It was also a day of celebration in the arena, for which the populace had been waiting. The games began with gladiatorial combat which the audience watched listlessly, bored because the deaths did not come fast enough or with enough suffering. After one combat an unpopular gladiator was condemned to death by the action of the crowd. His body was dragged from the arena and placed on the heap with those previously slain. Unfortunately for the crowd's amusement, the lion turned loose in the arena with Glaucus crept with a moan back into its cage. Before the lion could be prodded into action Sallust appeared demanding the arrest of Arbaces. A slave had called his attention to Nydia's letter, which he had thrown aside the night before. Reading it, he had hurried to lay his information before the praetor. The mob, not to be cheated after Glaucus had been set free, demanded that Arbaces be thrown to the lion.

Then the famous fatal eruption began. The whole gladiatorial scene became chaos as terrified thousands poured out of the doomed amphitheater, crushing the weakest in their hurry to escape. Looting began in the temples. Nydia reached Glaucus. Together they hurried to the house of Arbaces to discover and save Ione. It was too dark to see, but Nydia, accustomed to darkness, was able to lead Ione and Glaucus through the streets. Arbaces was killed in the earthquake. At last Glaucus, Ione, and Nydia gained the safety of the seaside and put out to sea in a small ship.

All night they slept in the boat. In the morning Glaucus and Ione discovered that before they had awakened, the heartbroken Nydia had cast herself into the sea.

THE LAST OF THE BARONS

Type of work: Novel
Author: Edward George Earle Bulwer-Lytton (1803-1873)
Type of plot: Historical romance
Time of plot: 1467-1471
Locale: England
First published: 1843

Principal characters:

EARL OF WARWICK, the kingmaker
ISABELLA, his older daughter
ANNE, his younger daughter
KATHERINE DE BONVILLE, his sister
EDWARD IV, King of England
WILLIAM DE HASTINGS, a royal chamberlain
ADAM WARNER, an alchemist
SIBYLL, his daughter
NICHOLAS ALWYN, a goldsmith
MARMADUKE NEVILE, kinsman of the Earl of Warwick

Critique:

The Last of the Barons is a complex, involved, and fascinating novel of a troubled period in English history. After the Wars of the Roses the House of York seemed secure, the leaders of the House of Lancaster being dead or in exile. Edward IV was a popular ruler who might have enjoyed a peaceful reign if he had not insulted the Earl of Warwick, the last of the great lords whose power overshadowed the king's. A dramatic moment in history has been recaptured by Bulwer-Lytton in this novel.

The Story:

Just outside London a crowd had gathered to watch an archery contest. Several shot at the white cloth on the butt, but no one hit the mark squarely. Then in a haughty and preoccupied way a commoner stepped up, fitted his arrow, and pierced the center of the white field. While his fellow tradesmen applauded, he dropped back into the crowd.

A young noble, who was not entered in the contest, borrowed a bow. With sure aim he hit fairly the little peg that secured the cloth to the butt. Gallantly he returned the bow and strode away. As he was leaving, the commoner who had hit the cloth stopped him. At once their recognition was mutual, and they began to talk delightedly of past times.

The commoner was Nicholas Alwyn, a goldsmith who had been the younger son of a good family. He had rejected the monk's habit, the usual lot of younger sons, and had chosen to go into trade. He was shrewd enough to see that the future greatness of England lay in the prosperous middle class and that the day of feudal nobility was nearly over. He had taken part in the tournament simply to advertise his profession, not through love of decadent sport. The young noble, who was his foster brother, was Marmaduke Nevile. He had come from his northern estate to seek service with his kinsman, the powerful Earl of Warwick, who was known as the kingmaker.

On Alwyn's advice, Marmaduke went up to Lord Montagu, the Earl of Warwick's brother, and made known his errand. The nobleman repulsed Marmaduke in full view of his retinue, for Marmaduke's father had fought on the side of Lancaster in the recent wars, and the Warwicks had successfully supported the Yorkists.

Feeling abashed, Marmaduke accompanied Alwyn into the city. Alwyn advised him to go to see the earl in person, and Marmaduke resolved to do so the very next day.

On the road to his inn he met a gentle girl surrounded by a screaming mob of women who earned their living by dancing and playing timbrels for fair crowds. Accusing the girl of trying to earn money by playing her gittern at the tournament, they would have harmed her if Marmaduke had not come to her rescue. He escorted the frightened girl away, but through faint-heartedness he did not take her all the way home. As soon as he left her, the women set upon her again. She was rescued by an older man, a true knight who saw her to her ruined dwelling.

It was dusk when Marmaduke left the city. Shortly afterward he was attacked by a band of robbers who slashed him severely and left him to die. He managed to make his way to a nearby house, and there he was cared for by the girl whom he had deserted a short time before. She was Sibyll Warner, daughter of Adam Warner, a philosopher and alchemist who spent all his time in his laboratory. He had, after years of labor, nearly completed a crude model of a small steam engine. In those superstitious days Adam was accounted a sorcerer and his daughter was suspected of witchcraft.

During his convalescence Marmaduke was greatly attracted to Sibyll, but her superior learning was a barrier between them. Alwyn, who came to the house many times, also fell in love with the girl. But Sibyll thought always of the great knight who had brought her to her door.

When Marmaduke was well and able to leave the house, he at once sought an audience with the mighty Earl of Warwick. Warwick welcomed him and made him a courtier. There he met Isabelle, Warwick's haughty older daughter, and Anne, her gentle young sister.

Warwick was preparing to go to France on a mission to the court of Louis XI. On Warwick's advice, King Edward IV had agreed to marry his sister Margaret to one of the French princes. During Warwick's absence Marmaduke served in the king's household.

As soon as Warwick had left the country, Edward's wife and all her kinsmen of the Woodville family began to work on the king's pride. The Woodvilles, intensely jealous of Warwick, encouraged the king to defy the kingmaker's power. They proposed that Edward hastily affiance his sister to the Duke of Burgundy. Edward, persuaded by his wife, at once invited the illegitimate brother of the Burgundian ruler to England and concluded the alliance.

Warwick, hurrying back when he heard the news, felt keenly the slight to his honor. When he found Edward at a hunting party, he immediately demanded Edward's reasons for his step. Edward was frightened, but he assumed an air of confidence and declared that he had followed what seemed the best policy of diplomacy. Although he was much mortified, Warwick magnanimously forgave the king and withdrew. His many followers sought him out and offered to rebel, but Warwick withdrew entirely from court and went into seclusion on his own estate.

Meanwhile Adam Warner had been brought to the court as alchemist to the Duchess of Bedford. Sibyll fitted in well with court life, and Lord Hastings became attached to her. In time they became engaged, and Lord Hastings awaited only the king's permission to marry her. Katherine de Bonville, Warwick's sister, had been his first love, but Warwick had refused his consent to a marriage because Lord Hastings then was not powerful enough to aspire to a connection with the Warwicks. Although Katherine had later married another, Lord Hastings still loved her; his attachment to Sibyll was only temporarily the stronger.

As Warwick had forseen, the Duke of Burgundy proved an unworthy ally of England and the incensed French king never ceased to make trouble for the

English. At last Edward had to confess that he could not rule the kingdom without Warwick to advise him. The king swallowed his pride and invited Warwick back to London with more honors and power than he had held before. The gallant earl, as a gesture of friendship, brought his daughter Anne to live in the queen's retinue.

Anne chose Sibyll as her companion and the two girls became close friends. One night the lecherous Edward accosted Anne in her bedroom. The girl screamed with fright and ran to Adam Warner for help. There the king found her and abjectly begged her pardon, but Anne was still hysterical. Marmaduke smuggled Anne out of the castle and told her father what had happened.

Warwick at once put Marmaduke at the head of a hundred men who tried to capture the king, but Edward stayed secure in his tower. Warwick then withdrew his followers from the court and embarked for France.

In London, Lord Hastings and Sibyll continued to meet. Then Katherine de Bonville's husband died and she was free once more. Lord Hastings' old love revived and he married her secretly in France.

Margaret of Anjou, the Lancastrian queen in exile, joined forces with Warwick in France. When the mighty earl returned to England, the people welcomed him and joined his cause. Edward fled without fighting a battle. Warwick restored Henry VI to the throne.

The success of his kingmaking made Warwick careless. Edward's power lay not with the nobles but with the merchants, and a coalition of the rich merchants and the adherents of the House of York soon put Edward back into power. On the battlefield of Barnet Warwick was killed and his chiefs were either executed or exiled. Somehow Adam Warner and Sibyll died together in the same fight. Alwyn, an adherent of Edward, took Marmaduke prisoner but later tried to secure his freedom. History does not tell whether he succeeded.

THE LAST OF THE MOHICANS

Type of work: Novel
Author: James Fenimore Cooper (1789-1851)
Type of plot: Historical romance
Time of plot: 1757
Locale: Northern New York State
First published: 1826

Principal characters:
- NATTY BUMPPO, a frontier scout known as Hawkeye
- CHINGACHGOOK, Hawkeye's Indian friend
- UNCAS, Chingachgook's son
- MAJOR DUNCAN HEYWARD, an English soldier, Hawkeye's friend
- MAGUA, a renegade Huron
- CORA MUNRO, daughter of the commander of Fort William Henry
- ALICE MUNRO, her sister

Critique:

The battles and exciting pursuits which constitute the plot of *The Last of the Mohicans* are rounded out by interesting Indian lore and the descriptive style of the author. In spite of Cooper's awkward characterizations, this novel remains the most popular of the Leatherstocking Tales, a classic story of the French and Indian wars.

The Story:

Major Duncan Heyward had been ordered to escort Cora and Alice Munro from Fort Edward to Fort William

Henry, where Colonel Munro, father of the girls, was commandant. In the party was also David Gamut, a Connecticut singing-master. On their way to Fort William Henry they did not follow the military road through the wilderness. Instead, they placed themselves in the hands of a renegade Huron known as Magua, who claimed that he could lead them to their destination by a shorter trail.

It was afternoon when the little party met the woodsman, Hawkeye, and his Delaware Mohican friends, Chingachgook and his son Uncas. To their dismay, they learned they were but an hour's distance from their starting point. Hawkeye quickly decided Magua had been planning to lead the party into a trap. His Mohican comrades tried to capture the renegade, but Magua took alarm and fled into the woods.

At Heyward's urging the hunter agreed to guide the travelers to their destination. The horses were tied and hidden among some rocks along a river. Hawkeye produced a hidden canoe from among some bushes and paddled the party to a rock at the foot of Glenn's Falls. There they prepared to spend the night in a cave.

That night a band of Iroquois led by Magua surprised the party. The fight might have been a victory for Hawkeye if their supply of powder and ball had held out. Unfortunately, their ammunition had been left in the canoe which, unnoticed until it was too late, was stolen by one of the enemy who had ventured to swim the swirling river. The only hope then lay in the possibility of future rescue, for the capture of the rock and the little group was a certainty. Hawkeye, Chingachgook, and Uncas escaped by floating downstream, leaving the girls and Major Heyward to meet the savages.

Captured, Cora and Alice were allowed to ride their horses, but Heyward and David were forced by their captors to walk. Although they took a road paralleling that to Fort William Henry, Heyward could not determine the destination the Indians had in mind. Drawing close to Magua, he tried to persuade him to betray his companions and deliver the party safely to Colonel Munro. The Huron agreed, if Cora would come to live with him among his tribe as his wife. When she refused, the enraged Magua had everyone bound. He was threatening Alice with his tomahawk when Hawkeye and his friends crept silently upon the band and attacked them. The Iroquois fled, leaving several of their dead behind them. The party, under David's guidance, sang a hymn of thanksgiving, and then pushed onward.

Toward evening they stopped at a deserted blockhouse to rest. Many years before it had been the scene of a fight between the Mohicans and the Mohawks, and a mound still showed where bodies lay buried. While Chingachgook watched, the others slept.

At moonrise they continued on their way. It was dawn when Hawkeye and his charges drew near Fort William Henry. They were intercepted and challenged by a sentinel of the French under Montcalm, who was about to lay siege to the fort. Heyward was able to answer him in French and they were allowed to proceed. Chingachgook killed and scalped the French sentinel. Then, through the fog which had risen from Lake George, and through the enemy forces which thronged the plain before the fort, Hawkeye led the way to the gates of the fort.

On the fifth day of the siege, Hawkeye, who had been sent to Fort Edward to seek help, was intercepted on his way back and a letter he carried was captured. Webb, the commander of Fort Edward, refused to come to the aid of Munro.

Under a flag of truce, Montcalm and Munro held a parley. Montcalm showed Webb's letter to Munro and offered honorable terms of surrender. Colonel Munro and his men would be allowed to keep their colors, their arms, and their baggage, if they would vacate the fort the next morning. Helpless to do otherwise, Munro accepted these terms. During one of the parleys Heyward was surprised to see Magua in the camp of the French. He had not been killed during the earlier skirmish.

The following day the vanquished English started their trip back to Fort Edward. Under the eyes of the French and their Indian allies they passed across the plain and entered the forest. Suddenly an Indian grabbed at a brightly-colored shawl worn by one of the women. Terrified, she wrapped her child in it. The Indian darted to her, grabbed the child from her arms, and dashed out its brains on the ground. Then under the eyes of Montcalm, who did nothing to discourage or to hold back his savage allies, a monstrous slaughter began.

Cora and Alice, entrusted to David Gamut's protection, were in the midst of the killing when Magua swooped down upon them and carried Alice away in his arms. Cora ran after her sister, and faithful David dogged her footsteps. They were soon atop a hill, from which they watched the slaughter of the garrison.

Three days later, Hawkeye, leading Heyward, Munro, and his Indian comrades, traced the girls and David with the help of Cora's veil which had caught on a tree. Heyward was particularly concerned for the safety of Alice. The day before the massacre he had been given her father's permission to court her.

Hawkeye, knowing that hostile Indians were on their trail, decided to save time by traveling across the lake in a canoe which he discovered in its hiding place nearby. He was certain Magua had taken the girls north, where he planned to rejoin his own people. Heading their canoe in that direction, the five men paddled all day, at one point having a close escape from some of their intercepting enemies. They spent that night in the woods and next day turned west in an effort to find Magua's trail.

After much searching Uncas found the trail of the captives. That evening, as the party drew near the Huron camp, they met David Gamut wandering about. He told his friends that the Indians thought him crazy because of his habit of breaking into song, and they allowed him to roam the woods unguarded. Alice, he said, was being held at the Huron camp. Cora had been entrusted to the care of a tribe of peaceful Delawares a short distance away.

Heyward, disguising his face with paint, went to the Huron camp in an attempt to rescue Alice, while the others set about helping Cora. Heyward was in the camp but a short time, posing as a French doctor, when Uncas was brought in, a captive. Called to treat an ill Indian woman, Heyward found Alice in the cave with his patient. He was able to rescue the girl by wrapping her in a blanket and declaring to the Hurons that she was his patient, whom he was carrying off to the woods for treatment. Hawkeye, attempting to rescue Uncas, entered the camp disguised in a medicine man's bearskin he had stolen. Uncas was cut loose and given the disguise, while the woodsman borrowed David Gamut's clothes. The singer was left to take Uncas' place while the others escaped, for Hawkeye was certain the Indians would not harm David because of his supposed mental condition. Uncas and Hawkeye fled to the Delaware camp.

The following day Magua and a group of his warriors visited the Delawares in search of their prisoners. The chief of that tribe decided the Hurons had a just claim to Cora because Magua wished to make her his wife.

Under inviolable Indian custom, the Huron was permitted to leave the camp unmolested, but Uncas warned him that in a few hours he and the Delawares would follow his trail.

During a bloody battle Magua fled with Cora to the top of a cliff. There, pursued by Uncas, he stabbed and killed the young Mohican, and was in his turn sent to his death by a bullet from Hawkeye's long rifle. Cora, too, was killed by a Huron. Amid deep mourning by the Delawares, she and Uncas were laid in their graves in the forest. Colonel Munro and Heyward conducted Alice to English territory and safety. Hawkeye returned to the forest. He had promised to remain with his sorrowing friend Chingachgook forever.

THE LAST PURITAN

Type of work: Novel
Author: George Santayana (1863-)
Type of plot: Social criticism
Time of plot: Early twentieth century
Locale: Connecticut, Massachusetts, England
First published: 1936

Principal characters:
OLIVER ALDEN, the last puritan
PETER ALDEN, his father
HARRIET ALDEN, his mother
FRAULEIN IRMA SCHLOTE, Oliver's governess
JIM DARNLEY, Oliver's friend
ROSE DARNLEY, Jim's sister
MARIO VAN DE WEYER, Oliver's cousin
EDITH VAN DE WEYER, another cousin
BOBBY, Jim's illegitimate son

Critique:

Although he is best known as a philosopher and essayist, George Santayana has invaded the field of fiction with great success. *The Last Puritan* is his first novel; but, unlike most first novels, it is the work of a mature mind. In the story of Oliver Alden, Santayana has given us a character sketch of an almost extinct type of American, a puritan.

The Story:

Young Peter Alden was educated in America but left Harvard before he had completed his studies and went abroad with a tutor. After he had come of age and had inherited his money he wandered aimlessly about the world, studying occasionally. He was in his early middle years before he completed any one course. Licensed to practice medicine, his practice was limited to himself, for he had burdened himself with many ills, some real but most of them imaginary. Once he consulted Dr. Bumstead, a psychiatrist whose main concern was Peter's money. Dr. Bumstead convinced Peter that a home and a wife would be the best treatment possible and, as a consequence, Peter married the doctor's daughter Harriet. Oliver was their only child.

Little Oliver was a puritan from the beginning. He accepted things as they were, never complaining, never wondering why. There were no other children with whom he could play because his mother feared that other children might be dirty or vulgar. And there were no stories, songs, or prayers for the boy, as Mrs. Alden would not have him filled with nonsensical ideas. His father was no more than a polite stranger to little Oliver, for he spent most of his time traveling about the world.

Fraulein Irma Schlote, a German, became Oliver's governess, and from her he had what little brightness there was in his childhood. On their long walks together, Irma instilled in Oliver his first love of nature and a love for the German language. But even with Irma, Oliver remained a stoical little puritan. If he were tired or his foot hurt, there was no use to complain. They had come for a walk, and they must finish that walk. One must do his duty, even an unpleasant one. As he grew older, Oliver hated human weakness with the hatred of a true puritan.

When Oliver was fifteen, he went to high school, where he excelled in scholarship and in athletics because it was his duty to keep his body strong and because it was his duty to do everything that the school demanded.

During one holiday season Oliver joined his father on his yacht. There he met Jim Darnley, the captain, who had been a British sailor before he became involved in a scandal. Jim was an entirely new type of person in Oliver's world. Oliver knew that the sailor was worldly and had no sense of duty, but strangely enough Oliver was always to consider Jim his dearest friend.

After his graduation from high school, Oliver joined his father and Jim in England. There, while visiting Jim's family, he learned to respect Jim's minister father and to enjoy the company of Rose, Jim's young sister. He learned also that Jim had an illegitimate child, Bobby, who lived with Mrs. Bowler, his tavern-keeping mother.

While in England, Oliver also met his distant cousin, Mario Van de Weyer, a worldly young man dependent upon his rich relatives for his education and livelihood. Mario also puzzled Oliver. Mario had nothing, not even much real intelligence, yet he was happy. Oliver, who had everything, was not consciously happy; he merely lived as he felt it his duty to live.

Before they left England, Oliver's father committed suicide. He felt that Oliver needed to be free of him and as much as possible of his own mother. Rather than see the boy torn between his conflicting duties to both parents, Peter took his own life.

Back in America, Oliver entered Williams College. While playing football, he broke his leg. In the infirmary he was visited by his cousin Mario and another cousin, Edith Van de Weyer. Mario, who attended Harvard on Oliver's money, seemed to feel no reluctance about living extravagantly on his cousin's bounty. Oliver began to think of Edith as a possible wife. Like his father, he did not consider love an important element in marriage, but he felt it his duty to marry and have children.

In his last year of college, Oliver transferred to Harvard University. There he spent much time with Mario, until that young man was forced to leave college because he had been found in his room with a young woman. When he went to Edith's home to tell her about Mario, Oliver found that Edith's family had already heard the story from Mario and had forgiven him. Oliver also learned that Edith had great affection for Mario. But because he thought a match between himself and Edith a sensible one, he proposed to her anyway, forgetting to mention love. Edith refused him. She knew that marriage with Oliver would be a dutiful experience only, and she wanted more than duty.

When he had finished college, Oliver took a cruise around the world. Then he settled in England and lived for a time near Jim Darnley's family. War was coming closer, but Oliver felt no duty toward either side. Mario enlisted at once, for Mario was romantic. The war became more personal for Oliver when he learned that Jim had been killed. Jim's death seemed proof of war's useless waste. More practically, Jim's death meant that Bobby and Rose were now Oliver's responsibility.

When the United States entered the war, Oliver felt that it was his duty to go home and join the army. After his training he was sent to France. Before he went to the front, he wrote to Rose Darnley, asking her to marry him at once, so that she would be his wife and would be cared for if he were killed. But Rose, like Edith, wanted love, and she refused to marry him. She knew, too, that Oliver should never marry, because love should be unreasoning and illogical at times, conditions which Oliver could never accept.

After Rose's refusal, Oliver seemed free for the first time. No one needed him any longer. Jim was dead. Mario was in the army and provided for in case of Oliver's death. Bobby had been made secure financially. Edith was engaged to be married. Rose was provided for in Oliver's will. All his life he had acted in accordance with duty, in his parental relations, in school, in the army. At least he would not be a dutiful husband. Now he need be true only to himself. That night he slept peacefully.

Oliver was killed, but not in battle. He was a post-Armistice casualty, the victim of a motorcycle accident. His will told the story of his life. He had left adequate, but not extravagant, provisions for Mario, Rose, Mrs. Darnley, Fraulein Irma, and Bobby. The bulk of his fortune he left to his mother because he had believed it his duty to provide for her.

So Oliver Alden ended his life a true puritan, doing what must be done without flinching, taking little pleasure in worldly things, yet not withdrawing from the world. He did not believe in puritanism, for he knew that those who lived selfishly were often more happy than he. He was not a prig. He had been a puritan in spite of himself, and for that reason, perhaps, the last true puritan.

THE LATE GEORGE APLEY

Type of work: Novel
Author: John P. Marquand (1893-)
Type of plot: Simulated biography
Time of plot: Late nineteenth and early twentieth centuries
Locale: Boston
First published: 1937

Principal characters:
George Apley, a proper Bostonian
John, his son
Eleanor, his daughter
Catharine, his wife
Mr. Willing, George Apley's biographer

Critique:

Satire has been said to require the utmost of great minds. In a sense it requires a man to have two visions: one of society as it might be and one as it is. The range between those two points offers the opportunity for satirical comparisons. In *The Late George Apley* the satire is double-edged because of the method of telling the story. The novel is sub-titled "A Novel in the Form of a Memoir." Mr. Willing, the supposed biographer of these memoirs, is as much a source of satire as George Apley himself, for without Mr. Willing, the staid, polished, and politely-dull annotator, the book would be only one more realistic novel.

The Story:

George William Apley was born on Beacon Hill, on January 25, 1866. The Apleys were an old family in Massachusetts. Thomas, known in the old records as Goodman Apley, had emigrated from England to America and settled in Roxbury in 1636. Goodman Apley's son, John, had graduated from Harvard in 1662. From his time there had been an

Apley in Harvard in each succeeding generation. John Apley's son, Nathaniel, established himself in Boston. A later Apley, Moses, became a shipping master and laid the foundation of the Apley fortune. Moses Apley was George Apley's grandfather.

George Apley grew up in a quiet atmosphere of wealth and social position. He learned his parents' way of living calmly and with fortitude. In an orderly way he was introduced to the polite world, at first through visits to relatives; later, through study at Harvard.

His Harvard days were probably the high point of his life. He was sent to Harvard to weld those qualities of gentlemanly behavior which private grammar school and parents together had tried to encourage. His parents were anxious that he should make friends with the right people. George was carefully instructed in the ways of high-minded gentlemen. His training was indicated by a theme in which he wrote a description of a Boston brothel in terms expressing his repulsion and shock. In the gymnasium George won distinction as a boxer. Moreover, he became a member of the Board of the Harvard *Lampoon.* He was taken into the Club, an honor his father appreciated greatly. In his junior and senior years he took part in the musical extravaganzas of the Hasty Pudding Club. In spite of these activities he never neglected his studies and he was known as a respectable student with grades placing him in the middle of his class at graduation.

While in college, he fell in love with an impossible girl, Mary Monahan. The affair was cut short by the Apleys and never referred to publicly. Shortly thereafter his family prescribed a sea voyage for him. When he returned home he took up the study of law, and became a member of the board for the Boston Waifs' Society.

George was instructed in the shrewd businesslike manners and knowledge of the Apleys. He was sent to work with his Uncle William for one summer. William sensed that his nephew would never make a good businessman and advised that George should be put into law or made a trustee of other peoples' money, not his own. As a result George, like many of his friends, never went actively into business, but spent his lifetime clipping coupons.

In February, 1890, George followed his parents' wishes and suitably became engaged to Catharine Bosworth. Both his father-in-law and his own father saw to it that the young couple had a summer cottage and a house for the winter. The two mothers were equally solicitous. George discovered that he had married not only Catharine but also her family.

As the years passed, George devoted his time to charitable groups, learned societies, and to writing for his clubs. One of his papers, "Jonas Good and Cow Corner," was said to be among the best papers read before the Browsers in fifty years.

His first child's name was a subject for debate in his own and Catharine's family. The name, John, common to both families, was finally chosen. His second child was a daughter, Eleanor.

Shortly after his sister Amelia's marriage, George's father died of an apoplectic stroke. He left a million dollars to Harvard, other large sums to his charities, and the remainder of his fortune in trust for his family. George had to pay a sum of money to a woman who claimed she had borne a son to his father. Although he did not believe the charge, he paid rather than cause scandal in the family.

George invested in a place known as Pequod Island and there he took his friends when he wanted to get away from Boston. On the island he and his friends condescended to share the campfire with their guides. Planned as a male retreat, the island was soon overrun with literary lights of the times invited by George's wife and sister.

As his son grew up, George noted

an increasing desire on the part of the younger generation to be wild and careless with money. Later, George began to realize that he and his generation had let much slip and that Boston was going to the Irish. He gave his name to the "Save Boston Association" as he considered his membership an Apley duty. He also interested himself in bird lore and philosophy and took as much personal concern as possible in the affairs of his children. When his mother died in 1908, George counted her death one of his most poignant tragedies.

When George's son entered Harvard, George took a new interest in the university and noted many changes he did not like.

Old Uncle William, now over eighty, still controlled the Apley mills and held out successfully against the new labor unions. One day the old man shocked his family by marrying his nurse, a Miss Prentiss.

His daughter Eleanor's marriage was completely unsatisfactory to George because she did not induce her husband to give up his job for a position in the Apley mills and to take up residence near her family. But George was proud of his son John for his service at the front. George himself belonged to the Home Guards. When John married a girl of good connections after the war, George was doubly pleased.

At last George came into opposition with a man named O'Reilly, whom George planned to have brought before criminal court on charges of extortion. However, O'Reilly tricked George into a scandal. George intended to have the whole case cleared in court, but before the trial he received a note from his one-time sweetheart, Mary Monahan. After an interview with her, he settled the case quietly and bought off his opponents.

In 1928 he became a grandfather. As soon as the baby had been born, George telegraphed Groton to include his grandson's name among the entrance applicants.

In his last years George took interest in the new novels, condemning those too blatant in their description of sex and fighting against the inclusion of some of them in the Boston libraries. His own copy of *Lady Chatterly's Lover* he hid in the silver safe to keep his daughter from seeing it. He defied prohibition as an abuse of his rights and kept a private bootlegger on principle because he thought it important to help break the prohibition law.

He thought, too, that the colossal fortunes being gathered by the uneducated should be handed over to the government. In the autumn of 1929 he and his wife made a trip to Rome, where they visited Horatio Apley, recently appointed to a diplomatic post there. George was absent from America when the stock market crash came. His financial affairs did not suffer greatly, but, his health breaking, he began to plan his will and his funeral.

George Apley died in December, 1933.

LAVENGRO

Type of work: Novel
Author: George Henry Borrow (1803-1881)
Type of plot: Simulated autobiography
Time of plot: Nineteenth century
Locale: England, Scotland, Ireland
First published: 1851

Principal characters:
Lavengro, a scholar, journalist, and tinker
John, his brother
Jasper Petulengro, his gipsy friend
Mrs. Herne, an old crone

THE FLAMING TINMAN, a bully of the roads
ISOPEL BERNERS, Lavengro's companion
PETER WILLIAMS, an evangelist
WINIFRED, his wife

Critique:

Lavengro; The Scholar—The Gipsy—The Priest is a long novel, in part fiction and in part the autobiography of its eccentric author, which gives an interesting and unusual picture of England during the early part of the last century. The autobiographical method of the narrative has aroused the interest of scholars as to what is fact in the book and what is pure imagination. To the general reader, *Lavengro* is most interesting for its accounts of nomadic gipsy life and character studies of tinkers, beggars, and thieves who roamed the English highways more than a hundred years ago.

The Story:

Lavengro was the son of an army officer who had fought against Napoleon, and the boy spent his early years at army garrisons in various parts of England, Scotland, Ireland, and Wales. When he was six years old, Lavengro discovered *Robinson Crusoe,* a book which stimulated his imagination and aroused in him a desire to read and to study languages. One day, wandering on the outskirts of a garrison town, he met a group of gipsies who threatened to do him harm. They drew back, however, when he showed them a tame snake which he was carrying. The gipsies, becoming friendly, nicknamed him Sapengro, or snake tamer. A young gipsy named Jasper declared that they would always be brothers. He met also at the gipsy camp a Romany whom he saw hanged fifteen years later at Newgate.

A few years later he began the study of Latin. About the same time his father was ordered to Edinburgh. In Scotland, Lavengro took part in several bickers, or fights, with his schoolmates and learned mountain climbing. Then in 1815 his father was ordered to Ireland. Lavengro went to a seminary at Clonmel and studied more Latin and Greek and, in an incidental fashion, learned to speak Irish. His brother John was made an ensign and transferred to a post some few miles away. After peace was signed with the French, opportunities for military employment were few. John had always wanted to paint; therefore, his father allowed him to go to London to study his art.

Lavengro again met Jasper, his gipsy friend, and discovered that Jasper's last name was Petulengro. Jasper was now a Romany Kral—or gipsy king—a horseshoer, pugilist, jockey, and soothsayer. Through Jasper, Lavengro made the acquaintance of a malignant old crone named Herne, who hated him because she believed that he was stealing the Romany tongue. It was Jasper who named him Lavengro, which means "word-master," because he learned the gipsy language so rapidly. All of the gipsies departed for London, except Mrs. Herne, who went to Yorkshire. Lavengro remained at home with his parents while his father tried to decide what to do with him. It was finally agreed that Lavengro would enter a solicitor's office to study law. But Lavengro neglected his Blackstone while he studied Welsh and translated the poetry of Ab Gwilym. About the same time, Lavengro obtained a Danish book and learned to read it by first studying the Danish Bible. One day Lavengro was sent to deliver a thousand pounds to a magistrate with whom he had a very entertaining conversation concerning the manly art of self-defense. In spite of the magistrate's fondness for boxing, however, he refused a place on his land for a match.

Lavengro met Jasper again and put on the gloves with him for a friendly bout. Later he returned home and discovered that his father was seriously ill. His brother John also arrived home just before his father died. Shortly afterward Lavengro went to London to seek his fortune as a writer, taking with him a letter of introduction to a noted publisher. The publisher seemed delighted to be able to employ him, but was not interested in such things as Lavengro's translations of the songs of Ab Gwilym and his translations of Danish songs. Lavengro was informed that the reading public scoffed at works like these. Instead, the publisher recommended a story somewhat along the line of *The Dairyman's Daughter*.

While walking through Cheapside one day, Lavengro climbed upon the balustrade of a bridge in order to see something below. An old woman selling apples nearby thought he was trying to commit suicide and begged him not to fling himself over. The old lady had a partiality for a book about the "blessed" Mary Flanders. Lavengro returned from time to time to see her and to talk with her.

Lavengro, invited to dinner at the publisher's house one Sunday, discovered that the publisher did not believe in eating meat or drinking wine. After dinner Lavengro heard what was to be his new assignment since the publisher had now decided not to publish anything like *The Dairyman's Daughter*. He was to prepare a collection of the stories of the lives and trials of famous criminals incarcerated at Newgate. In addition, he was to translate the publisher's book of philosophy into German and to write an article about it for the *Review*.

In the company of an acquaintance named Francis Ardry, Lavengro visited many of the underworld spots of London and this experience, together with the series on criminals which he was preparing, gave him a wide and practical knowledge of the underworld. Then Lavengro's brother came to London and introduced him to a painter of the heroic. The peculiar thing about this painter's pictures was the short legs of the people in his paintings. When Lavengro's stories of crime were finished, he took them to the publisher. But the publisher was displeased because Lavengro had omitted several of the publisher's favorite criminal histories.

Lavengro went to visit the apple-woman again and his despondent appearance led her to think that he had been caught stealing. The apple-woman never became aware of Lavengro's profession. He talked her into letting him read her cherished copy of the life of Mary Flanders.

The publisher's speculations failed and left Lavengro without money, but Lavengro finally obtained all the wages that were due him. Taggart, the publisher's assistant, told Lavengro that Glorious John, another printer, would publish his ballads and the songs of Ab Gwilym. But Lavengro never offered his ballads to Glorious John. In midwinter he went again to visit the apple-woman and found that she had moved her stall to the other side of the bridge. He promised to take her book and trade it in for a Bible. However, he lost the book and had nothing to trade. He decided to purchase a Bible and never let her know about his negligence.

About this time Lavengro saved an Armenian from pickpockets. The Armenian wished him to translate some Armenian fables into English, but Lavengro refused. The Armenian, who had inherited a hundred thousand pounds from his father, was intent upon doubling the amount through his speculation. The Armenian ran into a bit of luck and came into possession of two hundred thousand pounds. Lavengro's advice to the Armenian was to take his fortune and fight the Persians.

Lavengro decided, when his money got short, to do the translations for the Armenian but the man had already departed to invest his money in a war against the Persians.

Lavengro left London after having some small success writing fiction. He met and talked with many and various people on his travels about England. On his rambles he heard the stories concerning the Flaming Tinman, who held a great repute as a fighter and who had forced Jack Slingsby, another tinker, out of business on threats of death. Lavengro met Slingsby and bought him out. He decided to become a tinker himself in the hope of meeting the Flaming Tinman.

One day, while he was mending pots and pans, he encountered Mrs. Herne and Leonora, a thirteen-year-old girl who was traveling with the old woman. Leonora brought him cakes made by Mrs. Herne. He ate one of them and that night became seriously ill. When the evil old crone came to gloat over him, he realized that the cakes had been poisoned. Then the sound of wheels frightened the old woman away, and Lavengro was saved by the timely arrival of Peter Williams, a traveling Welsh preacher, and Winifred, his wife. Peter Williams told Lavengro the sad story of his life and related how he had been led to commit the sin against the Holy Ghost, a sin for which there was no redemption. Peter had become a preacher to warn other people against the unforgivable sin. Lavengro journeyed with Peter and his wife as far as the Welsh border, where he left them to join Jasper Petulengro and his band of gipsies.

Jasper told Lavengro how Mrs. Herne had hanged herself because of her failure to poison him. Since Jasper was a blood-kinsman of Mrs. Herne, it was required by Romany law that he obtain revenge from Lavengro. Lavengro, however, was really only indirectly responsible for the old woman's death, a fact of which Jasper was well aware. They retired to a place where they could fight, and there Jasper received full satisfaction when he made Lavengro's nose bleed.

Soon after his friendly tussle with Jasper, Lavengro met the Flaming Tinman, Moll, his wife, and Isopel Berners, child of a gipsy mother and a noble father and now a free woman of the roads. Isopel was responsible for Lavengro's victory in a brawl with the Flaming Tinman, for she had told him to use his right hand and to strike at the bully's face. The Flaming Tinman and Moll departed, leaving the territory to Lavengro the tinker, but Isopel remained behind with her belongings. The story of the Flaming Tinman's defeat was soon known throughout the neighborhood, and Lavengro became a hero of the roads. At a public house he met a priest whom he called the Man in Black. He and Lavengro had many conversations concerning religion and the attempt to establish Catholicism as the religion in England.

On a wild stormy night Isopel and Lavengro helped a coachman right his coach which had overturned. Later the coachman told them the story of his life, and his tale was proof that in those days romance journeyed on the highways and adventure waited around the turn of any English lane.

LIFE ON THE MISSISSIPPI

Type of work: Reminiscence
Author: Mark Twain (Samuel L. Clemens, 1835-1910)
Type of plot: Regional romance
Time of plot: Mid-nineteenth century
Locale: Mississippi River region
First published: 1883

Principal characters:
MARK TWAIN
MR. BIXBY, a river pilot

Critique:

It is extraordinary that a book with so many defects should have become one of the classics of our national heritage. There is, for example, a sharp and obvious division between the first twelve or fourteen chapters and the rest of the book. It is clear that it was not written all at one time, and the effects of bad composition are evident. The chapters are badly organized and there are many labored passages. Despite this lack of craftsmanship, *Life on the Mississippi* is a vivid, dramatic, and extremely interesting collection of reminiscences. Like the mighty river with which it is concerned, the book has become part of the American tradition, part of our national pride and history.

The Story:

When Mark Twain was a boy, he and his comrades in Hannibal, Missouri, had one great ambition; they hoped to become steamboatmen. They had other ambitions, too, such as joining the circus or becoming pirates, but these soon passed. Only the ambition to be a steamboatman remained, renewed twice each day when the upriver and the downriver boats put in at the rickety wharf and woke the sleepy village to bustling life. Through the years, boy after boy left the river communities, to return later, swaggering in his importance as a worker on a steamboat. Mark Twain saw these boys often, and the fact that some of them had been considered as undeniably damned in the eyes of the pious folk shook Twain's convictions profoundly. He wondered why these boys who flouted Sunday School maxims and ran away from home should win the rewards of adventure and romance that meeker town boys never knew.

Mark Twain, too, had this dream of adventure. His ambition was a lofty one. He determined to become a cub-pilot. While in Cincinnati, he heard that a government expedition was exploring the Amazon. With thirty dollars he had saved he took a boat bound for New Orleans. His intention was to travel on to the headwaters of the Amazon. But the ship was grounded at Louisville, and during the delay Mark came to the attention of Mr. Bixby, the most famous pilot on the Mississippi River. He prevailed upon Bixby to teach him how to navigate.

At first the adventure was a glorious one. But soon Mark found that the more he knew about the river, the less romantic it seemed. Though he was a dutiful student, he discovered that he could not remember everything Bixby told him, regardless of how important this information seemed to be. Furthermore, to his astonishment and despair, his instructor told him that the river was changing its course continually; that there were no such things as permanent landmarks; that the river channel was never the same, but always variable. There were times when the young cub-pilot was frightened, especially when he narrowly missed hitting another ship, or trimmed the boat too close to shore. But worse was the experience of piloting in the dead of night, with no landmarks to observe and only deep blackness all around.

Bixby claimed the secret of navigation was not to remember landmarks, which changed, but to learn the shape of the river, and then to steer by the shape in one's head.

It was undeniably an interesting life. The pilot had to be on the lookout for rafts sailing the river at night without lights. Often a whole family would be on a raft, and they would shout imprecations at the steamboat which had just barely missed dumping them all into the river. Then there was the fascinating behavior of the river itself. Prosperous towns would be isolated by a new cut-off and reduced to insignificance; towns and islands in one state would be moved up or down and into another state, or, as sometimes happened, into an area that belonged to no state at all!

The river pilot reigned supreme on his boat. The captain was theoretically the master; but as soon as the boat got under way, the pilot was in charge, and only a very foolhardy captain would have interfered. The importance of the pilot in river navigation eventually led to the formation of a pilots' association. At first the idea seemed ridiculous. But the union grew as, one by one, all the good pilots joined. As a result pilots could make their own terms with the owners. Not only were wages guaranteed, but pilots secured better working conditions, pensions, and funds for their widows and orphans. Within a few years the association was the most indestructible monopoly in the country. But its days were numbered. First of all, the railroads came in and river transportation was gradually abandoned in favor of rail traffic. Then, too, the Civil War reduced navigation to a mere trickle and dealt a deathblow to river commerce. The steamboat was no longer an important means of transportation.

From then on the river was different. It seemed very different to Mark Twain when he returned after many years away from it, and saw the changes with nostalgic regret. He traveled once more on the Mississippi, but this time as a passenger and under an assumed name. He listened tolerantly to the man who told him wild and improbable stories about the river, and to a fellow traveler who explained, very explicitly, how everything worked.

Mark Twain decided to search for a large sum of money left by a murderer whom he had met in Germany. He and his companions made plans about the ten thousand dollars soon to be in their possession, and they asked to get off their boat at Napoleon to look for it. Unfortunately, the Arkansas River, years before, had swept the whole town into the Mississippi!

On his return to the river, Mark Twain learned many things he had not known. He witnessed the vast improvements in navigation and in the construction of the boats, improvements that made navigation easier and safer. He talked to the inhabitants of Vicksburg, who described their life during the bombardment of the town by Union forces. He visited Louisiana and expressed horror at the sham castles that passed for good architecture. He read Southern newspapers and saw in them, as in so many Southern traditions, the romantic sentimentality of Sir Walter Scott, an influence that he regretted, hated, and held responsible for the South's lack of progress. He came in contact with a cheerful and clever gambler; he heard about senseless feuds that wiped out entire families; he saw new and large cities that had grown up since he had left the river; he met such well-known writers as Joel Chandler Harris and George W. Cable; he had an experience with a spiritualist who grew rich on the credulous and the superstitious; he witnessed tragedy, and lost friends in steamboat explosions.

The river would never be the same again. The age of mechanization had arrived to stay. The days of the old river pilots, such as Mr. Bixby, were now a thing of the past. America was growing up, and with that growth the color and romance of the Mississippi had faded forever.

LIFE WITH FATHER

Type of work: Short stories
Author: Clarence Day, Jr., (1874-1935)
Type of plot: Humorous satire
Time of plot: Late nineteenth century
Locale: New York City
First published: 1935

Principal characters:
Clarence Day, Sr.
Mrs. Clarence Day, his wife
Clarence Day, Jr., the narrator

Critique:

This narrative of personal recollections is a humorous commentary on American manners in the Victorian age. Father is a domestic tyrant whose bark is considerably worse than his bite. His crotchety behavior is the last resort of masculine aggressiveness in a woman-dominated world.

The Story:

The Day household existed under the eccentric domination of Clarence Day, Sr., a Wall Street businessman who was convinced that he was always right. His son stood in awe of him. The boy's greatest treat was to be taken to his father's office on Saturday mornings. With Father dressed formally in silk hat and tailed coat, they rode downtown on the elevated and the boy gaped curiously into the windows of flophouses and wished that he could enjoy the luxury and freedom of being a tramp. That ambition he did not reveal to his father. Once he ventured to suggest that he would like to be a cowboy, but Father retorted that cowboys were shiftless people.

Father's office seemed very mysterious to the boy, and he enjoyed the privilege of filling inkwells and running errands. Later there would be luncheon at Delmonico's. Father and his favorite waiter always chatted in French about the menu, and Father enjoyed himself greatly. But the boy did not think highly of the food. There was too little of it, scarcely enough to satisfy his appetite. Seeing the starved look on his face, Father would order a large chocolate éclair for him.

One of Father's chief worries was the fear of becoming fat. The members of his club recommended long walks, but Father was already taking long walks. Then they suggested horseback riding. Accordingly, Father became a member of the Riding Club on East Fifty-eighth Street. Apart from stabling conveniences, the club had a park for riding, really only a little ring. But it was tame enough for Father, who liked things to be orderly and suitably arranged for his use. In a very short time he felt as if the park belonged to him, and if the leaves were not raked, if papers were lying around, he would take the neglect as a personal affront.

The first horse Father bought was an independent, rebellious creature. There was little love lost between them. The climax came one morning when the horse refused to obey. It reared and reared until Father gave up in disgust and went back to the club. Since the rest of the family wanted a horse of their own, Father gave them that one. He bought another for himself.

Having never been sick, Father became very annoyed whenever anybody else was ill; and he had no sympathy whatever for people whose illnesses he considered to be simply imaginary. Whenever he was unlucky enough to catch a cold, his method of treating it was to blow his nose loudly or to sneeze. Whenever he had a sick headache, he would not eat. After he had starved out his illness, he would eat again and triumphantly light up a cigar.

Father's laws were regarded as edicts not to be challenged. Accordingly, young Clarence was amazed when anyone did not respond to Father's whims and orders. While out in the country one summer, the family ran out of ice. Because Father's wine must always be chilled, the crisis was a grave one. Nothing the family could do was successful. But when Father came home, he went down to the village, intimidated a dealer into selling him an icebox, provided he would somehow get it filled with ice, and argued the iceman into delivering a load immediately.

Father got things done in his own way. The family could never keep servants for very long. One day the cook left. Father stormed into an employment agency, looked over the assembled girls, and then, over the manager's protests, picked out the one he liked. Although she had not wanted to be a cook, the girl went with him meekly and stayed on in the Day household for twenty-six years. Her name was Margaret.

In the summer Margaret always stayed in New York to look after the house, and each year there arose the problem of a temporary cook during the time that the family was in the country. One year they hired Delia. Before long Father insisted that she was starving him to death. Delia was replaced by a Japanese. At the first meal prepared by the Japanese, Father moaned with pain and declared that he was poisoned. Margaret was hastily summoned from the city, and Father was happy again.

What really vexed Father was Mother's inability to keep household accounts according to the system he tried to teach her. The money always inexplicably disappeared, and the bills were always high. In addition, Mother was fond of charge accounts. It was so easy to buy things that way, and the first of the month seemed far off in the distance. When the bills came in, however, Father always raged—and then gave in.

When Mother went on a trip to Egypt, Father could not understand why she should want to go off to the far corners of the world just to see pyramids. When she came back with part of her expense money unaccounted for, Father was curious. At last Mother admitted that she had not spent it, but intended to keep it. Father, wanting to know what good it would do her to keep it, demanded its return. But again he lost out. Mother kept the money.

Young Clarence witnessed many examples of Father's behavior. He was urged to be prompt for breakfast and bribed with the offer of a watch. He suffered whenever Father opened his mail, particularly when the letters were from young ladies. Father could never understand that letters could ever be for anyone else. When Father finally agreed to have a telephone installed, he likewise assumed that all calls were for him. Once he was very perturbed when a young lady, thinking she was speaking to young Clarence, invited him to lunch.

Women, Father insisted, did not know anything about politics. When Mother came under the influence of Miss Gulick, an emancipated young woman, he snorted contemptuously. Though he liked to dine out with friends, he did not like company in his own house. Once he startled a group of Mother's friends by uttering a lone, monosyllabic word as he stamped past the dining-room on his way upstairs.

Because he had disliked some members of his family buried in the family plot in the cemetery, he did not wish to be buried there after his death. Mother reminded him that such matters are not important to the dead. But Father insisted that he was going to buy a new plot in the cemetery, one all for himself, and in a corner where he could get out. Mother looked at him in astonishment. She whispered to young Clarence that she almost believed he could do it.

LIGHT IN AUGUST

Type of work: Novel
Author: William Faulkner (1897-)
Type of plot: Psychological realism
Time of plot: Early twentieth century
Locale: Mississippi
First published: 1932

Principal characters:
JOE CHRISTMAS, a white Negro
DOC HINES, his grandfather
MR. MCEACHERN, his foster father
JOANNA BURDEN, his benefactress and mistress
JOE BROWN, alias Lucas Burch, his partner
LENA GROVE, mother of Brown's child
BYRON BUNCH, in love with Lena

Critique:

This novel makes a study of the race problem in the South and psychological obsession with the Civil War. It is a fascinating narrative told with little regard for strict time sequence. Sometimes the author's sentence structure becomes obscure; sometimes the exact meaning of his poetic compression is lost. But the novel is important in its vivid treatment of a theme of widespread social signficance.

The Story:

Joe Christmas was the illegitimate son of a circus trouper of Negro blood and a white girl named Milly Hines. Joe's grandfather, old Doc Hines, killed the circus man, let Milly die in childbirth, and put Joe—at Christmas time; hence his last name—into an orphanage, where the children learned to call him "Nigger." Doc Hines then arranged to have Joe adopted by a religious and heartless farmer named McEachern, whose cruelties to Joe were met with a matching stubbornness that made of the boy an almost subhuman being.

One day in town McEachern took Joe to a disreputable restaurant, where he talked to the waitress, Bobbie Allen. McEachern told the adolescent Joe never to patronize the place alone. But Joe went back. He met Bobbie at night and became her lover. Night after night, while the McEacherns were asleep, he would creep out of the house and hurry to meet her in town.

One night McEachern followed Joe to a country dance and ordered him home. Joe reached for a chair, knocked McEachern unconscious, whispered to Bobbie that he would meet her soon, and raced McEachern's mule home. There he gathered up all the money he could lay his hands on and went into town. At the house where Bobbie stayed he encountered the restaurant proprietor and his wife and another man. The two men beat up Joe, took his money, and left for Memphis with the two women.

Joe moved on. Sometimes he worked. More often he simply lived off the money women would give him. He slept with many women and nearly always told them he was of Negro blood.

At last he went to Jefferson, a small town in Mississippi, where he got work shoveling sawdust in a lumber mill. He found lodging in a long-deserted Negro cabin near the country home of Miss Joanna Burden, a spinster of Yankee origin who had few associates in Jefferson because of her zeal for bettering the lot of the Negro. She fed Joe and, when she learned that he was of Negro blood, planned to send him to a Negro

LIGHT IN AUGUST by William Faulkner. By permission of the author and the publishers, Random House, Inc.

school. Joe was her lover for three years. Her reactions ranged from sheer animalism to evangelism, in which she tried to make Joe repent his sins and turn Christian.

A young man who called himself Joe Brown came to work at the sawmill, and Joe Christmas invited Brown to share his cabin with him. The two began to sell bootleg whiskey. After a while Joe told Brown that he was part Negro; before long Brown discovered the relations of Joe and Miss Burden. When their bootlegging prospered, they bought a car and gave up their jobs at the lumber mill.

One night Joe went to Miss Burden's room half-determined to kill her. That night she attempted to shoot him with an antiquated pistol that did not fire. Joe cut her throat with his razor and ran out of the house. Later in the evening a fire was discovered in Miss Burden's house. When the townspeople started to go upstairs in the burning house, Brown tried to stop them. They brushed him aside. They found Miss Burden's body in the bedroom and carried it outside before the house burned to the ground.

Through a letter in the Jefferson bank, the authorities learned of Miss Burden's New Hampshire relatives, whom they notified. Almost at once word came back offering a thousand dollars reward for the capture of the murderer. Brown tried to tell the story as he knew it, putting the blame on Joe Christmas, so that he could collect the money. Few believed his story, but he was held in custody until Joe Christmas could be found.

Joe Christmas remained at large for several days, but at last with the help of bloodhounds he was tracked down. Meanwhile old Doc Hines had learned of his grandson's crime and he came with his wife to Jefferson. He urged the white people to lynch Joe, but for the most part his rantings went unheeded.

On the way to face indictment by the grand jury in the courthouse, Joe, handcuffed but not manacled to the deputy, managed to escape. He ran to a Negro cabin and found a gun. Some volunteer guards from the American Legion gave chase, and finally found him in the kitchen of the Reverend Gail Hightower, a one-time Presbyterian preacher who now was an outcast because he had driven his wife into dementia by his obsession with the gallant death of his grandfather in the Civil War. Joe had gone to Hightower at the suggestion of his grandmother, Mrs. Hines, who had had a conference with him in his cell just before he escaped. She had been advised of this possible way out by Byron Bunch, Hightower's only friend in Jefferson. The Legionnaires shot Joe down; then their leader mutilated him with a knife.

Brown now claimed his reward. A deputy took him out to the cabin where he had lived with Joe Christmas. On entering the cabin, he saw Mrs. Hines holding a new-born baby. In the bed was a girl, Lena Grove, whom he had slept with in a town in Alabama. Lena had started out to find Brown when she knew she was going to have a baby. Traveling most of the way on foot, she had arrived in Jefferson on the day of the murder and the fire. Directed to the sawmill, she had at once seen that Byron Bunch, to whom she had been sent, was not the same man as Lucas Burch, which was Brown's real name. Byron, a kindly soul, had fallen in love with her. Having identified Brown from Byron's description, she was sure that in spite of his new name Brown was the father of her child. She gave birth to the baby in Brown's cabin, where Byron had made her as comfortable as he could, with the aid of Mrs. Hines.

Brown jumped from a back window and ran away. Byron, torn between a desire to marry Lena and the wish to give her baby its rightful father, tracked Brown to the railroad grade outside town and fought with him. Brown escaped aboard a freight train.

Three weeks later Lena and Byron took to the road with the baby, Lena still searching for Brown. A truck driver gave them a lift. Byron was patient, but one night tried to compromise her. When she repulsed him, he left the little camp where the truck was parked. But next morning he was waiting at the bend of the road, and he climbed up on the truck as it made its way toward Tennessee.

LILIOM

Type of work: Drama
Author: Ferenc Molnar (1878-)
Type of plot: Fantasy
Time of plot: Early twentieth century
Locale: Budapest
First presented: 1909

Principal characters:

LILIOM, a merry-go-round barker
MRS. MUSKAT, his employer
JULIE, his wife
MARIE, her friend
WOLF, Marie's husband
MRS. HOLLUNDER, Julie's aunt
FICSUR, Liliom's friend
LINZMAN, the cashier whom Ficsur suggests robbing
LOUISE, daughter of Julie and Liliom

Critique:

This play is a popular favorite on the stages of Europe and America. The author's purpose was to tell a story of love and loyalty among the working classes. As literature the play is not profound, but as an entertainment piece it will probably enjoy a long life.

The Story:

Liliom was a barker for Mrs. Muskat's merry-go round at an amusement park on the edge of Budapest. As a barker he was a great success, for he had a stock of funny jokes that kept the customers laughing, and he had a playful way with the girls.

One day two young servant girls, Marie and Julie, came to the merry-go-round. To Mrs. Muskat's indignation, Liliom followed Julie onto the merry-go-round and put his arm around her. Mrs. Muskat warned Julie that if she ever came near the merry-go-round again she would be thrown out, as she did not wish to lose her license because of questionable behavior in the park. Liliom, however, told Julie to come back any time and she would be welcome. Although Mrs. Muskat was reluctant to let Liliom go, she could not ignore his insolence, and she dismissed him.

Liliom, to show his independence, announced that he was going to get some beer. While he was collecting his belongings, Marie disclosed to Julie that she was in love with a man in a uniform, a porter, however, not a soldier. When Liliom returned, he turned Marie away and began to discuss love with Julie, bragging and bullying all the while. Julie showed that she was deeply in love, for she had forfeited her job by staying out so late. Two policemen looking for vagrants interrupted their conversation. After asking routine questions and warning Julie that Liliom was a notorious ne'er-do-well, the policemen continued on their rounds. Though Julie protested that she did not love Liliom, it was obvious that she did. So they were married.

They moved into a run-down photographer's shop operated by the Hollunders, mother and son, at the edge of the park. Mrs. Hollunder, Julie's aunt, provided them not only with shelter but also with food and fuel. She grumbled all the time, but she was good-hearted beneath her gruffness. Marie, meanwhile, was falling more deeply in love with Wolf, the porter. One day, while the two girls were exchanging confidences, Mrs. Hollunder came in and said that Julie's other suitor, a widowed carpenter with two children and a respectable income, still wanted to take her out of the poverty in which she lived. Julie preferred to stay where she was. Then Mrs. Muskat came and offered to take Liliom back, but he refused. He and a friend named Ficsur had a scheme for getting a great deal of money; he was no longer interested in his old job at the merry-go-round.

Ficsur was planning a robbery. Each Saturday a cashier for a leather factory passed a nearby railway embankment, with the workmen's wages in a leather bag. Liliom was to accost the man and ask him what time it was while Ficsur was to come up from behind and stab the man. Ficsur encouraged Liliom to steal a knife from Mrs. Hollunder's kitchen. Julie, knowing that the two men were up to no good, begged Liliom not to go out with Ficsur, for she had arranged to have the carpenter come that evening and offer Liliom work. After Liliom had gone, Mrs. Hollunder missed her knife and suspected Liliom of taking it. Julie lied, saying that she had gone through Liliom's pockets and had found only a pack of cards.

Liliom and Ficsur arrived at the embankment just as the six o'clock train passed. Being early, they started a game of twenty-one and Ficsur won from Liliom his share in the loot they hoped to take from the cashier. Liliom accused Ficsur of cheating. Then their victim appeared and Liliom accosted him. As Ficsur was about to strike, however, the cashier seized Ficsur's arm. He pointed a pistol at Liliom's breast. Ironically, he had come from the factory, where he had just finished paying off the workers, and if Ficsur had killed him the robbers would have got no money. As the cashier called out to two policemen in the distance, Liliom broke away and stabbed himself with the kitchen knife.

The policemen attempted to take him to a hospital, but his condition was too critical. They took him back to the photographer's studio, where he died with Julie by his side holding his hand.

Dying, Liliom had a vision. Two heavenly policemen came to him and told him to follow them. They reminded him that death was not the end, that he was not through with earth until his memory had also passed away. Then they led him to the heavenly court assigned to suicide cases. There he learned that after a period of purification by fire, suicides were sent back to earth for one day to see whether they had profited by their purification. Liliom was sentenced to sixteen years in the fires.

At the end of that time Liliom returned to earth to find his wife and sixteen-year-old daughter Louise about to lunch in the garden of their dilapidated little house. Liliom was unrecognized. Julie gave him some food. He learned from Louise that her father, a handsome man, had gone to America before she was born, and had died there. When Liliom accused her husband of having struck her, Julie denied that he had ever mistreated her, and she dismissed Liliom as an ungrateful wretch. Liliom tried to please his daughter with card tricks and with a beautiful star which he had stolen from heaven, but Louise would have nothing more to do with him. As he left he struck her hard on the hand, but the blow felt as tender as a caress to her.

Her mother told her that there had been times when she, too, had experienced that sort of reaction from a blow. So Liliom left in the company of the two policemen, who shook their heads in profound regret at Liliom's failure.

THE LITTLE MINISTER

Type of work: Novel
Author: James M. Barrie (1860-1937)
Type of plot: Sentimental romance
Time of plot: Mid-nineteenth century
Locale: The village of Thrums in Scotland
First published: 1891

Principal characters:
GAVIN DISHART, the little minister of Thrums
MARGARET DISHART, his mother
MR. OGILVY, the schoolmaster, Margaret's second husband, and the narrator
ROB DOW, a drunkard converted by Gavin
BABBIE, a gipsy who loves Gavin
NANNY WEBSTER, an old woman saved from the poorhouse by Babbie
LORD RINTOUL, Babbie's guardian and her betrothed

Critique:

Barrie's sensitivity and deep appreciation of human values explain the popularity of this novel. The quiet, reserved humor appeals to the intellect and the heart rather than to a ludicrous sense of buffoonery, and the frequent note of sentiment is delicate and restrained. The book displays Barrie's gift for character portrayal and his lack of self-consciousness in his whimsical, ironic style.

The Story:

Mr. Ogilvy, the schoolmaster of Glen Quharity, had not seen Margaret Dishart for eighteen years until that day when he stood in the crowd that had gathered to welcome Gavin Dishart, the new minister of Auld Licht parish in Thrums. When the dominie saw Margaret again, he knew that all her happiness lay in her son Gavin. The schoolmaster did not allow Margaret to see him, as he never would even in the disturbed days to come. He knew that he was best out of her life, that he could bring her only unhappiness. When he heard Gavin deliver his first sermon at Auld Licht, the dominie knew that the little minister, who was just twenty-one, had indeed received the "call."

Lord Rintoul's castle stood in the Spittal on the hill above Glen Quharity. It was rumored that he had in his household a young girl whom he expected to marry soon, but no one had seen the girl except the sheriff of Thrums, who stopped at the castle to tell Lord Rintoul that a detachment of militia was coming to Thrums to arrest some insurgent weavers. Dressed as a gipsy, the young bride-to-be ran to the village to warn the people that soldiers were on their way.

Gavin Dishart met her that night as he was walking through Windyghoul toward Caddam. She ran dancing and singing, and laughed at him as she darted past him toward Thrums. When Gavin caught up with her, they became rivals as Gavin attempted to calm the workers whom the gipsy had aroused against the soldiers. Her activities on the night the militia came was a topic of discussion in Thrums for days afterward—this mysterious gipsy whose origin no one could guess. Even Gavin spent more hours than was proper pondering over the girl who had brazenly claimed, when the soldiers had tried to arrest her, that she was his wife.

Gavin's next meeting with the gipsy

THE LITTLE MINISTER by James M. Barrie. Published by Charles Scribner's Sons.

was in the cottage of old Nanny Webster, a parish charge. This story the schoolmaster heard through village gossip. The story of how Gavin had gone with Dr. McQueen to take old Nanny to the poorhouse, and how the gipsy girl, Babbie, interrupted the proceedings by offering to provide Nanny with an income for the old woman's support, reached the dominie only in rumor. Most of the villagers believed that the little minister had done the good work; few knew about the gipsy's part in the story.

Gavin could have avoided ever seeing Babbie again, but he did not. He even went so far as to tell her when he would be walking through Caddam woods. Babbie was not like the people of Thrums. She horrified old Nanny with her impertinence to the little minister of Auld Licht. She embarrassed Gavin by teasing him about his height, a fact which had caused him great distress all his life. Ever on the lookout for the pair was Rob Dow, who skulked among the pines of Windyghoul spying on his beloved minister and the witch who had cast a spell on Gavin. Rob, a drunkard whom Gavin had converted, feared for his minister after he had seen the gipsy nearly succeed in her attempt to make the minister kiss her. Rob jealously guarded his secret, for he was no gossip. To his death, Rob protected the little minister who had saved him from drink.

While the dominie feared lest Margaret be hurt by this woodland courtship, Gavin was troubled by his love for the brazen gipsy. As she gradually became aware of his devotion, the gipsy girl began to love him in turn. No one had ever loved her before. Lord Rintoul only played at watching her beauty. When Gavin stated that he would marry her, Babbie protested that he would be banished from Thrums and so break his mother's heart.

One night the lovers walked together through Windyghoul. Unknown to anyone, the dominie, Mr. Ogilvy, often strolled through the same wood so that he could gaze at the manse where Margaret lived. That night he met Gavin and Babbie. Immediately sensing their relationship and thinking only of Margaret, Ogilvy stepped into the affair and there he remained until it ended, not for Gavin's sake but for Margaret's protection. There were no words exchanged that night, but each knew that the dominie was aware of the love between Gavin and Babbie.

In Windyghoul, the next day, Babbie met Micah, Rob Dow's small son. Sobbing, the child told her that his father had taken to drink again because the little minister had been bewitched by the gipsy. If only she would go away, Rob could regain his faith in the minister and stop his drinking once more. Babbie realized then that Gavin's duty called him from her. She never laid eyes again on her lover until the terrible day of the great rain.

On the day of the great rain plans were being made at the Spittal for Lord Rintoul's wedding to his young bride. On this same day there was a fight in Thrums, and false news spread that Gavin had been killed by a drunken Highland piper. When the news traveled as far as the Spittal, Babbie, alarmed for Gavin and Margaret, ran to Mr. Ogilvy to ask his aid. The schoolmaster went with her to Windyghoul, where they encountered Gavin. When the two lovers were reunited, Babbie told Gavin that this was the day of her wedding to Lord Rintoul. Again Gavin asserted that he would marry her.

They hurried away to a gipsy camp and there the gipsy king married them over the tongs. Meanwhile Lord Rintoul, searching for his bride, had followed her in time to witness the ceremony. In the confusion of the gipsy camp, Babbie cried out to Gavin that she heard Lord Rintoul's voice. As Gavin rushed to encounter his rival, Babbie was suddenly snatched away. Assuming that Lord Rintoul would bring her back to the Spittal, Gavin headed toward Glen Quharity. The increasing rain drove him to Mr. Ogilvy's house for shelter.

The dominie ordered Gavin to end his fruitless pursuit, but the little minister insisted that he would take Babbie back to the manse as his bride. Then Mr. Ogilvy had to tell Gavin about Margaret. The schoolmaster—his name was Gavin also—had married Margaret after her first husband, Adam Dishart, had disappeared at sea. Six years after little Gavin's birth Adam Dishart had returned to claim his wife and little Gavin as his own. Mr. Ogilvy, perceiving the sorrow in Margaret's eyes as she faced the two men who claimed her, had disappeared and had sworn never to allow Margaret to know of his existence again. It was too late for the little minister and his real father to find any filial love after the schoolmaster's painful revelation. Gavin acknowledged his father, but he claimed that it was more God's will that he find Babbie again. As Gavin set out toward the Spittal, Mr. Ogilvy started toward Thrums to protect Margaret from village gossip that might reach her.

Babbie had not been captured by Lord Rintoul. Rob Dow, resolved to destroy the cause of his minister's downfall, had seized her. The gipsy eluded him during the severe storm, however, and ran to the manse to find Gavin.

Gavin, meanwhile, had lost all trace of Lord Rintoul in the rain-swept darkness. While he was making his way across the storm-flooded countryside, he came upon a ravine where some men shouted to him that Lord Rintoul was stranded on a small islet which was being washed away by the swiftly-flowing water. He could be saved if a man would jump down onto the island with a rope. Although he had no rope, Gavin jumped in the hope that he could help Lord Rintoul to maintain his foothold on the tiny piece of dwindling turf. As the villagers gathered at the brink of the ravine, their minister shouted to them that he had married Babbie the gipsy and that Mr. Ogilvy was to carry the news of his death to his mother and his wife. Then a man leaped into the ravine with a rope. It was Rob Dow, who performed his last living act to save the little minister whom he loved.

Gavin, followed by his admiring congregation, returned to the manse. There he found his mother and Babbie, who now could reveal herself, not as the wild gipsy of Windyghoul, but as the lady whom Lord Rintoul had planned to wed. Gavin and Babbie were married again under the prayers of a real minister, but Gavin always felt that he had really married her under the stars in the gipsy camp.

Mr. Ogilvy told the story of Gavin and Babbie to the eager little girl who was the daughter of the little minister and his wife. At the schoolmaster's request, Margaret Dishart had never learned of his part in Gavin's love affair. But after her death Gavin Ogilvy heard Babbie's and Gavin's daughter call him grandfather.

LITTLE WOMEN

Type of work: Novel
Author: Louisa May Alcott (1832-1888)
Type of plot: Sentimental romance
Time of plot: Nineteenth century
Locale: A New England village; New York City; Italy
First published: 1868

Principal characters:
MEG,
JO,
BETH, and
AMY, the March sisters

MRS. MARCH (MARMEE), their mother
MR. MARCH, their father
THEODORE LAWRENCE (LAURIE), a young neighbor
PROFESSOR BHAER, a tutor, in love with Jo

Critique:

Little Women is one of the best-loved books of all time, as popular today as when it was written eighty years ago. Although it is actually a children's book, it appeals to grownups as well, who see in it a mirror of their own childhood, or at least the childhood they would have preferred. The story is largely autobiographical, the March girls being Louisa's own sisters, with herself as Jo.

The Story:

The March family lived in a small house next door to the Lawrence mansion, where young Theodore Lawrence and his aged grandfather had only each other for company in the great house. Old Mr. Lawrence was wealthy and he indulged every wish of his grandson, but often Laurie was lonely. When the lamp was lit and the shades were up in the March house, he could see the four March girls with their mother in the center seated around a cheerful fire. He learned to know them by name before he met them, and in his imagination he almost felt himself a member of the family.

The oldest was plump Meg, who had to earn her living as governess of a group of unruly youngsters in the neighborhood. Next was Jo, tall, awkward, and tomboyish, who liked to write, and who spent all her spare time devising plays and entertainments for her sisters. Then there was gentle Beth, the homebody, content to sit knitting by the fire, or to help her mother take care of the house. The youngest was curly-haired Amy, a schoolgirl who dreamed of someday becoming a famous artist like Michelangelo or Leonardo da Vinci.

At Christmas time the girls were confronted with the problem of what to do with the dollar Marmee, as they called their mother, had said they might spend. At first each thought only of her own pleasure, but all ended by buying a gift for Marmee instead. On Christmas morning they insisted on sharing their breakfast with the Hummels, a poor family in the neighborhood, and for this unselfishness they were rewarded when rich Mr. Lawrence sent over a surprise Christmas feast consisting of ice cream, bonbons, and four bouquets of flowers for the table.

Many happy days followed, with Laurie, who had met Jo at a fashionable New Year's Eve dance, becoming a part of the March family circle. But in November of that same year a telegram brought a message that their father, an army chaplain in the Civil War, was critically ill. Mrs. March did not know what to do. She felt that she should go to her husband at once, but she had barely five dollars in her purse. She was hesitant about going to wealthy, irascible Aunt March for help. Jo solved the problem by selling her beautiful, long, chestnut hair, which was her only vanity, for twenty-five dollars. She made the sacrifice willingly, but that night, after the others had gone to bed, Marmee went to her daughter's room and found her weeping. Marmee asked if she were crying over her father's illness, and Jo sobbed that it was not her father she was crying for now, but for her hair.

During Marmee's absence dark days fell upon the little women. Beth, who had never been strong at best, contracted scarlet fever, and for a time it looked as if Jo were going to lose her dearest sister. Marmee was sent for, but by the time she arrived the crisis had passed and her little daughter was better. By the next

LITTLE WOMEN by Louisa May Alcott. Published by Little, Brown & Co.

Christmas, Beth was her old contented self again. Mr. March surprised them all when he returned home from the front well and happy. The little family was together once more.

Then John Brooke, Laurie's tutor, fell in love with Meg. This fact was disclosed when Mr. Brooke surreptitiously stole one of Meg's gloves and kept it in his pocket as a memento. Laurie discovered the glove and informed Jo. To his great surprise, she was infuriated at the idea that the family circle might be disturbed. But she was quite reconciled when, three years later, Meg became Mrs. Brooke.

In the meantime, Jo herself had grown up. She began to take her writing seriously, and even sold a few stories which helped with the family budget.

Her greatest disappointment came when Aunt Carrol, a relative of the Marches, decided she needed a companion on a European trip, and asked not Jo but the more lady-like Amy to accompany her. Then Jo, with Marmee's permission, decided to go to New York. She took a job as governess for a Mrs. Kirke, who ran a large boarding-house. There she met Professor Bhaer, a lovable and eccentric German tutor, who proved to be a good friend and companion.

Upon her return home, Laurie, who had always loved Jo, asked her to marry him. Jo, who imagined that she would always remain an old maid, devoting herself exclusively to her writing, tried to convince Laurie that they were not made for each other. He persisted, pointing out that his grandfather and her family both expected them to marry. When she made him realize that her refusal was final, he stamped off, and shortly afterward went to Europe with his grandfather. In Europe he saw a great deal of Amy, and the two became close friends, so that Laurie was able to transfer to her younger sister a great deal of the feeling he previously had for Jo.

In the meantime Jo was at home caring for Beth, who had never fully recovered from her first illness. In the spring, Beth died, practically in Jo's arms, and after the loss of her gentle sister Jo was lonely indeed. She tried to comfort herself with her writing, and with Meg's two babies, Daisy and Demi, but not until the return of Amy, now married to Laurie, did she begin to feel her old self again. When Professor Bhaer stopped off on his way to a university appointment in the Midwest, Jo was delighted. One day, under an umbrella he had supplied to shield her from a pouring rain, he asked her to marry him, and Jo accepted. Within a year old Aunt March died and willed her home, Plumfield, to Jo. She decided to open a boys' school, where she and her professor could devote their lives to instructing the young.

So the little women reached maturity, and on their mother's sixtieth birthday they all had a great celebration at Plumfield. Around the table, at which there was but one empty chair, sat Marmee, her children and her grandchildren. When Laurie proposed a toast to her, she replied by stretching out her arms to them all and saying that she could wish nothing better for them than this present happiness for the rest of their lives.

LOOK HOMEWARD, ANGEL

Type of work: Novel
Author: Thomas Wolfe (1900-1938)
Type of plot: Impressionistic realism
Time of plot: 1900 to 1920
Locale: North Carolina
First published: 1929

Principal characters:
EUGENE GANT
ELIZA GANT, his mother
OLIVER GANT, his father
BEN GANT, his brother
MARGARET LEONARD, his teacher
LAURA JAMES, his first sweetheart

Critique:

The work of Thomas Wolfe contains two invariable elements. One is a reliance on characters of exceptional brilliance and vitality. The other is the portrayal of a central character who is the sensitive artist isolated in a hostile world. The latter character is generally Thomas Wolfe himself. In his fiction Wolfe attempted to re-create the whole American experience in his own image, and beneath the sprawling, often chaotic mass of his novels there are firm outlines of the naked and innocent story of the American land and its people. Although his emotional range is limited to the adolescent and the romantic, he stands plainly in the succession of American writers who have expressed in their work the symbols of a haunted inner world of thought and feeling.

The Story:

Eugene, the youngest child in the Gant family, came into the world when Eliza Gant was forty-two years old. His father went on periodic drinking sprees to forget his unfulfilled ambitions and the unsatisfied wanderlust which had brought him to Altamont in the hills of old Catawba. When Eugene was born, his father was asleep in a drunken stupor.

Eliza disapproved of her husband's debauches, but she lacked the imagination to understand their cause. Oliver, who had been raised amidst the plenty of a Pennsylvania farm, had no comprehension of the privation and suffering which had existed in the South after the Civil War, the cause of the hoarding and acquisitiveness of his wife and her Pentland relations in the Catawba hill country.

Eliza bore the burden of Oliver's drinking and promiscuousness until Eugene was four years old. Then she departed for St. Louis, taking all the children but the oldest daughter, Daisy, with her. It was 1904, the year of the great St. Louis Fair, and Eliza had gone to open a boarding-house for her visiting fellow townsmen. The idea was abhorrent to Oliver. He stayed in Altamont.

Eliza's sojourn in St. Louis ended abruptly when twelve-year-old Grover fell ill of typhoid and died. Stunned, she gathered her remaining children to her and went home.

Young Eugene was a shy, awkward boy with dark, brooding eyes. He was, like his ranting, brawling father, a dreamer. He was not popular with his schoolmates, who sensed instinctively that he was different, and made him pay the price; and at home he was the victim of his sisters' and brothers' taunts and torments. His one champion was his brother Ben, though even he had been conditioned by the Gants' unemotional family life to give his caresses as cuffs. But there was little time for Eugene's childish daydreaming. Eliza believed early jobs taught her boys manliness and self-reliance. Ben got up at three o'clock every morning to deliver papers. Luke had been a *Saturday Evening Post* agent since he was twelve. Eugene was put under his wing. Although the boy loathed the work, he was forced every Thursday to corner customers and keep up a continuous line of chatter until he broke down their sales resistance.

Eugene was not yet eight when his parents separated. Eliza had bought the Dixieland boarding-house as a good investment. Helen remained at the old house with her father. Daisy married and left town. Mrs. Gant took Eugene with her. Ben and Luke were left to shift for themselves, to shuttle back and forth between the two houses. Eugene grew to detest his new home. When the Dixieland was crowded, there was no privacy, and Eliza advertised the Dixieland on printed cards which Eugene had to distribute to customers on his magazine route and to travelers arriving at the Altamont station.

But although life at the boarding-house was drabness itself, the next four years were the golden days of Eugene's youth, for he was allowed to go to the Leonards' private school. Margaret Leonard, the tubercular wife of the schoolmaster, recognized Eugene's hunger for beauty and love, and was able to find in literature the words that she herself had not the power to utter. By the time he was fifteen Eugene knew the best and the greatest lyrics almost line for line.

Oliver Gant, who had been fifty when his youngest son was born, was beginning to feel his years. Although he was never told, he was slowly dying of cancer.

Eugene was fourteen when the World War broke out. Ben, who wanted to join the Canadian Army, was warned by his doctor that he would be refused because he had weak lungs.

At fifteen, Eugene was sent to the university at Pulpit Hill. It was his father's plan that Eugene should be well on his way toward being a great statesman before the time came for old Oliver to die. Eugene's youth and tremendous height made him a natural target for dormitory horseplay, and his shy, awkward manners were intensified by his ignorance of the school's traditions and rituals. He roomed alone. His only friends were four wastrels, one of whom contributed to his social education by introducing him to a brothel.

That summer, back at the Dixieland, Eugene met Laura James. Sitting with her on the front porch at night, he was trapped by her quiet smile and clear, candid eyes. He became her lover on a summer afternoon of sunlit green and gold. But Laura went home to visit her parents and wrote Eugene that she was about to marry a boy to whom she had been engaged for nearly a year.

Eugene went back to Pulpit Hill that fall, still determined to go his way alone. Although he had no intimates, he gradually became a campus leader. The commonplace good fellows of his world tolerantly made room for the one who was not like them.

In October of the following year Eugene received an urgent summons to come home. Ben was finally paying the price of his parents' neglect and the drudgery of his life. He was dying of pneumonia. Eliza had neglected to call a competent doctor until it was too late, and Oliver, as he sat at the foot of the dying boy's bed, could think only of the expense the burial would be. As the family kept their vigil through Ben's last night, they were touched with the realization of the greatness of the boy's generous soul. Ben was given, a final irony, the best funeral money could buy.

With Ben went the family's last pretenses. When Eugene came back to the Dixieland after graduation, Eliza was in control of Oliver's property and selling it as quickly as she could in order to use the money for further land speculations. She had disposed of their old home. Oliver lived in a back room at the boarding-house. His children watched each other suspiciously as he wasted away, each concerned for his own inheritance. Eugene managed to remain unembroiled in their growing hatred of each other, but he could not avoid being a target for that hatred. Helen, Luke, and Steve had always resented his schooling. In September, before he left for Harvard to begin graduate work, Luke asked Eugene to sign a release saying that he had received his inheritance as tuition and school expenses. Though his father had promised him an education when he was still a child and Eliza was to pay for his first year in the North, Eugene was glad to sign. He was free, and he was never coming back to Altamont.

On his last night at home he had a vision of his dead brother Ben in the moonlit square at midnight; Ben, the unloved of the Gants, and the most lovable. It was for Eugene as well a vision of old, unhappy, unforgotten years, and in his restless imagination he dreamed of the hidden door through which he would escape forever the mountain-rimmed world of his boyhood.

LOOKING BACKWARD

Type of work: Novel
Author: Edward Bellamy (1850-1898)
Type of plot: Utopian romance
Time of plot: A.D. 2000
Locale: Boston, Massachusetts
First published: 1888

Principal characters:
JULIAN WEST, a traveler in time
EDITH BARTLETT, his nineteenth century fiancée
DR. LEETE, a twentieth century citizen
EDITH LEETE, his daughter

Critique:

The main value of *Looking Backward: 2000-1887* lies in its credible presentation of a socialist Utopia, and the book has served to introduce many famous people to the theory of socialism. Bellamy was not merely a follower of Marx and other economists; he rationalized for himself the case for economic revolution. The prophecies he makes for the world by A.D. 2000 are sometimes strikingly shrewd, and his judgments made of modern society are pointed and witty. Bellamy's idea was to present the ideas of socialism, as he saw them, in a way which would appeal to a wide reading public, both of yesterday and today.

The Story:

Julian West had a hard time sleeping. In order to have complete quiet he had built a sound-proof room with thick cement walls in the cellar of his house. He was also in the habit of having a quack doctor named Pillsbury put him to sleep by hypnosis.

One night he went to dinner with his fiancée's family and spent an enjoyable evening with Edith and her father, Mr. Bartlett. He went home, had the doctor give him a treatment, and went to sleep. He awoke to find strange people in the room. They asked him who he was, and when he had gone to sleep. Julian was amazed when he realized that he had been asleep one hundred and thirteen years, three months, and eleven days.

From much questioning, Julian learned what must have happened. During the night that he last remembered, his house had burned down except for the sealed room in which he slept; and apparently everyone assumed that he had died in the fire. Because of his hypnotic state, his body had remained the same. He was still a young man of thirty when he was discovered by Dr. Leete in the year 2000. Dr. Leete and his daughter, Edith, were very kind to their guest from the past and tried to explain the changes in the world since he had last seen it.

Boston was a new city with only the bay and the inlets as he remembered them. The city was beautiful, with attractive buildings and spacious parks.

The strikes and labor troubles of the nineteenth century had resulted in a bloodless revolution, and now a socialized government controlled all business. There was no smoke because all heating was done by electricity. All the people were healthy and happy.

Dr. Leete tried to explain the world of A.D. 2000. There was no money. The state gave everyone, no matter what his job, a card which contained the same amount of credit for a year's expenses. There was no chance, however, for anyone to spend his credit foolishly and starve. If a person proved incapable of handling his credit card intelligently, the government took care to see that he was supervised. Julian was taken to one of the big stores to see how goods were sold. The store had nothing but samples, representing every type of material made in or imported by the United States. The buyer picked out the items he wanted, called a clerk, gave the order, and the clerk relayed the order to the central warehouse from which the item was delivered to the buyer's home before he returned from the store. Julian was much impressed with this system.

He learned from Dr. Leete how education was handled. Everyone was given a full education until he was twenty-one. A broad cultural course was taught so that there was no intellectual snobbery among the people. At twenty-one, the student went into menial service for three years. During this time he waited on tables in the large public eating houses, or did some other simple task. After three years, he was given an examination to qualify him for one of the government professional schools. If he failed, he was helped to find the job for which he was best suited and which he would most enjoy. If this job proved to be the wrong one, he could change his position. In order that all necessary jobs would be chosen by enough people to do the essential work, the jobs were arranged so as to be equally attractive. If one job was so boring that few people would want to choose it, the hours were made shorter so that enough applicants could be found. Whether a citizen was a doctor or a bricklayer, he was given the same amount of credit for his work.

Crime was treated as a mental disease; criminals were put in hospitals and treated as mental cases. Julian learned that crime had been cut down amazingly as soon as money was abolished. Theft became silly when everyone had the right and power to own the same things. At the head of the government was the President, who was controlled by Congress. Education and medicine were controlled by boards made up of older professional advisers to the President. A woman chosen by the women of the country had the power to veto any bill concerning the rights of the female population. There was no public discontent with government, and there was wonderful international cooperation.

Julian asked Dr. Leete what he had done in life, and learned that the doctor had practiced medicine until he was forty-five years old. At that time he had retired. Now he studied and enjoyed various kinds of recreation.

Edith Leete took great pleasure in showing Julian the various advances the world had made in culture since his day. She showed him how music was carried into all the homes in the country by telephone. She showed him the public libraries in which Julian learned that his old favorites were still read. Dickens was especially popular, as the new world thought him one of the wisest men in judging the sadness of the old capitalistic system. When an author wrote a book, it was published at his own expense by the government. If it proved a success, he received royalties in additional credit cards. Works of art were voted on by the public in the same way. When Julian commented that this plan would not have worked in his day because of the lack of public taste, Edith told him that with general education the taste of the people had developed greatly. Julian became very fond of Edith, and thought how strange it was that she should have the same name as his long-dead fiancée.

When Julian became worried about a means of support, Dr. Leete told him that he had arranged for him to take a college lectureship in history, as Julian knew much about the past which even historians would be delighted to learn. Knowing that he was secure in this new world, Julian asked Edith to marry him. She told him that she had always loved him.

When Julian asked how this was possible, she explained that she was the great-granddaughter of Edith Bartlett. She had found some of Julian's old love letters to the other Edith, and had been charmed by them. She had always told her parents that she would marry only a man like the lover who had written them. Julian was pleased at this unexpected turn of affairs, and the two planned to marry and live happily in the wonderful world of the twenty-first century.

LORD JIM

Type of work: Novel
Author: Joseph Conrad (Teodor Józef Konrad Korzeniowski, 1857-1924)
Type of plot: Psychological romance
Time of plot: Late nineteenth century
Locale: Ports and islands of the East
First published: 1900

Principal characters:
LORD JIM, a British sailor
MARLOW, his friend
STEIN, a trader
DAIN WARIS, a native

Critique:

Lord Jim first ran as a magazine serial that puzzled many readers. Conrad claimed that he had planned the narrative as a novel. Critics claimed that he had written a short story which had run away from him. The fact remains that the story is told in a unique framework. At its beginning it seems to skip haphazardly backward and forward through time at no one's direction. It is told partly by Conrad, partly in narrative by Marlow, and partly through a letter written by Marlow. The reader must solve for himself the problem of Jim's character. Certainly, Conrad was attempting to illustrate in Jim's weakness and strength the mystery of human character and to reveal the hidden springs of human conduct.

The Story:

Jim was an outcast, a wanderer. Hired as water clerk in seaports throughout the East, he would keep his job only until his identity became known. Then he would move on. The story of Lord Jim began when he determined to leave home to go to sea. Accordingly, his father obtained a berth for him as an officer candidate and he began his service. Although he loved the sea, his beginning was not heroic. Almost at once he was injured and was left behind in an Eastern port. When he recovered, he accepted a berth as chief mate aboard an ancient steamer, the *Patna,* carrying Moslem pilgrims on their way to Mecca.

The steamer was unseaworthy, her German captain a gross coward, her chief engineer liquor-soaked. One sultry night in the Red Sea the ship struck a floating object. The captain sent Jim to check.

A month later Jim testified in court that when he went to investigate he found the forward hold rapidly filling with sea water. Hearing his report, the captain declared the *Patna* would sink quickly and gave orders to abandon ship. At first Jim was determined to stand by his post. At the last minute, on sudden impulse, he jumped to join the other white men in the lifeboat they had launched. The pilgrims were left aboard the sinking vessel.

But the *Patna* had not sunk. A French gunboat overtook the vessel and towed it and the abandoned passengers into port without its chief officers aboard.

Marlow, a white man, sat at the inquiry. Later, he took up the thread of the story as he had learned it from Jim. Something in Jim was fixed to Marlow's memory so that he was forced to recall the event and to tell the story to friends as long as he lived; it became a part of his own life.

It always began the same way. First there had come a cable from Aden telling that the *Patna,* abandoned by its officers, had been towed into port. Then two weeks later the captain, the two engineers, and Jim had come ashore, their boat having been picked up by a steamer of the Dale Line. They were whisked into court at once for the investigation. The captain lost his papers for deserting his ship, and he stormed away declaring that his disgrace did not matter; he would become an American citizen.

The chief engineer went to a hospital. There, raving in delirium tremens, he declared he had seen the *Patna* go down. The *Patna* was full of reptiles when she sank, he declared. He also declared that the space under his bed was crammed with pink toads. The second engineer, his arm broken, was also in the hospital. Neither was called to testify.

Jim, with his recollection of his family and his father's teaching, as well as his own deeply established sense of honor, was a marked man for the rest of his life. Marlow told how he had dinner with Jim during the trial. The boy seemed of a different stamp from the other officers of the *Patna.* Marlow was determined to fathom the boy's spirit, just as Jim was determined to regain his lost moral identity.

Jim told Marlow how the disgraceful affair had happened. After he had investigated the damage, he had felt that the ship could not remain afloat, for her plates were rust-eaten and unable to stand much strain. There were eight hundred passengers and seven boats, and not enough time to get into the boats the few passengers who could be carried to safety. Shortly afterward he discovered the captain and the engineers making ready to desert the ship. They insisted that he join them; the passengers were doomed anyway. The acting third engineer had a heart attack in the excitement and died. Jim never knew when—or why—he had jumped into the lifeboat the other officers had launched. Jim told Marlow how they had agreed to tell the same story. Actually, he and his companions thought that the *Patna* had gone down. Jim said that he had felt relief when he had learned that the passengers were safe. The whole story made sailor-talk in all ports where seamen met and talked. After the inquiry Marlow offered to help Jim, but Jim was determined to become a wanderer, to find out by himself what had happened to his soul.

Jim began his wanderings, to Bombay, to Calcutta, to Penang, Batavia, and the islands of the East. For a time he found work with an acquaintance of Marlow's, but he gave up his job when the second engineer of the *Patna* turned up unexpectedly. Afterward he became a runner for some ship chandlers, but he left them because he had heard one of the owners discussing the case of the *Patna.* He moved on, always toward the East, from job to job.

Marlow continued his efforts to help

Jim. He sought out Stein, a trader who owned a number of trading posts on the smaller islands of the East Indies. Stein made Jim his agent at Patusan, an out-of-the-way settlement where he was sure Jim might recover his balance. There, in that remote place, Jim tried to find some answer to his self-hatred. Determined never to leave Patusan, he associated with the natives, and by his gentleness and consideration became their leader. They called him Tuan Jim—Lord Jim. Dain Waris, the son of Doramin, the old native chief, was his friend.

The rumor spread in the ports that Jim had discovered a valuable emerald, and that he had presented it to a native woman. There was a story about a native girl who loved him and who had given him warning when some jealous natives came to murder him.

Marlow followed Jim to Patusan. When Marlow prepared to leave, Jim accompanied him part of the way. He explained to Marlow that at last he felt as though his way had been justified. Somehow, because the simple natives trusted him, he felt linked again to the ideals of his youth. Marlow felt there was a kind of desperateness to his conviction.

The end came when Gentleman Brown, a roving cutthroat, determined to loot Lord Jim's stronghold. He arrived while Jim was away. Led by Dain Waris, the natives isolated Brown and his marauders on a hilltop but were unable to capture them. Lord Jim returned and after a long talk with Brown became convinced that Brown would leave peaceably if the siege were lifted. He persuaded the reluctant natives to withdraw. The vicious Brown repaid Lord Jim's magnanimity by vengefully murdering Dain Waris. Lord Jim went unflinchingly to face native justice when he offered himself to the stern old chieftain as the cause of Dain Waris' death. Doramin shot Jim through the breast.

Marlow, who had watched Jim's life so closely, felt that Jim had at last won back his lost honor.

LORNA DOONE

Type of work: Novel
Author: R. D. Blackmore (1825-1900)
Type of plot: Historical romance
Time of plot: Late seventeenth century
Locale: England
First published: 1869

Principal characters:

John Ridd, yeoman of the parish of Oare in Somerset
Sir Ensor Doone, head of the outlaw Doone clan
Lorna Doone, his ward
Carver Doone, his son
Tom Faggus, a highwayman
Jeremy Stickles, king's messenger
Reuben Huckaback, John Ridd's great-uncle

Critique:

R. D. Blackmore, in his preface to *Lorna Doone: A Romance of Exmoor,* was content to call his work a "romance," because the historical element was only incidental to the work as a whole. Secret agents, highwaymen, clannish marauders, and provincial farmers figure against a background of wild moor country. A feeling for the old times, for great, courageous people, for love under duress made the novel popular with Victorian readers. People who have read it in their youth remember it with nostalgia, for the book has a penetrating simplicity. Told

LORNA DOONE by R. D. Blackmore. Published by Dodd, Mead & Co., Inc.

in the first person by John Ridd, the main character in the novel, it has an authentic ring, the sound of a garrulous man relating the adventures of his youth.

The Story:

John Ridd was engaged in a schoolboy fight in the yard of old Blundell's school when John Fry, employed by Ridd's father, called for the boy to summon him home. Before the two left, however, young John completed his fight by knocking out his opponent. On their way home through the moorlands they were nearly captured by members of the outlaw Doone band, who had been ravaging the countryside, stealing and killing. When John Ridd reached his father's farm, he learned that only a few days before, the Doones had set upon and murdered his father. This incident stimulated the desire for revenge by all the members of the parish of Oare, for the murdered man had been greatly respected.

John settled down to the responsibilities which the death of his father had thrust upon him. At first his time was greatly taken by farm work, as he grew and matured into the largest and strongest man in the Exmoor country. As he grew up, John learned much about the wild Doone clan. There was one Doone, however, for whom he felt no animosity. This was the beautiful child of the man supposed to be the murderer of John's father. At first sight John had been stirred by the beauty of Lorna Doone. Thereafter he was in great conflict when he understood that his passion was directed toward the girl whom he ought for his father's sake to hate.

When John's great-uncle, Master Reuben Huckaback, was attacked and robbed by the Doones, he went with John to swear out a warrant for their arrest, but he had no luck because the magistrates were unwilling to incur the enmity of the Doones.

John was drawn deeper into his relationship with Lorna Doone. At their secret meetings in Doone Valley she told him the story of her life with the outlaws; how she always had loved her grandfather, Sir Ensor Doone, but feared and lately had come to hate the rough, savage sons, nephews, and grandsons of Sir Ensor. This hatred was increased when Carver Doone cold-bloodedly murdered Lord Alan Brandir, a distant relative, who had come to take her away from the Doones.

About this time John was called to London to serve the cause of James II's tottering throne. There he disclosed all he knew of the Doones' activities and of the false magistrates who seemed to be in league with them. He was warned that Tom Faggus, a highwayman who was John's own cousin, might go to the gallows before long. He returned to his mother and his farm no penny richer or poorer than when he left, because of his refusal to accept bribes or to become the dupe of sly lawyers in the city.

In the meantime concern over Lorna, who had two suitors among the Doones themselves, had almost unhinged John's mind. He was delighted to discover that Lorna, still only seventeen, held off the two Doones. At the same time he feared more than ever his chance of winning the ward of the outlaws he was pledged to help the king destroy. However, he at last won Lorna over to his suit, and with her agreement he felt nothing could stop him.

At home the love of his sister Annie for her cousin, Tom Faggus, reminded John of his duties as his father's son and plunged him into the worries over his mother and Annie and the farm. John's mother had other plans for his marriage, but when he revealed the only course his love must take, he won her over. In the meantime Master Jeremy Stickles brought news of the rising of the Duke of Monmouth and of troubles brewing for the king.

Suddenly, Lorna's signals stopped. John made his will and descended into the Doone hideout and there at great risk discovered that Lorna had been kept in her rooms because she would not marry Carver Doone. John managed to talk to her and she pledged never to give in to her family. He narrowly escaped capture, and at the same time managed to save the life of Jeremy Stickles, king's messenger, by overhearing the outlaws as they plotted to kill Jeremy when he should be crossing the valley bridge. The Doones' plot to kill Stickles brought further plans for retaliation from the king's men.

Old Sir Ensor Doone was close to death. Before he died, he gave John Ridd and Lorna Doone his blessing and to Lorna he presented the glass necklace he had kept for her since childhood. Then John took Lorna home with him to his mother's farm. Jeremy Stickles went south to muster forces for the destruction of the Doone clan.

The counselor of the Doones took advantage of his absence to visit the Ridd farm in order to make a truce with John Ridd. His offer was rejected, but he threw trouble into the paths of the lovers by telling them that Lorna's father had murdered John's father and that his own father was the murderer of Lorna's father. Moreover, he tricked them out of Lorna's necklace, which by now, through the word of Tom Faggus, they knew to be made of diamonds.

Uncle Reuben Huckaback grew interested in having John marry his granddaughter Ruth, and took John to see the gold mine he had just bought. Upon his return, John learned that Lorna had disappeared. She had been taken away by the Dugals, who claimed her as their missing heiress.

When Tom Faggus joined the rebels against the king, John, at his sister Annie's request, went to find him and to bring him back to safety. John discovered Tom almost dead. John was taken prisoner and was nearly executed. He was saved only by the arrival of his friend, Jeremy Stickles.

John went to London and there saw Lorna. By good chance and virtue of his great strength he overcame two villains who were attempting to rob and kill a nobleman. The man happened to be Lorna's relative. In return for this deed, the king gave John the title of knight. Moreover, he had the court of heralds design a coat of arms for John's family. The coat of arms was soundly made and the queen herself paid for it, the king declining.

When John returned from London, covered with honors, he discovered the Doones had been raiding once more. Then came the long awaited revenge. The Doones were routed, their houses were burned, and their stolen booty was divided among those who put in claims for redress. The counselor revealed that it was Carver Doone who had killed John's father. The necklace was recovered.

Arrangements for the wedding of John and Lorna were made. At the end of the ceremony in the church, Carver Doone, out of his great jealousy, shot Lorna. Without a weapon in his hand, John rushed out in pursuit of Carver and found him at Barrow Down. There took place the greatest battle between two men ever told of in books. It was a fight of giants. As John felt his ribs cracking in Carver's tremendous hug, he fastened his own iron grip upon his enemy's arm and ripped it loose. Then he threw his crushed and bleeding enemy into the bog and saw Carver Doone sucked down into its black depths.

Thus the greatest enemy of John Ridd was at last destroyed and John returned to his bride to find that she might live. She did survive and in peace and plenty John Ridd lived among his friends to a hearty old age.

LOST HORIZON

Type of work: Novel
Author: James Hilton (1900-)
Type of plot: Adventure romance
Time of plot: 1931
Locale: Tibet
First published: 1933

Principal characters:
HUGH CONWAY, a British consul
RUTHERFORD, his friend
HENRY BARNARD, an American embezzler
MISS BRINKLOW, a missionary
CAPTAIN MALLISON, another British consul
CHANG, a Chinese lama
FATHER PERRAULT, the High Lama

Critique:

Shangri-La, the name for the setting of this novel, has come to mean to most Americans a place of peace and contentment. Such was the strange Utopia James Hilton described in *Lost Horizon,* making it seem like a real place, peopled by living beings, rather than the land of an impossible ideal.

The Story:

When Rutherford had found Hugh Conway, a former schoolmate, suffering from fatigue and amnesia in a mission hospital, Conway had related a weird and almost unbelievable story concerning his disappearance many months before.

Conway was a member of the consulate at Baskul when trouble broke out there in May, 1931, and he was considered something of a hero because of the efficiency and coolness he displayed while white civilians were being evacuated. When it was his turn to leave, he boarded a plane in the company of Miss Roberta Brinklow, a missionary; Henry Barnard, an American, and Captain Charles Mallison, another member of the consulate. The plane was a special high-altitude cabin aircraft provided by the Maharajah of Chandapore. Conway, thirty-seven years old, had been in the consular service for ten years. His work had not been spectacular and he was expecting to rest in England before being assigned to another undistinguished post.

After the plane had been in the air about two hours, Mallison noticed that their pilot was the wrong man and that they were not headed toward Peshawur, the first scheduled stop. Conway was undisturbed until he realized they were flying over strange mountain ranges. When the pilot landed and armed tribesmen refueled the plane before it took off again, Conway began to agree with Mallison and Barnard, who thought they had been kidnaped and would be held for ransom.

When Conway tried to question the pilot, the man only pointed a revolver at him. A little after midnight the pilot landed again, this time narrowly averting a crackup. Climbing out of the plane, the passengers found the pilot badly injured. Conway believed that they were high on the Tibetan plateau, far beyond the western range of the Himalaya Mountains. The air was bitterly cold, with no signs of human habitation in that region of sheer-walled mountains. The pilot died before morning, murmuring something about a lamasery called Shangri-La. As the little group started in search of the lamasery, they saw a group of men coming toward them.

When the men reached them, one introduced himself in perfect English; he was a Chinese named Chang. Following the men, Conway and his friends arrived at the lamasery of Shangri-La that evening. There they found central heat, plumbing, and many other luxuries more commonly found only in the Western Hemisphere. They were given fine rooms and excellent food. They learned that there was a High Lama whom they would not be privileged to meet. Although Chang told them porters would arrive in a few weeks to lead them back to the outer world, Conway had the strange feeling that their coming had not been an accident and that they were not destined soon to leave.

Presently Chang told them that Conway was to be honored by an interview with the High Lama. Mallison begged him to force the High Lama to provide guides for them, for Mallison had learned that Barnard was wanted for fraud and embezzlement in the United States and he was anxious to turn Barnard over to the British authorities. But Conway did not discuss their departure with the High Lama, whom he found a very intelligent, very old man. Instead, he listened to the lama's remarkable story of Father Perrault, a Capuchin friar lost in the mountains in 1734, when he was fifty-three years old. Father Perrault had found sanctuary in a lamasery and had stayed there after adopting the Buddhist faith. In 1789 the old man lay dying, but the miraculous power of some drugs he had perfected, coupled with the marvelous air on the plateau, prolonged his life. Later tribesmen from the valley helped him build the lamasery of Shangri-La, where he lived the life of a scholar. In 1804 another European came to the lamasery; then others came from Europe and from Asia. No guest was ever allowed to leave.

Conway learned then that the kidnaping of their plane had been deliberate. But, more important, he learned that the High Lama was Father Perrault and that he was two hundred and fifty years old. The old man told Conway that all who lived at Shangri-La had the secret of long life. He had sent the pilot for new people because he believed a war was coming which would destroy all known civilization and Shangri-La would then be the nucleus of a new world. His picture of life in the lamasery pleased Conway. He was content to stay.

Conway, knowing that the others would find it hard to accept the news, did not tell them that they could never leave. Mallison continued to talk of the coming of the porters, but Barnard and Miss Brinklow announced that they intended to pass up the first opportunity to leave Shangri-La and wait for a later chance. Barnard faced jail if he returned, and Miss Brinklow thought she should not miss the opportunity to convert the lamas and the tribesmen in the valley.

The weeks passed pleasantly for Conway. He met a Frenchman called Briac, who had been Chopin's pupil. He also met Lo-Tsen, a Chinese girl who seemed quite young, but Chang told him she was really sixty-five years old. Conway had more meetings with the High Lama; at one of them the old man told Conway that he knew he was going to die at last and that he wanted Conway to take his place as ruler of the lamasery and the valley and to act wisely so that all culture would not be lost after war had destroyed Western civilization.

While he was explaining these matters, the old lama lay back in his chair, and Conway knew he was dead. Conway wandered out into the garden, too moved to talk to anyone. He was interrupted by Mallison, with the news that the porters had arrived. Although Barnard and Miss Brinklow would not leave, Mallison had paid the porters to wait for him and Conway. Mallison said that the Chinese girl was going with them, that he had made love to her and that she wanted to stay with him. Conway tried to tell Mallison that the girl was really an old woman who would die if she left the valley, but Mallison refused to listen. At first Conway also refused to leave Shangri-La, but after Mallison and the girl started and then came back because they were afraid to go on alone, Conway felt that he was responsible for them as well and he left the lamasery with them. He felt that he was fleeing from the place where he would be happy for the rest of his life, no matter how long that life might be.

Rutherford closed his manuscript at that point, for Conway had slipped away and disappeared. Later Rutherford met a doctor who told him that Conway had been brought to the mission by a woman, a bent, withered, old Chinese woman. Perhaps, then, the story was true. Convinced that Conway had headed for the hidden lamasery, Rutherford hoped that his journey had been successful, that Conway had reached Shangri-La.

A LOST LADY

Type of work: Novel
Author: Willa Cather (1876-1947)
Type of plot: Regional realism
Time of plot: Late nineteenth century
Locale: Nebraska
First published: 1923

Principal characters:
Captain Forrester, a railroad constructor
Mrs. Forrester, his wife
Judge Pommeroy, his friend and legal adviser
Niel Herbert, the judge's nephew
Ivy Peters, a shyster lawyer

Critique:

This book, which is marked by a studied attention to form, achieves an epic-like tone. In part this is derived from the theme as well as from the viewpoint of the novel. The theme expresses a feeling of admiration which most Americans share for the builders who opened the West, a herculean task which could not be done twice. The viewpoint is that of a young man whose youth claims the right of sentimental ardor which makes youth so delightful. Moreover, Miss Cather captured the tone of many women of the generation about which she was writing. Mrs. Forrester possessed more valiant self-reliance than many of her contemporaries. As such she was able to be a lost lady and still keep her own personality intact.

The Story:

The Forrester home at Sweet Water was a stopping off place for railroad magnates riding through the prairie states along the Burlington line. Old Captain Forrester liked to drive his guests from the station and watch them as they approached his estate. He enjoyed their praise of his stock farm and their delight when his charming wife met them at the front door. Everyone from railroad presidents to the village butcher boy and the kitchen maids liked Mrs. Forrester; her manner was always one of friendliness and respect.

Niel Herbert's acquaintance with Mrs. Forrester began when he fell from a tree while playing with some village boys on the captain's property and Mrs. Forrester summoned a doctor. He did not know it at the time, but Mrs. Forrester had already singled him out from the others because he was Judge Pommeroy's nephew. After his recovery he was often invited to the Forrester home with his uncle.

The boy who had caused Niel's fall was Ivy Peters. He had winged a woodpecker and then had slit its eyes. The bird had fumbled back into its hole, and Niel was trying to reach the creature to put it out of its misery when he lost his balance and fell.

During a period of hard times Niel's father went out of business and left Sweet Water. Niel stayed on to read law in his uncle's office. A few days before Christmas, Mrs. Forrester invited Niel to her home to help entertain Constance Ogden, the daughter of one of the captain's friends, who was coming to spend the holidays with the Forresters. Also included in the party was Frank Ellinger, a bachelor of forty. The dinner was a gay one. Niel decided that Constance was neither pretty nor pleasant. It was plain that she had designs on Frank Ellinger.

The following day Niel was asked to stay with Constance during the afternoon, while Mrs. Forrester and Frank took the small cutter and went after cedar for the Christmas decorations. The Blum boy, out hunting, saw Mrs. Forrester and Frank after he came upon the deserted cutter beside a thicket, but he did not give away their secret. The doings of the rich were not his concern and Mrs. Forrester had been kind to him on many occasions.

During that winter Judge Pommeroy and his nephew often went to play cards with the Forresters. One night, during a snowstorm, Mrs. Forrester revealed to Niel how much she missed the excitement and glamour of former winters at fashionable resorts. She mocked the life of quiet domesticity in which she and the captain were living.

In the spring the captain went to Denver on business and while he was gone Frank Ellinger arrived for a visit. One morning Niel cut a bouquet of wild roses to leave outside the windows of Mrs. Forrester's bedroom. Suddenly he heard from the bedroom the voices of Mrs. Forrester and Frank Ellinger. The first illusion of his life was shattered by a man's yawn and a woman's laugh.

When the captain came home from Denver, he announced that he was a poor man. Having satisfied his creditors, he had left only his pension from the Civil War and the income from his farm. Shortly afterward the captain had a stroke.

Niel continued to visit the sick man and his wife. He realized that Mrs. Forrester was facing her new life with terror she tried to hide for her husband's sake. Niel, having decided to become an architect, left Sweet Water to spend two years at school in the East. When he returned, he learned that Ivy Peters, shrewd and grasping, had become an important person in the town. Niel, who despised Peters, was disappointed to learn that Peters, now the captain's tenant, had drained the marsh where the boys had gone fishing years before. The captain himself had become wasted and old. Most of the time he sat in his garden staring at a strange sundial he had made.

Niel learned that Mrs. Forrester, who seemed little older, was still writing to Frank Ellinger. He observed, too, that Mrs. Forrester treated Peters with easy familiarity, and he wondered how she could be on friendly terms with the pushing young lawyer.

That summer a storm flooded the fields along the creek. Niel went to Judge Pommeroy's office to read. He thought of an item he had seen in the Denver paper earlier in the day; Frank Ellinger had finally married Constance Ogden. Close to midnight Mrs. Forrester, drenched to the skin, appeared at the office. At her demand Niel made the telephone connection with Ellinger in Colorado Springs. Mrs. Forrester began to talk politely, as though complimenting Ellinger on his marriage. Then she became hysterical. When she began to scream reproaches, Niel cut the wires.

Mrs. Forrester recovered after her collapse, but the gossipy town telephone operator pieced together a village scandal from what she had managed to overhear.

Captain Forrester died in December. None of his wealthy friends attended the funeral, but old settlers and former employees came to do honor to the railroad pioneer who had been one of the heroes of the early West.

One day Mr. Ogden stopped in Sweet Water. He thought that Judge Pommeroy ought to send to Washington a claim to have Mrs. Forrester's pension increased. Niel was forced to explain that Mrs. Forrester had turned her affairs over to Ivy Peters.

After her husband's death Mrs. Forrester began to entertain Ivy Peters and other young men from the village. At her urging Niel went to one party, but he was disgusted with the cheap manners of both hostess and guests. He could not bear to see the old captain's home thus abused.

Niel felt that an era was ending. The great old people, such as the judge and the captain and their friends, were passing, the men who had built the railroads and the towns. The old men of gallant manners and their lovely ladies had gone forever. In their place was a new type of man, the shrewd opportunist, like Ivy Peters. On the day Niel saw Peters putting his arms around Mrs. Forrester, he decided to leave Sweet Water.

As long as his uncle lived, however, he had news of Mrs. Forrester. The judge wrote that she was sadly broken. Then his uncle died and Niel heard no more for many years.

A long time afterward a mutual friend told him what had happened to his lost lady. She had gone to California. Later, she had married a rich Englishman and had gone with him to South America. She had dyed her hair and had dressed expensively in an effort to keep her youth.

Finally, one year, the G.A.R. post received a letter from Mrs. Forrester's English husband. It enclosed money for the continued care of Captain Forrester's grave. His gift was a memorial to his late wife, Marian Forrester Collins.

THE LOST WEEKEND

Type of work: Novel
Author: Charles Jackson (1903-)
Type of plot: Psychological melodrama
Time of plot: Twentieth century
Locale: New York City
First published: 1944

Principal characters:
Don Birnam, an alcoholic
Wick, his brother
Helen, his friend

Critique:

Although *The Lost Weekend* is in some respects more a case history than a novel, it is nevertheless a vivid and convincing story of a maladjusted personality. Jackson shows considerable insight into alcoholism as a social problem without destroying the personal quality of his hero's experience and the desperation of his struggle during a long weekend when he is thrown upon his own resources. In this novel the drama remains objective; the underlying cause of Don Birnam's alcoholism is dramatized rather than analyzed.

The Story:

Don Birnam was an unsuccessful writer who drank too much. Time and again, his brother Wick and his friend Helen tried to break him of the habit. They kept money out of his reach so that he could not buy liquor. They warned neighbors and bartenders against his habits. They sent him to a rest farm for the cure. But even there he managed to get something to drink.

One weekend Don was left alone while Wick went to the country. As soon as his brother had gone, Don took the money Wick had left for the housekeeper and went out to buy liquor. He went into a bar and chatted with Gloria, the hostess. He told her about his life, about his wife who was frigid, his children, and other details all equally fantastic and imaginary. He asked Gloria to meet him later. After being convinced that he was not joking, she accepted.

That night Don went into another bar and began drinking heavily. While there, idly watching a young couple, he suddenly decided to steal the girl's purse. He would do it only as a joke, he told himself. Later he could return the purse and they would all laugh at his prank. He picked up the purse and slipped it under his coat, acting calmly and naturally all the time, but as he was walking out a waiter stopped him. Luckily, the girl did not want to press charges. Don was pushed out into the street.

He went from one bar to another. When he drifted back to Sam's bar, Gloria was angry because he had forgotten his date with her. He could not understand why she asked him about his wife and his children, because he had neither. Next morning he found that his money had disappeared and that there was no money in the apartment. He decided to pawn his typewriter. He walked up and down the streets, but all the pawnshops were closed because it was a Jewish holiday. He went home, changed his clothes, and borrowed ten dollars from a nearby merchant. He went out to drink again. Coming back, he fell down a flight of stairs and lost consciousness.

When he awoke, he was in the alcoholic ward of a hospital. With him were a doctor and Bim, a male nurse. He wanted his clothes, he insisted; he wanted to go home. At last the doctor told him that he could go if he would sign a paper absolving the hospital of all responsibility.

Leaving the hospital, Don went straight to his apartment, where he fell asleep. The ringing of the telephone awoke him. He could not remember when he had last eaten. When he tried to get up, he almost collapsed, and he sank, exhausted, into a chair. After a while he heard a key in the lock. It was Helen, coming to see how he was getting along while Wick was away. She helped him to get dressed and took him to her apartment. When the maid came in, Helen went out on an errand. Don tried to get the key to the closet, but the maid pretended that she had no idea where it was. Don was growing more and more desperate for liquor. Before Helen left the apartment, he had called to her in terror because he thought a bat was devouring a mouse in the room. His thirst was growing worse. Seeing Helen's fur coat, he seized it and ran out of the apartment. He pawned the coat for five dollars and bought several pints of whiskey. He went back to his own apartment. Afraid that Wick might return, he hid one bottle in the bathroom and suspended the other on a string outside his window.

He lay down on the bed and took a long drink of whiskey. He felt wonderful. The ordeal was over; he had come through once more. There was no telling what might happen the next time, but he saw no reason to worry now. He wondered why Wick and Helen made such a fuss about it all.

LOYALTIES

Type of work: Drama
Author: John Galsworthy (1867-1933)
Type of plot: Social criticism
Time of plot: Early 1920's
Locale: London
First presented: 1922

Principal characters:
FERDINAND DE LEVIS, a rich young Jew
CAPTAIN RONALD DANCY, D. S. O., retired
MABEL, his wife

Critique:

Loyalties is one of the first plays to deal honestly and openly with the problem of anti-Semitism. Galsworthy takes such pains to deal fairly with both sides of the question, however, that he comes close to destroying his own thesis. The most completely drawn character is probably Captain Dancy, a man of action trying to adjust himself to a static society and finding an outlet in anti-social behavior. Although he does not ask us to condone Dancy's behavior, Galsworthy certainly enables us to understand it.

The Story:

Having retired from His Majesty's service, young Captain Ronald Dancy, D.S.O., was at loose ends as to what to do with himself. Accustomed to a life of action, he at first absorbed himself in horses and women, but he found in neither the violent excitement he craved. His stable was so expensive that he was at last forced to give his Rosemary filly to his friend, Ferdinand De Levis, because he could no longer afford to keep her. As for his women, he decided to throw them all over and marry a woman who admired him, and who had the spirit which Ronny desired in his wife.

In spite of the fact that he was obviously penniless, Ronny managed to keep his memberships in his favorite London clubs, and friends invited him and his wife to their weekend parties in the country. At Meldon Court, the home of his old friend, Charles Winsor, Ronny discovered that De Levis had sold for a thousand pounds the horse Ronny had given him. He was naturally embittered by the discovery, and later in the evening his resentment prompted him to bet De Levis ten pounds that he could jump to the top of a bookcase four feet high. He won his bet, but De Levis was contemptuous of a man who would indulge in such parlor games for the sake of a little money.

Around midnight, Winsor and his wife were awakened by De Levis, who announced that the thousand pounds he had received for the sale of the filly had been stolen from under his pillow. De Levis demanded an investigation. The Winsors were reluctant to incriminate either their servants or their guests, but at the insistence of De Levis the police were called.

Ronny's friends immediately arrayed themselves against De Levis for his tactlessness in handling the matter. He instantly interpreted their attitude as the result of prejudice because he was a Jew, and Ronny substantiated his conclusion by taunting De Levis with his race. Although they tried desperately to be fair, Ronny's friends had to admit that De Levis had behaved badly, and they suddenly remembered that his father had sold carpets wholesale in the city. After all, De Levis was a little too pushing; in spite of his money he did not exactly belong to the Mayfair and country set.

De Levis carried into the club to which

both men belonged the enmity aroused by Ronny's insult to his race, and he openly accused Ronny of the theft. Ronny immediately challenged him to a duel, but since such barbaric customs were no longer tolerated among gentlemen, De Levis was saved.

Ronny urged his wife Mabel to go with him to Nairobi. But she, believing in her husband's innocence, begged him to remain and fight for his good name. Realizing that to do otherwise would be an admission of guilt, Ronny consulted a lawyer and entered a suit against De Levis for defamation of character. However, the lawyer selected to defend Ronny's case was the worst choice that a man in Ronny's position could possibly have made. Old Jacob Twisden, senior partner of the firm of Twisden and Graviter, was a lawyer of the old school who believed that simple justice should take precedence over all loyalties, whether they were racial, economic, social, political, or merely personal.

In addition to the fact that he had stolen De Levis's money, Ronny had also withheld from his wife and his friends his relations with an Italian girl before his marriage. The girl's father, a wine dealer named Ricardos, had threatened to inform Ronny's wife of the relationship unless he provided for the girl. Out of fear, Ronny had been prompted to make a daring jump from his room to that of De Levis to obtain the money with which to pay Ricardos. The stolen notes were eventually identified as having passed through these different hands. When Twisden learned the true circumstances on which the case he was defending were based, he advised Ronny to drop the suit and leave the country as soon as possible. In that proposal he was seconded by Ronny's own superior officer, General Canynge, who offered Ronny a way out with a billet in the Spanish war.

When De Levis discovered that the suit was to be dropped, he appeared willing to let bygones be bygones because he felt that he had been vindicated; he wanted no money in return. But Ronny's problems were still unsolved. When he confessed to his wife the truth about all that had happened, she at first refused to believe his story. At last she agreed to follow Ronny wherever he might choose to go. Before Ronny could make his escape, however, the police arrived with a warrant for his arrest. He fled to his room and called to the officers to come and get him. Before they could reach him, he had shot himself.

What Ronny never knew was that both he and De Levis were victims of social conventions. Because Ronny belonged, his friends had been loyal. But loyalty, as they now realized, was not enough.

MACBETH

Type of work: Drama
Author: William Shakespeare (1564-1616)
Type of plot: Romantic tragedy
Time of plot: Eleventh century
Locale: Scotland
First presented: 1606

Principal characters:
MACBETH, a Scottish thane
LADY MACBETH, his wife
DUNCAN, King of Scotland
MALCOLM, his son
BANQUO, a Scottish chieftain
MACDUFF, a rebel lord

Critique:

The Tragedy of Macbeth, one of Shakespeare's shortest dramas, is the story of a highly imaginative, ambitious and conscience-stricken nobleman whose wife drove him to murder. Macbeth, at first a man of honor and integrity, had one major flaw — ambition. When the opportunity for power was presented to him, he committed his first crime. Later he was forced into utter degradation in order to conceal that first evil step. The macabre settings of *Macbeth,* the gloomy castle and the eerie heath, are in keeping with the weird tone of the whole play.

The Story:

On a lonely heath in Scotland, three witches sang their riddling runes and said that soon they would meet Macbeth.

Macbeth was the noble thane of Glamis, recently victorious in a great battle against Vikings and Scottish rebels. For his brave deeds, King Duncan intended to confer upon him the lands of the rebellious thane of Cawdor.

But before Macbeth saw the king, he and his friend Banquo met the three weird witches upon the dark moor. The wild and frightful women greeted Macbeth by first calling him thane of Glamis, then thane of Cawdor, and finally, King of Scotland. Too, they prophesied that Banquo's heirs would reign in Scotland in years to come.

When Macbeth tried to question the three hags, they vanished. Macbeth thought very little about the strange prophecy until he met one of Duncan's messengers, who told him that he was now thane of Cawdor. This piece of news stunned Macbeth, and he turned to Banquo to confirm the witches' prophecy. But Banquo, unduped by the witches, thought them evil enough to betray Macbeth by whetting his ambition and tricking him into fulfilling the prophecy. Macbeth did not heed Banquo's warning; the words of the witches as they called him king had gone deep into his soul. He pondered over the possibility of becoming a monarch and set his whole heart on the attainment of this goal. If he could be thane of Cawdor, perhaps he could rule all of Scotland as well. But as it was now, Duncan was king, with two sons to rule after him. The problem was great. Macbeth shook off his ambitious dreams to go with Banquo to greet Duncan.

A perfect ruler, Duncan was kind, majestic, gentle, strong; Macbeth was fond of him. But when Duncan mentioned that his son, Malcolm, would succeed him on the throne, Macbeth saw the boy as an obstacle in his own path, and he hardly dared admit to himself how this impediment disturbed him.

On a royal procession, Duncan announced that he would spend one night at Macbeth's castle. Lady Macbeth, who knew of the witches' prophecy, was even more ambitious than her husband, and she saw Duncan's visit as a perfect opportunity for Macbeth to become king. She determined that he should murder Duncan and usurp the throne.

That night there was much feasting in the castle. After everyone was asleep, Lady Macbeth told her husband of her plan for the king's murder. Horrified at first, Macbeth refused to do the deed. But on being accused of cowardice by his wife, and having bright prospects of his future dangled before his eyes, Macbeth finally succumbed to her demands. He stole into the sleeping king's chamber and plunged a knife into his heart.

The murder was blamed on two grooms whom Lady Macbeth had smeared with Duncan's blood while they were asleep. But the deed was hardly without suspicion in the castle, and when the murder was revealed, the dead king's sons fled — Malcolm to England, Donalbain to Ireland. Macbeth was proclaimed king. But Macduff, a nobleman who had been Duncan's close friend, also carefully noted the murder, and when Macbeth was crowned king, Macduff suspected him of the bloody killing.

Macbeth began to have horrible dreams; his mind was never free from fear. Often he thought of the witches' second prophecy, that Banquo's heirs would hold the throne, and the prediction tormented him. Macbeth was so determined that Banquo would never share in his own hard-earned glory that he resolved to murder Banquo and his son, Fleance.

Lady Macbeth and her husband gave a great banquet for the noble thanes of Scotland. At the same time, Macbeth sent murderers to waylay Banquo and his son before they could reach the palace. Banquo was slain in the scuffle, but Fleance escaped. Meanwhile in the large banquet hall Macbeth pretended great sorrow that Banquo was not present. But Banquo was present in spirit, and his ghost majestically appeared in Macbeth's own seat. The startled king was so frightened that he almost betrayed his guilt when he alone saw the apparition. Lady Macbeth quickly led him away and dismissed the guests.

More frightened than ever, thinking of Banquo's ghost which had returned to haunt him, and of Fleance who had escaped but might one day claim the throne, Macbeth was so troubled that he determined to seek solace from the witches on the dismal heath. They assured Macbeth that he would not be overcome by man born of woman, nor until the forest of Birnam came to Dunsinane Hill. They warned him to beware of Macduff. When Macbeth asked if Banquo's children would reign over the kingdom, the witches disappeared. The news they gave him brought him cheer. Macbeth felt he need fear no man, since all were born of women, and certainly the great Birnam forest could not be moved by human power.

Then Macbeth heard that Macduff was gathering a hostile army in England, an army to be led by Malcolm, Duncan's son, who was determined to avenge his father's murder. So terrified was Macbeth that he resolved to murder Macduff's wife and children in order to bring the rebel to submission. After this slaughter, however, Macbeth was more than ever tormented by fear; his twisted mind had almost reached the breaking point, and he longed for death to release him from his nightmarish existence.

Before long Lady Macbeth's strong will broke. Dark dreams of murder and violence drove her to madness. The horror of her crimes and the agony of being hated and feared by all of Macbeth's subjects made her so ill that her death seemed imminent.

On the eve of Macduff's attack on Macbeth's castle, Lady Macbeth died, depriving her husband of all courage she had given him in the past. Rallying, Macbeth summoned strength to meet his enemy. Meanwhile, Birnam wood had moved, for Malcolm's soldiers were hidden behind cut green boughs, which from a distance appeared to be a moving forest. Macduff, enraged by the slaughter of his innocent family, was determined to meet Macbeth in hand-to-hand conflict.

Macbeth went out to battle filled with the false courage given him by the witches' prophecy that no man born of woman would overthrow him. Meeting Macduff, Macbeth began to fight him, taunting him at the same time about his having been born of woman. But Macduff had been ripped alive from his mother's womb. The prophecy was fulfilled. Macbeth fought with waning strength, all hope of victory gone, and Macduff, with a flourish, severed the head of the bloody King of Scotland.

McTEAGUE

Type of work: Novel
Author: Frank Norris (1870-1902)
Type of plot: Naturalism
Time of plot: 1890's
Locale: San Francisco and Death Valley
First published: 1899

Principal characters:
McTEAGUE, a dentist
TRINA, his wife
MARCUS SCHOULER, McTeague's friend and Trina's cousin

Critique:

McTeague, generally considered the best of Norris' novels, falls into the category of naturalism, a mode popular in the early 1900's. Two characteristics of this school were the hero of much brawn and few brains, and the influences of heredity and environment upon character. McTeague, Trina, and Marcus are drawn inevitably to catastrophe through their own inherited qualities acted upon by environmental forces. The novel is at once powerful and terrifying.

The Story:

McTeague, born in a small mining town, worked with his unambitious father in the mines. But his mother saw in her son a chance to realize her own dreams. The opportunity to send him away for a better education came a few years after McTeague's father had died. A traveling dentist was prevailed upon to take the boy as an apprentice.

McTeague learned something of dentistry, but he was too stupid to understand much of it. When his mother died and left him a small sum of money, he set up his own practice in an office-bedroom in San Francisco. McTeague was easily satisfied. He had his concertina for amusement and enough money from his practice to keep him well supplied with beer.

In the flat above McTeague lived his friend, Marcus Schouler. Marcus was in love with his cousin, Trina Sieppe, whom he brought to McTeague for some dental work. While they were waiting for McTeague to finish with a patient, the cleaning woman sold Trina a lottery ticket.

McTeague immediately fell in love with Trina. Marcus, realizing his friend's attachment, rather enjoyed playing the martyr, setting aside his own love in order that McTeague might feel free to court Trina. He invited the dentist to go with him to call on the Sieppe family. From that day on McTeague was a steady visitor at the Sieppe home. To celebrate their engagement, McTeague took Trina and her family to the theater. Afterward they returned to McTeague's flat, to find the building in an uproar. Trina's lottery ticket had won five thousand dollars.

In preparation for their wedding, Trina was furnishing a flat across from McTeague's office. When she decided to invest her winnings and collect the monthly interest, the dentist was disappointed, for he had hoped to spend the money on something lavish and exciting. But Trina's wishes prevailed. With that income and McTeague's earnings, as well as the little that Trina earned from her hand-carved animals, the McTeagues could be assured of a comfortable life.

Marcus slowly changed in his attitude toward his friend and his cousin. One day he accused McTeague of stealing Trina's affection for the sake of the five thousand dollars. In his fury he struck at his old friend with a knife. McTeague was not hurt, but his anger was thoroughly aroused.

In the early months after their wedding, McTeague and Trina were extremely happy. Trina was tactful in the changes she began to make in her husband. Gradually she improved his manners and appearance. They both planned for the time when they could afford a home of their own. Because of those plans they had their first real quarrel. McTeague wanted to rent a nearby house, but Trina objected to the high rent. Her thriftiness was slowly turning into miserliness. When McTeague, unknown to her, rented the house, she refused to move or to contribute to the payment of the first month's rent which signing of the lease entailed.

Some days later they went on a picnic to which Marcus was also invited. Outwardly he and McTeague had settled their differences, but jealousy still rankled in Marcus. When some wrestling matches were held, Marcus and the dentist were the winners in their bouts. It now remained for the two winners to compete. No match for the brute strength of McTeague, Marcus was thrown. Furious, he demanded another match. In that match Marcus suddenly leaned forward and bit off the lobe of the dentist's ear. McTeague broke Marcus' arm in his anger.

Marcus soon left San Francisco. Shortly thereafter an order from City Hall disbarred McTeague from his practice because he lacked college training. Marcus had informed the authorities.

Trina and McTeague moved from their flat to a tiny room on the top floor of the building, for the loss of McTeague's practice had made Trina more niggardly than ever. McTeague found a job making dental supplies. Trina devoted almost every waking moment to her animal carvings. She allowed herself and the room to become slovenly, she begrudged every penny they spent, and when McTeague lost his job she insisted that they move to even cheaper lodgings. McTeague began to drink, and drinking made him vicious. When he was drunk, he would pinch or bite Trina until she gave him money for more whiskey.

The new room into which they moved was filthy and cramped. McTeague grew more and more surly. One morning he left to go fishing and failed to return. That night, while Trina was searching the streets for him, he broke into her trunk and stole her hoarded savings. After his disappearance Trina learned that the paint she used on her animals had infected her hand. The fingers of her right hand were amputated.

Trina took a job as a scrub woman, and the money she earned together with the interest from her five thousand dollars was sufficient to support her. Now that the hoard of money that she had saved was gone, she missed the thrill of counting over the coins, and so she withdrew the whole of her five thousand dollars from the bank and hid the coins in her room. One evening there was a tap on her window. McTeague was standing outside, hungry and without a place to sleep. Trina angrily refused to let him in. A few evenings later, drunk and vicious, he broke into a room she was cleaning. When she refused to give him any money, he beat her until she fell unconscious. She died early next morning.

McTeague took her money and went back to the mines, where he fell in with another prospector. But McTeague was haunted by the thought that he was being followed. One night he stole away from his companion and started south across Death Valley. The next day, as he was resting, he was suddenly accosted by a man with a gun. The man was Marcus.

A posse had been searching for McTeague ever since Trina's body had been found, and as soon as Marcus heard about the murder he volunteered for the manhunt. While the two men stood facing each other in the desert, Mc-

Teague's mule ran away, carrying on its back a canteen bag of water. Marcus emptied his gun to kill the animal, but its dead body fell on the canteen bag and the water was lost. The five thousand dollars was also lashed to the back of the mule. As McTeague went to unfasten it, Marcus seized him. In the struggle McTeague killed his enemy with his bare hands. But as he slipped to the ground, Marcus managed to snap one handcuff to McTeague's wrist, the other to his own. McTeague looked stupidly around, at the hills about a hundred miles away, and at the dead body to which he was helplessly chained. He was trapped in the parching inferno of the desert that stretched away on every side.

MADAME BOVARY

Type of work: Novel
Author: Gustave Flaubert (1821-1880)
Type of plot: Psychological realism
Time of plot: Mid-nineteenth century
Locale: France
First published: 1857

Principal characters:
CHARLES BOVARY, a provincial doctor
EMMA, his wife
LÉON DUPUIS, a young lawyer
RODOLPHE BOULANGER, a wealthy landowner

Critique:

Flaubert's genius lay in his infinite capacity for taking pains, and *Madame Bovary,* so true in its characterizations, so vivid in its setting, so convincing in its plot, is ample testimony to the realism of his work. This novel was one of the first of its type to come out of France, and its truth shocked contemporary readers. Condemned on the one hand for picturing the life of a romantic adulteress, he was acclaimed on the other for the honesty and skill with which he handled his subject. Flaubert does not permit Emma Bovary to escape the tragedy which she brings upon herself. Emma finds diversion from the monotony of her life, but she finds it at the loss of her own self-respect. The truth of Emma's struggle is universal and challenging.

The Story:

Charles Bovary was a student of medicine who married for his own advancement a woman much older than himself. She made his life miserable with her nagging and groundless suspicions. One day Charles was called to the bedside of M. Rouault, who had a broken leg, and there he met the farmer's daughter, Emma, a beautiful but restless girl whose early education in a French convent had given her an overwhelming thirst for broader experience. Charles found his patient an excellent excuse to see Emma, whose charm and grace had captivated the young doctor. But his whining wife, Héloise, soon began to suspect the true reason for his visits to the Rouault farm. She heard rumors that in spite of Emma's peasant background, the girl conducted herself like a gentlewoman. Angry and tearful, Héloise made Charles swear that he would not visit the Rouault home again. Then Héloise's fortune was found to be non-existent. There was a violent quarrel over her deception and a stormy scene between her and the parents of Charles brought on an attack of an old illness. Héloise died quickly and quietly.

Charles felt guilty because he had so few regrets at his wife's death. At old Rouault's invitation, he went once more to the farm and again fell under the influence of Emma's charms. As old Rouault watched Charles fall more deeply in love with his daughter, he decided that the young doctor was dependable and perfectly respectable, and so he forced the young man's hand, told Charles he could have Emma in marriage, and gave the couple his blessing.

During the first weeks of marriage Emma occupied herself with changing their new home, and busied herself with every household task she could think of to keep herself from being utterly disillusioned. Emma realized that even though she thought she was in love with Charles, the rapture which should have come with marriage had not arrived. All the romantic books she had read during her early years had led her to expect more from marriage than she received, and the dead calm of her feelings was a bitter disappointment. The intimacy of marriage disgusted her. Instead of a perfumed, handsome lover in velvet and lace, she found herself tied to a dull-witted husband who reeked of medicines and drugs.

As she was about to give up all hope of finding any joy in her new life, a noble patient whom Charles had treated invited them to a ball at his chateau. At the ball Emma danced with a dozen partners, tasted champagne, and received compliments on her beauty. The contrast between the life of the Bovarys and that of the nobleman was painfully evident. Emma became more and more discontented with Charles. His futile and clumsy efforts to please her only made her despair at his lack of understanding. She sat by her window, dreamed of Paris, moped, and became ill.

Hoping a change would improve her condition, Charles took Emma to Yonville, where he set up a new practice and Emma prepared for the birth of a child.

When her daughter was born, Emma's chief interest in the child was confined to laces and ribbons for its dresses. The child was sent to a wet nurse, where Emma visited her, and where, accidentally, she met Léon Dupuis, a law clerk bored with the town and seeking diversion. Charmed with the youthful mother, he walked home with her in the twilight, and Emma found him sympathetic to her romantic ideas about life. Later Léon visited the Bovarys in company with Homais, the town chemist. Homais held little soirees at the local inn, to which he invited the townsfolk. There Emma's acquaintance with Léon ripened. The townspeople gossiped about the couple, but Charles Bovary was not acute enough to sense the interest Emma took in Léon.

Bored with Yonville and tired of loving in vain, Léon went to Paris to complete his studies. Broken-hearted, Emma deplored her weakness in not giving herself to Léon, fretted in her boredom, and once more made herself ill.

She had not time to become as melancholy as she was before, however, for a stranger, Rodolphe Boulanger, came to town. One day he brought his farm tenant to Charles for bloodletting. Rodolphe, an accomplished lover, saw in Emma a promise of future pleasure. When he began his suit, Emma realized that if she gave herself to him her surrender would be immoral. But she rationalized her doubts by convincing herself that nothing as romantic and beautiful as love could be sinful.

Deceiving Charles, Emma met Rodolphe, rode over the countryside with him, listened to his urgent avowals of love, and finally succumbed to his persuasive appeals. At first she felt guilty, but later she identified herself with adulterous heroines of fiction and believed that, like them, she had known true romance. Sure of Emma's love, Rodolphe no longer found it necessary to continue his gentle lover's tricks. He no longer bothered to maintain punctuality in his meetings with Emma; and though he continued to see her, she began to suspect that his passion was dwindling.

Meanwhile Charles became involved

in Homais' attempt to cure a boy of a clubfoot with a machine Charles had designed. Both Homais and Charles were convinced that the success of their operation would raise their future standing in the community. But after weeks of torment, the boy contracted gangrene, and his leg had to be amputated. Homais' reputation was undamaged, for he was by profession a chemist, but Bovary, a doctor, was looked upon with suspicion. His practice began to fall away.

Disgusted with Charles' failure, Emma, in an attempt to hold Rodolphe, scorned her past virtue, spent money recklessly on jewelry and clothes, and involved her husband deeply in debt. She finally secured Rodolphe's word that he would take her away, but on the very eve of what was to be her escape she received from him a letter so hypocritically repentant of their sin that she read it with sneers. Then, in horror over the realization that she had lost him, she almost threw herself from the window. She was saved when Charles called to her. But she became gravely ill with brain-fever, and lay near death for several months.

Her convalescence was slow, but she was finally well enough to go to Rouen to the theater. The tender love scenes behind the footlights made Emma breathless with envy. Once more, she dreamed of romance. In Rouen she met Léon Dupuis again.

This time Léon was determined to possess Emma. He listened to her complaints with sympathy, soothed her, and took her driving. Emma, whose thirst for romance still consumed her, yielded herself to Léon with regret that she had not done so before.

Charles Bovary grew concerned over his increasing debts. In addition to his own financial worries, his father died, leaving his mother in ignorance about the family estate. Emma used the excuse of procuring a lawyer for her mother-in-law to visit Léon in Rouen, where he had set up a practice. At his suggestion she secured a power of attorney from Charles, a document which left her free to spend his money without his knowledge of her purchases.

Finally, in despair over his debts, the extent of which Emma only partly revealed, Charles took his mother into his confidence and promised to destroy Emma's power of attorney. Deprived of her hold over Charles' finances and unable to repay her debts, Emma threw herself upon Léon's mercy with all disregard for caution. Her corruption was so complete that she had to seek release and pleasure or go out of her mind.

In her growing degradation, Emma began to realize that she had brought her lover down with her. She no longer respected him, and she scorned his faithfulness when he was unable to give her money she needed to pay her bills. When her name was posted publicly for a debt of several thousand francs, the bailiff prepared to sell Charles' property to settle her creditors' claims. Charles was out of town when the debt was posted, and Emma, in one final act of self-abasement, appealed to Rodolphe for help. He, too, refused to lend her money.

Knowing that the framework of lies with which she had deceived Charles was about to collapse, Emma Bovary resolved to die a heroine's death and swallowed arsenic bought at Homais' shop. Charles, returning from his trip, arrived too late to save her from a slow, painful death.

Charles, pitiful in his grief, could barely endure the sounds of the hammer as her coffin was nailed shut. Later, feeling that his pain over Emma's death had grown less, he opened her desk, to find there the carefully collected love letters of Léon and Rodolphe. Broken with the knowledge of his wife's infidelity, scourged with debt, and helpless in his disillusionment, Charles died soon after his wife, leaving a legacy of only twelve francs for the support of his orphaned daughter. The Bovary tragedy was complete.

MADEMOISELLE DE MAUPIN

Type of work: Novel
Author: Théophile Gautier (1811-1872)
Type of plot: Sentimental romance
Time of plot: Early nineteenth century
Locale: France
First published: 1835

Principal characters:
M. D'ALBERT, a young esthete
ROSETTE, his mistress
THÉODORE DE SÉRANNES, in reality Mademoiselle Madelaine de Maupin

Critique:

France, in the 1830's, was going through one of those occasional periods of high morality which at intervals excite the world, and Gautier, disgusted with the hypocrisy of many of the period's defenders, wrote this romance of passion as his challenge to the period. In a long and boastful preface he pleads the cause of moral freedom in art. The novel is highly sensual, its plot based partly on history and partly on Shakespeare's *As You Like It.*

The Story:

D'Albert was a young Frenchman of twenty-two, handsome, well-educated, artistic, and well-versed in the affairs of the world. He loved beauty, especially female beauty. All his life he had dreamed of women, but he had never met the girl of his dreams, who would combine the beauty of a Ruben's nude with that of a Titian nude. It was little wonder that he had not found her.

The one thing lacking in d'Albert's life was a mistress. One day his friend de C—— offered to take him around the town and discourse on the various ladies of his acquaintance so that d'Albert could make a choice. The expedition was a delightful one, as de C—— seemed to have precise and full information on every beauty, not only on her outward circumstances, but also on the very quality of her mind. D'Albert, after some hesitation, finally decided to lay siege to Rosette, a beautiful young woman who seemed the most likely to bring his romantic and poetic mind down to earth.

It did not take d'Albert long to win the love of Rosette, and they were soon acknowledged lovers. Rosette was pliable, versatile, and always entertaining. She did not let d'Albert alone long enough for him to go off into musing daydreams. Variety was the spice of their love.

For five months the two continued to be the happiest of lovers, but at last d'Albert began to tire of Rosette. As soon as she noticed the cooling of his ardor, Rosette knew that she must do something different if she wished to keep his love. If he were growing tired of her in the solitary life they were leading, perhaps he would regain his interest if he saw her among a group of people. For this reason Rosette took d'Albert to her country estate for a visit. There she planned parties, dinners, and visits to keep him amused, but he remained bored.

One day a visitor, an old friend of Rosette, arrived. The guest was an extremely handsome young man named Théodore de Sérannes, whose conversation, riding, and swordsmanship all entranced d'Albert. The two men met every day and went hunting together, and the more d'Albert saw of Théodore the more fascinated he became. In time d'Albert was forced to admit to himself that he was in love with Théodore.

He was in love with a man, and yet he always thought of him as a woman. D'Albert's mind grew sick with the problem of Théodore's true identity. Some days he would be sure that Théodore was a woman in disguise. Then, seeing him fencing or jumping his horse, d'Albert would be forced to conclude that Théodore was a man. Rosette, he knew, was also in love with Théodore, and her infatuation kept her from noticing d'Albert's interest in the same young man.

One day d'Albert mentioned that his favorite play was Shakespeare's *As You Like It.* The rest of the company immediately decided to present the play. At first Rosette was chosen for the part of Rosalind, the heroine who dressed as a man in order to escape from her uncle, but when she refused to wear men's clothes the part was given to Théodore.

As soon as d'Albert saw Théodore dressed in woman's clothes, he guessed rightly that Théodore really was a woman. What he did not know was that Théodore, who was really named Madelaine de Maupin, had decided that she would have nothing to do with men until she had found a good and noble lover. She knew that as a woman she would have no chance to see men as they really were, and so she had hit upon the device of learning about them by dressing as a man. But she had found perfidy and falseness in every man she met. Mademoiselle de Maupin had with amusement seen d'Albert fall in love with her, and she had watched the tortures of his mind when he could not decide whether she was male or female.

As the rehearsals of the play went on, the parallels between the play and real life became even more amusing to both d'Albert and Mademoiselle de Maupin. At last, after the play had been presented, d'Albert wrote Mademoiselle de Maupin a letter. In it he said that he was sure she was a woman, and that he loved her deeply.

She took so long to reply to his letter that d'Albert again became afraid that she really was a man. One night, however, as d'Albert stood at a window a hand gently touched his shoulder. He looked around and beheld Mademoiselle de Maupin dressed in her costume as Rosalind. He was struck dumb with amazement. Mademoiselle de Maupin told him her story, and said that since he was the first man to see through her disguise, he should be the man to first have her as a woman.

That night d'Albert learned that she was truly the woman of his dreams. In the morning he found himself alone. Mademoiselle de Maupin had gone, leaving a letter in which she told d'Albert and Rosette that they would never see her again. She wrote to d'Albert that they had known one perfect night. She had answered his dream, and to fulfill a dream once was enough. Her letter ended by telling d'Albert to try to console Rosette for the love she had wasted on the false Théodore, and she hoped that the two would be very happy for many years to come.

MAGGIE: A GIRL OF THE STREETS

Type of work: Novel
Author: Stephen Crane (1871-1900)
Type of plot: Social criticism
Time of plot: Late nineteenth century
Locale: New York
First published: 1893

Principal characters:
MAGGIE, a girl of the slums
JIMMY, her brother
PETE, Jimmy's friend and Maggie's lover
THE MOTHER

Critique:

The importance of *Maggie* is primarily historical, for it was the first novel to deal realistically and straightforwardly with the sordid life of the slums. It is, therefore, the first naturalistic novel in America of any real value, and in spite of its many faults of style and structure it gave rise to the naturalistic fiction of our day. For this contribution to our literature we owe Stephen Crane a great debt.

The Story:

In the slum section of New York City, Maggie and her two brothers grew up in the squalor and corruption, both moral and physical, of that poverty-stricken area. Her father usually came home from work drunk, and her mother, too, was fond of the bottle. The children were neglected. When the drunken parents ranted at each other, the children hid in terror under the table or the bed.

Somehow Maggie managed to remain untouched by that sordidness. Her younger brother died. Jimmy, her older brother, went to work after the father died. He fought, drank, and had many affairs with women. From time to time he was hounded by some of the women, who demanded support for themselves and the illegitimate children he had fathered. Jimmy brushed them aside.

When Jimmy brought his best friend home with him, Maggie fell in love. Pete, a bartender, was handsome, flashy, and exciting. One night he took her out to show her the night life of the city. Maggie's wonder knew no bounds, for to her the experience was the height of luxury. On the doorstep she allowed Pete to kiss her goodnight. Pete was disappointed, but not discouraged. He took Maggie out again. The next time she surrendered and went to live with him.

But Pete soon grew tired of Maggie, and she was compelled to return home. In furious indignation, her mother ordered her out of the house. She had done everything, the mother insisted, to bring Maggie up to be a fine, decent girl. She had been an excellent mother and had spared no pains to keep her daughter on the path of virtue. Now her daughter would be dead to her. The neighbors joined in, denouncing Maggie. Jimmy, the seducer of other men's sisters, became indignant. He and a companion went to the bar where Pete worked, intent upon beating him up. When they failed, Jimmy contented himself by shrugging his shoulders and condemning his sister.

Maggie was now homeless and penniless. She went to see Pete, but he sent her away, irritated and fearful lest he should lose his job. She turned to prostitution, plying her trade by night, accosting poor and wealthy alike. But she did not have much luck. One night she walked forlornly and unsuccessfully in the waterfront district. Resignedly she trudged on, toward the pier and the black, murky depths of the river.

A short time later, Jimmy came home from one of his prolonged absences. Maggie, the mother wailed, was dead. With the neighbors around her, she sobbed and moaned. What the Lord had given the Lord had taken away, the neighbors told her. Uncomforted, Maggie's mother shrieked that she forgave her daughter; oh yes, she forgave Maggie her sins.

THE MAGIC MOUNTAIN

Type of work: Novel
Author: Thomas Mann (1875-   )
Type of plot: Philosophical chronicle
Time of plot: 1907-1914
Locale: Davos, Switzerland
First published: 1924

Principal characters:
HANS CASTORP, a German engineer
JOACHIM ZIEMSSEN, his cousin
SETTEMBRINI, a patient at Davos
NAPHTA, Settembrini's friend
CLAVDIA, Hans' friend

Critique:

The Magic Mountain is a novel concerned with perspectives of history and philosophy in our time. In it the modern age has become the International Sanatorium Berghof high in the Swiss Alps, and to this institution gravitate various and conflicting currents of thought and activity in the persons of a group of invalids exiled by disease to a pinnacle of the "magic mountain." The magic it exercises in their lives is to cut them off from calendar time. Time flows through their days and years with quiet nothingness and perceptions of reality stretch into eternity. Modern ideologies and beliefs are represented by characters like the Italian humanist, the absolutist Jewish Jesuit, a German doctor, a Polish scientist, and hedonistic Mynheer Peeperkorn. The magic mountain is the sick world of Europe, and its people are various aspects of the modern consciousness.

The Story:

Hans Castorp had been advised by his doctor to go to the mountains for a rest. Accordingly, he decided to visit his cousin, Joachim Ziemssen, who was a patient in the International Sanatorium Berghof at Davos-Platz in the mountains of Switzerland. He planned to stay there for three weeks and then return to his home in Hamburg. Hans had just passed his examinations and was now a qualified engineer; he was eager to get started in his career. His cousin was a soldier by profession. His cure at the sanatorium was almost complete. Hans thought Joachim looked robust and well.

At the sanatorium, Hans soon discovered that the ordinary notions of time did not exist. Day followed day almost unchangingly. He met the head of the institution, Dr. Behrens, as well as the other patients, who, at dinner, sat in groups. There were, for instance, two Russian tables, one of which was known to the patients as the bad Russian table. A couple who sat at the latter table had the room next to Hans. Through the thin partitions, he could hear them—even in the daytime—chase each other around the room. Hans was rather revolted, inasmuch as he could hear every detail of their love-making.

There was another patient who interested him greatly, a gay Russian woman, supposedly married, named Clavdia Cauchat. Every time she came into the dining-room she would bang the door, an act which annoyed Hans a great deal. Hans also met Settembrini, an Italian, a humanist writer and philosopher. Settembrini introduced him to a Jew, Naphta, who turned out to be a converted Jesuit and a cynical absolutist. Because the two men spent their time in endless discussions, Settembrini finally left the sanatorium to take rooms in the village, in the house where Naphta lodged.

From the very first day of his arrival, Hans felt feverish and a bit weak. When his three weeks were almost up, he decided to take a physical examination. The examination proved that he had tuberculosis. So he stayed on as a patient. One day, defying orders, he went out skiing and was caught in a snowstorm. The exposure aggravated his condition.

His interest in Clavdia was heightened when he learned that Dr. Behrens, who liked to dabble in art, had painted her picture. Further, the doctor gave Hans an X-ray plate of Clavdia's skeletal structure. The plate Hans kept on his bureau in his room.

Most of his free time he spent with Joachim or with Settembrini and Naphta. The Italian and the Jesuit were given to all sorts of ideas, and Hans became involved in a multitude of philosophical discussions on the duration of time, God, politics, astronomy, and the nature of reality. Joachim, who was rather humorless and unimaginative, did not enjoy those talks. But Hans, since he himself had become a patient at the sanatorium, felt more at home and was not quite so attached to Joachim. Besides, it was Clavdia who interested him.

On the occasion of a carnival, when some of the restrictions of the sanatorium had been lifted, Hans declared his love for Clavdia. She thought him foolish and refused his proposal. The next day she left for Russia. Hans was in despair and became listless. Joachim grew even more impatient with the progress of his cure when the doctor told him that he was not yet well and would have to remain on the mountain for six more months. Wanting to rejoin his regiment, Joachim, in defiance of the doctor's injunctions, left the sanatorium. The doctor told Hans that he could leave too; but Hans knew that the doctor was angry when he said it, and he remained.

Before long Joachim returned, his condition now so serious that his mother was summoned to the sanatorium. He died shortly afterward. Clavdia Cauchat also returned. She had been writing to the doctor and Hans had heard of her from time to time. But she did not return alone. As a protector, she had found an old Dutchman named Mynheer Peeperkorn, an earthy, hedonistic planter from Java. Hans became very friendly with Peeperkorn, who soon learned that the young engineer was in love with Clavdia. The discovery did not affect their friendship at all, a friendship that lasted until the Dutchman died.

For a time the guests amused themselves with spiritualist seances. A young girl, a new arrival at the sanatorium, claimed that she was able to summon anyone from the dead. Hans took part in one meeting and asked that Joachim be called back from the dead. But Dr. Krokowski, the psychologist at the sanatorium, was opposed to the seances and the sessions broke up. Then Naphta and Settembrini got into an argument. A duel was arranged between the two dialecticians. When the time came, the Italian said he would fire into the air. When he did so, Naphta became more furious than ever. Realizing that Settembrini would not shoot at him, Naphta turned the pistol on himself and pulled the trigger. Dying, he fell face downward in the snow.

Hans Castorp had come to the sanatorium for a visit of three weeks. That stay turned out to be more than seven years. During that time he saw many deaths, many changes in the institution. He became an old patient, not just a visitor. The sanatorium became another home in the high, thin air of the mountaintop. For him time, as measured by minutes, or even years, no longer existed. Time belonged to the flat, busy world below.

Then an Austrian archduke was assassinated. Newspapers brought the world suddenly to the International Sanatorium Berghof, with news of war declared and troop movements. Some of the patients remained in neutral Switzerland. Others packed to return home. Hans Castorp said goodbye to Settembrini, who was his best friend among the old patients, and the disillusioned humanist wept at their parting. Hans was going back to Germany to fight. Time, the tragic hour of his generation, had overtaken him at last, and the sanatorium was no longer his refuge. Dodging bullets and bombs in a front line trench, he disappeared into the smoky mists that hid the future of Europe.

THE MAGNIFICENT OBSESSION

Type of work: Novel
Author: Lloyd C. Douglas (1877-1951)
Type of plot: Quasi-mysticism
Time of plot: Early twentieth century
Locale: Detroit and Europe
First published: 1929

Principal characters:
DR. WAYNE HUDSON, a famous brain surgeon
HELEN BRENT HUDSON, the doctor's second wife
JOYCE HUDSON, the doctor's daughter and Helen's school friend
ROBERT MERRICK, a physician
NANCY ASHFORD, superintendent at the Hudson Clinic

Critique:

The author accomplishes in *The Magnificent Obsession* one of the most difficult problems in novel-writing, the exposition of an idea, and he makes an excellent case for the theory of extending personality and gaining moral power by doing good for other individuals. The motive behind the novel is, of course, to prove that Christian teachings can be applied to modern life, even in the case of the selfish materialist.

The Story:

The staff at the Hudson Clinic was worried about the head of the hospital, Dr. Wayne Hudson. The doctor had suddenly become nervous and haggard, a bad condition for an eminent practicing surgeon, and his staff tried to advise the doctor to take six months away from his work. The doctor himself surprised his staff by announcing that he was about to marry his daughter's school friend, Miss Helen Brent. The couple were married within a short time and went to live at the doctor's lakeside cottage.

Soon afterward a shocking tragedy occurred at the lake. Dr. Hudson drowned because the inhalator that might have saved his life had been dispatched across the lake to resuscitate a wealthy young playboy, Robert Merrick.

While he was recuperating from his experience, young Merrick felt that the doctors and the nurses at the Hudson clinic resented him. He did not yet know that it was at the expense of the life of the hospital's chief surgeon that he himself was alive. He questioned the superintendent of the clinic, Nancy Ashford, who had been in love with her chief, Doctor Hudson, but Miss Ashford did not give him a satisfactory answer. Later, overhearing a conversation, Merrick discovered why the people at the hospital seemed to despise him. He talked again to Nancy Ashford, who told him the only way he could ever make amends would be to take Dr. Hudson's place in life by becoming a great surgeon.

After weeks of pondering on the idea of going to medical school, Merrick decided that he would try to fill Dr. Hudson's place. When he went back to Nancy Ashford to tell her of his plans, she told him the story of the doctor's

THE MAGNIFICENT OBSESSION by Lloyd C. Douglas. By permission of the author and the publishers, Houghton Mifflin Co.

many philanthropies. She also gave him a book which the doctor had written in code. After many days and nights of perseverance, the young man managed to break the cipher. When he had done so, it seemed to him that the doctor, whom he had come to look upon as an ideal, had been a lunatic, for the book was a strange, mystic tract about doing good. From Nancy Ashford he learned that the deceased doctor had been a great mystic, believing that his gift as a surgeon came to him from what he called the Major Personality. That power was earned by doing good unknown to others, philanthropy that would aid the recipient in leading a valuable life of service.

During the next few years Merrick attended the state medical school. One night, as he sat studying, he suddenly felt a call to go to a night club where he knew Joyce Hudson, the doctor's daughter, was to be. After rescuing her from a drunken scene, he took her home. There he met the doctor's widow.

That semester Merrick almost failed at medical school. Discouraged with his own efforts, he decided to experiment with the knowledge he had gained from the dead surgeon's manuscript. He aided a fellow student, Dawson, who was about to leave school because he lacked funds. Immediately he felt renewed hope and plunged into his work with enthusiasm.

Helen Hudson, the doctor's widow, had gone to Europe, where she remained three years. Near the end of that time she discovered that the cousin who was handling her affairs was dishonest. Needing funds, she wrote to Nancy Ashford to ask if her stock in the Hudson Clinic could be sold. Nancy told Merrick, now a doctor at the clinic. He sent Helen twenty-five thousand dollars and sold some of the stock for her. Toward the end of her stay in Europe Helen met Mrs. Dawson, wife of the medical student whom Merrick had helped through medical school. Merrick had asked Mrs. Dawson to learn something of Helen's financial losses so that he might put her affairs in order. After telling Mrs. Dawson her troubles, Helen discovered an envelope Mrs. Dawson had addressed to Merrick. Helen promptly disappeared.

Merrick went to the cousin who was managing Helen's financial affairs. The man had robbed Helen of about one hundred thousand dollars. Merrick made good the loss and sent the man out of the country, bringing no charges against him because he was related to Helen. Before the cousin left, he learned Merrick's theory of personality projection and made up his mind to lead an honest life.

Tired from overwork, Merrick took a vacation in the country for several weeks. Then he returned to his laboratory and began a program of hard work. His meals were returned to the kitchen almost untouched. His labors were at last successful, for he perfected a scalpel which automatically cauterized by electricity. The device opened a new field of brain surgery because it prevented hemorrhage as it cut into the tissue.

About Christmas Helen returned to the United States. In Detroit she went to her trust company and asked to see the shares of stock which they held in her name. As she suspected, they had been transferred from Merrick. When she left the bank, she did not know whether to feel thankful or insulted.

Helen went from the bank to the Hudson Clinic, where she asked to see Merrick immediately. Her confusion was even greater when he told her he could not take back the money. He tried to explain the transfer of her stock, but she was in no mood for explanations. As he took her to the door they met her stepdaughter. Joyce complicated the tense situation by proposing a theater party for the next day. In order not to create gossip, both Helen and Merrick agreed to go to dinner and the theater afterward. As he handed Helen into the taxi, Merrick managed to murmur that he loved her.

The next evening at dinner Merrick

asked Helen not to tell all she had done for a needy Italian family at Assisi. He added that the philanthropy would thereby lose its value if the story were told.

The following summer Merrick went to Europe to visit eminent surgeons in Vienna and to demonstrate his cauterizing scalpel to them. While he was in Paris he heard that Helen had been injured in a train wreck near Rome. Hurrying to Rome, he operated on the injured woman and saved her life. Then, in quixotic fashion, he left Rome before anyone could tell her who had performed the delicate operation. Helen guessed Merrick's identity, however, from the few words he had mumbled in her presence. Weeks later, when she discovered that he was planning to visit her, Helen, ashamed of her previous attitude toward his interest in her affairs, arranged to leave for the United States. But Merrick flew to Le Havre ahead of her, arranged for their marriage, and met her on the dock. When she saw him waiting, she walked into his arms. She did not have to be told why he had come.

MAIN STREET

Type of work: Novel
Author: Sinclair Lewis (1885-1951)
Type of plot: Social satire
Time of plot: c. 1910-1920
Locale: Small Midwestern town
First published: 1920

Principal characters:
CAROL KENNICOTT, an idealist
DR. WILL KENNICOTT, her husband

Critique:

To puncture the egos of smug, self-satisfied Americans who consider their home towns flawless, Sinclair Lewis wrote *Main Street,* a novel which deals with the life of Gopher Prairie, a fictitious, small, and supposedly typical Midwestern town in Minnesota. Carol Kennicott is intent upon reforming not only her husband, a doctor in Gopher Prairie, but also the town. Lewis speaks blunt truths about the inadequacies of small-town life, but his satire is rarely vicious; and if the reader sees himself or his town reflected in the author's pages, he cannot help admitting that much that Lewis says is true, uncomfortable as truth may be.

The Story:

When Carol Milford was graduated from Blodgett College in Minnesota, she determined to conquer the world. Interested in sociology, and village improvement in particular, she often longed to set out on a crusade of her own to transform dingy prairie towns to thriving, beautiful communities. When she met Will Kennicott, a doctor from Gopher Prairie, and listened to his praise of his home town, she agreed to marry him. He had convinced her that Gopher Prairie needed her.

Carol was essentially an idealist. On the train, going to her new home, she deplored the run-down condition of the countryside and wondered about the future of the northern Middle West. Will did not listen to her ideas sympathetically. The people were happy, he said. Through town after town they traveled, Carol noting with sinking heart the shapeless mass of hideous buildings, the dirty depots, the flat wastes of prairie surrounding everything, and she knew that Gopher Prairie would be no different from the rest.

Gopher Prairie was exactly like the

other towns Carol had seen, except that it was a little larger. The people were as drab as their houses, as flat as their fields. A welcoming committee met the newlyweds at the train. To Carol, all the men were alike in their colorless clothes; over-friendly, over-enthusiastic. The Kennicott house was a Victorian horror. But Will said he liked it.

Introduced to the townsfolk at a party held in her honor, Carol heard the men talk of motor cars, train schedules, "furriners," and praise Gopher Prairie as God's own country. The women were interested in gossip, sewing, and cooking, and most of them belonged to the two women's clubs, the Jolly Seventeen and the Thanatopsis Club. At the first meeting of the Jolly Seventeen, Carol brought wrath upon her head when she stated that the duty of a librarian was to get people to read. The town librarian staunchly asserted that her primary trust was to preserve the books.

Carol did many things which were to cause her great unhappiness. She hired a maid and paid her the over-generous sum of six dollars a week. She gave a party with an Oriental motif. Sometimes she even kicked off a slipper under the table and revealed her arches. The women frowned on her unconventional behavior. Worse, she redecorated the old Kennicott house and got rid of the mildew, the ancient bric-a-brac, the dark wallpaper. Will protested against her desire to change things.

Carol also joined the Thanatopsis Club, for she hoped to use the club as a means of awakening interest in social reform. But the women of Gopher Prairie, while professing charitable intentions, had no idea of improving social conditions. When Carol mentioned that something should be done about the poor people of the town, everyone firmly stated that there was no real poverty in Gopher Prairie. Carol also attempted to raise funds for a new city hall, but no one could see that the ugly old building needed to be replaced. The town voted against appropriating the necessary funds.

Will Kennicott bought a summer cottage on Lake Minniemashie. There Carol enjoyed outdoor life and during the summer months almost lost her desire for reform. But when September came she hated the thought of returning to Gopher Prairie.

Carol resolved to study her husband. He was well thought of in the town, and she romanticized herself as the wife of a hard-working, courageous country doctor. She fell in love with Will again on the night she watched him perform a bloody but successful operation upon a poor farmer. But Carol's praise of her husband had little effect. Will was not the romantic figure she had pictured. He accepted his duties as a necessary chore, and the thought that he had saved the life of a human being did not occur to him. His interest in medicine was identical with his interest in motor cars. Once more Carol turned her attention to Gopher Prairie.

Carol, trying to interest the Thanatopsis Club in literature and art, finally persuaded the members to put on an amateur theatrical. But enthusiasm soon waned. Carol's choice of a play, Shaw's *Androcles,* was vetoed, and *The Girl from Kankakee* put in its place. Carol considered even that choice too subtle for Gopher Prairie, but at least the town's interest in the theater had been revived.

After three years of marriage, Carol discovered that she was pregnant. Almost immediately the neighborhood became interested in her condition. When her son was born, she resolved that some day she would send little Hugh away from Gopher Prairie, to Harvard, Yale, or Oxford.

With a new son and the new status of motherhood, Carol found herself more a part of the town, but she devoted nine-tenths of her attention to Hugh and had little time to criticize the town. She wanted a new house, but she and Will could not agree on the type of building. He was satisfied with a square frame house. Carol had visions of a Georgian mansion, with stately columns and wide lawns, or a white cottage like those at Cape Cod.

Then Carol met a tailor in town, an artistic, twenty-five-year-old aesthete, with whom she imagined herself in love. She often dropped by his shop to see him, and one day Will warned her that the gossip in town was growing. Ashamed, Carol promised she would not see him again. The tailor left for Minneapolis.

Carol and Will decided to take a trip to California. When they returned three months later, Carol realized that her attempt to escape Gopher Prairie had been unsuccessful. For one thing, Will had gone with her. What she needed now was to get away from her husband. After a long argument with Will, Carol took little Hugh and went off to Washington, where she planned to do war work. But hers was an empty kind of freedom. She found the people in Washington an accumulation of the population of thousands of Gopher Prairies all over the nation. Main Street had merely been transplanted to the larger city. Disheartened by her discovery, Carol had too much pride to return home.

After thirteen months, Will went to get her. He missed her terribly, he said, and begged her to come back. Hugh was overjoyed to see his father, and Carol realized that inevitably she would have to return to Gopher Prairie.

Home once more, Carol found that her furious hatred for Gopher Prairie had burned itself out. She made friends with the clubwomen and promised herself not to be snobbish in the future. She would go on asking questions—she could never stop herself from doing that—but her questions now would be asked with sympathy rather than with sarcasm. For the first time she felt serene. In Gopher Prairie she felt at last that she was wanted. Her neighbors had missed her. For the first time Carol felt that Gopher Prairie was her home.

THE MALTESE FALCON

Type of work: Novel
Author: Dashiell Hammett (1894-   )
Type of plot: Mystery romance
Time of plot: Twentieth century
Locale: San Francisco
First published: 1930

Principal characters:
SAM SPADE, detective
BRIGID O'SHAUGHNESSY, his client
CASPER GUTMAN, her employer
WILMER, Gutman's bodyguard
JOEL CAIRO, Gutman's one-time agent
MILES ARCHER, Spade's partner
FLOYD THURSBY, Brigid's murdered accomplice

Critique:

The Maltese Falcon is a detective novel of the hard-boiled school. Its distinction lies in the fact that the detective himself becomes involved in crime through a large bribe. Written in racy, colloquial language, the book pretends to no more than pure entertainment, but it is a classic example of its type.

The Story:

Brigid O'Shaughnessy went to the office of Sam Spade and Miles Archer, detectives, to ask them to trail a Floyd Thursby. Archer, who undertook the job, was killed the first night. About an hour later Thursby himself was killed in front of his hotel. The police were inclined to suspect Spade of the murder of his partner, for it was known that Iva Archer had been wanting a divorce so that she could marry Spade.

Brigid left word at Spade's office that she wanted to see him. She had changed hotels because she was afraid. She said she could not tell Spade the whole story, but that she had met Thursby in the Orient and that they had arrived in San Francisco the week before. She said she did not know who killed Thursby.

When Spade returned to his office, Joel Cairo was waiting for him. He asked Spade where the statuette of the black bird was and offered five thousand dollars for the recovery of the ornament. That night Spade was trailed by a small young man in a gray overcoat and cap. Spade eluded his pursuer long enough to slip into Brigid's hotel unseen. There he learned that Brigid was connected in some way with a mysterious black bird, an image of a falcon. Later she went with Spade to his apartment, to meet Cairo. She told Cairo that she did not have the prize, that he would have to wait possibly a week for its return.

When the police arrived to question Spade about his relations with Iva, they discovered Cairo and Brigid in the apartment. Spade introduced Brigid as an operator in his employ and explained that he had been questioning Cairo about the murders of Archer and Thursby. After Cairo and the police had gone, Brigid told Sam that she did not know what made the falcon so important. She had been hired to get it away from a Russian named Kemidov in Constantinople.

Next morning, before Brigid was awake, Spade went out to get groceries for breakfast and incidentally to search her hotel room for the falcon, which he failed to find. He was certain that Brigid knew where the falcon was. Brigid was afraid of what Cairo might do, however, and Spade arranged for her to stay a few days at the home of his secretary.

Because, in explaining to Cairo how Thursby was killed, Brigid had outlined the letter G in the air, Spade knew that there was some special significance attached to the letter. He again saw the young man trailing him in the corridor of a hotel and went up to him. Spade said that someone would have to talk, and G might as well know it. Shortly afterward a Mr. Gutman called and asked Spade to go see him. Spade told him that Cairo was offering him ten thousand dollars, not five, for the return of the falcon. Gutman laughed derisively; the bird was obviously worth an enormous fortune. Angry because Gutman would tell him no more, Spade left, saying he would give Gutman until five-thirty to talk.

From a taxi driver Spade learned that Brigid had gone to the Ferry Building and not to his secretary's house and that she had stopped on the way to buy a newspaper. When he returned to Gutman's hotel, he learned that the falcon was an old ornament, made in Malta, encrusted with precious gems and covered with black enamel for protection. Gutman had traced it to the Constantinople home of Kemidov, where Gutman's agents had got it. Now Gutman was wondering where it was.

Next day Spade searched Cairo's hotel room and found that the ships' schedules had been torn out of a newspaper of the day before. He bought a copy of the paper and saw that the ship *La Paloma* had arrived from Hongkong. Remembering that Brigid had mentioned the Orient, he associated her going to the Ferry Building with the arrival of the ship. Later he learned that Cairo had checked out of his hotel room. Meanwhile Spade had gone aboard the *La Paloma* and had learned that Gutman, Cairo, the strange young man, and Brigid had had a long conference with Jacobi, the captain.

While Spade was telling his secretary of his discoveries, a man came in, held out a bundle to Spade, and dropped over dead. Spade opened the package and discovered the falcon. Spade was sure that the man was Jacobi. He had his secretary call the police while he checked the package in a station nearby. The key he mailed to his post-office box. He then went to answer a distress call from Brigid, but she was not in her room. Instead, Spade found Gutman's daughter, who sent him to the suburbs on a wild-goose chase. When he returned to his apartment, he met Brigid waiting outside, obviously frightened. Opening the door, he found Gutman, the young man, and Cairo waiting for him.

Spade realized that his wild-goose chase had been planned to get him out of the way long enough to give these people a chance to find Jacobi before he returned. Since they were all together, Spade said he would give them the falcon in return for ten thousand dollars and someone on whom to blame the murders. He suggested the young man, whose name was Wilmer, as the suspect. Spade explained that if Wilmer were hanged for the murder of Thursby, the district attorney would drop the case, taking it for granted that Jacobi had been murdered by the same person. Gutman, sure that Thursby had killed Archer, finally consented to make Wilmer the victim.

Gutman produced ten one-thousand-dollar bills. Then Spade called his secretary and asked her to get the claim check from the post-office and redeem the falcon. After she had delivered the package to Spade's apartment, Gutman untied it and, to make sure he had the genuine falcon, began to scratch away the enamel. The falcon was a lead imitation. Kemidov had tricked him. Spade gave back nine thousand dollars. Then he called the police and told them that Wilmer had killed Jacobi and Thursby.

Knowing that Gutman would tell about his and Brigid's part in the plot, Spade made Brigid confess to him that she had drawn Archer into an alley that first night and had killed him with a pistol borrowed from Thursby. He told Brigid that he intended also to turn her over to the police. He had to clear himself of suspicion of killing his partner, and he could not let a woman stand in his way.

THE MAN WITHOUT A COUNTRY

Type of work: Short story
Author: Edward Everett Hale (1822-1909)
Type of plot: Historical romance
Time of plot: Nineteenth century
Locale: United States and the high seas
First published: 1863

Principal character:
PHILIP NOLAN

Critique:

Written originally as propaganda for the bitterly-contested presidential campaign of 1864, *The Man Without a Country* has become a classic of our literature. No story better expresses the spirit of American nationalism. Cut off from his native land, Philip Nolan wished himself dead rather than to experience the exile which he was forced to endure because of his youthfully rash statement and deed.

The Story:

Few people noticed in the newspaper columns of 1863 the report of the death of Philip Nolan. Few people would have recognized his name, in fact, for since Madison's administration went out in 1817, it had never been mentioned in public by any naval officer and the records concerning his case had been destroyed by fire years before his death.

When he was a young officer in Texas, Philip Nolan met Aaron Burr and became involved in Burr's infamous plot against the United States Government. When Burr's treason was revealed and the rebels were brought to trial, Nolan was indicted along with some of the lesser figures of the plot. Asked at his trial whether he had any statement to make concerning his loyalty to the United States, Nolan, in a frenzy, cursed the name of his country. Shocked, Colonel Morgan, who was conducting the court-martial, sentenced Philip Nolan never again to hear the name of his native land.

The Secretary of the Navy was requested to place the prisoner aboard a naval ship with a letter to the captain explaining Nolan's peculiar punishment. For the remainer of his life Nolan and this letter went from one ship to another, Nolan traveling alone, speaking only to officers who guarded their country's name from his ears. None of the officers wanted to have him around because his presence prevented any talk of home or of politics. Once in a while he was invited to the officers' mess, but most of the time he ate alone under guard. Since he wore an army uniform with perfectly plain buttons, he became known as "Plain Buttons."

The periodicals and books he read had to be edited in order to delete any naming of or allusion to the United States. One incident was marked well by those who witnessed it. Some officers were gathered on deck one day reading aloud to one another Scott's *Lay of the Last Minstrel.* When it came his turn, Nolan took up the poem at the section which contained the lines, "This is my own, my native land!" He colored, choked, and threw the book into the water as he ran to his room. He did not emerge for two months.

Nolan altered considerably as time passed, and he lost the bragging air of unconcern he had assumed at first. After the incident of the poem he became shy and retiring, conversing with few people and staying in his quarters most of the time. He was transferred from ship to ship, never coming closer than a hundred miles to the land whose name he was forbidden to hear. Once Nolan came close to gaining his freedom from this bondage of silence. It happened during a naval battle with a British ship. A good shot from the enemy struck one of the ship's guns, killing the officer in charge and scattering the men. Unexpectedly Nolan appeared to take command of the gun, heroically ignoring his own safety and aiding in the defeat of the English ship. He was highly praised by the captain, who promised to mention him in his naval report. Nolan's case had been so forgotten in Washington that there seemed to be no orders concerning him. His punishment was being carried on simply by repetitious habit and naval form.

During his extensive studies Nolan kept scholarly notebooks. For diversion he began to collect organic specimens of wild life, which were brought to him by ship's men who went ashore. He was never known to be ill, and often he nursed those who were. So the expatriate passed his years, nameless, friendless, loveless. If there were any record of him in Washington, no evidence of such papers could ever be uncovered. So far as the government was concerned, Nolan did not exist. Stories about the lonely man circulated through mess halls, but many were untrue.

During the last fifteen years of his life Nolan aged rapidly. The men whom he had known when he first began his endless journey in 1807 had retired, and younger men took their places on the ships. Nolan became more reserved than ever, but he was always well regarded by those who knew him. It is said that young boys idolized him for his advice and for his interest in them.

Constantly the men were on guard never to reveal to their prisoner any news about the United States. This secrecy was often difficult to maintain, for the nation was growing rapidly. With the annexation of Texas there arose a strained incident. The officers puzzled over the removal of that state from Nolan's maps, but they decided that the change would give him a hint of westward expansion. There were other inconvenient taboos. When the states on the west coast joined the Union, the ships which bore Nolan had to avoid customary landings there. Although Nolan suspected the reason for this change in his habitual itinerary, he kept silent.

When Nolan lay dying, the captain of the ship came to see him. He found that Nolan had draped the stars and stripes around a picture of Washington. On one bulkhead hung the painting of an eagle grasping the entire globe in its claws, and at the foot of the bed was a map of the United States which Nolan had drawn from memory. When the dying man asked for news from home, the captain, who liked and pitied Nolan, told him about the progress of the United States during the more than fifty years of Nolan's exile. Seeing Nolan's joy at the news of his country, the captain could not bring himself, however, to tell the dying man that the United States was engaged in the Civil War.

Philip Nolan died in 1863. His last request was that he be buried at sea, his only home.

MANHATTAN TRANSFER

Type of work: Novel
Author: John Dos Passos (1896-)
Type of plot: Impressionistic realism
Time of plot: World War I
Locale: New York City
First published: 1925

Principal characters:
ELLEN THATCHER, an actress
CONGO, a French sailor who later became a wealthy bootlegger
GUS MCNIEL, a milkman who later became an assemblyman
JIMMY HERF, a newspaper reporter
GEORGE BALDWIN, a lawyer
JOE HARLAND, a drunk
JOE O'KEEFE, a young labor organizer
STAN EMERY, whom Ellen loves

Critique:

In this novel Dos Passos presents a panoramic portrait of New York City. The book is composed of many episodes in the lives of many different characters. Some of the episodes are connected; others stand by themselves. The author's style is abrupt; the scene shifts without warning. The complexity of the plot realistically reflects the complexity of metropolitan life.

The Story:

Ed Thatcher and his wife Susie had their first child, a girl named Ellen. After the birth of the child, Susie became neurotic; she wanted to die.

Congo and Emile, two French boys, came to New York to make their fortunes. Emile married a widowed Frenchwoman who owned a delicatessen. Congo did not like New York and went to sea again.

Gus McNiel, a milkman, was run over by a train. George Baldwin, a young lawyer, took Gus' case against the railroad and obtained a settlement for the injured man. While Gus was in the hospital recovering from the accident, George had an affair with Gus' wife, Nellie.

Jimmy Herf arrived from Europe with his widowed mother, who was in delicate health. One evening she had a heart attack; not long afterward she died. Jimmy's rich Uncle Jeff and Aunt Emily Merivale then became his legal guardians. One evening at their house Jimmy met Joe Harland, the drunken black sheep of the family, who had won and lost several fortunes on Wall Street.

Susie Thatcher died, and Ed worked hard for little Ellen. He stayed at the office until late each evening, working and dreaming of all the fine things he would do for his daughter some day. Ellen grew up, went on the stage, and married John Oglethorpe, a competent but lazy actor. Her married life was unhappy, for she discovered that her husband was a homosexual.

Jimmy Herf's Uncle Jeff tried to get him interested in business, but Jimmy would have none of it. He got a job as a reporter and became acquainted with Ruth Prynne, a young actress who lived in the boarding-house where Ellen and John Oglethorpe stayed.

George Baldwin had forgotten Nellie McNiel. He was now interested in Ellen. One afternoon, as he and Ellen sat together at tea, a drunken college boy stopped at their table. George introduced him to Ellen as Stan Emery.

Joe Harland, the black sheep relative of the Merivales and Jimmy Herf, was now forty-five and almost broke. He spent his last money on a few shots of whiskey to bring back memories of the old prosperous days on Wall Street.

Ellen and Stan fell in love. When she was with him, she was happy. But when she went home to John, she was miserable. Ellen decided that she and John could no longer live together. She packed her things and moved to a hotel.

Stan Emery came to Jimmy Herf's room. Stan was on a long drunk after being expelled from college. Later in the day they met John and Ellen drinking tea together. Stan left, but Jimmy stayed to talk with Ellen.

George Baldwin sat at breakfast with his wife, Cecily. He had married her for social position; they were not happy. Cecily knew of his other affairs. George did all he could to keep her from leaving home because a scandal would ruin him in the business world.

Ellen moved from her hotel to an apartment. She was supporting herself well now, for she had become a success on Broadway.

Joe Harland had finally got a job as a night watchman. One evening he was visited by a young labor organizer, Joe O'Keefe. The older man warned him against getting mixed up in labor troubles. But O'Keefe said that Gus McNiel, now an assemblyman, was on the side of labor.

Harry Goldweiser, a rich Broadway producer, fell in love with Ellen. He asked her to marry him. She refused, but in a friendly way, for her career depended upon Goldweiser.

Gus McNiel retained George Baldwin as his lawyer throughout his rise to political power. George warned him against getting mixed up with labor because, as a member of a conservative law firm, George could not help Gus with labor troubles.

Ellen wanted Stan to stop drinking so much, but he would not reform. Drink was the only means by which he could adjust himself to the world.

One evening Ellen went out to dinner with George Baldwin. Everyone was excited about the beginning of the World War. But George could think only of Ellen, and in a fit of rage he threatened her with a gun. Gus McNiel, who was nearby, took away the gun and hushed up the incident. Jimmy

Herf, who had been talking to the bartender, Congo, took Ellen outside and sent her home in a taxi.

Ellen finally obtained a divorce from John, and Harry Goldweiser renewed his attentions. One evening Ellen and Harry met Stan dancing with a girl named Pearline. Stan revealed that he and Pearline had been on a long drunk and had been married. Later Stan came home drunk, disgusted with his life and with Pearline. He poured kerosene around the apartment and set fire to it. Pearline returned just in time to see the firemen carry Stan from the burning building.

Ellen was crushed by Stan's death, for he was the only man she had really loved. To be with Jimmy Herf gave her some comfort because he had been Stan's friend. But Jimmy wanted to be more than a friend to Ellen; he still loved her. She told him that she was going to have Stan's baby; she wanted to leave show business and rear the child. But she had an abortion instead. Ellen and Jimmy went to Europe to do Red Cross work during the war. Finally they were married. They returned from France with their baby.

Joe O'Keefe came back from the war with a chip on his shoulder. He thought the veterans deserved a bonus because they had lost out on the big money at home. He had another reason for feeling bitter: somewhere overseas he had caught syphilis.

George Baldwin's home life was still troubled. Having post-war political ambitions, he turned against his old friend, Gus McNiel, and ran for mayor on a reform ticket. Meanwhile Jimmy and Ellen drifted apart. Jimmy became despondent and quit his job. George Baldwin finally got a divorce. He proposed to Ellen. Too weary of her muddled life to resist him, she accepted his proposal.

One night Jimmy Herf was walking the streets when a car drew up beside him and stopped. In it was the Frenchman, Congo, now a wealthy bootlegger. He took Jimmy home with him and tried to cheer him up. Late one evening after a party Jimmy Herf wandered down by the river. As he waited for a ferry to take him from Manhattan, he realized that he felt gay and happy for the first time in many months. Morning found him walking along a concrete highway, penniless but still happy. He did not know where he was going; he knew only that it would be a long way.

MANON LESCAUT

Type of work: Novel
Author: Abbé Prévost (Antoine François Prévost d'Exiles, 1697-1763)
Type of plot: Sentimental romance
Time of plot: 1700
Locale: France and New Orleans
First published: 1731

Principal characters:
MANON LESCAUT, a courtesan
THE CHEVALIER DES GRIEUX, her lover
TIBERGE, his friend
M. DE G— M—, a wealthy nobleman
M. LESCAUT, Manon's brother

Critique:

The Story of Manon Lescaut and the Chevalier des Grieux is an early example of the sentimental romance and as such it has had a considerable influence on romantic fiction in different literatures. The book is not widely read today, but the popular operatic version of the story is familiar enough. Despite its importance in the history of fiction, the modern reader is apt to be out of sympathy with its swashbuckling hero and its sentimental heroine. The Abbé Prévost would have the reader sympathize with these characters, but many readers will feel that the pair received much less misfortune than their conduct deserved.

The Story:

While the young Chevalier des Grieux was a student of philosophy at Amiens, he became friendly with a fellow student named Tiberge. One day he stood idly with his friend and watched the arrival of the Arras coach. Among the passengers was a beautiful young girl who attracted the chevalier's attention. Politely introducing himself, he learned that her name was Manon Lescaut and that she had come to Amiens under the protection of an elderly man. Against her will she was to enter a convent. She accepted the chevalier's offer to set her free from such an irksome life, and after skillfully and untruthfully disposing of her escort she went with the young student to an inn. On the morrow they planned to flee to Paris. Tiberge argued with his friend against this folly, but the chevalier was hopelessly infatuated. In Paris he and Manon took a furnished apartment, where for three weeks they were absorbed in each other.

The idyll came to an end when the young lover discovered that his mistress had also bestowed her affections on M. de B—. But the chevalier's love for Manon was so great he forgave her. Then three lackeys, sent by the chevalier's father, came to the apartment and took the young man home. There his father tried in vain to persuade him that Manon had behaved treacherously. Finally the father locked his son in his room for a period of six weeks. During this time Tiberge came to visit him, bringing him news that Manon was being kept at the expense of M. de B—. Finally Tiberge persuaded the young man to enroll at the Seminary of Saint-Supplice as a student of theology. With his father's permission, he entered the school where he became an outstanding student. Manon was present to hear his declamation at the public disputation at the Sorbonne, and after the ceremonies she came to visit him. A single passionate embrace made him forget his future in the Church. The chevalier escaped from school without any money; his mistress furnished the funds to set up quarters at Chaillot, outside Paris.

Then began a life of extravagance and riotous living far beyond their slender means. In Paris they met Manon's brother, M. Lescaut of the Royal Guards, who did not scruple to install himself in their house. When a fire destroyed all their money and possessions, the brother suggested that Manon sell her charms to some free-handed nobleman. The chevalier rejected this proposal, but consented to become a professional gambler in order to support Manon. He borrowed from Tiberge enough money to begin his career as a card cheat. For a time his luck held, but their period of prosperity ended when a maid and a valet fled with all the valuable possessions of the new household. Urged by her brother, Manon consented to become the mistress of the old and wealthy M. de G—M—, who had promised her a house, servants, and a large sum of money.

The young couple decided to play on Manon's protector by introducing the chevalier into the household as her brother. Having duped the man to make his settlement on Manon, they ran away with the jewels and money he had given her. But they were followed by the police, apprehended, and imprisoned—Manon at the Common Hospital; the chevalier at Saint-Lazare.

Once lodged at Saint-Lazare, the chevalier began to plan his escape. He cultivated his superiors and made a show of reading theology. M. de G—M—, hearing of the chevalier's studious habits, came to visit him. But when the young man heard, for the first time, that Manon was also imprisoned, he seized the old man by the throat and tried to throttle him. The monks stopped the fight and saved the old man's life.

The chevalier now wrote to Tiberge, asking his old friend to visit Saint-Lazare. To Tiberge he entrusted a note addressed to M. Lescaut. Using a pistol which Manon's brother brought him soon afterward, the chevalier escaped, killing a turnkey in his flight. Later, by bribing the attendants at the hospital, he was able to arrange for Manon's escape. Manon, wearing men's clothing, was safely conveyed to her brother's house, but just as the happy pair descended from the carriage M. Lescaut was shot by a man whose fortune the guardsman had won at cards. Manon and the chevalier fled to the inn at Chaillot to escape apprehension for the murder.

In Paris the next day the chevalier borrowed a hundred pistoles from Tiberge. He also met M. de T—, a friend, whom he invited to Chaillot for supper. During the meal the son of old M. de G—M— arrived at the inn. The impetuous young chevalier wanted to kill him at once to get revenge on the father, but M. de T— persuaded him rather to meet young de G—M— in a friendly manner over the supper table. The young man was charmed with Manon, and like his father offered to maintain her handsomely. But Manon and her lover had made plans to deceive the gullible young man, in order to get revenge on his father. She accepted his rich presents. The chevalier planned to have street ruffians capture and hold the infatuated young man while Manon and the chevalier enjoyed the supper and the bed de G—M— had arranged for himself and his mistress. But the young man's father learned of the scheme and Manon and the chevalier were surprised by the police, who hurried them off to the Chatelet.

The young chevalier then appealed to his father, whose influence was great enough to secure his son's release. He refused to interest himself in Manon, however, and she was sentenced to exile on the next shipload of convicts to be sent to the penal colony in Louisiana. After a feeble attempt to rescue her from the prison guards, the chevalier accompanied his mistress on the trip from the prison to Havre-de-Grace. He also gained permission to accompany her on the voyage to America. On shipboard and on their arrival in New Orleans they passed as man and wife.

In New Orleans they settled in a rude shelter. After the chevalier secured honorable employment, Manon desired above all things that they become legally man and wife. The chevalier appealed to the governor for permission to marry and admitted his earlier deceit. The governor refused, for his nephew M. Synnelet, had fallen in love with Manon. As a result, the chevalier fought a duel with Synnelet. Thinking that he had killed his opponent, he and Manon left the colony, but on the journey Manon, ill from fatigue, died in a lonely field. The chevalier was disconsolate.

Tiberge followed his friend to America and persuaded him to return to France. Back home, the chevalier resolved to turn to God in penance.

MAN'S FATE

Type of work: Novel
Author: André Malraux (1895-)
Type of plot: Social criticism
Time of plot: 1927
Locale: Shanghai, China
First published: 1933

Principal characters:
CH'EN, a Chinese terrorist
KYO, a Communist organizer of French and Japanese parentage

GISORS, Kyo's father
MAY, Kyo's German wife
BARON DE CLAPPIQUE, a French adventurer
KATOV, a Russian revolutionist
HEMMELRICH, a German revolutionist
FERRAL, a French businessman
KÖNIG, chief of Chiang Kai-shek's police

Critique:

Man's Fate is in part an eye-witness account of a troubled period of crisis in China's troubled history. Malraux, himself a revolutionary at the time, was first of all a literary artist in the writing of this novel. His characters are the melting pot of cosmopolitan Shanghai. The episodic plot is significant chiefly as an illustration of leftist dialectics in modern fiction.

The Story:

The Reds, a revolutionary group with a nucleus of Moscow agents, had made a temporary alliance with Chiang Kai-shek, their immediate object being to control Shanghai with the help of the Kuomintang. But the alliance was an uneasy one, for neither side trusted the other. The Reds had completed their plans to seize Shanghai, ostensibly as part of Chiang Kai-shek's campaign, but they intended to put a Communist in control before the Blue army arrived. On their part, the Blues hoped to use the Communists to seize the city and afterwards disperse the revolutionaries.

Ch'en, the terrorist, stood ready to strike through the mosquito netting and kill the sleeper in the bed. Nerving himself for his first murder, he plunged his dagger into the man's heart. Quickly from the dead man he took a paper which would authorize the delivery of arms now aboard the *Shantung,* at anchor in the harbor. The Reds counted on these arms to seize control of the city before government troops arrived.

Ch'en took the document to Hemmelrich's phonograph shop, where Kyo was waiting. There they all congratulated him, Kyo, Katov, and Hemmelrich. Kyo and Katov tested their new code of paralleled phonograph records. One record gave an innocent language lesson, the other gave a loud hiss which covered all but the key words on the first record. Satisfied with their work, they planned a final check of their revolutionary cells. Hemmelrich refused to go with them; his wife and child were sick.

Kyo and Katov visited their two hundred units. A general strike at noon would paralyze the city. At the same time saboteurs would wreck the railway so that the government could not send reinforcements from the battle front. Other groups would take over police stations and army posts and seize all firearms. With the grenades already on hand, they would be equipped to resist even tanks.

Kyo went to the Black Cat, a night club where he knew he could find de Clappique. The Frenchman was drunk, but he had to be trusted. De Clappique was commissioned to take a forged order to the *Shantung,* directing her to shift anchorage.

Tired and tense, Kyo went home. Gisors, his father, was still awake, and Kyo told him a few details of the plan. Then May, Kyo's wife, came home exhausted from her hospital work. She was one of the few women doctors in all Shanghai, a woman with advanced views on marriage relationships. She and Kyo quarreled because of her affair with another doctor. During the quarrel de Clappique came to report that the *Shantung* had moved. A messenger recalled Kyo to headquarters.

MAN'S FATE by André Malraux. Translated by Haakon M. Chevalier. By permission of the author's agent William Aspenwall Bradley, Paris, his publishers, Messrs. Gallimard, Paris, and of Random House, Inc.

Dressed as government soldiers, Kyo and Katov with ten others boarded the *Shantung* and got the arms, but only after seizing the captain and holding him prisoner. Now the revolutionaries could plan with confidence.

Meanwhile Ferral, head of the French Chamber of Commerce, decided to throw his support to Chiang Kai-shek. After giving orders to send funds to the Blues, he retired with his mistress Valérie. It was arranged that she would see him the following night at her hotel. He was to bring her a pet bird in a cage. At the appointed time Ferral asked for Valérie at the hotel desk. To his surprise, she was out. A young Englishman was also waiting for her with a caged bird. To revenge himself, Ferral bought the entire stock of a pet store —forty birds and a kangaroo, and set them loose in Valérie's room.

The uprising took place as planned. Ch'en seized one police station with ease and armed his small band. The second station was better defended, and grenades failed to dislodge officers barricaded on the top floor. Ch'en set fire to the building, killing the resisters as well as his own wounded comrades.

The feeble central government could not fight both Chiang and the Reds at the same time. While the government forces were occupied with the Blues, the Reds easily took control of the city.

Two days later the Blues under Chiang approached Shanghai. The general had been shrewd enough to send his first division, composed largely of Communists, to another front; consequently the Communists found themselves confronting an unsympathetic Blue army which in turn took over the city. Many of the Communists were arrested. When Moscow ordered all armed Communists to surrender their weapons to Chiang's police, dissension broke out among the Reds. Many of the Chinese deserted the Moscow party and embarked on a terroristic campaign of their own.

Ch'en conceived the idea that he must kill Chiang in order to free China. With two companions he lay in wait to throw a bomb into the general's car. His first attempt having failed, Ch'en went to Hemmelrich's shop. Hemmelrich refused to shelter him. In a second attempt, Ch'en threw himself with his bomb under the automobile. The car was wrecked and Ch'en was killed, but Chiang was not in the car.

Chiang's police destroyed Hemmelrich's shop, accidentally killing his wife and baby. Believing his cowardice was the cause of Ch'en's action and the subsequent riot, Hemmelrich seized a rifle and joined the rioters. He was quickly killed by Chiang's police.

Now in complete control, Chiang's police chief, König, began to round up the Communists, Katov among them. When the word went out that Kyo was to be arrested, Gisors begged de Clappique to intervene because the baron was König's good friend. Instead of warning Kyo, de Clappique lingered in a gambling house until after Kyo had been arrested. Later de Clappique went to König to ask for Kyo's release. The Frenchman was given only forty-eight hours to leave China.

In prison Katov gave his cyanide tablet to Kyo, who poisoned himself. Katov and his revolutionary group were executed.

Each of the survivors sought safety in his own way. Gisors returned to Japan to teach painting. May went to Moscow to practice medicine. By disguising himself de Clappique got aboard the same French liner that was taking Ferral back to France. So the Communists and their sympathizers were destroyed by relentless Chiang and the vacillating policy of Moscow. Yet there was good news from China for the survivors; the quiet work of revolution had already started again.

MANSFIELD PARK

Type of work: Novel
Author: Jane Austen (1775-1817)
Type of plot: Social criticism
Time of plot: Early nineteenth century
Locale: Northamptonshire, England
First published: 1814

Principal characters:
FANNY PRICE, a poor relation at Mansfield Park
SIR THOMAS BERTRAM, owner of Mansfield Park
LADY BERTRAM, his wife
TOM,
EDMUND,
MARIA, and
JULIA BERTRAM, Fanny's cousins
MRS. NORRIS, a busybody
HENRY CRAWFORD, a self-centered young gentleman
MARY CRAWFORD, his sister
MR. RUSHWORTH, Maria Bertram's suitor
MR. YATES, a young man of fashion

Critique:

Mansfield Park is the most obviously didactic of Jane Austen's novels: virtue is universally rewarded and vice just as certainly punished. The characterization, also, is inclined more to black and white than is true of her greater works. As always, the feminine characters are more convincing than the men. The heroine, Fanny Price, is appealing and sweet, while Mrs. Norris is a masterly satirical sketch of the universal type of busybody.

The Story:

Of the three Ward sisters, one had married very well to a baronet, one very badly to a lieutenant of the marines, and one neither too badly nor too well to a clergyman. The fortunate sister, Lady Bertram, agreed at the instigation of the clerical sister, Mrs. Norris, to care for one of the unfortunate sister's nine children. Accordingly, Fanny Price, ten years old, and a shy and sensitive child, came to make her home at Mansfield Park. Among her four Bertram cousins, Tom, Edmund, Maria, and Julia, Fanny found a real friend only in Edmund. The others usually ignored her except when she could be of use to them, but Edmund comforted her, and advised her. He alone seemed to recognize her good qualities—cleverness, grace, and a pleasant disposition. Besides Edmund's attentions, Fanny received some of a very different kind from her selfish and hypocritical Aunt Norris, who was constantly calling unnecessary attention to Fanny's dependent position.

When Fanny was fifteen, Sir Thomas Bertram went to Antigua to look after some business affairs. With him went his oldest son, who was inclined to extravagance and dissipation, and the family was left to Edmund's and Lady Bertram's care. During Sir Thomas' absence, his older daughter, Maria, became engaged to Mr. Rushworth, a young man who was rich and well-connected but extremely stupid.

Another event of importance was the arrival in the village of Mary and Henry Crawford, the sister and brother of Mrs. Grant, whose husband had become the rector after the death of Mr. Norris. Both of the Bertram girls liked Henry immensely, but since Maria was engaged, he rightfully belonged to Julia. They also became close friends with Mary Crawford, who in turn attracted both Tom, now returned from abroad, and Edmund.

Fanny regretted the Crawfords' coming, for she saw that Edmund, whom she herself loved, was falling in love with the shallow, worldly Mary, and that her cousin Maria was carrying on a most unseemly flirtation with Henry. The less observant, like Mrs. Norris, saw only what they wished to see and insisted that he was paying particular attention to Julia.

At the suggestion of Mr. Yates, a pleasure-loving friend of Tom, the young people decided to engage in some private theatricals and chose for their entertainment the sentimental "Lovers' Vows." Fanny opposed the scheme from the start, for she knew Sir Thomas would have disapproved. Edmund tried to dissuade the others, but finally let himself be talked into taking a part because there were not enough men for all the roles. Rehearsals and preparations went forward, the plan growing more elaborate as it progressed. However, the unexpected return of Sir Thomas put an end to the rehearsals. The house was soon cleared of all theatrical gear, including Mr. Yates, whose trifling, affected ways Sir Thomas had disliked immediately.

Maria, willing to break her engagement to Mr. Rushworth, had hoped her father's return would bring a declaration from Henry. Instead of declaring himself, he announced his departure for a stay in Bath. Although her pride was hurt, Maria resolved that Henry Crawford should never know she had taken their flirtation seriously. She was duly married to Mr. Rushworth.

Julia went to Brighton with the Rushworths. With both the Bertram sisters gone, Henry began an idle flirtation with Fanny and ended by falling in love with her. One of his plans for winning her favor was a scheme for getting her beloved brother William, who had just visited her at Mansfield Park, a promotion in the navy. Although Fanny was grateful for this favor, she refused him promptly when he proposed. In doing so, she incurred the serious displeasure of her uncle, Sir Thomas, who regarded as sheer perversity the sentiments which made her turn down such an advantageous match. Even Edmund encouraged her to change her mind, for he was too preoccupied with his attachment to Mary Crawford to guess that Fanny had more than a cousinly regard for him. Edmund had just been ordained as a clergyman, a step which Mary Crawford had ridiculed, and he was not sure she would accept him as a husband. He persisted in believing, however, that her frivolous dislike of the clergy was only a trait she had acquired from worldly friends, and that her opinion could be changed.

About this time Fanny went to Portsmouth to visit her family. The stay was a depressing one, for she found her family, with the exception of William, disorderly and ill-bred, by Mansfield Park standards. Also, several catastrophes occurred at Mansfield Park to make her long to be helpful there. Tom, the oldest son, had such a serious illness that his recovery was uncertain; Maria, now Mrs. Rushworth, ran away with Henry, who forgot his love for Fanny long enough to commit an irrevocable indiscretion; and Julia eloped with Mr. Yates. The Bertram family, crushed under this series of blows, at last realized Fanny's value and dearness to them, and welcomed her back to Mansfield Park with tenderness that touched her deeply.

Mrs. Norris, as spiteful as ever, said that if Fanny had accepted Henry Crawford as she should have, he would never have run away with Maria. But Sir Thomas gave Fanny credit for seeing Henry's character more clearly than he had, and forgave her for having refused Henry. He blamed himself for Maria's downfall, for he realized he had never taken the trouble to know his children well.

But good came from all this evil. Tom's illness sobered him, and he proved a better son thereafter. Mr. Yates, though not a great match for Julia, had more income and fewer debts than Sir Thomas had anticipated, and seemed inclined to settle down to quiet domesticity. Henry and Maria separated after spending a few unhappy months together. Sir Thomas refused to receive her at Mansfield Park, but provided a home for her in another part of the country. There Mrs. Norris went to live with her favorite niece, to the great relief of everyone at Mansfield Park.

Edmund had finally realized Mary Crawford's frivolous and worldly nature when she treated his sister's and her brother's affair quite lightly. Her levity shocked him, and made it easier for him to give up thoughts of an unsuitable marriage. Eventually he fell in love with Fanny, who had loved him so long. They were married and lived at the parsonage near Mansfield Park.

THE MARBLE FAUN

Type of work: Novel
Author: Nathaniel Hawthorne (1804-1864)
Type of plot: Allegorical romance
Time of plot: Mid-nineteenth century
Locale: Rome
First published: 1860

Principal characters:
MIRIAM, an artist
HILDA, another artist, friend of Miriam
KENYON, an American sculptor
DONATELLO, a young Italian

Critique:

A romance filled with moral and symbolic overtones and undertones, *The Marble Faun,* or, *The Romance of Monte Beni* exhibits Hawthorne's preoccupation with the problem of evil. Hawthorne himself was a complex person, and some of the psychological concerns of his own character are reflected in this novel. The book is a study of the birth of the human conscience, the consequences of a sin committed by a simple, pagan spirit who through his unthinking deed releases a new sense of intellectual and moral responsibility. *The Marble Faun* is one of the American classics, eloquent testimony to the ability and insight of one of our greatest native writers.

The Story:

Nothing at all was known about Miriam. In the artistic world of Rome, she lived without revealing anything about herself and without arousing the curiosity or suspicion of those living around her. With a New England girl, Hilda, and Kenyon, a sculptor, she enjoyed a friendship which even her mysterious origin did not shadow, so complete was their understanding and trust of one another.

One day the three friends, accompanied by Donatello, a young Italian, saw a statue of the faun by Praxiteles. Struck by the resemblance of the statue to Donatello, they asked jokingly to see if the Italian also had pointed ears under his golden locks. Indeed, Donatello was very much like a faun in his character. He had great agility, cheerfulness, and a sunny nature unclouded by melancholy or care. He was deeply in love with Miriam.

On another occasion, the trio went to visit the catacombs. While there, Miriam disappeared for a moment. When she came back, she returned with a strange individual whom she had met inside one of the tombs. This person followed her for months to come. No one knew anything about him. He and Miriam had conversations together, and he spoke of the hold he had on her, of their life together in a mysterious past. Miriam became more and more unhappy. She told Donatello—who was ever ready to defend her—that he must go away, for she would bring doom and destruction upon him. But Donatello stayed, as ardent as ever.

Her persecutor appeared everywhere, followed her wherever she went. One day Miriam went to Hilda and left a packet for Hilda to deliver on a certain date to the address she would find written on the outside. Shortly afterward, the friends went out one night and climbed the Tarpeian Rock, over which the old Romans used to throw their criminals. As they were getting ready to return home, Miriam's persecutor appeared. Miriam went with him, followed by Donatello. Donatello attacked the man and with the stranger secure in his grasp looked at Miriam. Her eyes gave him his answer. He threw the tormentor over a cliff to his death.

United by this crime, Miriam and Donatello also became united in love. But they did not know that Hilda had witnessed the murder, that she was suffering because of it. They had all agreed to visit the Church of the Capuchins the following afternoon in order to see a painting which supposedly bore a resemblance to Miriam's tormentor. But Hilda did not keep the appointment. The others went, to find a mass for the dead in progress. The dead man was Miriam's persecutor. Later, when Miriam went to see Hilda, the American girl told Miriam that their friendship was over.

Donatello, too, had changed. He was no longer the unworried faun, but a person with a very guilty conscience. He began to avoid Miriam, even to hate her. He left Rome and went back to his ancestral home. Kenyon went there to visit his friend. Hilda stayed in Rome by herself, lonely, distraught.

At Donatello's country home, Kenyon learned the local tradition about his friend's family, a legend that Donatello was, in fact, descended from a race of fauns who had inhabited the countryside in remote times. He learned, too, of Donatello's feeling of guilt, but he, unaware of the killing, did not know the reason for Donatello's changed spirit. When Miriam followed Donatello to his home, he would not see her. Kenyon told her Donatello still loved her, however, and she agreed to meet both of them later on. When they met in the city square, Miriam stood quietly, waiting for Donatello to speak. At last he spoke her name, and she went to him. So they were united once more, but the union was haunted by their sin.

In the meantime Hilda had gone to deliver the packet Miriam had left in her keeping. The address was that of one high in the affairs of the government. Kenyon looked for Hilda everywhere, for he had seen her but briefly since his return. Realizing at last that he was in love with her, he was worried about her disappearance. During the carnival season he met Donatello and Miriam, who promised him he would soon see Hilda again. He did, on the day the carnival was at its height and the streets were filled with a merry-making throng.

Hilda told him her story. Her knowledge of the crime had weighed so heavily upon her that at last she had gone to confession in St. Peter's and had poured out the tale to a listening priest. Later she had delivered the packet, as Miriam had requested her, and afterward she had been detained in a convent until the authorities were satisfied she had taken no part in the murder on the Tarpeian Rock. She had just been released from her strange captivity. While they stood talking, there was a commotion in the crowd nearby. The police had seized Donatello and were taking him to jail.

For his crime Donatello was sentenced to prison. Miriam was not brought to trial, for her only crime had been the look in her eyes which had told Donatello to murder her persecutor. But Miriam's history was finally revealed. Although she herself was innocent, her family had been involved in a crime which made its name infamous. She had gone to Rome and attempted to live down the past, but evil had continued to haunt her, and the past had reappeared in the form of a tormentor who had dogged her footsteps, threatening to make her identity known to the world, until Donatello had thrown him over the cliff.

Kenyon and Hilda were married. Once again they saw Miriam, kneeling in the Pantheon before the tomb of Raphael. As they passed, she stretched out her hands to them in a gesture that both blessed them and repulsed them. They left her to her expiation and her grief.

MARCHING ON

Type of work: Novel
Author: James Boyd (1888-1944)
Type of plot: Historical romance
Time of plot: The Civil War period
Locale: North Carolina
First published: 1927

Principal characters:
JAMES FRASER, a farm boy
STEWART PREVOST, a rich planter's daughter
COLONEL PREVOST, her father
CHARLES PREVOST, her brother

Critique:

When James Boyd wrote *Marching On,* he obviously had two motives: one, to depict the spirit of the soldiers who fought heroically for a lost cause, and, two, to show how the spirit of one boy, James Fraser, kept marching on to the point where he could hold up his head proudly among those he had once thought of as his superiors. Both parts of the plot have been developed in an interesting and challenging manner. *Marching On* is not one of the best-known Civil War novels, but it is a good story, well told.

The Story:

When James Fraser fell in love with Stewart Prevost, he loved her in a hopeless way. He was the son of a poor farmer who lived in the swamps of North Carolina, and Stewart was the daughter of Colonel Prevost, a gentleman planter. Although Colonel Prevost was always courteous and friendly with the Frasers, his friendliness was reserved; James knew that he must keep his place.

James loved his father and mother, both hard-working, God-fearing people who toiled endlessly with meager reward. But he felt that he must somehow rise above their station in life, that he must gain an equal footing with the planters and other gentlemen toward whom he was forced to show a servile attitude. On nights when he was filled with despair and confusion, he slipped out of the house and played his fiddle. Into his music he could pour his dreams without fear of ridicule.

James first saw Stewart when he delivered a load of wood to her father. She said only a few words in greeting, but to James the words were as beautiful as the ringing of bells. During the next weeks he saw her often; it seemed to him that she was always on the road leading to the plantation as he passed with a load of wood. When he was alone, he cursed himself for a fool; no girl in Stewart's position would purposely seek out an awkward, uncouth farm boy. He swore to himself that he would avoid her. At last Stewart began to talk with him about life. When he told her that he would like to go away and work on the railroad, she offered to give him money to start him on his way. He bitterly decided that she only wanted to get rid of him.

For a few days James avoided the plantation. Then his pride forced him to call at Stewart's home and ask to see her. Colonel Prevost answered the door and went to call Stewart. He returned to tell James that Stewart was busy—and would be busy in the future. Trying to save his dignity, the boy stumbled blindly down the steps. The next morning he told his father and mother that he was going away.

James went to Wilmington and took a job on the railroad. His interest in machines and his determination to succeed made him an excellent worker. He lived well and sent money home each week. He made friends, but the vision of Stewart would not leave him and he was lonely. The men with whom he associated were all concerned over the coming election, for they believed that there would be trouble if Abraham Lincoln were elected. Everywhere he went, abolition and war were the main topics of conversation. Not long after Lincoln had been elected, the Secession began.

In April, after Fort Sumter had been attacked, James went home to join the company being formed by Colonel Prevost. Stewart's brother Charles was to be the captain, for he had attended Virginia Military Institute. On the night before the company was to leave the plantation James wrote Stewart a note and asked her to meet him. His love was greater than his pride, and for that he would always be grateful; Stewart swore to him that her father had never told her that James had come to see her once before, and she said regretfully that her offer of money had been thoughtlessly given. She promised to write to him, and she asked him to look after her brother Charles, for she had a premonition that he would be killed.

The next three years were later to seem to James like one continuous nightmare. Their company engaged in battle with the Yankees only three or four times, but the men marched and marched until they slept as they walked. Most of the time they were starving. When their shoes wore out, they wrapped their swollen feet in rags. Still they went on. Charles was killed. Although James killed the men who had attacked Charles, he feared that Stewart would not forgive him for failing in his promise. He wrote her, but it was two years before her answer reached him. By that time he was a prisoner. Her letter was the only thing that kept him sane during his years in prison. All the prisoners were gaunt and sick, unbelievably thin and emaciated. The Yankees were fairly kind, but there was not enough food and clothing for anyone in those terrible years. James tried to keep a record of the number of days he had been a prisoner, but the problem was too great for his fuzzy mind. To him only Stewart's letter was real.

Released at last in an exchange of prisoners, James went immediately to the Prevost plantation. He was dirty and in rags and too weak to walk without help, but Stewart drew him like a magnet. When he climbed the long steps to her house, she was waiting for him at the top.

James stayed at the plantation until he was stronger. Stewart told him she loved him and would marry him. Although Colonel Prevost was courteous and gracious, James knew that the old gentleman still considered him little better than a poor white cracker and would be glad when he went to his own home. At last James went back to his father and mother.

James had been home only a short time before he learned that the Union army was attacking a town close to the plantation. Because the Fraser farm was off the main path of the soldiers, he went to the plantation to bring Stewart and her father home with him. The colonel could not believe that Southern troops would be defeated again and he did not want to leave his house. While James was there, the old man apologized for his attitude and told the boy that he was pleased that Stewart was going to marry him. He honored James by showing him a picture of Stewart's dead mother, his most prized treasure.

The town fell. James and Stewart went to his home, with the colonel's promise that he would follow them as soon as he had arranged for the protection of his slaves and overseers. But he never came. James returned to the plantation after he had taken Stewart to safety. There he found that Yankees had ransacked the house and killed the colonel as he tried to save his wife's picture. Filled with a desire to avenge the colonel's death, James started down the road after the troops. He wanted to kill any Yankee he saw. He had an opportunity to kill three of them, but he suddenly changed his mind when he saw that the men were released prisoners. They had fought for what they thought was right, just as he had. He could think of them only as brothers who had suffered in the same war. He put his gun away and gave them the little food he had. Then he started back to Stewart. He was going home.

THE MASTER OF BALLANTRAE

Type of work: Novel
Author: Robert Louis Stevenson (1850-1894)
Type of plot: Adventure romance
Time of plot: Mid-eighteenth century
Locale: Scotland, India, France, America
First published: 1889

Principal characters:
James Durrie, Master of Ballantrae
Henry Durrie, James' brother
Alison Graeme, Henry's wife
Mr. Mackellar, factor of Durrisdeer
Secundra Dass, James' servant

Critique:

The Master of Ballantrae: A Winter's Tale is considered by many to be Stevenson's best novel, although it probably is not as well known as *Treasure Island* or *Kidnapped*. The story is engrossing, moves with commendable speed, and generally does not seem incredible. However, the novel is lacking in background detail, the author's chief aim, apparently, being a delineation of character.

The Story:

When the Stuart Pretender landed in Scotland in 1745, to assert his right to the throne of England by force of arms if necessary, the Durries of Durrisdeer decided to steer a middle course. One son would fight for the exiled Stuart, the other would bide at home in loyalty to King George. James, Master of Ballantrae and his father's heir, won the toss of a coin and elected to join the Stuart cause. The younger son, Henry, stayed at Durrisdeer. By this means it was hoped by their shrewd old father that either way the struggle went, the family estate would remain intact.

Soon after came word of the defeat of the Scottish forces at Culloden and the news of James' death. Henry became the Master of Ballantrae. In 1748, he married Alison Graeme, who had been betrothed to James. But even after a daughter and a son had been born to them, their marriage was overshadowed by the spirit of the former Master of Ballantrae. James had been the favorite son. Old Lord Durrisdeer had denied him nothing, and Alison had loved him. This feeling led to domestic difficulties, and later the village gossips idolized James and accused Henry of selling out the Stuart cause.

Colonel Francis Burke, an Irishman, came into this strained situation and announced that he and James had escaped together from the field at Culloden. The old lord was exceedingly happy with this news; Henry felt frustrated; Alison seemed pleased. Burke's mission was to get money from the estate to take to James, who was living in France. Henry arranged to send him money by Burke.

Burke described his association with James and their adventures after leaving Scotland. The ship on which they escaped was boarded by pirates, and James and Burke were taken aboard the pirate ship. The pirates, under the leadership of Teach, their captain, were a drunken, incompetent, ignorant lot.

James bided his time, and when the ship put in for repairs, he escaped with Burke and several members of the crew, after robbing the store chest of money and treasure Teach had accumulated. With their spoils James and Burke eventually arrived in New York, where they met Chew, an Indian trader. They took off with him into the wilderness. When Chew died, they were left without a guide. James and Burke quarreled and separated. James buried the treasure he had and set off through the wilderness for Fort St. Frederick. When he arrived at the fort, he again met Burke, who welcomed him as a long-lost brother and paid his fare to France.

In France, James served in the French army and became a man of consequence at the French court because of his adeptness at politics, his unscrupulousness, and the money from his inheritance in Scotland. His demands finally put the estate in financial difficulties, for over a period of seven years he demanded and obtained a sum amounting to more than eight thousand pounds. Because he practiced strict economy to provide funds for his brother, Henry acquired a reputation as a miser and was upbraided by his wife. Then in 1756 Alison learned the true state of affairs from Mackellar, Henry's factor.

After that matters ran more smoothly in the household until James returned suddenly from France aboard a smuggler's lugger. His father was overjoyed to see his favorite son, who during his stay at Ballantrae was known as Mr. Bally. James' hatred for Henry was known only to Henry and Mackellar. In the presence of the household James seemed to be on the friendliest terms with his brother, but when no one was around he goaded Henry by subtle innuendoes and insinuations. Henry bore this state of affairs as best he could because James, even in exile, was the true Master of Ballantrae. As a further torment for his patient brother, James paid marked attention to Alison, and it really seemed she preferred his company to Henry's.

Matters came to a head one night when James casually mentioned to Henry that there never was a woman who did not prefer him when Henry was around. When this assertion was made, there was no one present but Mackellar, Henry, and James. Henry struck James and hot words quickly led to drawn swords. The brothers ordered Mackellar to carry candles into the garden. They went outside, Mackellar remonstrating all the while, but he could not stop the duel. The air was so still that the light of the candles did not waver as the brothers crossed swords. From the onset Henry became the aggressor, and it was not long before James realized he stood to lose the fight. He then resorted to trickery. As Henry lunged, James seized his brother's blade in his left hand. Henry saved himself from James' stroke by leaping to one side, and James, slipping to one knee from the force of his lunge, impaled himself on Henry's sword. Mackellar ran to the fallen James and declared him dead.

Henry seemed stupified and made off

toward the house at a stumbling pace. Mackellar took it upon himself to tell Alison and the old lord what had happened. The four decided that the first thing to do was to remove James' corpse. But when they arrived at the scene of the duel, the body had disappeared. They decided that smugglers, attracted by the light of the candles in the shrubbery, had found the body and taken it away, and their belief was confirmed by blood stains they found on the boat landing the next morning. Mr. Bally was reported in the neighborhood to have left Durrisdeer as suddenly as he had arrived.

As the affair turned out, James had been found alive but seriously wounded. He was taken aboard a smuggler's ship, and when he recovered he went to India. After he made a fortune there, he returned once more to Scotland in the company of an Indian named Secundra Dass.

They arrived at Durrisdeer early one morning. That night Henry with his wife and two children left the house secretly and took the next ship to New York. James, having learned of Henry's plans through the eavesdropping of Secundra Dass, sailed for New York three weeks later, and Mackellar, hoping to help his master, went with James and his servant. When they arrived in New York, Mackellar was pleased to learn that Henry had already taken precautions to forestall any claims which James might make.

When James' allowance from his brother proved insufficient for him to live in the style he desired, he set up shop as a tailor, and Secundra Dass employed himself as a goldsmith. Hatred for James gradually became an obsession with Henry. He reveled in the fact that after many years of humiliation and distress he had his wicked brother in his power.

To recoup his fortunes, James made plans to recover the treasure which he had previously hidden in the wilderness. He asked Henry to lend him the money to outfit an expedition, but Henry refused. Mackellar, although he hated James, could not bear to see a Durrie treated in such a haughty manner; therefore, he sent to Scotland for his own savings to assist James. But Henry had plans of his own, and he conspired with a man of unsavory reputation to guide James into the wilderness and there kill him. Again Secundra Dass overheard a chance conversation and warned his master of danger. Then James sickened and died. He was buried, and his guide returned to report his death to Henry.

Henry, however, believed his brother James to be in league with the devil, with the ability to die and return to life seemingly at will. With Mackellar and a small party, he set out for James' grave. They arrived one moonlit night in time to see Secundra Dass in the act of exhuming James' body and they gathered around to see what would happen. After digging through the frozen earth for a short distance, Secundra Dass removed his master's body from the shallow grave. Then the Indian began strange ministrations over the corpse. The moon was setting. The watchers imagined that in the pale light they saw the dead man's eyelids flutter. When the eyes opened and James looked full into his brother's face, Henry fell to the ground. He died before Mackellar could reach his side.

But the Indian trick of swallowing the tongue to give the appearance of death would not work in the cold American climate, and Secundra Dass failed to bring James completely to life. James, the Master of Ballantrae, and his brother were united in death in the wilderness of America.

THE MAYOR OF CASTERBRIDGE

Type of work: Novel
Author: Thomas Hardy (1840-1928)
Type of plot: Psychological realism
Time of plot: Nineteenth century
Locale: "Wessex," England
First published: 1886

Principal characters:
MICHAEL HENCHARD, the mayor of Casterbridge
SUSAN HENCHARD-NEWSON, his abandoned wife
ELIZABETH-JANE NEWSON, his stepdaughter
RICHARD NEWSON, a sailor
DONALD FARFRAE, a grain merchant
LUCETTA LE SUEUR, loved by Henchard, later Farfrae's wife

Critique:

Despite contrived events, the plot of *The Mayor of Casterbridge* works out well. Descriptions of the Wessex countryside are excellent. Hardy's simple country people are realistic and sometimes funny, if not always sympathetic. The modern reader is likely to question the melodramatic and spectacular opening scenes of the novel, in spite of Hardy's insistence that such occurrences did take place in rural districts during the last century. The plot illustrates Hardy's belief that "in fiction it is not improbabilities of incident but improbabilities of character that matter."

The Story:

One late summer afternoon, early in the nineteenth century, a young farm couple with their baby arrived on foot at the village of Weydon-Priors. A fair was in progress. The couple, tired and dusty, entered a refreshment tent where the husband proceeded to get so drunk that he offered his wife and child for sale. A sailor strange to the village bought the wife, Susan, and the child, Elizabeth-Jane, for five guineas. The young woman tore off her wedding ring and threw it in her drunken husband's face; then, carrying her child, she followed the sailor out of the tent.

When he awoke sober the next morning, Michael Henchard, the young farmer, realized what he had done. After taking an oath not to touch liquor for twenty years, he searched many months for his wife and child. In a western seaport he was told that three persons answering the description he gave had emigrated a short time before. He gave up his search and wandered on until he came to the town of Casterbridge. There he stayed to seek his fortune.

Richard Newson, the sailor, convinced Susan Henchard that she had no moral obligations to the husband who had sold her and her child. He married her and moved with his new family to Canada. Later they returned to England. Susan, meanwhile, had learned of the illegality of her marriage to Newson, but before she could make a positive move Newson was lost at sea. Susan and Elizabeth-Jane, now eighteen and attractive, returned to Weydon-Priors. There they heard that Henchard had gone to Casterbridge.

Henchard, in the intervening period, had become a prosperous grain merchant and the mayor of Casterbridge. When the women arrived in the town they heard that Henchard had sold some bad grain to bakers and restitution was expected. Donald Farfrae, a young Scots corn expert who was passing through Casterbridge, heard of Henchard's predicament and told him a method for partially restoring the grain. Farfrae so impressed Henchard and the people of the town that they prevailed on him to remain. Farfrae became Henchard's manager.

At the meeting of Susan and Henchard, it was decided Susan and her daughter would take lodgings and Henchard would pay court to Susan. Henchard, trusting young Farfrae, told the Scot of his philandering with a young woman named Lucetta Le Sueur, from Jersey. He asked Farfrae to meet Lucetta and keep her from coming to Casterbridge.

Henchard and Susan were married. Elizabeth-Jane developed into a beautiful young woman for whom Donald Farfrae had a growing attraction. Henchard wanted Elizabeth-Jane to take his name, but Susan refused his request, much to his mystification. He noticed that Elizabeth-Jane did not possess any of his personal traits.

Bad feeling came between Henchard and Farfrae over Henchard's harsh treatment of a simple-minded employee. Farfrae had succeeded Henchard in popularity in Casterbridge. The complete break came when a country dance sponsored by Farfrae drew all the populace, leaving Henchard's dance unattended. Farfrae, anticipating his dismissal, set up his own establishment but refused to take any of Henchard's business away from him. Henchard, antagonized, would not allow Elizabeth-Jane and Farfrae to see each other.

Henchard received a letter from Lucetta saying she would pass through Casterbridge to pick up her love letters. When Lucetta failed to keep the appointment, Henchard put the letters in his safe. Susan fell sick and wrote a letter for Henchard to open on the day Elizabeth-Jane was married. Soon afterward she died and Henchard told the girl that he was her real father. Looking for some documents to corroborate his story, he found the letter his wife had left in his keeping for Elizabeth-Jane. Henchard, unable to resist, read Susan's letter and learned that Elizabeth-Jane was really the daughter of Newson and Susan, his own daughter having died in infancy. His wife's reluctance to have the girl take his name was now clear, and Henchard's attitude toward Elizabeth-Jane became distant and cold.

One day Elizabeth-Jane met a strange woman at the village graveyard. The woman was Lucetta Templeman, formerly Lucetta Le Sueur, who had inherited property in Casterbridge from a rich aunt named Templeman. She took Elizabeth-Jane into her employ to make it convenient for Henchard, her old lover, to call on her.

Young Farfrae came to see Elizabeth-Jane, who was away at the time. He and Miss Templeman were immediately attracted to each other, and Lucetta refused to see Henchard after meeting Farfrae. Elizabeth-Jane overheard Henchard berate Lucetta under his breath for refusing to admit him to her house; she was made further uncomfortable when she saw that Farfrae had succumbed to Lucetta's charms. Henchard was now determined to ruin Farfrae. Advised by a weather prophet that the weather would be bad during the harvest, he bought grain heavily. When the weather stayed fair, Henchard was almost ruined by low grain prices. Farfrae bought cheap. The weather turned bad late in the harvest, and prices went up. Farfrae became wealthy.

In the meantime, Farfrae continued his courtship of Lucetta. Henchard, jealous, threatened to expose Lucetta's past unless she married him. Lucetta agreed. But an old woman disclosed to the village that Henchard was the man who had sold his wife and child years before. Lucetta, ashamed, left town. On the day of her return, Henchard rescued her and Elizabeth-Jane from an enraged bull. He asked Lucetta to give evidence to a creditor of their engagement. Lucetta confessed that in her absence she and Farfrae had been married. Henchard, utterly frustrated, again threatened to expose her. Elizabeth-Jane, upon learning of the marriage, left Lucetta's service.

The news that Henchard had sold his wife and child spread through the village. His creditors closed in, and he became a recluse. He and Elizabeth-Jane were reconciled during his illness. Upon his recovery he hired out to Farfrae as a common laborer.

Henchard's oath having expired, he began to drink heavily. Farfrae planned to set up Henchard and Elizabeth-Jane in a small seed shop, but the project did not materialize because of a misunderstanding. Farfrae became mayor of Casterbridge despite the desire of Lucetta to leave the village.

Jopp, a former employee of Henchard, blackmailed his way into the employ of Farfrae through Lucetta, whose past he knew, because he had lived in Jersey before he came to Casterbridge. Henchard, finally taking pity on Lucetta, gave Jopp the love letters to return to her. Before delivering them, Jopp read the letters aloud in an inn.

Royalty visited Casterbridge. Henchard, wishing to retain his old stature in the village, forced himself among the receiving dignitaries, but Farfrae pushed him aside. Later, Henchard got Farfrae at his mercy, during a fight in a warehouse loft, but the younger man shamed Henchard by telling him to go ahead and kill him.

The townspeople, excited over the letters they had heard read, devised a mummery employing effigies of Henchard and Lucetta riding back to back on a donkey. Farfrae's friends arranged to have him absent from the village during the mummers' parade, but Lucetta saw it and was prostrated. She died of a miscarriage that night.

Richard Newson, not lost after all, came to Casterbridge in search of Susan and Elizabeth-Jane. He met Henchard, who sent him away with the information that both Susan and Elizabeth-Jane were dead.

Elizabeth-Jane went to live with Henchard in his poverty. They opened a seed shop and began to prosper in a modest way. Farfrae, to the misery of the lonely Henchard, began to pay court to Elizabeth-Jane, and they planned to marry soon. Newson returned, obviously knowing he had been duped. Henchard left town but returned for the marriage festivities, bringing with him a goldfinch as a wedding present. When he saw that Newson had completely replaced him as Elizabeth-Jane's father, he went sadly away. Newson, restless, departed for the sea again, after Farfrae and his daughter were settled. Henchard pined away and died, ironically enough, in the secret care of the simple-minded old man whom he had once tyrannized.

MEDEA

Type of work: Drama
Author: Euripides (480-406 B.C.)
Type of plot: Classical tragedy
Time of plot: Remote antiquity
Locale: Corinth
First presented: 431 B.C.

Principal characters:
Medea, a sorceress
Jason, her lover
Creon, King of Corinth
Glauce, daughter of Creon
Aegeus, King of Athens

Critique:

Medea is justly one of the best known of Greek tragedies, for although it was written more than two thousand years ago it has meaning and significance today. Jason and Medea are purely human and even without the intervention of supernatural agencies, tragedy is implicit in their characters. Their story is a perennial caution against excess of emotion and a stern warning against bitter vengeance.

The Story:

When Medea discovered that Jason had deserted her and married Glauce, the daughter of Creon, she vowed a terrible vengeance. Her nurse, although she loved Medea, recognized that a frightful threat now hung over Corinth, for she knew that Medea would not let the insult pass without some dreadful revenge. She feared especially for Medea's two sons, since the sorceress included her children in the hatred which she now felt for their father.

Her resentment increased still further when Creon, hearing of her vow, ordered her and her children to be banished from Corinth. Slyly, with a plan already in mind, Medea persuaded him to allow her just one day longer to prepare herself and her children for the journey. She had already decided the nature of her revenge; the one problem that remained was a place of refuge afterward. Then Aegeus, King of Athens and a long-time friend of Medea, appeared in Corinth on his way home from a journey. Sympathetic with her because of Jason's brutal desertion, he offered her a place of refuge from her enemies in his own kingdom. In this manner Medea assured herself of a refuge, even after Aegeus should learn of the deeds she intended to commit in Corinth.

When the Corinthian women came to visit her, Medea told them of her plan, but only after swearing them to absolute secrecy. At first she had considered killing Jason, his princess, and Creon, and then fleeing with her children. But after she had considered, she felt that revenge would be sweeter should Jason live to suffer long afterward. Nothing could be more painful than to grow old without a lover, without children, and without friends, and so Medea planned to kill the king, his daughter, and her own children.

She called Jason to her and pretended that she forgave him for what he had done, recognizing at last the justice and foresight he had shown in marrying Glauce. She begged his forgiveness for her earlier rage, and asked that she be allowed to send her children with gifts for the new bride, as a sign of her repentance. Jason was completely deceived by her supposed change of heart, and expressed his pleasure at the belated wisdom she was showing.

Medea drew out a magnificent robe and a fillet of gold, presents of her grandfather, Helios, the sun god, but before she entrusted them to her children she smeared them with a deadly drug. Shortly afterward, a messenger came to Medea and told her to flee. One part of her plan had succeeded. After Jason and the children had left, Glauce had dressed herself in her wonderful robe and walked through the palace. But as the warmth and moisture of her body came in contact with the drug, the fillet and gown clung to her body and seared her flesh. She tried frantically to tear them from her, but the garments only wrapped more tightly around her, and she died in a screaming agony of flames. When Creon rushed in and saw his daughter writhing on the floor, he attempted to lift her, but was himself contaminated by the poison. His death was as agonized as hers had been.

Meanwhile the children had returned to Medea. As she looked at them and felt their arms around her, she was torn between her love for them and her hatred of Jason; between her desire for revenge and the commands of her mother-instinct. But the barbarian part of her nature—Medea being not a Greek, but a barbarian from Colchis—triumphed. After reveling in the messenger's account of the deaths of Creon and his daughter, she entered her house with the children and barred the door. While the Corinthian women stood helplessly outside, they listened to the shrieks of the children as Medea killed them with a sword. Jason appeared, frantically eager to take his children away lest they be killed by Creon's followers for having brought the dreadful gifts. When he learned Medea had killed his children, he was almost insane with grief. As he hammered furiously on the barred doors of the house, Medea suddenly appeared above, holding the bodies of her dead children, and drawn in a chariot which Helios, the sun god, had sent her. Jason alternately cursed her and pleaded with her for one last sight of his children as Medea taunted him with the loneliness and grief to which he was doomed. She told him that her own sorrow would be great, but it was compensated for by the sweetness of her revenge.

The chariot, drawn by winged dragons, carried her first to the mountain of the goddess Hera. There she buried her children. Then she journeyed to Athens, where she would spend the remainder of her days feeding on the gall and wormwood of her terrible grief and revenge.

MEMOIRS OF A FOX-HUNTING MAN

Type of work: Novel
Author: Siegfried Sassoon (1886-)
Type of plot: Social chronicle
Time of plot: 1895-1916
Locale: England and France
First published: 1929

Principal characters:
GEORGE SHERSTON, the fox-hunting man
AUNT EVELYN, with whom he lived
TOM DIXON, Aunt Evelyn's groom
DENIS MILDEN, George's friend and master at Ringwell, later at Packlestone
STEPHEN COLWOOD, George's schoolmate and friend
MR. PENNETT, George's trustee
DICK TILTWOOD, George's friend in the army

Critique:

Memoirs of a Fox-Hunting Man is the scarcely concealed autobiography of the author. The tone of the book is nostalgic. The passages concerning cricket and the more technical passages about fox hunting are somewhat tedious, but for the most part this sensitive record of a young man's quiet, well-ordered life in pre-war England is interesting and illuminating. The class distinctions may be difficult for an American reader to understand, but Sassoon indicates that later in life he himself came to be more liberal in his feeling about people of lower social ranks.

The Story:

George Sherston was orphaned so early that he could not remember when he had not lived with his Aunt Evelyn at Butley. At the age of nine he became the possessor of a pony, bought at the urgent request of Aunt Evelyn's groom, Tom Dixon. Aunt Evelyn would not let George go to school until he was twelve, and his early training was given him by an incompetent tutor, Mr. Star. Dixon, however, taught him to ride, and this training he valued more highly than anything Mr. Star taught him. Because George's early life was often lonely, he welcomed the diversion of riding.

At last Dixon thought George was ready to see some fox hunting. Since there was no hunting in the Sherston neighborhood, they had to ride some nine miles to the Dumborough Hunt, where George was thrilled by the color and excitement of the chase. He saw a boy of about his own age who carried himself well and was obviously one to be imitated. The next Friday at a dance George saw the boy again and was pleased that the boy, Denis Milden, remembered seeing him at the hunt.

After his first year in school at Ballboro' George was happy to be back at Aunt Evelyn's. Dixon met him at the station with the word that he had secured a place for George on the village cricket team, which would play next day at the Flower Show Match. George had played good cricket at school, but he did not know how he would show up facing players of long experience. The next day, learning that he was to be last at bat, he spent the afternoon trying to forget his nervousness. Once in the game, he suddenly gained confidence and brought his side the victory.

George's trustee and guardian, Mr. Pennett, was disturbed when his ward quit Cambridge without a degree. George settled down with Aunt Evelyn at Butley. He played some cricket and some golf. He ordered a great many books from London. Dixon began to revive George's interest in hunting, but Mr. Pennett would not give George the full amount of his annual income and so George could not afford the kind of horse he wanted. Dixon, however, soon found a suitable horse within the limits of George's budget, a hunter named Harkaway. The season was well on, and George was out only three days. Later in the spring he attended the Ringwell Hunt Point-to-Point Races, where Stephen Colwood, a friend whom he had known at Ballboro', won the Heavy-Weight Race.

The following autumn George made one of his rare trips to London. There he heard a concert by Fritz Kreisler and bought some clothes suitable for a fox-hunting man. His first hunting was with the Potford Hunt, an experience he found much more exciting than that he had known with the Dumborough. He also went down to Sussex to stay with Stephen at his father's rectory. While visiting Stephen, George bought another horse, Cockbird, in defiance of Mr. Pennett. When he returned to Butley with his new horse, his Aunt Evelyn, realizing that he could not afford the hunter, sold one of her rings and gave George the money for Christmas.

Cockbird was more than a satisfactory horse. Riding him with the Ringwell Hounds, George qualified for the Colonel's Cup Race. One of his competitors was riding a horse owned by Nigel Croplady, a noisy young braggart liked by very few people. Another competitor was his friend Stephen. During the race Stephen was forced to drop back, but he encouraged George so much that George came in to win. As the afternoon came to a close, someone drew his attention to the new master of the Ringwell Hounds. It was Denis Milden.

That summer George played in a number of cricket matches. Stephen, now in the artillery, spent a weekend at Butley. As autumn drew on, George became impatient for the hunting season to begin. Stephen, now stationed near his home, asked George to spend some time at the rectory and ride with the Ringwell Hounds. Nothing could have pleased George more, for he was a great admirer of Denis. The two became good friends, and George sometimes stayed at the kennels with Denis. Denis proved to be an excellent master, skillful in the hunt and careful and patient with his hounds.

Early in the following season, however, Denis resigned to become master of the Packlestone Hunt, and he insisted that George go up to the Midlands with him. To ride with the Packlestone Hounds would be an expense George knew he could not afford, but he went for the first season. He was always embarrassed, for he knew that his new friends were unaware of his economic limitations. The year was 1914.

War was declared. George, aware of his incompetency as a soldier, had turned down two opportunities to be an officer, and was serving in the army as a cavalryman. To have to salute Nigel Croplady made him feel silly. One day the horse George was riding threw him, and he broke his arm. Two months later he was sent home to allow his arm to heal. One afternoon he went to see his neighbor, Captain Huxtable, and asked that he be recommended for a commission in the infantry. The commission came through. George proceeded to his new camp. There he made friends with Dick Tiltwood, a pleasant young man not long out of school.

They crossed the Channel together and were assigned to a battalion coming back from the front for a rest. Dick and George spent many hours sightseeing and talking and reading. George took Dick out riding frequently. They would pretend they were fox hunting. George, assigned to headquarters, felt rather shaken when Dick was sent to the trenches without him. Word reached George that Stephen had been killed. Dixon, who was also in service and who wanted to be transferred to George's company, died of pneumonia. Then when George learned that Dick had died of a throat wound, he asked to be transferred to the trenches. There he served bravely, always angry at the war which had taken away his best friends.

MEMOIRS OF A MIDGET

Type of work: Novel
Author: Walter de la Mare (1873-)
Type of plot: Fantasy
Time of plot: Late nineteenth century
Locale: England
First published: 1921

Principal characters:
MISS M., a midget
MRS. BOWATER, her landlady
FANNY BOWATER, Mrs. Bowater's daughter
MRS. MONNERIE, Miss M.'s patroness
MR. ANON, a dwarf

Critique:

Memoirs of a Midget is a highly original novel which mingles poetry and social criticism. Exquisitely written, it has an unfailing charm and interest. Remarkable is the careful and exact use of the proper perspective throughout the thoughtfully executed work. Nor can the reader fail to note the veiled criticisms of society which the author puts into the mouth of tiny Miss M.

The Story:

Miss M., a perfectly-formed midget, was born to normal parents and in pleasant surroundings. Until her eighteenth year she was brought up in seclusion. Then her mother died, followed shortly thereafter by her father, and tiny Miss M. was left alone in the world. Her godmother offered to take her in, but the girl, having inherited a modest fortune, decided to take lodgings instead. She made her first humiliating excursion in public when she moved to her new home.

Her lodgings were in the home of Mrs. Bowater, a stern woman, who nevertheless had a great affection for her small roomer. At Mrs. Bowater's Miss M. met Fanny, the daughter of her landlady. A teacher in a girls' school, Fanny was both charming and clever. Because of the friendship between the two, the midget became involved in the love affair of Fanny Bowater and the curate, an affair which ended with the curate's suicide when Fanny rejected his suit.

After a time Miss M. began to go out in society. She became the friend of Lady Pollacke, whose friendship she was never to lose. At their home she met the wealthy Mrs. Monnerie, the youngest daughter of Lord B. Mrs. Monnerie took such a fancy to the tiny girl that she invited her for a vacation at Lyme Regis, a fashionable watering place in Dorsetshire.

Before she left on her vacation Miss M. accidentally met a new friend, Mr. Anon, a deformed and hunchbacked creature only a few inches taller than Miss M. Miss M., unaware of the ways of the world, introduced Mr. Anon to Mrs. Bowater, who approved of him in a grudging way. They saw each other frequently, and Miss M. once solicited his aid when she wanted to secure money for Fanny while she was away at Lyme Regis. Soon after they returned from their holiday, Mrs. Monnerie invited Midgetina, as she called Miss M., to visit at her elaborate town house in London.

Miss M. accepted the invitation and became another prized possession Mrs. Monnerie could exhibit to her guests. In London she met the niece and nephew of her patroness. Percy Maudlen was a languid, ill-mannered youth whom the small girl disliked. Susan Monnerie was a pleasant person of whom Miss M. became very fond. After a visit of six weeks, Miss M. returned briefly to Mrs. Bowater's. There she received a letter from Fanny, begging her to try to use her influence with Mrs. Monnerie to secure a position for Fanny as a governess. During Miss M.'s stay with Mrs. Bowater she again met Mr. Anon, who declared his love for her. The midget told him that she was not able to return his love.

Before long Miss M. returned to London, where her pampered way of living did much to spoil her. During her stay Mrs. Bowater came with the news that she was going to South America to nurse her sick husband, a sailor. Shortly afterward Miss M.'s solicitors informed her that her small inheritance had dwindled because of the gifts and trifles she had bought and because of her loans to Fanny. When Miss M. confessed her troubles to Sir Walter Pollacke, he consented to become both her guardian and financial adviser. Meanwhile, Miss M. had not forgotten Fanny Bowater's request. Through the little person's persuasion, Mrs. Monnerie found a place for Fanny as morning governess and invited the girl to stay with her.

Mr. Anon wrote and proposed marriage, but Miss M. was horrified at the idea of repeating the performance of Tom Thumb and Mercy Lavinia Bump Warren. Then it became evident that Mrs. Monnerie was no longer amused by her little charge, for Fanny had become her favorite. To celebrate Miss M.'s birthday, Percy Maudlen planned a banquet in her honor, but the party was a dismal failure so far as Miss M. was concerned. The menu disgusted her, and when Percy proposed a toast Miss M. responded by drinking down her glass of chartreuse at a single gulp and staggering drunkenly down the table. In this condition she hurled at Fanny a reference to the unfortunate suicide of the curate.

Such actions deserved punishment. Mrs. Monnerie sent Miss M. in disgrace to Monks' House, her summer place in the country. One afternoon Miss M. saw the caravans of a circus passing the gate. Because she knew that she could no longer count on Mrs. Monnerie for support, Miss M. was desperate and she suddenly decided to hire herself to the circus. The owner engaged her to ride a pony in the ring, and she agreed to appear for four nights for fifteen guineas. She also told fortunes. She was a great success, the most popular attraction of the circus.

Her solitude during the day at Monks' House was interrupted by the arrival of

Fanny Bowater. Fanny seemed to know of her escapades at the circus, and the two quarreled violently. Then Mrs. Monnerie arrived. She was in a high state of excitement over the news of the midget who was so popular at the circus. She had even made up a party to attend the performance on the last night. When Miss M. flatly refused to perform, Mrs. Monnerie sent her, like a child, to bed.

At the last minute Miss M. felt that she must appear at the circus to keep her contract. Setting out on foot, she encountered Mr. Anon, and they went on to the circus together. Although he tried to persuade her not to appear, she exhibited herself in the tent, unrecognized, in her disguise, by all of the members of Mrs. Monnerie's party except Fanny. Mr. Anon, determined that he would take her place in the riding act, put on her costume and rode into the ring. Thrown from the pony, he died in Miss M.'s arms.

Through a legacy from her grandfather, Miss M. became financially independent, and settled down at Lyndsey with Mrs. Bowater as her housekeeper. But one night Miss M. disappeared mysteriously, leaving a note saying that she had been called suddenly away. She was never seen again, and her memoirs were eventually presented to the public by her faithful friend, Sir Walter Pollacke.

MEMOIRS OF AN INFANTRY OFFICER

Type of work: Novel
Author: Siegfried Sassoon (1886-)
Type of plot: Social chronicle
Time of plot: 1916-1917
Locale: France and England
First published: 1930

Principal characters:
GEORGE SHERSTON, an infantry officer
DAVID CROMLECH, his friend
AUNT EVELYN, his aunt

Critique:

This novel—the second of a series which also includes *Memoirs of a Fox-Hunting Man* and *Sherston's Progress*—is almost a caricature of what many people regard as typical English behavior. The war is a very casual, very personal thing, almost devoid of import and strategy. The officers who meet Sherston briefly are men who exhibit just the right amount of detachment and regard for good form. Underneath the well-bred tolerance for the real discomfort and danger of trench warfare there is a thread of revolt which culminates in Sherston's letter informing his colonel that the war is needlessly being prolonged. Even the authorities, however, are too well-bred to take the letter seriously, and Sherston falls back into nonchalance. The book is quiet but effective satire on upper-class English life.

The Story:

Spring arrived late in 1916 in the trenches near Mametz. Sherston had made up his mind to die, because under the circumstances there seemed to be little else to do. The battle of the Somme had exhausted him. Colonel Kinjack could see that Sherston was looking for trouble and so, to forestall any unpleasantness, he sent Sherston to the Fourth Army School at Flixécourt for a month's training.

The beds at the school were clean and comfortable, and the routine was not too onerous. Sherston settled back to forget the war. He attended a big game hunter's lectures on sniping and practiced with a bayonet. To him it was a little incongruous to listen to advice from civilians and army men who had never been close to real war. All the instructors concentrated on open warfare; they were sure that the trenches would soon be abandoned.

One hot Saturday afternoon he went back to his outfit, where the talk was all of an impending raid. There seemed to be some jealousy involved, for a Canadian raid a short time before had been a great success.

Sherston, sure he would accompany the raiders, wrote a farewell letter to his Aunt Evelyn, a letter in which he slyly assumed the attitude of the "happy warrior." Entering a dugout, he was a little surprised to see the raiders putting burnt cork on their faces. Their appearance reminded him ridiculously of a minstrel show. Requested to take the raiders up to headquarters, he jumped at the opportunity to present his plea to the commanding officer.

To his disappointment, Colonel Kinjack brusquely told him he had to stay behind to count the raiders when they returned. So he was condemned to stand in the trench and wait.

As soon as the raiders were well over the parapet, the explosions began. The men struggled back defeated when the second belt of German wire proved invulnerable. They had all tossed their bombs and retired. Sherston began to go out into No Man's Land to bring in the casualties. A gray-haired lance corporal was glad of his wound, for he had been waiting eighteen months for a chance to go home. O'Brien, the major, was killed, and Sherston had to drag him out of a shell crater. Luckily the Germans, perhaps out of pity, stopped firing.

The result of the raid was two killed and ten wounded. In the newspapers, the account was somewhat changed. Aunt Evelyn read that the party entered the German trenches without difficulty, displayed admirable morale, and withdrew after twenty-five minutes of hand-to-hand fighting.

The big push, the summer offensive, was in the air. Before Sherston really had time to think much about impending events, he was given a leave. At first it was strange to be back in England, where everyone seemed to know about the projected onslaught. Out of deference to one who would take part in it, however, they seldom mentioned it. Aunt Evelyn soon found out about the raid when Sherston grandly announced that he was due for a military cross. She was horrified, for she thought her nephew was still in the transport service.

On his way back to France he stopped in the Army and Navy Store and bought two pairs of wire cutters. Then, because he was late in returning from leave, he bought a salmon and two bottles of brandy to appease his colonel.

When the offensive began, Sherston's company advanced fifteen hundred yards in four hours. Then the guides became confused, and all forward progress stopped. According to the General Staff, the Germans were supposed to be out of the Mametz Woods, but they were still there. The company waited.

Sherston was going along a communications trench when his companion, Kendle, was killed by a sniper. Furious at the unexpected killing, Sherston took a mills bomb in each hand and went over the top. After a while he was looking down into a well-ordered trench filled with Germans. Fortunately they were just leaving, and he jumped into Wood Trench, until lately the German front line. Then he lost his perspective. Not knowing what to do with the trench, he returned to his own lines. His colonel reproved him severely for not "consolidating" the trench or even reporting the incident.

During the battle of Bazentin Ridge

Sherston was kept in reserve in the transport lines. In this brief respite, he met his old friend, David Cromlech. For a while they shared experiences, but both were reluctant to talk about the battle of the Somme. David irritated the other officers greatly by his habit of making bold pronouncements about sacred things. For instance, he said that all sports except boxing, football, and rock climbing were snobbish and silly.

When Sherston was finally recalled to his battalion, it was with the expectation that he would go into action at once. As it turned out, however, he came down with enteritis before he arrived in the front lines. It was an escape, really, for he was removed to the base hospital and eventually was sent back to England.

At the military hospital in Oxford, Sherston recovered enough to go canoeing occasionally. By the end of August he was back with Aunt Evelyn on a month's sick leave with a possibility of extension. Several letters from fellow officers kept him informed about his battalion, mostly reports on men killed. He remained fairly cheerful, however, by riding in the local fox hunts. In February he went back to Rouen.

The Germans were retreating from the Hindenburg Line, and the British were on the offensive in the battle of Arras. To his surprise and gratification, Sherston was put in charge of a hundred bombers who were clearing the trenches. He carried out his task with great skill and bravery. When the mission was nearly accomplished, he was struck by a rifle bullet.

Back in England again, he rebelled against going into action a third time. With the help of Tyrrell, a pacifist philosopher, he composed a defiant letter to his colonel, saying that he refused to take part in the war any longer because he was sure it was being unnecessarily continued by those in power. He was sure, above all, that the Germans would surrender if the Allies would publish their war aims. Expecting to be court-martialed for this breach of discipline, he was resolved to accept even execution.

To his chagrin, the superiors refused to take him seriously. He went before a board which investigated his sanity. Then David Cromlech was called in to talk to him at Clitherland Camp. Unable to persuade him to recant by any other means, David finally told Sherston that if he refused to retract his statements he would be confined in a lunatic asylum for the duration of the war. Sherston knew David was only telling a friendly lie, but he did not want to see his friend proved a liar. He decided to admit his mistake and see the war through to its finish.

THE MERCHANT OF VENICE

Type of work: Drama
Author: William Shakespeare (1564-1616)
Type of plot: Tragi-comedy
Time of plot: Sixteenth century
Locale: Venice
First presented: c. 1596

Principal characters:
SHYLOCK, a Jewish money-lender
PORTIA, a wealthy young woman
ANTONIO, an impoverished merchant, Shylock's enemy, championed by Portia
BASSANIO, Portia's husband, Antonio's friend
NERISSA, Portia's waiting-woman
GRATIANO, Nerissa's husband, Bassanio's friend
JESSICA, Shylock's daughter
LORENZO, Jessica's husband

Critique:

Though the closing scenes of *The Merchant of Venice* keep it from becoming a tragedy, it is essentially a serious study of the use and misuse of wealth, of love and marriage. The encounter between the greedy, vengeful Jew, Shylock, and the wise and fine Portia, gives the play a theme of grave beauty.

The Story:

Bassanio, meeting his wealthy friend, Antonio, revealed that he had a plan for restoring his fortune, carelessly spent, and for paying the debts he had incurred. In the town of Belmont, not far from Venice, there lived a wealthy young woman named Portia, who was famous for her beauty. If he could secure some money, Bassanio declared, he was sure he could win her as his wife.

Antonio replied that he had no funds at hand with which to supply his friend, as they were all invested in the ships which he had at sea, but he would attempt to borrow some money in Venice.

Portia had many suitors for her hand. According to the strange conditions of her father's will, however, anyone who wished her for his wife had to choose among three caskets of silver, gold, and lead the one which contained a message that she was his. Four of her suitors, seeing that they could not win her except under the conditions of the will, departed. A fifth, a Moor, decided to take his chances. The unfortunate man chose the golden casket, which contained only a skull and a mocking message. For his failure he was compelled to swear never to reveal the casket he had chosen and never to woo another woman.

The Prince of Arragon was the next suitor to try his luck. In his turn he chose the silver casket, only to learn from the note it bore that he was a fool.

True to his promise to Bassanio, Antonio arranged to borrow three thousand ducats from Shylock, a wealthy Jew. Antonio was to have the use of the money for three months. If he should be unable to return the loan at the end of that time, Shylock was to have the right to cut a pound of flesh from any part of Antonio's body. In spite of Bassanio's objections, Antonio insisted on accepting the terms, for he was sure his ships would return a month before the payment would be due. He was confident that he would never fall into the power of the Jew, who hated Antonio because he often lent money to others without charging the interest Shylock demanded.

That night Bassanio planned a feast and a masque. In conspiracy with his friend, Lorenzo, he invited Shylock to be his guest. Lorenzo, taking advantage of her father's absence, ran off with the Jew's daughter, Jessica, who did not hesitate to take part of Shylock's fortune with her.

Shylock was cheated not only of his daughter and his ducats but also of his entertainment, for the wind suddenly changed and Bassanio set sail for Belmont.

As the days passed, the Jew began to hear news of mingled good and bad fortune. In Genoa, Jessica and Lorenzo were making lavish use of the money she had taken with her. The miser flinched at the reports of his daughter's extravagance, but for compensation he had the news that Antonio's ships, on which his fortune depended, had been wrecked at sea.

Portia, much taken with Bassanio when he came to woo her, would have had him wait before he tried to pick the right casket. Sure that he would fail as the others had, she hoped to have his company a little while longer. Bassanio, however, was impatient to try his luck. Not deceived by the ornateness of the gold and silver caskets, but philosophizing that true virtue is inward virtue, he chose the lead box. In it was a portrait of Portia. He had chosen correctly.

To seal their engagement, Portia gave Bassanio a ring. She declared he must never part with it, for if he did it would signify the end of their love.

Gratiano, a friend who had accompanied Bassanio to Belmont, spoke up. He was in love with Portia's waiting-woman, Nerissa. With Portia's delighted approval, Gratiano planned that both couples should be married at the same time.

Bassanio's joy at his good fortune was soon blighted. Antonio wrote that he was ruined, all his ships having failed to return. The time for payment of the loan being past due, Shylock was demanding his pound of flesh. In closing, Antonio declared that he cleared Bassanio of his debt to him. He wished only to see his friend once more before his death.

Portia declared that the double wedding should take place at once. Then her husband, with her dowry of six thousand ducats, should set out for Venice in an attempt to buy off the Jew.

After Bassanio and Gratiano had gone, Portia declared to Lorenzo and Jessica, who had come to Belmont, that she and Nerissa were going to a nunnery, where they would live in seclusion until their husbands returned. She committed the charge of her house and servants to Jessica and Lorenzo.

Instead of taking the course she had described, however, Portia set about executing other plans. She gave her servant, Balthasar, orders to take a note to her cousin, Doctor Bellario, a famous lawyer of Padua, in order to secure a message and some clothes from him. She explained to Nerissa that they would go to Venice disguised as men.

The Duke of Venice, before whom Antonio's case was tried, was reluctant to exact the penalty which was in Shylock's terms. When his appeals to the Jew's better feelings went unheeded, he could see no course before him except to give the money-lender his due. Bassanio also tried to make Shylock relent by offering him the six thousand ducats, but, like the Duke, he met only a firm refusal.

Portia, dressed as a lawyer, and Nerissa, disguised as her clerk, appeared in the court. Nerissa offered the duke a letter from Doctor Bellario. The doctor explained that he was very ill, but that Balthasar, his young representative, would present his opinion in the dispute.

When Portia appealed to the Jew's mercy, Shylock answered with a demand for the penalty. Portia then declared that the Jew, under the letter of the contract, could not be offered money in exchange for Antonio's release. The only alternative was for the merchant to forfeit his flesh.

Antonio prepared his bosom for the knife, for Shylock was determined to take his portion as close to his enemy's heart as he could cut. Before the operation could begin, however, Portia, examining the contract, declared that it contained no clause stating that Shylock could have any blood with the flesh.

The Jew, realizing that he was defeated, offered at once to accept the six thousand ducats, but Portia declared that he was not entitled to the money he had already refused. She stated also that Shylock, an alien, had threatened the life of a Venetian citizen. For that crime Antonio had the right to seize half of his property and the state the remainder.

Antonio refused that penalty, but it was agreed that one half of Shylock's fortune should go at once to Jessica and Lorenzo. Shylock was to keep the remainder, but it too was to be willed the couple. In addition, Shylock was to undergo conversion. The defeated man agreed to those terms.

Pressed to accept a reward, Portia took only a pair of Antonio's gloves and the ring which she herself had given Bassanio. Nerissa, likewise, managed to secure Gratiano's ring. Then the pair started back for Belmont, to be there when their husbands returned.

Portia and Nerissa arrived home shortly before Bassanio and Gratiano appeared in company with Antonio. Pretending to discover that their husbands' rings were missing, Portia and Nerissa at first accused Bassanio and Gratiano of unfaithfulness. At last, to the surprise of all, they revealed their secret, which was vouched for by a letter from Doctor Bellario. For Jessica and Lorenzo they had the good news of their future inheritance, and for Antonio a letter, secured by chance, announcing that some of his ships had arrived safely in port.

MESSER MARCO POLO

Type of work: Novelette
Author: Donn Byrne (1889-1928)
Type of plot: Exotic romance
Time of plot: Thirteenth century
Locale: Venice and China
First published: 1921

Principal characters:
MARCO POLO, the Venetian
KUBLA KHAN, Emperor of China
GOLDEN BELLS, Kubla Khan's daughter
LI PO, court poet
SANANG, court magician

Critique:

A mixture of three elements gives this simple tale a unique flavor. A modern Irishman tells the adventures of a Christian Italian in pagan China. Irish mysticism mingles with the mystery of the East to produce a romantic and tragic love story based upon the visit of Marco Polo to the court of Kubla Khan. The author succeeds in bringing together, in one framework, folk tale, history, and imagination. His simple narrative style is of a kind very rarely found among modern authors; it suggests the fireside stories and poems of the past which passed from generation to generation by word of mouth.

The Story:

On the first night of spring young Marco Polo deserted his work in his father's counting-house and wandered restlessly through the streets of Venice. He entered a wine shop in the hope of talking with some of the foreign people gathered there. The people inside were gambling and drinking, except for one man who sat by himself at a table. Marco recognized him as a Chinese sea captain and sat down to talk to him. In a friendly argument over the merits of their native countries, the sea captain got the better of young Marco by describing the beauty of Golden Bells, the daughter of Kubla Khan.

From that night on, the image of Golden Bells haunted Marco Polo. When his father and uncle, Nicholas and Matthew Polo, returned from China, Marco told them that he wished to go with them on their next trip. Kubla Khan had told the Polos to bring a Christian missionary back with them from Venice, and they chose young Marco to play the part. He was delighted, for he had convinced himself that it was his mission to convert Golden Bells to Christianity.

The wise old Pope gave his blessing to Marco as he started out for China, but he warned the young man not to expect to convert many pagans. Marco, his uncle, and his father set out with their camel caravan for the court of Kubla Khan. Marco saw on the way many strange countries and cities. At last the travelers came to the Desert of the Singing Sands. Many deserted or died until there were only six of the caravan left. When a great sandstorm came upon them, Marco struggled until his strength gave out and he lay down to die.

Meanwhile Golden Bells sat in the garden of Kubla Khan and talked with Li Po, the court poet. Sanang, the court magician, joined them. He told Golden Bells that he could see in his crystal ball the troubles of Marco Polo. Golden Bells felt pity for the young man and begged Sanang to save him from death in the Desert of the Singing Sands. Through his magic power Sanang called upon the Tartar tribesmen to rescue Marco. Golden Bells was joyful when the old magician assured her the young man had been saved. Li Po smiled and said he would write a marriage song for her. She said that she was in love with no one, but she refused to sing any more the sad "Song of the Willow Branches."

The desert tribesmen brought Marco before Kubla Khan and Golden Bells. The emperor asked him to tell something about the Christian religion. Marco quoted the Beatitudes and related the life of Christ, but Kubla Khan and his court were not impressed by that story of gentleness and love. Golden Bells alone, of all the court, told Marco that she was his convert.

Marco began to instruct Golden Bells and told her all the Bible stories he knew. She was charmed by his voice. He tried to explain to her what sin was, but she could not believe that the beauty of a woman was a curse. Finally, when he had told her all he knew of Christianity, he spoke of returning to Venice. Golden Bells was heartbroken. At last Marco took her in his arms.

For three years they lived happily; then Golden Bells died. Marco remained on for fourteen years in the service of the emperor. One evening Kubla Khan came to Marco with Li Po and Sanang and told him that he should return to Venice, for some of the people in the land were jealous of Marco's power. It was for his own good that he should return.

Marco refused to go. He did not wish to leave the place where he had been happy. Only a sign from the dead Golden Bells would make him leave. Then Sanang cast a magic spell and Li Po sang a magic song. A ghostly moonlight appeared at the end of the palace garden, and there, slim in the moonlight, stood Golden Bells. With her pleading eyes and soundless lips she begged Marco to return to Venice; then she disappeared. Marco was overcome with grief, but he promised to go. As he took leave of his three old friends, he said that he was going home to be an exile in his own land. The sunshine and the rain of China—and the memory of Golden Bells—would be always in his heart.

MICAH CLARKE

Type of work: Novel
Author: Arthur Conan Doyle (1859-1930)
Type of plot: Historical romance
Time of plot: Late seventeenth century
Locale: England
First published: 1888

Principal characters:
MICAH CLARKE, an English youth
JOSEPH CLARKE, his father
DECIMUS SAXON, an old soldier
REUBEN LOCKARBY, Micah's friend
SIR GERVAS, a Cavalier
THE DUKE OF MONMOUTH, pretender to the throne

Critique:

Micah Clarke is one of a group of historical romances by the writer who will always be best known for his creation of Sherlock Holmes. *Micah Clarke* is a stirring adventure story as well as a careful reconstruction of the events of 1685, when the Duke of Monmouth attempted to seize the English throne. The pictures of the determined Protestants who preferred death to a Catholic king are unforgettable.

The Story:

At Havant, near Portsmouth, young Micah Clarke grew up under the domination of his strong Puritan father, Joseph Clarke. He led a vigorous, active life, but he spent much time praying and hymn singing. From his father he heard many tales of Cromwell and the Puritans, for Joseph had fought in the wars of those troubled times. Save for a year at an Established Church school, Micah's education was taken in hand by his father himself. At the age of twenty, Micah was the strongest man in the village.

As was their custom, Micah and his good friend Reuben set out to fish in Langston Bay. They pulled up to their favorite fishing ground just as the sun was setting, threw out the large anchor stone, and set their lines. Not far away a king's ship stood in for the channel. The two youths watched her until their attention was drawn to a large brig not over a quarter mile distant. The ship seemed to be out of control, for she yawed as if there were no hand at the tiller. While they watched, they heard two musket shots aboard the brig. A few minutes later a cannon shot sounded and the ball passed close to their boat as the brig came about and headed down the channel. Reuben urged his friend to pull hard, for there was a man in the water. They could soon see him swimming easily along, and as they came alongside the swimmer expertly hoisted himself aboard. He was a tall, lean man, over fifty but wiry and strong. Their passenger looked them over coolly, drew out a wicked knife, and ordered them to head for the French coast. But when Micah lifted his oar and threatened to knock the man over the head, their passenger gave in meekly and handed over his knife with good grace. He told them that he had jumped overboard from the brig after he and his brother, the captain, had exchanged musket shots during a quarrel.

As they headed shoreward, the stranger heard Reuben use the name Clarke. Instantly the man became interested and asked Micah if he were the son of Joseph Clarke. When Micah replied that he was, the stranger pulled out his pouch and showed them that he carried a letter for Joseph Clarke, as well as for twenty others in the district. Reassured, Micah took the man home, where he learned that the stranger was Decimus Saxon, a mercenary soldier recruiting soldiers for the army of the Duke of Monmouth, the Protestant pretender who was coming to wrest his throne from Catholic King James. Joseph was too old to fight, but mindful of his duty he permitted Micah to go to the wars. With many prayers Micah set out in Saxon's company to meet Monmouth, who was soon to land somewhere in Devonshire. Even though he was a good member of the Church of England, Reuben went with them for friendship's sake.

Saxon soon threw off his sanctimonious manner, and to Micah's dismay showed himself a hardened man of the world. One night at an inn Saxon fought a king's officer over a card game and they were forced to flee, pursued by a body of horsemen and dogs. Only by stout courage and luck were they able to kill the dogs and go on their way.

That night they found shelter in the hut of a recluse, Sir Jacob Clancy. The hermit had lost all his estates through helping Charles II to gain his throne. Now renounced by the Stuart kings, he worked at his alchemy in solitude. When he heard that his guests were going to join the rebel Monmouth, he pressed on Micah some bars of gold to give to the Protestant pretender, and also a scroll on which was written:

"When thy star is in the trine
Between darkness and shine
Duke Monmouth, Duke Monmouth
Beware of the Rhine."

On another night the trio stayed at an inn kept by a buxom widow. The landlady cast sheep's eyes at Saxon, and that soldier seemed mightily interested. Reuben and Micah listened anxiously as he muttered to himself the advantages of keeping an inn. Saxon was shocked when a powdered and perfumed knight came into the tavern and kissed the widow heartily. In anger he left the table and the newly-arrived fop took his seat.

Micah soon learned that the newcomer was Sir Gervas, a London dandy who had gambled and drunk away all his estates. When Sir Gervas heard that Micah was going to join Monmouth, he nonchalantly agreed to go with them. Afterward Saxon returned to the dining-room. No longer thinking of settling down as an innkeeper, he welcomed Sir Gervas as a good recruit to the cause.

The Protestants were rallying at Taunton, the strong center of the Dissenters. The mayor, Stephen Timewell, was a wealthy wool merchant and a staunch enemy of Rome, and so in Taunton the ragged but rugged horde of Dissenters found a secure headquarters. On their arrival, Saxon was made a colonel and Micah and Reuben became captains of infantry. Sir Gervas headed a hundred musketeers. In all the turmoil of drill and inspections, the most prominent figures were the gowned clergy, who intoned prayers and hymns for the godly rebels who were to fight the Lord's battles against Papist King James.

Micah thrilled to see the arrival of Monmouth at the head of his small but growing army. Because of his strength and manly bearing, Micah soon found his way into Monmouth's inner circle. At a council meeting Micah gave over the gold and the scroll entrusted to him by Sir Jacob Clancy. Monmouth blanched at the prophecy, but after nervously exclaiming he would be fighting in England, not in Germany, he ignored the warning.

The Protestants needed at least one great and powerful lord to support their cause. So far Monmouth had rallied the peasants, the ministers, and a few reckless cavaliers. He knew, however, that his forces were too weak to meet the royal army. After prolonged debate the Protestants decided that the Duke of Beaufort was the most likely convert. Lord of all Wales, he had always been an enemy of Catholicism, and he was under obligations to Monmouth. Micah was chosen to bear a message to the noble lord.

Micah set off alone to make the long trip from Taunton to Bristol. Near the channel he half dozed on his horse during the night. Suddenly he was knocked from the saddle, bound, and dragged to a cave, where he learned that smugglers had kidnaped him because they had mistaken him for a tax collector. When he was able to establish his identity and errand, the smugglers changed their attitude; they even took him and his horse in a lugger up the channel to Bristol.

Micah tried to talk to Beaufort alone, but he was forced to deliver his papers in full sight of the duke's court. Beaufort became very angry at the idea of deserting King James and had Micah imprisoned in a dungeon. Expecting to be hanged as a traitor, Micah resigned himself to his last night on earth. But during the night a rope dropped mysteriously from an opening in the ceiling. Climbing up, Micah saw that his deliverer was Beaufort himself. The duke explained that he had not dared say anything in council, but if Monmouth could get to Bristol Beaufort would join him.

Micah carried the news back to Monmouth, who announced his immediate decision to march toward Bristol. The ragged army encamped at Sedgemoor and decided to make a stand there. As Monmouth looked over the battlefield, he was startled to hear the natives refer to a big ditch nearby as the "rhine." Indeed the rhine was an omen, for the small band of Protestant zealots proved no match for the king's men. As the battle raged, Monmouth fled in a vain attempt to save his own skin.

Micah himself was captured and sentenced to be sold as a slave. Saxon saved his life. Using money which he had blackmailed from Beaufort, Saxon bought Micah's release. Thankfully Micah set out for the continent to become a man-at-arms in the foreign wars.

MIDDLEMARCH

Type of work: Novel
Author: George Eliot (Mary Ann Evans, 1819-1880)
Type of plot: Psychological realism
Time of plot: Nineteenth century
Locale: England
First published: 1871-1872

Principal characters:

DOROTHEA BROOKE, an idealistic girl
EDWARD CASAUBON, her scholarly husband
WILL LADISLAW, Casaubon's cousin
TERTIUS LYDGATE, a doctor
ROSAMOND VINCY, whom he married
CELIA, Dorothea's sister
SIR JAMES CHETTAM, Celia's husband

Critique:

In this story of the provincial English life of the mid-nineteenth century, George Eliot has contrived a work of art that exemplifies a theme both noble and coherent. The lives of her characters, as she reveals them, indicate the truth of the writer's statement that ideals are often thwarted when applied to an imperfect social order. This novel is an ample picture of many aspects of English social life during the Victorian period.

The Story:

Dorothea Brooke and her younger sister, Celia, were young women of good birth, who lived with their bachelor uncle at Tipton Grange near the town of Middlemarch. So serious was Dorothea's cast of mind that she was reluctant to keep jewelry she had inherited from her dead mother, and she gave all of it to her sister. Upon reconsideration, however, she did keep a ring and bracelet.

At a dinner party where Edward Casaubon, a middle-aged scholar, and Sir James Chettam both vied for her attention, she was much more attracted to the serious-minded Casaubon. Casaubon must have had an inkling that his chances with Dorothea were good, for the next morning he sought her out. Celia, who did not like his complexion or his moles, escaped to other interests.

That afternoon Dorothea, contemplating the wisdom of the scholar, was walking and by chance encountered Sir James; he, in love with her, mistook her silence for agreement and supposed she might love him in return.

When Casaubon made his proposal of marriage by letter, Dorothea accepted him at once. Mr. Brooke, her uncle, thought Sir James a much better match; Dorothea's acceptance merely confirmed his bachelor views that women were difficult to understand. He decided not to interfere in her plans, but Celia felt that the event would be more like a funeral than a marriage, and frankly said so.

Casaubon took Dorothea, Celia, and Mr. Brooke to see his home so that Dorothea might order any necessary changes. Dorothea, intending in all things to defer to Casaubon's tastes, said she would make no changes in the house. During the visit Dorothea met Will Ladislaw, Casaubon's second cousin, who seemed to be hardly in sympathy with his elderly cousin's marriage plans.

While Dorothea and her new husband were traveling in Italy, Tertius Lydgate, an ambitious and poor young doctor, was meeting pretty Rosamond Vincy, to whom he was much attracted. Fred Vincy, Rosamond's brother, had indicated that he expected to come into a fine inheritance when his uncle, Mr. Featherstone, should die. Vincy, meanwhile, was pressed by a debt he was unable to pay.

Lydgate became involved in petty local politics. When the time came to choose a chaplain for the new hospital of which Lydgate was the head, the young doctor realized that it was to his best interest to vote in accordance with the wishes of Nicholas Bulstrode, an influential banker and founder of the hospital. A clergyman named Tyke received the office.

In Rome, Ladislaw encountered Dorothea and her middle-aged husband. Dorothea had begun to realize too late how pompous and incompatible she found Casaubon. Seeing her unhappiness, Ladislaw first pitied and then fell in love with his cousin's wife. Unwilling to live any longer on Casaubon's charity, Ladislaw announced his intention of returning to England and finding some kind of gainful occupation.

When Fred Vincy's note came due, he tried to sell a horse at a profit but the animal turned out to be vicious. Caleb Garth, who had signed his note, now stood to lose a hundred and ten pounds because of Fred's inability to raise the money. Fred fell ill, and Lydgate was summoned to attend him. Lydgate used his professional calls to further his suit with Rosamond.

Dorothea and her husband returned from Rome in time to hear of Celia's engagement to Sir James Chettam. Will Ladislaw included a note to Dorothea in a letter he wrote to Casaubon. This attention precipitated a quarrel which was followed by Casaubon's serious illness. Lydgate, who attended him, urged him to give up his studies for the time being. To Dorothea, Lydgate confided that Casaubon had a weak heart and must be guarded from all excitement.

Meanwhile all the relatives of old Mr. Featherstone were waiting impatiently for his death, but he hoped to circumvent their desires by giving his fortune to Mary Garth, daughter of the man who had signed Fred Vincy's note. When she refused it, he fell into a rage and died soon afterward. When his will was read, it was learned he had left nothing to his relatives; most of his money was to go to a Joshua Riggs, who was to take the name of Featherstone, and a part of his fortune was to endow the Featherstone Almshouses for old men.

Plans were made for Rosamond's marriage with Lydgate. Fred Vincy was ordered to prepare himself finally for the ministry, since he was to have no inheritance from his uncle. Mr. Brooke, having gone into politics, enlisted the help of Ladislaw in publishing a liberal paper. Mr. Casaubon had come to dislike Ladislaw intensely after his cousin had rejected further financial assistance, and he had forbidden Ladislaw to enter his house.

Casaubon died suddenly. A codicil to his will gave Dorothea all of his property as long as she did not marry Ladislaw. This strange provision caused Dorothea's friends and relatives some concern because if publicly given out, it would appear that Dorothea and Ladislaw had been indiscreet.

Mr. Brooke, on the advice of his Tory friends, gave up his liberal newspaper and thus cut off his connection with Ladislaw. The latter realized that Dorothea's family was in some way trying to separate him from Dorothea but he refused to be disconcerted about the matter. He resolved to stay on in Middlemarch until he was ready to leave. When he heard of the codicil to Casaubon's will, he was more than ever determined to remain so that he could eventually disprove the suspicions of the village concerning him and Dorothea.

Meanwhile Lydgate and Rosamond had married, and the doctor had gone deeply in debt to furnish his house. When he found that his income did not meet his wife's spendthrift habits, he asked her to help him economize. He and his wife began to quarrel. His practice and popularity decreased.

A disreputable man named Raffles appeared in Middlemarch. Raffles knew that Ladislaw's grandfather had amassed a fortune as a receiver of stolen goods and that Nicholas Bulstrode, the highly respected banker, had once been the confidential clerk of Ladislaw's ancestor. More than that, Bulstrode's first wife had been his employer's widow. Upon money inherited from her, money which should have gone to Ladislaw's mother, Bulstrode had built his own fortune.

Already blackmailed by Raffles, Bulstrode reasoned that the scoundrel would tell Ladislaw the whole story. To forestall trouble, he sent for Ladislaw and offered him an annuity of five hundred pounds and liberal provision in his will. Ladislaw, feeling that his relatives had already tainted his honor, refused, unwilling to be associated in any way with the unsavory business. Deciding to leave Middlemarch, Ladislaw went to London without the assurance that Dorothea loved him.

Lydgate drifted deeper into debt. When he wished to sell what he could and take cheaper lodgings, Rosamond managed to make him hold on, to keep up the pretense of prosperity a little longer. At the same time Bulstrode gave up his interest in the new hospital and withdrew his financial support.

Faced at last with the seizure of his goods, Lydgate went to Bulstrode and asked for a loan. The banker advised him to seek aid from Dorothea and abruptly ended the conversation. But when Raffles, in the last stages of alcoholism, returned to Middlemarch and Lydgate was called in to attend him, Bulstrode, afraid the doctor would learn the banker's secret from Raffles' drunken ravings, changed his mind and gave Lydgate a check for a thousand pounds. The loan came in time to save Lydgate's goods and reputation. When Raffles died, Bulstrode felt at peace at last. But it soon became common gossip that Bulstrode had given money to Lydgate and that Lydgate had attended Raffles in his final illness. Bulstrode and Lydgate were publicly accused of malpractice in Raffles' death. Only Dorothea took up Lydgate's defense. The rest of the town was busy with gossip over the affair. Rosamond was anxious to leave Middlemarch to avoid public disgrace. Bulstrode also was anxious to leave town after his secret, which Raffles had told while drunk in a neighboring village, became known. But he became ill and his doctors would not permit him to leave his bed.

Dorothea, sympathetic with Lydgate, determined to give her support to the hospital and to try to convince Rosamond that the only way Lydgate could recover his honor was by remaining in Middlemarch. Unfortunately, she came upon Will Ladislaw, to whom poor Rosamond was pouring out her grief. Afraid Rosamond was involved with Ladislaw, Dorothea left abruptly. Angered at the false position Rosamond had put him in, Ladislaw explained that he had always loved Dorothea, but from a distance. When Dorothea forced herself to return to Lydgate's house on the following morning, Rosamond told her of Ladislaw's declaration. Dorothea realized she was willing to give up Casaubon's fortune for Ladislaw's affection.

In spite of the protests of her family and friends, they were married several weeks later and went to London to live. Lydgate and Rosamond lived together with better understanding and prospects of a happier future. Fred Vincy became engaged to Mary Garth, with whom he had long been in love. For a time Dorothea's family disregarded her, but they were finally reconciled after Dorothea's son was born and Ladislaw was elected to Parliament.

THE MIKADO

Type of work: Comic opera
Author: W. S. Gilbert (1836-1911)
Type of plot: Social satire
Time of plot: Middle Ages
Locale: Titipu, Japan
First presented: 1885

Principal characters:
Ko-Ko, Lord High Executioner of Titipu
The Mikado of Japan
Nanki-Poo, his son, disguised as a minstrel
Pooh-Bah, Lord High Everything Else
Yum-Yum, Pitti-Sing, and Peep-Bo, wards of Ko-Ko
Katisha, an elderly lady in love with Nanki-Poo
Pish-Tush, a noble lord

Critique:

The Mikado, or *The Town of Titipu,* is one of the many works of the famous light opera collaborators, Sir William Gilbert and Sir Arthur Seymour Sullivan (1842-1900). Although they began their creative careers independently, their greatest fame is the result of the work they did as co-workers, Gilbert as librettist and Sullivan as composer, after 1871. *The Mikado* is a comic opera in two acts. Like most of the Gilbert and Sullivan productions, it contains much light humor and pointed satire.

The Story:

Ko-Ko had become the Lord High Executioner in the town of Titipu in old Japan, and to his courtyard came many knights and lords to flatter and cajole the holder of so dread and august an office.

One day a stranger appeared at Ko-Ko's palace, a wandering minstrel who carried his guitar on his back and a sheaf of ballads in his hand. The Japanese lords were curious about his presence there, for he was obviously not of noble birth and therefore could expect no favors from powerful Ko-Ko. At last Pish-Tush questioned him about his business with Ko-Ko. Introducing himself as Nanki-Poo, the minstrel announced that he sought Yum-Yum, the beautiful ward of Ko-Ko, with whom he had fallen in love while playing the second trombone in the Titipu town band a year before. He had heard that Ko-Ko was to be executed for flirting, a capital offense in the land of the Mikado, and since Ko-Ko was to die, he hoped that Yum-Yum would be free to marry him.

Pish-Tush corrected the rash young man, telling him that the Mikado had revoked the death sentence of Ko-Ko and raised him at the same time to the great and noble rank of the Lord High Executioner of Titipu. Nanki-Poo was crestfallen, for he realized that the ward of an official so important would never be allowed to marry a lowly minstrel.

Pooh-Bah, another nobleman, secretly resented the fact that he, a man of ancient lineage, had to hold minor office under a man like Ko-Ko, previously a mere tailor. But Pooh-Bah was interested in any opportunity for graft; he was even willing to betray the so-called state secret of Ko-Ko's intention to wed his beautiful ward. Pooh-Bah advised Nanki-Poo to leave Titipu and by all means to stay away from Yum-Yum.

Meanwhile, Ko-Ko had been preparing a list of the types of criminals he intended to execute—autograph hunters, people who insist upon spoiling tête-à-têtes, people who eat peppermint and breathe in one's face, the man who praises every country but his own, and apologetic statesmen.

Uncertain of the privileges of his new office, the Lord High Executioner consulted the Lord High Everything Else about the money to be spent on his impending marriage. Pooh-Bah advised him, first as Private Secretary, and gave one opinion; then as Chancellor of the Exchequer he expressed a contrary point of view. He had a different opinion for every one of his many offices and official titles. They were interrupted, however, by the appearance of Yum-Yum and her sisters Peep-Bo and Pitti-Sing. Ko-Ko attempted to kiss his bride-to-be, but she openly expressed her reluctance and distaste.

When the three sisters saw Nanki-Poo loitering nearby, they rushed to greet him, astonished to find him in Titipu. Ko-Ko, baffled and displeased by their schoolgirl mirth, demanded an introduction to the stranger.

When Yum-Yum and Nanki-Poo had a few moments alone with each other, the minstrel revealed his true identity as the son of the Mikado, and confessed the reasons for his flight from court. Katisha, a middle-aged woman in the court, had misunderstood acts of Nanki-Poo as overtures of romance. She mentioned them to the Mikado. He in turn misunderstood his son's conduct and requested that Nanki-Poo marry Katisha. Nanki-Poo, already in love with Yum-Yum, fled the court in the disguise of a minstrel and went to Titipu.

That same day Ko-Ko received from the Mikado a communication which instructed him to execute somebody within a month. Otherwise the office of Lord High Executioner would be abolished; Ko-Ko would be beheaded for neglecting his duties, and the city of Titipu would be ranked as only a village. Perplexed by this sudden and unhappy news, Ko-Ko saw no solution until he discovered Nanki-Poo carrying a rope with which to hang himself. Seeing a way of escape, Ko-Ko bargained with Nanki-Poo, promising him a luxuriant life for thirty days, if at the end of that time the minstrel would allow himself to be executed officially. Nanki-Poo agreed on the condition that he could marry Yum-Yum at once.

This acceptable solution was upset, however, by the arrival of Katisha, who recognized Nanki-Poo and tried to claim him for her husband. When she learned that he was to marry Yum-Yum, she attempted to reveal his true identity, but her voice was not heard above the singing and shouting instigated by Yum-Yum.

Hearing of the proposed marriage of Yum-Yum and Nanki-Poo, Pooh-Bah informed Ko-Ko that the wife of a beheaded man must be buried alive, a law which would mean Yum-Yum's death if Nanki-Poo were executed. Again lost as to a way out of his problem, Ko-Ko was spurred to action by the unexpected arrival of the Mikado himself. Desperate, he concealed Nanki-Poo and showed the Mikado a forged certificate of Nanki-Poo's execution.

But when the Mikado read the name of the victim, he announced that the heir-apparent had been executed. According to law, Ko-Ko's life must now be forfeited.

Luckily for Ko-Ko, Nanki-Poo and Yum-Yum appeared at that moment. Man and wife at last, they were ready to start on their honeymoon. Seeing his son happily married and not dead as he had supposed, the Mikado forgave everyone concerned in Ko-Ko's plot—the unfortunate Lord High Executioner, however, only after he had wed the jilted Katisha.

THE MILL ON THE FLOSS

Type of work: Novel
Author: George Eliot (Mary Ann Evans, 1819-1880)
Type of plot: Domestic realism
Time of plot: Nineteenth century
Locale: England
First published: 1860

Principal characters:
MR. TULLIVER, owner of the mill on the Floss
MRS. TULLIVER, his wife
TOM TULLIVER, their son
MAGGIE TULLIVER, their daughter
AUNT GLEGG, and
AUNT PULLET, sisters of Mrs. Tulliver
PHILIP WAKEM, Maggie's suitor
LUCY DEANE, cousin of Tom and Maggie
STEPHEN GUEST, Lucy's fiancé

Critique:

This book is more than a revelation of manners and conventions. It is the happy union of knowledge with sympathy, of understanding with determination to reveal some of the real differences between people. There is also bitterness in this book, a kind of grimness which is basic. People who get on in the book are those who are iron-willed, who go after what they want and subdue all emotions and desires that lie close to the heart. Those who try to live both by bread and by spirit end tragically, as do Tom and Maggie Tulliver, both unfitted for the roles life chose for them.

The Story:

Dorlcote Mill stood on the banks of the River Floss near the village of St. Ogg's. Owned by the ambitious Mr. Tulliver, it provided a good living for him and his family, but he dreamed of the day when his son Tom would climb to a higher station in life.

Mrs. Tulliver's sisters, who had married well, criticized Mr. Tulliver's unseemly ambition and openly predicted the day when his air castles would bring himself and his family to ruin. Aunt Glegg, richest of the sisters, held a note on his property, and when he quarreled with her over his plans for Tom's education, Mr. Tulliver determined to borrow the money and repay her.

For Tom, who had inherited the placid arrogance of his mother's people, life was not difficult. He was resolved to be just in all his dealings and to deliver punishment to whomever it was due. His sister Maggie grew up with an imagination beyond her years of understanding. Her aunts predicted she would come to a bad end because she was tomboyish, dark-skinned, dreamy, and indifferent to their wills. Frightened by ill luck in her attempts to please her brother Tom, her cousin Lucy, and her mother and aunts, Maggie ran away, determined to live with the gipsies. But she was glad enough to return. Her father scolded her mother and Tom for abusing her. Her mother was sure Maggie would come to a bad end because of the way Mr. Tulliver humored her.

Tom's troubles began when his father sent him to study at Mr. Stelling's school. Having little interest in spelling, grammar, or Latin, Tom found himself wishing he were back at the mill, where he might dream of someday riding a horse like his father's and giving orders to people around him. Mr. Stelling was convinced that Tom was not only obstinate but also stupid. Returning home for the Christmas holidays, Tom learned that Philip Wakem, son of a lawyer who was his father's enemy, would also enter Mr. Stelling's school.

Philip Wakem was a cripple, and so Tom was not able to beat him up as he should have liked at first. Philip could draw, and he knew Latin and Greek. After they overcame their initial reserve, the two boys became useful to one another. Philip admired Tom's arrogance and self-possession and Tom needed Philip's knowledge to help him in his studies. But their fathers' quarrel kept a breach between them. Tom felt that Philip needed to be watched, that he was the son of a rascal.

When Maggie came to visit Tom, she met Philip, and the two became close friends. Then, after Maggie had been sent away to school with her cousin Lucy, Mr. Tulliver became involved in a lawsuit. Because Mr. Wakem defended the opposition, Mr. Tulliver said his children should have as little as possible to do with Philip.

Mr. Tulliver lost his suit and stood to lose all his property as well. In order to pay off Aunt Glegg, he had borrowed money on his household furnishings. Now he hoped Aunt Pullet would lend him the money to pay the debt against which his household goods stood forfeit. He could no longer afford to keep Maggie and Tom in school. Then Mr. Tulliver learned that Mr. Wakem had bought up his debts, and the discovery brought on a stroke. Tom made Maggie promise never to speak to Philip Wakem again. Mrs. Tulliver wept because her household things were to be put up at auction. In the ruin which followed, Tom and Maggie rejected the scornful offers of help from their aunts.

Bob Jakin, a country lout with whom Tom had fought as a boy, turned up to offer Tom partnership with him in a venture where Tom's education would help Bob's native business shrewdness. But both were without capital. For the time being Tom took a job in a warehouse and studied bookkeeping each night.

Mr. Wakem bought the mill but permitted Mr. Tulliver to act as its manager for wages. It was Wakem's plan eventually to turn the mill over to his son. Tulliver, not knowing what else to do, stayed on as an employee of his enemy, but he asked Tom to sign a statement in the Bible that he would wish the Wakems evil as long as he lived. Against Maggie's entreaties, Tom signed his name. Finally Aunt Glegg gave Tom some money which he invested with Bob Jakin. Slowly Tom began to accumulate funds to pay off his father's debts.

Meanwhile Maggie and Philip had been meeting secretly in the glades near the mill. One day he asked Maggie if she loved him. She put him off. Later, at a family gathering, she betrayed her feeling for Philip in a manner which aroused Tom's suspicions. He made her swear on the Bible not to have anything more to do with Philip, and then he sought out Philip and ordered him to stay away from his sister.

Shortly afterward Tom showed his father his profits. The next day Mr. Tulliver thrashed Mr. Wakem and then suffered another stroke, from which he never recovered.

Two years later Maggie, now a teacher, went to visit her cousin, Lucy Deane, who was also entertaining young Stephen Guest in her home. One difficulty Lucy foresaw was that Philip, who was friendly with both her and Stephen, might absent himself during Maggie's visit. Stephen had already decided that Lucy was to be his choice for a wife, but at first sight he and Maggie were attracted to one another. Lucy, blind to what was happening, was pleased that her cousin Maggie and Stephen were becoming good friends.

Maggie asked Tom's permission to see Philip Wakem at a party Lucy was giving. Tom replied that if Maggie should ever consider Philip as a lover, she must expect never to see her brother again.

Tom stood by his oath to his father. He felt his dignity as a Tulliver, and he believed Maggie was apt to follow the inclination of the moment without giving consideration to the outcome. He was right. Lacking the iron will which marked so many of her relatives, Maggie loved easily and without restraint.

Meanwhile Lucy's father had promised to try to buy back the mill for Tom. Learning of this plan, Philip hoped to persuade his father to sell the mill. For this service Philip felt sure Tom would forget his old hatred.

At a dance Stephen Guest tried to kiss Maggie. She evaded him and the next day avoided Philip Wakem as well. She felt she owed it to Lucy not to allow Stephen to fall in love with her, and she felt that she owed it to her brother not to marry Philip.

She was carried along by the tide. Her relatives would not let her go back into teaching, for Tom's good luck continued and he repossessed his father's mill. Both Stephen and Philip urged her to marry them without the knowledge of each other's aims. Certainly, Lucy did not suspect Stephen's growing indifference to her.

One day Stephen took Maggie boating and tried to convince her to run away with him and be married. She refused his offer. Then the tide carried them beyond the reach of shore and they were forced to spend the night in the boat.

Maggie dared the wrath and judgment of her relatives when she returned and attempted to explain to Lucy and the others what had happened. They refused to listen to her. Tom turned her away from the mill house, with the word that he would send her money but that he never wished to see her again. Mrs. Tulliver resolved to go with Maggie, and Bob Jakin took them in.

Maggie slowly began to realize what ostracism meant, for one by one people deserted her. Only Aunt Glegg and Lucy offered any sympathy. Stephen wrote to her in agony of spirit, as did Philip. Maggie wanted to be by herself. She wondered if there could be love for her without pain for others.

That autumn a terrible flood ravaged St. Ogg's. Knowing that Tom was at the mill, Maggie attempted to reach him in a boat. The two were reunited and Tom took over the rowing of the boat. But the full force of the flood overwhelmed them and they drowned, together at the end as they had been when they were children.

THE MISANTHROPE

Type of work: Drama
Author: *Molière* (Jean Baptiste Poquelin, 1622-1673)
Type of plot: Comedy of manners
Time of plot: Seventeenth century
Locale: Paris
First presented: 1666

Principal characters:
Alceste, in love with Célimène
Philinte, friend of Alceste
Oronte, in love with Célimène
Célimène, a young widow
Éliante, cousin of Célimène

Critique:

Molière, born Jean Baptiste Poquelin, is the outstanding French writer of comedies, above all, comedies of manners; and he is sometimes compared in the breadth and humanity of his genius with Shakespeare. *The Misanthrope* is a comedy with a rather sad conclusion; but the merit of the play rests on its depiction of manners. We can see in *The Misanthrope* Molière's objective analysis of his own time, for he exposes to the public eye the frivolity and inconsistency of his contemporaries.

The Story:

Alceste had been called a misanthrope by many of his friends, and he took a rather obstinate delight in the name. This characteristic led him to quarrel heatedly with his good friend Philinte, who accepted uncritically the frivolous manners of the day. When Philinte warmly embraced a chance acquaintance, as was customary, Alceste maintained that such behavior was hypocritical, especially since Philinte hardly knew the man.

Philinte reminded Alceste that his lawsuit was nearly ready for trial, and that he would do well to moderate his attitude toward people in general. His opponents in the suit were doing everything possible to curry favor, but Alceste insulted everyone he met and made no effort to win over the judges.

Philinte also taunted Alceste on his love for Célimène, who, as a leader in society, was hypocritical most of the time. Alceste had to admit that his love could not be explained rationally.

Oronte interrupted the quarrel by coming to visit Alceste, who was puzzled by a visit from suave and elegant Oronte. Oronte asked permission to read a sonnet he had lately composed, as he was anxious to have Alceste's judgment of its literary merit.

After some affected hesitation, Oronte read his mediocre poem. Alceste, too honest to give false praise, condemned the verses and even satirized the poor quality of the writing. Oronte instantly took offense at this criticism, and a new quarrel broke out. Although the argument was indecisive, there were hints of a possible duel.

Alceste then went to call on Célimène. As soon as he saw her, he began perversely to upbraid her for her frivolous conduct and her hypocritical attitude toward other people. Although Célimène could slander and ridicule with a keen wit and a barbed tongue while a person was absent, she was all flattery and attention when talking with him. This attitude displeased Alceste.

The servant announced several callers, including Éliante. To Alceste's dismay, they all sat down for an interminable conversation. The men took great delight in naming over all their mutual acquaintances, and as each name was mentioned, Célimène made unkind remarks. The only gentle person in the room was Éliante, whose good sense and kind heart were in striking contrast with Célimène's caustic wit. Éliante was overshadowed, however, by the more brilliant Célimène. The men all declared they had nothing to do all day, and each swore to outstay the other, to remain longer with Célimène. Alceste determined to be the last to leave.

A guard appeared, however, to summon Alceste before the tribunal. Astonished, Alceste learned that his quarrel with Oronte had been noised about, and the authorities intended to prevent a possible duel. Loudly protesting that except for an order direct from the king nothing could make him praise the poetry of Oronte, Alceste was led away.

Arsinoé, an austere woman who made a pretense of great virtue, came to call on Célimène. She took the opportunity to warn Célimène that her conduct was creating a scandal, because her many suitors and her sharp tongue were hurting her reputation. Célimène spoke bitingly of Arsinoé's strait-laced character.

Arsinoé decided to talk privately with Alceste, with whom she was half in love. She comforted him as best she could for being so unfortunate as to love Célimène, and complimented him on his plain dealings and forthright character. Carried away by the intimacy of her talk, Arsinoé offered to do much for Alceste by speaking in his favor at court. But the two concluded that the love of Alceste for

Célimène, though unsuitable from almost every point of view, was a fast tie.

Éliante and Philinte were in the meantime discussing Alceste and his habit of antagonizing his friends through his frankness. Philinte told her of Alceste's hearing before the tribunal. He had insisted that Oronte's verses were bad, but he had nothing more to say. Éliante and Philinte began to discover a mutual liking. If Éliante ever lost her fondness for Alceste, Philinte intended to offer himself as a lover.

Alceste received an unflattering letter, purporting to come from Célimène, which described him in malicious terms. After much coy hesitation, Célimène admitted that she had sent the letter and expressed surprise at Alceste's indignation. Other suitors appeared, each holding a letter and each much upset. On comparing notes, they found that they had all been ridiculed and insulted.

Meanwhile, Alceste had made up his mind to ask Éliante to marry him, but reconsidered when he realized that his proposal would seem to spring from a desire to avenge himself on Célimène. To the misanthrope there seemed to be no solution except to go into exile and live a hermit's life.

When Célimène's suitors clamored for an explanation, she told them that she had written the letters because she was tired of the niceties of polite conversation. For once she decided to say what she really thought. This confession was shocking to the suitors who thought frankness and rudeness were unpardonable crimes. Hypocrisy, flattery, cajolery, extravagances—these were the marks of a gentle lady. Protesting and disdainful, they left together, never to return.

Only Alceste remained. Even the coquettish and malicious heart of Célimène was touched. When Alceste repeated his vows of fidelity and asked her once more to marry him, she almost consented. But when Alceste revealed that he wanted them to go into exile and lead quiet, simple lives, she refused. Célimène could never leave the false, frivolous society she loved.

Now completely the misanthrope, Alceste stalked away with the firm resolve to quit society forever, to become a hermit, far removed from the artificial sham of preciosity. Philinte and Éliante, more moderate in their views, however, decided that they would marry.

LES MISÉRABLES

Type of work: Novel
Author: Victor Hugo (1802-1885)
Type of plot: Social chronicle
Time of plot: About 1815 to 1835
Locale: France
First published: 1862

Principal characters:

Jean Valjean, also known as Father Madeleine
Fantine, a woman befriended by Valjean
Cosette, her daughter
M. Javert, inspector of police
Marius Pontmercy, in love with Cosette
M. Thénardier, known also as Jondrette, a rogue
Eponine Thénardier, his daughter

Critique:

Les Misérables is a romantic novel, packed with exciting incidents. It is also a sociological study of poverty and slum life. Victor Hugo spent fourteen years on the book, a fact which probably accounts for the numerous digressions and additions to the story. The core of this extremely long novel is the life story of a criminal, Jean Valjean, who serves as an example of the misery and contradictions of society with which the author was especially concerned at the time of writing. *Les Misérables* is both a powerful social document and an extremely interesting and dramatic narrative. Hugo's masterpiece, it is one of the great novels of the world.

The Story:

In 1815, in France, a man named Jean Valjean was released after nineteen years in prison. He had been sentenced to a term of five years because he stole a loaf of bread to feed his starving sister and her family, but the sentence was later increased because of his attempts to escape. During his imprisonment he astonished others by his exhibitions of unusual physical strength.

Freed at last, he started out on foot for a distant part of the country. Innkeepers refused him food and lodging because his yellow passport revealed that he was an ex-convict. Finally he came to the house of the Bishop of Digne, a saintly man who treated him graciously, fed him, and gave him a bed. During the night Jean stole the bishop's silverware and fled. He was immediately captured by the police, who returned him and the stolen goods to the bishop. Without any censure, the priest not only gave him what he had stolen, but also added his silver candlesticks to the gift. The astonished gendarmes let the prisoner go. Alone with the bishop, Jean was confounded by the churchman's attitude, for the bishop asked only that he use the silver as a means of living an honest life.

In Paris, in 1817, lived a beautiful girl named Fantine. She gave birth to an illegitimate child, Cosette, whom she left with M. and Mme. Thénardier to bring up with their own children. As time went on, the Thénardiers demanded more and more money for Cosette's support, yet treated the child cruelly and deprived her even of necessities. Fantine, meanwhile, had gone to the town of M— and obtained a job in a glass factory operated by Father Madeleine, a kind and generous man whose history was known to no one, but whose good deeds and generosity to the poor were public information. He had arrived in M— a poor laborer, and by a lucky invention he was able to start a business of his own. Soon he built a factory and employed many workers. After five years in the city he was named mayor and was beloved by all the citizens. He was reported to have prodigious strength. Only one man, Javert, a police inspector, seemed to watch him with an air of suspicion. Javert was born in prison. His whole life was influenced by that fact and his fanatical attitude toward duty made him a man to be feared. He was determined to discover the facts of Father Madeleine's previous life. One day he found a clue while watching Father Madeleine lift a heavy cart to save an old man who had fallen under it. Javert realized that he had known only one man of such prodigious strength, a former convict named Valjean.

Fantine had told no one of Cosette, but knowledge of her illegitimate child spread and caused Fantine to be discharged from the factory without the knowledge of Father Madeleine. Finally Fantine became a prostitute in an effort to pay the increasing demands of the Thénardiers for Cosette's support. One night Javert arrested her while she was walking the streets. When Father Madeleine heard the details of her plight, and learned that she had tuberculosis, he sent Fantine to a hospital and promised to bring Cosette to her. Just before the mayor left to get Cosette, Javert confessed that he had mistakenly reported to the Paris police that he suspected Father Madeleine of being the ex-convict, Jean Valjean. He said that the real Jean Valjean had been arrested at Arras under an assumed name. The arrested man was to be tried two days later.

That night Father Madeleine struggled with his own conscience, for he was the real Jean Valjean. Unwilling to let an innocent man suffer, he went to Arras for the trial and identified himself as Jean Valjean. After telling the authorities where he could be found, he went to Fantine. Javert came there to arrest him. Fantine was so terrified that she died. After a day in prison Jean Valjean escaped.

Valjean, some time later, was again imprisoned by Javert. Once more he made his escape. Shortly afterward he was able to take Cosette, a girl of eight, away from the Thénardiers. He grew to love the child greatly, and they lived together happily in the Gorbeau tenement on the outskirts of Paris. When Jarvert once more tracked them down, Valjean escaped with the child into a convent garden, where they were rescued by Fauchelevant, whose life Valjean had saved when the old peasant fell beneath the cart. Fauchelevant was now the convent gardener. Valjean became his helper, and Cosette was put into the convent school.

Years passed. Valjean left the convent and took Cosette, her schooling finished, to live in a modest house on a side street in Paris. The old man and the young girl were little noticed by their neighbors. Meanwhile the blackguard Thénardier had brought his family to live in the Gorbeau tenement. He now called himself Jondrette. In the next room lived Marius Pontmercy, a young lawyer estranged from his aristocrat grandfather because of his liberal views. Marius was the son of an officer whose life Thénardier had saved at the battle of Waterloo. The father, now dead, had asked his son some day to repay Thénardier for his deed. Marius never suspected that Jondrette was really his father's benefactor. When the Jondrettes were being evicted from their quarters, however, he paid their rent from his meager resources.

During one of his evening walks Marius met Cosette and Valjean. He fell in love with the girl as he continued to see her in the company of her white-haired companion. At last he followed her to her home. Valjean, noticing Marius, took Cosette to live in another house.

One morning Marius received a begging letter delivered by Eponine Jondrette. His neighbors were again asking for help, and he began to wonder about them. Peeping through a hole in the wall, he heard Jondrette speak of a benefactor who would soon arrive. When the man came, Marius recognized him as Cosette's companion. From Eponine he later learned Cosette's address, but before he saw Cosette again he overheard the Jondrettes plotting against the man whom he believed to be Cosette's father. Alarmed, he told the details of the plot to Inspector Javert.

Marius was at the wall watching when Valjean returned to give Jondrette money. While they talked, numerous heavily-armed men appeared in the room. Jondrette then revealed himself as Thénardier. Marius, horrified, did not know whom to protect, the man his father had requested him to befriend or the father of Cosette. Threatened by Thénardier, Valjean agreed to send to his daughter for more money, but he gave a false address. When this ruse was discovered, the robbers threatened to kill Valjean. Marius threw a note of warning through the hole in the wall as Javert appeared and arrested all but Valjean, who made his escape through a window.

Marius finally located Cosette. One night she told him that she and her father were leaving for England. He tried to get his grandfather's permission to marry Cosette. It was refused. In despair, he returned to Cosette and found the house where she had lived empty. Eponine met him there and told him that his revolutionary friends had begun a revolt and were waiting for him at the barricades. Because Cosette had disappeared, he gladly followed Eponine to the barricades, where Javert had been seized as a spy and bound. During the fighting Eponine gave her life to save Marius. As she died, she gave him a note which Cosette had given her to deliver. In it Cosette told him where she could be found.

In answer to her note, Marius wrote that his grandfather would not permit his marriage, that he had no money, and that he would be killed at the barricade. Valjean discovered the notes and set out for the barricades. Finding Javert tied up by the revolutionists, he freed the inspector. The barricades fell. In the confusion Valjean came upon the wounded Marius and carried him into the Paris sewers.

After hours of wandering he reached a locked outlet. There Thénardier, unrecognized in the dark, met him and agreed to open the grating in exchange for money. Outside Valjean met Javert, who took him into custody. Valjean asked only that he be allowed to take Marius to his grandfather's house. Javert agreed to wait at the door, but suddenly he turned and ran toward the river. Tormented by his conscientious regard for duty and his reluctance to return to prison the man who had saved his life, he drowned himself in the Seine.

When Marius recovered, he and Cosette were married. Valjean gave Cosette a generous dowry, and for the first time Cosette learned that Valjean was not her real father. Valjean told Marius only that he was an escaped convict, believed dead, and he begged to be allowed to see Cosette occasionally. But gradually Marius banished him from the house. Then Marius learned from Thénardier that it was Valjean who had rescued Marius at the barricade. Marius and Cosette hurried to Valjean's lodgings, to find him on his deathbed. He died knowing that his children loved him and that all his entangling past was now clear. He bequeathed the bishop's silver candlesticks to Cosette, with his last breath saying that he had spent his life in trying to be worthy of the faith of the Bishop of Digne. He was buried in a grave with no name on the stone.

MR. BRITLING SEES IT THROUGH

Type of work: Novel
Author: H. G. Wells (1866-1946)
Type of plot: Social criticism
Time of plot: World War I
Locale: England
First published: 1916

Principal characters:
Mr. Direck, an American
Mr. Britling, an English writer
Hugh, Mr. Britling's oldest son
Teddy, Mr. Britling's secretary
Letty, Teddy's wife
Cissie, Letty's sister and Mr. Direck's sweetheart
Heinrich, the Britling children's tutor

Critique:

In this book the author tries to show the effect of World War I upon the mind of one man. Mr. Britling passes from optimism to despair and back to optimism as he ponders questions of war, religion, morality, and social reform. For anyone who enjoys novels of theme this is a rewarding and inspiring book.

The Story:

Mr. Direck, secretary of a Boston cultural society, was in England for the purpose of persuading Mr. Britling, a famous writer, to deliver a series of lectures in the United States. Direck found England all that he had expected, as he traveled from London to Matching's Easy in Essex to meet Mr. Britling. However, Mr. Britling did not support the illusion. He neither dressed like an Englishman nor acted like an intellectual, and Direck was disappointed. But Mr. Britling's family and friends aroused his interest. Mr. and Mrs. Britling had three boys. The oldest, Hugh, was the son of Mr. Britling's first wife. In addition to the immediate family, an old aunt and a young German tutor, Heinrich, lived in the house. Mr. Britling's secretary Teddy, his wife Letty, and her sister Cissie, lived in a cottage nearby. Direck fell in love with Cissie, a vivacious and intelligent girl.

Largely because of Cissie, Direck entered with zest into the entertainments of the Britling household, and at times he almost forgot the real reason for his visit. Several times, however, he and his host had serious discussions. Once they spoke about possible war with Germany. Mr. Britling said the idea was nonsense; it had been expected for a long time and had never happened. Unknown to Direck and Mr. Britling, however, an attempt was at that moment being made to kill Archduke Francis Ferdinand of Austria. The fatal march of events had begun.

One morning Mr. Britling took Direck on a ride around the countryside. Mr. Britling, a poor driver, was involved in an accident with a motorcycle. He was not hurt, but Direck broke his wrist. He saw in the accident an opportunity to prolong his stay at Matching's Easy. Meanwhile, war brewed behind the scenes. France was unsettled. The British were troubled with civil war in Ireland. Heinrich anxiously questioned Mr. Britling about the war. Mr. Britling was still confident that Germany could not be so foolish as to fight the rest of the world.

When the time finally came for Direck to leave Matching's Easy, he decided that he could not go without confessing his love to Cissie. Because she had not yet made up her mind about her love for him, Direck left for a tour of Europe. He felt hopeful because Cissie had not definitely rejected him.

Mr. Britling, too, was involved in a love affair. He and his wife had ceased to love each other years before, but they cooperated admirably to run their pleasant household. Life ran smoothly at home. Away from home there was Mrs. Harrowdean, a widow. The love affair between her and Mr. Britling did not run smoothly. At the time they had ceased to see each other and were quarreling by mail.

The threat of war crept forward. Heinrich was called home for mobilization. He left sadly. He did not believe in war. The Britlings urged him to stay, but he said that he must serve his country.

Germany invaded France, and Russia invaded Germany. Although forced to readjust his thinking. Mr. Britling firmly believed that Germany could never win. With a troubled mind he drove into the country, half-determined to call on Mrs. Harrowdean, but on the way he began to think of what the war would mean to the world. Instead of going to see Mrs. Harrowdean, he returned home to his writing desk. The war had arrived to fill the mind of Mr. Britling to the exclusion of everything else.

When the Germans attacked Belgium, England declared war. Direck, who had been in Germany when war was declared, returned immediately to England, where he found Cissie thinking only of England and the war. Direck, being an American, remained only an interested spectator.

Gradually it dawned on Mr. Britling that Germany could not easily be beaten. The Britling household slowly became involved in the war. First Teddy volunteered, then Hugh. Mr. Britling at last got a job as a constable guarding bridges and public works. Mrs. Britling worked for the Red Cross. A Belgian refugee and his family came to live with them for a time. Later two squads of soldiers were billeted in their barn.

Mr. Britling did a lot of thinking in his attempt to adjust his mind to Germany's attitude in the war. To most Englishmen, the war was a game to be played and won against an honorable enemy; to many Germans, the war was a campaign of hate. Mr. Britling thought often of Heinrich. There had to be other Germans as good as Heinrich, for not all of them could be evil. Then he realized that the British were growing as cruel and hardened as the enemy. This war, after all, was no different from the ones that had gone before, and men on both sides were victims of their own foolishness and stupidity.

Hugh lied about his age and managed to be sent to the front in Flanders. Teddy was there too, and one day Letty received a telegram which said that he was missing. Mr. Britling was so disturbed that writing was now impossible. Direck, still a civilian, left for the continent to learn news of Teddy. Then a telegram announced that Hugh had been killed. The war was leaving its mark upon Mr. Britling of Matching's Easy.

Although Direck had found almost certain evidence that Teddy had been killed, Letty still believed him to be alive. Cissie tried to make her sister face the truth. Convinced, Letty went alone out into the fields with her grief. There she met Mr. Britling. He had become reconciled to Hugh's death because he had convinced himself that the boy had not died in vain. A better world was in the making; after the war things would be different.

Letty returned home, strangely quieted by what Mr. Britling had told her; she, too, had become reconciled to the idea of death. Suddenly she saw a familiar figure in front of the cottage. It was Teddy. He was alive, with one hand gone. Now it was Cissie who must begin to worry. Direck had volunteered in the Canadian Army.

Some weeks later Mr. Britling learned that Heinrich had died. He tried to compose a letter to Heinrich's parents, but the effort was useless. He wrote all night without being able to express what he felt. Hugh and Heinrich had both died for a reason. With the promise of a better world to come, now was not the time for despair. Mr. Britling rose from his desk and watched the morning begin. His mind was calm. It seemed as if the whole world was bathed in sunrise.

MR. MIDSHIPMAN EASY

Type of work: Novel
Author: Frederick Marryat (1792-1848)
Type of plot: Adventure romance
Time of plot: Napoleonic wars
Locale: Mediterranean Sea and European coastal waters
First published: 1836

Principal characters:
JACK EASY, a midshipman
GASCOIGNE, another midshipman
MESTY, an Ashantee Negro
AGNES REBIERA, Easy's Sicilian sweetheart

Critique:

Marryat wrote from experience, having himself been a captain in the British navy, and his book gives a fully detailed account of life aboard a war vessel, including vivid accounts of several battles at sea. Unlike many other stories about the British or American navy in the early nineteenth century, he did not charge the naval system of discipline with being too harsh. Rather, he tried to show that it developed the best that was in a man. Marryat thought poorly of the theories of equality which had been popularized in France during the French Revolution.

The Story:

Jack Easy was the son of a wealthy landowner in the county of Hampshire, England. Jack's father and mother had almost spoiled the boy for any good in the world, the former by his over-simplified philosophy of equality, and the latter by her doting. Fortunately for the young lad, the family physician, Doctor Middleton, rescued him from his home and put him in a school where he began to learn that the survival of the fittest was the way of the world. When he left school, it was decided he should go to sea as midshipman with Captain Wilson, a poor relation who was indebted to Mr. Easy for a loan of one thousand pounds and who was in command of the warship *Harpy*.

Jack soon made friends aboard the *Harpy* through the use of his fists in beating down bullies among the ship's company and through the obvious goodwill which the captain showed him. It was hard at first for the young man to become accustomed to life aboard the warship. The duties of a midshipman kept him busy, but the small living quarters and the discipline proved irksome to the son of a philosopher who preached a doctrine of equality.

Jack's first naval adventure occurred when the ship was not far from Tarragona. In command of a boat during the capture of a Spanish vessel by a boarding party, he was left behind when the *Harpy* sailed away. Captain Wilson thought that Easy's boat had been sunk with all hands. The following night Easy's boat captured another Spanish vessel by boarding. Easy ordered the crew and passengers, including an elderly Sicilian and his wife and two beautiful daughters, overboard into a small boat. A few days later, after Easy had vainly tried to find the *Harpy*, the crew landed on an island and refused to return to the captured ship. But an Ashantee Negro, Mesty, was loyal to Easy because the midshipman had befriended him and had treated him as an equal. Through the efforts of Mesty, the men were brought back on board in a docile condition and Easy again set sail to look for the *Harpy*. After a week had passed, Easy and his crew found the British warship engaged with a Spanish vessel. The timely aid of gunfire from Easy's prize helped the *Harpy* take its opponent. Everyone, including Captain Wilson, was amused at the flag which Easy had flown in the engagement. Having no British flag aboard the prize, he had hoisted a lady's green petticoat.

The first stop for the *Harpy* in the Mediterranean was at Malta. There Easy fought a duel. Thinking he had killed his man, he and a fellow midshipman, Gascoigne, ran away in a native boat they had hired. A storm drove their small craft to the Sicilian shore, where the two young sailors hid in a cart and there fell asleep. When they awakened they found themselves in the yard of a great house. Hearing loud cries, they rushed into the house in time to prevent the owner from being murdered by two relatives. The man and his family proved to be the passengers whom Easy had put into a small boat when he had taken his prize a month earlier. Before Don Rebiera sent them to Palermo, Easy had fallen deeply in love with the Sicilian nobleman's daughter, Agnes.

At Palermo the two midshipmen went aboard a British frigate which took them back to Malta to rejoin the *Harpy*. Since Easy's opponent in the duel had not died, Captain Wilson forgave their escapade.

A few weeks later the *Harpy* was sailing off the coast of Africa. In another battle to board a vessel, Easy distinguished himself a second time. The prize was taken back to Malta, where Captain Wilson learned that he had been promoted to the command of a larger ship, the *Aurora*. When he left the *Harpy*, Captain Wilson took Easy, Gascoigne, and Mesty with him.

Separated from the fleet during a storm, the *Aurora* was struck by lightning and set afire. Many of her officers and men were killed or injured. Both Easy and Gascoigne were heroic in their efforts to help stop the blaze and get the ship seaworthy enough to reach Malta for repairs. Back at Malta, Easy and Gascoigne had still further adventures. Chosen to accompany a Sicilian nobleman who was visiting the ship, they recognized him as one of the men who had tried to assassinate Don Rebiera. The impostor was arrested by the authorities and returned to Sicily.

Several weeks later the *Aurora* sighted a galley, filled with criminals, sinking off the Sicilian coast. A party was sent to release the prisoners and set them ashore. During the operation Easy recognized the man who had attempted to assassinate Don Rebiera and who had been sent to the galleys just a few weeks before. He notified Captain Wilson, who immediately informed the authorities on the island and then permitted Easy, Gascoigne, and Mesty to go ashore to warn their friends. Easy and his companions arrived at Don Rebiera's home in time to warn the household of its danger. A battle of a day and a night ensued. At the end of that time Sicilian troops arrived and rescued the besieged house and its defenders from the band of escaped galleyslaves under the leadership of Don Rebiera's enemy.

The next day Easy asked Agnes' father if he might marry her. The father, indebted to Easy and knowing that his daughter loved the young midshipman, could not give his permission immediately because of the Church. His family confessor threatened excommunication if the marriage took place.

Not to be daunted, Easy and Gascoigne, with the help of Mesty, pretended to have broken their legs in a carriage accident. Captain Wilson was forced to leave them behind to convalesce when the *Aurora* left port. As soon as the ship had sailed, Mesty was sent with a bribe to the confessor. The priest, in his turn, tried to get Mesty's aid in poisoning Easy in order to prevent the marriage. Mesty promised to help the priest but administered the poison to the confessor instead. Don Rebiera then withdrew his objection to the marriage if he could have the written permission of the midshipman's father, since Easy was still under age. Easy eagerly reported to the *Aurora* to resign from the navy and return to England to get his father's permission to marry.

Back in England, Easy learned that his mother had died and his father had become insane. While the son was straightening out the affairs of the family, the father also died, leaving Easy a large fortune. Since the seas were not a safe place to travel as a passenger in a merchant vessel, Easy bought a small ship. Armed with cannon and letters of marque, he sailed for Sicily. There he married Agnes.

He and his bride returned to England after Easy had helped to secure Gascoigne's resignation from the navy. Neither Easy nor Gascoigne went to sea again, but settled down as country gentlemen on Easy's large estate in Hampshire.

MISTER ROBERTS

Type of work: Novel
Author: Thomas Heggen (1919-1949)
Type of plot: Humorous satire
Time of plot: Last months of World War II
Locale: Southwest Pacific
First published: 1946

Principal characters:
DOUGLAS ROBERTS, First Lieutenant, U. S. S. *Reluctant*
CAPTAIN MORTON, skipper of the *Reluctant*
ENSIGN KEITH, USNR
BOOKSER, a seaman
FRANK THOMPSON, radio man

Critique:

Mister Roberts, first published serially in *The Atlantic Monthly,* became a national best seller soon after its appearance in book form. The subject matter offers relief from the general run of war literature; the style ranges from almost poetic prose to screaming farce. An air of lusty masculinity pervades the narrative. Heggen has perfectly reproduced the uninhibited idiom of men at war. The success of the novel led Heggen, with Joshua Logan, to dramatize it into an equally successful play. Heggen's artistic motive in writing the novel must surely have been his wish to show the public that the backwashes of the war also have their tragedy and comedy, and even their romance, despite their apparent lack of color.

The Story:

Douglas Roberts, First Lieutenant on the *Reluctant,* a U. S. Navy supply ship in the Pacific, was the guiding spirit of the crew's undeclared war against the skipper, Captain Morton, an officious, childish, and unreasonable officer. The *Reluctant* was non-combatant, plying among islands left in the backwash of the war. None of its complement had seen action, and none wanted action except Roberts, who had applied without success for transfer to a ship of the line.

In the continuously smoldering warfare between the captain and the other officers and the men of the ship, Roberts scored a direct hit on the captain's fundament with a wad of lead-foil shot from a rubber band while the captain was watching movies on board. Ensign Pulver, who spent most of his time devising ways of making the skipper's life unbearable, manufactured a giant firecracker to be thrown into the captain's cabin at night. The premature and violent explosion of the firecracker put the entire *Reluctant* on a momentary battle footing. Ensign Pulver was burned badly.

Ensign Keith came to the *Reluctant* by way of middle-class Boston, Bowdoin College, and accelerated wartime naval officer training. He was piped aboard in the blazing sunshine of Tedium Bay, hot in his blue serge uniform but self-assured because Navy Regulations prescribed blues when reporting for duty. Despite the discomfort of a perspiration-soaked shirt and a wilted collar, Ensign Keith immediately showed the crew that they would have to follow naval regulations if he had his way aboard ship. One night, however, while he was on watch, he came upon a drinking and gambling party presided over by Chief Dowdy. Keith was hoodwinked by the men into trying some of their drink. Not much later, under the influence of Chief Dowdy's "pineapple juice," Keith had become roaring drunk, all regulations and service barriers forgotten. His initiation completed, Ensign Keith never again referred to rules and regulations.

At a forward area island base, where the *Reluctant* had docked to unload cargo, the crew quickly learned that the military hospital was staffed by real live nurses. Every available binocular, telescope, and range-finder on board was soon trained on the nurses' quarters. Interest rose to fever-pitch when it was discovered that a bathroom window shade in quarters was never lowered. Officers and men soon came to know the nurses by their physical characteristics, if not by formal introduction. One day a nurse came aboard and overheard two seamen making a wager concerning her physical characteristics. That same day the bathroom shade was lowered, never to be raised again.

For days in advance the ship's complement planned their shore leave in Elysium, a civilized port of call. Seaman Bookser, the spiritual type, was the butt of many jokes concerning his liberty plans. At Elysium half of the men were given shore leave. From sundown until the following dawn they were brought back by jeep and truck. They had fought with army personnel, insulted local citizens, stolen government property, wrecked bars and saloons, and damaged the house of the French consul. Further shore leave was canceled. Bookser, the spiritual seaman, was driven up to the dock in a large car on the day of departure. Beside him was a beautiful young woman whom he kissed long and passionately before leaving her. Astonished at Bookser and proud of him at the same time, the crew made him the hero of the stop at Elysium.

Roberts listened to V-E Day reports on the ship's radio. The apathy of his fellow officers toward events happening in Europe led him to pitch the captain's pet potted palm overboard late that night. At the same time Roberts stirred up the noise-hating captain by slamming a lead stanchion against a stateroom bulkhead. Roberts was not caught, nor did he give himself up during the captain's mad search for the culprit. The crew manufactured a medal and presented it to Roberts for valor above and beyond the call of duty—a seaman had seen Roberts in action on V-E night.

Frank Thompson, a radio man and the ship's monopoly expert, was informed by wire that his baby, whom he had never seen, had died in California. Thompson, anxious to go to the funeral and to be with his wife, applied for permission to fly to the States. The captain refused. Roberts advised him to go to a nearby island to see the chaplain and the flag secretary. Thompson went, but he was told that no emergency leave could be permitted without his captain's approval. He then walked alone in a deserted section of the island for several hours before he returned to the *Reluctant* and took his usual place at the head of the monopoly table.

Not long after V-E Day, Roberts received orders to report back to the States for reassignment. The night before he left the *Reluctant* he spent with his special friends among officers and men, drinking punch made of crew-concocted raisin brew and grain alcohol from dispensary supplies. The effect of Roberts' leaving the ship was immediate. No longer was there a born leader aboard. All functions and activities in ship's routine went wrong; no longer was there any one man upon whom the officers could depend to maintain their balance in the tedium of a dull tropic supply run. No longer did the enlisted men have an officer upon whom they could depend as a link between them and the ship's authorities.

Roberts was assigned to duty aboard a destroyer which was part of a task force bombarding the Japanese home islands. Not long before V-J Day, Ensign Pulver received a letter from a friend aboard the same ship. The letter stated that a Japanese kamikaze plane had broken through anti-aircraft defenses and had crashed into the bridge of the destroyer. Among those killed in the explosion was Roberts, who was in the officers' mess drinking coffee with another officer. Mr. Roberts had seen action at last.

MRS. DALLOWAY

Type of work: Novel
Author: Virginia Woolf (1882-1941)
Type of plot: Psychological realism
Time of plot: 1920's
Locale: London
First published: 1925

Principal characters:
CLARISSA DALLOWAY
RICHARD DALLOWAY, her husband
PETER WALSH, a former suitor
ELIZABETH, Mrs. Dalloway's daughter
MISS KILMAN, Elizabeth's friend
SALLY SETON, an old friend of Clarissa and Peter

Critique:

Mrs. Dalloway is a cleverly written book. The author has used the stream-of-consciousness method, encompassing within a single day the activities of Clarissa Dalloway's life and the lives of other people as well. There is little action but much intense probing of memory.

The Story:

Mrs. Clarissa Dalloway went to make last-minute preparations for an evening party. During her day in the city she enjoyed the summer air, the many sights and people, the general bustle of London. She met Hugh Whitbread, now a court official, a handsome and sophisticated man. She had known Hugh since her youth, and she knew his wife, Evelyn, as well, but she did not particularly care for Evelyn. Other people came down to London to see paintings, to hear music, or to shop. The Whitbreads came down to consult doctors, for Evelyn was always ailing.

Mrs. Dalloway went about her shopping. While she was in a flower shop, a luxurious limousine pulled up outside. Everyone speculated on the occupant behind the drawn curtains of the car. Everywhere the limousine went, it was followed by curious eyes. Mrs. Dalloway, who had thought that the queen was inside, felt that she was right when the car drove into the Buckingham Palace grounds.

The sights and sounds of London reminded Mrs. Dalloway of many things. She thought back to her youth, to the days before her marriage, to her husband, to her daughter Elizabeth. Her daughter was indeed a problem and all because of that horrid Miss Kilman who was her friend. Miss Kilman was something of a religious fanatic, who scoffed at the luxurious living of the Dalloways and felt sorry for Mrs. Dalloway. Mrs. Dalloway hated her. Miss Kilman was not at all like the friend of her own girlhood. Sally Seton had been different. Mrs. Dalloway had really loved Sally.

Mrs. Dalloway wondered what love really was. She had loved Sally, but she had loved Richard Dalloway and Peter Walsh, too. She had married Richard, and then Peter had left for India. Later she learned that he had married someone he met on shipboard. She had heard little about his wife since his marriage.

But the day was wonderful and life itself was wonderful. The war was over and she was giving a party.

While Mrs. Dalloway was shopping, Septimus Smith and his wife were sitting in the park. Septimus had married Lucrezia while he was serving in Italy, and she had given up her family and her country for him. Now he frightened her because he acted so queerly and talked of committing suicide. The doctor said that there was nothing wrong with him, nothing wrong physically. Septimus, one of the first to volunteer for war duty, had gone to war to save his country, the England of Shakespeare. When he got back, he was a war hero and he was given a good job at the office. They had nice lodgings and Lucrezia was happy. Septimus began reading Shakespeare again. He was unhappy; he brooded. He and Lucrezia had no children. To Septimus the world was in such horrible condition that it was unjust to bring children into it.

When Septimus began to have visitations from Evans, a comrade who had been killed in the war, Lucrezia became even more frightened and she called in Dr. Holmes. Septimus felt almost completely abandoned by that time. Lucrezia could not understand why her husband did not like Dr. Holmes, for he was so kind, so much interested in Septimus. Finally she took her husband to Sir William Bradshaw, a wealthy and noted psychiatrist. Septimus had had a brilliant career ahead of him. His employer spoke highly of his work. No one knew why he wanted to kill himself. Septimus said that he had committed a crime, but his wife said that he was guilty of absolutely nothing. Sir William suggested a place in the country, where Septimus would be by himself, without his wife. It was not, Sir William said, a question of preference. Since he had threatened suicide, it was a question of law.

In the meantime Mrs. Dalloway returned home. Lady Bruton had invited Richard Dalloway to lunch. Mrs. Dalloway had never liked Millicent Bruton; she was far too clever. Then Peter Walsh came to call, and Mrs. Dalloway was surprised and happy to see him again. She introduced him to her Elizabeth. He asked Mrs. Dalloway if she were happy; she wondered why. When he left, she called out to him not to forget her party. Peter thought, Clarissa Dalloway and her parties! That was all life meant to her. He had been divorced from his wife and had come to England. For him, life was far more complicated. He had fallen in love with another woman, one who had two children, and he had come to London to arrange for her divorce and to get some sort of a job. He hoped Hugh Whitbread would find him one, something in the government.

That night Clarissa Dalloway's party was a great success. At first she was afraid that it would fail. But at last the prime minister arrived and her evening was complete. Peter was there, and Peter met Lady Rossetter. Lady Rossetter turned out to be Sally Seton. She had not been invited, but had just dropped in. She had five sons, she told Peter. They chatted. Then Elizabeth came in and Peter noticed how beautiful she was.

Later, Sir William Bradshaw and his wife entered. They were late, they explained, because one of Sir William's patients had committed suicide. For Septimus Smith, feeling altogether abandoned, had jumped out of a window before they could take him into the country. Clarissa was upset. Here was death, she thought. Although the suicide was completely unknown to her, she somehow felt it was her own disaster, her own disgrace. The poor young man had thrown away his life when it became useless. Clarissa had never thrown away anything more valuable than a shilling into the Serpentine. Yes, once she had stood beside a fountain while Peter Walsh, angry and humiliated, had asked her whether she intended to marry

Richard. And Richard had never been prime minister. Instead, the prime minister came to her parties. Now she was growing old. Clarissa Dalloway knew herself at last for the beautiful, charming, inconsequential person she was.

Sally and Peter talked on. They thought idly of Clarissa and Richard, and wondered whether they were happy together. Sally agreed that Richard had improved. She left Peter and went to talk with Richard. Peter was feeling strange. A sort of terror and ecstasy took hold of him, and he could not be certain what it was that excited him so suddenly. It was Clarissa, he thought. Even after all these years, it must be Clarissa.

MOBY DICK

Type of work: Novel
Author: Herman Melville (1819-1891)
Type of plot: Symbolic allegory
Time of plot: Early nineteenth century
Locale: The high seas
First published: 1851

Principal characters:
ISHMAEL, the narrator
QUEEQUEG, a savage harpooner
AHAB, captain of the *Pequod*
STARBUCK, the first mate
STUBB, the second mate
FEDALLAH, Captain Ahab's Parsee servant

Critique:

Moby Dick, or, *The White Whale* is undoubtedly one of the finest novels in American literature. On one level it has an appeal for children, and on another a deep and penetrating significance for all men. Melville intended to indicate in this work the disaster which must result when man constitutes himself a god and sets out to eliminate a force established by God throughout the universe. The whale symbolizes evil, but Ahab, in believing that alone he could hope to destroy it, was also evil. Here is a universal problem, handled with skill and understanding.

The Story:

Ishmael was a schoolmaster who often felt that he must leave his quiet existence and go to sea. Much of his life had been spent as a sailor, and his voyages were a means for ridding himself of the restlessness which frequently seized him. One day he decided that he would sign on a whaling ship, and packing his carpetbag he left Manhattan and set out, bound for Cape Horn and the Pacific.

On his arrival in New Bedford he went to the Spouter Inn near the waterfront to spend the night. There he found he could have a bed only if he consented to share it with a harpooner. His strange bedfellow frightened him when he entered the room, for Ishmael was certain that he was a savage cannibal. After a few moments, however, it became evident that the native, whose name was Queequeg, was a friendly person, for he presented Ishmael with an embalmed head and offered to share his fortune of thirty dollars. The two men quickly became friends, and decided to sign on the same ship.

After some difficulty, they were both signed on as harpooners aboard the *Pequod,* a whaler out of Nantucket. Although several people seemed dubious about the success of a voyage on a vessel such as the *Pequod* was reported to be, under so strange a man as Captain Ahab, neither Ishmael nor Queequeg had any intention of giving up their plans. They were, however, curious to see Captain Ahab.

For several days after the vessel had sailed there was no sign of the captain, as he remained hidden in his cabin. The running of the ship was left to Starbuck and Stubb, two of the mates, and although Ishmael became friendly with them, he learned very little more about Ahab. One day, as the ship was sailing southward, the captain strode out on deck. Ishmael was struck by his stern, relentless expression. In particular, he noticed that the captain had lost a leg and that instead of a wooden leg he now wore one cut from the bone of the jaw of a whale. A livid white scar ran down one side of his face and was lost beneath his collar, so that it seemed as though he were scarred from head to foot.

For several days the ship continued south looking for the whaling schools. The sailors began to take turns on masthead watches to give the sign when a whale was sighted. Ahab appeared on deck and summoned all his men around him. He pulled out an ounce gold piece, nailed it to the mast, and declared that the first man to sight the great white whale, known to the sailors as Moby Dick, would have the gold. Everyone expressed enthusiasm for the quest except Starbuck and Stubb, Starbuck especially deploring the madness with which Ahab had directed all his energies to this one end. He told the captain that he was like a man possessed, for the white whale was a menace to those who would attempt to kill him. Ahab had lost his leg in his last encounter with Moby Dick; he might lose his life in the next meeting. But the captain would not listen to the mate's warning. Liquor was brought out, and at the captain's orders the crew drank to the destruction of Moby Dick.

Ahab, from what he knew of the last reported whereabouts of the whale, plotted a course for the ship which would bring it into the area where Moby Dick was most likely to be. Near the Cape of Good Hope the ship came across a school of sperm whales, and the men busied themselves harpooning, stripping, melting, and storing as many as they were able to catch.

When they encountered another whaling vessel at sea, Captain Ahab asked for news about the white whale. The captain of the ship warned him not to attempt to chase Moby Dick, but it was clear by now that nothing could deflect Ahab from the course he had chosen.

Another vessel stopped them, and the captain of the ship boarded the *Pequod* to buy some oil for his vessel. Captain Ahab again demanded news of the whale, but the captain knew nothing of the monster. As the captain was returning to his ship, he and his men spotted a school of six whales and started after them in their rowboats. While Starbuck and Stubb rallied their men into the *Pequod's* boats, their rivals were already far ahead of them. But the two mates urged their crew until they outstripped their rivals in the race and Queequeg harpooned the largest whale.

Killing the whale was only the beginning of a long and arduous job. After the carcass was dragged to the side of the boat and lashed to it by ropes, the men descended the side and slashed off the blubber. Much of the body was usually demolished by sharks, who streamed around it snapping at the flesh of the whale and at each other. The head of the whale was removed and suspended several feet in the air, above the deck of the ship. After the blubber was cleaned, it was melted in tremendous try-pots, and then stored in vats below deck.

The men were kept busy, but their excitement increased as their ship neared the Indian Ocean and the probable sporting grounds of the white whale. Before long they crossed the path of an English whaling vessel, and Captain Ahab again demanded news of Moby Dick. In answer, the captain of the English ship held out his arm, which from the elbow down consisted of sperm whalebone. Ahab demanded that his boat be lowered at once, and he quickly boarded the deck of the other ship. The captain told him of his encounter, and warned Captain Ahab that it was foolhardy to try to pursue Moby Dick. When he told Ahab where he had seen the white whale last, the captain of the *Pequod* waited for no civilities, but returned to his own ship to order the course changed to carry him to Moby Dick's new feeding ground.

Starbuck tried to reason with the mad captain, to persuade him to give up this insane pursuit, but Ahab seized a rifle and in his fury ordered the mate out of his cabin.

Meanwhile, Queequeg had fallen ill with a fever. When it seemed almost certain he would die, he requested that the carpenter make him a coffin in the shape of a canoe, according to the custom of his tribe. The coffin was then placed in the cabin with the sick man, but as yet there was no real need for it. Queequeg recovered from his illness and rejoined his shipmates. He used his coffin as a sea chest and carved many strange designs upon it.

The sailors had been puzzled by the appearance early in the voyage of the Parsee, Fedallah. His relationship to the captain could not be determined, but that he was highly regarded was evident. Fedallah had prophesied that the captain would die only after he had seen two strange hearses for carrying the dead upon the sea, one not constructed by mortal hands, and the other made of wood grown in America. But he said that the captain himself would have neither hearse nor coffin for his burial.

A terrible storm arose one night. Lightning struck the masts so that all three flamed against the blackness of the night, and the men were frightened by this omen. It seemed to them the hand of God was motioning them to turn from the course to which they had set themselves and return to their homes. Only Captain Ahab was undaunted by the sight. He planted himself at the foot of the mast and challenged the god of evil which the fire symbolized for him. He vowed once again his determination to find and kill the white whale.

A few days later a cry rang through the ship. Moby Dick had been spotted. The voice was Captain Ahab's, for none of the sailors, alert as they had been, had been able to sight him before their captain. Then boats were lowered and the chase began, with Captain Ahab's boat in the lead. As he was about to dash his harpoon into the side of the mountain of white, the whale suddenly turned on the boat, dived under it, and split it into pieces. The men were thrown into the sea, and for some time the churning of the whale prevented rescue. At length Ahab ordered the rescuers to ride into the whale and frighten him away, so he and his men might be picked up. The rest of that day was spent chasing the whale, but to no avail.

The second day the men started out again. They caught up with the whale and buried three harpoons in his white flanks. But he so turned and churned that the lines became twisted, and the boats were pulled every way, with no control over their direction. Two of them were splintered, and the men hauled out of the sea, but Ahab's boat had not as yet been touched. Suddenly it was lifted from the water and thrown high into the air. The captain and the men were quickly picked up, but Fedallah was nowhere to be found.

When the third day of the chase began, Moby Dick seemed tired, and the *Pequod's* boats soon overtook him. Bound to the whale's back by the coils of rope from the harpoon poles they saw the body of Fedallah. The first part of his prophecy had been fulfilled. Moby Dick, enraged by his pain, turned on the boats and splintered them. On the *Pequod* Starbuck watched and turned the ship toward the whale in the hope of saving the captain and some of the crew. The infuriated monster swam directly into the *Pequod,* shattering the ship's timbers. Ahab, seeing the ship founder, cried out that the *Pequod*—made of wood grown in America—was the second hearse of Fedallah's prophecy. The third prophecy, Ahab's death by hemp, was fulfilled when rope from Ahab's harpoon coiled around his neck and snatched him from his boat. All except Ishmael perished. He was rescued by a passing ship after clinging for hours to Queequeg's canoe-coffin, which had bobbed to the surface as the *Pequod* sank.

A MODERN COMEDY

Type of work: Novel
Author: John Galsworthy (1867-1933)
Type of plot: Social chronicle
Time of plot: 1922-1926
Locale: England and America
First published: 1924, 1926, 1928

Principal characters:
SOAMES FORSYTE, the man of property
FLEUR MONT, his daughter
MICHAEL MONT, his son-in-law
JON FORSYTE, Fleur's former lover
MARJORIE FERRAR, an acquaintance of Fleur

Critique:

A Modern Comedy is part of the Forsyte Chronicles (1886-1926), in which Galsworthy pictures the life of a large, upper middle-class family against a carefully detailed background of English life. Solid and very readable, this novel is important as a social document aside from its value as literature. The volume is composed of three long sections—*The White Monkey, The Silver Spoon,* and *Swan Song*—originally published as separate novels, and two interludes. Galsworthy's social history is valuable as a record of the various currents of British life in the 1920's.

The Story:

Soames Forsyte was a member of the board of the Providential Premium Reassurance Society. Against his better judgment, the society had invested much of its holdings in foreign securities. Because the European exchange was so unstable, Soames insisted that the report to the stockholders be detailed. Not long afterward, Butterfield, a clerk in the P.P.R.S. office, overheard a conversation between Elderson, the manager, and a German. The German insisted that Elderson, who had received commissions on the society's investments in Germany, should see to it that the board made good any losses if the mark fell in value. Accused of bribery, Elderson denied the charge and dismissed Butterfield. When pressed, however, Elderson escaped to the continent. The stockholders were outraged that the board had permitted Elderson to get away. Although Soames explained that any early revelation of the manager's dishonesty would have been futile, he received very little support from his listeners. He resigned from the board.

Michael Mont, Soames' son-in-law, was a publisher. When Butterfield lost his job with the P.P.R.S., Soames asked Michael to give the clerk employment. Butterfield prospered as a salesman of special editions.

Michael's wife, Fleur, had been spoiled by her father. She was restless, passionate, and not in love with her husband. Wilfred Desert, an artist, was deeply in love with her, but she knew that he could provide only adventure, not love. Wilfred finally left the country for Arabia. For a time the relationship of Michael and Fleur appeared happier, and Fleur gave birth to a son, whom they named Christopher.

Before she married Michael, Fleur had been in love with her cousin, Jon Forsyte, but because of a family feud she could not marry him. Jon had gone to America, where he fell in love with a Southern girl, Anne Wilmot, and married her.

A year or so after Christopher's birth, Michael entered Parliament. To help her husband and to provide herself with diversion, Fleur entertained many prominent people. One night Soames overheard one of Fleur's guests, Marjorie Ferrar, speak of her as a snob. He asked Marjorie to leave the house. Fleur was impatient with her father for interfering, but she criticized Marjorie for creating an unpleasant scene. Marjorie demanded an apology. After an offer of settlement from Soames, Marjorie still insisted on the apology and took her suit into court, Soames and his lawyer managed to prove that Marjorie was a woman of irresponsible morals. Fleur won the case, but the victory brought her so many snubs from former friends that she was more unhappy than ever.

Francis Wilmot, whose sister Anne had married Jon, arrived from America to see what England was like. He stayed for a time with Fleur and Michael but, having fallen in love with Marjorie Ferrar, he moved out after the unpleasantness between Marjorie and Fleur. Marjorie refused to marry him, however, and go to what she felt would be a dull life in America. Francis contracted pneumonia in a lonely hotel and would have died but for the kindliness of Fleur. He recovered and went back to America.

Fleur, discontented with her life in London, persuaded Soames to take her on a trip around the world. Michael could not leave until the current session of Parliament had adjourned. He was fostering Foggartism—a plan for a return to the land and for populating the dominions with the children of the British poor—and he felt that he must remain in London. It was arranged that he would meet Fleur and Soames in Vancouver five months later. Meanwhile, little Christopher would be in the care of his grandmother, Soames' wife.

While in Washington, Fleur, Michael, and Soames stayed at the hotel where Jon Forsyte and his mother, Irene, were also staying. It was Soames' first sight of his divorced wife in many years. He kept discreetly in the background, however, and saw to it that Fleur did not encounter Jon.

Back in London, with the Marjorie Ferrar affair almost forgotten, Fleur was eager for activity. When the general strike of 1926 began, she opened a canteen for volunteer workers. One day she saw Jon there. He had come over from France to work during the strike. Jon's conscience would not let him fall in love again with Fleur, but she managed to be near him as often as she could. After a single night together, Jon wrote that he could not see her again.

Foggartism having met with high disfavor and unpopularity, Michael became interested in slum improvement. Fleur, still smarting from Jon's rebuff, established a country rest home for working girls. Michael's work had taught him that the poor would never have consented to part with their children, even though keeping them would always mean privation and suffering. He realized that he was well out of Foggartism.

Soames, unhappy in an environment of post-war confusion and family unrest, spent more and more time among his collection of great paintings. One night, awakened by the odor of smoke, he discovered that his picture gallery was on fire. With the aid of his chauffeur, he managed to save many of his pictures by tossing them out the window. At last, when they could stay in the room no longer, they went outside, where Soames directed the firemen as well as he could. Then he saw that one of his heavily framed pictures was about to fall from the window above. He also saw that Fleur was deliberately standing where the frame would fall on her. He ran to push her out of the way, and received the blow himself. He died from exhaustion and from the injury. Fleur was further desolated because she knew that her own desire for death had killed her father. The death of Soames brought her to her senses, however. Michael was assured that her affair with Jon was over forever.

MOLL FLANDERS

Type of work: Novel
Author: Daniel Defoe (1661?-1731)
Type of plot: Picaresque romance
Time of plot: Seventeenth century
Locale: England and the American colonies
First published: 1722

Principal characters:
MOLL FLANDERS, a female rogue
ROBIN, her first husband
A SEA CAPTAIN, Moll's half-brother and husband
JEMMY E., a rogue

Critique:

The complete original title of this remarkable volume was as follows: *The Fortunes and Misfortunes of the famous Moll Flanders, who was born in Newgate, and during a life of continued variety, for threescore years, besides her childhood, was twelve years a Whore, five times a Wife (thereof once to her own brother), twelve years a Thief, eight years a transported Felon in Virginia, at last grew rich, lived honest, and died a penitent. Written from her own Memorandums.* As this title suggests, the heroine of the story is perhaps the world's best-known female picaroon. Like the story of *Robinson Crusoe,* this book is so convincingly written, with such a wealth of intimate detail, the reader feels it must be true.

The Story:

When her mother was transported to the colonies as a felon, eighteen-month-old Moll Flanders was left without family or friends to care for her. For a time she was befriended by a band of gipsies, who deserted her in Colchester. There the child was a charge of the parish. Becoming a favorite of the wife and daughters of the mayor, Moll received gentle treatment and no little attention and flattery.

At the age of fourteen Moll Flanders was again left without a home. When her indulgent instructress died, she was taken in service by a kindly woman of means, receiving instruction along with the daughters of the family. In all but wealth Moll was superior to these daughters. During her residence there she lost her virtue to the oldest son of the family and secretly became his mistress. Later when Robin, the youngest son, made her a proposal of marriage, she accepted him. At the end of five years Robin died. Soon afterward Moll married a spendthrift draper, who quickly went through her savings and was imprisoned. In the meantime Moll took lodgings at the Mint. Passing as a widow, she called herself Mrs. Flanders.

Her next venture in matrimony was with a sea captain with whom she sailed to the Virginia colony. There she discovered to her extreme embarrassment that she was married to her own half-brother. After eight years of residence in Virginia she returned to England to take up her residence at Bath. In due time she became acquainted with a gentleman whose wife was demented. Moll helpfully nursed him through a serious illness. Later she became his mistress. When she found herself with child she made arrangements for her lying-in, sent the child to nurse, and rejoined her companion. During the six years in which they lived together, she gave birth to three children and saved enough money to support herself after the gentleman had regretted his indiscretions and left her.

Next the ambitious girl met a banker with whom she carried on a mild flirtation. However, she left him to marry an Irishman named Jemmy E., supposedly a very wealthy gentleman of Lancashire. Moll had allowed him to believe she had means. She soon learned that her new husband was penniless. He had played on her the same trick she had used on him. Both rogues, they were a congenial couple, but eventually they decided to separate; he to follow his unlawful profession of highway robbery, she to return to the city. After Jemmy had left her, Moll found that she was again to become a mother. Lying-in at the house of a midwife, Moll was delivered of a healthy boy who was boarded out.

In the meantime Moll Flanders had been receiving letters from her admirer, the bank clerk. They met at an inn and were married there. On the day after the ceremony she saw her Lancashire husband, the highwayman, in the courtyard of the inn, and she was able to save him from arrest. For five years, until his death, Moll lived with the banker in great happiness. After his death she sold her property and took lodgings. Forty-eight years old and with two children as dependents, she was prompted by the devil to steal a bundle from an apothecary shop. Next she stole a necklace from a pretty little girl on her way home from dancing school. Thus Moll Flanders embarked on a twelve-year period as a thief. Sometimes she disguised herself in men's clothing. A chance encounter with a gentleman at Bartholomew Fair resulted in an affair which the two carried on for some time. Moll became, after a period of apprenticeship, the richest thief in all England. Her favorite disguise was that of a beggar woman.

Finally she was seized while trying to steal two pieces of silk brocade and was imprisoned in Newgate prison. There she saw again her former husband, the highwayman, committed at Newgate for a robbery on Hounslow Heath. Before going up for trial and sentence, Moll repented of her sins; nevertheless she was sentenced to death by the court. But through the kind offices of a minister, Moll Flanders, now truly repentant, was given a reprieve. The next day she watched her fellow prisoners being carried away in carts for the fate which had been spared her. She was finally sentenced to transportation to America.

The highwayman, with whom she had become reconciled, was awarded a like sentence. The pair embarked for Virginia in the same ship, having made all arrangements for a comfortable journey, and stocked themselves with the tools and materials necessary for running a plantation in the new world. Forty-two days after leaving an Irish port they arrived in Virginia. Once ashore, Moll found that her mother had died. Her brother, whom she had once married, and her son were still living near the spot where she had disembarked.

Not yet wishing to meet her relatives, and not desiring to be known as a transported criminal in America, she arranged for transportation to the Carolina colony. After crossing Chesapeake Bay, she and the highwayman found the ship already overloaded. They decided to stay in Maryland and set up a plantation there. With two servants and fifty acres of land under cultivation, they soon prospered. Then Moll arranged an interview with her son in Virginia across the bay.

In due course she learned that her mother had willed her a plantation on the York River, a plantation complete with stock and servants. To her son she presented one of the stolen watches which she had brought from London. After five weeks she returned to Maryland, where she and her husband became wealthy and prosperous planters of good repute throughout all the colonies. This prosperity was augmented by the arrival of a second cargo of goods from England, for which Moll had arranged before she sailed. In the meantime the man who had been both brother and husband to Moll died and she was able to see her son without any embarrassment.

At the age of seventy years, Moll returned to England. Her husband soon joined her there, and they resolved to spend the rest of their lives in repentance for their numerous sins.

MONSIEUR BEAUCAIRE

Type of work: Novelette
Author: Booth Tarkington (1869-1946)
Type of plot: Period romance
Time of plot: Early eighteenth century
Locale: Bath, England
First published: 1900

Principal characters:

LOUIS-PHILLIPE DE VALOIS, Duke of Orleans, alias Victor, M. Beaucaire, and M. de Chateaurien; nephew of King Louis XV of France
DUKE DE WINTERSET, an English scoundrel
LADY MARY CARLISLE, a shallow aristocrat
MOLYNEAUX, a sympathetic Englishman
BEAU NASH, social arbiter of Bath

Critique:

Booth Tarkington achieved international fame with the appearance of this slight and romantic story of disguise and intrigue. The truism embodied in *Monsieur Beaucaire*—that a man's name is unimportant, that it is the man himself who is important—is proved delightfully enough, not by a nobody but by a real prince, and at the expense of a snobbish English aristocracy. Beaucaire duels twice in Tarkington's Bath; in the historical Bath dueling was outlawed by social arbiter Beau Nash. The story was dramatized in 1901.

The Story:

Victor, alias Monsieur Beaucaire, the barber of the French ambassador to England, gambled with the socially elite of Bath for any amount. It was the early eighteenth century, when Bath society was under the leadership of Beau Nash. One night M. Beaucaire caught the English Duke de Winterset cheating at his table. But instead of hush money, Beaucaire exacted Winterset's promise to take him, a barber in disguise, to Lady Malbourne's ball, and there to introduce him to the young and beautiful Lady Mary Carlisle.

Winterset was disgusted beyond words, for he was sure the barber would be recognized and he himself shamed before his acquaintances. Beaucaire then shed the disguise he wore and appeared before Winterset as an entirely different person. He declared that he would be Monsieur le Duc de Chateaurien.

It was dawn when the ball ended. The gallant M. de Chateaurien, assisting Lady Mary to her sedan chair, begged her for a rose. She refused but managed to drop a flower to the ground for him to retrieve. Within a short time

M. de Chateaurien became, along with Winterset, the cynosure of Bath society. But Winterset planned revenge for the way in which this upstart barber had blackmailed him. Unable to expose Beaucaire without ruining his own reputation, Winterset had a captain in his debt provoke M. de Chateaurien by insulting French womanhood. In the ensuing duel, Chateaurien was victorious; he sent Winterset a basket of roses. Another of Winterset's minions then daringly suggested that M. de Chateaurien was an impostor. The Frenchman, avowedly fighting to defend the honor of his sponsor, Winterset, was victorious a second time.

All the while M. de Chateaurien gained favor with Lady Mary. After a grand fête he was granted the privilege of riding beside her coach. As they talked, Lady Mary more than tacitly confessed her love for the supposed duke. Armed and masked horsemen suddenly attacked M. de Chateaurien and shouted that they intended to kill the barber. He defended himself skillfully, but was finally overcome by superior numbers. As he was being prepared for a lashing, his servants rode up in force and dispersed the attackers. Winterset, who was the leader of the attackers, returned to the coach and disclosed to Lady Mary that M. de Chateaurien was an impostor who had blackmailed Winterset into sponsoring his introduction to Bath society. To the horror of Lady Mary, M. de Chateaurien confessed that he was really a barber. Also he promised to see Winterset at the assembly in a week's time.

The assembly progressed under the watchful eye of Beau Nash. The Chateaurien affair was on every tongue, and Winterset, now the hero of Bath, was again Lady Mary's favorite. Beau Nash assured Winterset that the house and grounds were being guarded, that it would be impossible for the ridiculous barber to enter.

As the Marquis de Mirepoix, the French ambassador, and the Comte de Beaujolais entered the house, Lady Mary retired to a side room where she discovered Molyneaux, a Bath dandy, and M. de Chateaurien playing cards. She vilified Molyneaux for associating with a common barber, and she refused to heed M. de Chateaurien's plea to her to consider him not as a name, but as a man.

Winterset, upon being told of the barber's presence at the assembly, prepared to eject the impostor forcibly. The decorations and orders on the Frenchman's chest aroused indignation among the English gentry. Molyneaux returned from the ballroom with the Comte de Beaujolais, who addressed M. de Chateaurien as Phillipe. It soon became evident that M. de Chateaurien and de Beaujolais were brothers, and that de Beaujolais had come to England to escort Phillipe back to France now that certain family problems had been resolved.

M. de Chateaurien, or Prince Louis-Phillipe de Valois, Duke of Orleans, shamed the Englishmen present for their blindness. He said that the humblest French peasant would have recognized his high nobility if he had seen the sword fight of a week previous. He exposed Winterset as a base coward and a cheat. When Lady Mary asked the prince's forgiveness, he said that he would return to France and marry the lady that his uncle, King Louis XV, had chosen for him; he was sure that she would accept him whether he were Victor, the barber; M. Beaucaire, the gambler; M. Chateaurien, the gentleman, or Prince Louis-Phillipe, nephew of the king.

MONT-ORIOL

Type of work: Novel
Author: Guy de Maupassant (1850-1893)
Type of plot: Social satire
Time of plot: Mid-nineteenth century
Locale: Auvergne, France
First published: 1887

Principal characters:

CHRISTIANE ANDERMATT, a young married woman
PAUL BRETIGNY, Christiane's lover
WILLIAM ANDERMATT, Christiane's husband
GONTRAN DE RAVENEL, Christiane's brother
FATHER ORIOL, a wealthy peasant landowner
CHARLOTTE, and
LOUISE, Oriol's daughters

Critique:

There are two stories told in *Mont-Oriol.* One deals with the love intrigues of Christiane Andermatt, her brother, and her lover. The other describes the financial scheming of William Andermatt, Father Oriol, and the physicians at the health resort. The fact that the love affair carried on by Christiane and Paul Bretigny is often melodramatic and unconvincing is more than compensated for, however, by the skill and humor with which some of the minor characters, such as the crafty Oriol and Christiane's witty brother Gontran, are drawn.

The Story:

The Marquis of Ravenel, who was an enthusiastic patron of the baths at Enval, persuaded his young daughter Christiane and her husband, William Andermatt, to join him. On the advice of one of the doctors at the spring, Christiane agreed to take a series of baths, internal and external, in the hope that they would cure her childlessness.

When the young couple arrived, they were joined by Christiane's spendthrift brother Gontran and his friend, Paul Bretigny, who had come to the country to recover from a disappointing love affair. During their stay, learning that Father Oriol, a wealthy peasant landowner of the district, was going to blast out a huge rock which hindered cultivation of his fields, the party went to watch the event.

To everyone's surprise, a spring came gushing from the ground after the explosion. Andermatt decided that if the water were of medicinal value he would make Oriol an offer for it, for he hoped to build an establishment that would give the existing baths heavy competition. That same evening Andermatt, accompanied by Gontran, went to the Oriol house and placed his proposal before the peasant.

Oriol, whose bargaining ability was also one to be reckoned with, decided that he would have to be careful not to ask too much for the spring and the fields around it; on the other hand, he would not let the possibility of obtaining great wealth slip from his grasp. To inflame Andermatt's desire, he engaged a beggar named Clovis to help him. Clovis, who engaged in poaching by night and feigned rheumatism by day to escape the attentions of the police, was to bathe in the spring for an hour each day—for a fee. At the end of a month he was to be examined. If he were cured of his rheumatism, his condition would prove the medicinal value of the spring.

The unsuspecting Andermatt was enthusiastic about the projected plan, and he himself agreed to pay Clovis for undergoing treatment. Meanwhile he and Oriol agreed to sign a promise of sale.

In order that the Oriol family might be won over to his project, Andermatt decided to hold a charity fête and a lottery, in which the Oriol girls and Christiane would participate.

Andermatt returned to Paris, leaving Christiane at the baths. She and her family, accompanied by Paul Bretigny and the Oriol girls, made numerous excursions about the countryside. Paul began to confide in her, to tell her of his adventures, his love affairs. As their conversations became more intimate, she realized that he was paying court to her. To inflame his desire, she held him at arm's length until finally, as they were starting back from a jaunt at nightfall, he caught at her shawl while she walked in front of him and kissed it madly. She had all she could do to master her agitation before she joined the others in the carriage.

A few days later, when the party went to view the ruins of a nearby castle by moonlight, Paul threw himself at Christiane's feet and she submitted to him.

The following morning Andermatt returned. Losing no time, the financier set about reaching an agreement with Oriol. According to the terms decided upon after much discussion, the company which Andermatt had formed was assigned the lands along the newly-created stream and the crest and slope of the hill down which it ran. In return, Oriol was to receive one fourth of the profits to be made.

Andermatt rushed back to Paris after completing his arrangements. That night Paul went to Christiane's room. During Andermatt's absence they had nearly a month for uninterrupted lovemaking. It was a blow to both of them when they learned that Andermatt was arriving within a few days and that he was planning to take Christiane back to Paris with him when he left.

The financier brought several members of the newly-formed company with him. The terms of the purchase were read and signed before the village notary, and Andermatt was elected president of the company, over the dissenting votes of Oriol and his son. It was agreed that the baths should be known as Mont-Oriol.

That night Paul sorrowfully said goodbye to his love. He felt that, although they might meet later in Paris, part of the enchantment of their affair would be gone forever. Christiane, on the other hand, was full of plans for future meetings and ways of evading the notice of her servants.

The first of July in the following year was set as the dedication date for the new baths at Mont-Oriol. Christiane, big with child, walked with her father and brother and Paul to watch the dedication of the three new springs. They were to be known as the Christiane, Charlotte, and Louise springs, the latter two named after the Oriol girls. But Clovis, who had seemed so successfully cured the previous summer, was again doubled up by his assumed rheumatism. He threatened to become a serious menace to business, for he declared to the guests who would listen that the waters had ultimately done him more harm than good. At last Andermatt was forced to reckon with him, and Clovis finally agreed to undergo treatment every year. It was decided that his return annually for the same treatment would only prove to the public the medicinal value of the baths.

Andermatt had planned an operetta and a display of fireworks for that evening. Gontran, observing that his sister was suffering from the heat of the room in which the entertainment was beginning, sneaked out and set off the rocket which was the signal for the fireworks display to start. Everyone dashed out, to Andermatt's disgust, but he took advantage of the unexpected interlude to have a serious conversation with Gontran. Having been informed that Oriol intended to give the lands around Mont-Oriol as his daughters' dowries, Andermatt proposed that Gontran, who was deeply in debt, should recoup his finances by marrying either Charlotte or Louise. Gontran, after meditating for a few moments, announced that he would open the ball to be held later that evening by dancing with Charlotte Oriol, the younger and prettier of the two sisters.

Christiane, too, made use of the interruption. She proposed to Paul that they walk along the road on which they had said goodbye the previous year. At that time he had fallen to his knees and kissed her shadow. Her hopes that he would repeat the act were dashed, for although the child she was carrying was his, her shadow betrayed too clearly her changed form.

Gontran paid court to Charlotte Oriol at the ball and the news of his interest in her soon became common gossip at the springs. The innocent girl responded so freely that Christiane and Paul, who were fond of her, began to fear that she would eventually find herself compromised. They were satisfied, however, when Gontran confided to them his intention to ask for her hand. When he asked Andermatt to sound out Oriol, the crafty peasant, realizing that his younger daughter would be easier to dispose of than the older, said that he planned to endow her with the lands on the other side of the mountain. Because those lands were of no use to Andermatt at the moment, Gontran realized that he would have to change his tactics.

He persuaded Louise that he had courted Charlotte only to arouse the older sister's interest. He managed to meet her frequently at the home of one of the doctors and on walks, and when the time seemed ripe he sent Andermatt once more to talk to Oriol. As the reward for his efforts he received a signed statement which assured him a dowry and the promise of the girl's hand.

Paul, unaware of Gontran's and Andermatt's designs, had been incensed by the sudden desertion of Charlotte. Gradually his feeling grew to love. One day her father found them together. Partly because he was in love, and partly because he did not want to compromise Charlotte, his immediate reaction was to propose. When he agreed to sign a statement as to his satisfactory income, the peasant gave his consent to the marriage.

The next morning Christiane learned that Paul was to marry Charlotte. Her informant was the doctor who came to examine her, for she felt ill. As soon as she heard that her lover was to marry, she went into labor from the shock. Fifteen hours later a little girl was born. She would have nothing to do with the baby at first, but when Andermatt brought the child to her she found the infant irresistible, and wanted it kept near her.

Because there was no one else to nurse her, the doctor's wife was chosen to keep Christiane company during her recovery. The talkative woman knew the Oriols well, and Christiane was able to learn from her most of the details of Paul's courtship. Upset by the realization that he had given Charlotte the same attentions she had once received, she fell into a delirium for a day. The next day her condition began to improve.

When the baby was a few days old, Christiane asked that Paul be sent to see her. He went, planning to beg her pardon, but he found there was no need to do so. Christine, engrossed in the child, had only a few conventional words for him. Although he had hoped to see the infant that was partly his, he noted that the curtains of the cradle were significantly fastened in the front with some of Christiane's pins.

THE MOON AND SIXPENCE

Type of work: Novel
Author: W. Somerset Maugham (1874-)
Type of plot: Fictional biography
Time of plot: Nineteenth century
Locale: England, France, Tahiti
First published: 1919

Principal characters:
CHARLES STRICKLAND, an artist
DIRK STROEVE, his friend
BLANCHE STROEVE, Dirk's wife
ATA, Strickland's Tahitian wife
AMY STRICKLAND, Strickland's English wife

Critique:

A fictionalized biography of the French artist, Paul Gauguin, this novel attempts to portray the character of a pure artist, a man of renunciation. The material world meant nothing to Strickland; man meant nothing to him, either. He lived ruthlessly for his art. There is shrewd comment on the world's attitude toward a man who passes by the material and the sensual to fulfill some spiritual need. If by chance his intent is to help mankind, then he is proclaimed a saint; but if he is like Charles Strickland, and ignores mankind, he is vested with the spirit of the devil. Maugham passes no judgment on this painter. He merely presents him as he was.

The Story:

Charles Strickland, a dull stockbroker, lived in England with his wife and two children. Mrs. Strickland was a model mother, but her husband seemed bored with her and with his children. To everyone else, it was Strickland himself who seemed commonplace. The family had spent the summer at the seashore, and Strickland had returned ahead of his wife. When she wrote him that she was coming home, he had answered from Paris, simply stating that he was not going to live with her any more. With singleness of intention, Mrs. Strickland dispatched a friend to Paris to bring back her husband.

Strickland was living in a shabby hotel; his room was filthy, but he appeared to be living alone. Much to the discomfort of the friend, he candidly admitted his beastly treatment of his wife, but there was no emotion in his statements concerning her and her future welfare. When asked about the woman with whom he had allegedly run away, he laughed, explaining to Mrs. Strickland's emissary that he had really run off to paint. He knew he could if he seriously tried. The situation was incredible to Mrs. Strickland's friend. Strickland said he did not care what people thought of him.

Stubbornly, Strickland began to take art lessons. Although his teacher laughed at his work, he merely shrugged his shoulders and continued to paint in his own way. Back in England, the friend tried to explain to Mrs. Strickland the utter hopelessness of trying to reconcile her husband. She could not realize her defeat at first. If Strickland had gone off with a woman, she could have understood him. She was not able to cope with an idea.

Dirk Stroeve, a very poor painter with a delicate feeling for art, had married an Englishwoman and settled in Paris. Impossible as it seemed, Dirk, who had become acquainted with Strickland, thought the red-haired Englishman a great painter. But Strickland did not want any man's opinion. Indifferent to physical discomfort, he had not tried to sell his paintings in order to eat. When he needed money, he found odd jobs in and around Paris.

It was apparent that the Stroeves were very much in love. A buffoon and a fool, Dirk was constantly berating himself, but Blanche seemed to hold him in high esteem. When Strickland became very ill, Dirk rushed home to Blanche and pleaded with her to nurse the sick artist back to health. She bitterly professed her hatred of the man who had laughed at her husband's paintings, and she tearfully begged Stroeve not to bring that monster near her. Nevertheless, Dirk was able to persuade her to allow Strickland to come to their home.

Although she and Strickland rarely spoke to each other, Blanche proved a capable nurse. There seemed to be something electrifying in the air when they were together in the same room. Strickland recovered. Because he admired Strickland's work, Dirk was anxious that he stay and work in Dirk's studio. Strickland took possession of the studio. When Dirk finally gathered enough courage to ask him to leave, Blanche said that she would leave also. Dirk fell before her, groveling at her feet, and pleaded with her to stay, but his adoring demonstrations only bored her. When he saw that she would indeed return with Strickland to the filthy hovel which was the Englishman's studio, Dirk's generous soul could not bear to think that his beloved Blanche should live in such poverty. He said that she need not leave; he would go. Thanking her for having given him so much happiness, he left her with half of what he owned.

Dirk hung around Paris waiting for the time to come when Blanche would need him again after Strickland had tired of her. Once he followed her when she went shopping. He walked along with her, telling her of his devotion; she would not speak to him. Suddenly she slapped him in the face and walked away. One day the police informed Dirk that Blanche had swallowed oxalic acid. After she died, Dirk felt compelled to return to his studio. There he found a nude portrait of his wife, evidently the work of Strickland. In a mad passion of jealousy he started to hack at the picture with a knife, but he was arrested by the obvious fact that it was a wonderful piece of art. No matter what he felt, Dirk could not mutilate the painting. He packed his belongings and went back to Holland to live with his mother.

Strickland had taken Blanche Stroeve because he thought she had a beautiful body to paint. When he had finished the picture, he was through with her. Thinking that the picture was not satisfactory, he had left it in the studio. The death of Blanche and the misery of Dirk did not move him. He was an artist.

After Blanche's death Strickland went to Marseilles, and finally, after many wanderings, to Tahiti. There he painted his vivid awkward-looking pictures and left them with people all over the island in payment for lodging and food. No one thought the pictures worth anything, but years later some who had saved the pictures were pleasantly surprised to sell them for enormous sums of money to English and French collectors who came to the island looking for the painter's work.

At one of the hotels in Tahiti, Strickland had been befriended by a fat old woman, Tiare, who looked after his health and his cleanliness. She even found him a wife, a seventeen-year-old native girl named Ata. For three years Ata and her husband lived together in a bungalow just off the main road. These were perhaps the happiest years in Strickland's life. He painted, read, and loafed. Ata had a baby.

One day Ata sent to the village for a doctor. When the doctor came to the artist's bungalow, he was struck with horror, for to his experienced eye Strickland bore the thickened features of a leper. More than two years passed. No one went near Strickland's plantation, for the natives knew well the meaning of Strickland's disease. Only Ata stayed faithfully with him, and everyone shunned her just as they shunned Strickland. Two more years passed. One of Ata's children died. Strickland was now so crippled by the disease that he would not even permit the doctor to see him. He was painting on the walls of his bungalow when at last he went blind. He sat in the house hour after hour, trying to remember his paintings on the walls—his masterpieces. Caring nothing for the fame his art might bring, Strickland made Ata promise to destroy this work upon his death, a wish she faithfully carried out.

Years later a friend of Strickland, just returned from Tahiti, went to call on Mrs. Strickland in London. She seemed little interested in her husband's last years or his death. On the wall were several colored reproductions of Strickland's pictures. They were decorative, she thought, and went so well with her Bakst cushions.

THE MOONSTONE

Type of work: Novel
Author: Wilkie Collins (1824-1889)
Type of plot: Mystery romance
Time of plot: 1799-1849
Locale: India and England
First published: 1868

Principal characters:

JOHN HERNCASTLE, an adventurer
LADY VERINDER, his sister
RACHEL VERINDER, his niece
FRANKLIN BLAKE, Lady Verinder's nephew
GODFREY ABLEWHITE, a charity worker
DR. CANDY, a physician
SERGEANT CUFF, an inspector from Scotland Yard
ROSANNA SPEARMAN, a maid

Critique:

The Moonstone is often called the first and best of detective stories. The true story of the theft of the Moonstone is told by several different hands who were judged best able to describe the various phases of the solution of the plot. These papers have been brought together and studied by one of the suspects, and in due time the mystery is solved. There is not as much true detection in this novel as there is in the later detective story, but the fine characterization and the humor of the book compensate for any loss.

The Story:

In the storming of Seringapatam in India, in the year 1799, John Herncastle, a violent and cruel man, stole the sacred Hindu diamond called the Moonstone. The jewel had been taken years before from the forehead of the Moon-God in its Brahmin shrine, and Herncastle's theft was only one of a series. Since the stone had first been stolen three faithful Hindus had followed its trail, sworn to recover the gem and return it to the statue of the Moon-God. Herncastle took the gem to England and kept it in a bank vault. He saved himself from murder by letting the Hindus know that if he were killed the stone would be cut up into smaller gems, thus losing its sacred identity. Herncastle left the jewel to his niece, Rachel Verinder, at his death.

The stone was to be presented to

Rachel on her birthday following her uncle's death, and young Franklin Blake, Lady Verinder's nephew, was asked by Herncastle's lawyer to take the gift to his cousin. Franklin took the stone to his cousin's estate and barely missed death at the hands of the Hindus before reaching his destination. On the advice of Gabriel Betteredge, the Verinders' old family servant, Franklin put the gem in the vault of a bank nearby until the birthday arrived, as the Hindus had been seen in the neighborhood about three weeks before. Franklin and Rachel fell in love, and even the appearance of Godfrey Ablewhite, a handsome and accomplished charity worker, failed to weaken Rachel's affection. Godfrey had been asked to attend the birthday celebration, together with a number of guests, including Dr. Candy, the town physician, and Mr. Bruff, the family lawyer.

While the guests at the birthday dinner were admiring the beauty of the jewel, they heard the beating of a drum on the terrace. Three Hindus had appeared, disguised as jugglers. One of the guests was Mr. Murthwaite, a famous traveler in the Orient, and at a sharply spoken word from him the Indians retreated. Watchdogs were released to protect the house that night. There was no disturbance to alarm the household, however, and everyone thought all had gone well until Rachel announced the jewel had disappeared from an unlocked cabinet in her dressing-room.

Over Rachel's protests, Franklin Blake insisted the police be called in. The Hindus were arrested and put in jail, but to the astonishment of everyone they were able to prove an alibi for the entire night.

Little about the crime was discovered until Sergeant Cuff of Scotland Yard arrived. He decided that some fresh paint from the door in Rachel's dressing-room must have come off on someone's clothes. Rachel, for some unknown reason, refused to allow a search for the stained clothing. Sergeant Cuff suspected that Rachel had staged the theft herself, and her actions seemed to substantiate his theory. He also thought that Rosanna Spearman, a maid with a criminal record, was a party to the plot, for he learned that Rosanna had made a new nightdress shortly after the theft. Sergeant Cuff guessed it was to take the place of another dress which was stained. Because the Verinders opposed his efforts, he dropped the case. The only other clue he had was that Rosanna might have hidden something in the rocks by the seashore. He suspected it was the stained dress. Rosanna committed suicide soon afterward by throwing herself into a pool of quicksand. Betteredge discovered she had left a letter for Franklin, who had departed from the country by the time it was found.

Rachel went to London with her mother, and in time became engaged to Godfrey Ablewhite. When Mr. Bruff told her Godfrey had secretly learned the terms of her mother's will before asking for her hand, Rachel broke the engagement. Franklin returned to England later in the year and went to visit Betteredge, who told him about Rosanna's letter. Franklin got the letter and learned from it that she had thought him guilty of the crime. The letter also gave him directions for recovering a box which, as Sergeant Cuff had thought, she had buried by the sea. The box proved to have the stained nightgown in it, but it was not Rosanna's nightgown. On the contrary, it was Franklin's!

Unable to account for this strange fact, Franklin returned to London, where he had a long talk with Mr. Bruff about the case. Mr. Bruff informed Franklin that the Moonstone must be in a certain bank in London, deposited there by a notorious pawnbroker named Luker. A mysterious attack upon the money-lender seemed to confirm this belief. Franklin told Mr. Bruff of the strange discovery of the nightgown. Mr. Bruff planned a surprise meeting between Franklin and Rachel, at which Franklin learned that

Rachel had actually seen him come into the room and steal the stone. Because she loved him she had refused to let the investigation go on. Franklin tried to convince her he had no memory of the deed.

On Mr. Bruff's advice, Franklin returned to the country place and tried to discover what had happened to him that night. From Dr. Candy's assistant, Ezra Jennings, he learned that the doctor had secretly given him a dose of laudanum on the night of the theft, so that Franklin, suffering from insomnia, would get a good night's sleep. Jennings suggested administering a like dose to Franklin again, in the same setting, to see what he would do. Mr. Bruff and Rachel came down from London to watch the experiment.

With the help of Betteredge the scene was set and Franklin given the laudanum. Under its influence he repeated his actions on the night of the theft. Rachel watched him come to her room and take out a substitute stone. She was now convinced that his original act had been an attempt to protect her from the Hindus by removing the stone to another room. Before Franklin could recollect what he did with the stone after he left Rachel's room, however, the drug took full effect and he fell sound asleep.

The experiment explained how the stone disappeared from Rachel's room, but not how it got into a London bank through the hands of Luker. Mr. Bruff suggested that the gem might shortly be redeemed from Luker. Sergeant Cuff was called back into the case, and a watch set on the bank. One day Luker came into the bank and claimed the stone. On his way out he could have passed it to any of three people. All three men were followed. Two proved to be innocent citizens. Bruff's office boy trailed the third, a bearded man who looked like a sailor, to an inn where the suspect took lodgings for the night.

When Franklin and Sergeant Cuff arrived at the inn, they found the sailor dead and the box from the bank empty. Sergeant Cuff examined the dead man closely and then tore away a false wig and beard to expose the features of Godfrey Ablewhite. From Luker they learned that Godfrey had seen Franklin go into Rachel's room the night of the robbery, and that Franklin had given Godfrey the stone with instructions to put it in the bank. Since Franklin had remembered nothing of this request the next day, Godfrey kept the jewel. The mystery solved, Rachel and Franklin were happily reunited.

Several years later Mr. Murthwaite, the explorer, told them of a great festival in honor of the Moon-God which he had witnessed in India. When the idol was unveiled, he saw gleaming in the forehead of the stone image the long-lost treasure of the god—the sacred Moonstone.

LE MORTE D'ARTHUR

Type of work: Chronicle
Author: Sir Thomas Malory (1400?-1471)
Type of plot: Chivalric romance
Time of plot: Golden Age of chivalry
Locale: Britain
First published: 1485

Principal characters:
ARTHUR, King of Britain
QUEEN GUINEVERE, his wife
SIR MORDRED, his natural son
SIR LAUNCELOT,
SIR TRISTRAM, and
SIR GALAHAD, knights of the Round Table

Critique:

Le Morte d'Arthur is a monumental work which made the Arthurian cycle available for the first time in English. Malory took a body of legends which had gone from the folklore of Celtic Britain into French literature by way of Brittany, gave these tales a typically English point of view, and added, amended, and deleted for his own purposes, to produce a work which has had tremendous influence on literature ever since. Because of the episodic nature of its contents, the romance concerns itself at great length with figures associated with King Arthur, to the extent that Arthur, as a man, never quite materializes. But Arthur, as the symbol of knighthood at its full flower, pervades the book.

The Story:

King Uther Pendragon saw and loved Igraine, the beautiful and chaste Duchess of Cornwall. His desires being checked by Igraine's husband, King Uther made war on Cornwall and in that war the duke was killed. By means of magic, King Uther got Igraine with child; the couple were subsequently married. The child, named Arthur, was raised by a noble knight, Sir Ector. After the death of King Uther, Arthur proved his right to the throne by removing a sword from an anvil which was imbedded in a rock. From the Lady of the Lake he received his famous sword, Excalibur. When the independent kings of Britain rebelled and made war on the young king, they were defeated. Arthur ruled over all Britain.

King Arthur married Guinevere, the daughter of King Leodegrance, who presented to Arthur as a wedding gift the Round Table and a hundred knights. Merlin the magician was enticed by one of the Ladies of the Lake into eternal imprisonment under a rock.

Five foreign kings invaded Arthur's realm and were defeated after a long war. To show his gratitude to God for his victory, King Arthur founded the Abbey of the Beautiful Adventure at the scene of his victory.

Sir Accolon, the paramour of Morgan Le Fay, enchantress sister of King Arthur, fought Arthur with Excalibur, which Morgan had procured from Arthur by black magic. Arthur was nearly overcome, but in the fight their swords were accidentally exchanged and the king defeated Accolon.

King Lucius of Rome sent ambassadors to Britain to demand tribute of King Arthur. When Arthur refused to pay, he was promised aid in war by all of the knights of his realm. In the war that followed, the British defeated Lucius and conquered Germany and Italy. Arthur was crowned Emperor of Rome.

Back in England, Sir Launcelot, a knight of the Round Table and Queen Guinevere's favorite, set out on adventures to further the honor and glory of himself and of his queen. After many long and arduous adventures, all of them triumphant, Sir Launcelot returned to Camelot, the seat of King Arthur, and was acclaimed the first knight of all Christendom.

Elizabeth, queen of King Meliodas of Liones, died in giving birth to a son, who was named Tristram because of the sad circumstances surrounding his birth. Young Tristram was sent with his preceptor, Gouvernail, to France, where he was trained in all the accomplishments of knighthood. When the king of Ireland demanded tribute from King Mark of Cornwall, Sir Tristram, defending the sovereignty of King Mark, his uncle, slew the Irish champion, Sir Marhaus, but was wounded in the contest. He was nursed by Isolde, princess of Ireland. Tristram and Isolde fell in love and promised to remain true to each other. Later, King Mark commissioned Sir Tristram to return to Ireland to bring back Isolde, whom the king had contracted to marry.

LE MORTE d'ARTHUR by Sir Thomas Malory. Published by Appleton-Century-Crofts, Inc.

During the return voyage from Ireland to Cornwall, Tristram and Isolde drank a love potion and swore undying love. Isolde married King Mark, and Sir Tristram later married Isolde La Blanche Mains, daughter of King Howels of Brittany. But Tristram, unable to remain separated from Isolde of Ireland, joined her secretly. At last, fearing discovery and out of his mind for love of Isolde, Tristram fled into the forest. In a pitiful condition he was carried back to the castle, where a faithful hound revealed his identity to King Mark. King Mark then banished Tristram from Cornwall for ten years. The knight went to Camelot, where he won great renown at tourneys and in knightly adventures. King Mark, hearing of Tristram's honors, went in disguise to Camelot to kill Tristram. Sir Launcelot recognized King Mark and took him to King Arthur, who ordered the Cornish sovereign to allow Sir Tristram to return to Cornwall. In Cornwall, King Mark attempted unsuccessfully to get rid of Tristram. But Tristram managed to avoid all the traps set for him, and he and Isolde escaped to England and took up residence in Castle Joyous Guard.

An old hermit prophesied to King Arthur that a seat which was vacant at the Round Table would be occupied by a knight not yet born—one who would win the Holy Grail.

After Sir Launcelot was tricked into lying with Elaine, the daughter of King Pelles, the maid gave birth to a boy named Galahad. Some years later there appeared in a river a stone with a sword imbedded in it. A message on the sword stated that the best knight in the world would remove it. All the knights of the Round Table attempted to withdraw the sword, without success. Finally an old man brought a young knight to the Round Table and seated him in the vacant place at which the young knight's name, Sir Galahad, appeared magically after he had been seated. Sir Galahad withdrew the magic sword from the stone and set out, with other of Arthur's knights, in quest of the Holy Grail. During his quest, he was joined part of the time by his father, Sir Launcelot. Sir Launcelot tried to enter the Grail chamber and was stricken for twenty-four days as penance for his years of sin. A vision of Christ came to Sir Galahad, who, with his comrades, received communion from the Grail. They came to a near-Eastern city where they healed a cripple. Because of this miracle they were thrown into prison by the pagan king. When the king died, Sir Galahad was chosen king; he saw the miracle of the Grail and died in holiness.

There was great rejoicing in Camelot after the questing knights returned. Sir Launcelot forgot the promises he had made during the quest and began to consort again with Guinevere.

One spring, while traveling with her attendants, Guinevere was captured by a traitorous knight, Sir Meliagrance. Sir Launcelot rescued the queen and killed the evil knight. Enemies of Launcelot reported to King Arthur Launcelot's love for Guinevere. A party championing the king's cause engaged Launcelot in combat. All members of the party except Mordred, Arthur's natural son, were slain. Guinevere was sentenced to be burned, but Sir Launcelot and his party saved the queen from the stake and retired to Castle Joyous Guard. When King Arthur besieged the castle, the Pope commanded a truce between Sir Launcelot and the king. Sir Launcelot and his followers went to France, where they became rulers of that realm. King Arthur invaded France with the intent of overthrowing Sir Launcelot, and in Arthur's absence Mordred seized the throne of Britain and tried to force Guinevere to become his queen. Guinevere escaped to London, where she took refuge in the Tower. King Arthur, hearing of the disaffection of Sir Mordred, returned to England and in a great battle drove the usurper and his false knights back to Canterbury.

At a parley between King Arthur and Sir Mordred, an adder caused a knight to draw his sword. This action brought on a pitched battle in which Mordred was killed and King Arthur was mortally wounded. On his deathbed King Arthur asked Sir Bedivere to cast Excalibur back into the lake from which the sword had come. Sir Bedivere hid the sword twice, but was reproached by the king each time. Finally, Sir Bedivere threw the sword into the lake, where it was caught by a hand and withdrawn under the water.

King Arthur died and was carried on a barge down the river to the Vale of Avalon. When Sir Launcelot returned from France to avenge his king and queen, he learned that Guinevere had become a nun. Sir Launcelot retired to a hermitage and took holy orders. Sir Constantine of Cornwall was chosen king to succeed King Arthur.

MUTINY ON THE BOUNTY

Type of work: Novel
Authors: Charles Nordhoff (1887-1947) and James Norman Hall (1887-1951)
Type of plot: Adventure romance
Time of plot: Late eighteenth century
Locale: South Pacific and Tahiti
First published: 1932

Principal characters:
LIEUTENANT WILLIAM BLIGH, captain of H.M.S. *Bounty*
ROGER BYAM, a midshipman
FLETCHER CHRISTIAN, leader of the mutiny
GEORGE STEWART, midshipman friend of Byam
TEHANI, a Tahitian girl

Critique:

Written in the form of a novel and completely romantic in temper, *Mutiny on the Bounty* is a great story of adventure based upon actual fact. The story of the voyage of the *Bounty,* which sailed from England in 1787, the mutiny aboard her, the exploit of Captain Bligh in piloting a small boat across thirty-six hundred miles of open sea, the trial of the mutineers, and the final refuge of others on bleak Pitcairn Island, are all matters of record. The authors' free arrangement of their material is designed to give to factual narrative the drama and romantic atmosphere of fiction.

The Story:

In 1787 Roger Byam accepted Lieutenant Bligh's offer of a berth as midshipman on H. M. S. *Bounty,* a ship commissioned by the English government to carry the edible breadfruit tree of Tahiti to English possessions in the West Indies, to be used there as a cheap food supply for the black slaves of English planters. Byam's special commission was to work at the task of completing a study of Tahitian dialects for the use of English seamen. After filling the ship's roster and getting favorable weather, the *Bounty* set sail, and Midshipman Byam began to learn the ways of a ship at sea. He also began to learn, when only a few days from England, of the many traits of his captain which were to lead eventually to mutiny. Bligh's fanaticism rested on discipline, which he often enforced at the cost of justice through excessive floggings of the seamen aboard the *Bounty*. However, the principal objection the men had was their captain's exploitation of them and their rations for private graft.

When the *Bounty* arrived in Tahiti,

the crew was given the freedom it deserved. Making use of the native custom, each of the men chose for himself a taio, or special friend from among the natives, who, during the sailor's stay in Tahiti, would supply him with all the delicacies the island had to offer.

During the stay at Tahiti, Byam, living ashore, collected information for his language study. Most of the sailors found women with whom they lived and to whom some of them were later married. Fletcher Christian chose Maimiti, the daughter of Byam's taio. George Stewart chose a Tahitian girl named Peggy. Byam saw Tehani, later his wife, only once during his stay on the island, but from this one appearance he was highly impressed with the beauty of the princess.

Captain Bligh, on the *Bounty,* had continued to practice the cruelties which the men considered not only unfair but also illegal. One practice was the confiscation of gifts which the islanders had brought to the men on shipboard and which rightfully belonged to those men. The gifts he ordered to be put into the ship's stores. He had further placed the men on salt pork rations, amid all the plentiful fresh fruits of the island. Just before leaving Tahiti, Bligh falsely accused Christian of stealing a coconut.

Collection of the breadfruit trees was finally completed and the *Bounty* left for England, but not before four of the chagrined crewmen had attempted desertion. They were caught, returned, and flogged before the crew. This was one more incident to add to the already sullen attitude of the sailors. Feeling continued to run high against Bligh during the early part of the voyage, until that fateful night when a sudden impulse led Christian into mutiny. With his mutineering friends he gained control of the ship and subsequently set Bligh adrift in the *Bounty's* launch, in the company of as many of the loyal crewmen as that boat would hold. The launch was too small to hold all of the loyal hands and so seven had to stay behind, among them Byam and Stewart, his close friend. The mutiny left the *Bounty* manned by twenty-three men, including the seven loyal men.

With Christian in command, the *Bounty* sailed about in the South Seas, the mutineers searching for a suitable island on which to establish a permanent settlement. After several attempts, all balked by unfriendly natives, Christian returned with the crew to Tahiti. By a show of hands, the crew again split, some of the men continuing with Christian their search for a permanent home, the others, including Byam and Stewart, remaining at Tahiti. They expected eventually to be picked up by an English vessel and returned home to continue their naval careers.

After Christian and his crew had sailed to an unknown destination, Byam and his friend established homes on the island by marrying the native girls with whom they had fallen in love during the first visit to the island. Byam went to live in the home of Tehani, his wife, and there continued his language studies. During that idyllic year on the island, children were born to the wives of both Byam and Stewart. Then H. M. S. *Pandora* arrived, searching for the lost *Bounty*. Unaware that Bligh, who had miraculously reached England, had not distinguished between mutineer and loyal sailor among the men who remained on the *Bounty,* Byam and Stewart, anxious for some word of home, eagerly met the newly arrived ship. They were promptly placed in irons and imprisoned. They saw their wives only once after imprisonment, and had it not been for the ship's doctor on the *Pandora* they would have suffered greater hardship than they had experienced on the *Bounty*. The doctor made it possible for Byam to go on with his studies, a task which gave the prisoners something to do and kept them from losing their minds.

The *Pandora* sailed for England with

a total of seven prisoners, four of whom were not guilty of mutiny. They suffered many unnecessary hardships, the greatest occurring during a storm in which the *Pandora* was sunk. The captain delayed releasing the men from their irons until the last possible moment, an act which cost the life of Stewart, who was unable to get clear of the sinking *Pandora* and drowned.

The survivors, gathered on a small island, were forced into a decision to try to make the voyage to Timor, in the Dutch East Indies, the nearest island of call. Their experiences in open boats, with little or no water and food, were savagely cruel because of the tropic sun, the madness from lack of water, and the foolish attempts of the *Pandora's* captain to continue to treat the prisoners as prisoners. Eventually the group reached Timor and there found passage on a Dutch ship bound for England.

Returned to England, the prisoners awaited court-martial for mutiny. The loyal men, falsely accused, were Byam, Morrison, and Muspratt. Three of the mutineers with them were Ellison, Burkitt, and Millward, sailors who were convicted of their crime and hanged. The evidence concerning the innocent men finally reached a point where the decision rested upon the testimony of Robert Tinkler, another midshipman on the *Bounty*. Tinkler was believed lost at sea, but he turned up in time to save the lives of Byam, Muspratt, and Morrison.

Byam continued his naval career and eventually he became the captain of his own ship. In 1810 he returned to Tahiti. Tehani, his wife, was dead. His daughter he found alive and the image of her mother. In a last romantic gesture, he saw that he could not make himself known to her, and he left Tahiti without telling her he was her father. To him that beautiful green island was a place filled with ghosts of younger men, and young Midshipman Byam was one of them.

MY ÁNTONIA

Type of work: Novel
Author: Willa Cather (1876-1947)
Type of plot: Regional chronicle
Time of plot: Late nineteenth and early twentieth centuries
Locale: Nebraska prairie land
First published: 1918

Principal characters:
JIM BURDEN, the narrator and Antonia's friend
ÁNTONIA SHIMERDA, a Bohemian peasant girl

Critique:

Perhaps the most beautiful aspect of this book is its disarming simplicity. There are no witty phrases, no complicated characters; indeed, there is scarcely any plot. And yet there is a quiet, probing depth in Miss Cather's writing. *My Ántonia* is the story of a Bohemian girl whose family came from the old country to settle on the open prairies of Nebraska. While she lives on her farm and tills the soil, she is a child of the prairie, almost as much a part of her setting as the waving grass and the tall corn. But Ántonia goes also to the city, and there she knows heartbreak. She finds peace and meaning in life only after her return to the land which is her heritage.

The Story:

Jim Burden's father and mother died when he was ten years old, and the boy made the long trip from Virginia to his grandparents' farm in Nebraska in the company of Jake Marpole, a hired hand who was to work for Jim's grandfather. Arriving by train late at night in the prairie town of Black Hawk, the boy noticed an immigrant family huddled on the station platform. He and Jake were met by a lanky, scar-faced cowboy named Otto Fuchs, who drove them in a jolting wagon across the empty prairie to the Burden farm.

Jim grew to love the vast expanse of land and sky. One day Jim's grandmother suggested that the family pay a visit to the Shimerdas, an immigrant family just arrived in the territory. At first the newcomers impressed Jim unfavorably. The Shimerdas were poor and lived in a dugout cut into the earth. The place was dirty. The children were ragged. Although he could not understand her speech, Jim made friends with the oldest girl, Ántonia.

Jim found himself often at the Shimerda home. He did not like Ántonia's surly brother, Ambrosch, or her grasping mother, but Ántonia, with her eager smile and great, warm eyes won an immediate place in Jim's heart. One day her father, his English dictionary tucked under his arm, cornered Jim and asked him to teach the girl English. She learned rapidly. Jim respected Ántonia's father. He was a tall, thin, sensitive man, a musician in the old country. Now he was saddened by poverty and burdened with overwork. He seldom laughed any more.

Jim and Ántonia passed many happy hours on the prairie. Then tragedy struck the Shimerdas. During a severe winter, Mr. Shimerda, broken and beaten by the prairie, shot himself. Ántonia had loved her father more than any other member of the family, and after his death she shouldered his share of the farm work. When spring came, she went with Ambrosch into the fields and plowed like a man. The harvest brought money. The Shimerdas soon had a house, and with the money left over they bought plowshares and cattle.

Because Jim's grandparents were growing too old to keep up their farm, they dismissed Jake and Otto and moved to the town of Black Hawk. There Jim longed for the open prairie land, the gruff, friendly companionship of Jake and Otto, and the warmth of Ántonia's friendship. He suffered at school and spent his idle hours roaming the barren gray streets of Black Hawk.

At Jim's suggestion, his grandmother arranged with a neighbor, Mrs. Harling, to bring Ántonia into town as her hired girl. Ántonia entered into her tasks with enthusiasm. Jim saw a change in her. She was more feminine; she laughed oftener; and though she never shirked her duties at the Harling house, she was eager for recreation and gaiety.

Almost every night she went to a dance pavilion with a group of hired girls. There, in new, handmade dresses, the immigrant girls gathered to dance with the village boys. Jim Burden went, too, and the more he saw of the hired girls, the better he liked them. Once or twice he worried about Ántonia, who was popular and trusting. When she earned a reputation for being a little too gay, she lost her position with the Harlings and went to work for a cruel money-lender, Wick Cutter, who had a licentious eye on her.

One night, Ántonia appeared at the Burdens and begged Jim to stay in her bed for the night and let her remain at the Burdens. Wick Cutter was supposed to be out of town, but Ántonia suspected that, with Mrs. Cutter also gone, he might return and harm her. Her fears proved correct, for as Jim lay awake in Ántonia's bed Wick returned and went to the bedroom where he thought Ántonia was sleeping.

Ántonia returned to work for the

Harlings. Jim, eager to go off to college, studied hard during the summer and passed his entrance examinations. In the fall he left for the state university and although he found there a whole new world of literature and art, he could not forget his early years under the blazing prairie sun and his friendship with Ántonia. He heard little of Ántonia during those years. One of her friends, Lena Lingard, who had also worked as a hired girl in Black Hawk, visited him one day. He learned from her that Ántonia was engaged to be married to a man named Larry Donovan.

Jim went on to Harvard to study law, and for years heard nothing of his Nebraska friends. He assumed that Ántonia was married. When he made a trip back to Black Hawk to see his grandparents, he learned that Ántonia, deceived by Larry Donovan, had left Black Hawk in shame and returned to her family. There she worked again in the fields until her baby was born. When Jim went to see her, he found her still the same lovely girl, though her eyes were somber and she had lost her old gaiety. She welcomed him and proudly showed him her baby.

Jim thought that his visit was probably the last time he would see Ántonia. He told her how much a part of him she had become and how sorry he was to leave her again. Ántonia knew that Jim would always be with her, no matter where he went. He reminded her of her beloved father, who, though he had been dead many years, still lived nobly in her heart. She told Jim goodbye and watched him walk back toward town along the familiar road.

It was twenty years before Jim Burden saw Ántonia again. On a Western trip he found himself not far from Black Hawk, and on impulse he drove out in an open buggy to the farm where she lived. He found the place swarming with children of all ages. Small boys rushed forward to greet him, then fell back shyly. Ántonia had married well, at last. The grain was high, and the neat farmhouse seemed to be charged with an atmosphere of activity and happiness. Ántonia seemed as unchanged as she was when she and Jim used to whirl over the dance floor together in Black Hawk. Cusak, her husband, seemed to know Jim before they were introduced, for Ántonia had told all her family about Jim Burden. After a long visit with the Cuzaks, Jim left, promising that he would return the next summer and take two of the Cuzak boys hunting with him.

Waiting in Black Hawk for the train that would take him East, Jim found it hard to realize the long time that had passed since the dark night, years before, when he had seen an immigrant family standing wrapped in their shawls on the same platform. All his memories of the prairie came back to him. Whatever happened now, whatever they had missed, he and Ántonia had shared precious years between them, years that would never be forgotten.

THE MYSTERIES OF PARIS

Type of work: Novel
Author: Eugène Sue (1804-1857)
Type of plot: Mystery romance
Time of plot: Mid-nineteenth century
Locale: France and Germany
First published: 1842-1843

Principal characters:
RODOLPH, Grand Duke of Gerolstein
FLEUR-DE-MARIE, his daughter by Lady Sarah Macgregor
LADY SARAH MACGREGOR, his morganatic wife

CLÉMENCE D'HARVILLE, wife of one of Rodolph's friends
LA CHOUETTE, and
SCHOOLMASTER, two Paris criminals
JACQUES FERRAND, a hypocritical and cruel lawyer
MADAME GEORGES, befriended by Rodolph
RIGOLETTE, Fleur-de-Marie's friend

Critique:

The Mysteries of Paris is a novel which was written mainly to arouse public opinion for reform of the penal system and the poor laws. The descriptions of the poor, the needy, and the afflicted among the unfortunates of Paris are many and vivid. The novel is interspersed with short tales of misfortune and comments by the author as to how many of the difficulties could be remedied by new laws and new charities. The story which allows full freedom to the expression of these ideas is an amazing one. It contains almost a hundred main characters, to say nothing of the numerous minor character studies. Almost every minor plot contains enough material for a novel, and the major plot is intricate and detailed.

The Story:

Rodolph, the Grand Duke of Gerolstein, a small German state, was a handsome young man in his thirties in 1838. Behind him lay a strange past. As a youth he had been brought up in his father's court by an evil tutor named Polidori, who had done his best to warp and confuse the young prince's mind. Polidori had been urged on by the beautiful but sinister Lady Sarah Macgregor, who had been told in her youth that she was destined some day to be a queen.

Sarah had decided that Rodolph, heir to a duchy, would be the perfect husband for her, and with the aid of Polidori she had forced Rodolph into a secret morganatic marriage. In England, where she had fled, she gave birth to a daughter. Rodolph's father was furious, and he had the marriage annulled. One day, after he had threatened to kill his father, Rodolph was sent into exile. Before long Sarah lost all interest in her child and paid her Paris lawyer, Jacques Ferrand, to find a home for the girl. Ferrand gave the child into the care of some unscrupulous child-takers and after a few years falsely wrote to Sarah that the child had died. Sarah forwarded the letter to Rodolph.

Rodolph moved to Paris where he amused himself by roaming through the slums in disguise. Although he was strong, agile, and a fine fighter, the young duke was always followed by his faithful servant, Sir Walter Murphy. Together they ferreted out the secrets and mysteries of Paris streets. One night Rodolph chanced to save a young girl who was being attacked. When he had heard her story, he was so touched by it that he decided to help her. Fleur-de-Marie, as she was called, was an orphan who had been brought up by gangsters and had been in prison. Freed, she was recognized by her old tormentors and captured by them, drugged, made a prisoner, and compelled to suffer the greatest indignities. Feeling that she was really innocent of the crimes into which she had been forced, Rodolph took her to the farm of Madame Georges. The girl's beauty, her sad plight, and the fact that she was the age his dead daughter would have been, aroused his interest and pity.

Madame Georges was likewise a woman whom the duke had befriended. Her criminal husband had deserted her, taking their son with him. Rodolph had searched the streets of Paris for a clue to the whereabouts of Madame Georges' son. At the farm Fleur-de-Marie soon developed into a devout and delightful young woman.

Rodolph continued to live his double life. He attended diplomatic balls and the parties of thieves, and on both planes he found much to do to help people to live better lives. At last, in order to learn better the secrets of Paris, he took lodgings in a boarding-house in one of the poorer sections of town. There he met many needy families, and in countless ways he helped them all. One of the occupants of the house was a girl named Rigolette, who had been Fleur-de-Marie's friend in prison. Rigolette was hard-working and kind, and Rodolph learned a great deal about the people of the house from her.

One day he learned that Clémence d'Harville, the wife of one of his good friends, was involved in an intrigue with a lodger in the house. It did not take him long to discover that the person behind this affair, plotting the destruction of d'Harville and his wife, was Lady Sarah Macgregor. As soon as he could, Rodolph warned Clémence and saved her from her folly. Clémence was unfortunate in that she had been forced into marriage with d'Harville by her mother-in-law, for she did not love her husband. Because he and their daughter were subject to epileptic fits, her life was an unhappy one. D'Harville by chance learned of his wife's unhappiness, and contrived to commit suicide in such a way that everyone thought his death accidental. By this act he saved Clémence from greater unhappiness and atoned for the evil he had committed in marrying her.

While staying at the lodging-house, Rodolph had learned of the numerous evil deeds of the hypocritical lawyer, Jacques Ferrand. When Rodolph learned that Ferrand was planning the murder of Clémence's father, he and Sir Walter Murphy succeeded in thwarting the lawyer's evil scheme. Ferrand was also responsible for the imprisonment of Rigolette's lover. In order to get to the bottom of Ferrand's plans, Rodolph remembered Cicely, a beautiful woman who had once been married to his private doctor, but who later became a depraved creature. Rodolph secured her release from prison and had her introduced into Ferrand's household, where she could spy on his activities and learn his secrets.

Meanwhile Sarah had asked Ferrand to find a young girl whom she could claim was really her child by Rodolph, for she hoped that if she could produce the dead girl she could effect a reconciliation, now that Rodolph was the reigning duke of Gerolstein. Ferrand, learning the whereabouts of Fleur-de-Marie, hired La Chouette, an ugly one-eyed woman, and a criminal called the Schoolmaster to kidnap the girl from the farm of Madame Georges. When the Schoolmaster arrived at the farm, he discovered that Madame Georges was his wife, the woman he had deserted. He did not succeed in getting Fleur-de-Marie. Instead, she was put in jail for failing to give testimony concerning a crime she had witnessed before Rodolph had saved her from the slums. By chance, Clémence found the girl while on a charitable errand. Not knowing that Fleur-de-Marie knew Rodolph, she tried to make the girl's life more pleasant in prison.

When Sarah learned that Fleur-de-Marie had been under the care of Rodolph's friends, she became jealous and made arrangements to have her killed as soon as she could be released from the prison. Ferrand, entrusted with plans for her death, had her released from prison by an accomplice who pretended to be an agent of Clémence d'Harville. On leaving the prison, Fleur-de-Marie met Rigolette and told her old friend of her fortune. Rigolette, who knew Clémence through Rodolph, was pleased. After they parted, Fleur-de-Marie was seized by Ferrand's hirelings and taken into the country, where she was thrown into the river. But some passersby saw her in the water and pulled her ashore in time to save her life.

In the meanwhile La Chouette, learning that Fleur-de-Marie was really the daughter of Rodolph and Sarah, had hurried to Sarah with her information.

Sarah was shocked at the discovery. La Chouette, seeing a chance to make more money by killing Sarah and stealing her jewels, stabbed her protector. The attacker escaped with the jewels and returned to the Schoolmaster to taunt him with her success. The two got into a fight, and the Schoolmaster killed La Chouette. He was captured and put into prison.

Through Cicely, Rodolph had also learned that his daughter was not really dead. Cicely had had little difficulty in uncovering Ferrand's past. As soon as he knew what Sarah had done, Rodolph went to see her, and despite her terrible wound he accused her violently of the shameful and criminal neglect of her daughter.

On returning home, Rodolph was surprised to hear that Clémence had visited him. Clémence had had the fortune to find Fleur-de-Marie in the home where she had been cared for after her escape from drowning, and she had brought the girl to Rodolph. Clémence did not know that events had proved that Fleur-de-Marie was Rodolph's daughter, and so the reunion of father and child was not without pain as well as pleasure, for Clémence and Rodolph had long secretly known that they loved each other. Rodolph begged Clémence to marry him and be a mother to his child. He felt sure that Sarah would die, and the way would thus be clear for their happy life together.

Rodolph remarried Sarah on her deathbed so that their daughter could be called truly legitimate. Information that Rodolph had received from Cicely also made it possible for him to free Rigolette's lover from prison, and it turned out that he was the long-lost son of Madame Georges. With these problems solved, Rodolph planned to return to Germany. First, however, he used his knowledge of Ferrand's activities to force the lawyer to establish many worthy charities. His money gone, Ferrand went into a decline and died soon afterward. Rigolette's lover became administrator for one of the charities, and after their marriage he and Rigolette lived happily with Madame Georges.

Rodolph returned to Germany with Fleur-de-Marie as his legitimate daughter and Clémence as his wife. For a time the three lived together with great happiness. Then Rodolph noticed that Fleur-de-Marie seemed to have moods of depression. One day she explained, weeping, that his goodness to her was without compare, but that the evil life that she had led before he had rescued her from the slums preyed constantly on her mind. She begged to be allowed to enter a convent. Seeing that nothing he could say would change her mind, Rodolph gave his permission.

While serving as a novice at the convent, Fleur-de-Marie's conduct was so perfect that when she was admitted to the order she immediately became the abbess. This honor was too much for her gentle soul to bear, or for her weak, sick body to withstand, and that very night she died. Rodolph, noting that the day of her death was the anniversary of the day on which he had tried to kill his father, felt that the ways of fate are strange.

THE MYSTERIES OF UDOLPHO

Type of work: Novel
Author: Mrs. Ann Radcliffe (1764-1823)
Type of plot: Gothic romance
Time of plot: Late sixteenth century
Locale: France and Italy
First published: 1794

Principal characters:
EMILY ST. AUBERT, a young French aristocrat
SIGNOR MONTONI, a villainous Italian married to Emily's aunt
VALANCOURT, Emily's sweetheart
COUNT MORANO, a Venetian nobleman in love with Emily
MADAME MONTONI, Emily's aunt

Critique:

The Mysteries of Udolpho is the most famous of the Gothic novels extremely popular at the end of the eighteenth century. The mysterious elements of the story are always explained in some natural way, for Mrs. Radcliffe was too much of an eighteenth-century rationalist to succumb completely to the supernatural. The characters in the book are stilted both in action and conversation. Mrs. Radcliffe was at her best only when describing scenery, such as the rugged Pyrenees and Apennines, or when describing an atmosphere of suspense in creating her effects of terror.

The Story:

After the death of his wife, Monsieur St. Aubert, a French aristocrat, took his daughter on a trip in the Pyrenees Mountains. High on a mountain road the St. Auberts met a young nobleman dressed in hunting clothes. He was Valancourt, the younger son of a family with which M. St. Aubert was acquainted. Joining the St. Auberts on their journey, the young man soon fell in love with eighteen-year-old Emily St. Aubert, and the girl felt that she, too, might lose her heart to him.

St. Aubert became desperately ill and died in a cottage near the Chateau-le-Blanc, ancestral seat of the noble Villeroi family. After her father's burial at the nearby convent of St. Clair, Emily returned to her home at La Vallée and promptly burned some mysterious letters which her father had requested her to destroy. With the letters she found a miniature portrait of a beautiful unknown woman. Since she had not been told to destroy the portrait, she took it with her when she left La Vallée to stay with her aunt in Toulouse.

Valancourt followed Emily to Toulouse to press his suit. After some remonstrance, the aunt gave her permission for the young couple to marry. Then, a few days before the ceremony, the aunt married Signor Montoni, a sinister Italian, who immediately forbade his new niece's nuptials. To make his refusal doubly positive, he took Emily and her aunt to his mansion in Venice.

There Emily and Madame Montoni found themselves in unhappy circumstances, for it soon became apparent that Montoni had married in order to secure for himself the estates of his new wife and her niece. When he tried to force Emily to marry a Venetian nobleman, Count Morano, Emily was in despair. Suddenly, on the night before the wedding, Montoni ordered his household to pack and leave for his castle at Udolpho, high in the Apennines.

When the party arrived at Udolpho, Montoni immediately began to repair the fortifications of the castle. Emily did not like the dark, cold, mysterious castle from which the previous owner, Lady Laurentini, had disappeared under mysterious circumstances. Superstitious servants claimed that apparitions flitted about the halls and galleries of the ancient fortress.

Soon after Montoni and his household had settled themselves, Count Morano attempted to kidnap Emily. Foiled by Montoni, who wounded him severely in a sword fight, Morano threatened revenge.

A few days later Montoni tried to force his wife to sign over her estates to him. When she refused, he caused her to be locked up in a tower of the castle. Emily tried to visit her aunt that night. Terrified at finding fresh blood on the tower stairs, she believed her aunt murdered.

Ghostly sounds and shadows about Udolpho began to make everyone uneasy. Even Montoni, who had organized a band of marauders to terrorize and pillage the neighborhood, began to believe the castle was haunted. Emily heard that several hostages had been taken. She was sure that Valancourt was a prisoner because she had heard someone singing a song he had taught her and because one night a mysterious shadow had called her by name. Her life was made one long torment by Montoni's insistence that she sign away her estates to him, lest she suffer the same fate as her aunt.

The aunt had not been murdered, as Emily found out through her maid, but had become so ill because of harsh treatment that she had died and had been buried in the chapel of the castle.

Morano made another attempt to steal Emily away from the castle, this time with her assistance, as she was now afraid for her life. But Montoni and his men discovered the attempt in time to seize the abductors outside the castle walls. Shortly afterward Montoni sent Emily away, after forcing her to sign the papers which gave him control of her estates in France. At first she thought she was being sent to her death, but Montoni sent her to a cottage in Tuscany because he had heard that Venetian authorities were sending a small army to attack Udolpho and seize him and his bandits. His depredations had caused alarm after the villas of several rich Venetians had been robbed.

When Emily returned to the castle, she saw evidence that there had been a terrible battle. Emily's maid and Ludovico, another servant, disclosed to Emily on her return that a prisoner who knew her was in the dungeons below. Emily immediately guessed that the prisoner was Valancourt and made arrangements to escape with him. But the prisoner turned out to be Monsieur Du Pont, an old friend of her father. Emily, Monsieur Du Pont, the girl's maid, and Ludovico made their escape and reached Leghorn safely. There they took ship for France. Then a great storm drove the ship ashore close to the Chateau-le-Blanc, near which Emily's father had been buried.

Emily and her friends were rescued by Monsieur Villefort and his family. The Villeforts had inherited the chateau and were attempting to live in it, although it was in disrepair and said to be haunted. While at the chateau Emily decided to spend several days at the convent where her father was buried. There she found a nun who closely resembled the mysteriously missing Lady Laurentini, whose portrait Emily had seen at the castle of Udolpho.

When Emily returned to the chateau she found it in a state of turmoil because of weird noises that seemed to come from the apartments of the former mistress of the chateau. Ludovico volunteered to spend a night in the apartment. Although all the windows and doors were locked, he was not in the rooms the next morning. When the old caretaker came to tell Emily this news, she noticed the miniature Emily had found at La Vallée. The miniature, said the servant, was a portrait of her former mistress, the Marquise de Villeroi. More than that, Emily closely resembled the portrait.

Meanwhile Valancourt reappeared and once again made plans to marry Emily, but Monsieur Villefort told her of gambling debts the young man had incurred and of the wild life he had led in Paris while she had been a prisoner in Italy. Because of that report Emily refused to marry him. She returned in distress to her home at La Vallée to learn that Montoni had been captured by the Venetian authorities. Since he had criminally secured the deeds to her lands, the court now restored them to her, and she was once again a young woman of wealth and position.

While Emily was at La Vallée, the Villefort family made a trip high into the Pyrenees to hunt. Almost captured by bandits, they were rescued by Ludovico, who had so inexplicably disappeared from the chateau. He had been kidnaped by smugglers who had used the vaults of the chateau to store their treasure, and he disclosed that the noises in the chateau had been caused by the outlaws in an effort to frighten away the rightful owners.

Informed of what had happened, Emily returned to the chateau to see her friends. While there, she again visited the convent of St. Clair. The nun whom she had seen before, and who resembled the former mistress of Udolpho, was taken mortally ill while Emily was at the convent. On her deathbed the nun confessed that she was Lady Laurentini, who had left Udolpho to go to her former lover, the Marquis de Villeroi. Finding him married to M. St. Aubert's sister, she ensnared him once more and made him an accomplice in her plot to poison his wife. When the marquis, overcome by remorse, fled to a distant country and died there, she had retired to the convent to expiate her sins.

Emily's happiness was complete when Monsieur Du Pont, who had escaped with her from Udolpho, proved that Valancourt had gambled only to secure money to aid some friends who were on the brink of misfortune. Reunited, they were married and went to La Vallée, where they lived a happy, tranquil life in contrast to the many strange adventures which had parted them for so long.

NANA

Type of work: Novel
Author: Émile Zola (1840-1902)
Type of plot: Naturalism
Time of plot: 1860's
Locale: Paris and rural France
First published: 1880

Principal characters:
NANA, a beautiful courtesan
FAUCHERY, a dramatic critic
STEINER, a wealthy banker
GEORGE HUGON, a student
PHILIPPE HUGON, his brother, an officer
FONTAN, an actor
COUNT MUFFAT DE BEUVILLE,
SABINE, his wife
MARQUIS DE CHOUARD, and
COUNT XAVIER DE VANDEUVRES, well-known figures of the Parisian world of art and fashion

Critique:

Nana, one of Zola's Rougon-Macquart series of novels picturing French life and society in the period from 1852 to 1870, was written to portray a successful courtesan not sentimentally or romantically but realistically. As Zola presents her, Nana is moronic, vulgar, greedy, and cruel, and her story is a sermon warning men against a devotion to lust. The novel is a powerful indictment of the social decay which marked the reign of Napoleon III.

The Story:

M. Fauchery, theatrical reviewer for a Paris paper, was attending the première of *The Blonde Venus* at the Variety Theatre because he had heard rumors of Nana, Venus of the new play.

Smart Paris was well represented at

the theatre that night, and Fauchery and his cousin Hector de la Faloise noted a few of the more interesting people. In the audience were Steiner, a crooked but very rich banker who was the current lover of Rose Mignon, an actress in *The Blonde Venus;* Mignon, who served as procurer for his own wife; Daguenet, a reckless spender reputed to be Nana's lover for the moment; Count Xavier de Vandeuvres; Count Muffat de Beuville and his wife, and several of the city's well-known courtesans.

The play, a vulgar travesty on the life of the Olympian gods, was becoming boresome when Nana finally appeared, and with beautiful golden hair floating over her shoulders walked confidently toward the footlights for her feature song. When she began to sing, she seemed such a crude amateur that murmurs and hisses were beginning to sound. But suddenly a young student exclaimed loudly that she was stunning. Every one laughed, including Nana. It was as though she frankly admitted that she had nothing except her voluptuous self to offer. But Nana knew that was sufficient for her audience. As she ended her song she retired to the back of the stage amid a roar of applause. In the last act, Nana's body was veiled only by her golden locks and a transparent gauze. The house grew quiet and tense. Nana smiled confidently, knowing that she had conquered them with her marble-like flesh.

Thus Nana, product of the streets of Paris, started her career as mistress of the city. To get money for her scrofulous little son, Louis, and for her own extravagant wants, she sold herself at varying prices to many men. She captivated Steiner, the banker, at an all-night party after her initial success as Venus. He bought her a country place, La Mignotte, a league from Les Fondettes, home of Madame Hugon, whose seventeen-year-old son George had called Nana stunning the opening night of *The Blonde Venus* and who had been enraptured with her at Nana's party. Nana, making no pretense of belonging exclusively to Steiner, invited a number of friends to visit her at La Mignotte.

Madame Hugon entertained Count Muffat, his wife Sabine, and their daughter Estelle at her home in September. George, who had been expected several times during the summer, suddenly came home. He had invited Fauchery and Daguenet for a visit. M. de Vandeuvres, who had promised for five years to come to Les Fondettes, was likewise expected. Madame Hugon was unaware of any connection between the coming of Nana to La Mignotte and the simultaneous visits of all these men to Les Fondettes.

George escaped from his doting mother and went in the rain to Nana, who found him soaking wet as she was gathering strawberries in her garden. While his clothes were drying, he dressed in some of Nana's. Despite Nana's feeling that it was wrong to give herself to such an innocent boy, she finally submitted to George's entreaties — and she was faithful to him for almost a week.

Muffat, who had lived a circumspect life for forty years, became increasingly inflamed by passion as he paid nightly visits to Nana's place, only to be rebuffed each time. He talked with Steiner, who likewise was being put off by Nana with the excuse that she was not feeling well. Meanwhile Muffat's wife attracted the attention of Fauchery, the journalist.

Eleven of Nana's Parisian friends arrived in a group at La Mignotte. George was seen with Nana and her friends by his mother, who later made him promise not to visit the actress, a promise he had no intention of keeping. His brother Philippe, an army officer, threatened to bring him back by his ears if he had anything more to do with Nana.

Being true to George was romantically pleasing, but financially it was unwise, and Nana at last gave herself to the persistent Muffat the night before she returned to Paris to see whether she could recapture the public that had acclaimed her in *The Blonde Venus*.

Three months later Muffat, who had taken the place of castoff George, was involved in financial troubles. During a quarrel with Nana he learned that his wife Sabine and Fauchery were making a cuckold of him. Nana, by turns irritated or bored by Muffat and then sorry for him, chose this means of avenging herself on Fauchery, who had written a scurrilous article entitled *The Golden Fly,* obviously about Nana herself.

Having broken with Muffat and Steiner, Nana gave up her place in the Boulevard Haussmann and went to live with the actor Fontan. But Fontan became increasingly difficult and even vicious, beating her night after night and taking all her money. Nana returned to her old profession of streetwalking to pick up a few francs. After a close brush with the police, Nana grew more discreet. Also, she left the brutal Fontan and sought a part as a grand lady in a new play at the Variety Theatre. Given the part, she failed miserably in it; but she began to play the lady in real life in a richly decorated house which Muffat purchased for her. Despite Nana's callous treatment of him, Muffat could not stay away from her.

In her mansion in the Avenue de Villiers Nana squandered money in great sums. Finding Muffat's gifts insufficient, she added Count Xavier de Vandeuvres as a lover. She planned to get eight or ten thousand francs a month from him for pocket money. George Hugon reappeared, but he was less interesting than he had once been. When Philippe Hugon tried to extricate his young brother from Nana's net, he also was caught. Nana grew bored. From the streets one day she picked up the slut Satin, who became her vice.

In a race for the Grand Prize of Paris at Longchamps, Nana won two thousand louis on a horse named for her. But de Vandeuvres, who owned the filly Nana as well as the favorite Lusignan, lost everything through some crooked betting. He set fire to his stable and died with his horses.

Muffat found Nana in George's arms one evening in September and from that time he ceased to believe in her sworn fidelity. Yet he became more and more her abject slave, submitting meekly when Nana forced him to play woolly bear, horse, and dog with her, and then mocked his ridiculous nudity. Muffat was further degraded when he discovered Nana in bed with his father-in-law, the ancient Marquis de Chouard.

George, jealous of his brother Philippe, stabbed himself in Nana's bedroom when she refused to marry him. He died of his self-inflicted wound and Nana was briefly sorry for him. This utterly evil woman also broke Philippe. He was imprisoned for stealing army funds to spend on her.

Nana thrived on those she destroyed. It was fate which caught her at last. Visiting her dying son after a long absence and many conquests in foreign lands, she caught smallpox from him and died horribly in a Paris hospital. The once-beautiful body which had destroyed so many men lay like a rotting ruin in a deserted room as outside there sounded the French battlecry. The Franco-Prussian war of 1870 had begun.

THE NARRATIVE OF ARTHUR GORDON PYM

Type of work: Short story
Author: Edgar Allan Poe (1809-1849)
Type of plot: Adventure romance
Time of plot: Early nineteenth century
Locale: High seas
First published: 1838

Principal characters:
ARTHUR GORDON PYM, an adventurer
AUGUSTUS BARNARD, his friend
DIRK PETERS, a sailor

Critique:

Presented as the journal of Arthur Gordon Pym, this story is one of those celebrated literary hoaxes so well suited to Poe's talents and taste. The model of the story is the Gothic tale of horror, and in its effects of terror and the unbelievable it equals any other of Poe's tales. It includes such matters as the eating of human flesh and the discovery of human life in regions where the map of the world shows only sea waste. In all other respects the story illustrates the remarkable ability of the writer to simulate the truth when dealing with the unnatural or the supernatural.

The Story:

Arthur Gordon Pym was born the son of a respectable trader at Nantucket. While still young he attended an academy and there met Augustus Barnard, the son of a sea captain, and the two became close friends. One night after a party Augustus awoke Pym from his sleep and together they set off for the harbor. There, Augustus took charge of a small boat and they headed out to sea.

Before long, Pym, seeing that his companion was unconscious, realized the sad truth of the escapade. Augustus had been drunk, and now in the cold weather was lapsing into insensibility. As a result their boat was run down by a whaler and the two narrowly escaped with their lives. They were taken aboard the ship which had run them down and returned to port at Nantucket.

The two friends became even more intimate after this escapade. Captain Barnard was at that time preparing to fit out the *Grampus,* an old sailing hulk, for a voyage on which Augustus was to accompany him. Against his father's wishes, Pym planned to sail with his friend. Since Captain Barnard would not willingly allow Pym to sail without his father's permission, the two boys decided to smuggle Pym aboard and hide him in the hold until the ship should be so far at sea the captain would not turn back.

At first everything went according to schedule. Pym was hidden below in a large box with a store of water and food to last him approximately four days. Great was his consternation to discover, at the end of the fourth day, that his way to the main deck was barred. His friend Augustus did not appear to rescue him. In that terrible state he remained for several days, coming each day closer to starvation or death from thirst.

At last his dog, which had followed Pym aboard the ship, found his way to his master. Tied to the dog's body was a paper containing a strange message concerning blood and a warning to Pym to keep silent if he valued his life.

Pym was sick from hunger and fever when Augustus at last appeared. The story he had to tell was a terrible one. Shortly after the ship had put to sea the crew had mutinied, and Captain Barnard had been set adrift in a small boat. Some of the crew had been killed, and Augustus himself was a prisoner of the mutineers. Pym and Augustus located a place of comparative safety where it was agreed Pym should hide.

Pym now began to give his attention to the cargo, which seemed not to have been stowed in accordance with the rules for safety. Dirk Peters, a drunken mutineer, helped both Pym and Augustus and provided them with food.

When the ship ran into a storm, some of the mutineers were washed overboard. Augustus was once more given free run of the ship. Augustus, Pym, and Peters planned to overcome the other mutineers and take possession of the ship. To frighten the mutineers during a drunken brawl, Pym disguised himself to resemble a sailor recently killed. The three killed all of the mutineers except a sailor named Parker. Meanwhile a gale had come up, and in a few hours the vessel was reduced to a hulk by the heavy seas. Because the ship's cargo was made up of empty oil casks, there was no possibility of its sinking from the violence of the heavy seas. When the storm abated, the four survivors found themselves weak and without food or the hope of securing stores from the flooded hold. One day a vessel was sighted, but as it drew near those aboard the *Grampus* saw that it was adrift and all of its passengers were dead.

Pym tried to go below by diving, but he brought up nothing of worth. His companions were beginning to go mad from strain and hunger. Pym revived them by immersing each of them in the water for awhile. As their agony increased, a ship came near, but it veered away without coming to their rescue.

In desperation the men considered the possibility of eating one of their number. When they drew lots, Parker was chosen to be eaten. For four days the other three lived upon his flesh.

At last they made their way into the stores and secured food. Rain fell, and the supply of fresh water, together with the food, restored their hope. Augustus, who had suffered an arm injury, died. He was devoured by sharks as soon as his body was cast overboard.

A violent lurch of the ship threw Pym overboard, but he regained the ship with Peters' help just in time to be saved from sharks. The floating hulk having overturned at last, the two survivors fed upon barnacles. Finally, when they were nearly dead of thirst, a British ship came to their rescue. It was the *Jane Guy* of Liverpool, bound on a sealing and trading voyage to the South Seas and Pacific.

Peters and Pym began to recover. Within two weeks they were able to look back upon their horrible experiences with almost the same feeling with which one recollects terrible dreams.

The vessel stopped at Christmas Harbor, where some seals and sea elephants were killed for their hides. The captain was anxious to sail his vessel into Antarctica on a voyage of exploration. The weather turned cold. There was an adventure with a huge bear which Peters killed in time to save his companions. Scurvy afflicted the crew. Once the captain decided to turn northward, but later he foolishly took the advice of Pym to continue on. They sailed until they sighted land and encountered some savages whom they took aboard.

The animals on the island were strange, and the water was of some peculiar composition which Pym could not readily understand. The natives on that strange coast lived in a state of complete savagery. Bartering began. Before the landing party could depart, however, the sailors were trapped in what seemed to be an earthquake, which shut off their passage back to the shore. Only Pym and Peters escaped, to learn that the natives had caused the tremendous earth slide by pulling great boulders from the top of a towering cliff. The only white men left on the island, they were faced by the problem of evading the natives, who were now preparing to attack the ship. Unable to warn their comrades, Pym and Peters could only watch helplessly while the savages boarded the *Jane Guy* and overcame the six white men who had remained aboard. The ship was almost demolished. The savages brought about their own destruction, however, for in exploring the ship they set off the ammunition and the resulting explosion killed about a thousand of them.

In making their escape from the island Pym and Peters discovered ruins similar in form to those marking the site of Babylon. When they came upon two unguarded canoes, they took possession of one and pushed out to sea. Savages chased them but eventually gave up the pursuit. They began to grow listless and sleepy when their canoe entered a warm sea. Ashy material fell continually around and upon them. At last the boat rushed rapidly into a cataract, and a human figure, much larger than any man and as white as snow, arose in the pathway of the doomed boat. So ended the journal of Arthur Gordon Pym.

NATIVE SON

Type of work: Novel
Author: Richard Wright (1909-)
Type of plot: Social criticism
Time of plot: 1930's
Locale: An American city
First published: 1940

Principal characters:

- BIGGER THOMAS, a young Negro
- MR. DALTON, Bigger's employer
- MRS. DALTON, Mr. Dalton's wife
- MARY DALTON, their daughter
- JAN ERLONE, Mary's sweetheart
- BRITTEN, Dalton's private detective
- BESSIE MEARS, Bigger's mistress
- BUCKLEY, state prosecutor
- BORIS A. MAX, Bigger's lawyer

Critique:

Written in simple, unadorned English, *Native Son* succeeds in unfolding human emotions of the most primitive and sensuous nature. Richard Wright attempts in this story to create mutual understanding between his own race and the white. Bigger Thomas is not merely one twenty-year-old boy; he is an entire race. *Native Son* shows that the underprivileged Negro is either the church-loyal, praying, submissive type or the embittered, criminal type. The sociological pleading of the novel is subordinate, however, to the drama of a boy who finds freedom through killing and who learns the meaning of life by facing death.

The Story:

In a one-room apartment Bigger Thomas lived with his brother, sister, and mother. Always penniless, haunted by a pathological hatred of white people, driven by an indescribable urge to make others cringe before him, Bigger had retreated into an imaginary world of fantasy.

Through the aid of a relief agency he obtained employment as a chauffeur for a wealthy family. His first assignment was to drive Mary Dalton, his employer's daughter, to the university. Mary, however, was on her way to meet Jan Erlone, her sweetheart. The three of them, Mary and Jan, white people who were crusading with the Communist Party to help the black people, and Bigger, a reluctant ally, spent the evening driving and drinking. When Bigger brought Mary home, she was too drunk to take herself to bed. With a confused medley of hatred, fear, disgust, and revenge playing within his mind, Bigger helped her to her bedroom. When Mary's blind mother entered the room, Bigger covered the girl's face with a pillow to keep her from making any sound that might arouse Mrs. Dalton's suspicions. The reek of whiskey convinced Mrs. Dalton that Mary was drunk, and she left the room. Then

Bigger discovered that he had smothered Mary to death. To delay discovery of his crime, he took the body to the basement and stuffed it into the furnace.

Bigger began a weird kind of rationalization. The next morning in his mother's home he began thinking that he was separated from his family because he had killed a white girl. His plan was to involve Jan in connection with Mary's death.

When Bigger returned to the Dalton home, the family was worrying over Mary's absence. Bigger felt secure from incrimination because he had covered his activities by lying. He decided to send ransom notes to her parents, allowing them to think Mary had been kidnaped. But there were too many facts to remember, too many lies to tell. Britten, the detective whom Mr. Dalton had hired, tried to intimidate Bigger, but his methods only made Bigger more determined to frame Jan, who in his desire to protect Mary lied just enough to help Bigger's cause. When Britten brought Bigger face to face with Jan for questioning, Bigger's fear mounted. He went to Bessie, his mistress, who wrung from him a confession of murder. Bigger forced her to go with him to hide in an empty building in the slum section of the city. There he instructed her to pick up the ransom money he hoped to receive from Mr. Dalton.

Bigger was eating in the Dalton kitchen when the ransom note arrived. Jan had already been arrested. Bigger clung tenaciously to his lies. It was a cold day. Attempting to build up the fire, Bigger accidentally drew attention to the furnace. When reporters discovered Mary's bones, Bigger fled. Hiding with Bessie in the deserted building, he realized that he could not take her away with him. Afraid to leave her behind to be found and questioned by the police, he killed her and threw her body down an air shaft.

When Bigger ventured from his hideout to steal a newspaper, he learned that the city was being combed to find him. He fled from one empty building to another, constantly buying or stealing newspapers so that he could know his chances for escape. Finally he was trapped on the roof of a penthouse by a searching policeman. Bigger knocked him out with the butt of the gun he had been carrying with him. The police finally captured Bigger after a chase across the rooftops.

In jail Bigger refused to eat or speak. His mind turned inward, hating the world, but he was satisfied with himself for what he had done. Three days later Jan Erlone came to see Bigger and promised to help him. Jan introduced Boris A Max, a lawyer from the Comunist front organization for which Jan worked.

Buckley, the prosecuting attorney, tried to persuade Bigger not to become involved with the Communists. Bigger said nothing even after the lawyer told him that Bessie's body had been found. But when Buckley began listing crimes of rape, murder, and burglary which had been charged against him, Bigger protested, vigorously denying rape and Jan's part in Mary's death. Under a steady fire of questions from Buckley, Bigger broke down and signed a confession.

The opening session of the grand jury began. First Mrs. Dalton appeared as a witness to identify one of her daughter's earrings, which had been found in the furnace. Next Jan testified, and under the slanderous anti-Communist questioning, Max rose in protest against the racial bigotry of the coroner. Max questioned Mr. Dalton about his ownership of the high-rent rat-infested tenements where Bigger's family lived. Generally, the grand jury session became a trial of the race relations which had led to Bigger's crime rather than a trial of the crime itself. As a climax to the session the coroner brought Bessie's body into the courtroom in order to produce evidence that Bigger had raped and murdered his Negro sweetheart. Bigger was returned to jail after Max had promised to visit him. Under the quiet questioning of Max, Bigger at last was able to talk about his crime, his feelings, his reasons. He had been thwarted by white people all his life, he said, until he had killed Mary Dalton; that act had released him.

At the opening session of the trial Buckley presented witnesses who attested Bigger's sanity and his ruthless character. The murder was dramatized even to the courtroom reconstruction of the furnace in which Mary's body had been burned. Max refused to call any of his own witnesses or to cross-examine, promising to act in Bigger's behalf as sole witness for the defense. The next day in a long speech Max outlined an entire social structure, its effect on an individual such as Bigger, and Bigger's particular inner compulsions when he killed Mary Dalton. Pleading for mitigation on the grounds that Bigger was not totally responsible for his crime, he argued that society was also to blame.

After another race-prejudiced attack by Buckley, the court adjourned for one hour. It reopened to sentence Bigger to death. Max's attempts to delay death by appealing to the governor were unsuccessful.

In the last hours before death Bigger realized his one hope was to communicate his feelings to Max, to try to have Max explain to him the meaning of his life and his death. Max helped him see that the men who persecuted Negroes, poor people, or others, are themselves filled with fear. Bigger could forgive them because they were suffering the same urge that he had suffered. He could forgive his enemies because they did not know the guilt of their own social crimes.

THE NAZARENE

Type of work: Novel
Author: Sholem Asch (1880-)
Type of plot: Religious chronicle
Time of plot: First and twentieth centuries
Locale: Poland, Italy, Palestine
First published: 1939

Principal characters:

PAN VIADOMSKY, a learned man, an antiquarian, who believes himself a reincarnation of Cornelius the Ciliarch, Hegemon of Jerusalem
A JEWISH STUDENT
YESHUA, Jesus
PONTIUS PILATE
JUDAH ISH-KIRIOT, a disciple of Yeshua
MIRIAM OF MIGDAL, Mary Magdalene
BAR ABBA, a rebel robber

Critique:

The Nazarene attempts to tell the story of Christ as an eyewitness account, and the author's knowledge of historical background and his consummate artistry in handling character, plot, and action make for one of the better novels of our time. Part one is related by Pan Viadomsky, who believes himself to be the reincarnation of Cornelius the Ciliarch, the military governor of Jerusalem under Pontius Pilate. Part two purports to be the Gospel according to Judas Iscariot. Part three is narrated by a young Jewish scholar whom Pan Viadomsky calls Josephus, who later imagines himself a reincarnation of Jochanan, a student under Nicodemon.

THE NAZARENE by Sholem Asch. Translated by Maurice Samuel. By permission of the author and the publishers, G. P. Putnam's Sons. Copyright, 1939, by Sholem Asch.

The Story:

Pan Viadomsky had a peculiar reputation in Warsaw. He was generally accounted a great classical scholar—and a trickster. He earlier had been a frequent contributor to the journals of Latin and Greek, and often he settled controversial matters with a curiously minute and cunning knowledge of the ancients. But after several years he went too far: he talked and wrote of hidden or obscure events with a maddening air of superiority. He announced the discovery of ancient manuscripts, but he would allow no competent scholar to examine the documents.

On an expedition to Mediterranean lands, Pan Viadomsky pretended that he had found old documents of great worth. Some of his colleagues, however, found him in the company of a notorious forger. The learned world then began to discount Pan's scholarship, and gradually many people thought of him as a simple trickster.

Still, Jochanan the Jew was glad to work with Pan, even though he was a vindictive anti-Semite, after the Jew had heard of Pan's Hebrew manuscript and of his desire for a Hebrew scholar to read it with him. Jochanan became well acquainted with the famous Pan, even indispensable to him, and little by little a strange friendship grew between them. On his side Pan sneered at all Jews but he sometimes made an exception for Jochanan; on his side Jochanan was awe-struck by Pan's detailed knowledge of Jewish history, particularly of the time of Christ.

One day, almost against his will, Pan told part of his secret, the source of his detailed and exact knowledge. He announced that he was in reality the reincarnation of the Hegemon of Jerusalem, Pontius Pilate's right hand man! At first Jochanan took the story for an old man's babbling, but he listened to the tale with increasing belief.

Pontius Pilate had been a great soldier of Rome, one of the best lieutenants of Germanicus. But in Rome Pilate discredited his former commander, and doughty Germanicus retired from official life a ruined man. Then Pilate cast covetous eyes on Judea, a poor place, but a land where he could get rich through bribery. He sought and won the hand of Claudia, the debauched daughter of Tiberius Caesar. After the marriage Pilate was appointed Procurator of Judea. He took with him his friend, a young soldier, as Hegemon of Jerusalem.

Once in Jerusalem Pilate ordered the Hegemon to display the hated Roman eagle in the sacred temple of the Jews. The pious Jews were astounded and aroused, for by law Roman authority did not extend to religious matters. But Pilate was firm and the Hegemon cruelly beat back the attempts of the Jews to storm his fortress. At last the Jews gave in, and the crafty High Priest of the Temple paid an enormous bribe to Pilate.

Afterward the Hegemon visited around in Judea a great deal. He met and was drawn to the great courtesan and dancer, Miriam of Migdal. He was in the castle of Herod Antipater that infamous night when Salome danced, and the Hegeman saw the head of Jochanan the Baptist brought in on a platter. He visited K'far Nahum and heard the new Rabbi Yeshua preach. The Hegemon was strangely drawn to this young rabbi of Nazareth, but a real Roman could not deign to listen to a poor Jew, the fanatical son of a carpenter.

Jochanan had to believe Pan, this scholar who knew so much. Pan Viadomsky was really the Hegemon come back to life!

Now that the secret was out, Pan finally showed him his great manuscript. Jochanan looked at the strange document with wonder, and then he examined it with searching care. There could be no doubt that it was in fact what Pan said it was. Jochanan had before him the true manuscript that had been carefully deposited in the tomb-cave of Sepphoris in Galilee. It was the record of Judah Ish-Kiriot, written with his own hand, the story of Judah's time with Yeshua! Through reading it, Jochanan learned more of the great story.

Judah was young and impetuous, and he followed his Rabbi Yeshua with much love. In return Yeshua made Judah treasurer for the little band of disciples.

Judah went everywhere with Yeshua. He even went on that terrible journey into Zidon, where Yeshua was appalled at the sin and suffering and shame of the gentiles. On their return to Jerusalem Yeshua preached with more learning and with more purity than before. When Yeshua preached before Pharisees and Saduccees he was especially inspired.

The small band of twelve grew in number. Miriam, Yeshua's mother, came to be near her son, and Miriam of Migdal repented of her sins and ministered to the needs of Yeshua. But always there was fear among them. Was Yeshua really the Messiah? Would he deliver Judea from the Romans?

Here the manuscript broke off. When he had finished the reading, Jochanan was troubled. Why did these scenes seem so real? Pan Viadomsky's face peered forth through a haze, and Pan's look was triumphant. So that was it! Jochanan had a vivid racial memory of that other Jochanan, the young pupil of Nicodemon.

With the transformation backward in time, Jochanan and the Hegemon finished together, from their joint memories, the story of Yeshua.

Judah had been one of Rabbi Nicodemon's pupils, but he spent more and more time with Yeshua. Judah was sure Yeshua was the Messiah, and that impetuous feeling finally led him to point out Yeshua for the Romans. Judah did it merely to test his rabbi; he expected Yeshua to annihilate the Romans.

The Hegemon had been perturbed by Yeshua. He thought the rabbi was inciting the people to rebellion. The Hegemon went to the High Priest and demanded that Yeshua be tried for treason. Both the Pharisees and the Sadducees agreed that Yeshua was innocent of any crime, but under the urging of the Hegemon, the High Priest brought Yeshua before Pilate. Pilate, little aware of what was going on, hesitated to order Yeshua's crucifixion. He decided to let the people choose whether Yeshua or Bar Abba, a robber, should be released. When the crowd shouted for the release of Bar Abba, Pilate had no choice. He ordered the Hegemon to crucify Yeshua. With zest and Roman thoroughness, the Hegemon carried out the sentence.

Now the story was over. Pan Viadomsky sank back exhausted. Jochanan was still in a whirl, trying to separate the old from the new.

Then Pan confessed the rest of his secret. At the crucifixion Yeshua had conquered the Hegemon's spirit. As retribution and penance the Hegemon's soul remained on earth, inhabiting different bodies. Now Pan Viadomsky was ready to die, but his spirit would stay on in another body. The Hegemon of Jerusalem had to live forever.

THE NEW GRUB STREET

Type of work: Novel
Author: George Gissing (1857-1903)
Type of plot: Social criticism
Time of plot: Nineteenth century
Locale: England
First published: 1891

Principal Characters:
JASPAR MILVAIN, a writer
ALFRED YULE, a literary hack

MARIAN YULE, Alfred's daughter
AMY REARDON, Alfred's niece
EDWIN REARDON, Amy's husband
DORA MILVAIN, and
MAUD MILVAIN, Jaspar's sisters

Critique:

Jaspar Milvain may be classed as an egoist. At any rate, he is a mercenary whose literary aspirations tend only toward the material but pretend to be striving for the artistic. The new Grub Street portrayed by Gissing is not a place for talented but poor writers; it is a ruthless contest among moneymongers.

The Story:

There had been three Yule brothers. John, the oldest, had gone into a profitable paper manufacturing business; he abhorred the relatively impoverished state of his brother Alfred, a writer. Edmund Yule, the third brother, died, leaving only a small income to his wife, his daughter Amy, and his son John. Amy married Edwin Reardon, a man with much promise as a writer, but who had little success after his first book. Jaspar Milvain was Edwin's friend. Jaspar spent most of his time writing small pieces for different publications and making friends among people who counted in the world of letters. He believed, as Amy did, that Edwin would some day become financially successful in his work.

Alfred Yule had married a poor woman of a lower class, who, because of her lack of breeding, had become a drawback to his career. An unfortunate quarrel with an editor named Fadge had caused Alfred to hate Fadge and those associated with him. When Jaspar Milvain accepted his first literary appointment from Fadge, Alfred did not want to invite the young man to call at his home in London, although Marian, his daughter, wished him to do so.

Jaspar's mother died, leaving his two sisters, Dora and Maud, with no means of support, so Jaspar brought the girls to London to live with him. When his sisters arrived in London, Jaspar called at Alfred Yule's home to ask Marian if she would become friends with them. Marian was happy to meet Dora and Maud, as she had no close friends of her own.

Because of her calls on his sisters, Jaspar was able to see Marian frequently. Aware of their brother's selfishness, Dora and Maud viewed with trepidation their new friend's affection toward Jaspar. He was looking for a rich wife to support him while he made his way in the world of letters. If Marian suspected Jaspar's mercenary motives, she did not admit them to herself. Her great sorrow was that her father hated Jaspar along with his enemy, Fadge.

Edwin Reardon's personality was such that he succumbed easily to adversity. When he became discouraged, Amy, who loved her husband, tried to push him back to work. Edwin became irritable, and depended more and more for inspiration on Amy's love. They began to quarrel until they hardly spoke a civil word to one another.

One day Amy and Edwin realized that they would be starving within a month, for there was no hope that Edwin could produce a profitable story in time to save them. Edwin felt he could no longer write. Having been, before his marriage, a clerk in a charitable institution, he resumed his former occupation as a means of saving himself from ruin, both spiritual and financial. Amy was furious to think her husband would degrade himself by accepting the position of a mere clerk. She had believed that she had married a clever writer; Edwin as a clerk did not appeal to her. Finally they parted, Amy to return to her mother's home, and Edwin to assume his clerical job.

Jaspar hesitated to become too much involved with Marian Yule. Although he found her well suited to himself in temperament and intellect, he could not marry her because she was poor.

Suddenly fortune fell upon all these confused people. John Yule died, leaving a large sum of money to his nieces, Amy and Marian. Jaspar immediately proposed to Marian. Convincing herself that Jaspar's proposal came from the love he bore her rather than from her new wealth, Marian promised to marry him. Her greatest problem was to reconcile Alfred to his future son-in-law.

Amy was so stunned by the money that John had left her that at first she failed to realize her problems were at an end. The legacy would make it possible for her to return to Edwin, who could now write with no fear of poverty resulting from literary failure. But Edwin refused her aid. In the first place, he was sure he had lost his ability to write. Furthermore, his pride would not allow him to accept Amy's kindness, since he felt he had lost her love. His health broke. When he retired at last to his bed because of a serious congestion in his lungs, he would not allow his friends to tell Amy of his condition. He did not want her to come to him out of pity, or through a sense of duty.

Marian soon saw Jaspar's love put to a test when she learned that because of unfortunate investments she could receive only a small part of the original inheritance. Jaspar, hearing the news, said they should not consider marriage until he could establish himself. Meanwhile Alfred Yule learned his eyesight was failing, so that in a short while he would be blind and incapable of earning enough money to support his wife and his daughter. Planning to retire to a small institution with his wife, he called Marian to him and told her that henceforth she must try to earn her own income in anticipation of the time when he could no longer support her.

Edwin received a telegram from Amy, asking him to come to her immediately because their son, Willie, was sick. Edwin went back to his wife. The two, in their sorrow over their son's danger, were reconciled. Willie died, and Amy went with Edwin to nurse him in his own illness. His last few days were lightened by her cheerfulness and devotion.

Jaspar's situation became more uncomfortable; Marian without her money was a luxury impossible for him to contemplate. While his sister Dora disdainfully looked on, Jaspar secretly proposed to another woman of his acquaintance, a woman who had both money and connections. When the woman refused his proposal, Jaspar went to Marian and insisted that she marry him immediately. Because her blind father was now totally dependent upon Marian for support, Jaspar hoped to break the engagement by forcing Marian to make a decision between him and her parents. Marian desperately tried to hold the love she had always imagined that Jaspar had for her. But at last she saw him as he really was and broke their engagement.

A posthumous publication of the works of Edwin Reardon occasioned a very complimentary criticism from the pen of Jaspar Milvain, and a series of grateful letters from Amy Reardon sealed the friendship which had once existed between Jaspar and the wife of his former friend. Jaspar realized that he must have wealth to attain his goals in the literary world, and Amy recognized that a successful man must know how to use his social and financial advantages. They were married after a very brief courtship.

With Amy's help and with Jaspar's wise manipulations, the Milvains soon achieved the success which Jaspar had coldly calculated when he had proposed to Marian Yule. Shortly after their marriage, Jaspar was appointed to the editorship which Fadge had vacated. Jaspar and Amy accepted with mutual admiration and joy their unexpected success in life together, both satisfied that they were perfectly mated.

THE NEWCOMES

Type of work: Novel
Author: William Makepeace Thackeray (1811-1863)
Type of plot: Social criticism
Time of plot: Early nineteenth century
Locale: England
First published: 1854-1855

Principal characters:

COLONEL THOMAS NEWCOME, Anglo-Indian soldier
CLIVE NEWCOME, the colonel's son
BRIAN NEWCOME, the colonel's half-brother
HOBSON NEWCOME, another half-brother
LADY ANN, Brian's wife
BARNES, Brian's son
ETHEL, Brian's daughter
LADY KEW, Lady Ann's mother
JAMES BINNIE, the colonel's friend
MRS. MACKENZIE, Binnie's half-sister
ROSEY, Mrs. Mackenzie's daughter
LADY CLARA, Barnes' wife

Critique:

In true Victorian style Thackeray tells this story with zest and skill. The ladies are either virtuous or wicked. Many admirers of Thackeray have insisted that Colonel Newcome is the most perfect gentleman in fiction. Thackeray meant to show the reader the evil effect of certain social conventions of the nineteenth century, such as parental marriage choices, the over-indulgence in the accumulation of wealth, and the worldliness of the upper classes. Ethel, the heroine, goes through all these experiences, but withal she emerges at the end a happy woman.

The Story:

The elder Thomas Newcome married his childhood sweetheart, who died after bearing him one son, named for his father. Thomas remarried, and his second wife bore two sons, Brian and Hobson. Young Thomas proved to be a trial to his stepmother. When he was old enough, he went to India where he later became a colonel. He married and had a son, Clive, whom he loved with a passion far beyond the normal devotion of a father. Having lost his mother, little Clive was sent to England to begin his education.

Brian and Hobson Newcome had inherited their mother's wealthy banking house. Brian married Lady Ann, who was well-known in London for her lavish parties. When little Clive had spent about seven years in England, his impatient father crossed the ocean to join him. He expected to receive a warm welcome from his two half-brothers, Brian and Hobson. Much to the colonel's bewilderment, the bankers received him politely but coldly and passed on the responsibility of entertaining him to young Barnes, Brian's son, a youthful London swell and a familiar figure at the city's clubs.

Colonel Thomas Newcome's late wife had a sister and a brother. The sister, Miss Honeyman, ran a boarding-house in Brighton, where little Alfred and Ethel came with their mother, Lady Ann, for a vacation. There Colonel Newcome and Clive had also arrived for a visit. Mr. Honeyman lived in another house in Brighton, where the keeper's young son, John James Ridley, delighted in drawing pictures from the story-books which he found in Mr. Honeyman's room. While Clive, who aspired to be an artist, delighted in Ridley's drawings, Ethel became extremely fond of the colonel and his unaffected mannerisms. The colonel's great love for children caused him to be a favorite with all the Newcome youngsters, but it was fair-haired little Ethel who won the colonel's heart with her simple, adoring ways and her sincerity.

Colonel Newcome bought a house in London, where he lived with Clive and Mr. James Binnie, the colonel's friend. Clive was given a tutor, but the young man neglected his studies to sketch everything he saw and everyone he knew. If the colonel was disappointed by Clive's choice of career, he said nothing, but allowed Clive to attend art school with his friend Ridley. Clive was becoming a kind, generous and considerate young man. The colonel himself was satisfied that his son was growing up to be the fine man that the retired officer wished him to be. He spent a great deal of money fitting up a well-lighted studio for Clive in a house not far from his own. Meanwhile Mr. Binnie had taken a fall from a horse and was laid up in bed. Binnie's widowed half-sister, Mrs. Mackenzie, and her daughter, Rosey, came to stay with the bedridden Binnie in the colonel's house.

After a time the colonel found himself financially embarrassed. Realizing that he could no longer live on his income in London, he planned to return to India until he reached a higher grade in the army. Then with the increased pension he could afford to retire in London.

Ethel Newcome grew into a beautiful and charming young lady, and the colonel dreamed of a match between Ethel and Clive, but Lady Ann placed an early prohibition on such a match. She told her brother-in-law that Ethel had been promised to Lord Kew, a relative of Lady Kew, Lady Ann's mother. The other Newcomes thought that Rosey Mackenzie would be a fine wife for Clive.

After Colonel Newcome had returned to India, leaving Clive with a substantial income, Clive and Ridley, now a successful artist, went to Baden. There Clive met Ethel and the other Newcome children vacationing without the dampening presence of Lady Ann or her aristocratic mother. Ethel and Clive enjoyed a short period of companionship and innocent pleasure, and Clive fell in love with his beautiful cousin. When Lady Ann and Lady Kew arrived, Clive was warned that he must not press his suit with Ethel any longer, for Ethel must marry in her own station of life. Clive was reminded that the family had assumed him to have found in Miss Rosey Mackenzie a woman of his own social level. Bitterly Clive took his leave and went to Italy with Ridley.

Ethel, beginning to rebel against the little niche that had been assigned to her in society, defied social custom and defended Clive against the charges her brother Barnes repeatedly hurled at him. Finally she broke her engagement to young Lord Kew. When Clive learned of the broken betrothal, he returned to England to press his own suit once more.

In London Clive had little time for his art. He was fast becoming a favorite in London society, whose fashionable hostesses thought him the only son of a wealthy officer in India. Against the wishes of her grandmother, Lady Kew, Ethel arranged frequent meetings with Clive, and at last Clive proposed marriage. But Ethel sadly explained that she would not inherit Lady Kew's fortune unless she married properly. Ethel claimed that her younger brothers and sisters were in need of the money, for after her father's death Barnes Newcome had selfishly kept the family fortune for himself. Meanwhile Lady Kew was wooing Lord Farintosh for Ethel.

After three years' absence Colonel Newcome returned to London. During his absence the colonel had amassed a large fortune for his son, and armed with this wealth Colonel Newcome went to Barnes with a proposal of marriage between Ethel and Clive. Barnes was polite but non-committal. Shortly afterward Lady Kew announced Ethel's engagement to Lord Farintosh. Then, suddenly, Lady Kew died, leaving her immense fortune to Ethel, whose only concern was that the money should go to her younger brothers and sisters.

Barnes' marriage to Lady Clara Pulleyn had never been happy. Soon after they were married he had begun to mistreat his wife, who at last decided that she could no longer stand his bullying treatment. She ran off with her first lover, leaving her small children behind. The shock of the scandal and the subsequent divorce opened Ethel's eyes to dangers of loveless marriages. Realizing that she could never be happy with Lord Farintosh because she did not love him, she broke her second engagement.

Ethel retired from her former social life to rear Barnes' children. Clive, meanwhile, had succumbed to the wishes of Mr. Binnie and his own father. Before the news of Ethel's broken engagement with Lord Farintosh had reached the colonel and his son, Clive had married sweet-faced Rosey Mackenzie.

Clive's marriage was gentle but bare. The colonel was Rosey's chief protector and her greater admirer. Clive tried to be a good husband, but inwardly he longed for more companionship. Once he admitted to his father that he still loved Ethel.

The colonel had been handling the family income very unwisely since his return from India. Shortly after the birth of Clive's son, Thomas, an Indian company in which the colonel had heavy investments failed, and he went bankrupt. Clive, Rosey, and Colonel Newcome were now nearly penniless. Rosey's mother, Mrs. Mackenzie, descended upon them, and in a few months she began ruling them with such tyranny that life became unbearable for the colonel. With the help of some friends he retired to a poorhouse and lived separated from his beloved son. Clive faithfully stayed with Rosey under the forceful abuse of his mother-in-law. He was able to make a meager living by selling his drawings.

When Ethel learned of the pitiful condition of the old colonel, whom she had always loved, and of Clive's distress, she contrived a plan whereby she was able to give them six thousand pounds without their knowing that it came from her. Rosey had been very ill. One night Ethel visited Clive, and Mrs. Mackenzie raised such an indignant clamor that Rosey was seriously affected. She died the following day. The colonel, broken in spirit, also grew weaker from day to day, and soon afterward he too died.

Clive had never lost his love for Ethel through all the years of his unfortunate marriage to Rosey. Many months after the death of his wife, he went once more to Baden with little Thomas. There it was said, by observers who knew the Newcomes, that Clive, Ethel, and little Tommy often were seen walking together through the woods.

THE NIBELUNGENLIED

Type of work: Saga
Author: Unknown
Type of plot: Heroic epic
Time of plot: The Siegfried story is legendary. The Burgundian story is based on historical events of about 437.
Locale: North Central Europe
First transcribed: c. 1200

Principal characters:
SIEGFRIED, son of Siegmund and Sieglind
KRIEMHILD, Burgundian princess, Siegfried's wife
GUNTHER,

GERNOT, and
GISELHER, brothers of Kriemhild
HAGEN, their retainer
BRUNHILD, wife of Gunther
ETZEL (ATTILA), Kriemhild's second husband
DANKWART, Hagen's brother

Critique:

Chief among the battle sagas of Germanic peoples, *The Nibelungenlied* has merged and remerged with countless other legends and myths. In it are echoes of the ancient worship of the pagan gods as well as Christian ritual. In it are tales, like the battle of Siegfried and the dragon, that go back to prehistoric myths. In it are names and themes that seem to run into the substructure of Western civilization. Even in modern times the saga persists in poetry and music. Its revelation of hatred and greed, of honor and glory, stands changeless, indifferent to the passing of time.

The Story:

In Burgundy there lived a noble family which numbered three brothers and a sister. The sons were Gunther, who wore the crown, Gernot, and Giselher; the daughter was Kriemhild. About them was a splendid court of powerful and righteous knights, including Hagen of Trony, his brother Dankwart and mighty Hunold. Kriemhild dreamed one night that she reared a falcon which then was slain by two eagles. When she told her dream to Queen Uta, her mother's interpretation was that Kriemhild should have a noble husband but that unless God's protection followed him he might soon die.

Siegfried was born in Niderland, the son of King Siegmund and Queen Sieglind. In his young manhood he heard of the beautiful Kriemhild, and, although he had never seen her, he determined to have her for his wife. Undeterred by reports of her fierce and warlike kinsmen, he made his armor ready for his venture. Friends came from all parts of the country to bid him farewell, and many of them accompanied him as retainers into King Gunther's land. When he arrived at Gunther's court, Hagen, who knew his fame, told the brothers the story of Siegfried's first success, relating how Siegfried had killed great heroes and had won the hoard of the Nibelung, a treasure of so much gold and jewels that five score wagons could not carry all of it. He also told how Siegfried had won the cloak of invisibility from the dwarf Albric, and how Siegfried had become invincible from having bathed in the blood of a dragon he had slain.

Gunther and his brothers admitted Siegfried to their hall after they had heard of his exploits, and the hero stayed with them a year. But in all that time he did not once see Kriemhild.

The Saxons led by King Ludger threatened to overcome the kingdom of the Burgundians. Siegfried pledged to use his forces in overcoming the Saxons, and in the battle he led his knights and Gunther's troops to a great victory. In the following days there were great celebrations at which Queen Uta and her daughter Kriemhild appeared in public. On one of these occasions Siegfried and Kriemhild met and became betrothed.

King Gunther, wanting to marry Brunhild, Wotan's daughter, told Siegfried that if he would help him win Brunhild then he might wed Kriemhild. Gunther set out at the head of a great expedition, all of his knights decked in costly garments in order to impress Brunhild. But her choice for a husband was not for a well-dressed prince but for a hero. She declared that the man who would win her must surpass her in feats of skill and strength. With Siegfried's aid Gunther overcame Brunhild, and she agreed to go with Gunther as his bride.

Siegfried was sent on ahead to announce a great celebration in honor of the coming marriage of Gunther to Brunhild. A double ceremony took place, with Kriemhild becoming the bride of Siegfried at the same time. At the wedding feast Brunhild burst into tears at the sight of Kriemhild and Siegfried together. Gunther tried to explain away her unhappiness. But once more Gunther needed Siegfried's aid, for Brunhild had determined never to let Gunther share her bed. Siegfried went to her chamber and there overpowered her. She, thinking she had been overcome by Gunther, was thus subdued to Gunther's wit and will.

Brunhild bore a son who was named for Siegfried. As time passed she wished once more to see Siegfried, who had returned with Kriemhild to his own country. Therefore, she instructed Gunther to plan a great hunting party to which Siegfried and Kriemhild should be invited.

At the meeting of the two royal families there was great rivalry between Brunhild and Kriemhild. They vied with each other by overdressing their attendants and then fell to arguing as to the place each should have in the royal procession. Finally, Kriemhild took revenge when she told Brunhild the true story of her wedding night. Accusing Brunhild of acting the part of a harlot, she said that Brunhild had slept first with Siegfried, then with her husband, Gunther. For proof, she displayed Brunhild's ring and girdle, both of which Siegfried had won from Brunhild the night he had overcome her. Brunhild, furious and desirous of revenge, sought out her husband and confronted him with the story of her humiliation and betrayal.

Gunther and Siegfried soon settled to their own satisfaction the wanton quarrel between the two women. But Hagen, the crafty one, stirred up trouble among Gunther's brothers with his claim that Siegfried had stained the honor of their house, and they plotted to trap Siegfried and destroy him. When it was reported that the Saxons were to attack Gunther's knights, Kriemhild unwittingly revealed Siegfried's one vulnerable spot. While bathing in the dragon's blood, he had failed to protect a portion of his body the size of a linden leaf because a leaf had fallen down between his shoulders. The villainous Hagen asked her to sew a token on the spot so that he could protect Siegfried during the fighting.

Hagen sent men to say that the Saxons had given up the attack. Then, the fear of battle over, Gunther rode out to hunt with all his knights. There, deep in the forest, as Siegfried was bending over a spring to drink, he was struck in the fatal spot by an arrow from Hagen's bow. Before he died Siegfried cursed the Burgundians and their tribe forever. Indifferent to the dying man's curse, Hagen carried home the body of the dead hero.

He placed Siegfried's body in the path where Kriemhild would see it on her way to church, but a chamberlain discovered the body before she passed. Kriemhild knew instinctively whose hand had done the deed. A thousand knights headed by Siegmund, his father, mourned the dead hero, and everyone claimed vengeance. The widow gave vast sums of money to the poor in honor of Siegfried. When Siegmund prepared to leave for Niderland, he asked Kriemhild to go with him, but she refused, allowing him, however, to take Siegfried's son with him. She herself was determined to stay with the Burgundians. Queen Brunhild, however, offered no compassion. The Nibelungen hoard was given to Kriemhild, for it was her wedding gift. However, by order of Hagen, who planned to get possession of the treasure, all of it was dropped to the bottom of the Rhine. In the years that followed Kriemhild remained in mourning for Siegfried.

At last the mighty Etzel, King of the Huns, sought to marry Kriemhild. After a long courtship he won Kriemhild and took her to his land to be his wife. Etzel was rich and strong, and after her long years of mourning Kriemhild again occupied a position of power and honor. Now she began to consider how she might avenge herself for the death of Siegfried. Hoping to get Hagen in her power, she sent a messenger to her brothers, saying that she longed to see all of them again.

When they received her message, the brothers and Hagen set out. Old Queen Uta told them that in a dream she had seen a vision of dire foreboding, but the Burgundians refused to heed her warning. Furthermore, Hagen received a token from some mermaidens, who said none of the knights would return from Hunland. He disregarded the prediction. Then a quarrel broke out among the Burgundians, and Dankwart slew Gelfrat. Three evil omens now attended the coming journey, but still the brothers refused to turn back. At last the Burgundians came to Etzel's castle.

Gunther and his brothers were put into separate apartments. Dankwart and Hagen were sent to other quarters. Warned by Sir Dietrich that Kriemhild still plotted vengeance for Siegfried's death, Hagen urged them all to take precaution. When Kriemhild asked them to give her their weapons, Hagen replied that it could not be. The Burgundians decided to post a guard to prevent a surprise attack while they slept.

The court went to mass. At the services the Huns were displeased to see that Gunther and his party jostled Queen Kriemhild.

In honor of the Burgundians, a great tournament was held for all the knights. So bad was the feeling between the Burgundians and the Huns that King Etzel was forced to intervene in order to keep the peace. To appease the brothers, Etzel gave them Kriemhild's small son, Ortlieb, as a hostage. But Sir Bloedel pressed into Dankwart's quarters demanding justice for Kriemhild.

In a few minutes he had aroused the anger of Dankwart, who rose from his table and killed Bloedel. For this deed the angered Huns killed Dankwart's retainers. Dankwart, at bay, ran to Hagen for help. Hagen, knowing that he would not live to seek his vengeance on Kriemhild later, slaughtered the little prince, Ortlieb. Then followed a mighty battle in which Hagen and Gunther managed to kill most of their adversaries.

Kriemhild now urged her heroes to kill Hagen. The first to take up the challenge was Iring. After he had wounded Hagen, he rushed back to Kriemhild for praise. Hagen recovered quickly and sought Iring to kill him.

The battle continued, many knights from both sides falling in the bloody combat. Outnumbered, the Burgundians fell one by one. Kriemhild herself slew Hagen, the last of the Burgundians to survive. He died without revealing the location of the treasure.

King Etzel grieved to see so many brave knights killed. At a sign from him, Hildebrand, one of his retainers, lifted his sword and ended the life of Kriemhild as well.

So died the secret of the new hiding place of the Nibelungen treasure hoard.

A NIGHT IN THE LUXEMBOURG

Type of work: Novelette
Author: Remy de Gourmont (1858-1915)
Type of plot: Rationalized mysticism
Time of plot: Early twentieth century
Locale: Paris
First published: 1906

Principal characters:
M. James Sandy Rose, a journalist
"He"
Elise

Critique:

Remy de Gourmont was accused of blasphemy and indecency as a result of this book. Certainly de Gourmont lacked no honesty in presenting his views of the world based upon personal observation of certain facts. In any case, immorality and indecency depend upon the point of view of the reader. For those readers who think and who are not disturbed at facing the reality of ideas this book could well be a revelation.

The Story:

When James Sandy Rose, foreign correspondent for the *Northern Atlantic Monthly*, died, the newspapers printed only a part of the circumstances surrounding his death. Among his personal affects was a diary which threw more light upon his private experience and belief. In this diary Rose related how he had gone to the Luxembourg and had noticed a peculiar light shining through the windows of the Church of Saint-Sulpice. His curiosity aroused, he went into the church and discovered a man standing before the statue of the Virgin. At first glance the man was very ordinary looking, but when he looked at Rose there was something striking and attractive in his appearance. Rose merely called the man "He" in long passages of the diary that reported a discussion between them on philosophical and religious subjects.

Little by little, it became apparent to Rose that this strange man was really Christ. Rose followed the man out into the garden, which had suddenly become clothed in summer foliage. There they met three beautiful women, one of whom was called Elise. In that pastoral setting their conversations concerning divinity, religion, and philosophy continued. In a short interlude between discussions Rose and Elise had an affair.

"He" informed Rose that Epicurus and Spinoza were nearer to "Him" than anyone else, including the saints. "He" told the reporter also that the gods are superior but not immortal—they merely live longer. Destiny is the creator and the regulator of the world. There is no truth because the world is perpetually changing. The Acts of the Apostles were no more miraculous than those in "Aladdin and the Marvelous Lamp," but the men who wrote of those Acts touched God with their hands. Man's superiority to the animal world, particularly the termites, was brought about by the lowering of the world's temperature. Civilizations came into being because of the discoveries of fire and leisure. Lucretius' poem concerning Epicurus would have been a greater book for mankind than the Bible. Men will perhaps never recover from the wound given them by Christianity. Great hypocrites are always the chosen masters of the world. Suicide is not an act of cowardice. Happiness for men is not possession but desire. The difference between the girl of a public harem and a goddess is only a difference created by social custom and its conception of sin.

When "He" departed, Rose took Elise with him and went to his lodgings. There Rose died mysteriously, leaving no trace as to the exact manner of his death. In his rooms there were evidences of the presence of a woman but nothing else of importance except the diary he had written.

A NIGHT IN THE LUXEMBOURG by Remy de Gourmont. By permission of the publishers, John W. Luce & Co.

NIGHTMARE ABBEY

Type of work: Novel
Author: Thomas Love Peacock (1785-1866)
Type of plot: Social satire
Time of plot: Early nineteenth century
Locale: England
First published: 1818

Principal characters:
CHRISTOPHER GLOWRY, master of Nightmare Abbey
SCYTHROP, his son
MR. FLOSKY, a visitor
MARIONETTA, Glowry's niece
MR. TOOBAD, Glowry's friend
CELINDA, his daughter
LISTLESS, a dandy

Critique:

Peacock is one of the interesting minor novelists of his time. Apart from his own writings, he is remembered for his friendship with Shelley. Many of the literary figures of his time are but thinly disguised in his novels. Peacock, in *Nightmare Abbey,* has written light comedy with a heavy touch, and has satirized many of the customs of his day. The title of the novel suggests the influence of the popular Gothic horror tale.

The Story:

Refused by one young lady in his youth, Glowry immediately married another. His wife was cold and gloomy, and Nightmare Abbey was a fitting name for her house. Glowry found relief from his unhappy life in food and drink, and when his lady died, he was easily consoled by increasing his consumption of food and wine. She left one son, Scythrop, who was gloomy enough to suit his father and Nightmare Abbey. A university education had so stripped Scythrop of his thin veneer of social graces that he was rapidly becoming a country boor like his father.

While his father was away in London attending to an important lawsuit, Scythrop amused himself by constructing miniature dungeons, trapdoors, and secret panels. One day he discovered by chance an apartment in the main wing of the abbey which had no entrance or exit; through an error in construction, the apartment had remained hidden for many years. He imported a dumb carpenter and together they constructed a cunning secret panel through which one could step from the library into the hidden apartment. Then, Scythrop had a private refuge for his gloomy meditations.

Miss Emily Girouette declined decidedly to marry Scythrop. In consequence, when his cousin Marionetta came to visit, she rapidly conquered the heart of that sad young man. But Marionetta had no fortune, and Glowry refused to hear of the marriage. Scythrop, however, grew more enamored daily of his coquettish cousin.

Glowry viewed the increasing attachment of Scythrop and Marionetta with great concern. Finally, he told Scythrop the girl would have to leave. Furious, Scythrop rushed to his tower and filled a human skull with Madeira wine. Confronting his father and holding high the skull, he declared in ringing tones that if Marionetta ever left Nightmare Abbey except of her own free will, he would drink the potion. Convinced that the skull contained poison, his father consented to have Marionetta stay on as a guest. Scythrop drank the wine with gusto.

Glowry confided his troubles to his friend, Toobad, who agreed that marriage with Marionetta was unsuitable in every way. He proposed his own daughter

Celinda, a young woman then studying abroad, as a good match for Scythrop. With Glowry's hearty approval Toobad went to London to meet his daughter and return with her to Nightmare Abbey. But Celinda, refusing to have a husband chosen for her, fled from her domineering father. Toobad appeared at the abbey and left again, vowing to all that he would find his unruly daughter.

The house party at Nightmare Abbey grew larger. Mr. Flosky, a poet of the supernatural, came and spread confusion with his metaphysical paradoxes. Listless, a bored dandy, came with Fatout, his French valet, who was the guardian of his mind and body. Another addition to the party was Mr. Asterias the ichthyologist, engaged in tracing down rumors of mermaids in the vicinity of the abbey. It was not clear what a mermaid would do in the fens around the abbey, but Mr. Asterias had faith. That faith was rewarded one night when dimly Mr. Asterias perceived the form of a woman clad in black. As he rushed across the moat, the mysterious figure disappeared.

Scythrop took as much delight as he could in Marionetta's company. But Listless was the gayest person in the room when Marionetta was present. As far as his languid airs would permit, he followed her about with great eagerness.

Watching Scythrop's affection for Marionetta, Glowry decided that he had been too harsh with his son, and he suddenly announced his approval of their betrothal. To his father's surprise, Scythrop stammered that he did not want to be too precipitate. So the generosity of the father went unrewarded.

There was some mystery about Scythrop. For some time he had been more distraught than usual; now he practically refused marriage with his beloved. More than that, every time Glowry went to his son's rooms, he found the door locked and Scythrop slow in answering his knock. Always, before the door opened, a strange, heavy thud sounded in the room.

One evening, while the whole company was sitting in the drawing-room, a tall and stately figure wearing a bloody turban suddenly appeared. Listless rolled under the sofa. Glowry roared his alarm in Toobad's ear, and Toobad tried to run away. But he mistook a window for a door, and fell into the moat below. Mr. Asterias, still looking for a mermaid, fished him out with a landing net.

These mysteries went back to the night Mr. Asterias thought he saw the mermaid. Scythrop was sitting alone in his library when the door opened softly and in stepped a beautiful, stately woman. She looked at Scythrop carefully, and reassured by what she saw, she sat down confidently. The bewildered man could only sit and stare. Gently the mysterious stranger asked him if he were the illustrious author of the pamphlet, "Philosophical Gas." Flattered, Scythrop acknowledged his authorship of that profound work, only seven copies of which had been sold. Then the girl asked his protection from a marriage that would make her the slave of her sex. Already smitten, Scythrop agreed to hide her in his secret apartment.

Then Scythrop began his dual romance. The serious girl, who called herself Stella, talked night after night of the German metaphysicians and quoted German tragedy. On the other hand, Marionetta was always gay and lively. Scythrop did not know whom to choose.

One night his father demanded entry into his room while Stella was there. Stella decided to show herself, regardless of consequences. Toobad recognized his long-lost daughter Celinda. Scythrop now had to choose either Celinda or Marionetta. But he hesitated to make a choice, feeling that he could not relinquish either. The next day, however, the decision was made for him. Marionetta had accepted Listless and Celinda would soon be Mrs. Flosky. Stoically, Glowry reminded his son that there were other maidens. Scythrop agreed, and ordered the Madeira.

NO NAME

Type of work: Novel
Author: Wilkie Collins (1824-1889)
Type of plot: Domestic romance
Time of plot: Mid-nineteenth century
Locale: England
First published: 1862

Principal characters:
ANDREW VANSTONE, a country gentleman
MRS. VANSTONE, his wife
NORAH, and
MAGDALEN, their daughters
NOEL VANSTONE, a cousin, whom Magdalen married
CAPTAIN WRAGGE, a distant relative
MISS GARTH, a nurse
MR. CLARE, a neighbor
FRANK CLARE, his son
CAPTAIN KIRKE, Magdalen's second husband

Critique:

No Name rivaled *The Woman in White* and *The Moonstone* in popularity among readers of Collins' own day. Judged by modern taste, the novel is still one which diverts the reader and offers an excellent picture of Victorian customs and manners, domestic life, and morals. Its effectiveness lies chiefly in its presentation of character and in its realistic criticism of laws which often worked to the disadvantage of those whom they should have served. Magdalen Vanstone is presented as a headstrong but capable girl who fights for rights she believes are hers. Her sister Norah, a quiet, less determined girl, works out her future according to her own nature. The amiable Captain Wragge is one of the most delightful rogues in English fiction.

The Story:

The Vanstone house at Combe Raven was one of contentment and ease. In it were two lovely and charming daughters—Norah and Magdalen—Andrew Vanstone and his wife, and a wise, kindly nurse and governess, Miss Garth. It was a household in which cook and servants enjoyed immunity from scolding, pets were allowed to range freely, and the affairs of the house ran as smoothly as an old but trustworthy clock.

One morning Mr. and Mrs. Vanstone broke the quiet routine of the household with the announcement that they must go immediately to London on urgent but secret business. This announcement came after the arrival of a letter postmarked New Orleans. They were gone for almost a month. On their return they refused to reveal by any statement or hint the nature of their trip.

Shortly after their return a stranger made his appearance in the neighborhood. The girls learned only that his name was Captain Wragge and that he was distantly connected with Mrs. Vanstone's family. She sent him away without revealing to her husband the circumstances of his arrival or departure. It was apparent that Captain Wragge was attempting to obtain money from his kinswoman.

The Vanstones had an eccentric and surly neighbor, Mr. Clare, a scholar and cynic who frequently asserted that he hated most of mankind. Frank, his son, had been the childhood playmate of Magdalen Vanstone, and for him Mr. Vanstone had secured a position in a commercial house in London. Mr. Clare held a low opinion of his son's abilities; consequently he was not disappointed when Frank was dismissed by his employers as being of little account in the business. In spite of his shortcomings, however, Magdalen was still attracted to her old playmate. Mr. Clare commented ironically that some people always flocked after the worthless of the world—a view he felt confirmed when Mr. Vanstone arranged to have Frank given another chance in the business firm in London, rather than have him sent to China to work in the tea and silk trade.

Magdalen and Frank played in some private theatricals given in one of the country houses nearby. Magdalen did so well in her role that a theatrical agent who saw her performance gave her his card as a reference in case she should ever decide upon a career in the theater.

Mr. Vanstone was unexpectedly killed in a train wreck. His wife, overcome by grief, died before she could put her name to a paper which her husband's lawyer was anxious to have her sign.

Then the mystery of the Vanstones came to light. Mr. and Mrs. Vanstone had been married during their hurried trip to London. They had not been able to do so before because of Mr. Vanstone's earlier marriage to an adventuress whose death had been reported at last from New Orleans. Because Mr. Vanstone had died before he could make a new will, the legitimacy of his daughters was not recognized in the English courts; therefore the Vanstone fortune reverted to an uncle, a selfish and bad-tempered old man who refused to recognize his brother's daughters or to share the inheritance with them.

Frank Clare could no longer look forward to marriage with Magdalen after she had lost her fortune. Without Mr. Vanstone to back him, he was forced to take the offer of work in China.

Miss Garth took Norah and Magdalen with her to her sister's home for a time. There it was decided that the girls should find employment as governesses. One day Magdalen suddenly disappeared. Captain Wragge discovered her after a reward had been offered for news of her whereabouts, but instead of claiming the reward he took her home to Mrs. Wragge, a sad giantess of a woman. Learning of Magdalen's desire to be an actress, he promised to train her and act as her manager.

The uncle who had inherited the Vanstone fortune died. Magdalen, disguised to resemble Miss Garth, went to see his son, Noel Vanstone. He proved to be a weak, miserable creature, as miserly as his father had been.

At last Magdalen received a letter from Frank Clare, a cruel whining message in which he reproached her for allowing him to leave England and repudiated his engagement to her. Magdalen went on the stage. Without revealing her whereabouts or her occupation, she corresponded infrequently with Norah and with Miss Garth. Norah, in the meantime, had hired out as a governess.

Having been hurt by Frank Clare's selfish and spiteful letter, Magdalen decided to marry Noel Vanstone and thus secure the fortune she believed rightfully hers and her sister's. Using the money she had earned as an actress, she established Captain Wragge in a cottage near Noel's house. She herself passed as Miss Bygrave, the captain's niece.

Noel was completely under the influence of his housekeeper, Mrs. Le Count, who was suspicious of the supposed Miss Bygrave from the beginning. Convinced that the girl was the person who had impersonated the elderly Miss Garth some time before, the woman was unable to confirm her suspicions. She was successful, however, in thwarting Magdalen's attempt to win a proposal from Noel. At last Captain Wragge tricked the housekeeper into going to Zurich to visit a supposedly dying brother. Before she departed, Mrs. Le Count learned from Captain Wragge's stupid wife the details of the conspiracy in which the captain was involved, and she wrote Noel a letter to warn him against Magdalen. Captain Wragge intercepted the letter. A date for the wedding was set. As that day approached Magdalen shrank from carrying through the scheme she had so carefully planned, but at the last minute she stiffened her resolution and married Noel.

Mrs. Le Count arrived in Zurich and there realized the trick played on her. She returned to England and began a search for Noel. Tracing him to Scotland, she arrived there shortly after Magdalen had gone to London to see her sister. Noel was shocked when the housekeeper revealed the conspiracy of which he had been a victim. Never in good health, he grew rapidly worse and died after making a new will which gave his fortune to Admiral Bartram, a distant kinsman. Mrs. Le Count had also persuaded him to write a codicil by which George Bartram, the admiral's nephew, was to inherit the money if he married, within a specified time, a woman approved by the admiral. Magdalen, notified that her husband had died suddenly without providing for her, was also informed that the will was valid only if the codicil were properly executed.

Meanwhile George Bartram had met Norah and had become engaged to her. His uncle had no objections to his nephew's marriage to Norah, but the inquiries he made so hurt the girl's pride that she refused to marry George within the time specified in the codicil. The delay made Noel's will invalid.

Not knowing the nature of the codicil but hoping that its terms might work to her advantage, Magdalen hired out as a parlormaid in the admiral's household in order to search for the document. She found it eventually, but by that time the situation had grown even more complicated. Admiral Bartram died and left his fortune, including his inheritance from Noel Vanstone, to his nephew. Too proud to ask for her share of the money and without funds, she contracted a fever and was desperately ill. While she was being taken to a London hospital, she was recognized by Captain Kirke, an admirer little regarded when she was planning to marry Noel for his money. He provided for her until word of her illness could be carried to her sister and Miss Garth.

Good fortune came to her during her convalescence. Norah wrote to say that the codicil had been discovered and that by its terms the money bequeathed by Noel Vanstone was legally hers. Captain Wragge appeared to announce that he had grown prosperous through the manufacture of a patent medicine. Mr. Clare wrote to say that Frank had married a wealthy widow. Magdalen felt that Frank's marriage broke her last tie with her unhappy past. She could look forward to the future as Captain Kirke's wife.

NOCTURNE

Type of work: Novel
Author: Frank Swinnerton (1884-)
Type of plot: Domestic romance
Time of plot: Twentieth century
Locale: London
First published: 1917

Principal characters:
JENNY BLANCHARD, a milliner's assistant
EMMY BLANCHARD, her sister
PA BLANCHARD, their invalid father
ALF RYLETT, Jenny's suitor
KEITH REDINGTON, Jenny's beloved

Critique:

Nocturne is almost a play, for the entire novel is written in the form of duologues. Swinnerton has adhered strictly to the classical dramatic unity of time and only a little less strictly to the unities of place and action. The author reveals a shrewd insight into the psychological kinship in frustration of two sisters who had nothing in common in the way of physical appearance, personality, or character. The form of this compact novel is so fascinating that it sometimes obscures the content and the sympathetic picture of human experience presented.

The Story:

At six o'clock one afternoon Jenny Blanchard, a milliner's assistant, returned on the tram from her place of work in London's West End to her home in Kennington Park, a suburb south of the Thames River. As the tram passed over the dark Thames, she felt a sense of great unhappiness and frustration; but the mysterious quality of her reflection in the tram window gave her momentary satisfaction.

The Blanchard house was one of a row of identical houses in Kennington Park. There Jenny and her sister Emmy took care of their semi-invalid father, who lived on a pension and on money that Jenny earned at the milliner's shop. Emmy, older than Jenny, was the housekeeper; she stayed at home to prepare meals and to look after Pa Blanchard. The sisters were quite different in personality, character, and appearance. Jenny was thin, tall, rather beautiful, and of an independent nature. Emmy was plain, domestic, and dependent. The sisters shared, however, a frustration brought on by commonplace routine and dull existence.

Jenny began a quarrel when she expressed her intense dislike for their supper of stew and bread pudding; she felt, somehow, that she was entitled to better fare, but she was sure that the colorless Emmy enjoyed stew and pudding. Jealousy and frustration gave rise to bitter words between the two. Emmy was upset, too, because Jenny kept company with Alf Rylett, whom she herself wanted. Jenny, disdainfully offering Emmy her share of Alf, said that she kept company with him only for diversion.

After supper, as Jenny was preparing to remake a hat, Alf entered and told her that he had two tickets to the local theater. Jenny tricked Alf into asking Emmy to go with him. While Emmy was changing, Jenny parried Alf's protestations of love. Emmy, appearing actually lovely after her change, swallowed her pride and went with Alf, whom she idolized. It was eight o'clock.

Jenny put Pa to bed and resumed work on her hat. She rationalized her throwing over of Alf by saying to herself that she wanted adventure and that steady Alf was not the man to satisfy her dreams of romance. Besides, Emmy was the marrying kind, not she. While Jenny was wishing ardently for something thrilling to happen in her drab life, a knock sounded at the door. A liveried servant handed her a letter and waited. The letter, which was signed Keith, bade her to come to him immediately. Apprehensively, she left Pa alone and rode in a large car to the Thames. There she met Keith Redington, whom she had known only three days during a seaside vacation. He rowed her out to a yacht anchored in the river. The yacht, of which Keith was the captain, belonged to a wealthy lord. It was nine o'clock.

On the yacht Jenny found supper set for two. She was suspicious of Keith's intentions and annoyed at his confidence that she would come. The couple, little more than strangers, gradually warmed to each other; Jenny discarded her suspicions in her desire for happiness. Keith told her of his life, of three women he had loved, one of whom had been his wife, and of his desire to marry Jenny. Jenny, hungry for an entirely different story, was hurt, but Keith's enthusiasm in explaining his romantic plans for the two of them completely mollified her. The romantic dream of going off to Alaska or to Labrador was crushed, however, when Jenny thought of Pa. At midnight she left Keith and was driven home by the liveried chauffeur.

Meanwhile, Alf and Emmy had gone to the theater. The demure and domestic little Emmy having provoked startling reactions in Alf's mind and heart, they took the long way home after the show and Alf quickly came to the conclusion that Emmy was, after all, the girl for him. They kissed and decided to marry as soon as possible. Emmy invited Alf into the house for a late supper.

In the kitchen they stumbled over the body of Pa, who had fallen and struck his head in an attempt to get at his beer, which was kept on a high shelf. As they revived Pa, Jenny entered. Later Emmy, glowing with happiness, revealed to Jenny what had happened between her and Alf; Jenny then told Emmy about Keith and the yacht and their plans to run away to a romantic land. In spite of her distrust of Keith, Emmy, in her happiness, expressed approval. The sisters retired in the early hours of the morning, both lost in the utter completeness of the day. But Jenny, in bed, became conscious-stricken because she had left Pa and because she had given up her independence and freedom by admitting her love for Keith. The romantic nocturne was fading into common day.

O PIONEERS!

Type of work: Novel
Author: Willa Cather (1876-1947)
Type of plot: Regional chronicle
Time of plot: 1880-1910
Locale: Nebraska
First published: 1913

Principal characters:
ALEXANDRA BERGSON, a homesteader
OSCAR,
LOU, and
EMIL, her brothers
CARL LINDSTRUM,
MARIE TOVESKY, and
FRANK SHABATA, neighbors
CRAZY IVAR, a hired man

Critique:

O Pioneers! is more of a literary landmark than many of its readers realize. Aside from its plot and the fact that it deals with an important part of American history, there is the matter of the author's concept of her art. In this novel we find both the old chronological arrangement of circumstances and evidences of newer writing freedoms. It is a novel of local color and realistic reporting. In comparison with another book on the pioneer theme, *Giants in the Earth,* this book stands on a completely different plane. *Giants in the Earth* is more mystical. *O Pioneers!* is a realistic study of people who made a success of their efforts and who fathered a new nation that was both heroic and mediocre.

The Story:

Hanover was a frontier town huddled on the windblown Nebraska prairie. One winter day young Alexandra Bergson and her small brother Emil went into town from their new homestead. The Bergsons were Swedes. Their life in the new country was one of hardship because the father was sick and the children were too young to do all the work on their prairie acres. Alexandra went to the village doctor's office to get some medicine for her father. The doctor told her there was no hope for Bergson's recovery.

Emil had brought his kitten to town with him. He was crying on the street because it had climbed to the top of the telegraph pole and would not come down. When Alexandra returned, she met their neighbor, Carl Lindstrum, who rescued the cat. The three rode toward home together and Carl talked of his drawing. When Alexandra and Emil arrived home, their supper was waiting and their mother and father were anxious for their return. Shortly afterward Bergson called his family about him and told them to listen to Alexandra, even though she was a girl, for she had proved her abilities to run the farm capably. Above all, they were to keep the land.

Alexandra was still a girl when her father died, but she assumed at once the family's domestic and financial troubles; she guided everything the family did, and through her resourcefulness she gained security and even a measure of wealth for her brothers and herself.

Emil, the youngest brother, remained the dreamer of the family, in his mooning over Marie Tovesky, whom he had first loved as a little child. Marie had married Frank Shabata. Frank was wildly possessive and mistrusted everyone who showed the slightest kindness to Marie.

Alexandra was in love with Carl Lindstrum, whose father gave up his farm because the new, stubborn land seemed too hard to subdue. He returned to more settled country and took Carl with him to learn the engraver's trade.

Alexandra depended upon Crazy Ivar for many things. He was a hermit, living in a hole dug into the side of a river bed. The kinder Swedes claimed he had been touched by God. Those who were unsympathetic were sure he was dangerous. Actually, he was a kindhearted mystic who loved animals and birds and who let his beard grow according to the custom of ancient prophets. Through his lack of concern for worldly matters he lost his claim, and Alexandra gave him shelter on her own farm, much to the dismay of her brothers and their wives. They demanded that she send Crazy Ivar to an institution, but she refused. She respected Crazy Ivar as she did few other people.

In the same way, Alexandra defended Carl Lindstrum. After an absence of sixteen years he came back to their settlement. He had studied much, but in the eyes of the thrifty Swedes his life was a failure because he had not married, because he had no property, because he seemed willing to marry Alexandra, who was by now quite wealthy. Her brothers, Oscar and Lou, told Alexandra that she must not marry Carl, and she ordered them from her house. Carl, hearing of the disagreement, set out for the West at once.

Alexandra applied herself to new problems. She paid passage for other Swedes to come to America; she experimented with new farming methods. She became friendlier with Marie Shabata, whose husband was growing more jealous. She saw to it that Emil received an education, let him go off to the university despite the criticism of the other brothers. By now Emil knew he loved Marie Shabata, and he went away to study because he felt that if he stayed in the community something terrible would happen. Even attending the university did not help him. Other girls he met seemed less attractive. His secret thoughts were always about Marie.

Frank Shabata discharged hired hands

because he suspected them. He followed Marie about everywhere. Even at the Catholic Church he was at her heels scowling at every one to whom she talked. His jealousy was like a disease. At the same time he treated her coldly and insulted her publicly in front of their friends. She, on her part, was headstrong and defiant.

At last Emil returned from college. His friend Amédée became ill while working in his wheat fields and died shortly afterward. Following the funeral, Emil resolved to see Marie, to say good-bye to her before leaving the neighborhood permanently. He found her in her orchard under the mulberry tree. There for the first time they became lovers.

Frank returned from town slightly drunk. Finding a Bergson horse in his stable, he took a weapon and went in search of Emil. When he saw the two he fired, killing both. Then Frank, mad with horror, started to run away.

Crazy Ivar discovered the dead bodies and ran with the news to Alexandra. For the next few months Alexandra seemed in a daze and spent much of her time in the cemetery. She was caught there during a terrible storm, and Crazy Ivar had to go after her. During the storm she regained her old self-possession. Frank Shabata, who had been captured soon after the shooting, had been tried and sentenced to prison. Alexandra determined to do what she could to secure his freedom. If she could no longer help her brother, she would help Frank.

While trying to help Frank, she heard that Carl Lindstrum had returned. He had never received her letter telling of the tragedy, but on his return from Alaska he had read of the trial and had hurried to Alexandra. His mine was a promising venture. The two decided that they could now marry and bring their long separation to an end.

THE ODYSSEY

Type of work: Poem
Author: Homer (c. Ninth century B. C.)
Type of plot: Heroic epic
Time of plot: Years immediately following Trojan War
Locale: Greece and Mediterranean lands
First transcribed: Sixth century B. C.

Principal characters:
ODYSSEUS, the wandering hero of the Trojan War
PENELOPE, his faithful wife
TELEMACHUS, his son

Critique:

Such a wealth of material has grown around the name of Homer that the legendary blind bard might just as well himself be included in the Greek pantheon of gods about whom he wrote so well. The *Iliad,* an epic poem concerned with an incident in the Trojan War, and the *Odyssey,* concerned with Odysseus' difficulties in getting home after the war had been won by the Greeks, are the great epic masterpieces of Western literature and a storehouse of Greek folklore and myth. The *Odyssey,* with its sagacious and always magnificent hero, its romantic theme, and its frequent change of scene, has enjoyed greater popularity through the ages than has the *Iliad.*

The Story:

Of the Greek heroes who survived the Trojan War only Odysseus had not returned home, for he had been detained by the god Poseidon because of an offense that he had committed against the god of the sea.

At a conclave of the gods on Olympus,

Zeus decreed that Odysseus should be allowed at last to return to his home and family in Ithaca. The goddess Athene was sent to Ithaca where, in disguise, she told Telemachus, Odysseus' son, that his father was alive. She advised the youth to rid his home of the great number of suitors suing for the hand of his mother, Penelope, and to go in search of his father. The suitors refused to leave the house of Odysseus, but they gave ready approval to the suggestion that Telemachus begin a quest for his father, since the venture would take him far from the shores of Ithaca.

The youth and his crew sailed to Pylos, where the prince questioned King Nestor concerning the whereabouts of Odysseus. Nestor, a wartime comrade of Odysseus, advised Telemachus to go to Lacedaemon, where Menelaus, who reigned there as king, could possibly give him the information he sought. At the palace of Menelaus and Helen, for whom the Trojan War had been waged, Telemachus learned that Odysseus was a prisoner of the nymph Calypso on her island of Ogygia, in the Mediterranean Sea.

Meanwhile Zeus sent Hermes, the messenger of the gods, to Ogygia, with orders that Calypso was to release Odysseus. When the nymph reluctantly complied, the hero constructed a boat in four days and sailed away from his island prison. But Poseidon, ever the enemy of Odysseus, sent great winds to destroy his boat and to wash him ashore on the coast of the Phaeacians. There he was found by Nausicaä, daughter of King Alcinoüs of the Phaeacians, when she went down to the river mouth with her handmaidens to wash linen. The naked Odysseus awoke, saw Nausicaä and her maidens, and asked them where he was. Frightened at first by this stranger hiding behind the shrubbery, Nausicaä soon perceived that he was no vulgar person. She told him where he was, supplied him with clothing, and gave him food and drink. Then she conducted him to the palace of King Alcinoüs and Queen Arete. The royal pair welcomed him and, at his asking, promised to provide him with passage to his native land. At a great feast the minstrel Demodocus sang of the Trojan War and of the hardships suffered by the returning Greeks, and Alcinoüs saw that the stranger wept during the singing. At the games which followed the banquet and songs, Odysseus was goaded by a young Phaeacian athlete into revealing his great strength. Later, at Alcinoüs' insistence, Odysseus told the following story of his wanderings since the war's end.

When Odysseus left Ilium he was blown to Ismarus, the Cicones' city, which he and his men sacked. Then they were blown by an ill wind to the land of the Lotus-eaters, where Odysseus had difficulty in getting his men to leave a slothful life of ease. Arriving in the land of the Cyclops, the one-eyed monsters who herded giant sheep, Odysseus and twelve of his men were caught by a Cyclops, Polyphemus, who ate the men one by one, saving Odysseus until last. But the wily hero tricked the giant into a drunken stupor, blinded him with a sharpened pole, and fled back to his ship. On an impulse, Odysseus disclosed his name to the blinded Polyphemus as he sailed away. Polyphemus called upon his father, Poseidon, to avenge him by hindering the return of Odysseus to his homeland.

Odysseus' next landfall was Aeolia, where lived Aeolus, the god of the winds. Aeolus gave Odysseus a sealed bag containing all the contrary winds, so that they could not block his homeward voyage. But the crew, thinking that the bag contained treasure, opened it, releasing all the winds, and the ship was blown to the land of the Laestrigonians, half-men, half-giants, who plucked members of the crew from the ship and devoured them. Most managed to escape, however, and came to Aeaea, the land of the enchantress Circe. Circe changed the crew members into swine, but with the aid of the herb, Moly, which Hermes gave him, Odysseus withstood Circe's magic and forced her to change his crew back into men. Reconciled to the great leader, Circe told the hero that he could not get home without first consulting the shade of Teiresias, the blind Theban prophet. On the shore Odysseus dug a deep pit and in it sacrificed sheep. Thereupon appeared spirits from Hades, among them the shade of Teiresias, who warned Odysseus to beware of danger in the land of the sun god.

On his homeward way Odysseus was forced to sail past the isle of the Sirens, maidens who by their beautiful voices drew men to their death on treacherous rocks. By sealing the sailors' ears with wax and by having himself tied to the ship's mast, Odysseus passed the Sirens safely. Next, he sailed into a narrow sea passage guarded by the monsters, Scylla and Charybdis. Scylla's six horrible heads seized six of the crew, but the ship passed safely through the narrow channel. On the island of the sun god, Hyperion, the starving crew slaughtered some of Hyperion's sacred cows, despite a warning from their leader. The sun god caused the ship to be wrecked in a storm, all of the crew being lost but Odysseus, who was ultimately washed ashore on Ogygia, the island of Calypso.

His story finished, Odysseus received many gifts from Alcinoüs and Arete. They accompanied him to a ship they had provided for his voyage to Ithaca and bade him farewell, and the ship brought him at last to his own land.

Odysseus hid in a cave the vast treasure he had received from his Phaeacian hosts. The goddess Athene appeared to him and counseled him on a plan by which he could avenge himself on the rapacious suitors. The goddess, after changing Odysseus into an old beggar, went to Lacedaemon to arrange the return of Telemachus from the court of Menelaus and Helen.

Odysseus went to the rustic cottage of his old steward, Eumaeus, who welcomed the apparent stranger and offered him hospitality. The faithful servant disclosed the unpardonable behavior of Penelope's suitors and told how Odysseus' estate had been greatly reduced by their greed and love of luxury.

Meanwhile, Athene advised Telemachus to leave the ease of the Lacedaemon court and return home. On his arrival he went first to the hut of Eumaeus in order to get information from the old steward. There, Athene having transformed Odysseus back to his heroic self, son and father were reunited.

After pledging his son to secrecy, Odysseus described his plan of attack. Eumaeus and Odysseus, again disguised as a beggar, went to Odysseus' house where a meal was in progress. Reviled by the suitors, who had forgotten that hospitality to a stranger was a practice demanded by Zeus himself, Odysseus bided his time, even when arrogant Antinoüs threw a stool which struck Odysseus on the shoulder.

Odysseus ordered Telemachus to lock up all weapons except a few which were to be used by his own party; the women servants were also to be locked in their quarters. Penelope questioned Odysseus concerning his identity but Odysseus deceived her with a fantastic tale. When Eurycleia, ancient servant of the king, washed the beggar's feet and legs, she recognized her master by a scar above the knee, but she did not disclose his secret.

Penelope planned an impossible feat of strength to free herself of her suitors. One day, showing the famous bow of Eurytus, and twelve battle-axes, she said that she would give her hand to the suitor who could shoot an arrow through all twelve ax handles. Telemachus, to prove his worth, attempted, but failed to string the bow. One after another the suitors failed even to string the bow. Finally Odysseus asked if an old beggar might attempt the feat. The suitors laughed scornfully at his presumption. Then Odysseus strung the bow with ease and shot an arrow through the twelve ax hafts. Throwing aside his disguise, he next shot Antinoüs in the throat. There ensued a furious battle, in which all the suitors were killed by Odysseus and his small party. Twelve women servants who had been sympathetic with the suitors were hanged in the courtyard.

Penelope, in her room, heard what Odysseus, the erstwhile beggar, had done, and husband and wife were happily reunited after years of separation.

OEDIPUS TYRANNUS

Type of work: Drama
Author: Sophocles (495?-406 B. C.)
Type of plot: Classical tragedy
Time of plot: Remote antiquity
Locale: Thebes
First presented: c. 429 B. C.

Principal characters:
OEDIPUS, king of Thebes
JOCASTA, his wife
CREON, Jocasta's brother
TEIRESIAS, a seer

Critique:

Oedipus Tyrannus is Sophocles' masterpiece and considered by many the greatest of classic Greek tragedies. Aristotle referred to it continually in his *Poetics,* pointing out features of the ideal tragic poem. Character and action are in nearly perfect harmony. The fall of the king is made doubly horrifying by Sophocles' extremely effective use of dramatic irony. The play probably was written for production at one of the periodic drama competitions held in Athens.

The Story:

Thebes having been stricken by a plague, the people asked King Oedipus to deliver them from its horrors. Creon, brother of Jocasta, Oedipus' queen, returned from the oracle of Apollo and disclosed that the plague was punishment for the murder of King Laius, Oedipus' immediate predecessor, to whom Jocasta had been wife. Creon further disclosed that the citizens of Thebes would have to discover and punish the murderer before the plague would be lifted. The people, meanwhile, mourned their dead, and Oedipus advised them, in their own interest, to search out and apprehend the murderer.

Asked to help find the murderer, Teiresias, the ancient, blind seer of Thebes, told Oedipus that it would be better for all if he did not tell what he knew. He said that coming events would reveal themselves. Oedipus raged at the seer's reluctance to tell the secret until the old man, angered, said that Oedipus was the one responsible for the afflictions of Thebes, that Oedipus was the murderer, and that the king was living in intimacy with his nearest kin. Oedipus accused the old man of being in league with Creon, whom he suspected of plotting against his throne. Teiresias answered that Oedipus would be ashamed and horrified when he learned the truth about his true parentage, a fact Oedipus did not know. Oedipus defied the seer, saying that he would welcome the truth as long as it freed his kingdom from the plague. Suspicious, Oedipus threatened Creon with death, but Jocasta and the people advised him not to do violence on the strength of rumor or momentary passion. Oedipus yielded, and Creon was banished.

Jocasta, grieved by the enmity between her brother and Oedipus, told her husband that an oracle had informed King Laius that he would be killed by his own child, the offspring of Laius and Jocasta. Jocasta declared Laius could not have been killed by his own child because soon after the child was born it was abandoned on a deserted mountainside. When Oedipus heard from Jocasta that Laius had been killed by robbers at the meeting place of three roads, he was deeply disturbed. Learning that the three roads met in Phocis, he began to suspect that he was, after all, the murderer. Hesitating to reveal his crime, he became more and more convinced of his own guilt.

Oedipus told Jocasta he had believed himself the son of Polybus of Corinth and Merope, until at a feast a drunken man had announced that the young Oedipus was not really Polybus' son. Disturbed, he had gone to consult the oracle of Apollo, who had told him he would sire children by his own mother and he would kill his own father. Leaving Corinth, at a meeting place of three roads, Oedipus had been offended by a man in a chariot. He killed the man and all of his servants but one. Thereafter he had come to Thebes and had become the new king by answering the riddle of the Sphinx, a riddle which asked what went on all fours before noon, on two legs at noon, and on three legs after noon. Oedipus had answered, correctly, that Man walks on all fours as an infant, on two legs in his prime, and with the aid of a stick in his old age. With the kingship, he also won the hand of Jocasta, King Laius' queen.

The servant who had reported that King Laius had been killed by robbers was summoned. Oedipus awaited his arrival fearfully. Jocasta assured her husband that the entire matter was of no great consequence, that surely the prophecies of the oracles would not come true.

A messenger from Corinth announced that Polybus was dead and that Oedipus was now king. Because Polybus had died of sickness, not by the hand of his son, Oedipus and Jocasta were at ease for the time being. Oedipus told the messenger he would not go to Corinth for fear of siring children by his mother, Merope, thus fulfilling the prophecy of the oracle.

The messenger then revealed that Oedipus was not really the son of Polybus and Merope, but a foundling whom the messenger, at that time a shepherd, had taken to Polybus. The messenger related how he had received the baby from another shepherd, who was a servant of the house of King Laius. Jocasta, realizing the dreadful truth, did not wish any longer to see the old servant who had been summoned, but Oedipus, desiring to have the matter out regardless of the cost, called again for the servant. When the servant appeared, the messenger recognized him as the herdsman from whom he had received the child years before. The old servant then confessed he had been ordered by King Laius to destroy the boy, but out of pity he had given the infant to the Corinthian to raise as his foster son.

Oedipus, now all but mad from the realization of what he had done, entered the palace to discover that Jocasta had hanged herself by her hair. He removed her golden brooches and with them pierced his eyes. Blinded, he would not be able to see the results of the horrible prophecy. Then he displayed himself, blind and bloody and miserable, to the Thebans and announced himself as the murderer of their king and the defiler of his own mother's bed. He cursed the herdsman who had saved him from death years before.

Creon, having returned, ordered the attendants to lead Oedipus back into the palace. Oedipus asked Creon to have him conducted out of Thebes where no man would ever see him again. Also, he asked Creon to give Jocasta a proper burial and to see that the sons and daughters of the unnatural marriage should be cared for and not be allowed to live poor and unmarried because of any shame attached to their parentage. Creon led the wretched Oedipus away to his exile of blindness and torment.

OF HUMAN BONDAGE

Type of work: Novel
Author: W. Somerset Maugham (1874-)
Type of plot: Naturalism
Time of plot: Early twentieth century
Locale: England
First published: 1915

Principal characters:

PHILIP CAREY, an orphan boy
WILLIAM CAREY, his uncle
LOUISA CAREY, his aunt
MISS WILKINSON, Philip's first love
MILDRED ROGERS, a waitress
THORPE ATHELNY, Philip's friend
SALLY ATHELNY, his daughter

Critique:

Without question, *Of Human Bondage* is one of the few classics of the present day. In this novel Maugham tells of a young man's search for a way of life. It is the story of the thoughts and actions of a bitter, confused, warped boy, and it is a story told with the mature wisdom of an author who had suffered some of the same tangled emotions in his own youth. Maugham tells us that the emotions are his own, with the events and situations drawn partly from his own life and partly from experiences of his friends. Many critics believe that *Of Human Bondage* is Maugham's greatest contribution to prose fiction.

The Story:

Philip Carey was nine years old when his mother died and he was sent to live with his aunt and uncle at the vicarage of Blackstable, forty miles outside London. Uncle William Carey was a penny-pinching smugly religious man who made Philip's life miserable. Having been born with a clubfoot, Philip was extremely sensitive about his deformity, and he grew up bitter and rebellious. The only love he was shown was given to him by his Aunt Louisa, who had never been able to have children of her own.

At school Philip's clubfoot was a source of much ridicule, for children are cruel. Philip was so sensitive that any reference to his foot, even a kind reference, caused him to strike out at the speaker.

When he was eighteen, Philip, with a small inheritance of his own, went to Berlin to study. He took rooms in the home of Professor and Frau Erlin. There he studied German, French, and mathematics with tutors from the University of Heidelberg. He met several young men, among them Weeks, an American, and Hayward, a radical young Englishman. From their serious discussions on religion Philip decided that he no longer believed in God. This decision made him feel free, for in discarding God he subconsciously discarded his memories of his cold and bitter youth at the vicarage.

Shortly after his return to the Blackstable, Philip became involved with a spinster twice his age, a Miss Emily Wilkinson who was a friend of his Aunt Louisa. She was not attractive to him, but he thought a man of twenty should experience love. It was typical of Philip's attitude that even after they became lovers he continued to call the woman Miss Wilkinson.

Not long after that affair Philip went to London to begin a career as a clerk in an accounting firm. Dissatisfied, he worked only a year; then he went to Paris to study art. But two years later he gave up the idea of becoming an artist and returned to London for his third great start on a career. He had decided to study medicine.

In London, Philip met Mildred Rogers, a waitress. She was really nothing more than a wanton, but in spite of the fact that Philip saw her for what she was, he loved her and desired her above all else. He gave her presents which were extravagant for his small income. He neglected his studies to be with her. She gave him nothing in return. When he asked her to marry him, for it seemed that that was the only way he could ever possess her, she told him bluntly that he did not have enough money for her and that she was marrying someone else. Philip loved her and hated her so much that he was almost consumed by his emotions.

He had begun to forget Mildred, in his affection for another girl, when she returned to London. Alone and penniless, she told him that the other man had not married her, that he already had a wife and children. She was pregnant. Philip forgot the other girl and took Mildred back again. He paid her hospital bill and her lodging bills and sent her to the coast to rest. Mildred repaid him by going off for a holiday with a man Philip considered his good friend. They used Philip's money to pay their expenses. Despising himself, he begged Mildred to come back to him after her trip with the other man; he could not overcome his insane desire for her. But Mildred did not come back.

Philip forced himself to study harder than ever then. He met Thorpe Athelny, a patient in the hospital where he was studying, and the two men became good friends. Philip visited the Athelny home almost every Sunday. It was a noisy house, filled with happy children and with love and kindness, and the cheerful atmosphere filled an empty place in Philip's heart.

One evening Philip saw Mildred again. She was highly painted and overdressed, and she was sauntering slowly down the street with a vulgar swing of her hips. She had become a common street-walker. Although Philip knew then that he had lost his desire for her, out of pity he took her and her child into his home. Mildred was to act as his housekeeper. Because Philip's funds were small, they were forced to live frugally. Mildred once again took all he had to offer and gave him nothing in return. Her only payment was an unknowing one, for Philip loved her child very much and he had many hours of pleasure holding the baby girl in his arms. Mildred tried again and again to resume their old relationship, but each time Philip repulsed her. At last she became insanely angry and left his apartment with her baby. Before she left, however, she completely wrecked the apartment, ripped his clothing and linens with a knife, smashed furniture and dishes, and tore up his pictures.

A short time later Philip lost what little money he had in a bad investment. The Athelny family took him into their home, and Thorpe obtained work for him as a window dresser in the store where Thorpe himself was employed. Philip had to give up his studies at the hospital because of lack of money. Then, when he was thirty, his Uncle William died and left him enough money to finish his medical education. When he walked down the steps with his diploma in his hand, Philip thought that he was ready at last to begin his real life. He planned to sign on as a ship's doctor and sail around the world before he settled down to a permanent practice.

But before he accepted a position, Philip went on a holiday trip with the Athelnys. While on that holiday he realized with a distinct shock that one of the Athelny girls whom he had always thought of as a child had definitely grown up. As they walked home together one night, he and Sally Athelny became lovers. Back in London, a few weeks later, Sally told him that she thought she was pregnant. Philip immediately gave up his dreams of traveling over the world and accepted a small-salaried practice in a little fishing village, so that he and Sally could be married. But Sally's fears proved groundless. Free to travel and be his own master, Philip suddenly realized that what he really wanted was a home and a family and security. He had never been normal because of his deformity, and he had never done what he wanted to do but always what he thought he should do. He had always lived in the future. Now he wanted to live in the present. And so he asked Sally to marry him, to go with him to that little fishing village. He offered her nothing but his love and the fruit of the lessons he had learned from hard teachers, but Sally accepted his proposal. Philip felt that he was his own master after his bleak, bitter years of mortal bondage.

OF MICE AND MEN

Type of work: Novel
Author: John Steinbeck (1902-)
Type of plot: Sentimental melodrama
Time of plot: Twentieth century
Locale: Salinas Valley, California
First published: 1937

Principal characters:

LENNIE SMALL, a simple-minded giant
GEORGE MILTON, his friend
CANDY, swamper on the ranch on which George and Lennie worked
CURLEY, the owner's son
SLIM, the jerkline skinner on the ranch
CROOKS, the colored stable buck

Critique:

Written in terms of theatrical melodrama, the compact, tragic story of *Of Mice and Men* spins itself out in only three days. In that brief time Curley has his hand smashed, his wife is murdered, the old swamper's dog is killed, Lennie loses his life, and George shoots his best friend. The effect of the tightly-knit story is heightened by the naturalness of the setting and the men's talk, and by the underlying sympathy Steinbeck has for all of his creations, even the meanest.

The Story:

Late one hot afternoon two men carrying blanket rolls trudged down the path that led to the bank of the Salinas River. One man—his companion called him George—was small and wiry. The other was a large, lumbering fellow whose arms hung loosely at his sides. After they had drunk at the sluggish water and washed their faces, George sat back with his legs drawn up. His friend Lennie imitated him.

The two men were on their way to a ranch where they had been hired to buck barley. Lennie had cost them their jobs at their last stop in Weed, where he had been attracted by a girl's red dress. Grabbing at her clothes, he had been so frightened by her screaming that George had been forced to hit him over the head to make him let go. They had run away to avoid a lynching.

After George had lectured his companion about letting him talk to their new employer when they were interviewed, Lennie begged for a story he had already heard many times. It was the story of the farm they would own one day. It would have chickens, rabbits, and a vegetable garden, and Lennie would be allowed to feed the rabbits.

The threat that Lennie would not be allowed to care for the rabbits if he did not obey caused him to keep still when they arrived at the ranch the next day. In spite of George's precautions, their new boss was not easy to deal with. He was puzzled because George gave Lennie no chance to talk.

While the men were waiting for the lunch gong, the owner's son Curley came in, ostensibly looking for his father, but actually to examine the new men. After he had gone, Candy, the swamper who swept out the bunkhouse, warned them that Curley was a prizefighter who delighted in picking on the men and that he was extremely jealous of his slatternly bride.

Lennie had a foreboding of evil and wanted to leave, but the two men had no money with which to continue their wanderings. But by evening Lennie was happy again. The dog belonging to Slim, the jerkline skinner, had had pups the night before, and Slim had given one to simple-minded Lennie.

Slim was easy to talk to. While George played solitaire that evening, he told his new friend of the incident in Weed. He had just finished his confidence when Lennie came in, hiding his puppy inside his coat. George told Lennie to take the pup back to the barn. He said that Lennie would probably spend the night there with the animal.

The bunkhouse had been deserted by all except old Candy when Lennie asked once more to hear the story of the land they would some day buy. At its conclusion the swamper spoke up. He had three hundred and fifty dollars saved, he said, and he knew he would not be able to work many more years. He wanted to join George and Lennie in their plan. George finally agreed, for with Candy's money they would soon be able to buy the farm they had in mind.

Lennie was still grinning with delighted anticipation when Curley came to the bunkhouse in search of his wife. The men had been taunting him about her wantonness when he spied Lennie's grin. Infuriated with the thought that he was being laughed at, Curley attacked the larger man. Lennie, remembering George's warnings, did nothing to defend himself at first. Finally he grabbed Curley's hand and squeezed. When he let go, every bone had been crushed.

Curley was driven off to town for treatment, with instructions from Slim to say that he had caught his hand in a machine. Slim warned him that the truth would soon be known if he failed to tell a convincing story.

After the others had started to town with Curley, Lennie went to talk to Crooks, the colored stable buck, who had his quarters in the harness room instead of the bunkhouse. Crooks' coolness quickly melted before Lennie's innocence. While Lennie told the colored man about the dream of the farm, Candy joined them. They were deep in discussion of the plan when Curley's wife appeared, looking for her husband. The story about her husband and the machine did not deceive her, and she hinted that she was pleased with Lennie for what he had done. Having put an end to the men's talk, she slipped out noiselessly when she heard the others come back from town.

Lennie was in the barn petting his puppy. The other workmen pitched horseshoes outside. Lennie did not realize that the dog was already dead from the mauling he had innocently given it. As he sat in the straw, Curley's wife came around the corner of the stalls. He would not speak to her at first, afraid that he would not get to feed the rabbits if he did anything wrong, but the girl gradually managed to draw his attention to her and persuaded him to stroke her hair.

When she tried to pull her head away, Lennie held on, growing angry as she tried to yell. Finally he shook her violently and broke her neck.

Curley's wife was lying half-buried in the hay when Candy came into the barn in search of Lennie. Finding Lennie gone, he called George, and while the latter went off to get a gun the swamper spread the alarm. The opportunity to catch the murderer was what Curley had been looking for. Carrying a loaded shotgun, he started off with the men, George among them.

It was George who found Lennie hiding in the bushes at the edge of a stream. Hurriedly, for the last time, he told his companion the story of the rabbit farm, and when he had finished Lennie begged that they go at once to look for the farm. Knowing that Lennie could not escape from Curley and the other men who were searching for him, George put the muzzle of his gun to the back of his friend's head and pulled the trigger. Lennie was dead when the others arrived.

OF TIME AND THE RIVER

Type of work: Novel
Author: Thomas Wolfe (1900-1938)
Type of plot: Impressionistic realism
Time of plot: 1920's
Locale: Harvard, New York, France
First published: 1935

Principal characters:
EUGENE GANT, a young student and writer
BASCOM PENTLAND, his uncle
FRANCIS STARWICK, a friend
ANN, and
ELINOR, Starwick's friends
ROBERT WEAVER, Eugene's friend

Critique:

With this novel, his second, Thomas Wolfe became a more mature craftsman. The book is a happy blend of the best aspects, the enthusiasm and freshness of *Look Homeward, Angel* and of Wolfe's growing ability as a writer. Thomas Wolfe had his limitations. Yet what he gave contains some of the best writing America has produced. Wolfe was not a sophisticated novelist. He wrote of life, of the pains, hungers, sorrows, of the common people. More than any other writer in America, he has succeeded in vividly describing the sights, smells, fears, and hopes of our nation and our people. *Of Time and the River* is a masterpiece of which Americans can be proud.

The Story:

Eugene Gant was leaving Altamont for study at Harvard. His mother and his sister Helen stood on the station platform and waited with him for the train that would take him north. Eugene felt that he was escaping from his strange, unhappy childhood, that the train would take him away from sickness and worry over money, away from his mother's boarding-house, the Dixieland, away from memories of his gruff, kind brother Ben, away from all ghosts of the past. While they waited, they met Robert Weaver, who was also on his way to Harvard. Mrs. Gant said that Robert was a fine boy, but that there was insanity in his family. She told Eugene family scandals of the town before the train came puffing in.

Eugene broke his trip in Baltimore to visit his father, who was slowly dying of cancer. Old Gant spent much of his time on the sunlit hospital porch, dreaming of time and of his youth.

At Harvard, Eugene enrolled in Professor Hatcher's drama class. Hungry for knowledge, he browsed in the library, pulling books from the library shelves and reading them as he stood by the open stacks. He wrote plays for the drama workshop. Prowling the streets of Cambridge and Boston, he wondered about the lives of people he met, whose names he would never know.

One day he received a note from Francis Starwick, Professor Hatcher's assistant, asking Eugene to have dinner with him that night. As Eugene had made no friends at the university, he was surprised by Starwick's invitation. Starwick turned out to be a pleasant young man who welcomed Eugene's confidences but returned none.

In Boston Eugene met his uncle, Bascom Pentland, and his wife. Uncle Bascom had once been a preacher, but he had left the ministry and was now working as a conveyancer in a law office.

One day Eugene received a telegram telling him that his father was dying. He had no money for a ticket home, and so he went to see Wang, a strange, secretive Chinese student who roomed in the same house. Wang gave him money and Eugene went back to Altamont, but he arrived too late to see his father alive. Old Gant died painfully and horribly. Only with his death did his wife and children realize how much this ranting, roaring old man had meant in their lives.

Back at Harvard, Eugene and Starwick became close friends. Starwick always confused Eugene when they were together; Eugene had the feeling that everything Starwick did or said was like the surface of a shield, protecting his real thoughts or feelings underneath.

One night Robert Weaver came to Eugene's rooms. He was drunk and shouting at the top of his voice. He wanted Eugene to go out with him, but Eugene finally managed to get him to bed on a cot in Wang's room.

Eugene dreamed of becoming a great playwright. After he had completed his course at Harvard, he went back to Altamont and waited to have one of his plays accepted for production on Broadway. That was a summer of unhappiness and suspense. His plays were rejected. While visiting a married sister in South Carolina, he ran into Robert Weaver again. The two got drunk and landed in jail.

In the fall Eugene went to New York to become an English instructor at a city university. After a time Robert Weaver appeared. He had been living at a club, but now he insisted that Eugene get him a room at the apartment hotel where Eugene lived. Eugene hesitated, knowing what would happen if Weaver went on one of his sprees. The worst did happen. Weaver smashed furniture and set fire to his room. He also had a mistress, a woman who had married her husband because she knew he was dying and would leave her his money. One night the husband found his wife and Weaver together. There was a scuffle. The husband pulled a gun and attempted to shoot Weaver before he collapsed. It looked very much as if Eliza Gant's statement about insanity in the Weaver family were true.

Eugene also renewed a college friendship with Joel Pierce, the son of a wealthy family. At Joel's invitation he went to visit at the magnificent Pierce estate along the Hudson River. Seeing the fabulously rich close at hand for the first time, Eugene was both fascinated and disappointed.

At vacation time Eugene went abroad,

first to England, where he lived with the strange Coulson family, and then to France. In Paris he met Starwick again, standing enraptured upon the steps of the Louvre. Starwick was doing Europe with two women from Boston, Elinor and Ann. Elinor, who had left her husband, was mistakenly believed by her friends to be Starwick's mistress. Eugene went to see the sights of Paris with them. Ann and Elinor paid all of Starwick's bills. One night, in a cabaret, Starwick got into an argument with a Frenchman and accepted a challenge to duel. Ann, wanting to end the ridiculous affair, paid the Frenchman money to satisfy him for damages to his honor.

Eugene attempted to make love to Ann, but when she resisted him he realized that she was in love with Starwick. What made the affair even more tragic was Eugene's discovery that Ann's love was wasted because Starwick was a homosexual.

Disgusted with the three, Eugene went to Chartres by himself. From Chartres he went to Orleans. There he met an eccentric old countess who believed that Eugene was a correspondent for the New York *Times*, a journalist planning to write a book of travel impressions. She secured for him an invitation to visit the Marquise de Mornaye, who was under the mistaken impression that Eugene had known her son in America.

Eugene went to Tours. There in that old town of white buildings and narrow, cobble-stoned streets, memories of America suddenly come flooding back to him. He remembered the square of Altamont on a summer afternoon, the smell of woodsmoke in the early morning, the whistle of a train in the mountain passes. He remembered the names of American rivers, the parade of the states that stretched from the rocky New England coastline across the flat plains and the high mountains to the thunder of the Pacific slope, the names of battles fought on American soil. He remembered his family and his own childhood. He felt that he had recaptured the lost dream of time itself.

Homesick, he started back to America. One day he caught sight of Starwick and his two women companions in a Marseilles café, but he went away before they saw him.

He sailed from Cherbourg. On the tender taking passengers out to the great ocean liner he suddenly heard an American voice above the babble of the passengers grouped about him. He looked. A woman pointed eagerly toward the ship, her face glowing with an excitement as great as that Eugene himself felt. A woman companion called her Esther. Watching Esther, Eugene knew that she was to be his fate.

THE OLD AND THE YOUNG

Type of work: Novel
Author: Luigi Pirandello (1867-1936)
Type of plot: Historical chronicle
Time of plot: 1891-1892
Locale: Sicily and Rome
First published: 1913

Principal characters:
FLAMINIO SALVO, a Sicilian capitalist
CAPOLINO, a politician friend
ROBERTO AURITI, Capolino's political opponent
PRINCE GERLANDO LAURENTANO, Auriti's cousin, a Socialist
PRINCE IPPOLITO LAURENTANO, Gerlando's father and fiancé of Salvo's sister
DIANELLA SALVO, Salvo's daughter
AURELIO COSTA, Dianella's lover
MAURO MORTARA, an old man who had followed Garibaldi

Critique:

The story of *The Old and the Young* is as hectic as the bitter politics of Italy were at the end of the nineteenth century, when families were still divided because of the revolutions of 1848 and 1860. Outstanding passages in the novel are the scene in which a mob seizes and destroys two victims and the scene which describes the visit of two Socialists to a cemetery where they are allowed to inspect the bodies of several people slain by troops during a Socialist-incited demonstration.

The Story:

As late as the last decade of the nineteenth century the political air of Italy and Sicily was troubled by the events of the Garibaldi uprisings of 1848 and 1860. There were still people of influence who looked back a half century to the time when the Bourbons had dominated Italy. There were also those who had followed Garibaldi in his revolution, and now, among the younger people, there were those who had become Socialists and took to heart all the preachings of that doctrine. Italian politics were as confused as they were corrupt.

In Sicily, where a representative to the Chamber of Deputies had died, a campaign was under way for a successor to represent the district of Girgenti. One of the candidates was Roberto Auriti, who at twelve years of age had been with Garibaldi in Rome and whose father had been a Garibaldist leader. Auriti was opposed by Capolino, who was backed by the clerical party and Flaminio Salvo, a capitalist who owned the coal and sulphur mines in the district.

The situation was particularly strained for Salvo because he wanted to marry his spinster sister to Auriti's uncle, Prince Ippolito Laurentano, an old man who still believed in the Bourbon influence and lived apart from the world on his Sicilian estate. Salvo's plans for the marriage were blocked because the old man refused to submit to the civil ceremony of a government he had never recognized. The prince swore he would have only the Church officiate at his wedding. Salvo was also disturbed because the old man's grown son, Gerlando Laurentano, declared that he would not attend his father's wedding, thus withholding his sanction. Since Salvo was after money and power, it was necessary for his honor that young Laurentano be at his father's second marriage ceremony.

To complicate the affairs of Salvo even more, there was a real effort to foster discontent among his workers by the Socialists, under the leadership of Gerlando Laurentano. His activities did not endear young Laurentano to the financier, who stood to lose much by the young man's refusal to agree to terms that Salvo thought reasonable and proper.

When the election returns had been counted and the excitement of the election had begun to die down, it was found that Capolino had been elected to represent the district in which Salvo's interests were located. Salvo was soon to discover, however, that the government did not take kindly to his candidate because of the backing which Capolino had also received from the clericals. Capolino was reduced to a place among the minority opposition in the Chamber of Deputies.

Meanwhile Capolino's wife, Nicoletta, a woman much younger than her husband, had formed an attachment for another deputy, a scapegrace named Corrado Selmi, who owed a great deal of money and who had been Auriti's backer in the election. In addition to being a source of trouble to her husband, Nicoletta was a source of vexation to Salvo, her husband's patron.

After the election most of the principals returned to Rome, where further

THE OLD AND THE YOUNG by Luigi Pirandello. Translated by C. K. Scott-Moncrieff. By permission of the publishers, E. P. Dutton & Co., Inc. Copyright, 1928, by E. P. Dutton & Co., Inc.

intrigues, political and amorous, began to develop. During the election Auriti's mother, who had not seen her brother, Prince Ippolito Laurentano, for over forty years, had gone to him and asked him to support her son. The prince had refused because of the marriage pending between himself and Salvo's sister. In Rome it developed that there was in existence an incriminating letter which would make Auriti responsible for forty thousand lira misappropriated by Corrado Selmi, who was about to be impeached by his fellow deputies for bribery and misuse of government funds. Giulio, Roberto Auriti's brother, appealed to Capolino and then to his cousin, Gerlando Laurentano, for aid. Both refused to have anything to do with the affair, despite the protestations of old Mauro Mortara. Mortara was an aged Garibaldist, a comrade of Gerlando Laurentano's grandfather and Roberto Auriti's father, when all three had followed Garibaldi in '48 and '60. The old veteran could not realize that the descendants of his old revolutionary comrades were so divided in their politics that they would not aid each other when they were in need.

Selmi committed suicide and left a note admitting his guilt in the matter of the forty thousand lira. But Auriti had already been imprisoned. When his mother learned of the dishonor to the Auriti family, she died of grief.

Meanwhile the Socialists planned a coup in Sicily. When a strike had been called in the district of Girgenti, Salvo had closed his mines in an attempt to starve out the workers. His superintendent, Aurelio Costa, had been summoned to Rome to receive orders. Costa had been befriended by Salvo after he had saved the capitalist from drowning. Dianella Salvo, his daughter, was in love with Costa, but Salvo refused to permit their marriage because Costa had no money. In an effort to be rid of the superintendent, Salvo sent Costa back to Sicily to face the angry strikers. Planning to leave Salvo's employ, Costa returned to Sicily with the wife of Deputy Capolino. On their return they were murdered before Costa could explain to the mob that he wanted to join forces with the strikers.

When word of the double murder reached Rome, Capolino rushed to Salvo's home and told Dianella Salvo what her father had done by forcing Costa to return. Dianella went mad and had to be locked up. The only person who could calm her was old Mauro Mortara, who had become friendly with the woman during the election campaign.

Gerlando Laurentano had become more deeply embroiled in Socialist activities in Italy and Sicily. When word came of the strike at Girgenti, he went with members of a committee of his party to investigate the trouble in Sicily and to learn how the Socialists might benefit from the strike. He was horrified at the hunger and poverty among the strikers.

In spite of Socialist attempts to aid the peasants, the people did not want a Socialist government. At mass meetings the workmen carried pictures of the king and queen and images of the cross. The government, on the other hand, took advantage of the rioting to send troops and police to quell all disturbances.

Gerlando Laurentano was finally forced to flee from Sicily at night because the authorities had discovered that he was a Socialist organizer. During his flight he encountered Mauro Mortara. The old veteran was ashamed that the grandson of a Garibaldist leader would be involved in Socialist troubles. Shot when troops opened fire on a crowd, the dying Mortara wondered what was wrong in Italy, since even in his old age the peace and freedom for which he and his generation had fought were not secure. The young people seemed to have made just as great a turmoil in his native land as had his own revolutionary generation.

THE OLD MAID

Type of work: Novel
Author: Edith Wharton (1862-1937)
Type of plot: Social criticism
Time of plot: The 1850's
Locale: New York
First published: 1924

Principal characters:
DELIA RALSTON, a New York matron
JAMES RALSTON, her husband
CHARLOTTE LOVELL, Delia's cousin
JOE RALSTON, James' cousin
TINA LOVELL, Delia's ward

Critique:

Edith Wharton was justly famous for her ability to portray characters and scenes simply and accurately. In the brief space of *The Old Maid* she presented a woman whose life was extremely conventional, but who longed to live more fully and more emotionally than circumstances permitted. At the same time Mrs. Wharton told the story of a woman who had lived emotionally and for that reason was forced to live her middle and old years in the most conventional manner possible, to atone for her sinful youth. Both characters were carefully and interestingly depicted, and their life together has given us a novel which not only interests us, but also gives us a view of American society in the genteel decades.

The Story:

Among the leading families in New York in the 1850's, none was more correct or more highly regarded than the Ralstons. Their ancestors had come to America not for religious freedom but for wealth. By the time Delia Lovell married James Ralston, the Ralstons considered themselves the ruling class, with all their thoughts and actions dictated by convention. They shunned new ideas as they did strange people, and the sons and daughters of the numerous branches of the family married only the sons and daughters of similar good families.

Delia was conventional and correct by birth as well as by marriage. Before her marriage she had been in love with Clement Spender, a penniless young painter. But since he would not give up his proposed trip to Rome and settle down to a disciplined life in New York, it was impossible for a Lovell to marry him.

Delia often, against her will, imagined herself married to Clement. But the image was only momentary, for Delia had no place in her life for strong emotions or great passions. Her life with James and their two children was perfect. She was glad, too, that her cousin, Charlotte Lovell, was going to marry James' cousin, Joe Ralston, for at one time she had feared that Charlotte might never have a suitable proposal.

Charlotte was a strange girl who had become quite prudish in the years since she made her debut. At that time she had been gay and beautiful. Then a sudden illness had caused her to go to Georgia for her health. Since her return, she had been colorless and drab, spending all of her time with the children of the poor. She had set up a little nursery where she cared for the children, and to this nursery had come a baby who had been abandoned by a veiled woman whom no one could identify. Charlotte seemed especially fond of the orphan child and favored her with better toys and clothes than those given the other children.

One day Charlotte came to Delia and told her that she was not going to marry Joe Ralston. She told Delia that the orphaned baby in the nursery was her own, that she had gone to Georgia to give birth to the child. It was true that Charlotte was ill; she had a racking cough that often caused a hemorrhage, but it was not the cough that caused Charlotte to worry. Joe insisted upon her giving up her work with the children after they were married. Since her baby had no known parents, it would be placed in an orphanage. Charlotte could not think of her child in a charity home.

Joe, being a Ralston, would never marry Charlotte and accept her child if he knew the truth. Delia did not know what action to suggest until she learned that the baby's father was Clement Spender. Charlotte had always loved Clement, who, when he returned from Rome and found Delia married, had turned to Charlotte. When he went back to Rome, Charlotte had not told him of the baby, for she knew that he still loved Delia.

Although Delia thought she cared nothing for Clement now, she too could not bring herself to let his child be placed in an orphanage. She persuaded her husband to provide a home for Charlotte and the baby, telling him and the rest of the family that Charlotte and Joe should not marry because of Charlotte's cough. Joe, who wanted healthy children, was not hard to convince.

After Charlotte and the baby, Tina, had been established in a little house, Charlotte's health improved. In fact, she became quite robust, and each day grew more and more into an old maid. After James Ralston was killed by a fall from a horse, Delia took Charlotte and the little girl into her home. Tina grew up with the Ralston children and copied them in calling Delia "Mother" and Charlotte "Aunt."

Delia's children made proper marriages, and at last she and Charlotte and Tina were left alone in the house. Charlotte often seemed to resent Delia's interest in Tina and the fact that the young girl went to Delia's room for private talks, but she dared not give any hint that Tina owed her love or affection.

When Delia learned that the sons of the good families would not marry Tina because she had no family background, she asked Charlotte to let her adopt the girl and give her the Ralston name. Both women feared that Tina might make the same mistake Charlotte had made if she continued to see young men who loved her but would not marry her. Soon afterward, Delia made Tina her legal daughter and the girl became engaged to a correct young man, for the Ralston tie was one that all families wanted.

Tina was delighted with her new status as the daughter of Delia, for she had long thought of her as a mother. The two made endless plans for Tina's wedding. On the night before the wedding, Delia wanted to go up to Tina's room to tell the girl all the things a mother usually tells her daughter on the eve of her wedding. But Charlotte flew into a rage. She accused Delia of having helped her and Tina only because she wanted revenge for Charlotte's affair with Clement. She told Delia that she knew Delia still loved Clement, that she had turned to Delia in her need years ago because she knew that Delia would help her for Clement's sake. Charlotte had been carrying her hatred for Delia in her heart for many years, thinking always that Delia was trying to take Tina from her real mother. Charlotte declared fiercely that on her wedding eve Tina should talk with her real mother, and she started up to the girl's room.

When Charlotte had gone, Delia realized that there was some truth in what Charlotte had said. She had chosen James and the Ralston life willingly and knowingly, but she had often unconsciously wished for a life that was filled with love and unpredictable passions. And she knew, too, that she had made Tina her own child, thus leaving Charlotte nothing for herself.

Delia started up to her room. She wanted to see Tina, but she thought that Charlotte deserved this one night with her daughter. Delia met Charlotte coming downstairs. Charlotte had not been with Tina, for she knew that the girl would prefer her adopted mother. There was nothing an old maid aunt could say to a bride unless she were to tell her the truth, and that Charlotte could never do. And so Delia had her talk with Tina. She did not stay long, for she knew that Charlotte was alone and unhappy. As she kissed Tina goodnight, she asked one favor. On the morrow, for Delia's sake, Tina was to give her last goodbye kiss to her Aunt Charlotte.

OLD MORTALITY

Type of work: Novel
Author: Sir Walter Scott (1771-1832)
Type of plot: Historical romance
Time of plot: 1679
Locale: Scotland
First published: 1816

Principal characters:
HENRY MORTON, the heir of Milnwood
LADY MARGARET BELLENDEN, of Tillietudlem
EDITH, her granddaughter
COLONEL GRAHAME OF CLAVERHOUSE, later Viscount of Dundee
LORD EVANDALE, a royalist
JOHN BALFOUR OF BURLEY, a Covenanter
BASIL OLIFANT, a renegade Covenanter

Critique:

The man who gives his name to this novel appears only briefly in the story. Ostensibly a device to get the story under way, he was a native of Dumfries who traveled about Scotland caring for the tombstones of the Covenanters who fell in the rebellion of 1679. The assumed narrator of the story pretends to have gathered some of his facts from the old man. First published in the series called *Tales of My Landlord, Old Mortality* is one of Scott's better novels, the plot being dramatized with considerable skill and the characters ably drawn and presented.

The Story:

Henry Morton had the misfortune of being a moderate man, a man who could see both sides of a question. During the rebellion of the Covenanters against the crown in 1679, his position became an exceedingly precarious one. His uncle and guardian was the Squire of Milnwood, by faith a Covenanter and by nature a miser, and Henry's dead father had commanded a troop of horse when he fought for the Covenanters at Marston Moor. The story of his family was frequently cause for comment among the cavalier gentry of the district, especially at the tower of Tillietudlem, the home of Lady Margaret Bellenden and Edith, her granddaughter.

Henry and Lord Evandale contested as marksmen at a wappenschaw, and Edith Bellenden was among the spectators when Henry defeated his opponent. Declared the victor at this festival of the popinjay, Henry bowed his respects to Edith Bellenden, who responded with embarrassed courtesy under the watchful eyes of her grandmother.

After the shooting Henry went with friends to a tavern where some dragoons of Claverhouse's troop, under Sergeant

Francis Bothwell, were also carousing. Bothwell, a descendant of the Stuart kings through the bar sinister line, was a man of domineering disposition. After Henry and his friends had drunk a health to the king, Bothwell, intending to humiliate the Covenanters, resolved that they should drink also to the Archbishop of St. Andrew's. A stranger in the company proposed the toast to the archbishop, ending with the hope that each prelate in Scotland would soon be in the same position as his grace.

Henry and the stranger left the inn soon afterward, before word came that the archbishop had been assassinated. Realizing then that the stranger must have been one of the plotters in the deed, Bothwell ordered a pursuit.

Meanwhile Henry had learned that his companion was John Balfour of Burley, a Covenanter leader who had saved the life of Henry's father at Marston Moor. That night Henry gave Balfour lodging at Milnwood without his uncle's knowledge and next morning showed the fugitive a safe path into the hills. Bothwell and his troops arrived shortly afterward. Henry was arrested and taken away.

In company with Henry in his arrest were Mause Headrigg, a staunch Covenanter, and her son Cuddie. The prisoners were taken to Tillietudlem Castle, where Claverhouse sentenced Henry to execution. He was saved, however, by the intercession of Edith and Lord Evandale.

Lord Evandale brought information that a group of Covenanters was gathering in the hills, and Claverhouse gave orders to have his troops advance against them. At a council of war Lord Evandale, among others, suggested a parley in which both sides could air their grievances. Claverhouse sent his nephew, Cornet Grahame, to carry a flag of truce to the Covenanters. Balfour and a small group met Cornet Grahame, but the Covenanters refused to meet Claverhouse's demands. After an interchange of words, Balfour, to the surprise and suppressed indignation of all, shot Cornet Grahame in cold blood.

The killing of the young officer was the signal for a general fight. Bothwell and Balfour met beard to beard, and Balfour killed Bothwell with his sword as the dragoon stood defenseless, his sword arm broken by a kick of a horse. In the fray Henry saved the life of Lord Evandale after the young nobleman's horse had been shot from under him.

Victorious, Balfour's rebels next laid plans to capture Castle Tillietudlem. Claverhouse left a few of his men to defend the place under the command of Major Bellenden, brother-in-law of Lady Margaret.

Balfour, who had taken Henry Morton from the troops of Claverhouse on the battlefield, wanted Henry to join with the rebels but Henry still held back. Trying to convince Henry of the righteousness of his cause, Balfour took him to a council of war, where Henry was elected one of a council of six through Balfour's insistence.

Major Bellenden refused to surrender the castle to the insurgents, who then decided to starve out the small garrison. Balfour, realizing that Henry wished to remain in the vicinity of the castle because he was concerned for Edith's safety, sent the young man to Glasgow, the objective of the main Covenanter army. Claverhouse, who had retreated to Glasgow, laid careful plans for the defense of the city. Henry returned to Milnwood with Cuddie in order to learn what was happening at Tillietudlem. Hearing that Lord Evandale had been captured during a sortie from the castle, Henry once again saved Lord Evandale's life from Balfour's rough justice. Then Henry drew up a document stating the grievances of and the conditions offered by the Covenanters and sent Lord Evandale with the paper to the castle. Edith and Lady Margaret escaped from the castle, and Henry raised the flag of the Covenanters to the castle tower.

The Covenanters were finally defeated at the battle of Bothwell Bridge. In the retreat from the field Henry was taken prisoner by a party of Covenanter fanatics, who believed him to have deserted their cause. He was sentenced to death. Cuddie Headrigg caught a horse and escaped. He rode to Claverhouse and explained Henry's predicament. Since Henry's death was decreed on a Sabbath day, his captors decided he could not be executed until after midnight. This decision gave Claverhouse and his men time to rescue Henry. With the Covenanters' revolt now broken, Claverhouse agreed to put Henry on a parole of honor. Henry accepted exile from Scotland, promising to remain in banishment until the king's pleasure allowed his return. Henry went to Holland.

There he lived in exile for several years, until William and Mary came to the throne. When he returned to Scotland, he called upon Cuddie, who had married Jenny Dennison, Edith's maid. From Cuddie he learned of all that had occurred during his absence. He was informed that a man named Basil Olifant, a turncoat kinsman of Lady Margaret, had seized Tillietudlem and that Lady Margaret and Edith were forced to depend upon the charity of friends. Henry also learned that Balfour was still alive and that Lord Evandale was soon to marry Edith Bellenden. Henry set out to find Balfour and get from him a document which would place once more in Edith's possession the Ballenden estates. But Balfour burned the document and then threatened to fight Henry to the death. Henry refused, however, to fight with the man who had saved his father's life, and he made his escape from Balfour's fury by leaping across a ravine.

Meanwhile Edith had definitely refused marriage to Lord Evandale because she had caught a glimpse of Henry Morton as he passed her window. Later, at an inn, Henry overheard a plot to murder Lord Evandale, the murderers hoping to obtain a substantial sum from Basil Olifant for so doing. Henry scribbled a note of warning to Lord Evandale and sent his message by Cuddie. Then he went to Glasgow, intending to find Wittenbold, a Dutch commander of dragoons, and get help from him to protect Lord Evandale. Cuddie, however, tarried too long at an ale-house and forgot that the letter was to be delivered to Lord Evandale. Instead, he asked for Lady Margaret, and then, refused admittance, he stumbled away bearing the letter with him. Thus Lord Evandale was not warned of his danger.

A party of horsemen, led by Basil Olifant, came to kill Lord Evandale. Cuddie, knowing the danger, warned him too late. Shots were exchanged and Lord Evandale fell. Olifant ordered Lord Evandale murdered in cold blood just before Henry arrived with a magistrate and a detachment of dragoons.

The troopers quickly dispersed the attackers and Olifant fell during the charge. Balfour, attempting to escape, was swept to his death in a flooded stream. Henry hurried to the side of Lord Evandale, who recognized him and made signs that he wished to be carried into Lady Margaret's house. There he died, surrounded by his weeping friends. His last act was to place Edith's hand in that of Henry Morton. Several months later, to the great joy of the countryside, Henry married the young heiress of Tillietudlem. In the meantime, Basil Olifant having died without a will, Lady Margaret had recovered her castle and her estates.

THE OLD WIVES' TALE

Type of work: Novel
Author: Arnold Bennett (1867-1931)
Type of plot: Naturalism
Time of plot: Nineteenth century
Locale: England and Paris
First published: 1908

Principal characters:
CONSTANCE BAINES POVEY, and
SOPHIA BAINES SCALES, sisters
JOHN BAINES, their father
MRS. BAINES, their mother
SAMUEL POVEY, Constance's husband
GERALD SCALES, Sophia's husband
CYRIL POVEY, son of Constance and Samuel

Critique:

The Old Wives' Tale is a highly satisfying novel because of its excellent craftsmanship and its characterization of two strikingly different women. Although the book is long, the continuity of the narrative is sustained by the common family background of Constance and Sophia Baines and by the changes that time brings to their very different lives. The book contains many colorful details of the period between the age of crinolines and the industrial era, but its emphasis is not historical. Events such as the siege of Paris are used primarily as background for the development of character. The theme of the novel is time and the effects of its passing upon human life.

The Story:

Constance Baines at sixteen was a plump, pleasant girl with a snub nose. Sophia, aged fifteen, was a handsome girl with imagination and daring. The first symptoms of her rebelliousness, of her strong individuality, came when she announced her desire to be a teacher. That was in 1864.

Mr. and Mrs. Baines owned a draper's shop, and their income was adequate. They were most respectable, and were therefore horrified at their daughter's unconventional plan, for it had been taken for granted that she, as well as Constance, would assist in the shop. When Sophia was four years old, John Baines, the father, had suffered a stroke of paralysis which had left him a hopeless invalid whose faculties were greatly impaired. Prodded by his capable wife, he joined in forbidding Sophia to think of school teaching, but his opposition only strengthened Sophia's purpose.

One day, when Sophia had been left alone to care for her father, she saw a handsome young man, representative of a wholesale firm, enter the store. She instantly invented an errand to take her into the shop. His name, she learned, was Gerald Scales. When Sophia returned to her father's room he had slipped off the bed, had been powerless to movè himself, and had died of asphyxia. Mr. Baines' old friend, Mr. Critchlow, was called immediately, and he, having seen Sophia in the shop with Gerald, instantly accused her of killing her father. Presumably as a gesture of repentance but actually because she hoped for an opportunity to see Gerald again, Sophia offered to give up her plans to teach.

Sophia worked in millinery while Constance assisted Samuel Povey, the clerk, a small quiet man without dignity and without imagination. He and Constance gradually fell in love.

After two years Gerald returned. By artful contriving, Sophia managed to meet him alone and to initiate a correspondence. Mrs. Baines, recognizing Sophia's infatuation sent her off to visit her Aunt Harriet. Several weeks later Sophia ran off with Gerald Scales. She wrote her mother that they were married and planning to live abroad. A short time later Constance and Samuel Povey were married. Mrs. Baines turned over to them the house and shop, and went to live with her sister.

The married life of Constance held few surprises, and the couple soon settled to a routine tradesman's existence. Nothing further was heard of Sophia except for an occasional Christmas card giving no address. After six years of marriage a son, Cyril, was born. Constance centered her life about the baby, more so since her mother died shortly after his birth. Povey also devoted much attention to the child, but he made his wife miserable by his insistence on discipline. When, after twenty years of marriage, Povey caught pneumonia and left Constance a widow, she devoted herself entirely to Cyril. He was a charming, intelligent boy, but he seemed indifferent to his mother's efforts to please him. When he was eighteen years old, he won a scholarship in art and was sent to London. His mother was left alone.

Life had not dealt so quietly with Sophia. In a London hotel room, after her elopement, she had suffered her first disillusionment when Gerald began to make excuses for delaying their marriage. But after Sophia refused to go to Paris with him except as his wife, he reluctantly agreed to the ceremony. Gerald had inherited twelve thousand pounds. In Paris he and Sophia lived lavishly. Gerald's weakness, his irresponsibility, and lack of any morals or common sense soon became apparent. Realizing that Gerald had little regard for her welfare, Sophia took two hundred pounds in bank notes from his pocket and hid them against an emergency. As Gerald lost more at gambling, they lived in shabbier hotels, wore mended clothes, and ate sparingly. When their funds were nearly exhausted, Gerald suggested that Sophia should write to her family for help. When Sophia refused, Gerald abandoned her.

The next day she awoke ill and was visited by Gerald's friend, Chirac, who had come to collect money Gerald had borrowed from him. Chirac had risked his own reputation by taking money from the cash box of the newspaper where he was employed. Sophia unhesitatingly used some of the notes she had taken from Gerald to repay Chirac. When she again became ill, Chirac left her in the care of a middle-aged courtesan, Madame Faucault, who treated Sophia kindly during her long illness.

Madame Faucault was deeply in debt. Sophia rented Madame Faucault's flat and took in roomers and boarders. At that time France was at war with Germany, and soon the siege of Paris began. Food was scarce. Only by hard work and the most careful management was Sophia able to feed her boarders. She grew hard and businesslike. When the siege was lifted and Paris returned to normal, Sophia bought the pension Frensham at her own price. This pension was well-known for its excellence and respectability, and under Sophia's management it prospered. She did not hear from her husband again. By the Exhibition year she had built up a modest fortune from the two hundred pounds she had stolen from Gerald.

One day a young Englishman who was Cyril Povey's friend came to stay at the pension Frensham. Sophia's beauty and dignity intrigued him, and he learned enough about her to recognize her as his friend's aunt. On his return to England he hastily informed both Cyril and Constance of Sophia's situation.

Constance immediately wrote Sophia a warm, affectionate letter begging her to come to England for a visit. Meanwhile, in Paris, Sophia had suffered a slight stroke; when she was offered a large sum for the pension Frensham she reluctantly let it go. Soon afterward, she visited England.

Although Sophia had intended to make only a short visit, the sisters lived together for nine years. On the surface they got along well together, but Sophia had never forgiven her sister for her refusal to move from the ugly, inconvenient old house. Constance, on her part, silently resented Sophia's domineering ways.

Their tranquil existence was interrupted by a telegram to Sophia, informing her that Gerald Scales was very ill in a neighboring town. She went to him at once, but on her arrival she learned that he was already dead. He was shabby and thin and old. Seeing Gerald was a great shock to Sophia, and part of her shock was the fact that she no longer had any feeling for the man who had both made and ruined her life. On the drive home she suffered another stroke and lived but a few hours. Cyril was left all of Sophia's money. He had continued to live in London on an allowance, completely absorbed in his art, still secretive and indifferent in his attitude toward his mother. When Constance died several years later, he was abroad and did not return in time for the funeral. When the servants went off for Constance's burial, only Sophia's old poodle was left in the house. She waddled into the kitchen to see if any food had been left in her dish.

OLIVER TWIST

Type of work: Novel
Author: Charles Dickens (1812-1870)
Type of plot: Sentimental romance
Time of plot: Early nineteenth century
Locale: English provinces and London
First published: 1837-1839

Principal characters:

OLIVER TWIST, a workhouse waif
MR. BROWNLOW, Oliver's benefactor
MRS. MAYLIE, who also befriended Oliver
ROSE MAYLIE, her adopted daughter
FAGIN, a thief-trainer
BILL SIKES, his confederate
NANCY, in love with Sikes
MONKS (EDWARD LEEFORD), Oliver's half-brother
BUMBLE, a workhouse official

Critique:

The plot of this novel, written when Dickens was in his twenties, forecasts the extremely complicated plots he invented later. The action moves forward in a natural way, achieved by an artistic change of pace. Because the story was first published serially, there are switches of scene at moments of tension. Sentimentality abounds, perhaps unavoidably, because of the nature of the theme and because of Dickens' deep concern for the conditions of the underprivileged masses in the Great Britain of his day.

The Story:

Oliver Twist was born in the lying-in room of a parochial workhouse about seventy-five miles north of London. His mother's name was not known. She had been found unconscious by the roadside, exhausted by a long journey on foot, and she died leaving as the only tokens of her child's identity a locket and a ring. These were stolen by old Sally, a pauper present at her death.

Oliver owed his name to Bumble, the parish beadle and a bullying official of the workhouse, who always named his unknown waifs in the order of an alphabetical system he had devised. Twist was the name between Swubble and Unwin on Bumble's list. Oliver Twist he was named.

An offered reward of ten pounds failing to discover his parentage, he was sent to a nearby poor farm, where he passed his early childhood in neglect and near starvation. At the age of nine he was moved back to the workhouse. Always hungry, he asked one day for a second serving of porridge. The scandalized authorities put him in solitary confinement and posted a bill offering five pounds to some master who would take him off the parish.

Oliver was apprenticed to one Sowerberry, a casket maker, to learn a trade. Sowerberry employed little Oliver, dressed in miniature mourning clothing, as attendant at children's funerals. Another Sowerberry employee, Noah Claypole, teased Oliver about his parentage. Oliver, goaded beyond endurance, fiercely attacked Claypole and was subsequently locked in the cellar by Mrs. Sowerberry. Sowerberry released Oliver, who, that night, bundled up his meager belongings and started out for London.

In a London suburb Oliver, worn out from walking and weak from hunger, met Jack Dawkins, sharp-witted slum gamin. Dawkins, known as the Artful Dodger, offered Oliver lodgings in the city, and Oliver soon found himself in the midst of a gang of young thieves, led by a miserly old Jew, Fagin. Oliver was trained as a pickpocket. On his first mission he was caught and taken to the police station. There he was rescued by kindly Mr. Brownlow, the man whose pocket Oliver was accused of having picked. Mr. Brownlow, his gruff friend Grimwig, and the old housekeeper, Mrs. Bedwin, cared for the sickly Oliver. They marveled at the resemblance of the boy to a portrait of a young lady in Mr. Brownlow's possession. Recuperated, Oliver was one day given some books and money to take to a bookseller. Grimwig wagered that Oliver would not return. Meanwhile Fagin and his gang had been on constant lookout for the boy's appearance, and he was intercepted by Nancy, a young street girl associated with the gang.

Bumble, in London on parochial business, saw Mr. Brownlow's advertisement for word leading to Oliver's recovery. Hoping to profit, he hastened to Mr. Brownlow and reported that Oliver was incorrigible. After receiving this information, Mr. Brownlow refused to have Oliver's name mentioned in his presence.

Once more Oliver was in the hands of Fagin. During his absence the gang had been studying a house in Chertsey, west of London, preparatory to breaking into it at night. The time came for the adventure, and Oliver, much to his horror, was chosen to participate. He and Bill Sikes, brutal young co-leader of the gang, met Toby Crackit, another housebreaker, and the trio, in the dark of early morning, pried open a small window of the house. Oliver entered, determined to warn the occupants. The robbers were discovered, and the trio fled, Oliver wounded by gunshot.

In fleeing, Sikes threw the wounded Oliver into a ditch and covered him with a cape. Toby Crackit, the other housebreaker, returned and reported to Fagin. The old thief-trainer was more than ever interested in Oliver after an important conversation with one Monks. This discussion, overheard by Nancy, concerned Oliver's parentage and Monks' wish to have the boy made a youthful felon.

Oliver crawled feebly to the house into which he had gone the night before. He was taken in by the owner, Mrs. Maylie, and Rose, her adopted daughter. Oliver's story aroused their sympathy and he was saved from police investigation by Dr. Losberne, friend of the Maylies. Upon his recovery the boy went with the doctor to seek out Mr. Brownlow, but it was learned that the old gentleman, his friend Grimwig, and Mrs. Bedwin had gone to the West Indies.

Meanwhile Bumble courted the widow Corney. During one of their conversations, Mrs. Corney was called out to attend the death of old Sally, who had stood by at the death of Oliver's mother. After old Sally died, Mrs. Corney removed a pawn ticket from her hand. In Mrs. Corney's absence, Bumble appraised her property to his satisfaction. He proposed marriage.

The Maylies moved to the country, where Oliver studied gardening, read, and took long walks. During this holiday Rose Maylie fell sick and nearly died. After her recovery, Harry Maylie, wastrel son of Mrs. Maylie, joined the group. Harry, in love with Rose, asked for her hand in marriage. Rose refused on two grounds; she could not marry him before she discovered who she was, and she could not marry him unless he mended his ways. One night Oliver was frightened when he saw Fagin and Monks peering through the study window.

Bumble had discovered that married life with the former Mrs. Corney was not all happiness, for she dominated him completely. When Monks went to the workhouse seeking information about Oliver, he met with Mr. and Mrs. Bumble and learned that Mrs. Bumble had redeemed a locket and a wedding ring with the pawn ticket she had recovered from old Sally. Monks bought the trinkets from Mrs. Bumble and threw them in the river.

Monks told Fagin that he had disposed of the tokens of Oliver's parentage. Again Nancy overheard the two villains. After drugging Bill Sikes, whom she had been nursing to recovery from gunshot wounds received in the ill-fated venture at Chertsey, she went to see Rose Maylie, whose name and address she had overheard in the conversation between Fagin and Monks. Nancy told Rose everything she had heard concerning Oliver. Rose was unable to understand fully the various connections of the plot nor could she see Monks' connection with Oliver. She offered the miserable girl the protection of her own home, but Nancy refused, knowing that she could never leave Bill Sikes. The two young women agreed on a time and place for later meetings. Rose and Oliver went to call on Mr. Brownlow, whom Oliver had glimpsed in the street. The reunion of the boy, Mr. Brownlow, and Mrs. Bedwin was a joyous one. Even old Grimwig gruffly expressed his pleasure at seeing Oliver again. Rose told Mr. Brownlow Nancy's story.

Noah Claypole and Charlotte, maidservant of the Sowerberrys, had in the meantime, run away from the casket maker and arrived in London, where they went to the public house which was the haunt of Fagin and his gang. Fagin flattered Noah into his employ, Noah's job being to steal small coins from children on household errands.

At the time agreed upon for her appointment with Rose Maylie, Nancy was unable to leave the demanding Bill Sikes. Noticing Nancy's impatience, Fagin decided that she had tired of Sikes and that she had another lover. Fagin hated Sikes because of the younger man's power over the gang, and he saw this situation as an opportunity to rid himself of Sikes. Fagin set Noah on Nancy's trail.

The following week Nancy got free with the aid of Fagin. She went to Rose and Mr. Brownlow and revealed to them the haunts of all the gang except Sikes. Noah, having overheard all this, secretly told Fagin, who in turn told Sikes. In his rage Sikes brutally murdered Nancy, never knowing that the girl had been faithful to him. He fled, pursued by the vision of murdered Nancy's staring eyes. Frantic from fear, he attempted to kill his dog, whose presence might betray him. The dog ran away.

Apprehended, Monks confessed to Mr. Brownlow the plot against Oliver. Oliver's father, Edward Leeford, had married a woman older than himself. Their son, Edward Leeford, was the man now known as Monks. After several years of unhappiness, the couple separated, Monks and his mother staying on the continent and Mr. Leeford returning to England. Later Leeford met a retired naval officer and fell in love with his seventeen-year-old daughter. There was another daughter aged three. Leeford contracted to marry the girl, but before the marriage could be performed he was called to Rome, where an old friend had died. On the way to Rome he stopped at the house of Mr. Brownlow, his best friend, and left a portrait of his betrothed. He himself fell sick in Rome and died. His former wife seized his papers. When Leeford's young wife-to-be, who was pregnant, heard of Leeford's death, she ran away to hide her condition. Her father died soon afterward and the younger sister was eventually adopted by Mrs. Maylie. She was Rose Maylie, Oliver's aunt. Monks lived a prodigal life. When his mother died, he went to the West Indies, where Mr. Brownlow had gone in search of him. But Monks had already returned to track down Oliver, whose part of his father's settlement he wished to keep from his young half-brother. It was Monks who had offered the reward at the workhouse for information about Oliver's parentage, and it was Monks who had paid Fagin to see that the boy remained with the gang as a common thief.

After Fagin and the Artful Dodger had been seized, Bill Sikes and the remainder of the gang met on Jacob's Island in the Thames River. They intended to stay there in a deserted house until the hunt had died down. But Sikes' dog led their pursuers to the hideout. Bill Sikes hanged himself accidentally with the rope he was using as a means of escape. The other robbers were captured. Fagin was hanged publicly at Newgate after he had revealed to Oliver the location of papers concerning the boy's heritage. Monks had entrusted these papers to the Jew for safekeeping.

Harry Maylie, who had become a minister, married Rose Maylie. Mr. Brownlow adopted Oliver and took up residence near the church of the Reverend Harry Maylie. Mr. and Mrs. Bumble lost their parochial positions and soon became inmates of the workhouse which once had been their domain. Monks, allowed to retain his share of his father's property, went to America and eventually died in prison. Oliver's years of hardship and unhappiness were at an end.

OMOO

Type of work: Novel
Author: Herman Melville (1819-1891)
Type of plot: Adventure romance
Time of plot: Early 1840's
Locale: Tahiti and the South Seas
First published: 1847

Principal characters:

HERMAN MELVILLE, an American sailor
DOCTOR LONG GHOST, his companion in his adventures
CAPTAIN BOB, a jovial Tahitian jailer

Critique:

The title of this book, a sequel to Melville's earlier *Typee,* was borrowed from the native dialect of the Marquesas Islands. The word signifies a person who wanders, like the narrator of the book, from one island to another. Melville's object in writing *Omoo* was twofold. He wished to relate his own adventures in the Society Islands and to make people realize the effects promiscuous social intercourse with white men, generally, and missionaries, particularly, had had upon the Polynesians. The natives were better off, Melville felt, as unsophisticated but sincere pagans than as the hypocritical pseudo-Christians of the missionary schools.

The Story:

Rescued from the cannibal island of Typee by the crew of a British whaler, Herman Melville agreed to stay on the ship as a deckhand until it reached the next port, where he was to be placed ashore. But the *Julia* was not a well-managed vessel, and soon after Melville joined it several of the men made an attempt to desert. These unfortunates were recovered quickly, however, by the timely aid of the islanders and the crew of a French man-of-war.

In the weeks of cruising that followed this adventure, Melville, relieved from duty because of a lameness in his leg, spent his time reading the books of the ship's doctor and playing chess with their owner. Those were not weeks of pleasure. In that time two of the men in the forecastle died and the entire crew lived under the most abominable conditions, in the rat-infested, rotten old ship which should have been condemned years before. Finally, when the captain himself fell ill, the ship changed its course to Tahiti, the nearest island.

Having convinced themselves that when the captain left the ship they would no longer be bound by the agreements they had signed, the crew intended to leave the ship when she arrived in the harbor at Papeetee. The captain attempted to prevent their desertion by keeping the ship under way just outside the harbor while he went ashore in a small boat. Only Doctor Long Ghost's influence prevented the men from disregarding orders and taking the vessel into the harbor to anchor her. The crew did, however, protest their treatment in a letter sent to the British consul ashore by means of the Negro cook. Unfortunately, the acting consul in Papeetee and the captain of the *Julia* were old acquaintances, and the official's only action was to inform the men they would have to stay with the ship and cruise for three months under the command of the first mate. The captain himself would remain in Tahiti. But after a Mauri harpooner attempted to wreck the ship, the drunken mate decided to take the whaler into the harbor, regardless of consequences.

In Papeetee the acting consul had the men, including Melville and Doctor Long Ghost, imprisoned on a French frigate. After five days aboard the French ship, they were removed and were once more given an opportunity to return to their ship. When they refused, the mutineers were taken in custody by a Tahitian native called Captain Bob, who took them to an oval-shaped thatched house which was to be their jail.

There they were confined in stocks, two timbers about twenty feet long serving to secure all the prisoners. Each morning the jailer came to free the men and supervise their baths in a neighboring stream. The natives, in return for hard ship's biscuit from the *Julia,* fed the men baked breadfruit and Indian turnips. Sometimes the kindly jailer led the men to his orange grove, where they gathered fruit for their meals. This fruit diet was precisely what they needed to regain the health they had lost while eating sea rations of salt pork and biscuit.

The prisoners in the thatched hut were in sight of Broom Road, the island's chief thoroughfare. Since they were easily accessible, the idle, inquisitive Tahitians were constantly visiting, and they did not lack for company.

Within a few days, their jailer freed the sailors from the stocks during the daytime, except when white men were in the vicinity. Once this leniency was granted, the men roamed the neighborhood to take advantage of the natives' hospitality. Doctor Long Ghost always carried salt with him, in case he found some food to flavor.

When the consul sent a doctor to look at the prisoners, all the sailors pretended to be sick. Shortly after the doctor had made his examinations and departed, a native boy appeared with a basket of medicines. The sailors discarded the powders and pills, but eagerly drank the contents of all the bottles which smelled the least bit alcoholic.

British missionaries on the island took no notice of the sailors from the *Julia* other than sending them a handful of tracts. Three French priests, however, came to see the men. The natives, it seemed, looked upon the priests as magicians, and so they had been able to make only a few converts among the islanders. The priests were popular with the sailors because they gave freshly baked wheat bread and liquor to the prisoners.

Three weeks after arriving in the port of Papeetee, the captain of the *Julia* sailed away with a new crew recruited from beachcombers idling about the island. After his departure the mutineers were no longer confined to their jail, but continued to live there because the building was as convenient as any other thatched dwelling in the neighborhood. They existed by foraging the surrounding country and smuggling provisions from visiting ships with the aid of the sailors aboard.

Melville found this life not unpleasant at first, but after a time he grew bored. He even went to a native church to hear the missionary preach. The theme of the sermon was that all white men except the British were bad and so were the natives, unless they began to contribute more baskets of food to the missionary's larder. Melville did not go to the missionary church again.

Several weeks after the *Julia* had sailed, Melville met two white men who informed him that a plantation on a neighboring island was in need of laborers. Melville and Doctor Long Ghost, introduced to the planters as Peter and Paul, were immediately hired. One moonlight night the pair boarded the boat belonging to their employers. They left their former shipmates without ceremony, lest the authorities prevent their departure.

The planters lived by themselves in an inland valley on the mosquito-infested island of Imeeo. The prospect of plying a hoe in the heat of the day amid swarms of insects did not appeal to the two sailors, and so at noon of the first day in the fields Doctor Long Ghost pretended illness. He and Melville agreed to do as little work as possible. After a few days they gave up farming for good and went afoot to Tamai, an inland village unspoiled by missionaries or other white men. There they saw a dance by native girls, a rite which had been banned as pagan by the missionaries on the island. A day or two later, while the two white men were considering settling permanently at Tamai, the natives forced them to flee, for a reason they were never able to discover.

The next adventure they contemplated was an audience with the queen of Tahiti. Traveling by easy stages from one village to the next, afoot or by canoe, they made their way to Partoowye, where the island queen had her residence. They met a runaway ship's carpenter who had settled there and who kept busy building boxes and cabinets for the natives. From him they learned that a whaler was in the local harbor. But when they talked to the crew of the vessel, they were told that it was not a good ship on which to sail, and they gave up all thought of shipping away from the islands aboard the whaler.

After five weeks in the village, Doctor Long Ghost and Melville finally obtained admittance to the queen through the good offices of a Marquesan attendant at her court. When they came into the queen's presence, she was eating, and she waved them out of her palace in high-handed fashion, at the same time reprimanding their guide. Disappointed by their reception at court, the two travelers again decided to go to sea. They made friends with the third mate of the whaler, which was still in the harbor. The mate reassured them concerning conditions aboard the ship. The other sailors, knowing the ship could not sail away from the pleasant islands without more men in the crew, had deliberately lied.

Having confidence in the mate, Doctor Long Ghost and Melville then approached the captain and asked to sign on as members of the crew. The captain, however, would not accept Doctor Long Ghost as a deckhand or as the ship's doctor. Reluctantly Melville shipped alone on the voyage which would take him to the coast of Japan and, he hoped, eventually home.

THE ORDEAL OF RICHARD FEVEREL

Type of work: Novel
Author: George Meredith (1828-1909)
Type of plot: Tragi-comedy
Time of plot: Mid-nineteenth century
Locale: England
First published: 1859

Principal characters:

Richard Feverel, the young heir to Raynham Abbey
Sir Austin Feverel, his father
Adrian Harley, Sir Austin's nephew
Ripton Thompson, Richard's playmate and friend
Blaize, a neighboring farmer
Lucy Desborough, Blaize's niece
Clare, Richard's cousin, in love with him

Critique:

The Ordeal of Richard Feverel tells what happened when a disillusioned, woman-hating father tried to rear his son according to a scientific system of education in which women were to play a very minor part. Readers of the book will of course learn, as Sir Austin himself did, the futility of such attempts to control nature's processes. Some modern readers find an artificiality in the dialogue and a certain pseudo-intellectualism in the characterization. However, any artificial qualities of the book are more than redeemed by the idyllic romance of Lucy and Richard. Their story has undeniable appeal; if Meredith strained for his effect in other aspects of the novel, his treatment of young love was simple and sincere.

The Story:

Richard Feverel was the only son of Sir Austin Feverel, of Raynham Abbey. After Sir Austin's wife left him, the baronet became a woman-hater who was determined to rear his son according to a System, which, among other things, virtually excluded females from the boy's life until he was twenty-five. Then, Sir Austin thought, his son might marry, providing a girl good enough for the youth could be found.

Because of the System, Richard's early life was carefully controlled. The boy was kept from lakes and rivers so that he would not drown; from firecrackers so that he would not be burned; from cricket fields so that he would not be bruised. Adrian Harley, Sir Austin's nephew, was entrusted with Richard's education.

When he was fourteen, the Hope of Raynham, as Adrian called his charge, became restless. It was decided that he needed a companion — masculine, of course — near his own age. The candidate for this position was young Ripton Thompson, the none-too-brilliant son of Sir Austin's lawyer. In their escapades around Raynham Abbey together, Richard led and Ripton followed.

In spite of Ripton's subordinate position, he apparently had much to do with corrupting his companion and weakening Sir Austin's System. Soon after Ripton arrived at Raynham, the two boys decided to go shooting. A quarrel arose between them when Ripton, not a sportsman by nature, cried out as Richard was aiming his piece at a bird. Richard called his companion a fool, and a fight ensued. Richard won because he was a scientific boxer. The two boys soon made up their differences but their state of harmony was short-lived. The same afternoon they trespassed on the farm of a neighbor named Blaize, who came upon them after they had shot a pheasant on his property.

Blaize ordered the boys off his land, and when they refused to go he horsewhipped them. Richard and Ripton were compelled to retreat. Ripton suggested that he stone the farmer, but Richard refused to let his companion use such ungentlemanly tactics. The two boys did, however, speculate on ways to get even with farmer Blaize.

Richard was in disgrace when he returned to Raynham because his father knew of his fight with Ripton. Sir Austin ordered his son to go to bed immediately after supper; but he later discovered that Richard had gone, not to bed, but to meet Ripton, and the boys were overheard talking mysteriously about setting something on fire. Shortly afterward, when Sir Austin discovered that farmer Blaize's hayricks were on fire, he suspected Richard. Sir Austin was chagrined, but he did not try to make his son confess. Adrian Harley suspected both Richard and Ripton, who was soon sent home to his father.

The next day a laborer named Tom Bakewell was arrested on suspicion of committing arson. Tom really had set fire to Blaize's property, Richard having bribed him to do so, but he refused to implicate Richard. Conscience-stricken and aware of the fact that a commoner was shielding him, Richard was persuaded to go to Blaize and confess that he was responsible for Tom's action.

Blaize was not surprised by Richard's visit, for Sir Austin had already called and paid damages. Richard was humiliated by the necessity of apologizing to a farmer. He told Blaize that he had set fire to the farmer's grain stacks; and Blaize implied that Richard was a liar because the farmer had a witness, a dull-witted fellow, who said that Tom Bakewell had done the deed. Richard insisted that he himself was responsible, and he succeeded in confusing Blaize's star witness. Richard, however, left the farmer's place in a most irritated frame of mind, not even noticing the farmer's pretty little thirteen-year-old niece, Lucy Desborough, who had let the young man in and out of Blaize's house.

At Tom's trial, Blaize's witness was so uncertain about the identity of the arsonist that the accused was released. Thereafter Tom became Richard's devoted servant.

When Richard reached the age of eighteen, Sir Austin set about finding a prospective wife for the Hope of Raynham, a girl who could be trained for seven years to be a fit mate for Sir Austin's perfect son. Richard, however, could not wait seven years before he at least showed an interest in women, partly because they had no place in the System. He was attracted first to his cousin Clare, who adored him and dreamed of marrying the handsome young man, but in a single afternoon Richard completely forgot Clare. Boating on the weir, he came upon a young lady in distress and saved her boat from capsizing. In that instant the System collapsed completely. She introduced herself as farmer Blaize's niece, Lucy Desborough. Richard was immediately smitten with her, and she with him. Every day they met in the meadow by the weir.

Sir Austin, meanwhile, thought that he had found in London the perfect mate for his son, a young girl named Carola Grandison. Informed by Adrian and his butler that Richard was secretly meeting Lucy, Sir Austin ordered his son to come to London immediately in order to meet Carola. Richard at first refused to obey his father, but Adrian tricked Richard into going to London by saying that Sir Austin had apoplexy.

Richard found his father physically well, but mentally disturbed by the young man's interest in Lucy. He told Richard that women were the ordeal of all men, and though he hoped for a confession of Richard's affair with Lucy, he got none. Sir Austin, however, refused to let the young man return to Raynham as soon as Richard would have liked. Richard met the Grandisons, listened to his father's lectures on the folly of young men who imagined themselves in love, and moped when, after two weeks, Lucy mysteriously stopped writing.

When Sir Austin and his son finally returned to the abbey, Richard found that Lucy had been sent away to school against her will by her uncle so that she would not interfere with Sir Austin's System. Although the farmer did not object to Richard, he refused to have his niece brought back because of his promise to Sir Austin.

After his unsuccessful attempt to have his sweetheart returned to him, Richard decided upon drastic measures. Sir Austin unwittingly aided his son's designs, when he sent Richard to London to see the Grandisons. Tom Blaize, destined by Sir Austin and her uncle to be Lucy's husband, went to London by the same train. Richard got in touch with his old friend, Ripton Thompson, and asked him to get lodgings for a lady. While in London, Richard came upon Adrian Harley, Clare's mother, and Clare, who had picked up a wedding ring which Richard had dropped. Tom Blaize was tricked into going to the wrong station to find Lucy, and Richard met her instead. He installed her with Mrs. Berry in lodgings in Kensington and married her soon afterward, good-hearted Mrs. Berry giving them her own wedding ring to replace the one Richard had lost.

When Adrian learned of Richard's marriage, he admitted that the System had failed. Ripton himself broke the news to Sir Austin, who remarked bitterly that he was mistaken to believe that any System could be based on a human being. Actually Sir Austin objected not so much to the marriage of his son as to the deception involved.

Efforts were made to reconcile Richard and his father, but to no avail. Richard was uneasy because he had not heard from his father, and Sir Austin was too proud to take the first step. While Richard and Lucy were honeymooning in the Isle of Wight, he was introduced to a fast yachting crowd, including Lord Mountfalcon, a man of doubtful reputation, whom Richard naïvely asked to watch over Lucy while Richard himself went to London to see his father and ask his forgiveness.

In London he met a woman Lord Mountfalcon had bribed to bring about Richard's downfall, for his plan was to win Lucy for himself by convincing her of Richard's infidelity. Richard did not know that Mrs. Mount, as she was called, was being bribed to detain him and that while she kept him in London Lord Mountfalcon was attempting to seduce Lucy.

Because he could not bear separation from his son any longer, Sir Austin consented to see Richard. Relations between Richard and his father were still strained, however, for Sir Austin had not yet accepted Lucy. Since she could not have Richard, Clare, meanwhile, had married a man much older than she. Shortly after her marriage, she died and was buried with her own wedding ring and Richard's lost one on her finger.

The death of Clare and the realization that she had loved him deeply shocked Richard. Moreover, his past indiscretions with Mrs. Mount made him ashamed of himself; unworthy, he thought to touch Lucy's hand. He did not know that Mrs. Berry had gone to the Isle of Wight and had brought Lucy back to live with her in Kensington. Richard himself had gone to the continent, where he traveled aimlessly, unaware that Lucy had borne him a son. Then an uncle who disbelieved in all systems returned to London. Learning of Lucy and her child, he bundled them off to Raynham Abbey, and prevailed on Sir Austin to receive them. Then he went to the continent, found Richard, and broke the news that he was a father. Richard rushed back to Raynham to be with Lucy and to become completely reconciled with his father.

The reunion between Lucy and Richard was brief. Richard saw his son and received from his wife complete forgiveness for his past misdeeds. A letter from Mrs. Mount to Richard had revealed how Lord Mountfalcon had schemed so that his lordship could see Lucy and separate her from Richard. Knowing Lucy's innocence and Mountfalcon's villainy, Richard went immediately to France, where he was slightly wounded in a duel with Lord Mountfalcon. The news of the duel was, however, fatal for Lucy. She became ill of brain fever and died of shock, crying for her husband. Richard was heartbroken. Sir Austin was grieved too, but his closest friend often wondered whether he had ever perceived any flaws in his System.

THE OREGON TRAIL

Type of work: Record of travel
Author: Francis Parkman (1823-1893)
Type of plot: Travel and adventure sketches
Time of plot: 1846
Locale: The Oregon Trail
First published: 1849

Principal characters:
FRANCIS PARKMAN, a young man just out of college
QUINCY SHAW, his friend
HENRY CHATILLON, their guide
DESLAURIERS, their muleteer

Critique:

This book is one of the great documents of the West. Very few travelers wrote much about the country beyond the Mississippi as early as the 1840's, and those who did write seldom approached their subject with the objective and unbiased point of view from which Francis Parkman wrote in his account of a region he had known and enjoyed. His motive was to set down for posterity what he had observed on his trip to the Rocky Mountains. He realized only too well that the Indian, the trading post, the mountain man, and the great buffalo herds were passing figures in history. He wanted to leave a record of them, for he saw in them something of glamour and interest which, once gone, could never return.

The Story:

In the spring of 1846, Francis Parkman and his friend, Quincy Shaw, traveled by railroad from the East to St. Louis. From St. Louis they went by river steamer up the Missouri River to Kansas, then called Kanzas, about five hundred miles from the mouth of the river. Their object was a trip to the Rocky Mountains, a very unusual excursion in the 1840's.

Disembarking, the two young men

went by wagon to Westport to get horses and guides for their journey. At Westport they met three acquaintances with whom they agreed to travel; two British army officers and another gentleman, who were planning a hunting expedition on the American prairies. Pleased to have companions on their dangerous journey, the two Easterners were also glad they did not need to travel with a train of emigrants, for whom Parkman expressed the utmost contempt.

The journey began inauspiciously for the five travelers. The Britishers decided to start by a trail other than the one which had been previously decided upon. The result was that the party discovered, after several days of travel, that they had gone far out of their way. The party then rode northward to the Oregon Trail, which they decided to follow to Fort Laramie, seven hundred miles away.

On the twenty-third of May the party arrived on the Oregon Trail, where they saw the first human being they had met in eight days of travel. He was a straggler from a caravan of emigrants. At the end of three weeks Parkman and his companions, the Englishmen and a small group of emigrants who had joined them, reached the Platte River. They were still four hundred miles from Fort Laramie. The journey to the Platte River had been a muddy one, for each night the party was drenched by a terrific thunderstorm. During the day they also ran into numerous showers as they made their way westward across the uninteresting country east of the Platte, a country almost devoid of any game except for a few birds.

At the Platte the party entered the buffalo country. Parkman and Shaw were fascinated by those animals, and they slaughtered hundreds, mostly bulls, before their journey ended. When they entered the buffalo country they also entered the first territory where they were likely to encounter hostile Indians. A few days after crossing the Platte, Parkman, Shaw, and their guide went on a sortie after buffalo. Parkman became separated from his companions and spent several anxious hours before he found his solitary way back to the camp. Shortly after that adventure the party met the chief of the trading station at Fort Laramie, who was on his way downstream on the Platte with a shipment of skins. He warned them to watch out for Pawnees, in whose country the party was then traveling.

While traveling up the river, the Englishmen made themselves obnoxious to Parkman and his friend by encouraging emigrants to join the party and by camping at any time of the day they pleased without consulting the Americans. Since Parkman and Shaw had a definite schedule which they wished to keep, they left the Englishmen and pushed on ahead with Henry Chatillon, their guide, and a muleteer named Deslauriers. Not many days afterward Parkman and his group reached Fort Laramie, at that time a trading outpost and not a military fort.

At Fort Laramie the travelers introduced themselves and gave the factor in charge a letter they had brought from his superiors in St. Louis. They were entertained and housed in the best fashion possible at the fort. Parkman and his friend spent the next few days visiting the Indian villages outside the fort, talking with the trappers, and occasionally looking in on emigrant trains which were on their way to the Oregon country. Using a small chest of medical supplies he carried with him, Shaw gained some little reputation as a medicine man by doctoring a few of the more important Indians.

The most decisive news which came to Parkman and Shaw at the fort was that the Dakota Indians were preparing to make war upon their traditional enemies of the Snake tribe. Parkman and his friend decided that they would accompany the Dakotas on the raid, since their guide, Henry Chatillon, was married to a Dakota squaw and could, through her, promise the protection of the Dakota tribe. The travelers felt that it would be an unusual opportunity to study Indians and their customs.

On June twentieth Parkman's party, now augmented by two traders of Indian and French descent, left Fort Laramie to join the village of a Dakota chief named The Whirlwind. A few days later, reaching a point on Laramie Creek where the Indians would pass, they decided to camp and await the arrival of The Whirlwind and his village. While they waited, two misfortunes broke upon them. Parkman fell seriously ill with dysentery and word came that Chatillon's Indian wife, who was a member of The Whirlwind's village, was dying. Chatillon went ahead to meet the Indians and see his wife before she died. When the Indians failed to arrive, Parkman, recovered from his illness, went back to Fort Laramie. There he discovered that the Dakota war-spirit had lessened, so that there was some doubt as to whether the tribe would take the war-trail.

Parkman and Shaw decided to follow The Whirlwind's village of Dakotas. A day or two after they started, however, they received word that a trader was going to the Indian rendezvous and wished Parkman and Shaw to accompany him. They never did find the trader, but pushed on by themselves to the place where they expected to find the Indians camped before they went on the warpath.

Arriving at the rendezvous, Parkman and Shaw found no Indians. Since Shaw was not particularly interested in studying the Indians, Parkman took one man, who was married to an Indian, and set off by himself to find The Whirlwind's village. It was a dangerous undertaking, for there was some risk of bad treatment from all the Indians in the vicinity, both friendly and hostile.

After many days of lonely travel, Parkman and his companion came upon a Dakota village hunting in the foothills of the Rockies. They learned that The Whirlwind had left this village with a few families. A Frenchman named Reynal lived in the village, however, and Parkman gained the protection of Reynal and his squaw's relatives. Without ceremony Parkman and his man Raymond went to live in the lodge of Chief Big Crow, who was honored that the white men would come to live with him.

Until the first of August Parkman lived with Big Crow and shared the tribal life of the village. With his host or with other Indians he went on hunting expeditions after buffalo, antelope, and other game. It was a dangerous life, but Parkman enjoyed it in spite of the many risks.

That summer was a perilous time for the Indians. In search of a large herd of buffalo needed to get skins for the repair of their worn tepees, they had deeply penetrated the hunting grounds of their enemies. At last, after a successful hunt, the village turned eastward toward Fort Laramie, to rejoin the other Indians who had not dared to accompany them. Parkman and his man traveled part of the way with the tribe. But in order to reach Fort Laramie by the date he had set, Parkman found that he had to push ahead by himself, for the Indian village traveled too slowly. Women, children, and dogs reduced their rate of travel considerably.

Back at Fort Laramie, where he rejoined Shaw, Parkman prepared for the return journey to St. Louis. They left the fort on the fourth of August, accompanied by several traders who had promised to go with them for part of the journey. These men left the party, however, before it reached the Platte. Parkman and Shaw made most of the return journey with only their two hired men. At Bent's Fort, a small trading post, they were joined by a volunteer who had left the army because of sickness. This man gave them the first news of the Mexican War that Parkman and Shaw had received, for the war had begun after they had left civilization behind them. From that time on, the travelers met many wagon trains and columns of troops on their way westward to fight the Mexicans. Because of the many troop units in the territory, the small party had no difficulty with any of the Indian bands they encountered.

Early in September the four men rode into Westport, where they sold their horses and camping equipment. Parkman and Shaw traveled by boat downstream to St. Louis. There they discarded the buckskins they had been wearing for many weeks.

It had been an amazing vacation. For five months they had traveled through the heart of the Indian country, far from the protection of the government and the army. They had seen many Indians, but without loss of valuables or life. The only casualty had been an old mule that died as a result of a snake bite. The good fortune of Parkman and his friends was pointed up by the hostilities which began shortly after they left the frontier region. Three weeks after their return to civilization, Comanches and Pawnees began raiding the trail over which they had traveled. The raids were so methodical that not a single party passed over the Oregon Trail in the next six months.

ORLANDO

Type of work: Novel
Author: Virginia Woolf (1882-1941)
Type of plot: Biographical fantasy
Time of plot: 1588-1928
Locale: England
First published: 1928

Principal characters:

Orlando, first a man, then a woman
Sasha, a Russian princess loved by Orlando
Nicholas Greene, a poet pensioned by Orlando
Archduchess Harriet of Roumania, an admirer of Orlando
Marmaduke Bonthrop Shelmerdine, Esquire, Orlando's husband

Critique:

Orlando is a fantasy which traces in straightforward biographical manner the life of a hero-heroine, a boy who was sixteen years old in 1588 and a woman of thirty-six in 1928. The novel is really three centuries of English history presented symbolically through the family heritage of Victoria Sackville-West, English poet and novelist. Mrs. Woolf's method gives the impression of time passing and the present merging with the past, a fantasy that is a free release of the creative imagination, unhampered by calendar time and compelling that "willing suspension of disbelief" which we make also in stories of the supernatural.

The Story:

One day in 1588 young Orlando was slashing at the head of a Moor tied to the rafters in his ancestral castle. His forefathers had been of noble rank for centuries and had lived out their lives in action, but Orlando was inclined toward writing. Bored by his play in the attic, he went to his room and wrote for a while on his poetic drama, "Aethelbert: A Tragedy in Five Acts." Tiring of poetry before long, he ran out of doors and up a nearby hill, where he threw himself down under his favorite oak tree and gave himself over to contemplation.

He was still lying there when he heard trumpet calls announcing the arrival of Queen Elizabeth. He hurried to the castle to dress in his finest clothes to serve Her Majesty. On the way to his room he noticed a shabbily-dressed man in the servants' quarters, a man who looked like a poet, but he had no time to stop for inquiry. The man's image was to haunt him the rest of his life. Having dressed, he dashed down to the banquet hall and, kneeling before the queen, offered a bowl of rose water for her to wash her hands after her journey. Elizabeth was so taken with the boy that she deeded to his father a great house. Two years later she summoned Orlando to court, where in time he was made her treasurer and steward. One day, however, she saw Orlando kissing a girl of the court and became so angry that Orlando lost her royal favor.

Orlando had many adventures with women. He had decided finally, to marry at the time of the Great Frost in 1604. That year the Thames was frozen so deeply that King James had the court hold carnival on the ice. There Orlando met and fell in love with Sasha, a Russian princess, with whom he skated far down the river. They went aboard a Russian ship to get something for Sasha, who remained below so long that Orlando went to investigate. He found her sitting on the knee of a common seaman. Sasha was able to reconcile Orlando, however, and the two planned an elopement. While waiting for her that night, Orlando began to feel raindrops; the thaw had set in. After waiting two hours, he dashed down to the river bank, where he saw great pieces of ice crashing down the flooded waters. Far out to sea he saw the Russian ship sailing for home. Sasha had betrayed him.

For six months Orlando lived in grief. One morning in June he failed to get out of bed as usual. He slept for seven days. When he awoke at last, he seemed to have forgotten much of the past. He began to think a good deal about the subject of death, and enjoyed reading from Sir Thomas Browne's *Urn Burial*. He read, thought, and wrote a great deal.

He summoned Mr. Nicholas Greene, a poet, to visit him. Greene talked to him almost incessantly about the poets, about life, about literature. Orlando was so grateful to Greene that he settled a generous pension on the poet. Greene, however, could not endure the quiet country, and one morning he went back to his beloved London.

Still wondering what life was all about, Orlando decided to try filling his life with material achievement. First he set about refurbishing his great house. He spent a great part of his fortune and traveled into distant countries in his search for precious ornaments. The time was that of the Restoration, when Charles II was king.

One day, while Orlando was working on a long poem, "The Oak Tree," he was interrupted by a large, ugly woman, the Archduchess Harriet of Roumania. She had heard of Orlando and wanted to meet him. She stayed so long in his vicinity that Orlando asked King Charles to send him to Constantinople as Ambassador Extraordinary.

His duties in the Turkish capital were so formal and arid that he became extremely bored and began to wander about the city in disguise. While he was abroad, the King of England made him a member of the Order of the Bath and granted him a dukedom by proxy.

The next morning Orlando could not be awakened, and for seven days he slept soundly. When at last he did rouse himself, he was no longer a man. He had become a beautiful woman. In confusion Orlando left Constantinople and joined a gipsy tribe. Although Orlando spent many happy days in the gipsy camp, she could not bring herself to settle down among them. Selling some of the pearls she had brought with her from Constantinople, she set sail for England.

She noticed a difference in attitudes while on the ship. She who had been a man now received courteous attention from the captain, and she saw that her new role would require new responsibilities and bring new privileges. Back in England, she learned that all her estates were in chancery, for she was considered legally dead. At her country house she was received courteously by her servants. Again she was haunted by the Archduchess Harriet, who now, however, had become a man, the Archduke Harry, but at last she managed to rid herself of his attentions.

Orlando went to London to get a taste of society. The reign of Queen Anne was a brilliant one. Conversation flowed freely, and dinners and receptions were entertaining affairs. Addison, Dryden, and Pope were the great names of the age. After a time, however, intercourse with the great wits began to pall, and Orlando went looking for adventure. She began to associate with women of the streets and pubs and found their earthiness a welcome change from the formalities of the drawing-room. But the company of women without men soon grew dull and repetitive.

At last came the darkness and doubt of the Victorian era. Orlando saw that marriage, under Victoria's influence, was the career toward which most women were striving. Orlando married a man named Marmaduke Bonthrop Shelmerdine, Esquire, who took off immediately on a sea voyage. A wedding ring on her left hand, however, was Orlando's emblem of belonging to accepted society. Orlando's lawsuits had been settled in her favor, but they had been so expensive that she was no longer a rich woman.

She went into London, where she saw her old friend Greene, now a prominent literary critic. He offered to find a publisher for her poem, "The Oak Tree." London itself had become a roaring metropolis. It was October 11, 1928. Orlando began to muse over her long heritage. She recalled Sasha, the archduchess, Constantinople, the archduke, the eighteenth century, and the nineteenth. She saw herself now as the culmination of many influences.

She drove back to her country house and walked out to the great oak tree where, more than three hundred years before, she had watched the arrival of Queen Elizabeth. The stable clock began to strike twelve. She heard a roar in the heavens. Shelmerdine, now a sea captain of renown, was arriving home by plane.

ORPHEUS AND EURYDICE

Type of work: Classical myth
Source: Folk tradition
Type of plot: Allegory of grief
Time of plot: The Golden Age
Locale: Thrace and the Underworld
First transcribed: Unknown

Principal characters:
ORPHEUS, a musician
EURYDICE, his wife

Critique:

Although there exists a large body of literature called Orphic poems because of the claim that Orpheus composed them, it is now believed that these compositions date from the worship of Orpheus in Thrace. The story of Orpheus and Eurydice is concerned with beauty in music, as well as an assurance of immortality. As in many myths, a love of beauty and a recognition of the deeply spiritual exist side by side with cruelty and barbarism, and it is well to remember that this story partakes of both civilized virtues and savage vices.

The Story:

Orpheus, son of Apollo and the muse Calliope, grew up in Thrace, a land long noted for the purity and richness of its divine gift of song. His father presented him with a lyre and taught him to play it. So lovely were the songs of Orpheus that the wild beasts followed him when he played, and even the trees, the rocks and the hills gathered near him. It was said his music softened the composition of stones.

Orpheus charmed Eurydice with his music, but to their wedding Hymen brought no happy omens. His torch smoked so that tears came to their eyes. Passionately in love with his wife, Orpheus became mad with grief when Eurydice died. Fleeing from a shepherd who desired her, she had stepped upon a snake and died from its bite.

Heartbroken, Orpheus wandered over the hills composing and singing melancholy songs of memory for the lost Eurydice. Finally he descended into the Underworld and made his way past the sentries by means of his music. Approaching the throne of Proserpine and Hades, he sang a lovely song in which he said love had brought him to the Underworld. He complained that Eurydice had been taken from him before her time and if they would not release her, he himself would not leave Hades. Proserpine and Hades could not resist his pleas. They agreed to set Eurydice free if Orpheus would promise not to look upon her until they should safely reach the Upperworld.

The music of Orpheus was so tender that even the ghosts shed tears. Tantalus forgot his search for water; Ixion's wheel stopped; the vulture stopped feeding on the giant's liver; the daughters of Danaus stopped drawing water, and Sisyphus himself stopped to listen. Tears streamed from the eyes of the Furies. Eurydice then appeared, limping. The two walked the long and dismal passageway to the Upperworld and Orpheus did not look back toward Eurydice. At last, forgetting his vow, he turned, but as they reached out their arms to embrace Eurydice disappeared.

Orpheus tried to follow her, but the stern ferryman refused him passage across the River Styx. Declining food and drink, he sat by the River Strymon and sang his twice-felt grief.

As he sang his melancholy songs, so sad that oaks moved and tigers grieved, a group of Thracian maidens attempted to console him, but he repulsed them. One day, while they were observing the sacred rites of Bacchus, they began to stone him. At first the stones fell without harm when they came within the sound of the lyre. However, as the frenzy of the maidens increased, their shouting drowned out the notes of the lyre so that it no longer protected Orpheus. Soon he was covered with blood.

Then the savage women tore his limbs from his body and hurled his head and his lyre into the river. Both continued singing sad songs as they floated downstream. The fragments of Orpheus' body were buried at Libethra, and it is said that nightingales sang more sweetly over his grave than in any other part of Greece. Jupiter made his lyre a constellation of stars in the heavens. Orpheus himself joined Eurydice in the Underworld, and there, happy at last, they wandered through the fields together.

OTHELLO

Type of work: Drama
Author: William Shakespeare (1564-1616)
Type of plot: Romantic tragedy
Time of plot: Early sixteenth century
Locale: Venice and Cyprus
First presented: 1604

Principal characters:
OTHELLO, the Moor of Venice
DESDEMONA, his wife
IAGO, a villain
CASSIO, Othello's lieutenant
EMILIA, Iago's wife

Critique:

The Tragedy of Othello, The Moor of Venice is one of the four great tragedies written in what literary historians call Shakespeare's period of despair, a time when the bard seemed to be preëminently concerned with the struggle of evil and good in the human soul. Alone of the four tragedies—*Othello, Hamlet, King Lear,* and *Macbeth*—*Othello* might be said to be ill-motivated. Iago, the villain of the piece, is perhaps the most sadistic and consummately evil character in any literature. In *Othello,* love triumphs over evil and hate, and the love of one woman for another is instrumental in bringing the villain to poetic justice.

The Story:

Iago, an ensign serving under Othello, Moorish commander of the armed forces of Venice, was passed over in promotion, Othello having chosen Cassio to be his chief of staff. In revenge, Iago and his follower, Roderigo, aroused from his sleep Brabantio, senator of Venice, to tell him that his daughter Desdemona had stolen away and married Othello. Brabantio, incensed that his daughter would marry a Moor, led his serving-men to Othello's quarters.

Meanwhile, the Duke of Venice had learned that armed Turkish galleys were preparing to attack the island of Cyprus and in this emergency he had summoned Othello to the senate chambers. Brabantio and Othello met in the streets, but postponed any violence in the national interest. Othello, upon arriving at the senate, was commanded by the duke to lead the Venetian forces to Cyprus. Then Brabantio told the duke that Othello had beguiled his daughter into marriage without her father's consent. When Brabantio asked the duke for redress, Othello vigorously defended his honor and reputation, and he was seconded by Desdemona, who appeared during the proceedings. Othello, clear of all suspicion, prepared to sail for Cyprus immediately. For the moment, he placed Desdemona in the care of Iago, with Iago's wife, Emilia, to be attendant upon her during the voyage to Cyprus.

A great storm destroyed the Turkish fleet and scattered the Venetians. One by one the ships under Othello's command put into Cyprus until all were safely ashore and Othello and Desdemona were once again united. Still vowing revenge, Iago told Roderigo that Desdemona was in love with Cassio. Roderigo, himself in love with Desdemona, was promised all of his desires by Iago if he would engage Cassio, who did not know him, in a personal brawl while Cassio was officer of the guard.

Othello declared the night dedicated to celebrating the destruction of the enemy, but he cautioned Cassio to keep a careful watch on Venetian troops in the city. Iago talked Cassio into drinking too much, so that when the lieutenant was provoked later by Roderigo, Cassio lost control of himself and engaged Roderigo. Cries of riot and mutiny spread through the streets. Othello, aroused by the commotion, demoted Cassio for permitting a fight to start. Cassio, his reputation all but ruined, welcomed Iago's promise to secure Desdemona's good-will and through her have Othello restore Cassio's rank.

Cassio impatiently importuned Iago to arrange a meeting between him and Desdemona. While Cassio and Desdemona were talking, Iago brought Othello into view of the pair, and spoke vague innuendoes to his commander. Afterward Iago would, from time to time, ask questions of Othello in such manner that he led Othello to believe that there may have been some intimacy between Cassio and Desdemona before Desdemona had married him. These seeds of jealousy having been sown, Othello began to doubt the honesty of his wife.

When Othello complained to Desdemona of a headache, she offered to bind his head with the handkerchief which had been Othello's first gift to her. She dropped the handkerchief, inadvertently, and Emilia picked it up. Iago, seeing an opportunity to further his scheme, took the handkerchief from his wife and hid it later in Cassio's room. When Othello asked Iago for proof that Desdemona was untrue to him, threatening his life if he could not produce any evidence, Iago said that he had slept in Cassio's room and had heard Cassio speak sweet words in his sleep to Desdemona. He reminded Othello of the handkerchief and said that he had seen Cassio wipe his beard that day with the very handkerchief. Othello, completely overcome by passion, vowed revenge. He ordered Iago to kill Cassio, and he appointed the ensign his new lieutenant.

Othello asked Desdemona to account for the loss of the handkerchief, but she was unable to explain its disappearance. She was mystified by Othello's shortness of speech, and his dark moods.

Iago continued to work his treachery on Othello to the extent that the Moor fell into fits resembling epilepsy. He goaded Othello by every possible means into mad rages of jealousy. In the presence of an envoy from Venice, Othello struck Desdemona, to the consternation of all except Iago. Emilia swore to the honesty of her mistress, but Othello, in his madness, could no longer believe anything good of Desdemona, and he reviled and insulted her with harsh words.

One night Othello ordered Desdemona to dismiss her attendant and to go to bed immediately. That same night Iago persuaded Roderigo to waylay Cassio. When Roderigo was wounded by Cassio, Iago, who had been standing nearby, stabbed Cassio. In the scuffle Iago stabbed Roderigo to death as well, so as to be rid of his dupe. Then a strumpet friend of Cassio came upon the scene of the killing and revealed to the assembled crowd her relationship with Cassio. Although Cassio was not dead, Iago hoped to use this woman to defame Cassio beyond all hope of regaining his former reputation. Pretending friendship, he assisted the wounded Cassio to return to Othello's house. They were accompanied by Venetian noblemen who had gathered after the fight.

Othello, meanwhile, entered his wife's bedchamber and smothered her, after telling her, mistakenly, that Cassio had confessed his love for her and had been killed. Then Emilia entered the bedchamber and reported that Roderigo had been killed, but not Cassio. This information made doubly bitter for Othello his murder of his wife. Othello told Emilia that he had learned of Desdemona's guilt from Iago. Emilia could not believe that Iago had made such charges.

When Iago and other Venetians arrived at Othello's house, Emilia asked Iago to refute Othello's statement. Then the great wickedness of Iago came to light and Othello learned how the handkerchief had come into Cassio's possession. When Emilia gave further proof of her husband's villainy, Iago stabbed her. Othello lunged at Iago and managed to wound him before the Venetian gentlemen could seize the Moor. Emilia died, still protesting the innocence of Desdemona. Mad with grief, Othello plunged a dagger into his own heart. The Venetian envoy promised that Iago would be tortured to death at the hands of the governor-general of Cyprus.

OUR TOWN

Type of work: Drama
Author: Thornton Wilder (1897-)
Type of plot: Domestic romance
Time of plot: 1901-1913
Locale: New Hampshire
First presented: 1938

Principal characters:
DR. GIBBS, a physician
MRS. GIBBS, his wife
GEORGE, and
REBECCA, their children
MR. WEBB, a newspaper editor
MRS. WEBB, his wife
EMILY, and
WALLY, their children
SIMON STIMSON, director of the choir

Critique:

This play won the Pulitzer Prize in 1938. Portraying typical American small-town life, the play employs a minimum of scenery. A stage manager remains informally on the stage throughout the play and helps to explain much of the action. The tender and simple love story of George Gibbs and Emily Webb is the thread upon which the plot is strung. *Our Town* is an exceptionally fresh retelling of a timeless, nostalgic story.

The Story:

Early one morning in 1901 Dr. Gibbs returned to his home in Grover's Corners, New Hampshire. He had just been across the tracks to Polish Town to deliver Mrs. Goruslowski's twins. On the street he met Joe Crowell, the morning paper boy, and Howie Newsome, the milkman. The day's work was beginning in Grover's Corners.

Mrs. Gibbs had breakfast ready when her husband arrived, and she called the children, George and Rebecca, to the table. After breakfast the children left for school in the company of the Webb children, Wally and Emily, who lived across the way.

After the children had gone, Mrs. Gibbs stepped out to feed her chickens. Seeing Mrs. Webb stringing beans in her back yard, she crossed over to talk with her. Mrs. Gibbs had been offered three hundred and fifty dollars for some antique furniture; she would sell the furniture, she had decided, if she could get Dr. Gibbs to take a vacation with her. But Dr. Gibbs had no wish to take a vacation; if he could visit the Civil War battlegrounds every other year, he was satisfied.

The warm day passed, and the children began to come home from school. Emily Webb walked home alone pretending she was a great lady. George Gibbs, on his way to play baseball, stopped to talk to Emily and told her how much he admired her success at school. He could not, he insisted, imagine how anyone could spend so much time over homework as she did. Flattered, Emily promised to help George with his algebra. He said that he did not really need school work, because he was going to be a farmer as soon as he graduated from high school.

When George had gone, Emily ran to her mother and asked if she were pretty enough to make boys notice her. Grudgingly, her mother admitted that she was, but Mrs. Webb tried to turn Emily's mind to other subjects.

That evening, while Mrs. Webb and Mrs. Gibbs were at choir practice, George and Emily sat upstairs studying. Their windows faced each other, and George called to Emily for some advice on his algebra. Emily helped him, but she was more interested in the moonlight. When she called George's attention to the beautiful night, he seemed only mildly interested.

The ladies coming home from choir practice gossiped about their leader, Simon Stimson. He drank most of the time, and for some reason he could not adjust himself to small-town life. The ladies wondered how it would all end. Mr. Webb also wondered. He was the editor of the local paper; and, as he came home, he met Simon roaming the deserted streets. When Mr. Webb reached his home, he found Emily still gazing out of her window at the moon—and dreaming.

At the end of his junior year in high school George was elected president of his class, and Emily was elected secretary-treasurer. When George walked home with Emily after the election, she seemed so cold and indifferent that George asked for an explanation. She told him that all the girls thought him conceited and stuck-up because he cared more for baseball than he did for his friends. She expected men to be perfect, like her father and his.

George said that men could not be perfect, but that women could—like Emily. Then Emily began to cry, insisting that she was far from perfect. George offered to buy her a soda. As they drank their sodas, they found that they really had liked each other for a long time. George said he thought he would not go away to agricultural school, after all. When he graduated from high school, he would start right in working on the farm.

After a time Dr. and Mrs. Gibbs learned that George wanted to marry Emily as soon as he left high school. At first it was a shock to them, for they could not imagine that George was anything but a child. They wondered how he could provide for a wife; whether Emily could take care of a house. Then Dr. and Mrs. Gibbs remembered their own first years of married life. They had had troubles, but now they felt that the troubles had been overshadowed by their joys. They decided that George could marry Emily if he wished.

On the morning of his wedding day George dropped in on Mr. and Mrs. Webb, and Mrs. Webb left the men alone so that her husband could advise George. But all that Mr. Webb had to say was that no one could advise anyone else on matters as personal as marriage.

When George had gone, Emily came down to her last breakfast in her parents' home. Both she and Mrs. Webb cried. Mrs. Webb had meant to give her daughter some advice on marriage, but she was unable to bring herself to it.

At the church, just before the ceremony, both Emily and George felt as if they were making a mistake; they did not want to get married. By the time the music started, however, both of them were calm. The wedding ceremony was soon over. And Grover's Corners lost one of its best baseball players.

Nine years passed; it was the summer of 1913. Up in the graveyard above the town the dead lay, resting from the cares of their lives on earth. Now there was a new grave; Emily had died in childbirth and George was left alone with his four-year-old son.

It was raining as the funeral procession wound its way up the hill to the new grave. Then Emily appeared shyly before the other dead. Solemnly they welcomed her to her rest. But she did not want to rest; she wanted to live over again the joys of her life. It was possible to do so, but the others warned her against trying to relive a day in her mortal life.

Emily chose to live over her twelfth

birthday. At first it was exciting to be young again, but the excitement wore off quickly. The day held no joy, now that Emily knew what was in store for the future. It was unbearably painful to realize how unaware she had been of the meaning and wonder of life while she was alive. Simon Stimson, a suicide, told her that life was like that, a time of ignorance and blindness and folly. He was still bitter in death.

Emily returned to her resting place. When night had fallen, George approached full of grief and threw himself on Emily's grave. She felt pity for him and for all the rest of the living. For now she knew how little they really understood of the wonderful gift that is life itself.

THE OX-BOW INCIDENT

Type of work: Novel
Author: Walter Van Tilburg Clark (1909-)
Type of plot: Regional realism
Time of plot: 1885
Locale: Nevada
First published: 1940

Principal characters:
GIL CARTER, a ranch hand
CROFT, his friend
CANBY, a saloon keeper
TETLEY, a rancher
GERALD, his son
DAVIES, an old storekeeper
MARTIN, a young rancher

Critique:

The Ox-Bow Incident begins as a Western horse-opera with all the stage settings and characters of a cowboy thriller, but it ends as a saga of human misery. The novel has the action and the pace of a classic drama. The mob assumes the nature of a Greek chorus, now on one side, now on the other. The story rises toward an inevitable climax and as it does so it states a harsh truth forcibly—the law of survival is linked to an incredible curse of relentless cruelty. Clark has made the Western thriller a novel of art.

The Story:

Gil Carter, a cow puncher, and his friend Croft rode into the little frontier town of Bridger's Wells. At Canby's saloon they reined in their horses. Canby was alone at the bar, and he served Gil and Croft with silent glumness.

Canby told them that Rose Mapen, the girl Gil sought, had gone to Frisco. He also told the two cowboys that all the local cowhands and their employers were on the lookout for rustlers who were raiding the ranches in the valley. More than six hundred head of cattle had been stolen and the ranchers were even regarding one another with suspicion. Gil and Croft felt suspicion leveled at them when a group of riders and town men came into the bar.

Gil began to play poker and won hand after hand. The stakes and the bad feeling grew higher until finally Gil and a man named Farnley closed in a rough row. Gil downed his opponent but was himself knocked unconscious when Canby hit him over the head with a bottle.

A rider rode up to the saloon with the word that rustlers had killed Kinkaid, Farnley's friend. Farnley did not want to wait for a posse to be formed, but cooler heads prevailed, among them old Davies, a storekeeper, and Osgood, the Baptist minister. Everyone there joined in the argument, some for, some opposed to, immediate action.

Davies sent Croft and a young cowboy named Joyce to ask Judge Tyler to swear in a posse before a lawless man hunt began. The judge was not eager to swear in a posse in the absence of Risley, the sheriff, but Mapes, a loud, swaggering, newly appointed deputy, demanded that he be allowed to lead the posse.

Meanwhile the tempers of the crowd began to grow sullen. Ma Grier, who kept a boarding-house, joined the mob. Then Judge Tyler arrived and his long-winded oration against a posse stirred the men up more than anything else could have done. Davies took over again and almost convinced the men they should disband. But at that moment Tetley, a former Confederate officer and an important rancher, rode up with word that his Mexican herder had seen the rustlers.

Mob spirit flared up once more. Mapes deputized the men in spite of Judge Tyler's assertion that a deputy could not deputize others. The mob rode off in the direction of Drew's ranch, where Kinkaid had been killed.

There the riders found the first trace of their quarry. Tracks showed that three riders were driving forty head of cattle toward a pass through the range.

Along the way Croft talked to Tetley's sullen son, Gerald. Gerald was not cut out to be a rancher, a fact ignored by his stern, domineering father. Croft thought the boy appeared emotional and unmanly.

The stagecoach suddenly appeared over a rise. In the darkness and confusion, the driver thought that the riders were attempting a holdup. He fired, hitting Croft high in the chest. When he learned his mistake, he pulled up his horses and stopped. One of the passengers was Rose Mapen, the girl Gil had hoped to find in Bridger's Wells. She introduced the man with her as her husband. Gil was furious.

Croft had his wound doctored and continued on with the posse. On a tip from the passengers, the posse headed for the Ox-Bow, a small valley high up in the range.

Snow was falling by the time the riders came to the Ox-Bow. Through the darkness they saw the flicker of a campfire and heard the sound of cattle. Surrounding the campfire, they surprised the three men sleeping there, an old man, a young, dark-looking man, and a Mexican. The prisoners were seized and tied.

The dark-looking young man insisted there was some mistake. He said that he was Donald Martin and that he had moved into Pike's Hole three days before. But one of the members of the posse, a man from Pike's Hole, claimed he did not know Martin or anything about him. Martin began to grow desperate. He demanded to be taken to Pike's Hole, where his wife and two children were. The members of the posse were contemptuous.

Only Davies tried to defend Martin, but Mapes soon silenced the old storekeeper. The cattle were proof enough. Besides, Martin had no bill of sale. He claimed that Drew, who had sold him the cattle, had promised to mail a bill of sale later.

The posse was for an immediate hanging. Tetley wanted to force a confession, but most of the riders said it was no kindness to make the three wait to die. Martin told them that the Mexican was only his rider, that he did not know much about him because the man spoke no English. The old man was a simple-minded fellow who had agreed to work for Martin for very little pay.

Martin was permitted to write a letter to his wife. Shortly afterward it was discovered that the Mexican possessed Kinkaid's gun. He began to speak

English. He claimed that he had found Kinkaid's gun.

Tetley appointed three of the posse to lead the horses out away from the men, whose necks would then be caught in the nooses of the ropes tied to the overhanging limb of a tree. He insisted that his milksop son was to be one of the three. Farnley was another. Ma Grier was the third.

Martin became bitter and unforgiving. He made Davies promise to look after his wife and he gave Davies the letter and a ring. A fine snow continued to fall.

The three were executed. The Mexican and the old man died cleanly. Martin, whose horse had been slowly started by Gerald, had to be shot by Farnley. Tetley felled his son with the butt of his pistol for bungling the hanging. Then the posse rode away.

As they rode out of the Ox-Bow they met Sheriff Risley, Judge Tyler, Drew, and Kinkaid, who was not dead after all. The judge shouted that every member of the posse would be tried for murder. The sheriff, however, said that he could not arrest a single man present for the murders because identity was uncertain in the swirling snow. He asked for ten volunteers to continue the search for the real rustlers.

Only old Davies seemed moved by the affair, more so after he learned that Martin's story was true and that the cattle had been bought from Drew without a bill of sale. Nearly maddened, he gave the ring and letter to Drew, who promised to look after Martin's widow.

After Croft and Gil had returned to Canby's saloon, Davies began to moan to Croft. Davies now had the idea that he himself had caused the hanging of the three men. Gil got drunk. That day Gerald Tetley hanged himself. A few hours later Gerald's father also committed suicide. The cowhands took up a collection for Martin's widow. In their room at Canby's, Gil and Croft could hear Rose laughing and talking in the bar. They decided to leave town.

PAMELA

Type of work: Novel
Author: Samuel Richardson (1689-1761)
Type of plot: Sentimental romance
Time of plot: Early eighteenth century
Locale: England
First published: 1740-1741

Principal characters:
- Pamela Andrews, a servant girl
- Mr. B—, her master
- Mrs. Jervis, Mr. B—'s housekeeper
- Mrs. Jewkes, caretaker of Mr. B—'s country home
- Lady Davers, Mr. B—'s sister

Critique:

Pamela, or, Virtue Rewarded is a romantic tale that created, in effect, the epistolary form of the novel. Richardson's obvious absorption in preaching a moral does not hold our attention today, but the work is valuable for the picture it presents of life in the eighteenth century and of the code of morals to which people then held. The device of letter writing to tell a story does not always stand up under the test of reality, but its failure is more a matter for amusement than for condemnation. Richardson was a pioneer of the English novel, and he wrote with a moral earnestness and innocence of technique impossible for the modern writer.

The Story:

Pamela Andrews had been employed

from a very young age as the servant girl of Lady B—, at her estate in Bedfordshire. Because she had grown very fond of her mistress, the letter to her parents telling of her ladyship's death expressed her deep sorrow. Her own plans were uncertain. But it soon became clear that Lady B—'s son wanted her to remain in his household. Taking her hand before all the other servants, he had said that he would be a good master to Pamela for his dear mother's sake if she continued faithful and diligent. Mrs. Jervis, the housekeeper, put in a friendly word as well, and Pamela, not wishing to be a burden upon her poor parents, decided to remain in the service of Mr. B—. Shortly, however, she began to doubt that his intentions toward her were honorable. And when, one day, he kissed her while she sat sewing in a summerhouse, she found herself in a quandary as to what to do.

Once again she discussed the situation with the good Mrs. Jervis, and decided to stay if she could share the housekeeper's bed. Mr. B— was extremely annoyed at this turn of affairs. He tried to persuade Mrs. Jervis that Pamela was in reality a very designing creature who should be carefully watched. When he learned that she was writing long letters to her parents, telling them in great detail of his false proposals and repeating her determination to keep her virtue, he had as many of her letters intercepted as possible.

In a frightening interview between Mr. B—, Pamela, and Mrs. Jervis, he intimidated the housekeeper by his terrifying manner and told Pamela to return to her former poverty. After talking the matter over with her friend, however, Pamela decided that Mr. B— had given up his plan to ruin her and that there was no longer any reason for her to leave. But another interview with Mr. B— convinced her that she should return to her parents upon the completion of some household duties entrusted to her. When Mr. B— discovered that she was indeed planning to leave, a furious scene followed, in which he accused her of pride beyond her station. That night he concealed himself in the closet of her room. When she discovered him, she threw herself on the bed and fell into a fit. Both Pamela and Mrs. Jervis served notice. In spite of Mr. B—'s threats on the one hand and his cajolings on the other, Pamela remained firm in her decision to return home. The housekeeper was reinstated in her position, but Pamela set out by herself in the coach Mr. B— had ordered to return her to her parents.

What she had thought Mr. B—'s kindness was but designing trickery. Instead of arriving at her parents' humble home, Pamela now found herself a prisoner at Mr. B—'s country estate, to which the coachman had driven her. Mrs. Jewkes, the caretaker, had none of Mrs. Jervis' kindness of heart, and Pamela found herself cruelly confined. It was only by clever scheming that she could continue to send letters to her parents. She was aided by Mr. Williams, the village minister, who smuggled her mail out of the house. The young man soon confessed his love for Pamela and his desire to marry her. Pamela refused his offer, but devised with his help a plan to escape. Unfortunately, Mrs. Jewkes was too wily a jailer. When she suspected that the two were secretly planning for Pamela's escape, she wrote to Mr. B—, who was still in London. Pamela's persecutor, aided by his agents, contrived to have Mr. Williams thrown into jail on a trumped-up charge.

Although her plot had been discovered, Pamela did not allow herself to be discouraged. That night she dropped from her window into the garden. But when she tried to escape from the garden, she found the gate padlocked. Mrs. Jewkes discovered her cringing in the woodshed. From that time on her warder's vigilance and cruelty increased.

Mr. B— at length arrived, and frightened Pamela still further with his threats.

With the help of Mrs. Jewkes, he attempted to force himself upon her, but opportunely Pamela was seized by fits. Mr. B— expressed his remorse and promised never to attempt to molest her again. And now Pamela began to suspect that her virtue would soon be rewarded, for Mr. B— proposed marriage to her. But as she was enjoying the thought of being Mrs. B—, an anonymous warning arrived, suggesting that she beware of a sham marriage. Pamela was greatly upset. At her request, a coach was called and she set out to visit her parents. On the way, however, letters arrived from Mr. B— entreating her to return to him, and offering an honorable proposal of marriage.

Pamela returned immediately to Mr. B—'s hall, for in spite of all that had passed she found that she was in love with Mr. B—. He, in turn, was delighted with her beauty and goodness. She and Mr. B— were married by Mr. Williams before a few witnesses. Mr. Andrews, Pamela's father, was present and great was the rejoicing in the Andrews household when he returned and told of his daughter's virtue, and of the happiness it had brought her.

Pamela readily adapted herself to her new role as the wife of a gentleman. With typical virtue, she quickly forgave Mrs. Jewkes for her former ill-treatment. The only flaw in her married state was the fact that Lady Davers, Mr. B—'s sister, was angry with her brother because of his marriage to a servant girl. Pamela was alone when Lady Davers arrived. She so insulted Pamela that the poor girl fled to her husband for consolation. A terrible scene took place between Mr. B— and Lady Davers, but Pamela soon won the love and respect of that good woman when she showed her the letters she had written about her earlier sufferings.

One day Mr. B— told Pamela of a previous love affair with Miss Sally Godfrey and took her to see his daughter, who had been placed in a boarding-school in the neighborhood. Pamela liked the little girl and asked to have the pretty child under her care at some later date.

Mr. and Mrs. Andrews were pleased with Pamela's accounts of her happiness and of Mr. B—'s goodness to her. He gave the old people a substantial gift of money and thus enabled them to set themselves up in a small but comfortable business.

Lady Davers' correspondence with Pamela continued at a great length, and more and more she expressed her approval of Pamela's virtue and her disgust with her brother's attempts to dishonor her. During a visit she paid the young couple, Mr. B— expressed his regret for his earlier unmannerly conduct toward the one who had become his dearly beloved wife.

Mr. B—'s uncle, Sir Jacob Swynford, paid his nephew a visit, prepared to detest the inferior creature Mr. B— had married. But Pamela's charm, beauty, and virtue won his heart completely, and the grumpy old man left full of praises for his lovely niece.

At last Mr. B— and Pamela decided to leave the country and return to London. Although her husband was still as attentive and thoughtful as ever, Pamela began to suspect that he might be carrying on an intrigue with another woman. She was particularly distressed that she could not accompany him to the theater and other places of amusement as she was about to bear a child. The scene of the christening of their son was very gay, for besides the family, tenants from the estate arrived to express their joy that Mr. B— now had a son and heir.

But Pamela's suspicions after all had been justified. An anonymous note informed her that the business trip which Mr. B— had taken was in reality a journey to a neighboring city with a countess with whom he was having an affair. Pamela controlled her passions, and when Lord B— returned he was so overcome by this further evidence of her kindness and understanding that he begged her forgiveness and promised to remain faithful to her from that day on. Pamela made good use of the letters she had written to Lady Davers during this trying period by sending them to the countess that she might learn from them and turn away from the path of license.

True to her earlier wish, Pamela decided to take in Sally Godfrey's child and bring her up as a sister for her own son, Billy. Mr. B— was faithful to his resolve to devote himself only to his wife, and he spent the remainder of his days admiring and praising her virtue.

PARADISE LOST

Type of work: Poem
Author: John Milton (1608-1674)
Type of plot: Epic
Time of plot: The Beginning
Locale: Heaven, Hell, and Earth
First published: 1667

Principal characters:
God The Father
Christ The Son
Lucifer, called Satan
Adam
Eve

Critique:

John Milton prepared himself for many years for the creation of an epic poem in English that would rank with the epics of Homer and Virgil. He had planned to write it on the Arthurian Cycle, but after his identity with the Puritans and with individual liberty during the struggle between King and Parliament, he chose the fall of man as his subject. *Paradise Lost* is the epic of mankind, the story of Paradise lost and sought for in the life of every man.

The Story:

In Heaven Lucifer, unable to abide the supremacy of God, led a revolt against divine authority. Defeated, he and his followers were cast into Hell, where they lay nine days on a burning lake. Lucifer, now called Satan, arose from the flaming pitch and vowed that all was not lost, that he would have revenge for his downfall. Arousing his legions, he reviewed them under the canopy of Hell and decided his purposes could be achieved by guile rather than by force.

Under the direction of Mulciber, the forces of evil built an elaborate palace in which Satan convened a congress to decide on immediate action. At the meeting, Satan reasserted the unity of those fallen, and opened the floor to a debate on what measures to take. Moloch advised war. Belial recommended a slothful existence in Hell. Mammon proposed peacefully improving Hell so that it might rival Heaven in splendor. His motion was received with great favor until Beelzebub, second in command, arose and informed the conclave that God had created Earth, which he had peopled with good creatures called humans. It was Beelzebub's proposal to investigate this new creation, seize it, and seduce its inhabitants to the cause of the fallen angels.

Announcing that he would journey to the Earth to learn for himself how matters were there, Satan flew to the gate of Hell. There he encountered his daughter, Sin, and his son, Death. They opened the gate and Satan winged his way toward Earth.

God, in His omniscience, beheld the meeting in Hell, knew the intents of the evil angels, and saw Satan approaching the Earth. Disguised as various beasts, Satan acquainted himself with Adam and Eve and with the Tree of Knowledge, which God had forbidden to Man.

Uriel, learning that an evil angel had broken through to Eden, warned Gabriel, who appointed two angels to hover about the bower of Adam and Eve. The guardian angels arrived too late to prevent Satan, in the form of a toad, from beginning his evil work. He had influenced Eve's dreams.

Upon awaking, Eve told Adam that in her strange dream she had been tempted to taste of the fruit of the Tree of Knowledge. God, seeing danger to Adam and Eve was imminent, sent the angel Raphael to the garden to warn them. At Adam's insistence, Raphael related in detail the story of the great war between the good and the bad angels and of the fall of the bad angels to eternal misery in Hell. At Adam's further inquiries, Raphael told of the creation of the world and of how the Earth was created in six days, an angelic choir singing the praises of God on the seventh day. He cautioned Adam not to be too curious, that there were many things done by God which were not for Man to understand or to attempt to understand. Adam then told how he had been warned against the Tree of Knowledge of Good and Evil, how he had asked God for fellowship in his loneliness, and how Eve was created from his rib.

After the departure of Raphael, Satan returned as a mist to the garden and entered the body of a sleeping serpent. In the morning, as Adam and Eve proceeded to their day's occupation, Eve proposed that they work apart. Adam, remembering the warning of Raphael, opposed her wishes, but Eve prevailed, and the couple parted. Alone, Eve was accosted by the serpent, which flattered her into tasting the fruit of the Tree of Knowledge. Eve, liking what she tasted, took a fruit to Adam, who was horrified when he saw what Eve had done. But in his love for Eve, he also ate the fruit.

Having eaten, the couple knew lust for the first time, and after their dalliance they knew sickening shame. The guardian angels now deserted the transgressors and returned to God, who approved them, saying they could not have prevented Satan from succeeding in his mission.

Christ descended to Earth to pass judgment. Before Adam and Eve, who had been reluctant, in their shame, to come out of their bower to face him, Christ sentenced the serpent to be forever a hated enemy of mankind. He told Eve that her sorrow would be multiplied by the bearing of children and that she would be the servant of Adam to the end of time. Adam, said Christ, would eat in sorrow; his ground would be cursed and he would eat bread only by toiling and sweating.

Meanwhile, Death and Sin, having divined Satan's success, left the gates of Hell to join their father on Earth. Within sight of Earth, they met Satan, who delegated Sin and Death as his ambassadors on Earth. Back in Hell, Satan proudly reported his accomplishments to his followers. But he was acclaimed by hisses as his cohorts became serpents, and Satan himself was transformed into a serpent before their reptilian eyes. Trees similar to the Tree of Knowledge appeared in Hell, but when the evil angels tasted the fruit, they found their mouths full of ashes.

God, angered at the disaffection of Adam and Eve, brought about great changes on Earth. He created the seasons to replace eternal spring, and the violence and misery of storms, winds, hail, ice, floods, and earthquakes. He caused all Earth's creatures to prey upon one another.

Adam and Eve argued bitterly until they realized they must face their common plight together. Repenting their sins, they prayed to God for relief. Although Christ interceded for them, God sentenced them to expulsion from Eden and sent the angel Michael to Earth to carry out the sentence. Adam and Eve, lamenting their misfortune, contemplated suicide, but Michael gave them new hope when he brought to Adam a vision of life and death; of the rise and fall of kingdoms and empires; of the activities of Adam's and Eve's progeny through their evil days to the flood, when God destroyed all life except that preserved by Noah in the ark; and of the subsequent return to evil days and Christ's incarnation, death, resurrection, and ascension as mankind's redeemer.

Despite the violence and evil and bloodshed in the vision, Adam and Eve were pacified when they saw that mankind would be saved. They walked hand in hand from the heights of Paradise to the barren plains below.

A PASSAGE TO INDIA

Type of work: Novel
Author: E. M. Forster (1879-)
Type of plot: Social criticism
Time of plot: About 1920
Locale: India
First published: 1924

Principal characters:
Dr. Aziz, a young Indian surgeon
Mrs. Moore, a visiting Englishwoman, Dr. Aziz's friend
Ronald Heaslop, the City Magistrate, Mrs. Moore's son
Adela Quested, Ronald's fiancée, visiting India with Mrs. Moore
Cecil Fielding, Principal of the Government College, Dr. Aziz's friend

Critique:

A Passage to India has two aspects, political and mystic. Politically it deals with the tension between the natives and the British (now solved by the withdrawal of the British), and also with the tension between Hindus and Moslems (now solved by the creation of the two Dominions of India and Pakistan). Mystically it is concerned with the search after the infinite and the eternal, so characteristic of Oriental religion, and with the illogical and inexplicable element in human life. The visit to the Marabar Caves illustrates the malignant side of mysticism, the Temple-Festival at the close illustrates its benignity. The three sections into which the book is divided correspond to the three seasons of the Indian year—the Cold Weather, the Hot Weather, the Rains.

The Story:

Dr. Aziz had been doubly snubbed that evening. He had been summoned to the civil surgeon's house while he was at supper, but when he arrived he found that his superior had departed for his club without bothering to leave any message. In addition, two Englishwomen emerged from the house and took their departure in his hired tonga without even thanking him.

The doctor started back toward the city of Chandrapore afoot. Tired, he stopped at a mosque to rest and was furiously angry when he saw a third Englishwoman emerge from behind its pillars with, as he thought, her shoes on. Mrs. Moore, however, had gone barefoot to the mosque, and in a surge of friendly feeling Dr. Aziz engaged her in conversation.

Mrs. Moore had newly arrived from England to visit her son, Ronald Heaslop, the City Magistrate. Dr. Aziz found they had common ground when he learned that she did not care for the civil surgeon's wife. Her disclosure prompted him to tell of the usurpation of his carriage. The doctor walked back to the club with her, although as an Indian, he himself could not be admitted.

At the club, Adela Quested, Heaslop's prospective fiancée, declared she wanted to see the real India, not the India which came to her through the rarified atmosphere of the British colony. To please the ladies one of the members offered to hold what he whimsically termed a bridge party and to invite some native guests.

The bridge party was a miserable affair. The Indians retreated to one side of a lawn and although the conspicuously reluctant group of Anglo-Indian ladies went over to visit the natives, an awkward tension prevailed.

There was, however, one promising result of the party. The principal of the Government College, Mr. Fielding, a man who apparently felt neither rancor nor arrogance toward the Indians, invited Mrs. Moore and Adela to a tea at his house. Upon Adela's request, Mr. Fielding also invited Professor Godbole, a teacher at his school, and Dr. Aziz.

At the tea Dr. Aziz charmed Fielding and the guests with the elegance and fine intensity of his manner. But the gathering broke up on a discordant note when the priggish and suspicious Heaslop arrived to claim the ladies. Fielding had taken Mrs. Moore on a tour of his school, and Heaslop was furious at him for having left Dr. Aziz alone with his prospective fiancée.

Adela, irritated by Heaslop's callous priggishness during her visit, informed him she did not wish to become his wife, but before the evening was over she changed her mind. In the course of a drive into the Indian countryside, a mysterious figure, perhaps an animal, loomed out of the darkness and nearly upset the car in which they were riding. Their mutual loneliness and a sense of the unknown drew them together and Adela asked Heaslop to disregard her earlier rejection.

The one extraordinary thing about the city of Chandrapore was a phenomenon of nature known as the Marabar Caves, located several miles outside the city. Mrs. Moore and Adela accepted the offer of Dr. Aziz to escort them to the caves; but the visit proved catastrophic for all. Entering one of the caves, Mrs. Moore realized that no matter what was said the walls returned only a prolonged booming, hollow echo. Pondering that echo while she rested, and pondering the distance that separated her from Dr. Aziz, from Adela and from her own children, Mrs. Moore saw that all her Christianity, all her ideas of moral good and bad, in short, all her ideas of life, amounted only to what was made of them by the hollow, booming echo of the Marabar Caves.

Adela entered one of the caves alone. A few minutes later she rushed out, terrified, claiming she had been nearly attacked in the gloom, and that Dr. Aziz was the attacker. The doctor was arrested.

There had always been a clear division between the natives and the Anglo-Indian community, but as the trial of Dr. Aziz drew nearer, the temper of each group demanded strict loyalty. When Mrs. Moore casually intimated to her son that she was perfectly certain Dr. Aziz was not capable of the alleged crime, he had her shipped off to a coastal port of embarkation at once. And when Fielding expressed an identical opinion at the club, he was promptly ostracized.

The tension which marked the opening of the trial had a strange resolution. The first sensational incident occurred when one of Dr. Aziz's friends pushed into the courtroom and shouted that Heaslop had smuggled his mother out of the country because she would have testified to the doctor's innocence. When the restless body of Indian spectators heard the name of Mrs. Moore, they worked it into a kind of chant as though she had become a deity. The English colony was not to learn until later that

Mrs. Moore had already died aboard ship.

The second incident concluded the trial. It was Adela's testimony. The effects of the tense atmosphere of the courtroom, the reiteration of Mrs. Moore's name, and the continued presence of a buzzing sound in her ears which had persisted since the time she left the caves, combined to produce a trance-like effect upon Adela. She virtually relived the whole of the crucial day as, under the interrogation of the prosecuting attorney, she recollected its events. When she reached the moment of her lingering in the cave, she faltered, dramatically changed her mind, and withdrew all charges.

Chandrapore was at once and for several hours thereafter a great bedlam. Anglo-India sulked while India exulted. As for Adela, so far as Anglo-India was concerned she had crossed the line. Heaslop carefully explained that he could no longer be associated with her. After accepting Fielding's hospitality for a few weeks, she returned home. In spite of Dr. Aziz's increased Anglophobia, Fielding persuaded him not to press Adela for legal damages.

Two years later the Mohammedan Dr. Aziz was court physician to an aged Hindu potentate who died on the night of the Krishna Festival. The feast was a frantic celebration and the whole town was under its spell when Fielding arrived on an official visit. During the two years he had married again, and Dr. Aziz, assuming he had married Adela Quested, tried to avoid his old friend. When he ran into him accidentally, however, he found out it was Mrs. Moore's daughter, Stella, whom Fielding had married. The doctor's shame at his mistake only caused him to become more distant.

Before they parted for the last time, Dr. Aziz and Fielding went riding through the jungles. The misunderstanding between them had now been cleared up, but they had no social ground on which to meet. Fielding had cast his lot with his countrymen by marrying an Englishwoman. The rocks which suddenly reared up before them, forcing their horses to pass in single file on either side, were symbolic of the different paths they would travel from that time on. The affection of two men, however sincere, was not sufficient to bridge the vast gap between their races.

THE PATHFINDER

Type of work: Novel
Author: James Fenimore Cooper (1789-1851)
Type of plot: Historical romance
Time of plot: 1756
Locale: Lake Ontario and surrounding territory
First published: 1840

Principal characters:
SERGEANT DUNHAM, of the Oswego garrison
MABEL DUNHAM, his daughter
CHARLES CAP, Mabel's uncle
NATTY BUMPPO, called Pathfinder, a frontier scout
JASPER WESTERN, Pathfinder's friend
LIEUTENANT DAVY MUIR, garrison quartermaster

Critique:

The Pathfinder portrays Natty Bumppo, wilderness scout, at the height of his powers. Here, too, Natty falls in love for the first and only time, but he relinquishes his claim in deference to the man his beloved really loves. This novel, written in the tradition of the romantic novel, is the third in the series of the

Leatherstocking Tales. The account of the fort at Oswego, one of the westernmost British frontier posts, is historical. The action, however, is completely fictional.

The Story:

Mabel Dunham and Charles Cap, her seaman uncle, were on their way to the home of her father, Sergeant Dunham. They were accompanied by Arrowhead, a Tuscarora Indian, and his wife, Dew-of-June. When they reached the Oswego River, they were met by Jasper Western and Natty Bumppo, the wilderness scout known as Pathfinder among the English and as Hawkeye among the Mohican Indians. Pathfinder led the party down the Oswego on the first step of the journey under his guidance. Chingachgook, Pathfinder's Mohican friend, warned the party of the presence of hostile Indians in the neighborhood. They hid from the Indians and had a narrow escape when they were discovered. Arrowhead and Dew-of-June disappeared; it was feared they had been taken captives. Chingachgook was captured by the Iroquois but escaped. On the lookout for more hostile war parties, they continued their journey to the fort, where Mabel was joyfully greeted by her father after her dangerous trip through the wilderness.

The sergeant tried to promote a feeling of love between Mabel and Pathfinder — his real purpose in bringing Mabel to the frontier. When Major Duncan, commander of the post, proposed Lieutenant Davy Muir as a possible mate for Mabel, the sergeant informed the major that Mabel was already betrothed to Pathfinder. Muir came to the major and learned that he had been refused, but he did not give up hope. Actually Mabel and Jasper were in love with each other.

A passage of arms was proposed to test the shooting ability of the men at the post. Jasper scored a bull's-eye. Muir shot from a strange position and it was believed by all that he had missed, but he said he had hit Jasper's bullet. Pathfinder used Jasper's rifle and also struck the bullet in the bull's-eye. The next test of marksmanship was to drive a nail into a tree with a bullet. Jasper almost drove the nail into the tree; Pathfinder did. The next test was shooting at a potato tossed into the air. Muir failed, but Jasper hit the potato in the center. A silken calash was the prize, and Jasper wanted it greatly as a present for Mabel. When he mentioned the desire to Pathfinder, the scout was able only to cut the skin of the potato. After he had lost the match, Pathfinder could not resist killing two gulls with one bullet. Then Mabel knew how Jasper had won the calash. In appreciation she gave Pathfinder a silver brooch.

An expedition was sent to one of the Thousand Islands to relieve the garrison there. The party was to leave in the *Scud,* a boat captured by Jasper. Before departing, however, Major Duncan had received a letter which caused him to suspect that Jasper was a French spy. Pathfinder refused to believe the charge against his friend, but when the *Scud* sailed under the command of Jasper he was kept under strict surveillance by Sergeant Dunham and Charles Cap. On the way, the *Scud* overtook Arrowhead and his wife and they were taken aboard. When Pathfinder began to question the Tuscarora, Arrowhead escaped in a canoe the *Scud* was towing astern. Becoming suspicious, Sergeant Dunham removed Jasper from his command and sent him below, and Charles Cap took over the management of the boat. But Cap, being a salt-water sailor, was unfamiliar with fresh-water navigation. When a storm came up, it was necessary to call upon Jasper to save the ship. The *Scud* escaped from *Le Montcalm,* a French ship, and Jasper brought the *Scud* safely to port.

Pathfinder had really fallen in love with Mabel, but when he proposed to her she refused him. Muir had not given up his own suit. He admitted to Mabel that he had had three previous wives.

Sergeant Dunham decided to take some of his men and harass a French supply boat. Starting out with his detachment, he left six men at the post, Muir among them, with orders to look after the women. Soon after her father's departure, Mabel went for a walk and met Dew-of-June, who warned her of danger from Indians led by white men. Muir was unmoved by this intelligence when Mabel informed him. Mabel then went to MacNab, a corporal, and told her story, but he treated Dew-of-June's warning lightly. While they talked, a rifle cracked in the nearby forest and MacNab fell dead at her feet. Mabel ran to the blockhouse. The attacking party was composed of twenty Indians led by the Tuscarora renegade, Arrowhead. Those who escaped the ambush were Mabel, Cap, and Muir, all of whom survived through the help of Dew-of-June. Cap and Muir were captured a little later. Mabel discovered Chingachgook, who had been spying about the fort. She acquainted him with all the details of the situation.

Pathfinder arrived secretly at the blockhouse. He had not been fooled by dead bodies of the massacred people that had been placed in lifelike manner along the river bank by the Indians. Then the relief party of soldiers under Sergeant Dunham was ambushed, but the sergeant, seriously wounded, managed to reach the blockhouse. Cap escaped from the Indians and also gained the protection of the blockhouse. The small group then fought off the Indians during the night. Jasper arrived with men in time to relieve the situation. But Muir ordered Jasper bound, basing his action on the suspicion that Jasper was a spy. Arrowhead stabbed Muir and disappeared into the bushes, hotly pursued by Chingachgook, who later killed him. Muir died and Captain Sanglier, the white leader of the Indians, admitted that Muir had been the French spy, not Jasper. On his deathbed Sergeant Dunham, thinking Jasper to be Pathfinder, took Jasper's hand, placed it in that of Mabel, and gave the two his blessing. He died before the surprised witnesses could correct his error. Deciding that Mabel really loved Jasper, Pathfinder relinquished his claim on her. Pathfinder disappeared into the wilderness with his Indian friend Chingachgook, and was seen no more by Jasper and Mabel. From time to time Indian messengers came to the settlement with gifts of furs for Mrs. Jasper Western, but no name ever accompanied these gifts.

PAUL BUNYAN

Type of work: Short stories
Author: James Stevens (1892-)
Type of plot: Folklore
Time of plot: From the Winter of the Blue Snow to the Spring That the Rain Came Up From China
Locale: North America
First published: 1925

Principal characters:
PAUL BUNYAN, a mighty hero
BABE, the Blue Ox
HELS HELSEN, Paul's friend
JOHNNY INKSLINGER, the surveyor
SOURDOUGH SAM, a cook
HOT BISCUIT SLIM, another cook, Sourdough Sam's son
KING BOURBON, King of Kansas
SHANTY BOY, a storyteller

Critique:

In this collection of stories about the fabulous Paul Bunyan, Stevens has tried to catch the flavor of the north woods. Bunyan and his Blue Ox, Babe, whose horns were forty-two ax handles and a plug of chewing tobacco apart, have become a part of American folklore. The Paul Bunyan tales, which originated along the Canadian border about 1837, have the hearty tall story exaggeration of the wide West and the virile Northwest. They will be popular with readers of all ages for years to come.

The Stories:

That winter the blue snow fell. It frightened the moose so that they fled from the section of Canada where Paul Bunyan lived to the far North. The herds made so much noise that all the bears woke up from their hibernation and fled too. Some of the bears went so far North that they turned white and became polar bears. Some only went far enough to turn gray, and some were merely so frightened that they stayed small. When Paul Bunyan discovered the blue snow on the ground, he was surprised, but not as surprised as he was to find that his moose hound, Niagara, had followed the herds, and was no longer there to bring his food for him. Walking around, he saw a blue calf of an amazing size. Because it seemed ill, he took it home to his cave and fed it. Shortly afterward he dreamed that he and the calf were to invent and practice the art of logging.

So with the help of Babe, who had grown up to be a huge Blue Ox, Paul Bunyan set up a lumber camp. When Paul had to do the paper work for the camp, he invented the multiplication table, the cube root, and algebra. As boss of the logging, Paul was lucky to meet a man, almost as big as he was, named Hels Helsen. Hels was a wonderful worker and Paul's friend, but they fought after Paul decided to cut the trees on the Mountain That Stood On Its Head. When Paul found that his men could not hang upside down from the sides of the mountain and cut the down-growing trees with ease, he loaded his gun with plates of iron and shot it at the overhanging sides. The discharge cut off the trees so that they fell down and buried their tops in the plain below. Hels got angry at Paul for being so smart, and the two of them had a terrible fight on the top, which was really the bottom, of the mountain. Paul won, and from then on there was never any trouble between them.

Then the camp moved to a place where Paul found trees planted in perfect rows, and all of the same size. Paul's men cut down the trees. Soon afterward Paul met Johnny Inkslinger, the great surveyor, and learned that Johnny had planted the trees for surveying stakes. In recompense, Paul made Johnny, who also was almost as big as Paul, his bookkeeper.

Feeding the huge lumber camp was a great problem. At first Paul had a cook who would serve only pea soup. One day he threw the peas in a lake and boiled the lake water to make the soup. Then Paul got a new cook named Sourdough Sam. Sam served only sourdough, and he was convinced that it was good for everything. He advised it as a shoe polish, an emetic, liniment, and toothache medicine. Once he put some sourdough in Johnny Inkslinger's ink, in hopes that it would treble the amount. Unfortunately the ink blew up, and Sourdough Sam lost an arm and leg. Sam's son, Hot Biscuit Slim, then took over the cookhouse, and after demanding and getting a tremendous amount of equipment from Paul, he made mealtimes the happiest hours of the loggers' day.

Paul's loggers amused themselves at night by listening to songs and stories.

Shanty Boy, of Bunkhouse 1, was the best storyteller in the camp. Once, when the men were feeling sad, Shanty Boy ran out of stories to cheer them up, and he told them some lies. The men believed all Shanty Boy's lies until he told the story of Jonah and the whale. Then Paul had to be called in to keep the men from beating up Shanty Boy for telling what they thought was a whopper. Paul told them that the story was true. They believed Paul, but from that time on no logger ever told another lie.

Paul took his camp to Utah to cut down the stonewood trees there. The men grew so tired, and their axes got so dull, that they almost gave up. In disgust, Paul himself started cutting down the trees. He worked so hard that he sweated tremendous drops of water, which later became Salt Lake.

His men, frightened by the flood Paul's sweat caused, ran away to Kansas. There everything was perfect. All anyone did was gamble and drink. One day a duke planned a revolution against King Bourbon of Kansas. He had all the bars serve very strong drinks, and everyone but the duke and his friends fell down in a stupor. The duke, who wanted to get rid of drink and gambling forever, told all the men, including Paul's loggers, that they had sinned mightily. Paul finally turned up and forgave his men for running away. He also hitched Babe to Kansas and turned it over. He left Kansas flat, and hid forever the wonderful cigarette grass, beervines, and whiskey trees.

One day Babe became ill. Johnny Inkslinger tried several cures. He took the camp to the West Coast, where they captured whales and fed Babe whale's milk, but the treatment did little good. Finally Johnny whispered over and over in Babe's ear that Babe was really well. Johnny drank whiskey to keep his voice clear. After a few days, he fell in a faint. Babe drank some of the liquor and began to get well. Whiskey, not whale's milk, was the medicine for the Blue Ox.

Next the camp went to New Iowa, where Paul left them. The scenery was so beautiful that the men did nothing but write poetry. Paul had to come back and take them to the He-Man country to get them out of the habit. In the He-Man country it was so cold in the wintertime that words froze in the air, and you could not hear them until they thawed out in the spring. The men grew so virile after a winter of that hard life that all they did was fight one another. One day they stopped fighting because they seemed to be knee-deep in blood. After a while Paul discovered that it was not blood but red rain which had fallen up through the earth from China.

After the rain from China, the gang moved into the Nowaday Valley. There Paul discovered that the men were singing about women, a subject he could dimly remember having heard mentioned before. Paul also had trouble with one of his workers, who discovered machines which could do what only Paul and the Blue Ox had been able to perform before. Paul was afraid that his days were over. At last women appeared near the camp, and Paul's men disappeared. Paul went to look for them and met a woman. He picked her up in his hand and looked at her. Completely unconcerned, she powdered her nose. Paul was dumbfounded. Late that night he started out across the hills with his Blue Ox. He was never heard from again.

THE PEASANTS

Type of work: Novel
Author: Ladislas Reymont (1868-1925)
Type of plot: Social chronicle
Time of plot: Late nineteenth century
Locale: Poland
First published: 1902-1909

Principal characters:

MATTHIAS BORYNA, a well-to-do peasant
ANTEK, Matthias' son
DOMINIKOVA, a widow
YAGNA, her daughter
HANKA, Antek's wife

Critique:

The Peasants is epic in the sweep and significance of its story. The problem of Europe is contained in this novel—the problem of overpopulation, of poor and overworked soil, of ignorance, of imperialism. The novel is at once a text on the subject of mass sociology and a human, heart-warming narrative. In keeping with the seasonal movement of its story, Reymont's masterpiece is divided into four sections: *Autumn, Winter, Spring,* and *Summer*.

The Story:

It was autumn and the peasants of Lipka village were hurrying to finish the harvest before winter. In Boryna's barnyard the villagers gathered to see a cow that had been chased from manor lands and was now dying of colic. Hanka, Matthias Boryna's daughter-in-law, took the loss most to heart when old Kuba, the lame stableman, said that he could do nothing for the stricken cow.

That night Matthias, charged with having fathered a servant girl's child, went to visit the voyt, the headman of the village, to ask about his trial. The voyt, after assuring him that he would get off easily in court, flattered Matthias and told him he should marry again, now that his second wife was dead. Matthias pretended he was too old, but he knew all the time he was hopeful of marrying Yagna, the daughter of Dominikova. Yagna would some day inherit three acres of land.

The next morning the case against Matthias was dismissed. After the trial Matthias met Dominikova and tried to sound her out on her plans for her daughter.

On the day of the autumn sale Matthias went off to sell some hogs and Hanka her geese. Old Matthias, pleased when Yagna accepted some bright ribbons, asked her hand in marriage. He did not know that his son Antek, husband of Hanka, was secretly in love with Yagna. When Matthias settled six acres upon Yagna in return for the three she brought with her marriage portion, Antek and his father fought and Matthias ordered his son off the farm. Antek and Hanka moved with their children into the miserable cabin of Hanka's father.

The wedding of Matthias and Yagna was a hilarious affair. In the midst of the merriment Kuba, poaching on manor lands, was shot in the leg by a gamekeeper. Fearing the hospital, he cut off his own leg and died from loss of blood.

Winter came swiftly, and wolves lurked near the peasant's stock barns. That winter Hanka and Antek had to sell their cow to keep themselves in food. At last Antek took work with men building a new sawmill. Matthew, the foreman, was his enemy, for Matthew also loved Yagna. One day Antek overheard

THE PEASANTS by Ladislas Reymont. Translated by Michael H. Dziewicki. By permission of the publishers, Alfred A. Knopf, Inc.

Matthew's brag that he had been with Yagna in her bedroom. Antek, in a great fury, struck Matthew so hard that the carpenter broke several ribs when he fell over the railing and into the river.

At Christmas there was great rejoicing in Matthias' house, for Yagna was with child. At the midnight mass on Christmas Eve, Yagna and Antek saw each other for a moment. Antek asked her to meet him behind the haystack.

That winter the peasants of the village came to Matthias to report that a part of the forest which the peasants used for gathering wood had been sold by the manor people. Unhappily, Matthias allowed himself to be dragged into the dispute. While Matthias was away, Antek went to his father's farm to see Yagna. Returning, Matthias nearly caught them together.

One night at the inn Antek, drunk, ignored his wife and asked Yagna to dance with him. Matthias arrived, seized Yagna, and took her away. Later, on his way home, Antek found his wife almost dead in the snow. From that time on Matthias treated Yagna like a servant girl.

Antek lost his job and Hanka was forced to go with the paupers seeking firewood in the forest. Walking home through the storm, Hanka was given a ride by old Matthias. He insisted that Hanka come back to his farm the next day.

That night Antek took Yagna into the orchard. Coming upon them, old Matthias lit up a straw stack in order to see them. Antek and the old man fought. Then Antek fled and the fire spread, threatening the whole village. Yagna fled to her family. Everyone avoided Antek and refused to speak to him.

At last old Matthias took Yagna back, but only as a hired girl. Hanka was with him much of the time. When Yagna began to see Antek again, the old man took no notice.

Word came that the squire was cutting timber on land the peasants claimed. The next morning a fight took place in the forest as the villagers tried to protect their trees. Antek thought he might kill his own father in the confusion, but when he saw Matthias struck down, he killed the woodcutter who had wounded his father. Antek walked alongside as Matthias was carried home.

Spring came. Many of the villagers, Antek among them, were in jail after the fight in the forest. Fields went unplowed. Old Matthias lay insensible. Yagna had now begun to consort with the voyt. It seemed as if the devil himself had possessed the village.

Easter was a sad season because the men were still in prison. Word went around that the squire, who had been ordered to stop the sale of his land, was in desperate straits for money and vowing revenge upon the peasants. Shortly after Easter Hanka gave birth to a male child who was named Roch. Gifts were given out but in Antek's absence the christening did not seem complete.

At last the peasants were set free. Their homecoming was a happy occasion in every cabin but that of Matthias, for Antek had not been released. Yagna was also unhappy. Even Matthew, the carpenter who had once loved her, now ignored her for younger Teresa.

One night old Matthias arose from his stupor. For hours he wandered about the fields as if about to sow his land. In the morning he fell over and died.

Summer brought additional woes to the peasants. There were quarrels over Matthias' land. Some Germans came to occupy the squire's land, but the peasants threatened them and they went away. Then the squire made arrangements to parcel out the land to the peasants and some of them bought new land for homesteading.

Old Dominikova and Simon, one of her sons, had quarreled, and Simon bought his own land from the squire. Simon and his wife Nastka received many gifts from the villagers who wanted to spite old Dominikova. When the voyt's accounts were found to be short, the villagers blamed Yagna.

Released from prison, Antek returned to work on the farm. He was still attracted to Yagna, but the duties of his farm and the possibility that he still might be sent to Siberia pressed even harder upon him. That summer the organist's son, Yanek, came home from school. In a short time he and Yagna were seen together. At last the peasants put Yagna on a manure cart and told her never to return to the village.

The summer was dry and the harvest scanty. One day a wandering beggar stopped at Nastka's house. He gave her some balm for Yagna, who had taken refuge there. As the sound of the Angelus rose up through the evening air, he strode away. For the food Nastka had given him he called down God's blessing on her peasant home.

PEER GYNT

Type of work: Drama
Author: Henrik Ibsen (1828-1906)
Type of plot: Satiric fantasy
Time of plot: Mid-nineteenth century
Locale: Norway
First presented: 1867

Principal characters:

- PEER GYNT, a Norwegian farm lad
- ASE, his mother
- SOLVEIG, a Norwegian girl whose love for Peer remains constant
- THE GREAT BOYG, a troll monster
- THE BUTTON MOULDER, who threatens to melt Peer in his ladle

Critique:

A satire on Man, that contradictory creature with an upright body and groveling soul, *Peer Gynt* is an example of Ibsen's symbolic treatment of the theme of individualism. This drama is a long episodic fantasy, with a picaresque, jaunty, boastful, yet lovable hero. Into the fabric of the drama Ibsen weaves folklore and satire combined with symbolism that imparts a dramatic effect rich in emotional impact. The unorthodox and untheatrical design, however, make stage presentation difficult. The play deals with the degeneration of the human soul, yet the triumphant note at the end, the redeeming power of love, keeps it from being tragic in dramatic effect.

The Story:

Peer Gynt, a young Norwegian farmer with a penchant for laziness and bragging, idled away his hours in brawling and dreaming. Upbraided by his mother, Ase, for his willingness to waste his time, he answered that she was perfectly right. She ridiculed him further by pointing out that had he been an honest farmer, Hegstad's daughter would have had him, and he would have been a happy bridegroom. He told her that he intended to break the marriage of Hegstad's daughter, a wedding planned for that night. When his mother protested, he seized her in his arms and set her on the roof of their house, from where her unheeded cries followed him up the road to Hegstad's home.

At the wedding he was scorned by everyone present except Solveig, a girl unknown to him. But even she avoided him as soon as she heard of his base reputation. Peer became drunk and began to tell fantastic tales of adventure, stories that bridged an embarrassing gap in the marriage ceremony when the bride locked herself in the storeroom and refused to come out. In desperation, the bridegroom appealed to Peer for help. As Peer left for the storeroom, his mother, who had been released from the roof, arrived. Suddenly the bridegroom cried out and pointed toward the hillside. Rushing to the door, the guests saw Peer scrambling up the mountain with the bride over his shoulder.

Peer quickly abandoned the bride and penetrated more deeply into the wilderness. Eluding the pursuit of Hegstad and his neighbors, he married and deserted the daughter of the elf-king of the mountains. He encountered the Great Boyg, who represented the riddle of existence in the figure of a shapeless, grim, unconquerable monster. Time and again, Peer tried to force his way up the mountain, but the Boyg blocked his way. When Peer challenged the Boyg to a battle, the creature replied that though he conquered everyone he did not fight.

Exhausted, Peer sank to the ground. The sky was dark with carnivorous birds that were about to swoop down upon him. Suddenly he heard the sound of church bells and women's voices in the distance. The Boyg withdrew, admitting defeat because Peer had the support of women in his fight.

An outlaw for having carried off Hegstad's daughter, Peer built himself a hut in the forest, to which Solveig came to keep him company. Their happiness was brief, however, for one day Peer met the elf-king's daughter, whom he had deserted. With her was an ugly troll, Peer's son; unable to drive them off, he himself went away after telling Solveig that she must wait for him a little while.

Before leaving the country, he paid a farewell visit to his dying mother. With his arms around her, Peer lulled her into her last sleep. Over her dead body he uttered thanks for all his days, all his lullabies, all his beatings.

He went adventuring over the world. In America he sold slaves; in China, sacred idols. He did a thriving business in rum and Bibles. After being robbed of his earthly goods, he went to the African desert and became a prophet. Prosperous once more, he set himself up in Oriental luxury. One day he rode into the desert with Anitra, a dance girl. Stopping to rest, he could not resist the urge to show off by proving to Anitra that he was still young in spirit and body. While he was performing, she stole his moneybag and horse and galloped away. Solveig had grown middle-aged while she waited for Peer Gynt's return. Peer Gynt, on the other hand, still struggled on with his planless life, still drifted around the all-consuming Boyg of life without any apparent purpose in mind.

On his way back to Norway at last, his ship was wrecked. Peer clung to a spar which could hold only one man. When the ship's cook attempted to grasp the spar also, Peer thrust him into the ocean. He had saved his own life, but he doubted whether he had been successful in saving himself from his aimless existence.

On his return to Norway, he decided, however, that he was through with wandering, and he was willing to settle down to the staid life of a retired old man. One day on the heath he met a Button Moulder, who refused to let the aged Peer realize his dream of peace and contentment. Informed that he was to go into the Button Moulder's ladle to be melted, Peer became frantic. To lose his soul, his identity, was an end he had not divined for himself despite his aimless and self-centered life. He pleaded with the Button Moulder to relent. He was at worst a bungler, he cried, never an exceptional sinner. The Button Moulder answered that Peer, not bad enough for hell nor good enough for heaven, was fit only for the ladle. Peer protested, but the Button Moulder remained adamant. Peer was to be melted into the ladle of nonentity unless he could prove himself a sinner worthy of hell. Hell being a more lenient punishment than mere nothingness, Peer desperately enlarged upon his sins. He had trafficked in slaves, cheated people and deceived them, and had saved his life at the expense of another. The Button Moulder ironically maintained that these iniquities were mere trifles.

While they argued, the Button Moulder and Peer came to a house where Solveig stood in the doorway ready for church, a psalm book under her arm. Peer flung himself at her feet, begging her to cry out his sins and trespasses, but she answered that he was with her again, and that was all that mattered. She was shocked when Peer asked her to cry out his crime to her; she said that it was he who had made life beautiful for her. Hearing her words, the Button Moulder disappeared, prophesying that he and Peer would meet again.

Peer Gynt buried his face in Solveig's lap, safe and secure with her arms to hold him and her heart to warm him. Solveig's own face was bathed in sunlight.

PEG WOFFINGTON

Type of work: Novel
Author: Charles Reade (1814-1884)
Type of plot: Sentimental romance
Time of plot: Eighteenth century
Locale: England
First published: 1853

Principal characters:
PEG WOFFINGTON, a famous actress
HARRY VANE, her admirer
MABEL VANE, Harry's wife
SIR CHARLES POMANDER, another admirer of Mrs. Woffington
COLLEY CIBBER, actor and critic
TRIPLET, a painter and playwright

Critique:

This touching story reveals a keen insight into human nature. Much too sentimental to be credible to modern readers, the story of Mrs. Woffington is nevertheless a witty revelation of life behind the scenes in the theater. The dialogue between the critics and the artists is delightful, and the attack on critics follows a long tradition in our literature. The principal character of the story was a celebrated Irish actress.

The Story:

Mr. Harry Vane had come from Shropshire to London on business affairs. Having completed his business, he ventured to remain in London for pleasure, for he had seen Mrs. Woffington on the stage and had fallen in love with her. From his box seat at the theater, where he sat night after night, he sent her anonymous notes and flowers and waited for some sign that his attentions had awakened her interest. One night he sent a corsage with a note asking her to wear the flowers in her hair if the gentleman's notes had interested her. In the final act of the evening's performance, she appeared with the flowers in her hair. Vane was more determined than ever to meet the actress personally.

From the audience Sir Charles Pomander, whom Vane knew slightly, had seen Vane in his box for many evenings. Curiosity being one of Sir Charles' greatest weaknesses, he watched to detect signs in Mrs. Woffington or in Vane to learn whether the gentleman's suit was being successful. That night, observing Vane's conduct, Sir Charles joined that gentleman in his box and invited Vane to accompany him to a gathering of people in the green room backstage.

One of the group backstage was Mr. Colley Cibber, known in his more youthful days as a great actor and playwright.

When Vane questioned the famed actor concerning Mrs. Woffington's ability as an actress, Cibber scoffed and claimed that acting is the art of copying nature. He added that in his day there was a much finer actress, Mrs. Bracegirdle. Mrs. Woffington overheard his slighting remarks. In order to disprove Cibber's pompous claims, she disguised herself as the elderly Mrs. Bracegirdle and appeared among the backstage visitors as that famous old lady of the stage. So well did she fool everyone that Cibber was forced to admit his own deception by Mrs. Woffington's play-acting.

Sir Charles was still watching Vane for signs of the degree to which his suit of Mrs. Woffington had advanced. But the actress wore her feelings behind a mask. Vane himself was too astounded by his first visit backstage to reveal anything to Sir Charles, who was also pursuing Mrs. Woffington. Unfortunately, Sir Charles had to leave London for a few weeks. The next time Vane saw Mrs. Woffington, she openly expressed her admiration for him. Soon Mrs. Woffington revealed to Vane that he was her ideal of goodness and perfection. Vane himself was deeply in love.

Triplet, the playwright, scene painter, and poet, could find no market for his talents, and his wife and children were almost starving. One day when he was at the theater trying to get Mr. Rich, the manager, to read his latest tragedies, Mrs. Woffington recognized him as a man who had been kind to her when she was a poor little Irish girl selling oranges on the streets. When she learned of his plight, she promised to sit for a portrait and to persuade Mr. Rich to read his plays.

When Sir Charles returned from his trip, he immediately continued his suit of Mrs. Woffington, who haughtily refused him. Jealous of his rival's success, he set about to ruin Vane's romance and bribed Mrs. Woffington's servant to report to him whatever Mrs. Woffington did. One afternoon, suspecting that she had gone to spend the day with a lover, Sir Charles persuaded Vane to accompany him in a search for her. Trailing her to a strange apartment, they discovered her with Triplet's family, whom she had rescued from starvation when she had gone to sit for her portrait. Vane was dismayed at his own lack of trust in Mrs. Woffington, but she readily forgave him.

While he was journeying through the countryside, Sir Charles had seen a beautiful woman in a carriage. Arrested by her beauty, he had sent a servant to inquire about her identity. Soon after the incident in Triplet's apartment, Sir Charles learned that the beautiful woman was Vane's wife, Mabel, who was on her way to join her husband in London. When Mabel Vane arrived at her husband's house, there was a gay party in session. Although Mabel was a simple country girl, she discerned the meaning of Mrs. Woffington's presence, especially after Sir Charles had described her husband's conduct at the theater. True to his crude character, Sir Charles offered to comfort Mabel by making love to her, but she coldly sent him away. Sitting alone in the parlor, Mabel had to endure the unhappy circumstance of overhearing her husband pleading with Mrs. Woffington to forgive him. Thus the devoted and beautiful Mabel learned that her husband no longer loved her.

Learning Mabel's identity, the actress fled from Vane's house. Seeking comfort and diversion, she went to Triplet's studio and told him that she had come to sit for her portrait. While she was sitting, Triplet received word that some of his theatrical friends were coming to his studio to view the portrait. Knowing that the critics Snarl and Soaper were vicious and that Colley Cibber would sneer at Triplet's work, Mrs. Woffington contrived a plan to fool the arrogant men. She cut a hole in the portrait just large enough to fit round her head. When the critics saw the picture, they believed it to be a painting, while in reality it was merely a setting around the real head of Mrs. Woffington. True to their usual form, the critics sneered at the artist's lack of success in his endeavor to reproduce the head of Peg Woffington. Laughing at her own deception, Mrs. Woffington stepped forward and revealed the trick to the critics. Only Colley Cibber was able to take the joke with good nature. The others left in chagrin.

Mrs. Woffington told Triplet of Harry Vane's wife, and he warned her that two rival women were a dangerous combination. While they were talking, Mabel Vane entered the apartment. She had come to see Mrs. Woffington. The actress' vanity and pride had been cut to the quick, but Mabel's sweet and generous nature softened her heart. She promised Mabel that she would not only return Vane to his wife but also prove to her that the heart of her husband had never really deserted his wife. Mabel was so grateful to her that she swore to call Mrs. Woffington her sister, and the two women embraced.

The Vanes were reunited, for Harry truly loved his wife. Mabel Vane and Peg Woffington remained steadfast friends, seeing each other often in London and writing numerous letters.

PENDENNIS

Type of work: Novel
Author: William Makepeace Thackeray (1811-1863)
Type of plot: Social satire
Time of plot: Mid-nineteenth century
Locale: England
First published: 1848-1850

Principal characters:
Arthur Pendennis (Pen), a snob
Helen Pendennis, his mother
Major Arthur Pendennis, his uncle
Laura Bell, Mrs. Pendennis' ward
Emily Costigan, an actress
Blanche Amory, an heiress
Henry Foker, Pen's friend

Critique:

The History of Pendennis is a long, loosely organized novel, in which the author, between events, stops to chat and philosophize with the reader. There is present a strong emphasis on morality, on goodness and truth, as opposed to a selfish, scheming, attitude which stresses material wealth and social advancement. The most consistent theme, brought out with piercing irony, is the self-conscious, rigid snobbery between classes in England, and the unceasing efforts of the middle class to become gentlemen and aristocrats. This theme is epitomized in the character of Major Pendennis, but it is also illustrated in the experiences of young Arthur Pendennis, who is torn between his uncle's efforts to help him to rise socially and his mother's efforts to keep him natural and unspoiled.

The Story:

Major Arthur Pendennis, a retired army officer, impeccably dressed, dignified, yet affable, sat in his London club looking over his mail and considering which of several invitations would be most advantageous to accept. He left until last a letter from his sister-in-law, begging him to come to Fairoaks because her son Arthur, who was known to the family as Pen, had become infatuated with an actress twelve years older than himself, and insisted on marrying the woman. Helen Pendennis implored the major, who was young Pen's guardian, to use his influence with the sixteen-year-old boy.

John Pendennis, Pen's father, though of an old family, had been forced to earn his living as an apothecary and surgeon. He prospered financially, and at the age of forty-three married Helen Thistlewood, a distant relative of one of his aristocratic patrons. His own life's aim was to be a gentleman, and by fortunate transactions he was able to buy the small estate of Fairoaks. He acquired family portraits, and was henceforth known as Squire Pendennis. He referred proudly to his brother the major, who associated with well-known aristocrats. John Pendennis had died while his son was still a schoolboy. After that melancholy event, Pen took first place in the family. His mother was especially solicitous for his welfare and happiness. She had already planned that he should marry Laura Bell, his adopted sister and the orphan of the Reverend Francis Bell, whom Helen had loved years before.

Helen Pendennis was horrified at Pen's infatuation with an actress, but Pen, blind with youthful romance, saw Emily Costigan as the ideal of all womanhood. She was beautiful, and her reputation was unquestioned, yet she was crude and unintelligent. Pen was introduced to her father, Captain Costigan, by Henry Foker, a dashing, wealthy young schoolmate. The captain was a shabby, rakish Irishman who was constantly finding his daughter's income insufficient for the drinks he required. He assumed that Pen was a wealthy young aristocrat and urged Emily to accept his proposal of marriage. On the other hand, Emily regarded Pen as a child, but at the same time she was flattered by the serious attentions of a landed young gentleman.

When the major arrived at Fairoaks, Pen had almost won his indulgent mother's consent. The major handled the situation adroitly. Using many references to his aristocratic friends, he hinted that Pen, too, could be received in their homes if only he made a brilliant marriage. Then he called on Captain Costigan and informed him that Pen was dependent on his mother and that his prospects were only five hundred pounds a year. The captain wept over the deceitfulness of man and gave up Pen's letters and verses in return for a small loan. Emily wrote Pen a short note that Pen thought would drive him to distraction. But it did not. Meanwhile the major arranged through his aristocratic and influential friends to give Emily an opportunity to play an engagement in London. Pen, suffering over his broken love affair, was so restless and moody it seemed wise for him to join his friend, Henry Foker, and attend the University of Oxbridge.

He entered the university posing as a moneyed aristocrat. His mother by her own rigid economies gave him an adequate allowance, and Pen entered enthusiastically into all sorts of activities. His refined and diversified tastes led him into expenditures far beyond his means. As a result, he ended his third year deeply in debt. He was made still more miserable when he failed an important examination. Overcome by remorse at his reckless spending and his thoughtlessness of his devoted mother, he went to London. There Major Pendennis did not hesitate to show cold disapproval, and ignored his nephew. But his mother welcomed him home with affection and forgiveness. Laura Bell offered a solution by suggesting that the money left her by her father be turned over to Pen to clear his debts. It was Laura, too, who induced him to return to the university. When he received his degree, he came back to Fairoaks, still restless and depressed, until an event of local interest aroused him.

Clavering Park, the mansion owned by Sir Francis Clavering, was reopened. Sir Francis was a worthless spendthrift whose title was his only claim to respect. After living many years abroad, he had made an advantageous marriage to Jemima Amory, a widow recently returned from India. She had been left a large fortune, and, though uneducated, she was well liked because of her generous and good nature. In addition to the Claverings' young son, the heir to the now great Clavering fortune, Lady Clavering had by a previous marriage a daughter named Blanche. Although extremely pretty, Blanche was a superficial, self-centered girl whose demure appearance disguised a hard and cruel disposition. Pen and Laura soon became friendly with their new neighbors, and Pen imagined himself in love with Blanche. In the meantime, Helen confided to Pen her dearest wish that he should marry Laura. Pen, conscious of the sacrifices his mother had made for him and of Laura's generosity, made a grudging offer of marriage, which Laura spiritedly refused.

His dignity hurt, he decided he would make a place for himself in the world and so he went to London to read for the law. But in spite of his good resolutions he was unable to settle down to serious study. He became a young man about town, and he took pride in the variety of his acquaintances. He shared rooms with George Warrington, a philosophic man whom Pen came to respect and love. At last, through Warrington's influence, Pen began to earn his own living by writing. Eventually he published a successful novel. So Pen read law, wrote for a living, and spent his evenings at dinners and balls.

His disordered life finally resulted in a serious illness, and his mother and Laura went to London to nurse him. Later, accompanied by George Warrington, they went abroad. There Helen Pendennis, worn out with worry over Pen, became ill and died, and the party returned to Fairoaks for her burial. Then the estate was rented. Pen, now heir to the small fortune his mother had left, returned to London. During his residence in London, his uncle had again become actively interested in him. Feeling that Pen should improve his station in life, the shrewd major had decided the Claverings could be useful to Pen and he had encouraged his nephew to cultivate the family once more.

One night Pen and the major were invited to a dinner given by the Claverings. While the men were sitting over cigars and wine, Colonel Altamont appeared. He was drunk. It was known that for some mysterious reason Sir Francis Clavering had given this man large sums of money. Major Pendennis, who during his career in the army had been stationed in India, immediately recognized Altamont as Mr. Amory, the first husband of Lady Clavering. The major did not divulge his knowledge to anyone but Sir Francis, to whom he issued the ultimatum that Sir Francis must go to live abroad and that he must give his place in Parliament to Pen. If he refused, the major threatened to expose the fact that Amory was still alive and that the marriage of Sir Francis and Lady Clavering was illegal. Another point the major made was that Clavering Park should be left to Blanche Amory. Sir Francis had no choice but to agree.

Major Pendennis continued his intrigue by urging Pen to marry Blanche. Pen, with some uneasiness, fell in with his uncle's plans. He did not know how his place in Parliament had been secured, but he did know that he was not in love with Blanche. He became engaged to her, however, and began to campaign for his seat in Parliament. Laura, who had been abroad as companion to Lady Rockminster, returned to the vicinity. When Pen saw her again, he began to regret his plan to marry Blanche.

In the meantime the major's valet, Morgan, had learned of the Claverings' complicated marriage situation and planned blackmail on his own account. After a violent quarrel with the major, Morgan told Pen how Major Pendennis had forced Sir Francis to give up his seat in Parliament in favor of Pen. Pen was shocked by this news and by his uncle's unethical methods. He and Laura agreed that he should give up his candidacy for the district, but that he must, even though he loved Laura, go on with his plans to marry Blanche, after his proposal to her. However, this sacrifice to honor proved unnecessary, for Pen discovered that Blanche had forsaken him for his old friend, Henry Foker, who had just inherited a large fortune. Their marriage left Pen free to marry Laura. Because Lady Rockminster held Laura in great affection, the marriage was approved even by the class-conscious major.

So the simple wedding of Pen and Laura replaced the fashionable one which had been planned for Clavering Church. Blanche did not marry Foker. When Foker learned by chance that her father was still alive and that Blanche had kept the knowledge from him, he dropped his plans to marry her. Blanche became the wife of a French count. Lady Clavering, who had truly believed her husband dead, was horrified to learn that Amory was still alive, but the legality of her marriage to Sir Francis was established when it was learned that Amory had contracted several marriages before the one with her.

Meanwhile Pen and Laura lived happily. Laura had expectations from her friend and patroness, Lady Rockminster, and Fairoaks had increased in value because the new railroad bought rights through it. Later, when Sir Francis died, Pen was elected to Parliament. He had almost forgotten how to be a snob.

PENGUIN ISLAND

Type of work: Novel
Author: Anatole France (Jacques Anatole Thibault, 1844-1924)
Type of plot: Fantasy
Time of plot: Ancient times to the present
Locale: Mythical Alca
First published: 1908

Principal characters:
MAËL, a missionary monk
KRAKEN, an opportunist penguin
OBEROSIA, Kraken's mistress
TRINCO, a conqueror
PYROT, a scapegoat
M. CÉRÈS, a cabinet minister
EVELINE, his wife
M. VISIRE, Prime Minister of Penguinia

Critique:

Penguin Island is a satiric and ironic burlesque of history. Although the narrative is doubly enjoyable to those who know the history of France, the story can be appreciated by everyone. In an amusing way, the author seriously criticizes politics, the Church, and other social institutions.

The Story:

In ancient times Maël, a Breton monk, was diligent in gathering converts to the Church. One day the devil caused Maël to be transported in a boat to the North Pole, where the priest landed on an island inhabited by penguins. Being somewhat snow-blind, he mistook the birds for men, preached to them, and, taking their silence as a sign of willingness, baptized them into the Christian faith.

This error of the pious Maël caused great consternation in Paradise. God called all the saints together, and they argued whether the baptisms were valid. At last they decided that the only way out of the dilemma was to change the penguins into men. After this transformation had taken place, Maël towed the island back to the Breton coast so that he could keep an eye on his converts.

Thus began the history of Penguinia on the island of Alca. At first the penguins were without clothes, but before long the holy Maël put clothes on the females. Because this covering excited the males, sexual promiscuity was enormously increased. The penguins began to establish the rights of property—by knocking each other over the head. Greatank, the largest and strongest penguin, became the founder of power and wealth. A taxation system was set up by which all penguins were taxed equally. This system was favored by the rich, who kept their money to benefit the poor.

Kraken, a clever penguin, withdrew to a lonely part of the island and lived alone in a cave. Finally he took as his mistress Oberosia, the most beautiful of penguin women. Kraken gained great wealth by dressing up as a dragon and carrying off the wealth of the peaceful penguins. When the citizens banded together to protect their property, Kraken became frightened. It was predicted by Maël that a virgin would come to conquer the dragon. Kraken and Oberosia fashioned an imitation monster. Oberosia appeared to Maël and announced herself as the destined virgin. At an appointed time she revealed the imitation monster. Kraken sprang from a hiding place and pretended to kill it. The people rejoiced and thenceforth paid annual tribute to Kraken. His son, Draco, founded the first royal family of Penguinia.

Thus began the Middle Ages on the island of Alca. Draco the Great, a descendant of the original Draco, had a monastery established in the cave of Kraken in honor of Oberosia, who was now a saint. There were great wars between the penguins and the porpoises at that time, but the Christian faith was preserved by the simple expedient of burning all heretics at the stake.

The history of the penguins in that far time was chronicled by a learned monk named Johannes Talpa. Even though the battles raged about his very ears, he was able to continue writing in his dry and simple style. Little record was left of the primitive paintings on the isle of Alca, but later historians believed that the painters were careful to represent nature as unlike herself as possible.

Marbodius, a literary monk, left a record of a descent into hell similar to the experience of Dante. Marbodius interviewed Virgil and was told by the great poet that Dante had misrepresented him. Virgil was perfectly happy with his own mythology and wanted nothing to do with the God of the Christians.

The next recorded part of Penguinian history treated of modern times, when rationalistic philosophers began to appear. In the succeeding generation their teachings took root; the king was put to death, nobility was abolished, and a republic was founded. The shrine of St. Oberosia was destroyed. However, the republic did not last long. Trinco, a great soldier, took command of the country; with his armies he conquered and lost all the known world. The penguins were left at last with nothing but their glory.

Then a new republic was established. It pretended to be ruled by the people, but the real rulers were the wealthy financiers. Another republic of a similar nature, new Atlantis, had grown up across the sea at the same time. It was even more advanced in the worship of wealth.

Father Agaric and Prince des Boscenos, as members of the clergy and nobility, were interested in restoring the kings of Alca to the throne. They decided to destroy the republic by taking advantage of the weakness of Chatillon, the admiral of the navy. Chatillon was seduced by the charms of the clever Viscountess Olive, who was able to control his actions for the benefit of the royalists. An immense popular anti-republican movement was begun with Chatillon as its hero; the royalists hoped to reinstate the king in the midst of the uproar. But the revolution was stopped in its infancy, and Chatillon fled the country.

Eveline, the beautiful daughter of Madame Clarence, rejected the love of Viscount Clena, after she had learned that he had no fortune. She then accepted the attentions of M. Cérès, a rising politician. After a short time they were married. M. Cérès received a portfolio in the cabinet of M. Visire, and Eveline became a favorite in the social gatherings of the politicians. M. Visire was attracted by her, and she became his mistress. M. Céres learned of the affair, but he was afraid to say anything to M. Visire, the Prime Minister. Instead, he did his best to ruin M. Visire politically, but with little success at first. Finally M. Visire was put out of office on the eve of a war with a neighboring empire. Eveline lived to a respectable old age and at her death left all her property to the Charity of St. Oberosia.

As Penguinia developed into an industrial civilization ruled by the wealthy class, the one purpose of life became the gathering of riches; art and all other non-profit activities ceased to be. Finally the downtrodden workmen revolted, and a wave of anarchy swept over the nation. All the great industries were demolished. Order was established at last, and the government reformed many of the social institutions, but the country continued to decline. Where before there had been great cities, wild animals now lived.

Then came hunters seeking the wild animals. Later shepherds appeared and after a time farming became the chief occupation. Great lords built castles. The people made roads; villages appeared. The villages combined into large cities. The cities grew rich. An industrial civilization developed, ruled by the wealthy class. History was beginning to repeat itself.

PEREGRINE PICKLE

Type of work: Novel
Author: Tobias Smollett (1721-1771)
Type of plot: Picaresque romance
Time of plot: Early eighteenth century
Locale: England and the continent
First published: 1751

Principal characters:

PEREGRINE PICKLE, a reckless young man
GAMALIEL PICKLE, his father
GRIZZLE PICKLE, his aunt, later Mrs. Trunnion
COMMODORE HAWSER TRUNNION, an old sea dog, Peregrine's godfather
LIEUTENANT HATCHWAY, the commodore's companion
TOM PIPES, a companion and servant
EMILIA GAUNTLET, Peregrine's sweetheart

Critique:

Traditional criticism claims that the character of Peregrine Pickle undergoes no change in the course of this novel, that at the conclusion of his adventures with folly he is still unconvinced about the wisdom of a sober and useful life. This tradition does not take into consideration the nature of eighteenth-century manners or the temper of Smollett's mind. It must be noted that Smollett was anxious to reveal the chicaneries of his time and to satirize the manners and morals of society in general. Viewed in this light, the character of the writer's unheroic hero is in keeping with the theme and purpose of the novel. In addition, the inclusion of the disputed memoirs of the lady of quality complements the story of Peregrine's picaresque career.

The Story:

Mr. Gamaliel Pickle was the son of a prosperous London merchant who at his death bequeathed his son a fortune of no small degree. Later, having lost a part of his inheritance in several unsuccessful ventures of his own, Mr. Pickle prudently decided to retire from business and to live on the interest of his fortune rather than risk his principal in the uncertainties of trade. With his sister Grizzle, who had kept his house for him since his father's death, he went to live in a mansion in the country.

In the region to which he retired, Mr. Pickle's nearest neighbor was Commodore Hawser Trunnion, an old sea dog who kept his house like a seagoing ship and who possessed an endless list of quarterdeck oaths he used on any occasion against anyone who offended him. Other members of his household were Lieutenant Hatchway, a one-legged veteran, and a seaman named Tom Pipes.

Shortly after he had settled in his new home Mr. Pickle met Miss Sally Appleby, daughter of a gentleman in a nearby parish, and after a brief courtship the two were married. Before long Mr. Pickle discovered that his wife was determined to dominate him completely. Peregrine was the oldest son of that ill-starred union. During her pregnancy Mrs. Pickle took such a dislike to Grizzle that she tried in every way possible to embarrass and humiliate her sister-in-law. Realizing that she was no longer wanted in her brother's household, Grizzle began a campaign to win the heart of old Commodore Trunnion.

Ignoring his distrust of women in general, she won out at last over his obstinacy. The wedding was not without humor, for on his way to the church the commodore's horse ran away with him and carried him eleven miles with a hunting party. Upset by his experience, he insisted that the postponed ceremony be performed in his own house. The wedding night was also not without excitement when the ship's hammocks in which the bride and groom were to sleep collapsed and catapulted them to the floor. The next morning, wholly indifferent to her husband's displeasure, Mrs. Trunnion proceeded to refurnish and reorganize the commodore's house according to her own notions.

In order to silence his protests, Mrs. Trunnion conceived the idea of pretending to be pregnant. But the commodore's hopes for an heir were short-lived; his wife employed her ruse only to make herself absolute mistress of the Trunnion household. Lacking an heir of his own, the gruff but kindly old seaman turned his attention to young Peregrine Pickle, his nephew and godson. Peregrine was an unfortunate child. While he was still very young, his mother had taken an unnatural and profound dislike to him, and the boy was often wretched from the harsh treatment he received. Weak-willed Mr. Pickle, under the influence of his wife, did little to improve that unhappy situation. As a result, Peregrine grew into a headstrong, rebellious boy who showed his high spirits in all kinds of pranks that mortified and irritated his parents. Sent away to school, he rebelled against his foolish and hypocritical teachers, and at last he wrote to the commodore asking that he be removed from the school. Feeling pity for the boy and admiring his spirit of independence, the commodore took him out of school and adopted him as his son and heir.

When Peregrine's pranks and escapades became more than his indulgent uncle could stand, the boy was sent to Winchester School, with Pipes accompanying him as his servant. Aware of his uncle's kindness, Peregrine studied and made steady progress until he met Miss Emilia Gauntlet and fell in love with her. Emilia was visiting in Winchester; her own home was in a village about a day's journey away. So great was Peregrine's infatuation that soon after she had returned home he ran away from school and took lodgings in the village in order to be near her. His absence having been reported by the school authorities, Hatchway was sent to look for him. The boy was summoned to attend his uncle, who was alarmed by his heir's interest in a penniless girl. Peregrine's mother grew even more spiteful and his father disowned him for his youthful folly. Indignant at the parents' harsh treatment of their son, the commodore sent Peregrine to Oxford to continue his studies. There he encountered Emilia again and renewed his courtship. Because he hoped to make a good match for his nephew, the commodore attempted to end the affair by sending Peregrine on a tour of the continent. Aware of his uncle's purpose in sending him abroad, Peregrine visited Emilia before his departure and vowed eternal devotion.

Shortly thereafter, warned by the commodore that his reckless behavior would lead only to disaster, Peregrine set out for France. Faithful Pipes went with him as his servant and he was also accompanied by a mentor who was supposed to keep a check on Peregrine's behavior. All efforts in that direction were fruitless. Peregrine had barely set foot on French soil before he made gallant advances to Mrs. Hornbeck, the wife of a traveling Englishman. In Paris he encountered the lady again and eloped with her, an escapade that ended when the British ambassador intervened to send the lady back to her husband. On one occasion Peregrine was imprisoned by the city guard. At another time he fought a duel with a musketeer as the result of an amorous adventure. He quarreled with a nobleman at a masked ball and was sent to the Bastille in company with an artist friend. After Pipes had discovered his whereabouts and had secured his release, Peregrine was ordered to leave France within three days.

On his way back to England, Peregrine became embroiled with a knight of Malta, quarreled with Pipes, and was captivated by a lady he met in a carriage. Shortly afterward he lost his carriage companion and resumed his earlier affair with Mrs. Hornbeck. Her husband interposed and once more Peregrine was thrown into prison. After his release the travelers proceeded to Antwerp and from there to England. His uncle, who still retained his affection for his wayward nephew, received him with great joy.

On his return Peregrine called on Emilia, whom he found indifferent to his attentions. He wasted no time in pining over a lost love but continued to disport himself in London and Bath, until he was called home by the final illness of his uncle. The old commodore was buried according to his own directions and he was remembered with great affection and respect by his nephew. To Peregrine his uncle willed a fortune of thirty thousand pounds and his house. After a vain attempt to reach a friendly understanding with his parents, Peregrine left the house to the tenancy of Hatchway and returned to London.

As a handsome, wealthy young bachelor, he indulged in extravagance and dissipation of all kinds. After exaggerated reports of his wealth had been circulated, he was pursued by matchmaking mothers whose efforts merely amused him but whose designs gave him entrance into the houses of the fashionable and the great.

Meeting Emilia again, he began the same campaign to win her that had been successful with his other light and casual loves. Disappointed in his attempts to seduce her, he took advantage of the confusion attending a masquerade ball to try to overcome her by force. He was vigorously repulsed, and her uncle denied him the privilege of seeing Emilia again.

He became the friend of a notorious lady of quality who gave him a copy of her memoirs. The woman was Lady Vane, whose affairs with many lovers had created a great scandal in London.

Peregrine had a friend named Cadwallader who assumed the character of a fortune-teller and magician. In that way Peregrine was able to learn the secrets of the women who came to consult Cadwallader. Having acquired a reputation as a clever man and a wit, Peregrine used his knowledge to advance his own position.

Grizzle Trunnion died and Peregrine attended her funeral. On the road he met a vulgar young female beggar whom he dressed in fashionable clothes and taught a set of polite phrases. It amused him to introduce the girl into his own fashionable world. When his contemptuous joke was at last exposed, he lost many of his fine friends.

Peregrine now decided to retrench. He cut down his foolish expenses and made loans at a good rate of interest. He was persuaded to stand for Parliament. This decision was taken after he had met Emilia at her sister's wedding and he had begged the sister to intercede for him. But his political venture cost more money than he had expected. Having lost the election, he was for the first time in his life faced with the need for mature reflection on himself and his world.

His affairs went from bad to worse. A mortgage that he held proved worthless. A friend for whom he had endorsed a note defaulted. Reduced at last to complete ruin, he tried to earn money by writing translations and satires. He was again thrown into jail after the publication of a satire directed against an influential politician.

His old friends, Hatchway and Pipes, remained loyal to him in his adversity. Each brought his savings to the Fleet prison and offered them to Peregrine, but he refused to accept their aid. It was his intention to earn money for his release by his writing or else starve in the attempt.

About that time Emilia's brother, Captain Gauntlet, learned that he had been promoted to his rank largely through Peregrine's services in the days of his prosperity. Discovering Peregrine's plight, he set about to relieve his benefactor. Peregrine had an unexpected bit of luck when one of his debtors returned a loan of seven hundred pounds. Emilia, having inherited ten thousand pounds, offered the money and her hand to Peregrine. Touched by her generosity and forgiveness, he reluctantly refused to burden her with his debts and degradation.

Peregrine was saved at last by the death of his father, who died intestate. Legal heir to his father's fortune, he was able to leave Fleet prison and take immediate possession of his estate. Having settled an allowance upon his mother, who had gone to live in another part of the country, Peregrine hastened to ask for Emilia's hand in marriage. With his bride he settled down to lead the life of a country squire.

PERSUASION

Type of work: Novel
Author: Jane Austen (1775-1817)
Type of plot: Comedy of manners
Time of plot: Early nineteenth century
Locale: Somersetshire and Bath, England
First published: 1818

Principal characters:

SIR WALTER ELLIOT, owner of Kellynch Hall
ELIZABETH ELLIOT, his oldest daughter
ANNE ELLIOT, his second daughter
MARY MUSGROVE, his youngest daughter
CHARLES MUSGROVE, her husband
HENRIETTA, and

LOUISA, Charles Musgrove's sisters
CAPTAIN FREDERICK WENTWORTH, a naval officer
MRS. CLAY, Elizabeth Elliot's friend
WILLIAM ELLIOT, Sir Walter's cousin; heir to Kellynch Hall

Critique:

Persuasion may be called an autumnal novel. It is Jane Austen's last work, and the tone is mellow. Even the satire is gentler than in her other works. Anne Elliot is Jane Austen's sweetest heroine. The book has a certain melancholy throughout, even though the final outcome is a happy one.

The Story:

Sir Walter Elliot, a conceited man, vain of both his good looks and his title, lived at his countryseat, Kellynch Hall, with two of his daughters, Elizabeth and Anne. Elizabeth, handsome and much like her father, was the oldest and her father's favorite. Anne, sweet, self-effacing, and quietly intelligent, was ignored, neglected, and underrated by both. Mary, the youngest daughter, was married to an agreeable young man named Charles Musgrove, and lived in an untidy house at Uppercross, three miles from Kellynch Hall.

Living beyond his means had brought financial disaster upon Sir Walter, and on the advice of his solicitor and of a family friend, Lady Russell, he was persuaded to rent Kellynch Hall and take a smaller house in Bath. Anne would have preferred to take a modest house near home, but as usual her father and sister had their way in the matter.

Reluctantly, Sir Walter let his beloved countryseat to Admiral and Mrs. Croft. Mrs. Croft was the sister of a former suitor of Anne, Captain Frederick Wentworth of the navy. Anne and Captain Wentworth had fallen in love when they were both very young, but the match had been discouraged. Anne's father felt that the young man's family was not good enough for his own and Lady Russell considered the engagement unwise because Captain Wentworth had no financial means beyond his navy pay. Also, she did not like or understand Captain Wentworth. Anne had followed their advice and broken the engagement. But it had been poor advice, for Wentworth had advanced and had become rich in the navy, just as he had said he would. Anne, at twenty-seven, had not forgotten her love at nineteen. No one else had taken Captain Wentworth's place in her affection.

With all arrangements completed for the renting of Kellynch Hall, Sir Walter, Elizabeth, and her friend, Mrs. Clay, were off to Bath. Before they departed, Anne warned Elizabeth that Mrs. Clay's was not a disinterested friendship, and that she was scheming to marry Sir Walter if she could. Elizabeth would not believe such an idea, nor would she agree to dismiss Mrs. Clay.

Anne was to divide her time between her married sister, Mary Musgrove, and Lady Russell until Christmas. Mary and her family lived also near her husband's father and mother and their two daughters, Henrietta and Louisa. During her visit to the Musgroves, Anne met Captain Wentworth again, while he was staying with his sister at Kellynch Hall. She found him little changed by eight years.

The Musgroves at once took the Crofts and Captain Wentworth into their circle, and the captain and Anne met frequently. He was coldly polite to Anne, but his attentions to the Musgrove sisters were such as to start Mary matchmaking. She could not decide, however, whether he preferred Henrietta or Louisa. When Louisa encouraged Henrietta to resume a former romance with a cousin, Charles Hayter, it seemed plain that Louisa was destined for Captain Wentworth.

The likelihood of such a match was increased when, during a visit to friends of Captain Wentworth at Lyme Regis,

Louisa suffered an injury while the captain was assisting her to jump down a steep flight of steps. The accident was not his fault, for he had cautioned Louisa against jumping, but he blamed himself for not refusing her firmly. Louisa was taken to the home of Captain Wentworth's friends, Captain and Mrs. Harville, and Captain Benwick. Anne, quiet, practical, and capable during the emergency, had the pleasure of knowing that Captain Wentworth relied on her strength and good judgment, but she felt certain of a match between him and the slowly recovering Louisa.

Anne reluctantly joined her family and the designing Mrs. Clay at Bath. She was surprised to find that they were glad to see her. After showing her the house, they told her the news — mainly about how much in demand they were, and about a cousin, Mr. William Elliot, who had suddenly appeared to make his peace with the family. Mr. William Elliot was the heir to Sir Walter's title and estate, but he had fallen out with the family years before because he did not marry Elizabeth as Sir Walter and Elizabeth felt he should have. Also, he had affronted Sir Walter's pride by speaking disrespectfully of his Kellynch connections.

Now, however, these matters were explained away, and both Sir Walter and Elizabeth were charmed with him. Anne, who had seen Mr. Elliot at Lyme Regis, wondered why he chose to renew a relationship so long neglected. She thought it might be that he was thinking of marrying Elizabeth, now that his first wife was dead; Lady Russell thought Anne was the attraction.

About that time news came of Louisa Musgrove's engagement to Captain Benwick. Joy, surprise, and a hope that Captain Wentworth had lost his partiality for Louisa were mingled in Anne's first reaction. Shortly after she had heard the news, Captain Wentworth arrived in Bath. After a few meetings Anne knew that he had not forgotten her. She also had the pleasure of knowing that he was jealous of Mr. Elliot. His jealousy was groundless.

Even if Anne had felt any inclination to become Lady Elliot, the ambition would have been short-lived, for Mr. Elliot's true character now came to light. Anne learned from a former schoolmate, who had been friendly with Mr. Elliot before he basely ruined her husband, that his first design in renewing acquaintance with Sir Walter's family was to prevent Sir Walter from marrying Mrs. Clay and thus having a son who would inherit the title and estate. Later, when he met Anne, he had been genuinely attracted to her. This information was not news to Anne, since Mr. Elliot had proposed to her at a concert the night before. She, of course, gave him no encouragement.

Her patience in waiting for Captain Wentworth was soon to be rewarded. Convinced that Anne still loved him as he did her, he poured out his heart to her in a letter, and all was settled happily between them. Both Musgrove girls were also married shortly afterward. Neither of their husbands was as rich as Anne's, much to Mary's satisfaction. Mrs. Clay, sacrificing ambition for love, left Bath with Mr. William Elliot, and went to live under his protection in London. Perhaps she hoped some day to be Lady Elliot, though as the wife of a different baronet.

PETER IBBETSON

Type of work: Novel
Author: George du Maurier (1834-1896)
Type of plot: Historical romance
Time of plot: Mid-nineteenth century
Locale: France and England
First published: 1891

Principal characters:
PETER IBBETSON, a confessed murderer
COLONEL IBBETSON, his guardian
MIMSY SERASKIER, his dearest friend; later the Duchess of Towers
MR. LINTOT, his employer
MRS. DEANE, a widow

Critique:

Peter Ibbetson has become a minor classic in its particular field. It is a story composed of the elements of love, friendship, and kindness, but they are so mixed that we have a completely new plot. It is difficult to be sure of the author's purpose in writing this story. Certainly it was not to question the creation or eternity. Perhaps it was merely to show what might be possible if the world would "dream true." The story has been dramatized both for the stage and motion pictures, and it is also the subject of a popular opera.

The Story:

(After his death in a criminal lunatic asylum, Peter Ibbetson's autobiography was given to his cousin, Madge Plunket, who arranged for the publication of the manuscript. Through her efforts the strange and beautiful story was preserved.)

Peter Pasquier moved from England to Paris when he was five years old. His father was a dreamy-eyed inventor, his mother a soft-spoken woman devoted to her family. During his childhood Peter had many friends, but the dearest were Mimsy Seraskier and her beautiful mother, who lived nearby. Mimsy was a delicate, shy child, as plain as her mother was beautiful. She and Peter were inseparable friends, making up their own code language so that no one could intrude on their secret talks.

When Peter was twelve years old, his father was killed in an explosion, and his mother died giving birth to a stillborn child less than a week later. His mother's cousin, Colonel Ibbetson, came from England to take Peter home with him. Peter wept when he took leave of his friends, and Mimsy was so ill from her grief that she could not even tell him goodbye.

Colonel Ibbetson gave Peter his name, and he became Peter Ibbetson. The colonel sent him to school, where he spent six years. Events at the school touched him very little, as he spent most of his time dreaming of his old life in Paris.

When he left school, Peter spent some time with Colonel Ibbetson. The colonel's only request was that Peter become a gentleman, but Peter began to doubt that the colonel himself fitted the description. He learned that Colonel Ibbetson had a very poor reputation among his acquaintances, due largely to his vanity and gallantry. His latest victim was Mrs. Deane, a woman he had ruined with malicious lies. The colonel seemed also to derive great pleasure from telling scandalous tales about everyone he knew, and Peter grew to hate him for this habit. After a time he ran away to London and joined the cavalry for a year. Following his term in the army, he was apprenticed to Mr. Lintot, an architect whom he had met through Colonel Ibbetson. He took rooms in Pentonville and there began a new chapter in his life.

He worked industriously for Mr. Lintot and achieved some success, but his outer life was lonely and dull. The only real joy he found was in the arts, and of these only music inspired him deeply. He saved carefully that he might occasionally attend a concert. His nightly dreams were still of his childhood in Paris and of Mimsy, but his dreams were becoming blurred.

Viewing with skepticism the belief in a creator and a life after death, Peter believed man would have to work back to the very beginning of time before he could understand anything about a deity.

He believed it was possible to go back, if only he knew the way. His ideas on sin were unorthodox, for to Peter the only real sin was cruelty to the mind or body of any living thing.

During this period of his life his only acquaintances were the friends of Mr. and Mrs. Lintot, for Peter was a shy young man, too much concerned with his speculations and dreams for social gaiety. At one party, however, he saw a great lady who was to be his guiding star for the rest of his life. He was told she was the Duchess of Towers, and although he was not presented to her, he saw her looking at him in a strange manner, almost as if she found his a familiar face.

Some time after his first sight of the Duchess of Towers, Peter revisited Paris, where he found his old home and those of his friends replaced with modern bungalows. The only news he had of his old friends was that Madame Seraskier had died and Mimsy and her father had left Paris many years ago. He returned to his hotel that night, exhausted emotionally from the disappointments of the day.

But that night his real and true inner life began, for he learned how to dream true. When he fell asleep, the events of the day passed before him in distorted fashion. He found himself surrounded by demon dwarfs. As he tried to escape them, he looked up and saw standing before him the Duchess of Towers. She took his hand and told him he was not dreaming true, and then a strange thing happened.

He was transported back to the happy days of his childhood, and he saw himself as he was then. But at the same time he retained his present identity. He was two people at the same time, his adult self looking at his child self. The duchess told him he could always transport himself into any scene he had experienced if he would only dream true. To do this he must lie on his back with his arms over his head, and as he went to sleep he must never cease thinking of the place he wanted to be in his dreams. Also, he must never forget in his dream who and where he was when awake; in this way his dream would be tied to reality. She had learned the trick from her father and could revisit any place she chose.

When he awoke, he knew that at last one of his greatest desires had come true; he had looked into the mind of the duchess. But the matter puzzled him, for he had always thought such a fusion would be possible only between two people who knew and loved each other. The duchess was a stranger to him.

He returned to Pentonville and outwardly resumed his normal life. But his inner self was his real life, and he mastered the art of dreaming true and reliving any experience he wished. He visited with his mother and Mimsy frequently in his dreams, and his life was no longer bleak and lonely.

One day he again met the Duchess of Towers in his outer life. Then he discovered why she had been in his true dream. She was Mimsy, grown and married to a famous duke. She had had the same dream as he when she had rescued him from the dwarfs, and she too had been unable to understand why a stranger had invaded her dreams.

Although he did not again meet the grown Mimsy in his dreams, Peter saw the child Mimsy almost every night. So his life went along without interruption until he met Mrs. Gregory, formerly Mrs. Deane, whom Colonel Ibbetson had tried to ruin with slander. She told him that Colonel Ibbetson had told her and many others that he was Peter's real father. The recorded marriage and birth dates proved he was lying; the story was another product of the colonel's cruel mind. Peter was so enraged he went to the colonel's house to force an apology. The two men fought, and Peter in his fury struck blindly at Colonel Ibbetson and killed him.

Peter was tried and sentenced to be hanged for the murder of his uncle.

While he was in prison, the grown Mimsy came into his dream again and told him his sentence had been changed to life imprisonment because of the circumstances under which the murder had been committed. She promised Peter she would continue to come to him in his dreams and thus they would spend the rest of their lives together.

Peter in his prison cell was the happiest man in England. Attendants were kind to him during the day, and at night he was with Mimsy. At last they learned they were distant cousins, and then they discovered that they could project themselves into the past through the character of any of their direct ancestors. Either of them, not both at once, could become any ancestor he chose, and thus they relived scenes in history which had occurred hundreds of years before. They went back to the days when monsters roamed the earth and might have gone back to the beginning of time, but Mimsy died.

She came back to Peter seven times after she had died, urging him to continue his search for the beginning of time. She could come to him now only because he was the other half of her soul. She asked him to write down his method and to urge others to follow him, and she gave him some books in their secret code, telling him of things she had learned.

But before he could begin to write the secrets she told him, he died in his cell, and his cousin, Madge Plunket, felt that she would remember until her own death the look of happiness and peace upon his face.

PETER WHIFFLE

Type of work: Novel
Author: Carl Van Vechten (1880-)
Type of plot: Simulated biography
Time of plot: 1907-1919
Locale: New York, Paris, Italy
First published: 1922

Principal characters:
PETER WHIFFLE, a would-be writer
CARL VAN VECHTEN, his friend
EDITH DALE, friend of Peter and Carl
MAHALAH WIGGINS, Peter's friend

Critique:

A first reading of *Peter Whiffle* may leave the impression that here is an ordinary biographical novel of a pseudo-sophisticated young man who did not know what he wanted from life. But there is more to the story than that. Peter Whiffle learned, before he died, that not everyone is meant to accomplish great things, that some are meant to enjoy and appreciate the work of others. To tell his readers this fact was apparently Van Vechten's motive for writing the story.

The Story:

Carl Van Vechten saw Peter Whiffle for the first time in Paris, in the spring. They were both young. Carl was naïve and unworldly; Peter was sophisticated and knowing. Theirs was a strange friendship. Often they did not see one another for several years. But Carl knew that he was one of the few people whom Peter called his friend. They had spent many enjoyable hours in Paris that spring and together had seen all the famous places of which they had read. Peter wanted to write, and at that point in his life he thought that subject was unimportant, that style and form were the only important things. In fact, it was his plan to write a book containing nothing but lists of Things. When he wrote, he used colored papers to express his moods.

After that spring in Paris, six years passed before Carl saw Peter again. Carl was back in New York at the time, and while walking in the Bowery one night he met Peter. He hardly recognized his friend when he saw Peter in rags, unshaven and unkempt. Carl learned that the rags were only another phase of Peter's life, for Peter was a rich man. After he had learned Peter's history, Carl began to understand him better.

Peter Whiffle, the son of a banker, was born and raised in Toledo, Ohio. From infancy, Peter found it almost impossible to make decisions. Whether to do this or that was a problem that he could seldom solve, and so, preferring inactivity to decision, he usually did nothing. But there was one thing about which he knew his own mind. He hated work in any form. When Peter could no longer stand his work in his father's bank, he left home and went to New York. There he often slept in the park and went for days without food. He took a few odd jobs in order not to starve. He lived in this fashion until his mother's brother died and left him a fortune. On the night he learned of his inheritance he decided to become a writer. A few days later he left for Paris.

When they met in New York, Carl learned from Peter that although he was still a wealthy man he had joined a group of Socialists and with them was plotting an American revolution against capitalism. He was full of plans to barricade the rich in their homes and starve them to death, or bomb them, or hang them. Carl was not much disturbed, for he recognized this idea as another stage in Peter's life. When Carl asked Peter about his book, he learned that Peter now believed subject, rather than style or form, was all-important. He was planning to write about the revolution, to have as his heroine a girl with a clubfoot, a harelip, and a hunched back. The book would be bloody and dirty, for that was the way life was.

When Carl took Peter to see Edith Dale, a woman of wealth, Peter and Edith became friends. At Edith's house Peter met Mahalah Wiggins, a young girl whom he found interesting. But he could not make up his mind whether he wanted to marry her, and so he did nothing. He did change his living habits, however, and the next time Carl saw him Peter was clean and neat in appearance. He still talked of the revolution, but half-heartedly, and Carl knew another phase of Peter's life was almost over.

Deciding at last to marry Mahalah, Peter asked Carl to be his attendant. But on the wedding day Peter sent Carl a note saying that he could not go through with the wedding; it was too big a decision for him to make. Instead, Peter went to Africa.

Four months later Carl was in Italy, visiting Edith Dale at her villa in Florence. One night, while they were dining in the city, they saw Peter again. His father had died and his mother was traveling with him. Peter told them that he had almost died in Africa, that while he lay at the point of death he had had a vision. An angel from hell and an angel from heaven had waited for him to make up his mind about the place to which he wanted to go when he died. It had been a terrible moment, until he remembered that he did not have to make a decision; he could stay right where he was. Then he recovered.

He had again changed his mind about the book he planned to write. He claimed that everything about the characters must be put down, but he admitted that it would be quite a task to record all emotions, impressions, actions, and speech. Having sent his mother home, Peter went to stay with Carl and Edith. The days at the villa were peaceful and happy ones, so happy, in fact, that one day Peter told Carl that he was going to leave the villa at once, without telling Edith goodbye. He wanted to leave in the midst of his happiness so that his memory would not have one blot on it. He could not tell Carl where he was going because he had not yet made up his mind.

A few months later Carl found Peter sitting on a park bench in New York. Peter did not want Edith to learn that he was there, for he was in the middle of a new experiment and Edith might distract him. Interested in black magic, Peter was trying to discover the mystery of life and death. He took Carl to his apartment and showed him his laboratory. He also persuaded Carl to join him in an experiment. The magic brew exploded and they woke up in the hospital.

Carl sustained only minor injuries and left the hospital before Peter, who was dangerously hurt. But Peter recovered and returned to Toledo with his mother. Carl did not see him again until after the war, in 1919. By that time Peter was very ill from some incurable disease. He never mentioned his illness, but Carl knew that his friend's time was not long. One afternoon in December, while the two friends were in Peter's apartment, Carl learned that Peter had at last found himself. He told Carl that his book had never become a reality because he had attempted to do something that he was never intended to do. He was not meant to be a writer or a worker—he was meant only to appreciate and love the work of others, the art, the literature, the ability. He would make art greater and people better by bestowing upon them his appreciation and his affection. He would never have to make a decision; he would be himself. He told Carl that now he was happy and that he was a success. Then he closed his eyes. When Carl spoke to him again, Peter Whiffle did not answer.

PHAÈDRA

Type of work: Drama
Author: Jean Baptiste Racine (1639 1699)
Type of plot: Classical tragedy
Time of plot: Remote antiquity
Locale: Troezen, in Ancient Greece
First presented: 1677

Principal characters:
THESEUS, King of Athens
PHAÈDRA, his wife
HIPPOLYTUS, Theseus' son
ARICIA, an Athenian princess

Critique:

Phaèdra represents the classic tradition of the French stage. In the seventeenth century France, then at her apex, demanded great things of her artists to support the glory of the armies and the royal house, and the writers of the period assaulted the past in an effort to arouse the minds of their contemporaries to past glories and to stimulate them to greater efforts. The vast storehouse of classic legends became the source of countless plots and themes. In whole or in part, ancient plays and myths were constructed into plays which adhered as closely as possible to the classic tradition. Racine stands foremost among the neo-classicists of his century.

The Story:

After the death of his Amazon queen, Theseus, slayer of the Minotaur, married Phaèdra, the young daughter of the King of Crete. Phaèdra, seeing in her stepson, Hippolytus, all the bravery and virtue of his heroic father, but in more youthful guise, fell in love with him. In an attempt to conceal her passion for the son of Theseus, she treated him in an aloof and spiteful manner until at last Hippolytus decided to leave Troezen and go in search of his father, absent from the kingdom. To his tutor, Theramenes, he confided his desire to avoid both his stepmother and Aricia, an Athenian princess who was the daughter of a family which had opposed Theseus.

Phaèdra confessed to Oenone, her nurse, her guilty passion for Hippolytus, saying that she merely pretended unkindness to him in order to hide her real feelings.

Word came to Troezen that Theseus was dead. Oenone talked to Phaèdra in an attempt to convince the queen that her own son, not Hippolytus, should be chosen as the new king of Athens. Aricia hoped that she would be chosen to rule.

Hippolytus, a fair-minded young man, told Aricia that he would support her for the rule of Athens. He felt that Phaèdra's son should inherit Crete and that he himself should remain master of Troezen. He also admitted his love for Aricia, but said that he feared the gods would never allow it to be brought to completion. When he tried to explain his intentions to his stepmother, she in turn dropped her pretense of hatred and distrust and ended by betraying her love for Hippolytus. Shocked, he repulsed her, and she threatened to take her own life.

The people of Athens, however, chose Phaèdra's son to rule over them, to the disappointment of Aricia. There were also rumors that Theseus still lived. Hippolytus gave orders that a search be made for his father.

Phaèdra, embarrassed by all she had told Hippolytus, brooded over the injury she now felt, and wished that she had never revealed her love. Phaèdra was proud, and now her pride was hurt beyond recovery. Unable to overcome her passion, however, she decided to offer the kingdom to Hippolytus so that she might keep him near her. Then news came that Theseus was returning to his home. Oenone warned Phaèdra that now she must hide her true feeling for Hippolytus. She even suggested to the queen that Theseus be made to believe that Hippolytus had tempted Phaèdra to adultery.

When Theseus returned, Phaèdra greeted him with reluctance, saying that she was no longer fit to be his wife. Hippolytus made the situation no better by requesting permission to leave Troezen at once. Theseus was greatly chagrined at his homecoming.

When scheming Oenone told the king that Hippolytus had attempted to dishonor his stepmother, Theseus flew into a terrific rage. Hippolytus, knowing nothing of the plot, was at first astonished by his father's anger and threats. When accused, he denied the charges, but Theseus refused to listen to him and banished his son from the kingdom forever. When Hippolytus claimed he was really in love with Aricia, Theseus, more incensed than ever, invoked the vengeance of Neptune upon his son.

Aricia tried to convince Hippolytus that he must prove his innocence, but Hippolytus refused because he knew that the revelation of Phaèdra's passion would be too painful for his father to bear. The two agreed to escape together. Before Aricia could leave the palace, however, Theseus questioned her. Becoming suspicious, he sent for Oenone to demand the truth. Fearing that her plot had been uncovered, Oenone committed suicide.

Meanwhile, as Hippolytus drove his chariot near the seashore, Neptune sent a horrible monster, part bull and part dragon, which destroyed the son of Theseus.

When news of his death reached the palace, Phaèdra confessed her guilt and drank poison. Theseus, glad to see his guilty queen die, wished that memory of her life might perish with her. Sorrowfully he sought the grief-stricken Aricia to comfort her.

PICKWICK PAPERS

Type of work: Novel
Author: Charles Dickens (1812-1870)
Type of plot: Comic romance
Time of plot: Nineteenth century
Locale: England
First published: 1836-1837

Principal characters:

Mr. Pickwick, founder of the Pickwick Club
Mr. Winkle,
Mr. Snodgrass, and
Mr. Tupman, members of the club
Mr. Wardle, owner of Manor Farm
Rachael Wardle, his sister
Emily Wardle, his daughter
Mrs. Bardell, Mr. Pickwick's housekeeper
Mr. Perker, a lawyer
Sam Weller, Mr. Pickwick's servant
Arabella Allen, in love with Mr. Winkle
Mr. Alfred Jingle, a rascal

Critique:

Mr. Pickwick, the lovable, generous old gentleman of Dickens' novel, is one of the best-known characters of fiction. Mr. Pickwick benignly reigns over all activities of the Pickwick Club, satisfied, under every circumstance, that he has helped his fellow creatures by his well-meaning efforts. The height of this Dickensian comedy, however, lies in Sam Weller and his father. Sam's imperturbable presence of mind and his ready wit are indispensable to the Pickwickians. The novel has importance beyond humorous incident and characterization. It is the first novel of a literary movement to present the life and manners of lower and middle-class life.

The Story:

Samuel Pickwick, Esquire, was the founder and perpetual president of the justly famous Pickwick Club. To extend his own researches into the quaint and curious phenomena of life, he suggested that he and three other Pickwickians should make journeys to places remote from London and report on their findings to the stay-at-home members of the club. The first destination decided upon was Rochester. As Mr. Pickwick, Mr. Tracy Tupman, Mr. Nathaniel Winkle, and Mr. Augustus Snodgrass went to their coach, they were waylaid by a rough gang of cab drivers. Fortunately the men were rescued by a stranger who was poorly dressed but of a magnificently friendly nature. The stranger, who introduced himself as Alfred Jingle, appeared to be going to Rochester also, and the party mounted the coach together.

After they had arrived at their destination, Mr. Tupman's curiosity was aroused when Mr. Jingle told him that there was to be a ball at the inn that very evening and that many lovely young ladies would be present. Because his luggage had gone astray, said Mr. Jingle, he had no evening clothes and so it would be impossible for him to attend the affair. This was a regrettable circumstance because he had hoped to introduce Mr. Tupman to the many young ladies of wealth and fashion who would be present. Eager to meet these young ladies, Mr. Tupman borrowed Mr. Winkle's suit for the stranger. At the ball Mr. Jingle observed a doctor in faithful attendance upon a middle-aged lady. Attracting her attention, he danced with her, much to the anger of the doctor. Introducing himself as Dr. Slammer, the angry gentleman challenged Mr. Jingle to a duel.

The next morning a servant, identifying Mr. Winkle from the description given of the suit the stranger had worn, told Mr. Winkle that an insolent drunken man had insulted Dr. Slammer the previous evening and that the doctor was awaiting his appearance to fight a duel. Mr. Winkle had been drunk the night before, and he decided he was being called out because he had conducted himself in an unseemly manner which he could no longer remember. With Mr. Snodgrass as his second, Mr. Winkle tremblingly approached the battlefield. Much to his relief, Dr. Slammer roared that he was the wrong man. After much misunderstanding, the situation was satisfactorily explained and no blood was shed.

During the afternoon the travelers attended a parade, where they met Mr. Wardle in a coach with his two daughters and his sister, Miss Rachael Wardle, a plump old maid. Mr. Tupman, being quite taken with the elder Miss Wardle, accepted for his friends Mr. Wardle's invitation to visit his estate, Manor Farm. The next day the four Pickwickians departed for the farm, which was a distance of about ten miles from the inn where they were staying. Having difficulties with their horses, they arrived at Manor Farm in a disheveled state, but they were soon washed and mended under the kind assistance of Mr. Wardle's daughters. In the evening they played a hearty game of whist, and Mr. Tupman squeezed Miss Wardle's hand under the table.

The next day Mr. Wardle took his guests rook hunting. Mr. Winkle, who would not admit himself unable to cope with any situation, was given the gun to try his skill. He proved it by accidentally shooting Mr. Tupman in the arm. Miss Wardle offered her aid to the stricken man. Observing that their friend was in good hands, the others went off to a neighboring town to watch the cricket matches. There Mr. Pickwick unexpectedly encountered Mr. Jingle, and Mr. Wardle invited the fellow to return to Manor Farm with his party.

Convinced that Miss Wardle had a great deal of money, Mr. Jingle misrepresented Mr. Tupman's intentions to Miss Wardle and persuaded the spinster to elope with him. Mr. Wardle and Mr. Pickwick pursued the couple to London. There, with the assistance of Mr. Wardle's lawyer, Mr. Perker, they went from one inn to another in an attempt to find the elopers. Finally, through a sharp-featured young man cleaning boots in the yard of the White Hart Inn, they were able to identify Mr. Jingle. They indignantly confronted him as he was displaying a marriage license. After a heated argument, Mr. Jingle resigned his matrimonial designs for the sum of one hundred and twenty pounds. Miss Wardle went tearfully back to Manor Farm. The Pickwickians returned to London, where Mr. Pickwick engaged as his servant Sam Weller, the sharp, shrewd young bootblack of the White Hart Inn.

Mr. Pickwick was destined to meet the villainous Mr. Jingle soon again. A Mrs. Leo Hunter invited the learned man and his friends to a party. There Mr. Pickwick spied Mr. Jingle, who, upon seeing his former acquaintance, disappeared into the crowd. Mrs. Hunter told Mr. Pickwick that Mr. Jingle lived at Bury St. Edmonds. Mr. Pickwick set out in pursuit in company with his servant, Sam Weller, for the old gentleman was determined to deter the scoundrel from any fresh deceptions he might be planning. At the inn where Mr. Jingle was reported to be staying, Mr. Pickwick learned that the rascal was planning to elope with a rich young lady who stayed at a boarding-school nearby. Mr. Pickwick fell in with the suggestion that in order to rescue the young lady he should hide in the garden from which Mr. Jingle was planning to steal her. When Mr. Pickwick sneaked into the garden, he found nothing of a suspicious nature; in short, he had been deceived, and the blackguard had escaped.

Mr. Pickwick had for housekeeper Mrs. Bardell, a widow. When he was about to hire Sam Weller, Mr. Pickwick had spoken to her in such a manner that she had mistaken his words for a proposal of marriage. One day Mr. Pickwick was resting in his rooms when he received notice from the legal firm of Dodgson and Fogg that Mrs. Bardell was suing him for breach of promise. The summons was distressing, but first Mr. Pickwick had more important business to occupy his time. After securing the services of Mr. Perker to defend him, he went to Ipswich upon learning that Mr. Jingle had been seen in that vicinity. The trip to Ipswich was successful. The Pickwickians were able to catch Mr. Jingle in his latest scheme of deception and to expose him before he had carried out his plot.

At the trial for the breach of promise suit brought by Mrs. Bardell, lawyers Dodgson and Fogg argued so eloquently against Mr. Pickwick that the jury fined him seven hundred and fifty pounds. When the trial was over, Mr. Pickwick told Dodgson and Fogg that even if they put him in prison he would never pay one cent of the damages, since he knew as well as they that there had been no true grounds for suit.

The Pickwickians shortly afterward went to Bath, where fresh adventures awaited Mr. Pickwick and his friends. On that occasion Mr. Winkle's weakness for the fair sex involved them in difficulties. In Bath the Pickwickians met two young medical students, Mr. Allen and Mr. Bob Sawyer. Mr. Allen hoped to marry his sister, Arabella, to his friend, Mr. Sawyer, but Miss Allen professed extreme dislike for her brother's choice. When Mr. Winkle learned that Arabella had refused Mr. Sawyer because another had won her heart, he felt that he must be the fortunate man because she had displayed an interest in him when they had met earlier at Manor Farm. Kindly Mr. Pickwick arranged to have Mr. Winkle meet Arabella in a garden, where the distraught lover could plead his suit.

Mr. Pickwick's plans to further his friend's romance were interrupted, however, by a subpoena delivered because he had refused to pay money to Mrs. Bardell. Still stubbornly refusing to pay the damages, Mr. Pickwick found himself returned to London and lodged in Fleet Street prison. With the help of Sam Weller, Mr. Pickwick arranged his prison quarters as comfortably as possible and remained deaf to the entreaties of Sam Weller or Mr. Perker, who thought that he should pay his debt and regain his freedom. Dodgson and Fogg proved to be of lower caliber than even Mr. Pickwick had suspected. They had taken Mrs. Bardell's case without fee, gambling on Mr. Pickwick's payment to cover the costs of the case. When they saw no payment forthcoming, they had Mrs. Bardell arrested also and sent to the Fleet Street prison.

While Mr. Pickwick was trying to decide what to do, Mr. Winkle with his new wife, Arabella, came to the prison and asked Mr. Pickwick to pay his debts so that he could visit Mr. Allen with the news of Mr. Winkle's marriage to Arabella. Arabella herself felt that Mr. Pickwick was the only person who could arrange a proper reconcilliation between her brother and her new husband. Kindness prevailed; Mr. Pickwick paid the damages to Mrs. Bardell so that he would be free to help his friends in distress.

Winning Mr. Allen's approval of the match was not difficult for Mr. Pickwick, but when he approached the elder Mr. Winkle, the bridegroom's father objected to the marriage and threatened to cut off his son without a cent. To add to Mr. Pickwick's problems, Mr. Wardle came to London to tell him that his daughter Emily was in love with Mr. Snodgrass and to ask Mr. Pickwick's advice. Mr. Wardle had brought Emily to London with him.

The entire party came together in Arabella's apartment. All misunderstandings happily ended for the two lovers, and a jolly party followed. The elder Mr.

Winkle paid a call on his new daughter-in-law. Upon seeing what a charming and lovely girl she was, he relented his decision to disinherit his son, and the family was reconciled.

After Mr. Snodgrass had married Emily Wardle, Mr. Pickwick dissolved the Pickwick Club and retired to a home in the country, with his faithful servant, Sam Weller. Several times Mr. Pickwick was called upon to be a godfather to little Winkles and Snodgrasses, but for the most part he led a quiet life, respected by his neighbors and loved by all his friends.

THE PICTURE OF DORIAN GRAY

Type of work: Novel
Author: Oscar Wilde (1856-1900)
Type of plot: Fantasy
Time of plot: Late nineteenth century
Locale: England
First published: 1891

Principal characters:
DORIAN GRAY, a Faustian young man
LORD HENRY WOTTON, his tempter
BASIL HALLWARD, an artist
SIBYL VANE, an actress
JAMES VANE, her brother

Critique:

The Picture of Dorian Gray is definitely a period piece, but the central idea of the story is so typical of its author and the elements of the plot are so carefully worked out that the novel is sure to attract readers for many years to come. Wilde has written that there is no such thing as a moral or unmoral book, that a book can be judged only as it is well written or badly written. *The Picture of Dorian Gray* should be judged with this statement in mind.

The Story:

One day, in his London studio, Basil Hallward was putting a few last finishing touches on a portrait of his handsome young friend, Dorian Gray. Lord Henry Wotton, a caller, indolently watched the painter at work. In reply to his friend's admiration for the painting, the artist explained that Dorian was his ideal of youth. For this reason he asked Lord Henry never to meet Dorian because the older man's influence on the boy would be absolute and evil.

While they were talking, Dorian himself came to the studio, and he and Lord Henry met, much against Hallward's wishes. Half seriously, half jokingly, Sir Henry began to exert his influence on Dorian. Hallward signed the portrait and announced it was finished. When Lord Henry offered to buy the picture, the painter said it was not his property, that it belonged to Dorian, to whom he was presenting it. Looking at his portrait, after listening to Lord Henry's witty conversation, Dorian grew sad. He would become old and wrinkled, he said, while the picture would remain the same. He wished, instead, that the portrait might grow old while he remained forever young. He said he would give his soul to keep his youth.

Dorian and Lord Henry became close friends. One of the gifts Lord Henry gave the boy was a book about a young man who attempted to realize in his brief lifetime all the passions of man's history. Dorian made the book a pattern for his own life, and the first lesson from its pages was the lesson of love. In a third-rate theater he saw Sibyl Vane, a young

THE PICTURE OF DORIAN GRAY by Oscar Wilde. Published by The Viking Press, Inc.

actress who played the role of Juliet with such sincerity and charm that he fell in love with her on the spot. After he had met her, Dorian dreamed of taking her away from the cheap theatrical troupe and making her a great actress who would thrill the world. One night he took Lord Henry to watch her performance. That night Sibyl was listless and wooden, so uninspired in her acting that the audience hissed her. When Dorian went to her dressing-room after the final curtain, she explained that before meeting him she had thought acting her only reality. Now, she said, Dorian's love had taught her what reality actually was, and she could no longer act. Dorian coldly and cruelly told her she had killed his love and he never intended to see her again.

In the meantime, Hallward had delivered the painting to Dorian. When the young man returned to his home after the theater that night he saw that the appearance of his portrait had changed. There was a new, faint line of cruelty about the mouth. Looking at his own features in a mirror, he found no such line on his own lips. His wish had evidently been granted. He would remain young and untouched — the portrait would take on an appearance of experience and age.

Disturbed, he resolved to reform, to see no more of Lord Henry, to ask Sibyl Vane's forgiveness and marry her. Accordingly, he wrote her a passionate letter declaring his love. Before he could post the letter, however, Lord Henry visited him the next morning, bringing the news that Sibyl had killed herself in her dressing-room the night before.

After his friend had gone, forgetting all his good resolutions Dorian decided on a life of sensation and pleasure. The portrait only was to bear the burden of his shame. That night he attended the opera with Lord Henry. The next day, when Basil Hallward attempted to reason with him over scandalous reports beginning to circulate, Dorian refused to show any emotion over Sibyl's suicide. His part in her tragic story would never be revealed, for she had known him only as Prince Charming. Before he left, Hallward asked to see his painting. Dorian refused to show it. In sudden rage, he shouted that he never wished to see Hallward again. Later he hung the portrait in an old schoolroom upstairs, locked the door, and put the key where only he could find it.

London continued to gossip about the friendship of Lord Henry and Dorian Gray. The young man was suspected of strange vices, and gentlemen walked out of their club rooms when he entered them. He was invited to fewer balls and parties at country houses. Many of his former friends refused to recognize him when they met. It was reported he had been seen in low dives with drunken sailors and thieves. Meanwhile Dorian's features did not change; only the portrait reflected his life of crime and debauchery. For Dorian's life, like that of the hero in the book Lord Henry had given him, became a frenzied quest for fresh experiences and new sensations. In turn, he became interested in religious rituals, perfumes, music, jewels. He frequented opium dens. He had sordid affairs with women. His features in the portrait became the terrible record of his life.

On the eve of Dorian's thirty-eighth birthday, Basil Hallward visited him again. Though the two had been estranged for years, Hallward came in a last attempt to persuade Dorian to change his dissolute ways. He was still unable to believe many of the stories he had heard about Dorian. With a bitter laugh, Dorian said that Hallward should see what he had truly become. He took Hallward to the schoolroom and unveiled the portrait. The artist was horrified, for only by signature could he identify his own handiwork. In anger that he had betrayed his true self to his former friend, Dorian seized a knife which lay nearby and stabbed Hallward in the neck and back.

Dorian relocked the door and went

down to the drawing-room. Because Hallward had intended to leave for Paris that night, Dorian knew the painter would not be missed for some time. Removal of the body, he decided, was not enough. He wanted it completely destroyed. Suddenly he thought of Alan Campbell, a young chemist who had once been his intimate. By threatening the young scientist with exposure for some secret crime, Dorian forced Campbell to destroy the body with fire and chemicals. After that night, the hands of the portrait were smeared with blood.

Late one night, commonly dressed, Dorian visited an opium den. As he was leaving the place, a drunken woman addressed him as Prince Charming. A sailor followed him out. The sailor was James Vane, Sibyl's brother, who had sworn revenge on his sister's betrayer. The sailor would have killed Dorian but for the fact that he looked so young. Sibyl had committed suicide eighteen years before, and Dorian seemed no more than twenty years old. When Vane, convinced that Dorian could not have known his sister, returned to the den, the woman told him that Dorian Gray had ruined her many years before, and that he had not changed in appearance since then.

Some time later, at his country home, Dorian saw James Vane watching him outside a window. During a hunt on the estate Vane was accidentally shot and killed. In the meantime, Alan Campbell had committed suicide under strange circumstances, and Basil Hallward's disappearance was being investigated.

Back in London, Dorian, having decided to destroy the picture which stood as an awful record of his guilt, went to the old schoolroom. The portrait now had an appearance of cunning and triumph. Using the knife with which he had murdered Basil Hallward, Dorian stabbed the frightful portrait. The servants in the house heard a horrible cry of agony. When they forced open the locked door of the room, they found, hanging on the wall, a fine portrait of their master as he had always looked. On the floor was a dead body, withered, wrinkled, in evening dress, with a knife in its breast. Only by his jewelry did they recognize Dorian Gray, who, in his desperate attempt to kill his conscience, had killed himself.

THE PILGRIM'S PROGRESS

Type of work: Novel
Author: John Bunyan (1628-1688)
Type of plot: Religious allegory
Time of plot: Any time since Christ
Locale: Anywhere
First published: 1678

Principal characters:
CHRISTIAN
FAITHFUL
HOPEFUL
MR. WORLDLY WISEMAN
EVANGELIST
DESPAIR
IGNORANCE
APOLLYON, a giant devil

Critique:

This famous story of man's progress through life to heaven or hell has often been rated next to the Bible in importance as a Christian document. In any case, it remains one of the most pleasing allegories of the Christian way ever written. Bunyan, an early Puritan, wished to write a book which would be popular with the common people as well as with intellectuals. His characters are more than simple symbols; they are real people. The story can be read as a symbolic narrative, a picaresque romance, and a realistic novel.

The Story:

One day, according to Bunyan, he lay down in a den to sleep, and in his sleep dreamed that he saw a man standing in a field and crying out in pain and sorrow because he and his whole family as well as the town in which they lived were to be destroyed. Christian, for that was his name, knew of this catastrophe because he had read about it in the book he held in his hands, the Bible. Evangelist, the preacher of Christianity, soon came up to Christian and presented him with a roll of paper on which it was written that he should flee from the wrath of God and make his way from the City of Destruction to the City of Zion. Running home with this hope of salvation, Christian tried to get his neighbors and family to go away with him, but they would not listen and thought he was either sick or mad. Finally, shutting his ears to his family's entreaties to stay with them, he ran off toward the light in the distance. Under the light he knew he would find the wicket gate which opened into Heaven.

On his way he met Pliant and Obstinate, who so distracted Christian that he fell in a bog called the Slough of Despond. He could not get out because of the bundle of sins on his back. Finally Help came along and aided Christian out of the sticky mire. Going on his way, he soon fell in with Mr. Worldly Wiseman, who tried to convince Christian he would lead a happier life if he gave up his trip toward the light and settled down to the comforts of a burdenless town life. Fearing that Christian was about to be led astray, Evangelist came up to the two men and quickly showed the errors in Mr. Worldly Wiseman's arguments.

Soon Christian arrived at a closed gate where he met Good-Will, who told him that if he knocked the gate would be opened to him. Christian did so. Invited into the gatekeeper's house by the Interpreter, he learned from him the meaning of many of the Christian mysteries. He was shown pictures of Christ and Passion and Patience; Despair in a cage of iron bars; and finally a vision of the Day of Judgment, when evil men will be sent to the bottomless pit and good men will be carried up to Heaven. Having seen these things, Christian was filled with both hope and fear. Continuing on his journey, he came to the Holy Cross and the Sepulchre of Christ. There his burden of sins fell off, and he was able to take to the road with renewed vigor.

Soon he met Sloth, Simple, Presumption, Formalism, and Hypocrisy, but he kept to his way and they kept to theirs. Later Christian lay down to sleep for a while. When he went on again, he forgot to pick up the roll of paper Evangelist had given him. Remembering it later, he ran back to find it. Running to make up the time lost, he suddenly found himself confronted by two lions. He was afraid to pass by them until the porter of the house by the side of the road told him that the lions were chained, and that he had nothing to fear. The porter then asked Christian to come into the house. There he was well-treated and shown some of the relics of Biblical antiquity by four virgins, Discretion, Prudence, Piety, and Charity. They gave him good advice and sent him on his journey armed with the sword and shield of Christian faith.

In the Valley of Humiliation, Christian was forced to fight the giant devil, Apollyon, whose body was covered with the shiny scales of pride. In this battle Christian was wounded, but after he had chased away the devil, he healed his wounds with leaves from the Tree of Life which grew nearby. After the Valley of Humiliation came the Valley of the Shadow of Death in which Christian had to pass one of the gates to Hell. In order to save himself from the devils who issued out of that terrible hole, he recited some of the verses from the Psalms.

Having passed through this danger, he had to go by the caves of the old giants, Pope and Pagan, and when he had done so he caught up with a fellow traveler, Faithful. As the two companions went along, they met Evangelist, who warned them of the dangers in the town of Vanity Fair.

Vanity Fair was a town of ancient foundation which since the beginning of time had tried to lure men away from the path to Heaven. Here all the vanities of the world were sold, and the people who dwelt there were cruel and stupid and had no love for travelers such as Christian and Faithful. Having learned these things, the two companions promised to be careful and went on down into the town. There they were arrested and tried because they would buy none of the town's goods. Faithful was sentenced to be burned alive and Christian was put in prison. When Faithful died in the fire, a chariot came down from Heaven and took him up to God. Christian escaped from the prison. Accompanied by a young man named Hopeful, who had been impressed by Faithful's reward, he set off once more.

They passed through the Valley of Ease, where they were tempted to dig in a silver mine free to all. As they left the valley, they saw the pillar of salt which had once been Lot's wife. Becoming lost, they were captured by a giant, Despair, who lived in Doubting Castle, and were locked in the vaults beneath the castle walls. There they lay until Christian remembered he had a key called Promise in his pocket, and with this they escaped from the prison.

They met the four sheperds, Knowledge, Experience, Watchful, and Sincere, who showed them the Celestial Gate and warned them of the paths to Hell. Then the two pilgrims passed by the Valley of Conceit, where they were met by Ignorance and other men who had not kept to the straight and narrow path. They passed on to the country of Beulah. Far off they saw the gates of the city of Heaven glistening with pearls and precious stones. Thinking that all their troubles were behind them, they lay down to rest.

When they went on toward the city, they came to the River of Death. They entered the river and began to wade through the water. Soon Christian became afraid, and the more afraid he became the deeper the waters rolled. Hopeful shouted to him to have hope and faith. Cheered by these words, Christian became less afraid, the water became less deep, and finally they both got across safely. They ran up the hill toward Heaven. Shining angels led them through the gates.

THE PILOT

Type of work: Novel
Author: James Fenimore Cooper (1789-1851)
Type of plot: Historical romance
Time of plot: Revolutionary War
Locale: Northeastern coast of England
First published: 1823

Principal characters:

Lt. Richard Barnstable, commander of the *Ariel*
Mr. Edward Griffith, an officer aboard an American frigate
Long Tom Coffin, coxswain of the *Ariel*
Mr. Merry, a midshipman
Mr. Gray, the pilot, in reality John Paul Jones
Colonel Howard, a Tory
Katherine Plowden, his niece

CECILIA HOWARD, another niece of Colonel Howard
CAPTAIN MANUAL, an officer of the Marine Corps
CAPTAIN BORROUGHCLIFFE, a British officer
CHRISTOPHER DILLON, kinsman of Colonel Howard
ALICE DUNSCOMBE, friend of Katherine and Cecilia

Critique:

While a number of earlier poems and stories had presented fragmentary pictures of seafaring life and some details of the handling of ships, it was not until 1823, when Cooper's sea romance appeared, that the first genuine sea novel was published. For the technical material of his story Cooper drew upon his six years of service in the United States Navy. Since the time of its publication the novel has been popular with readers of many lands and all ages. While Cooper never names the pilot whose activities give the novel its title, it is generally understood that the unknown seaman was John Paul Jones.

The Story:

Toward the close of a bleak wintry day during the American Revolution, a small schooner and a frigate sailed through shoal waters off the northeastern coast of England and anchored in a small bay beneath some towering cliffs. As darkness settled, a whaleboat was put ashore from the schooner *Ariel*. The boat was in charge of the *Ariel's* commander, Lieutenant Richard Barnstable, who had been ordered to make a landing near the cliffs and bring off a pilot known only as Mr. Gray.

With the aid of a weather-beaten old Nantucket whaler, Long Tom Coffin, Barnstable climbed the cliff and there met his mysterious passenger, a man of middle height and sparing speech. Before he had completed his mission, however, he also encountered Katherine Plowden, his fiancée, who gave him a letter and a signal book. The girl was staying temporarily at the St. Ruth's Abbey manor house, the home of her uncle, Colonel Howard, a wealthy South Carolina Tory who had fled from America at the outbreak of the war. From her Barnstable learned that another niece, Cecilia Howard, and her friend, Alice Dunscombe, were also guests at the abbey. Cecilia was in love with Lieutenant Edward Griffith, first officer aboard the frigate. Alice Dunscombe was reported to be in love with the mysterious pilot, but she refused to marry him because she was completely Loyalist in her sympathies.

Darkness had fallen by the time the pilot had been put aboard the deck of the frigate, and a storm was rising. Captain Munson of the frigate alone knew the pilot's identity, a secret concealed from everyone else aboard the ship and its escort, the *Ariel*. Captain Munson, seeing the pilot by the light of the battle-lanterns on deck, thought him greatly changed in appearance since their last meeting.

As the storm rose, the pilot guided the frigate safely through dangerous, wind-lashed shoal waters and out to open sea. At sunrise the frigate signaled the *Ariel* and ordered Barnstable to go aboard the larger ship for a council of war. There plans were made to harass the English by sending landing parties ashore to raid the mansions and estates of the gentry in the neighborhood.

Barnstable wanted these expeditions to serve another purpose, for he hoped to rescue Katherine Plowden and Cecilia Howard from the abbey, where they lived unhappily with Colonel Howard, their uncle and guardian.

Meanwhile, at the abbey, Colonel Howard was holding a conference with Christopher Dillon, a kinsman, and Captain Borroughcliffe, a British officer in charge of a small detachment of troops stationed at the abbey. Dillon, an impoverished gentleman, hoped to marry, with the colonel's approval, one of his wealthy cousins. The three men discussed the progress of the American Revolution, other political questions, and the piracies of John Paul Jones. They agreed that extra precautions should be taken, for there were rumors that Jones himself had been seen in the neighborhood.

That night Griffith and the pilot, accompanied by a Marine Corps captain named Manual, went ashore on a scouting expedition. Because of Griffith's imprudent conduct, they were seen and seized. When a sentry reported the arrest of strange seamen lurking in the neighborhood, Captain Borroughcliffe ordered them brought to the abbey for examination.

On their arrival at the abbey the prisoners would say only that they were seamen out of employment, a suspicious circumstance in itself. When the seamen offered no further information of any consequence, they were imprisoned to await Borroughcliffe's pleasure. Katherine and Cecilia bribed the sentry on duty and obtained permission to visit the prisoners. They recognized Griffith in disguise. Alice Dunscombe also went to visit the pilot, whom she recognized. After drinking too much wine at dinner, Borroughcliffe began to interview the men and in his intoxicated condition unwittingly helped them to escape.

Believing that the men had come from a ship lying offshore, Dillon mounted a horse and rode to a neighboring bay, where the war cutter *Alacrity* lay at anchor. Alarmed at the possible presence of an American ship in the neighborhood, the cutter put out to sea, with Dillon among its volunteer crew. Barnstable and Long Tom Coffin, waiting in the *Ariel's* whaleboat, engaged the cutter in a furious battle that ended when Coffin pinned the captain of the cutter to the mast with his whaler's harpoon. Dillon was among the prisoners taken. Frightened, he offered to return to the abbey and, in return for his own freedom, secure the release of the Americans held there.

After their escape, the pilot left Griffith and Manual, who rejoined a party of marines that had remained in hiding while their captain went with Griffith and the pilot to reconnoiter the abbey. Attacked by Borroughcliffe and his troops, the marines were surrounded. Griffith was recaptured and Manual was forced to surrender.

Trusting Dillon's word of honor, Barnstable had sent Long Tom Coffin with Dillon to the abbey to arrange for the transfer of prisoners. But Dillon, dishonoring his parole, had Coffin held prisoner while he and Borroughcliffe planned to trap Barnstable and his men. When Borroughcliffe boasted of his intentions, Coffin made a surprise attack upon him and seized and bound the British officer. He then followed Dillon to the apartments of Katherine and Cecilia and there took Dillon prisoner. He succeeded in getting Dillon aboard the *Ariel* as a British battery on the shore opened fire on the schooner. A lucky shot wrecked her mainmast as the schooner put out to sea, where a heavy storm completed the *Ariel's* destruction.

Before the schooner sank, Barnstable, a true captain, decided to go down with his ship, and he ordered Mr. Merry, a midshipman, to take charge of the crew and lower the boats. Coffin threw Barnstable overboard and in this manner saved his commander's life. The ship went down with Coffin and Dillon aboard. When Dillon's body was later washed up by the sea, Barnstable ordered his burial.

Shortly afterward Mr. Merry appeared at the abbey in the disguise of a peddler. Barnstable himself signaled by means of flags to Katherine, using signals from the code book which she had given him. Later they met secretly and laid plans for surprising the abbey and the soldiers who guarded it. Borroughcliffe had wind of the plot, however, and Barnstable walked into Borroughcliffe's ambush. But at this juncture the pilot arrived with a party of marines from the frigate and made prisoners of the Tories and the British.

Later Griffith released Borroughcliffe and his soldiers because Borroughcliffe had behaved in an honorable manner toward his prisoners. There was a final interview between Alice Dunscombe and the pilot. During their talk she addressed him as John and said that if she should speak his real name the whole countryside would ring with it. The pilot insisted that he would continue his activities for the cause of patriotism, regardless of the unsavory reputation it might gain for him in England. Colonel Howard and his two nieces were taken aboard the frigate for the return voyage to America.

But the American ship was not yet out of danger. The next morning a man-of-war broke through the morning mists, her decks cleared for action. There was tremendous activity aboard the frigate in preparation for the battle, and the women were taken below for safety as the English ship of the line blazed a three-tiered broadside at the American vessel. One shot struck Captain Munson and cut him down. Griffith, who now knew the pilot's identity begged for permission to reveal it to the crew, to encourage them in the fight, but the pilot refused. Meanwhile the British ship had been reinforced by two others, but the Americans were lucky enough to disable the smallest of their attackers. Then, as the other ships closed in upon the battered American ship, the pilot took the wheel and daringly guided her through the shoal waters that only he knew well. Out-maneuvered, the pursuing British ships dropped behind.

Colonel Howard, wounded during the engagement, lived long enough to see his nieces married by the ship's chaplain to their lovers. He died insisting that he was too old to change his politics and blessing the king.

The frigate sailed to Holland, where the pilot was put ashore. To all but Griffith, among those who watched his small boat dwindling to a speck against the horizon, his identity remained a mystery.

THE PIONEERS

Type of work: Novel
Author: James Fenimore Cooper (1789-1851)
Type of plot: Historical romance
Time of plot: 1793
Locale: New York State
First published: 1823

Principal characters:
JUDGE TEMPLE, a frontier landowner
ELIZABETH TEMPLE, his daughter
NATTY BUMPPO, an old hunter, sometimes called Leatherstocking
OLIVER EDWARDS, in reality Edward Oliver Effingham, Natty's young friend
INDIAN JOHN, Natty's Indian companion
HIRAM DOOLITTLE, a local magistrate

Critique:

The Pioneers, or The Sources of the Susquehanna was the first of the Leatherstocking Tales written by Cooper. A romantic story of life in upstate New York ten years after the Revolutionary War, it has historical importance as the first true romance of the frontier in American literature. The novel is filled with scenes of hunting and trapping life, the description of Templeton being drawn from Cooper's memories of his own boyhood in Cooperstown. Although romantic in effect, the novel presents with considerable realism the character of Natty Bumppo, the old hunter and frontiersman. His fate and the death of Indian John point to the tragedy of the Indian and the wilderness scout; neither had a place in the life of a developed frontier.

The Story:

On a cold December day in 1793, Judge Temple and his daughter Elizabeth were traveling by sleigh through a snow-covered tract of wilderness near the settlement of Templeton. Elizabeth, who had been away from her home attending a female seminary, was now returning to preside over her father's household in the community in which he had been a pioneer settler after the Revolutionary War. Hearing the baying of hounds, the judge decided that Leatherstocking, an old hunter, had started game in the hills, and he ordered his coachman to stop the sleigh so he could have a shot at the deer if it came in his direction. A few minutes later, as a great buck leaped into the road, the judge fired both barrels of his fowling piece at the animal, but apparently without effect. Then a third report and a fourth were heard, and the buck dropped dead in a snowbank.

At the same time Natty Bumppo, the old hunter, and a young companion appeared from the woodland. The judge insisted that he had shot the buck, but Leatherstocking, by accounting for all the shots fired, proved the judge could not have killed the animal. The argument ended when the young stranger revealed that he had been wounded by one of the shots fired by the judge. Elizabeth and her father then insisted that he accompany them into the village in their sleigh, so he could have his wound dressed as soon as possible.

The young man got into the sleigh with obvious reluctance and said little during the drive. In a short time the party arrived at the Temple mansion, where his wound was treated. In answer to the judge's questions, he gave his name as Oliver Edwards. His manner remained distant and reserved. After he had departed, a servant in the Temple home reported that Edwards had appeared three weeks before in the company of old Leatherstocking and that he lived in a nearby cabin with the hunter and an Indian known as Indian John.

Judge Temple, wishing to make amends for having accidentally wounded Edwards, offered him a position as his secretary. When Elizabeth added her own entreaties to those of her father, Edwards finally accepted the judge's offer, with the understanding that he would be free to terminate his employment at any time. For a while he attended faithfully and earnestly to his duties in Judge Temple's mansion during the day, but his nights he spent in Leatherstocking's cabin. So much secrecy surrounded his comings and goings, and the reserve of Leatherstocking and his Indian friend, that Richard Jones, the sheriff and a kinsman of the judge, became suspicious. Among other things, he wondered why Natty always kept his cabin closed and never allowed anyone except the Indian and Edwards to enter it. Jones and some others decided that Natty had discovered a mine and was working it. Jones also suspected that Edwards was an Indian half-breed, his father a Delaware chief.

Hiram Doolittle, the local magistrate, prowled around the shack and set free the dogs guarding it. In the meantime Elizabeth and Louisa Grant, the minister's daughter, went walking in the woods. There they were attacked by a savage panther and were saved only by the timely arrival of Leatherstocking, who shot the animal. But Natty had also shot a deer, in defiance of Judge Temple's strict game laws. With the charge that the old hunter had killed a deer out of season as his pretext, Doolittle persuaded Judge Temple to sign a warrant so that the magistrate could gain entrance to the cabin and search it. Jones was more convinced than ever that Leatherstocking was secretly smelting ore he had mined.

But when Doolittle went to the cabin, Leatherstocking, rifle in hand, refused him entrance. Then the magistrate attempted to force his way over the threshold, but the old hunter seized him and threw him twenty feet down an embankment. As the result of his treatment of an officer, Leatherstocking was arrested. Found guilty, he was given a month's jail sentence, a fine, and placed in the stocks for a few hours. When Elizabeth went to see what assistance she could give the humiliated old woodsman, she learned he was planning to escape. Edwards, who had given up his position with the judge, was planning to flee with his aged friend; he had provided a cart in which to carry the old hunter to safety. Elizabeth promised to meet Leatherstocking the following day on the top of a nearby mountain and to bring with her a can of gunpowder he needed.

The next day Elizabeth and her friend Louisa started out on their expedition to meet Leatherstocking. On the way Louisa changed her mind and turned back, declaring that she dared not walk unprotected through the woods where they had lately been menaced by a panther. Elizabeth went on alone until she came to a clearing in which she found old Indian John, now dressed in the war costume and feathers of a great Mohican chief. When she stopped to speak to the Indian, she suddenly became aware of dense clouds of smoke drifting across the clearing and discovered that the whole mountainside was ablaze. At that moment Edwards appeared, followed by Leatherstocking, who led them to a cave in the side of the mountain. There the old Indian died of exhaustion, and Elizabeth learned that he had been in earlier days Chingachgook, a great and noble warrior of the Mohican tribe.

When danger of the fire had passed, Edwards conducted Elizabeth down the mountainside until she was within hearing of a party of men who were looking for her. Before they parted, Edwards promised he would soon reveal his true identity.

The next day the sheriff led a posse up the mountain in search of Leatherstocking and those who had aided him in his escape from jail. Leatherstocking was again prepared to defend with his rifle the cave to which he had taken Elizabeth the day before, but Edwards declared that the time had now come to let the truth be known. He and Natty brought from the depths of the cave an old man seated in a chair. The stranger's face was grave and dignified, but his vacant eyes showed that his mind was gone. Edwards announced that the old man was really the owner of the property on which they stood. Judge Temple interrupted with a shout of surprise and greeted the old man as Major Effingham.

The young man told his story. His name, he said, was Edward Oliver Effingham, and he was the grandson of the old man who sat before them. His own father had been, before the Revolutionary War, a close friend of Judge Temple. They had gone into business together, but the outbreak of the war found them on opposite sides during the struggle. Judge Temple had some money entrusted to him by his friend, money which actually belonged to his friend's father, but when he received no reply to letters he wrote to the Effinghams he at last decided that all the family had been lost in a shipwreck off Nova Scotia. The money he had invested in his own enterprises.

The judge had never met Major Effingham; he would not have recognized him if he had seen the helpless old man who had for years been hidden in the cabin on the outskirts of Templeton. During those years he was nursed faithfully by Leatherstocking and his Indian friend; by Leatherstocking because he had served with the major on the frontier years before, by Indian John because the major was an adopted member of the Mohican tribe.

Judge Temple ordered that the old man be carried to the Temple mansion at once, where he would receive the best of care. Old Major Effingham thought himself back home once more, and his eyes gleamed with joy. He died, happy and well cared for, soon afterward.

Edward Effingham also explained his belief that Judge Temple had stolen his father's property and the money left in trust years before. In his resentment he had come to Templeton to assist his grandfather and regain in some manner the property which he believed Judge Temple had unrightfully possessed. Now the judge was happy to return that part of the property which belonged to the Effinghams, and there was a reconciliation between the two men. As it turned out, however, the property stayed in the family, for Elizabeth and Edward Effingham were married within a short time.

Elizabeth and Edward Effingham wanted to build a new cabin for Leatherstocking, but the old hunter refused their offer. He intended to go off into the woods to hunt and trap in the free wilderness until he died. Settlements and towns were not for him. He would not listen to their pleas but set out soon afterward on his long journey, pausing only long enough to view the stone tablet on Indian John's grave, a monument Edward Effingham had erected. Then he trudged off toward the woods, his long rifle over his shoulder. Elizabeth and her husband watched him go. Tears were in their eyes as they waved a last farewell to the old hunter just before he disappeared into the forest.

THE PIT

Type of work: Novel
Author: Frank Norris (1870-1902)
Type of plot: Naturalism
Time of plot: 1890's
Locale: Chicago
First published: 1903

Principal characters:
CURTIS JADWIN, a speculator in wheat
LAURA DEARBORN, later his wife
SHELDON CORTHELL, an artist in love with Laura
MR. AND MRS. CRESSLER, friends of the Jadwins
GRETRY, Jadwin's broker

Critique:

The Pit, A Story of Chicago, is an exciting story about the Board of Trade in Chicago and a man who for a time cornered the wheat market of the world. Norris, who intended to write a trilogy about wheat, completed the first two books. The second novel of the planned trilogy, *The Pit* tells how wheat is bought and sold on the Board of Trade. Along with the interest in the financial explorations of the novel, there is presented a moving love story of two strong but very human characters.

The Story:

From the first evening that Laura Dearborn met Curtis Jadwin she knew that she interested him. She had attended the opera with her sister Page and her Aunt Wess, as the guests of some very old friends, the Cresslers. Jadwin had also been a guest that evening, and she found the marked attention which he paid her so flattering that she listened only absently to avowals of love from her old and devoted suitor, Sheldon Corthell. Corthell was an artist. The life of the capitalist who made and broke fortunes and human lives from the floor of the Board of Trade seemed to Laura more romantic than painting.

The next day Mrs. Cressler told Laura part of Jadwin's story. He had been born into a poor family, had worked to educate himself. When, in default of a loan, he gained possession of some land in Chicago, he sold it, bought more real estate, and by shrewd dealings now owned a portion of one of the wealthiest sections of real estate in Chicago. He was also speculating in the wheat market, and he was a familiar figure on the floor of the Board of Trade.

Jadwin, stopping by the Board of Trade one morning in answer to the summons of his broker, Gretry, paused in the Pit—the huge room downstairs in which all the bidding took place—to watch the frenzied excitement of bidders and sellers. Gretry had advance information that in a few days the French government would introduce a bill placing heavy import duties on all foreign goods. When this news became widespread, the price of wheat would drop considerably. Gretry urged Jadwin to sell his shares at once and Jadwin agreed.

The deal was a tremendous success. Jadwin pocketed a large profit. The Cresslers tried to persuade Jadwin to stop his speculating. Mr. Cressler had almost ruined himself at one time through his gambling with wheat, and he feared that the same thing might eventually happen to his friend.

But Jadwin was too much interested in Laura to pay attention to the warning or even to hear the words of his friends. One evening at the Cresslers he asked Laura to marry him. Laura, in a capricious mood, said that although she loved no one as yet she might some day come to love him. She had given Sheldon Corthell the same encouragement. That night, ashamed of her coquetry, she wrote to both men telling them that she did not love either, and that if they were to continue friends they must never speak of love to her again. Corthell accepted her refusal and left for Europe. Jadwin came to call on Laura while she was out and refused to leave until he had spoken to her. He was successful in his suit and they were married in July.

The early years of their marriage were completely happy. Their home was a mansion, exquisitely furnished and with beautiful grounds. At first Laura found it difficult to adjust herself to her luxurious surroundings, but as time passed she found great pleasure in satisfying her interest in art, decorating her home, and entertaining her friends.

Jadwin, caught up once more in the excitement of the Pit, invested all his money in successful speculative enterprises. For some time he had aligned himself with the bears in the wheat market. But now, as he saw that the country was becoming more prosperous and the wheat crops were increasing, he decided to change to the side of the bulls. He resolved to buy as much wheat as he could and, if possible, to corner the market. Luck was with him. One year, when European crops were very poor, Jadwin bought a tremendous amount of wheat at a low price and determined to hold it until he could ask his own price.

Laura was worried by his constant attendance at the Board of Trade, and he promised to give up speculating as soon as he concluded an important deal.

One evening Laura had dinner with Sheldon Corthell, who had returned from Europe. Late that night Jadwin came home with the announcement that the deal had been concluded and that he had cleared five hundred thousand dollars. He kept his promise to give up speculating in the Pit, but within a short time he grew restless. He began again to try his luck in the wheat market.

Because he kept his activities hidden from the public, he was spoken of as the unknown bull. After he had purchased as much wheat as he could, it suddenly became evident that he was in a position to corner the world's wheat and name his own price. Cressler, meantime, had been drawn into speculation by the group of bears who were certain that they could break the unknown bull. He had no idea that the bull was his own friend, Jadwin.

Weeks went by while Laura saw her husband only at breakfast. He spent his days and many of his nights at the board. Laura, lonely and unhappy, began to see more and more of Corthell.

Corthell, still in love with Laura, finally declared his feelings to her. Laura was kind in her dismissal, but she still loved her husband.

In cornering the market, Jadwin had risen upon a wave of power and prosperity. But he began to have strange, irritating headaches which he attempted to ignore, just as he disregarded his moods of loneliness and depression.

Mrs. Cressler confided that her own husband was not well. She invited Laura to call on her one afternoon. When Laura arrived, Mrs. Cressler was not yet home. She wandered into the library and saw Mr. Cressler sitting there. He had shot himself through the temple.

Jadwin was horrified when he realized that Cressler had lost all his money in speculation with the bears, and he felt that he was responsible for his friend's death. But Jadwin himself was in a tight spot. Having forced the price of wheat to a new high, he was now faced by the necessity of cornering a bumper crop in addition to the millions of bushels he already owned. His enemies were waiting for the time when the unknown bull could buy no more wheat. At that moment the price would drop considerably. Jadwin put every penny he owned into his attempt to keep wheat cornered, but he was defeated by the wheat itself. The grain flowed in, millions of bushels at a time. Almost out of his mind, he bought and bought, and still the wheat harvest continued. He no longer controlled the market. He was ruined.

He walked into his home one night a broken man. Laura nursed him through days and nights of illness. When he was well enough, the two set out for the West to begin life again. Although they had lost their money, the Jadwins were much happier than they had been for many years.

THE PLAYBOY OF THE WESTERN WORLD

Type of work: Drama
Author: John Millington Synge (1871-1909)
Type of plot: Realistic comedy
Time of plot: Early twentieth century
Locale: County Mayo, Ireland
First presented: 1907

Principal characters:
Christopher Mahon, a braggart
Old Mahon, his father
Margaret Flaherty (Pegeen Mike), his sweetheart
Widow Quin, a villager
Shawn Keogh, a young farmer in love with Pegeen

Critique:

This play is the most outstanding of John Millington Synge's Irish dramas, and in it Synge has used the beautiful lyrical Irish language to the finest effect. *The Playboy of the Western World* is tender, ironical, and humorous drama.

The Story:

One evening a young man arrived at a small inn on the wild Mayo coast of Ireland and announced that he had run away from home. He said his name was Christopher Mahon and that he was running away because he had killed his father during a fight. The farmers who were passing the time in the inn were very much pleased by his exhibition of courage. Christopher was especially admired by Pegeen, the pretty young daughter of Michael Flaherty, the innkeeper. She, along with the others, pressed the young man to tell his story over and over again.

At home Christopher had been a meek and obedient son, domineered by his father. He accepted the insults of his parent until the latter tried to force him into marrying a rich old woman. At last, in desperation, he hit his father over the head with a loy. Seeing the old man fall, Christopher presumed that he was dead.

The experience at the inn was something new for Christopher, who for the first time in his life was looked upon as a hero. When the news of his story spread among the villagers, they flocked to look at this paragon of bravery. The young women were particularly interested in him—and the not so young as well. Dame Quin, a middle-aged widow, was much taken with the young taproom hero.

But Christopher was attracted to pretty Pegeen. He was flattered by her admiration, and in an attempt to live up to her opinion of him he began to adopt an attitude of bravado. Before long he himself believed that he had done a courageous deed.

Each year the village held a festival in which the men competed with each other in various sports. Christopher was naturally expected to take part. His early timidity having long since disappeared, he made every effort to appear a hero in the eyes of Pegeen, to whom he was now openly betrothed. She had broken her engagement with a young farmer, Shawn Keogh, soon after Christopher arrived on the scene.

While her Playboy, as Pegeen called him, was taking part in the sports, an old man came to the inn. He was looking for a young man whose description fitted Christopher's appearance. Dame Quin, who still had designs on the boy, deliberately misdirected the stranger. But when the man returned from his wild goose chase, he arrived in time to see Christopher hailed as a hero because he had just won the mule race. Old Mahon, not dead from Christopher's blow, recognized his son and flew into a rage. He insisted that Christopher go home with him, and by his angry tirade he humiliated his son in front of the spectators.

But the Playboy had enjoyed too long the thrill of being a hero. He did not give in timidly as he would have done at an earlier time. Much to his father's astonishment, he struck the old man over the head. Once again it appeared that old Mahon was dead. But the reaction of the people was not at all what Christopher might have expected. Killing one's father some miles away was one thing. Killing him in front of a number of spectators who might be involved in the affair was another. The people muttered angrily among themselves, and even Pegeen joined with them in denouncing the murderer.

Deciding at last that the only thing to do was to hang Christopher for his crime, they tied up the struggling young man and prepared to lead him away. But Old Mahon had proved himself a tough fellow once before, and he did so again. The first blow that Christopher had given him had only stunned him, so that soon after the boy ran away his father was able to follow him to the village. Now the second blow had merely knocked him unconscious for a short time. As Christopher struggled and the noose was slipped over his head, Mahon crawled through the door on his hands and knees.

While the villagers stood around dumbfounded, he walked over to his son and quickly untied him. Far from being angry with Christopher for hitting him, he was pleased to discover that his son was not the timid weakling he had thought him to be. The two left the inn, arm in arm, deaf to the pleas of Pegeen, both of them jeering at the foolishness of the people on the Mayo coast.

POINT COUNTER POINT

Type of work: Novel
Author: Aldous Huxley (1894-)
Type of plot: Social criticism
Time of plot: 1920's
Locale: England
First published: 1928

Principal characters:
PHILIP QUARLES, a novelist
ELINOR, Philip's wife
SIDNEY QUARLES, Philip's father
RACHEL, Philip's mother
JOHN BIDLAKE, Elinor's father
MRS. BIDLAKE, her mother
LITTLE PHILIP, Philip's and Elinor's son
BURLAP, editor of *Literary World*
BEATRICE GILRAY, his mistress
SPANDRELL, a cynic
EVERARD WEBLEY, a disciple of force
WALTER BIDLAKE, Elinor's brother
MARJORIE CARLING, Walter's mistress
LUCY TANTAMOUNT, Walter's infatuation

Critique:

Point Counter Point contains a novel within a novel. Within the framework of the outer novel, Huxley places a novelist who observes the activities of his own world of fictional characters and then plots a novel that is constructed exactly as Huxley has written *Point Counter Point.* From one set of individuals to another the focus of the novel moves, balancing each life against its counterpoint. The lives of these people repeat the same patterns in different forms, while Philip Quarles plots a novel based on their lives. It is apparent that Quarles is Huxley himself plotting *Point Counter Point.* Huxley would have us believe that the theme of this novel is one of variations on a single theme, the struggle of natural sexual desire and escapism against the bond of marriage.

The Story:

John Bidlake was an artist with an artist's temperament. He had been married three times. The first marriage had ended in bitter resentment. The second marriage had been idyllic for him, but Isabelle had died two years later, leaving her husband with a void that he had tried to erase by pretending that he had never known a woman named Isabelle. His third marriage had lasted, although John had not lived with his wife for many years. He merely maintained a home where he went whenever he became ill enough to need his wife's nursing skill.

The children of his third marriage, Walter and Elinor, had not been too successful in their own experiments with marriage as a social institution. Walter had been living with a married woman named Marjorie Carling for a year and a half, and he was growing tired of her. Worse than his moral ties to Marjorie was the fact that she tenaciously tried to possess him, rejecting his proposal that they live together as close friends, each going his own free direction with whomever he pleased. Now Marjorie was going to have a baby, and her whining jealousy toward his latest infatuation, Lucy Tantamount, was pricking Walter's conscience. It annoyed him immensely that he was making Marjorie unhappy by going to a party at Tantamount House without her.

Elinor and Philip Quarles were traveling abroad, having left little Philip behind under the care of a governess and his grandmother, Mrs. Bidlake. Philip was a novelist. As he traveled through life, he jotted down in his notebook incidents and thoughts that might make rich material for his next novel. His mind was turned inward, introspective, and his self-centered interests gave him little time for emotional experience. Elinor, wishing that he could love her as much as she loved him, resigned herself to the unhappy dilemma of being loved as much as Philip could possibly love any woman.

Denis Burlap, editor of the *Literary World,* flattered himself with the just conceit that although his magazine was not a financial success, it as least contributed to the intellectual life of his time. When Walter, who was one of his chief contributors, asked for more pay, Burlap hedged until Walter felt ashamed of his demands. Burlap was attracted to Beatrice Gilray, a pathetic figure who had feared the very touch of a man ever since she had been attacked by her uncle while riding in a taxicab. Burlap hoped eventually to seduce Beatrice. Meanwhile they were living together.

Another significant member of this set was Spandrell, an indolent son of a doting mother who supported him. There was also Everard Webley, a friend of Elinor and an active political figure.

Philip's parents still lived together. Sidney Quarles pretended that he was writing a long history, but he had not progressed far beyond the purchase of office equipment. Rachel Quarles, assuming the burden of managing their affairs, endured with patience Sidney's whims and mild flirtations. Now it was someone in London, for Sidney made frequent trips to the British Museum to gather material for his history. The girl in London with whom Sidney had been having an affair appeared one day at his country house and in loud and furious language informed her paramour that she was going to have a baby. When Mrs. Quarles appeared, Sidney quietly left the room. The girl threatened Rachel and then returned to London. Later the affair was settled quietly.

Marjorie appealed to Walter's pity enough to cause him some degree of anguish because of his association with Lucy Tantamount. Lucy herself was not much interested in Walter. Becoming tired of London, she went to Paris.

Elinor and Philip returned from abroad to find little Philip faring well under the care of his governess and his grandmother. John Bidlake, having learned that he was dying of cancer, had returned to his wife's home. He had become a cantankerous patient and treated little Philip with alternate kindness and harshness.

With Lucy in Paris, Philip had persuaded Walter to take Marjorie to the Quarles home in the country, in the hope that some sort of reconciliation would come about from this association. Rachel Quarles began to like Marjorie, and the pregnant woman found herself gaining cheer under this new affection. Shortly after she and Walter had come to the Quarles estate, Walter received a letter from Lucy in Paris, telling him that she had found a new lover who had seduced her in a shabby Parisian studio. With her newly-acquired content, Marjorie felt sympathetic toward Walter, who was crestfallen at the cruel rejection he had received from Lucy.

Everard Webley had long been in love with Elinor. Sometimes she wondered whether Philip would care if she went to another man, and she decided that it would be Philip's own fault if she turned to Everard. She felt that a breach was forming between herself and Philip, but she could not seem to gain enough attention or concern from him to make him realize what was happening.

She arranged a rendezvous with Everard.

Behind the scenes of love-making and unfaithfulness lurked the political enmity of Spandrell and Everard. Perhaps it was the lack of a useful purpose in his life that allowed Spandrell's plan to grow in his mind. Elinor Quarles was home alone awaiting Everard's call when Spandrell and a telegram arrived simultaneously. The telegram urged Elinor to come to her father's home, for little Philip was ill. Elinor asked Spandrell to wait and tell Everard that she could not keep her appointment with him. Spandrell agreed. When Everard arrived at Elinor's home, Spandrell attacked him and killed him. Spandrell lugged the dead body into an automobile and drove it away. Later that evening he met Philip and told him his son was ill.

Philip arrived at the Bidlake estate the next day in time to hear the doctor say that young Philip had meningitis. For days Elinor stayed by the child's side, waiting for the crisis to pass. One night the sick boy opened his eyes and told his parents that he was hungry. They were overjoyed at his apparent recovery, but later that night he died suddenly. As they had done in the past, Elinor and Philip escaped their unpleasant world by going abroad.

For a long while the Webley murder baffled the police. Spandrell, haunted by his own conscience, sent the police a note which stated that Everard's murderer would be found at a certain address at a certain hour. On their arrival, the police found Spandrell dead with a letter of confession in his hands.

Burlap was the only happy man among these sensualists and intellectuals. One night he and Beatrice pretended they were children and splashed merrily taking their bath together. Happiness was like misery in the modern world, it seemed—lustful, dull, selfish.

POOR WHITE

Type of work: Novel
Author: Sherwood Anderson (1876-1941)
Type of plot: Psychological realism
Time of plot: 1880-1900
Locale: Missouri and Ohio
First published: 1920

Principal characters:
HUGH MCVEY, an inventor and manufacturer
SARAH SHEPARD, his foster mother
STEVE HUNTER, his partner
TOM BUTTERWORTH, his father-in-law
CLARA BUTTERWORTH, his wife

Critique:

Poor White is a significant novel, an early study of pioneer rural America invaded by industrialism. It is also the story of one man's rise from decadent, poor white folk to a life of creation and self-realization. Anderson graphically described, not only the growth of America, but also the conflicts and frustrations between man and the machine, a conflict that is today one of the major problems in our culture.

The Story:

As a young boy in Missouri, Hugh McVey was incredibly lazy. Hour after hour he would lie on the grass by the river doing absolutely nothing. Not having gone to school, he was ignorant and his manners were rude.

When the railroad came to town, Hugh got work sweeping the platform and doing odd jobs. His boss, Henry Shepard, took an interest in him, and bought him clothes. Soon Hugh went to live with

Henry and his wife Sarah. Sarah, who was from New England, always preserved her memory of quiet Eastern villages and large industrial cities. Determined to educate Hugh, she lavished on him the discipline and affection she would have given her own child.

The situation was difficult, at first, for both of them. But Sarah Shepard was a determined woman. She taught Hugh to read, to write, to wonder about the world beyond the little town. She instilled within him the belief that his family had been of no account, so that he grew to have a repulsion toward the poor white farmers and workers. Always she held out before him the promise of the East, the progress and growth of that region. Gradually, Hugh began to win his fight against natural indolence and to adjust himself to his new way of life. When the Shepards left town, Hugh was appointed station agent for the railroad.

He kept the job for a year. During that time the dream of Eastern cities grew more and more vivid for Hugh. He gave up his job and traveled east, working wherever he could. Always lonely, always apart from people, he felt an impenetrable wall between him and the rest of the world. He kept on, through Illinois, Indiana, Ohio.

Hugh was twenty-three when he settled down in Ohio. By accident, he got the job of a telegraph operator, just a mile from the town of Bidwell. There he lived alone, a familiar and puzzling figure to the people of the town. The rumor began to spread that he was an inventor working on a new device. Others suggested that he was looking over the town for a possible factory site. But Hugh was doing neither as yet. Then during his walks around the farmlands, he became fascinated by the motions of the farmers planting their seeds and their crops. Slowly there grew in his mind an idea for a crop-setting machine that would save the labor of the farmers and their families.

Steve Hunter, who had just come back from school in Buffalo, was another dreamer. He dreamed of being a manufacturer, the wealthiest in Bidwell. He succeeded in convincing the town's important people that Hugh was his man, and that he was working on an invention that would make them both rich. He persuaded them to invest in a new company which would build a factory and promote Hugh's invention. Steve went to see Hugh, who had progressed so that the blueprint for a plant-setting machine was complete. The two young men came to an agreement.

The town idiot, who had skill in woodworking, made models of the machine, and the machine itself was finally constructed in an old building carefully guarded from the curious. When the machine was not successful, Hugh invented another, his mind more and more preoccupied with the planning of devices and machines. A factory was then built and many workers were hired. With the factory, Bidwell's industrialization began.

What was happening in Bidwell was the same growth of industrialism that was changing the entire structure of the nation. It was a period of transition. Bidwell, being a small town, felt the effects of the new development keenly. Workers became part of the community, in which there had been only farmers and merchants.

Joe Wainsworth, the harness-maker, had invested his life-savings in Hugh's invention, and he had lost them. An independent man, a craftsman, he came to resent the factory, the very idea of the machine. People came into his shop less often. They were buying machine-made harness. Joe became a broken man. His employee, Jim Gibson, a spiritual bully, really ran the business, and Joe submitted meekly.

Meanwhile, Clara Butterworth came back to Bidwell after three years at the university in Columbus. She too was lonely, unhappy. When she returned, she saw that the old Bidwell was gone, that her father, Tom Butterworth, was wealthier than before, that the growth of the town was due primarily to one person, Hugh McVey. A week after she met Hugh, he walked up to the farm and asked her to marry him. They eloped and were married that night.

For four years they lived together in a strange, strained relationship. During those four years Joe Wainsworth's fury against Steve Hunter, against the new age of industry which had taken his savings, increased. One day he heard Jim Gibson brag about his hold over his employer. That night Joe Wainsworth killed Jim Gibson. As he fled from the scene, he met Steve Hunter and shot him.

Clara, Hugh, and Tom Butterworth were returning from a drive in the family's first automobile when they learned what had happened. Two men had captured Joe, and when they tried to put him into the automobile to take him back to town, Joe jumped toward Hugh and sank his fingers into his neck. It was Clara who broke his grip upon her husband. Somehow the incident brought Hugh and Clara closer together.

Hugh's career as an inventor no longer satisfied him. Joe Wainsworth's attack had unnerved him, made him doubt the worth of his work. It did not matter so much if someone in Iowa had invented a machine exactly like his, and he did not intend to dispute the rights of the Iowan. Clara was bearing his child, an individual who would struggle just as he had. Clara told him of the child one night as they stood listening to the noises of the farm and the snoring of the hired hand. As they walked into the house side by side, the factory whistles blew in the night. Hugh hardly heard them. The dark Midwestern nights, men and women, the land itself —the full, deep life current would go on in spite of factories and machines.

PORGY

Type of work: Novel
Author: DuBose Heyward (1885-1940)
Type of plot: Regional romance
Time of plot: Early twentieth century
Locale: Charleston, South Carolina
First published: 1925

Principal characters:
PORGY, a crippled Negro beggar
CROWN, a stevedore
BESS, his woman

Critique:

Porgy tells of Negroes living in a society dominated by whites, and the Negroes are presented as being elemental, emotional, amoral, and occasionally violent. Heyward develops in the reader a sympathy not only for the crippled Porgy, whose goatcart excites so much amusement among the whites, but also for Bess, who comes to live with him. Bess honestly tries to be true to Porgy, but she knows the weakness of her will and flesh when the brutal Crown touches her or when she has had liquor or dope. The story was dramatized in 1927 by Heyward and his wife Dorothy. The novel was also the basis for the opera *Porgy and Bess* (1935), for which Heyward wrote the book and, with Ira Gershwin, the lyrics.

The Story:

Porgy, a crippled Negro beggar, lived in a brick tenement called Catfish Row, once a fine old Southern mansion in Charleston, South Carolina. Different from the eager, voluble beggars of his race, Porgy sat silent day by day, acknowledging only by lifting his eyes the coins dropped in his cup. No one knew how old he was, and his large, powerful hands were in strange contrast to his frail body. His single vice was gambling. In a gambling session one evening in April he witnessed the brutal murder of Robbins by Crown, a stevedore who thought he had been cheated.

In May Porgy made his first trip by homemade goatcart through the city streets, to the mocking amusement of the white folks. The goatcart gave Porgy a new freedom. He no longer had to stay at one stand all day; but he could roam at will and take in more money than before.

In June Crown's woman, Bess, came to live with Porgy, and the cripple became a new man. He seemed less an impassive observer of life and he developed a tender affection for children. Bess left off her evil ways and became in truth Porgy's woman.

On the day of the grand parade and picnic of "The Sons and Daughters of Repent Ye Saith the Lord," Crown came upon Bess cutting palmetto leaves for the picnic on Kittiwar Island. He took her to his hut. At the end of the day he let her return to Porgy with the promise that in the fall, when cotton shipments would provide stevedoring work in Savannah, she would again be Crown's Bess.

In September, while the "Mosquito Fleet" was at the fishing banks, the hurricane flag was up over the custom house. Jake's wife, Clara, shuddered with fear for her husband whom she had warned not to go out that day in his boat, the *Seagull*. After an ominous calm the hurricane struck the city. The water of the bay, driven by the shrieking wind, rose above the sea wall, crossed the street, and invaded the ground floor of Catfish Row. Forty frightened Negroes huddled in the great second-story ballroom of the old mansion. During a lull in the storm Clara saw the wreck of her husband's boat near the wharf. Leaving her baby with Bess, Clara went out into the flood. A few minutes later she was overwhelmed during a sudden return of the storm's great fury. Bess and Porgy kept Clara's baby.

In October drays loaded with heavy bales of cotton came rumbling down the street. In Catfish Row there was excitement and happiness, for stevedoring jobs and money would be plentiful again. But the coming of the cotton seemed to Porgy to portend disaster. He asked Bess whether she was his woman or Crown's. His, she answered, unless Crown put his hot hands on her again as he did that day of the picnic. She could not answer for herself if that happened again. Porgy assured her he would not let Crown take her away from him. When Crown broke into their room one midnight not long afterward, Porgy stabbed him. Next day the body was found in the river nearby. The police got nowhere in their questioning of the occupants of Catfish Row, and there was a kind of communal sigh of relief when the officers left without having made any arrests. But when one of the buzzards that had fed upon Crown's body lighted on the parapet above Porgy's room, the frightened little cripple felt that doom was in store for him. The next day Porgy, having been asked to identify Crown's body at the morgue, fled in terror in his goatcart, hotly pursued by a patrol wagon full of officers. Passersby laughed uproariously at the ridiculously one-sided race. Porgy was caught at the edge of town, but by the time he had been brought downtown he was no longer needed since another Negro had identified the body. Crown was declared to have come to his death at the hands of a person or persons unknown. Porgy was jailed for five days for contempt of court.

When he returned from jail and found

Serena Robbins holding Jake's and Clara's orphan baby, Porgy suspected the worst. From a neighbor he learned that some stevedores had gotten Bess drunk and taken her off to Savannah. Porgy knew she would never return. Serena had adopted the baby. Porgy had for one brief summer known the joys that come to other people. Now he was just a pitiful old man sitting sadly in a goat-cart with the morning sunlight shining upon him.

THE PORTRAIT OF A LADY

Type of work: Novel
Author: Henry James (1843-1916)
Type of plot: Psychological realism
Time of plot: About 1875
Locale: England, France, Italy
First published: 1881

Principal characters:

Isabel Archer, an American heiress
Gilbert Osmond, her husband
Ralph Touchett, her cousin
Madame Merle, her friend and Osmond's former mistress
Pansy Osmond, Osmond's daughter
Lord Warburton, Isabel's English suitor
Caspar Goodwood, Isabel's American suitor
Henrietta Stackpole, American newspaper correspondent, Isabel's friend

Critique:

With the exception of the English Lord Warburton, *The Portrait of a Lady* contains a gallery of Americans who work out their destinies against a European background. The influence of European culture is seen most closely as it affects the heroine, high-minded Isabel Archer. By means of careful penetration into her mental processes, the steps which lead to her marriage with the dilettante, Gilbert Osmond, are delineated, as well as the consequent problems which arise from this marriage. The novel is an excellent example of the Jamesian method of refracting life through an individual temperament.

The Story:

Isabel Archer, upon the death of her father, had been visited by her aunt, Mrs. Touchett. She proved so attractive to the older woman that Mrs. Touchett decided to give her the advantage of more cosmopolitan experience, and Isabel was quickly carried off to Europe so she might see something of the world of culture and fashion.

On the day the women arrived at the Touchett home in England, Isabel's sickly young cousin, Ralph Touchett, and his father were taking tea in the garden with their friend, Lord Warburton. When Isabel appeared, Warburton had been confessing to the two men his boredom and his distaste for his routine existence. The young nobleman was much taken with the American girl's grace and lively manner.

Isabel had barely settled at Gardencourt, her aunt's home, before she received a letter from an American friend, Henrietta Stackpole, a newspaper woman who was writing a series of articles on the sights of Europe. At Ralph's invitation, Henrietta went to Gardencourt to spend some time with Isabel and to obtain material for her writing.

Soon after Henrietta's arrival, Isabel heard from another American friend. Caspar Goodwood, a would-be suitor, had followed her abroad. Learning her whereabouts from Henrietta, he wrote to ask if he might see her. Isabel was much irked by his aggressiveness, and she decided not to answer his letter.

On the day she received the letter from

Goodwood, Lord Warburton proposed to her. Not wishing to seem indifferent to the honor of his proposal, she asked for time to consider it. At last she decided she could not marry the young Englishman, for she wished to see considerably more of the world before she married. She was afraid that marriage to Warburton, although he was a model of kindness and thoughtfulness, would prove stifling.

Because Isabel had not seen London on her journey with Mrs. Touchett and since it was on Henrietta Stackpole's itinerary, the two young women, accompanied by Ralph Touchett, went to the capital. Henrietta quickly made the acquaintance of a Mr. Bantling, who undertook to squire her around. When Caspar Goodwood visited Isabel at her hotel, she again refused him, though his persistence made her agree that if he still wished to ask for her hand he might visit her again after two years had passed.

While the party was in London a telegram came from Gardencourt. Old Mr. Touchett was seriously ill of the gout, and his wife was much alarmed. Isabel and Ralph left on the afternoon train. Henrietta remained under the escort of her new friend.

During the time Mr. Touchett lay dying and his family was preoccupied, Isabel was forced to amuse herself with a new companion. Madame Merle, an old friend of Mrs. Touchett, had come to Gardencourt to spend a few days. She and Isabel, thrown together a great deal, exchanged many confidences. Isabel admired the older woman for her ability to amuse herself, for her skill at needlework, at painting, at the piano, and for her ability to accommodate herself to any social situation. On the other hand, Madame Merle spoke enviously of Isabel's youth and intelligence, lamenting the life which had left her, at middle age, a widow with no children and no visible success in life.

When her uncle died, he left Isabel, at her cousin's instigation, one-half of his fortune. Ralph, greatly impressed with his young kinswoman's brilliance, had persuaded his father that she should be given an opportunity to fly as far and as high as she might. For himself, he knew he could not live long because of his pulmonary illness, and his legacy was enough to let him live in comfort.

As quickly as she could, Mrs. Touchett sold her London house and took Isabel to Paris with her. Ralph went south for the winter to preserve what was left of his health. In Paris the new heiress was introduced to many of her aunt's friends among American expatriates, but she was not impressed. She thought their indolent lives worthy only of contempt. Meanwhile Henrietta and Mr. Bantling had arrived in Paris, and Isabel spent much time with them and Edward Rosier. She had known Rosier when both were children and she was traveling abroad with her father. Rosier was another dilettante, living on the income from his inheritance. He explained to Isabel that he could not return to his own country because there was no occupation there worthy of a gentleman.

In February Mrs. Touchett and her niece went to the Palazzo Crescentini, the Touchett house in Florence. They stopped on the way to see Ralph, who was staying in San Remo. In Florence they were joined once more by Madame Merle.

Unknown to Isabel or her aunt, Madame Merle also visited her friend, Gilbert Osmond, another American who lived in voluntary exile outside Florence with his art collection and his young, convent-bred daughter, Pansy. Madame Merle told Osmond of Isabel's arrival in Florence saying that as the heir to a fortune, Isabel would be a valuable addition to Osmond's collection.

The heiress who had rejected two worthy suitors did not refuse the third. She was quickly captivated by the charm of the sheltered life Gilbert Osmond had created for himself. Her friends were against the match. Henrietta Stackpole, who was inclined to favor Caspar Goodwood, was convinced that Osmond was interested only in Isabel's money, as was Isabel's aunt. Mrs. Touchett had requested Madame Merle, the good friend of both parties, to discover the state of their affections; she was convinced that Madame Merle could have prevented the match. Ralph Touchett was disappointed that his cousin should have fallen to the ground from her flight so quickly. Caspar Goodwood, learning of Isabel's intended marriage when he revisited her after the passage of the two years agreed upon, could not persuade her to reconsider her step. Isabel was indignant when he commented on the fact that she did not even know her intended husband's antecedents.

After her marriage to Gilbert Osmond, Isabel and her husband established their home in Rome, in a setting completely expressive of Osmond's tastes. Before three years had passed, Isabel began to realize that her friends had not been completely wrong in their objections to her marriage. Osmond's exquisite taste had made their home one of the most popular in Rome, but his ceaseless effort to press his wife into a mold, to make her a reflection of his own ideas, had not made their marriage one of the happiest.

He had succeeded in destroying a romance between Pansy and Edward Rosier, who had visited the girl's stepmother and found the daughter attractive. He had not succeeded, however, in contracting the match he desired between Pansy and Lord Warburton. Warburton had found Pansy as pleasing as Isabel had once been, but he had dropped his suit when he saw that the girl's affections lay with Rosier.

Ralph Touchett, his health growing steadily worse, gave up his wanderings on the continent and returned to Gardencourt to die. When Isabel received a telegram from his mother telling her that Ralph would like to see her before his death, she felt it her duty to go to Gardencourt at once. Osmond reacted to her wish as if it were a personal insult. He expected that, as his wife, Isabel would want to remain at his side, and that she would not disobey any wish of his. He also made it plain that he disliked Ralph.

In a state of turmoil after her conversation with her husband, Isabel met the Countess Gemini, Osmond's sister. The countess, visiting the Osmonds, had seen how matters lay between her brother and Isabel. An honest soul, she had felt more sympathy for her sister-in-law than for her brother. To comfort Isabel, she told her the story of Gilbert's past. After his first wife had died, he and Madame Merle had an affair that lasted six or seven years. During that time Madame Merle, a widow, had borne him a child, Pansy. Changing his residence, Osmond had been able to pretend to his new circle of friends that the original Mrs. Osmond had died in giving birth to the child.

With this news fresh in her mind, and still determined to go to England, Isabel stopped to say goodbye to Pansy, who was staying in a convent where her father had sent her to recuperate from her affair with Rosier. There, too, she met Madame Merle. Madame Merle, with her keen perception, had no difficulty realizing that Isabel knew her secret. When she remarked that Isabel would never need to see her again, that she would go to America, Isabel was certain Madame Merle would also find in America much to her own advantage.

Isabel was in time to see her cousin before his death. She stayed on briefly at Gardencourt after the funeral, long enough to bid goodbye to Lord Warburton, who had come to offer condolences to her aunt, and to reject a third offer from Caspar Goodwood, who knew of her husband's treatment. When she left to start her journey back to Italy, Isabel knew what she must do. Her first duty was not to herself, but to put her house in order.

A PORTRAIT OF THE ARTIST AS A YOUNG MAN

Type of work: Novel
Author: James Joyce (1882-1941)
Type of plot: Psychological realism
Time of plot: 1882-1903
Locale: Ireland
First published: 1916

Principal characters:
STEPHEN DEDALUS, an Irish student
SIMON DEDALUS, his father
EMMA, his friend

Critique:

In telling the story of his own youth under a thin disguise of fiction, Joyce has written one of the most compelling and forceful of recent autobiographies. He tried to show the beginnings of his artistic compulsion, and the events that led him to think and to act as he did. Highly descriptive, the book moves from incident to incident in an unhurried way, sketching in all the important moments and thoughts of Joyce's youth as he remembered them. This novel is a forerunner of Joyce's more significant and experimental *Ulysses.*

The Story:

When Stephen Dedalus went to school for the first time, his last name soon got him into trouble. It sounded too Latin, and the boys teased him about it. Seeing that he was sensitive and shy, the other boys began to bully him. School was filled with unfortunate incidents for Stephen. He was happy when he became sick and was put in the infirmary away from the other boys. Once, when he was there just before the Christmas holidays, he worried about dying and death. As he lay on the bed thinking, he heard the news of Parnell's death. The death of the great Irish leader was the first date he remembered—October 6, 1891.

At home during the vacation he learned more of Parnell. His father, Simon Dedalus, worshiped the dead man's memory and defended him on every count. Stephen's aunt, Dante Riordan, despised Parnell as a heretic and a rabble-rouser. The fierce arguments that they got into every day burned themselves into Stephen's memory. He worshiped his father, and his father said that Parnell had tried to free Ireland, to rid it of the priests who were ruining the country. Dante insisted that just the opposite was true. A violent defender of the priests, she leveled every kind of abuse against Simon and his ideas. The disagreement between them became a problem which, in due time, Stephen would have to solve for himself.

Returning to school after the holidays, Stephen got in trouble with Father Dolan, one of the administrators of the church school he attended. Because he had broken his glasses, Stephen could not study until a new pair arrived. Father Dolan saw that Stephen was not working, and thinking that his excuse about the glasses was false he gave the boy a beating. The rest of the boys for once were on Stephen's side, and they urged him to complain to the head of the school. With fear and trembling, Stephen went to the head and presented his case. The head understood, and promised to speak to Father Dolan about the matter. When Stephen told the boys about his conversation, they hoisted him in their arms like a victorious fighter, and called him a hero.

Afterward life was much easier for Stephen. Only one unfortunate incident marked the term. In a spirit of fun, one of his professors announced in class that Stephen had expressed heresy in one of his essays. Stephen quickly changed the offending phrase and hoped that the mistake would be forgotten. After class, however, several of the boys accused him not only of being a heretic but also of liking Byron, whom they considered an immoral man and therefore no good as a poet. In replying to their charges, Stephen had his first real encounter with the problems of art and morality. They were to follow him throughout his life.

On a trip to Cork with his father, Stephen was forced to listen to the often-told tales of his father's youth. They visited the places his father had loved as a boy. Each night Stephen was forced to cover up his father's drunkenness and sentimental outbursts. The trip was an education in everything Stephen disliked.

At the end of the school year Stephen won several prizes. He bought presents for everyone, started to do over his room, and began an ill-fated loan service. As long as the money lasted, life was wonderful. Then one night, when his money was almost gone, he was enticed into a house by a woman wearing a long pink gown. At sixteen he learned what love was.

Not until the school held a retreat in honor of Saint Francis Xavier did Stephen realize how deeply conscious he was of the sins he had committed with women. The sermons of the priests about heaven and hell, especially about hell, ate into his mind. At night his dreams were of nothing but the eternal torture which he felt he must endure after death. He could not bear to make confession in school. At last he went into the city, to a church where he was unknown. There he opened his unhappy mind and heart to an understanding and wise old priest, who advised him and comforted his soul. After the confession Stephen promised to sin no more, and he felt sure that he would keep his promise.

For a time Stephen's life followed a model course. He studied Aquinas and Aristotle and won acclaim from his teachers. One day the director of the school called Stephen into his office and, after a long conversation, asked him if he had ever thought of joining the order of the Jesuits. Stephen was deeply flattered. Priesthood became his life's goal.

When Stephen entered the university, however, a change came over his thinking. He began to doubt, and the longer he studied, the more confused and doubtful he became.

His problems drew him closer to two of his fellow students, Davin and Lynch and farther away from Emma, a girl for whom he had felt affection since childhood. With Davin and Lynch he discussed his ideas about beauty and the working of the mind. Because he would not sign a petition for world peace, Stephen won the enmity of many of the fellows. They called him anti-social and egotistic. Finally neither the peace movement, the Irish Revival, nor the Church itself could claim his support.

Davin was the first to question Stephen about his ideas. When he suggested to Stephen that in everything Ireland should come first, Stephen answered that to him Ireland was an old sow that ate her own children.

One day Stephen met Emma at a carnival, and she asked him why he had stopped coming to see her. He answered that he had been born to be a monk. When Emma said that she thought him a heretic instead of a monk, his last link with Ireland seemed to be broken. At least he was not afraid to be alone. If he wanted to find beauty, and to understand beauty, he had to leave Ireland, where there was nothing in which he believed. The prayers of his friends asking that he return to the faith went unanswered. Stephen got together his things, packed, and left Ireland, intending never to return. He did intend, some day, to write a book that would make clear his views on Ireland and the Irish.

THE POSSESSED

Type of work: Novel
Author: Fyodor Mikhailovich Dostoevski (1821-1881)
Type of plot: Psychological realism
Time of plot: Mid-nineteenth century
Locale: Russia
First published: 1867

Principal characters:

STEPAN VERHOVENSKY, a provincial patriot and mild progressive
PYOTR, his nihilist son
VARVARA STAVROGIN, a provincial lady and employer of Stepan
NIKOLAY, her son, a victim of materialism
MARYA, his idiot wife
SHATOV, the independent son of one of Varvara's serfs

Critique:

The Possessed is Dostoevski's answer to Turgenev's treatment of Russian nihilism in *Fathers and Sons*. By means of a large number of characters representing all classes of Russian society, Dostoevski shows how an idle interest in nihilism brought on robbery, arson, and murder in one Russian community. The plot is exceedingly complex, but this very complexity tends to emphasize a similar quality in nineteenth-century Russian life, which convulsed violently when it concerned itself with denial of an ordering principle in the universe.

The Story:

Stepan Verhovensky, a self-styled progressive patriot and erstwhile university lecturer, was footloose in a provincial Russian town until Varvara Stavrogin hired him to tutor her only son, Nikolay. Although Stepan's radicalism, which was largely a pose, shocked Varvara, the two became friends. When Varvara's husband died, Stepan even looked forward to marrying the widow. They went together to St. Petersburg, where they moved daringly in radical circles. After attempting without success to start a literary journal, they left St. Petersburg, Varvara returning to the province and Stepan, in an attempt to assert his independence, going to Berlin. After four months in Germany, Stepan, realizing that he was Varvara's thrall emotionally and financially, returned to the province in order to be near her.

Stepan became the leader of a small group that met to discuss progressive ideas. Among the group were Shatov, the independent son of one of Varvara's serfs, a liberal named Virginsky, and Liputin, a man who made everyone's business his business.

Nikolay Stavrogin, whom Stepan had introduced to progressivism, went on to school in St. Petersburg and from there into the army as an officer. He resigned his commission, however, returned to St. Petersburg, and went to live in the slums. When he returned home, at Varvara's request, he proceeded to insult the members of Stepan's group. He bit the ear of the provincial governor during an interview with that dignitary. Obviously mentally unbalanced, Nikolay was committed to bed. Three months later, apparently recovered, he apologized for his actions and again left the province.

Months later Varvara was invited to visit a childhood friend in Switzerland, where Nikolay was paying court to her friend's daughter, Lizaveta. Before the party returned to Russia, however, Lizaveta and Nikolay broke their engagement because of Nikolay's interest in Dasha, Varvara's servant woman. In Switzerland, Nikolay and Stepan's son, Pyotr, met and found themselves in sympathy on political matters.

THE POSSESSED by Fyodor Mikhailovich Dostoevski. Published by The Modern Library, Inc.

In the province, meanwhile, there was a new governor, one von Lembke. Stepan, lost without Varvara, visibly deteriorated during her absence. Varvara arranged with Dasha, who was twenty, to marry Stepan, who was fifty-three. Dasha, who was the sister of Shatov, submitted quietly to her mistress' wishes. Stepan reluctantly consented to the marriage, but he balked when he discovered from a member of his group that he was being used to cover up Nikolay's relations with the girl.

New arrivals in the province were Captain Lebyadkin and his idiot, crippled sister, Marya. One day Marya attracted the attention of Varvara in front of the cathedral, and Varvara took the cripple home with her. Nikolay, she learned, had known the Lebyadkins in St. Petersburg. Pyotr assured Varvara, who was suspicious, that Nikolay and Marya Lebyadkin were not married.

By his personal charm and a representation of himself as a mysterious revolutionary agent returned from exile, Pyotr began to dominate Stepan's liberal friends and became, for his own scheming purposes, the protégé of Yulia, the governor's wife. Nikolay at first followed Pyotr in his political activities, but he turned against the revolutionary movement and warned Shatov that Pyotr's group was plotting to kill Shatov because of information he possessed. Nikolay confessed to Shatov that on a bet he had married Marya Lebyadkin in St. Petersburg.

As a result of a duel between Nikolay and a local aristocrat who hated him, a duel in which Nikolay emerged victorious without killing his opponent, Nikolay became a local hero. He continued intimate with Dasha, Lizaveta having announced her engagement to another man. Pyotr, meanwhile, sowed seeds of dissension among all classes in the town; he disclosed von Lembke's possession of a collection of radical manifestoes; he caused a break between his father and Varvara, and he secretly incited the working people to rebel against their masters.

Yulia led the leaders of the town in preparations for a grand fête. Pyotr saw in the fête the opportunity to bring chaos into an otherwise orderly community. He brought about friction between von Lembke, who was an inept governor, and Yulia, who actually governed the province through her salon.

At a meeting of the revolutionary group, despair and confusion prevailed until Pyotr welded it together with mysterious talk of orders from higher revolutionary leaders. He talked of many other such groups engaged in like activities. Shatov, who attended the meeting, denounced Pyotr as a spy and a scoundrel and walked out. Pyotr disclosed to Nikolay his nihilistic beliefs and proposed that Nikolay be brought forward as the Pretender when the revolution had been accomplished.

Blum, von Lembke's secretary, raided Stepan's quarters and confiscated all of Stepan's private papers, among them some political manifestoes. Stepan went to the governor to demand his rights under the law and witnessed in front of the governor's mansion the lashing of dissident workers who had been quietly demonstrating for redress of their grievances. Von Lembke appeased Stepan by saying that the raid on his room was a mistake.

The fête was doomed beforehand. Many agitators without tickets were admitted. Liputin read a comic and seditious poem. Karmazinov, a great novelist, made a fool of himself by recalling the follies of his youth. Stepan insulted the agitators by championing the higher culture. When an unidentified agitator arose to speak, the afternoon session of the fête became a bedlam, so that it was doubtful whether the ball would take place that night. Abetted by Pyotr, Nikolay and Lizaveta eloped in the afternoon to the country house of Varvara.

The ball was not canceled, but few of the landowners of the town or countryside appeared. Drunkenness and brawling soon reduced the ball to a rout which came to a sorry end when fire was discovered raging through some houses along the river. Captain Lebyadkin, Marya, and their servant were discovered murdered in their house, which remained unburned in the path of the fire. When Pyotr informed Nikolay of the murders, Nikolay confessed that he had known of the possibility that violence would take place, but that he had done nothing to prevent it. Horrified, Lizaveta went to see the murdered pair; she was beaten to death by the enraged townspeople because of her connections with Nikolay. Nikolay left town quickly and quietly.

When the revolutionary group met again, all mistrusted one another. Pyotr explained to them that Fedka, an ex-convict, had murdered the Lebyadkins for robbery, but he failed to mention that Nikolay had all but paid Fedka to commit the crime. He warned the group against Shatov and said that a fanatic named Kirillov had agreed to cover up the proposed murder of Shatov. After Fedka denounced Pyotr as an atheistic scoundrel, Fedka was found dead on a road outside the town.

At the same time, Marie, Shatov's wife, returned to the town. The couple had been separated for three years; Marie was ill and pregnant. When she began her labor, Shatov procured Virginsky's wife as midwife. The couple were reconciled after Marie gave birth to a baby boy, for the child served to regenerate Shatov and make him happy once more.

Shatov left his wife and baby alone in order to keep an appointment with the revolutionary group, an appointment made for the purpose of separating himself from the plotters. Attacked and shot by Pyotr, his body was weighted with stones and thrown into a pond. After the murder Pyotr went to Kirillov to get Kirillov's promised confession for the murder of Shatov. Kirillov, who was Shatov's neighbor and who had seen Shatov's happiness at the return of his wife, at first refused to sign, but Pyotr finally prevailed upon him to put his name to the false confession. Kirillov, morally bound to end his life, shot himself. Pyotr left the province.

Stepan, meanwhile, left the town to seek a new life. He wandered for a time among peasants and at last became dangerously ill. Varvara went to him, and the two friends were reconciled before the old scholar died. Varvara disowned her son. Marie and the baby died of exposure and neglect when Shatov failed to return home. One of the radical group broke down and confessed to the violence that had been committed in the town at the instigation of the completely unmoral Pyotr. Liputin escaped to St. Petersburg, where he was apprehended in a drunken stupor in a brothel.

Nikolay wrote to Dasha, the servant, suggesting that the two of them go to Switzerland and begin a new life. Before Dasha could pack her things, however, Nikolay returned home secretly and hanged himself in his room.

POWER

Type of work: Novel
Author: Lion Feuchtwanger (1884-)
Type of plot: Historical novel
Time of plot: Mid-eighteenth century
Locale: Germany
First published: 1925

Principal characters:
JOSEF SÜSS OPPENHEIMER, a court favorite
RABBI GABRIEL, his uncle
NAEMI, his daughter

KARL ALEXANDER, the Duke
MARIE AUGUSTE, the Duchess
WEISSENSEE, a politician
MAGDALEN SIBYLLE, his daughter

Critique:

What is a Jew? What causes a Jew, in the midst of disdain, antipathy, and persecution, to remain a Jew? Feuchtwanger deals with this problem through his fictional minister, Josef Süss Oppenheimer, the half-Christian Jew who chose to remain a Jew until his death. Subtly, Feuchtwanger shows us the metamorphosis of a rank materialist. At first Süss chose to remain a Jew because he wanted to be the greatest Jew in Germany. As a Christian he could never be at the top. At the end, he chose Judaism because he found inspiration in its teachings. The outer Süss was no more than a moneymonger, but the inner man was sensitive and human.

The Story:

All of Prussia rejoiced, and European courts lost their best topic of scandal when Duke Eberhard Ludwig broke with the countess who had been his mistress and returned to his wife to beget another heir to the throne. The countess had been his mistress for thirty years, bleeding the country with her extravagant demands for wealth and jewels. Ludwig was too vain, however, to remain her lover when she grew fat and middle-aged.

The countess sent for Isaac Landauer, the wealthy international banker who was her financial agent. Unable to advise her as to the means by which she could keep her hold on the duke, he offered to liquidate her possessions and send them to another province. But the countess, who had a strong belief in black magic, insisted that Landauer must bring to her the Wandering Jew to help cast a spell on Ludwig.

Landauer went to his young friend, Joseph Süss Oppenheimer, and offered half of what his dealings with the countess would bring him, if the young man would aid Landauer in the countess' scheme. The so-called Wandering Jew was an uncle of Süss, Rabbi Gabriel, whose melancholy demeanor and mystic ways had caused people to think that he was the legendary Wandering Jew. Süss considered the offer. It was tempting, but for some unknown reason the young man was half afraid of his uncle, whose presence always instilled in his nephew a feeling of inferiority. Furthermore, Rabbi Gabriel was rearing motherless, fourteen-year-old Naemi, the daughter whom Süss wished to conceal from the rest of the world. But at last he sent for Rabbi Gabriel.

Penniless Prince Karl Alexander came to Wildbad in hopes of gaining the grant of a substantial income from the duke. Süss, discovering the poverty of the prince, made himself the financial adviser of that destitute nobleman. Although Landauer warned him that Karl Alexander was a poor risk, Süss continued his association with the prince merely because he hoped to ingratiate himself with the nobility. Half in gratitude, half in jest, the prince granted Süss admission to his levees.

On his arrival in Wildbad, Rabbi Gabriel told Süss that he intended to bring Naemi to his nephew. But Landauer no longer needed Gabriel to help carry out the countess' scheme, and the rabbi returned to his home. The countess had been banished from the duchy, taking with her the money procured by Landauer.

Süss became the favorite of Prince Karl Alexander. To Wildbad also came Prince Anself Franz of Thurn and Taxis and his daughter, Princess Marie

Auguste. Their mission was to urge Prince Karl Alexander to marry the princess and turn Catholic. Angry because the duke had refused to give him a pension, the prince consented.

Duke Eberhard Ludwig died suddenly, and Karl Alexander, now a Catholic, inherited the duchy. Süss became a court favorite, appointed by the new duchess to be keeper of her privy purse. Although Jews were forbidden to live in the duchy, the people had to acknowledge that the duke should be allowed his private court Jew.

Rabbi Gabriel had bought a little white house where he lived with Naemi and a servant. For three days, while the uncle was away, Süss went to Hirsau to visit his daughter. Then he returned to his duke. Since Karl Alexander's succession Süss had slyly directed him in measures which were resulting in a complete control of Swabia by the duke himself. The Constitution and the Parliament were powerless. Great noblemen had been ruined. Although his income was enormous, Süss himself refrained from holding any office. Süss had picked one former cabinet member, Weissensee, as President of the Ecclesiastical Council. One night he gave a party to which Weissensee brought his daughter, Magdalen Sibylle. Süss, noting the duke's attentiveness toward the girl, enticed her into his bedroom, where the duke followed. After that evening, the duke sent gifts to Magdalen Sibylle, his declared mistress, and Weissensee was promoted to a high office. Hating Süss, Weissensee secretly hoped to bring the favorite into disfavor at court. Learning that Süss had a daughter, he planned to place the Jew in the same position that Süss had placed him on the night Karl Alexander had taken Magdalen Sibylle.

The murder of a child revived the old legend that Jews sacrificed a Christian child at the Passover feast, and a Jew, Reb Jeckeskel Seligmann, was arrested for the crime. Pressure was put on Süss to use his power to save the innocent man, but he refused because of the danger to his position at court. Then Rabbi Gabriel sent word to Süss that Naemi had heard rumors of his wickedness. At last Süss decided that he would help the arrested man. In rescuing Seligmann, he felt anew his power as the court Jew. Soon afterward, at the request of Rabbi Gabriel, he went to visit his mother. From her he learned that his real father had been a great Christian marshal in the German army. Confused, Süss finally decided that he was a Jew and would remain so.

Convinced at last that Süss was a swindler, the duke threatened to dismiss and dishonor him. But when Süss offered his own fortune in exchange for proof of any financial trickery, the duke changed his mind and roared his anger at the enemies of Süss. Realizing that the favorite now had more power than ever, Weissensee continued to plot his revenge. Arranging for the duke to spend some time at his home in Hirsau while Rabbi Gabriel was not at home, Weissensee took the duke to Süss' daughter. With visions of a heavenly rescue, the quiet, lonely child climbed to the roof of the house to escape from her attacker. She fell from the roof to her death.

Outwardly Süss professed forgiveness toward the duke, but he pocketed more and more funds from the ducal treasury. His personality altered. Instead of ingratiating himself at court, he criticized and ridiculed his acquaintances. Filling the duke's head with dreams of conquest, Süss inveigled him into leading a new military coup. At the same time he planned the duke's destruction. While Karl Alexander lay dying at the scene of his defeat, Süss rained over his head a torrent of pent-up abuse. His enemies ordered his arrest.

For many months the case against Süss dragged on. Finally he was put into a stinking, rat-infested hole, where every day the authorities plied him for a confession, but he remained stubbornly alive and sane. Sentenced to hang, he assailed the court with icy, cutting words. He could have freed himself by declaring his Christian birth. He kept silent.

On the day of the hanging Süss died with the name "Adonai," the Hebrew name for God, on his lips, and the word was echoed by all the Jews who had gathered to watch him die.

THE PRAIRIE

Type of work: Novel
Author: James Fenimore Cooper (1789-1851)
Type of plot: Historical romance
Time of plot: 1804
Locale: Western Plains of the United States
First published: 1827

Principal characters:
- NATTY BUMPPO, an old frontiersman
- ISHMAEL BUSH, a desperado
- ESTHER BUSH, his wife
- ELLEN WADE, Esther's niece
- ABIRAM WHITE, Esther's brother
- DR. BATTIUS, a naturalist
- PAUL HOVER, Ellen's lover
- CAPTAIN MIDDLETON, of the United States Army
- INEZ, Middleton's wife
- HARD-HEART, a Pawnee chief

Critique:

This novel, the fifth and last volume of Cooper's familiar Leatherstocking series, closes the career of his famous frontiersman and scout, Natty Bumppo. The plot is full of incident, but it depends too much on coincidence to seem realistic to many modern readers. The character portrayal is not vivid; the women, especially, seem dull and unreal. Much of the action is slowed down by the stilted dialogue. Yet, in spite of these defects, *The Prairie* catches much of the spirit of the old West.

The Story:

Shortly after the time of the Louisiana Purchase the family of Ishmael Bush traveled westward from the Mississippi River. Ishmael was accompanied by his wife, Esther, and their sons and daughters. Also in the caravan were Ellen Wade, a niece of Esther; Abiram White, Esther's brother; and Dr. Battius, a physician and naturalist. As this company searched for a camping place one evening, they met an aged trapper, Natty Bumppo, and his dog. The trapper directed them to a nearby stream.

After night had fallen, Bumppo discovered Ellen in a secret meeting with her lover, Paul Hover, a wandering bee hunter. The three were captured by a band of Sioux. While the Indian raiders stole all the horses and cattle from Ishmael's party, the captives made their escape. Unable to proceed across the prairie, the emigrant family occupied a naturally fortified hilltop shown to them by Bumppo.

A week later, Paul, Bumpoo, and Dr. Battius were gathered at Bumppo's camping ground. They were soon joined by a stranger, who introduced himself as Captain Middleton of the United States Army. Bumppo was delighted to find that Middleton was the grandson of an old friend whom he had known in the days of the French and Indian wars. The young officer had come to find his wife, Inez, who had been kidnaped by Abiram White shortly after her marriage. She was now a captive in Ishmael's camp.

Paul, Bumppo, and Dr. Battius agreed to help Middleton rescue her.

On the same day Ishmael and his sons left their camp to hunt buffalo. That evening they returned with meat, but Asa, the oldest son, did not return with the rest of the hunters. In the morning the entire family set out to search for him. At last his dead body was found in a thicket; he had been shot in the back with one of Bumppo's bullets. His family buried him and returned to camp. There they found that both Ellen and Inez were gone.

The girls, who had been rescued by Middleton and his friends, were rapidly making their escape across the prairie, when their progress was interrupted by a meeting with a Pawnee warrier, Hard-Heart. After the Indian had galloped away on his horse, the travelers found themselves in the path of a stampeding herd of buffalo. The group was saved from being trampled to death at the last moment by the braying of Dr. Battius' donkey, for at the strange sound the buffalo turned aside. However, Middleton's party was soon captured by a band of Sioux pursuing the buffalo herd. They were the same Indians who had captured Bumppo, Paul, and Ellen once before. At the same time Ishmael and his sons approached on foot in search of the two girls. The Indians remounted and gave horses to their captives so that all could ride to Ishmael's camp while he and his sons were away. During the Indian raid on the camp, Bumppo helped his friends escape on horseback.

They rode as far as possible before making camp for the night. But in the morning they found that the Sioux had followed them and had set fire to the prairie in order to drive them into the open. Bumppo rescued the party by burning off the nearby prairie before the larger fire reached it. As they started off, they met the lone Hard-Heart again. From him they learned that the Sioux and Ishmael's family had joined forces in order to search for them. Since Hard-Heart and the little band had a common enemy in the Sioux, he agreed to take them to his Pawnee village for protection.

In order to evade their pursuers, the fugitives crossed a nearby river. As they reached the far bank the Sioux appeared on the opposite shore. That night the fugitives remained free, but snow fell and made it impossible for them to escape without being tracked. They were captured and taken to the Sioux village.

Hard-Heart, Paul, and Middleton were bound by their savage captors. Out of respect for his age, Bumppo was allowed to roam freely, but he declined to leave his friends. The women were placed in the lodge of the Sioux chief.

Using Bumppo as an interpreter, the Sioux chief asked Inez to be his wife. At the same time Ishmael asked the chief to hand over to him Inez, Ellen, and Bumppo, as had been previously agreed. When the chief refused, Ishmael departed angrily.

The Indians then gathered in council to decide the fate of Hard-Heart, and many wished to torture him to death. But an old warrier stepped forward and declared that he wished to make the Pawnee his adopted son. Hard-Heart, however, refused to become a member of the Sioux tribe. The Sioux began their torture, but in the midst of it Hard-Heart escaped and joined a war party of his own Pawnees, who arrived on the scene at that moment.

Leaving their women to guard the prisoners, the Sioux prepared to fight. The braves of the two tribes gathered on the opposite banks of a river, neither side daring to make the first move. Then Hard-Heart challenged the Sioux chief to single combat.

Meanwhile, Bumppo helped the rest of the captives to escape. Shortly afterward they fell once more into the hands of Ishmael.

Hard-Heart was victorious in the single-handed combat, and his warriors put the Sioux to flight in the battle which followed.

The next morning Ishmael held a court of justice in order to deal with his captives. He realized his mistake in carrying Inez away from her husband and allowed the couple their freedom. He gave Ellen her choice of remaining with his family or going with Paul. She chose to go with her lover. Ishmael allowed Dr. Battius his freedom because he did not think the scientist worth bothering about. Then Bumppo came up for judgment.

Ishmael still believed that Bumppo had shot his son, Asa. Bumppo, however, revealed that it was really Abiram who had done the cowardly deed. Abiram confessed his crime and then fainted. Ishmael was reluctant to pronounce judgment on his brother-in-law, but he felt it his duty to do so. That evening he gave Abiram the choice of starving to death or hanging himself. Late that night Ishmael and Esther returned to find that Abiram had hanged himself. They buried him and continued on their way back to the frontier settlements.

Middleton, Paul, and the girls invited Bumppo to return to the settlements with them, where they would make comfortable his last days. He refused, giving as his reason his desire to die away from civilization. He chose to remain in the Pawnee village with Hard-Heart.

A year later, when Middleton's duties as an army officer brought him near the Pawnee village, he determined to pay Bumppo a visit. Arriving at the camp, Middleton found the old trapper near death. It was late afternoon. Bumppo revived enough to greet his old friend. At sundown, however, he seemed to be breathing his last. As the sun sank beneath the horizon, he made one last tremendous effort. He rose to his feet and, as if answering a roll call, he uttered a loud and firm "Here"— then fell back dead into the arms of his friends.

PRECIOUS BANE

Type of work: Novel
Author: Mary Webb (1881-1927)
Type of plot: Regional romance
Time of plot: Mid-nineteenth century
Locale: England
First published: 1924

Principal characters:
PRUDENCE SARN, a harelipped girl
GIDEON, her brother
WIZARD BEGUILDY, an evil neighbor
JANCIS BEGUILDY, his daughter
KESTER WOODSEAVES, the weaver

Critique:

Just as Prudence Sarn seemed to view the past events of her life through a veil, so she tells her story. The story is not autobiographical, but into it Mrs. Webb put many experiences of her own youth. In this novel man seems to be controlled by forces of nature. The Bane, the poison that was in Gideon Sarn, moved him even to murder, for powers outside him drove him beyond his will. But when nature was satisfied, the Bane was exorcised; and peace came to the Sarns.

The Story:

The country people said there had been something queer about the Sarn family ever since old Timothy Sarn was struck by forked lightning. The lightning seemed to have gone into Timothy and into all the Sarns. In Prue's father the lightning took the form of a raving temper, and in Prue's brother Gideon the lightning was the more frightening because it was quiet but deadly. Dogs and horses turned away from Gideon's gray eyes. Prue understood her brother better than most, but even she was frightened when Gideon offered to be the sin-eater at their father's funeral. For a sin-eater took the sins of the dead person and sold his soul for a price. Gideon's price was the farm which would have been his mother's. Mrs. Sarn feared to accept the terms, for a sin-eater's destiny was dreadful; but she feared more to let her husband go to his grave with all his sins, and so she gave Gideon the farm.

On the night after the funeral, Gideon told Prue his plans. They were going to become rich, own a house in town, and have fine clothes and beautiful furniture. Gideon promised Prue that for her help he would give her fifty pounds to get her harelip cured. He warned her, however, that he would work her as he would an animal. Because Prue had hated her harelip for many years, she consented to his terms. They signed an agreement and took an oath on the Bible that Gideon would be the master and Prue his servant.

Prue was also to learn to read and write and do sums so that she could keep the farm accounts. Her teacher would be Wizard Beguildy, a neighbor who was preached against in church because he earned his living by working spells and charms. Wizard was the father of Jancis Beguildy, a childhood friend of Prue and Gideon.

During the next four years Prue and Gideon slaved long hours in the field. Prue grew thinner and thinner and their mother became quite feeble. She was compelled to watch the pigs, for Gideon would let no one be idle. The farm prospered.

One part of Gideon's plan did not work out, however, as he had arranged. In love with Jancis Beguildy, he decided that he would make his fortune and then marry her. Jancis did not want to wait that long, but Gideon would not change his mind.

Gideon and Jancis were handfasted and Jancis had a love-spinning, even though her father swore that she could never marry Gideon. At the love-spinning Prue first saw Kester Woodseaves, the weaver. When Kester came into the room, it seemed to Prue that a beautiful mist surrounded her. Then she turned sadly away. Gideon had told her often enough that no man would love a girl with a harelip.

A few days after the spinning Jancis went to tell Gideon that her father threatened either to sell her to a rich squire for his pleasure or to hire her out for three years as a dairymaid. Her only salvation was immediate marriage to Gideon. But Gideon told her that he had not made enough money, that she must be bound over for three years. Even Jancis' tears would not move him. Jancis was sent to work for Mr. and Mrs. Grimble.

After several months Jancis ran away from the Grimble farm. Because Gideon had a good crop of grain coming up, he promised to marry her after the harvest. Wizard Beguildy still swore that there would be no wedding, and Prue was afraid.

One day, as Prue was walking through the fields, Kester met her. When she tried to hide her face, Kester took her by the shoulders and looked straight into her eyes. He did not laugh, but talked to Prue as a man talks to a woman who is beautiful and attractive. His words were almost more than Prue could bear.

Never had there been such a harvest. Gideon's crop was piled in high ricks, and all the neighbor folks who had helped with the harvest came to the house to dance and feast. As soon as the grain buyer came to buy the crop, Jancis and Gideon would be married. But Gideon, unable to wait until their wedding, went to Jancis' home to be with her. Mrs. Beguildy tricked her husband into leaving so that the lovers could be together. Wizard Beguildy, arriving home early, found Jancis and Gideon in bed together, and the two men quarreled. Prue was more frightened than ever.

Prue had reason for her premonition of danger, for that night Wizard set the ricks on fire and everything burned except the house and the barn. Gideon was like a madman. When Jancis tried to comfort him, he said she was cursed by her father's blood, and he drove her away. He tried to get to Wizard to kill him, but Prue prevented this deed by having Wizard arrested. Gideon cursed the Beguildy family, even Jancis. Jancis swooned and lay for days in a trance. She and her mother were put off their farm, for no landowner would have the family of an arsonist on his land.

Gideon began to rebuild his dream, but Jancis was no longer a part of it. He worked himself and Prue and their mother almost to death. When the mother became too weak to work, Gideon put poison into her tea, for he would feed no one who could not earn her way. Prue knew that her brother's mind was deranged after the fire, but she had not known that he would kill for money.

Jancis returned with Gideon's baby. When Gideon drove her out of the house, Jancis took her baby to the pond and drowned herself and her child. Gideon began to see visions. He told Prue often that he had seen Jancis or his mother, and sometimes he heard Jancis singing. He talked queerly about the past, about his love for Jancis. He no longer wanted the money that had been his whole life. One day he rowed out on the pond and threw himself into the water and drowned. Prue was left alone.

Her vow to Gideon ended, Prue decided to leave the farm. When she rounded up the livestock and went into the village to sell them, the people called her a witch and blamed all the trouble on her harelip. They said that the forked lightning was in her worse than in all the other Sarns, and they put her in the ducking chair and ducked her in the pond until she was senseless. When she awakened, Kester was beside her, to lift her upon his horse and take her away to be his wife. Prue knew then that the forked lightning was not in her; the curse of the Sarns had been lifted.

PRIDE AND PREJUDICE

Type of work: Novel
Author: Jane Austen (1775-1817)
Type of plot: Comedy of manners
Time of plot: Early nineteenth century
Locale: Rural England
First published: 1813

Principal characters:
Mr. Bennet, father of five daughters
Mrs. Bennet, his wife
Elizabeth Bennet, her father's favorite
Jane Bennet, the family beauty
Mary,
Catherine (Kitty), and
Lydia Bennet, younger sisters
Mr. Bingley, an eligible bachelor
Caroline Bingley, his sister
Mr. Darcy, a proud gentleman, Bingley's friend
Mr. Collins, a conceited bore
Lady Catherine de Bourgh, Collins' arrogant patroness

Critique:

Elizabeth Bennet, one of the most delightful heroines of all time, would be enough to make *Pride and Prejudice* outstanding among English novels. In addition, the book has a beautifully symmetrical plot in which the action rises and falls as inevitably as does an ocean wave. Many of the other characters besides Elizabeth are superbly drawn. Jane Austen's delicate but telling satire of the English country gentlefolk of her day—and indeed of her neighborhood—remains a delightful commentary upon the little foibles of human nature.

The Story:

The chief business of Mrs. Bennet's life was to find suitable husbands for her five daughters. Consequently she heard with elation that Netherfield Park, one of the great houses of the neighborhood, had been let to a London gentleman named Mr. Bingley. Gossip such as Mrs. Bennet loved reported him a rich and altogether eligible young bachelor. Mr. Bennet heard the news with his usual dry calmness, suggesting in his mild way that perhaps Bingley was not moving into the county for the single purpose of marrying one of the Bennet daughters.

Mr. Bingley's first public appearance in the neighborhood was at a ball. With him were his two sisters, the husband of the older, and Mr. Darcy, Bingley's friend. Bingley was an immediate success in local society, and he and Jane, the oldest Bennet daughter, a pretty girl of sweet and gentle disposition, were attracted to each other at once. His friend, Darcy, however, created a bad impression, seeming cold and extremely proud. In particular, he insulted Elizabeth Bennet, a girl of spirit and intelligence and her father's favorite. He refused to dance with her when she was sitting down for lack of a partner, and he said in her hearing that he was in no mood to prefer young ladies slighted by other men. On future occasions, however, he began to admire Elizabeth in spite of himself. At a later ball she had the satisfaction of refusing him a dance.

Jane's romance with Bingley flourished quietly, aided by family calls, dinners, and balls. His sisters pretended great fondness for Jane, who believed them completely sincere. The more critical and discerning Elizabeth suspected them of hypocrisy, and quite rightly, for they made great fun of Jane's relations, especially her vulgar, garrulous mother and her two ill-bred officer-mad younger sisters. Miss Caroline Bingley, who was eager to marry Darcy and shrewdly aware of his growing admiration for Elizabeth, was especially loud in her ridicule of the Bennet family. Elizabeth herself became Caroline's particular target when she walked three muddy miles to visit Jane, who was sick with a cold at Netherfield Park after a ride through the rain to accept an invitation from the Bingley sisters. Until Jane was able to be moved home, Elizabeth stayed to nurse her. During her visit Elizabeth received enough attention from Darcy to make Caroline Bingley long sincerely for Jane's recovery. Nor were her fears ill-founded. Darcy admitted to himself that he would be in some danger from the charm of Elizabeth, if it were not for her inferior family connections.

Elizabeth now acquired a new admirer in the person of Mr. Collins, a ridiculously pompous clergyman and a distant cousin of the Bennets, who would some day inherit Mr. Bennet's property because that gentleman had no male heir. Mr. Collins' patroness, Lady Catherine de Bourgh, had urged him to marry, and he, always obsequiously obedient to her wishes, hastened to comply. Thinking to alleviate the hardship caused the Bennet sisters by the entail which gave their father's property to him, Mr. Collins first proposed to Elizabeth. Much to her mother's displeasure and her father's joy, she firmly and promptly rejected him. He almost immediately transferred his affections to Elizabeth's best friend, Charlotte Lucas, who, twenty-seven and somewhat homely, accepted at once his offer of marriage.

During Mr. Collins' visit, the younger Bennet sisters, Kitty and Lydia, on one of their many walks to Meryton, met a fascinating new officer, Mr. Wickham, stationed with the regiment there. Outwardly charming, he became a favorite among the ladies, even with Elizabeth. She was willing to believe the story that he had been cheated out of an inheritance left him by his godfather, Darcy's father. Her suspicions of Darcy's arrogant and grasping nature deepened when Wickham did not come to a ball given by the Bingleys, a dance at which Darcy was present.

Soon after the ball, the entire Bingley party suddenly left Netherfield Park. They departed with no intention of returning, as Caroline wrote Jane in a short farewell note which hinted that Bingley might soon become engaged to Darcy's sister. Jane accepted this news at face value and believed that her friend Caroline was telling her gently that her brother loved elsewhere, and that she must cease to hope. Elizabeth, however, was sure of a plot by Darcy and Bingley's sisters to separate him and Jane. She persuaded Jane that Bingley did love her and that he would return to Hertfordshire before the winter was over. Jane almost believed her until she received a letter from Caroline assuring her that they were all settled in London for the winter. Even after Jane told her this news, Elizabeth remained convinced of Bingley's affection for her sister, and deplored the lack of resolution which made him putty in the hands of his designing friend.

About that time Mrs. Bennet's sister, Mrs. Gardiner, an amiable and intelligent woman with a great deal of affection for her two oldest nieces, arrived for a Christmas visit. She suggested to the Bennets that Jane return to London with her for a rest and change of scene and — so it was understood between Mrs. Gardiner and Elizabeth — to renew her acquaintance with Bingley. Elizabeth, not too hopeful for the success of the plan, pointed out that proud Darcy would never let his friend call on Jane in the unfashionable London street on which the Gardiners lived. Jane accepted the invitation, however, and she and Mrs. Gardiner set out for London.

The time drew near for the wedding of Elizabeth's friend, Charlotte Lucas, to the obnoxious Mr. Collins. Charlotte asked Elizabeth to visit her in Kent. In spite of her feeling that there could be little pleasure in such a visit, Elizabeth promised to do so. She felt that in taking such a husband Charlotte was marrying simply for the sake of an establishment, as was indeed the case. Since she herself could not sympathize with her friend's action, Elizabeth thought their days of real intimacy were over. As March approached, however, she found herself eager to see her friend, and she set out with pleasure on the journey with Charlotte's father and sister. On their way, the party stopped in London to see the Gardiners and Jane. Elizabeth found her sister well and outwardly happy, though she had not seen Bingley and his sisters had paid only one call. Elizabeth was sure Bingley had not been told of Jane's presence in London and blamed Darcy for keeping it from him.

Soon after arriving at the Collins' home, the whole party was honored, as Mr. Collins repeatedly assured them, by a dinner invitation from Lady Catherine de Bourgh, Darcy's aunt and Mr. Collins' patroness. Elizabeth found Lady Catherine a haughty, ill-mannered woman and her daughter thin, sickly, and shy. Lady Catherine was extremely fond of inquiring into the affairs of others and giving them unasked advice. Elizabeth turned off the meddling old woman's questions with cool indirectness, and saw from the effect that she was probably the first who had dared to do so.

Soon after Elizabeth's arrival, Darcy came to visit his aunt and cousin. He called frequently at the parsonage, and he and Elizabeth resumed their conversational fencing matches. His rather stilted attentions were suddenly climaxed by a proposal of marriage, but one couched in such proud and condescending terms that Elizabeth indignantly refused him. When he requested her reason for such an emphatic rejection, she mentioned his part in separating Bingley and Jane, and also his mistreatment of Wickham. Angry, he left abruptly, but the next day brought a letter answering her charges. He did not deny his part in separating Jane and Bingley, but he gave as his reasons the improprieties of Mrs. Bennet and her younger daughters, and also his sincere belief that Jane did not love Bingley. As for his alleged mistreatment of Wickham, he proved that he had in reality acted most generously toward the unprincipled Wickham, who had repaid his kindness by attempting to elope with Darcy's young sister. Elizabeth, at first incensed at the proud tones in which he wrote, was at length forced to acknowledge the justice of all he said, and her prejudice against him began to weaken. Without seeing him again, she returned home.

She found her younger sisters clamoring to go to Brighton, where the regiment formerly stationed at Meryton had been ordered. When an invitation came to Lydia from a young officer's wife, Lydia was allowed to accept it over Elizabeth's protests. Elizabeth herself was asked by the Gardiners to go with them on a tour which would take them into Derbyshire, Darcy's home county. She accepted, reasoning that she was not very likely to meet Darcy merely by going into the same county with him. While they were there, however, Mrs. Gardiner decided they should visit Pemberly, Darcy's home. Elizabeth made several excuses, but her aunt was insistent. Then, learning that the Darcy family was not at home, Elizabeth consented to go.

At Pemberly, an unexpected and most embarrassing meeting took place between Elizabeth and Darcy. He was more polite than Elizabeth had ever known him to be, and asked permission for his sister to call upon her. The call was duly paid and returned, but the pleasant intercourse between the Darcys and Elizabeth's party was suddenly cut short when a letter came from Jane telling Elizabeth that Lydia had run away with Wickham. Elizabeth told Darcy what had happened, and she and the Gardiners left for home at once. After several days the runaway couple was located and a marriage arranged between them. When Lydia came home as heedless as ever, she told Elizabeth that Darcy had attended her wedding. Elizabeth, suspecting the truth, learned from Mrs. Gardiner that it was indeed Darcy who brought about the marriage by giving Wickham money.

Soon after Lydia and Wickham left, Bingley came back to Netherfield Park, and with him came Darcy. Elizabeth, now more favorably inclined to him than ever before, hoped his coming meant that he still loved her, but he gave no sign. Bingley and Jane, on the other hand, were still obviously in love with each other, and became engaged, to the great satisfaction of Mrs. Bennet. Soon afterward Lady Catherine paid the Bennets an unexpected call. She had heard it rumored that Darcy was engaged to Elizabeth. Hoping to marry her own daughter to Darcy, she had charged down with characteristic bad manners to order Elizabeth not to accept his proposal. The spirited girl was not to be intimidated by the bullying Lady Catherine and coolly refused to promise not to marry Darcy. She was far from certain she would have another chance, but she had not long to wonder. Lady Catherine, unluckily for her own purpose, repeated to Darcy the substance of her conversation with Elizabeth, and he knew Elizabeth well enough to surmise that her feelings toward him had greatly changed. He returned to Netherfield Park, and he and Elizabeth became engaged. Pride had been humbled and prejudice dissolved.

THE PRISONER OF ZENDA

Type of work: Novel
Author: Anthony Hope (Sir Anthony Hope Hawkins, 1863-1933)
Type of plot: Adventure romance
Time of plot: 1880's
Locale: "Ruritania"
First published: 1894

Principal characters:

RUDOLF RASSENDYLL, an English gentleman
LADY ROSE BURLESDON, his sister-in-law
RUDOLF, King of Ruritania
MICHAEL, DUKE OF STRELSAU, King Rudolf's half-brother
ANTOINETTE DE MAUBAN, in love with Michael
PRINCESS FLAVIA, betrothed to King Rudolf
FRITZ VON TARLENHEIM, a loyal subject of the king
COLONEL SAPT, another loyal subject

Critique:

Many novels have been written about the intrigues and plots of royalty, but few hold the reader's attention as does *The Prisoner of Zenda.* In its pages we meet kings and would-be kings, beautiful ladies, loyal subjects, and those who would sell out their leader for the promise of gold or power. There are thrills and excitement enough for all: murder, duels at midnight, trysts, daring rescues. If Anthony Hope's desire was to give his readers a few hours of pure enjoyment, and it seems to have been his sole purpose in writing this novel, he was successful. His success is confirmed by the fact that the story is almost as popular today as it was when first published.

The Story:

To his sister-in-law, Lady Rose Burlesdon, Rudolf Rassendyll was a great disappointment. In the first place, he was twenty-nine years old and had no useful occupation. Secondly, he bore such a striking resemblance to the Elphbergs, ruling house of Ruritania, that Rose thought him a constant reminder of an old scandal in which her husband's family had been involved. More than a hundred years before, a prince of the country of Ruritania had visited England and had become involved with the wife of one of the Rassendyll men. There was a child, who had the red hair and the large straight nose of the Elphbergs. Since that unfortunate event, five or six descendants of the English lady and the Ruritanian prince had had the characteristic nose and red hair of their royal ancestor. Rose thought Rudolph's red hair and large nose a disgrace for that reason.

Rassendyll himself, however, had no concern over his resemblance to the Ruritanian royal family. A new king was to be crowned in that country within a few weeks, and he decided to travel to Ruritania for the coronation, in order to get a close view of his unclaimed relatives. Knowing that his brother and sister-in-law would try to prevent his journey, he told them that he was going to take a tour of the Tyrol. After he left England, his first stop was Paris, where he learned something more about affairs in the country he was to visit. The new king, also called Rudolf, had a half-brother, Michael, Duke of Strelsau. Michael would have liked to become king, and it was hinted that he would try to prevent the coronation of Rudolf. Rassendyll also learned that there was a beautiful lady, Antoinette de Mauban, who loved Michael and had his favor. She, too, was traveling to Ruritania for the coronation.

When he reached Ruritania and found the capital city crowded, Rassendyll took lodging in Zenda, a small town some fifty miles from the capital, and prepared to go by train for the coronation. Zenda was part of Michael's domain, his hunting lodge being only a few miles from the inn where Rassendyll stopped. Rassendyll learned also that King Rudolf was a guest at his half-brother's hunting lodge while waiting for the coronation. There were more rumors of a plot against the king and talk that Black Michael, as he was called, planned to seize the throne.

Rassendyll walked every day through the woods near the hunting lodge. One day he heard two men discussing how much he resembled the king. The men introduced themselves as Fritz von Tarlenheim and Colonel Sapt, faithful friends of King Rudolf. While they talked, the king himself appeared. The king had shaved his beard, but otherwise he and Rassendyll were identical. Pleased to meet his distant cousin, the king invited Rassendyll to the lodge. There the king drank so much that Fritz and Sapt could not wake him the next morning.

This was the day of the coronation, and as the king slept in his stupor Fritz and Sapt proposed a daring plan to Rassendyll. They knew that if the king did not appear for the coronation Black Michael would seize the throne. Their plan was to shave Rassendyll's beard and dress him in the king's clothes and have him crowned in the king's place. By the time the ceremonies were over, the king would have recovered, would take his rightful place, and no one would be the wiser. It was a dangerous gamble, for exposure would mean death, but Rassendyll agreed to the plot.

Fritz and Sapt locked the king in the wine cellar and left a servant to tell him of the plan when he awoke. Rassendyll, with Fritz and Sapt, proceeded to the palace. With the two men to help him, he carried off the deception, even convincing the Princess Flavia that he was the real king. His role with Flavia was the most difficult for Rassendyll, for he must be gracious and yet not commit the king too far.

The success of the conspirators was not to last. When they returned that night to the lodge, they found the servant murdered and the real king gone. Black Michael's men had worked well. Black Michael knew that the supposed king was an impostor, and Rassendyll, Fritz, and Sapt knew that Black Michael had the real king. But neither group dared call the other's hand. Rassendyll's only chance was to rescue the rightful king. Black Michael's hope was to kill both Rassendyll and the king and thus seize the throne and Princess Flavia for himself. Rassendyll was attacked and almost killed many times. Once he was saved by a warning from Antoinette de Mauban, for although she loved Michael she would not be a party to murder. Also, she did not want Michael to be successful, for his coup would mean his marriage to Flavia. Michael learned of her aid to Rassendyll and held her a semi-prisoner in the hunting lodge where he had hidden the king.

Playing the part of the king, Rassendyll was forced to spend much time with Flavia. He wanted to tell her his real identity, but Fritz and Sapt appealed to his honor and persuaded him that all would be ruined if Flavia learned that he was not the true king.

When they learned that King Rudolf was dying, Rassendyll, Fritz, and Sapt knew that they must take a daring chance to rescue him. They and part of the king's army attacked the lodge. Those not aware of the deception were told that Black Michael had imprisoned a friend of the king. There was a bloody battle both outside and inside the lodge. Black Michael was killed and King Rudolf wounded before the rescue was completed. When he knew that the king would live, Rassendyll realized that his part in the deception was over. The king sent for him and thanked him for his brave work in saving the throne. Princess Flavia also sent for him. She had been told the whole story, but her only concern was to learn whether Rassendyll had spoken for himself or the king when he had given her his love. He told her that he would always love only her and begged her to go away with him. But she was too honorable to leave her people and her king, and she remained in Ruritania, later to marry the king and rule with him.

Rassendyll left Ruritania and spent a few weeks in the Tyrol before returning to England. His sister-in-law, still trying to get him to lead a more useful life, arranged through a friend to get him a diplomatic post. When he learned the post would be in Ruritania, he declined it. Rassendyll resumed his former idle life, with one break in his monotonous routine. Each year Fritz and Rassendyll met in Dresden, and Fritz always brought with him a box containing a rose, a token from Flavia.

PROMETHEUS BOUND

Type of work: Drama
Author: Aeschylus (525-456 B.C.)
Type of plot: Classical tragedy
Time of plot: Remote antiquity
Locale: A barren cliff in Scythia
First presented: 470 B.C.

Principal characters:

PROMETHEUS, a Titan
HEPHAESTUS, his kinsman and the god of fire
KRATOS, Might
BIA, Force
OCEANUS, god of the sea
IO, daughter of Inachus, a river god
HERMES, the winged messenger of the gods

Critique:

Displaying perfectly the Aeschylean pattern, *Prometheus Bound* is a dramatic treatment of the legend of Prometheus, the Fire-Bearer. The spectacle of a demigod in conflict with his destiny, defiant in the face of severe punishment, makes for compelling drama. The mood is one of sharp irony and deep reflection, for the suffering of Prometheus is a symbol of man's inhumanity to man.

The Story:

Condemned by Zeus for giving fire to mere mortals, the Titan Prometheus was brought to a barren cliff in Scythia by Hephaestus, the god of fire, and two guards, Kratos and Bia. There he was to be bound to the jagged cliffs with bonds as strong as adamant. Kratos and Bia obeyed willingly the commands of Zeus, but Hephaestus experienced pangs of sorrow and was reluctant to bind his kinsman to the storm-beaten cliff in that waste region where no man came, where Prometheus would never hear the voice or see the form of a human being. He grieved that the Titan was doomed forever to be guardian of the desolate cliff. But he was powerless against the commands of Zeus, and so at last he chained Prometheus to the cliff by riveting his arms beyond release, thrusting a biting wedge of adamant straight through his heart, and putting iron girths on both his sides with shackles around his legs. After Hephaestus and Bia departed, Kratos remained to hurl one last taunt at Prometheus, asking him what possible aid mankind might now offer their benefactor. The gods who gave Prometheus his name, Forethinker, were foolish, Kratos pointed out, for Prometheus required a higher intelligence to do his thinking for him.

Alone and chained, Prometheus called upon the winds, the waters, mother earth, and the sun, to look on him and see how the gods tortured a god. Admitting that he must bear his lot as best he could because the power of fate was invincible, he was still defiant. He had committed no crime, he insisted; he had merely loved mankind. He remembered how the gods first conceived the plan to revolt against the rule of Kronos and seat Zeus on the throne. At first Prometheus did his best to bring about a reasonable peace between the ancient Titans and the gods. Failing, and to avoid further violence, he had ranged himself on the side of Zeus, who through the counsel of Prometheus overthrew Kronos. Once on the throne, Zeus parceled out to the lesser gods their share of power, but ignored mortal man with the ultimate plan in mind of destroying him completely and creating instead another race which would cringe and be servile to Zeus' every word. Among all the gods, only Prometheus objected to this heartless proposal, and it was Prometheus' courage, his act alone, which saved man from burial in the deepest black of Hades. It was he who taught blind hopes to spring within man's heart, and gave him the gift of fire. Understanding the significance of these deeds, he had sinned willingly.

Oceanus, brother of Prometheus, came to offer aid out of love and kinship, but he first offered Prometheus advice and preached humility in the face of Zeus' wrath. Prometheus remained proud, defiant, and refused his offer of help on the grounds that Oceanus himself would be punished were it discovered that he sympathized with a rebel. Convinced by Prometheus' argument, Oceanus took sorrowful leave of his brother.

Once more Prometheus recalled that man was a creature without language, ignorant of everything before Prometheus came and told him of the rising and setting of stars, of numbers, of letters, of the function of beasts of burden, of the utility of ships, of curing diseases, of happiness and lurking evil, of methods to bring wealth in iron, silver, copper, and gold out of the earth. In spite of his torment, he rejoiced that he had taught all arts to humankind.

Io, a young girl changed into a heifer and tormented by a stinging gadfly, came to the place where Prometheus was chained. Daughter of Inachus, a river god, she was beloved by Zeus. His wife, Hera, out of jealousy, had turned Io into a cow and set Argus, the hundred-eyed monster, to watch her. When Zeus had Argus put to death, Hera sent a gadfly to sting Io and drive her all over the earth. Prometheus prophesied her future wanderings to the end of the earth, predicting that the day would come when Zeus would restore her to human form and together they would conceive a son named Epaphus. Before Io left, Prometheus also named his own rescuer, Hercules, who with his bow and arrow would kill the eagle devouring his vital parts.

Hermes, messenger of Zeus, came to see Prometheus and threatened him with more awful terrors at the hands of angry Zeus. Prometheus, still defiant, belittled Hermes' position among the gods and called him a mere menial. Suddenly there was a turbulent rumbling of the earth, accompanied by lightning, thunder, and blasts of wind, as angry Zeus shattered the rock with a thunderbolt and hurled Prometheus into an abysmal dungeon within the earth. Such was the terrible fate of the Fire-Bearer who defied the gods.

PROMETHEUS UNBOUND

Type of work: Poem
Author: Percy Bysshe Shelley (1792-1822)
Type of plot: Lyric drama
Time of plot: Remote antiquity
Locale: Asia
First published: 1820

Principal characters:
PROMETHEUS, a Titan
EARTH, his mother
ASIA, his wife
JUPITER, king of the gods
DEMOGORGON, supreme power, ruling the gods
MERCURY, messenger of the gods
HERCULES, hero of virtue and strength
PANTHEA, and
IONE, the Oceanides

Critique:

This poem, called a lyric drama by the author, is more lyric than dramatic. The poem owes its form to Shelley's study of Greek drama, however, and the characters are drawn from Greek mythology. Through the combined mediums of drama and poetry Shelley expounds his idea that universal love is the one solution to mankind's ills. *Prometheus Unbound* is valuable as a key to Shelley's philosophy; it is also enjoyable as a work of art.

The Story:

Prometheus, the benefactor of mankind, was bound to a rocky cliff by order of Jupiter, who was jealous of the Titan's power. Three thousand years of torture Prometheus suffered there, while heat and cold and many torments afflicted him. An eagle continually ate at his heart. But Prometheus still defied the power of Jupiter.

At last Prometheus asked Panthea and Ione, the two Oceanides, to repeat to him the curse he had pronounced upon Jupiter when Jupiter had first begun to torture him. But neither Earth, his mother, nor the Oceanides would answer him. At last the Phantasm of Jupiter appeared and repeated the curse. When Prometheus heard the words, he repudiated them. Now that he had suffered tortures and found that his spirit remained unconquered, he wished pain to no living thing. Earth and the Oceanides mourned that the curse had been withdrawn, for they thought Jupiter had at last conquered Prometheus' spirit.

Then Mercury approached with the Furies. Mercury told the captive that he would suffer even greater tortures if he did not reveal the secret which Prometheus alone knew — the future fate of Jupiter. Jupiter, afraid, wished to avert catastrophe by learning the secret, and Mercury promised that Prometheus would be released if he revealed it. But Prometheus refused. He admitted only that he knew Jupiter's reign would come to an end, that he would not be king of the gods for all eternity. Prometheus said that he was willing to suffer torture until Jupiter's reign ended. Although the Furies tried to frighten him by describing the pains they could inflict, they knew they had no power over his soul.

The Furies mocked Prometheus and mankind. They showed him visions of blood and despair on earth; they showed the Passion of Christ and men's disregard for His message of love. Fear and hypocrisy ruled; tyrants took the thrones of the world.

A group of spirits appeared and prophesied that Love would cure the ills of mankind. They prophesied also that Prometheus would be able to bring Love to earth and halt the reign of evil and grief.

When the spirits had gone, Prometheus acknowledged the power of Love, for his love for Asia, his wife, had enabled him to suffer pain without surrendering.

While Asia mourned alone in a lovely valley for her lost husband, Panthea appeared to tell of two dreams she had had. In one, she saw Prometheus released from bondage and all the world filled with sweetness. In the other dream she had received only a command to follow. Just then the echoes in the valley broke their silence. They called Asia and Panthea to follow them. The listeners obeyed.

Asia and Panthea followed the echoes to the realm of Demogorgon, the supreme power ruling the gods. They stopped on a pinnacle of rock, but spirits beckoned them down into Demogorgon's cave. There he told them that he would answer any question they put to him. When they asked who had made the living world, he replied that God had created it. Then they asked who had made pain and evil. Prometheus had given knowledge to mankind, but mankind had not eradicated evil with all the gifts of science. They asked whether Jupiter was the source of these ills, the evil master over man.

Demogorgon answered that nothing which served evil could be master, for only eternal Love ruled all. Asia asked when Prometheus would gain his freedom and bring Love into the world to conquer Jupiter. Demogorgon then showed his guests the passage of the Hours. A dreadful Hour passed, marking Jupiter's fall; the next hour was beautiful, marking Prometheus' release. Asia and Panthea accompanied this spirit of the Hour in her chariot and passed by Age, Manhood, Youth, Infancy, and Death into a new paradise.

Meanwhile, Jupiter, who had just married Thetis, celebrated his omnipotence over all but the soul of man. Then Demogorgon appeared and pronounced judgment on Jupiter. Jupiter cried for mercy, but his power was gone. He sank downward through darkness and ruin.

At the same time Hercules approached Prometheus. In the presence of Asia, Panthea, the Spirit of the Hour, and Earth, the captive was set free. Joyfully, Prometheus told Asia how they would spend the rest of their days together with Love. Then he sent the Spirit of the Hour to announce his release to all mankind. He kissed Earth, and Love infused all of her animal, vegetable, and mineral parts.

The Spirit of Earth came to the cave where Asia and Prometheus lived and told them of the transformation that had come over mankind. Anger, pride, insincerity, and all the other ills of man had passed away. The Spirit of the Hour reported other wonders that took place. Thrones were empty, and each man was king over himself, free from guilt or pain. But he was still subject to chance, death, and mutability, without which he would oversoar his destined place in the world.

Later in a vision Panthea and Ione saw how all the evil things of the world lay dead and decayed. Earth's happiness was boundless, and even the moon felt the beams of Love from Earth as snow melted on its bleak lunar mountains. Earth rejoiced that hate, fear, and pain had left mankind forever. Man was now master of his fate and of all the secrets of Earth.

PROSERPINE AND CERES

Type of work: Classical myth
Source: Folk tradition
Type of plot: Allegory of fertility and death
Time of plot: Remote antiquity
Locale: Mediterranean region
First transcribed: Unknown

Principal characters:

CERES, goddess of fertility
PROSERPINE, her daughter
HADES, king of the underworld
VENUS, goddess of love
CUPID, her son
TRIPTOLEMUS, builder of a temple to Ceres
ARETHUSA, a fountain nymph
ALPHEUS, a river god
DIANA, goddess of the hunt
JUPITER, king of the gods
MERCURY, messenger of the gods

Critique:

Prominent in popularity among the legends created by the Greeks and the Romans is the story of Proserpine and Ceres. As a fable which identifies itself with the simplest explanation of the seasons, it has lived by being transferred in oral legend, in poetry, and in prose from generation to generation. Although the story has changed in certain details, its basic structure remains. Its hold upon the imagination of the Western world lies in its appeal as a record of man's search for a beautiful interpretation of grief.

The Story:

One of the Titans, Typhoeus, long imprisoned for his part in the rebellion against Jupiter, lay in agony beneath Mount Aetna on the island of Sicily in the Mediterranean Sea. When Typhoeus groaned and stirred, he shook the sea and the island of Sicily so much that the god of the underworld, Hades, became frightened lest his kingdom be revealed to the light of day.

Rising to the upper world to make entrance to his kingdom, Hades was discovered by Venus, who ordered her son Cupid to aim one of his love darts into the breast of Hades and so cause him to fall in love with Proserpine, daughter of Ceres, goddess of fertility.

Proserpine had gone with her companions to gather flowers by the banks of a stream in the beautiful vale of Enna. There Hades, stricken by Cupid's dart, saw Proserpine, seized her, and lashed his fiery horses to greater speed as he carried her away. In her fright the girl dropped her apron, full of flowers she had gathered. At the River Cyane, Hades struck the earth with his scepter, causing a passageway to appear through which he drove his chariot and took his captive to the underworld.

Ceres sought her daughter everywhere. At last, sad and tired, she sat down to rest. A peasant and his daughter found her in her disguise as an old woman, took pity on her, and urged her to go with them to their rude home. When they arrived at the house they found that their only son, Triptolemus, was dying. Ceres first gathered some poppies. Then, kissing the child, she restored it to health. The happy family bade her join them in their simple meal of honey, cream, apples, and curds. Ceres put some of the poppy juice in the boy's milk and that night when he was sleeping she placed the child in the fire. The mother, awakening, seized her child from the flames. Ceres assumed her proper form and told the parents that it had been her plan to make the boy immortal. Since the mother had hindered that plan, she would teach him the use of the plow.

Then the goddess mother continued her search for Proserpine until she returned to Sicily. There, at the very spot Hades had entered the underworld, she asked the river nymph if she had seen anything of her daughter. Fearful of being punished, the river nymph refused to tell what she had seen but gave to Ceres the belt of Proserpine, which the girl had lost in her struggles.

Ceres decided to take revenge upon the land, to deny it further gift of her favors so that herbage and grain would not grow. In an effort to save the land which Ceres was intent upon cursing, the fountain Arethusa told the following story to Ceres. Arethusa had been hunting in the forest, where she was formerly a woodland nymph. Finding a stream, she decided to bathe. As she sported in the water, the river god Alpheus began to call her. Frightened, the nymph ran, the god pursuing.

The goddess Diana, seeing her plight, changed Arethusa into a fountain which ran through the underworld and emerged in Sicily. While passing through the underworld, Arethusa saw Proserpine, now queen of the dead, sad at the separation from her mother but at the same time bearing the dignity and power of the bride of Hades.

Ceres immediately demanded help from Jupiter, ruler of the gods. The king of the gods said that Proserpine should be allowed to return to the valley of Enna from which she had been abducted only if in the underworld she had taken no food.

Mercury was sent to demand Proserpine for her mother. But Proserpine had eaten of a pomegranate. Because she had eaten only part of the fruit, a compromise was made. Half of the time she was to pass with her mother and the rest with Hades. Ceres, happy over the return of Proserpine during one half of each year, caused the earth to be fertile again during the time Proserpine lived with her.

Ceres remembered her promise to the peasant boy, Triptolemus. She taught him to plow and to plant seed, and he gathered with her all the valuable seeds of the earth. In gratitude the peasant's son built a temple to Ceres in Eleusis where priests administered rites called the Eleusinian mysteries. Those rites surpassed all other Greek religious celebrations because in the mysteries of nature, men saw symbolized the death of man and the promise of his revival in future life.

THE PURPLE LAND

Type of work: Novel
Author: W. H. Hudson (1841-1922)
Type of plot: Adventure romance
Time of plot: Nineteenth century
Locale: Uruguay and Argentina
First published: 1885

Principal characters:
RICHARD LAMB, an English adventurer
PAQUITA, his wife
DOÑA ISIDORA, her aunt
LUCERO, a horse tamer
MARCOS MARCO, General Coloma
MARGARITA, his daughter
DON PERALTA, a mad landowner
DEMETRIA PERALTA, his daughter

Critique:

The Purple Land is a story of romantic adventure, perhaps not quite so entertaining as *Green Mansions,* but with merits of its own. The reader gets an insight into the lives and environment of the people of an unhappy far-off purple land in revolutionary South America. Hudson is one of the great masters of sensuous prose. Perhaps the reason for this stylistic skill is the fact that he was a botanist and the keenness of observation required in scientific writing is reflected in his choice of adjectives and verbs.

THE PURPLE LAND by W. H. Hudson. Published by E. P. Dutton & Co., Inc.

The Story:

Richard Lamb married Paquita without her father's consent and eloped with her to Montevideo. There they went to see Doña Isidora, a relative of Paquita, and stayed with her for some time. Doña Isidora gave Lamb a letter to the overseer of the *Estancia de la Virgen de los Desamparados,* a ranch called in English Vagabond's Rest.

Lamb departed with the letter, and in the Florida department he began to learn the history of the unhappy land of Uruguay. The Argentines and Brazilians interfered in the country's politics, and, as if the foreign influences were not enough to cause trouble, there was constant friction between the country and the town districts. At a pulpería, or tavern, he met Lucero, a horse tamer, and went to stay at his house; but he soon left Lucero and continued his journey to the estancia.

Lamb took advantage of rustic hospitality throughout his journey. One night he stayed at a house in which lived a family with many children. The children were all named after particular Christian concepts, such as Conception and Ascension. However, there were far too many insects infesting the house for his comfort, and he departed early the next day. Lamb continued his journey through Lucuarembó department and then entered the county of his destination. There he discovered that Doña Isidora's letter meant nothing; there was no employment for him.

During his stay at the estancia he had a fight with a man called Barbudo and gained a reputation for being a great fighter. When he discovered that his reputation as a fighter would only lead to more and bloodier fights, he decided to return to Montevideo.

At Toloso, Lamb met a group of English expatriates in a pulpería, and he remained with his fellow countrymen for a time. Finally he found them to be quite worthless and quarreled with them. Then he headed once more for Montevideo. In the Florida department he met a lovely girl named Margarita and helped her get her doves from a branch in a tree. Margarita was so different from the rest of her family that Lamb could not help wondering how she came to be born into such a rough, coarse family. There he met Anselmo, who was an indefatigable talker and teller of pointless tales. There, too, he met Marcos Marco.

Lamb and Marcos started out to go to Montevideo together, but on the way they were captured by an army detail and taken prisoners because Lamb had neglected to get a passport. They were taken before a justice of the peace at Las Cuevas. Through the machinations of the justice's fat wife, Lamb was free to move about until his trial. Marcos, however, was imprisoned. Lamb talked the fat wife into giving him the key to the fetters which bound his friend Marcos. Lamb freed his friend so that Marcos would be able to sleep comfortably in his captivity, but Marcos took advantage of his opportunity and escaped during the night. Lamb, being a lover of nature, captured a small snake and used it as a means to ward off the attentions of the justice's wife. He was finally released.

Later, at the estate of Alday, he first heard of General Santa Coloma, who in reality was Marcos Marco. He told Anita, an orphan living with the Aldays, the story of Alma, who wanted a playmate, and Little Niebla. Anita wanted a playmate too and the next morning she ran off to find one. Monica, the daughter of the household, searched for and found Anita. Monica then asked Lamb to tell her a story out of the great store of anecdotes he knew.

Lamb was taken to see General Coloma, whom he recognized as his friend Marcos. He joined the general and fought in the battle of San Paulo. The general explained to Lamb the mystery of Margarita; she was Coloma's daughter.

When the battle of San Paulo ended badly for the general's army, Lamb escaped. At a pulpería he met Gandara, who wanted to take him prisoner because he had been a member of General Coloma's army. Lamb shot Gandara and escaped. He stayed for a time at the home of an expatriate Scotsman named John Carrickfergus, but soon he continued his journey to Montevideo.

His next important stop was at the home of Don Peralta, who was demented. Don Peralta had lost a son, Calixto, who had been killed in battle several years before. Demetria Peralta, the daughter, was the heir to the estate, but she and everyone else were under the thumb of Don Hilario, the supervisor of the estate. When Lamb rode away, he left with Santos, a servant, who told him the history of the Peralta family. Demetria wished to marry Lamb and thus be able to take over and administer the property which was really hers. Lamb could not marry her, but he arranged to abduct her and take her to Montevideo, where she would be safe from Hilario. When they arrived safely in Montevideo, Paquita looked after Demetria as if she were her own sister. From Montevideo they went to Buenos Aires, where the unsanctioned marriage of Lamb and Paquita promised to give still more trouble for the young couple.

QUALITY STREET

Type of work: Drama
Author: James M. Barrie (1860-1937)
Type of plot: Comedy of manners
Time of plot: Napoleonic wars
Locale: English provincial village
First presented: 1902

Principal characters:
Miss Phoebe Throssel, a spinster
Miss Susan Throssel, her sister
Valentine Brown, loved by Phoebe

Critique:

This play contains acute if not very penetrating observations on the problem of a wartime love affair in which the lovers are apart for ten years, during which time both change superficially. Most of the action is based on the heroine's successful attempt to bring her lover to his senses. Barrie employs dramatic irony quite effectively throughout and the minimum of privacy in the lives of people in a small village is brought out with good comic effect.

The Story:

In the days of the Napoleonic wars, two sisters, Phoebe and Susan Throssel, lived in a little house in Quality Street, the main thoroughfare of a provincial English village. Both were single, both were pretty. One day they entertained a needlework party in their charming blue and white parlor. One of the ladies present repeated a rumor that a gentleman of the village had enlisted to go to the wars. All wondered who the gentleman could be.

Phoebe told her sister that Valentine Brown, a dashing doctor who had come to the village two years before, had walked with her in the street, and had said that he wanted to tell her something important. The retiring Phoebe had asked Brown to come to the house to tell her. Both sisters assumed that Brown was coming to propose marriage to Phoebe, a likely conclusion since a venture in which Brown had invested their savings had failed and he would naturally feel responsible for their welfare. In anticipation of his proposal, Susan gave Phoebe a wedding dress which she had made for her own marriage, a wedding which had never materialized.

But to Phoebe's disappointment and humiliation, Brown said nothing of marriage. Instead, he told them that he was the man who had enlisted. He declared his friendship for both sisters and his liking for the little blue and white parlor, but he gave no indication of love for Phoebe, who had given her heart to him. Ironically, Phoebe revealed her disappointment by telling Brown that she had thought he was going to announce his marriage and that they were curious to know the name of the fortunate young lady. The sisters, out of pride, did not mention that the loss of their investment left them all but destitute. They planned to set up a school in their house.

Ten years later Susan and Phoebe were still conducting their school, which had prospered in spite of their many shortcomings as teachers. They were loved, but hardly respected by the older children. Dancing and the more gentle acquirements they taught with pleasure, but they detested Latin, and would teach algebra only at the request of their pupils' parents. They could not bring themselves to whip the older boys, most of whom they feared.

The wars were over at last, and everywhere people were celebrating the victory at Waterloo. On Quality Street all but Susan and Phoebe were preparing for a village ball that night. While Phoebe was out of the house, Captain Valentine Brown, who had lost his left hand during a battle on the continent, came to call on his dear old friends. Disappointed at the disappearance of the delightful blue and white parlor, he paid his respects to Miss Susan and asked to see Phoebe of the ringlets and the dancing eyes. When Phoebe returned, Captain Brown could not hide his dismay at the way she had changed into a drab, mouselike spinster. Phoebe was hurt by his unconcealed feelings. She was further hurt later in the day when a former pupil, now Ensign Blades and a veteran, asked her, under duress, to attend the ball with him. Miserable, Phoebe declined. But Phoebe was only thirty and tired of teaching. Inspired by Susan and by Patty, the maid, she transformed herself into the Phoebe of ten years before. When Brown came again, he failed to recognize Phoebe, and he was told that she was the sisters' niece. Completely taken in and charmed by "Miss Livvy," he asked her to accompany him to the ball. "Livvy" teased him, to his discomfort, about his gray hairs.

At later balls and parties of the victory celebration, "Livvy" continued to capture the fancy of all the young men of the village. Difficulties posed by the dual existence of Phoebe-"Livvy" were met by the explanation that Phoebe or "Livvy" was either out or indisposed.

At one ball the swains hovered about "Livvy" constantly, but Captain Brown stoutly held his place as her escort. The sisters' gossipy spinster neighbors, who lived across the street and observed their comings and goings, began to suspect that something was not quite right. They were almost in a position to expose Phoebe at the ball, but Susan saved the day by lending another young lady "Livvy's" coat. Captain Brown, alone with "Livvy," told her of his love for Phoebe, explaining that he had fallen in love with Phoebe during the balls because of "Livvy's" resemblance to the Phoebe of days gone by. "Livvy," the flirt, had made Captain Brown realize that he was no longer twenty-five and that he preferred, after all, the retiring, modest, quiet Phoebe.

School over, the parlor was redecorated with its blue and white frills for the summer holiday. Phoebe, tiring of her dual role, announced that "Livvy" had been taken sick, and became the tired schoolteacher again. The gossips who came to call were more suspicious than ever because no doctor had visited "Livvy." They almost discovered that there was no one in the sick room, but they prudently did not go beyond the partly opened door.

That day Captain Brown came to propose to Phoebe. When the sisters left the parlor for a moment, he entered the sick room and found it empty. Then he heard the entire story from Patty, the maid. Captain Brown was amused, but carried on the masquerade when "Livvy" came out of the sick room and announced her recovery. The sisters were stupefied when he offered to take "Livvy" to her home twenty miles away. They stepped out of the parlor to have a hurried consultation, but they knew that Captain Brown had found them out when they heard him talking to a "Livvy" he devised with pillows and a shawl and which he carried out to a waiting coach, to the satisfaction of the gossips who were watching from their windows.

Miss Susan Throssel announced the forthcoming marriage of her sister Phoebe to Captain Valentine Brown. The reopening of school was quite forgotten.

QUENTIN DURWARD

Type of work: Novel
Author: Sir Walter Scott (1771-1832)
Type of plot: Historical romance
Time of plot: 1468
Locale: France and Flanders
First published: 1823

Principal characters:
QUENTIN DURWARD, a Scottish cadet
LUDOVIC LESLEY (LE BALAFRÉ), his maternal uncle
ISABELLE, Countess of Croye, disguised as Jacqueline, a servant
LADY HAMELINE, her aunt
KING LOUIS XI
COUNT PHILIP DE CRÈVECOEUR, of Burgundy
CHARLES, Duke of Burgundy
WILLIAM DE LA MARCK, a Flemish outlaw
HAYRADDIN MAUGRABIN, a Bohemian

Critique:

Quentin Durward was one of the many Scotsmen who sought their fortunes abroad in the service of foreign kings, and the story of his adventures is the first of Scott's novels with a foreign setting. There is no doubt in the mind of the reader that Scott liked this Scotsman very much because the character of the hero is the idealized younger son who goes out to seek fortune with nothing but his own wit and bravery. *Quentin Durward* is among the best of Scott's novels, its authenticity little marred by some slight reorganization of actual events to implement the plot.

The Story:

When Quentin Durward, a young Scottish gentleman, approached the ford of a small river near the castle of Plessis-les-Tours, in France, he found the river in flood. Two people watched him from the opposite bank. They were King Louis XI in his common disguise of Maitre Pierre, a merchant, and Tristan l'Hermite, marshal of France. Quentin entered the flood and nearly drowned. Arriving on the other side and mistaking the king and his companion for a respectable burgher and a butcher, he threatened the two with a drubbing because they had not warned him of the deep ford. Amused by the lad's spirit and daring, Maitre Pierre took him to breakfast at a nearby inn to make amends. At the inn Quentin met a beautiful young peasant girl, Jacqueline. Actually, Jacqueline was Isabelle, Countess of Croye. Quentin tried to learn why the merchant, Maitre Pierre, acted so much like a noble. He saw many other things which aroused his curiosity but for which he found no explanation.

Shortly afterward Quentin met Ludovic Lesley, known as Le Balafré, his maternal uncle, who was a member of King Louis' Scottish Archers. Le Balafré was exceedingly surprised to learn that Quentin could read and write, something which neither a Durward nor a Lesley had heretofore been able to do.

Quentin discovered the body of a man hanging from a tree. When he cut the man down, he was seized by two officers of Tristan l'Hermite. They were about to hang Quentin for his deed when he asked if there were a good Christian in the crowd who would inform Le Balafré of what was taking place. A Scottish archer heard him and cut his bonds. While the two were defending themselves from the mob, Le Balafré rode up with some of his men and took command of the situation, haughtily insisting that Quentin was a member of the Scottish Archers and beyond the reach of the marshal's men. Quentin had not joined the guards as yet, but the lie saved his life. Le Balafré took Quentin to see Lord Crawford, the commander of the guards, to enroll him. When the Scottish Archers were summoned to the royal presence, Quentin was amazed to see that Maitre Pierre was King Louis.

Count Philip de Crèvecoeur arrived at the castle and asked audience with the king in the name of his master, the Duke of Burgundy. When the king admitted de Crèvecoeur, the messenger presented a list of wrongs and oppressions, committed on the frontier, for which the Duke of Burgundy demanded redress. The duke also requested that Louis cease his secret and underhand dealings in the towns of Ghent, Liège and Malines, and, further, that the king send back to Burgundy, under safeguard, the person of Isabelle, Countess of Croye, the duke's ward, whom he accused the king of harboring in secret. Dissatisfied with the king's replies to these demands, de Crèvecoeur threw his gauntlet to the floor of the hall. Several of the king's attendants rushed to pick it up and to accept the challenge, but the king ordered the Bishop of Auxerre to lift the gauntlet and to remonstrate with de Crèvecoeur for thus declaring war between Burgundy and France. The king and his courtiers then left to hunt wild boars.

During the chase Quentin Durward saved the king's life by spearing a wild boar when Louis slipped and fell before the infuriated beast. The king decided to reward Quentin with a special mission. He was ordered to stand guard in the room where the king entertained de Crèvecoeur and others, and at a sign from the king Quentin was to shoot the Burgundian. But the king changed his mind; the signal was not given. Then the king made Quentin the personal bodyguard of Isabelle and her aunt, Lady Hameline, on their way to seek the protection of the Bishop of Liège.

Quentin set out with the ladies to conduct them to Liège. In the party was Hayraddin Maugrabin, a Bohemian, whose brother it was whom Quentin had cut down earlier. On the road they were assaulted by the Count de Dunois and the Duke of Orleans. Quentin defended himself with great courage and received timely help from his uncle, who arrived with a body of Scottish Archers. Le Balafré took de Dunois prisoner. Nothing untoward occurred until the small party reached Flanders. There Quentin discovered, by following Hayraddin, that a plot had been hatched to attack his party and carry off the women to William de la Marck, the Wild Boar of Ardennes. Quentin frustrated these plans by going up the left bank of the Maes instead of the right. He proceeded safely to Liège, where he gave over the women into the protection of the bishop at his castle of Schonwaldt. Four days later William de la Marck attacked the castle and captured it during the night. Lady Hameline escaped. In the bishop's throne room in the castle William de la Marck murdered the churchman in front of his own episcopal throne. Quentin, aroused by the brutality of William, stepped to the side of Carl Eberson, William's son, and placed his dirk at the boy's throat, threatening to kill the lad if William did not cease his butchery. In the confusion Quentin found Isabelle and took her safely from the castle in the disguise of the daughter of the syndic of Liège. They were pursued by William's men, but were rescued by a party under Count de Crèvecoeur, who conducted them safely to the court of the Duke of Burgundy at Peroune.

The king came to the castle of the Duke of Burgundy, asserting the royal prerogative of visiting any of his vassals. Disregarding the laws of hospitality, the duke imprisoned Louis and then held a council to debate the difficulties between France and Burgundy. Hayraddin appeared as a herald from William de la Marck, who had married the Lady Hameline. But Toison d'Or, the duke's herald, unmasked Hayraddin because he knew nothing of the science of heraldry. The duke released Hayraddin and set his fierce boar hounds upon him, but ordered the dogs called off before they tore Hayraddin to shreds. Then he ordered that Hayraddin be hanged with the proper ceremony.

The king and the duke also debated the disposal of Isabelle's hand and fortune. But Isabelle had fallen in love with Quentin and announced that she preferred the cloister to any other alliance. The duke solved the problem, at least to his satisfaction, by declaring that Isabelle's hand would be given to the man who brought him the head of William de la Marck.

The king and the duke joined forces to assault Liège. Their combined forces gallantly besieged the city but were forced to go into bivouac at nightfall. That night William made a foray but was driven back into the city. Next day the forces of the king and the duke attacked once more, made breaches in the wall, and poured into the city. Quentin came face to face with William de la Marck, who rushed at him with all the fury of the wild boar for which he was named. Le Balafré stood by and roared out for fair play, indicating that this should be a duel of champions. At that moment Quentin saw a woman being forcibly dragged along by a French soldier. When he turned to rescue her, Le Balafré attacked de la Marck and killed him.

Le Balafré was announced as the man who had killed de la Marck, but he gave most of the credit to Quentin's valiant behavior and deferred to his nephew. While it was agreed that Quentin was responsible for de la Marck's death, there was still the question of his lineage, which the duke questioned. Indignant, Le Balafré recited the pedigree of Quentin and thereby proved his gentility. Without more ado, Quentin and the Countess Isabelle were betrothed.

QUO VADIS

Type of work: Novel
Author: Henryk Sienkiewicz (1846-1916)
Type of plot: Historical novel
Time of plot: c. A. D. 64
Locale: Rome
First published: 1895

Principal characters:
VINICIUS, a young Roman patrician
LYGIA, a foreign princess whom Vinicius loves
PETRONIUS, Vinicius' uncle, intimate friend of Nero
NERO, the Roman emperor
CHILO, a Greek sycophant
PETER, leader of the Christians
TIGELLINUS, Petronius' enemy, Nero's friend

Critique:

Quo Vadis is a tremendous achievement, both as a historical re-creation and as a vivid and dramatic work of fiction. Those who enjoy learning history by reading novels will find it extremely satisfactory. Others who are willing to settle for a good story will be moved by its sharply depicted characters, its tremendous tensions and energy. No one has succeeded better than Sienkiewicz in portraying the broad panorama of Roman civilization in the last, degenerate days of the Empire, and no one else has so credibly presented the early Christians as real, live people.

The Story:

When Vinicius returned to Rome, after duty in the colonies, he called on his uncle, Petronius, who was one of the most influential men in Rome. A friend of the Emperor Nero, Petronius owned a beautiful home, choice slaves, and numerous objects of art. Petronius had no delusions about the emperor. He knew quite well that Nero was coarse, conceited, brutal, thoroughly evil.

Petronius was happy to see his handsome young nephew. Vinicius had fallen in love with Lygia, daughter of a foreign king, now living with Aulus Plautius and Pomponia. He asked his uncle to help him get Lygia as his concubine. Petronius spoke to Nero, and Lygia was ordered brought to the palace. The giant Ursus was sent as Lygia's devoted servant by her foster parents.

At a wild orgy in the palace, Vinicius attempted to make love to Lygia. Through the watchfulness of Acte, who was a Christian and a former concubine of Nero, he did not succeed. Lygia herself was a Christian and she feared both the lust of Vinicius and that of the emperor himself. Then Acte received information that Lygia would be handed over to Vinicius. At the same time, the daughter of the Empress Augusta died. The empress and her circle believed that Lygia had bewitched the child. Alarmed at the dangers threatening the girl, Acte and Ursus planned Lygia's escape.

That night the servants of Vinicius came and led Lygia away from the palace. Meanwhile Vinicius waited at his house, where a great feast was to take place in honor of his success in securing Lygia. But Lygia never arrived, for on the way to his house a group of Christians had suddenly attacked the servants of Vinicius and rescued the girl. Her rescuers took Lygia outside the city walls to live in a Christian colony.

Vinicius was furious. Petronius sent some of his own men to watch the gates of the city. Day after day Vinicius grew more and more upset. Finally, Chilo, a Greek who passed as a philosopher, offered for a sufficient reward to find Lygia. By pretending to be a convert, he learned where the Christians met in secret. He and Vinicius, together with a giant named Croton, went there, and then followed Lygia to the house where she was staying. When they attempted to seize the girl, Ursus killed Croton. Vinicius was injured in the scuffle. For a few days he stayed with the Christians who took care of him. Lygia herself nursed him until she became aware of her love for the pagan patrician. Afterward, rather than succumb to temptation, she left him to the attentions of others.

Vinicius had heard the Christians speaking at their meeting. While recuperating, he was amazed at their goodness, at their forgiveness, at their whole religious philosophy. He heard their leader, Peter, talk of Christ and of Christ's miracles, and his mind became filled with odd and disturbing thoughts. He realized that he must either hate the God who kept Lygia from him, or love Him. Strangely enough, he became convinced that he no longer had the desire to take Lygia by force. He maintained his contacts with the Christians. At last, after he had accepted their faith, Lygia agreed to marry him.

In the meantime Nero had gone to Antium. There the noble Tigellinus planted in his mind the idea that he should burn Rome in order to write and sing a poem about the tremendous catastrophe. Accordingly, Nero fired Rome, and almost all of the city was destroyed. Vinicius rushed from Antium to save Lygia. Luckily, she had left the city before the fire gained headway. The populace was angry and violent about the fire. Rebellion was in the air. The empress and the Jews at court persuaded Nero to blame the Christians for the fire. Chilo, who had been befriended by the Christians and whose abominable crimes had been wiped away by Christian forgiveness, turned traitor. He gave the emperor all the information he had about the Christians and led the guards to the hiding places of the sect. Cruel persecutions began.

Petronius tried desperately to stop Nero and save Vinicius. Failing in his attempt, he knew that his own days were numbered. The Christians were crammed first into prisons and then brought into the arena for the entertainment of the populace. Virgins were raped by the gladiators and then fed to starving lions. Christians were crucified, burned alive. After Lygia had been seized and imprisoned, Vinicius failed in an attempt to rescue her.

At last her turn came to be led into the arena to amuse the brutal populace. Stripped, she was tied to the back of a raging bull. When the bull was sent running into the arena, Ursus rushed forward and locked his strong arms around the animal. To the astonishment of all, the bull yielded and died. Then the people demanded that Lygia and Ursus be set free, and the emperor had to obey the public clamor. Petronius advised Vinicius that they should all leave the city, for Nero had subtle ways of removing people who had offended him.

The persecutions continued, the spectacles in the arena growing more and more ghastly. At last the people sickened of the bestial tortures. One of the dying Christians looked straight at Nero and accused him of all his infamous crimes. While Glaucus, a martyr, was being burned alive, he looked at Chilo, the Greek who had betrayed them. Glaucus, who had been left for dead by Chilo, forgave the Greek who had caused the Christian's wife and children to be sold into slavery. Moved by the dying man's mercy, Chilo cried out in a loud voice that the Christians were innocent of the burning of Rome, that the guilty man was Nero. Despairing of his own fate, Chilo was on the point of complete collapse. But Paul of Tarsus took him aside and assured him that Christ was merciful to even the worst of sinners. Then he baptized the Greek. When Chilo went back home, he was seized by the emperor's guards and led away to his death in the arena.

Vinicius and Lygia escaped to Sicily. When Petronius heard that the emperor had ordered his own death, he invited some of the patricians to his house at Cumae, where he had gone with Nero and the court. There at a great feast he read an attack against Nero and astounded everyone by his foolhardiness. Then he and Eunice, a slave who loved him, stretched out their arms to a physician. While the party continued and the astonished guests looked on, Petronius and Eunice bled to death in each other's arms.

Nero returned to Rome. His subjects hated him more than ever. A rebellion broke out at last, and he was informed that his death had been decreed. He fled. With some of his slaves around him, he attempted to plunge a knife into his throat. But he was too timid to complete the deed. As some soldiers approached to arrest him, a slave thrust the fatal knife into his emperor's throat.

THE RAINBOW

Type of work: Novel
Author: D. H. Lawrence (1885-1930)
Type of plot: Psychological realism
Time of plot: Nineteenth and early twentieth centuries
Locale: England
First published: 1915

Principal characters:
TOM BRANGWEN, a farmer
LYDIA LENSKY, his wife
ANNA LENSKY, Lydia's child by her first husband
WILL BRANGWEN, Anna's husband
URSULA BRANGWEN, Anna's and Will's daughter
ANTON SKREBENSKY, Ursula's lover

Critique:

The Rainbow has been the center of much controversy. The author used it as a lever to bring intelligent consideration of basic human relations into the open, where those relationships could be reviewed in a clear-eyed, objective manner, and in doing so he made use of the sexual aspects of marriage and love. The book is essentially a comparison of the matings of three successive generations. The book was not well received when it appeared. The author was ostracized and the novel was suppressed for a time by the police. That such a tempest was occasioned by *The Rainbow* is hard for the reader to understand today, for by present standards the book can be read and appreciated for what it is, an excellent psychological study.

The Story:

Tom Brangwen was descended from a long line of small landholders who had owned Marsh Farm in Nottinghamshire for many generations. Tom was a man of the soil, living alone on his farm with only an old woman for his company and housekeeper. Then a Polish widow, Lydia Lensky, became the housekeeper of the vicar of the local church. She brought her small daughter, Anna, with her. Within a few months Tom Brangwen found enough courage to present the widow with a bouquet of daffodils one evening in the vicar's kitchen and to ask the woman to be his wife.

Their marriage was a satisfactory one, judged by the standards of the world. Tom was kind to his stepdaughter. Later he had two sons by his wife. But knowing his stepdaughter was easier for him than knowing Lydia. The fact that they were of different nationalities, cultures, and even languages kept the couple from ever becoming intellectually intimate with one another. There were times when either one or both felt that the marriage was not what it should be for them, that they were not fulfilling the obligations which their mating had pressed upon them. On one occasion Lydia even suggested to her husband that he needed another woman.

Little Anna was a haughty young girl who spent many hours imagining herself a great lady or even a queen. In her eighteenth year a nephew of Tom Brangwen came to work in the lace factory in the nearby village of Ilkeston. He was only twenty years old; the Brangwens at Marsh Farm looked after him and made him welcome in their home.

Anna Lensky and young Will Brangwen fell in love, with a naïve, touching affection for each other. They soon announced to Tom and Lydia that they wished to be married. Tom leased a home in the village for the young couple and gave them a present of twenty-five hundred pounds so they would not want because of Will's small salary.

The wedding was celebrated with rural pomp and hilarity. After the ceremony the newly-married couple spent two weeks alone in their cottage, ignoring the world and existing only for themselves. Anna was the first to come back to the world of reality. Her decision to give a tea party both bewildered and angered her husband, who had not yet realized that they could not continue to live only for and by themselves. It took him almost a lifetime to come to that realization.

Shortly after the marriage Anna became pregnant, and the arrival of the child brought to Will the added shock that his wife was more a mother than she was a married lover. Each year a new baby came between Will and Anna. The oldest was Ursula, who was always her father's favorite. The love which Will wished to give his wife was given to Ursula, for Anna refused to have anything to do with him when she was expecting another child, and she was not satisfied unless she was pregnant.

In the second year of his marriage Will Brangwen tried to rebel. He met a girl at the theater and afterward took her out for supper and a walk. After that incident the intimate life of Will and Anna began to gain in passion, intense enough to carry Will through the daytime when he was not necessary to the house until the nighttime when he could rule his wife. Gradually he became free in his own mind from Anna's domination.

Since Ursula was her father's favorite child, she was sent to high school. That privilege was a rare thing for a girl of her circumstances in the last decade of the nineteenth century. She drank up knowledge in her study of Latin, French, and algebra. But before she had finished, her interest in her studies was shared by her interest in a young man. The son of a Polish friend of her grandmother's was introduced into the house, young, blond Anton Skrebensky, a lieutenant in the British Army. During a month's leave he fell in love with Ursula, who was already in love with him. On his next leave, however, she drove him away with the love she offered to him. He became afraid of her because of that love; it was too possessive.

After finishing high school, Ursula took an examination to enter the university. Having passed the examination, she decided to teach school for a time, for she wanted to accumulate money to carry her through her education without being a burden to her parents. Anna and Will were furious when she broached the subject of leaving home. They compromised with her, however, by securing for her a position in a school in Ilkeston. Ursula spent two friendless, ill-paid, and thankless years teaching at the village elementary school. At the end of that time she was more than ready to continue her education. She decided to become a botanist, for in botany she felt she was doing and learning for herself things which had an absolute truth.

Then one day, after the Boer War ended, Ursula received a letter which upset her completely. Anton Skrebensky had written that he wished to see her again while he was in England on leave. Within a week he arrived in Nottingham to visit her at school. Their love returned for each of them with greater intensity than they had known six years before. During the Easter holidays they went away for a weekend at a hotel, where they passed as husband and wife. They went to the continent as soon as Ursula had finished classes for the summer. Even then, however, Ursula did not want to marry Skrebensky; she wanted to return to college to take her degree. But Skrebensky continued to press increasingly for marriage. He wanted Ursula to leave England with him when he returned to service in India.

Meanwhile Ursula had so neglected her studies that she failed her final examinations for her degree and had to study to take them over again before the summer was finished. When Ursula failed her examinations a second time, Skrebensky urged her to marry him immediately. In India, he insisted, her degree would mean nothing anyway. In the meantime they went to a house party, where they realized that there was something wrong in their mating, that they could not agree enough to make a successful marriage. They left the party separately and a few weeks later Skrebensky was on his way to India as the husband of his regimental commander's daughter.

After he had gone, Ursula learned that she was pregnant. Not knowing that he was already married, she wrote to Skrebensky and promised to be a good wife if he still wished to marry her. Before his answer came from India, Ursula contracted pneumonia and lost the child. One day, as she was convalescing, she observed a rainbow in the sky. She hoped that it was the promise of better times to come.

THE RAPE OF THE LOCK

Type of work: Poem
Author: Alexander Pope (1688-1744)
Type of plot: Mock-heroic epic
Time of plot: Early eighteenth century
Locale: London
First published: 1712

Principal characters:
BELINDA, Miss Arabella Fermor
LORD PETRE, Belinda's suitor
THALESTRIS, Belinda's friend
ARIEL, a sprite
UMBRIEL, a gnome

Critique:

The Rape of the Lock, generally considered the most popular of Pope's writings as well as the finest satirical poem in the English language, was written at the suggestion of John Caryll, Pope's friend, ostensibly to heal a family row which resulted when an acquaintance of Pope, Lord Petre, playfully clipped a lock of hair from the head of Miss Arabella Fermor. Pope's larger purpose in writing the poem, however, was to ridicule the social vanity of his day and the importance that was attached to affected manners.

The Story:

At noon, when the sun was accustomed to awaken both lap dogs and lovers, Belinda was still asleep. She dreamed that Ariel appeared to whisper praises of her beauty in her ear. He said that he had been sent to protect her because something dreadful — what, he did not know — was about to befall her. He also warned her to beware of jealousy, pride, and, above all, men.

After Ariel had vanished, Shock, Belinda's lap dog, thought that his mistress had slept long enough, and he awakened her by lappings of his tongue. Rousing herself, Belinda spied a letter on her bed. After she had read it, she promptly forgot everything that Ariel had told her, including the warning to beware of men.

Belinda, aided by her maid, Betty, began to make her toilet. Preening before her mirror, she was guilty of the pride against which Ariel had cautioned her.

The sun, journeying across the sky, witnessed its brilliant rival, Belinda, boating on the Thames with her friends and suitors. All eyes were upon her, and like the true coquette she smiled at her swains but favored no one more than another.

Lord Petre, one of Belinda's suitors, admired a lock of her hair and vowed that he would have it by fair means or foul. So set was he on getting the lock that before the sun rose that morning he had built an altar to Love and had thrown on it all the trophies received from former sweethearts, meanwhile asking Love to give him soon the prize he wanted and to let him keep it for a long time. But Love granted him only half his prayer.

Everyone except Ariel seemed happy during the cruise on the Thames. That sprite summoned his aides, and reminded them that their duty was to watch over the fair Belinda, one sylph to guard her fan, another her watch, a third her favorite lock. Ariel himself was to guard Belinda's lap dog, Shock. Fifty sylphs were dispatched to watch over the maiden's petticoat, in order to protect her chastity. Any negligent sylphs, warned Ariel, would be punished severely.

After her cruise on the Thames, Belinda, accompanied by Lord Petre and the rest of the party, visited one of the palaces near London. There Belinda decided to play ombre, a Spanish card game, with two of her suitors, including Lord Petre. As she played, invisible sylphs sat on her important cards to protect them.

Coffee was served after the game. Sylphs guarded Belinda's dress to keep it from being spotted. The fumes from the coffee sharpened Lord Petre's wits to the point where he thought of new stratagems for stealing Belinda's lock. One of his cronies handed him a pair of scissors. The sylphs, aware of Belinda's danger, attempted to warn her before Lord Petre could act, but as the maid bent her head over her coffee cup he clipped the lock. Even Ariel was unable to warn Belinda in time.

At the rape of her lock, Belinda shrieked in horror. Lord Petre cried out in triumph. He praised the steel used in the scissors, comparing it with the metal of Greek swords that overcame the Trojans. Belinda's fury was as tempestuous as the rage of scornful virgins who have lost their charms. Ariel wept bitterly and flew away.

Umbriel, a melancholy gnome, took advantage of the human confusion and despair to fly down to the center of the earth to find the gloomy cave of Spleen, the queen of all bad tempers and the source of every detestable quality in human beings, including ill-nature and affectation. Umbriel asked the queen to touch Belinda with chagrin, for he knew that, if she were gloomy, melancholy and bad temper would spread to half the world. Spleen granted Umbriel's request and collected in a bag horrible noises such as those uttered by female lungs and tongues. In a vial she put tears, sorrows, and griefs. She gave both containers to Umbriel.

When the gnome returned to Belinda's world, he found the girl disheveled and dejected. Pouring the contents of the magic bag over her, Umbriel caused Belinda's wrath to be magnified many times. One of her friends, Thalestris, fanned the flames of the maiden's anger by telling her that her honor was at stake and that behind her back her friends were talking about the rape of her lock. Thalestris then went to her brother, Sir Plume, and demanded that he confront Lord Petre and secure the return of the precious lock. Sir Plume considered the whole episode much magnified from little, but he went to demand Belinda's lock. Lord Petre refused to give up his prize.

Next Umbriel broke the vial containing human sorrows, and Belinda was almost drowned in tears. She regretted the day that she ever entered society and also the day she learned to play ombre. She longed for simple country life. Suddenly she remembered, too late, that Ariel had warned her of impending evil.

In spite of Thalestris' pleas, Lord Petre was still adamant. Clarissa, another of Belinda's circle, wondered at the vanity of women and at the foolishness of men who fawn before them. Clarissa felt that both men and women need good sense, but in making her feelings known she exposed the tricks and deceits of women and caused Belinda to frown. Calling Clarissa a prude, Thalestris gathered her forces to battle with Belinda's enemies, including Clarissa and Lord Petre. Umbriel was delighted by this Homeric struggle of the teacups. Belinda pounced upon Lord Petre, who was subdued when a pinch of snuff caused him to sneeze violently. She demanded the lock, but it could not be found. Some thought that it had gone to the moon, where also go love letters and other tokens of tender passions. But the muse of poetry saw it ascend to heaven and become a star.

RASSELAS

Type of work: Novel
Author: Samuel Johnson (1709-1794)
Type of plot: Philosophical romance
Time of plot: Eighteenth century
Locale: Abyssinia and Cairo
First published: 1759

Principal characters:
RASSELAS, Prince of Abyssinia
NEKAYAH, his sister
PEKUAH, her maid
IMLAC, a poet

Critique:

The History of Rasselas, Prince of Abyssinia, one of the most popular works of Samuel Johnson during his own lifetime, is still widely read. However, it is a weighty novel, ponderous in style and slow moving. There is almost no narrative, for the plot deals with the efforts of four people to find a working philosophy by which they can guide their lives. The age in which Johnson lived was characterized by superficial optimism, and this novel is an attack on that optimism. There is a popular theory that Johnson wrote *Rasselas* in one week, in order to pay his mother's funeral expenses, but many scholars refute this theory. The novel shows that Johnson hated pretense of any kind, and he used his pen to fight it at every opportunity.

The Story:

It was the custom in Abyssinia for the sons and daughters of the emperor to be confined in a remote place until the order of succession to the throne was established. The spot in which Rasselas and his brothers and sisters were confined was a beautiful and fertile valley situated between high mountains. In the valley was everything needed for a luxurious life. Entertainers were brought in from the outside world to help the royal children pass the time pleasantly. These entertainers were never allowed to leave, for the outside world was not to know how the royal children lived before they were called on to rule.

It was this perfection which caused Rasselas in the twenty-sixth year of his life to become melancholy and discontented. He was unhappy because he had everything to make him happy; he wanted more than anything else to desire something which could not be made available to him. When he talked of his longing with an old philosopher, he was told that he was foolish. The old man told him of the misery and suffering of the people outside the valley and cautioned him to be glad of his present station. But Rasselas knew that he could not be content until he had seen the suffering of the world.

For many months Rasselas pondered on his desire to escape from the valley. He took no action, however, for the valley was carefully guarded and there was no chance for anyone to leave. Once he met an inventor who promised to make some wings for him so that he could fly over the mountains, but the experiment was a failure. In his search for a way to escape, his labor was more mental than physical.

In the palace there was a poet, Imlac, whose lines pleased Rasselas by their intelligence. Imlac was also tired of the perfect life in the valley, for in the past he had traveled over much of the world. He had observed the evil ways of mankind and had learned that most wickedness stemmed from envy and jealousy. He had noticed that people envy others with more worldly goods and oppress those who are weak. As he talked, Rasselas longed more than ever to see the world and its misery. Imlac tried to discourage him, for he believed that Rasselas would long for his present state should he ever see the violence and treachery which abounded in the lands beyond the mountains.

But when Imlac realized he could not deter the prince, he agreed to join him in his attempt to leave the perfect state. Together the two men contrived to hew a path through the side of a mountain. When they were almost ready to leave, Rasselas saw his sister Nekayah watching them. She begged to accompany the travelers for she too was bored with the valley and longed to see the rest of the world. Because she was the favorite sister of Rasselas, he gladly allowed her and her maid, Pekuah, to join them. The four made their way safely through the path in the mountainside. They took with them enough jewels to supply them with money when they reached a city of trade. They were simply dressed and no one recognized them as royalty.

In Cairo they sold some of their jewels and rented a magnificent dwelling. They entertained great men and began to learn the customs of people different from themselves. It was their object to observe all possible manners and customs so that they could make their own choices about the kind of life each wanted to pursue. But they found many drawbacks to every form of living.

Rasselas and Nekayah believed that it was only necessary to find the right pursuit to know perfect happiness and contentment. Imlac knew that few men lived by choice but rather by chance and the whims of fortune. But Rasselas and Nekayah believed that their chance birth had at least given them the advantage of being able to study all forms of living and thus to choose the one most suitable for them to pursue. So it was that the royal pair visited with men of every station. They went into the courts and into the fields. They visited sages of great fame and hermits who had isolated themselves to meditate. Nowhere did they find a man completely happy and satisfied, for each desired what the other had and thought his neighbor more fortunate than he.

Only once did Rasselas find a happy man. This man was a philosopher who preached the doctrine of reason. He stated that by reason man can conquer his passions and disappointments and thus find true happiness. But when Rasselas called on the sage the following day, he found the old man in a fit of despair. His daughter had died in the night, and the reason which he had urged others to use failed completely in his own life.

Imlac and Nekayah spent long hours discussing the advantages of one kind of life over another. They questioned the state of marriage as compared with celibacy and life at court as compared with pastoral pleasures, but at no time could they find satisfactory solutions for their questions. Nowhere could they find people living in happiness. Imlac suggested a visit to the pyramids so that they might learn of people of the past. While they were in a tomb, Pekuah was stolen by Arabs, and it was many months before she was returned to Nekayah. Pekuah told her mistress that she had spent some time in a monastery while she waited for her ransom, and she believed that the nuns had found the one truly happy way of life.

Their search continued for a long period. Often they thought they had found a happy man, but always they would find much sorrow in the life they thought so serene. Nekayah at one time decided that she would cease looking for happiness on earth and live so that she might find happiness in eternity. A visit to the catacombs and a discourse on the soul prompted her decision.

When the Nile flooded the valley, confining them to their home for a time, the four friends discussed the ways of life which promised each the greatest happiness. Pekuah wished to retire to a convent. Nekayah more than anything desired knowledge and wanted to found a woman's college, where she could both teach and learn. Rasselas thought he wanted a small kingdom where he could rule justly and wisely. Imlac said he would be content to drift through life, with no particular goal. Because all knew their desires would never be fulfilled, they began to look forward to their return to the Abyssinian valley where everyone seemed happy and there was nothing to desire.

REBECCA

Type of work: Novel
Author: Daphne du Maurier (1907-)
Type of plot: Mystery romance
Time of plot: 1930's
Locale: England
First published: 1938

Principal characters:

MAXIM DE WINTER, owner of Manderley
MRS. DE WINTER, Maxim's wife and the narrator
MRS. DANVERS, the housekeeper at Manderley
FRANK CRAWLEY, estate manager of Manderley
JACK FAVELL, Rebecca's cousin
COLONEL JULYAN, a magistrate

Critique:

Rebecca is an excellent example of the suspense novel. From the time the drab little companion marries Maxim de Winter, the reader is aware that there is something wrong with the situation at Manderley, the fine house where Rebecca was formerly the mistress. All through the novel there are hints that some startling disclosure about Rebecca is to come, a revelation which will explain many strange events. In development of situation and in character portrayal there is ample evidence of the author's technical skill.

The Story:

Manderley was gone. Since the fire which had destroyed their home, Mr. and Mrs. de Winter had lived in a secluded hotel away from England. Occasionally Mrs. de Winter recalled the circumstances which had brought Manderley and Maxim de Winter into her life.

A shy, sensitive orphan, she had been traveling about the continent as companion to an overbearing American social climber, Mrs. Van Hopper. At Monte Carlo Mrs. Van Hopper forced herself upon Maxim de Winter, owner of Manderley, one of the most famous estates in England. Before approaching him, Mrs. Van Hopper had informed her companion that Mr. de Winter was recovering from the shock of the tragic death of his wife, Rebecca, a few months previously.

During the following days the young girl and Mr. de Winter became well acquainted; when Mrs. Van Hopper decided to return to America, Maxim de Winter unexpectedly proposed to her companion. Already deeply in love with him, the girl accepted and they were married shortly afterward.

After a long honeymoon in Italy and southern France, Mr. and Mrs. de Winter returned to Manderley. Mrs. de Winter was extremely nervous, fearing that she would not fit into the life of a great estate like Manderley. The entire staff had gathered to meet the new mistress. Mrs. Danvers, the housekeeper, had been devoted to her former mistress and immediately began to show her resentment toward the new Mrs. de Winter.

Gradually Mrs. de Winter pieced together the picture of Rebecca. She learned that Rebecca had been a beautiful, vivacious woman, a charming hostess. As she became acquainted with the relatives and friends of her husband, she became convinced that they found her lacking in those qualities which had made Rebecca so attractive and gracious. One day she went secretly to the closed rooms Rebecca had occupied. Everything was as Rebecca had left it before her fatal sail in her boat. Mrs. Danvers suddenly appeared and forced her to view Rebecca's lovely clothes and other personal possessions.

When the bishop's wife suggested that the traditional Manderley fancy dress ball be revived, Mr. de Winter gave his consent. Mrs. de Winter announced her intention of surprising them all with her costume. At Mrs. Danvers' suggestion, she planned to dress as an ancestress whose portrait hung in the hall at Manderley. But as Mrs. de Winter descended the stairs that night a silence fell over the guests, and her husband turned angrily away without speaking. Realizing that something was wrong, Mrs. de Winter returned to her room. Beatrice, Mr. de Winter's sister, went to her immediately and explained that Rebecca had worn the identical costume to her last fancy dress ball. Again Mrs. Danvers had humiliated her new mistress. Although Mrs. de Winter reappeared at the ball in a simple dress, her husband did not speak to her all evening; and her belief that he had never ceased to love Rebecca became firmly established in her mind.

The next day a steamer ran aground in the bay near Manderley. A diver sent down to inspect the damaged steamer discovered Rebecca's boat and in its cabin the remains of a human body. Mr. de Winter had previously identified the body of a woman found in the river as that of Rebecca.

Unable to keep silent any longer, Mr. de Winter told his wife the whole story of Rebecca and her death. The world had believed their marriage a happy one, but Rebecca had been an immoral woman, incapable of love. To avoid the scandal of a divorce, they made a bargain; Rebecca was to be outwardly the fitting mistress of Manderley, but she would be allowed to go to London periodically to visit her dissolute friends. All went well until she began to be careless, inviting her friends to Manderley and receiving them in the boathouse. Then she began to plague Frank Crawley, the estate manager of Manderley, and Giles, Mr. de Winter's brother-in-law. There had been gossip after Frank and others had seen Rebecca's cousin, Jack Favell, at the boathouse with her. One evening Mr. de Winter had followed her to the boathouse to tell her that their marriage was at an end. Rebecca taunted him, suggesting how difficult it would be to prove his case against her, asserting that should she have a child it would bear his name and inherit Manderley. She assured him with a smile that she would be the perfect mother as she had been the perfect wife.

She was still smiling when he shot her. Then he put her in the boat and sailed out on the river. There he opened the seacocks, drilled holes with a pike, and, leaving the boat to sink, rowed back in the dinghy.

Mrs. de Winter was horrified, but at the same time she felt a happiness she had not known before. Her husband loved her; he had never loved Rebecca. With that discovery, her personality changed. She assured her husband that she would guard his secret.

A coroner's inquest was held, for the body in the boat was that of Rebecca. At the inquest it was established that a storm could not have sunk the boat; evidence of a bolted door, the holes, and the open seacocks pointed to the verdict of suicide which the coroner's jury returned.

That night Jack Favell, drunk, appeared at Manderley. Wildly expressing his love for Rebecca and revealing their intimate life, he tried to blackmail Mr. de Winter by threatening to prove that de Winter had killed his wife. Mr. de Winter called the magistrate, Colonel Julyan, to hear his case. Favell's theory was that Rebecca had asked her husband to free her so that she could marry Jack, and that de Winter, infuriated, had killed her.

From Rebecca's engagement book it was learned that she had visited a Doctor Baker in London on the last day of her life. Colonel Julyan and Mr. and Mrs. de Winter, with Jack Favell following in his car, drove to London to see Doctor Baker. On checking his records, the doctor found that he had examined a Mrs. Danvers on the day in question. They realized that Rebecca had assumed the housekeeper's name. Doctor Baker explained that he had diagnosed Rebecca's ailment as cancer in an advanced stage. The motive for suicide established, Colonel Julyan suggested that the matter be closed.

Driving back to Manderley after leaving Colonel Julyan at his sister's home, Mr. de Winter told his wife that he believed that Colonel Julyan had guessed the truth. He also realized that Rebecca had intimated that she was pregnant because she had been sure that her husband would kill her; her last evil deed would be to ruin him and Manderley. Mr. de Winter telephoned Frank from the inn where they stopped for dinner, and the estate manager reported that Mrs. Danvers had disappeared. His news seemed to upset Mr. de Winter. At two o'clock in the morning they approached Manderley. Mrs. de Winter had been sleeping. Awaking, she thought by the blaze of light that it was dawn. A moment later she realized that she was looking at Manderley, going up in flames.

THE RED AND THE BLACK

Type of work: Novel
Author: Stendhal (Marie-Henri Beyle, 1783-1842)
Type of plot: Psychological realism
Time of plot: Early nineteenth century
Locale: France
First published: 1830

Principal characters:
JULIEN SOREL, an opportunist
M. DE RÊNAL, mayor of Verrières
MADAME DE RÊNAL, his wife
MATHILDE DE LA MOLE, Julien's mistress
FOUQUÉ, Julien's friend

Critique:

This novel is unusual in that its chief character is a villain. He is an interesting villain, however, for Stendhal analyzes the psychological undercurrents of his

THE RED AND THE BLACK by Stendhal. Published by Liveright Publishing Corp.

nature in an attempt to show clearly how struggle and temptation shaped his energetic but morbidly introspective character. The author analyzes the actions of Julien's loves in the same way. This method of writing slows down the action of the plot considerably, but on the other hand it makes the characters real and understandable and shows much of the sordid conditions of French society at the end of the Napoleonic wars.

The Story:

Julien Sorel was the son of a carpenter in the little town of Verrières, France. Napoleon had fallen, but he still had many admirers, and Julien was one of these. Julien pretended to be deeply religious. Now that Napoleon had been defeated, he believed that the church rather than the army was the way to power. Because of his assumed piety and his intelligence, Julien was appointed as tutor to the children of M. de Rênal, the mayor of the village.

Madame de Rênal had done her duty all her life; she was a good wife and a good mother. But she had never been in love with her husband, a coarse man who would hardly inspire love in any woman. Madame de Rênal was attracted to the pale young tutor and fell completely in love with him. Julien, thinking it his duty to himself, made love to her in order to gain power over her. He discovered after a time that he had really fallen in love with Madame de Rênal.

When Julien went on a holiday to visit Fouqué, a poor friend, Fouqué tried to persuade Julien to go into the lumber business with him. Julien declined; he enjoyed too much the power he held over his mistress.

The love affair was revealed to M. de Rênal by an anonymous letter written by M. Valenod, the local official in charge of the poorhouse. He had become rich on graft and he was jealous because M. de Rênal had hired Julien as a tutor. He had also made unsuccessful advances to Madame de Rênal at one time.

The lovers were able to smooth over the situation to some extent. M. de Rênal agreed to send Julien to the seminary at Besançon, principally to keep him from becoming tutor at M. Valenod's house. After Julien had departed, Madame de Rênal was filled with remorse. Her conscience suffered because of her adultery and she became extremely religious.

Julien did not get on well at the seminary, for he found it full of hypocrites. The students did not like him and feared his sharp intelligence. His only friend was the Abbé Pirard, a highly moral man.

One day Julien went to help decorate the cathedral and by chance found Madame de Rênal there. She fainted, but he could not help her because his duties called him elsewhere. The experience left him weak and shaken.

The Abbé Pirard lost his position at the seminary because of his opposition to the local bishop; he had supported the Marquis de La Mole, who was engaged in lawsuits against the bishop. When the Abbé Pirard left the seminary, the marquis obtained a living for him in Paris. He also hired Julien as his secretary.

Julien was thankful for his chance to leave the seminary. On his way to Paris he called secretly upon Madame de Rênal. At first she repulsed his advances, conscious of her great sin. But at last she yielded once again to his pleadings. M. de Rênal became suspicious and decided to search his wife's room. To escape discovery, Julien jumped out the window, barely escaping with his life.

Finding Julien a good worker, the marquis entrusted him with many of the details of his business. Julien was also allowed to dine with the family and to mingle with the guests afterward. He found the Marquise de La Mole to be extremely proud of her nobility. Her daughter, Mathilde, seemed to be of the same type, a reserved girl with beautiful eyes. Her son, the Comte de La Mole, was an extremely polite and pleasant young man. However, Julien found Parisian high society boring. No one was allowed to discuss ideas.

Julien enjoyed stealing volumes of Voltaire from the marquis' library and reading them in his room. He was astonished when he discovered that Mathilde was doing the same thing. Before long they began to spend much of their time together, although Julien was always conscious of his position as servant and was quick to be insulted by Mathilde's pride. The girl fell in love with him because he was so different from the dull young men of her own class.

After Julien had spent two nights with her, Mathilde decided that it was degrading to be in love with a secretary. Her pride was an insult to Julien. Smarting, he planned to gain power over her and, consequently, over the household.

Meanwhile the marquis had entrusted Julien with a diplomatic mission on behalf of the nobility and clergy who wanted the monarchy reestablished. On this mission Julien met an old friend who advised him how to win Mathilde again. Upon his return he put his friend's plan into effect.

He began to pay court to a virtuous lady who was often a visitor in the de La Mole home. He began a correspondence with her, at the same time neglecting Mathilde. Then Mathilde, thinking that Julien was lost to her, discovered how much she loved him. She threw herself at his feet. Julien had won. But this time he would not let her gain the upper hand. He continued to treat Mathilde coldly as her passion increased. In this way he maintained his power.

Mathilde became pregnant. She was joyful, for now, she thought, Julien would know how much she cared for him. She had made the supreme sacrifice; she would now have to marry Julien and give up her place in society. But Julien was not so happy as Mathilde over her condition, for he feared the results when Mathilde told her father.

At first the marquis was furious. Eventually, he saw only one way out of the difficulty; he would make Julien rich and respectable. He gave Julien a fortune, a title, and a commission in the army. Overwhelmed with his new wealth and power, Julien scarcely gave a thought to Mathilde.

Then the Marquis received a letter from Madame de Rênal, whom Julien had suggested to the marquis for a character recommendation. Madame de Rênal was again filled with religious fervor; she revealed to the marquis the whole story of Julien's villainy. The marquis immediately refused to let Julien marry his daughter.

Julien's plans for glory and power were ruined. In a fit of rage he rode to Verrières, where he found Madame de Rênal at church. He fired two shots at her before he was arrested and taken off to prison. There he promptly admitted his guilt, for he was ready to die. He had his revenge.

Mathilde, still madly in love with Julien, arrived in Verrières and tried to bribe the jury for the trial. Fouqué arrived and begged Julien to try to escape. But Julien paid no attention to the efforts his friends made to help him.

Tried, he was found guilty and given the death sentence, even though his bullets had not killed Madame de Rênal. In fact, his action had only rekindled her passion for him. She visited him and begged him to appeal his sentence. The two were as much in love as they had been before. When M. de Rênal ordered his wife to come home, Julien was left again to his dreams. He had lost his one great love — Madame de Rênal. The colorless Mathilde only bored and angered him by her continued solicitude.

Julien went calmly to his death on the appointed day. The faithful Fouqué obtained the body in order to bury it in a cave in the mountains, where Julien had once been fond of going to indulge in his daydreams of power.

A woman had loved a famous ancestor

of Mathilde with an extreme passion. When the ancestor was executed, the woman had taken his severed head and buried it. Mathilde, who had always admired this family legend, did the same for Julien. After the funeral ceremony at the cave, she buried Julien's head with her own hands. Later, she had the cave decorated with Italian marble.

Madame de Rênal did not go to the funeral. But three days after Julien's death she died in the act of embracing her children.

THE RED BADGE OF COURAGE

Type of work: Novel
Author: Stephen Crane (1871-1900)
Type of plot: Impressionistic realism
Time of plot: Civil War
Locale: A Civil War battlefield
First published: 1895

Principal characters:
HENRY FLEMING, a young recruit
JIM CONKLIN, a veteran
WILSON, another veteran

Critique:

Most war stories are epic histories of generals and victories or defeats. In *The Red Badge of Courage* we follow only the personal reactions of a soldier; we do not even know what battle is being fought or who the leaders are. We know only that Henry Fleming was motivated, not by the unselfish heroism of more conventional and romantic stories, but first by cowardice, then by fear, and finally by egoism. The style of narrative of the novel belongs to a late period in English prose fiction. The stream of Henry's thought tells a story, and the reader must perceive the hero's environment through the subjective consciousness of the young man. This novel set the pattern for the treatment of war in modern fiction.

The Story:

The tall soldier, Jim Conklin, and the loud soldier, Wilson, argued bitterly over the rumor that the troops were about to move. Henry Fleming was impatient to experience his first battle, and as he listened to the quarreling of the seasoned soldiers he wondered if he would become frightened and run away under gunfire. He questioned Wilson and Conklin, and each man stated that he would stand and fight no matter what happened.

Henry had come from a farm, where he had dreamed of battles and longed for army life. His mother had held him back at first. When she saw that her son was bored with the farm, she packed his woolen clothing and with a warning that he must not associate with the wicked kind of men who were in the military camps sent him off to join the Yankee troops.

One gray morning Henry awoke to find that the regiment was about to move. With a hazy feeling that death would be a relief from dull and meaningless marching, Henry was again disappointed. The troops made only another march. He began to suspect that the generals were stupid fools, but the other men in his raw regiment scoffed at his idea and told him to shut up.

When the fighting suddenly began, there was very little action in it for Henry. He lay on the ground with the other men and watched for signs of the enemy. Some of the men around him were wounded. He could not see what was going on or what the battle was about. Then an attack came. Immediately Henry forgot all his former confused thoughts, and he could only fire his rifle over and over; around him men behaved in their strange individual manner as they were wounded. Henry felt a close comradeship with the men at his side who were firing at the enemy with him.

Suddenly the attack ended. To Henry, it seemed strange that the sky above should still be blue after the guns had stopped firing. While the men were recovering from the attack, binding wounds, and gathering equipment, another surprise attack was launched from the enemy line. Unprepared and tired from the first fighting, the men retreated in panic. Henry, sharing their sudden terror, ran, too.

When the fearful retreat had ended, the fleeing men learned that the enemy had lost the battle. Now Henry felt a surge of guilt. Dreading to rejoin his companions, he fled into the forest. There he saw a squirrel run away from him in fright. The fleeing animal seemed to vindicate in Henry's mind his own cowardly flight; he had acted according to nature whose own creatures ran from danger. Then, seeing a dead man lying in a clearing, Henry hurried back into the retreating column of wounded men. Most were staggering along in helpless bewilderment and some were being carried on stretchers. Henry realized that he had no wound and that he did not belong in that group of staggering men. There was one pitiful-looking man, covered with dirt and blood, wandering about dazed and alone. Everyone was staring at him and avoiding him. When Henry approached him, the young boy saw that the soldier was Jim Conklin. He was horrified at the sight of the tall soldier. He tried to help Jim, but with a wild motion of despair Jim fell to the ground dead. Once more Henry fled.

His conscience was paining him. He wanted to return to his regiment to finish the fight, but he thought that his fellow soldiers would point to him as a deserter. He envied the dead men who were lying all about him. They were already heroes; he was a coward. Ahead he could hear the rumbling of artillery. As he neared the lines of his regiment, a retreating line of men broke from the trees ahead of him. The men ran fiercely, ignoring him or waving frantically at him as they shouted something he could not comprehend. He stood among the flying men, not knowing what to do. One man hit him on the head with the butt of a rifle.

Henry went on carefully, the wound in his head paining him a great deal. He walked for a long while until he met another soldier, who led Henry back to his regiment. The first familiar man Henry met was Wilson. Wilson, who had been a terrible braggart before the first battle, had given Henry a packet of letters to keep for him in case he were killed. Now Henry felt superior to Wilson. If the man asked him where he had been, Henry would remind him of the letters. Lost was Henry's feeling of guilt; he felt superior now, his deeds of cowardice almost forgotten. No one knew that he had run off in terror. Wilson had changed. He no longer was the swaggering, boastful man who had annoyed Henry in the beginning. The men in the regiment washed Henry's head wound and told him to get some sleep.

The next morning Wilson casually asked Henry for the letters. Half sorry that he had to yield them with no taunting remark, Henry returned the letters to his comrade. He felt sorry for Wilson's embarrassment. He felt himself a virtuous and heroic man.

Another battle started. This time Henry held his position doggedly and kept firing his rifle without thinking. Once he fell down, and for a panicky moment he thought that he had been shot, but he continued to fire his rifle blindly, loading and firing without even seeing the enemy. Finally someone shouted to him that he must stop shooting, that the battle was over. Then Henry looked up for the first time and saw that there were no enemy troops before him. Now he was a hero. Everyone stared at him when the lieutenant of the regiment complimented his fierce fighting. Henry realized that he had behaved like a demon.

Wilson and Henry, off in the woods looking for water, overheard two officers discussing the coming battle. They said that Henry's regiment fought like mule drivers, but that they would have to be used anyway. Then one officer said that probably not many of the regiment would live through the day's fighting. Soon after the attack started, the color-bearer was killed and Henry took up the flag, with Wilson at his side. Although the regiment fought bravely, one of the commanding officers of the army said that the men had not gained the ground that they were expected to take. The same officer had complimented Henry for his courageous fighting. He began to feel that he knew the measure of his own courage and endurance.

His outfit fought one more engagement with the enemy. Henry was by that time a veteran, and the fighting held less meaning for him than had the earlier battles. When it was over, he and Wilson marched away with their victorious regiment.

THE RED ROVER

Type of work: Novel
Author: James Fenimore Cooper (1789-1851)
Type of plot: Historical romance
Time of plot: Mid-eighteenth century
Locale: Newport, Rhode Island and the Atlantic Ocean
First published: 1827

Principal characters:

HARRY WILDER, formerly Henry Ark, actually Henry de Lacy
THE RED ROVER, captain of the *Dolphin*
DICK FID, and
SCIPIO AFRICA, seamen, Harry Wilder's friends
GERTRUDE GRAYSON, General Grayson's daughter
MRS. WYLLYS, her governess

Critique:

Cooper, who knew the sea quite well, wrote this novel to repeat the success of *The Pilot*. His characters, as is customary with him, are types, and there is little character development. The plot is simple and plausible until the end of the story, when Cooper unravels the mystery surrounding Henry Ark and the Red Rover by proving improbable relationships among the characters. However, few novels of the sea contain a better record of life and work aboard a sailing ship.

The Story:

While in the town of Newport, Rhode Island, Harry Wilder saw in the outer harbor a ship, the *Dolphin,* which interested him greatly. He decided to try to secure a berth on her for himself and his two friends, Dick Fid and Scipio Africa, a Negro sailor. His determination was strengthened after meeting a stranger who in effect dared him to try to obtain a berth there. That night the three men rowed out to the ship lying at anchor, in order to give the vessel a closer inspection. Hailed by the watch on deck, Wilder went aboard her. There he learned that he had been expected and that if he were interested in sailing with her, he might go to see the captain. The captain was the mysterious, mocking stranger whom Wilder had met that afternoon in the town. But before Wilder signed on as a member of the ship's crew, the captain revealed the true nature of the ship and admitted that he himself was the Red Rover, the scourge of the sea. Wilder, who had formerly been an officer in the British Navy, was given the post of second in command. He persuaded the captain to sign on Dick and Scipio as well. He then returned to shore to settle his affairs in the town. The other two men remained aboard the *Dolphin*.

At the same time the *Royal Caroline*, a merchantman trading along the coast and between the colonies and England, lay in the inner harbor ready to embark on the following day. Two ladies, Gertrude Grayson and her governess, Mrs. Wyllys, were to take passage on her to Charleston, South Carolina, Gertrude's home. Wilder met the ladies as if by chance and tried to dissuade them from sailing aboard the *Royal Caroline*. He hinted that the *Royal Caroline* was unsafe, but his words were discredited by an old seaman who insisted that there was nothing wrong with the ship. The ladies decided to sail in spite of Wilder's warnings. Then the master of the *Royal Caroline* fell from a cask and broke his leg, and a new captain had to be found immediately. The Red Rover sent a message ordering Wilder to apply for the vacant position. He did, and was immediately hired.

The voyage of the *Royal Caroline* began with difficulties which continued as time went on. They were not long out of port when a ship was sighted on the horizon. It continued to keep its distance in approximately the same position, so that all aboard the *Royal Caroline* suspected that it was following them. In trying to outdistance the other ship, Wilder put on all sail possible, in spite of the threatening weather. A storm struck the ship and left her foundering in heavy seas. When Wilder commanded the crew to man the pumps, they refused and deserted the sinking ship in one of the boats. Only Wilder and the two women were left aboard the helpless *Royal Caroline*. Hoping to make land, they embarked in a longboat, but the wind blew them out to sea. They were sighted and picked up by the *Dolphin*.

Gertrude and Mrs. Wyllys were not long aboard the *Dolphin* before the true state of affairs became apparent to the women in spite of the kindly treatment afforded them. Mrs. Wyllys realized also that Roderick, the cabin boy, was in reality a woman. But this mystery was nothing when compared with that of Harry Wilder.

Dick Fid told the story of Harry Wilder's past history to the two ladies and the Red Rover, thus explaining the affection Wilder, Dick, and Scipio held for each other. Some twenty-four years earlier, Dick and Scipio had found a child and a dying woman, apparently a nurse, aboard an abandoned ship. After the woman died, the two seamen took care of the boy. They had only one clue to follow in their efforts to locate the child's relatives. This was the name Ark of Lynnhaven which had been painted on a ship's bucket and which Scipio had tattooed on Dick's arm. But there was no ship of that name in any port registry, and so the search for the child's relatives was abandoned.

As Dick finished his story, another ship was sighted. It was the *Dart*, a British naval vessel on which Wilder, Dick, and Scipio had previously sailed. Wilder wanted the Red Rover to flee, but the captain had another plan for dealing with the *Dart*. After showing British colors, the Red Rover was invited by Captain Bignall of the *Dart* to come aboard his ship. There the pirate captain learned that Henry Ark, alias Harry Wilder, was absent from the *Dart* on a dangerous secret mission. The Red Rover realized that he had betrayed himself to his enemy. He went back to the *Dolphin* and then sent Wilder, Dick, Scipio, and the two women to the *Dart*.

Wilder had informed the Red Rover that once aboard his own ship, the *Dart,* he would be duty bound to reveal the true nature of the *Dolphin.* But in telling Captain Bignall his story, Wilder begged for mercy for both the master and the crew of the pirate ship. Bignall agreed and sent Wilder back to the *Dolphin* with lenient terms of surrender. The Red Rover refused them and told Wilder that if there were to be a fight Captain Bignall would have to start it. As the *Dart* attacked the pirate ship, a sudden storm gave the *Dolphin* an unexpected advantage. Its crew boarded the *Dart,* killed Captain Bignall, and captured the ship. The crew of the *Dolphin* demanded the lives of Wilder, Dick, and Scipio as traitors, and the Red Rover handed them over to the crew. When the chaplain who was aboard the *Dart* came forward to plead for their lives, he saw the tattoo on Dick's arm. He told the story of the *Ark of Lynnhaven* and revealed that Harry Wilder must be the son of Paul de Lacy and Mrs. Wyllys, who had kept the marriage a secret because of parental disapproval and later because of Paul's death. Mrs. Wyllys then begged for the life of her son, whom she had thought dead all these years. The Red Rover dismissed his crew until the next morning, when he would announce his decision concerning the fate of the prisoners.

The next morning, the Red Rover put his crew and all the gold aboard the *Dolphin* into a coaster and sent them ashore. The crew of the *Dart,* Wilder, Dick, Scipio, and the women were put aboard the *Dart* and told to sail off. When they were some distance away, they saw the *Dolphin* catch fire and burn. None had been left aboard her but the Red Rover and Roderick. Some aboard the *Dart* thought they saw a small boat putting off from the burning ship, but none could be sure because of the billowing smoke.

Twenty years later, after the colonies had won their independence from England, the Red Rover, a veteran of the Revolutionary War, reappeared in Newport and made his way to the home of Captain Henry de Lacy, who had previously called himself Henry Wilder. Admitted, he identified himself as the long-lost brother of Mrs. Wyllys. Shortly thereafter the Red Rover, pirate and patriot, died.

REMEMBRANCE OF THINGS PAST

Type of work: Novel
Author: Marcel Proust (1871-1922)
Type of plot: Psychological realism
Time of plot: Late nineteenth, early twentieth centuries
Locale: France
First published: 1913-1927

Principal characters:

MARCEL, the narrator
MARCEL'S GRANDMOTHER, a kind and wise old woman
M. SWANN, a wealthy broker and esthete
MME. SWANN, formerly a cocotte, Odette de Crécy
GILBERTE, their daughter, later Mme. de Saint-Loup
MME. DE VILLEPARISIS, a friend of Marcel's grandmother
ROBERT DE SAINT-LOUP, her nephew, Marcel's friend
BARON DE CHARLUS, another nephew, a Gomorrite
MME. VEDURIN, a vulgar social climber
THE PRINCE and PRINCESS DE GUERMANTES, and
THE DUKE and DUCHESS DE GUERMANTES, members of the old aristocracy

Critique:

Remembrance of Things Past is not a novel of traditional form. Symphonic in design, it unfolds without plot or crisis as the writer reveals in retrospect the motifs of his experience, holds them for thematic effect, and drops them, only to return to them once more in the processes of recurrence and change. This varied pattern of experience brings together a series of involved relationships through the imagination and observation of a narrator engaged in tracing with painstaking detail his perceptions of people and places as he himself grows from childhood to disillusioned middle age. From the waking reverie in which he recalls the themes and characters of his novel to that closing paragraph with its slow, repeated echoes of the word *Time,* Proust's novel is great art distilled from memory itself, the structure determined entirely by moods and sensations evoked by the illusion of time passing, or seeming to pass, recurring, or seeming to recur. The title shows Proust's twofold concern as a novelist: time lost and time recalled. To the discerning reader it is plain that for Proust the true realities of human experience were not contained in a reconstruction of remembered scenes and events but in the capture of physical sensations and moods re-created in memory. The seven novels which make up *Remembrance of Things Past* are *Swann's Way, Within a Budding Grove, The Guermantes Way, Cities of the Plain, The Captive, The Sweet Cheat Gone,* and *The Past Recaptured.*

The Story:

All his life Marcel found it difficult to go to sleep at night. After he had blown out the light, he would lie quietly in the darkness and think of the book he had been reading, of an event in history, of some memory from the past. Sometimes he would think of all the places in which he had slept—as a child in his great-aunt's house in the provincial town of Combray, in Balbec on a holiday with his grandmother, in the military town where his friend, Robert de Saint-Loup, had been stationed, in Paris, in Venice during a visit there with his mother.

He remembered always a night at Combray when he was a child. M. Swann, a family friend, had come to dinner. Marcel had been sent to bed early, where he lay for hours nervous and unhappy until at last he heard M. Swann leave. Then his mother had come upstairs to comfort him.

For a long time the memory of that night was his chief recollection of Combray, where his family took him to spend a part of every summer with his grandparents and aunts. Years later, while drinking tea with his mother, the taste of a small sweet cake suddenly brought back all the impressions of his old days at Combray.

He remembered the two roads. One was Swann's way, a path that ran beside M. Swann's park where the lilacs and hawthorns bloomed. The other was the Guermantes way, along the river and past the chateau of the Duke and Duchess de Guermantes, the great family of Combray. He remembered the people he saw on his walks. There were familiar figures like the doctor and the priest. There was M. Vinteuil, an old composer who died broken-hearted and shamed because of his daughter's friendship with a woman of bad reputation. There were the neighbors and friends of his grandparents. But best of all he remembered M. Swann, whose story he pieced together slowly from family conversations and village gossip.

M. Swann was a wealthy Jew accepted in rich and fashionable society. His wife was not received, however, for she was his former mistress, Odette de Crécy, a cocotte with the fair, haunting beauty of a Botticelli painting. It was Odette who had first introduced Swann to the Vedurins, a vulgar family that pretended to despise the polite world of the Guermantes. At an evening party given by Mme. Vedurin, Swann heard played a movement of Vinteuil's sonata and identified his hopeless passion for Odette with that lovely music. Swann's love was an unhappy affair. Tortured by jealousy, aware of the vulgarity and pettiness of the Vedurins, determined to forget his unfaithful mistress, he went to Mme. de Sainte-Euvert's reception. There he heard Vinteuil's music again. Under its influence he decided, at whatever price, to marry Odette.

After their marriage Swann drifted more and more into the bourgeois circle of the Vedurins. When he went to see his old friends in Combray and in the fashionable Faubourg Saint-Germain, he went alone. Many people thought him both ridiculous and tragic.

On his walks Marcel sometimes saw Mme. Swann and her daughter, Gilberte, in the park at Combray. Later, in Paris, he met the little girl and became her playmate. That friendship, as they grew older, became an innocent love affair. Filled also with a schoolboyish passion for Mme. Swann, Marcel went to Swann's house as much to be in her company as in Gilberte's. But after a time his pampered habits and brooding, neurasthenic nature began to bore Gilberte. His pride hurt, he refused to see her for many years.

Marcel's family began to treat him as an invalid. With his grandmother, he went to Balbec, a seaside resort. There he met Albertine, a girl to whom he was immediately attracted. He met also Mme. de Villeparisis, an old friend of his grandmother and a connection of the Guermantes family. Mme. de Villeparisis introduced him to her two nephews, Robert de Saint-Loup and Baron de Charlus. Saint-Loup and Marcel became close friends. While visiting Saint-Loup in a nearby garrison town, Marcel met his friend's mistress, a young Jewish actress named Rachel. Marcel was both fascinated and repelled by Baron de Charlus; he was not to understand until later the baron's corrupt and depraved nature.

Through his friendship with Mme. de Villeparisis and Saint-Loup, Marcel was introduced into the smart world of the Guermantes when he returned to Paris.

One day, while he was walking with his grandmother, she suffered a stroke. The illness and death of that good and unselfish old woman made him realize for the first time the empty worldliness of his smart and wealthy friends. For comfort he turned to Albertine, who came to stay with him in Paris while his family was away. But his desire to be humored and indulged in all his whims, his suspicions of Albertine, and his petty jealousy, finally forced her to leave him and go back to Balbec. With her, he had been unhappy; without her, he was wretched. Then he learned that she had been accidentally killed in a fall from her horse. Later he received a letter, written before her death, in which she promised to return to him.

More miserable than ever, Marcel tried to find diversion among his old friends. They were changing with the times. Swann was ill and soon to die. Gilberte had married Robert de Saint-Loup. Mme. Vedurin, who had inherited a fortune, now entertained the old nobility. At one of her parties Marcel heard a Vinteuil composition played by a musician named Morel, the nephew of a former servant and now a protegé of the notorious Baron de Charlus.

His health breaking down at last, Marcel spent the war years in a sanitarium. When he returned to Paris, he found still greater changes. Robert de Saint-Loup had been killed in the war. Rachel, Saint-Loup's mistress, had become a famous actress. Swann was also dead, and his widow, remarried, was a fashionable hostess who received the Duchess de Guermantes. Prince de Guermantes, his fortune lost and his first wife dead, had married Mme. Vedurin for her money. Baron de Charlus had grown senile.

Marcel went to one last reception at the Princess de Guermantes' lavish house. Meeting there the daughter of Gilberte de Saint-Loup, he realized how time had passed, how old he had grown. In the Guermantes library, he happened to take down the novel by George Sand which his mother had read to him that remembered night in Combray, years before. Suddenly, in memory, he heard again the ringing of the bell that announced M. Swann's departure and knew that it would echo in his mind forever. He saw then that everything in his own futile, wasted life dated from that far night in his childhood, and in that moment of self-revelation he saw also the ravages of time among all the people he had ever known.

THE RETURN OF THE NATIVE

Type of work: Novel
Author: Thomas Hardy (1840-1928)
Type of plot: Romantic tragedy
Time of plot: Mid-nineteenth century
Locale: Egdon Heath, in southern England
First published: 1878

Principal characters:
DIGGORY VENN, a reddleman
DAMON WILDEVE, proprietor of the Quiet Woman Inn
THOMASIN YEOBRIGHT, betrothed to Wildeve
MRS. YEOBRIGHT, Thomasin's guardian
CLYM YEOBRIGHT, Mrs. Yeobright's son
EUSTACIA VYE, a designing woman

Critique:

In this novel Thomas Hardy created two strong and opposing forces: Egdon Heath, a somber tract of wasteland symbolic of an impersonal fate, and Eustacia Vye, a beautiful young woman representing the opposing human element. Throughout the book Eustacia struggles against the Heath, but in vain. Of course, her failure to overcome her environment would seem to prove Hardy's view that man is not the master of his fate. But in attempting to minimize the importance of the individual in this life, Hardy has created in the character of Eustacia Vye a person of great strength and marked individuality. Indeed, the reader, contemplating her, feels that Eustacia herself, not fate alone, is responsible for her tragic end.

The Story:

Egdon Heath was a gloomy wasteland in southern England. Against this majestic but solemn, brooding background a small group of people were to work out their tragic drama in the impersonal presence of nature.

Fifth of November bonfires were glowing in the twilight as Diggory Venn, the reddleman, drove his van across the Heath. Tired and ill, Thomasin Yeobright lay in the rear of his van. She was a young girl whom Diggory loved, but she had rejected his proposal in order to marry Damon Wildeve, proprietor of the Quiet Woman Inn. Now Diggory was carrying the girl to her home at Blooms-End. The girl had gone to marry Wildeve in a nearby town, but the ceremony had not taken place because of an irregularity in the license. Shocked and shamed, Thomasin had asked her old sweetheart, Diggory, to take her home.

Mrs. Yeobright, Thomasin's aunt and guardian, heard the story from the reddleman. Concerned for the girl's welfare, she decided that the wedding should take place as soon as possible. Mrs. Yeobright had good cause to worry, for Wildeve's intentions were not wholly honorable.

Later in the evening, after Wildeve had assured the Yeobrights, rather casually, that he intended to go through with his promise, his attention was turned to a bonfire blazing on Mistover Knap. There old Cap'n Vye lived with his beautiful granddaughter, Eustacia. At dusk the girl had started a fire on the Heath as a signal to her lover, Wildeve, to come to her. Though he had intended to break with Eustacia, he decided to obey her summons.

Eustacia, meanwhile, was waiting for Wildeve in the company of young Johnny Nunsuch. When Wildeve threw a pebble in the pond to announce his arrival, Eustacia told Johnny to go home. The meeting between Wildeve and Eustacia was unsatisfactory for both. He complained that she gave him no peace. She, in turn, resented his desertion. Meanwhile Johnny Nunsuch, frightened by strange lights he saw on the Heath, went back to Mistover Knap to ask Eustacia to let her servant accompany him home, but he kept silent when he came upon Eustacia and Wildeve. Retracing his steps, he stumbled into a sand pit where stood the reddleman's van. From the boy, Diggory learned of the meeting between Eustacia and Wildeve. Later, he overheard Eustacia declare her hatred of the Heath to Wildeve, who asked her to run away with him to America. Her reply was vague, but the reddleman decided to see Eustacia without delay to beg her to let Thomasin have Wildeve.

Diggory's visit to Eustacia was fruitless. He then approached Mrs. Yeobright, declared again his love for her niece, and offered to marry Thomasin. Mrs. Yeobright refused the reddleman's offer because she felt that the girl should marry Wildeve. She confronted the innkeeper with vague references to another suitor, with the result that Wildeve's interest in Thomasin awakened once more.

Shortly afterward Mrs. Yeobright's son, Clym, returned from Paris, and a welcome-home party gave Eustacia the chance to view this stranger about whom she had heard so much. Uninvited, she went to the party disguised as one of the mummers. Clym was fascinated by this interesting and mysterious young woman disguised as a man. Eustacia dreamed of marrying Clym and going with him to Paris. She even broke off with Wildeve, who, stung by her rejection, promptly married Thomasin to spite Eustacia.

Clym Yeobright decided not to go back to France. Instead he planned to open a school. Mrs. Yeobright strongly opposed her son's decision. When Clym learned that Eustacia had been stabbed in church by a woman who thought that Eustacia was bewitching her children, his decision to educate these ignorant people was strengthened. Much against his mother's wishes, Clym visited Eustacia's home to ask her to teach in his school. Eustacia refused because she hated the Heath and the country peasants, but as the result of his visit Clym fell completely in love with the beautiful but heartless Eustacia.

Mrs. Yeobright blamed Eustacia for Clym's wish to stay on the Heath. When bitter feeling grew between mother and son, he decided to leave home. His marriage to Eustacia made the break complete. Later Mrs. Yeobright relented somewhat and gave a neighbor, Christian Cantle, a sum of money to be delivered in equal portions to Clym and Thomasin. Christian foolishly lost the money to Wildeve in a game of dice. Fortunately, Diggory won the money from Wildeve, but, thinking that all of it belonged to Thomasin, he gave it to her. Mrs. Yeobright knew that Wildeve had duped Christian. She did not know that the reddleman had won the money away from the innkeeper, and she mistakenly supposed that Wildeve had given the money to Eustacia. Meeting Eustacia, she asked the girl if she had received any money from Wildeve. Eustacia was enraged by the question and in the course of her reply to Mrs. Yeobright's charge she said that she would never have condescended to marry Clym had she known that she would have to remain on the Heath. The two women parted angrily.

Eustacia's unhappiness was increased by Clym's near-blindness, a condition brought on by too much reading, for she feared that this meant she would never get to Paris. When Clym became a wood-cutter, Eustacia's feeling of degradation was complete. Bored with her life, she went by herself one evening to a gipsying. There she accidentally met Wildeve and again felt an attachment for him. Seeing Eustacia and Wildeve together, the reddleman told Mrs. Yeobright of the meeting and begged her to make peace with Eustacia for Clym's sake. She agreed to try.

But Mrs. Yeobright's walk at noon across the hot, dry Heath to see her son and daughter-in-law proved fatal. When she arrived in sight of Clym's house, she saw her son from a distance as he entered the front door. Then, while she rested on a knoll near the house, she saw another man entering, but she was too far away to recognize Wildeve. After resting for twenty minutes, Mrs. Yeobright went on to Clym's cottage and knocked. No one came to the door. Heartbroken by what she considered a rebuff by her own son, Mrs. Yeobright started home across the Heath. Overcome by exhaustion and grief, she sat down to rest and a poisonous adder bit her. She died without knowing that inside her son's house Clym had been asleep, worn out by his morning's work. Eustacia did not go to the door because, as she later explained to her husband, she had thought he would answer the knock. The real reason for Eustacia's failure to go to the door was fear of the consequences, should Mrs. Yeobright find Eustacia and Wildeve together.

Clym awoke with the decision to visit his mother. Starting out across the Heath toward her house, he stumbled over her body. His grief was tempered by bewilderment over the reason for her being on the Heath at that time. When Clym discovered that Eustacia had failed to let his mother in and that Wildeve had been in the cottage, he ordered Eustacia out of his house. She went quietly because she felt in part responsible for Mrs. Yeobright's death.

Eustacia took refuge in her grandfather's house, where a faithful servant thwarted her in an attempt to commit suicide. In utter despair over her own wretched life and over the misery she had caused others, Eustacia turned to Wildeve, who had unexpectedly inherited eleven thousand pounds and who still wanted her to run away with him. One night she left her grandfather's house in order to keep a prearranged meeting with the innkeeper, but in her departure she failed to receive a letter of reconciliation which Thomasin had persuaded Clym to send to her. On her way to keep her rendezvous with Wildeve she lost her way in the inky blackness of the Heath and either fell accidentally or jumped into a small lake, and was drowned. Wildeve, who happened to be near the lake when she fell in, jumped in to save her and was drowned also.

(Originally *The Return of the Native* ended with the death of Eustacia and of Wildeve; but in order to satisfy his romantic readers, in a later edition Hardy made additions to the story. The faithful Diggory married Thomasin. Clym, unable to abolish ignorance and superstition on the Heath by teaching, became in the end an itinerant preacher.)

THE REVOLT OF THE ANGELS

Type of work: Novel
Author: Anatole France (Jacques Anatole Thibault, 1844-1924)
Type of plot: Fantasy
Time of plot: Early twentieth century
Locale: France
First published: 1914

Principal characters:
MAURICE D'ESPARVIEU, a lazy young man
ARCADE, his guardian angel
MONSIEUR JULIEN SARIETTE, a librarian
MADAME GILBERTE DES AUBELS, Maurice's mistress

Critique:

Anatole France was a revolutionary. Opposed to the Church and the state, he wrote many bitter novels ridiculing those institutions. *The Revolt of the Angels* is one of the most abusive satires of this century. It is a fantasy, telling the story of an angel who read so widely in the field of science that he lost his faith in God. He aroused thousands of angels, and they planned to take over the Kingdom of Heaven for Satan. In this satire France attacked almost every established institution in the world, but in his desire to ridicule he often sacrificed sincerity and thus effectiveness. His greatest personal conviction, as reflected in this satire, was his love for and his faith in the little people of the world. This factor is the greatest positive quality of the novel.

The Story:

Because their fabulous library was so large and valuable, the d'Esparvieu family employed Monsieur Julien Sariette to look after the three hundred thousand volumes. The books were the most precious charge that Sariette had ever had, and he guarded them as if they were jewels. There were rare first editions, some with notations in the handwriting of famous men of history. There were several unpublished manuscripts written on sheepskins and sycamore tablets. It was no more difficult to steal an emerald than to borrow one of those precious books or manuscripts from Sariette.

One morning he entered the library to find many of the books in complete disorder. Some of the finest specimens were among the desecrated books, and for a time the old librarian could not comprehend what his eyes saw. But he was even more disturbed when he realized that some of the books were gone. When he reported the theft to his master, he was told that he had probably left them lying carelessly around. Sariette was completely upset.

For more than two months the thefts continued. Locks were changed, and a detective was employed, but all precautions failed. Sariette hid himself in the library one night, and what he saw there frightened him more than ever. He had fallen asleep. When he awoke, he saw that the room was filled with a queer, phosphorescent light. A book he held in his hand opened, and he could not close it. When he tried to force it shut, the book leaped up and struck him over the head, knocking him unconscious.

From that time on Sariette could neither sleep nor eat. He was at the point of insanity when young Maurice d'Esparvieu, who lived in the garden pavilion and who had not heard of the losses, asked him why so many of the books from the library were piled in his rooms. Sariette rushed to the pavilion.

THE REVOLT OF THE ANGELS by Anatole France. Translated by Mrs. Wilfrid Jackson. By permission of the publishers, Dodd, Mead & Co., Inc.

There lay his precious books, scattered around but all complete. He carefully carried them back into the house and put them on the shelves again.

The books continued to disappear each night and appear in the pavilion the next morning. Sariette knew no more than he did before. One day a fine talcum scattered on the floor revealed a strange footprint. Some thought it the print of a fairy, others that of a small, dainty woman.

While these events were disrupting the peace of the d'Esparvieu household, Maurice was having a love affair with Madame Gilberte des Aubels. While she was visiting him in his pavilion one evening, they were startled by the sight of a nude man who suddenly appeared. Gilberte, thinking him a burglar, offered him her money and jewels, but the stranger announced in a calm voice that he was Arcade, Maurice's guardian angel. He explained his appearance by telling them that angels could take human form when they pleased. He had come to the earth at Maurice's birth, but had remained invisible, as all good guardian angels do. Because Maurice was a lazy young man, Arcade had found time heavy on his hands, and he had gone into the d'Esparvieu library to find something to read. He had studied the great books on philosophy, theology, and science, and the scientific approach to the creation of the universe had impressed him so much that he had decided to assume human form and lead the angels into revolt against God.

In his explanation to Gilberte and Maurice he acknowledged that God existed, but he denied that He was the creator of the universe. Arcade now considered God, or Ialdabaoth, as He was called in Heaven, as only one of the strong men of that kingdom. Ialdabaoth and Satan had battled for the supremacy of that beautiful and rich land, and Ialdabaoth had won. Now there were many other angels on earth who had also assumed human form, thus disobeying Ialdabaoth, and they too were ready to revolt. Arcade was determined to join the rebel angels and lead them to victory against Ialdabaoth.

Gilberte and Maurice were shocked. They begged Arcade to renounce his wicked ways and return to God, but he was firm in his decision. Not wishing to leave his angel in a nude state, Maurice secured some clothes for him before Arcade left the pavilion.

Arcade found many revolutionary angels to plan with him for the final battle. There was Prince Istar, the chemist, who spent his time manufacturing bombs. Zita was a female angel, as willing to go to war as any of the males. Théophile was not a revolutionary and did not want to go to war against Ialdabaoth. Théophile was a fallen angel who had succumbed to the lust he felt for a mortal woman, but he still believed in God and would not join in plans for the revolt. While they were gathering recruits, most of the angels enjoyed the pursuits of mortal men. Many of them took lovers; Arcade seduced Gilberte in Maurice's pavilion, after Maurice had brought the angel home with him. Arcade tried to enlist the help of Sophar, an angel who had become a Jewish banker named Max Everdingen, but Sophar would not give them money for the revolution. He offered to sell them munitions, however, and to finance the purchases at his bank.

While the angels were preparing for the final attack, Gilberte and Maurice continued their affair, for Maurice had forgiven Arcade and Gilberte. Sariette, among his books, was happy because Arcade, busy with the revolution, no longer stole the precious volumes. But through a mishap, *Lucretius,* one of the most precious of the rare editions, was taken from the library and lost. This final blow drove Sariette to madness.

At last all was in readiness for the revolt. Hundreds of thousands of rebel angels joined Arcade and presented themselves to Satan, asking him to lead them into the battle against Ialdabaoth. Satan asked them to wait until the next day for his answer. That night he had a dream. He dreamed that he led the rebels against Ialdabaoth, and that they were victorious. Satan was crowned king, and he banished Ialdabaoth as He had banished Satan millions of years ago. But Satan dreamed that as he received the praises of mankind and the angels, he became like the other God, Ialdabaoth, and lost his sympathy for humanity.

Satan awoke from his dream, and called the leaders of the angels around him. He told them that they would not conquer Heaven, that one war always brings on another because the vanquished seek constantly to regain what they have lost. He told them that he did not want to be God, that he loved the earth and wanted to stay on earth and help his fellow men. And he told the angels that they had done much already to destroy God on earth, for they had been slowly destroying ignorance and superstitions concerning the false religion taught by God. Satan told the angels to stay on earth to spread the doctrine of love and kindness; in this way they would triumph over God and bring peace to heaven and earth.

RICEYMAN STEPS

Type of work: Novel
Author: Arnold Bennett (1867-1931)
Type of plot: Social criticism
Time of plot: 1919
Locale: Riceyman Steps, a suburb of London
First published: 1923

Principal characters:
HENRY EARLFORWARD, a bookseller
MRS. VIOLET ARB, owner of a nearby shop
ELSIE, maid for both Earlforward and Mrs. Arb
JOE, Elsie's friend

Critique:

Riceyman Steps is a novel both amusing and tragic. Bennett's gifts for satire, for ironic comment and incident, and for character development, combine in this novel to create an excellent comedy of manners. But, as in all of Bennett's work, the note of tragedy is, in the last analysis, the important one and it is not absent in *Riceyman Steps.* Henry Earlforward and his wife, as well as Elsie and Joe, are the victims of selfishness and greed.

The Story:

Henry Earlforward owned a bookstore left to him by his uncle, T. T. Riceyman. It was cluttered, dusty, badly lighted. Earlforward lived in a back room of the shop, the upstairs of the building being filled with old books.

One night Elsie, his cleaning girl, came into the shop. She told Henry that she also worked for Mrs. Arb, who owned the confectioner's shop next door, and that Mrs. Arb had sent her for a cookbook. Henry found one containing recipes for making substantial meals out of practically no food at all. A little later Elsie returned and said that Mrs. Arb thanked him, but the book was too expensive.

His curiosity aroused, he himself went to Mrs. Arb's shop. Even though he marked down the price of the book, Mrs. Arb still refused to buy it. Henry became more interested, for it was clear that Mrs. Arb was no spendthrift. The following Sunday they went for a walk, and from then on they became close friends.

At last Violet Arb sold her shop and agreed to marry Henry. When Violet asked him about a wedding ring, he seemed surprised, for he had supposed the one she already owned would do. He got a file, sawed off the ring, sold it, and bought another, all without really spending a penny. They were married one morning and for a honeymoon spent the day in London.

They visited Madame Tussaud's Waxworks and the Chamber of Horrors. Henry, who had thought the wedding breakfast expensive enough, was distressed at being forced to spend more money. He wondered if he had been deceived, if Violet were not a spendthrift after all. He began to complain about his lame foot. Violet was dismayed; she had wanted to see a motion picture. But Henry could not be persuaded to change his mind. He did not, he said, want a painful leg on his wedding day.

When they passed by the shop that night, Henry thought the place was on fire. It was glowing with light, and men were working inside. Violet explained that the men had been engaged to clean the dirty, cluttered shop. She had planned the work as her wedding gift to him, but he had spoiled the surprise by coming home before the men had finished their task. Henry showed Violet a safe that he had bought to safeguard her valuables and her money.

Violet soon discovered that miserly Henry would not light a fire, would have no electric light, would eat practically nothing. On their first morning together she cooked an egg for him but he refused to eat it. Later Elsie ate it in secret. At another time Violet had Elsie cook steaks, but Henry would not touch them. There was an argument in which Violet called him a miser who was starving her to death. He left the room and his steak. That night Elsie ate it.

When Violet discovered that Elsie had eaten the steak, there was another row. But Elsie began to eat more and more when nobody was there to observe her. The girl was half-starved in the miserly household. To stop Elsie's thefts of food, Henry went to bed, called Elsie to his room, announced he was seriously ill, and asked if she thought it right to steal food while he lay dying. Elsie was glum and frightened.

A short time later Henry actually became ill. Elsie, in defiance of the Earlforwards, managed to get Dr. Raste to examine Henry. The doctor said that the sick man would have to go to the hospital. Then the doctor discovered that Violet was also ill. At first Henry refused to go to the hospital, but Violet finally persuaded him to go. When the doctor called the next morning, it was Violet, however, who went to the hospital. Henry stayed at home in the care of Elsie.

In the meantime Elsie had been hoping for the return of Joe, her sweetheart. He had been employed by Dr. Raste, had been ill, and had wandered off. Elsie was sure he would return some day.

One night Elsie wanted to send a boy to the hospital to inquire about Violet. When she asked Henry for sixpence for the messenger, he said she could go herself. Not wanting to leave him, she picked up his keys, went downstairs, and opened the safe. Amazed to find so much money there, she borrowed sixpence and put an I. O. U. in its place. Then she dashed out to find a boy to carry her note. When she came back, she found Joe waiting for her. He was shabbily dressed and sick.

Elsie quietly carried Joe up to her room and took care of him, taking pains so that Henry would not suspect his presence in the house. When Joe began to improve, he told her he had been in jail. Elsie did not care. She continued to take care of Henry, promising him that she would never desert him. The hospital informed them that Violet was to have an operation. That night Elsie went next door to the confectioner's shop. Mrs. Belrose, the wife of the new proprietor, telephoned the hospital and was told that Violet had died because her strength had been sapped through malnutrition.

Henry seemed to take the news calmly enough, but he grew steadily worse. Dr. Raste came again and said that he must go to a hospital, but Henry refused. Without Elsie's knowledge, he got up and went downstairs, where he discovered with dismay Elsie's appropriation of the sixpence. He sat down at his desk and began to read his correspondence.

Elsie was in her room taking care of Joe. To the neighbors the house seemed quite dark. Accordingly, Mrs. Belrose insisted that her husband go over to inquire about the sick man. He discovered Henry's body lying in the shop.

A relative came from London and sold the shop to Mr. Belrose. Joe recovered and went back to work for Dr. Raste. Because Elsie intended to marry Joe, she also went to work for Dr. Raste.

THE RIME OF THE ANCIENT MARINER

Type of work: Poem
Author: Samuel Taylor Coleridge (1772-1834)
Type of plot: Ballad fantasy
Time of plot: Late medieval period
Locale: A voyage around the Horn into the Pacific and thence home
First published: 1798

Principal characters:
The Ancient Mariner
A Hermit
A Wedding Guest

Critique:

According to Coleridge, his aim in writing *The Ancient Mariner* was to make the supernatural seem real. For the poem he chose as his verse form the old four-line ballad stanza and an archaic style. Especially noteworthy is the division of the poem into parts, each part ending with a striking sentence which serves as a high point in the story.

The Story:

Three young gallants on their way to a wedding were stopped by an old gray-headed sailor who detained one of them. The Ancient Mariner held with his glittering eye a young man whose next of kin was being married in the church nearby and forced him to listen, against his will, to the old seaman's tale. The Ancient Mariner told how the ship left the home port and sailed southward to the equator. In a storm the vessel was blown to polar regions of snow and ice.

When an albatross flew out of the frozen silence, the crew hailed it as a good omen. The sailors made a pet of the albatross and regarded it as a fellow creature. One day the Ancient Mariner killed the bird with his crossbow. The superstitious sailors believed bad luck would follow.

Fair winds blew the ship northward until it reached the equator, where it was suddenly becalmed and lay for days without moving. The thirsty seamen blamed the Ancient Mariner and hung the dead albatross about his neck as a sign of his guilt.

In the distance a ship appeared, a skeleton ship which moved on the still sea where no wind blew. On its deck Death and Life-in-Death were casting dice for the crew and the Ancient Mariner. As a result of the cast, Death won the two hundred crew members, who dropped dead one by one. As the soul of each dead sailor rushed by, the Ancient Mariner was reminded of the whiz of his crossbow when he shot the albatross. Life-in-Death had won the Ancient Mariner, who must now live on to expiate his sins. Furthermore, the curse lived on in the eyes of the men who died accusing him. One night the Ancient Mariner, observing the beauty of the water snakes around the ship, blessed these creatures in his heart. The spell was broken. The albatross fell from his neck into the sea.

At last the Ancient Mariner was able to sleep. Rain fell to quench his thirst. The warped vessel began to move, and the bodies of the dead crew rose to resume their regular duties as the ship sailed quietly on, moved by a spirit toward the South Pole.

The Ancient Mariner fell into a trance. He awoke to behold his own country, the very port from which he had set sail. Then the angelic spirits left the dead bodies of the crew and appeared in their own forms of light. Meanwhile, the pilot on the beach had seen the lights and he rowed out with his son and a holy Hermit to bring the ship in to harbor.

Suddenly the ship sank, but the pilot pulled the Ancient Mariner into his boat. Once ashore, the old man asked the Hermit to hear his confession and give him penance. The Ancient Mariner told the Wedding Guest that at uncertain times since that moment, the agony of his guilt returned and he must tell the story of his voyage to one who must be taught love and reverence for all things God has made and loved.

The merry din of the wedding had ceased, and the Wedding Guest returned home a sadder and a wiser man.

THE RING AND THE BOOK

Type of work: Poem
Author: Robert Browning (1812-1889)
Type of plot: Dramatic monologues
Time of plot: Seventeenth century
Locale: Italy
First published: 1868-1869

Principal characters:
PIETRO COMPARINI, an aged Roman
VIOLANTE, Pietro's wife
POMPILIA, the Comparini's adopted daughter
GUIDO FRANCESCHINI, Pompilia's husband
GIUSEPPE CAPONSACCHI, a priest

Critique:

This poem reveals Browning's deep perceptive and poetic powers at their greatest heights. Based upon a murder trial in the city of Florence in 1698, the poem attempts to probe the inner motivations of the people involved in that old, sordid tale of passion and crime. A series of dramatic characterizations and episodes carries the reader to the magnificent conclusion. Pompilia and Caponsacchi are among Browning's most notable creations. Too long to be one of the widely read poems of Browning, yet too penetrating to be disregarded by any of his admirers, *The Ring and the Book* is written with tremendous power of language.

The Story:

Count Guido Franceschini, descended from an ancient house of Aretine, had married Pompilia Comparini, a young and beautiful Roman girl. Unhappy with her husband, the young wife fled back to Rome in the company of a young priest, Giuseppe Caponsacchi. Guido and four accomplices followed her, and on Christmas night he found his wife at the home of her parents, Pietro and Violante. He murdered the seventy-year-old man and woman and fatally wounded seventeen-year-old Pompilia.

The aged parents were laid in the church where the people of Rome came to stare and to speculate. The Comparini had been childless until somehow Violante had tricked Pietro into thinking that she had given birth to the child she had secretly bought. It was Violante's mischief which had led to evil, asserted the Roman people. She had spied Guido, of a noble family, and had persuaded him to take Pompilia for his wife. Then all three, parents and daughter, had moved to his estate in Arezzo and there learned of Guido's poverty. Leaving Pompilia behind, the Comparini returned to Rome. Back in Rome, Violante confessed to Pietro that she had bought the child from a prostitute, and by disowning her parentage the aged couple denied Guido his dowry rights. Pompilia, meanwhile, wrote a letter to the archbishop in Rome, telling him that since her parents' departure life in Arezzo had become unbearable. In Arezzo, Pompilia had begun a flirtation with Caponsacchi, the Roman gossipers related, and at last had run away with him. As the guilty pair neared Rome, Guido overtook them and brought them to Rome and to the Pope. The couple declared themselves innocent and disavowed love letters which Guido claimed had passed between them. When the court treated the case as a slight marriage quarrel, Guido returned to Arezzo and the taunts of his townsmen. Soon afterward news reached him that Pompilia, who had returned to the Comparini, had given birth to a son. Then Guido took four men, went to Rome, killed the parents, and left Pompilia dying. The Romans excitedly awaited the trial, for Caponsacchi would be one of the witnesses.

Another group of spectators in Rome took a different view of the murderer and his wife. Pompilia had been a blessing to her foster parents, no matter how she came to them. They had considered it a blessing when Guido married their daughter, only to reach horrible disillusionment when they went to Arezzo and saw his cruelty and poverty. She was Guido's victim, these gossips said.

The tribunal tried to determine the truth in the case. Pietro and Violante had been poor, struggling creatures. When the mother of Pompilia was with child, Violante had bargained with her for the baby and deceived her husband by pretending that it was she who was pregnant. Her act was judged criminal. When Guido came to Rome to find a wife to bear him sons, and a dowry to pay his debts, Pietro and Violante gave him their daughter so that she could rise in name and fortune. When they learned that Guido was penniless, they cried that they had been cheated. Meanwhile it was Pompilia who suffered between the rival factions of parents and husband. She was tricked by Guido to trace letters to Caponsacchi, which were offered at the trial. But Guido's friends claimed that he could not have so mistreated his young wife, that she must have written the letters herself.

Guido told his own story. His family had once been wealthy and great, but in his lifetime they had known only poverty. His brothers were priests; he alone remained to carry on the Franceschini name. His brother Paul, a priest in Rome, had advised him that Pompilia would make a suitable wife. He was to give the girl his name and state in return for her dowry and her son. But Pompilia shirked her wifely duties from the first. One day she caught the eye of Caponsacchi at the opera. Afterward Caponsacchi's way to church led him past Guido's house, past Pompilia's window. Then one night Pompilia drugged Guido and all the servants and fled with her priest to the inn where Guido located them. He found some letters Caponsacchi had exchanged with her, letters which she claimed had been forged. He brought them to court to have his marriage annulled, but the court upheld the marriage and sent Caponsacchi away for a short confinement. Pompilia returned to Pietro and Violante and there she had a child which Guido believed Caponsacchi's. He had no other course, he said, but to go to Rome and cleanse his family name, and he threw himself upon the justice of the court.

Caponsacchi took the stand to describe his first sight of Pompilia at the opera. Not long after he received a letter, signed by Pompilia, confessing love and asking him to come to her window. Suspecting the letter to be a forgery, he answered it with a refusal. He received more letters. At last he became curious and went to stand outside Guido's house. Pompilia, seeing him, rebuked him for his unseemly letters to her, a married woman. They decided that they were victims of Guido's plot. Pompilia begged Caponsacchi to take her to her parents in Rome. His heart softening at her plight, he arranged for her to go away with him.

Pompilia, Caponsacchi said, had been victimized by her cruel husband. The testimony of dying Pompilia upheld what Caponsacchi had said. At the time of her marriage she had been only thirteen years old. She had been brought to Arezzo, to an impoverished home where Guido's brother had tried to seduce her. For three years she lived in misery. Then she received letters from Caponsacchi. She tried to understand the mystery, knowing that somehow she was being tricked, but finally she sent for the priest because she had decided to seek help from the outside world.

The testimony of others followed, some in defense of Guido, others exposing his carefully laid plot to rid himself of Pompilia. Testimony of Pompilia's innocence was also presented. The Pope, condemning Guido for the crime, pronounced Pompilia innocent of guilt and told the court of the tremendous burden of justice that a Pope must carry on his shoulders. Guido and his four accomplices were sentenced to be hanged.

Humbled and fearful of death, Guido made one last plea for his life. Pride and self-love colored his statements as he confessed his crime but rationalized his motive. He was to be pitied; he wanted to live. He pleaded for mercy which was not granted.

THE RISE OF SILAS LAPHAM

Type of work: Novel
Author: William Dean Howells (1837-1920)
Type of plot: Domestic realism
Time of plot: Nineteenth century
Locale: New England
First published: 1885

Principal characters:

Silas Lapham, a self-made manufacturer
Mrs. Lapham, his wife
Penelope, and
Irene, his daughters
Tom Corey, the Laphams' friend
Mr. Rogers, Mr. Lapham's former partner

Critique:

According to many critics, *The Rise of Silas Lapham* is the most important book William Dean Howells ever wrote. Howells, a prolific though never a brilliant writer, attempted to deal conscientiously with the everyday experiences of rather ordinary people. By presenting character and situation in a straightforward manner, he wrote novels characterized chiefly by their moral atmosphere and authentic domestic realism.

The Story:

Silas Lapham was being interviewed

for a Boston paper. The journalist was secretly mocking Lapham's way of life, but Lapham, content with his success, paid little attention to his interviewer as he proudly exhibited a photograph of his two daughters and his wife. He told how he had been brought up in a large family, how he had gone West with his brothers, how he had returned, bought a stage route, married the village schoolteacher and finally hit upon making paint from a mineral his father had discovered on his farm.

The story of his success was a story of determination and hard work. During the Civil War his wife had kept the paint works going and after the war he had taken a man named Rogers as a partner for a short time.

After the interview Lapham and his wife drove out to see the site of a house they were building in a more fashionable part of Boston. Although both looked with pride upon the place soon to be their residence, they pretended not really to want the house at all. They merely suggested the new home would be a greater advantage for Penelope and Irene when their friends came to call.

But neither Penelope nor Irene anticipated with any great joy their coming change of living. They said they felt the present house was more convenient to the horsecars. Secretly, both realized that their parents were awkward in social life. At the same time they themselves had never been brought up to feel comfortable in the presence of people whose families had been accustomed to wealth for generations.

One day, as Mr. and Mrs. Lapham were dismounting from their carriage, Lapham's former partner appeared unexpectedly. Rogers had furnished money to help Lapham get started, but later Lapham had crowded Rogers out. Lapham insisted that what he had done had merely been good business. But Mrs. Lapham maintained that she never felt quite right about what had happened to Rogers, and seeing him again took all the happiness out of her plans for the new house.

The next time the family ventured out to visit the partly-completed house, Irene was surprised by the arrival of Tom Corey, a young man who had shown some interest in her. Immediately Mr. Lapham took over the occasion, and by his bragging greatly embarrassed his daughters.

That evening young Corey talked to his father about the Laphams. Bromfield Corey did not agree with his son's easy acceptance of the Laphams, but he did not object when his son announced his intention to apply for a position in Lapham's firm.

Young Corey visited Lapham in his office in order to ask for a job. Lapham was so pleased that he invited Corey to go with him to Nantasket where Mrs. Lapham and the girls were expecting Lapham for the weekend. At the Nantasket cottage the girls and their mother could not understand what had brought young Corey for the weekend visit. They had thought Lapham's bragging would have kept him away forever.

That evening Lapham discussed Corey with his wife. Mrs. Lapham contended that Corey was interested not in the paint but in Irene. Her husband commented that unless the young man were interested in the paint he would never get a chance to be interested in Irene. When Lapham said he intended to give the young man a chance, Mrs. Lapham warned him that he was playing with a situation which was bound to bring trouble.

Tom Corey's mother was concerned when she heard what her son had done. She admitted she would not object if he made a fortune from the paint business, but she did not want him to fall in love with either of the Lapham girls.

After Corey entered Lapham's employ, he was invited frequently to the Lapham home, for Irene was beginning to fall in love with him. Bromfield Corey grew more and more curious about the

Laphams. He decided that he would encourage his wife to give a dinner for them in the autumn.

The cost of the new house worried Mrs. Lapham, and she asked her husband to stop his lavish spending. She learned he had given a substantial loan to Rogers, his former partner.

When Mrs. Corey returned from Bar Harbor, she debated a long time about giving a dinner party for the Laphams. In the first place, the Laphams were newcomers. On the other hand, she wanted to give public recognition of the new connection between her son and the Lapham family. She finally decided to give a formal dinner early in the season, before her more prominent friends returned to the city.

On the night of the dinner the Laphams tried to appear at ease. Penelope had refused to attend, thus causing her mother considerable embarrassment. Lapham watched the other men carefully, feeling sure he had not made too many social blunders. The next day, however, he was not so sure, for he had taken too much wine at dinner.

At the office Lapham sought out Corey and mentioned with embarrassment his behavior of the night before. He offered Corey his liberty to seek another job, a position among gentlemen, but Corey refused to go, saying that Lapham's tipsy talk had been only an unfortunate accident. When they parted, Corey insisted that Lapham's conduct had been proper and entertaining.

That night, feeling that he had actually patronized Lapham, Corey resolved to go to his employer and apologize. Lapham was out, but Penelope received Corey. At the end of a long talk he stammeringly confessed his love for her. In great confusion he left without waiting to speak to Lapham.

The next day Mrs. Lapham informed her husband that Corey had been coming to see Penelope all the time. She could only imagine what the shock would do to Irene. They felt, however, that Penelope would never permit Corey to become her suitor, for Penelope was convinced he belonged to Irene.

Irene was informed of the situation by her mother that evening. Immediately she carried to her sister's room every memento of Corey's attentions she possessed. After a few days Lapham took her to his boyhood village in Vermont.

Corey called on the Laphams to present his explanation, saying that he had cared more for Penelope all the time. Penelope refused to give him any satisfaction. She said she owed more to her sister's hurt feelings.

At the same time Lapham's finances were troubling him greatly. People who owed him money were unable to pay; his own creditors were pressing him. Lapham determined to take a trip west to inspect some mills held as security for his loan to Rogers. When he returned he was even more concerned. Rogers had drawn him into a trap with his securities, for a railroad controlled the value of the property. Lapham decided it would be necessary to sell the new house unfinished. Learning of Lapham's difficulties, Corey offered to lend his employer thirty thousand dollars, but Lapham rejected the offer.

Lapham's affairs took a turn for the worse. An added blow was the destruction of the unfinished Back Bay house. Wandering through the house one night, he decided to test one of the chimneys and made a fire from blocks and shavings the workmen had left scattered about. He thought the fire had burned out before he left. That night the house burned to the ground. The insurance policy had expired a week before.

Determined to raise money by selling everything he could, Lapham visited his competitors who were working on a new mineral paint. They were willing to merge with him if he could raise money to help develop their plant. While he was trying to secure a loan, he learned from Rogers that some English gentlemen were interested in buying the property which Rogers had put up as security and which Lapham had thought valueless. Lapham refused to sell the mills however, because he believed a sale would be unethical as long as the railroad controlled their value.

He asked for time to think over the proposition. Shortly afterward the railroad forced him to sell the mills at a ruinous figure. Lapham felt that his honesty, which had kept him from selling the property to the Englishmen, had been unjustly abused. Rogers claimed Lapham had made it impossible for him to recover his losses. Lapham was now ruined, for he could not raise capital to merge with the rival paint firm.

Tom Corey was determined to marry Penelope in spite of her father's impending ruin. He did marry her after Lapham went into bankruptcy, and his family accepted her for their own sake as well as for his. Irene, who had returned as soon as she heard of her father's troubles, was pleased with her sister's happiness.

Lapham managed to save a part of his fortune, but more important to him was the belief that he had acted honestly in all his business dealings.

THE RIVALS

Type of work: Drama
Author: Richard Brinsley Sheridan (1751-1816)
Type of plot: Comedy of manners
Time of plot: Eighteenth century
Locale: Bath, an English watering place
First presented: 1775

Principal characters:

CAPTAIN JACK ABSOLUTE (ENSIGN BEVERLEY), a young officer in love with Lydia Languish
SIR ANTHONY ABSOLUTE, his father
FAULKLAND, his friend, in love with Julia
BOB ACRES, a country squire
SIR LUCIUS O'TRIGGER, a fiery Irishman
LYDIA LANGUISH, an heiress
MRS. MALAPROP, her aunt
JULIA MELVILLE, her cousin

Critique:

One of the most popular of the English comedies of manners, *The Rivals* is most successful in character portrayal. All the great characters are here — Mrs. Malaprop, whose misuse of words gave the word malapropism to the language; Bob Acres, the bumptious but lovable country squire trying to behave like a gentleman; romantic Lydia Languish with her head stuffed with nonsense from current novels. The play is Sheridan's satire on the pretentiousness and sentimentality of his age, satire which in many respects is applicable to our own day.

The Story:

To beautiful and wealthy young Lydia Languish, who had been brought up on romantic novels, the only lover worth considering was one whose position in life was in complete contrast to her own. To this end she had fallen in love with a penniless young ensign named Beverley. But to this same Beverley, her aunt, Mrs. Malaprop, raised serious objections. Her antipathy to young Mr. Beverley was partly aroused by letters which the ensign had written to Lydia, letters which made uncomplimentary references to her aunt's age and appearance. Mrs. Malaprop had

THE RIVALS by Richard Brinsley Sheridan. Published by The Macmillan Co.

some moments of extreme discomfiture, when she wondered whether she did resemble the she-dragon to which Beverley had compared her.

Mrs. Malaprop herself had fallen hopelessly in love with a quixotic Irishman named Sir Lucius O'Trigger, who presumably returned her affection. Sir Lucius, who had never seen Mrs. Malaprop, had been hoodwinked by a maidservant into believing that the romantic creature with whom he was exchanging love letters was Lydia herself.

The situation was further complicated by the fact that Beverley was in reality young Captain Jack Absolute, the son of Sir Anthony Absolute, and as wealthy and aristocratic as Lydia herself. Jack very early sensed that he would get nowhere if he wooed the romantic Lydia in his own person, and so he assumed a character more nearly resembling the heroes of the novels with which Lydia's pretty but silly head was stuffed.

Nor did Jack's friend, Faulkland, fare any better in his own romantic pursuit of Lydia's cousin, Julia Melville. In fact, it might be thought that he fared worse, for unlike Jack, he was forever placing imaginary obstacles between himself and his beloved. Whenever they were separated, Faulkland imagined all kinds of horrible catastrophes which might have befallen her, and when he found that she was alive and well he tormented himself with the thought that she could not be in love and remain so happy. At last Jack Absolute lost patience with his friend's ridiculous behavior, and even Julia became a little tired of her lover's unfounded jealousy. This curious love tangle reached a crisis when Sir Anthony Absolute informed his son that he had selected the woman for him to marry, threatening, if he refused, to cut him off without a penny. Not having the faintest idea as to the identity of the woman his father had picked out for him, and conjuring up pictures of some homely heiress his father intended to force on him against his will, Jack rebelled. He declared that, whatever the consequences, he would have nothing to do with his father's choice.

Having been quite a connoisseur of pretty women in his youth, and being not exactly immune to their charms in his old age, Sir Anthony Absolute was not the man to saddle his son with an unattractive wife. He had made an agreement with Mrs. Malaprop for the bestowal of her niece's hand upon his son. Mrs. Malaprop, in turn, was only too glad to save Lydia from a foolish marriage to Beverley. But when Jack refused to marry anyone not of his own choosing, Sir Anthony flew into a rage and insisted that the marriage take place regardless of what the lady might be like.

By chance, however, Jack discovered that the girl Sir Anthony had selected as his bride was Lydia Languish, the identical girl he himself had been wooing as Ensign Beverley. He immediately assured his father that he would be willing to marry anyone of his choosing. Sir Anthony, not used to such tractability on Jack's part, became suspicious and a little worried. Nevertheless, he made arrangements for his son to meet his bride-to-be, thus placing Jack in a neat dilemma.

Jack realized that Lydia would have none of him as Sir Anthony Absolute's son. Finally the supposed Ensign Beverley pretended to Lydia that in order to gain access to her aunt's house, he would be forced to pose as Jack Absolute.

Lydia had another suitor in the person of Bob Acres, a wealthy country squire and a neighbor of Sir Anthony, who had ambitions to become a man about town. Before Sir Anthony proposed his son as a husband for her niece, Mrs. Malaprop had favored Bob Acres as a likely candidate for Lydia's hand. When Acres discovered he had a rival in Ensign Beverley, he was disheartened. Encouraged by his friend, Sir Lucius O'Trigger, he challenged Beverley to a duel. Never having seen young Beverley, he was forced to give the challenge to the ensign's friend, Jack Absolute, to deliver.

The great crisis in Jack's love affairs came when he was forced to face Lydia in the company of his father. With his true identity revealed, Lydia's dreams of a romantic elopement with a penniless ensign vanished. She dismissed Jack from her life forever. Chagrined by his abrupt dismissal, Jack accepted with positive gusto another challenge to a duel from Sir Lucius O'Trigger. Sir Lucius named the place as King's Mead Fields at six o'clock that very evening, when he had an appointment to act as a second to his friend, Acres, in a duel with a certain Ensign Beverley.

When Lydia learned that Jack had involved himself in a duel on her account, he became a different person in her eyes, and she hurried with her aunt to King's Mead Fields in an effort to halt the duel. Meanwhile Sir Lucius O'Trigger had alarmed Acres with his bloodthirsty stories of dueling, so that when Acres recognized his opponent as his old friend, Jack Absolute, he heaved a distinct sigh of relief.

With the arrival of Lydia and Mrs. Malaprop, the whole situation was quickly explained. Sir Lucius, much to his chagrin, was forced to realize that the writer of tender love letters to whom he addressed his own impassioned correspondence was not Lydia but Mrs. Malaprop. Faulkland was content to accept Julia's love for the whole-hearted thing it was. Lydia at last saw Ensign Beverley and Jack Absolute as the same person with whom she was in love. And Bob Acres, happy because he would not be forced to fight a duel with anyone, ordered fiddles and entertainment for all in the fashionable parlors of Bath.

RIVER OF EARTH

Type of work: Novel
Author: James Still (1906-)
Type of plot: Regional romance
Time of plot: Early twentieth century
Locale: Kentucky
First published: 1940

Principal characters:
BRACK BALDRIDGE, a Kentucky mountaineer
ALPHA BALDRIDGE, his wife
BRACK'S OLDEST BOY, the narrator
EULY, the narrator's sister
GRANDMOTHER MIDDLETON, Alpha's mother
UNCLE JOLLY, Alpha's brother

Critique:

It is obvious that James Still is a poet as well as a novelist, for his words almost sing as he describes the Kentucky hills and the people who inhabit them. He tells the story of the *River of Earth* through the words of a very young boy, and through the eyes of that boy shows us the tiny, barren farms; the smoky, sooty mining towns; the bat-filled schoolhouses; the local jails where a prisoner could have company for as many days as he wished. Although the boy did not understand all that he saw and heard, he makes us understand what the author is trying to say—that life flows as a river flows and that the cycle of life is never finished but goes on and on.

The Story:

When the mines closed in March, there was very little food left in the house. It was still a long time before the garden crops would be ready, and Alpha wanted Brack to tell his two cousins, Harl and Tibb Logan, to leave the house and find food for themselves. But the father said that as long as he had food in his house, he would never turn his blood kin away. Then Uncle Samp came to live with them, and the mother saw her four children getting hungrier and leaner. Knowing that the kin would leave if there were no place for them to sleep, she calmly set fire to the house, first moving the children and the skimpy furniture to the smokehouse.

All spring, while the family lived in the smokehouse, they ate less and less and waited for the first vegetables. When the beans were almost ready and the whole family dreamed of having their stomachs full, three men came from the mining town to beg food for their families. Unable to turn down starving people, Brack sent the men into his garden. When they came out, the boy saw that they had taken every bean from the patch. He turned away, wanting to cry.

In May, Brack took the boy with him when he went to help a neighbor deliver a colt. The boy expected to get the colt for his own, as his father's fee, but the neighbor's son told him that no Baldridge was going to get the colt, that the Baldridges were cowards, and that after their Grandpa Middleton had been killed by Aus Coggins no Baldridge had done anything about it. The boy fought with the neighbor's son. When the fight was over, they found that the colt was dead.

One day Uncle Jolly arrived and brought them a pair of guineas from Grandmother Middleton. Uncle Jolly spent as much time in jail as out. It was said that he was avenging Grandpa's death by tormenting Aus Coggins—cutting his fences, breaking his dam, and doing other mischief.

Soon after Uncle Jolly left, Brack wanted to move the family down to Blackjack, for the mines were going to open again. The mother did not want to go because the smoky valley would be a bad place for her sickly baby. But she resigned herself to her husband's wishes.

In the middle of August the boy and his sister Euly started to school. They were anxious to learn to read and write, the boy especially, for he did not want to be a miner. He hoped that some day he could be an animal doctor, as his father had always wanted to be. But it seemed to the boy and Euly that the most important thing they learned in school was how to smoke bats out of the building.

In late September the boy was sent to stay with his Grandmother Middleton while Uncle Jolly served a term in jail. He was to stay with her only until Uncle Luce came, but the corn was husked and the other grain harvested before Uncle Luce arrived. The boy was astonished at his grandmother's ability to do heavy work, for she was very old. When she learned that Uncle Jolly had been sentenced to two years in the state penitentiary, she asked the boy to stay with her during the winter. As soon as the crops were in she spent a great deal of time in bed. She spent hours telling him about her children and her husband. It was easy to see that Jolly was her favorite.

In January Uncle Jolly came home. There had been a fire at the penitentiary, and Jolly had been so brave in helping to fight the fire that the governor had pardoned him. Grandmother Middleton said nothing when Uncle Jolly told her that he had started the fire.

Uncle Jolly also brought the news that the boy's family had moved at last to Blackjack, but there was no other word of his family. Visitors were scarce in the hills.

Spring and summer passed pleasantly for the boy. In October Uncle Jolly was in jail again, this time for fighting. Uncle Toll came to bring Grandmother Middleton the news and he took the boy back to Hardin Town with him. They found Jolly content to be in jail except that he was lonesome. Uncle Toll begged him not to break out, for one more jailbreak would send him to the penitentiary for a long time. Toll left the boy at the jail so that Uncle Jolly would not break out for lack of companionship. The boy slept in the hall outside his uncle's cell. When Uncle Jolly thought he would have to break out of jail or die, he stole the keys from the deputy and told the boy to take the key of Jolly's cell to his mother and ask her to keep it until the remaining days of the sentence were served. In that way the boy went back to his family.

In March the family moved from Blackjack again, this time to a little rented farm on a hillside. There the baby died of croup. Another garden was planted, and in the summer they had a funeral for the baby. The boy saw more relatives than he had known he had. At the end of summer Brack decided to go back to the mines and moved his family to Blackjack and into a house with windows.

Uncle Samp and Harl and Tibb Logan came back to live with the family. Harl and Tibb worked in the mine, but Uncle Samp had never worked and did not intend to start now. Soon the mines began to close down, and men everywhere were laid off again. Brack was kept on, with only one or two days of work each week.

Harl and Tibb, angry because they were laid off, dynamited one of the veins. At first it was thought that they were trapped in the mine and had died, but Uncle Samp and Brack rescued them. They left the Baldridge house after Harl and Tibb were kicked out by the mine boss and Uncle Samp married a fortuneteller.

Food was scarce again, and the mother sickly most of the time, her stomach swollen terribly. In March Uncle Jolly brought Grandmother Middleton's body to the house. The old lady had died at last, and Jolly was taking her to her old home to be buried. While they were sitting with the body in the front room of the house, the boy noticed his father looking constantly at the closed door behind which the mother had been taken by a neighbor woman. In the morning the boy knew what his father had been waiting for and why his mother had been so swollen. As he stood looking at the tracks the wagon had made as it carried his grandmother's body away for the last time, he heard a baby begin to cry.

ROAN STALLION

Type of work: Poem
Author: Robinson Jeffers (1887-)
Type of plot: Symbolic melodrama
Time of plot: 1920's
Locale: Carmel Coast, California
First published: 1925

Principal characters:
CALIFORNIA, a farm wife
JOHNNY, her husband
CHRISTINE, their daughter

Critique:

Roan Stallion is a powerful and highly symbolic narrative poem. Jeffers is a decentralist who believes that the only salvation for man lies in his escaping from himself and his fellow men to a communion with nature. In this poem he employs the roan stallion as a symbol of the rejection of man and the embracing of the natural life. It is a brutal story, but its difficult theme is handled with delicacy and power.

The Story:

California was the daughter of a Scottish father and a Spanish and Indian mother. From her mother she had inherited a dark beauty and a passionate nature. When she was still very young she married a farmer, Johnny, and at twenty-one her features were already beginning to show the marks of hard work.

Johnny spent much of his time away from the farm drinking and gambling. One evening he brought home a splendid roan stallion he had won. It was shortly before Christmas, and California, pleased with his good fortune, decided to go into town to buy some Christmas presents for her young daughter, Christine. Johnny delayed her departure in the morning so that it was quite late before she could hitch their old mare to the buggy and set out for Monterey. By nightfall, when she was ready to return home, a heavy rainstorm had started. The water was high when she reached the ford. Before trying to cross in the darkness, she lashed the presents around her body and hoped that they would keep dry. Refusing to cross the swollen stream, the mare floundered back to shore. California soothed the mare and tried once more to guide her across the ford, but the animal was still frightened. Desperate, California prayed for light. Suddenly the heavens lit up brilliantly and she saw in them the face of a child over whom hovered angels. The mare, startled by the light, scrambled back to shore. Sobbing, California climbed out of the buggy, fastened the presents securely to her back, and mounted the horse. By the light of the heavens she was able to guide the mare across the stream and reach home safely.

California thought she hated the roan stallion, but she could not forget the magnificent beast. When she told young Christine of the miraculous light at the ford and described the birth of Christ, she could hardly restrain herself from identifying God and the stallion. She knew that outside Johnny was mating the stallion with a neighbor's mare.

That evening Johnny went down the valley to the home of a neighbor. After Christine was asleep, California stole out to the stable. She leaned against the fence, listening to the far-off cries of the coyotes and watching the moon rise over the hill. Once before she had seen God. If she were to ride to the top of the hill, perhaps she might see Him again. She hurried down to the corral. The stallion heard her as she approached. She caressed his flanks, wishing that nature had not made it impossible for him to possess her. Then she sprang upon his back and reveled in the feel of his muscles as he galloped up the hillside. At the top they halted, and she tethered him lightly to a tree. Overwhelmed by his majesty and her desire, she threw herself at his feet.

The following night California could not bear the thought of being with Johnny. He had brought home some wine and, half drunk, he ordered her to drink some. Revolted at the thought of the night ahead, California stole to the door, opened it, and fled. Excited by the prospect of a chase, Johnny called to his dog to help him. When California heard them approaching, she crawled under the fence into the corral, the dog close behind her. The stallion plunged, frightened by the snarling, snapping dog. Johnny climbed into the corral, where the fierce stallion trampled him to death.

In the meantime Christine had awakened. Frightened by the lonely house, she made her way to the corral. When she saw her father's body she ran back to the house for the rifle. California took the gun and shot the dog. While she watched, the stallion struck again at Johnny's body. Then, prompted by a remnant of fidelity to the human race, she raised the rifle and shot the stallion. It was as though she had killed God.

ROB ROY

Type of work: Novel
Author: Sir Walter Scott (1771-1832)
Type of plot: Historical romance
Time of plot: 1715
Locale: Northumberland and Glasgow
First published: 1818

Principal characters:
MR. WILLIAM OSBALDISTONE, of the firm of Osbaldistone & Tresham
FRANK OSBALDISTONE, his son
SIR HILDEBRAND OSBALDISTONE, Frank's uncle
RASHLEIGH OSBALDISTONE, his son
SIR FREDERICK VERNON, a Jacobite
DIANA VERNON, his daughter
ROB ROY MACGREGOR CAMPBELL, a Scottish outlaw

Critique:

Rob Roy MacGregor Campbell is not the hero of this novel; he is the man behind the scenes. The novel itself concerns the fortunes of Frank Osbaldistone and his adventures with Rob Roy, the Scottish Robin Hood. Scott, as he usually does, manipulates Scottish history to suit his purpose. The story is told by Frank Osbaldistone, writing to his friend, Tresham. Always a popular Waverley novel, it has been dramatized several times and was the subject of an opera by Flotow.

The Story:

Frank Osbaldistone was recalled from France where he had been sent to learn his father's mercantile business. Disappointed in his son's progress, the angry parent ordered the young man to Osbaldistone Hall, home of his uncle, Sir Hildebrand Osbaldistone, in northern England. His father gave him fifty guineas for expenses and instructions to learn who among Sir Hildebrand's sons would accept a position in the trading house of Osbaldistone and Tresham.

On the road Frank fell in with a traveler named Morris, who was carrying a large sum of money in a portmanteau strapped to his saddle. That evening they stopped at the Black Bear Inn, in the town of Darlington, where they were joined at dinner by Mr. Campbell, a Scotsman. Campbell was Rob Roy, the Scottish outlaw. The next morning Campbell and Morris left together, and at a secluded spot along the road the men were halted and a highwayman robbed Morris of his saddlebag. Frank, meanwhile, rode toward Osbaldistone Hall. As he neared the rambling old mansion, he saw a fox hunt and met Diana Vernon, Sir Hildebrand's niece. Outspoken Diana told Frank that his cousins were a mixture of sot, gamekeeper, bully, horse-jockey, and fool, these characteristics being mixed in varying proportions in each man. Rashleigh, she said, was the most dangerous of the lot, for he maintained a private tyranny over everyone with whom he came in contact.

It was Rashleigh, however, who was prevailed upon to accept Frank's vacant position. The cousins disliked each other. One night, while drinking with the family, Frank became enraged at Rashleigh's speech and actions and struck him. Rashleigh never forgot the blow, although to all intents and purposes he and Frank declared themselves friends after their anger had cooled.

Shortly after Frank's arrival he was accused of highway robbery and he went at once to Squire Inglewood's court to defend himself and to confront his accuser, who turned out to be Morris. Rob Roy, however, appeared at the squire's court of justice and forced Morris to confess that Frank had not robbed him.

When Rashleigh departed to go into

business with Frank's father, Frank became Diana's tutor. Their association developed into deep affection on both sides, a mutual attraction marred only by the fact that Diana was by faith a Catholic and Frank a Presbyterian.

One day Frank received a letter from his father's partner, Mr. Tresham. The letter informed him that his father, leaving Rashleigh in charge, had gone to the continent on business, and that Rashleigh had gone to Scotland, where he was reported involved in a scheme to embezzle funds of Osbaldistone and Tresham.

Frank, accompanied by Andrew Fairservice, Sir Hildebrand's gardener, set off for Glasgow in an attempt to frustrate Rashleigh's plans. Arriving in the city on Sunday, they went to church. As Frank stood listening to the preacher, a voice behind him whispered that he was in danger and that he should not look back at his informant. The mysterious messenger asked Frank to meet him on the bridge at midnight. Frank kept the tryst and followed the man to the Tolbooth prison. There he found his father's chief clerk, Mr. Owen, who had been arrested and thrown into prison at the instigation of MacVittie and MacFin, Glasgow traders who did business with his father. Frank learned that Campbell had been his mysterious informant and guide, and for the first time he realized that Campbell and Rob Roy were one and the same.

Shortly thereafter Frank saw Morris, MacVittie, and Rashleigh talking together. He followed them and when Morris and MacVittie departed, leaving Rashleigh alone, Frank confronted his cousin and demanded an explanation of his behavior. As their argument grew more heated, swords were drawn, but the duel was broken up by Rob Roy, who cried shame at them because they were men of the same blood. Rob Roy considered both men his friends. Frank learned also that his father's funds were mixed up with a Jacobite uprising, in which Sir Hildebrand was one of the plotters. He suspected that Rashleigh had robbed Morris on information supplied by Rob Roy.

Frank and Andrew were arrested by an officer on their way to meet Rob Roy, and the officer who searched Frank discovered a note which Rob Roy had written to him. On the road the company was attacked by Scotsmen under the direction of Helen, Rob Roy's wife, who captured or killed all the soldiers. Helen, a bloodthirsty creature, ordered the death of Morris, who had fallen into the hands of the Highlanders. In the meantime, Rob Roy had also been captured but had made his escape when one of his captors rode close to Rob Roy and surreptitiously cut his bonds. Rob Roy threw himself from his horse into the river and swam to safety before his guards could overtake him.

With a Highland uprising threatening, Frank thought he had seen Diana for the last time. But he met her soon afterward riding through a wood in the company of her father, Sir Frederick Vernon, a political exile. She gave him a packet of papers which Rashleigh had been forced to give up; they were notes to the credit of Osbaldistone and Tresham. The fortune of Frank's father was safe.

In the Jacobite revolt of 1715, Rashleigh became a turncoat and joined the forces of King George. At the beginning of the revolt Sir Hildebrand had made his will, listing the order in which his sons would fall heir to his lands. Because Rashleigh had betrayed the Stuart cause, he substituted Frank's name for that of Rashleigh in the will. Sir Hildebrand was captured by the royal forces and imprisoned at Newgate, where he died. His four sons died in various ways and Frank inherited all the lands and properties belonging to Sir Hildebrand. When Frank went to Osbaldistone manor to take over, Rashleigh showed up with a warrant for Diana and her father. But he obtained no end that he desired, for he was killed in a fight with

Rob Roy. Frank became the lord of Osbaldistone Hall. At first Frank's father did not like the idea of having his son marry a Papist, but at last he relented and Frank and Diana were married.

ROBINSON CRUSOE

Type of work: Novel
Author: Daniel Defoe (1661?-1731)
Type of plot: Adventure romance
Time of plot: 1651-1705
Locale: An island off the coast of South America, and the Several Seas
First published: 1719

Principal characters:
ROBINSON CRUSOE, a castaway
FRIDAY, his faithful servant

Critique:

The Life and Strange Surprising Adventures of Robinson Crusoe as Defoe called his novel, is read as eagerly today as when it was first published. At times the narrative seems too detailed, since the routine of Crusoe's life on the island was much the same. But Defoe knew the theatrical device of timing, for no sooner do we begin to tire of reading the daily account of his hero's life than a new situation breaks the monotony of Crusoe's life and of our reading. The book has attained a high place in the literature of the world, and justly so.

The Story:

Robinson Crusoe was the son of a middle-class English family. Although his father desired that Robinson go into some business and live a quiet life, Robinson had such longing for the sea that he found it impossible to remain at home. Without his parents' knowledge he took his first voyage. The ship was caught in a great storm, and Robinson was so violently ill and so greatly afraid that he vowed never to leave the land again should he be so fortunate as to escape death.

But when he landed safely, he found his old longing still unsatisfied, and he engaged as a trader, shipping first for the coast of Africa. The ship on which he sailed was captured by a Turkish pirate vessel, and he was carried a prisoner into Sallee, a Moorish port. There he became a slave, and his life was so unbearable that at the first opportunity he escaped in a small boat. He was rescued by a Portuguese freighter and carried safely to Brazil. There he bought a small plantation and began the life of a planter.

When another English planter suggested they make a voyage to Africa for a cargo of slaves, Robinson once more gave way to his longing and sailed again. This voyage was destined to be the most fateful of all, for it brought him his greatest adventure.

The ship broke apart on a reef near an island off the coast of South America, and of the crew and passengers only Robinson was saved. The waves washed him ashore, where he took stock of his unhappy plight. The island seemed to be completely uninhabited, and there was no sign of wild beasts. In an attempt to make his castaway life as comfortable as possible, he constructed a raft and brought away food, ammunition, water, wine, clothing, tools, sailcloth, and lumber from the broken ship.

He first set up a sailcloth tent on the side of a small hill. He encircled his refuge with tall, sharp stakes and entered his shelter by means of a ladder which he drew up after him. Into this area he carried all of the goods he had salvaged, being particularly careful of the gunpowder. His next concern was his food supply. Finding that there was little which had not been ruined by rats or by water, he ate sparingly during his first days on the island.

Before long, having found some ink and a quill among the things he had brought from the ship, he began to keep a journal. He also added the good and evil of his situation and found that he had much for which to thank God. He began to make his shelter permanent. Behind his tent he found a small cave which he enlarged and braced. With crude tools he made a table and a chair, some shelves, and a rack for his guns. He spent many months on the work, all the time able to find wild fowl or other small game which kept him well supplied with food. He also found several springs and so was never in want for water.

His life for the next twenty-four years was spent in much the same way as his first days upon the island. He explored the island and built what he was pleased to call his summer home on the other side of it. He was able to grow corn, barley, and rice. He carefully saved the new kernels each year until he had enough to plant a small field. With these grains he learned to grind meal and bake coarse bread. He caught and tamed wild goats to supply his larder and parrots for companionship. He made better furniture and improved his cave, making it even safer from intruders, whom he still feared, even though he had seen no sign of any living thing except small game and fowl and goats. From the ship he had brought also three Bibles, and he had time to read them carefully. At a devotional period each morning and night, he never failed to thank God for delivering him from the sea.

In the middle of Robinson's twenty-fourth year on the island, an incident occurred which altered his way of living. About a year and a half previously he had observed some savages who had apparently paddled over from another island. They had come in the night and gorged themselves on some other savages, obviously prisoners. Robinson had found the bones and the torn flesh the next morning and had since been terrified that the cannibals might return and find him. Finally a band of savages did return. While they prepared for their gruesome feast, Robinson shot some of them and frightened the others away. Able to rescue one of the prisoners, he at last had human companionship. He named the man Friday after the day of his rescue, and Friday became his faithful servant and friend.

After a time Robinson was able to teach Friday some English. Friday told him that seventeen white men were prisoners on the island from which he came. Although Friday reported the men well-treated, Robinson had a great desire to go to them, thinking that together they might find some way to return to the civilized world. He and Friday built a canoe and prepared to sail to the other island, but before they were ready for their trip another group of savages came to their island with more prisoners. Discovering that one of the prisoners was a white man, Robinson managed to save him and another savage, whom Friday found to be his own father. There was great joy at the reunion of father and son. Robinson cared for the old man and the white man, who was a Spaniard, one of the seventeen of whom Friday had spoken. A hostile tribe had captured Friday's island, and thus it was that the white men were no longer safe.

Robinson dispatched the Spaniard and Friday's father to the neighboring island to try to rescue the white men. While waiting for their return, Robinson saw an English ship one day at anchor near shore. Soon he found the captain of the ship and two others, who had been set ashore by a mutinous crew. Robinson and Friday and the three seamen were able to retake the ship, and thus Robinson was at last delivered from the island. He disliked leaving before the Spaniard and Friday's father returned, and he determined to go back to the island some day and see how they had fared. Five of the mutinous crew chose to remain rather than be returned to England to hang. And so Robinson and Friday went to England, Robinson returning to his homeland after an absence of thirty-five years. He arrived there, a stranger and unknown, in June of 1687.

But he was not through with adventure. When he visited his old home, he found that his parents had died, as had all of his family but two sisters and the two children of one of his brothers. Having nothing to keep him in England, he went to Lisbon to inquire about his plantation. There he learned that friends had saved the income of his estate for him and that he was now worth about five thousand pounds sterling. Satisfied with the accounting, Robinson and Friday returned to England, where Robinson married and had three children.

After his wife died, Robinson sailed again in 1695 as a private trader on a ship captained by his nephew and bound for the East Indies and China. The ship put in at his castaway island, where he found that the Spaniards and the English mutineers had taken native wives from an adjoining island, so that the population was greatly increased. Robinson was pleased with his little group and gave a feast for them. He also presented them with gifts from the ship.

After he had satisfied himself that the colony was well cared for, Robinson and Friday sailed away. On their way to Brazil some savages attacked the ship and Friday was killed. From Brazil Robinson went around the Cape of Good Hope and on to the coast of China. At one port, after the sailors had taken part in a massacre, Robinson lectured them so severely that the crew forced their captain, Robinson's nephew, to set him ashore in China, as they would have no more of his preaching. There Robinson joined a caravan which took him into Siberia. At last he reached England. Having spent the greater part of fifty-four years away from his homeland, he was glad to live out his life in peace and in preparation for that longer journey from which he would never return.

RODERICK RANDOM

Type of work: Novel
Author: Tobias Smollett (1721-1771)
Type of plot: Picaresque romance
Time of plot: Eighteenth century
Locale: England
First published: 1748

Principal characters:
Roderick Random, an adventurer
Tom Bowling, his uncle
Strap, Tom's friend and companion
Miss Williams, an adventuress
Narcissa, Roderick's sweetheart

Critique:

The Adventures of Roderick Random is unique in being the first English novel to describe with any detail life on a British warship. For this material Smollett drew upon his own experience as a ship surgeon. There is little structure to the book. The success of the novel lies in Smollett's ability to narrate and describe incident after incident and to keep his readers interested and, usually, amused. The central character of Roderick Random is used, as in a picaresque novel, to unite the incidents into a story and to provide a reason for the development of the climax. Roderick's adventures provide an opportunity for satire on the follies and affectations of the age.

The Story:

Although Roderick Random came from a wealthy landowning family of Scotland, his early life was one of vicissitudes. Roderick's father had married a servant in the Random household, and for that reason he had been disowned without a penny. Soon after Roderick's birth his mother died. When his father disappeared, heartbroken, the grandfather was prevailed upon to send the lad to school for the sake of the family's reputation.

At school Roderick was the butt of the masters, although a great favorite with the boys his own age. His whippings were numerous, for he could be used as a whipping boy when something had gone wrong and the real culprit could not be determined. In Roderick's fourteenth year, however, there was a change in his fortunes. His mother's brother, Tom Bowling, a lieutenant in the navy, came to visit his young nephew.

Lieutenant Bowling remonstrated with his nephew's grandfather over his treatment of Roderick, but the old man was firm in his refusal to do anything beyond what necessity dictated for the offspring of the son whom he had disinherited. When the grandfather died, he left Roderick nothing. Tom Bowling sent the lad to the university, where Roderick made great progress. Then Tom Bowling became involved in a duel and was forced to leave his ship. This misfortune cut off the source of Roderick's funds and made it necessary for him to leave the university.

Casting about for a means of making a livelihood, Roderick became a surgeon's apprentice. He proved to be so capable that before long his master sent him to London with a recommendation to a local member of Parliament, who was to get Roderick a place as surgeon's mate in the navy.

Securing a place on a man-of-war was a difficult task. To keep himself in funds, Roderick worked for a French chemist in London. In the shop he met Miss Williams, with whom he fell in love, but much to his chagrin he discovered one day that she was a prostitute trying to better her fortune. Soon afterward Roderick was accused of stealing and was dismissed by his employer. While he was leading a precarious existence, waiting for his navy warrant, he learned that Miss Williams lived in the same lodging-house. He won the everlasting gratitude of the young woman by acting as her doctor while she was ill.

One day, while walking near the Thames, Roderick was seized by a press-gang and shanghaied aboard the man-of-war *Thunder*, about to sail for Jamaica. Roderick, who had found friends on the ship, was made a surgeon's mate.

The voyage to Jamaica was a terrible one as the commanding officer, Captain Oakhum, was a tyrant who came very close to hanging Roderick and another surgeon's mate because one of the ship's officers claimed he had heard them speaking ill of both the surgeon and the captain. Thinking that Roderick's Greek notebook was a military code, the captain threatened again to hang him as a spy.

After seeing action against the Spanish at Cartagena, Roderick secured a billet as surgeon's mate aboard the *Lizard,* a ship returning to England with dispatches. On the way the captain died and Lieutenant Crampley, an officer who greatly disliked Roderick, took command of the ship. Crampley, being a poor officer, ran the ship aground off the Sussex coast. The crew robbed and tried to kill Roderick when they reached the shore, but an old woman befriended him, cured him of his wounds, and found him a place as footman with a spinster gentlewoman who lived nearby.

Roderick spent several months in her service. He found his way into his employer's good-will by his attention to his duties and by showing a knowledge of literature, even to the extent of explaining passages from Tasso's Italian poetry to her. The spinster had a niece and a nephew living with her. Narcissa, the niece, was a beautiful girl of marriageable age to whom Roderick was immediately attracted. Her brother, a drunken, fox-hunting young squire, was determined that she should marry a wealthy knight in the neighborhood.

One day Roderick prevented the girl's brutal suitor from forcing his attentions on her and beat the man severely with a cudgel. While he was deliberating on his next move, he was taken prisoner by a band of smugglers who for their own safety carried him to Boulogne in France. There Roderick found his uncle, Tom Bowling, and assured him that he would be safe if he returned to England, for the man Bowling believed he had killed in a duel was very much alive.

Roderick set out for Paris in company with a friar who robbed him one night and left him penniless. Meeting a band of soldiers, Roderick enlisted in the army of King Louis XIV and saw service at the battle of Dettingen. After the battle his regiment went into garrison and Roderick unexpectedly met a boyhood companion, Strap, who was passing as Monsieur D'Estrapes and who was friendly with a French nobleman. Strap befriended Roderick and secured his release from onerous service as a private in the French army.

Strap and Roderick schemed for a way to make their fortunes and finally hit upon the idea of setting up Roderick as a wealthy gentleman. They hoped that he would marry, within a short time, some wealthy heiress.

The two men went to Paris, where Roderick bought new clothes and became acquainted with the ways of a man about town. Then they went to London. There Roderick quickly became acquainted with a group of young men who were on the fringe of fashionable society.

Roderick's first attempt to become intimate with a rich woman was a dismal failure, for she turned out to be a woman of the streets. On the second attempt he met Melinda, a young woman of fortune, who won many pounds from him at cards and then refused to marry him because he did not have an independent fortune of his own. Finally one of Roderick's friends told him of a cousin, Miss Snapper, who was a wealthy heiress. The friend promised that he would help Roderick in his suit in return for Roderick's note for five hundred pounds, due six months after the marriage.

Falling in with this suggestion, Roderick immediately started out for Bath in company with the young woman and her mother. On the way he saved them from being robbed by a highwayman, a deed which established him in the good graces of both mother and daughter. At Bath, Roderick squired the young woman about day and night. Although she was crippled and not good-looking, the thought of her fortune was greater in his mind than her appearance. Besides, she was an intelligent and witty young woman.

All went well with the plan until Roderick caught sight of Narcissa, the young girl he had known while he was employed as a footman by her aunt. Realizing that he was in love with her, he promptly deserted Miss Snapper.

Narcissa soon revealed to Roderick that she returned his love. The young squire, her brother, had no objections to Roderick because he thought that Random was a wealthy man. Unfortunately Roderick's former love, Melinda, arrived in Bath and caught the attention of Narcissa's brother. At a ball she spread evil reports about Roderick because he had left her. The result was that Roderick first fought a duel with Lord Quiverwit, one of Narcissa's admirers, and then saw his Narcissa spirited away by her brother. The only thing that kept Roderick's hope alive was the fact that he knew Narcissa loved him and that her maid, the Miss Williams whom Roderick had long before befriended, was eternally grateful to him and would help him in any way which lay in her power.

Returning to London, Roderick again met his uncle, Tom Bowling, who had been appointed to take a merchant ship on a mysterious trip. He proposed to take Roderick with him as ship surgeon, and he gave Roderick a thousand pounds with which to buy goods to sell on the voyage. He also made out a will leaving all his property to Roderick in case he should die.

The mysterious trip proved to be a voyage to the Guinea Coast to pick up Negro slaves for the Spanish American trade. The slaves and the cargo, including the goods shipped by Roderick, were sold at a handsome profit. While their ship was being prepared for the return voyage, Roderick and his uncle spent several weeks ashore, where they were entertained by people they met and with whom they did business. One of their acquaintances was a rich Englishman known as Don Rodrigo, who invited them to visit him on his estate. During their stay it was discovered that the man was Roderick's father, who had gone to America to make his fortune after having been disinherited because of his marriage to Roderick's mother.

The voyage back to England was a happy one. Roderick was full of confidence, for he had made a small fortune out of the voyage and had expectations of quite a large fortune from the estates of his father and his uncle. He immediately paid his addresses to Narcissa, who accepted his offer of marriage in spite of her brother's opposition. They were married shortly afterward and went to live in Scotland on the Random estate, which Roderick's father had bought from his bankrupt elder brother.

ROGUE HERRIES

Type of work: Novel
Author: Hugh Walpole (1884-1941)
Type of plot: Historical chronicle
Time of plot: 1730-1774
Locale: England
First published: 1930

Principal characters:
FRANCIS HERRIES, the Rogue
MARGARET HERRIES, his first wife
MIRABELL STARR, his second wife
DAVID HERRIES, his son
DEBORAH HERRIES, his daughter
ALICE PRESS, his mistress
SARAH DENBURN, David's wife

Critique:

Rogue Herries is the first novel of a tetrology which traces in detail the story of an English family over a period of two hundred years. The story of the Herries becomes also the story of England through the Georgian, Victorian, and modern periods, largely upon the domestic level of morals and manners. There is a growing complexity to the novel as new generations appear and succeed one another, but Hugh Walpole keeps the narrative within bounds by relating the action to the descendants of the notorious Rogue Herries. Throughout there is a fairly successful capturing of the flavor of the period.

The Story:

In the year 1730 Francis Herries brought his family from the roistering life of Doncaster to live in a long-deserted family house—called Herries—at

Rosthwaite not far from Keswick in Cumberland. In addition to his wife and three children, he brought along the most recent of his many mistresses, Alice Press, who, under pretense of being the children's governess, had actually been unkind and overbearing with them and insolent to their mother. The family rested for a period at the Keswick inn, and met Francis' oldest brother and his wife. After an uncomfortable journey on horseback over a scarcely discernible road, the party reached Herries.

Francis Herries had led a life of dissipation. His respectable relatives, of whom there were a great many, looked on him as the black sheep of the family and avoided him. His wife Margaret he had married more for pity than for love. But she had brought him some money. The one person whom Francis really loved was his son David. And David returned his love.

One day Francis, now tired of Alice Press, came upon her berating his wife. Although he did not love Margaret, he loved Alice less. He tried from that day to make Alice leave the house, but she refused. When he took David to Keswick to a fair, they saw Alice Press. Furious, Francis told Alice that she must not return to Herries. At last he began to shout, announcing that Alice was for sale. People were shocked and astounded. Then a man threw down a handful of silver. Francis picked up a token piece and walked away. David felt that his father was possessed of a devil.

Francis became notorious throughout the district for his escapades and before long acquired the epithet of Rogue Herries. One Christmas night, at a feast in a friend's house, he was challenged to a duel by young Osbaldistone. Francis had won money from him gambling in Keswick and had also paid some attention to a young woman that Osbaldistone fancied. In the course of the duel, Francis had the advantage. Then, when Francis' guard was down, Osbaldistone slashed him from temple to chin. The resulting scar marked Rogue Herries for the rest of his life.

One evening in the spring following, Francis came in from working on his land and found Margaret ailing. They had never had any warmth of feeling between them, but even in the moment of her death she felt that he would be at a loss without her. After making David promise never to leave his father, she called for Francis and died in his arms.

In 1745 Francis had a strange adventure. After a long walk through the hills near his home, he lay down to rest and fell sound asleep. When he awoke he was bound hand and foot. His mysterious captor untied his bonds after questioning him as to his identity and led him to a cave where he saw several desperate-looking men and a lovely young girl. One of the men gave him a cross and chain which the girl's mother had left for him at her death. Years before, he had seen her shuddering with cold by the roadside and had given her his cloak. Fascinated now by the girl, he talked kindly to her and learned that her name was Mirabell Starr. The men with whom she lived were thieves and smugglers.

In November Francis took David to Carlisle. The Young Pretender had landed in Scotland and was marching toward London. At an inn in Carlisle, Francis saw Mirabell with a young man of her own age. He was jealous, for he knew that he loved Mirabell despite the great difference in their ages. He also saw that an ugly man of considerable age was jealous of Mirabell's lover. During the siege of the city all able men were pressed into service. When Carlisle fell to the Pretender's forces, the city became quiet once more. On a dark night Francis, out for a walk, saw Mirabell and the young man walking ahead of him. He also saw the ugly man of the inn approach the pair. He yelled a warning too late. The boy Harry dropped dead. Mirabell escaped in the darkness.

In the summer of 1756 David and his sister Deborah attended a ball in Keswick. At the dance Deborah fell in love with a young clergyman. When they arrived home next day, they were met by their father, who explained to them that Mirabell had arrived and had promised to marry him. After her hard life on the roads Mirabell had come to offer herself to Francis in return for food and protection.

In 1758 David was thirty-eight. On a business trip he met and fell in love with a girl named Sarah Denburn, a frank, friendly girl of more than average beauty. Her uncle-guardian intended her for another man, but David carried her off one night after killing his rival.

For about two years David and Sarah lived at Herries. Mirabell hated Sarah. At last David bought a house not far off and moved with his wife to it. Deborah went to Cockermouth to wed her clergyman. Alone with his young wife, Francis unsuccessfully tried to teach her to read and write and to love him. Mirabell had something of the gipsy in her. One day she ran away. From then on most of Francis' life was devoted to traveling over England looking for Mirabell.

Meanwhile David and Sarah, settled at Uldale, had three children and became well established in the community. Sarah loved the society of the people of Uldale and David prospered.

After many years of wandering, Francis at last saw Mirabell again among a troupe of players in Penrith. She promised to meet him after the play, but did not. Francis searched the town in vain. As he returned to his inn, he fell ill of an old ailment, a fever, and was forced to stay there for six months. When at last he returned home, he found Mirabell waiting for him. She explained that she could not desert the acting company on that fateful night because the leader, her lover, had threatened to kill himself if she deserted him, and his death would have left his children friendless orphans. But at last he had run away with a younger woman, and Mirabell had come back to Francis once more for protection. She tried to make him understand that the only man she had ever truly loved was the boy killed in Carlisle.

In 1774 an old woman from a nearby village came in to cook for Francis and Mirabell, for at last Mirabell was going to have a baby. Francis, stricken again by his fever, was in bed in the next room as Mirabell gave birth to a daughter and died. Francis, in a final spasm of vigor, rose from his bed and then fell back, he thought, into Mirabell's arms. He too was dead. Only the new-born child and the old woman were alive in the house on that stormy winter night.

THE ROMANTIC COMEDIANS

Type of work: Novel
Author: Ellen Glasgow (1874-1945)
Type of plot: Humorous satire
Time of plot: 1920's
Locale: Richmond, Virginia
First published: 1926

Principal characters:
JUDGE GAMALIEL BLAND HONEYWELL, a widower of sixty-five
ANNABEL, his second wife, a girl of twenty-three
MRS. UPCHURCH, Annabel's mother
EDMONIA BREDALBANE, the judge's sister
AMANDA LIGHTFOOT, the judge's childhood sweetheart

Critique:

The Romantic Comedians presents the age-old problem of the old man who marries a young girl. But symbolized in these two people is the struggle between two diverse eras in American culture. The man represents the faded Victorianism of the American South in the last third of the nineteenth century. The girl represents the generation of Southern Americans in the decade after the first World War. Since Ellen Glasgow's purpose was to present the new South, the novel succeeds because it reflects the forces which pervade that section of our country today.

The Story:

As Judge Honeywell walked home from church on the first Easter morning after his wife's death, he was surprised by his own reactions to the Virginia springtime. He felt quite young, for sixty-five, and life with his wife, now dead, seemed so remote as never to have happened. In fact, he felt relieved, for his first wife had seldom let him lead an existence of his own.

The judge looked after Mrs. Upchurch and her daughter Annabel in a friendly way because they were kinswomen of his late wife. But shortly after that memorable Easter morning he began to think of twenty-three-year old Annabel in quite another way. His changed attitude began because he was secretly sorry for her. She had been engaged to a young man who had left her almost at the altar. It had hurt her bitterly, as the judge and her mother knew.

As time passed the judge found himself thinking more and more of Annabel Upchurch and of Amanda Lightfoot, his childhood sweetheart. Unfortunately, the judge's sister, Mrs. Bredalbane, tried to convince him that falling in love with Amanda would be the sensible thing for him to do. The judge, like most men, promptly closed his mind to Amanda and began thinking more of Annabel, who had asked the judge if he would help her to open a flower shop.

Soon the judge had purchased a house with a large garden for Mrs. Upchurch and her daughter, so that Annabel might practice landscape gardening. When he told the girl, he added that he only expected the reward of seeing her happy. But when she left, he kissed her.

By the time that Mrs. Upchurch and Annabel were settled in their new home, the judge knew he was in love with the girl, who was more than forty years younger than he. He bought new clothes and had his hair and beard trimmed to lessen the amount of gray which had appeared. He felt that he could give Annabel everything she needed—love, tenderness, security, and wealth.

The number and quality of the judge's gifts soon made apparent to Annabel and her mother what was in the old man's mind. Annabel thought at first that it would be more suitable for him to marry her mother. But, as she informed her mother, marrying an older man was certainly better than living in an atmosphere of shabby gentility. Annabel decided to visit Amanda Lightfoot. Knowing that Amanda had never married because she had been in love with the judge, Annabel wished to find out if the older woman still loved him. If she did not, Annabel decided, she herself would marry him. But the older woman almost refused to say anything at all. Annabel was disappointed but secretly relieved. When she arrived home, Judge Honeywell was waiting with a present for her, a sapphire bracelet. Before he left the house he told her he loved her, and she accepted him.

After the marriage the judge and Annabel traveled in Europe and in England. The judge felt that he was as fine a man as he had been at thirty-five, although his nerves were jarred a little when some one occasionally referred to Annabel as his daughter. That she often danced with young men did not bother him. He felt no envy of their youth;

after all, she was his wife.

The judge was glad to be back in his home in Virginia after the honeymoon. His dyspepsia soon disappeared after he began to eat familiar cooking once more, and he felt at peace to be living in the familiar old house which had not been refurnished in over thirty years.

The couple dined out frequently and went to many dances. The judge, after noting how silly his contemporaries appeared on the dance floor, abstained from any dancing, but he encouraged Annabel to enjoy herself. He always went with her, not from jealousy but because he felt that he had to keep up with her life. It cost him a great deal of effort, for on those evenings he sometimes thought that he had never before known what fatigue was really like.

At home, Annabel had brought changes into the house. While he did not approve, the judge said nothing until she tried to change the furniture in his own room. She learned then, although it cost him a ring she had admired, that he would not let her meddle with his own privacy.

When the judge came down with bronchitis, Annabel proved an able and attentive nurse. During his convalescence, however, she found it difficult to remain at home reading night after night. He, noticing her restlessness, told her to begin going out again, even though he could not go with her. When Annabel went out, her mother or the judge's sister would come to have dinner and stay with him during the evening.

The passing weeks brought in Annabel a change which many people noticed. Noted for her boisterous spirits and lack of reticence, she surprised them by becoming more vague about her comings and goings. At the same time they complimented the judge on how happy she seemed. The compliments made the old gentleman content, for, as he said, Annabel's happiness was what he wanted most.

Slowly the judge began to feel that all was not right in his home. Annabel was distant in her manner. When he talked with his sister and Annabel's mother, both reassured him of the girl's devotion. Still, he knew something was not right. He received proof one day when he found Annabel kissing a young man. Dabney Birdsong belonged to an old family in the community. Annabel had resolved to have him, cost what it might. To the judge, his greatest sorrow was that it might be only an infatuation which would not make Annabel happy. The girl, on the other hand, thought if she did not have Dabney she would die.

Annabel and her lover ran away and went to New York. The judge followed them to the city. Unable to understand his young wife, he felt sorry for her because she defied convention, and he thought that he himself was to blame for what had happened. After a talk with Annabel he left New York, defeated, to return to Virginia.

The rain and the draughty train gave the judge a cold which turned into influenza, and he was in bed for several weeks in a serious condition. During his convalescence he discovered that spring had once more arrived. With the stirring in nature, he felt a resurgence of life in his weary body. Like many an old man before him, the season of freshness and greenery gave him the feeling of youth that he had had on the previous Easter Sunday morning. He found himself beginning to look with new, eager interest at the young nurse who was attending him during his illness.

THE ROMANY RYE

Type of work: Novel
Author: George Henry Borrow (1803-1881)
Type of plot: Simulated autobiography
Time of plot: Nineteenth century
Locale: England
First published: 1857

Principal characters:
LAVENGRO, a scholar gipsy
ISOPEL BERNERS (BELLE), his companion
JASPER PETULENGRO, a gipsy
JACK DALE, a horse-trader
MURTAGH, an Irishman and Lavengro's childhood friend
THE COACHMAN

Critique:

The Romany Rye continues without a break the story of *Lavengro*. The novel is a collection of stories about the people Lavengro met, together with his many side remarks and observations on gipsy customs, English fairs, religion, and literature. *The Romany Rye* is unevenly written, but its pictures of English life in the first half of the nineteenth century are at all times vivid and dramatic.

The Story:

In those days, Lavengro and Isopel Berners traveled the English highroads together. Lavengro was a scholar who had become a gipsy tinker, and Isopel, whom he called Belle, was a strapping woman of the roads and dingles. One night they rescued a coachman whose carriage had overturned in a swollen stream, and, while they waited for daylight, he entertained them with the story of his life. In the morning Lavengro forged a new linch-pin for the broken wheel, and the coachman continued on his way. The Man in Black, a Catholic priest whom Lavengro had met before, visited Lavengro again that evening, and the two of them discussed and argued the merits of Catholicism and Protestantism, with an occasional remark from Belle.

The next morning Lavengro informed Belle that Jasper Petulengro and his band of gipsies had camped nearby during the night and that he was going to invite Mr. and Mrs. Petulengro for breakfast. Lavengro's gipsy friend refused his invitation, however, saying that he and his wife would pay a visit later in the day when they were better settled. On the next Sunday they all went to church together. Following the service, Jasper and Lavengro began a lengthy discussion on morals.

Belle had indicated to Lavengro that she thought it about time their paths separated. When she informed him she was going on a journey, he feared she was leaving for good, but she told him she would come back before too long. One evening while she was gone Lavengro had a long talk with Ursula, Mrs. Petulengro's sister, and thus he learned her story. She had been married some years previously. Her husband, escaping from a constable, had met with an unfortunate accident and had drowned. She had been a widow until just two days before, when she had married Sylvester, another member of the gipsy band and a widower with two children. Lavengro and Ursula discussed many subjects, including morals, virtue, marriage customs, and words. It was about the meanings of some of the gipsy words that Lavengro wanted most to talk with Ursula.

Belle returned that night and the next day Lavengro, who had thought the matter over in her absence, asked Belle to marry him and to migrate with him to

America. When she told him that she could not give him her answer immediately, he planned to attend a fair in a nearby village the next day. Belle agreed to consider his proposal during his absence and to give him her reply when he returned. At the fair Lavengro saw a horse which he desired, but he did not have the money to buy the animal and he refused to borrow the money from Jasper, who was willing to lend it to him.

When Lavengro returned to the dingle, Belle had disappeared. At first he thought she had gone only on a short journey, but when two days went by and she did not appear, he began to fear she would not return. A few days later he received a letter from her, telling him that on her previous short journey she had made arrangements to dispose of all her goods and to go to America. When he proposed to her, she had been tempted to accept his offer, but after thinking it over carefully she had decided that her first plan would be the best after all. Lavengro never saw her again.

That night, at a nearby public house, Lavengro again saw the horse he had admired at the fair and learned the animal could be bought for fifty pounds. Jasper insisted on giving Lavengro the money with which to buy the horse, and Lavengro reluctantly agreed. He and Jasper planned to meet about ten weeks later. Lavengro departed the following morning. On his way he met an old man who had just had his mule taken away from him by force. Lavengro rode after the offender and returned the mule.

One afternoon, as Lavengro and his horse were resting at the door of an inn, he met his old friend, the coachman, and through him obtained a job in the hostelry as a keeper of accounts in exchange for room and board for himself and his horse.

After a short while at the inn, Lavengro decided it was time for him to be on his way again. He had decided to go to Horncastle, a town at a distance of about one hundred and twenty-five miles. There he hoped to sell his horse at a good profit. He journeyed at a leisurely pace for several days and was nearing Horncastle late one evening when his horse, frightened by a light on a gig, threw him and knocked him unconscious. When he recovered consciousness, he found himself in the home of the man who owned the gig. The man informed him that his horse was safe and uninjured in the barn. A surgeon came soon after to examine Lavengro and to bandage his injured arm. While recuperating, Lavengro learned his host's story, how at the shattering of all his hopes for happiness with the death of his beloved, he had turned to the study of Chinese as a way to occupy his mind. Through this man, Lavengro learned much of the character of Chinese language and writing.

The surgeon finally declared Lavengro well enough to continue to the fair and gave him a letter to an innkeeper in Horncastle, so that he might find room and board for both himself and his horse. He proceeded to Horncastle, and the next morning, after displaying his horse's abilities to the best advantage, he sold him to Jack Dale, a horse-trader, who was acting as a representative for a Hungarian. Later that evening Lavengro and the Hungarian began a discourse in German, and Lavengro learned much of the history of Hungary. He also heard Jack Dale's life story. Jack, the son of a forger, had experienced a difficult and unhappy childhood. His life had been made even harder because of his physical ugliness. After his father was convicted and sent away to serve a prison sentence, Jack decided to live an upright life, as he had promised his father he would do. After much struggling, he had finally achieved a respectable place in the community.

While walking through the town the next morning, Lavengro saw a thimblerigger chased off by Jack Dale. Lavengro recognized the thimblerigger as a boyhood friend, Murtagh, and followed him. After much recollection of old times he gave Murtagh five pounds to return to Ireland and become a priest, a profession for which Murtagh had studied as a young man, but in which he had never been ordained because of difficulties over card playing.

Lavengro left Horncastle and walked eastward. He continued his journey for two days until he came to a large town. There, on the outskirts, he was accosted by a recruiting sergeant who tried to get him to join the Honorable East India Company and to go to India to fight. Lavengro was struck by the similarity of words the sergeant used and those of the gipsies. But when the sergeant noticed that Lavengro's hair was beginning to turn gray, he withdrew his offer. All of his life Lavengro was to wonder what new adventures he might have encountered if he had gone to India.

ROME HAUL

Type of work: Novel
Author: Walter D. Edmonds (1903-)
Type of plot: Regional romance
Time of plot: 1850
Locale: Erie Canal
First published: 1929

Principal characters:
DAN HARROW, a newcomer on the canal
MOLLY LARKINS, his cook
FORTUNE FRIENDLY, a canal character
GENTLEMAN JOE CALASH, a canal highwayman
JOTHAM KLORE, a canal bully

Critique:

There is a native tang and sharpness to this novel, which reclaims a segment of the American past in its picture of life along the Erie Canal. The book is vivid in its painstaking detail. The description of a flock of geese becomes more than description for pictorial effect; it becomes a symbol of the passing of a season and a passing of a way of life. There is poignancy and passion in the lives of people like Dan and Molly, Mrs. Gurget and Sol, and even Gentleman Joe Calash, who lived on the big ditch before the railroads destroyed its free, picturesque life. *Rome Haul* is authentic Americana.

The Story:

It was early summer. A young man carrying a carpetbag was walking to Boonville, New York, when a peddler named Jacob Turnesa picked him up. The young man said his name was Dan Harrow, lately a farmhand and now looking for work on the Erie Canal. A farm woman stopped them for news and gave them some root beer. She and Turnesa talked about Gentleman Joe Calash, a highwayman on the canal.

While Dan was looking for lodgings in one of the taverns, he saw Gentleman Joe Calash quarreling with Jotham Klore, canal bully. The highwayman struck Klore with his revolver and rode off in the darkness. Dan made no effort to give the alarm, not even for the two thousand dollars reward. Inwardly he felt sympathy for the robber, who was, like himself, alone and without friends.

Looking for work, Dan went to the *Ella-Romeyn,* the canal boat of Hector Berry. He found Berry playing cards with Sol Tinkle and Mrs. Gurget, Sol's cook. Mrs. Gurget was enormously fat and addicted to rum noggins with lots of lemon in them. Mrs. Berry was away, and so Hector, who could make no decisions without his wife, could only offer Dan a job for the short haul to

Rome. Later that day Mrs. Berry came aboard. She was suspicious of Dan because he was a stranger. Dan left the boat on reaching Rome.

At Rome he went to Hennessy's Saloon to see Julius Wilson about a job. While he waited he overheard more talk of Gentleman Joe Calash and of the reward for capturing him. Then Molly Larkins, a pretty canal cook, joined him. Molly cooked for Jotham Klore. When Klore came in, he accused Dan of getting too familiar with Molly. Angry, Dan hit Klore. Gentleman Joe suddenly appeared, knocked out Klore, and held Molly and Dan with his weapon. When they promised not to give the alarm, he made his escape.

A little later Wilson hired Dan for the haul to Albany on his boat, the *Xerxes*. Ben Rae was the captain and William Wampy, the cook and fiddler. Near Utica they saw a tall thin man running from a crowd that chased him into a haymow. They learned that the man was a traveling preacher who had been paid for six sermons but had tried to sneak out without giving the last one. Cornered, the minister preached a fire-and-brimstone sermon from the mow. After he had finished, Ben Rae took the minister aboard. He explained that though he had been trained for the ministry he was not really a preacher. His name was Fortune Friendly.

At the next stop Dan went ashore and encountered Molly Larkin again. She had given up her job with Klore and was going to Lucy Cashdollar's place to get a new position. Later that night Dan got into another fight with Klore and was knocked out. When he came to, he found that someone had carried him to the boat. He caught a glimpse of Gentleman Joe.

At Albany Samson Weaver, captain of the *Sarsy Sal*, hired him to drive his team. On the first day of their haul they saw a burning canal boat condemned because of cholera. Samson claimed he was not afraid of cholera, but he began to drink hard. Ill, he asked Dan to use his money for a doctor, but before Dan could get a doctor Samson died. While looking for an undertaker, Dan found a funeral director who offered him ten dollars for Samson's corpse. He took the money because he could not afford to pay for Samson's funeral.

Deciding to carry on alone, he headed for Lucy Cashdollar's agency. Lucy supplied girls as cooks for lonely canal men. Whether they married the canal men was no concern of hers, but usually she was glad if they did. By nightfall Molly was installed as the cook aboard the *Sarsy Sal*.

Mr. Butterfield, the agent for whom Samson had worked, offered to keep Dan hauling for him at the rates he had paid Samson. Together they planned to reclaim Samson's body from the surgeon to whom the undertaker had sold it, and give it decent burial.

On the wharf Dan saw old Fortune Friendly again and hired him as a driver. Molly and Friendly talked about Jotham Klore and agreed that sooner or later there would have to be a show-down fight between Klore and Dan. Molly and Dan found Samson's money hidden aboard the *Sarsy Sal*, over eight hundred dollars. Dan thought it was enough to start a small farm.

When Dan decided to buy a pair of horses at the Utica fair, Molly, Sol Tinkle, Mrs. Gurget, Hector Berry, and Mrs. Berry went with him. While Molly and Dan shopped for a suit for Dan, the clerk treated them as man and wife. Dan almost asked Molly to marry him, but he lost his chance when Hector hurried them along so that his wife could witness the hanging of a woman who had browbeaten her husband and finally killed him. Hector hoped the hanging would be a lesson to his nagging wife. At the fair Dan purchased two well-matched horses.

Autumn was in the air, and soon the canal would be closed for the season. Jotham Klore had not appeared. His fight with Dan would be postponed until spring. Dan and Molly saw Gentleman Joe again, and the highwayman gave them a jeweled pin as a memento. Dan had always linked himself with Gentleman Joe, feeling that neither he nor the highwayman was really part of the canal.

That winter Dan and Molly realized that the initial warmth of their feeling for each other was over. Molly confided to her friends that she intended to stay on the canal and that if Dan decided to go back to the land she would leave him. When spring came, Dan received an offer to work on a farm, but the offer was good only if he were not married. Not knowing what to do and unwilling to desert Molly, Dan headed the *Sarsy Sal* west on the canal. At the Lansing Kill they met Jotham Klore's boat coming toward the lock. Dan and Klore fought on a square of grass that the excited, shouting boaters marked off beside the locks. It was a battle that men talked about on the Erie for years afterward, Dan and Klore pummeling each other under the hot sunshine while Molly Larkin stood by to see what the outcome would be. Dan won, and he and Molly started west once more. But the feeling between them was no longer the same. Dan felt that she was pitying Klore, the beaten bully of the canal.

Then Gentleman Joe was caught and killed, and for the first time Dan saw the highwayman's cruel, mean face. Somehow, he felt that the highwayman's death freed him from life on the canal. One day Molly left him to go back to Klore. Dan took the farm job that had been offered him. He knew that he belonged in the farm country from which he had come.

ROMEO AND JULIET

Type of work: Drama
Author: William Shakespeare (1564-1616)
Type of plot: Romantic tragedy
Time of plot: Fifteenth century
Locale: Verona, Italy
First presented: c. 1595

Principal characters:

Romeo, son of the house of Montague
Juliet, daughter of the house of Capulet
Friar Lawrence, a Franciscan
Mercutio, Romeo's friend
Tybalt, Lady Capulet's nephew

Critique:

This story of two star-crossed lovers is one of Shakespeare's tenderest dramas. Shakespeare was evidently quite sympathetic toward Romeo and Juliet, and in attributing their tragedy to fate, rather than to a flaw in their characters, he raised them to heights near perfection. They are both sincere, kind, brave, loyal, virtuous, and desperately in love, and their tragedy is greater because of their innocence. The feud between the lovers' families represents the fate which Romeo and Juliet are powerless to overcome. The lines capture in poetry the youthful and simple passion which characterizes the play.

The Story:

Long ago in Verona, Italy, there lived two famous families, the Montagues and the Capulets. These two houses were deadly enemies, and their enmity did not stop at harsh words, but extended to bloody duels and sometimes death.

Romeo, son of old Montague, thought himself in love with haughty Rosaline, a beautiful girl who did not return his affection. Hearing that Rosaline was to attend a great feast at the house of Capulet, Romeo and his trusted friend, Mercutio, donned masks and entered the great hall as invited guests. But Romeo was no sooner in the ballroom than he noticed the exquisite Juliet, Capulet's daughter, and instantly forgot his disdainful Rosaline. Romeo had never seen Juliet before, and in asking her name he aroused the suspicion of Tybalt, a fiery member of the Capulet clan. Tybalt drew his sword and faced Romeo. But old Capulet, coming upon the two men, parted them, and with the gentility that comes with age requested that they have no bloodshed at the feast. Tybalt, however, was angered that a Montague should take part in Capulet festivities, and afterward nursed a grudge against Romeo.

Romeo spoke in urgent courtliness to Juliet and asked if he might kiss her hand. She gave her permission, much impressed by this unknown gentleman whose affection for her was so evident. Romeo then begged to kiss her lips, and when she had no breath to object, he pressed her to him. They were interrupted by Juliet's nurse, who sent the young girl off to her mother. When she had gone, Romeo learned from the nurse that Juliet was a Capulet. He was stunned, for he was certain that this fact would mean his death. He could never give her up. Juliet, who had fallen instantly in love with Romeo, discovered that he was a Montague, the son of a hated house.

That night Romeo, too much in love to go home to sleep, stole to Juliet's house and stood in the orchard beneath a balcony that led to her room. To his surprise, he saw Juliet leaning over the railing above him. Thinking herself alone, she began to talk of Romeo and wished aloud that he were not a Montague. Hearing her words, Romeo could contain himself no longer, but spoke to her. She was frightened at first, and when she saw who it was she was confused and ashamed that he had overheard her confession. But it was too late to pretend reluctance, as was the fashion for sweethearts in those days. Juliet freely admitted her passion, and the two exchanged vows of love. Juliet told Romeo that she would marry him and would send him word by nine o'clock the next morning to arrange for their wedding.

Romeo then went off to the monastery cell of Friar Lawrence to enlist his help in the ceremony. The good friar was much impressed with Romeo's devotion. Thinking that the union of a Montague and a Capulet would dissolve the enmity between the two houses, he promised to marry Romeo and Juliet.

Early the next morning, while he was in company with his two friends, Benvolio and Mercutio, Romeo received Juliet's message, brought by her nurse. He told the old woman of his arrangement with Friar Lawrence and bade her carry the word back to Juliet. The nurse kept the secret and gave her mistress the message. When Juliet appeared at the friar's cell at the appointed time, she and Romeo were married. But the time was short and Juliet had to hurry home. Before she left, Romeo promised that he would meet her in the orchard underneath the balcony after dark that night.

That same day, Romeo's friends, Mercutio and Benvolio, were loitering in the streets when Tybalt came by with some other members of the Capulet house. Tybalt, still holding his grudge against Romeo, accused Mercutio of keeping company with the hateful and villainous young Montague. Mercutio, proud of his friendship with Romeo, could not take insult lightly, for he was as hot-tempered when provoked as Tybalt himself. The two were beginning their heated quarrel when Romeo, who had just returned from his wedding, appeared. He was appalled at the situation because he knew that Juliet was fond of Tybalt, and he wished no injury to his wife's people. He tried in vain to settle the argument peaceably. Mercutio was infuriated by Romeo's soft words, and when Tybalt called Romeo a villain, Mercutio drew his sword and rushed to his friend's defense. But Tybalt, the better swordsman, gave Mercutio a mortal wound. Romeo could ignore the fight no longer. Enraged at the death of his friend, he rushed at Tybalt with drawn sword and killed him quickly. The fight soon brought crowds of people to the spot. For his part in the fray, Romeo was banished from Verona.

Hiding out from the police, he went, grief-stricken, to Friar Lawrence's cell. The friar advised him to go to his wife that night, and then at dawn to flee to Mantua until the friar saw fit to publish the news of the wedding. Romeo consented to follow this good advice. As darkness fell, he went to meet Juliet. When dawn appeared, heartsick Romeo left for Mantua.

Meanwhile, Juliet's father decided that it was time for his daughter to marry. Having not the slightest idea of her love for Romeo, the old man demanded that she accept her handsome and wealthy suitor, Paris. Juliet was horrified at her father's proposal but dared not tell him of her marriage because of Romeo's part in Tybalt's death. She feared that her husband would be instantly sought out and killed if her family learned of the marriage.

At first she tried to put off her father with excuses. Failing to persuade him, she went in dread to Friar Lawrence to ask the good monk what she could do. Telling her to be brave, the friar gave her a small flask of liquid which he told her to swallow the night before her wedding to Paris. This liquid would make her appear to be dead for a certain length of time; her seemingly lifeless body would then be placed in an open tomb for a day or two, and during that time the friar would send for Romeo, who should rescue his bride when she awoke from the powerful effects of the draught. Then, together, the two would be able to flee Verona. Juliet almost lost courage over this desperate venture, but she promised to obey the friar. On the way home she met Paris and modestly promised to be his bride.

The great house of the Capulets had no sooner prepared for a lavish wedding than it became the scene of a mournful funeral. For Juliet swallowed the strong liquid and seemed as lifeless as death itself. Her anguished family sadly placed her body in the tomb.

Meanwhile Friar Lawrence wrote to Romeo in Mantua, telling him of the plan by which the lovers could make their escape together. But these letters failed to reach Romeo before word of Juliet's death arrived. He determined to go to Verona and take his last farewell of her as she lay in her tomb, and there, with the help of poison procured from an apothecary, to die by her side.

Reaching the tomb at night, Romeo was surprised to find a young man there. It was Paris, who had come to weep over his lost bride. Thinking Romeo a grave robber, he drew his sword. Romeo, mistaking Paris for a hated Capulet, warned him that he was desperate and armed. Paris, in loyalty to Juliet, fell upon Romeo, but Romeo with all the fury of his desperation killed him. By the light of a lantern, Romeo recognized Paris and, taking pity on one who had also loved Juliet, drew him into the tomb so that Paris too could be near her. Then Romeo went to the bier of his beautiful bride. Taking leave of her with a kiss, he drank the poison he had brought with him and soon died by her side.

It was near the time for Juliet to awaken from her deathlike sleep. The friar, hearing that Romeo had never received his letters, went himself to deliver Juliet from the tomb. When he arrived, he found Romeo dead. Juliet, waking, asked for her husband. Then, seeing him lying near her with an empty cup in his hands, she guessed what he had done. She tried to kiss some of the poison from his lips that she too might die, but failing in this, she unsheathed his dagger and without hesitation plunged it into her breast.

By this time a guard had come up. Seeing the dead lovers and the body of Paris, he rushed off in horror to spread the news. When the Capulets and Montagues arrived at the tomb, the friar told them of the unhappy fate which had befallen Romeo and Juliet, whose only sin had been to love. His account of their tender and beautiful romance shamed the two families, and over the bodies of their dead children they swore to end the feud of many years.

ROMOLA

Type of work: Novel
Author: George Eliot (Mary Ann Evans, 1819-1880)
Type of plot: Historical romance
Time of plot: 1492-1498
Locale: Italy
First published: 1863

Principal characters:
BARDO, a Florentine scholar
ROMOLA, his daughter
TITO MELEMA, an adventurer
TESSA, a peasant girl
BALDASARRE CALVO, Tito's benefactor

Critique:

Romola is the story of a thoroughly good woman and a thoroughly wicked man. It is not an easy novel to read, for the author has attempted a work involving more than literary craftsmanship. She has dipped into the history of an age of political intrigue and mystical religious personalities, and often the plot of the story becomes lost in the maze of its own environment. But if the plot of this novel fails to stand out clearly from its background, the characters themselves can carry the burden of brilliant development.

The Story:

Tito Melema arrived in Florence penniless and unknown, but the sale of some rare jewels in his possession soon brought him into the circle of the wealthy, learned men of the city, among them the blind antiquarian, Bardo. Bardo was a great scholar who continued his annotations of Greek and Roman books through the eyes of his beautiful daughter, Romola. Bardo's only interest in life was his library and museum, and he had brought up his daughter in innocence of the outside world. Bardo accepted Tito eagerly, for he was always eager to meet a scholar and a man who had traveled much. He also told Tito of a son whom he had lost.

Tito's fortune had at last come to him with the sale of all his jewels except a single ring. He recalled that the money properly belonged to Baldasarre Calvo, the man who had been almost a father to him, the man who might now be a slave in the hands of the Turks. If Baldasarre were really alive, Tito told himself, he would spend the money for the old man's ransom. But he was not sure his foster father still lived.

Quickly Tito entrenched himself in the learned society of Florence. At the yearly festival of San Giovanni, patron saint of Florence, Tito, while sitting at a window with a friend, fancied that he saw in the crowd below a monk who gazed upon him with a malicious glance. Also glancing up at Tito from below was the beautiful Tessa, daughter of a milk vendor, whom Tito had met on the day of his arrival in Florence.

Later as he walked through the crowded streets, he rescued Tessa from some jostling revelers. When he had left her, he met the strange monk who had gazed at him from the crowd earlier in the afternoon. The monk, Fra Luca, gave him a note that had been brought from a pilgrim in the Near East. The note was from Baldassare, who pleaded that Tito should rescue him from slavery. Tito wondered what was so familiar about the Fra's face.

Attracted by the lovely, grave Romola, Tito spent many hours reading and writing manuscripts with her blind father. One day, when Tito had the opportunity to be alone with Romola for a brief moment, he declared his love to her, and Romola shyly confessed her love for him. That same day Monna Brigida paid a call on her cousin Bardo. When she accidentally mentioned the name of a Dominican monk, Dino, Tito discovered that the lost son of Bardo was not dead, but banished from his father's house. Realizing that Fra Luca was Dino, Tito feared exposure of his benefactor's slavery. He felt the time ripe for asking the old man for permission to marry Romola. Bardo readily consented.

Tito learned that Fra Luca was dangerously ill at Fiesole. One evening Romola told him that her dying brother had sent for her. Tito feared that Fra Luca would tell her the story which Tito had hoped would die with him. In despair, he wandered through the city and accidentally met Tessa. In a ribald ceremony which amused the gaping crowd, Tito allowed Tessa to believe that he had really married her. Unwilling to undeceive her, he made her promise to keep the marriage a secret. Meanwhile Dino died without revealing to Romola the story of Baldassare and the ungrateful Tito. Tito and Romola were married.

Bardo died, leaving Romola to carry on his scholarly work. Meanwhile political events in Florence helped to advance Tito's fortunes; he became an interpreter in negotiations with the French. On the day the French king arrived in the city, the soldiers led through the streets a group of prisoners who begged their ransoms from the Florentines. The mocking mob cut an old man loose from his fetters and allowed him to escape into the crowd. The prisoner ran blindly into Tito, who stood with a group of dignitaries on the steps of San Marco. Tito turned and found himself looking into the face of Baldasarre Calvo, who then disappeared into the crowd.

Fearing Baldasarre's revenge, Tito bought a coat of mail to wear under his clothes as a defense against the thrust of a knife or a spear. Tito begged Romola to sell her father's library and leave Florence with him. When Romola refused, he secretly sold the library and the antiquities it contained.

In his search for a place to stay, Baldasarre came by chance to the house where Tessa and her children by Tito lived with a deaf old peasant woman. The woman gave the old man permission to sleep in the loft. Tessa eagerly confided in Baldasarre. Tito had not abandoned her after their mock-marriage. At first he had been too flattered by her innocent admiration to tell her they were not man and wife. Instead, he had sent her to live with the old peasant woman, whom he paid well for the care she gave Tessa and his children, and he had sworn the two women to secrecy. While Baldasarre lay in the hayloft, Tito came to see Tessa. Suspecting from her description the identity of the old man, Tito went to his foster father to ask his forgiveness. He had decided that Baldasarre should come to live with him and share his comfort. But the old man did not forgive. He threatened to expose Tito and ruin him.

At a dinner in Florence, Baldasarre appeared to denounce Tito before his political friends. The trembling old man was pronounced mad and sent to prison. During a plague the jails were emptied to make room for the sick, and Baldasarre was released. He spied upon Tito until he learned that the youth had two wives, one noble and brave, the other timid and stupid. He approached Romola to expose Tito. When he told Romola of Tito's betrayal, she was able to piece together all the suspicions she had felt toward her husband, his long absences from home, his strange moods, and his secret fears. One day she found little Lillo, Tessa's son, wandering lost in the streets. She took the child to his home, and there she realized that she had discovered Tito's Tessa.

The final blow came to Romola when her godfather, Bernardo Del Nero, the only person in the world she still loved, was arrested. The Medici had been plotting to return to Florence, and Bernardo was a member of the committee which plotted their return. Romola knew Tito had been a spy for both political factions; he had gained his own safety by betraying others. Romola revealed to Tito her knowledge of Baldasarre's story and the truth of the old man's accusation against him. Then, disillusioned and sorrowful at the execution of Bernardo, she fled from Florence.

Tito also planned to flee from Florence, for his double dealings had been discovered. A mob followed him out of the city. To escape his pursuers, he threw away his money belt, and while the crowd scrambled for it, he jumped into the river. Weakly he pulled himself ashore on the opposite side. There Baldasarre, now a starving beggar, found him. In a final effort the old man threw himself upon his exhausted enemy and strangled him.

After passing many months in another city, Romola returned to Florence to learn of her husband's murder at the hands of an old man who had long been his enemy. Romola understood the justice of Tito's violent end. She found Tessa and the children and brought them to live with her. Hers was the one good deed that resulted from Tito's false and guilty life.

ROUGHING IT

Type of work: Record of travel
Author: Mark Twain (Samuel L. Clemens, 1835-1910)
Type of plot: Travel sketches and autobiography
Time of plot: Mid-nineteenth century
Locale: The West
First published: 1872

Principal characters:
MARK TWAIN, a tenderfoot
BRIGHAM YOUNG, the Mormon leader
SLADE THE TERRIBLE, a Western desperado
HANK ERICKSON, a correspondent of Horace Greeley

Critique:

Mark Twain's recollections are interesting because they present a picture of the still expanding Western frontier. Although the book is badly organized, it is excellent for its eye-witness accounts of Virginia City and the Nevada mining camps, Mormonism, early San Francisco, and the Hawaiian Islands. Always, of course, the book is enlivened by Mark Twain's boisterous, native humor.

The Story:

When Mark Twain traveled West with his brother, he had no idea that he would stay out there for any long period of time. His brother had been appointed Secretary of the Nevada Territory, and Twain went along as his secretary, with no salary. Instead of the three months he intended to stay, however, he was six years away from home.

The trip itself was exciting. There were many inconveniences, naturally, as well as danger from the Indians and attacks by highwaymen. But Twain saw the country and enjoyed the adventure, nonetheless. On the way he came face to face with Slade the Terrible. Slade was foreman of the stagecoach workers, a man who would kill anyone if crossed, a man whose repute went far and wide. To Twain he seemed very polite, a gentleman, and quite harmless. But Slade's days were numbered. The vigilantes were after him. Although he was warned, he was drunk at the time, and so was unable to avoid capture. Brought to trial by a vigilante court, he was found guilty and ordered hanged. He died without having seen his wife, probably a fortunate circumstance for the vigilantes. At an earlier time, with blazing six-shooters flaming from under her petticoats, she had rescued Slade from a similar situation.

Twain also met Brigham Young, the Mormon leader, who bemoaned the fact that he had so many wives, wives who were jealous and argumentative. Out of curiosity Twain also read the Mormon Bible.

Twain and some companions set out to prospect for gold in the Nevada mountains. Once they were caught in a snowstorm and seemingly doomed to die. Each of them renounced a particular vice. Twain threw away his pipe, another his cigarettes, and the third his bottle of whiskey. But they did not die. At dawn they discovered that they had been but a few yards away from an inn. Then Twain was sorry he had thrown away his pipe. He found it in the snow and sneaked behind the barn for a smoke. There he came upon one of his comrades drinking from the whiskey bottle and the other rolling a cigarette.

At first they had no luck in their search for gold. True, they found places where there was gold, but the operations needed to extract it were too complicated and expensive. Finally they had real luck. When they found rock that would yield millions of dollars for them, they claimed it and dreamed of spending their lives in luxury. The law specified that some work must be done on each new claim within ten days; otherwise the claimants lost their right to the claim and anyone else could get control of it. Twain left, having confidence that his partners would work the new claim. But each thought the other would do the work, and so none was done. At the end of ten days the mine was claimed by others. Twain and his partners were relegated to a common, working existence.

He wandered from place to place, working for newspapers, being fired from them, and moving on. Eventually he landed in San Francisco and went from there to the Hawaiian Islands, where he visited the spot on which Captain Cook had been killed by natives. At first the natives had treated the British explorer kindly. Cook, in turn, had made them believe that he was a god, and he had treated them brutally. One day, injured, he showed his pain. Convinced by his hurt that he was not divine, but a man like themselves, the natives killed him — rightly, according to Twain, for he had returned their kindness with cruelty.

Then there was Hank Erickson, the crazy stranger. Erickson had once written a letter to Horace Greeley. A widow had a son who liked turnips. She wanted to find out if turnips sometimes grew into vines. This was the question Erickson asked in the letter he wrote to Greeley. Greeley replied, but the handwriting was so illegible that nothing could be made of it. In fact, every time Erickson read the letter it seemed different, but always meaningless. Finally he deciphered it and became convinced that Greeley had insulted him. Erickson wrote to Greeley again. The publisher had a clerk copy the letter, which turned out to be informative and not at all insulting. Twain slyly maintained that he never found out why Erickson was crazy.

Twain decided to try his luck at lecturing. At his first appearance he was afraid that nobody would laugh at his jokes. He gave free tickets to various people, and told them to laugh at the right moments. When he got to the auditorium the seats were empty. He sat in the wings and felt sad. However, he soon heard the noise of voices and came out of his dream to find that the hall was crowded. His lecture was a great success; people even laughed when his talk was not funny.

When he returned to San Francisco from Hawaii, Twain planned a trip to Japan. Later he abandoned the idea to go back home. He traveled to New York by way of Panama. So ended his Wild West and Hawaiian adventures.

SALAMMBÔ

Type of work: Novel
Author: Gustave Flaubert (1821-1880)
Type of plot: Historical romance
Time of plot: Third century B.C.
Locale: Carthage
First published: 1862

Principal characters:
HAMILCAR, Suffete of Carthage
SALAMMBÔ, his daughter
MATHÔ, a Libyan chief
SPENDIUS, a Greek slave
NARR' HAVAS, a Numidian chief

Critique:

Salammbô is a monumental description of Carthage while that city-republic was still a great power. Into this novel Flaubert put five years of reading, years when he read every scrap of information he could find about Carthage during the Punic Wars. The result is a vast, erudite reconstruction for which there are few parallels. Flaubert was a careful, slow worker, and this novel demonstrates his exact style. Character analysis is scant and the plot little more than animated history, but critical opinion accords it a distinguished place because of its faithful picture of the people and the times.

The Story:

Inside the walls of Carthage a vast army of mercenaries gathered in the gardens of Hamilcar. There were Ligurians, Lusitanians, nomadic barbarians from North Africa, Romans, Greeks, Gauls, and Egyptians. A feast for these thousands of hired warriors was in preparation. Odors of cooking food came from Hamilcar's kitchens, and the Council of Elders had provided many oxen to roast over the open fires in the gardens. The men, tired from their defeat at the hands of the Romans and weary from the sea journey over the Mediterranean, waited with ill-concealed impatience for the feasting to begin.

More than that, they were in an ugly mood because they had not been paid. Hamilcar, their beloved leader even in defeat, had promised them their pay many times. The elders, however, parsimonious and afraid of this huge assembly of fierce foreigners, withheld their pay. Offers of token payment had been angrily refused.

While the revelry was at its height, many men were emboldened by drink and began to pillage the palace of Hamilcar. In a private lake, surrounded by a heavy hedge, they found fish with jewels in their gill flaps. With joy they ruthlessly tore off the gems and boiled the sacred fish for their feast. The slaves brought new foods and fresh casks of wine for the drunken revelers. Then above them on a high balcony appeared Salammbô, the priestess of the moon goddess and daughter of Hamilcar. Her great beauty stilled the wild barbarians. She called down a malediction on their heads and in a wailing refrain lamented the sad state of Carthage.

Among those who watched the young

girl, none was more attracted than Narr' Havas, a Numidian chief who had been sent by his father to Carthage to serve with Hamilcar. Although he had been in Carthage six months, this was his first sight of Salammbô. Also watching her keenly was Mathô, a gigantic Libyan. He had heard of Salammbô, and already loved her. With Mathô was Spendius, a former Greek slave who, tricky and shrewd, played the jackal to brave Mathô. Spendius had been long in service to Carthage, and he whispered the delights of Salammbô to his master.

The elders gave each soldier a piece of gold if he promised to go to Sicca and wait for the rest of his money to be sent to him. The gold and the solemn promises enticed many, and finally all the mercenaries and barbarians joined the march to Sicca. Many of their leaders distrusted the words of the elders, but they were sure of better treatment when Hamilcar returned to Carthage.

Mathô lay in his tent all day long at Sicca. He was in love, and since he had no prospect of ever seeing Salammbô again, he despaired. Finally the wily Spendius profited greatly by Mathô's inaction and ingratiated himself with the Libyan.

At Sicca the enormous Hanno appeared in his costly litter. Hanno, one of the Council of Elders, was tremendously fat; the fat on his legs even covered his toenails and his body was covered with weeping sores. Pompously he addressed the crowd, telling them of Carthage's intent to pay later and urging them all to return to their homes. But the Gauls and the Campanians and the rest understood not a word of Punic. Spendius leaped up beside Hanno and offered to translate. Falsely he told the soldiers that Hanno was exalting his own gods and reviling theirs. The mob became unruly and Hanno barely escaped with his life.

Soon the inflamed barbarians were on the march again, this time to besiege Carthage. At their head rode Mathô, Narr' Havas, and Spendius, now a leader.

The mob camped at the gates of Carthage. The city sent Gisco, a famous warrior, to treat with them. In fear the Carthaginians raised a little money and began to pay the soldiers. They felt powerless without Hamilcar. But the payment was slow. Gisco had insufficient funds, and many barbarians claimed more pay than they merited.

As the unrest grew, Spendius went to Mathô with a project of his own. He was sure he had found a way into the city, and if Mathô would follow his lead and help him in his own private errand, he would take Mathô to Salammbô.

Outside the walls Spendius had found a loose stone in the pavement over the aqueduct that supplied the city with water. Mathô with his giant strength lifted the stone, and the two swam with the current in the darkness until they came to a reservoir inside the city itself. Then Spendius revealed his project. He and Mathô were to steal the zaïmph, the mysterious veil of Tanit, goddess of the moon. Since the Carthaginians put their trust in Tanit, and Tanit's strength lay in the veil, Spendius hoped to cripple the morale of the city. Mathô was fearful of committing sacrilege, but he was forced to consent in order to see Salammbô.

While the female guards slept, the two stole into Tanit's sanctuary and Mathô seized the veil. Then quietly Spendius led the trembling Mathô, who wore the sacred robe, into Salammbô's sleeping chamber.

As Mathô advanced with words of love to Salammbô's bed, the terrified girl awoke and shouted an alarm. Instantly servants came running. Mathô had to flee, but while he wore the sacred veil no one dared to lay a hand on him. So Mathô left the city and returned to the barbarians with his prize.

Hamilcar returned to Carthage in time to organize the defense of the city, and the siege melted away. Because the barbarians were short of food, they marched to Utica to demand supplies. Only loosely bound to Carthage, Utica was glad to harass Carthage by aiding its enemies.

Newly supplied with arms and food, the barbarians were a more formidable host. Hamilcar, however, had brought his army out of Carthage and joined the battle on the plain. Although the Carthaginians were few in number, they were disciplined and well led. They engaged the barbarians several times, always indecisively. Finally, by a stroke of luck, the army of Hamilcar was trapped, and the barbarian's surrounded the city's defenders.

Meanwhile Salammbô was goaded by the high priest into retrieving the sacred veil. Disguised and with a guide, she made her way into the barbarian camp, under priestly injunction to do whatever might be necessary to reclaim the robe. Finding Mathô's tent, she went in and asked for the veil which hung among his trophies of war. Mathô was thunderstruck and stammered eager protestations of love. Remembering the commands of the priest, Salammbô submitted to Mathô. While the Libyan slept, she took the veil and went unmolested into her father's camp.

Hamilcar noticed immediately that the thin golden chain linking her ankles was broken, and in his shame he promised her to Narr' Havas, who had long since deserted the barbarians and returned to help Hamilcar. But the marriage was delayed until after the final defeat of Hamilcar's enemies.

Hamilcar, wary of the stalemate in the battle, led his followers back to Carthage and the barbarians again laid siege to the city. Spendius sought to end the siege by breaking the aqueduct. Thirst and famine threatened the city from within. When pestilence broke out, the children of Carthage were burned in sacrifice to Moloch. Moloch was appeased, and torrential rains saved the city.

With help from his allies, Hamilcar began to reduce the forces of the enemy. A large part of the army was trapped in a defile in the mountains and left to starve. Mathô was taken prisoner.

On the wedding day of Narr' Havas and Salammbô, Mathô was led through the city and tortured by the mob. Still alive but with most of his flesh torn away, he staggered up to the nuptial dais of Salammbô. There he fell dead. Salammbô recalled how he had knelt before her, speaking gentle words. When the drunken Narr' Havas embraced her in token of possession and drank to the greatness of Carthage, she lifted a cup and drank also. A moment later she fell back on the wedding dais, dead. So died the warrior and the priestess who by their touch had profaned the sacred robe of Tanit.

SANCTUARY

Type of work: Novel
Author: William Faulkner (1897-)
Type of plot: Psychological melodrama
Time of plot: 1929
Locale: Mississippi and Memphis, Tennessee
First published: 1931

Principal characters:
Popeye, a racketeer
Horace Benbow, a lawyer
Temple Drake, a girl attacked and held by Popeye
Tommy, a moonshiner killed by Popeye
Lee Goodwin, a moonshiner accused of Tommy's murder
Ruby Lamar, Goodwin's woman
Reba Rivers, madam of a Memphis bawdy house
Gowan Stevens, a college student

Critique:

Sanctuary is a harsh and brutal book which on one level reads like a sensational and motiveless recital of horrors enacted by a sinister cast of grotesques and perverts. Beneath its surface violence, however, the novel has a deeper meaning for which an interesting allegorical interpretation has been suggested: The social order of the old South has been corrupted and defiled by progressive modernism and materialistic exploitation, represented by Popeye and his bootlegging activities, so that historic tradition, symbolized by Horace Benbow, is powerless to act because it is opposed by middle-class apathy and inbred violence which victimizes both the Negro and poor white trash. Viewed in this light, *Sanctuary* is a social document which has its proper place in William Faulkner's tragic legend of the South.

The Story:

Horace Benbow, on his way to Jefferson one afternoon, stopped to drink from a spring on the Old Frenchman place. When he rose he saw an undersized man in a black suit watching him, the man's hand in a pocket which held his gun. Satisfied at last that the lawyer was not a revenue officer, Popeye led Benbow to the gaunt, gutted ruins of a plantation house. That night the lawyer ate with Popeye, several moonshiners, and a blind and deaf old man, the father of Lee Goodwin, one of the moonshiners. They were fed by Ruby, Goodwin's woman. Later Benbow was given a lift into Jefferson on a truck loaded with whiskey on its way to Memphis.

The next afternoon, at his widowed sister's home, Benbow watched her walking in the garden with young Gowan Stevens. Stevens left that evening after supper because he had a date with a girl at the State University the following night. The girl was Temple Drake.

After a dance Stevens got drunk. He awoke the next morning in front of the railroad station. A special train taking university students to a baseball game had already left. Driving rapidly, Stevens caught up with the train in the next town. Temple jumped from the train and climbed into his car. Disgusted with his disheveled appearance, she ordered him to drive her back to the university. Stevens insisted that he had promised to drive her to the game. On the way he decided to stop at Goodwin's place to buy more whiskey.

Stevens wrecked his car when he struck a barrier across the lane leading to the house. Popeye took Temple and Stevens to the house. Temple went into the kitchen, where Ruby sat smoking and watching the door.

When she saw Stevens again, he was drunk. Then Popeye refused to drive them back to town. Temple was frightened. Ruby told Temple to go into the dining-room to eat with the men.

One of the men tried to seize her and Temple ran from the room. Tommy, one of the moonshiners, followed her with a plate of food. The men began to quarrel and Stevens was knocked unconscious and carried into the house. Goodwin and a moonshiner named Van tussled until Popeye stopped them. When Van found Temple in one of the bedrooms, Goodwin knocked him down.

Then began a series of comings and goings in the bedroom. Ruby came to stand quietly in the darkness. Later Popeye appeared and stood silently over the girl. After he had gone, Goodwin entered to claim a raincoat in which Temple had wrapped herself. Popeye returned once more, followed noiselessly by Tommy, who squatted in the dark beside Ruby. When the men finally left the house to load the truck for its run to Memphis, Ruby took Temple out to the barn and stayed with her until daylight.

Stevens awoke early and started out for the nearest house to hire a car. Feeling that he could not face Temple again after his drunken night, he paid a farmer to drive to the house for Temple, while he thumbed a ride into town.

Learning that Stevens had already gone, Temple went into the kitchen with Ruby. When she left the house again, she saw the shadowy outline of a man who was squatting in the bushes and watching her. She returned to the house. Seeing Goodwin coming toward the house, she ran to the barn and hid in the corncrib.

Watching, Popeye saw Goodwin looking from the house toward the barn. In the barn Popeye found Tommy at the door of the corncrib. While Tommy stood watching Goodwin, Popeye shot him. A short time later Goodwin told Ruby that Tommy had been shot. He sent her to the nearest house to phone for the sheriff.

Benbow stayed with his sister for two days. When Goodwin was brought in, charged with Tommy's murder, Benbow agreed to defend the prisoner. Goodwin, afraid of Popeye, claimed only that he had not shot Tommy. It was Ruby who told Benbow that Popeye had taken Temple away in his car.

Benbow attempted to trace the girl's whereabouts. State Senator Snopes told him that Judge Drake's daughter was supposed to be visiting an aunt in Michigan after an attempted runaway marriage.

A week before the opening of the court session Benbow met Senator Snopes again. For a price the politician was willing to reveal that Temple was in Reba Rivers' bawdy house in Memphis. Benbow went at once to see the girl. Temple, although reluctant to talk, confirmed many details of Ruby's story. The lawyer realized that without the girl's testimony he could not prove that Goodwin was innocent of Popeye's crime.

One morning Temple bribed Reba's colored servant to let her out of the house to make a phone call. That evening she managed to sneak out again, just as a car with Popeye in it pulled up at the curb. When she refused to go back to her room, he took her to the Grotto, where Temple had arranged to meet a young man called Red, whom Popeye had taken to her room.

At the Grotto she danced with Red while Popeye played at the crap table. She begged Red to take her away with him. Later in the evening two of Popeye's henchmen forced Temple into a car waiting outside. As they drove away, Temple saw Popeye sitting in a parked car.

Red's funeral was held in the Grotto. For the occasion the tables had been draped in black and a downtown orchestra had been hired to play hymns. Drinks were on the house.

The night before the trial Benbow learned from Reba Rivers that Popeye and Temple had left her house. Ruby took the witness stand the next day and she told the story of Tommy's murder. She and Benbow spent that night in the jail cell with Goodwin, who was afraid that Popeye might shoot him from one of the buildings across the street.

Temple, located through the efforts of Senator Snopes, was called to testify the next morning. She indicated that Goodwin was the man who had first attacked her on the day of Tommy's murder. Goodwin was convicted. That night a mob dragged the prisoner from the jail and burned him.

Popeye, on his way to Pensacola, was arrested for the murder of a policeman in Birmingham. The murder had occurred the same night Red was shot outside the Grotto. Popeye made no defense, and his only claim was that he knew nothing about the Birmingham shooting. Convicted, he was executed for a crime he had not committed.

Judge Drake took his daughter to Europe. In the Luxembourg Gardens with her father, listening in boredom to the band, Temple sat in quiet, sullen discontent.

SAPPHO

Type of work: Novel
Author: Alphonse Daudet (1840-1897)
Type of plot: Naturalism
Time of plot: Nineteenth century
Locale: Paris
First published: 1884

Principal characters:
JEAN GAUSSIN, a student
FANNY LEGRAND, his mistress
IRÈNE, his fiancée
BOUCHEREAU, a famous physiologist
DÉCHELETTE, a wealthy engineer
LAGOURNERIE, a poet
DE POTTER, a composer
ROSA, de Potter's mistress
FLAMANT, convict engraver
CÉSAIRE, Jean's uncle

Critique:

To many people Daudet's name is a synonym for naturalism, and in some respects Daudet is the outstanding representative of his school. His writing is carefully documented; his style releases a sustained emotion. Above all Daudet is an intuitive psychologist. *Sappho,* concerned with the half-world of prostitutes and crime, is generally considered a surprisingly delicate and sure study of a distasteful milieu.

The Story:

Déchelette, a vigorous though aging engineer, spent all but two months of the year on construction projects far from Paris. Each summer, however, he returned to the gay city to compress into two months enough pleasure to make up for his enforced absences. To one of his masquerade parties came Jean Gaussin, a young student from the south of France. Jean was bewildered at the extravagant ball. Unhappy and lost, he wandered into a gallery and found there a woman dressed as an Egyptian.

When he was ready to leave, the woman stopped him and asked him to take her to his room. In this way he became her lover. Her name, she told him, was Fanny Legrand.

She continued to come to his room frequently. When he finally visited her apartment, he was astonished at the luxury of the place. In the morning before he was up, the servant announced a visitor. Fanny went into another room to see the early caller, and Jean was horrified to overhear a violent quarrel. Fanny was shouting insults and curses at the man in the language of the gutter. Finally the man began to sob and pressed money on Fanny. He begged her not to dismiss him, whatever else she did. Jean went back to his classes much disturbed.

Unable to end the affair, he rented an apartment and set up housekeeping with Fanny. She proved to be a capable housewife and a demanding mistress. Jean felt settled and at ease. He made good progress in his consular studies.

The following summer he met Déchelette and Caoudal, a sculptor, at a café and learned the past history of his mistress. Thirty years before, she had lived with Caoudal and had been the model for his well-known figure of Sappho. She had lived with Déchelette at various times and LaGournerie, the poet, had kept her for some years. Jean felt nauseated when he came to understand that she owed her imaginative diction to LaGournerie, her graceful gestures to Caoudal, her ample spending money to Déchelette. One of her latest lovers had been Flamant. The poor man, an engraver, had counterfeited some bank notes and had been sentenced to prison. Jean learned that Fanny was nearly fifty, almost thirty years older than he.

When he taxed Fanny with his knowledge, she readily admitted her past. When she protested her love for him alone, Jean asked for her box of keepsakes. In her letters he traced her history of loose love for nearly thirty years. The farewell letter from Flamant asked Fanny to look after his young son. Jean suspected that the child was Fanny's also. But in spite of this knowledge, Jean could not leave his mistress after Fanny meekly submitted to his reproaches. They continued to live together.

Césaire, Jean's uncle, came to Paris with news that Jean's family had been ruined by failure of the grape crop and that he had been sent to Paris to collect an old debt of eight thousand francs. With Fanny's help, Césaire collected the money but soon lost it gambling. Fanny volunteered to get more money from Déchelette. Jean and Césaire awaited her return anxiously. Jean tortured himself by imagining how she would get it. After some hours Fanny returned with the money. Césaire left for home, loudly asserting the goodness of Fanny and promising to keep silent about Jean's loose life.

With the decline in the Gaussin fortunes, Jean and Fanny decided to separate. Fanny went to work managing an apartment for Rosa, mistress of the wealthy composer, de Potter. She and Jean were together each Sunday on her day off. After reckoning his decreased allowance, Jean found that they could take a small hut in the country. He was sure they could exist there for another year, and then he would be through with his course of study. But Jean hated their life in the country. The grumbling old servant Fanny hired had been revealed as Fanny's mother. Her father, a dissolute cab driver, came to visit them. Flamant's child, a savage boy of six, lived with them. Jean counted on an appointment to a consular office to break away from Fanny.

On his trips into town, he became acquainted with Bouchereau, the eminent physiologist. Then he met and fell in love with Bouchereau's niece, Irène. Jean hoped that he would receive an appointment in South America and that Irène would go with him as his wife.

As he was gradually permitted to see Irène more often, Jean became troubled. Her innocent enjoyment of simple things was disturbing, for he had become so satiated with his experienced courtesan that other women had little attraction for him. When he told Fanny of his approaching marriage, a furious quarrel broke out.

Shortly afterward Jean met de Potter, who congratulated him on his approaching marriage. De Potter's story was a horrible warning to Jean; the composer had never been able to get away from his mistress, and the attraction of her flesh had held him fast for many years. De Potter's wife rarely saw him; his children were almost strangers. De Potter was bitter about his wasted life, but he could not leave the aging Rosa, whom he supported in luxury.

Despite de Potter's example, despite his engagement to Irène, Jean resolved to keep Fanny. On the eve of his departure for his post in South America, he broke his engagement to Irène and wrote to Fanny to join him in Marseilles. Waiting with tense expectancy in a hotel room in the Mediterranean port, Jean received a letter from Fanny. She had gone back with Flamant on his release from prison. Fanny was too old to go traveling about. She could not leave her beloved Paris.

THE SCARLET LETTER

Type of work: Novel
Author: Nathaniel Hawthorne (1804-1864)
Type of plot: Psychological romance
Time of plot: Early days of the Massachusetts Colony
Locale: Boston
First published: 1850

Principal characters:
HESTER PRYNNE, a woman convicted of adultery
ARTHUR DIMMESDALE, a minister of the community
ROGER CHILLINGWORTH, a physician, and Hester's husband
PEARL, Hester's daughter

Critique:

Critics have called *The Scarlet Letter* the greatest book ever written in the Western Hemisphere. The theme of the novel is the universal subject of sin. Specifically, Hawthorne traces the effect of one particular sin on the lives of four people. In the pages of *The Scarlet Letter* we watch the almost beneficial effect of her sin upon Hester Prynne, who wears her shame openly for all the world to see; upon the Reverend Arthur Dimmesdale, who is killed by the distressing secret which he keeps hidden in his own breast; upon Roger Chillingworth, who becomes a devil incarnate; and upon little Pearl, who develops into a capricious, wayward child, but still sympathetic and lovable.

The Story:

On a summer morning in Boston, in the early days of the Massachusetts Colony, a throng of curious people had gathered outside the jail in Prison Lane. They were there to watch for Hester Prynne, who had been found guilty of adultery by a court of stern Puritan judges. Condemned to wear on the breast of her gown the scarlet letter, the A which stood for adulteress, she was to stand on the stocks before the meeting house, so that her shame might be a warning and a reproach to all who saw her. The crowd waited to see her ascend the scaffold with her child in her arms, and there for three hours bear her shame alone.

At last, escorted by the town beadle, the woman appeared. She moved serenely to the steps of the scaffold and stood quietly under the staring eyes that watched her public disgrace. It was whispered in the gathering that she had been spared the penalty of death or branding only through the intercession of the Reverend Arthur Dimmesdale, into whose church she had brought her scandalous sin.

While Hester stood on the scaffold, an elderly, almost deformed man appeared from the edge of the forest. When her agitation made it plain that she had recognized him, he put his finger to his lips as a sign of silence.

Hester's story was well-known in the community. She was the daughter of an ancient house of decayed fortune, and when she was young her family had married her to a husband who had great repute as a scholar. For some years they had lived in Antwerp. Two years before, the husband had sent his wife alone across the ocean to the Massachusetts Colony, intending to follow her as soon as he could put his affairs in order. There had been news of his departure, but his ship had never been heard of again. Hester, a young, attractive widow, had lived quietly in Boston until the time of her disgrace.

The scaffold of the pillory on which Hester stood was situated next to the balcony of the church where all the dignitaries of the colony sat to watch her hu-

THE SCARLET LETTER by Nathaniel Hawthorne. Published by Houghton Mifflin

miliation. The ministers of the town called on her to name the man who with herself was equally guilty, and the most eloquent of those who exhorted her was the Reverend Arthur Dimmesdale, her pastor. Still Hester refused to name the father of her child, and she was led back to the prison after her period of public shame had ended.

On her return to prison Hester was found to be in a state of great nervous excitement. When at last medical aid was called, a man was found who professed knowledge of medicine. His name was Roger Chillingworth, he told the jailer, recently arrived in town after a year of residence among the Indians. Chillingworth was the stranger who had appeared so suddenly from the forest while Hester stood on the scaffold that afternoon, and she knew him as her husband, the scholar Prynne. His ship had been wrecked on the coast and he had been captive among the Indians for many months.

He also asked Hester to name the father of her child. When she refused, he stated that he would remain in Boston to practice medicine, swearing at the same time that he would devote the rest of his life to discovering the identity of the man who had dishonored him. He commanded Hester not to betray the relationship between them, and she swore she would keep his secret.

When Hester's term of imprisonment was over, she found a small house on the outskirts of town, far removed from other habitation. There with her child, whom she had named Pearl, she settled down to earn a living from needlework, an outcast from society and still wearing the scarlet emblem on her breast.

Hester Prynne dressed her child in bright highly-ornamented costumes, in contrast to her own sober dress. As she grew up, Pearl proved to be a capricious, wayward child, hard to discipline. One day Hester called on Governor Bellingham to deliver a pair of embroidered gloves. She also wanted to see him about the custody of Pearl, for there was a movement afoot among the strict church members to take the child away from her. In the garden of the governor's mansion, Hester found the governor, Dimmesdale, and old Roger Chillingworth. Because the perverse Pearl would not repeat the catechism, the governor was about to separate the child from her mother. Dimmesdale saved the situation, however, by a persuasive speech which resulted in the decision to let Hester keep Pearl, who seemed to be strangely attracted to the minister.

Roger Chillingworth had become intimately acquainted with Arthur Dimmesdale both as his parishioner and his doctor, for the minister had been in ill health ever since the physician had come to town. As the two men lodged in the same house, the physician came to know Dimmesdale's inmost thoughts and feelings. The minister was much perturbed by thoughts of conscience and guilt, but when he expressed these ideas in generalities to his congregation, the people thought him only the more righteous. Slowly in Chillingworth the conviction grew that Dimmesdale was Pearl's father, and he conjured up for the sick man visions of agony, terror, and remorse.

One night, unable to sleep, Dimmesdale walked to the pillory where Hester Pyrnne had stood in ignominy. He went up the steps and stood for a long time in the same place. A little later Hester, who had been watching at a deathbed, came by with little Pearl. The minister called them to the scaffold, saying that they had been there before when he lacked courage to stand beside them. Thus the three stood together, Dimmesdale acknowledging himself as Pearl's father and Hester's partner in sin. This striking tableau was not unobserved. Roger Chillingworth watched them from the shadows.

Hester Prynne was so shocked by Dimmesdale's feeble and unhealthy condition that she determined to see her former husband and plead with him to free the sick minister from his evil influence.

One day she met the old physician gathering herbs in the forest and begged him to be merciful to his victim. But Chillingworth was inexorable; he would not forego his revenge on the man who had wronged him. Hester then advised him that she would tell Arthur Dimmesdale their secret and warn him against his physician. A short time later, Hester and Pearl intercepted Dimmesdale in the forest as he was returning from a missionary journey to the Indians. Hester confessed her true relation with Chillingworth and warned the minister against the physician's evil influence. She and the clergyman decided to leave the colony together in secret, to take passage in a ship then in the harbor and return to the Old World. They were to leave four days later, after Dimmesdale had preached the Election Sermon.

Election Day, on which the new governor was to be installed, was a holiday in Boston, and the port was lively with the unaccustomed presence of sailors from the ship in the harbor. In the crowd was the captain of the vessel, with whom Hester had made arrangements for her own and Dimmesdale's passage. During the morning the captain informed Hester that Roger Chillingworth had also arranged for passage on the ship. Filled with despair, Hester turned away and went with Pearl to listen to Dimmesdale's sermon.

Unable to find room within the church, she stood at the foot of the scaffold where at least she could hear the sound of his voice. As the procession left the church, everyone had only words of praise for the minister's inspired address. Dimmesdale walked like a man in a dream and once he tottered and almost fell. When he saw Hester and Pearl at the foot of the scaffold, he stepped out of the procession and called them to him. Then, taking them by the hand, he climbed the steps of the pillory. Almost fainting, but with a voice terrible and majestic, the minister admitted his guilt to the watching people. With a sudden motion he tore the ministerial band from across his breast and sank dying to the platform. When he thus exposed his breast, witnesses said that the stigma of the scarlet letter A was seen imprinted on the flesh above his heart.

Chillingworth, no longer able to wreak his vengeance on Dimmesdale, died within the year, bequeathing his considerable property to Pearl. For a time Hester disappeared from the colony, but years later she returned alone to live in her humble thatched cottage and to wear as before the scarlet emblem on her breast. But the scarlet letter, once her badge of shame, became an emblem of her tender mercy and kindness — an object of veneration and reverence to those whose sorrows she alleviated by her deeds of kindness and mercy. At her death she directed that the only inscription on her tombstone should be the letter A.

THE SCHOOL FOR SCANDAL

Type of work: Drama
Author: Richard Brinsley Sheridan (1751-1816)
Type of plot: Comedy of manners
Time of plot: Eighteenth century
Locale: London
First presented: 1777

Principal characters:
Sir Peter Teazle, an elderly nobleman
Lady Teazle, his young wife
Maria, Sir Peter's ward
Sir Oliver Surface, Sir Peter's friend

JOSEPH SURFACE, and
CHARLES SURFACE, Sir Oliver's nephews
LADY SNEERWELL, Lady Teazle's friend
ROWLEY, Sir Peter's servant

Critique:

The School for Scandal contains elements of Restoration comedy as well as the usual sentimentalism of the comedy of sensibility. There are two plots: Lady Sneerwell's love for Charles and her scandalous tales about Lady Teazle and the latter's relations with Joseph, and Sir Oliver Surface's tests to discover the worthier of his two nephews. Sheridan brilliantly brings the two plots together in the famous screen scene, which demonstrates his adeptness as a writer of comedy. *The School for Scandal,* revived from time to time as a costume play, continues to hold the interest of audiences everywhere.

The Story:

Lady Sneerwell, who in her youth was the target of slander, had set her life upon a course to reduce the reputations of other women to the level of her own. Aided by her intimate, Snake, she was intriguing to involve the Teazles in scandal, to bring Joseph Surface's true character to light, to wreck the love of Charles and Maria, and to gain Charles for herself along with Sir Oliver's fortune. To her the world was nothing but scandal and scandalous intrigues, and she did her best to make her vision a reality. But when she abused Charles Surface, Maria, Sir Peter Teazle's ward, refused to listen to her. Instead, Maria trustingly confided in Lady Candour, whose defense of a reputation insured its complete annihilation.

Sometimes Sir Peter Teazle pondered the wisdom of his marriage to Lady Teazle, doubting the judgment of an old bachelor in marrying a young wife. Lady Teazle was a country-bred girl who was extravagantly enjoying London life to the full. Sir Oliver Surface was concerned about his two nephews, his problem being the disposal of his great fortune. Sir Oliver, having been abroad for the past fifteen years, felt that he did not know their real natures, and he hoped by some stratagem to catch them unawares and test their characters.

One day Sir Peter and Lady Teazle quarreled because Sir Peter objected violently to her attendance at the home of Lady Sneerwell. Lady Teazle accused Sir Peter of wishing to deprive her of all freedom and reminded him that he had promised to go to Lady Sneerwell's with her. He retorted that he would do so for only one reason, to look after his own character. When he arrived, Lady Sneerwell's rooms were full of people uttering libelous remarks about their enemies and saying even worse things about their friends. Sir Peter escaped as soon as possible.

When the rest of Lady Sneerwell's guests retired to the card room, leaving Maria and Joseph alone, Joseph once more pressed his suit for Maria's hand. He insinuated that she was in love with Charles and was thus running counter to Sir Peter's wishes. Lady Teazle interrupted as Joseph was on his knees avowing his honest love. Surprised, Lady Teazle told Maria she was wanted in the next room. She then asked Joseph for an explanation. Joseph informed her that he was pleading with Maria not to tell Sir Peter of his tender concern for Lady Teazle.

Sir Oliver consulted Rowley, Sir Peter's shrewd and observing servant, in an attempt to learn more of his nephews' characters. Rowley himself believed that Joseph had less good character than his reputation seemed to indicate and that Charles had more. Sir Peter was also

THE SCHOOL FOR SCANDAL by Richard Brinsley Sheridan. Published by The Macmillan Co.

consulted. He declared that he was ready to stake his life on Joseph's honor. He was much put out, therefore, when Maria once more refused to marry Joseph.

Sir Peter, Sir Oliver, and Rowley planned to test the worthiness of the nephews. Charles, as usual, was in dire need of money. Since Moses, a Jew, was going to see Charles, Sir Oliver was to accompany him as Mr. Premium, a man who could supply the money Charles needed.

When they arrived at Charles' lodging, a drinking party was in progress. Some of the guests were at games of dice. Sir Oliver was not at all impressed with Trip, Charles' footman, who gave himself the airs of a fashionable man about town. Upon investigation, Sir Oliver discovered that Charles had turned his inherited possessions into cash with the exception of the portraits of his ancestors. Convinced that Charles was a scamp, Sir Oliver, still calling himself Premium, agreed to buy the paintings, and he purchased each picture as presented except his own, which Charles would not sell for any amount of money. Sir Oliver was pleased by this fact and discounted Charles' reputation for extravagance. Charles received a draft for eight hundred pounds for the portraits and immediately sent one hundred pounds to Mr. Stanley, a poor relation in even more straitened circumstances.

During an assignation between Joseph Surface and Lady Teazle in Joseph's library, he advised her to give her husband grounds for jealousy rather than suffer his jealousy without cause. He argued that to save her reputation she must ruin it and that he was the man best able to help her. Lady Teazle said that such a doctrine was very odd.

While they were talking, Sir Peter arrived unexpectedly, and Lady Teazle hid behind the screen which Joseph ordered placed against the window. Joseph pretended to be reading when Sir Peter walked in. The purpose of Sir Peter's call was to inform Joseph of his suspicions that Lady Teazle was having an affair with Charles, and he showed Joseph two deeds he had brought with him. One deed settled eight hundred pounds a year upon Lady Teazle for her independent use, the other gave her the bulk of his fortune at his death. Joseph's dissimulation before Sir Peter and Sir Peter's generosity to her were not lost on Lady Teazle. Then Sir Peter began to discuss Joseph's desire to wed Maria. Hidden, Lady Teazle realized that Joseph had been deceiving her.

Below stairs, Charles inopportunely demanded entrance to the house to see his brother. Not wishing to see Charles, Sir Peter asked where he could hide. Sir Peter caught a glimpse of a petticoat behind the screen, but Joseph assured him that the woman was only a French milliner who plagued him. Sir Peter hid in a closet; Lady Teazle remained behind the screen.

When Charles came in, he and Joseph discussed Lady Teazle and Sir Peter's suspicion that Charles was her lover. Charles mentioned that he believed Joseph to be her favorite and recounted all the little incidents which led him to think so. Embarrassed by this turn in the conversation, Joseph interrupted to say that Sir Peter was within hearing. Placed in a difficult position, Charles explained to Sir Peter that he was merely playing a joke on Joseph. Sir Peter knew a good joke on Joseph, too, he said; Joseph was having an affair with a milliner. Charles decided that he would have a look at the milliner and threw down the screen. Joseph was undone because Lady Teazle refused to agree with any excuses he made. She angrily informed her husband of the whole nature of Joseph's intentions and departed. Sir Peter followed her, leaving Joseph to his own conscience.

Sir Oliver, masquerading as Mr. Stanley and badly in need of assistance, gained admittance to Joseph's apartment. Joseph refused to help Mr. Stanley, saying that he received very little money from Sir Oliver and claiming that he had advanced all his funds to Charles. After Sir Oliver left, Rowley, who was a party to the whole scheme, came to tell Joseph that Sir Oliver had arrived in town.

Sir Oliver went again to see Joseph. Still believing that his uncle was Mr. Stanley, Joseph was showing him out just as Charles entered. Charles, surprised to see Mr. Premium in his brother's apartment, also insisted that he leave. But at that moment Sir Peter Teazle arrived and addressed Sir Oliver by his right name. Both Sir Oliver and Sir Peter were now aware of Joseph's real character. Charles, promising to try to reform, got Maria and his uncle's inheritance as well. Then Lady Sneerwell was exposed by Snake, who was paid double to speak the truth, and Lady Teazle returned her diploma to the School for Scandal of which Lady Sneerwell was president. Everyone was happy except Lady Sneerwell and Joseph Surface.

THE SEA OF GRASS

Type of work: Novel
Author: Conrad Richter (1890-)
Type of plot: Regional romance
Time of plot: 1885-1910
Locale: The Southwest
First published: 1936

Principal characters:
COLONEL JIM BREWSTER, a pioneer rancher
LUTIE, his wife
HAL, his nephew
BRICE CHAMBERLAIN, a lawyer

Critique:

The Sea of Grass conveys within its brief framework the whole atmosphere of space and freedom of the West, the sweeping drama of the cow country at the end of the last century, when cattlemen fought to hold their free range against the homesteader's fence and plow. For a few years an empire was available. Whether the ranchers had a greater right to it than the nesters is open to dispute, but the battle they fought was frontier history in brief passage. In this novel Conrad Richter has reclaimed a dramatic segment of the American past.

The Story:

Hal Brewton never forgot the day he stood on the railroad platform at Salt Fork, where he waited to meet Lutie Cameron, who was arriving from St. Louis to marry his uncle, Colonel Jim Brewton, owner of the vast Cross B Ranch. At present Colonel Brewton was involved in a range war with nesters coming to rip the sod off the grazing lands in order to raise wheat.

On the day of Lutie's arrival two of the colonel's cowhands were being tried for shooting at a homesteader on the Brewton range. Although the colonel's lawyer, Henry McCurtin, won the case, the opposition lawyer, young Brice Chamberlain, protested indignantly that the victory would not be permanent. Colonel Brewton was contemptuous of the lawyer's warnings.

Lutie Cameron was a lovely woman, too lovely for that still-wild territory. When men saw her, she won them completely. Only Hal refused to be moved by her charm. All that winter in an academy at Lexington, Missouri, he thought of her as part of the destruction coming from the East to destroy the sea of grass he loved.

The following summer he returned to a changed ranch house. Lutie had filled it with furniture and flowers and had planted a row of cottonwoods and tamarisks about it. Guests from the whole territory came and went. Officers from the Army posts, officials of the railroad companies, neighboring ranch men—all found ample welcome at the home of Colonel and Mrs. Brewton.

The old-timers who had known the colonel before he had married Lutie hoped she would settle down after her babies came. The babies were born, two boys and a girl; however, Lutie did not settle down. The third baby was scarcely in its cradle before she was dancing with Brice Chamberlain as her favored partner. Colonel Brewton ignored the gossip which was whispered about Lutie.

Local politics shifted with the administration in Washington, for the territory depended upon appointments to its judicial staffs. For a while Brice Chamberlain had influential support from Washington. Then, during another administration, the forces which backed Colonel Brewton were in power, and the incoming tide of settlers seemed to be checked. Hal read of the change with great pleasure, but when he returned to Salt Fork he discovered that Chamberlain was still in his law office on the Salt Fork plaza. He learned that hundreds of settlers were waiting nearby for a change in government which would permit them to stake claims upon the miles of land held by men like Colonel Brewton.

Then Lutie calmly announced that she was leaving her husband and children. She explained that she had had enough of the flat grass country and the fighting between ranchers and homesteaders. She claimed she would be able to get possession of her three children, Jimmy, Brock, and Sarah Beth later, by court action.

The town was informed that Mrs. Brewton was leaving for a visit in St. Louis. Most of the people knew better. Their feelings were confirmed when they saw Brice Chamberlain with a bag packed, ready to head east on the same train. But the colonel paced the station platform, a gun belt buckled under his broadcloth coat. Chamberlain did not board the train.

A few days later the colonel sent Hal to Denver, to give Lutie a thousand dollars. He knew that his wife's cowardly lover had no intention of following her. But Hal could find no trace of Lutie in Denver. At the same time a new administration appointed Chamberlain a judge of the district court. Back in Salt Fork, Hal saw the white-covered wagons of the emigrant trains moving westward into the range country.

When Colonel Brewton planned to run the homesteaders off his land, a troop of cavalry from Fort Ewing was sent to guard him until all chances of his stopping the land-grabbers were gone.

Studying for his medical degree, Hal spent three more years away from Salt Fork. When he returned, he discovered that his sea of grass had been hopelessly despoiled. His uncle seemed much older. The Brewton children were growing up wild, for their mother had never sent for them.

One day Hal saw Jimmy and Brock fighting in the dusty Salt Fork street. Then a nester among the onlookers called out that he was betting on the Chamberlain brat. So Hal heard for the first time the rumor that Brock was not his uncle's son. Hal fired at the nester but missed. When Colonel Brewton appeared, the crowd, even the jeering nesters, grew quiet.

As young Brock grew older, he became the image of Brice Chamberlain. It was obvious that he realized the truth and resented it. He took to gambling, drinking, and barroom brawling. At last he was caught cheating in a card game. For that disgrace Colonel Brewton could not forgive him, but he continued to indulge the boy and pay his debts.

By that time Hal was practicing medicine in Salt Fork. He was glad when Sarah Beth, who had been away at school, returned and began to look after her father.

One day Brock shot and killed Dutch Charley, who had accused Brock of using a woman to help him cheat at cards. Brock was locked up, but Brice Chamberlain soon got him out of jail. When Brock returned home, he defied Colonel Brewton and said he was leaving the Brewton ranch to go to work for Brice Chamberlain's interests. This last blow to the colonel's pride permanently wrecked his health.

Brock now took the name of Chamberlain, an act which cut the old colonel still more. Brock began to ride wild, shooting up towns and staging reckless holdups. He became the talk of the Southwest for his daring lawlessness. At last he was trapped by a posse of homesteaders and held at bay in a cabin by twenty or thirty vigilantes.

That same day Lutie Brewton unexpectedly returned. She was fifteen years older, but she still carried herself with quiet self-possession. Lutie immediately assumed her place in her household as though she had been away fifteen days, not fifteen years.

Meanwhile the colonel rode out to the cabin where Brock was holding off the sheriff and the armed and angry nesters. With Hal, who had been summoned to attend a wounded deputy, he broke through to Brock, who lay dying from a bullet wound in his lung. They brought his body back across desolate country scorching in raw sunlight, with nesters' families huddled about sagging shacks and plows rusting in fields where wheat would not grow in hot, rainless summers. Sand was beginning to drift among dugouts and rotting fence posts.

Brock was buried on the Brewton ranch. The stone inscribed with the name "Brock Brewton" was the old colonel's challenge to all gossip and speculation around Salt Fork. He and Lutie took up their life where she had broken it off years before, and no one ever dared ask either the colonel or his wife where she had been. It seemed to Hal that the colonel had found peace at last.

THE SEA WOLF

Type of work: Novel
Author: Jack London (1876-1916)
Type of plot: Adventure romance
Time of plot: 1904
Locale: Pacific Ocean, Bering Sea
First published: 1904

Principal characters:
- HUMPHREY VAN WEYDEN (HUMP), an unwilling sailor aboard the *Ghost*
- WOLF LARSEN, captain of the *Ghost*
- MUGRIDGE, ship's cook
- MAUD BREWSTER, a survivor picked up at sea

Critique:

Jack London began his career as a sailor, and on shipboard he observed the sea life that he later described. A teller of two-fisted yarns, he wrote brilliant description to go with tailor-made plots. Enormously popular with American readers, many of his books have been filmed and many of them republished year after year. In *The Sea Wolf* London told an impossible story with such gusto and fervor that he created reality all his own within his limited, specialized world of violent action and masculine interests.

The Story:

When the ship in which he was a passenger sank in a collision off the coast of California, Humphrey Van Weyden was picked up by the crew of Wolf Larsen's ship, the *Ghost,* a sailing vessel headed for seal hunting ranges in the Bering Sea. Wolf Larsen was a brute. Van Weyden witnessed the inhuman treatment of a sick mate who died shortly afterward. He saw a cabin boy badly beaten. In his own interview with the captain, he fared little better. Instead of promising to help him return to San Francisco, Wolf demanded that Van Weyden sign as cabin boy and stay with his ship.

The crew set to work taking in the topsails and jibs. From that moment Hump, as the crew called Van Weyden, learned life the hard way. He had to get his sea legs and he had to learn the stoical indifference to pain and suffering which the sailors seemed to have mastered already. As cabin boy, he peeled potatoes and washed greasy pots and pans. Mugridge, the cook, abused him and robbed him of his money.

Only one man, Louis, seemed to share Hump's feelings about the captain and his ship. Louis predicted many deaths would result from this voyage. He said that Wolf Larsen was a violent, dangerous man, that the crew and seal hunters were vicious outcasts. Wolf did seem mad. He varied from moods of wild exultation to spells of extreme depression. In his cabin were classic books of literature, and when he spoke he chose either to use excellent English or the lingo of the sailors. Sometimes he amused himself by arguing with Hump. He claimed that life was without meaning.

During a southeaster Hump badly dislocated his knee, and Wolf unexpectedly allowed Hump to rest for three days while he talked to him about philosophy and literature. When Hump returned to the galley, the cook was whetting his knife. In return, Hump obtained a knife and began whetting it also. His actions so frightened the cowardly cook that Hump was no longer the victim of his abuse.

Louis talked of the coming season with the seals. Moreover, he hinted that trouble would come if the *Macedonia,* a sealing steamer, came near. Captained by Death Larsen, the brother and enemy of Wolf, the *Macedonia* was a certain menace. As a prelude to things to come, an outbreak of fury took place aboard the *Ghost.* First, Wolf Larsen and the mate beat a seaman named Johnson to a pulp because he complained of ill treatment; then Leach, the former cabin boy, beat the cook. Later two hunters exchanged shots, severely wounding each other, and Wolf beat them because they had crippled themselves before the hunting season began. Afterward Wolf suffered from one of his periodic headaches. To Hump, life on shipboard was a tremendous experience in human cruelty and viciousness.

A few days later the men tried to mutiny. In the row which followed, Johansen, the mate, was drowned and Wolf was nearly killed. While Hump dressed Wolf's wounds, Wolf promoted him to mate in Johansen's place. Both Leach and Johnson would have killed Wolf in a second, but he remained too wary for them.

At the seal hunting grounds a terrific storm cost them the lives of four men. The ship itself was beaten, its sails torn to shreds and portions of the deck swept into the sea.

When Leach and Johnson deserted in a small skiff, Wolf started out in pursuit. On the morning of the third day an open boat was sighted. The boat contained a young woman and four men, survivors from a sinking steamer. Wolf took them aboard, planning to make sailors of the men as he had of Hump. Shortly afterward the *Ghost* overtook Johnson and Leach. Refusing to pick them up, Wolf let them struggle to get aboard until their small craft capsized. He watched them drown without comment and then ordered the ship's course set for a return to the seal hunting grounds.

The woman survivor was Maud Brewster, a rich woman and a poet, as weak physically for a woman as Hump had been for a man. Wolf resented the intimacy which sprang up at once between Maud Brewster and Hump, but he took out his resentment by deciding to give the cook the first bath the cook had ever been known to take.

At his orders Mugridge was thrown into the water with a tow rope slung about his middle. First, however, the cook fled madly about the ship, causing one man to break a leg and another to be injured in a fall. Before Wolf was ready to bring Mugridge back aboard ship, a shark bit off the cook's right foot at the ankle. Dragged aboard, Mugridge in his fury tried to bite Wolf's leg, and the captain almost strangled him. Then Hump bandaged the wounded man's leg. Maud Brewster looked on, nearly fainting.

The *Macedonia* appeared one day and robbed Wolf's hunters of their day's catch of seals by cutting off the line of approach to the *Ghost*. In revenge, Wolf set his men to work capturing hunters from the *Macedonia*. When the *Macedonia* gave chase, Wolf sailed his ship into a fog bank.

That night Wolf tried to seize Maud, but Hump, awakening, ran his knife into Wolf's shoulder. At the same time, Wolf was overcome by one of his headaches, this seizure accompanied by blindness. Hump helped him to his bunk and under cover of darkness he and Maud made their escape in an open boat. After days of tossing they came to a small island. Using supplies they had taken from the *Ghost,* they set about making themselves houses and gathering food for the coming winter.

One morning Hump saw the wreck of the *Ghost* lying offshore. Going aboard, he discovered Wolf alone, his crew having deserted him to go aboard Death Larsen's ship. Wolf seemed nearly insane, and had only a sick man's desire to sleep. Hump stole some pistols and food which he took to the island.

Hump, planning to repair the masts of the *Ghost,* began work on the crippled ship. That night Wolf undid all Hump's work, and cast the masts off the vessel.

Hump and Maud began anew to refit the ship. One day Wolf attempted to murder Hump, but during the struggle he had one of his spasms and fainted. While he was still unconscious, they handcuffed him and shut him in the hold.

Then they moved aboard the *Ghost* and the work of refitting the vessel went forward. Wolf became more than a prisoner. He had a stroke which paralyzed the right side of his body.

Hump continued to repair the vessel. At last it was able to sail. Wolf Larsen finally lost the use of his muscles and lay in a coma. When he died, Hump and Maud buried him at sea. By that time they were deeply in love. When a United States revenue cutter discovered them one day, they felt that their dangerous odyssey was at an end. But they were about to begin another, less perilous journey, together.

A SENTIMENTAL EDUCATION

Type of work: Novel
Author: Gustave Flaubert (1821-1880)
Type of plot: Naturalism
Time of plot: Nineteenth century
Locale: France
First published: 1869

Principal characters:
Frederic Moreau, a young student
M. Arnoux, a businessman
Mme. Arnoux, his wife
M. Dambreuse, a banker
Mme. Dambreuse, his wife
Rosanette, mistress of many
Deslauriers, Frederic's friend
Louise Roque, Frederic's neighbor

Critique:

This novel by Flaubert illustrates well his style. Flaubert's writing is always exact, concise, and detailed. His fame rests on a rather small number of works, of which the best known are *Madame Bovary* and *Salammbô,* all of them exhibiting the careful, labored work of a superb craftsman. *A Sentimental Education,* like the others, is a careful piece of work. Although the plot interest is slight, there are many impressive analyses of French character.

The Story:

In 1840 the boat down the Seine to Nogent had among its passengers Frederic Moreau, who was returning home after finishing his course at the College de Sens. Frederic, with the prospect of a long vacation before beginning his law studies, saw on the boat an older man whose conversation was eagerly followed by a group of admirers.

Frederic drew closer to hear what was being said. M. Arnoux was holding forth on the subject of women; his remarks were worldly in the extreme. Noticing Frederic in the circle, he made the young man's acquaintance and the two promenaded for some time. Arnoux invited Frederic to call when he arrived in Paris. Frederic went up to the first-class deck to sit and reflect on his homecoming. There he saw a woman knitting. Frederic thought her the most beautiful woman he had ever seen. She was a little older than he and demure of manner; she never once looked directly at him.

They were alone on the deck. Frederic moved several times to see her from different angles. Finally she dropped her ball of yarn. When Frederic retrieved it, her murmur of thanks was pleasant to hear. A few minutes later a little girl came up, and he knew the child was her daughter. Then Arnoux appeared on deck, and Frederic learned that the woman was his wife. When the boat docked, he watched them drive away.

Mme. Moreau, a widow, was glad to see her son, for all her hopes were in his future career in diplomacy. As soon as he decently could, Frederic went out to meet his friend Deslauriers, an older boy also planning a legal career. The two friends discussed at great length their plans for Paris in the fall.

A neighbor of the Moreaus, M. Roque, gave Frederic a letter for M. Dambreuse, a rich banker in Paris. Mme. Moreau advised her son to call on Dambreuse as soon as he could; the banker could be of great help to a young lawyer. Bidding goodbye to his relatives and Louise Roque, a girl who had become his special friend during the summer, Frederic left for Paris and his studies at the university.

Deslauriers and Frederic took an apartment together and began to attend lectures in law. Frederic, however, found great difficulty in keeping his mind on his studies, for he thought most of the time of Mme. Arnoux. He finally received an invitation to the Arnoux store, a big establishment dealing in paintings and other works of art. He was patient enough to become intimate with Arnoux, and he lived in hopes of meeting his wife.

One night Arnoux invited Frederic to a ball. At the masquerade Arnoux introduced him to Rosanette, an attractive woman called la Maréchale by her friends. Frederic was sure that Rosanette was Arnoux's mistress. He was glad to learn about the liaison; he had more hopes of becoming friendly with Mme. Arnoux.

When Frederic was finally invited to dine at the Arnoux home, he was happy to learn that Mme. Arnoux remembered him perfectly. She was a friendly woman, but as time went on Frederic saw little chance of ever becoming more intimate with her. Even when he was regularly included in gatherings at their country house, he made no progress. At last Frederic had to conclude that his friends were right; Mme. Arnoux was an honest woman.

So great was his preoccupation with the pursuit of Mme. Arnoux that Frederic failed his examinations that spring. Before he left for home he called at the Dambreuse home, where he was well received. He vowed to study hard, to forget about Mme. Arnoux, and to try his luck in public life under the sponsorship of M. Dambreuse. For a time Frederic studied diligently, cultivated the Dambreuse family, and went only occasionally to see Mme. Arnoux. Having passed his examinations, he was admitted to the bar.

Before leaving Paris, he was included in a picnic in honor of Mme. Arnoux's birthday. During the party she seemed put out with her husband. Arnoux shrugged off his wife's pique and sent her back to the city with Frederic. As they left, Arnoux gave his wife a bouquet which she surreptitiously threw away. Thinking she had dropped it, Frederic picked it up and gave it to her in the carriage. As soon as they had started the trip, she begged him to throw the flowers out the window. Frederic had never felt so close to her.

At Nogent Frederic had bad news. His mother's income had dwindled considerably because of the troubled politics of monarchial France, and she had been forced to sell some of her lands. Henceforth she would have only enough for a frugal living. A worse blow fell when Frederic's rich uncle in Le Havre announced that he would not leave his wealth to Frederic. Feeling that he was ruined, with no income and no expectations, Frederic resigned himself to a dull life in Nogent and spent three years in almost complete idleness. His only friend was Louise Roque, who had grown into an attractive woman.

At last a telegram came. The uncle in Le Havre had died intestate and Frederic was his only heir. Hastily Frederic prepared to return to Paris, in spite of his mother's remonstrances. He declared his love for Louise before he left, but all the while he was thinking of Mme. Arnoux.

In Paris, Frederic took a fashionable apartment and settled down to a life of ease. He became an intimate of the Arnoux household and renewed his friendship with Deslauriers. He agreed to furnish the money to found a journal of political opinion, his intention being to give employment to Deslauriers and at the same time control a paper that would support his own future career in politics. But when he learned that Arnoux was pressed financially, he lent money to him on Arnoux's promise of repayment in a few days. But Arnoux never repaid the money, and in disappointment Deslauriers broke off their friendship. Frederic consoled himself by his increasing intimacy with Mme. Arnoux.

Little by little Arnoux lost most of his money, and an oil company he had founded went bankrupt. He began to spend less time at home and more with various mistresses. His wife, becoming aware of his many affairs, turned to Frederic for sympathy. At last she agreed to meet him and spend the afternoon in his company.

With high hopes Frederic rented a

room for their rendezvous and filled it with expensive trinkets. He was to meet Mme. Arnoux between two and four, and on the appointed day he went to the meeting place at one-thirty. He waited until six-thirty, but she did not appear. In despair he went to see Rosanette, for to him it seemed a just retaliation to make Arnoux's mistress his own.

Mme. Arnoux had not kept the appointment because her son was ill. Taking his illness as a sign from heaven, she was much ashamed of her interest in Frederic.

During the riots which attended the overthrow of the monarchy and the establishment of the republic, Frederic spent the time agreeably enough in the country with Rosanette. He returned to Paris only after he received word that one of his friends had been wounded. Louise Roque went to Paris with her father, chiefly to see what had happened to Frederic. When she finally met him, she understood that he no longer was interested in her.

In spite of his affair with Rosanette, Frederic took another mistress, Mme. Dambreuse. When the banker died, Frederic decided to marry his widow. But in his will, canny Dambreuse had left his money to his niece. Frederic gave up all thought of the proposed marriage.

Although Frederic had many loves, none was permanent. When he was nearly fifty, Mme. Arnoux went to see him. They agreed that they had been right not to love carnally. Deslauriers had been for twenty-five years a lawyer in Nogent. He came to visit Frederic, and they talked over the past. Deslauriers had married Louise Roque, but she had run away with a singer. To the old friends it seemed that love was fickle, selfish, unhappy — like life itself.

A SENTIMENTAL JOURNEY

Type of work: Novel
Author: Laurence Sterne (1713-1768)
Type of plot: Novelized autobiography
Time of plot: 1760's
Locale: France
First published: 1768

Principal characters:
Mr. Yorick, a sentimental traveler
Madame de L—, a fellow traveler
Madame de R—, Madame de L—'s friend
Count de B—, an admirer of Englishmen
La Fleur, a servant
Maria, a country girl

Critique:

Sterne called his book *A Sentimental Journey Through France and Italy,* but the title of this unconventional mixture of autobiography, travel impressions, and fiction is misleading. Sterne told of his travels through France, but he died of tuberculosis before he had written the Italian section of his narrative. Sentimental, as the title implies, outrageous and eccentric in its humorous effects, the novel entertains the reader with delightful accounts and observations of whatever came into the author's mind. Like *Tristram Shandy,* the book broadened the scope of prose fiction for later writers by demonstrating that form and unified plot are not necessary for a successful novel.

The Story:

With all the different kinds of travelers, the Idle Travelers, the Inquisitive Travelers, the Travelers of Necessity, the

Simple Travelers, and the rest, Mr. Yorick felt no kinship. He was a Sentimental Traveler. As such, he collected sentimental adventures as other tourists collected postcards of the points of interest they visited. Mr. Yorick had started his journey because a man had asked him, with a sneer, if he had ever been in France. Yorick had just made some statement on the French and did not like being answered so tartly merely because he did not have first-hand experience. The same evening he packed some clothes and left by boat for Calais.

While he was having supper at an inn in Calais, a poor monk approached him and begged alms for his monastery. Yorick rebuffed him with caustic and witty remarks. A little later Yorick saw the monk talking with an attractive woman who was also staying at the inn. Afraid the monk might tell her how rudely he had behaved, Yorick approached the couple, apologized to the monk, and offered his shell snuffbox to him as a peace offering. Having made friends with the monk and the lady, Yorick planned to ask the lady to travel with him to Paris. Her name, he learned, was Madame de L—.

Proposing to make the trip to Paris in a private carriage, Yorick invited the lady to go with him to look over some of the vehicles for sale in a nearby courtyard. Their admiration of each other grew with unusual rapidity. Before Yorick had a chance to ask her to travel with him, however, she was called away by a message that her brother, Count L—, had arrived. He had come to take her back to Belgium with him. Yorick was brokenhearted.

In parting, Madame de L— asked Yorick to visit her in Belgium if he passed through that country. She also gave him a letter of introduction to a good friend in Paris, Madame de R—.

The next day Yorick set off in a small carriage for Paris. His baggage fell out of the chaise several times, and he had a most uncomfortable trip to Montriul. There an innkeeper suggested he needed a servant, and Yorick saw that the man was quite right. He hired a young boy named La Fleur, whose greatest accomplishments were playing the flute and making love to the girls. La Fleur was delighted at the prospect of traveling around Europe with a generous and unpredictable English milord; his only sadness on leaving home was the necessity to say goodbye to all his village sweethearts. Yorick was pleased with the lad's quickness and wit, as he was sure that the young Frenchman would be equal to any emergency arising along the way.

The first problem the travelers met on their journey was a dead ass lying in the middle of the road. The horses refused to pass the carcass, and La Fleur's horse threw him and ran away. Proceeding to the next town, they met and talked with the owner of the poor dead beast. He had taken the ass with him from Germany to Italy, and was very unhappy at its death, not so much because the beast had been a help to him, but because he felt sure that the ass had loved him dearly and had been a good friend to him for many years.

In Paris, Yorick went to the opera. A quotation from Shakespeare popping into his mind, he suddenly decided to go and buy the works of that writer. He went into a bookstore and found a set on the counter. Unfortunately they were not for sale, but had been sent to be rebound for Count de B—, a great lover of English authors and Englishmen. In the shop Yorick saw a most attractive young girl who, he decided, must be a chambermaid. When she left the shop, he followed her and began a conversation about the book she had bought. Yorick was surprised and pleased to discover that the young girl belonged to the household of Madame de R—. He told her to inform her mistress that he would call the next day.

On returning to his rooms, Yorick learned from La Fleur that the police wanted to see him. In his rush out of

England he had forgotten to get a passport, and he had overlooked completely the fact that England and France were at war. Since he did not wish to be put in jail, he decided that he would have to get a passport. But he did not know how these matters were arranged in France. Madame de R— was the only person in Paris to whom he carried a letter of introduction, and he did not want to bother the lady about the matter. The only other chance of help was from Count de B—, who at least liked Englishmen.

It took Yorick some time to get in to see the count, but when he did the count was most polite. As an amusing way to introduce himself, Yorick opened one of the volumes of Shakespeare, which had just been sent from the bookseller's. Turning to *The Tragedy of Hamlet* and pointing to the passage about the jester Yorick, he said that was his name. The count was overcome with pleasure at meeting so famous a person, and Yorick could say nothing that would change the count's mind. The count left the room and did not return for a long while. When he did, he presented Mr. Yorick with a passport which called him the King's Jester. Realizing that he could not correct the mistake without losing his passport, Yorick thanked the count and returned to his rooms.

The next day Madame de R—'s chambermaid called to see why Mr. Yorick had not visited her mistress as he had promised. Yorick explained about the passport and asked her to present his apology. Some hours later, after the girl had gone, the manager of the hotel came in and objected to Yorick's having young ladies in his room. In order to keep from being evicted from the hotel, Yorick had to buy some lace from a young woman. He suspected that the manager pocketed most of the profits from such sales.

On Sunday La Fleur appeared in a fine suit of clothes which he had bought second-hand. He asked if he might be allowed to have the day off, as he had been able to make friends with a young woman he would like to see again that day. Yorick asked him to bring some food before he left for the day. Wrapped about the butter, which La Fleur brought with Yorick's dinner, was a piece of paper which bore on it some old printing. Yorick became interested in the story it told and spent the whole day translating the faded characters to read the story of a luckless notary. But he was never to know the ending of the tale, for La Fleur had used the rest of the paper to wrap up a bouquet for his new ladylove.

Yorick had a fine time at parties to which he was invited by Count de B— and the count's friends. He agreed with everyone to whom he talked, and made no remarks of his own, and so he was thought the finest wit in Paris. After several minor sentimental adventures, Yorick and La Fleur set out to travel through southern France. At Moulines, Yorick stopped to see Maria, a poor unhappy girl who wandered about the country grieving for her dead father. He had heard of the girl from his old friend, Mr. Toby Shandy, who had met her several years before. Yorick sat down on a rock with Maria and, moved by her purity and sadness, shed a few tears with her.

Before ascending Mount Taurira, Yorick stopped and had dinner with a pleasant peasant family. That night he was forced to stay in a roadside inn. There was only one room in the inn, and Yorick had to share it with a French lady and her maid. In the room there were two large beds standing beside each other and, in a closet connected to the room, a cot. After much deliberation, the lady and Yorick took the big beds and sent the maid into the closet. Yorick had to promise to stay in his bed all night, and not to say a word. Unable to sleep, both Yorick and the lady began talking. Afraid that something untoward might occur, the maid come out of the closet and, unseen, stood between the two beds. Yorick stretched out his hand. With this sentimental gesture Sterne ended abruptly the story of his sentimental journey.

SEVENTEEN

Type of work: Novel
Author: Booth Tarkington (1869-1946)
Type of plot: Humorous romance
Time of plot: Early twentieth century
Locale: Small Midwestern town
First published: 1916

Principal characters:
WILLIAM SYLVANUS BAXTER, aged seventeen
MRS. BAXTER, his mother
JANE BAXTER, his sister
MISS PRATT, a summer visitor

Critique:

Seventeen is the hilarious story of William Sylvanus Baxter, just seventeen, who is in love with Miss Pratt, a summer visitor in the neighborhood. There is nothing weighty in this book to arrest the reader's thought, nothing sublime, but everything ridiculous. The adolescent antics of a small-town Lothario are beguiling and utterly harmless, and the completely normal but demoniacal actions of Jane, William's pesky younger sister, are foolish and delightful. The only really sane person in the tale is Mrs. Baxter, who sadly tries to keep up with her children's whims and moods.

The Story:

William Sylvanus Baxter had at last reached the impressive age of seventeen, and as he emerged from the corner drug store after indulging in two chocolate and strawberry sodas, he tried to impress the town with his lofty air of self-importance. But no one noticed him except his friend, Johnny Watson, who destroyed William's hauteur in one breath by calling him "Silly Bill." At that moment William saw a feminine vision in pink and white. A stranger in town, she carried her parasol and her little white dog with easy grace. William, not daring to speak, managed only an insincere yawn. The vision, taking no apparent notice of William, spoke in charming lisps to her little dog Flopit, and disappeared around the corner.

William went home in a daze, hardly bothering to speak to his outrageous little sister, Jane, who greeted him between mouthfuls of applesauce and bread. Scorning her, he went up to his room, his heart full of the mystery of love, and composed a poem to his new and unknown lady. He was interrupted by his mother, who asked William to go with Genesis, the Negro handyman, to pick up some laundry tubs from the second-hand store. The errand, to William, was worse than being seen in public with a leper, for he looked on Genesis as a ragged, bedraggled, down-at-the-heels pariah, whose presence was an unwholesome reproach to the whole neighborhood.

Genesis was in reality a wise old philosopher, despite his semi-nudity and the ubiquitous presence of his mongrel dog, Clematis. But William was in no mood to be tolerant. His worst fears were realized when, on the way home, he heard behind him the silvery voice of the fair stranger referring to Clematis as a nasty old dog. William was hidden by the laundry tub he carried over his head, but his invisibility in no way diminished his growing horror at being taken for a companion of Genesis and the owner of the dreadful Clematis. Clematis, meanwhile, was fascinated by Flopit, and when William heard the yips and barks of the two dogs, he ran away, still hidden under his protecting tub.

The young vision in pink and white was the summer visitor of May Parcher. Her name, William learned, was Miss Pratt. Soon the boys in the neighborhood collected on the Parcher porch and swarmed around the adorable girl every evening after supper, much to the disgust of Mr. Parcher, who lay awake for hours in his room over the porch and listened reluctantly to the drivel of conversation below. William had an advantage over the other suitors, for he borrowed his father's dress suit without his parents' knowledge and arrived each night in splendid attire.

During the day William could not escape his sister Jane, who insisted on appearing in dirty summer sunsuits, her face smeared with her favorite repast of applesauce and bread, just at the moment when William would be walking by the house with Miss Pratt. His angry demands that his sister present a more ladylike appearance irritated Jane to a calm, smouldering intent to get even with William. She knew that William wore his father's dress suit every evening when he visited Miss Pratt. She also knew that Mr. Parcher was nearly crazy over the nightly sessions on his front porch. Putting these facts together, she coldly repeated to her mother some of Mr. Parcher's comments. Mrs. Baxter was horrified that William had worn out his welcome at the Parcher's, and when she discovered Mr. Baxter's dress suit under William's window seat she took it to a tailor and had it altered to fit only Mr. Baxter. William could not go to see Miss Pratt without the dress suit. He was not among Miss Pratt's evening admirers thereafter.

As a reward to Jane, who had immediately told him of her part in decreasing by one the population of his front porch, Mr. Parcher sent her a five-pound box of candy, much to the amazement of the whole Baxter household. No one suspected Jane's perfidy.

Feeling herself to blame for William's gloomy moods, Mrs. Baxter decided to have a tea for her son's friends, with Miss Pratt as guest of honor. The great day arrived, swelteringly hot. Upstairs, William had no sooner broken his only collar button on his fifth and last white shirt than he had the misfortune to tear his white trousers. Another suit was splattered by Jane's paints. By the time he found a heavy winter suit in a trunk in the attic, the guests had gone. Angry and miserable, William sat down on Jane's open, wet paint box.

The time came for Miss Pratt to return home. As a farewell party, the relieved Parchers scheduled a picnic in their guest's honor. To impress Miss Pratt, William bought a package of Cuban cigarettes. But coy Miss Pratt gave all her attention to George, a braggart who stuffed himself with food to impress the beauty with his gustatory prowess. Lunch over, William offered George his cigarettes. Before long he had the satisfaction of seeing George disappear behind a woodpile. William was blissful once more.

When Miss Pratt unexpectedly granted the weary Parchers the privilege of her company for another week, they gave a final farewell dance in her honor. Mrs. Baxter had her husband's dress suit again altered to fit William. Resplendent, but late as usual, William arrived at the dance to find all Miss Pratt's dances taken, and he was forced to spend the evening with a lonely wallflower. His dignity suffered another blow when Genesis, serving sandwiches, not only greeted William with familiarity but also chided him about the dress suit. His evening was a dismal failure.

The next day William went down to the train to see Miss Pratt off. Laden with candy and lush poetry, he found her surrounded by her many admirers. He had the uncomfortable sensation that they were all laughing at him, for they were pointing derisively in his direction. Turning, he saw Jane, who had deliberately come to torment him in company with an equally disreputable female companion. The two pranksters were walking with a vulgar strut that William abhorred. So flustered was he that he merely waved to Miss Pratt and went sadly home, forgetting that he still carried under his arm the box of candy and the poem intended for the pink and white beauty who was going out of his life forever.

SHADOWS ON THE ROCK

Type of work: Novel
Author: Willa Cather (1876-1947)
Type of plot: Historical chronicle
Time of plot: Late seventeenth century
Locale: Quebec, Canada
First published: 1931

Principal characters:
EUCLIDE AUCLAIR, the apothecary in Quebec
CÉCILE AUCLAIR, his daughter
COUNT FRONTENAC, governor of New France and Auclair's patron
PIERRE CHARRON, a Canadian woodsman

Critique:

Shadows on the Rock is a very human story about a little-known segment of North American history, the early colonies in Canada. Unlike many fictional French people in the literature of Britain and America, Willa Cather's characters maintain personalities and enlist the sympathies of the Anglo-Saxon reader. The author has divested them of any alien spirit, so that they become members of the human family rather than members of a different national stock. The book is also a mine of information on life in Quebec at the end of the seventeenth century. The author noted in great detail the customs, habits, and daily routine of the people whom she described, even to the food they ate and the homes in which they lived.

The Story:

Late in October of 1697 the last ship left Quebec to return to France, and the colony of New France was isolated from the world until the arrival of the fleet in June or July of the following year. One of the persons who watched as the last vessel passed out of sight down the St. Lawrence River was Euclide Auclair, the apothecary in Quebec.

Auclair lived on the street which wound up the slope and connected the Upper Town on the cliff with the Lower Town that clustered along the shore of the river at the foot of the mountain. In his home behind his shop, Auclair and his daughter Cécile did their best to re-create the atmosphere they had known in France. So successful were they that many people came to the shop merely to visit and snatch a breath of the France they had left behind.

Cécile was only thirteen years old and her mother had been dead for several years. Although she was content to remain in Canada, her father seemed to live only for the time when he could return to France with his patron, the governor of the colony, Count Frontenac. Auclair, who had served the count for many years, was a trusted friend of the governor as well as his apothecary.

A few weeks after the last ship had departed, Cécile went to see the count to ask his aid in obtaining some shoes for a little orphan boy. The governor was glad to see her, for too many of the people who came to him were anxious only to help themselves. He said that when he made his will he would leave the girl a bowl of glass fruit she had always admired.

The first days of December brought a heavy fall of snow which ushered in the deepest reality of life in Canada, the long, dark winter. The snow also reminded Cécile of the boxes of Christmas presents which had been sent to her by aunts in France the previous summer. On the twenty-fourth of December the Auclairs brought the boxes out of their storage place. In one was a crèche to be set up in their living room. The crèche was the crowning point of Christmas for many of their friends, for the French colonists were, as a rule, very devout.

One day in March Father Hector Saint-Cyr put in his appearance. The priest spent several evenings recounting to the Auclairs stories of the missionaries, the Indians, and the hardships of backwoods life. When he left, Euclide Auclair wondered if, after all, the gifts of an educated man like Father Saint-Cyr might not be going to waste in misplaced heroisms among the Canadian missions to the Indians.

About the middle of March the weather changed. There was a continuous downpour of rain which the snow soaked up as if it were a gigantic sponge. Even the ice in the St. Lawrence broke up and floated downstream in huge gray blocks. It was a season of sickness, and the apothecary was busy from morning until night acting as doctor to many of the inhabitants of the town. Cécile herself caught a cold and was in bed for several days.

One evening while Cécile was ill, Auclair had a strange visit with a misshapen hunchback who secured water and wood for the Auclairs in return for a bowl of soup and a small glass of brandy each evening. Blinker, as the hunchback was called, told Auclair that as a boy he had been an apprentice to the king's torturer at Rouen. While an apprentice, Blinker had tortured an old woman into admitting that she had murdered her son. Some months after her execution the son had returned. The shock of what he had done was too great for the apprentice. He ran away, took ship, and went to Quebec to begin a new life. But visions of the old woman haunted him so that he could not sleep. Filled with sympathy, the apothecary gave Blinker some laudanum so that he might have a little untroubled rest.

One day, while Cécile was regaining her strength, her father wrapped her in a blanket and carried her to the door. There, outside the door, Cécile saw the first swallow hunting for its old nest in the wall of the cliff that rose sharply to the chateau above. As soon as she was well, Cécile hurried to inform old Bishop Laval of the bird's appearance. The old man had kept a record of the changing seasons for thirty-eight years and he had always included the date of the first swallow's arrival.

On the first day of June the leaves began to bud and the hunters arrived from the woods with their loads of pelts. Among the first hunters to reach Quebec was Pierre Charron, an old friend of the apothecary and his daughter. Pierre, the son of a rich family in Montreal, had been disappointed in love. His sweetheart had decided to build a chapel with her dowry and enter the Church as a recluse. After she had taken her vows, Pierre had become a hunter traveling through the wilderness as far as Michilimackinac and Lake Superior in his quest for furs and forgetfulness. During the spring Pierre Charron took Cécile with him to visit some friends on the Isle d'Orleans, in the St. Lawrence some miles below Quebec. The squalid and primitive life there disgusted Cécile.

Early in July the ships from France arrived. The count had requested the king to recall him from Canada, and he had promised that he would take the Auclairs back to France with him. As each ship arrived through the summer, the Auclairs looked for the governor's recall. Toward the end of summer the count called Euclide Auclair to the chateau to warn him that the king's request would never come. When the count offered to send the Auclairs back to France, Euclide refused, assuring the count that he could not leave while his patron was forced to remain in Quebec.

The last ship left Quebec in October. Shortly afterward Count Frontenac became ill. Euclide Auclair knew that his patient could not live through the winter. When the count died, Euclide carried out his patron's last wish. He sealed the count's heart in a lead box and sent it with a missionary priest to the English colonies in the south. From there it was returned to France for burial.

The death of the count was a great blow to the Auclairs, for security seemed to have gone from their lives. Thinking to return to France that year, they had not even laid in a proper supply of food to last through the winter. Fortunately for them, Pierre Charron arrived in Quebec with an offer of help. Later he married Cécile. Charron had not the authority of documents and seals which the count had had to protect them, but he had his knowledge of the woods and the people, which was as good or better in the wilds of Canada. The future was safe.

SHE

Type of work: Novel
Author: H. Rider Haggard (1856-1925)
Type of plot: Adventure romance
Time of plot: Late nineteenth century
Locale: Africa
First published: 1887

Principal characters:
Ludwig Horace Holly, a teacher
Leo Vincey, his ward
She, a beautiful ageless woman, in love with Leo
Job, Holly's servant
Ustane, a woman also in love with Leo
Billali, an old man of the Amahagger tribe

Critique:

She contains such deft allusions to real events and places that the reader frequently finds himself wondering if the whole invention could not be true. This story of a land presided over by an ageless white queen and of the fire which enabled her to live for thousands of years is in the tradition of adventure romance and fantasy.

The Story:

Late one night in his rooms at Cambridge, Ludwig Holly received an urgent visit from a fellow student named Vincey. The man was dying of a lung condition, and because he had no living relatives he asked Holly to undertake the guardianship of his young son after his death. Vincey explained that the boy would be the last representative of one of the oldest families in the world. He could trace his ancestry back to the ancient Egyptians, to a priest of Isis named Kallikrates, who had broken his vows and fled the country with an Egyptian princess. Kallikrates had been murdered by the queen of a savage tribe, but his wife had escaped and had borne a son, from whom the boy was descended.

Holly agreed to rear the boy. It was understood that he was to be tutored at home, where he would be taught Greek, mathematics, and Arabic. On his twenty-fifth birthday he was to receive an iron box which Vincey would leave with

Holly; at that time he could decide whether he wanted to act upon its contents.

The following morning Vincey was found dead in his rooms. Shortly afterward five-year-old Leo Vincey went to live with his guardian.

Twenty years passed happily for Leo and for the man whom he called his uncle. Then, on the morning of the youth's twenty-fifth birthday, the iron chest was opened. Inside was an ebony box which, in turn, contained a silver chest. Within the silver chest was a potsherd inscribed by the wife of the ill-fated Kallikrates. A message to her son, it declared that the queen who had murdered Kallikrates had shown them both the Pillar of Life. The message ended by begging that he, or some brave descendant, should try to find the Pillar of Life and slay the evil queen.

There was also a letter to Leo from his father in the inmost chest. He wrote that he had journeyed to Africa to find the land which his ancestors had visited, but had gone only as far as the coast. There, suffering a shortage of provisions, he had been forced to turn back. Before he could plan another trip, he had been taken with his fatal illness.

Leo determined at once that he would carry on from the point where his father had been forced to give up his quest. Three months later, he, Holly, and their servant, Job, were on their way to Africa.

Their destination was a rock shaped like a Negro's head, which reared as a landmark on the eastern coast of Central Africa. As they drew near shore the little party readied the whaleboat which they planned to use for travel inland. The boat was tied onto the large dhow that carried them down the coast. Suddenly a squall came up, and huge waves wrecked the dhow. The three white men and an Arab named Mahomed managed to launch the small boat and reach the shore.

The men found themselves at the mouth of a river whose teeming marshy banks were crowded with crocodiles. After refreshing themselves, the little party started inland in the whaleboat. Holly and his companions traveled without much difficulty for five days, but at the end of that time the river grew too shallow to continue farther and they were forced to branch off into another stream, which proved to be an ancient canal.

During the next four days the trip became increasingly more difficult. Because the canal was full of weeds, the boat had to be towed. While the exhausted men were resting, on the fourth evening, they were suddenly attacked by a party of about fifty tall, light-colored men who spoke Arabic. They would have been slain on the spot, had not the old man who was the leader of the natives ordered that their lives be spared. He explained that word had come from some one whom he called "She-who-must-be-obeyed" that any white men who wandered into the country were to be brought to her. The man, whose name the adventurers later learned was Billali, decreed that Mahomed's life should also be spared. In litters the prisoners were carried to a cave village of the Amahagger tribe. There Billali left them with his people while he went on to report to She-who-must-be-obeyed.

The next four days passed peacefully. The men were well-treated, and Ustane, one of the Amahagger women, took Leo for her husband by the simple ceremony of throwing her arms around him and kissing him.

On the fourth night the three white men and Mahomed were invited to a party. The only refreshment served was a fermented drink. After the brew had been passed around several times, a terrible thing occurred. Suddenly a woman slipped a rope around Mahomed's body. At the same time some of the men reached into the fire around which they were sitting, dragged out a red-hot pot, and tried to slip it on the Arab's head. Holly, realizing that the natives were preparing to kill and eat Mahomed, drew his gun and shot the woman. The bullet passed through her body and killed the Arab as well. In the furious struggle that followed Leo was seriously wounded in the side. The situation was growing desperate when Billali appeared to restore order.

Three days later, when Leo's wound had barely healed, the three white men, accompanied by Billali and Ustane, were taken to meet She in her hidden city of Kôr. The way led through deep swamps which at last gave way to spreading plains. The next day the travelers reached a tunneled mountain. Their guides led Holly and his friends, blindfolded, through the tunnel to a great plain that had once been a lake. There the blindfolds were removed, and the men were taken to some apartments cut into the solid rock.

After he had refreshed himself, Holly was taken to the apartments of the heavily-veiled queen. She, asking about the ancient Greeks and Egyptians, explained that she had been living in the mountain for the past two thousand years. Holly wondered at the strange power which had enabled her to live untouched, apparently, by time or death. She declared that she stayed with the Amahagger only to await the return of the man she had once loved, for he was destined to be born again. Ayesha, as she asked Holly to call her, removed her veil. She was exceedingly beautiful.

That night Holly could not sleep from excitement. Wandering in the passages which led off from his room, he saw Ayesha uttering curses over a fire. They were, he discovered, directed against an Egyptian woman. Near the fire, on a stone shelf, lay a corpse with a shroud over it. Holly, fearful for his own life if he were discovered, crept back to his room.

The next day the savages who had plotted Mahomed's death were brought before Ayesha and condemned to death by torture. In the evening Ayesha went to visit Leo, who was ill with a fever and near death. When she saw his face, the queen staggered back with a scream. Leo had the face of the dead Kallikrates. It was he whose arrival Ayesha awaited.

She quickly forced some life-giving fluid down the young man's throat. In her jealousy she would have killed Ustane, had not Holly reminded her of the suffering she had had to bear for killing Kallikrates so long ago. Ustane was sentenced to leave the mountain.

On the following evening the three white men were invited to attend a dance performed by natives dressed in animal skins. The caves were honeycombed by preserved human bodies, and these were used to illuminate the proceedings, for when a torch was applied to them they burned brightly.

Ustane, who had not been able to bear the parting from Leo, was one of the dancers. She revealed herself to Leo when he strolled to a dark corner of the room, but she was discovered by Ayesha before she could flee with him. When Ustane refused to leave Leo's side, Ayesha killed her with a fierce look.

Ayesha led Leo and Holly to the place where Holly had seen her uttering her incantations. Drawing back the shroud which covered the corpse, she disclosed the body of Kallikrates. Then over it she poured some acid that destroyed it quickly. With Leo present in the flesh, she explained, she had no more need for the body of the dead man.

Leo quickly fell under Ayesha's spell and forgot Ustane. That night the queen and the three white men started their journey to the place where Leo was to bathe in the fire of the Pillar of Life and so be assured of thousands of years of existence.

Traveling across the plain, through the ruins of the ancient city of Kôr, the party reached a steep mountain. At its foot they left the litter bearers in the charge of Billali, who had accompanied them, and began the ascent. When, by difficult stages, they reached the top, they were forced to walk a plank across a deep chasm to reach the cave which held the pillar of fire, the Pillar of Life.

When Leo hesitated to immerse himself in that spiraling flame, Ayesha, to show that there was nothing to fear, walked into it. As she stood in its rising flame, a sudden change came over Ayesha. Her face and limbs began to shrivel until finally, before the horrified onlookers, she shrank into a little old monkey-like creature and died. Whether her death was caused by some fatal quality which had crept into the flame, or whether her earlier immersion in it had been neutralized, the men did not know. Shaken to their depths, Holly and Leo started back to Billali. They left Job, who had died of shock, in the cave with the remains of Ayesha.

Informed of Ayesha's fate, Billali hurried to lead the white men back through the swamps toward the coast, before the Amahagger tribe learned they no longer had to fear their dread queen. Much the worse for wear, Holly and Leo managed to make their way to Delagoa Bay after leaving the old native at the edge of the swamp country. Though they had only spent three weeks in the interior, Leo's hair had turned white.

The two men eventually arrived in England and resumed their old existence. However, as he sat alone at night, Holly frequently wondered what the next step in the drama he had witnessed would be, and what, some day, would be the role of the Egyptian princess whom Kallikrates had loved.

SHE STOOPS TO CONQUER

Type of work: Drama
Author: Oliver Goldsmith (1728-1774)
Type of plot: Comedy of situation
Time of plot: Eighteenth century
Locale: England
First presented: 1773

Principal characters:
Mr. Hardcastle, an English gentleman
Mrs. Hardcastle, his wife
Tony Lumpkin, Mrs. Hardcastle's son
Kate Hardcastle, Mr. Hardcastle's daughter
Constance Neville, Tony's cousin
Marlow, Kate's reluctant suitor
Hastings, in love with Constance
Sir Charles, Marlow's father

Critique:

This charming play has entertained audiences for more than one hundred and seventy-five years. Conditions of society on which the comedy is based have long since ceased to exist, but the gaiety of the plot and the racy dialogue are still amusing. Designed to satirize the sentimental comedy of Goldsmith's day, *She Stoops to Conquer* far outshines the exaggerated sentimentality of the author's contemporary stage.

The Story:

Mrs. Hardcastle, the wife of Mr. Hardcastle by a second marriage, had by her first husband a son, Tony Lumpkin. Tony was a lazy, spoiled boy, but his mother excused his actions by imagining him to be sickly. Mr. Hardcastle vowed that his stepson looked the picture of good health.

Kate Hardcastle, Mr. Hardcastle's daughter, was headstrong. To overcome his daughter's wish to be a lady of importance, Mr. Hardcastle had struck a bargain with her whereby she wore ordinary clothes and played a country girl during part of the day; at other times she was allowed to appear in fine clothes. Knowing it was time for his daughter to marry, Mr. Hardcastle sent for Mr. Marlow, the son of his closest friend, to meet Kate. Kate was pleased by her father's description of the young man in all features except one. She did not like the fact that he was considered shy and retiring.

Mrs. Hardcastle hoped to arrange a match between Tony and Constance Neville, her ward and Kate's best friend. The two young people mutually hated each other but pretended otherwise for Mrs. Hardcastle's sake. On the day of Mr. Marlow's expected arrival, Constance identified the prospective bridegroom as the friend of Hastings, the man whom Constance really loved. Constance described Marlow as being very shy with fashionable young ladies but quite a different character with girls of lower station.

En route to the Hardcastle home, Hastings and Marlow lost their way and arrived at an ale-house where Tony was carousing with friends. Recognizing the two men, Tony decided to play a trick on his stepfather. When Hastings and Marlow asked the way to the Hardcastle home, Tony told them that they were lost and would be wise to stop at an inn a short distance up the road. Marlow and Hastings arrived at their destination but thought it the inn Tony had described. Hardcastle, knowing nothing of their misconception, treated them as guests, while Hastings and Marlow treated him as an innkeeper, each party thinking the other extremely rude. Hardcastle decided that Marlow's apparent character was in contradiction to the modest personage who had been described to him.

When Hastings met Constance, she quickly recognized Tony's hand in the mischief, but Hastings and Constance kept the secret to themselves. Hastings explained to Marlow that the two young ladies had arrived at the inn after a long journey through the country. When Tony came home, Hastings took him aside and explained his desire to marry Constance, an arrangement quite satisfactory to the rascal. He promised to help the lovers and even to try to secure Constance's jewelry, which was in Mrs. Hardcastle's keeping. The bargain having been made, Tony went to his mother's room and stole the gems. He gave them to Hastings. When Constance asked for the jewels, Tony whispered to his mother that she should tell Constance they had been lost. Thinking it a capital plan, Mrs. Hardcastle complied with Tony's suggestion, only to discover later that the gems actually were gone. Meanwhile, Kate, according to her agreement with her father, had put on a pleasant, simple dress.

Learning of Marlow's mistaken idea that he was at an inn, Kate decided to keep him in error. Marlow, seeing Kate in her simple dress, thought she was a serving-girl, and revealed himself as a flirtatious dandy. As he was trying to kiss her, Mr. Hardcastle entered the room, and Marlow fled. Mr. Hardcastle remarked to Kate that obviously she now had proof that Marlow was no modest young man. Kate vowed she would convince her father Marlow had the kind of personality pleasing to them both. However, Marlow's continued impudence aroused Hardcastle to such an uncontrollable state that he ordered him to leave his house. Kate, thinking the time had come to enlighten her deceived suitor, told Marlow about the trick Tony had played. Marlow, still unaware of Kate's real identity, found himself more and more attracted to her, while Kate was discovering him to be a fine and honest person.

Hastings had given Marlow the jewels which Tony had stolen from Mrs. Hardcastle. To protect the valuables, Marlow had sent them to Mrs. Hardcastle, supposing her to be the innkeeper's wife. The servants, under Tony's instructions, then explained to the distraught lady that the jewels had been mislaid because of some confusion in the household.

Mrs. Hardcastle discovered that Hastings planned to elope with Constance. Enraged, she decided to punish Constance by sending her to visit her Aunt Pedigree. To add to the confusion, news came that Sir Charles, Marlow's father, was on his way to the Hardcastle home.

Tony offered to drive the coach for Mrs. Hardcastle, but instead of taking the ladies to the house of Aunt Pedigree, he drove them around in a circle for three hours until Mrs. Hardcastle believed they were lost. After hiding his terrified mother in the bushes, Tony took Constance back to Hastings. But Constance was determined not to leave without her jewels. When Mrs. Hardcastle at last discovered Tony's trick, she was furious.

Sir Charles, on his arrival, was greatly amused by Hardcastle's account of Marlow's mistake. Hardcastle assured Sir Charles that Marlow loved Kate, but Marlow insisted he was not interested in Miss Hardcastle. Kate promised the two fathers she would prove that Marlow loved her, and she told them to hide while she talked with Marlow. Still under the impression that Kate was a serving-girl, the wretched young man told her he loved her and wanted to marry her. Sir Charles and Hardcastle emerged from their hiding place satisfied that the marriage would be arranged. Marlow was upset to learn that the serving-girl with whom he had behaved so freely was really Miss Hardcastle.

Mrs. Hardcastle reminded her husband that she had full control of Constance's fortune until Tony married her when he became of age. But if he should refuse her, Constance would be given control of her inheritance. It was then announced that Tony's real age had been hidden in the hope that the lad would improve his character. Informed that he was already of age, Tony refused to marry Constance. Sir Charles assured Mrs. Hardcastle that Hastings was a fine young man, and Constance obtained her jewels from her guardian.

So Kate married Marlow, and Constance married Hastings. And Tony gained his freedom from his mother.

THE SHELTERED LIFE

Type of work: Novel
Author: Ellen Glasgow (1874-1945)
Type of plot: Social criticism
Time of plot: Twentieth century
Locale: Virginia
First published: 1932

Principal characters:
General Archbald, a Southern gentleman
Jenny Blair Archbald, his granddaughter
George Birdsong, his neighbor
Eva Birdsong, George's wife

Critique:

Ellen Glasgow, at a time when many writers of her generation and section of the United States saw fit to write in experimental patterns, kept to established traditions of writing. The result was a lucid, realistic approach to the problem of Southern society in the early twentieth century. A tragedy that is the necessary outcome of folly is presented clearly and with distinction in *The Sheltered Life.* There can be no criticism of Miss Glasgow's logic. The novel is a revealing picture of manners and morals.

The Story:

The Archbalds and the Birdsongs

were the last of the old families left on once-fashionable Washington Street, and they clung to it along with their passion for the gentility of the past decades in an effort to keep things as they had always known them. They not only disliked change; they also forbade it on their premises.

Jenny Blair Archbald was five when her father died. A short time later her mother had gone to live with her husband's father and his two unmarried daughters, Etta and Isabella.

At the end of the block lived Eva and George Birdsong. Eva, after twelve years of marriage, was still the acknowledged beauty among her wide circle of friends. They had no doubt that had she so chosen she might have been a famous prima donna or a great actress. Her husband, however, was not successful; he lost his inheritance, he drank, and he was unfaithful to her.

Jenny Blair Archbald wanted new roller-skates. Her grandfather, General Archbald, promised to give her a penny a page for reading *Little Women,* but Jenny Blair found the book dull reading. She would rather have been investigating Canal Street against her mother's wishes.

Aunt Etta was having one of her spells. Doomed to a single life by her unpopularity with men, Etta suffered all sorts of nervous disorders. Isabella, having just broken off an engagement, was currently allowing herself to talk frequently with Joseph Crocker, a carpenter.

Jenny Blair finally took her old roller-skates and skated in the direction of Canal Street. There she stumbled and was taken in by Memoria, the Birdsong's mulatto laundress. While she was recovering she saw George Birdsong, who took her home but made sure that she promised to tell no one where she had met him.

The Peytons were giving a ball which Jenny Blair was to attend, although she and young Bena Peyton were to keep out of sight and out of the way. Her aunts were preparing to go. Eva Birdsong was making over an old gown for the affair and was planning to dance only two dances, the first and the last, both with her husband.

At the dance Eva saw George walking in the garden with Delia Barron. She promptly fainted, recovered in the children's nursery, and had to be carried home by her husband.

Seven years passed. Old General Archbald, now eighty-three, mused over his life and that of his relatives. He had always surrendered the things he wanted most for the things he had felt were his duty. Now he wondered what he had done with his life. Isabella had broken two engagements to marry Joseph Crocker, a man socially beneath her. Jenny Blair's mother had loved his son and his son had died while fox hunting. Eva Birdsong had given up everything for a husband who was indifferent to her beauty and her wit. And now Eva, whom he admired greatly, was being operated on.

Eva was past the age when she was likely to have children, but she had hidden the nature of her illness as long as possible until now her life was in danger. For many long hours the old general relived in his memories the fleeting events of his life.

The general visited Eva in the hospital. Eva seemed despondent. She made him promise to look after George and retold many amusing old tales about her life with her husband. As he left the sick woman's room, the old man wondered how he could help her or if there were any help on earth for her.

Now old enough to make her appearance in the formal society of the dignified old city, Jenny Blair rebelled against her mother's formal plans. Instead, she and Bena Peyton hoped to go to New York. Jenny Blair thought that she wanted to be an actress.

One day George Birdsong waited for Jenny Blair outside the hospital, where they talked as the sun was setting. Suddenly, before she knew what had happened, George seized her and kissed her. Jenny Blair was unsure of her emotions, although George pretended it was the kind of a kiss he had always given her —a sort of little girl's kiss. But this kiss, she was positive, was different.

When she accompanied her grandfather home, she told him that she thought she would give up going on the stage or even going to New York.

The old man was puzzled and tired. Cora, Jenny Blair's mother, mixed a mint julep for him in an effort to revive him, but he felt that the drink had little effect. As he went upstairs to dress for dinner he saw his sick daughter Etta reading in bed one of her endless French love stories. He wished in vain she might have had some of Isabella's charm so that she might have married.

At the hospital the next day Jenny Blair left a kimono for Eva to wear. Old General Archbald listened with disgust to George Birdsong's exhibition of grief for his wife's suffering. Then, just as the operation was about over, the old man had a heart attack which he kept secret.

Jenny Blair had become infatuated with George Birdsong, or thought she was, and to her that was the same thing. She pretended to be angry with him, but when he took his wife away for a rest after her illness Jenny Blair counted the days until he should return. She wondered why she had ever wanted to go to New York, and she decided that she hated Eva's cousin, John Welch, a doctor, because he seemed to understand her strange moods better than she herself understood them.

When George Birdsong returned alone, Jenny Blair sought him out and admitted she loved him. George, somewhat surprised, tried to put her off. Finally he kissed her as she desired him to do, but he tried to make her see that she was being very foolish.

When autumn came and the Archbalds returned from their summer vacation, Jenny Blair was glad because she could see George Birdsong again. At the same time she visited Eva, who seemed to get no better.

George had shot some ducks and tied cards to their necks with bits of Eva's green ribbon, for he intended to give them away to his friends. That evening Jenny Blair and George stood together in the garden of the Birdsong home. As George bent to embrace her, they heard Eva, who had arisen from her bed. George went into the house at his wife's insistence. A few minutes later there was a shot. When John Welch called Jenny Blair into the house, she saw George dead from a gunshot wound and Eva with a strangely vacant look on her face. The dead ducks and George's gun were lying in the hall. John insisted that the shooting had been an accident. Old General Archbald, when he arrived, asserted also that it had been an accident. Jenny Blair, in terror and shame, found refuge in hysteria.

SILAS MARNER

Type of work: Novel
Author: George Eliot (Mary Ann Evans, 1819-1880)
Type of plot: Domestic realism
Time of plot: Early nineteenth century
Locale: England
First published: 1861

Principal characters:
SILAS MARNER, a weaver
EPPIE, his adopted daughter
AARON WINTHROP, whom Eppie married

Godfrey Cass, Eppie's father
Dunstan Cass, his wastrel brother
Nancy Lammeter, whom Godfrey married

Critique:

George Eliot's intent in writing *Silas Marner: the Weaver of Raveloe* was to show that good things come to pure, natural people. In contrast to the deadly serious nature of the hero are the simple and humorous village characters. Silas does not belong to the realm of important literary characters. He is merely a symbol of patience, pathos, and goodness; the victim of an injustice which he does nothing to rectify. He waits for sixteen years until justice, the abstraction, conquers, and Silas, the man, reaps his deserved harvest.

The Story:

In the small community of Raveloe lived the linen-weaver, Silas Marner. Long years at his spinning-wheel had left Silas extremely near-sighted so that his vision was limited to only those objects which were very bright or very close to him. Because of an unjust accusation of theft, Silas had left his former home at Lantern Yard and had become a recluse. For fifteen years the lonely, shriveled man had lived for no purpose but to hoard the money he received in payment for his weaving. Night after night he took his golden hoard from its hiding place in the floor of his cottage and let the shining pieces run through his fingers.

The leading man in Raveloe was Squire Cass, who had one fine son, Godfrey, and one wastrel son, Dunstan. It was said that Godfrey would marry Nancy Lammeter. But Godfrey had become involved in Dunstan's gambling debts. He had lent his spendthrift brother some of the squire's rent money, which Dunstan had lost in gambling. Since neither brother could raise the money, they decided that Dunstan must sell Godfrey's favorite horse, Wildfire, at a nearby fair. Godfrey's one fear was that this affair would harm his reputation in the neighborhood and his chance with Nancy. Another thing that weighed on Godfrey's conscience and prevented his declaration to Nancy was the fact that he was already married. Once he had been drunk in a tavern in a distant hamlet, and in that condition he had married a low-bred, common woman. Sober, he had fled back to Raveloe and kept his marriage a secret.

Dunstan rode Wildfire across the fog-dimmed fields and crippled the animal on a high jump. With no means of raising the money, half-drunk and fear-driven, Dunstan came to Silas Marner's cottage. He knew the neighborhood gossip that the weaver had a hoard of gold hidden away. The cottage was empty, and instinct soon led the drunken boy to the hiding place of the gold. Stealing out of the cabin with his prize and stumbling through the night, Dunstan fell into an abandoned quarry pit and was killed.

The robbery of Silas' cottage furnished gossip for the entire community. Another mystery was the disappearance of Dunstan Cass. Godfrey was forced now to tell his father about the rent money he had given Dunstan and about the loss of the valuable horse, which had been found dead. Silas began to receive visitors from the neighborhood. One of his most frequent callers was Dolly Winthrop and her son Aaron, a charming little boy. Yet Silas could not be persuaded to come out of his hermitage; he secretly mourned the loss of his gold.

On New Year's Eve a destitute woman died in the snow near Silas' cottage. She had with her a little yellow-haired girl who made her way toward the light shining through the cottage window and entered the house. Returning from an errand, Silas saw a golden gleam in front of his fireplace, a gleam which he mistook for his lost gold. On closer examination, he discovered a sleeping baby. Following the child's tracks through the snow, he came upon the body of the dead woman.

Godfrey was dancing happily with Nancy when Silas appeared to say that he had found a body. Godfrey went with the others to the scene and saw to his horror that the dead woman was his estranged wife. He told no one of her identity, and had not the courage to claim the baby for his own. Silas, with a confused association between the golden-haired child and his lost hoard, tenaciously clung to the child. After Dolly Winthrop spoke up in favor of his proper attitude toward children, the villagers decided to leave the baby with the old weaver.

Years passed. Under the spell of the child who in her baby language called herself Eppie instead of the Biblical Hephzibah that Silas had bestowed upon her, the cottage of the weaver of Raveloe took on a new appearance. Lacy curtains decorated the once drab windows, and Silas himself outgrew his shell of reticence. Dolly brought her son to play with Eppie. Silas was happy. Even his blighted past was cleared, for Eppie caused Silas to return to Lantern Yard, where he found evidence that proved his innocence.

Godfrey Cass married Nancy, but it was a childless union. For sixteen years Godfrey secretly carried with him the thought of his child growing up under the care of Silas. At last the old stone quarry was drained and workmen found a skeleton identified by Dunstan's watch and seals. Beside the skeleton was Silas' lost bag of gold, stolen on the night of Dunstan's disappearance. With this discovery, Godfrey's past reopened its sealed doors. He felt that the time had come to tell Nancy the truth. When he confessed the story of Eppie's birth, Nancy agreed with him that they should go to Silas and Eppie with their tale. Hearing this strange story of Eppie's parentage, the unselfish weaver opened the way for Eppie to take advantage of her wealthy heritage; but Eppie fled to the arms of the man who had been a father and a mother to her when no one else would claim her.

There was one thing remaining to complete the weaver's happiness. Eppie married Aaron Winthrop, her childhood playmate, while Silas beamed happily on the scene of her wedding.

SISTER CARRIE

Type of work: Novel
Author: Theodore Dreiser (1871-1945)
Type of plot: Naturalism
Time of plot: 1889
Locale: Chicago and New York
First published: 1900

Principal characters:
CARRIE MEEBER, a small-town girl
CHARLES DROUET, her first lover
G. W. HURSTWOOD, Drouet's friend and Carrie's second lover

Critique:

Dreiser's first novel is, in some ways, somewhat superior to much of his later work. As usual, his characters are vivid and lifelike, sympathetically portrayed. Unlike some of the later novels, *Sister Carrie* is well-unified, the style more fluent and natural. A companion piece to Stephen Crane's *Maggie*—and a comparison between the two books is always interesting and revealing—it is also historically significant as a pioneer work of the naturalistic movement in American literature.

The Story:

When Carrie Meeber left her home town in Wisconsin, she had nothing but a few dollars and a certain unspoiled beauty and charm. Young, inexperienced, she was going to Chicago to live with her sister and to find work. While on the train, she met Charles Drouet, a genial, flashy traveling salesman. Before the train pulled into the station, they had exchanged addresses, and Drouet promised to call on Carrie at her sister's house.

When she arrived at her sister's home, Carrie discovered that her life there would be far from the happy, carefree existence of which she had dreamed. The Hansons were hard-working people, grim and penny-pinching, allowing themselves no pleasures, and living a dull, conventional life. It was clear to Carrie that Drouet could not possibly call there, not only because of the unattractive atmosphere, but also because the Hansons were sure to object to him. She wrote and told him that he was not to call, that she would get in touch with him later.

Meanwhile Carrie went job-hunting and finally found work in a small shoe factory. Of her first wages, all but fifty cents went to her sister and brother-in-law. Then she fell ill and lost her job. Once again she had to look for work. Day after day she trudged the streets, without success. It seemed as if she would have to go back to Wisconsin, and the Hansons encouraged her to do so. If she could not bring in money, they did not want her.

One day, while Carrie was looking for work, she met Drouet and told him her troubles. He offered her money which, with reluctance, she finally accepted. The money was for clothes she needed, but she did not know how to explain the source of the money to her sister. Drouet solved the problem by suggesting that he rent a room for her, where she could keep her clothing. A few days later Carrie went to live with Drouet, who had promised to marry her as soon as he had completed a business deal.

In the meantime Drouet introduced her to a friend, G. W. Hurstwood. Hurstwood had a good job as the manager of a saloon, a comfortable home, a wife, and two grown children. More than twice Carrie's age, he nevertheless accepted Drouet's suggestion that he look in on her while the salesman was out of town on one of his trips. Before long Hurstwood was passionately in love with her. When Drouet came back, he discovered from a chambermaid that Carrie and Hurstwood had been going out together frequently. A scene followed. Carrie was furious when Drouet told her that Hurstwood was already married. She blamed Drouet for her folly, saying that he should have told her that Hurstwood was a married man.

Meanwhile, Mrs. Hurstwood had become suspicious of her husband. Drouet had secured for Carrie a part in a theatrical entertainment which a local lodge was presenting. Hurstwood, hearing that Carrie was to appear, persuaded many of his friends to go with him to the show. Mrs. Hurstwood learned of the affair and heard, too, that her husband had been seen riding with an unknown woman. She confronted Hurstwood and told him that she intended to sue for divorce. Faced with social and financial ruin, Hurstwood was in despair. One night he discovered that his employer's safe was open. He robbed it of several thousand dollars and went to Carrie's apartment. Drouet had just deserted her. Pretending that Drouet had been hurt, Hurstwood succeeded in getting Carrie on a train bound for Montreal. In Montreal Hurstwood was approached by an agent of his former employer, who urged him to return the money and to settle the issue quietly. Hurstwood returned all but a relatively small sum.

Under the name of Wheeler, he and Carrie were married, Carrie being all the while under the impression that the ceremony was legal. Then they left for New York. There Hurstwood looked for work, but with no success. Finally he bought a partnership in a small tavern. After a time the partnership was dissolved and he lost all his money. Every day he went looking for work. Gradually he grew less eager for a job, and began staying at home all day. When bills piled up, he and Carrie moved to a new apartment to escape their creditors.

Carrie set out to find work and was lucky enough to get a job as a chorus girl. With a friend, she took an apartment and left Hurstwood to himself. Soon Carrie became a well-known actress, and a local hotel invited her to become a guest there, at a nominal expense. Carrie had many friends and admirers. She had money and all the comforts and luxuries which appealed to a small-town girl.

Hurstwood had not fared so well. He could find no work. Once he worked as a scab, during some labor troubles, but he left that job because it was too hazardous. He became a bum, living in Bowery flophouses and begging on the streets. One day he went to see Carrie. She gave him some money, largely because she had seen Drouet and had learned for the first time of Hurstwood's theft in Chicago. She believed that Hurstwood had kept his disgrace a secret in order to spare her feelings.

Although Carrie was a toast of the town, she was not happy in spite of her success. She was invited to give performances abroad. In the meantime Hurstwood died and, unknown to Carrie, was buried in the potter's field. As Carrie was sailing for London, Hurstwood's ex-wife, daughter, and prospective son-in-law were coming into the city, eager for pleasure and social success, a success made possible by the daughter's coming marriage and by Hurstwood's divorce settlement, which had given the family all of his property.

SMOKE

Type of work: Novel
Author: Ivan Turgenev (1818-1883)
Type of plot: Social criticism
Time of plot: 1862-1865
Locale: Germany and Russia
First published: 1867

Principal characters:
Grigóry Litvínoff, a serious Russian
Tánya Shestoff, his fiancée
Kapitólina Shestoff, Tánya's aunt
Irína, a fashionable lady
General Ratmíroff, her husband
Potúgin, a retired clerk

Critique:

Smoke has for background the nihilistic movement in Russian politics just after the emancipation of the serfs. In background of period and place it is comparable to *Fathers and Sons*. But *Smoke* is different from its predecessor in time in that it is a pleasant, unencumbered love story, a novel of deftly drawn characters. The political theme of *Smoke* is not intrusive; few modern readers will even be aware of the political tensions involved. The character of Irína was modeled from a mistress of Alexander II.

The Story:

At Baden Grigóry Litvínoff decided to enjoy a few days of vacation. The fashionable German watering place was full of Russians, and there, in a week or so, Litvínoff was to meet Tánya Shestoff, his fiancée, who was coming to Baden with her Aunt Kapitólina.

Litvínoff was poor, comparatively speaking. His father owned a large farm with forests, meadows, and a lake, but Russian farming was so unproductive that he could barely make ends meet. After his university days, Litvínoff had decided to learn progressive farming, but because Russia was so far behind in agriculture he had to go abroad to study. He had been in the Crimea, in France, Switzerland, and England. Everywhere his keen mind had absorbed the latest agricultural methods, and he was particularly impressed by the superiority of the few pieces of American machinery he had seen. Full of ideas, his life was planned; he would make a model farm. But first, he would marry Tánya.

Quite by chance he ran into Bambáeff, a former acquaintance. Bambáeff was an ebullient person, filled with windy politics and intimate with the most advanced thinkers in Baden. When Bambáeff took Litvínoff to meet Gubaryóff, the idol of the liberals, Litvínoff was repelled by the company he met in Gubaryóff's room. They all talked long and loud in their assertions that Russia produced nothing good, that all virtue resided in Europe proper, that the emancipation of the serfs was a foolish step. He met Bindásoff, a choleric boor who borrowed a hundred roubles from him; he never repaid the debt, although Litvínoff later watched him win four hundred roubles with the money. Only one man in the gathering was quiet; he sat unnoticed in a corner.

The next morning the quiet man came to Litvínoff's room and presented himself; he was Potúgin, a former clerk in Moscow. They talked agreeably for a long time. Both men disliked very much their compatriots who were so sure that nothing good came out of Russia, and they both agreed that by hard work Russia could advance. At last, as Potúgin rose to go, he excused himself by saying that he had a girl with him. Seeing Litvínoff's look of polite blankness, he explained that he was looking after a little child who had no parents.

After a short walk Litvínoff returned to his hotel. He had a letter from Tánya to read, and as he read he was bothered by a heavy sweet smell. Looking around, he saw a bunch of fresh heliotrope in a glass. Here was a mystery. The servant said that a lady had given him two gulden to get into the room. She must have left the flowers. Suddenly he remembered Irína.

Ten years before Litvínoff had been a student in Moscow. He was poor, and he visited frequently another poor family, the Osínins. The family was of the real nobility, but for generations the Osínins had declined, until they existed only on a small pension the father received from some obscure sinecures. Litvínoff was attracted greatly to Irína, the seventeen-year-old daughter of the household, but for a long time Irína paid little heed to the poor student. One day her haughtiness suddenly changed. Pliant and cheerful, she talked eagerly with Litvínoff of his ambitions. When he declared his love, Irína was pleased and grateful. Without any formal understanding, Litvínoff became her accepted suitor.

By a trick of fate, Prince Osínin, her father, received an invitation to the court ball. Now that Irína was grown, he decided to accept, to show his daughter in fine society. Litvínoff urged Irína to go to the ball. She repeated many times that she was going only at Litvínoff's insistence.

On the night of the ball, Litvínoff brought her a bunch of heliotrope to wear. She took the flowers and kissed him passionately. The next day Irína had a headache and refused to see him. Two days after the ball Irína had gone to St. Peterburg with Count Reisenbach, a distant cousin of her mother.

The explanation was brief and tragic. The count needed an ornament in his household. Grasping and ambitious as she was, Irína had accepted and had gone to stay with her debauched cousin. Litvínoff put her out of his mind; he had almost forgotten the incident until the heliotrope appeared mysteriously in his room.

Litvínoff wrestled with his conscience and decided not to see Irína again. He held to his resolve until Potúgin came to him with a pressing invitation to visit the home of General Ratmíroff. At the party he met Irína again, now the wife of General Ratmíroff, a vain, cruel aristocrat. Litvínoff was as much repelled by the empty smart set as he had been by the empty liberals he had met in Baden.

Irína would not let him ignore her. She begged her former suitor to love her again, and when she came to his rooms he admitted his love had never died.

Tánya and her Aunt Kapitólina appeared. Even naïve Tánya saw at once that something had happened to her fiancé; she was not wholly unprepared when he confessed his affair with Irína.

Potúgin tried his best to get Litvínoff to abandon Irína. He had good reason to do so. For love of Irína, he had agreed to marry a friend of hers who was soon to bear an illegitimate child. Although the girl fell ill and the marriage never took place, Potúgin was burdened with the care of the little girl. He had acted because of his hopeless infatuation for Irína, and he warned Litvínoff that only evil could come of leaving Tánya for the shallow aristocrat.

In his despair Litvínoff made a compact. He would not become Irína's secret lover; she must go away with him and be his alone. He named the train on which he would leave. Irína was not at the station and Litvínoff sadly took his seat. Just then he saw Irína, dressed in her maid's costume, rush to the platform. He motioned her to come aboard; she understood, but she refused by gesture and motioned him to dismount. She stood in a hopeless attitude on the platform as the train pulled out.

Litvínoff recovered almost wholly from his hurt. He was too quiet for his years, but he was fairly happy. He found his father's farm in bad shape, with not even enough income to keep up the house. His father, pathetically glad to see him, abandoned the control of the estate to his son. That end accomplished, he died content. For a long time there was no opportunity to introduce new methods; Litvínoff had all he could do to remain solvent.

After three years he learned that Tánya was living on a farm a day's journey away. Resolved to mend his life, he decided to go to her and ask her forgiveness. He found Tánya ready to forget as well as forgive, and she was even embarrassed by his penitence. They were soon married.

Irína continued to attract admirers in St. Petersburg, for, in spite of her thirty years, she retained the freshness of youth. Although many gallants were in attendance upon her, she never singled out a special admirer. The society ladies all agreed that Irína was not generally liked; she had such an ironical turn of mind.

SNOW-BOUND

Type of work: Poem
Author: John Greenleaf Whittier (1807-1892)
Type of plot: Pastoral idyl
Time of plot: Early nineteenth century
Locale: Haverhill, Massachusetts
First published: 1866

Principal characters:
MEMBERS OF THE WHITTIER FAMILY
THE SCHOOLMASTER
A GUEST

Critique:

Snow-Bound, Whittier's popular idyl, is one of the most beautiful pastorals in American literature. The harshness of winter life on a New England farm is scarcely suggested, for the glow of the aging poet's memory gives the impression that in his youth life was serene, secure, and joyful. The title suggests a nature poem, but the poet's chief interest is not in the external world. He dwells upon the people who were dear to him, picturing a family circle which represents an idealization of the American home.

The Story:

One December day a wind from the east and a leaden sky forecast snow. As night came on, the members of the Whittier family brought in firewood, littered the cattle stalls with fresh straw, and fed the stock. All night the storm raged, and in the morning the Whittiers looked upon a world of fleecy snow. The elder Whittier, a man of action, ordered a path dug to the barn, and his sons merrily turned to the work, making a crystal-walled tunnel through the deepest drift. Though the snow no longer fell, all day a north wind drove bits of sleet against the windows of the house. Again, as night fell, wood was brought in for the great fireplace around which the family gathered. While the moon shone on the snow outside and the north wind still battered the house, the family stayed snug and warm inside.

As the poet recalled this happy scene of long ago, he paused a moment to think of the many changes which had later taken place. Only he and his brother now remained; death had taken all the others. Again his memory went back to the old fireside, the stories told there, the puzzles and riddles solved, the poems recited. The elder Whittier told of adventures he had had with the Indians, of fishing trips, and of the witches reputed to have inhabited the land in olden days. The mother told of Indian raids and of the happy times she had had as a girl. To these stories from her own life she added some which she had read in books by famous and revered Quakers. Next the poet called to mind the tales of the world of nature told by his uncle, a man unschooled in a formal way but seemingly filled with a boundless knowledge of moons and tides, of weather signs, of birds and beasts. The memory of the poet's maiden aunt brought her also vividly before him. He remembered how she lived for others instead of bewailing her lonely maidenhood. He saw again his elder sister whose rich, full nature had prompted many deeds of self-sacrifice. Tenderly he recalled his dearly loved younger sister, who had been with him until a year ago, but whose body now lay with the others in the earth.

From the members of his family, the poet turned to the young schoolmaster, a boarder in the Whittier home. The son of a poor man, the schoolmaster had as a boy learned independence. As a student he had helped to pay his way through Dartmouth College by taking varied jobs. Later as a teacher he had, when school was out, joined in schoolboy sports. In the schoolroom he was the earnest shaper of youthful minds. The poet prayed that Freedom might have many young apostles like him.

Another guest of the Whittier household on that night of long ago came to the poet's mind. A strange woman, half-feared, half-welcome, she was as well-known for her violent temper as she was for her eccentric devotion to religion. Leaving her home, she later went to Europe and the Near East, prophesying everywhere the imminent second coming of Christ. The poet asked His mercy upon the poor woman whose mind had seemed so odd to her neighbors.

As the hour grew late the group about the fire retired for the night. The next morning teamsters came to clear the snow-filled roads. The young folks played in the snowbanks. Later, along the cleared road came the neighborhood doctor on his rounds. A week passed before the mailman finally delivered a newspaper to tell of happenings beyond the Whittiers' snow-bound world.

The poet shut the covers of his book of memory upon these happy scenes of the past, and he put the book away with the hope that readers in the future might pause with him to view for a little while these Flemish pictures of old days.

SO RED THE ROSE

Type of work: Novel
Author: Stark Young (1881-)
Type of plot: Historical romance
Time of plot: 1860-1865
Locale: Mississippi
First published: 1934

Principal characters:
MALCOLM BEDFORD, owner of Portobello
MRS. SARAH TAIT BEDFORD, his wife
DUNCAN,
MARY HARTWELL, and
FRANCES, their children
VALETTE, an adopted daughter
MIDDLETON, an orphaned nephew
HUGH MCGEHEE, owner of Montrose
AGNES MCGEHEE, his wife, Malcolm Bedford's sister
EDWARD, and
LUCINDA (LUCY), their children
SHELTON TALIAFERRO, a distant relative of the McGehees
CHARLES, his son
ZACH MCGEHEE, Hugh's nephew
AMELIE BALFOUR, Zach's fiancée

Critique:

Stark Young takes rather long to set the stage for the action in this novel. The gradual unfolding of character and scene is necessary, however, because the book is not so much a story of the political and military aspects of the Civil War as it is a study of the effects of the war upon those who stayed at home. The book presents an excellent picture of the background of plantation life prior to the Civil War, tells of people's thoughts at the time, and shows what happened to the civilian population during the war years.

The Story:

Malcolm Bedford was the owner of Portobello plantation, where he lived with his second wife, Sarah, and their three children, an adopted daughter, Valette, and an orphaned nephew, Middleton. Malcolm's sister Agnes had married Hugh McGehee, and they and their two children occupied a neighboring plantation, Montrose. Plantation life in Mississippi flowed easily in those days just preceding the Civil War, with frequent parties and visits between families to provide hospitality and entertainment. But other happenings, less pleasant, gradually intruded upon the serenity of plantation life. Talk of secession, states' rights, slavery, emancipation, Lincoln, and war began to be more seriously discussed and argued whenever a group of people assembled. Hugh McGehee and his son Edward discussed these problems and Edward's possible enlistment when the latter returned home for a short visit from the Louisiana Seminary of Learning and Military Academy.

Duncan Bedford was also in school, at Washington College in Virginia. In love with Valette, he accused her of leading other young men on. When he went back to college, they were no longer on friendly terms.

Shelton Taliaferro, a distant relative of the McGehees, and his son Charles came to visit Montrose. Edward was home for a visit at the time, and the two young men became friends. They spent a short time together at the seminary until Charles resigned. It was this young man, to whom life seemed to flow generously, who attached himself to Edward. A year after his first visit to Montrose he and Edward enlisted under General Beauregard. Shelton Taliaferro, his father, and Edward McGehee were the only two people for whom Charles cared, to the disappointment of Lucy, who had fallen in love with him. Duncan also enlisted, but without first coming home. He wrote a letter to Valette to tell her of his enlistment and to assure her that he still loved her.

About a year later, at the time of the battle of Pittsburg Landing, Agnes received a letter from her son. It was dated three days earlier and according to his letter the battle would be taking place at that moment she was reading the letter. Feeling instinctively that Edward was dead, she ordered William Veal, the butler, to hitch up the wagon so that they might set out for the battlefield and bring home the body of her dead son. When she returned, she brought with her Edward's body and those of two other boys of the neighborhood. She also brought word that the body of Charles Taliaferro had not been found, although it was almost certain that he was dead since he was not with the survivors of the desperate fighting. Lucy was heartbroken.

After the Emancipation Proclamation on January 2, 1863, many of the slaves deserted their former owners to flee to the Union lines. A short time later Malcolm Bedford, who had been helping to strengthen the defenses at Vicksburg, came home with a very bad case of dysentery from which he never recovered. He died, on the day Vicksburg fell, claiming that with the fall of Vicksburg the doom of the South was sealed.

Life went on at both plantations under much altered circumstances. Natchez, the nearest town, had been bombarded and occupied. Federal soldiers swarmed over the countryside, burning, looting, and carrying off horses, food, and clothing. More slaves ran away to the protection of Federal troops in Natchez, and many joined the Federal army to help fight against their former masters. But when disease broke out in the Natchez stockades, where the Negroes were confined, some of the former slaves, especially the older ones, began to return to the plantations, the only place they had ever known security.

Sherman, on a visit to Natchez, rode out to see the McGehees because he had known their son Edward when he was superintendent of the seminary Edward had attended. He was very much of an enigma to the McGehees, as he was to many. His kindness and personal interest could not be reconciled with his toleration of plunder and destruction by his troops. Shortly after his visit Montrose was destroyed by a mob of former slaves under the direction of a few white officers. They burned the place to the ground, after permitting the family to save only what could be rescued in twenty minutes. After the fire the family moved into a five-room cottage on the plantation.

The Bedfords at Portobello were having their own difficulties. One night a group of Confederate soldiers hanged three Federals on the trees not far from the house. A fourth soldier escaped, injured, and he was taken into the house and cared for until a way could be found to smuggle him out. The three Union soldiers were quickly buried to avoid reprisals.

There had been no word of Duncan for many months, and the Bedfords at Portobello believed that he must be dead. Now that the war was over, they thought that they should at least have a letter from him if he were still alive. Then one day Duncan, without any previous warning, walked in. He had been taken prisoner but had been booked for exchange soon afterward. A Union officer had spoken insultingly of General Lee, however, and Duncan had struck him. His order for exchange was immediately revoked and he was placed in irons, charged with having struck an officer of the United States Army. When peace was declared and all prisoners were released, Duncan's charge still stood. But at his trial the judge, who felt that a great injustice had been done Duncan, dismissed the case.

The South was beginning to feel the vengeance of the North. Many of the plantations had been burned and many of the men had been killed. The slave labor gone, there was no one to work the plantations. Heavy taxes were imposed to make the South pay for its military government. Negroes were insolent and destructive and carpetbaggers were beginning to buy up mortgages on the plantations, thus gaining control of huge amounts of property. Mrs. Bedford and Duncan decided that they would not mortgage their property but would try to make the land productive once more. During those grim years Duncan found Valette kinder and more understanding than she had been in the proud old days at Portobello.

Amelie Balfour and Zach McGehee, nephew of Hugh, were to be married. Amelie convinced Valette that they should make it a double wedding. Their plans were all made on the spur of the moment, and the next evening at Homewood, the home of Amelie's aunt, Duncan and Valette were married. They were to have a honeymoon in New Orleans and then return to Portobello to live.

THE SONG OF BERNADETTE

Type of work: Novel
Author: Franz Werfel (1890-1945)
Type of plot: Religious chronicle
Time of plot: 1858-1875
Locale: Lourdes, France
First published: 1941

Principal characters:
BERNADETTE SOUBIROUS, a religious mystic
LOUISE SOUBIROUS, her mother
FRANÇOIS SOUBIROUS, her father
DEAN PEYRAMALE, the parish priest
SISTER MARIE THERESE, Bernadette's teacher and superior

Critique:

Franz Werfel wrote this book as a fulfillment of a vow he made while hiding from the Nazis at the beginning of World War II. Every fact he records is absolutely true, but from the records of the actual apparition at Lourdes he has produced a novel of great interest and emotional power. Franz Werfel did not write a purely religious story; his book is a story of people who have the same emotions, the same hopes and fears, that all men and women share. For that reason *The Song of Bernadette* is a masterful work, haunted by shadows of the unknown, filled with delicate beauty and a strong affirmation of man's essential goodness.

The Story:

In Lourdes the Soubirous family had fallen into pitiful poverty. François Soubirous, having lost the mill whose products provided a livelihood for his family, was reduced to taking odd jobs that he could beg from the prosperous citizens of the little French village. His wife Louise helped out by taking in washing. But their combined earning, scant and irregular, were insufficient for the care of the children. The family lived in the *Cachot,* a dank, musty building that had been abandoned as a jail because it was unhealthy.

The oldest Soubirous child, Bernadette, was weak and suffered from asthma. At school she was considered, both by her schoolmates and her teacher, Sister Marie Therese, to be the most ignorant and stupid of all the children. Her ignorance extended even to religion. Although fourteen years old and the daughter of Catholic parents, she did not understand the meaning of the Holy Trinity. It was clear that little could be expected from the daughter of the poor and uneducated Soubirous family.

One day the children were sent out to gather firewood near the grotto of Massabielle. Close to the grotto ran a small stream into which the offal of the town was emptied. Carcasses of dead beasts were swept along by the current, and earlier that day François Soubirous had dumped there a cartload of amputated limbs and filthy bandages from the contagion ward of the local hospital. It was rumored that the spot had once been the scene of pagan religious ceremonies.

Slower than the rest, Bernadette became separated from the other children and went to the cave alone. Suddenly, to her great astonishment, a strange light shone at the mouth of the grotto. She was unable to believe her eyes when a beautiful lady appeared before her. Dressed in blue, her face shining with brilliant light, her bare feet twined with roses, the lady smiled at the frightened child. Bernadette threw herself on her knees and prayed.

When the other children came upon her they found her kneeling on the ground. After making the others promise to keep her secret, Bernadette told of her vision. But the children told and soon the whole town was laughing at stupid Bernadette. The next day she returned to the grotto and saw the lady once more. The vision told her to return each day for fifteen days.

When she returned again and again to the grotto, the townspeople were aroused. To the local intellectuals and the atheists, Bernadette's vision was an example of ignorant superstition. To government officials, it was a plot of the Church against the state. To the Church, it was a dangerous event that could lead to disaster for Catholics. No one in authority believed Bernadette, but the common people became more and more interested. Soon many went with her when she made her daily visits. At last the authorities tried every method to make the girl confess that her vision was a hoax, but without success.

One day the lady told Bernadette to ask Dean Peyramale to build a chapel on the site of the grotto. When Bernadette told the dean of the request, he angrily asked who the lady was. If she were truly a heaven-sent vision, persisted the dean, let her give some sign that would prove it. Let her make the rose bush in the cave bloom with roses in February.

The lady smiled when she heard the dean's message. She beckoned to Bernadette, wanting her to come forward. The girl moved toward the lady, bent down, and kissed the rose bush, scratching her face on the thorns. Then the lady told her to go to the spring and drink from it. When Bernadette started for the stream, the lady shook her head and told the girl to dig with her hands. In a short while, Bernadette reached moist soil. Scooping it up with her hands, she tried to drink the little water in it. The earth that she swallowed made her ill, however, and she vomited.

The crowd that had followed her was disgusted. To the people her actions had seemed those of a lunatic because they had seen no lady there, only the gray stone walls of the cave and its opening. They scoffed when Bernadette was taken away.

A few days later one of the townspeople went to the grotto. There, where Bernadette had dug, water had begun to flow. He scooped up some of the moist soil and applied it to his blind eye. After a while he could see; his blindness was gone. Local experts swore that there could be no spring there, that no water could flow from solid rock. By that time both the Church and the government were thoroughly aroused. Bernadette was forbidden to visit the grotto, and the place was barred to the public.

Reluctantly the dean began to wonder whether a miracle had occurred. After he discovered that roses were indeed blooming in the cave, he persuaded the Church authorities to set up a commission to investigate the whole affair. The dean was at last convinced that Bernadette had seen the Blessed Virgin. The commission agreed with his views. Finally the emperor ordered that the public be allowed to visit the grotto.

Throughout all the excitement Bernadette remained calm and humble. After the Church had given its sanction to her vision, she agreed to enter a convent. There her immediate superior was her former teacher, Sister Marie Therese. The nun, proud, arrogant, skeptical, refused to believe in Bernadette's vision.

As a nun Bernadette won the hearts of everyone by her humility, her friendliness, her genuine goodness. The prosperity of Lourdes, where pilgrims came from all over the world to be healed by the miraculous water, did not matter to her. When her family came to visit her, she was glad to see them, especially her father; but she was relieved when they left. For more than seventeen years she lived in the convent.

At last a tumor of the leg afflicted her with a long and agonizing illness. As she lay dying, Sister Marie Therese admitted her error and confessed belief in the miracle. In Lourdes, the town atheist was converted. Dean Peyramale, disappointed and sad because the Church authorities had ignored him in the establishment of a shrine built at the grotto, went to visit Bernadette during her last moments. Her death was peaceful and serene.

After her death the fame of Lourdes became world-wide. Bernadette has been canonized and is now a saint of the Roman Catholic Church.

THE SONG OF HIAWATHA

Type of work: Poem
Author: Henry Wadsworth Longfellow (1807-1882)
Type of plot: Legendary romance
Time of plot: Aboriginal period
Locale: Indian territory around Lake Superior
First published: 1855

Principal characters:
HIAWATHA, an Indian hero
MINNEHAHA, whom he married
NOKOMIS, his grandmother
MUDJEKEEWIS, the West Wind, Hiawatha's father

Critique:

Longfellow based his story on traditional legend among North American Indians of a warrior hero sent to clear the rivers, forests, and lakes, and to unite the tribes in peace. With this legend the poet combined other Indian traditions. Of particular interest are the folklore stories of the way the woodpecker got a red streak on his tuft of feathers, the introduction of picture writing, the gift of corn to man, and the origin of the peace pipe.

The Story:

Weary of the constant fighting of his people, the Great Spirit called together all Indian tribes to reprimand them for their foolish ways. He had given them fertile lands, abundant streams, and forests, but they had continued to hunt each other. He promised to send a prophet who would guide and teach them. Should they fail to follow his counsel, they would perish. Breaking off a piece of a red-stone precipice, he molded a pipe as a symbol of peace among them. He told the warriors to plunge themselves into the stream and wash the war paint from their faces, the bloodstains from their hands.

One evening in twilight the beautiful Nokomis fell to earth from the full moon. There among the ferns and mosses she bore a daughter, Wenonah. As Wenonah grew tall and lovely, Nokomis feared for her daughter and warned her to beware of Mudjekeewis, the West Wind. When Wenonah failed to heed the warning and succumbed to his wooing, she bore a son, Hiawatha. Deserted by the false and faithless Mudjekeewis, Wenonah died grieving for his love.

Hiawatha grew up in the wigwam of Nokomis. From boyhood he was skilled in the craft of hunters, in sports and manly arts and labors. He was a master of speed and accuracy with a bow and arrow. He had magic deerskin mittens which gave him great physical power. Upon his feet he wore magic moccasins which allowed him to stride a mile with each step.

Aroused by the story of his father's treachery, he vowed to visit Mudjekeewis and seek revenge. In the land of the West Wind the two fought for three days. At last Mudjekeewis told Hiawatha that it would be impossible for him to kill his immortal father. Pleased with the boy's courage, however, Mudjekeewis sent him back to his people as the prophet who had been promised. On his long journey home Hiawatha stopped in the land of the Dacotahs to purchase arrowheads from an old man. There he saw Minnehaha, the arrow-maker's lovely daughter.

When Hiawatha returned to his people, he built a wigwam in the forest and went there to fast. On the fourth day of his fast, as he lay exhausted on his couch, Hiawatha saw a youth dressed in green and yellow garments with green plumes over his forehead. The stranger informed Hiawatha that his prayers had been heard and that they would be answered should Hiawatha overcome him. In spite of his weakness, Hiawatha struggled bravely until the young stranger yielded himself. He ordered Hiawatha to strip his green and yellow garments and bury him, and then to guard his grave until he leaped again into the sunshine. Hiawatha faithfully guarded the grave until a green shoot appeared, then the yellow silk, and finally the matured ear of corn which was to feed his people.

Hiawatha next shaped a canoe from the birch tree. Then he set out with his strong friend, Kwasind, and cleared the rivers of roots, sandbars, and dead trees, to make the streams safe for the people. At another time he rid the lake of its greatest menace, the sturgeon.

Nokomis then bade Hiawatha to undertake the destruction of Pearl-Feather, the magician, who was responsible for fever, pestilence, and disease. Hiawatha prepared to battle the dozen serpents that guarded the entrance to the wizard's domain. As he approached, he killed them with his arrows. A woodpecker helped Hiawatha to overcome the magician by telling him to aim his arrows at the roots of the wizard's hair. Hiawatha rewarded the woodpecker by dabbing his tuft of feathers with the magician's blood, which the woodpecker wears to this day.

When Hiawatha told Nokomis that he intended to make Minnehaha his wife, Nokomis urged him to marry a woman of his own tribe. Hiawatha refused to listen to her arguments, however, and assured her that the marriage would unite the two tribes. On his return with Minnehaha, they were honored at a huge banquet at which Hiawatha's beloved friend, Chibiabos, sang his famous love songs, and Iagoo related his fanciful tales.

Hiawatha's people prospered in peace and raised abundant crops of corn. In order to keep a record of their tribal history, Hiawatha invented picture writing to tell their story.

One winter famine struck Hiawatha's people. Snow covered the forests and lakes so deeply that it was impossible for hunters to seek food. Hiawatha's people were starving and dying of fever. When Minnehaha died, Hiawatha mourned her death for seven days.

At last came the warmth and fertility of spring, and life began to return to the earth. There were rumors of the approach of white men in large canoes with sails. Hiawatha confirmed the rumors, for he had seen the white men in a vision. He urged his people to welcome the strangers and be friendly, adding that if they ignored his counsel the tribes would only destroy themselves.

As Hiawatha stood by the wigwam of Nokomis one evening, three white men approached, one of them a priest. Hiawatha welcomed them and invited his people to hear the stories the priest told of the Saviour. That night, as the white men lay sleeping, Hiawatha told Nokomis that the time for him to leave had arrived. Having fulfilled his promises, he left to travel through the portals of the Sunset, to the Land of the Hereafter.

THE SONG OF ROLAND

Type of work: Tale
Author: Unknown
Type of plot: Chivalric romance
Time of plot: About 800
Locale: Western Europe
First transcribed: Medieval manuscript

Principal characters:
ROLAND, prince in Charlemagne's court
OLIVER, his friend
CHARLEMAGNE, the Holy Roman Emperor
OGIER THE DANE, Roland's friend
GANELON, a wicked courtier
BERTHA, Roland's mother

Critique:

The Song of Roland is the latest of great hero tales. As a result it incorporates all of those which go before. In its narrative framework are legends of the Greeks and the Germans, and a fusing of historical accounts from the dark ages of Europe with folklore from the Far East. Poetic legends of the troubadours, the tales of Virgil, Dante, and Hebrew testament all blend together in this vast fabrication of chivalric ideals and romantic lore.

The Story:

The boy Roland grew up far from his home country and lived with his penniless mother in a cave formerly occupied by a lonely monk. Nevertheless, his mother had taught him that some day he should be a brave hero like his father, Milon, and serve with the great army of Charlemagne. When he asked his mother to tell him the story of his birth, he learned that through his father he was descended from great heroes of old, Trojan Hector on one side and Wotan, king of the Norse gods, on the other. His father, Milon, having incurred the wrath of Charlemagne for taking the king's sister, the Princess Bertha, as his wife, had come to Italy and there had died fighting pagans in single-handed combat.

One summer, when he was still only a lad, his friend Oliver, the son of a local prince, met him and the two watched the coming of the great Charlemagne into Italy, where the king was to receive the blessing of the Pope at Rome.

Roland was impressed by the royal pageant but not overawed. That night he walked into Charlemagne's banquet hall and demanded his rights for himself and his mother. Amused by the boy's daring, Charlemagne ordered that Bertha be brought to him. When the emperor recognized his long-lost sister, he rejoiced and gave her and her son a place of honor in his court.

Roland's boyhood years passed quickly and with increasing honors. At first he was merely a page in the court, his duties being to attend the ladies, to carry messages, and to learn court etiquette. He was permitted to accompany the king's knights during war with the Saxons, and he was present when the swan knight, of the race of Lohengrin, appeared at the court of Charlemagne.

When Roland was fourteen years old, he became a squire and made the acquaintance of Ogier the Dane, a hostage prince at Charlemagne's court. The two boys became great friends. Then, urged by a new queen, Ogier's father, Duke Godfrey, planned a revolt against Charlemagne. In retaliation Charlemagne threatened to kill Ogier. Roland intervened and saved his friend's life.

In the meantime barbarians attacked Rome. In an effort to save the Pope, Charlemagne ignored the rebellion of the Danes and set off to the south, taking Ogier with him as a prisoner. The great army was assisted on its passage across the Alps when a magnificent white stag appeared to lead the army through the mountain passes.

In the battles which followed, Charlemagne's army was divided. One force, led by the cowardly son of Charlemagne and the false knight Alory, attempted to retreat and placed the emperor's life in jeopardy. Roland and Ogier, aided by other squires, donned the garments of the cowards and saved the day. Charlemagne knighted them upon the battlefield.

One of the pagan knights proposed a personal combat. In this encounter Charlot, a son of Charlemagne, and Ogier met two barbarians, Prince Sadone and Karaheut. The pagans trapped Ogier and threatened to put him to death, but Charlot escaped. Karaheut, who was to have fought Ogier, rebelled against the unchivalrous action of his pagan prince and gave himself up to Charlemagne, to be treated exactly as Ogier would be treated. Reinforcements came to the pagans, among them the giant king of Maiolgre. In a dispute over the marriage of Glorianda, a Danish prisoner, Ogier fought for Glorianda and put his enemy to rout. Charlemagne attacked at the same time. Ogier and Roland were reunited. The Pope was restored to his throne.

Roland was invested with royal arms. His sword was the famous Durandal; his battle horn was the horn of his grandfather, Charles the Hammer. None but Roland could blow that horn. His armor was the best in the kingdom.

A new war began when Count Gerard refused homage to the emperor. Oliver, grandson of the count, was among the knights opposed to Charlemagne. After the French had besieged the fortress of Viana for seven months, it was decided to settle the war by encounter between a champion from each army. Roland was chosen to fight for Charlemagne. Unknown to him, his adversary was to be Oliver, his boyhood friend. When the two discovered each other's identity, they embraced.

A few weeks later Charlemagne on a boar hunt near Viana was captured by Count Gerard. The two leaders declared a truce and Count Gerard agreed to be a faithful liegeman of the emperor thereafter. Roland met Oliver's sister, Alda, and became betrothed to her.

At Christmas time the Princess of Cathay arrived with her brothers at Charlemagne's court. She proposed a contest between a Christian knight and her brother Argalia. If one of Charlemagne's knights were the victor, he should have her hand in marriage. If the knight were defeated, he should become a hostage. Malagis, the wizard, discovered that the princess and her brothers really sought by sorcery to destroy Charlemagne. He visited the apartment of the foreigners but was discovered by them. They complained and Charlemagne, not understanding the wizard's desire to help him, sentenced Malagis to be imprisoned in a hollow rock beneath the sea forever.

The jousts began. After Argalia had defeated the first knight, Ferrau, the fierce Moor, began combat. Unhorsed, the Moor fought Argalia on foot and overpowered him. Then the princess became invisible, and Argalia rode away, the Moor in pursuit.

In the forest of Ardennes the Moor discovered Argalia sleeping, killed him without honor, and seized his wonderful helmet. Roland, having followed them, discovered the murder of Argalia, and sought the Moor to punish him for his unknightly deed.

Reinold of Montalban found the Princess of Cathay in the forest after he had drunk from the waters of the fountain of Merlin, and the effect of this water was to make him see the princess as an ugly crone. She thought him handsome, but he felt disgust and hurried away. Roland discovered the Moor and challenged him to combat, but the Moor suddenly remembered that his liege lord in Spain was in need of his help and did not remain to fight with Roland.

When the Princess of Cathay saw the Moor wearing her brother's helmet, she knew a tragedy had occurred and she transported herself by magic to her father's kingdom.

Roland went on a quest to the Far East in search of the complete armor of Trojan Hector. Whether by chance or by evil design he came to a fountain and there drank the water of forgetfulness. He was rescued by the Princess of Cathay and fought many a battle for her sake, even though she was a pagan princess.

At last he came to the castle of the fairy queen, Morgan the Fay, where the armor of Trojan Hector was said to be hidden. Overcome for the first time, he failed to gain the armor and was ordered to return to the court of Charlemagne.

He arrived home in time to help the Danes resist an invasion of their country. When Ogier's father, Duke Godfrey, summoned help, Ogier and Roland set out for Denmark. The invaders fled. At the same time Ogier's father died, but Ogier, on the advice of Morgan the Fay, renounced his rights to his father's holdings in favor of his younger brother.

On his way back to France, Roland heard of a fierce orc said to be the property of Proteus. The orc devoured one beautiful maiden each day until Roland overcame it and was rewarded by Oberto, the king of Ireland, whose daughter he had saved.

In the meantime Charlemagne's forces were being attacked by Saracens, and Roland set out to help Charlemagne's knights. On the way he was trapped in a wizard's castle. From this captivity he was saved by Bradamant, a warrior maiden. She, having won a magic ring from the Princess of Cathay, overcame the wizard and released all of the knights and ladies held prisoner in the wizard's castle.

Ferrau, the Moorish knight, lost the helmet he had stolen from Argalia and vowed he would never again wear a helmet until he should wear that of Roland. By trickery he managed to get Roland's helmet.

Roland was set upon by Mandricardo, the fierce knight to whom fortune had awarded the arms of Trojan Hector. They fought for the possession of Durandal, Roland's sword, the only part of Trojan Hector's equipment which Mandricardo did not possess. At last Mandricardo was forced to flee for his life.

Roland visited the forest where the Princess of Cathay and Medoro, a Moorish prince, had fallen in love. Some declared it was jealousy for the princess but others declared it was sheer exhaustion which caused Roland now to lose his mind. He cast his armor away from him and went wandering helplessly through the forest. Mandricardo seized Durandal and made Roland his prisoner.

Astolpho and Oliver set out from the court of Charlemagne to save Roland. Astolpho journeyed on the back of a flying horse to the fabulous land of Prester John. Having freed Prester John from a flock of harpies, Astolpho journeyed to the rim of the moon and there saw stored up all the things lost on earth. There he found Roland's common sense, which he brought back with him and returned to Roland so that the knight became his former self.

In a battle against the Saracens the wicked Ganelon betrayed the knights of Charlemagne and they, greatly outnumbered, fell one by one to their enemies.

Roland, unwilling to call for help, refused to use his famous horn to summon aid, and he died last of all. Charlemagne, discovering the dead hero, declared a great day of mourning. Alda, the betrothed of Roland, fell dead and was buried with many honors. Then Charlemagne died and was buried with great pomp. Only Ogier the Dane, remained, and it is said that Morgan the Fay carried him to Avalon where he lives in company with Arthur of the Round Table.

It is said also that Charlemagne dwells inside a vast mountain cave with all his heroes gathered around him. There they wait for the day when they shall march out to avenge the wrongs of the world.

THE SONG OF SONGS

Type of work: Novel
Author: Hermann Sudermann (1857-1928)
Type of plot: Naturalism
Time of plot: Early twentieth century
Locale: Germany
First published: 1909

Principal characters:
LILLY CZEPANEK, daughter of a music master
FRITZ REDLICH, a student
COLONEL VON MERTZBACH, Lilly's elderly first husband
WALTER VON PRELL, Lilly's first lover
RICHARD DEHNICKE, Lilly's lover and later her husband
KONRAD RENNSCHMIDT, Lilly's great love

Critique:

The Song of Songs belongs to the naturalistic movement in European literature. In its detailed study of a woman's fall from virtue, the novel resembles in many ways the novels of Balzac and Zola. There is no mistaking the critical purpose and the symbolism behind Sudermann's frank study of social hypocrisy and vice.

The Story:

Lilly Czepanek was fourteen years old when her temperamental father, a music master, disappeared from home. The girl and her mother became destitute, but they looked forward every day to Czepanek's return since he had left behind his cherished musical composition, *The Song of Songs,* around which the entire family had built its hopes for success.

Lilly grew into an attractive young woman. She attended school in preparation for a career as a governess. Meanwhile Mrs. Czepanek, beginning to lose her mind, projected mad schemes to regain her social position. One day, in a fit of rage, she attacked Lilly with a bread knife and was subsequently committed to an asylum. Lilly, now alone, took work as a clerk in the circulating library of Mrs. Asmussen; she assuaged her loneliness by reading voraciously. She admired a high-minded young student, Fritz Redlich, who spurned her because he misunderstood her overtures of friendship.

Mrs. Asmussen's two worldly daughters, home after having failed to find their fortunes elsewhere, coached Lilly in the ways of catching a man. Lieutenant von Prell, attached to the local regiment, came to the library, saw Lilly, and was overwhelmed by her simple charm. His visit was followed by the visits of many young officers and men of fashion of the town. The sisters, Lona and Mi, jealous of Lilly, hated her for her ability to attract men without even venturing out of the Asmussen house.

When Colonel von Mertzbach, the commander of the regiment, offered Lilly a job as his secretary and reader in order to save her from such sordid surroundings, she declined because she was suspicious of his intentions. She received dozens of fine Christmas gifts from the colonel, but she returned them all. At the colonel's request, Lilly went to his quarters, where he proposed after revealing his passion for her. Seeing a chance for freedom and luxury, Lilly accepted and became his wife. Soon she discovered, however, that the colonel had only a physical attraction for her and that she was little more than his chattel. Their wedding trip to Italy was interrupted when the colonel, who was extremely jealous, saw Lilly take a passive interest in a young man who shared their compartment.

The couple went to East Prussia to the colonel's castle. The colonel, retired from military service, devoted his time to molding Lilly into an aristocratic Junker lady, and in this task he was assisted by the housekeeper, Miss von Schwertfeger.

Von Prell, who had resigned his commission, was now employed on the estate of his former commanding officer. He taught Lilly to ride, and on one of their jaunts together into the countryside she surrendered herself to him. Having access to the castle, he made his way to her room secretly at night. One night the colonel returned home unexpectedly from one of his frequent trips to the nearby town and almost surprised the two together. Miss von Schwertfeger covered up Lilly's infidelity, however, and later told her mistress that she hated von Mertzbach because he had forced her for years to be a party to mad orgies which had taken place in the castle. But she forbade any further relations between Lilly and von Prell.

Later Lilly, hearing that von Prell was philandering in the town, went to his lodge. The colonel discovered them together, and ordered Lilly off the estate. She went to Berlin; von Prell went to the United States.

Lilly, now divorced, assisted a maker of lampshades until, being herself proficient, she opened her own shop. When her business venture proved unsuccessful, she went to Dehnicke, a friend of von Prell, who was a bronze statuary manufacturer and who, von Prell had assured her, would help any friend of his. To escape Dehnicke's attentions, Lilly left him and went to Kellermann, a glass painter, whom Dehnicke recommended to her. Kellermann made advances, but Lilly immediately made him understand that she was there only to learn glass painting. As she produced transparencies, Dehnicke took them and acted as her agent in selling them. One day Dehnicke gave Lilly a large check drawn on an American bank and sent to her, he said, by von Prell. With her new wealth, Lilly was able to establish her studio in a fine apartment in a decent part of the city. But soon she lost interest in her transparencies and began to live as Dehnicke's creature. She toured the bronze factory, but was barred from entering one small storeroom.

Lilly, now virtually a prisoner in the luxurious surroundings provided by Dehnicke, grew morose and melancholy. She and Dehnicke attended an elaborate carnival at Kellermann's studio. There she learned that not one of her transparencies had sold, that the forbidden storeroom in the factory was their repository.

One day Dehnicke, a bachelor and very much under the influence of his mother, announced to Lilly that at his mother's insistence he intended to marry an heiress. Lilly, confused and helpless, yielded herself to Kellermann. But Dehnicke gave up the heiress and returned to Lilly; their old way of life was resumed. Still Lilly grew more lonely and waited for the one man in her life to appear.

After several years in Berlin, Lilly again met Fritz Redlich. Seeing that the former student was a failure and in extreme poverty, she prepared to dedicate her life to regenerating him. She fed and clothed him, made him a frequent guest at her table, and finally secured for him a position as tutor in another part of Germany. Still misunderstanding her interest in him, he refused to have dinner with her the night before he was to leave for his new job.

Lilly next met Konrad Rennschmidt, a young student of art history. There was an immediate sympathy between the two, and Lilly knew what she thought was real happiness at last. Because Konrad did not know all the true facts of Lilly's past, she told him many lies in her frantic desire to keep his friendship. At last she surrendered herself to Konrad and drifted away from Dehnicke, whose mother still had hopes that her son would marry well.

Konrad had a rich uncle who came to Berlin to meet Lilly when he heard that his nephew planned to marry her. The old uncle, an adventurer of sorts, tricked Lilly into disclosing her true tortured and fallen soul to him. Sure that Lilly would do Konrad no good and that his family and friends would not accept her, he persuaded Lilly never to see Konrad again.

Having never been essentially evil, and seeing little hope of happiness in her life, Lilly attempted to throw herself in the River Spree after her last great disappointment. But she failed even in that attempt. She did, however, throw *The Song of Songs* into the river. For years she had guarded the musical composition as a symbol of all that was fine and good in life. At last, when his mother had resigned herself to the inevitable, Dehnicke again asked Lilly to marry him. She accepted. It seemed to her by this time that Dehnicke was her fate.

SONS AND LOVERS

Type of work: Novel
Author: D. H. Lawrence (1885-1930)
Type of plot: Psychological realism
Time of plot: Late nineteenth century
Locale: England
First published: 1913

Principal characters:
GERTRUDE MOREL, a devoted mother
WALTER MOREL, her husband, a collier
WILLIAM, her oldest son
ANNIE, her daughter
PAUL, her favorite son
ARTHUR, another son
MIRIAM LEIVERS, Paul's sweetheart
CLARA DAWES, Paul's mistress
BAXTER DAWES, Clara's husband

Critique:

Sons and Lovers is a realistic novel developing two significant psychological themes. The first is the story of Paul Morel's beautiful but terrible relationship with his mother, who gives to him all her warmth of feeling because her husband has denied her the love she craves. The second is a study of attraction and repulsion in love, presented through Paul's relations with two quite different women, Clara and Miriam. It is, on the whole, a tragic story of work, love, and despair. Lawrence's psychological insight and the poetry of his style make this novel one of the great landmarks in modern autobiographical fiction.

The Story:

Walter Morel, a collier, had been a handsome, dashing young man when Gertrude had married him. But after a few years of marriage he proved to be an irresponsible breadwinner and a drunkard, and his wife hated him for what he had once meant to her and for what he now was. Her only solace lay in her children, William, Annie, Paul, and Arthur, for she leaned heavily upon them for companionship, lived in their happiness. She was a good parent; her children loved her. The oldest son, William, was successful in his work but he longed to go to London, where he had promise of a better job. After he had gone, Mrs. Morel turned to Paul for the companionship and love she had found in William.

Paul liked to paint. More sensitive than his brothers and sister, he was closer to Mrs. Morel than any of the others. William brought a girl named Lily home to visit, but it was apparent that she was not the right kind of girl for him; she was too shallow and self-centered. Before long, William himself became aware of that fact, but he resigned himself to keeping the promise he had made to his fiancée.

When William became ill, Mrs. Morel went to London to nurse her son and was with him there when he died. Home once more after she had buried her first son, Mrs. Morel could not bring herself out of her sorrow. Not until Paul became sick did she realize that her duty lay with the living rather than with the dead. After that she centered all her attention upon Paul. The two other children were capable of carrying on their affairs without the constant attention that Paul demanded.

At sixteen Paul went to visit some friends of Mrs. Morel. The Leivers were a warm-hearted family, and Paul easily gained the friendship of the Leivers children. Fifteen-year-old Miriam Leivers was a strange girl, but her inner charm attracted Paul. Mrs. Morel, like many others, did not care for Miriam. Paul went to work at a stocking mill, where he was successful in his social relationships and in his work. He continued to draw. Miriam watched over his work and with quiet understanding offered judgment concerning his success or failure. Mrs. Morel sensed that some day her son would become famous for his art.

By the time Miriam and Paul had grown into their twenties, Paul realized that Miriam loved him deeply and that he loved her. But for some reason he could not bring himself to touch her. Then through Miriam he met Clara Dawes. For a long while Mrs. Morel had been urging him to give up Miriam, and now Paul tried to tell Miriam that it was all over between them. He did not want to marry her, but he felt that he did belong to her. He could not make up his own mind.

Clara Dawes was separated from her husband, Baxter Dawes. She was five years Paul's senior, but a beautiful woman whose loveliness charmed him. Although Clara became his mistress, she refused to divorce her husband and marry Paul. Sometimes Paul wondered whether he could bring himself to marry Clara if she were free. She was not what he wanted. His mother was the only woman to whom he could turn for complete understanding and love, for Miriam had tried to possess him and Clara maintained a barrier against him. Paul continued to devote much of his time and attention to making his mother happy. Annie had married and gone to live with her husband near the Morel home, and Arthur had married a childhood friend who bore him a son six months after the wedding.

Baxter Dawes resented Paul's relationship with his wife. Once he accosted Paul in a tavern and threatened him. Paul knew that he could not fight with Baxter, but he continued to see Clara. Paul had entered pictures in local exhibits and had won four prizes. With encouragement from Mrs. Morel, he continued to paint. He wanted to go abroad, but he could not leave his mother. He began to see Miriam again. When she yielded herself to him, his passion was ruthless and savage. But their relationship was still unsatisfactory. He turned again to Clara.

Miriam knew about his love affair with Clara, but the girl felt that Paul would tire of his mistress and come back to her. Paul stayed with Clara, however, because he found in her an outlet for his unknown desires. His life was a great conflict. Meanwhile Paul was earning enough money to give his mother the things her husband had failed to provide. Mr. Morel stayed on with his wife and son, but he was no longer accepted as a father or a husband.

One day it was revealed that Mrs. Morel had cancer and was beyond any help except that of morphine and then death. During the following months Mrs. Morel declined rapidly. Paul was tortured by his mother's pain. Annie and Paul marveled at her resistance to death, wishing that it would come to end her suffering. Paul dreaded such a catastrophe in his life, although he knew it must come eventually. He turned to Clara for comfort, but she failed to make him forget his misery. Then, visiting his mother at the hospital, Paul found Baxter Dawes recovering from an attack of typhoid fever. For a long time Paul had sensed that Clara wanted to return to Dawes, and now, out of pity for Dawes, he brought about a reconciliation between the husband and wife.

When Mrs. Morel's suffering had mounted to a torturing degree, Annie and Paul decided that anything would be better than to let her live in agony. One night Paul gave her an overdose of morphine, and Mrs. Morel died the next day.

Left alone, Paul was lost. He felt that his own life had ended with the death of his mother. Clara, to whom he had turned before, was now back with Dawes. Because they could not bear to stay in the house without Mrs. Morel, Paul and his father parted, each taking different lodgings.

For a while Paul wandered helplessly trying to find some purpose in his life. Then he thought of Miriam, to whom he had once belonged. He returned to her, but with the renewed association he realized more than ever that she was not what he wanted. Once he had thought of going abroad. Now he wanted to join his mother in death. Leaving Miriam for the last time, he felt trapped and lost in his own indecision. But he also felt that he was free from Miriam after many years of passion and regret.

His mother's death was too great a sorrow for Paul to cast off immediately. Finally, after a lengthy inner struggle, he was able to see that she would always be with him and that he did not need to die to join her. With his new found courage he set out to make his own life anew.

THE SORROWS OF YOUNG WERTHER

Type of work: Novel
Author: Johann Wolfgang von Goethe (1749-1832)
Type of plot: Sentimental romance
Time of plot: Mid-eighteenth century
Locale: Germany
First published: 1774

Principal characters:
WERTHER, a sentimental young man
CHARLOTTE (LOTTE), his beloved
ALBERT, betrothed to Charlotte

Critique:

Many teachers of literature consider *The Sorrows of Young Werther* the starting point of a certain phase of the romantic movement which in England reached its peak in the early nineteenth century and which at a later date left its mark upon the novels of Charles Dickens and others. The interest in landscape, in excessive emotion, and in despairing passion developed more freely and earlier on the continent, but when such books reached England they found immediately a sympathetic audience of readers and many imitators among the writers of the period. Today, however, the novel belongs almost exclusively to poets, scholars, and special readers of one kind or another. Perhaps it will always appeal to the very young in spirit.

The Story:

Young Werther, having left his former home, wrote to his friend Wilhelm to describe the secluded region where he had gone to forget the unhappiness of his earlier years. He had discovered a pleasant cottage surrounded by a lovely garden, and he felt that in his peaceful retreat he could live in happy solitude forever.

A few days later he reported that his soul had recovered in his rustic surroundings. He did not want books or the companionship of his old friends, for he had been transported into a new world of kinship with nature. He mentioned a nearby hamlet called Walheim and the village inn where he could drink good coffee, sit in solitude, and read his Homer. Several letters to Wilhelm told the same story of Werther's simple life among scenes of natural beauty.

Suddenly there was a break in his letters. Then he wrote to tell his friend that he had met an angel. At a ball he had been introduced to Charlotte S., the daughter of a judge who had retired to a hunting lodge not far from Walheim. Charlotte was a beautiful and charming girl, and in spite of the fact that she was betrothed to another, Werther had fallen deeply in love with her at first sight.

Perhaps his passion ran all the more deeply because he had been warned not to fall in love with her, since she was betrothed to a young man not present at the ball. The warning went unheeded. At the dance Werther had demanded much of her attention. He had begun to ask her some questions about the Albert to whom she was betrothed when a storm suddenly interrupted the dance. The hostess led the guests into a room protected by curtains and shutters. There they played a game called counting. Once Werther kissed Charlotte's hands. When the party broke up at sunrise, he took her to her home through a dazzling world of raindrops and morning sun.

From that time on he called every day on Lotte, as he referred to her in his letters. He grieved over their separation when she went to attend a sick woman whom she knew. One day he went with her to visit an old pastor; he noted that her youthful presence seemed to bring new life to the old man as well.

Because he could not bear to have her out of his sight, Werther began to object to the time Lotte gave to sick friends and to other acquaintances. A glimpse of her as she rode away on some errand was enough to set his head spinning and his heart beating wildly. If her finger accidentally touched his, the blood pounded through his veins. To his friend he confessed that he had done little of the painting he had intended; all of his time was taken up with his love for Charlotte.

After his friend Wilhelm had written, advising him either to press his suit for Lotte or else to give up his hopeless passion, Werther decided to see the girl less frequently. His decision was further strengthened when Albert returned to Walheim. Jealous of Albert, Werther wrote nevertheless that he admired his rival's fine character. In answer to further urging from his friend, Werther replied that he could neither give up Lotte nor hope to win her from Albert.

Werther grew more and more melancholy. Because he could hope to possess Lotte only in his dreams, he was plunged into gloom and despair. At last, deciding that he must leave Walheim, he asked Wilhelm to secure a government post for him. When Wilhelm suggested a post with an ambassador, Werther postponed his acceptance or refusal of the position. But Wilhelm obtained the appointment without waiting to hear from his friend, and so Werther's course was decided for him. During the two last hours he spent with Lotte and Albert, he pretended all the time that he was not going away. He felt that their farewells would be more than he could bear.

At first the official duties of his new position kept Werther from brooding over his sorrows. But as time passed he began to dislike the ambassador under whom he worked. No longer interested in government affairs, he reproached Wilhelm for securing his appointment. He chafed constantly at the responsibilities he was forced to assume.

At last he wrote a letter to Lotte. Albert wrote to him in reply and informed him that the two had been married some time before.

Meanwhile Werther had resigned his position at court. Failing in his attempt to enter the army, he accepted the offer of a young prince to spend the summer on his estate. When he failed to find in the nobleman's household the peace and calm for which he had hoped, he decided at last to return to Walheim in order to be near Lotte.

His first encounter with Albert and Lotte threw him into such a state that his letter to Wilhelm was almost incoherent. He could not understand why Albert did not look more distractedly happy. Lotte pitied Werther and Albert sympathized with him, but they were unable to help him. At the same time Werther was concerned with the fate of a peasant who had been convicted of murder. Failing to save the man from his fate, Werther was more wretched than ever. At last, following her husband's suggestion, Lotte suggested that Werther visit her house less frequently. In despair, he wrote that when he could bear his sorrows no longer he intended to end his life.

The rest of his story was told by others. One night, while Albert was away from home, Werther went to Lotte's house. Frightened by his speech and appearance, she asked him to read aloud some passages from Ossian. After he had seized her in a wild embrace, she fled and locked herself in her room. He stood outside the door and begged her to speak so that he could hear her voice for the last time.

The next day he sent a servant to Albert and asked for the loan of a brace of pistols to take with him on an unexpected journey. He shot himself that night, but he was not quite dead when his servant found him the next morning. He died at noon without regaining consciousness. Charlotte, hearing of his death, fell into a swoon so deep that her life was despaired of. Workmen of the village carried Werther's body to its resting place under the lime trees at Walheim.

THE SOUND AND THE FURY

Type of work: Novel
Author: William Faulkner (1897-)
Type of plot: Psychological realism
Time of plot: 1910-1928
Locale: Mississippi
First published: 1929

Principal characters:
MRS. COMPSON, the mother
BENJAMIN, her idiot son
QUENTIN, another son
CANDACE, her daughter
JASON, another son
SYDNEY HERBERT HEAD, Candace's husband
QUENTIN, Candace's daughter
DILSEY, a Negro servant

Critique:

Beneath its involved and difficult technique, *The Sound and the Fury* is a compelling study of the dissolution of an old southern family gone to seed. The members of the Compson family are victims of lust, incest, suicide. The story is told through the minds of the various characters, and the scene jumps from 1928 to 1910 without so much as a change of sentence. The lack of punctuation is effective, but confusing, for it is difficult to tell where reality ends and memory begins. The book is divided into four parts, but only in the last two parts does the story fall into a clear pattern. Then the pieces of the puzzle begin to fit into place and the reader finds that he is experiencing stark tragedy and horrible reality. The novel is not easy to read, but it is powerful work that will haunt the reader for many days after the last page has been turned.

The Story:

The Compson family had once been a good one, but the present generation had done everything possible to ruin the name of Compson for all time. In the little Mississippi town in which they lived everyone laughed and made slighting remarks when the name Compson was mentioned.

Mrs. Compson had come from what she considered good stock, but she thought she must have sinned terribly in marrying a Compson and now she was paying for her sins. For eighteen years she had been saying that she did not have long to live and would no longer be a burden to her family. Benjamin was her greatest cross. He was an idiot who moaned and cried and slobbered all day long. The only person who could quiet Benjamin was Candace, his sister. When they were small, Candace loved Benjamin very much and made herself his protector. She saw to it that the other children of the family and the Negro servants did not tease him. As Candace grew up, she continued to love Benjamin, but she also loved every man she met, giving herself freely to any man who would have her. Mrs. Compson thought Candace was another cross she had to bear and did very little to force her daughter to have better morals.

Quentin, another son, was a moody, morose boy whose only passion was his sister Candace. He loved her not as a sister, but as a woman, and she returned his love. Quentin was sent to school at Harvard. But although she loved Quentin in the spirit, Candace could not keep away from other men. Sydney Herbert Head was the one serious lover she had. He wanted to marry her. Head, a banker, promised to give her brother Jason a job in his bank after they were married. When Quentin learned that Candace was in a condition which made her marriage necessary, he was wild. He lied to his father and told him that he had had incestuous relations with Candace and that she must not be allowed to marry. His father did not believe him, and the family went along with their plans for the wedding. At last Quentin could stand no more. On the day of his sister's wedding he drowned himself in the Charles River in Cambridge, Massachusetts. Mrs. Compson resigned herself to one more cross.

When Candace had a baby too soon, Head threw her out of his house with her child. Her mother and father and her brother Jason would not let her come home, but they adopted the baby girl, Quentin. Jason believed that Quentin was the child of his brother Quentin and Candace, but the rest of the family refused to face such a fact and accept it. They preferred to believe, and rightly, that Quentin was the child of some other lover who had deserted Candace. Candace stayed away from the little town for many years.

Quentin was as wild as her mother as she grew up. She, too, gave herself to any man in town and was talked about as her mother had been. Every month Candace sent money to Mrs. Compson for Quentin's care. At first Mrs. Compson burned the checks, for she would have none of Candace's ill-gotten money. When Mr. Compson died, Jason became the head of the family. He blamed Quentin for his not getting the job in the bank, for if the child had not been born too soon Head would not have left Candace and would have given Jason the job. Hating his sister, he wrote checks on another bank and gave those to his mother in place of the checks Candace had sent. The old lady was almost blind and could not see what she burned. Jason then forged her signature on the real checks and cashed them, using the money to gamble on the cotton market.

Quentin hated her Uncle Jason as much as he hated her, and the two were always quarreling. He tried to make her go to school and keep away from the men, but Mrs. Compson thought he was too cruel to Quentin and took the girl's part.

A show troupe came to town and Quentin took up with one of the performers. Jason locked her in her room each night, but she climbed out the window to meet her lover. One morning she did not answer when old Dilsey, the colored mammy who had cared for the family for years, called her to breakfast. Jason went to her room and found that all her clothes were gone. He also found that the three thousand dollars he had hidden in his room had been stolen. He tried to get the sheriff to follow the girl and the showman, but the sheriff wanted no part of the Compson family affairs. Jason set out to find the fugitives, but he had to give up his search when a severe headache forced him to return home for medicine.

Jason felt more than cheated. His money was gone and he could not find Quentin so that he could punish her for stealing it. He forgot that the money really belonged to Quentin, for it was part of the amount he had saved from the money Candace had sent for the girl's care. There was nothing left for Jason but blind rage and hatred for everyone. He believed that everyone laughed at him because of his horrible family—because Benjamin was an idiot, Candace a lost woman, Quentin a suicide, and the girl Quentin a village harlot and a thief. He forgot that he, too, was a thief and that he had a mistress. He felt cursed by his family as his mother was cursed.

When he saw Benjamin riding through town in a carriage driven by one of the colored boys, he knocked the colored boy down and struck Benjamin with all his force, for there was no other way for him to show his rage. Benjamin let out a loud moan, then settled back in the carriage. He petted a wilted flower and his face assumed a calm, quiet, blankness, as if all the strife in the world were over and things were once more serene. It was as if he had understood what old Dilsey meant when she said she had seen the beginning and the end of life. Benjamin had seen it all, too, in the pictures he could never understand but which flowed endlessly through his disordered mind.

THE SPOILERS

Type of work: Novel
Author: Rex Beach (1877-1949)
Type of plot: Adventure romance
Time of plot: The Alaska gold rush
Locale: The Yukon
First published: 1906

Principal characters:
Roy Glenister, the owner of the Midas gold mine
Bill Dextry, Glenister's partner
Mr. McNamara, a politician
Helen Chester, the girl with whom Glenister is in love
Judge Stillman, her uncle
Cherry Malotte, a notorious woman in love with Glenister
Mr. Struve, a dishonest lawyer

Critique:

The Spoilers is a lusty book about a raw new land filled with adventurers and gamblers of all kinds. Blood and thunder leap forth from every page. The real fault of the novel is the number of coincidences. In his scenes of action the author is at his best. His descriptions and dramatic incidents, like the battle at the mines or the epic bare-handed duel between the hero and the villain, are his best work. The merit of the book lies in such, not in the loosely-planned plot or the love story.

The Story:

Trouble began for Glenister and Dextry, the owners of the Midas mine, the moment they started from Seattle back to the frozen North. First of all a young woman, Helen Chester, enlisted their aid in stowing away aboard their ship. Then Roy Glenister fell in love with her. After they were aboard Dextry told Glenister that the government was sending a court to institute law and order in the gold country and warned him that they would have to be careful lest they lose their claim to the Midas mine.

In Nome Helen delivered a packet of documents to the law firm of Struve and Dunham and then went with the two partners up to the Midas mine. There was no place else for her to go for the time being.

Two weeks later her uncle, Judge Stillman, arrived in Nome with a politician named McNamara. Stillman had been appointed the first Federal judge in Nome, Alaska. Trouble soon brewed for the owners of the mines on Anvil Creek, including Glenister and Dextry. Their claims were relocated and possession of the mines was given to McNamara as a receiver appointed by the court until the claims could legally be cleared. Convinced that the receivership was dishonest, Glenister and Dextry robbed their mine of ten thousand dollars in gold with which to send their attorney to San Francisco. By the time the attorney had made the trip and returned, all the mine owners on Anvil Creek realized that there was collusion between Judge Stillman and McNamara. When the attorney tried to serve an injunction which would force the judge to return the mines to the owners, Stillman refused to recognize the writ from the San Francisco court. Glenister and Dextry immediately smuggled their attorney aboard a ship bound for San Francisco, with a request that United States marshals be sent to Nome to serve the writ and arrest Stillman for contempt of court.

Meanwhile Glenister and Dextry spied on McNamara and discovered the part Helen Chester had played in bringing in the documents which had made possible the theft of the mines by McNamara. Cherry Malotte also told Glenister that Helen had informed McNamara of the money Glenister and Dextry had at their camp. The last straw for Glenister was the announcement that McNamara and Helen were to be married.

Deciding to repossess their mines by violence, the owners on Anvil Creek formed a vigilante committee with the intention of lynching McNamara and tarring and feathering the judge.

After spreading the word that troops were going to guard the mines, McNamara laid a trap for the vigilantes at his office in Nome. He thought that the mine owners, not daring to attack the troops, would attack his own office. To his surprise, the owners attacked the mines and seized them after a short, sharp battle. They discovered that the defending force had been only a few guards posted by McNamara.

In the meantime Helen Chester had gone to Struve to discover what she could about the dealings of her uncle and McNamara. At a deserted hotel outside Nome he tried to bargain with the girl for the documents he had, papers which would incriminate himself, the judge, and McNamara of collusion to rob the mines. After Helen had read the papers, he tried to attack her. As he was about to overpower her, a gambler—Helen's long-lost brother—appeared on the scene and shot Struve. Helen and her rescuer set out through a terrific storm to return to Nome and turn over the incriminating documents to Glenister and other mine owners.

A few hours after they had left, Glenister himself came to the hotel and discovered the wounded man. Struve told

Glenister that Helen had left the hotel with a cheap gambler. Furious, Glenister rode back to Nome. He resolved to hunt down McNamara and the gambler and to kill them both.

When Glenister arrived in Nome early the following morning, he found McNamara alone in his office. Glenister laid aside his coat and gun to fight the man hand-to-hand. In their struggle they demolished the office. A crowd gathered to watch them. Feeling himself slipping, McNamara tried to reach for a pistol. As he did so, Glenister seized him in a hammerlock and slowly broke his arm. At that moment Judge Stillman arrived at the office with several soldiers and put Glenister under arrest.

As he was being led away to jail, a ship sailed into the harbor. Shortly afterward Glenister's attorney came ashore with several United States marshals and the court orders from San Francisco. With Stillman's power broken, Glenister was quickly released. When he returned to his cabin to rest, Dextry told him that his fight with McNamara was the talk of the town, for no one had ever seen a combat like it in all the rugged North country. Glenister, too tired to care, stumbled into his bunk and fell asleep.

He was finally awakened when Helen and her gambler brother entered his cabin. Helen told Glenister of the gambler's real identity and tried to prove to him that she had not willingly been a partner in the plot to rob the mine owners of Anvil Creek. What she told him convinced Glenister that she was telling the truth. She also told him that she had seen his fight with McNamara, that she could never marry a man who was more of a brute animal than a civilized human being.

The next day all was again peaceful in Nome. Glenister planned to return to his mine and resume operations there. While he was preparing to leave, Dextry walked into his cabin. Dextry told him that he was going to sell his share of the Midas mine and leave Nome. His excuse was that law and order had finally come to Alaska, so that the country was growing too civilized for an old frontiersman like himself.

After Dextry left, Glenister wandered down toward the beach, too downhearted to finish his preparations for going to the mine. Helen Chester saw him on the beach. Calling him to her, she told him that she finally understood why he could be as brutal as he was, for her own battle with Struve had shown her how thin the veneer of civilization was in the far North, where life had to be fought for against both men and the elements. Glenister pretended not to understand what she meant, and asked her when she was leaving. Her reply to him was that she did not intend to leave, unless he sent her away.

THE SPY

Type of work: Novel
Author: James Fenimore Cooper (1789-1851)
Type of plot: Historical romance
Time of plot: 1780; 1812
Locale: New York State
First published: 1821

Principal characters:
HARVEY BIRCH, a peddler
MR. HARPER, General George Washington
MR. WHARTON, a Loyalist sympathizer
FRANCES, his daughter
SARAH, another daughter
HENRY, his son

MAJOR PEYTON DUNWOODIE, an American officer
CAPTAIN LAWTON, another American officer
COLONEL WELLMERE, a British officer

Critique:

Judged by modern standards, *The Spy: A Tale of the Neutral Ground* is still a satisfactory historical novel. As Cooper remarked in the introduction to his novel, however, his purpose in *The Spy* is frankly patriotic. If the reader bears this fact in mind, he can understand that Peyton Dunwoodie is supposed to represent the ideal American soldier and officer; Frances Wharton, the ideal of American womanhood; and Washington, of course, the ideal father of his country, combining Roman strength and vigor with American humanity and humility. This understanding will help the reader to appreciate Cooper's point of view. The great historical novelist of the early nineteenth century was an intensely nationalistic individual who, conscious of the past achievements and potentialities of his country, looked forward eagerly to the development of a great nation.

The Story:

At the beginning of the Revolutionary War, Harvey Birch, a peddler, became a spy against the British. Because of the extremely secret nature of Birch's work, few Americans were aware of his true mission. As a matter of fact, they suspected that he was a British spy, and they denounced him as a bold and shameless Tory.

At the time, Westchester County in New York was considered common ground for both the rebels and the Loyalists, and the inhabitants of the county affected a neutrality they did not feel. This was the case of Mr. Wharton, a British sympathizer, who at the outbreak of hostilities had retired to his country estate with his two daughters, Sarah and Frances, and their aunt, Miss Jeanette Peyton.

One evening as a storm was approaching a horseman rode up to the Wharton house, The Locusts. He was a tall man of powerful frame, military in his bearing but plain and sober in his dress. After being let into the house by the Whartons' Negro servant, Caesar Thompson, the traveler introduced himself as Mr. Harper and asked for shelter from the storm. Mr. Wharton courteously granted the traveler's request, and the two men were soon engaged in conversation concerning the progress of the war. Mr. Wharton expressed his views cautiously in order to determine Mr. Harper's sentiments, but the stranger remained tight-lipped and uncommunicative in his replies.

The conversation between the two men was interrupted by the arrival of Henry Wharton, Mr. Wharton's son and a captain in the British army. The young man wore a disguise because he had been compelled to cross the American lines in order to visit his home. He was disconcerted when Mr. Harper recognized him, despite the disguise.

Later Harvey Birch, the peddler believed by all in the neighborhood to be a royalist spy, came to the Wharton home, bringing with him laces for the ladies, tobacco for Mr. Wharton, and news of the war — news which included a report of the hanging of Major André. During Birch's visit, Caesar, the colored servant, remarked to his master that he had heard voices in Mr. Harper's room. There seemed to be no reason why the traveler and the peddler should have matters to talk over in private.

With the return of fair weather, Mr. Harper said goodbye to his host. Before he departed he promised to help Henry Wharton, if the latter ever needed help, in return for Mr. Wharton's hospitality. Shortly after Mr. Harper left, the Wharton home was surrounded by a troop of Virginia cavalry looking for a man answering Mr. Harper's description. When the American soldiers entered Mr. Wharton's house, they discovered Henry, whose disguise was so hastily assumed that Captain Lawton, in command of the troop, was able to discover the deception. The captain was certain that Henry was a spy because he knew that Birch, whom he believed a British spy, had recently been visiting the Whartons.

Not certain what course he should follow with Henry, Captain Lawton consulted his superior, Major Peyton Dunwoodie, who was interested not only in Henry Wharton but also in Henry's sister, Frances. She pleaded with her lover for Henry's release, but when Henry was found to have a pass signed by General Washington, Major Dunwoodie thought that the case warranted Henry's arrest.

Further investigation by Major Dunwoodie into the matter was halted by a report that British troops were in the neighborhood. The major rushed to his command, leaving Henry guarded by two soldiers.

In the confusion Henry escaped. He reported to his superior, Colonel Wellmere, leader of the advancing British troops, who professed to be in love with Sarah Wharton. When Henry advised the colonel to be wary of Major Dunwoodie and his Americans, Wellmere scorned the advice and determined to force a fight with the rebels. In the brief engagement which followed the British were routed and Captain Lawton succeeded in recapturing Henry, who was returned under guard to his father's home. Colonel Wellmere, also taken prisoner, was slightly wounded in the action. Chagrined by his defeat and capture, he gave the impression that his injuries were mortal, much to the distress of Sarah Wharton.

Birch was watching Major Dunwoodie's success from a distant hill when he was sighted by Captain Lawton, who determined to capture the spying peddler dead or alive. In the pursuit, Captain Lawton overtook Birch, but he fell from his horse and found himself at the peddler's mercy. Birch, however, spared Captain Lawton's life, and for that act of magnanimity the captain would not allow his men to overtake the peddler.

A price was put on Birch's head. One night his house was ransacked and burned by a band of lawless men called Skinners, who surprised the peddler and his dying father. They then delivered Birch to Captain Lawton and claimed their reward. Major Dunwoodie, who was also present when the peddler was brought in, accused him of treason. Although Birch possessed a paper which would have cleared him of the charge, he swallowed it rather than betray the confidence of his secret employer. Captain Lawton paid the Skinners in gold for their captive, but he also ordered them whipped for burning, robbing, and murdering.

Birch was put in jail, but that night he escaped in the guise of a washerwoman who visited his cell. The next morning, on the outskirts of the American camp, he confronted Major Dunwoodie again. With a gun pointed at the officer, to prevent recapture, the peddler warned him to be on guard against danger to the Whartons. Major Dunwoodie was alarmed by the thought of danger threatening Frances Wharton. He was also much disturbed because he felt that he could never win Frances if her brother were executed as a spy. Major Dunwoodie's troubles were magnified when, after assuring Frances that he would try to get General Washington's help for her brother, she turned from him coldly because she believed that he was in love with Isabella Singleton, the sister of an American officer who was recuperating at The Locusts from injuries sustained in the battle.

Meanwhile Sarah Wharton had accepted Colonel Wellmere's proposal of marriage, and a date for the wedding had been set, the night when there was to be an exchange of prisoners at the Wharton house. Major Dunwoodie and Captain Lawton were among the guests during the truce arranged for the exchange and the wedding. The ceremony was suddenly interrupted, however, by the appearance of Birch, who told the colonel that the Englishman's wife had crossed the ocean to meet him. Sarah fainted. Captain Lawton challenged Colonel Wellmere to a duel. The Englishman missed his mark, but Captain Lawton was prevented from killing his adversary when the Skinners leaped upon him and overpowered him. Colonel Wellmere fled the scene, and Captain Lawton was able to escape his enemies only after a fierce struggle.

The Skinners then proceeded to burn Mr. Wharton's house. Captain Lawton returned to the scene with troops he had met on the road, and after routing the Skinners he rescued Frances from the blazing house. Birch rescued Sarah and again Captain Lawton permitted the peddler to escape. A bullet fired at Captain Lawton from the darkness, apparently by the Skinners, struck Isabella Singleton and wounded her mortally. On her deathbed she confessed to Frances her love for Major Dunwoodie but said that he thought of her only as a friend.

At his trial Henry Wharton admitted that he had used a disguise in order to pass through the American lines, but he insisted that his reason for doing so had been for the one purpose of visiting his family, especially his aged father. Major Dunwoodie himself vouched for Henry's character. Frances, however, ruined her brother's chances for acquittal when she confessed that Henry had had dealings with Birch, who, she told the court, had given her brother his disguise. Henry's fate seemed certain. He was found guilty and sentenced to be hanged on the following day.

Major Dunwoodie declared that he would go to General Washington to make an appeal for the life of his friend. His attempt was unsuccessful, however, for the commander-in-chief was not at his headquarters.

Soon afterward a tall, gaunt man in clerical dress appeared and announced himself as a minister from a nearby village, come to offer spiritual comfort to the condemned man. Admitted to Henry's cell, he revealed himself as Harvey Birch. He helped Henry to disguise himself as Caesar Thompson, the faithful black servant of the Whartons, and led the young officer past the unsuspecting sentinel with the remark that the black servant was being sent on an errand for his master.

Frances, hearing of the escape, thought that her brother and the peddler would probably hide in a cabin not far away. Stealing away from the American lines, she set out to join them. But to her surprise, she found the cabin occupied by Mr. Harper, who was poring over an outspread map. Recalling his promise to help her brother, she told him the whole story. He reassured her that all would be well and told her to return to headquarters to await Major Dunwoodie.

Orders from General Washington arrived in time to relieve Major Dunwoodie of the necessity of tracking down Henry, who was thus allowed to escape. Several days later Birch saw him safely aboard a British man-of-war in New York harbor.

Frances and Major Dunwoodie decided to be married immediately. Within a short time, however, their bliss was tempered by the news that Captain Lawton had fallen in battle with the British.

Some time later Birch appeared at the headquarters of the American army in a New Jersey town. There he had a long interview with a grave and noble man whom the Whartons would have recognized as Mr. Harper. The peddler called him General Washington. During their talk the general attempted to reward his faithful spy by giving him money. The peddler refused to accept payment for his services to his country, but he did welcome a letter of approbation from his commander-in-chief. It was agreed that the peddler's real mission as an American spy should remain a secret which only they would share.

Thirty-two years later, in the War of 1812, a gaunt old peddler appeared on the Canadian border and carried word of British troop movements to the American lines. There he met Captain Wharton Dunwoodie, the son of Major Peyton Dunwoodie and his wife Frances. To him the peddler acknowledged his earlier acquaintanceship with the young officer's parents.

A few days later, during a battle, the old peddler threw away his pack and with a musket seized from a fallen soldier rushed into the fight. After the battle Captain Dunwoodie found the old man's body and on his person a letter, signed by George Washington, which revealed Harvey Birch, not as a despicable spy but as a loyal, heroic, and long-suffering patriot.

STATE FAIR

Type of work: Novel
Author: Phil Stong (1899-)
Type of plot: Regional romance
Time of plot: Early 1930's
Locale: Iowa
First published: 1932

Principal characters:

- Abel Frake, a prosperous farmer
- Melissa Frake, his wife
- Wayne, his son
- Margy, his daughter
- Eleanor, Wayne's friend
- Harry Ware, Margy's friend
- Emily, a girl Wayne met at the fair
- Pat Gilbert, a newspaperman
- The Storekeeper, a local philosopher
- Blue Boy, a prize boar

Critique:

In *State Fair* Phil Stong has accurately and sympathetically shown us the reactions of a typical Midwestern family to that most important event of the year, the state fair. The members of the Frake family might be any of our neighbors, and the storekeeper the cracker-barrel sage at whom all small towns smile indulgently. *State Fair* has no lesson to teach or moral to point up. It is interesting in characterization and entertaining in story and therefore achieves the purpose for which it was written.

The Story:

Abel Frake knew that this year Blue Boy would be judged the finest boar at the state fair. As he discussed his hog with the men loafing in the store one Saturday night, he found the storekeeper as pessimistic as usual.

The storekeeper believed that something intangible was always working to see that things did not go too well for most people. What it was he could not exactly say, but he was willing to bet Abel five dollars that it would either keep him from winning the blue ribbon or let him win because some other catastrophe would occur later. Abel, accustomed to the storekeeper's gloom, went home with his confidence in Blue Boy unshaken.

As Abel and his wife Melissa made plans for the next day's start for the fair, their son and daughter were not so carefree. Wayne was with Eleanor, home from her first year in college. But she was changed. Before she went away she had always been his girl; now she did not want to be committed to any promises for the future. Wayne drove home in gloomy silence. When he pulled into the farmyard, he found his sister Margy and Harry Ware sitting in his convertible. Harry was begging Margy to marry him as soon as she came home from the fair. But Margy, like Eleanor, did not know whether it was Harry she wanted.

Sunday was spent in making last-minute preparations for their departure. Melissa checked the jars of pickles she intended to exhibit at the fair. Abel could do nothing except groom Blue Boy.

That evening they started out in the farm truck. The pickles and Blue Boy were given most consideration in the packing, for they were to win honors for the family. Abel drove all night and reached the fairgrounds in Des Moines on Monday morning. Blue Boy was taken at once to the stock pavilion, and the family set up their tent in an area reserved for fair visitors.

As soon as Wayne could get away, he went to the fairgrounds to look for a barker who had cheated him the year before. During the past year Wayne had practiced throwing hoops, and he almost cleaned out the barker before he stopped throwing. When the barker threatened to call the police, a girl who had been watching called his bluff and walked away with Wayne. Her name was Emily; she was the daughter of a stock-show manager. She and Wayne visited other booths together. In the afternoon they went to the horse races and Emily won some money for them to spend.

While Wayne was busy with Emily, Margy strolled around the fairgrounds and looked at the exhibits. That night she and Wayne planned to visit the midway, but they became separated and Margy went on alone. On the roller coaster she met Pat Gilbert, a reporter for a Des Moines paper. Margy found that she could talk easily with Pat.

On Wednesday Melissa's pickles won three blue ribbons. A photographer who was with Pat took pictures of Melissa and Margy. Neither Wayne nor Margy had told their family about their new friends, and Margy had to pretend that she did not see Pat at the exhibit. As soon as she could get away, she and Pat went again to the roller coaster. As they walked back to the tent grounds that night, they stopped in a grassy spot that was hidden from the walks and paths. Pat took Margy in his arms and kissed her, and she gave herself to him willingly.

On Thursday the most important event was the judging of the hogs. Although Abel was nervous and at times had doubts of his victory, he was not really much surprised when Blue Boy had the blue ribbon pinned on his stall. The judges declared him the finest boar they had ever seen, and from then on the fair was over for Abel. In fact, the judging over, he and Melissa had little interest in the remainder of the week.

That evening Wayne and Emily went to a stage show in the city, and Wayne thought it the most wonderful show he had ever seen. Afterward Emily took Wayne to her hotel room and gave him a drink of whiskey. He had never tasted liquor before; it gave him a wonderful, warm feeling inside. Emily went into another room to change from her evening gown. Wayne was not surprised when she returned wearing only a thin kimona. He had known what to expect when he had gone to the hotel with her.

On Friday evening Pat asked Margy to marry him right away. He loved her and wanted to keep her with him. But she knew that a marriage between them would never work out. Pat was restless and wanted to see the world. He thought now that he would gladly settle down in Des Moines for the rest of his life if he could have Margy with him, but she knew that he would grow restless again and be unhappy with her. When she told him goodbye, she knew she would not see him again.

That same night Wayne told Emily that he loved her and asked her to marry him and go back to the farm with him. Emily also refused. She, like Pat, could never stand quiet life on the farm. She was not a wild girl, but she still wanted to enjoy the pleasures of youth.

The next morning the family packed their truck and went back home. On Sunday Eleanor and Harry came to dinner as though nothing had happened that made this Sunday different from any other. The storekeeper drove out and paid his five dollars to Abel, conceding that nothing would happen in the next two months to make him win the bet. But as he looked at Wayne and Margy, he smiled, as if he saw that something had already happened.

THE STORY OF A BAD BOY

Type of work: Novel
Author: Thomas Bailey Aldrich (1836-1907)
Type of plot: Regional romance
Time of plot: Nineteenth century
Locale: New Hampshire
First published: 1869

Principal characters:
TOM BAILEY ALDRICH, the narrator
CAPTAIN NUTTER, his grandfather
MISS ABIGAIL, the captain's sister
KITTY COLLINS, the Nutter maid
BILL CONWAY, and
SETH RODGERS, Tom's enemies
SAILOR BEN, Tom's friend; Kitty's missing husband
PHIL ADAMS,
PEPPER WHITCOMB, and
BINNY WALLACE, Tom's friends

Critique:

The Story of a Bad Boy is one of the most fascinating and amusing accounts of the life of an American boy in the early part of the nineteenth century. Acknowledged by the author to be largely autobiographical, it is an adult recapture of childhood experience. The fictional Rivermouth is Portsmouth, New Hampshire, the author's childhood home.

The Story:

Tom, the son of a banker, was born at Rivermouth in New England. When he was eighteen months old, however, his family moved to New Orleans, and there he lived until he was ten, growing up in almost complete ignorance of everything that was not Southern. In his tenth year, he was sent North to live with his Grandfather Nutter. Tom soon learned to admire his hale, cheery grandfather and to respect his great-aunt, Miss Abigail. The fourth member of the household was Kitty Collins, the maid, an Irish girl happily married to a sailor until he sailed away one day and failed to return.

Tom's grandfather sent him to school immediately — to keep him out of mischief. At the Temple Grammar School he made friends with many boys and incurred the enmity of two, Bill Conway and Seth Rodgers. Tom's friends decided to put on a play, *William Tell,* in Tom's barn. Pepper Whitcomb, as Walter Tell, balanced an apple on his head, while Tom played the part of William. Tom's arrow missed the apple and struck Pepper in the mouth. The theatricals ceased abruptly.

Bill Conway's tyranny finally drove

Tom to make preparations to fight his tormentor, and Phil Adams tutored Tom in the manly art of self-defense. The fight did not occur, however, until after Tom had experienced several more adventures.

As the Fourth of July approached, the boys in the Temple Grammar School could not concentrate on their studies. One of the boys placed a torpedo under the cloth on the desk, at the exact spot where Mr. Grimshaw usually struck with his heavy ruler. The resultant explosion created quite a commotion and nearly caused the strangulation of Charley Marden, who was at the water pail getting a drink.

On the night before the Fourth, Tom slipped out of bed and used Kitty's clothesline to escape from his bedroom. He did not tie knots in the rope and, as a result, burned his hands in his descent. He went to the square, where a big bonfire was to be lit. When the fire burned down after a while, Tom and his friends took an old stagecoach from Ezra Wingate's barn and used the vehicle as fuel. The boys were caught and put in jail, but they escaped. The next day Ezra collected three dollars from the family of each boy who had aided in the theft. Ezra made a good profit, for he had previously offered the coach to anyone who would pay seventy-five cents for it. During the celebration of the Fourth, Tom accidentally stepped on a mine and was blown into the air and knocked unconscious. As a result, he was a hero among his friends for about two weeks.

Shortly after this experience, Tom was initiated into the mysterious order of the Centipedes, an organization notorious for the pranks of its members. One of these pranks was the stealing of the druggist's gilt mortar and pestle, which the Centipedes placed over the Widow Conway's front door. On the drug store window shutters they tacked a sign advertising for a seamstress. The town laughed, because everyone except Mr. Meeks himself knew that Widow Conway had set her cap for the mild-mannered druggist.

One day after school, Tom found Bill Conway tormenting Binny Wallace. Tom lowered his head and swung right and left as he prepared to give Conway a thrashing. Tom pummeled the school pump for twenty seconds before he discovered that Conway had already retired.

Miss Abigail could not stand the odor of tobacco. When she took over as housekeeper for her brother, she restricted his smoking to the barn. One morning during a very cold winter Grandfather Nutter descended the steps with a clay pipe in his mouth. Abigail objected strenuously but the captain merely removed the pipe from his lips and blew a cloud into the hall, where the temperature was two degrees below zero. Miss Abigail fainted dead away. When she was revived, Grandfather Nutter told her that there had been no tobacco in the pipe and that she had seen only his congealed breath in the frosty hallway.

At Slatter's Hill, the North-End boys and the South-End boys met for a snowball fight at specified times during the week. But the fights became too dangerous because frozen snowballs were used, and parents and police put an end to the snow battles.

One summer Tom bought a boat called the *Dolphin,* and he and three of his friends planned a day's trip to Sandpeep Island. When the boys landed on the island, they found that they had left the lemons in the boat. Binny Wallace volunteered to get them. The boat, after he stepped into it, broke loose from its mooring-place and floated away. Binny drifted farther and farther out to sea. A rising squall developed into a full-sized storm, and the boys waited through it, hoping that Binny would be rescued. However, such was not to be. He was drowned.

One day Tom saw Sailor Ben, whom he had met during his voyage north from New Orleans. The old sailor failed to recognize Tom because he had grown so tall. When Tom took Sailor Ben home with him, Kitty at once recognized the sailor as her long-lost husband and the two were reunited. Grandfather Nutter broke out a fresh decanter of Madeira and they all celebrated the happy occasion. Deciding to quit the sea, Sailor Ben bought a small cottage near the wharf. Kitty remained as the Nutter maid, but spent her free time with her husband.

Silas Trefethen bought all the cannon available in Rivermouth because he thought that war with England was imminent. When he died, still thinking so, the cannon rusted and became unfit for any use except as monuments. Tom and his gang decided to have some fun with the cannon after they found several pieces near the wharf and cleaned them. Everything went well with their plan to set them off, except that Tom and his conspirators could not make the proper fuse. Sailor Ben, learning of their plan, told them how to prepare the fuse. When everything was in readiness, the Centipedes drew lots to determine who would fire the cannon. The chance fell to Tom. That night he slipped out of bed, lit the fuse, and returned to his room before the first cannon went off. The operation succeeded as planned. Everyone was aroused from bed by the explosions. The only casualty was Sailor Ben's chimney. No one was ever able to solve the mystery of the explosions.

With Primrose Hall, a girls' school, close by, it was not surprising that Tom should fall in love, but he was unsuccessful with the girls attending the seminary. Tom finally fell in love with Nelly Glentworth, who came to visit his grandfather, but she scorned him, and so for some time Tom rather enjoyed the pangs of unrequited love.

In New Orleans the yellow fever broke out, causing the death of Tom's father. His mother came north and settled in New York, where Tom was offered a position with an uncle in his counting-house. Ready at last to make his own way in the world, Tom left Rivermouth regretfully. He felt that the happiest days of his life were over.

THE STORY OF A COUNTRY TOWN

Type of work: Novel
Author: Edgar Watson Howe (1853-1937)
Type of plot: Social criticism
Time of plot: Mid-nineteenth century
Locale: The Middle West
First published: 1883

Principal characters:
NED WESTLOCK, a boy on the Middle Border
REV. JOHN WESTLOCK, his father
JOE ERRING, his uncle
MATEEL SHEPHERD, Joe Erring's sweetheart
CLINTON BRAGG, Joe Erring's rival for Mateel

Critique:

This novel is the earliest of a number of books that sounded a revolt against the popular conception that the American small town was an idyllic place in which to live. In it Howe drew a deadly picture of village life — the shallowness of thought, the materialism, the ever-present sense of failure and the underlying spirit of petty and mischievous enmity. Through all of the book rings a note of sincerity which makes Howe's iconoclastic efforts valid, giving his novel depth and lasting value as a social document.

The Story:

The Westlocks had gone west to grow up with the country. They lived first on a farm near a church where the father acted as the volunteer preacher. It was a life of toil and privation on the bleak prairie. Days began early and ended soon after supper, when fatigue drove the Westlocks to bed. There were four of them, John Westlock and his wife, their son Ned, and Mrs. Westlock's younger brother, Joe Erring. The only real amusement Ned had was visiting a nearby miller with his young uncle. The miller, Mr. Barker, had been a sailor in early life and he regaled the boys with stories of his travels.

When Ned was eleven years old a minister was sent from the East to take charge of the country church where Mr. Westlock had been acting as preacher. Erring immediately fell in love with Mateel Shepherd, the daughter of the new preacher, but he found no favor in her eyes because he was uneducated and crude. With the miller's help he began to improve himself. The miller became so fond of Erring that he took him on as an apprentice who would some day take over the mill. This was a great opportunity for the seventeen-year-old boy. The only flaw in his happiness then was that Mateel Shepherd was being courted by a young lawyer named Clinton Bragg.

Shortly after Erring left the farm, Mr. Westlock sold his farm and bought the almost defunct paper in the town of Twin Mounds. When the Westlocks moved into town, Ned went to the office every day to learn the printing trade and to help his father in the newspaper office.

Twin Mounds was an unprepossessing village with a post-office, several stores, a jail, and about six hundred people. The only pleasures in which the people seemed to indulge, so far as Ned could see, were drinking, gossiping, and fighting. Although the Westlocks lived in a large stone house, the father had Ned stay at the newspaper office in the company of one of the printers, under whom he was learning the trade.

Erring, apprenticed to the miller, made such excellent progress that after a year or so the community subscribed to a fund so that he could build a mill of his own, the growing population justifying a second mill in the district. He was also successful in his suit with Mateel Shepherd, who had promised to marry him when his mill was completed and in operation.

One day the quiet life of the Westlock family was rudely shattered. Mr. Westlock left the deeds to all his property in the custody of Ned and his mother and ran away with another woman. Ned took over the newspaper, which became more profitable under his management than it had been under his father, for the people in the community had not liked Mr. Westlock. He had been too solitary and strange to suit their natures.

The family gradually began to grow out of the feeling of disgrace which had fastened itself upon them when the father disappeared. Their friends did what they could for them and rallied in support of Mrs. Westlock and her son. At times it seemed as if the disappearance of Mr. Westlock were of more benefit than harm. Ned was left with some valuable property and a chance to make a name for himself at a very early age.

The following Christmas Eve Erring married Mateel Shepherd. Just before the marriage he and Ned had a long talk, in which he told Ned that in some way he was not as anxious for the marriage as he had been when he first met Mateel. What Erring did not realize was that he had been so zealous in getting an education that he had not only reached Mateel's level but he had already passed her. It was not a happy wedding. Only a handful of guests came to the wedding supper, and those who stayed away did not bother to send their regrets. The Shepherds were not popular in the community.

After the marriage of Mateel and Erring, life in the community of Twin Mounds settled into a quiet routine for everyone. Ned was more disappointed than ever in the town. Its people seldom thought out anything for themselves, and every opinion they had was made for them, often by Ned's own editorials. Their shallowness and smugness irked him.

One cold winter night Erring appeared at the door of the Westlock home. Nervous and disheveled, he had come because he felt the need to talk to someone whom he could trust. He had found a letter which his wife had written to his rival before her marriage, a letter disclosing Mateel's belief that she could never love any man but Bragg. This idea rankled in Erring's mind. He had been thoughtful and tender with his wife, but she had always been distant and cool to him, in keeping with the vow she had made in her letter to Bragg.

Ned listened to his uncle's story and then took him back to the mill and Mateel. After Erring had confronted his wife with what he had discovered, he and Ned sat up all night, unable to sleep. Clinton Bragg disappeared from Twin Mounds within a few days, apparently afraid of Mateel's husband.

That same winter Ned's father returned to Twin Mounds and accidentally met his son on the street at a late hour. He told Ned that he had been faced with misfortune ever since he had left his wife and son. The woman with whom he had run away had not really loved him and had deserted him soon after she learned that he had left his money and property in Ned's hands. John Westlock was a pathetic and broken figure, unwilling to face the wife he had deserted. Ned gave him the little money he happened to have in his pocket, and the older man then turned away into the snowy night and was soon lost to sight. Ned knew that he had seen his father for the last time.

Meanwhile matters between Erring and his wife had gone from bad to worse. He had taken a vow never to speak to his wife or touch her again, and Mateel began to fade quickly under his harsh treatment. At last she asked Erring to let her return to her father's home. He agreed. A day later Bragg drove up in a buggy to take the girl back to her father and mother. It was a bitter experience for Erring to see another man carry his wife away from his house. Ned was with his uncle and left only when the older man had fallen asleep, exhausted.

When Ned arrived home he discovered that his mother had died in his absence. Always quiet and subdued, she had died as she had lived, asking nothing from anyone.

In the spring Ned braved a heavy rainstorm to visit his uncle. He arrived to find the mill deserted. Suddenly the door opened and Erring walked in, carrying Mateel, who was unconscious. In a calm voice he told Ned how he had lain in wait along the road until Bragg and Mateel had come along in a buggy. He had dragged his rival from the vehicle and killed him with his bare hands while Mateel looked on. Then he had carried Mateel back to the mill. Unable to face the fact that Mateel had divorced him and married Bragg, he felt it was better to murder and then to die himself than to live with Mateel married to another.

Erring surrendered quietly to the authorities and was taken to jail. He was never tried, however, because one night he took poison. The jailer discovered him with a letter for Ned clutched in his hand.

After Erring's burial, Ned stopped at the Shepherd home to ask about Mateel. The poor girl was demented. While he was in the house she came into the room and mistook Ned for Erring. She drew a dagger from her dress and told Ned she had gone by the mill that day to have one last look at the place where she had been happy. Now she intended to kill herself. Her mother led her away. That same night she died, shortly after telling her father and mother she hoped to see Joe Erring soon.

THE STORY OF AN AFRICAN FARM

Type of work: Novel
Author: Olive Schreiner (1855-1920)
Type of plot: Social criticism
Time of plot: 1880's
Locale: South Africa
First published: 1883

Principal characters:
TANT' SANNIE, a Boer farm woman
LYNDALL, her stepdaughter
EM, Lyndall's cousin
WALDO, son of a German overseer
BONAPARTE BLENKINS, a hypocrite
GREGORY ROSE, a young Englishman

Critique:

The Story of an African Farm was an early attempt to present realistically the problem of a woman's place in the world. The struggle of Lyndall to find power and freedom in a world of strict moral conventions and restricted social opportunities foreshadows woman suffrage struggles still to come. The novel is also noteworthy for its finely wrought passages concerning religious doubts and moral independence.

The Story:

Just before the Englishman had died he had married Tant' Sannie, so that there would be someone to take care of his farm and his motherless daughter, Lyndall. Tant' Sannie, a heavy, slow simple Boer woman, took over the farm and the care of Lyndall and her cousin, Em. Most of the hard work was done by an old German, who lived with his young son in a small house nearby. The boy, Waldo, watched over the sheep and helped his father take charge of the black natives who did the heaviest work.

The farm lay in a dreary flat plain of red sand that was sparsely dotted with pale bushes. The sun always glittered in a blinding way on the zinc roofs of the buildings and on the stone walls of the enclosures for the animals. Life was monotonous and deadly. Tant' Sannie sat in the farmhouse drinking coffee; the children played in a half-hearted way; young Waldo did his chores, and the German went about seeing that things were as they should be.

Tant' Sannie had been asked by the Englishman to see that the two girls were educated, but she, believing only in the Bible, paid no attention to their demands for books. The two girls and Waldo found some old histories, and studied them when they could. Lyndall learned rapidly, for she was a quick, serious girl, fascinated especially by the story of Napoleon. Em was more quiet and reserved.

Waldo was the strangest of the three. His father was deeply devout, with an innocent faith in the goodness of man and the mercy of God. He had filled the boy's head with ideas which were frightening and overpowering.

One day a visitor came to the farm and asked for a night's lodging. He introduced himself as Bonaparte Blenkins, but because he was English-speaking Tant' Sannie would have nothing to do with him. The old German interceded for the visitor, however, and finally won Tant' Sannie's grudging permission for him to spend the night. The German could not bear to pass up an opportunity to practice Christian charity.

Blenkins soon won the German over completely with his fantastic tales of adventure and travel, and he even conquered Tant' Sannie by the wonderful way he read and preached the service on Sunday. But the children were not fooled. Lyndall knew that the man was lying when he talked, and that his religion was all hypocrisy. But Blenkins was soon installed on the farm as tutor to the children. After a few days, Lyndall walked out of class and refused to return.

Slowly Blenkins gained Tant' Sannie's esteem, until he felt that it was safe to try to get rid of the German and take over his job. With a trumped-up charge, he accused the overseer to his mistress, and stood by happily as the old German was ordered off the farm. Shocked the more deeply because of the support he had given Blenkins, the German went to his house to pack up and leave. It was not in his nature to argue or fight for his rights; what God sent must be accepted. In his grief he died that night.

Bonaparte Blenkins took over the farm. Like his namesake, he loved power and took advantage of his new position. He ordered Waldo about, beat him, and destroyed the model for a sheep-shearing machine the boy had made. None of these matters made any impression on Tant' Sannie. She thought that Blenkins had a wonderful sense of humor, and daily he grew more and more valuable to her. She hoped some day to be his wife.

A visit by one of Tant' Sannie's nieces disillusioned her. The niece was young, only a little overweight, and wealthy. One day Tant' Sannie climbed up to the loft to see if everything there was neat and let her maid take the ladder away. While she was there, Blenkins came into the room below with the niece and began to make love to her. Furious at Blenkins' deception, Tant' Sannie dropped a barrel of salt meat on his head, almost knocking him out, and drenching him with pickle-water. His stay on the farm was over.

When the children grew up, Lyndall had her way about going to the city to work and study. Waldo began to doubt the God he had so terribly feared in his childhood, and Em grew to attractive, if not beautiful, womanhood. Tant' Sannie rented part of the farm to a young Englishman named Gregory Rose, who soon fell in love with Em. It was the first time anyone had paid much attention to the girl, and she was enraptured at the prospect of marriage. Tant' Sannie thought she herself might as well marry again, and she sent out word to the surrounding farms that she was looking for a husband.

Waldo eagerly awaited Lyndall's return from the city. He wanted to know what she had found out about the world and to tell her of his own problems. He had learned wood carving. One day, while he was watching the sheep, a stranger had come up and talked with him. After looking at one of Waldo's carvings, the traveler told the boy a story of a man who searched for Truth but found merely a creed until, just before his death, he caught a glimpse of his goal. The meeting was short but unforgettable. Waldo wanted to go out into the world, to find the man again, to learn more about the search for Truth.

When Lyndall returned, she was a different person. Waldo found that he could not talk with her as he had before. She had learned the problems a woman faces in the world, and she refused to be held down by the laws and restrictions which bound her. Neither Em nor Gregory Rose, her fiancé, could understand Lyndall. Gregory disliked her at first, but as time passed he became more attracted to her. At Tant' Sannie's wedding feast, for she had found a widower who wanted to marry again, Em discovered that she did not really love Gregory, and she asked him to forget the plans they had made.

When Lyndall asked him to marry her—just to give her his name—Gregory consented. It was a long time before he discovered the reason. Lyndall had made a friend in the city, a man who wanted her to marry him, but she could not stand the idea of being tied down by legal marriage. She wanted freedom, not bondage. She felt that if she could threaten her lover with marriage to another man, she could get what she wanted from him. Her plan worked. When he received a letter telling of her plans, he set out at once to see her. Lyndall met her friend secretly at the farm and went away to live with him, but not as his wife.

Since Waldo, too, had gone off to seek his way in the world, the farm was quiet for a time. Gregory did not know what to do about Lyndall's disappearance. The longer she was away, the more he felt he loved her. At last he started out to learn what had become of her.

As Gregory tracked Lyndall from town to town, he learned the story of a slowly fading love between the two people he was following. In time he found Lyndall, lying sick in a hotel room, deserted by her lover. She had had a child, but it had died shortly after birth. Seeing her so weak and sick, Gregory wanted to be near her, to care for her. Dressed as a woman, he was hired as Lyndall's nurse. When she died, he took her body back to the farm for burial.

One night Em was startled by a knock on the door. Waldo had returned. He had traveled much, but had learned little. Once he had seen the stranger who had talked to him so wonderfully about Truth, but the man, not recognizing him, had turned away. The first thing Waldo did was to sit down and begin a letter to Lyndall. When Em learned what he was doing, she told him that Lyndall was dead.

Gregory still thought of Lyndall and kept as his greatest treasure the one letter he had received from her, a letter which advised him to marry Em. In time he asked Em again to be his wife, and she accepted. Waldo knew that Em felt she would have only half a husband, but he also knew that she had never learned to hope for much, as he had, as Lyndall had. Waldo kept one of Lyndall's dancing shoes in his blouse. He spent much of his time wandering about the farm watching the insects, looking at the flowers. He wanted to be like them, to die, to sleep in the same earth with Lyndall. One day, lying in the warm sunshine, he died.

THE STORY OF GÖSTA BERLING

Type of work: Novel
Author: Selma Lagerlöf (1858-1940)
Type of plot: Picaresque romance
Time of plot: Early nineteenth century
Locale: Sweden
First published: 1894

Principal characters:
Gösta Berling, formerly a minister
The Countess Elizabeth, Gösta's wife
Margareta Samzelius, the major's wife
Marianne Sinclair, in love with Gösta
Christian Bergh, Gösta's crony

Critique:

The Story of Gösta Berling has remained since its publication a great favorite, and the esteem in which it is held is due to several noteworthy qualities of the novel. Selma Lagerlöf has recreated much of the warm, emotional tone of Swedish country life. The use of the almost supernatural, which can be explained reasonably, is unique. The moral theme of Gösta's redemption is a powerful one. In addition, the tale is told with a light, sure touch that adds to the delight of the reader. The novelist takes the point of view of an old resident who recalls with difficulty the tales of long ago, a process which gives an air of realism.

The Story:

Gösta Berling stood in the pulpit on what was a critical Sunday for him, for the bishop was present to make a strict investigation of his ministry. Gösta drank far too much and too often. With his crony, Christian Bergh, he spent more and more time in tavern taprooms, and brandy had become for him a necessity. The congregation had complained of his conduct to the bishop, and now Gösta felt himself on trial.

That morning he preached his sermon as if inspired by God Himself. At the end of the service, the bishop stood up and asked for complaints against the minister, but no one would say a word. In his heart Gösta felt love for his flock.

As he sat up that night, thinking of the wonder that had happened, Bergh came to his window to assure him that the bishop would never trouble him again. Thinking to help his drinking crony, Bergh had driven the bishop and his attendant priests in his carriage. He took them on a wild ride, up and down hill and over plowed fields at top speed. Then, as he drew up at the inn which was their destination, he warned the bishop not to bother Gösta thereafter. The bishop did not come to see Gösta any more on any errand, nor did any other bishop, for Gösta was dismissed from the church.

He became a beggar. In the winter he had only rags on his feet. He met the twelve-year-old daughter of the wicked clergyman of Bro. Neglected by her father, she was hauling a heavy sled with a sack of meal for her own food. Gösta took hold of the rope with her. When she left him in charge of the sled, he promptly bartered both sled and meal for brandy.

Awaking from a drunken sleep, Gösta saw Margareta Samzelius, the major's wife, looking at him; out of compassion she intended to help Gösta. Margareta, strong and rough, ruled Ekeby and six estates. She had been betrothed to a young man named Altinger, but her parents made her take the major while she was waiting the five years for Altinger to make his fortune. Then Altinger came back rich and famous and Margareta became his mistress. At his death he left his lands ostensibly to the major, but in reality to Margareta.

After great urging, Gösta became a pensioner, one of the group of merry wastrels who existed handsomely on the bounty of Margareta. On Christmas Eve the pensioners had a great party, with much to drink. Then Sintram, who was so evil that he thought himself the chosen of Satan, came in dressed as the devil. He said he was going to renew his pact with Margareta. The half-drunk pensioners thought uneasily of Margareta's great wealth and power. Surely something supernatural had helped her. It was said that she held her power by sacrificing the soul of one pensioner to the devil each year.

In a frightening bit of nonsense the pensioners made a pact with the devil; no one of their number was to die that year. Once in charge of Ekeby and the six estates, the pensioners agreed to conduct themselves as masters in a manner pleasing to Satan himself.

The next day when the grouse was passed at the Christmas feast, Bergh called the birds crows and threw them one by one against the wall. Margareta ordered him out of the house. In his wrath, Bergh accused her of having been Altinger's mistress with the compliance of her husband. Margareta proudly confessed the truth of what he said. Then, to save his honor, the major disowned his wife. All the pensioners, who owed her so much, turned their faces when she asked for help. Margareta left her home to become a beggar.

That year the pensioners were in

charge at Ekeby. The major, indifferent to the estates, returned to his own farm. Gösta learned that Anna Stjärnhok, the rich and beautiful belle of the district, had broken her engagement to a timid man named Ferdinand to become engaged to a rich old man with a bald head.

Determined to bring Anna back to Ferdinand, Gösta harried her so much at a ball that she slapped his face. But that slap revealed the truth; Anna really loved Gösta. Forgetting his duty to Ferdinand, Gösta set out with Anna for Ekeby. But on the way their sleigh was followed by wolves and they were forced to stop at Ferdinand's home for protection. So Gösta involuntarily brought Anna back to Ferdinand, and so he was saved from committing a sin.

Ferdinand, however, soon died, and Anna went through a marriage ceremony with his corpse. Ever after she concealed her love for Gösta.

At a ball at Ekeby, Gösta and Marianne Sinclair took part in a tableau presenting them as lovers. Marianne, succumbing to the charm of Gösta, kissed him after the tableau. Later, at the gaming table, Gösta won all the money Marianne's father had, and then, in jest, won his consent to a betrothal with Marianne. When the father discovered that Gösta, a drunkard and an unfrocked minister, was in earnest, he was furious with his daughter.

After the ball the pensioners found Marianne locked out by her father and half-frozen. Supposedly asleep in the guest room at Ekeby that night, the girl heard Margareta, who had returned full of wrath against her pensioners, plan a riot to drive the wastrels out. Marianne ran to a bear hunter and enlisted his aid, and succeeded in breaking up the riot.

But Marianne contracted smallpox on her errand, and the scars greatly marred her beauty. Not wishing Gösta to see her, she returned to her father, and Gösta thought she had discontinued their romance. Too proud to go after her, he soon forgot her.

Countess Elizabeth Dohna, at twenty, was a gay, sympathetic girl married to a stupid husband. At a dance Gösta asked her for a polka. She refused because she had heard that Gösta had caused the death of Ebba, her husband's sister, who had died in sorrow after hearing the story of Gösta's life. Angry at her refusal, Gösta and his friends abducted the countess and took her home. There the stupid husband sided with Gösta. The poor girl led a miserable life. Finally she ran away to live as a peasant, and the count had the marriage annulled. After she was legally a single woman again, she bore a child. Not wishing to have an unnamed baby, she asked Gösta to marry her. Gösta accepted, awed and grateful, for he loved the countess.

Gösta, helped by his wife, turned over a new leaf, and all the pensioners followed his lead. Ekeby rang with the smith's hammer; walls and docks were repaired. When Margareta came back after the death of the major, she reëntered Ekeby as mistress of a prosperous estate.

Gösta and his wife retired to a modest cottage where Gösta could earn his living as a carpenter and help all who were in trouble, and the countess could serve the sick. So Gösta became, after many years, a good man.

STRIFE

Type of work: Drama
Author: John Galsworthy (1867-1933)
Type of plot: Social criticism
Time of plot: Early twentieth century
Locale: Industrial town near London
First presented: 1909

Principal characters:

JOHN ANTHONY, chairman of the Trenartha Tin Plate Works
EDGAR ANTHONY, his son
FRANCIS UNDERWOOD, manager of the plant
ENID UNDERWOOD, his wife, and John Anthony's daughter
SIMON HARNESS, a Trades Union official
DAVID ROBERTS, leader of the strike
ANNIE ROBERTS, David's wife

Critique:

Galsworthy wrote this play at a time when the rights of laborers were only beginning to be asserted. *Strife* presents a picture of both sides of the strike question, for Galsworthy was always an impartial realist. Aside from its social implications, the play is also notable for several very real and forceful characters, Roberts and old Anthony among them.

The Story:

The strike at the Trenartha Tin Plate Works had lasted so long without any sign of a settlement that the directors had begun to fear for their dividends. They had all gathered at the Underwood home at the request of the workers, and at first there was some talk of compromise. Facing them, however, was the stern figure of the chairman of the board, seventy-five-year-old John Anthony, who refused to consider any plan for compromise.

Anthony belonged to the old school of businessmen who refused to move with the times. For him there could be only one master at the plant, and that was John Anthony himself. He had defeated four strikes in his thirty-two years as chairman of the board, and he was certain that a little more perseverance would defeat the strikers once more.

The other directors were a little uneasy under his stern refusal. In his report Underwood, the plant manager, had made no attempt to disguise the terrible suffering of the striking workers and their families. The directors were also aware that if the strike lasted much longer their stockholders would begin to protest strongly.

Although the union had withdrawn support from the strikers because two of their conditions exceeded the prevailing standards, Simon Harness, a Trades Union official, had been sent to attempt mediation between the board and the workers. His interview with the directors accomplished nothing because of Anthony's obstinacy. The meeting between the representatives of the workers and the directors was equally unhappy. Roberts, the leader of the striking workmen, was just as unyielding on his side as Anthony was on his. Both sides faced a deadlock.

Conditions among the workers were so terrible that many of them were ready to give in, but Roberts remained adamant. Mrs. Roberts was dying; her weak heart could not stand the cold and hunger which the strike imposed upon them all. At one time she had been the maid in Underwood's home, and one afternoon Enid Underwood went to visit her. Mrs. Underwood had tried to send food to Mrs. Roberts, but the strike leader was too proud and too stubborn to accept help from the daughter of John Anthony. Mrs. Underwood tried to plead with Roberts, asking him, for his wife's sake, to give in and end the strike. But he was fanatic in his certainty that in the end the workmen could bring their employers to terms.

At a meeting of the men and Harness, the Trades Union official, it became evident that most of the strikers were willing to compromise, to accept the union suggestions. A few were willing to give in completely. When Roberts appeared at the meeting, the men did not wish to hear him speak. But Roberts was a powerful orator, and as he talked to them again about the eventual victory which they could win if they refused to give in now, they were once more moved and convinced by his oratory. As he was speaking, a young woman approached the platform and told him that his wife had died. With this tragedy as an example of what they must expect if they continued to resist, the men decided to accept the terms of the union compromise.

The news of Mrs. Roberts' death was a blow to the directors. Edgar Anthony, in spite of the respect which he had for his father, now faced his colleagues and accused them of responsibility for the woman's condition and death. They felt uncomfortably that what he said was very close to the truth. Old Anthony, weak and unwell as he was, still insisted that the company should not yield. But the directors had decided to act in spite of him, although they knew that should they decide to accept the union terms, Anthony would resign.

That evening the meeting between the workers, Harness, and the directors was painful in the extreme. Anthony found himself outvoted by his colleagues. Wearily, with an acknowledgement of his defeat, he resigned. Roberts, who knew nothing of the action which his men had decided to take after he had left the meeting, arrived at the Underwood home in time to watch Harness complete the settlement. The terms agreed upon were those which the union had suggested to both sides before the strike began, but it had needed months of suffering to bring agreement in the dispute. The two leaders stared at each other, both deserted by their supporters, both defeated by the compromise. As they recognized the courageous battle which each had put up, their expression of hate turned to one of grudging admiration and mutual respect.

A STUDY IN SCARLET

Type of work: Novel
Author: Arthur Conan Doyle (1859-1930)
Type of plot: Mystery romance
Time of plot: Nineteenth century
Locale: London
First published: 1887

Principal characters:
SHERLOCK HOLMES, the detective
DR. JOHN WATSON, his friend
JEFFERSON HOPE, an American cab driver
TOBIAS GREGSON, of Scotland Yard
LESTRADE, of Scotland Yard

Critique:

A Study in Scarlet was the first of the many adventures of Sherlock Holmes, the most delightful as well as the most durable of fictional detectives. No ordinary criticism can apply to the canon of Sherlock Holmes. From 1887 until Doyle's death in 1930 the amazing Holmes appeared in a total of sixty novels and short stories. Many of the plots are incredible; many of the deductions are improbable; all of Doyle's Americans are people from another planet. Dr. Watson's bullet wound was sometimes in his shoulder, sometimes in his leg, and he was married and widowed at Doyle's convenience. These matters are irrelevant. Let us have a puzzle, let us have Holmes to solve it, let us have Watson foı a foil, and we are all content.

The Story:

To many the Afghan wars brought

fame and promotion, but to John H. Watson, M.D., they brought only misfortune. He was wounded by a Jezail bullet, and during his convalescence was struck down with enteric. After months of suffering he was invalided home on eleven shillings and sixpence a day.

At first Watson lived in a hotel, but his pension scarcely covered his bills. By chance he met Stamford, an old friend, and confided his difficulties. Through him he learned of an amateur scientist, Sherlock Holmes, who had rooms at 221B Baker Street and was looking for some one to share them. On the spot Watson arranged to have Stamford bring them together. Stamford warned that Sherlock Holmes pursued no orthodox studies; one day Stamford had found him beating a cadaver to see if bruises could be produced after death. Holmes had a queer habit of making deductions from trifling, often personal things. Watson grew curious about Sherlock Holmes. Soon after their first meeting Watson went to share Holmes' rooms in Baker Street.

Watson never went out; consequently he spent much time studying his new friend. He found Holmes an amazingly contradictory man who knew nothing at all of literature, philosophy, or astronomy, but who had a profound knowledge of chemistry, anatomy, and sensational crime stories. He also played the violin. From time to time Holmes had visitors, but Watson never knew why they came.

One day at breakfast Watson learned a good deal more about his friend. Holmes showed Watson a letter from Tobias Gregson, a Scotland Yard investigator, who asked help in a case of murder. A gentleman identified by his visiting cards as Enoch J. Drebber, Cleveland, Ohio, U. S. A., had been found murdered in a deserted house in Lauriston Gardens. Holmes then explained his profession; he was a consulting detective. Whenever an unusual case, outside police jurisdiction or too difficult for Scotland Yard, came up, Holmes was asked to step in and help solve the mystery.

Holmes and Watson took a cab to Lauriston Gardens to look into the affair. Holmes spent a long time outside in the road and in the yard. Watson was impatient at the delay, but Holmes examined everything carefully. Inside the house Gregson and Lestrade, another detective from Scotland Yard, greeted them and pointed out the body of Drebber, surrounded by spatters of blood. Holmes went over the body painstakingly.

As the orderlies were carrying out the corpse, a woman's wedding ring fell to the floor. The Scotland Yard men were sure a woman was involved, and Lestrade was triumphant when he found the word *Rache* printed in letters of blood on the wall. As Sherlock Holmes left the room, he announced his findings to the detectives. The murderer was over six feet in height and florid; he wore square-toed boots; and he smoked a Trichinopoly cigar. He had long nails on his right hand. He had driven up to the house in a four-wheeler drawn by a horse with a new shoe on his off forefoot. The murder was done by poison, and *Rache* was not short for Rachel but was rather the German word for revenge.

The cigar ashes, the tracks, the height of the writing, and the scratches during the writing on the wall had told their story to Holmes. The blood on the floor came from a nosebleed, indicating the ruddy coloring of the murderer. But after uncovering these initial clues Holmes was balked for a time. He advertised the wedding ring as lost, and an old woman came to claim it. When the old woman eluded him, he knew that he was searching for a clever opponent.

The trail of Drebber led to his secretary, Stangerson. Gregson was sure that if Stangerson could be found, he would have the murderer. But a short time later Stangerson was found dead, stabbed through the heart, in his hotel room. The case seemed impenetrable, at least to Scotland Yard.

Gregson and Lestrade came to Holmes one night, and the three detectives and Watson went over their difficulties. Holmes was tying up a trunk preparatory to sending it away. He called a cab to deliver it, and when the bell rang he asked the cabbie up to help with the ropes. As the man bent down, Holmes quickly slipped handcuffs over the cabbie's wrists. The cabbie was a large, vigorous man who fought as if possessed, but finally the four men subdued him. With a theatrical flourish, Holmes presented him—Jefferson Hope, the murderer of Drebber and Stangerson!

Hope calmed down. He told the men he had nothing to fear and he asked Watson to feel his pulse. Watson detected an aneurism immediately. He agreed that Hope had not long to live. Indeed, Hope never came to trial, for he died in less than a week; but from him the English officers learned his strange story.

On the great alkali plain in Utah, John Ferrier and little Lucy were the only survivors of a wagon train. But the two were providentially picked up by Mormons, who under the leadership of Brigham Young were on their way to a new settlement in the wilderness. Ferrier had to agree to adopt the Mormon faith, and in return he and Lucy were taken along.

Ferrier prospered as a Mormon and soon became a rich man; Lucy grew up to be a beautiful woman. But Ferrier, although a Mormon, refused to take wives, and he made a vow that Lucy should never marry a Mormon. When a traveler named Jefferson Hope stopped at their house on his way to the silver mines, an attraction soon developed between him and Lucy. After Hope left, the blow fell. The Mormon elders decreed that before thirty days should elapse, Lucy must choose a husband. She could marry either Drebber or Stangerson, who already had several wives, but she must marry.

In his dilemma, Ferrier sent word to Hope, who returned on the last day of grace. At night Hope, Ferrier, and Lucy stole out of the Mormon village and rode furiously toward the mountains.

When he judged that they were safely away, Hope left Ferrier and Lucy in camp while he went hunting. On his return, he saw his error. Ferrier had been murdered, and Lucy was gone. Hope hid near the Mormon village in the hope of rescuing Lucy, but he was balked by the strong, watchful Latter-day Saints. Lucy was given in marriage to Drebber. She survived only a month. While the women watched at night over her coffin, Hope stormed in, kissed his dead love, and took the wedding ring from her finger. Then he vanished.

Shortly afterward both Drebber and Stangerson renounced Mormonism and moved to Cleveland. When Hope took up the trail again, he became a nemesis. Drebber and Stangerson were wealthy and afraid, for they knew Hope was after them. They fled to Russia and Germany, and finally ended up in London. Hope followed them from place to place.

To exist, Hope took a job as cab driver, and as such he could follow his prey conveniently. Drebber engaged him one night when he was drunk, and Hope drove him to the deserted house. There he showed Drebber the wedding ring. Taking from his pocket a small box containing two pills, one harmless and one deadly, he forced Drebber to choose one and swallow it. Hope put the other in his own mouth. Hope felt that Lucy's spirit guided the choice; it was Drebber who died. On impulse, Hope had scribbled *Rache* on the wall with the blood which had gushed from his nose in his excitement. Later, finding Stangerson in his hotel room, Hope offered him the fatal choice. When Stangerson had attacked him, Hope had killed him with a knife. He refused to give the name of the old woman who had appeared to claim the ring.

On the day he was to appear in court Hope died from the bursting of the aneurism in his heart. His work was done; Lucy was avenged.

THE SUN ALSO RISES

Type of work: Novel
Author: Ernest Hemingway (1898-)
Type of plot: Social criticism
Time of plot: 1920's
Locale: Paris and Pamplona, Spain
First published: 1926

Principal characters:
JAKE BARNES, an American newspaper man
LADY BRETT ASHLEY, one of the lost generation
ROBERT COHN, a young writer
MICHAEL CAMPBELL (MIKE), Brett's fiancé
BILL GORTON, Jake's friend
PEDRO ROMERO, a Spanish bullfighter

Critique:

This early Hemingway novel reflects the period following the first World War, a period of maladjustment and despair on the part of a war-weary generation for whom life had lost its significance. The opening quotation from Gertrude Stein and the quotation from *Ecclesiastes,* from which the title of the novel is taken, clearly point to this theme. Such reference is not necessary, however, once the reader has started the book. *The Sun Also Rises* describes realistically life among American expatriates on the Left Bank in Paris and the color and excitement of a Spanish fiesta. Above all, the skillful character analysis, sketched in so rapidly by Hemingway, will make the reader feel that he has really lived with the disillusioned people who appear in the novel.

The Story:

Jake Barnes knew Robert Cohn in Paris shortly after the first World War. Somehow Jake always thought that Cohn was typical of the place and the time. Cohn, the son of wealthy Jewish parents, had once been the middleweight boxing champion of Princeton. He never wanted anyone to forget that fact. After leaving college, he had married and had lived incompatibly with his wife until she ran off with another man. Then in California he met some writers and decided to start a little, arty review of his own. He also met Frances Clyne, who became his mistress, and when Jake knew Cohn the two were living unhappily in Paris, where Cohn was writing his first novel. Cohn wrote and boxed and played tennis, and he was always careful not to mix his friendships. A man named Braddocks was his literary friend. Jake Barnes was his tennis friend.

Jake Barnes was an American newspaperman who had fought with the Italians during the war. His own private tragedy was a war wound which had emasculated him so that he could never marry Lady Brett Ashley, a young English war-widow with whom he was in love. In order not to think too much about himself, Jake spent a lot of time listening to the troubles of his friends and drinking heavily. When he grew tired of Paris, he went on fishing trips to the Basque country or to Spain for the bullfights.

One night, feeling lonely, Jake asked Georgette, a girl of the streets, to join him in a drink at the Café Napolitain. They dined on the Left Bank, where Jake met a party of his friends, including Robert Cohn and Frances Clyne. Later Brett Ashley came in with a group of young men. It was evident that Cohn was attracted to her, and Frances was jealous. Brett refused to dance with Cohn, however, saying that she had a date with Jake in Montmartre. Leaving a fifty-franc note with the café proprietor for Georgette, Jake left in a taxi with Brett for a ride to the Parc Montsouris. They talked for a time about themselves without mentioning what was in both their minds, Jake's injury. At last Brett asked Jake to drive her back to the Café Select.

The next day Cohn cornered Jake and asked him questions about Brett. Later, after drinking with Harvey Stone, another expatriate, on the terrace of the Café Select, Jake met Cohn and Frances, who announced that her lover was dismissing her by sending her off to London. She abused Cohn scornfully and taunted him with his inferiority complex while he sat quietly without replying. Jake was embarrassed. The same day Jake received a telegram from his old friend, Bill Gorton, announcing his arrival on the *France*. Brett went on a trip to San Sebastian with Robert Cohn. She thought the excursion would be good for him.

Jake and Bill Gorton had planned to go to Spain for the trout fishing and the bullfights at Pamplona. Michael Campbell, an Englishman whom Brett was to marry, had also arrived in Paris. He and Brett arranged to join Jake and Bill at Pamplona later. Because Cohn had gone to San Sebastian with Brett and because she was staying now with Mike Campbell, everyone felt that it would be awkward if Cohn accompanied Jake and Bill on their trip. Nevertheless, he decided to join them at Bayonne. The agreement was that Jake and Bill would first go trout fishing at Burguete in the mountains. Later the whole party would meet at the Montoya Hotel in Pamplona for the fiesta.

When Jake and Bill arrived in Bayonne, they found Cohn awaiting them. Hiring a car, they drove on to Pamplona. Montoya, the proprietor of the hotel, was an old friend of Jake's because he recognized Jake as a true *aficionado*—one who is passionate about the bullfight. The next morning Bill and Jake left by bus for Burguete, both riding atop the ancient vehicle with several bottles of wine and an assortment of Basque passengers. At Burguete they enjoyed good fishing in the company of an Englishman named Wilson-Harris.

Once back in Pamplona, the whole party had gathered for the festival of San Fermin. The first night they went to see the bulls come in, to watch the men let the savage bulls out of the cages one at a time. Much wine made Mike Campbell loquacious and freed his tongue so that he harped constantly on the fact that Cohn had joined the group, although he knew he was not wanted. At noon on Sunday the fiesta exploded. The carnival continued for seven days. Dances, parades, religious processions, the bullfights—these and much wine furnished the excitement of that hectic week. Also staying at the Montoya Hotel was Pedro Romero, a bullfighter about twenty years old, who was extremely handsome. At the fights Romero acquitted himself well, and Brett fell in love with him, a fact she admitted with embarrassment to Jake. Brett and the young man met at the hotel; Romero soon became interested in her.

Besides the bullfights, the main diversion of the group was drunken progress from one drinking spot to another. While they were in the Café Suizo, Jake told Cohn that Brett had gone off with the bullfighter to his room. Cohn swung at both Mike and Jake and knocked them down. After the fight Cohn apologized, crying all the while. He could not understand how Brett could go off with him to San Sebastian one week and then treat him like a stranger when they met again. He planned to leave Pamplona the next morning.

The next morning Jake learned that after the fight Cohn had gone to Pedro Romero's room, where he found Brett and the bullfighter together. Cohn had beaten Romero badly. But that day, in spite of his swollen face and battered body, Romero performed beautifully in the ring, dispatching a bull which had recently killed another torero. That night, after the fights, Brett left Pamplona with Romero. Jake got very drunk.

The fiesta over, the party dispersed. Bill Gorton went back to Paris, Mike Campbell to Saint Jean de Luz. Jake was in San Sebastian when he received a wire from Brett asking him to come to the Hotel Montana in Madrid. Taking the express, Jake met her the next day. Brett was alone. She had sent Pedro Romero away, she said, because she thought she was not good for him. Then, without funds, she had sent for Jake. She had decided to go back to Mike, she told Jake, because the Englishman was her own sort.

After dinner Jake and Brett rode around in a taxi, seeing the sights of Madrid. This, Jake reflected wryly, was one of the few ways they could ever be alone together—in bars and cafés and taxis. Both knew the ride was as purposeless as the war-wrecked world in which they lived, as aimless as the drifting generation to which they belonged.

THE SWISS FAMILY ROBINSON

Type of work: Novel
Author: Johann Rudolf Wyss (1781-1830)
Type of plot: Adventure romance
Time of plot: Late eighteenth century
Locale: An island near New Guinea
First published: 1813

Principal characters:
MR. ROBINSON, a shipwrecked Swiss gentleman
MRS. ROBINSON, his wife
FRITZ,
ERNEST,
JACK, and
FRANCIS, their sons
EMILY MONTROSE, an English girl, also shipwrecked

Critique:

The adventures of the Robinson family are familiar to most school children, for the account of their life on an uninhabited island has long been a favorite. For adults the story moves rather slowly; the events are related in such detail that they become tiring at times. All ages, however, can admire the perfect harmony in which the Robinsons lived. Obedience to parental wishes and love for one's family are points the author apparently wished to stress in the story.

The Story:

Of all the passengers and crew on board the ship, only the Robinson family was saved when the vessel broke apart on a reef and the crew and other passengers jumped into lifeboats without waiting for the little family to join them. As the ship tossed about, the father prayed that God would spare them. There was plenty of food on board, and after they had eaten the boys went to sleep, leaving the father and the mother to guard them.

In the morning their first concern was to get to the island they could see beyond the reef. With much effort, they constructed a vessel out of tubs. After they had filled the tubs with food and ammunition and all other articles of value they could safely carry, they rowed toward the island. Two dogs from the ship swam beside them, and the boys were glad they would have pets when they reached their new home.

Their first task on reaching the island was to erect a tent of sailcloth they had brought from the ship. They gathered moss and dried it, so that they would have some protection from the ground when they slept. They were able to find a lobster and to shoot some game, and thus to add fresh food to their supplies. Since they had no utensils for eating, they used shells for spoons, all dipping out of the iron kettle which they had brought from the ship. They had released some geese and pigeons while they were still on the ship and had brought two hens and two cocks with them. The father knew that they must prepare for a long time on the island, and his thoughts were as much on provisions for the future as for their immediate wants.

The father and Fritz, the oldest son, spent the next day exploring the island. They found gourds from which they would make dishes and spoons, and many edible fruits and roots. Coconuts, growing in abundance, provided a treat for the mother and the younger boys. Fritz captured a small monkey which he took back for a pet. The younger boys were enchanted with the mischievous little animal.

The Robinsons spent the next few days securing themselves against hunger and danger from wild animals. The father and Fritz made several trips to the ship in their efforts to bring ashore everything that they could possibly use. The domesticated animals on the ship were towed back to the island. There was also a great store of firearms and ammunition, hammocks for sleeping, carpenter's tools, lumber, cooking utensils, silverware, and dishes.

While the father and Fritz were salvaging these supplies, the mother and the younger boys were working on the shore, sowing seeds, examining the contents of the kegs which floated to shore, and in every way possible making the tent home more livable. The mother and boys also explored the island to find a spot for a more permanent home. When the father and Fritz could join them, the whole family helped to construct a tree house which would give them protection from wild animals which they feared might dwell on the island.

Through the following weeks each day brought a new adventure of some kind. There were encounters with wild birds and terrifying animals. Ernest, the second son, had studied nature with great interest before their ill-fated voyage, and it was he who identified many of the animals and birds. They found some food which they considered luxuries, sugarcane, honey, potatoes, and spices. They fenced in a secluded area for their cattle, so that they might have a constant supply of milk and fresh meat. Several new dwellings were constructed to provide homes on all sides of the island. The father found a tree which contained long threads, and after he had constructed a loom the mother was able to weave cloth for new clothing. Jack and Francis, the younger boys, contributed to the welfare of the family by helping their mother to care for the animals and thresh the grain grown from seeds brought from the ship.

Many times the little band found their labor destroyed by forces they could not control. Goats ate the bark off young fruit trees they had planted. Monkeys robbed their food stores frequently, and jackals and serpents killed some of their pets. But the family would not be too discouraged, for they knew that they had been very fortunate to be saved on an island which provided food and shelter in such abundance.

About a year later they discovered a cave which became a home and a storage place for their supplies. In it they were protected from the rains and their supplies were safe from intruders. They spent many enjoyable evenings reading books they salvaged from the ship. The father and mother had found a way to make candles from the sap of a native tree. Altogether, their lives were agreeable and happy, and each morning and evening they thanked God for His goodness.

Ten years passed. The boys had become young men, and Fritz often sailed long distances in the canoe he had constructed. One day he captured a wounded albatross and found attached to it a note, written in English, asking someone to help an English girl who was in a cave near a volcano. The father and Fritz decided that Fritz must try to find her without telling the rest of the family of the note or the proposed search. Fritz, successful in his search, found a young girl, Emily Montrose, who had also been shipwrecked as she was sailing from India to her home in England. The members of the Robinson family accepted Emily as a daughter and a sister who was able to help the mother in her duties and give the boys much joy with her stories of life in India. Her own mother was dead. Emily had lived in India with her father, an army officer, who had sailed back to England on a different ship. She knew he would be worried about her, but there was no way for her to communicate with him.

One morning, a few months later, the castaways were astonished to hear the sound of three cannon shots. Not knowing whether the sound came from a friendly ship or from a pirate vessel, they loaded their small boat with firearms and sailed out to investigate the noise. There they found an English ship which had been driven off her course by a storm. It was impossible for this ship to take Emily back to England, but the captain promised to notify her father and to send a ship back for her. A captain, his wife and two children, who were on board, were so enchanted with the island that they asked to be allowed to stay. It seemed as if a little colony would grow there.

Six months later the ship sent by Emily's father arrived. Fritz and Jack had a great longing to see their homeland again, and since they were now mature young men, their mother and father allowed them to return with Emily. Before he left Fritz told his father that he loved Emily and intended to ask her father's permission to propose marriage to her. The Robinsons, who loved Emily dearly, gave their blessing to their son.

The father, who had prepared a manuscript relating their adventures, gave it to Fritz before the boy sailed, in the hope that their story might be of interest to the rest of the world. The father and mother wanted to spend their remaining days on the island. Now that their island was known, commerce would begin and a colony could grow there. The father prayed that the little colony would increase in prosperity and piety, and continue to deserve and receive the blessings of the merciful God who had cared for them all so tenderly in the past.

A TALE OF TWO CITIES

Type of work: Novel
Author: Charles Dickens (1812-1870)
Type of plot: Historical romance
Time of plot: French Revolution
Locale: France and England
First published: 1859

Principal characters

DR. MANETTE, a former prisoner in the Bastille
LUCIE MANETTE, his daughter
MR. LORRY, an agent of Tellson & Co.
CHARLES DARNAY, Marquis St. Evrémonde

SYDNEY CARTON, a lawyer's clerk
MISS PROSS, a servant
MADAME DEFARGE, a French revolutionary
M. DEFARGE, her husband

Critique:

Dickens is a remarkable story-teller. Although one may complain of the many characters in his stories, each character is necessary to complete the pattern of the Dickens plot. In this novel of the French Revolution, Dickens' treatment of his complicated plot, every event of which draws toward one great climax against the greater drama of history, is both delightful and fascinating to experience.

The Story:

The early rumbling of the French Revolution was echoing across the English Channel. In Paris a lonely old man waited in an attic for his first meeting with a daughter whom he had not seen since she was a baby. With the aid of Mr. Jarvis Lorry, an agent for the Franco-British banking house of Tellson & Co., the lovely Lucie Manette had been brought to Paris to find her father, imprisoned for eighteen years in the Bastille. Above the wine shop of Madame and M. Defarge, Dr. Manette was kept secretly until his rescuers could take him safely back to England. Day after day Madame Defarge sat outside her wine shop, knitting into a long scarf strange symbols which would later spell out a death list of hated aristocrats.

Five years later Lucie Manette sat beside her father in the courtroom of the Old Bailey, where Charles Darnay, a teacher of languages, was on trial for treasonable activities which involved his passing between France and England on secret business. A man named John Barsad had brought charges against him. Lucie and her father had testified they had met Darnay on the boat when they had traveled from France five years earlier. But an unusual circumstance saved the prisoner. Mr. Stryver, the prisoner's counsel, pointed across the courtroom to another man who so resembled the prisoner that legal identification of Darnay was shaken. The other man was Sydney Carton, and because of the likeness between the two Mr. Stryver secured an acquittal for the prisoner. Carton's relationship to Stryver was that of the jackal to the lion, for the alcoholic, aimless Carton wrote the cases which Stryver pleaded in court.

Lucie and her father lived in a small tenement under the care of their maid, Miss Pross, and their kindly friend, Mr. Lorry. Jerry Cruncher, porter at Tellson & Co., and a secret resurrectionist, was often helpful. Darnay and Carton became frequent callers in the Manette household, after the trial which had brought them together.

In France the fury of the people grew. Monseigneur the Marquis St. Evrémonde, was driving in his carriage through the countryside when he carelessly killed a child of a peasant named Gaspard. The nobleman returned to his castle to meet his nephew, who was visiting from England. Charles Darnay's views differed from those of his uncle. Darnay knew that his family had committed grave injustices, for which he begged his uncle to make amends. Monseigneur the marquis haughtily refused. That night the marquis was murdered in his bed.

Darnay returned to England to seek Dr. Manette's permission to court Lucie. In order to construct a bond of complete honesty, Darnay attempted to tell the doctor his true French name, but Manette fearfully asked him to wait until the morning of his marriage before revealing it. Carton also approached Lucie with a proposal of marriage. When Lucie refused, Carton asked her always to remember that there was a man who would give his own life to keep a life she loved beside her.

Meanwhile in France Madame Defarge knitted into her scarf the story of the hated St. Evrémondes. Gaspard had been hanged for the assassination of the marquis; monseigneur's house must be destroyed. John Barsad, the spy, brought news that Lucie Manette would marry Charles Darnay, nephew of the marquis. This news disturbed Defarge, for Dr. Manette, a former prisoner of the Bastille, held a special honor in the eyes of the Revolutionists.

Lucie and Darnay were married. Sydney Carton became a loyal friend of the family. Time passed, and tiny Lucie arrived. When the child was six years old, in the year 1789, the French people stormed the Bastille. At the Bastille Defarge went to the cell where Dr. Manette had been a prisoner and extracted some papers hidden behind a stone in the wall.

One day, while Darnay was talking to Mr. Lorry at Tellson & Co., a letter addressed to the Marquis St. Evrémonde was placed on Mr. Lorry's desk. Darnay offered to deliver it to the proper person. When he was alone, he read the letter. It was from an old family servant who had been imprisoned by the Revolutionists. He begged the Marquis St. Evrémonde to save his life. Darnay realized that he must go to Paris. Only Dr. Manette knew of Darnay's family name, and the doctor had been sworn to secrecy.

Darnay and Mr. Lorry went to Paris, the latter to look after the French branch of Tellson & Co. Shortly after his arrival Darnay was seized as an undesirable immigrant after Defarge had ordered his arrest. Mr. Lorry was considerably upset when Lucie and Dr. Manette suddenly arrived in Paris. Some of the doctor's friends had informed him of Darnay's arrest. The old man felt that his own imprisonment in the Bastille would win the sympathy of the Revolutionists and enable him to save his son-in-law.

After fifteen months of waiting, Darnay was brought to trial. Able to prove his innocence of harming the French people, he was freed, but forbidden to leave France. A short time later he was again arrested, denounced by Defarge and one other person whose name the officer refused to disclose.

While shopping one day in the Paris market, Miss Pross and Jerry Cruncher, who were in Paris with Lucie and Mr. Lorry, met a man who caused Miss Pross to scream in amazement and Jerry to stare in silent astonishment. The man was Solomon, Miss Pross' lost brother. Jerry remembered him as John Barsad, the man who had been a spy-witness at the Old Bailey. Carton arrived on the scene at that moment, and he was able to force Barsad to come with him to the office of Tellson & Co. for a private conference. Barsad feared detection of his duplicity for he was now an employee of the Republican French Government. Carton and Jerry threatened to expose him as a former spy for the English government, the enemy of France. Carton made a deal with Barsad.

When Darnay was once more brought before the tribunal, Defarge testified against him and named Dr. Manette as the other accuser. Defarge produced the papers which he had found in Dr. Manette's cell in the Bastille. Therein the doctor had written the story of his arrest and imprisonment because he had learned of a secret crime committed by a St. Evrémonde against a woman of humble birth and her young brother. His account was enough to convict Darnay. Sentenced for the crimes of his ancestors, Darnay, the young St. Evrémonde, was condemned by the tribunal to the guillotine.

Now Sydney Carton began to act. He visited the Defarge wine shop, where he learned that Madame Defarge was the sister of the woman ruined by St. Evrémonde years before. Then with the help of the false Barsad, he gained admittance to the prison where Darnay had been taken. There he drugged the prisoner and, still aided by the cowed Barsad, had him carried from the cell. Carton remained. The resemblance between the two would allow him to pass as Darnay and prevent discovery of the aristocrat's escape.

Madame Defarge went to the lodgings of Lucie and Dr. Manette to denounce them. Only Miss Pross was there; the others, including Darnay, were already on their way to safety. To keep Madame Defarge from learning of their escape, Miss Pross struggled with the furious woman demanding admittance to Lucie's apartment. Madame Defarge was killed when her pistol went off. Miss Pross was deaf for the rest of her life.

Lucy and Darnay returned safely to England. Sydney Carton died at the guillotine, giving his own life for the happiness of his dear friends.

TAMAR

Type of work: Poem
Author: Robinson Jeffers (1887-)
Type of plot: Psychological melodrama
Time of plot: World War I
Locale: Carmel Coast Range, California
First published: 1924

Principal characters:
TAMAR CAULDWELL, a neurotic girl
LEE CAULDWELL, her brother
DAVID CAULDWELL, her father
JINNY CAULDWELL, David's idiot sister
STELLA MORELAND, sister of David's dead wife
WILL ANDREWS, Tamar's suitor

Critique:

Tamar is one of the greatest of Jeffers' long narrative poems. In powerful and rugged language he outlines the turbulent lives of the Cauldwell family and their terrible but inevitable destruction. The symbol which he employs to indicate humanity's absorption in itself is incest and its resulting miseries. *Tamar* is a violent and powerful story told against the harshly magnificent background of the Carmel coastline range. It is at once thrilling and moving.

The Story:

Injured when his horse stumbled and fell over a sea cliff, young Lee Cauldwell was nursed back to health by his sister Tamar. Lee, who had lived a wild and dissolute life, vowed to give up his drinking and debauchery. He and Tamar became devoted to each other during his convalescence, so much so that Lee jealously warned a former suitor of his sister to stay away from her. Old David Cauldwell feared what might result from the isolation of his family. His fears were confirmed when the brother and sister, after swimming in the river, were drawn to each other against their wills.

The Cauldwell family was a peculiar group. Besides the father and the two children, it contained two old women. Aunt Jinny, an idiot sister of David Cauldwell, was cared for by Aunt Stella, the sister of David's dead wife. Through the confused mumblings of Jinny, Tamar realized that an incestuous relationship had occurred between David and his own sister Helen.

A short time later, Tamar discovered that she was pregnant. Rather than admit that Lee was the father of her child, she deliberately sought out and seduced her former suitor, Will Andrews. Disgust and revulsion grew in her until she hated her two lovers and, most of all, herself. She felt that she would lose her mind unless she talked to someone.

Aunt Stella was a medium through whom the voices of the dead sometimes spoke. In desperation, Tamar appealed to her to let her speak to Helen. That evening she and Stella, with the imbecile Jinny between them, stole down to the seashore, so that they would not be discovered by the men. Stella gradually fell into a trance, and through her lips Tamar heard the voice of a man who told her that the coastline country had been the land of the Indians, where their gods used to come to them. He ordered Tamar to strip and dance so that the gods would come again. Against her will, Tamar danced to strange guttural chants from the lips of the tranced woman. After a while the chanting ceased and Tamar returned slowly to her senses. Then through the lips of Stella she heard the voice of Helen taunting her for the shameful orgy. The voice, after warning Tamar that she would lose her child, told her that a fire Tamar had earlier set in the cabin would be quenched before it fulfilled its purpose of destroying the corruption of the Cauldwell family. Then in a mournful voice Helen told Tamar of the horror of death, of her longing for life, and of her need to haunt Tamar as long as she lived, because she possessed life. On the shore, unassisted by anyone and in great agony, Tamar lost her baby.

Back in the cabin once more, Tamar could scarcely restrain the hatred she felt for her family. All pity had left her, and all love. In order to revenge herself on Helen, she tempted her old father with her beauty. Through the medium of Stella, Helen cursed Tamar and pleaded with her not to commit that ultimate folly.

Lee, who had returned to his drinking, enlisted in the army, but Tamar was determined not to let him go. She told him that the child had not been his but the child of Will Andrews, who had visited her late at night after she had set a lighted lamp in her window as a signal. Tamar taunted Lee until he lashed her with a whip.

When Will Andrews came to the cabin that night, Tamar told him that Lee would leave the following day for the army and would like to say goodbye to him. The meeting between the two men was cool but amiable. But while Lee was out of the room, Tamar showed Will her whip-lash wounds and told him that she had lost his child through outrages which both her father and Lee had perpetrated upon her. When Lee returned with his father, Will accused him of those atrocities. In turn, Lee accused Will of having attempted to set fire to their home. Tamar, who herself had been responsible, said nothing but goaded on the fight with her smiles and wordless encouragement to Will. Lee stabbed Will horribly and fatally.

Helen, through the person of Stella, tried to save old David Cauldwell from the destroying forces of hate and evil, but he refused to heed her warnings. Downstairs the idiot Jinny, alone and disturbed, was attracted by the light of a candle. She carried it to the window, where the flame set fire to the blowing curtains. Her dying shrieks attracted the attention of those upstairs.

Lee tried to run to her, but Tamar clung to him and would not let him go. Will, dying, dragged himself as far as the window. Stella rushed out into the flaming hall and perished. The old man prayed brokenly, groveling on the floor. Lee made one last effort to escape, but Tamar, glorying in the destruction of her three lovers, embraced him until the flames consumed them all.

TAMBURLAINE THE GREAT

Type of work: Drama
Author: Christopher Marlowe (1564-1593)
Type of plot: Romantic tragedy
Time of plot: Fourteenth century
Locale: Asia
First presented: c. 1587

Principal characters:
TAMBURLAINE, the Scythian conqueror
ZENOCRATE, his wife
BAJAZETH, Emperor of the Turks
CALLAPINE, his son
MYCETES, King of Persia
COSROE, his brother
THERIDAMAS,
TECHELLES, and
USUMCASANE, followers of Tamburlaine
ORCANES, King of Natolia

Critique:

A study of driving ambition, *Tamburlaine the Great* is also notable for the dignity and beauty of Marlowe's lines. The poetry of the play is all the more remarkable in view of the fact that it was among the first written in English blank verse. Marlowe wrote so well, with so much original invention, that for a time many scholars believed him the author of some plays now attributed to Shakespeare. It is safe to say that Marlowe is the best of pre-Shakespearean playwrights.

The Story:

When Mycetes became king of Persia, his brother, Cosroe, blatantly told the new king that he was not fit for the office. Among Mycetes' greatest concerns were the raids of Tamburlaine, the Scythian bandit, upon the Persian people. Because it was rumored that this robber chief aspired to rule the East, Mycetes sent Theridamas with a thousand troops to capture Tamburlaine, and ordered another lord named Menaphon to follow Theridamas. Cosroe sarcastically pointed out to the king that Menaphon was needed in Babylon, where the province was about to revolt against such an inferior sovereign as Mycetes. At this insult Mycetes vowed to revenge himself against his brother.

Menaphon asked Cosroe if he were not afraid of the king's threat, but Cosroe assured the Persian lord that there was a plot afoot to make Cosroe emperor of Asia, explaining that it hurt him to witness the scorn now being directed toward the Persian monarchy, which had formerly awed the entire world. Shortly afterward there was a revolt, and the rebellious lords offered Cosroe the crown. Cosroe set out to annex the thousand troops of Theridamas in order to conquer his brother Mycetes.

Meanwhile, on a Scythian hill, Tamburlaine held Zenocrate, the daughter of the sultan of Egypt. To her the former shepherd spoke grandly of kingdoms he would conquer. Techelles and Usumcasane echoed his boasts, vowing to follow Tamburlaine to the death. To Zenocrate the ambitious leader promised all the wealth and power in his kingdom; he was in love. Suddenly the thousand horse troops of Mycetes attacked the five hundred foot soldiers of Tamburlaine. When Theridamas accosted the Scythian, he was so impressed by the appearance of the former shepherd that Tamburlaine was able to persuade Theridamas to become an ally. Visions of mighty kingdoms and power had persuaded Theridamas.

Cosroe, smugly discussing Tamburlaine's personality and latest conquest, was preparing to send troops to join Tamburlaine and Theridamas by the river Araris, there to engage the forces of Mycetes, who was fuming with rage at the revolt. Meander, a follower of Mycetes, conceived the idea that he who could conquer Tamburlaine would be offered the province of Albania, and whoever took Theridamas could have Media, but Mycetes asked that Cosroe be captured alive. Mycetes was convinced that the followers of the bandit Tamburlaine could be bribed to desert their leader, who had purchased them by bribes in the first place.

When Cosroe met Tamburlaine, the Scythian boasted of his great future; Theridamas indicated to Cosroe that he believed in Tamburlaine's ability. Certain of victory, Cosroe promised Techelles and Usumcasane rewards for their deeds.

Mycetes was defeated. After the victory, Tamburlaine bribed Theridamas, Techelles, and Usumcasane with a promise of kingdoms of their own if they would attack Cosroe. Marveling at Tamburlaine's arrogant daring, Cosroe prepared for battle. Cosroe was wounded in battle, and Tamburlaine, gloating over his easy conquest, proclaimed himself king of Persia.

At the court in Algiers, the kings of Fez, Morocco, and Algiers fumed at the bandit who had taken Persia and who now was forcing them to raise their siege of Greek Constantinople. Bajazeth, king of the Turks, dispatched a message to Tamburlaine and offered threats if the Scythian conqueror dared set foot in Africa. Meanwhile the kings planned to take Greece by siege.

Zenocrate had grown slowly to admire Tamburlaine, who was now plotting the conquest of the Turkish kings. Zabina, wife of Bajazeth, sneered at Zenocrate and called her a concubine. When he had subdued Bajazeth, Tamburlaine made Zabina Zenocrate's attendant slave.

The next victim of the Scythian's lust for power was the sultan of Egypt, Zenocrate's father. To show his might, Tamburlaine had put Bajazeth in a cage and subjected him to base ridicule by using his prisoner as a footstool. Still Bajazeth and Zabina courageously insulted their master by hurling disdainful remarks and threats at him.

As Tamburlaine's armies prepared to take Damascus, Zenocrate gently asked her paramour to deal kindly with the city of her father, but he refused. Zenocrate grieved until Tamburlaine promised not to harm her father when Damascus fell. By now the Scythian conqueror loved Zenocrate dearly, and while he ordered three emissaries from Damascus to be killed, he thought of his beloved's beauty and tenderness. Zenocrate herself was torn between her conscience, which revolted against her lord's cruelty, and her love for him.

When Tamburlaine brought the sultan alive to Zenocrate, the conqueror promised to give the sultan's kingdom back to him if Zenocrate would accept the title of Queen of Egypt. She readily accepted this condition and Tamburlaine planned his wedding with Zenocrate.

Bajazeth and Zabina had killed themselves by dashing their heads against the bars of the cage in which Tamburlaine had imprisoned the Turkish monarch.

Orcanes, king of Natolia, preparing for a battle with Sigismund, king of Hungary, learned that Tamburlaine was mustering for an attack. He sent for all the Christian rulers of Europe to form an alliance against an invasion by the Scythian. The former enemies, Sigismund and Orcanes the Mohammedan, entered into a pact of friendship with the rulers of Buda and Bohemia.

Callapine, son of Bajazeth and a prisoner of Tamburlaine, was guarded by Almeda, whom the young prince bribed with offers of wealth and power if he would help Callapine to escape. Tamburlaine by now had three sons, Calyphas, Amyras, and Celebinus. Calyphas expressed a desire to lead a peaceful life with his mother Zenocrate.

The treaty of the monarchs against Tamburlaine did not hold. When the Mohammedan Orcanes withdrew his troops from his campaign against the Christians, Sigismund was urged by his allies to attack Orcanes. Orcanes was trapped, for he was at the same time preparing to attack Tamburlaine. The betrayed monarch, crying for his enemies' Christ to help him defeat the traitors, prepared to defend himself. Sigismund was killed in the fighting, and Orcanes was the victor in the battle.

Zenocrate had become ill, and when she died, Tamburlaine was overcome with such grief that he would not have her buried until after his own death.

Escaping with the aid of Almeda, Callapine returned to his father's kingdom and marshaled the allies to defeat Tamburlaine and revenge Bajazeth's death. Inconsolable in his grief for Zenocrate, Tamburlaine prepared to fight the forces of Callapine. The Scythian's sons, Amyras and Celebinus, were eager for battle, but Calyphas, disliking his father's career of bloodshed, refused to join the fighting.

After he had vanquished his Turkish enemies, Tamburlaine returned to his camp and wrathfully stabbed Calyphas, who had remained in his tent all the while. The Turkish monarchs were bridled like horses, and under Tamburlaine's whip, forced to pull his carriage. The conqueror then planned to take Babylon. After this city was taken, terrible plunder, rape, and murder followed. Tamburlaine was now mad with lust and power. Only Callapine was still free to oppose him.

Tamburlaine fell ill with some mysterious malady, and his physician declared that he was dying. After the dying conqueror had crowned his son Amyras monarch of his empires, he sent for Zenocrate's hearse. Bidding his son to reign with power, Tamburlaine, the scourge of God, died leaning over his beloved Zenocrate's coffin.

TAPS FOR PRIVATE TUSSIE

Type of work: Novel
Author: Jesse Stuart (1907-)
Type of plot: Regional romance
Time of plot: Twentieth century
Locale: Kentucky
First published: 1943

Principal characters:
GRANDPA TUSSIE, head of the Tussie clan
GRANDMA TUSSIE, his wife
GEORGE TUSSIE, his brother
UNCLE MOTT TUSSIE, his son
UNCLE KIM TUSSIE, his deceased son
AUNT VITTIE TUSSIE, Kim's wife
SID SEAGRAVES TUSSIE, a grandson

Critique:

Jesse Stuart, who came into sudden fame with his book of Kentucky poems, *Man With a Bull-Tongue Plow,* has continued to use this familiar background in the series of novels and short stories which have followed. Stuart displays a great understanding for the people about whom he writes in *Taps for Private Tussie.* In this novel of the Kentucky mountain people the plot is unimportant; the characters are the story. Stuart's treatment of this region grows out of his deep familiarity with the place and its people. He himself has lived the life about which he writes.

The Story:

There was trouble at Grandpa Tussie's. In the coal shed behind the schoolhouse where the Tussies lived, Uncle Kim's body was beginning to smell. Kim Tussie had been killed in the war. The government had sent his body home, and now the Tussie clan had gathered for the funeral. Kim's folks, Grandpa and Grandma Tussie, comforted Aunt Vittie, Kim's wife, who was screaming and wailing. Uncle Mott, Kim's brother, was telling how he had identified the body. Sid, Kim's young nephew, was just excited. There had not been so much going on since he could remember. The noise the Tussie kin made as they carried the coffin up the mountainside could not soon be forgotten by a young boy.

Uncle Kim had left Aunt Vittie ten thousand dollars in government insurance, and the day after the funeral she rented the Rayburn mansion and filled it with new furniture, all ready for Grandpa and Grandma, Uncle Mott, and Sid to move in. It was the biggest and best house any of the Tussies had ever seen. Uncle Mott flicked the electric lights off and on all day. Sid used the bathroom over and over. Aunt Vittie bought them all new clothes to go with the house. To Sid it was all wonderful, but his happiness was spoiled a little when he realized Uncle Kim had to die in order for the rest of them to have that splendor.

The next few weeks were really a miracle in the lives of the Tussies. Grandpa continued to get his relief groceries and Aunt Vittie bought more groceries at the store. Grandpa began to look for more of the Tussies to come when they heard about the money. Grandpa thought his brother George would be the first. Brother George had been married five times. He could play a fiddle till it made a man cry.

Grandpa was right. When George heard about the money, he decided to come home to die. Uncle Mott hoped that that time would come soon, but Aunt Vittie looked at George and smiled. George played his fiddle far into the night, playing tunes Aunt Vittie asked for, and Grandpa knew George had come to stay. Aunt Vittie bought George new clothes, too, and Uncle Mott began to look mean.

Then more Tussies came, first Uncle Ben, then Dee, then Young Uncle Ben, then Starkie, then Watt, then Sabie, then Abe, all with their wives and young ones. The mansion was ready to burst. Only Grandpa knew them all. When Grandma counted forty-six of them, she would stand for no more.

The money began to go fast. Sid knew now why Grandpa and Grandma had not cried at Kim's funeral. They had known Aunt Vittie would get the money and all the Tussies would live high. Brother George's fiddle playing had Aunt Vittie looking as she had never looked before. Uncle Mott was losing out and he looked dangerous.

Grandpa knew things were bound to change. He was right. First the government man came and stopped their relief. It hurt Grandpa to lose his relief. He had had it for years and had expected it to go on forever. Then George Rayburn came to inspect his house. When he saw the floor full of nail holes, the broken windowpanes, the charcoal and pencil marks on the walls, he threatened to bring suit if the Tussies did not leave at once. But the uncles and the brothers and the cousins twice removed refused to leave. It was not until Sheriff Whiteapple came with the law papers that they knew they were whipped. That night there was the grandest dance of all. Aunt Vittie kissed Brother George and then she kissed Uncle Mott, but not very hard. It looked as if George were winning.

The next day the Tussies began to leave. Grandpa and Grandma, Aunt Vittie, Brother George, Uncle Mott, and Sid were the last to go. Aunt Vittie had bought fifty acres of land and an old shack with the last of her money, and she put the farm in Grandpa's name. They had no furniture, no sheets, no dishes, since Rayburn had attached everything to pay for damages to his house. There was only Grandpa's old-age pension check to look forward to. But Uncle Mott and Brother George made a table and sapling beds and Sid found their old dishes in the gully by the old schoolhouse, and the Tussies began living as they had always lived.

Then came the worst blow of all. Someone had reported that Grandpa now owned land, and his old-age pension was stopped. Sometimes there was not enough to eat. Uncle Mott and George began to look dangerous. Sid knew bad trouble was coming. After Brother George and Vittie were married, Uncle Mott stayed in town most of the time, drinking bootleg and getting mean drunk.

Grandpa knew his time on earth was about up, but he felt something was going to happen that he did not want to miss. And he was right again. Uncle Mott came home from town one day and told them that he had found Young Uncle Ben and Dee and had shot them for reporting Grandpa to the relief agency. As Uncle Mott talked, Brother George began to stroke his fiddle, and he played a note of death. Uncle Mott, cursing the fiddle for being the cause of all his trouble, shot the fiddle from George's hands. George drew his gun and shot Uncle Mott through the head.

Aunt Vittie had been to town, too, begging food for Grandpa and the rest, and now they saw her coming, walking close beside a strange man. That is, he was a stranger until he came nearer, and then they saw that it was Uncle Kim, who was supposed to be buried on the mountainside. When George saw the ghost, he went through the windowpane. But it was simple for Sheriff Whiteapple, when he came a little later, to follow his footprints in the snow.

After Kim had explained that he had not been killed after all, they began to understand what had happened. Uncle Mott had always wanted Aunt Vittie, and it had been easy for him to identify a body as Kim's. And Kim told more. He told Sid that he was Aunt Vittie's son, that she had been wronged by a rich man who paid Kim to marry her, and that now Sid would be their son.

That night it was as if nothing had happened, except for Uncle Mott's body in the shack. To Sid it was like a dream, but a dream with life in it. For the first time he began to feel really good. Peace had come to the Tussies.

TARAS BULBA

Type of work: Novel
Author: Nikolai V. Gogol (1809-1852)
Type of plot: Historical romance
Time of plot: Fifteenth century
Locale: Russia
First published: 1835

Principal characters:
Taras Bulba, a Cossack warrior
Ostap, Taras' older son
Andríi, Taras' younger son
Yankel, a Jewish merchant
Daughter of the Polish Waiwode, Andríi's sweetheart

Critique:

Taras Bulba is a prose poem in praise of the Cossack warrior, celebrating, as it does, the brave deeds of those hardy fighters. Presenting the life of the Cossack band on the march and in battle, Gogol uses a theme which is truly epic.

Certainly Gogol intended this heroic tale as a romantic commentary of the dullness of life in his own day. Its application for our own time is just as apt.

The Story:

When the two sons of Taras Bulba returned home after finishing their studies at the Royal Seminary in Kiev, their father ridiculed their monastic garb. Ostap, the older of the two, insisted that any insult must be avenged, and father and son began to exchange blows. Taras, learning in this manner that Ostap was a stout contender, embraced him heartily. The father would have liked also to try the mettle of his younger son, Andrii, but his wife intervened, preventing any more fisticuffs.

In honor of his sons' arrival Taras entertained all the local officers of the Zaporozhian Cossacks. Under the stimulus of corn brandy, Taras resolved to take his sons the next day to the Setch, the permanent camp of the fighting Cossacks. The mother was heartbroken to hear that she must part with her sons, but Taras was firm. Before the party left for the encampment, all sat down, even the servants, while the mother blessed her sons and gave them holy pictures to wear around their necks.

Taras Bulba and his sons rode off together across the steppes, each concerned with his own thoughts. Taras was a Cossack leader imbued with the old fashioned ideas that the only good life was that of the soldier. Ostap, when first enrolled at the seminary, had found life there unbearable; but he gradually grew accustomed to scholastic life and became a good student. Though not a leader at the seminary, he was willing to follow other boys whose main interests, like his own, were war and revelry. Andrii was of a different sort. He was a willing student, a better leader, but was also passionately fond of women, who came in his dreams to trouble his sleep. He remembered a beautiful girl who one day had laughed from her window. Learning that she was the daughter of the Polish Waiwode of Koven, Andrii daringly visited the girl in her bedroom the following night. To his regret she left the city with her father soon afterward.

Three days later Taras and his sons reached the suburb of the Setch, where the workmen and merchants for the great encampment were located. Finally they came to the Setch itself, and the Cossacks uproariously greeted Taras, their old comrade-in-arms. The only requirements for admission to the Setch were belief in Christ, the Holy Trinity, and the Church. If the members lacked money, they simply plundered the merchants in the suburb. Andrii and Ostap fitted well into this wild life and soon they gained recognition among the Cossacks for their bravery and daring.

Not wanting his sons to be idle, Taras consulted the Cossack leader about the possibility of stirring up some bold enterprise. Taras suggested attacking the Turks, but he was told that a treaty of peace had been signed with the sultan. Sly Taras then arranged for a meeting of the whole encampment, at which Kirdyaga, a close friend, was chosen as the new leader. The next day Kirdyaga called the group together and harangued them into voting for a raid on the coasts of Anatolia.

Immediately the Setch became active with preparations for the march. Before arrangements were completed, however, a group of Cossacks appeared in a barge and reported persecution and defeat at the hands of the Poles. The Jews were also accused, and so the enraged Cossacks threw the Jewish merchants into the Dnieper River. Only one escaped, a trader named Yankel, who was saved by the intercession of Taras Bulba.

The Zaporozhti began their trek of pillage and plunder throughout southeast Poland. Arriving at the city of Dubno, they found it heavily garrisoned and walled. The Zaporozhti then surrounded Dubno, cutting off all food supplies from the surrounding district, and gave themselves up to pillage and drunken revelry.

Both of Taras' sons were bored with this inactivity. One night Andrii was awakened by a Tatar serving-woman. She told him that her mistress was the beautiful daughter of the waiwode, the girl whom he had encountered at Kiev. Having seen him from the walls, the girl had sent her servant through a secret gate to ask Andrii to visit her in the city and to bring food for her starving family. Andrii stole a sack of bread and accompanied the Tatar into Dubno. When he met the waiwode's daughter, she seemed more beautiful to his sight than ever; in her embrace he forgot home, honor, country, loyalty, and Church.

A short time later Taras learned of his son's treachery from Yankel, who had been inside the city walls. The old Cossack was furious at Andrii, but proud of Ostap, who had been raised in rank and put in command of a large unit. Then news came that the Setch had been invaded by the Tatars. Half of the Cossacks departed to pursue the Tatars, while the others remained at the siege of Dubno, Taras and Ostap among them. Taras, to bolster the courage of his warriors, gave the Cossacks a large supply of wine he had brought along for just such a purpose.

One day there was a great battle, a fight in which most of the Cossacks were killed or captured. Toward the end of the fray Andrii appeared, richly attired, to fight against his own people. Taras, who saw him come into the battle, maneuvered his men so that he and his son met alone. Taras shot Andrii, who died with the name of the waiwode's daughter on his lips. The victorious Poles captured Ostap, who had distinguished himself in the battle. After receiving a serious wound, Taras was rescued by a faithful servant. He regained consciousness on the way back to the Setch, where he learned that not another man who had been on the expedition had returned.

Unable to forget Ostap, now a prisoner of the Poles, Taras set out for the city of Ouman. There he found Yankel, who for a large sum was persuaded to conduct Taras to the hostile city of Warsaw in search of Ostap. Hidden under a load of bricks, Taras entered the city, but he was unable to see Ostap before the day the Cossack prisoners were led out for torture and death. When Ostap called out for his father, Taras was unable to endure the sight of his son's torture in silence. Taras answered him so that Ostap knew his father was close by at his death.

Thus discovered, Taras was pursued but escaped to the Ukraine, where he became the leader of a Cossack band. When the Zaporozhian chiefs made peace with the Poles, Taras broke away with a band of his followers and raided towns and cities through all Poland. Finally, pursued by five regiments, he was taken prisoner. Crucified to a burning tree, Taras Bulba died calling to his comrades to carry on their fight for freedom.

TARTARIN OF TARASCON

Type of work: Novel
Author: Alphonse Daudet (1840-1897)
Type of plot: Satiric romance
Time of plot: Nineteenth century
Locale: France and North Africa
First published: 1872

Principal characters:
TARTARIN, a huntsman
BAÏA, a Moorish beauty
PRINCE GREGORY OF MONTENEGRO
BARBASSOU, captain of the *Zouave*

Critique:

The saying is that words fly so quickly in southern France because the air is so light and buoyant. Indeed the Midi is renowned for its braggarts. Tartarin was a real braggart, but in this story he made good his boasts — to a certain extent. *Tartarin of Tarascon* was written with the sure touch of a humorist combined with the fantastic imagination of the Provençal poet. In his understanding of people and in his method of character portrayal, Daudet is often compared with Dickens.

The Story:

In the little town of Tarascon in the Midi, Tartarin enjoyed an enviable reputation which was based first of all on his garden. But Tartarin grew no plants of France. He had banana trees, palm trees, cacti, and all the most exotic plants he could find.

To understand the second reason for Tartarin's fame one must know the town of Tarascon. The Tarasconese were mighty hunters and all the men had ample arsenals. Tartarin's study contained a complete collection of deadly weapons. He had rifles, carbines, blunderbusses, Malayan krishes, and Indian tomahawks. It was too bad that there was no game at all for many leagues around the town, for in order to indulge their passion for the chase, the Tarasconese had to hunt their own caps. A man would throw his cap in the air and fire while it was still in flight. Tartarin had the distinction of ruining more caps than all his rivals put together.

The third reason for his fame came from the custom of each Tarasconese to sing his own particular song at all social events. Tartarin had no particular song, for he could sing them all. It was a brave thing to hear Tartarin sing "NO, NO, NO" in a duet with Mme. Bezuquet. True, all Tartarin could sing was "No," but this he sang with enviable gusto.

Fourth, Tartarin had once been offered a job as clerk in the Shanghai office of a French importing firm. Although he had not taken the job, it was almost the same to him in later years, when he talked in a knowing way of the mysterious customs of the Far East. Even if he had never stayed overnight outside of Tarascon, he was a true cosmopolite.

Often he would roam the poorer streets of Tarascon looking for those stealthy people who carry on international intrigue and thuggery. He would arm himself with knuckle dusters, his bowie knife, his trusty forty-five, and then fearlessly seek adventure. Every one he met, unfortunately, was a harmless citizen who greeted him by name. However, one never knew when something unusual might happen.

One night a member of the club came running to announce that a carnival had brought a lion to Tarascon. Tartarin bravely affixed a bayonet to his elephant gun and went to the carnival. It was an inspiring sight to see Tartarin swagger in front of the lion's cage, and he never flinched no matter how the lion roared.

This experience, coupled with his own ability at telling tales, soon gave Tartarin a reputation as a great lion hunter, and in some way the impression grew that Tartarin was actually going to Africa to hunt lions. It must be admitted that Tartarin enjoyed the story and actually talked about his coming trip. But as the months went by he showed no signs of leaving. He could not bring himself to give up his regular hot chocolate.

Finally even the Tarasconese could no longer stand the suspense. When Commander Bravida told Tartarin that he must go, Tartarin, with uneasy heart, put on his costume of full white linen trousers, a cummerbund two feet wide, and a gigantic red fez. On each shoulder he carried a heavy gun, in his belt a hunting knife, and on his hip a revolver. In his two copper-lined chests were his reserve weapons. Other boxes contained drugs, pemmican for emergency rations, and a shelter tent. Thus attired and supplied, he put on his spectacles and left, amid the hurrahs of the town.

On the trip across the sea the good ship *Zouave* was unsteady, and Tartarin's great fez was often inclined over the rail. But in Algeria he still had strength to go on deck, where to his horror, he saw the ship invaded by hordes of natives he mistook for Algerian pirates. Taking out his sheath knife, he courageously rushed upon the invaders. Luckily Captain Barbassou caught him around the middle before he could harm the startled porters.

The first morning in Algiers Tartarin arose at daybreak and prepared to hunt lions. Dashing out into the road, he met hunters with game bags filled with rabbits. Tartarin pushed on over the desert country. By nightfall he was in a thicket. Uttering cries to imitate a stray kid, he settled down to wait. Before long he saw a lion bearing down upon him. Up went his trusty gun. Two shots rang out, and the wounded lion thrashed away. Not daring to move for fear the female would come to the aid of her mate, Tartarin sat uneasily until dawn.

Then to his dismay he found himself sitting in a garden among rows of beets. He had killed no lion, but there in a ditch lay a donkey with two bullet holes in him.

Tartarin decided to go back to Algiers, get his equipment, and head south. On the bus he was stricken by the bold glance of a Moorish lady. Losing his head, he started on a conquest of love.

After weeks of fruitless searching, Prince Gregory of Montenegro, whom he had met aboard the *Zouave,* helped Tartarin find the beautiful Moor. She was Baïa, a widow of twenty and sister of a pipe seller in the bazaar. Prince Gregory kindly offered to placate the brother by buying his pipes. The smitten Tartarin gave his friend enough money over several weeks to buy gross after gross of pipes before the matter was arranged to the satisfaction of all.

Tartarin took a house in the native quarter with his Baïa. At first glance Baïa seemed much fatter than the lady in the bus, but Tartarin put down such base suspicions. Now he was known as Sidi Tart'ri ben Tart'ri. All day he puffed his narghilé and ate sweetmeats flavored with musk. Baïa entertained her lord by singing monotonous airs through her nose or dancing the stomach dance. The only flaw in the household was that Baïa spoke no French and Tartarin no Arabic.

One day Tartarin met Barbassou by chance. The cynical captain warned Tartarin against all Montenegrin princes and expressed doubt that Baïa knew no French. Although Tartarin disdained the suspicions of Barbassou, the sight of a fellow Tarasconese again recalled lion hunting to his mind. He stoutly resolved to leave his bliss and go south to hunt the terrible lion.

After two days of rough jolting in an obsolete coach, Tartarin entered the city of Milianah, where on a street corner he saw a degrading sight. A lion had been trained to hold a bowl in his mouth and beg for alms. Incensed at this debasement of the most noble of beasts, Tartarin seized the bowl from the lion's jaws and dashed it on the ground. Thinking him a robber, the two Negro attendants set on him with clubs. A riot was averted by the arrival of suave Prince Gregory, who had hurried south after his friend.

Now with a proper caravan made up of the prince, Tartarin, and one camel, Tartarin wandered for nearly a month. Each time they entered a town, the prince would visit the military post, the commander would extend full hospitality to Tartarin, and Tartarin would pay the bill. But he found no lions anywhere.

Finally, on a notable night, Tartarin was hiding in a copse of oleanders when he heard a lion cough. Giving his purse to the prince to hold, he lay in wait. No lion appeared. The prince vanished. Without lion or money, Tartarin sat in despair on the steps of a saint's tomb. To his great astonishment, a noble lion advanced down the path. Tartarin fired twice, and bagged his lion at last.

But the lion was a holy, blind lion belonging to a Mohammedan convent, and Tartarin had to pay a fine of twenty-five hundred francs. He was forced to sell all his fine weapons to pay the sum, but he skinned the lion and sent the skin to Tarascon.

In disgust Tartarin walked back to Algeria, followed by his faithful camel, which had formed a liking for him. Tartarin could not shake off the beast. The camel swam the Mediterranean behind the *Zouave* and trotted behind the train from Marseille to Tarascon.

So the great hero of Tarascon came home. The story of how he killed twenty lions was told over and over again.

TARTUFFE

Type of work: Drama
Author: Molière (Jean Baptiste Poquelin, 1622-1673)
Type of plot: Comedy
Time of plot: Seventeenth century
Locale: Paris
First presented: 1664

Principal characters:

ORGON, a wealthy ex-officer of the King's Guard
MADAME PERNELLE, his mother
ELMIRE, his wife
DAMIS, his son
MARIANE, his daughter
VALÈRE, Mariane's lover
DORINE, Mariane's maid
CLÉANTE, Orgon's brother-in-law
TARTUFFE, a hypocrite

Critique:

It is almost impossible for a modern reader to realize the disturbance *Tartuffe, or the Hypocrite* caused when it was originally produced. Molière was attacked for undermining the very basis of religion in his portrait of the hypocrite. For moderns, the comedy is valuable mainly as the ancestor of similar satiric portraits, ranging from Dickens' Mr. Pecksniff to Sinclair Lewis' Elmer Gantry. Molière's Tartuffe is hardly convincing to us, however, because we do not know why or how he became what he was.

The Story:

Orgon's home was a happy one. He himself was married to Elmire, a woman much younger than he, who adored him. His two children by a former marriage were fond of their stepmother, and she of them. Mariane, the daughter, was engaged to be married to Valère, a very eligible young man, and Damis, the son, was in love with Valère's sister.

Then Tartuffe came to live in the household. Tartuffe was a penniless scoundrel whom the trusting Orgon had found praying in church. Taken in by his cant and his pose of fervent religiousness, Orgon had invited the hypocrite into his home. As a consequence, the family was soon demoralized. Once established, Tartuffe proceeded to change their normal, happy mode of life to a strictly moral one. He set up a rigid puritan regimen for the family, and persuaded Orgon to force his daughter to break her engagement to Valère in order to marry Tartuffe. He said she needed a pious man to lead her in a righteous life.

Valère was determined that Mariane would marry no one but himself, but unfortunately Mariane was too spineless to resist Tartuffe and her father. Confronted by her father's orders, she remained silent and remonstrated only weakly. As a result, Tartuffe was cordially hated by every member of the family, including Dorine, the saucy, outspoken servant, who did everything in her power to break the hold that the hypocrite had secured over her master. Dorine hated not only Tartuffe but also his valet, Laurent, for the servant imitated the master in everything. In fact, the only person besides Orgon who liked and approved of Tartuffe was Orgon's mother, Madame Pernelle, who was the type of puritan who wished to withhold from others pleasures she herself could not enjoy. Madame Pernelle highly disapproved of Elmire, maintaining that in her love for clothes and amusements she was setting her family a bad example which Tartuffe was trying to correct. Actually, Elmire was merely full of the joy of living, a fact that her mother-in-law was unable to perceive. Orgon himself was little better. When Elmire fell ill, and he was informed of this fact, his sole concern was for the health of Tartuffe. Tartuffe, however, was in fine fettle, stout and ruddy-cheeked. For his evening meal, he consumed two partridges, half a leg of mutton, and four flasks of wine. He then retired to his warm and comfortable bed and slept soundly until morning.

Tartuffe's designs were not really for the daughter, Mariane, but for Elmire herself. One day, after Orgon's wife had recovered from her illness, Tartuffe appeared before her. He complimented Elmire on her beauty, and even went so far as to lay his fat hand on her knee. Damis, Orgon's son, observed all that went on from the cabinet where he was hidden. Furious, he determined to reveal to his father all that he had seen. Orgon refused to believe him. Wily Tartuffe had so completely captivated Orgon that he ordered Damis to apologize to Tartuffe. When his son refused, Orgon, violently angry, drove him from the house and disowned him. Then to show his confidence in Tartuffe's honesty and piety, Orgon signed a deed of trust turning his estate over to Tartuffe's management, and announced his daughter's betrothal to Tartuffe.

Elmire, embittered by the behavior of this imposter in her house, resolved to unmask him. She persuaded Orgon to hide under a cloth-covered table and see and hear for himself the real Tartuffe. Then she enticed Tartuffe to make love to her, disarming him with the assurance that her foolish husband would suspect nothing. Emboldened, Tartuffe poured out his heart to her, leaving no doubt as to his intention of making her his mistress. Disillusioned and outraged when Tartuffe asserted that Orgon was a complete dupe, the husband emerged from his hiding place, denounced the hypocrite, and ordered him from the house. Tartuffe defied him, reminding him that the house was now his according to Orgon's deed of trust.

Another matter made Orgon even more uneasy than the possible loss of his property. This was a casket given him by a friend, Argas, a political criminal now in exile. It contained important state secrets, the revelation of which would mean a charge of treason against Orgon and certain death for his friend. Orgon had foolishly entrusted the casket to Tartuffe, and he feared the use that villain might make of it. He informed his brother-in-law, Cléante, that he would have nothing further to do with pious men; that in the future he would shun them like the plague. But Cléante pointed out that such rushing to extremes was the sign of an unbalanced mind. Because a treacherous vagabond was masquerading as a religious man was no good reason to suspect religion.

The next day Tartuffe made good this threat, using his legal right to force Orgon and his family from their house. Madame Pernelle could not believe Tartuffe guilty of such villainy, and she reminded her son that in this world virtue is often misjudged and persecuted. But when the sheriff's officer arrived with the notice for evacuation, even she believed that Tartuffe was a villain.

The crowning indignity came when Tartuffe took to the king the casket containing the state secrets. Orders were issued for Orgon's immediate arrest. But fortunately the king recognized Tartuffe as an imposter who had committed crimes in another city. Because of Orgon's loyal service in the army, however, the king annulled the deed Orgon had made covering his property and returned the casket unopened.

THE TEMPEST

Type of work: Drama
Author: William Shakespeare (1564-1616)
Type of plot: Romantic fantasy
Time of plot: Fifteenth century
Locale: An island in the sea
First presented: 1611

Principal characters:

PROSPERO, the rightful Duke of Milan
MIRANDA, his daughter
FERDINAND, son of the King of Naples
ARIEL, a spirit, Prospero's servant
CALIBAN, Prospero's slave
ALONSO, King of Naples
SEBASTIAN, Alonso's brother
ANTONIO, Duke of Milan, Prospero's brother
GONZALO, a philosopher who saved the lives of Prospero and Miranda

Critique:

The Tempest, written toward the close of Shakespeare's career, is a work of fantasy and courtly romance. The story of a wise old magician, his beautiful, unworldly daughter, a gallant young prince, and a cruel, scheming brother, it contains all the elements of a fairy tale in which ancient wrongs are righted and true lovers live happily ever after. The play is also one of poetic atmosphere and allegory. Beginning with a storm and peril at sea, it ends on a note of serenity and joy. No other of Shakespeare's dramas holds so much of the author's mature reflection on life itself.

The Story:

When Alonso, King of Naples, was returning from the wedding of his daughter to a foreign prince, his ship was overtaken by a terrible storm. In his company were Duke Antonio of Milan and other gentlemen of the court. As the gale rose in fury, and it seemed certain the vessel would split and sink, the noble travelers were forced to abandon ship and trust to fortune in the open sea.

The tempest was no chance disturbance of wind and wave. It had been raised by a wise magician, Prospero, as the ship sailed close to an enchanted island on which he and his lovely daughter Miranda were the only human inhabitants. Theirs had been a sad and curious history. Prospero was rightful Duke of Milan. Being devoted more to the study of philosophy and magic than to affairs of state, he had given much power to ambitious Antonio, his brother, who twelve years before had seized the dukedom with the aid of the crafty Neapolitan king. The conspirators set Prospero and his small daughter adrift in a boat, and they would have perished miserably had not Gonzalo, an honest counsellor, secretly stocked the frail craft with food, clothing, and the books Prospero valued most.

The helpless exiles drifted at last to an island which had been the refuge of Sycorax, an evil sorceress. There Prospero found Caliban, her son, a strange, misshapen creature of brute intelligence, able only to hew wood and draw water. Also obedient to Prospero's will were many good spirits of air and water, whom he had freed from torments to which the sorceress Sycorax had condemned them earlier. Ariel, a lively sprite, was chief of these.

Prospero, having used his magic arts to draw the ship bearing King Alonso and Duke Antonio close to his enchanted island, ordered Ariel to bring the whole party safely ashore, singly or in scattered groups. Ferdinand, King Alonso's son, was moved by Ariel's singing to follow the sprite to Prospero's rocky cell. Miranda, who remembered seeing no human face but her father's bearded one, at first sight fell deeply in love with the handsome young prince, and he with her. Prospero was pleased to see the young people so attracted to each other, but he concealed his pleasure, spoke harshly to them, and to test Ferdinand's mettle commanded him to perform menial tasks.

Meanwhile Alonso, Sebastian, Antonio, and Gonzalo wandered sadly along the beach, the king in despair because he believed his son drowned. Ariel, invisible in air, played solemn music, lulling to sleep all except Sebastian and Antonio. Drawing apart, they planned to kill the king and his counsellor and make Sebastian tyrant of Naples. Watchful Ariel awakened the sleepers before the plotters could act.

On another part of the island Caliban, carrying a load of wood, met Trinculo, the king's jester, and Stephano, the royal butler, both drunk. In rude sport they offered drink to Caliban. Tipsy, the loutish monster declared he would be their slave forever.

Like master, like servant. Just as Sebastian and Antonio had plotted to murder Alonso, so Caliban, Trinculo, and Stephano schemed to kill Prospero and become rulers of the island. Stephano was to be king, Miranda his consort; Trinculo and Caliban would be viceroys. Unseen, Ariel listened to their evil designs and reported the plan to Prospero.

Meanwhile Miranda had disobeyed her father to interrupt Ferdinand's task of rolling logs and, the hidden magician's commands forgotten, the two exchanged lovers' vows. Satisfied by the prince's declarations of devotion and constancy, Prospero left them to their own happy company. He, with Ariel, went to mock Alonso and his followers by showing them a banquet which vanished before the hungry castaways could taste the rich dishes. Then Ariel, disguised as a harpy, reproached them for their conspiracy against Prospero. Convinced that Ferdinand's death was punishment for his own crime, Alonso was moved to repentance for his cruel deed.

Returning to his cave, Prospero released Ferdinand from his hard toil. While spirits dressed as Ceres, Iris, Juno, nymphs, and reapers entertained Miranda and the prince with a pastoral masque, Prospero suddenly remembered the schemes which had been devised by Caliban and the drunken servants. Told to punish the plotters, Ariel first tempted them with a display of kingly garments; then, urging on his fellow spirits in the shapes of fierce hunting dogs, he drove them howling with pain and rage through bogs and brier patches.

Convinced at last that the King of Naples and his false brother Antonio had repented the evil deed they had done him years before, Prospero commanded Ariel to bring them into the enchanted circle before the magician's cell. Ariel soon returned, luring by strange, beautiful music the king, Antonio, Sebastian, and Gonzalo. At first they were astonished to see Prospero in the appearance and dress of the wronged Duke of Milan. Prospero confirmed his identity, ordered Antonio to restore his dukedom, and severely warned Sebastian not to plot further against the king. Finally he took the repentant Alonso into the cave, where Ferdinand and Miranda sat playing chess. There was a joyful reunion between father and son at this unexpected meeting, and the king was completely captivated by the beauty and grace of Miranda. During this scene of reconciliation and rejoicing, Ariel appeared with the master and boatswain of the wrecked ship; they reported the vessel safe and ready to continue the voyage. The three grotesque conspirators were driven in by Ariel, and Prospero released them from their spell. Caliban was ordered to prepare food and set it before the guests. Prospero invited his brother and the King of Naples and his train to spend the night in his cave.

Before he left the island, Prospero dismissed Ariel from his service, leaving that sprite free to wander as he wished. Ariel promised calm seas and auspicious winds for the voyage back to Naples and Milan, where Prospero would journey to take possession of his lost dukedom and to witness the marriage of his daughter and Prince Ferdinand.

THE TENANT OF WILDFELL HALL

Type of work: Novel
Author: Anne Brontë (1820-1849)
Type of plot: Domestic romance
Time of plot: Early nineteenth century
Locale: England
First published: 1848

Principal characters:
HELEN GRAHAM, in reality Helen Huntingdon, the tenant
FREDERICK LAWRENCE, her landlord
ARTHUR HUNTINGDON, her first husband
GILBERT MARKHAM, her second husband

Critique:

The story of *The Tenant of Wildfell Hall* is told in a series of letters written by Gilbert Markham to his brother-in law, Mr. Halford. This epistolary device, so common to fiction writers of the eighteenth and nineteenth centuries, gives a certain psychological value to Anne Brontë's study of marital difficulties. There is keen irony here, as well, for Arthur Huntingdon's male superiority and brutal dominance is offset in large measure by the inherent priggishness and short-sightedness of the woman whom he should never have married. Huntingdon, the attractive but drunken profligate, is generally identified with Bramwell Brontë, brother of the writer.

The Story:

Gilbert Markham, a young man of good family, was mildly interested when the strange tenant came to Wildfell Hall. Mrs. Graham, as her neighbors knew her, was young and beautiful, and her demand for seclusion stimulated the interest of the gentry of the neighborhood.

She was particularly criticized for the way in which she was caring for her small son, Arthur, whom she would not allow out of her sight. Gilbert's mother declared the child would become the worst of milksops.

On his first visit to Wildfell Hall, Gilbert learned that Mrs. Graham was a landscape painter of considerable ability and that she was concealing her whereabouts from her former friends. Her air of secrecy aroused both his curiosity and sympathy.

Hoping to avoid the attentions of a local girl for whom he had at one time shown a preference, Gilbert spent much of his time in the company of the young widow. He accompanied her and young Arthur on long walks to find scenes for Mrs. Graham to paint. His friends, however, attempted to discourage his attentions to the tenant of Wildfell Hall. Rumor spread that she was having an affair with Frederick Lawrence, her landlord, and Lawrence assured Gilbert that he would fail in his attentions to Mrs. Graham. When he tried to tell her of his growing affection, Mrs. Graham herself insisted that Gilbert regard her simply as a friend.

After the vicar of the parish had accused the widow of improper conduct, Gilbert overheard Mrs. Graham deep in a mysterious discussion with her landlord. Suspecting that the rumors about them were true, Gilbert resolved to have no more to do with her. On his next encounter with Lawrence, Gilbert struck his rival and wounded him severely.

A short time later Gilbert met Mrs. Graham and she gave him a copy of her journal to read. The journal, beginning in 1821, told the story of Helen Graham's life for the past six years. It opened with an account of her meeting with Arthur Huntingdon, whom she loved in spite of her aunt's claim that the young man was wild and wayward. Her aunt, with whom she made her home, had taken her away so that she might see no more of the objectionable Huntingdon. But by a miscalculation her unwelcome suitor was invited to their summer home for partridge hunting. That autumn the two were married, and shortly afterward the young wife discovered that her husband's true character was exactly that which her aunt had described. He was a drunkard, a man incapable of high principle or moral responsibility. She began to be contemptuous of him, and he responded by growing indifferent to her. More and more frequently he began to absent himself from his home, and during his absences she had no way of knowing where he was.

Several years passed. When Helen bore a child, a boy, she hoped that her husband's conduct would improve. But Huntingdon absented himself again and again. Each time she welcomed him back because she still loved him.

When Helen's father died, she was greatly disturbed by her husband's callous attitude toward her grief. Then a reconciliation took place, and for a time Huntingdon seemed to reform. One day, however, she discovered her husband making love to Lady Lowborough, a visitor in their house. When she demanded a separation for herself and her child, Huntingdon refused. To keep the affair from becoming known to others, Helen decided at last to stay on with her husband.

Lord Lowborough also learned of the affair Helen's husband was having with Lady Lowborough. Indifferent to public scandal, Huntingdon kept up his wild hunting parties and filled his house with drunken, riotous men. Helen began to make her plans for escape. All that time she had to fight off a would-be lover of her own, a Mr. Hargrave, who was determined to win her. She hoped to find refuge in a place where her husband could not find her and legally take her child from her. Her pride kept her from appealing to her brother or her uncle and aunt.

Helen's husband learned of her plan when he read her journal. From that time on he had her closely watched. He refused to let her have any money in her possession.

Her position became unendurable, however, when Huntingdon brought his mistress into the house on the pretext of providing a governess for young Arthur. Helen determined to make her escape without money or resources. The diary ended with the arrival of Helen at Wildfell Hall.

Reading the journal, Gilbert realized that Frederick Lawrence was the brother mentioned several times in the diary. He at once sought out Helen to renew his suit, but in spite of his entreaties she insisted that they should not see each other again. Gilbert then went to see her brother, whom he had treated so roughly at their last meeting. The reconciliation between the two men was prompt and sincere.

A short time later the whole community learned the secret of the tenant of Wildfell Hall. Huntingdon had a fall from his horse and his wife, learning of his serious condition, went to his house at Grassdale to look after him. Frederick Lawrence told Gilbert that Huntingdon had received her ungraciously, but that she was determined to stay with him out of a sense of duty.

In spite of her care, however, Huntingdon secured a bottle of wine and drank it in defiance of his doctor's orders. His indiscretion brought on a relapse which ended in his death.

Several months later Gilbert heard that Helen's uncle had died and that she had gone to live with her aunt at Staningley. More than a year passed before he dared to go to her. He found her at Staningley, and the welcome of young Arthur was as joyous as Helen's was warm and gracious. She and Gilbert were married a short time later.

TESS OF THE D'URBERVILLES

Type of work: Novel
Author: Thomas Hardy (1840-1928)
Type of plot: Philosophical realism
Time of plot: Late nineteenth century
Locale: England
First published: 1891

Principal characters:
Jack Durbeyfield, a poor worker
Tess, his daughter
Alec d'Urberville, her betrayer
Angel Clare, her husband

Critique:

Thomas Hardy's *Tess of the d'Urbervilles* has become a modern classic. In it Hardy concerned himself with the question of fate and its influence upon the lives of most people. If Tess's father had not learned that he was a d'Urberville, if Angel had found the letter Tess slipped under the door, her life would have been much different. But fate ruled that these things were to happen, and so determined the course of Tess's life. Hardy called Tess a pure girl, and so she was. He believed that she was not responsible for her actions, and he forces us to agree with him.

The Story:

It was a proud day when Jack Durbeyfield learned that he was descended from the famous d'Urberville family. Durbeyfield had never done more work than was necessary to keep his family supplied with meager food and himself with beer, but from that day on he ceased doing even that small amount of work. His wife joined him in thinking that such a high family should live better with less effort, and she persuaded their oldest daughter, Tess, to visit the Stoke-d'Urbervilles, a wealthy family who had assumed the d'Urberville name because no one else claimed it. It was her mother's hope that Tess would make a good impression on the rich d'Urbervilles and perhaps a good marriage with one of the sons.

When Tess met her supposed relatives, however, she found only a blind mother and a dapper son who made Tess uncomfortable by his improper remarks to her. The son, Alec, tricked the innocent young Tess into working as a poultry maid, not letting her know that his mother was unaware of Tess's identity. After a short time Tess decided to look for work elsewhere to support her parents and her numerous brothers and sisters. She was innocent, but she knew that Alec meant her no good. Alec, more clever than she, at last managed to get her alone and then possessed her.

When Tess returned to her home and told her mother of her terrible experience, her mother's only worry was that Alec was not going to marry Tess. The poor girl worked in the fields, facing the slander of her associates bravely. Her trouble was made worse by the fact that Alec followed her from place to place, trying to possess her again. By going about to different farms during the harvest season, Tess managed to elude Alec long enough to give birth to her baby without his knowledge. The baby did not live long, however, and a few months after its death, Tess went to a dairy farm far to the south to be dairymaid.

At the dairy farm Tess was liked and well treated. Also at the farm was Angel Clare, a pastor's son who had rejected the ministry to study farming. It was his wish to own a farm some day, and he was working on different kinds of farms, so that he could learn something of the many kinds of work required of a general farmer. Although all the dairymaids were attracted to Angel, Tess interested him the most. He thought her a beautiful and innocent young maiden, as she was, for it was her innocence which had caused her trouble with Alec.

Tess felt that she was wicked, however, and rejected the attentions Angel paid to her. She urged him to turn to one of the other girls for companionship. It was unthinkable that the son of a minister would marry a dairymaid, but Angel did not care much about family tradition. In spite of her pleas, he continued to pay court to Tess. At last, against the wishes of his parents, Angel asked Tess to be his wife. Not only did he love her, but also he realized that a farm girl would be a help to him on his own land. Although Tess was in love with Angel by this time, the memory of her night with Alec caused her to refuse Angel again and again. At last his insistence, coupled with the written pleas of her parents to marry someone who could help the family financially, won her over, and she agreed to marry him.

On the night before the wedding, which Tess had postponed many times because she felt unworthy, she wrote Angel a letter, telling everything about herself and Alec. She slipped the letter under his door, sure that when he read it he would renounce her forever. But in the morning Angel acted as tenderly as before and Tess loved him more than ever for his forgiving nature. When she realized that Angel had not found the letter, she attempted to tell him about her past. Angel only teased her about wanting to confess, thinking that such a pure girl could have no black sins in her history. They were married without Angel's learning about Alec and her dead baby.

On their wedding night Angel told Tess about an evening of debauchery in his own past. Tess forgave him and then told about her affair with Alec, thinking that he would forgive her as she had him. But such was not the case. Angel was at first stunned, and then so hurt that he could not even speak to Tess. Finally he told her that she was not the woman he loved, the one he had married, but a stranger with whom he could not live, at least for the present. He took her to her home and left her there. Then he went to his home and on to Brazil, where he planned to buy a farm. At first neither Tess nor Angel told their parents the reason for their separation. When Tess finally told her mother, that ignorant woman blamed Tess for losing her husband by confessing something he need never have known.

Angel had left Tess some money and some jewels which had been given to him by his godmother. The jewels Tess put in a bank; the money she spent on her parents. When it was gone, her family went hungry once more, for her father still thought himself too high-born to work for a living. Tess again went from farm to farm, doing hard labor in the fields in order to get enough food to keep herself and her family alive.

While she was working in the fields,

she met Alec again. He had met Angel's minister father and, repenting his evil ways, had become an itinerant preacher. The sight of Tess, for whom he had always lusted, caused a lapse in his new religious fervor, and he began to pursue her once more. Frightened, Tess wrote to Angel, sending the letter to his parents to forward to him. She told Angel that she loved him and needed him, that an enemy was pursuing her. She begged him to forgive her and to return to her.

The letter took several months to reach Angel. Meanwhile Alec was so kind to Tess and so generous to her family that she began to relent in her feelings toward him. At last, when she did not receive an answer from Angel, she wrote him a note saying that he was cruel not to forgive her and that now she would not forgive his treatment of her. Then she went to Alec again, living with him as his wife.

It was thus that Angel found her. He had come to tell her that he had forgiven her and that he still loved her. But when he found her with Alec, he turned away, more hurt than before.

Tess, too, was bitterly unhappy. She now hated Alec because once again he had been the cause of her husband's repudiation of her. Feeling that she could find happiness only if Alec were dead, she stabbed him as he slept. Then she ran out of the house and followed Angel, who was aimlessly walking down a road leading out of the town. When they met and Tess told him what she had done, Angel forgave her everything, even the murder of Alec, and they went on together. They were happy with one another for a few days, even though Angel knew that the authorities would soon find Tess.

When the officers finally found them, Tess was asleep. Angel asked the officers to wait until she awoke. As soon as she opened her eyes, Tess saw the strangers and knew that they had come for her and that she would be hanged, but she was not unhappy. She had had a few days with the husband she truly loved, and now she was ready for her punishment. She stood up bravely and faced her captors. She was not afraid.

THADDEUS OF WARSAW

Type of work: Novel
Author: Jane Porter (1776-1850)
Type of plot: Historical romance
Time of plot: Late eighteenth century
Locale: Poland and England
First published: 1803

Principal characters:
THADDEUS SOBIESKI, a patriotic young Pole
COUNT SOBIESKI, his grandfather
GENERAL KOSCIUSKO, a Polish leader
PEMBROKE SOMERSET, Thaddeus' English friend
GENERAL BUTZOU, another Polish patriot
MARY BEAUFORT, Somerset's cousin, whom Thaddeus married

Critique:

This novel combines factual history with considerable imaginative invention. The Englishman of the early nineteenth century was already familiar with the spectacle of the political refugee. Pity for the plight of the exile who must adapt himself to a different land and strange customs is one of the chief themes of Miss Porter's novel.

The Story:

Thaddeus Sobieski was educated in the palace of Count Sobieski, his grandfather, an enlightened nobleman of Warsaw. On the evening of Thaddeus' eighteenth birthday, his mother gave him a letter in which she revealed that his father, an Englishman, had deserted his mother in Italy before Thaddeus was born. The man's name was Sackville. Thaddeus' mother had returned to Poland and her father maintained the fiction that she had married and had been widowed within two months. None knew of the deception save the king. At the end of the letter Thaddeus' mother begged him to be honorable always for the sake of his grandfather and the illustrious Sobieski name.

In 1792 the Poles began a war of independence against Russia. Before Thaddeus and his grandfather set off to the war, Thaddeus heard the story of how Count Sobieski and General Butzou had long ago saved the life of King Stanislaus of Poland. Both the knowledge of his own past and the story of his grandfather's bravery helped to shape Thaddeus' character into heroic mold.

Later, Thaddeus met General Kosciusko and was filled with hope for Poland. In one of the skirmishes with the enemy Thaddeus displayed both bravery and intelligence. With dismay he learned that the Poles were immediately to retreat, for they were outnumbered by the Russians. His grandfather was injured during the retreat but refused to let Thaddeus attend him. He ordered him to stay with the troops.

Thaddeus took a prisoner, an Englishman named Pembroke Somerset, who had joined the Russian army for the sake of adventure. Somerset and Thaddeus became close friends. Thaddeus gained Somerset's freedom, and when Thaddeus returned to his mother's home Somerset accompanied him.

The tremendous patriotism and the sense of honor existing in Thaddeus now transferred themselves to Somerset, who in his letters home wrote of his great admiration of the Poles. Somerset soon returned home to England, at the insistence of his family.

Count Sobieski had greater cares, for Poland was falling under the Russian attack. When the Germans broke their treaties of assistance, the king decided that organized resistance was useless. He surrendered for his people. In Warsaw the sons of the nobles vowed eternal resistance to the enemy, and Thaddeus was among those taking the sacred oath.

Poland in November, 1793, was shorn of her best lands and her nobles were humbled. In the meantime Thaddeus led troops into the south, where resistance continued. He managed to join with General Kosciusko and so brought a measure of hope to the Poles.

Thaddeus managed to free his grandfather from a Russian prison. Later Thaddeus led the other nobles in the surrender of all his personal property for the continuation of the war. In a battle fought soon afterward, Thaddeus' grandfather was killed. With his last breath he made Thaddeus promise never to take any name other than Sobieski.

Devastation spread over Poland as the fighting continued. In one of the last campaigns of the war Thaddeus found a moment to talk to his mother, who said she would not survive the destruction of Poland. She made him promise to go to England if Poland should fall. The Sobieski palace was burned to the ground. Thaddeus, along with General Butzou, watched as the towers of Villanow crumbled. Inside lay the dead body of his mother, who had died during the battle. Taking his farewell of the defeated king, Thaddeus left Poland forever.

True to his promise, he went to England. In London he took lodgings under the name of Mr. Constantine and then became ill with a slow and disastrous fever which threatened his life. His landlady, Mrs. Robson, had become quite attached to him because of his gentle manners and deep courtesy and she watched over him during his illness. When he recovered he sold his jewelry in order to pay his bills. He tried also to sell some original drawings but was insulted by the merchant to whom he showed them, and he refused to do business with the man.

Mrs. Robson's sick grandson died in spite of the care that Thaddeus gave the child. Dr. Vincent, suspecting that Thaddeus had a large fortune, sent a huge bill for his services. Thaddeus promised to raise the money for the medicine and for the burial, but he had not a shilling in his pocket. He was forced to sell more of his possessions.

Thaddeus tried to contact Somerset, but without success. About the same time he found General Butzou in the greatest distress of poverty and took him to his lodgings with Mrs. Robson. Thaddeus now began to earn enough for the expenses of himself and the penniless general by means of his drawings. Once he saw Pembroke Somerset on the street, but Somerset passed without noticing him.

One day Thaddeus saved a woman, Lady Tinemouth, from ruffians in Hyde Park. Out of gratitude, Lady Tinemouth took Thaddeus in hand and found employment for him as a tutor in German. At the same time her friend, Lady Sara Ross, attempted to involve him in a love affair, but she found him indifferent.

The old general was going mad. The doctor whom Thaddeus called in was Dr. Cavendish, a good man who would not take the payment when he heard the cause of the old general's illness.

Thaddeus went to the home of Lady Dundas, where he was to serve as a tutor. Lady Dundas proved to be a bore and her daughters ill-favored and ill-mannered. Attracted by Thaddeus' noble appearance, the two girls, Diana and Euphemia, determined to study hard. Euphemia Dundas and Lady Sara Ross pursued him.

A visitor in the Dundas household was Miss Mary Beaufort, a gentle girl who saw at once the noble nature of Thaddeus and tried to ease the slights and rebuffs he received from the rich and vulgar Lady Dundas on the one hand and the embarrassing attentions of Euphemia Dundas on the other. In the meantime Mary Beaufort occupied herself with trying to discover the true name of Mr. Constantine.

One day some of Lady Tinemouth's friends were discussing the tutor. One laughed at Euphemia for her interest in a man no better than a mere schoolmaster. But Mary Beaufort defended him. Lady Tinemouth remained silent, for to her alone Thaddeus had confessed his true identity. Shortly afterward gossip caused Lady Tinemouth to receive unpleasant notice from her relatives that her attentions to Mr. Constantine were intolerable. Lady Tinemouth planned to leave London. In her letter announcing her departure she told Thaddeus that Mary Beaufort was deeply interested in him.

When old General Butzou died, Thaddeus realized that one of Poland's bravest sons was dead. In order to meet the death expenses, Thaddeus, who still had not received any payment from Lady Dundas, was forced to sell his last tokens. The same pawnbroker took them, but the amount gained was not enough to pay his debts and Thaddeus was put in Newgate prison.

Hearing of his misfortune, Mary Beaufort searched out his apartment and learned from Mrs. Robson the story of his imprisonment. Mary's plan to aid Thaddeus was interrupted by the arrival of Pembroke Somerset, her cousin, and by the betrayal of Euphemia. Euphemia declared that Thaddeus had made passionate love to her. Euphemia's mother screamed for revenge and announced her intention of sending her daughter to Scotland.

Somerset, not knowing that Mr. Constantine was really his old friend Thaddeus, paid the debt of the tutor at Mary's request, but he did not so much as look at Thaddeus.

When Thaddeus returned to his room, he discovered a note in which Lady Dundas called him a rogue. Before he could demand an explanation for the note, the whole group had left London. He then took a stage to the place where Lady Tinemouth had found refuge.

At Lady Tinemouth's home Thaddeus and Somerset met again and Somerset revealed that he actually had not seen Thaddeus on the occasion of their meeting on a London street.

This meeting also brought about a reunion between Thaddeus and Mary Beaufort. A more surprising revelation was the discovery that Somerset's father was the same Sackville who was the father of Thaddeus. To right the old wrong, Thaddeus was given a large inheritance from the Somerset estate. With this fortune he married Mary Beaufort and spent the rest of his days happily with his wife and the half-brother whom he had found after many strange adventures.

THE THIN MAN

Type of work: Novel
Author: Dashiell Hammett (1894-)
Type of plot: Mystery romance
Time of plot: 1930's
Locale: New York
First published: 1934

Principal characters:
MIMI JORGENSEN, Clyde Wynant's ex-wife
DOROTHY WYNANT, her daughter
GILBERT WYNANT, her son
CHRISTIAN JORGENSEN, her present husband, Wynant's former associate
NICK CHARLES, a detective
NORA CHARLES, his wife
HERBERT MACAULAY, Wynant's attorney
MORELLI, a gangster
ARTHUR NUNHEIM, an ex-convict

Critique:

As detective fiction, this novel presents a picture of sophisticated New York life at the end of the prohibition era. The plot itself follows the pattern set by Poe in *The Murders of the Rue Morgue* in 1841 and by Arthur Conan Doyle in his Sherlock Holmes stories. Here are the astute detective, the somewhat obtuse and distrustful police, the questioning companion, the dropping of clues to give the reader a chance to solve the mystery, and the final explanation by the detective.

The Story:

Nick Charles, one-time detective and now a California lumberman, arrived in New York with his wife Nora for the Christmas holidays. He was drawn into investigation of a murder case because the dead woman, Julia Wolf, was the secretary of Nick's old client, a lunatic-fringe inventor whose wife had divorced him in order to marry a man named Christian Jorgensen. Clyde Wynant, the inventor, was reported to be out of town, working on some new project. Herbert Macaulay, attorney for Wynant, had told police that he had not seen Wynant since October, when Wynant had given the lawyer power of attorney.

Suspicion fell on Mimi Jorgensen, just returned from Europe, for she had gone to see Julia on the afternoon of the murder, had arrived, in fact, in time for Julia to die in her arms. She had wanted, she said, to get her husband's address, for she needed more money to support his two children, twenty-year-old Dorothy and eighteen-year-old Gilbert, since Jorgensen had run through the large settlement Wynant had made on Mimi at the time of their divorce.

Suspicion fell on Jorgensen, who turned out to be a man formerly known as Kelterman, with whom Wynant had worked several years before. He thought that Wynant had not treated him fairly. Then it was discovered that Jorgensen had a wife living in Boston and that he had married Mimi only to get Wynant's money.

Suspicion fell on Morelli, a gangster who had been fond of Julia. When he learned that Nick was on the case, Morelli went to Nick's apartment and, as the police arrived, shot Nick in the chest, a glancing shot that did not produce a serious wound. Nick told the police he would not press charges, for the man was apparently in enough trouble. Although the police beat up Morelli, they could find no reason for holding him. He was released the same day.

Suspicion fell on Gil Wynant, for the members of the Wynant family did not have much love for one another. Gil was an odd young man who asked Nick about bizarre subjects such as incest and cannibalism. He was frequently found at keyholes listening to private conversations.

Suspicion fell on Arthur Nunheim, who identified Julia Wolf's body. When Nick went with Guild, a detective, to see Nunheim, they found him living in an extremely untidy apartment with a big, frowzy blonde. In the presence of their callers, Nunheim and the blonde insulted each other until the woman left him. Nunheim escaped from Nick through a back window. He was reported murdered a little while later.

Suspicion fell on Wynant himself, for Macaulay reported that Wynant had made an appointment with him on the day the murder was committed, but had failed to appear. During the course of the investigation several people received from Wynant communications which seemed to throw suspicion on Mimi and Jorgensen. One day Wynant was reported to have tried to commit suicide in Allentown, Pennsylvania. The report was false, however, for the man was not Wynant.

On First Avenue Wynant had maintained a shop which the police had given a cursory examination. Nick insisted that they return and tear it apart if necessary, for he felt sure that some clue was to be found there. The police discovered a section of the cement floor newer than the rest. When they tore it up, they found the bones of a dead man, with a cane, some clothes apparently for a larger man than Wynant and a key chain bearing the initials D.W.Q.

At last Nick accused Macaulay of murdering Wynant, Julia, and Nunheim. He believed that Macaulay and Julia had joined forces to get Wynant's money, that Wynant had gone to Macaulay's house in Scarsdale to accuse Macaulay of the plot, and that Macaulay had killed his client there. Then, Nick reasoned, Macaulay had dismembered the body and brought it back to the workshop, where he discharged the two mechanics and buried the body under new cement. The cane, the large-size clothes, and the key chain were intended to prevent identification of the body.

Macaulay, according to Nick, had renewed the lease on the shop and kept it vacant while with a forged power of attorney and Julia's help he began to transfer Wynant's fortune to his own accounts. Then Mimi had come back from Europe with her children and had asked for Wynant. When Nick had arrived for his Christmas holiday and had agreed to help Mimi find the missing inventor, Macaulay felt he would be safer with Julia dead. Later he sent letters to members of Wynant's family, and even to himself, supposedly from Wynant. Nick thought Macaulay had killed Nunheim because the ex-convict had been near Julia's apartment and had probably heard the shots that killed her. When

Nunheim had demanded hush money from Macaulay, the lawyer had murdered him also to keep him permanently quiet.

So Nick outlined his case. But on the day he made the accusation, Gilbert Wynant received a letter, supposedly from his father, telling him to use the enclosed key, go to Julia's apartment, and look for an important paper between the pages of a certain book. Following the instruction in the letter, Gilbert entered the apartment, where a plainclothesman struck him, fettered him, and took him to police headquarters. The boy showed the officials and Nick the letter that he had received. The book and paper had been invented. When Nick took Gilbert home, he learned from Mimi that Wynant had just been there to leave with Mimi ten thousand dollars in bonds.

As it turned out, Macaulay, knowing that the police would be in Julia's apartment, had sent the letter to Gilbert in an attempt to shift the suspicion back to Wynant once more. Also, Macaulay himself had brought Wynant's bonds to Mimi, making her promise to say that Wynant had brought them and thus give credence to his own story that Wynant was in town. Nick forced Mimi to admit the truth by explaining that Macaulay now had possession of Wynant's fortune and that if she played his game she would have to be satisfied with comparatively small sums occasionally, whereas if she were to stop shielding Macaulay — however innocent of Wynant's death—she would, through her children, have control of her ex-husband's entire fortune. Jorgensen, meanwhile, had gone back to his legal wife in Boston.

After Nick had explained the whole case to Nora, she could not help feeling that the business of a detective, based as it is on so much probability, is at best unsatisfactory.

THE THIRTY-NINE STEPS

Type of work: Novel
Author: John Buchan (1875-1940)
Type of plot: Adventure romance
Time of plot: 1914
Locale: England and Scotland
First published: 1915

Principal characters:

Richard Hannay, a retired mining engineer
Franklin Scudder, a private investigator
Sir Walter, a government official
The Black Stone, espionage agents

Critique:

Well-told spy stories are always exciting, and *The Thirty-Nine Steps* is no exception to the rule. Both as fiction and in motion picture versions, the novel has survived with remarkable popularity the time for which it was written. Buchan's style was always crisp and lively, a fact which helps to explain the widespread appeal of his novels during the first three decades of this century.

The Story:

Richard Hannay was a mining engineer who had made a modest fortune in South Africa and returned to England to retire. Before long he found himself bored beyond belief with the conversations and actions of the Englishmen he met. He had just about decided to return to South Africa when a strange series of events provided him with ample excitement.

As he was unlocking the door of his flat, he was startled by the sudden appearance of Franklin Scudder, another tenant in the building. Scudder, obviously a badly frightened man, begged Hannay to give him refuge in his flat. After the two men were settled comfortably, Scudder told Hannay a fantastic tale. He said that a plot to start a war between England and Germany was being hatched. A Greek diplomat, Karolides, the only really strong man in Europe, was to visit London on June fifteenth. At that time his assassination would create an excuse for a declaration of war.

Scudder told Hannay that a group called The Black Stone were the agents arranging for the assassination. This group of men knew that Scudder had learned of their plot, and they had tried several times to kill him. He had now planted a body in his flat, hoping that the murderers would think the body his. He asked Hannay to let him stay with him until plans could be made to prevent the assassination.

Impressed by the sincerity of Scudder's story, Hannay gave him sanctuary. One day he returned to his flat to find Scudder with a knife through his heart. Hannay knew then that The Black Stone had found Scudder and that his own life was in danger. The police, too, would want Hannay for questioning.

When he saw two men strolling in front of his flat, he decided that they were part of the enemy group. By a ruse he exchanged clothes with the milkman and left his flat, taking with him a little black book in which he had seen Scudder making notes. He was afraid to go to any government office with his fantastic story. His plan was to disappear for the three weeks remaining before June fifteenth, and at the last minute to try to get to someone in authority to listen to him.

He went to Scotland, thinking that he could hide more easily there. But the London papers carried the story of the murder of Scudder and Hannay's description. He had several narrow escapes from local Scottish police. The Black Stone had also traced him. When an airplane flew low over his refuge, obviously on the lookout for him, he took shelter in an inn until The Black Stone found him there and he was forced to flee again. In every spare moment he studied Scudder's little black book. Deciphering the code, he learned that Scudder had told him only part of the truth. The murder of Karolides was only a small part of the plot. The main threat of the plan was an invasion of England without warning. Airfields were already laid out and mines had been placed to line the shores at a given signal. The time for invasion was to be determined after The Black Stone intercepted a French envoy who was coming to London to secure the plans which showed the arrangement of the British fleet. When the enemy learned where the ships were, they could lay mines in strategic positions and destroy a great portion of the fleet. The only clue Hannay could find about the time and place of the enemy operation was a reference to thirty-nine steps and a high tide at 10:17 P. M.

By luck, Hannay met a man who had an uncle in an influential position in the government. This man believed the story and promised to write his uncle and ask him to talk to Hannay and to help in thwarting the plot. Hannay traveled carefully, for the police and The Black Stone were still after him. Once he was captured by a member of The Black Stone, but he blew up the building in which he was held and escaped. At last he reached Sir Walter, the uncle of his friend, and Sir Walter listened carefully to Hannay's report. At first he dismissed Scudder's story as that of a loyal but overly anxious young man. But when he received a call informing him that Karolides had been killed, he knew that Scudder's information had been right, and he promised to take Hannay's information to the proper authorities.

Although Hannay was not to be allowed to attend the secret conference of government officials, he had the uneasy feeling that his presence there was of utmost importance, that only he could find out how the highly confidential information about the French envoy's visit had leaked out to the enemy. Against Sir Walter's orders, he went to the house where the officials were meeting. As he sat in the hall waiting to be admitted, one of the officials came out of the meeting room. Realizing that the man had recognized him and that he had seen the official elsewhere, he burst into the room and told the astonished officials that the man who had just left was an impostor.

They thought him mad, for the man was the First Lord of the Admiralty and they knew him well. But at Hannay's insistence they called the official's home and learned that he was there. Then they remembered that the impostor had scanned the drawings and figures carefully and could have memorized them. If he left the country, the whole plan of defense would be in the hands of the enemy. The only hope was to capture him. But there were hundreds of small ports where a little boat could leave English shores; not all could be watched.

By checking isolated spots along the coast, Hannay finally found a small cove where the tide was high at 10:17 P. M. and nearby a house with thirty-nine steps leading down to the cove. Accompanied by police, he went to the house. There he found three Englishmen on a vacation. Their actions were so natural that he doubted that they could be spies. Only the presence of a fast yacht in the water close to the cove supported his suspicions. But an unconscious finger tapping by one of the vacationers identified him as the enemy agent who had once captured Hannay. Hannay and the police were able to capture two of the men. The third escaped to the ship, but as it had already been boarded by English police, he too was taken.

The murder charge against Hannay had been dropped, and he was safe for the first time in many weeks. Three weeks later war was declared between England and Germany. But the war was not fought on English soil and there was no surprise invasion. Hannay enlisted in the army, but he knew that he had done his greatest service for his country before he put on a uniform. The Black Stone was no more and Scudder's murder was avenged.

THIS ABOVE ALL

Type of work: Novel
Author: Eric Knight (1897-1943)
Type of plot: Sentimental romance
Time of plot: Summer, 1940
Locale: England
First published: 1941

Principal characters:
Clive Briggs, a soldier
Prue Cathaway, in love with Clive
Monty, Clive's friend
Dr. Cathaway, Prue's father

Critique:

This Above All is a story of great emotional conflict between a girl who knew and loved the England of hunting, cricket, and afternoon tea, and a man who knew and hated the England of slums, mines, starvation, and disease. The author attempted to show what war can mean to a civilian as well as to a front-line soldier.

The Story:

Home on rest leave, after the disaster of Dunkirk, Clive Briggs went first to Leaford and then to Gosley, both resort towns on the coast of England. At a band concert in Gosley he met Prudence Cathaway, who was stationed nearby with the women's army corps. Prue was of an upper middle-class family and Clive was from the slums, but they were attracted to each other and became lovers the second time they were together.

Prue told him of her family. Her grandfather had been a general in the last war and felt unwanted and useless in this one; her father was a doctor, a famous brain specialist. She told him of her Aunt Iris, who wanted only to get to America and who pretended that she wanted her children to be safe when it was really for herself she feared. Iris' brother was in America, buying steel for the British government. Prue also told Clive that she had broken her engagement to a conscientious objector, and because she was ashamed for him she had joined the W. A. A. F.

Clive seemed reluctant to talk about himself, other than to say he had been born in the slums. In fact, it was many days before Prue knew he was in the army and had been in the rear-guard action at Dunkirk.

When they found that Prue could get a leave which would give them ten days together, they went to Leaford. Most of the time they were quite happy but each time Prue mentioned the War Clive became angry and sullen and seemed to get pleasure from taunting her about her family. Sometimes they quarreled without knowing the reason and were reconciled only because of their desire for each other.

During the last five days of their stay, Clive's friend Monty joined them. Monty was also slum-born. It was Monty who told Prue of Clive's heroism at Dunkirk. Monty's story puzzled Prue more than ever. She could understand even less why Clive was so bitter.

While they were at Leaford, air raids became frequent. One night during a heavy raid Clive told Prue why he would not go back to the army, why he intended to desert. He told her of his childhood, of his illegitimate birth and of his sordid remembrances of childhood in the slums. He asked her if a country that ignored its poor were worth fighting for. England was still fighting a gentleman's war, he said, and the leaders were asking the slum boys to win the war and then go back to the mines and the factories and the mills from which they had come. He was through. Prue tried to tell him that he must go back to save himself. She said it was his pride that had brought him up from the filth, and his pride and that of the others like him would change all the conditions of which he had told her. He would not listen to her.

At the end of the leave Prue returned to her camp. Clive, true to his word, did not go back to the army at the end of his furlough. He wandered along the coast while trying to decide what he really wanted to do. Once he went into a church and talked with the pastor, but he scoffed when the minister told him that we fight because we have faith in our ability to build a better life than we have had. He accused the minister and all the churches of betraying Christ and His teachings because the rich who support the church must not be told of their sin in neglecting their fellow men. Before he left the church the minister told him that realism and reasoning like his had brought war and hunger and cruelty, and that only faith could restore human dignity and freedom throughout the world.

At last Clive tired of running away; there was no place for him to go. Finally he decided to give himself up, to let the army decide for him whether he was wrong, for he was too exhausted to decide his problem for himself. Perhaps Prue and the minister had been right; perhaps faith in himself meant faith in his country and the willingness to die for it.

On the train to London, Clive suddenly remembered something Prue had said, a remark which had no meaning at the time. Now he knew she was going to have a baby. He felt that he could not give himself up before he saw Prue and asked her to marry him. He managed to evade the military police in London and call Prue. They arranged to meet at the station in London and to marry as soon as possible. Clive knew at last that he loved Prue, and he was determined that his child would never know the hurt an illegitimate child must always feel.

While he was waiting for Prue's train, a bomb fell on a nearby building. As he tried to help rescue a woman trapped in the basement of the building, the wall collapsed on him. He regained consciousness with Prue sitting beside him in a hospital room. Monty and her father had helped her find him. Prue's father was honest with her. He had tried to save Clive's life with an emergency operation, but part of the brain tissue was gone and there was no hope that Clive would live. During one of his periods of consciousness Clive told Prue that he had risked his life to save a strange woman, because he knew at last that he did have faith in himself and his country.

Clive died in the night during a heavy bombing raid. Afterward Prue walked along the streets of London and saw the volunteer firemen and the Cockney policemen performing their duties among the wreckage, and she knew why Clive had died. Feeling the child stir within her, she hoped that by sacrifices like Clive's his child and all children might have the chance to live in a good and free world.

THE THREE BLACK PENNYS

Type of work: Novel
Author: Joseph Hergesheimer (1880-)
Type of plot: Period chronicle
Time of plot: c. 1750-1910
Locale: Pennsylvania
First published: 1917

Principal characters:
HOWAT PENNY, son of the owner of Myrtle Forge
LUDOWIKA WINSCOMBE, in love with Howat Penny
JASPER PENNY, Howat Penny's great-grandson
SUSAN BRUNDON, Jasper's sweetheart
HOWAT PENNY, Jasper's and Susan's grandson
MARIANA JANNAN, Howat's cousin
JAMES POLDER, Mariana's lover

Critique:

The Three Black Pennys is, in an unusual way, the history of American culture, the first of the Pennys representing the beginning of a culture, the second representing the essential crudeness of the early nineteenth century, and the last Penny representing the effete qualities of a Victorian generation which passed away without ever understanding the modern society supplanting it. The author aptly named the three sections of his book The Furnace, The Forge, and The Metal, in keeping with a story dealing with a family engaged in the steel industry in Pennsylvania. The symbolism is obvious. The characterization is excellent, as is the description. Two of the highlights of the book are the descriptions of an all-night raccoon hunt in the eighteenth century and the tapping of an open-hearth converter in a twentieth-century steel mill.

The Story:

The Penny family was English, except for a Welsh ancestor whose blood cropped out from time to time among his descendants. Those who showed the Welsh strain were called black Pennys by their relatives in an attempt to describe the mental make-up of individuals to whom it was applied. Howat was the first black Penny in over a hundred years; the last one had been burned to death as a heretic by Queen Elizabeth, long before the family had emigrated to the Colonies.

Living at Myrtle Forge, on the edge of the Pennsylvania Wilderness, Howat Penny was far more interested in the deep woods than he was in becoming an ironmaster. Nor did the appearance of Ludowika Winscombe make him any more satisfied or contented with his life.

Ludowika Winscombe, the young Polish wife of an elderly British envoy, had been left at the Penny home while her husband traveled through the Colonies on the king's business. Before long Howat Penny fell in love with her. Ludowika warned him, however, that she was a practical person who felt it was best for her to remain married to her husband rather than to run away with a young frontiersman. Howat stubbornly told her that she would have to marry him, for he would permit nothing to stand in the way of their happiness.

Winscombe returned ill to Myrtle Forge and Howat Penny found himself acting as Winscombe's nurse. It was an ironic situation filled with tension. Howat Penny waited for the old man to die. Ludowika was torn between two desires. She wanted Howat Penny, but she hated to face a life with him in the wilderness. The climax came late one night while Howat and Ludowika sat by the sick man's bed while Winscombe made a gallant effort to remain alive. Howat and Ludowika dared not even look at each other for fear of what they might see behind each other's eyes. Early in the morning the old man died. As they faced each other in the gray dawn Howat and Ludowika realized that she was destined to remain with him in Pennsylvania and never to see London again.

Three generations later the Welsh Penny blood again appeared in the person of Howat's great-grandson, Jasper. By that time the forge, which had been the beginning of the Penny fortune, had been replaced by a great foundry with many furnaces. Jasper Penny was a rich man, steadily growing richer by supplying the tremendous amounts of iron needed for the new railroads in the United States.

Jasper Penny had never married. Like his great-grandfather Howat, he was a man of great passions whose energies were spent in building up his foundry and fortune. He was still painfully reminded, however, of his earlier indiscretions with a woman who had borne him an illegitimate daughter. The woman hounded Jasper for money and he found it easier to give her money than it was to refuse her demands.

He saw very little of Eunice, his daughter, for he assumed that she would be cared for by her mother as long as he paid all expenses. One day in Philadelphia Jasper decided, on impulse, to visit Eunice. He discovered her, ill-clothed and underfed, in the home of a poor family, and, horrified, he took her away with him. Not knowing what to do with her, he finally placed her in a school in New York.

In Philadelphia Jasper had also met Susan Brundon, mistress of a girls' school and friend of a distant branch of Jasper's family. Jasper fell in love with her and in his abrupt fashion proposed marriage. Being honest, he told her that he had an illegitimate child. Susan refused to marry Jasper because she felt that his first duty was to Eunice's mother.

Shortly after his proposal Jasper was involved in a murder. Eunice's mother had killed another lover and suspicion fell on Jasper Penny. He hated to involve Susan Brundon in the sordid affair, but he found that the only way he could clear himself was through her testimony that he had been with her when the crime was committed.

After the trial Susan told Jasper that she could not marry him until Eunice's mother was dead, that she could not have the past intruding itself upon her love for him after they were married. Almost a decade passed before they were finally able to marry.

The last of the black Pennys was also the last of the family name, for the family died out with the second Howat Penny, the grandson of Jasper Penny and Susan Brundon. Howat was a bachelor who lived alone in the country near the site of the original Penny forge. Interested in music and art, he had never married, and the management of the Penny foundries had gone out of his hands. Possessed of a comfortable fortune, he had in the closing years of his life the companionship of Mariana Jannan, a cousin. She was a young woman in her twenties and little understood by old-fashioned Howat.

He did not understand Mariana because he could not understand her generation. Because Jasper's son and grandson had never had anything to do with that branch of the family descended from Jasper's illegitimate daughter, Howat was horrified when Mariana told him that she was in love with James Polder, a distant cousin.

Howat thought Mariana mad to fall in love with James Polder, who had begun working in the Penny foundries as a boy. The fact that he had worked his way up to a position of importance failed to redeem him in old Howat's eyes.

Polder finally ran away with an actress. Three years after his marriage, Mariana and Howat Penny called on him and his wife. Polder, unhappy with his slatternly wife, had begun drinking heavily. Howat, at Marianna's insistence, invited Polder to visit his home in the country. Polder accepted. Shortly afterward he learned that his wife had deserted him and returned to the stage. He no longer cared; in love once more, he and Mariana realized they should never have permitted family differences to come between them.

Mariana's relatives, shocked by the affair, protested to Howat. Howat himself said nothing, for he now felt that he was too old and understood too little of modern life to intrude in the affairs of Mariana and Polder. Although he was as much Mariana's friend as ever, he could not understand how she was able to live with Polder as his mistress while they waited for his wife to divorce him. Howat believed until the end of his life that women should be protected from reality. Even when he knew he was dying, he said nothing to Mariana, who sat reading by his side. The delicacy of his sensibilities prevented him from shocking her with the fact of his approaching death and kept him from saying goodbye to her when he died, the last of the three black Pennys.

THE THREE-CORNERED HAT

Type of work: Novel
Author: Pedro Antonio de Alarcón (1833-1891)
Type of plot: Comedy of intrigue
Time of plot: Early nineteenth century
Locale: Spain
First published: 1874

Principal characters:
Lucas, a miller
Frasquita, his wife
Don Eugenio, the corregidor
Doña Mercedes, the corregidor's wife

Critique:

This novel is based on a famous folk tale that could belong to every age and almost every people. The plot is simple yet satisfying; the characters lack complexity but are delightful and real. Although the story is set in a particular place and time, it is basically universal, for the cuckold is an invariable subject for humor in all nations. This story is among the most delightful on the subject ever written.

The Story:

The early years of the nineteenth century were calm ones for Spain. Life there still followed the old pattern, and an almost medieval attitude toward government existed. The Church was a great power, and government officers treated their commands like petty kingdoms. Corregidor Don Eugenio was a fine example. He ruled one of the Andalusian cities like a little Caesar.

Near the city was a famous old flour mill. Lucas was its owner. There the military and the gentry visited every day to eat the miller's good food and to talk with the miller's beautiful wife, Frasquita.

These daily visits the miller shrewdly put to good use. He did not give his food without recompense, although he was never so blunt as to demand anything for his hospitality. If he needed some wood, a word to the bishop would secure him the right to cut some on the bishop's grounds, or if he needed to have his taxes lowered, a word to Don Eugenio, the corregidor, would suffice. Life for him was pleasant and fruitful. His wife Frasquita was a beautiful woman who loved him deeply and sincerely despite the miller's ugly face and the slight hump on his back. They joked together, and tried to outdo one another in kindness. Only children were lacking to make their love complete.

To those who met every day under the shady grape arbor outside the mill, it became obvious that Don Eugenio had fallen in love with Frasquita. There was nothing unusual in this, for everyone who knew her was in love with her. Fortunately, the miller was not jealous of his wife; she had never given him any reason to be so. Yet where so important a person as Don Eugenio was concerned, suspicion was certain to arise.

Don Eugenio was a sight to see. He wore a huge black three-cornered hat, a scarlet cape, white stockings, and black shoes with gold buckles. His face was deeply wrinkled, for he had no teeth. On his back was a hump much larger than the miller's, and in his breast a heart much smaller. But he was the corregidor, and everyone bowed to him when he passed, with his bailiff, Weasel, following always at his heels.

One day Don Eugenio came to the mill much earlier than usual, and the miller, spying him at a distance, plotted to surprise him. Knowing that Don Eugenio would try to make love to Frasquita, the miller hid in the grape arbor above the spot where the corregidor would sit. He told his wife to act as if she knew nothing of his presence there.

Don Eugenio began to talk of love, but when he tried to take one of Frasquita's hands in his own she knocked over his chair in pretended confusion. At that moment the miller fell from the arbor. Don Eugenio was furious. The couple pretended that the miller, asleep in the arbor, had not overheard the silly love scene. Although the affair seemed to pass off easily, Don Eugenio planned revenge.

That night, as the miller and his wife were preparing for bed, they heard a knock at the door. It was a messenger from the mayor, demanding that the miller go at once to testify in an important case. The miller, guessing correctly that this request was part of Don Eugenio's plot, told Frasquita to bolt the door and not to let anyone in after he had gone.

When the miller arrived at the mayor's home, he found that his testimony was not needed. The mayor insisted, however, that he go up to the loft and spend the night, to be on hand for the trial the next morning. The miller pretended to go to bed, but shortly afterward he let himself down from the window, got his mule, and started back to the mill. On his way he passed another rider whose mule neighed at his and received an answer. Alarmed, the miller turned aside from the road. When he arrived at the mill, he found the doors all open. Furious, he got a gun and crept up to the bedroom. Peeking through the keyhole, he saw Don Eugenio in his bed. The miller did not know what to do. He wanted to kill his wife and Don Eugenio, but he knew he would be hanged for the crime. He went downstairs, where Don Eugenio's clothes were scattered about on chairs in front of the fire. An idea came to the miller. Turn about is fair play. He dressed in Don Eugenio's clothes and set out for town.

What had actually happened was different from what the miller suspected. Don Eugenio had come to the house, but Frasquita had let him in only after he had fallen into the millpond. When he had tried to make love to her, she threatened him with a gun. Then she had called the bailiff, who was waiting outside, and told him to put his master to bed. Saying that she was going for a doctor, she had started out to get her husband. It had been her mule that had alarmed the miller on his way to the house. Don Eugenio had sent the bailiff away at the moment the miller arrived home and judged the circumstances so falsely.

Arriving at the mayor's house, Frasquita learned that her husband had fled. Together she and the mayor set out for the mill. They arrived in time to meet Don Eugenio leaving in the miller's clothes. The bailiff had returned, noticed that his master's clothes were gone, and guessed that the miller had taken them. The whole group, for different reasons, started out for Don Eugenio's house.

On their arrival the maid, insisting that Don Eugenio had returned home some time before, refused to admit them. Don Eugenio angrily demanded entrance, and at last his wife told the maid to admit the party. They all went upstairs.

Doña Mercedes refused to recognize Don Eugenio until she had learned what he had been doing. Frasquita would not speak to the miller. Doña Mercedes ordered her husband to leave the room. Then she told Frasquita that she had found the miller hiding under her bed. At first she had been furious, but after she heard his story she had become angry at her husband. Frasquita, reconciled with the miller, proved her own innocence by telling him about the neighing mules, and he apologized for doubting her honor.

When Don Eugenio returned to the room, Doña Mercedes refused to tell him anything about what had happened that night and ordered him never to come to her room again. There was nothing his guilty conscience would allow him to say. The miller and his wife went home.

The next day the bishop and the other officials came to the mill as usual, for they did not want anyone to feel that the night's happenings had anything to do with the miller's reputation. But Don Eugenio never came to the mill again. The miller and his wife both lived to a happy and prosperous old age.

THE THREE MUSKETEERS

Type of work: Novel
Author: Alexandre Dumas, father (1802-1870)
Type of plot: Historical romance
Time of plot: 1626
Locale: France
First published: 1844

Principal characters:

D'ARTAGNAN, a Gascon adventurer
ATHOS,
PORTHOS, and
ARAMIS, the three musketeers
CONSTANCE BONACIEUX, the queen's seamstress
LADY DE WINTER, Cardinal Richelieu's agent
CARDINAL RICHELIEU, minister of state

Critique:

Of all the stories by Dumas, this is probably the best. It is true that today we may find it too melodramatic, but once we accept the fact that the novel is a romance, we can read it as such and enjoy it. For it is a highly interesting story, full of adventure and intrigue, considered a classic of its type by all who admire historical romances of love and intrigue.

The Story:

In the spring of 1625 a young Gascon named D'Artagnan, on his way to Paris to join the musketeers, proudly rode up to an inn in Meung. He was mounted on an old Béarn pony given him by his father, along with some good advice and a letter of introduction to the captain of the musketeers. In Meung he showed his fighting spirit by fiercely challenging to a duel a stranger who seemed to be laughing at his orange horse. Before continuing his journey to Paris he had another encounter with the stranger, identified by a scar on his face, and the stranger's companion, a young and beautiful woman.

Athos, Porthos, and Aramis were the three best blades in the ranks of the Musketeers of the Guard, in the service of Louis XIII. D'Artagnan became a fourth member of the group within three months of his arrival in Paris. He had made himself loved and respected by the others when he challenged each in turn to a duel and then helped them drive off Cardinal Richelieu's guards, who wished to arrest them for brawling.

D'Artagnan was not made a musketeer at once; he had to serve an apprenticeship as a cadet in a lesser company of guards before being admitted to the musketeer ranks. Athos, Porthos, and Aramis looked forward to the day he would become their true comrade in arms and each took turns accompanying him when he was on guard duty. D'Artagnan was curious about his friends, but could learn nothing about them. Athos looked like a nobleman. He was reserved, never mentioned women, and it was said that a great treachery had poisoned his life. Porthos was a squire of dames, bragging incessantly of his loves. Aramis, who always dressed in black, insisted that he was a musketeer only temporarily, that he was a churchman at heart and soon would enter a monastery and exchange his plumed hat for a monk's cowl.

The three musketeers had been rewarded in gold by the timid king for their bravery against the cardinal's guards, but had since spent all their money. They were trying to figure a way out of their difficulties when Bonacieux, D'Artagnan's landlord, came to D'Artagnan because he had heard that his tenant was a brave man. He said that his wife Constance, who was a seamstress to the queen and whose devotion to the queen was well-known, had been abducted. He suggested that D'Artagnan find and rescue Constance in payment for long-overdue rent and for financial compensation.

When Bonacieux described the abductor, D'Artagnan recognized him as the man he had challenged at Meung. On these two scores, the Gascon was willing to help the stricken husband. But he was even more eager when he discovered that the purpose of the abduction was to force Constance to tell what she knew of a rumored romance between the queen and the Duke of Buckingham.

Constance escaped her abductors and returned to her home, where the cardinal's men again tried to seize her, only to be attacked and scattered by D'Artagnan who had overheard the struggle. Later that evening D'Artagnan met Constance who was hurrying along alone on the streets at a late hour. He questioned her, but she would not say where she was going. He told her that he loved her, but she gave him no encouragement. Still later that evening he encountered her again as she was leading the Duke of Buckingham, in disguise, to the queen.

The queen had sent for Buckingham to beg him to leave the city where his life was in danger. As they talked she confessed her love for him, and gave him as a memento a rosewood casket containing twelve diamond studs that the king had given her.

Richelieu, through his spies, learned of the gift and suggested to the king that he should give a fête and ask the queen to wear her diamond studs. The cardinal then ordered Lady de Winter who was in London, to snip off two of the studs from Buckingham's clothing. This deed gave him a chance to strike at the king, the queen, and also Buckingham. Learning of this scheme, Constance went to D'Artagnan. Because he loved Constance and because he wanted to serve his queen, he undertook to recover the jewels. With his three comrades he started out for London. Only D'Artagnan arrived there, for when the cardinal's agents ambushed the comrades the three musketeers were wounded and left behind. D'Artagnan reached the duke in time to recover the studs and return to Paris with them. Richelieu's plot was foiled.

After D'Artagnan had received the thanks of the queen he was to meet Constance that evening, but Constance was again seized and imprisoned by the cardinal's spies, one of whom was identified as the man from Meung. D'Artagnan decided he needed the help of his three friends and, accompanied by his servant Planchet, he went to find them. First he called at the inn where he had left Porthos and found him still there, recovering from his wounds. Later he found Aramis talking with some doctors of theology and about to renounce the world. Athos had barricaded himself in a wine-cellar. Drunk, he related a story about a friend of his, a count, who, when he was young, had married a beautiful girl and had made her the first lady in his province. However, he had later discovered that she was branded on the shoulder with the fleur-de-lis, the brand for a convicted criminal, and he had hanged her on a tree, leaving her for dead.

Once again the four friends were together. Then D'Artagnan, who had followed Porthos into a church, saw a beautiful woman whom he recognized as the companion of the man he had met at Meung. He followed her out of church and saw her get into her coach. Later he and his friends took the same road her coach had taken and encountered the coach by the side of the road. The lady was talking to a young man who, D'Artagnan discovered, was her brother-in-law, Lord de Winter. D'Artagnan became a friend of Lord de Winter after sparing his life in a duel; the lord introduced him to his sister-in-law. D'Artagnan fell in love with Lady de Winter.

But she loved another, a M. de Wardes, who, unknown to her, had been killed.

D'Artagnan deceived her one night into believing she had an assignation with de Wardes. D'Artagnan presented himself to her as de Wardes that night and she gave him a magnificent sapphire ring. When D'Artagnan showed the ring to Athos, he recognized it as the one which had belonged to his mother and which he had given to his wife. Athos began to suspect that his wife was not dead, but was Lady de Winter.

D'Artagnan overheard Lady de Winter make slurring remarks about him because he had spared the life of her brother-in-law. She was Lord de Winter's heir. D'Artagnan also realized that Lady de Winter was the cardinal's spy. At his next meeting with her, D'Artagnan, as himself, confessed his duplicity to her and she angrily struck a blow which caused him to step on her dress. The dress pulled from her shoulder, exposing the brand of the fleur-de-lis. As D'Artagnan realized the truth, Lady de Winter attacked him with a knife and screamed that she would get revenge. D'Artagnan fled to Athos.

The war between England and France was reaching a climax, and the siege of La Rochelle was of particular political importance. The four friends prepared to go to La Rochelle. Before they left, D'Artagnan was called for an interview with the cardinal. Richelieu tried to bribe D'Artagnan to enter his own guards, but D'Artagnan refused and left with the knowledge that his refusal might mean his death. In La Rochelle two young soldiers tried to kill D'Artagnan. From them he learned that they had been hired by Lady de Winter to kill him, and he also learned that she was responsible for the imprisonment of Constance.

The musketeers did not have much to do with the siege and led a carefree life. One evening they encountered two horsemen on a lonely road. One was the cardinal on his way to a nearby inn. The cardinal ordered the musketeers to go with him. Lady de Winter was at the inn and the musketeers overheard the cardinal instruct her to go to London, where she was to tell Buckingham that unless he ended the war his affair with the queen would be exposed. If he refused, Lady de Winter was to poison him. As her reward Lady de Winter asked to have two of her enemies killed. These two were Constance, who had been conveyed to a convent by an order the queen had obtained from the king, and D'Artagnan. Richelieu then wrote out a safe-conduct for Lady de Winter.

A few minutes later, Athos, who had recognized her voice, was in Lady de Winter's room. There he revealed himself as the Count de la Fère, her husband. She was terrified, for she had thought him dead as well. Athos took from her the cardinal's letter of safe-conduct and ordered her to leave France at once under threats of exposure.

The four friends returned to the siege of La Rochelle, where they conducted themselves with such bravery that they again drew notice from the cardinal. When the cardinal spoke of them to him, their captain said that D'Artagnan was not in the service of the musketeers. The cardinal then gave orders that D'Artagnan was to be made a musketeer, and this news, when relayed to D'Artagnan, made him very happy. The friends now wrote out a message to warn Lord de Winter against his sister-in-law and sent Planchet to deliver it. They also sent a message to a cousin of Aramis, and learned from her the name of the convent in which Constance had been confined.

When Lady de Winter arrived in England, she was held a prisoner by Lord de Winter. But her pretense of religious fervor and her beauty convinced her young Puritan jailer of her innocence. After she had told him a fantastic tale to the effect that her downfall had been caused by Buckingham, he helped her to escape. To avenge her he then went to Buckingham and stabbed him. De Winter, who discovered her escape also hurried to Buckingham, but arrived too late to save his life. Before he died, a messenger from Paris brought Buckingham word from the queen of her faithful love.

Lady de Winter escaped to France, to the convent where Constance was staying. There she managed to poison Constance and flee again before the four companions arrived to rescue the queen's faithful servant. Lord de Winter, also in pursuit of Lady de Winter, arrived a few minutes after they had discovered Constance. Continuing their pursuit of Lady de Winter, they overtook her and held a trial. They condemned her to die. She was executed by the public executioner of Lille, who had branded her for her crimes, many years before.

On his return to La Rochelle, D'Artagnan was arrested and taken to the cardinal. The man who took him prisoner was the stranger D'Artagnan had met at Meung, identified now as the Chevalier de Rochefort. The cardinal charged D'Artagnan with treason, but D'Artagnan interrupted and named the long list of crimes of the woman who had charged him. Then he informed the cardinal of her death and produced the safe-conduct pass, signed by the cardinal, which Athos had taken from the woman. D'Artagnan told Richelieu that as bearer of the pass he should be allowed to go free. The cardinal was so pleased by the Gascon's cleverness that he could not be angry. Instead, he offered D'Artagnan a commission in the musketeers. D'Artagnan offered it to his friends, but each refused it, insisting that he deserved the rank, an honor great nobles often sought in vain.

La Rochelle surrendered to the French and the faithful four disbanded. Athos returned to his estate, Porthos married a rich widow, and Aramis became a monk. D'Artagnan became a famous soldier. He and de Rochefort, his old enemy at Meung, fought three times, but finally became good friends.

THREE SOLDIERS

Type of work: Novel
Author: John Dos Passos (1896-)
Type of plot: Social criticism
Time of plot: 1917-1919
Locale: France
First published: 1921

Principal characters:
DAN FUSELLI, an American soldier from San Francisco
CHRISFIELD, an American soldier from Indiana
JOHN ANDREWS (ANDY), an American soldier from Virginia
GENEVIÈVE ROD, Andrews' friend

Critique:

This novel attempts to do for World War I what Stephen Crane's *The Red Badge of Courage* did for the Civil War; that is, to destroy the myth of glamour and glory and to expose the brutal reality of war. Unlike the hero of *The Red Badge of Courage,* who deserts in fright and returns proudly to battle, John Andrews of *Three Soldiers* can only take a self-respecting step by deserting after months of ignominious conformity. The novel succeeds best in its presentation of the tedium, de-humanizing regimentation, and the physical horrors of war. As such, it is a vividly realized social document.

The Story:

Private Dan Fuselli was anxious to become Corporal Dan Fuselli. He had seen movies of Huns spitting Belgian babies on their bayonets and then being chased like rabbits by heroic Yankee soldiers who were later rewarded with embraces by the pretty and picturesque Belgian milkmaids. He looked forward to the time when his girl, Mabe, writing from San Francisco, his home town, would address her letters to Corporal Dan Fuselli.

Private First Class Fuselli of the Medical Corps hated the Army and everything about it, but he knew that to become a corporal he must keep clean, keep his mouth shut, obey the brass, and continually cajole the sergeant. He was infuriated one night when he went to town to see Yvonne and learned that the sergeant had taken her over. Then, when he returned to camp, he heard that the consumptive corporal was back, the one in whose absence Fuselli had been made acting corporal. But Private Fuselli kept his mouth shut. Someday he would be a corporal, perhaps even a sergeant; but now he kept his mouth shut.

Finally, after a setback doing endless K. P. and following his recovery from a venereal disease, after the Armistice, he did become Corporal Dan Fuselli. But by that time his girl had married a naval officer.

Matters worked out differently for Chrisfield. The Army was not as easy-going as life in the Indiana farm country had been. The officers shouted at you, made you do things you hated. You had to take it. One night Chrisfield was so furious he pulled a knife on a sergeant named Anderson, but his friends held him back and nothing happened. In Europe, things were not much better. Occasionally he had a talk about the stars and the fields with his educated buddy, John Andrews. Mostly, however, the war was awful.

The marches were endless, and his shoulders ached from his heavy pack. When bombardments came, the marchers scattered face down in a field. Once Chrisfield asked Andrews to speak French for him to a French girl at an inn, but nothing came of it.

One day, walking alone through a wood near the front, Chrisfield found a dead German lying prone. When he kicked the body over, he saw that it had no face, only a multicolored, pulpy mass with green flies hovering around it. In the man's hand was a revolver—he was a suicide. Chrisfield ran off panting.

Chrisfield was high-strung. When he was sitting thinking, a soldier prodded him and asked him what he was dreaming about. Chrisfield punched the fellow in the nose. He and Andy hated the Y. M. C. A. men who were always telling the men at the front what brutes the Huns were and urging them in the name of Old Glory to kill Germans. Chrisfield was court-martialed when he announced that he intended to kill Sergeant Anderson after the war was over.

One day he went wandering and made his way silently into the kitchen of a house near the front. Looking into the next room, he saw a man in a German uniform. He reached into his pocket, pressed the spring on the grenade he had, withdrew it, and tossed it into the room. Not long afterward he came across Anderson, now a lieutenant, seated wounded in a deserted section of the wood. Chrisfield had two more grenades in his pocket, and he threw them at the man he hated.

After the Armistice, the rumor that he had killed Anderson somehow leaked out. Afraid, Chrisfield went A. W. O. L. and became a refugee in France, eternally on the move.

John Andrews was a Harvard graduate and a would-be composer. The Queen of Sheba section of Flaubert's *Temptation of Saint Anthony* kept recurring to his mind as he washed the barracks windows, and he thought how fine the subject would be for a musical composition. He cursed the Army for slowly stamping him into its iron mold. Overseas, he saw action and was more convinced than ever that war was needless butchery. He felt happiest away from the regiment. One day he walked away from his company in order to be alone. He was looking at little frogs in a pool when a shell burst near him. He awoke on a stretcher.

For a while the hospital was a relief from the endless orders and general mechanization of Army routine. Lying in his bed, he began to realize that he had respect for himself only when he thought of rebelling against the system, of going A. W. O. L. Soon the tedium of the hospital began to gall him. After his leg healed, he rejoined his company reluctantly and full of rebellion. The Armistice had been signed. When he heard that he could go to a French University through a school detachment being set up, he lied, secured some recommendations, and found himself in Paris.

In Paris he met Geneviève Rod, a young Frenchwoman who admired his piano playing and his artistic tastes. She thought of artists as men who, because of their special sensitivity, should be exempt from the horrors of war. Andrews disagreed; one worker was like another; it was the whole of humanity that should be exempt. One day he left Paris without official leave for a country trip with Geneviève. An MP picked him up and took him to a local office where he was beaten by several MP's. He was sent to a labor battalion loading concrete for a stadium being presented by the Americans to the French. It was crushing work. Convinced that Army life was a menace to human freedom, Andrews decided to desert, for one man less in the system made it weaker by that much. One night he leaped from a plank and swam out to a barge in the Seine.

The barge family cared for him for a few days. They sank his uniform in the river, bought him new clothes, and as anarchists proclaimed their solidarity with him. He went back to Paris to find Geneviève, and stayed for a while with Chrisfield and a group of other concealed deserters. Then, hearing that Geneviève was at her country place, he joined her there.

At first he did not tell her of his desertion. He lived in an inn nearby and began composing, not about the Queen of Sheba, but about John Brown, liberator of slaves. When he finally confessed his plight to Geneviève, a noticeable reserve crept into her attitude toward him. Perhaps, she suggested, he should give himself up. She could not comprehend the social motive in his rebellion.

One day he heard an American officer's voice at the door of the inn below his window. He thought of the prison sentence he must face. Too late he discovered that the landlady, experienced in the ways of impecunious Americans who were possible deserters, had stolen his revolver. As the MP's took him away, the wind blew in through the window of his room and the music papers on which he had been working fluttered one by one to the floor.

THE TIME MACHINE

Type of work: Novel
Author: H. G. Wells (1866-1946)
Type of plot: Fantasy
Time of plot: Late nineteenth century
Locale: England
First published: 1895

Principal characters:
THE TIME TRAVELER
WEENA, a woman the Time Traveler meets in the future

Critique:

The Time Traveler's description of the people of the future, the weak Eloi and the predatory Morlocks, has its roots in some interesting scientific hypotheses. This speculative chronicle of a space-time concept and a picture of life in the world of the future is so exciting, however, that it may be read merely as an adventure story. The book is a mixture of fantasy and pseudo-scientific romance.

The Story:

After dinner, one evening, the Time Traveler led the discussion to the subject of the relationship of time and space. It was his theory that time was a fourth dimension, and that his concept could be proved. To the astonishment of his guests, he exhibited a model of his Time Machine, which, he declared, could travel backward or forward in time. One of the guests was invited to touch a lever. To the amazement of all, the machine disappeared. The Time Traveler explained that the instrument was no longer visible because it was traveling into the past at such great speed that it was below the threshold of visibility.

The following week the Time Traveler was not at home to greet his dinner guests when they arrived, but he had left word that they were to proceed without him. Everyone was at the table when their host came in, dirty from head to toe, limping, and with a cut on his chin. After he had changed his clothes and dined, he told his friends the story of the day's adventures.

That morning he had taken off on his Time Machine. As he reeled through space, the days shot past him like minutes, the rapid alternation of light and darkness hurting the Time Traveler's eyes. Landing and falling from his machine when he braked too suddenly, he found himself on the side of a hill. In the misty light he could see the figure of a winged sphinx on a bronze pedestal. As the sun came out, the Time Traveler saw enormous buildings on the slope. Some figures were coming toward him. One was a little man about four feet tall. Regaining his confidence, the Time Traveler waited to meet this citizen of the future.

Soon a group of these creatures gathered around the voyager. Without a common language, he and his new acquaintances had to communicate with signs. After they had examined the Time Machine, from which he had the presence of mind to remove the levers, one of them asked him if he had come from the sun.

The Time Traveler was led to one of the large buildings, where he was seated upon a cushion and given fruit to eat. Everyone was a vegetarian, animals having become extinct. When he had eaten, he tried to learn his new friends' language, but without much success. These people, who called themselves the Eloi, were not able to concentrate and tired quickly.

Free to wander about, the Time Traveler climbed a hill and from the crest saw the ruins of an enormous granite structure. Looking at some of the creatures who were following him, he realized that all wore similar garb and had the same soft, rounded figures. Children could be distinguished only by their size.

The Time Traveler realized that he was seeing the sunset of humanity. In the society of the future there was no need for strength. The world was at peace and secure. The strong of body or mind would only have felt frustrated.

As he looked about to find a place to sleep, he saw that his Time Machine had disappeared. He tried to wake the people in the building in which he had dined, but he succeeded only in frightening them. At last he went back to the lawn and there, greatly worried over his plight, fell asleep.

The next morning he managed to trace the path the Time Machine made to the base of the sphinx, but the bronze doors in the pedestal were closed. The Time Traveler tried to intimate to some of the Eloi that he wished to open the doors, but they answered him with looks of insult and reproach. He attempted to hammer in the doors with a stone, but he soon stopped from weariness.

Weena, a young girl he rescued from drowning, became the Time Traveler's friend and guide. On the fourth morning, while he explored one of the ruins, he saw eyes staring at him from the dark. Curious, he followed a small, ape-like figure to a well-like opening, down which it retreated. He was convinced that this creature was also a descendant of man, a subterranean species that worked below ground to support the dwellers in the upper world.

Convinced that the Morlocks, as the subterranean dwellers were called, were responsible for the disappearance of his Time Machine and hoping to learn more about them, he climbed down into one of the wells. At its bottom he discovered a tunnel which led into a cavern in which he saw a table set with a joint of meat. The Morlocks were carnivorous. He was able to distinguish, too, some enormous machinery.

The next day the Time Traveler and Weena visited a green porcelain museum containing animal skeletons, books, and machinery. Since they had walked a long distance, he planned to sleep in the woods that night with Weena and to build a fire to keep the dark-loving Morlocks away. When he saw three crouching figures in the brush, however, he changed his mind and decided he and Weena would be safer on a hill beyond the forest. He started a fire to keep their enemies at a distance.

When he awoke the fire had gone out, his matches were missing, and Weena had vanished. A fire he had started earlier was still burning, and while he slept it had set the forest on fire. Between thirty and forty Morlocks perished in the blaze while the Time Traveler watched.

When daylight returned, the Time Traveler retraced his steps to the sphinx. He slept all day and in the evening prepared to ram open the doors in the pedestal with the lever he had found in the porcelain palace. He found the doors open, his machine in plain view. As a group of Morlocks sprang at him, he took off through space.

The Time Traveler had his encounter with the Morlocks and the Eloi in the year 802,701. On his next journey he moved through millions of years, toward that time when the earth will cease rotating. He landed on a deserted beach, empty except for a flying animal, which looked like a huge white butterfly, and some crab-like monsters. On he traveled, finally halting thirty million years after the time he had left his laboratory. In that distant age the sun was setting. It was bitter cold and it began to snow. All around was deathly stillness. Horrified, the Time Traveler started back toward his present.

That evening, as he told his story, his guests grew skeptical. In fact, the Time Traveler himself had to visit his laboratory to make sure his machine existed. The next day, however, all doubts ceased, for one of his friends watched him depart on his vehicle. It was this friend who wrote the story of the Time Traveler's experiences three years later. The Time Traveler had not reappeared during that time, and his friends speculated on the mishap which had made him a lost wanderer in space and time.

THE TIME OF MAN

Type of work: Novel
Author: Elizabeth Madox Roberts (1886-1941)
Type of plot: Regional romance
Time of plot: Early twentieth century
Locale: Kentucky
First published: 1926

Principal characters:
ELLEN CHESSER, a farm girl
NELLIE, her mother
HENRY, her father
JASPER KENT, her husband
JONAS, her fiancé

Critique:

The Time of Man is a farm story that strikes a nice balance between the sordid and the romantic. Here we have the life of the migrant Kentucky farmer as it is, unvarnished and plain. But deeper, we see the springs from which these people draw their strength. They lived in poverty, with little hope of security. But in their love for the soil and in their fierce independence they find meaning for their lives. To call this novel a story of local color would be true but inadequate. The regionalism of *The Time of Man* is but a convenient frame for the depiction of human and enduring values.

The Story:

Henry and Nellie Chesser had been on the road a long time. People sometimes called the Chessers and their friends gipsies, and they did tell fortunes and swap horses and mules. But Henry liked the earth, and he worked as a tenant for different farmers from time to time. Only his restless spirit kept him from settling somewhere permanently.

One day Henry's wagon broke down. The others could not wait for the Chessers, and Henry haunted the smithy, hoping to speed repairs. But when Hep Bodine offered him twenty dollars a month, a tenant house, and a garden spot, he accepted. The house had only one room and a loft, but it was better than sleeping outside.

Henry's daughter, Ellen, was greatly disappointed. She hated to leave Tessie, her great friend, the fortune-teller. Ellen knew no one on the Bodine farm, nor did she make friends easily. Mrs. Bodine even ordered her out of the berry patch. Only Joe Trent, home from college, noticed her.

Joe was elegant, always wearing shoes and clothes of different kinds of cloth. He would joke with Ellen as she got in the firewood. She was growing up, and Joe awakened some spark of longing in her thin body. Then one day Joe drove past her with Emphira Bodine. He pretended not to see Ellen in her skimpy skirt above her bare feet and legs. After that, Joe would stand behind a big bush where the men from the house could not see him and call to Ellen. Ellen was ashamed. She was glad when her father decided to move over to the Wakefield farm.

Their new house was better; even the loft had once been papered. Miss Tod Wakefield let Ellen look after the turkeys for money wages. So with setting out tobacco plants, getting in the firewood, and going regularly to the big barnyard, she settled into a pleasant routine. By fall Nellie was able to get Ellen a store dress and new shoes.

In an old abandoned barn where she went to look for turkey eggs she often noticed Amanda Cain waiting in the hay loft for Scott MacMurtrie, who was married to Miss Cassie. All the field workers knew of the affair, and they discussed eagerly how Miss Cassie would lay into Scott when she learned he was carrying on with her cousin Amanda, for Miss Cassie was strong and independent. One day Scott and Amanda disappeared. That night Ellen was awakened by the tolling bell on the MacMurtrie place. She hurried over, outdistancing her father, who thought the barn must be on fire. Ellen found the old Negress pulling the bell rope in a frenzy. Miss Cassie had hanged herself.

Dorine moved into one of the tenant houses. She was merry and gay and attracted others to her. She and Ellen became friends. At her house Ellen went to her first party. Shy, she hoped desperately that no one would notice her. But in her agony of timidity she sang a ballad her father had taught her, and she was accepted as one of the group. At their dances and games and on their Sunday walks she went sometimes with Jonas Prather but more often with Sebe Townley. Sebe was kind and gentle, but she liked Jonas better.

Jonas took little part in their gay dances. He would call the figures and then retire with the old folks. He seemed to withdraw from contact with girls; some even said he had got religion.

One night Jonas told Ellen he wanted her to marry him. When he went away to work for wages, he promised to come back during the summer to get married. Ellen had a letter from him and she wrote him a letter in return. But the summer wore on and Jonas did not come. At last she heard that Jonas had married Sallie Lou.

When Henry rented a patch of twenty-five acres called the Orkeys place, Ellen felt a sense of escaping from her troubles. Their new home had once been a toll house. It contained three rooms on one floor, and Ellen's bedroom was weather-tight.

The nearest neighbors were on the Wingate place. Old Mrs. Wingate, half mad, sat suspiciously in her house all day long and Jasper Kent worked her farm on half shares. Albert Wingate, the son, seldom came to the farm, and when he did appear he would often be roaring drunk. He would beg or steal money from his mother and sometimes he would turn the house upside down looking for more. When he began driving off cattle in which Jasper had a half interest, Jasper felt his anger mount.

Although Jasper prudently kept his own pigs in a corral far from the house, Albert discovered them. One morning Jasper found the corral empty; Albert had sold the pigs to a passing trader. That night Albert and Jasper fought in the barn. Jasper was stronger than his opponent. Then Albert drew a gun. Jasper wrested it away and threw it in the brush. But in the fighting Jasper forgot his lantern on the barn floor. When the building went up in flames, Jasper fled. He had been in jail before, and he was afraid.

He found work on the Phillips farm. Joe Phillips offered a house to Jasper. So Jasper and Ellen were married and set up housekeeping in their own place. Their house was tight, and Joe promised to add a room. Ellen was carrying her first child and was very content with her marriage.

The letter they had been dreading came, an indictment for arson drawn up against Jasper for the burning of the Wingate barn. Henry was Jasper's witness and Jasper was freed. At last Ellen and Jasper seemed to be free of all care; they had only to work the land and raise their family. Each year they had another child.

Following the custom of the migrant people, they left the Phillips farm. It became a matter of indifference to Ellen where she lived; a year on the Goodrich place, a year on the McKnight farm—it was all the same. Then they moved back to the Phillips farm. Joe Phillips, greatly attracted to Ellen, spoke sweet words to her. When Jasper began to go off for all-night carouses, Ellen accepted Joe's attentions. She did not tell Jasper right away about the new baby she was carrying. When she did, Jasper was bitter and swore it was Joe's. But when the sickly child was born, Jasper was very fond of it. The baby died in its third year.

When a nearby barn burned, suspicion unjustly fell on Jasper. One night masked raiders came to their home, seized Jasper while he slept, and bound him with ropes. They beat him savagely. Ellen brought him in and washed his bleeding welts. Jasper was greatly shamed.

The family loaded all their goods on the wagon and set out. They scarcely knew where they were going, but it would be far away. As they went they dreamed of a homeplace of land they could call their own. Perhaps they could even set out trees for an orchard, somewhere, someday.

THE TITAN

Type of work: Novel
Author: Theodore Dreiser (1871-1945)
Type of plot: Naturalism
Time of plot: 1890's
Locale: Chicago
First published: 1914

Principal characters:

FRANK ALGERNON COWPERWOOD, a multimillionaire and financial genius
AILEEN COWPERWOOD, his mistress and then his wife
PETER LAUGHLIN, his business partner
STEPHANIE PLATOW, Cowperwood's mistress
BERENICE FLEMING, Cowperwood's protégée and mistress

Critique:

Dreiser's full-length portrait of a great financial wizard is one of the triumphs of the naturalistic school of writers. Between 1890 and the publication of this book scores of novels dealing with the American financier were published, but none approached the thoroughness and the psychological insight of *The Titan,* which continues the psychological and sociological study of Cowperwood begun by Dreiser in *The Financier*. While the man Dreiser portrays is wholly without a conventional moral code, he is nevertheless a strong man with a purpose. The author makes no effort to judge his character, and the reader feels that it is best if he, too, refrains from passing judgment.

The Story:

Released from a Pennsylvania prison in the 1870's, Frank Algernon Cowperwood, still young and a millionaire, went to Chicago to begin a new life with Aileen Butler, his mistress. Within a short time Cowperwood made friends among influential businessmen there.

Divorced by his first wife, Cowperwood finally married Aileen. He prepared to increase his fortune, to become a power in the city, and to conquer its society. To this end, he sought an enterprise which would quickly yield him heavy returns on his investment. His first battle among the financial barons of Chicago was to gain control of the gas companies.

At the same time the Cowperwoods

made their first attack on Chicago society, but with little success. Aileen Cowperwood was too high-spirited and lacking in the poise which would win her social success. Then Cowperwood became involved in several lawsuits and his earlier political-economic disgrace in Philadelphia was exposed in the Chicago newspapers. But after a long battle Cowperwood was able to force the rival gas companies to buy out his franchises at a profit to himself.

Unfortunately, the deal brought social defeat, at least temporarily, to the Cowperwoods, for his rivals in finance were the social powers of Chicago at that time. Cowperwood turned once again to a mistress, but the affair ended when Aileen attempted to kill her rival.

For several years a cable-car system of street railways claimed most of Cowperwood's time. He bought control of the horsecar company which served the north side of Chicago. Then the naturally promiscuous temperament of Cowperwood intruded itself when he met dark, lush Stephanie Platow. Ten years younger than his wife and interested in art, literature, and music, she was able to occupy a place in his life Aileen could never fill.

While involved in that affair, Cowperwood coerced the west side street railway company into giving its franchise to him. But the sweetness of his victory was partially lost by the exposure of Stephanie as another man's lover. Meanwhile financial forces were at work against Cowperwood. Through two city bosses, these forces hoped to play the city politicians against Cowperwood, for without the support of the city council to aid him with franchises and grants the financier would find himself helpless to merge all the street railways of the city under his control.

The first battle was fought in an election to gain possession of the Chicago city council. It was far more painful for Cowperwood to learn at this time that his wife had been unfaithful to him than to discover that he had arrayed the whole financial and social element of the city against himself. The loss of the election proved no permanent setback to Cowperwood, however, nor did his wife's infidelity. From the latter he recovered, and the first was soon undone by his opponents because they did not pave the way with favors and money when they tried to push bills through the new reform council. Even the new mayor was soon an ally of Cowperwood.

Soon afterward Cowperwood met Berenice Fleming, daughter of a procuress, who was being prepared in a fashionable boarding-school for a career in society. Taking her and her family under his wing, Cowperwood became her lover with some misgivings, for the girl was but seventeen and he was fifty-two at the time. By this time his enemies were trying to gain franchises for elevated lines powered by electricity.

This new effort by his financial rivals meant that his own street railways had to be converted to electricity, and he had to compete for at least a share of the elevated lines to prevent his ruin. The south side "L" was already a tremendous success because of the World's Fair of 1893, and the whole city was now clamoring for better transportation service. Cowperwood's opponents held control over the city banks, which prevented those institutions from lending him funds needed to begin his operations. When he attempted to secure funds in the East, Cowperwood discovered that his assets were in question. But by one master stroke the financier wiped out any question of his ability and his credit; he donated three hundred thousand dollars to the local university for a telescope and observatory.

Even with unlimited credit, the problem of gaining franchises was not easy. He was determined to keep control of the Chicago transportation system, but he began to realize that neither he nor his wife could ever become socially acceptable there. He decided to build a mansion in New York to hold his collection of art and be his card of entry into society.

Meanwhile, having obtained his franchises, he began work on Chicago elevated lines. Cowperwood's enemies planned to let him overreach himself, so that they could force him out of Chicago financially as well as socially. Then the collapse of the American Match Corporation, partially engineered by Cowperwood, began a series of runs on the Chicago banks controlled by his enemies. When their attempts to recall the enormous loans made to Cowperwood failed, he emerged from the affair stronger than ever.

The final battle, the climax of Cowperwood's financial career in Chicago, was the one he waged to secure fifty-year franchises for his growing transportation system. This project was made doubly difficult because of Cowperwood's latest property, the Union Loop, by which he controlled the elevated lines. This loop of elevated track, encircling the downtown business district, had to be used by all the lines in the city. The moneyed interests opposed Cowperwood because he was not with them; the newspapers, because they wanted to see better and cheaper facilities. In the face of the opposition, even the most reckless of the city's aldermen feared to grant the franchises Cowperwood wanted, regardless of the money and power he was prepared to give to them. Then his lawyers informed Cowperwood that the state constitution prevented the city from granting such long-term franchises, even if the city council could be coerced into approving them.

Cowperwood's next idea was to have a transportation commission set up by bribery in the state legislature. In the bill which set up the commission was a clause extending existing franchises for a period of fifty years. The bill, passed by the legislature, was vetoed by the governor.

Meanwhile the New York mansion had been completed, and Aileen Cowperwood moved in. She met with no social success, except among the Bohemian set. Berenice Fleming was settled at the same time with her family in a mansion on Park Avenue. The next step in Cowperwood's personal affairs was to be his second divorce. Then Aileen heard of his affair with Berenice Fleming. When he asked her for the divorce, she tried to commit suicide but failed.

Cowperwood again tried to force his bill through the Illinois Legislature, but the legislators returned it to the city council. There, as before, Cowperwood lost. The people and the newspapers frightened the aldermen so that they dared not grant what the financier wished, despite his fantastic bribes.

With his hope of controlling the Chicago transportation system gone, Cowperwood sold his interests. Admitting defeat, he and Berenice went to Europe. The Titan's empire had fallen.

TO THE LIGHTHOUSE

Type of work: Novel
Author: Virginia Woolf (1882-1941)
Type of plot: Psychological realism
Time of plot: c. 1910-1920
Locale: The Isle of Skye in the Hebrides
First published: 1927

Principal characters:

MR. RAMSAY, a professor of philosophy
MRS. RAMSAY, his wife
JAMES, their son
CAMILLA, their daughter

Mr. Tansley, Mr. Ramsay's guest and friend
Lily Briscoe, an artist
Mr. Carmichael, a poet

Critique:

Set in the out-of-the-way Hebrides Islands, this book has an other-world quality. There is an air of unreality about it, achieved, perhaps, by the odd structure of the book. Virginia Woolf learned a great deal from James Joyce about the psychological novel. Although her stream of consciousness does not get out of hand or lead the story into hidden depths, it does dominate the entire novel and make good its effect. The past has, throughout the novel, an effect upon the present action, and this mingling of past and present is the secret of the book's unity.

The Story:

Mrs. Ramsay promised James, her seven-year-old son, that if the next day were fair he would be taken on a visit to the lighthouse they could see from the window of their summer home on the Isle of Skye. James, the youngest of Mrs. Ramsay's eight children, was his mother's favorite. The father of the family was a professor of philosophy whose students often thought that he was inspiring and one of the foremost metaphysicians of the early twentieth century; but his own children, particularly the youngest, did not like him because he made sarcastic remarks.

Several guests were visiting the Ramsays at the time. There was young Mr. Tansley, Ramsay's student, who was also unpopular with the children because he seemed to delight in their discomfiture. Tansley was mildly in love with his hostess, despite her fifty-five years and her eight children. There was Lily Briscoe, who was painting a picture of the cottage with Mrs. Ramsay and little James seated in front of it. There was old Mr. Carmichael, a ne'er-do-well who amused the Ramsay youngsters because he had a white beard and a mustache tinged with yellow. There was also Mr. Bankes, a young man in love with Prue, the prettiest of the Ramsay daughters.

The afternoon went by slowly. Mrs. Ramsay went to the village to call on a sick woman. She spent several hours knitting stockings for the lighthouse keeper's child, whom they were planning to visit. Many people wondered how the Ramsays, particularly the wife, managed to be as hospitable and as charitable as they were, for they were not rich; Mr. Ramsay could not possibly make a fortune by expounding Locke, Berkeley, and Hume to students or by publishing books on metaphysics.

Mr. Carmichael, pretending to read, had actually fallen asleep early after lunch. The children, except for James, who was busy cutting pictures out of a catalogue, had busied themselves in a game of cricket. Mr. Ramsay and Mr. Tansley had passed the time in a pointless conversation. Miss Briscoe had only made a daub or two of paint on her canvas. For some reason the lines of the scene refused to come clear in her painting. Prue and Mr. Bankes had gone walking along the shore.

Even the dinner went by slowly. The only occasion of interest to the children, which was one of tension to their mother, came when Mr. Carmichael asked the maid for a second bowl of soup, thereby angering his host, who liked to have meals dispatched promptly. As soon as the children had finished, their mother sent the younger ones to bed. Mrs. Ramsay hoped that Prue would not fall in love with Mr. Bankes, and that Lily Briscoe, who always became seasick, would not want to accompany them in the small sailboat if they should go to the lighthouse the following day. She thought also about the fifty pounds needed to make some necessary repairs on the house.

After dinner Mrs. Ramsay went upstairs to the nursery. James had a boar's skull which his sister detested. Whenever Camilla tried to remove it from the wall and her sight, he burst into a frenzy of screaming. Mrs. Ramsay wrapped the skull in a handkerchief. Afterward she went downstairs and joined her husband in the library, where they sat throughout the evening, she knitting and Mr. Ramsay reading. Before they went to bed it was agreed that the trip for the next day would have to be canceled. The night had turned stormy.

Night followed night. The trip to the lighthouse was never made that summer, nor did the Ramsays return to their summer home for some years. In the meantime Mrs. Ramsay died quietly in her sleep. Prue was married, although not to Mr. Bankes, and died in childbirth. The first World War began. Andrew Ramsay enlisted and was sent to France, where he was killed by an exploding shell.

Time passed. The wallpaper in the house came loose from the walls. Books mildewed. In the kitchen a cup was occasionally knocked down and broken by old Mrs. McNab, who came to look after the house from time to time. In the garden the roses and the annual flowers grew wild or died.

Mr. Carmichael brought out a volume of poems during the war. About the time his book appeared, daffodils and violets bloomed on the Isle of Skye. Mrs. McNab looked longingly at a warm cloak left in a closet. She wished the cloak belonged to her.

At last the war ended. Mrs. McNab received a telegram requesting that the house be put in order. For several days the housekeeper worked, aided by two cleaning women, and when the Ramsays arrived the cottage was in order once more. Several visitors came again to share a summer at the cottage. Lily Briscoe returned for a quiet vacation. Mr. Carmichael, the successful poet, also arrived.

One morning Lily Briscoe came down to breakfast and wondered at the quiet which greeted her. No one had been down ahead of her, although she had expected that Mr. Ramsay and the two youngest children, James and Camilla, would have eaten early and departed for the long-postponed sail to the lighthouse, to which the youngsters had been looking forward with joyful anticipation. Within a few minutes the three straggled down, all having slept past the time they had intended to arise. After a swift breakfast they disappeared toward the shore, their going watched by Lily Briscoe, who had set up her canvas with the intention of once again trying to paint her picture of the cottage.

The journey to the island where the lighthouse stood was not as pleasant as the children had expected. They had never really liked their father; he had taken too little time to understand them. He was short and sharp when they did things which seemed foolish to him, though those actions were perfectly comprehensible to his son and daughter. James, especially, expected to be blamed caustically and pointlessly if the crossing were slow or not satisfactory in some other way, for he had been delegated to handle the sheets and the tiller of the boat.

Mr. Ramsay strode down to the beach with his offspring, each carrying a paper parcel to take to the keepers of the lighthouse. They soon set sail and pointed the prow of the sailboat toward the black and white striped pillar of the lighthouse in the hazy distance. Mr. Ramsay sat in the middle of the boat, along with an old fisherman and his son. They were to take over the boat in case of an emergency, for Mr. Ramsay had little trust in James as a reliable seaman. In the stern sat James himself, nerves tingling lest his father look up from his book and indulge in unnecessary and hateful criticism. But his nervous tension was needless, for within a few hours the little party reached the lighthouse, and, wonderful to relate, Mr. Ramsay sprang ashore like a youngster, smiled back at his children, and praised his son for his seamanship.

TOBACCO ROAD

Type of work: Novel
Author: Erskine Caldwell (1903-)
Type of plot: Social melodrama
Time of plot: 1920's
Locale: Georgia
First published: 1932

Principal characters:
JEETER LESTER, a poor white
ADA, his wife
DUDE, his son
ELLIE MAY, his daughter
PEARL, another daughter
LOV BENSEY, Pearl's husband
BESSIE, a backwoods evangelist

Critique:

The uproarious, Rabelaisian episodes of *Tobacco Road* make the novel appear to be a burlesque on rural life of the southern United States. Granted the exaggeration for effect, the book deals truthfully, in the main, with a human element which is in evidence in the eastern piedmont from Virginia to Georgia. The character of Jeeter Lester, although repulsive in many respects, is nevertheless a curiously moving one. In creating Jeeter, Caldwell gave the world another minor hero, a man whose futile hopefulness attracts the sympathy of the sentimental and the social-minded.

The Story:

Lov Bensey, husband of Pearl, fifteen-year-old daughter of Jeeter Lester, felt low in his mind when he stopped by the Lester house on his way home with a bag of turnips. Pearl, he complained, refused to have anything to do with him; she would neither sleep with him nor talk to him.

The Lesters lived in a one-room shack which was falling apart. They had nothing to eat but pork-rind soup. Jeeter was trying to patch an inner tube so that the Lester car, a nondescript wreck which had been refused even by the junk dealer, could be used to carry firewood to Augusta. Jeeter's harelipped daughter Ellie May charmed Lov away from his bag of turnips. While she and Lov were dallying in the yard in front of the shack, the other Lesters pounced upon the bag of turnips. Jeeter grabbed it and ran into the scrub woods, followed by his worthless son Dude. Jeeter ate his fill of turnips. He gave Dude several and even saved a handful for the rest of the family. They returned from the woods to find Lov gone. Sister Bessie, a woman preacher, had come for a visit. Bessie, middle-aged, and Dude, sixteen, were attracted to each other. Bessie, upon leaving, promised to return to take Dude away to be her husband.

The Lesters were starving. Jeeter had long since been unable to get credit at the local stores in order to buy seed, fertilizer, and food. His land was exhausted and there was no chance of re-

TOBACCO ROAD by Erskine Caldwell. By permission of the author and the publishers, Duell, Sloan & Pearce, Inc. Copyright, 1932, by Erskine Caldwell.

claiming it because of Jeeter's utter laziness. Jeeter and his wife Ada had had seventeen children. Twelve of them survived, but all except Ellie May and Dude had left home.

Bessie returned and announced that God had given her permission to marry Dude, but Dude refused to listen until Bessie said that she was planning to buy a new car with some money that her late husband had left her. She and Dude went to town and bought a new Ford, the loud horn of which Dude highly approved. At the county courthouse, over the mild protestations of the clerk because of Dude's youth, Bessie got a marriage license. Back at the Lester shack, Bessie, using her authority as preacher, married herself to Dude.

The newlyweds went for a ride in their new car; they returned to the tobacco road at sundown with one fender of the car completely ruined. They had run into a farm wagon on the highway and had killed a Negro whom they left lying by the roadside.

Jeeter, anxious to get food and snuff, persuaded Bessie and Dude to take him to Augusta with a load of firewood. Their arrival in Augusta was delayed, however, by the breakdown of the car. A gallon and a half of oil poured into the crank case enabled them to get to the city, where Jeeter failed to sell one stick of wood. The trio sold the car's spare tire, for which they could see no use, and bought food. They mistook a house of ill-repute for a hotel; Bessie was absent from Jeeter and her young husband most of the night.

During the return trip to the tobacco road, Jeeter unloaded the wood beside the highway and set fire to it. He was about to suggest another trip in the car, but Bessie and Dude rode away before he could stop them.

As the car rapidly fell apart, the warmth between Bessie and her young husband cooled. In a fight between Bessie and the Lesters over Jeeter's right to ride in the car again, Dude sided with his wife. After all, the car still ran a little.

Meanwhile Pearl ran away from Lov; she had managed to escape after he had tied her to their bed. Jeeter advised Lov not to look for Pearl, but to take Ellie May in her place. He asked Ellie May to bring back victuals and clothes from Lov's house. The grandmother, who had been run over by Bessie's Ford, died in the yard.

Jeeter anticipated seeding time by burning the broomsedge off his land. A wind blew the fire to the house while Jeeter and Ada were asleep. The destitute sharecroppers were burned to death on the land that Jeeter's family had once owned as prosperous farmers.

TOM CRINGLE'S LOG

Type of work: Novel
Author: Michael Scott (1789-1835)
Type of plot: Adventure romance
Time of plot: Nineteenth century
Locale: West Indies
First published: 1833

Principal characters:
Tom Cringle, a young midshipman
Mary Palma, his cousin and wife
Obadiah, a smuggler and pirate
Captain Transom, of the *Firebrand*

Critique:

There is almost no plot in *Tom Cringle's Log* and even little connection between episodes. Great numbers of people appear briefly in disconnected incidents and then disappear, for the novel is, as the name implies, a recital of one man's experience as an officer on various British warships during the Napoleonic wars. Although the book gives the reader some first-hand accurate accounts of minor actions in the war with Napoleon and many sidelights on the War of 1812 with America, Scott emphasizes merry bibulous exploits ashore rather than the business of fighting.

The Story:

Tom Cringle, aged thirteen and four feet four inches tall, looked upon himself as a successor to Nelson. In pursuing his aim, he pestered his relative, Sir Barnaby Blueblazes, to such lengths that at last Tom was appointed midshipman aboard the frigate *Breeze* and ordered to report for foreign duty in four days.

Poor Tom had envisioned a period of months ashore after his appointment, time to strut his uniform before all his friends. His time being so short, he hardly knew whether he wanted to go to sea after all, and his widowed mother wept and begged him not to leave. But on the appointed day Tom went aboard his ship, bound for action.

He had a trip to the Bay of Biscay on the *Breeze,* and a tour of duty on the *Kraaken.* Then, an old hand, Tom boarded the *Torch,* an eighteen-gun sloop bound for the North Sea.

Near Cuxhaven the ship's boat was lowered and Tom was put second in command of a party to enter the harbor. The captain was sure no French were near; consequently the party shoved off with light hearts. To their astonishment they were challenged by French sentries. In trying to regain the ship, Tom's boat was hit by a shell from a shore battery, and subsequently he was taken prisoner.

A resident of Hamburg went surety for Tom and took him to his own country house. The next day the Russians advanced and drove out the French. In the confusion Tom and the Hamburg family escaped and safely boarded the *Torch.*

The *Torch* stood off Cork, where Tom played the part of a spy. By a clever tale he induced a group of British seamen to rendezvous in a small tavern. There they were captured and pressed into service. Then with her full complement the *Torch* left for Caribbean waters, where Tom was to spend many years. In the West Indies the French, Spaniards, English, and Americans were all privateering, and there was much work for a British man-of-war, in escorting merchantmen, keeping a lookout for American marauders, and trying to keep slavery and smuggling within bounds.

Tom had an early introduction to the horrors of piracy the day a London merchantman was sighted behaving erratically. With great difficulty a boarding party captured the ship after subduing a pirate crew. In the main cabin of the merchantman the British found a terrifying situation. The captain had been tied on the table, his throat so savagely slashed that he was almost decapitated. Tied in a chair was a prosperous gentleman very nearly hysterical. On the sofa was the man's wife, violated by the pirates. The poor lady was mad with shame and fright and spent her last days in an asylum. The leader of the pirates, who subsequently escaped, was a tall, handsome Spaniard. Tom learned much later that his name was Francesco Cangrejo.

During a violent hurricane the *Torch* went down, and Tom, believing himself the only survivor, spent three terrible days in an open boat. At last thirst and privation overcame him. When he regained consciousness he was on shore, tended by Lieutenant Splinter, the only other crew member to escape. Captain Deadeye, of the *Torch,* was stretched out under a canvas on the beach. Scarcely had Tom recovered his senses when they were taken prisoners by a Spanish platoon. When Tom and Splinter had satisfactorily established their identity, they were freed, but they were stranded in the tiny port of Cartagena, far from the British forces.

On the beach Tom made the acquaintance of a black pilot, Peter Musgrave, who was wanted by the Admiralty for running a British ship aground. Tom agreed to act as Peter's friend at court, and in turn Peter would procure passage to Jamaica.

Peter went aboard a suspiciously decrepit small craft in the harbor and returned with the American mate of the vessel. Obadiah, the mate, took them aboard, and the black captain consented to take the Englishmen to Jamaica for a reasonable fee. As soon as they were at sea, however, some astonishing changes took place. Obadiah assumed the captaincy, and under his directions the villainous but alert crew re-rigged the worn sails and mounted guns on deck. Then the truth dawned on Tom; he was aboard a pirate ship.

Two British men-of-war bore down on the ship, but Captain Obadiah, refusing to heave to, held his course in the face of almost certain suicide. By clever seamanship the pirate craft outran its pursuers, although many of the crew were killed or wounded. Making a landfall in Cuba, the pirates put in to a small river, and after a narrow passage came to anchor in a secluded lagoon a mile in diameter. The lagoon was filled with armed craft of many types. Tom was in the secret den of the West Indian pirates.

When the *Firebrand,* an English warship, engaged a pirate felucca near the river's mouth, Tom escaped with the help of Peter. Going aboard the *Firebrand,* to which he had been assigned by dispatch, Tom took part in the capture of the whole pirate band. Obadiah, who was a renegade Englishman, as Tom learned later, was shot as he tried to swim away. For his bravery in the engagement Tom was promoted to the rank of lieutenant.

Captain Transom of the *Firebrand* proved to be a genial commander with many friends in the islands. Tom spent much time ashore indulging in high jinks. One trip ashore, however, was a somber one. Tom served as interpreter at the trial of the pirates, who were all condemned to death. One of the prisoners, Tom found, was Francesco Cangrejo, who cut a brave figure in the dock in spite of his confessed career of villainy. At the pirate's request, Tom took his miniature and crucifix to deliver to the pirate's betrothed.

In Kingston, where Tom called on his relatives, the Palmas, he was most cordially received. There he met and fell in love with Mary Palma, his cousin. When he was called away on duty, it was with the understanding that they would be married after his next promotion.

At Santiago Tom went ashore to visit Ricardo Campana, a rich merchant. There a priest who met him and Ricardo on the street seemed much upset. Tom could hear the name Cangrejo mentioned and learned that Maria, Francesco's sweetheart, was dying. The party hastened to the Cangrejo house in time for Tom to have a few words with Maria before she died. Tom was saddened when he heard of Francesco's early promise and reflected on the Spaniard's later death for piracy.

On a trip out from Santiago, Tom was ordered to take command of the small schooner *Wave.* At twenty-three, Tom Cringle, lieutenant, became master of his own ship. Sent to patrol for suspicious vessels, Tom sighted a large schooner that failed to heed his signals. After a two days' chase the *Wave* closed with the heavily-armed, larger ship. Displaying great courage at close quarters, the gallant crew of the *Wave* boarded the schooner, which proved to be a slaver. Unable to land the ship with a prize crew, Tom had the slaver shelled until it caught fire and sank. Tom rescued as many slaves as the *Wave* could carry and put them ashore.

Tom was afterward trusted with many missions, including one to Panama. Since he was always diligent in doing his duty and since he had always displayed great courage in battle, he received his second epaulet. Tom Cringle, one time midshipman, became Commander Cringle.

At dinner in Kingston, wearing his two epaulets, Tom was surprised that none of the Palmas remarked on his promotion. Mary herself was quite agitated and left the table. In his embarrassment Tom had the misfortune to drink a glass of catsup. But in spite of all his awkwardness, Tom managed to see Mary alone and win her consent to an immediate marriage.

TOM JONES

Type of work: Novel
Author: Henry Fielding (1707-1754)
Type of plot: Comic epic
Time of plot: Early eighteenth century
Locale: England
First published: 1749

Principal characters:
TOM JONES, a foundling
SQUIRE ALLWORTHY, his foster father
BRIDGET, Allworthy's sister
MASTER BLIFIL, Bridget's son
MR. PARTRIDGE, the schoolmaster
MR. WESTERN, an English squire
SOPHIA WESTERN, his daughter

Critique:

It is difficult to determine whether greater pleasure is derived from the narrative parts of *The History of Tom Jones, a Foundling,* as Fielding titled his novel, or from the essays written at the beginning of each book. The story itself is a long, involved plot in which Tom finally wins the confidence of those he loves. Most of the humor in this novel lies in Fielding's exaggerated dramatic emphasis and in his lengthy, delicate dissections of the motives of his characters. It must be remembered that Fielding had few examples of the novel form from which to learn, but his novels are so far advanced in development over their predecessors that Fielding must be recognized as a literary innovator. The author knew the follies of human nature, and he attempted to laugh mankind out of its own weaknesses.

The Story:

Squire Allworthy lived in retirement in the country with his sister Bridget. Returning from a visit to London, he was considerably surprised upon entering his room to find an infant lying on his bed. His discovery caused much astonishment and consternation in the household, for the squire himself was a childless widower. The next day Miss Bridget and the squire inquired in the community to discover the baby's mother, and their suspicions were shortly fixed upon Jenny Jones, who had spent many hours in the squire's home while nursing Miss Bridget through a long illness. The worthy squire sent for the girl and in his gentle manner reprimanded her for her wicked behavior, assuring her, however, that the baby would remain in his home under the best of care. Fearing malicious gossip of the neighborhood, Squire Allworthy sent Jenny away.

Jenny Jones had been a servant in the house of a schoolmaster named Mr. Partridge, who had educated the young woman during her four years in his house. Mrs. Partridge, because of Jenny's comely face, was jealous of her. Neighborhood gossip soon convinced Mrs. Partridge that her husband was the father of Jenny's son, whereupon Squire Allworthy called the schoolmaster before him and talked to him at great length concerning morality. Mr. Partridge, deprived of his school, his income, and his wife, also left the country.

Not long afterward Captain Blifil won the heart of Bridget Allworthy. Eight months after their nuptials Bridget bore a son. The squire thought it would be well to rear the foundling and his sister's child together. The foundling had been named Jones, after his mother.

Squire Allworthy became exceedingly fond of the foundling. Captain Blifil died during his son's infancy, and Master Blifil grew up as Squire Allworthy's acknowledged heir. Otherwise, he remained on even terms with the foundling so far as opportunities for advancement were concerned. But Tom was such a mischievous lad that he had but one friend among the servants, the gamekeeper, Black George, an indolent man with a large family. Hired to instruct the lads were Mr. Thwackum and Mr. Square, who considered Tom a wicked soul. Tom's many deceptions were always discovered through the combined efforts of Mr. Thwackum, Mr. Square, and Master Blifil, who as he grew older disliked Tom more and more. It had been assumed by all that Mrs. Blifil would dislike Tom, but at times she seemed to show greater affection for him than for her own son. In turn, the compassionate squire took Master Blifil to his heart and became censorious of Tom.

Mr. Western, who lived on a neighboring estate, had a daughter whom he loved more than anyone else in the world. Sophia had a tender fondness for Tom because of a deed of kindness he had performed for her when they were still children. At the age of twenty, Master Blifil had become a favorite with the young ladies, while Tom was considered a ruffian by all but Mr. Western, who admired his ability to hunt. Tom spent many evenings at the Western home, with every opportunity to see Sophia, for whom his affections were increasing daily. One afternoon Tom had the good fortune to be nearby when Sophia's horse ran away. Tom, in rescuing her, broke his arm. He was removed to Mr. Western's house, where he received medical care and remained to recover from his hurt. One day he and Sophia had occasion to be alone in the garden, where they exchanged confessions of love.

Squire Allworthy became mortally ill. Assuming that he was dying, the doctor sent for the squire's relatives. With his servants and family gathered around him, the squire announced the disposal of his wealth, giving generously to Tom. Tom was the only one satisfied with his portion; his only concern was the impending death of his foster father and benefactor. On the way home from London to see the squire, Mrs. Blifil died suddenly. When the squire was pronounced out of danger, Tom's joy was so great that he became drunk through toasting the squire's health, and quarreled with young Blifil.

Sophia's aunt, Mrs. Western, perceived the interest her niece showed in Blifil, for Sophia, wishing to conceal her affection for Tom, gave Blifil the greater part of her attention when she was with the two young men. Informed by his sister of Sophia's conduct, Mr. Western suggested to Squire Allworthy that a match be arranged between Blifil and Sophia. When Mrs. Western told the young girl of the proposed match, Sophia thought that she meant Tom, and she immediately disclosed her passion for the foundling. But it was unthinkable that Mr. Western, much as he liked Tom, would ever allow his daughter to marry a man without a family and a fortune, and Mrs. Western forced Sophia to receive Blifil under the threat of exposing the girl's real affection for Tom. Sophia met Tom secretly in the garden and the two lovers vowed constancy. Discovering them, Mr. Western went immediately to Squire Allworthy with his knowledge.

Blifil, aware of his advantage, told the squire that on the day he lay near death

Tom was out drinking and singing. The squire felt that he had forgiven Tom any wrongs, but his show of unconcern for the squire's health infuriated the good man. He sent for Tom, reproached him, and banished him from his house.

With the help of Black George, the gamekeeper, and Mrs. Honour, Sophia's maid, Tom and Sophia were able to exchange love letters. When Sophia was confined to her room because she refused to marry Blifil, she bribed her maid to flee with her from her father's house. Tom, setting out to seek his fortune, went to an inn with a small company of soldiers. A fight followed in which he was severely injured, and a barber was summoned to treat his wound. When Tom had told the barber his story, the man surprisingly revealed himself to be Partridge, the schoolmaster, banished years before because he was suspected of being Tom's father. When Tom was well enough to travel, the two men set out together on foot.

Before they had gone far they heard screams of a woman in distress and came upon a woman struggling with a soldier who had beguiled her to that lonely spot. Promising to take her to a place of safety, Tom accompanied the unfortunate creature to the nearby village of Upton, where the landlady of the inn refused to receive them because of the woman's torn and disheveled clothing. But when she heard the true story of the woman's misfortune and had been assured that the woman was the lady of Captain Waters, a well-known officer, she relented. Mrs. Waters invited Tom to dine with her so that she could thank him properly for her rescue.

Meanwhile a lady and her maid arrived at the inn and proceeded to their rooms. They were followed, several hours later, by an angry gentleman in pursuit of his wife. Learning from the chambermaid that there was a woman resembling his wife in the inn, he burst into Mrs. Waters' chambers, only to confront Tom Jones. At his intrusion, Mrs. Waters began to scream. The gentleman, abashed, identified himself as Mr. Fitzpatrick and retreated with apologies. Shortly after this disturbance had subsided, Sophia and Mrs. Honour arrived at the inn. When Partridge unknowingly revealed Tom's relation with Mrs. Waters and the embarrassing situation which Mr. Fitzpatrick had disclosed, Sophia, grieved by Tom's fickleness, decided to continue on her way. Before leaving the inn, however, she had Mrs. Honour place on Tom's empty bed a muff which she knew he would recognize as hers.

Soon after setting out, Sophia overtook Mrs. Fitzpatrick, who had arrived at the inn early the previous evening and who had fled during the disturbance caused by her husband. Mrs. Fitzpatrick was Sophia's cousin, and they decided to go on to London together. In London Sophia proceeded to the home of Lady Bellaston, who was known to her through Mrs. Western. Lady Bellaston was sympathetic with Sophia's reasons for running away.

Unable to overtake Sophia, Tom and Partridge followed her to London, where Tom took lodgings in the home of Mrs. Miller, whom Squire Allworthy patronized on his visits to the city. The landlady had two daughters, Nancy and Betty, and a lodger, Mr. Nightingale, who was obviously in love with Nancy. Tom found congenial residence with Mrs. Miller, and he became friends with Mr. Nightingale. Partridge was still with Tom in the hope of future advancement for himself. Repeated visits to Lady Bellaston and Mrs. Fitzpatrick finally gave Tom the opportunity to meet Sophia during an intermission at a play. There Tom was able to allay Sophia's doubts as to his love for her. During his stay with the Millers, Tom learned that Mr. Nightingale's father objected to his marrying Nancy. Through the kindness of his heart Tom persuaded the elder Nightingale to permit the marriage, to Mrs. Miller's great delight.

Having learned Sophia's whereabouts from Mrs. Fitzpatrick, Mr. Western came to London and took Sophia from Lady Bellaston's house to his own lodgings. When Mrs. Honour brought the news to Tom, he was in despair. Penniless, he could not hope to marry Sophia, and now his beloved was in the hands of her father once more. Then Partridge brought news that Squire Allworthy was coming to London, bringing with him Master Blifil to marry Sophia. In his distress Tom went to see Mrs. Fitzpatrick, but encountered her jealous husband on her doorstep. In the duel which followed, Tom wounded Fitzpatrick and was carried off to jail.

There he was visited by Partridge, the friends he had made in London, and Mrs. Waters, who had been traveling with Mr. Fitzpatrick ever since their meeting in Upton. When Partridge and Mrs. Waters met in Tom's cell, Partridge recognized her as Jenny Jones, Tom's reputed mother. Horrified, he revealed his knowledge to everyone, including Squire Allworthy, who by that time had arrived in London with Blifil.

In Mrs. Miller's lodgings so many people had praised Tom's goodness and kindness that Squire Allworthy had almost made up his mind to relent in his attitude toward the foundling when news of his conduct with Mrs. Waters reached his ears. But fortunately the cloud was soon dispelled by Mrs. Waters herself, who assured the squire that Tom was no son of hers but the child of his sister Bridget and a student the squire had befriended. Tom's true father having died before his son's birth, Bridget had concealed her shame by putting the baby on her brother's bed upon his return from a long visit to London. Later she had paid Jenny liberally to let suspicion fall upon her former maid.

Squire Allworthy also learned that Bridget had claimed Tom as her son in a letter written before her death, a letter Master Blifil had destroyed. There was further proof that Blifil had plotted to have Tom hanged for murder, although Fitzpatrick had not died. That gentleman recovered sufficiently to acknowledge himself the aggressor in the duel, and Tom was released from prison.

Upon these disclosures of Blifil's villainy, Squire Allworthy dismissed Blifil and made Tom his true heir. Tom's proper station having been revealed, Mr. Western withdrew all objections to his suit. Reunited, Tom and Sophia were married and retired to Mr. Western's estate in the country.

TOM SAWYER

Type of work: Novel
Author: Mark Twain (Samuel L. Clemens, 1835-1910)
Type of plot: Adventure romance
Time of plot: Nineteenth century
Locale: St. Petersburg on the Mississippi River
First published: 1876

Principal characters:
TOM SAWYER
AUNT POLLY, Tom's aunt
HUCKLEBERRY FINN, and
JOE HARPER, Tom's friends
BECKY THATCHER, Tom's girl
INJUN JOE, a murderer
MUFF POTTER, a village ne'er-do-well

Critique:

Rich native humor and shrewd observation of human character make *The Adventures of Tom Sawyer* one of the greatest boys' books ever written. More

TOM SAWYER by Mark Twain. Published by Harper & Brothers.

than a book for boys, it is an idyl of America's golden age, of that pastoral time and scene which had already vanished when Mark Twain re-created St. Petersburg from memories of his own boyhood. Of a lesser greatness and different in purpose from *The Adventures of Huckleberry Finn,* the story of Tom Sawyer's adventures is true to both the fantasies of boyhood and adult nostalgia. Tom's pirate gang, cures for warts, the white-washing of the fence, Jackson's island, Becky Thatcher, Injun Joe, and Huck Finn — American literature would be poorer without them.

The Story:

Tom Sawyer lived securely with the knowledge that his Aunt Polly loved him dearly. When she scolded him or whipped him, he knew that inside her breast lurked a hidden remorse. Often he deserved the punishment he received, but there were times when he was the victim of his tale-bearing half-brother, Sid. Tom's cousin, Mary, was kinder to him. Her worst duty toward him was to see to it that he washed and put on clean clothes, so that he would look respectable when Aunt Polly took Tom, Sid, and Mary to church on Sunday.

A new family had moved into the neighborhood. Investigating Tom saw a pretty, blue-eyed girl with lacy pantalets. She was Becky Thatcher. Instantly the fervent love he had felt for Amy Lawrence fled from his faithless bosom, to be replaced by devotion to the new girl he had just beheld.

She was in school the next day, sitting on the girls' side of the room with an empty seat beside her. Tom had come late to school that morning. When the schoolmaster asked Tom why he had been late, that empty seat beside Becky Thatcher caught Tom's eye. Recklessly he confessed he had stopped to talk with Huckleberry Finn, son of the town drunk. Huck wore castoff clothing, never attended school, smoked and fished as often as he pleased, and slept wherever he could. For associating with Huck, Tom was whipped by the schoolmaster and ordered to sit on the girls' side of the room. Amid the snickers of the entire class, he took the empty seat next to Becky.

Tom first attracted Becky's attention by a series of drawings on his slate. At length he wrote the words, "I love you," and Becky blushed. Tom urged her to meet him after school. Sitting with her on a fence, he explained to her the possibilities of an engagement between them. Innocently she accepted his proposal, which Tom insisted must be sealed by a kiss. In coy resistance she allowed Tom a brief chase before she yielded to his embrace. Tom's happiness was unbounded. But when he mentioned his previous tie with Amy Lawrence, the brief romance ended. Becky left her affianced with a haughty shrug of her pretty shoulders.

That night Tom heard Huck's whistle below his bedroom window. Sneaking out, Tom joined his friend, and the two went off to the cemetery, Huck dragging a dead cat behind him. They were about to try a new method for curing warts. The gloomy atmosphere of the burial ground filled the boys with apprehension, and their fears increased still more when they spied three figures stealing into the graveyard. They were Injun Joe, Muff Potter, and Doctor Robinson. Evidently they had come to rob a grave. When the two robbers had exhumed the body, they began to quarrel with the doctor about money, and in the quarrel Potter was knocked out. Then Injun Joe took Potter's knife and killed the doctor. When Potter recovered from his blow, he thought he had killed Robinson, and Injun Joe allowed the poor old man to believe himself guilty.

Terrified, Tom and Huck slipped away from the scene they had just witnessed, afraid that if Injun Joe discovered them he would kill them too.

Tom brooded on what he and Huck had seen. Convinced that he was ill,

Aunt Polly dosed him with Pain Killer and kept him in bed, but he did not seem to recover. Becky Thatcher had not come to school since she had broken Tom's heart. Rumor around town said that she was also ill. Coupled with this sad news was the fear of Injun Joe. When Becky finally returned to school, she cut Tom coldly. Feeling that there was nothing else for him to do, he decided to run away. He met Joe Harper and Huck Finn. Together they went to Jackson's Island and pretended to be pirates.

For a few days they stayed happily on the island and learned from Huck how to smoke and swear. One day they heard a boat on the river, firing cannon over the water. Then the boys realized that the townspeople were searching for their bodies. This discovery put a new aspect on their adventure; the people at home thought they were dead. Gleeful, Tom could not resist the temptation to see how Aunt Polly had reacted to his death. He slipped back to the mainland one night and into his aunt's house, where Mrs. Harper and Aunt Polly were mourning the death of their mischievous but good-hearted children. When Tom returned to the island, he found Joe and Huck tired of their game and ready to go home. Tom revealed to them an attractive plan which they immediately decided to carry out.

With a heavy gloom overhanging the town, funeral services were held for the deceased Thomas Sawyer, Joseph Harper, and Huckleberry Finn. The minister pronounced a lengthy eulogy about the respective good characters of the unfortunate boys. When the funeral procession was about to start, Tom, Joe, and Huck marched down the aisle of the church into the arms of the startled mourners.

For a while Tom was the hero of all the boys in the town. They whispered about him and eyed him with awe in the schoolyard. But Becky ignored him until the day she accidentally tore the schoolmaster's book. When the irate teacher demanded to know who had torn his book, Tom confessed. Becky's gratitude and forgiveness were his reward.

After Muff Potter had been put in jail for the murder of the doctor in the graveyard, Tom and Huck had sworn to each other they would never utter a word about what they had seen. Afraid Injun Joe would murder them for revenge, they furtively sneaked behind the prison and brought Muff food and other cheer. But Tom could not let an innocent man be condemned. At the trial he appeared to tell what he had seen on the night of the murder. While Tom spoke, Injun Joe, a witness at the trial, sprang from the window of the courtroom and escaped. For days Tom worried, convinced that Injun Joe would come back to murder him. But as time went by and nothing happened, he gradually lost his fears. With Becky looking upon him as a hero, his world was filled with sunshine.

Huck and Tom decided to hunt for pirates' treasures. One night, ransacking an old abandoned house, they watched, unseen, while Injun Joe and a companion unearthed a chest of money buried under the floorboards of the house. The two frightened boys fled before they were discovered. The next day they began a steady watch for Injun Joe and his accomplice, for Tom and Huck were bent on finding the lost treasure.

When Judge Thatcher gave a picnic for all the young people in town, Becky and Tom were supposed to spend the night with Mrs. Harper. One of the biggest excitements of the merrymaking came when the children went into a cave in the riverbank. The next day Mrs. Thatcher and Aunt Polly learned that Tom and Becky were missing, for Mrs. Harper said they had not come to spend the night with her. Then everyone remembered that Tom and Becky had not been seen since the picnickers had left the cave. Meanwhile the two, having lost their bearings, were wandering in the cavern. To add to Tom's terror, he discovered that Injun Joe was also in the cave. Miraculously, after spending five days in the dismal cave, Tom found an exit that was five miles from the place where they had entered. Again he was a hero.

Injun Joe starved to death in the cave. After searchers had located his body, Tom and Huck went back into the cavern to look for the chest which they believed Injun Joe had hidden there. They found it and the twelve thousand dollars it contained.

Adopted shortly afterward by the Widow Douglas, Huck planned to retire with an income of a dollar a day for the rest of his life. He never would have stayed with the widow or consented to learn her prim, tidy ways if Tom had not promised that he would form a pirates' gang and make Huck one of the bold buccaneers.

TONO-BUNGAY

Type of work: Novel
Author: H. G. Wells (1866-1946)
Type of plot: Social criticism
Time of plot: Late nineteenth and early twentieth centuries
Locale: England, West Africa, Bordeaux
First published: 1908

Principal characters:
George Ponderevo, a young scientist and the narrator
The Honorable Beatrice Normandy, an aristocrat
Edward Ponderevo, George's uncle
Susan Ponderevo, George's aunt
Marion Ramboat, George's wife

Critique:

Tono-Bungay is a spirited novel, interesting from several points of view. The references to early stages of aviation have a quaint charm for the modern reader, and the use of science as a motive of fiction throws light upon the intellectual development of the period. The manufacture and sale of patent medicine becomes a symbol of disintegrating society. Frequently unconvincing, the novel is still good reading, if only for the Dickensian characters it presents. Wells' critical views are always relieved by humor and a shrewd analysis of human motives.

The Story:

George Ponderevo grew up in the shadow of Bladesover House, where his mother was the housekeeper. In that Edwardian atmosphere the boy soon became aware of the wide distinctions between English social classes, each according to their station and degree, for the neighborhood around Bladesover was England in miniature, a small world made up of the quality, the church, the village, the laborers, and the servants. Although George spent most of his time away at school, he returned to Bladesover for his vacations. During one of his vacations he learned for the first time the class he himself represented—the servants.

His lesson came as the result of the arrival at Bladesover House of the Honorable Beatrice Normandy, a child of eight, and her snobbish young half-brother, Archie Garvell. Twelve-year-old George Ponderevo fell in love with the little aristocrat that summer. Two years later their childish romance ended abruptly when George and Archie fought each other. George was disillusioned because the Honorable Beatrice did not come to his aid. In fact, she betrayed him, abandoned him, and lied about him, picturing George as an assailant of his social betters.

When George refused flatly to apologize to Archie Garvell, he was taken to Chatham and put to work in the bakery of his mother's brother, Nicodemus Frapp. George found his uncle's family dull, cloddish, and over-religious. One night, in the room he shared with his two cousins, he told them in confidence that he did not believe in any form of revealed religion. Traitorously, his cousins reported George's blasphemy to their father. As a result, George was called upon in a church meeting to acknowledge his sins. Humiliated and angry, he ran away to his mother at Bladesover House.

Mrs. Ponderevo then took him to live with another uncle, his father's brother, Edward Ponderevo, at Wimblehurst, in Sussex. There George worked in his uncle's chemist shop out of school hours. Edward Ponderevo was a restless, dissatisfied man who wanted to expand, to make money. Aunt Susan Ponderevo was a gentle, patient woman who treated George kindly. His mother died during his years at Wimblehurst.

But George's pleasant life at Wimblehurst was brought suddenly to an end. By foolish investments Edward Ponderevo lost everything of his own, including the chemist shop and also the small fund he was holding in trust for George. The Ponderevos were forced to leave Wimblehurst, but George remained behind as an apprentice with Mr. Mantell, the new owner of the shop.

At the age of nineteen George went up to London to matriculate at the University of London for his Bachelor of Science degree. On the trip his uncle, now living in London, showed him the city and first whispered to him the name of Tono-Bungay, an invention on which the older Ponderevo was working.

When George finally arrived in London to begin his studies he was nearly twenty-two, and in the meantime he had decided to accept a scholarship at the Consolidated Technical Schools at South Kensington instead of the one offered at the university. One day he met an old schoolfellow, Ewart, an artist who exerted a broadening influence on the young man. He also met Marion Ramboat, the girl who was later to become his wife. Because of these influences, George began to neglect his studies. When he saw a billboard which advertised Tono-Bungay, he remembered the hints his uncle had thrown out several years before. A few days later his uncle sent George a telegram in which he offered the young man a job at three hundred pounds a year.

Tono-Bungay was a patent medicine, a stimulant most inexpensive to make and only slightly injurious to the person who took it. After a week of indecision, George joined the firm. One factor that helped to sway him was the thought that Marion Ramboat might be persuaded to marry him if his income were greater. Using new and bold methods of advertising, George and his exuberant uncle made Tono-Bungay a national product. The enterprise was highly successful; both George and his uncle became wealthy. At last Marion consented to marry George but their marriage was unsuccessful. They were divorced when Marion learned that her husband had gone off for the weekend with Effie Rink, one of the secretaries in his office. After his divorce George devoted himself to science and research. He became interested in flying.

Edward Ponderevo, in the meantime, branched out into many enterprises, partly through the influence of the wealthy Mr. Moggs, with whom he became associated. His huge corporation, Domestic Utilities, became known as Do-Ut, and his steady advancement in wealth could be traced by the homes in which he lived. The first was the elaborate suite of rooms at the Hardingham Hotel. Next came a gaunt villa at Beckenham; next, an elaborate estate at Chiselhurst, followed by the chaste simplicity of a medieval castle, Lady Grove, and finally the ambitious but uncompleted splendor of the great house at Crest Hill, on which three hundred workmen were at one time employed. While his uncle was buying houses, George was absorbed in his experiments with gliders and balloons, working in his special workshop with Cothope, his assistant. The Honorable Beatrice Normandy was staying near Lady Grove with Lady Osprey, her stepmother. She and George became acquainted again and after a glider accident she nursed him back to health. Although the two fell in love, Beatrice refused to marry him.

Suddenly all of Edward Ponderevo's world of top-heavy speculation collapsed. On the verge of bankruptcy, he clutched at anything to save himself from financial ruin and the loss of his great, uncompleted project at Crest Hill.

George did his part by undertaking a voyage to Mordet Island in the brig *Maude Mary,* to secure by trickery a cargo of quap, an ore containing two new elements valuable to the Ponderevos largely because they hoped to use canadium—one of the ingredients—for making a new and better lamp filament. The long, difficult voyage to West Africa was unpleasant and unsuccessful. After the quap had been stolen and loaded on the ship, the properties of the ore were such that the ship sank in mid-ocean. Rescued by the *Portland Castle,* George learned of his uncle's bankruptcy as soon as he came ashore at Plymouth.

To avoid arrest, George and his uncle decided to cross the channel at night in George's airship, and escape the law by posing as tourists in France. The stratagem proved successful, and they landed about fifty miles from Bordeaux. Then Uncle Ponderevo became dangerously ill at a small inn near Bayonne, and a few days later he died, before his wife could reach his side. Back in England, George had a twelve-day love affair with Beatrice Normandy, who still refused to marry him because she said she was spoiled by the love of luxury and the false pride of her class.

George Ponderevo, by that time a severe critic of degeneration in England, became a designer of destroyers.

THE TOWER OF LONDON

Type of work: Novel
Author: William Harrison Ainsworth (1805-1882)
Type of plot: Historical romance
Time of plot: Sixteenth century
Locale: England
First published: 1840

Principal characters:
DUKE OF NORTHUMBERLAND
GUILFORD DUDLEY, Northumberland's son
LADY JANE GREY, Dudley's wife
CUTHBERT CHOLMONDELEY, Dudley's squire
CICELY, in love with Cuthbert
LAWRENCE NIGHTGALL, the jailer
SIMON RENARD, Spanish ambassador
QUEEN MARY
PRINCESS ELIZABETH, Mary's sister
EDWARD COURTENAY, Earl of Devonshire

Critique:

Fictionalized history holds a twofold interest for the reader. First it tells a romantic story; secondly it tells a partly true story. *The Tower of London* brings one more factor to the reader, a lively description of one of the most famous structures in England. The story proper is concerned with Queen Mary's troubled reign, one of the least understood by students of history and literature.

The Story:

At the death of King Edward the Sixth, there were several claimants to the English throne, among them Mary, Elizabeth's older sister, and Lady Jane Grey, wife of Lord Guilford Dudley, who was supported by her father-in-law, the Duke of Northumberland. According to custom, Lady Jane was brought to the Tower of London for her coronation. There the supporters of Mary, while pretending to be in accord with Northumberland, waited to betray Lady Jane.

Among those present was Cuthbert Cholmondeley, Dudley's squire, who having seen a beautiful young girl in the Tower, had fallen in love with her. From inquiries among his servants, Cuthbert learned that she was the adopted daughter of Peter the pantler and Dame Potentia Trusbut, the true circumstances of Cicely's birth being unknown. The chief jailer of the Tower, Lawrence Nightgall, also loved Cicely. When Simon Renard, the Spanish ambassador, and Lord Pembroke, Mary's supporters, conspired to assassinate Cuthbert because they knew him to be Dudley's favorite, Nightgall eagerly agreed to help them.

Nightgall told Cicely that her new lover had been taken from the Tower and that she would never see him again. Meanwhile, a prisoner in a dungeon below the Tower, Cuthbert was accosted by a strange woman who cried out that she wanted her child to be returned to her. When Nightgall visited Cuthbert, the prisoner asked his jailer about the woman, but Nightgall evaded the question by stating that the woman was mad.

An old woman, Gunnora Broase, had at Northumberland's command administered a dose of poison to the late boy-king, Edward the Sixth. She was directed by a strange man to reveal Northumberland's part in the murder and thus to defeat his intention to place Lady Jane on the throne of England.

Simon Renard and Lord Pembroke had effected a rupture between Lady Jane and Northumberland by convincing Lady Jane that she should not consent to make Dudley a king. Northumberland desired this distinction for his son, but Lady Jane believed that making her husband a king would cause too much dissention in the kingdom. In anger at this slight from his wife, Dudley left the Tower. Surrounded by intrigue, Lady Jane was convinced that Renard and Lord Pembroke were her friends and that Northumberland was her enemy. Lord Pembroke next persuaded Lady Jane to send Northumberland against Mary's forces, which were reported advancing on London. With Northumberland separated from Lady Jane, Lord Pembroke and Renard were certain that they could destroy her rule. Lady Jane was easily persuaded because she did not suspect the treachery of her two advisers.

Cuthbert Cholmondeley escaped from his dungeon. Dudley returned to his wife and his queen in time to convince her of the treachery of Lord Pembroke and Renard, whom Lady Jane ordered imprisoned. Cicely came to Dudley and Lady Jane with the tale of what had happened to Cholmondeley. Soon after the imprisonment of Lord Pembroke and Renard, Nightgall helped them to escape from the Tower. Meanwhile Lady Jane had made Cicely a lady-in-waiting.

Gunnora Broase came to Lady Jane for an audience. The old woman declared that Northumberland had poisoned Edward and that his purpose in marrying his son to Lady Jane was to elevate Dudley to the throne, after which Lady Jane was to be poisoned. Meanwhile Cuthbert had found his way from the lower dungeons and he and Cicely were reunited. He was present when the Duke of Suffolk, Lady Jane's father, urged her to save her head by abdicating. Dudley, however, persuaded his wife not to surrender the crown. Mary was proclaimed queen, and Lady Jane was placed in prison with Cicelv and Cuthbert. Dudley was separately confined. Gunnora Broase sneaked into Lady Jane's cell and secreted her from the prison with the promise that Dudley would follow shortly. But when Northumberland disbanded his forces and acknowledged Mary as queen, Lady Jane surrendered herself and returned to her cell in the Tower.

The people acclaimed Mary when she entered London. The new queen's first act was to release all Catholic prisoners and replace them with her former enemies. When Northumberland was arrested and condemned to the scaffold, he pleaded for mercy for Lady Jane because he had been the chief proponent of her pretension to the throne. Although the duke publicly embraced Catholicism in the mistaken belief that his life would be spared, he was executed by Mary's order.

Mary put pressure upon Lady Jane and Dudley to embrace Catholicism as Northumberland had done in order to save their heads, but Lady Jane was determined to die a Protestant.

Released from custody, Cuthbert returned to Dame Trusbut seeking Cicely, but she was nowhere to be found. Cuthbert did find the strange madwoman again. She was lying in a cell, dead.

Among the prisoners Mary had released from the Tower was Edward Courtenay, the Earl of Devonshire. The young nobleman was really in love with Elizabeth, although, covetous of Mary's throne, he pretended to love Mary. Without scruple, he was able to win Mary's promise that she would make him her husband. Renard, however, lurked menacingly in the background. When Courtenay went to Elizabeth with one last appeal of love, Mary and Renard were listening behind a curtain and overheard the conversation. In anger Mary committed Courtenay to the Tower and confined Elizabeth to her room. Then, on Renard's advice, Mary affianced herself to Philip, King of Spain. Later Mary's counselors persuaded her to release Elizabeth.

Moved by compassion for the innocent Lady Jane, Mary issued a pardon for the pretender and her husband. The couple retired to the home of Lady Jane's father, where Dudley began to organize a new plot to place his wife on the throne. Seeing that Dudley was fixed in his design, Lady Jane, faithful to her husband, consented to follow him in whatever he did. Another revolt was led by Sir Thomas Wyat, a fervent anti-Catholic, supported by those who opposed an alliance between England and Spain. The rebellion was quelled, and Wyat and Dudley were captured. Lady Jane and Cuthbert surrendered themselves to Mary, Lady Jane to plead for the life of her husband in exchange for her surrender. The only condition on which Mary would grant Dudley's life was that Lady Jane should embrace Catholicism. When she refused, she was sentenced to death along with Dudley. Elizabeth was brought to the Tower, Mary planning to do away with Courtenay and her sister after she had completed the destruction of Lady Jane and Dudley.

Nightgall, still suffering from jealousy over Cicely's love for Cuthbert, had held the girl in prison since the fall of Lady Jane. Meanwhile Nightgall had been hired by the French ambassador to assassinate Renard. Renard and Nightgall met in Cuthbert's cell after the squire had been tortured, and in the ensuing fight Cuthbert escaped and ran to find Cicely. Renard succeeded in killing Nightgall, who lived long enough to prove Cicely's noble birth. She was the daughter of the unfortunate madwoman, Lady Grace Mountjoy. Before her execution, Lady Jane requested that Cicely and Cuthbert be allowed to marry. Mary, with strange generosity, pardoned them and granted their freedom.

At the scene of her execution, even the enemies of Lady Jane shuddered at the sight of so good and fair a woman about to die. On the block she reaffirmed her Christian faith as the ax descended upon one of the most ill-fated of English monarchs.

THE TRAVELS OF MARCO POLO

Type of work: Record of travel
Author: Marco Polo (1254-1324), as set down by the scribe, Rustigielo
Type of plot: Adventure romance
Time of plot: 1260-1295
Locale: Greater Asia
First transcribed: Fourteenth-century manuscript

Principal characters:
Nicolo Polo, a Venetian merchant
Maffeo Polo, his brother
Marco Polo, Nicolo's son
Kublai Khan, Emperor of China

Critique:

The story of Marco Polo's Asiatic journey is the most astounding of all travel books of Western civilization. One reason for its popularity is that Marco Polo did not mind mixing some real facts with his fiction. Another is that he possessed in high degree a quality few travelers have ever had; he was able to see more objectively than the many who have described lands visited only in terms of their home countries. His book is the record of a merchant-gentleman who sets forth his own observations and at the same time reveals the medieval viewpoint — its interest in alchemy and enchantments, its concern with mystery, and its sound, logical way of thinking beneath the surface superstition and credulity of the age.

The Story:

Marco Polo's father and uncle set forth on their first trip East in 1260, with a cargo of merchandise for Constantinople. From there Nicolo and Maffeo Polo ventured on into the lands of the Tartar princes. Having at last reached the court of Kublai Khan, they managed to ingratiate themselves into his highest favor. During their stay the khan questioned them about the Catholic faith and asked them to return to Europe and to request the Pope to send missionaries to his distant land. In the year 1269, the two Polos arrived in Venice, to learn that Pope Clement was dead and that Nicolo Polo's wife had also died after giving birth to a son, Marco Polo.

There was a long delay in the naming of a new Pope. At last the Polos decided to return to Kublai Khan and to take young Marco with them. Scarcely had they left Italy, however, when word followed them that Gregory the Tenth had been elected in Rome. The Polos at once asked the new Pope to send missionaries to Kublai Khan, and Gregory appointed two priests to accompany the merchants. Before their arrival at the khan's court, the priests turned back when confronted by strange lands and unknown dangers. Young Marco Polo remembered that the journey to the land of Kublai Khan took three and a half years.

Kublai Khan received them graciously and appointed Marco one of his attendants. In a short time Marco Polo had learned four different languages and he was sent by Kublai Khan on various important missions.

For seventeen years the Polos remained at the court of Kublai Khan before they finally expressed a desire to return to their own country with their wealth. They felt that if the great khan should die they would be surrounded by envious princes who might harm them. The khan was unwilling to part with the Polos, but they managed to get his permission by offering to transport some barons to the East Indies. Fourteen ships were made ready for the homeward voyage. The expedition arrived at Java after about three months. Eighteen months more were required for the voyage to the territory

THE TRAVELS OF MARCO POLO by Marco Polo. Published by Doubleday & Co., Inc.

of King Argon in the Indian seas. During the voyage six hundred of the crew were lost as well as two of the barons. From there the Polos took an overland route to Trebizond. En route they learned that the great Kublai Khan was dead. The three arrived home safely in 1295, in possession of their wealth and in good health.

When the time came for him to dictate to the scribe, Rustigielo, the story of his travels, Marco Polo remembered that Armenia was divided into two sections, the lesser and the greater. In Armenia Major was the mountain said to have been Mount Ararat, where Noah's ark came to rest. Near this place was a fountain of oil so great that caravans of camels hauled away the oil, which was used for an unguent as well as for heat and light.

At the boundaries of the province of Georgiania, Alexander the Great had caused a gate of iron to be constructed. This gate, though not all of iron, was commonly said to have enclosed the Tartars between two mountains.

At Teflis was a fountain wherein hundreds of fish made their appearance from the first day of Lent until Easter Eve. During the remainder of the year they were not to be seen.

Baudas, or Baghdad, anciently known as Babylon, lay along the river that opened out upon the Sea of India. The city was one of the great cities of the world, and its ruler one of the richest men of all time. He lost his life through his unwillingness to spend a penny of his wealth for its protection. His captor locked him up in his tower where he starved to death surrounded by gold. In that region also a Christian cobbler had caused a mountain to move and by his miracle converted many Arabs to Christianity.

In Irak Marco Polo visited a monastery in which the monks wove woolen girdles said to be good for rheumatic pains. He also visited Saba, from whence were said to have come the three Magi who adored Christ in Bethlehem. At Kierman, on the eastern confines of Persia, Marco saw the manufacture of steel and products in which steel was used. Much rich embroidery was also found there as well as splendid turquoises. The Karaunas of the region had learned the diabolical art of producing darkness in order to obscure their approach to caravans they intended to rob.

At Ormus he encountered a land-wind so hot that people exposed to it died. A whole army was once wiped out by the wind and the inhabitants, seeking to bury the invaders, found the bodies baked so hard that they could not be moved. Bitter, undrinkable water, the tree of the sun, and the old man of the mountain were all of that region. The old man of the mountain used to administer drugs to young men to make them think they were truly in Paradise. At his orders they assassinated any one not of the true faith. His followers held their own lives of little worth, convinced that they would return to Paradise upon their deaths.

On the overland route to Cathay, Marco met Nestorian Christians as well as people who were part Christian and part Mohammedan. There too he found a miraculous pillar said to remain upright without any visible means of support. In Peyn he discovered chalcedony and jasper and also peculiar marriage customs. Passing over a desert, he heard the strange sounds attributed to evil spirits but since explained as the sounds of shifting sand dunes. At Kamul he discovered the primitive hospitality of turning over houses and wives for the entertainment of strangers. At Chinchitalas he discovered the use of material which would not burn; it was asbestos.

On the borders of the Gobi the Polos gathered supplies for their trip through the desert. They passed close to the land of Prester John and heard the history of the war between Prester John and Genghis Khan. He saw the land of Tenduk, governed by the princes of the race of Prester John.

Kublai Khan was a great king who had rewarded generously those who had aided him in the conquest of other nations. Each noble so favored received a golden tablet inscribed by the khan for the protection of its wearer. Kublai Khan had four principal wives, plus a number of women who were given to him each year. He had some fifty sons, all of whom were appointed to high places in the empire. In the winter the khan lived in Peking, in a magnificent palace that was eight miles square. His personal bodyguard consisted of twelve thousand horsemen.

Greatest in interest among his people were the Tibetans, who produced the scent of musk, used salt for money, and dressed in clothes of leather. Gold dust was found in their rivers and among their inhabitants were many said to be sorcerers. Karazan was known for its huge serpents, or crocodiles, which the natives killed for hides and gall. This gall was a medicine for bites from mad dogs.

In Kardandan, Marco observed fathers who took over the nursing of babies. In the city of Mien he saw two towers, one of silver and one of gold. Bengal he found rich in cotton, spikenard, galangal, ginger, sugar, and many drugs. The region also supplied many eunuchs.

For a time Marco Polo held the government of the city of Yan-Gui upon orders of the khan. Nicolo and Maffeo Polo aided the khan in overcoming the city of Sa-Yan-Fu, the two Venetians having designed a catapult capable of hurling stones weighing as much as three hundred pounds.

Marco thought the city of Kin-sai, or Hang-chau, so beautiful that the inhabitants might imagine themselves in Paradise. There were twelve thousand bridges over the canals and rivers of the city, and the houses were well-built and adorned with carved ornaments. The streets were paved with stone and brick. The people were greatly concerned with astrology. Moreover, the inhabitants had provided for fire fighters who kept a constant guard throughout the city. From it the khan received revenue of gold, salt, and sugar.

In the kingdom of Kon-cha, Marco found people who ate human flesh. He also found there a kind of chicken covered with black hair instead of feathers. He observed with much interest the manufacture of Chinese porcelain.

In his travels he saw the merchant ships of India, which were large and built in sections so that if one section sprang a leak, it could be closed off while repairs were made. On the island of Java he obtained pepper, nutmegs, spikenard, galangal, cubebs, cloves, and gold. Idolators lived there as well as cannibals. Elephants, rhinoceroses, monkeys, and vultures were in abundance. He also discovered the practice of the natives which was to pickle certain monkeys so that they resembled dead pygmies. These creatures were then sold as souvenirs to sailors and merchants.

In Lambri he saw what he thought were men with tails. He also saw the sago tree from which the natives made flour. On the island of Nocueran he visited people living like naked beasts in trees. They possessed the red and white sandal wood, coconuts, sapanwood, and cloves. At Angaman he saw more cannibals. In Ceylon he found rubies, sapphires, topazes, amethysts, and garnets. The grave of Adam was believed to be on a high mountain in Ceylon.

Marco thought India the noblest and richest country in the world. Pearls were found in abundance. The kingdom of Murphili was rich in diamonds. In the province of Lac he heard that people often lived to the age of one hundred and fifty years and managed to preserve their teeth by a certain vegetable they chewed. In Kael he found people chewing a leaf called tembul, sometimes mixed with camphor and other aromatic drugs as well as quicklime. At Cape Comorin he found apes of such a size as to appear like men. At Malabar he found gold brocades, silk, gauzes, gold, and silver. At Guzzerat he discovered pirates of the worst character. In Bombay he bought incense and horses.

Marco visited the island of Madagascar, where the inhabitants reported a bird so large it was able to seize an elephant in its talons. He thought the women of Zanzibar the ugliest in the world. The people did business in elephant teeth and tusks.

Marco recalled how Kublai Khan and his nephew, Kaidu, fought many battles for the possession of Great Turkey. Over a hundred thousand horsemen were brought to fight for each side. At first Kaidu was victorious. Kaidu had a mannish daughter, Aigiarm, who battled with any man who wanted her for a bride. At last she seized the man of her choice from the hosts of enemies in battle.

Marco believed that Russia was a region too cold to be pleasant. He spoke of trade in ermine, arcolini, sable, marten, fox, silver, and wax among the natives, who were included in the nation of the king of the Western Tartars.

Marco Polo gave thanks to God that the travelers were able to see so much and return to tell about the marvels of many lands.

TRAVELS WITH A DONKEY

Type of work: Record of travel
Author: Robert Louis Stevenson (1850-1894)
Type of plot: Sketches and impressions
Time of plot: 1878
Locale: The Cévennes, French Highlands
First published: 1879

Principal characters:

ROBERT LOUIS STEVENSON, the traveler
MODESTINE, a donkey
FATHER APOLLINARIS, a Trappist monk

Critique:

Stevenson said that every book is a circular letter to the friends of him who wrote it. *Travels with a Donkey in the Cévennes* takes much of its merit from the warm-hearted spirit of Stevenson himself. Throughout the narrative the reader is led by Stevenson's voice as if Stevenson were talking in the same room for the enjoyment of his reader. More vivid than either his account of the people or his account of the history made in the Cévennes is Stevenson's way of describing the countryside and its variations in mood.

The Story:

In twelve days, from September 22, 1878, until October 3, 1878, Robert Louis Stevenson walked from Le Monastier to St. Jean du Gard in the Cévennes. His only companion was Modestine, a donkey. He traveled as his fancy led him, stopping to sleep whenever occasion offered. One morning after a night's sleep out of doors Stevenson scattered coins along the road upon the turf in payment for his night's lodging.

Modestine, the donkey, demanded that her owner exercise all his ingenuity. At first he loathed her for her intractable differences of opinion displayed concerning the rate of travel to be maintained. Repeated blows seemed not to influence her until he learned to use the magical word "Proot" to get her moving. Later he obtained a real goad from a sympathetic innkeeper at Bouchet St. Nicolas. Modestine was dainty in her eating. She seemed to prefer white bread, but she learned to share half of Stevenson's brown loaves with him.

Modestine and her owner quarreled about a short cut. She hacked, she reared; she even brayed in a loud, aggrieved tone. However, he forced her to give in. A few days later Stevenson began to understand his strong-willed donkey; he came to understand her stupidity, and he overlooked her flights of ill-judged light-heartedness.

Stevenson, like many who buy at the insistence of others and sell at their own pleasure, was eager to dismiss the matter of Modestine's cost. He had paid sixty-five francs and a glass of brandy for her, but he sold her for thirty-five francs. Stevenson commented that the pecuniary gain was not obvious, but that he had bought freedom into the bargain.

More absorbing than the pleasure with which Stevenson contrasted his vagabond life and that of deeply-rooted monks and peasants was his interest in long-remembered, local conflicts. Such a conflict was that struggle at Pont de Montvert where Camisards, led by Pierre Seguier, murdered the Archpriest of the Cévennes. Seguier was soon taken and his right hand cut off. He himself was then burned alive. Stevenson also identified the characteristic elements in the landscape as he went along. He thought the Cévennes remarkably beautiful.

Stevenson's account of the local peasantry was less appreciative than his account of the landscape. He described two mishaps. In the first place, the peasants looked with suspicion upon a traveler wandering on their bleak high hills with very little money and no obvious purpose other than to stare at them. At his approach to one village the people hid themselves. They barricaded their doors and gave him wrong directions from their windows. Secondly, two girls whom he termed "impudent sly sluts" bade him follow the cows. For these reasons, Stevenson came to feel sympathy for the infamous beast of Gevauden, who, according to tradition, ate about a hundred children of the district.

During his travels he visited Our Lady of the Snows Monastery. Approaching the monastery, he encountered Father Apollinaris, who, clad in the white robe of his order, greeted him and led him to the entrance of the monastery. He felt the atmosphere of his environment and portrayed it in descriptions of the monks at their duties, the feel of the highland wind on his face, the cheerless, four-square buildings which were bleak and too new to be seasoned into the place. The belfry and the pair of slatted gables seemed plain and barren. When he departed after a day of quiet repose, the lonely Trappist, Father Apollinaris, accompanied him, holding Stevenson's hands in his own.

Stevenson continued on to St. Jean du Gard. He lost his way and found it again. Modestine learned to wait patiently when he wanted to stop to talk with someone. The procession of days took him through gullies, along river beds, and over high ridges. At St. Jean du Gard he parted from Modestine. Then, seated by the driver en route to Alais through a rocky gully past orchards of dwarf olive trees, Stevenson began to reflect what Modestine had become in his life. She had been patient and she had come to regard him as a god. She had eaten from his hand. He felt that he had parted from his best friend.

TREASURE ISLAND

Type of work: Novel
Author: Robert Louis Stevenson (1850-1894)
Type of plot: Adventure romance
Time of plot: 1740's
Locale: England and the Spanish Main
First published: 1883

Principal characters:
JIM HAWKINS, cabin boy of the *Hispaniola*
DR. LIVESEY, a physician and Jim's friend
SQUIRE TRELAWNEY, a wealthy landowner

MR. SMOLLETT, captain of the *Hispaniola*
LONG JOHN SILVER, leader of the mutineers
BEN GUNN, a pirate

Critique:

Since its publication, this novel has been a favorite of boys everywhere. With action moving swiftly from beginning to end, the story is told in the first person for the most part by the boy hero; the rest is told in the person of Doctor Livesey. The character of John Silver dominated Stevenson so completely that the outcome is not entirely acceptable from a conventionally moral point of view. The book, according to Stevenson, was born out of his fascination with a water-color map he himself drew of an imagined treasure island.

The Story:

Young Jim Hawkins always remembered the day the strange seaman, Bill Bones, came looking for lodgings at his father's inn, the Admiral Benbow. He came plodding up to the inn door, where he stood for a time and looked around Black Hill Cove. Jim heard him singing snatches of an old sea song:

"Fifteen men on the dead man's chest,
Yo-ho-ho, and a bottle of rum."

When he learned from Jim's father that the inn was a quiet one with little trade, he declared it was just the berth for an old seaman. From that time the strange guest—a retired captain he called himself—kept watch on the coast and the land road by day and made himself free in the taproom of the inn at night. There he drank and sang and swore great oaths while he told fearsome tales of the Spanish Main. Wary of all visiting seamen, he paid Jim Hawkins to be on the lookout for a one-legged sailor in particular. He was so terrible in his speech and manners that Jim's father, sick man that he was, never had the courage to ask for more than the one reckoning Bill Bones had paid the day he came to the inn. He stayed on without ever clinking another coin into the inn till for his meals and lodging.

The one-legged sailor never came to the inn, but another seaman named Black Dog did. The two men fought in the inn parlor, to the terror of Jim and his mother, before Captain Bones chased his visitor up the road and out of sight. He fell down in a fit when he came back to the inn, and Doctor Livesey, coming in to attend Jim's father, cautioned Captain Bones to contain himself and drink less.

Jim's father died soon afterward. On the day of the funeral a deformed blind man named Pew tapped his way up to the door of the Admiral Benbow. The man forced Jim to lead him to the captain. Bill Bones was so terrified when the blind man gave him the Black Spot, the pirates' death notice, that he had a stroke and died.

Jim and his mother took the keys to his sea chest from the dead man's pocket and opened it to find the money due them. As they were examining the contents, they heard the tapping of the blind man's stick on the road. Jim pocketed an oilskin packet and he and his mother left hurriedly by the back door of the inn as a gang of men broke in to search for Captain Bones' chest. Mounted revenue officers arrived and scattered the gang. Blind Pew was trampled to death by the charging horses.

Jim gave the packet to Dr. Livesey and Squire Trelawney. The three discovered that it contained a map locating the hidden treasure of the bloody buccaneer, Captain Flint. Squire Trelawney, intrigued, decided to outfit a ship in which to sail after the treasure. The doctor threw in his lot and invited Jim to come along as cabin boy.

In Bristol Trelawney purchased a schooner, the *Hispaniola,* and hired one Long John Silver as ship's cook. Silver promised to supply a crew. Jim went to Bristol and met Silver, who had but one leg. He was alarmed when he saw Black

Dog again in the inn operated by Silver, but Silver's smooth talk quieted Jim's suspicions.

After the *Hispaniola* had sailed, Captain Smollett, hired by Squire Trelawney to command the ship, expressed his dislike of the first mate and the crew and complained that Silver had more real authority with the crew than he did. One night Jim, in a barrel after an apple, overheard Silver discussing mutiny with members of the crew. Before Jim had a chance to reveal the plot to his friends, the island was sighted.

The prospects of treasure on the island caused the disloyal members of the crew to pay little heed to Captain Smollett's orders; even the loyal ones were hard to manage. Silver shrewdly kept his party under control. Wisely, the captain allowed part of the crew to go ashore; Jim smuggled himself along in order to spy on Silver and the men on the island. Ashore, Silver killed two of the crew who refused to join the mutineers. Jim, alone, met Ben Gunn, who was with Captain Flint when the treasure was buried. Gunn told Jim that he had been marooned on the island three years before.

While Jim was ashore, Dr. Livesey went to the island and found Captain Flint's stockade. Hearing the scream of one of the men Silver murdered, he returned to the *Hispaniola,* where it was decided that the honest men would move to the fort within the stockade. Several dangerous trips in an overloaded boat completed the move. During the last trip the mutineers aboard the ship unlimbered the ship's gun. Squire Trelawney shot one seaman from the boat.

In the meantime the gang ashore saw what was afoot and made efforts to keep Jim's friends from occupying the stockade. The enemy repulsed, Squire Trelawney and his party took their posts in the fort. The mutineers on the *Hispaniola* fired round shot into the stockade, but did little damage.

After leaving Ben Gunn, the marooned seaman, Jim made his way to the stockade. The *Hispaniola* now flew the Jolly Roger skull and crossbones. Carrying a flag of truce, Silver approached the stockade and offered to parley. Admitted by the defenders, he demanded the treasure chart in exchange for the safe return of Squire Trelawney's party to England. Captain Smollet would concede nothing and Silver returned to his men in a rage. The stockade party prepared for the coming battle. A group of the pirates attacked from two sides, swarmed over the paling and engaged the defenders in hand-to-hand combat. In the close fighting the pirates were reduced to one man, who fled back to his gang in the jungle. The loyal party was reduced to Squire Trelawney, Dr. Livesey, Captain Smollett, and Jim.

During the lull after the battle, Jim sneaked off and borrowed Ben Gunn's homemade boat. In this he rowed out to the *Hispaniola* under cover of darkness and cut the schooner adrift. In trying to return to shore, he was caught offshore by coastal currents. Daylight having come, Jim saw that the *Hispaniola* was also aimlessly adrift. When the ship bore down upon him, he jumped to the bowsprit. Ben Gunn's little boat was smashed. Jim found himself on board alone with pirate Israel Hands, wounded in a fight with another pirate. Jim took command and proceeded to beach the ship. Pursued by Hands, he climbed quickly to a crosstree just before Hands threw his knife into the mast not more than a foot below Jim as he climbed. Jim had time to prime and reload his pistols, and he shot the pirate after he had pinned the boy to the mast with another knife throw.

Jim removed the knife from his shoulder, made the ship safe by removing the sails, and returned to the stockade at night, only to find it abandoned by his friends and now in the hands of the pirates. When Silver's parrot, Captain Flint, drew attention to the boy's presence, the pirates captured him. Silver's men, dissatisfied with the buccaneer's methods of gaining the treasure, grumbled. One attempted to kill Jim, who had bragged to them of his exploits in behalf of his friends. But Silver, for reasons of his own, took the boy's side and swore he would take the part, also, of Squire Trelawney. Silver's disaffected mates met and gave Silver the Black Spot, deposing him as their chief. The pirate leader talked his way out of his difficulty by showing them, to Jim's amazement and to their delight, Captain Flint's chart of Treasure Island.

Dr. Livesey came under a flag of truce to the stockade to administer to the wounded pirates. He learned from Jim that Silver had saved the boy's life. And Jim heard, to his mystification, that the doctor had given Captain Flint's chart to Silver.

Following the directions of the chart, the pirates went to find the treasure. Approaching the hiding place, they heard a high voice singing the pirate chantey, "Yo ho ho, and a bottle of rum." Also, the voice spoke the last words of Captain Flint. The men were terrified until Silver recognized Ben Gunn's voice. Then the pirates found the treasure cache opened and the treasure gone. When they uncovered only a broken pick and some boards, they turned on Silver and Jim. At this moment Jim's friends, with Ben Gunn, arrived to rescue the boy.

Early in his stay on the island Ben Gunn had discovered the treasure and carried it to his cave. After Dr. Livesey had learned all this from Gunn, the stockade was abandoned and the useless chart given to Silver. Squire Trelawney's party moved to Gunn's safe and well-provisioned quarters.

The *Hispaniola* having been floated by a tide, the group left Treasure Island, leaving on it three escaped buccaneers. They sailed to a West Indies port where, with the connivance of Ben Gunn, John Silver escaped the ship with a bag of coins. A full crew was taken on, and the schooner voyaged back to Bristol. There the treasure was divided among the survivors of the adventure. "Drink and the devil had done for the rest."

A TREE GROWS IN BROOKLYN

Type of work: Novel
Author: Betty Smith (1904-)
Type of plot: Domestic romance
Time of plot: Early twentieth century
Locale: Brooklyn, New York
First published: 1943

Principal characters:
FRANCIE NOLAN, a Brooklyn girl
NEELEY NOLAN, her brother
KATIE NOLAN, her mother
JOHNNIE NOLAN, her father

Critique:

A Tree Grows In Brooklyn is the story of a young girl affected by the realities and mysteries of life. The setting of Brooklyn tenement life in the early 1900's makes full use of local color. Francie's struggles to overcome poverty and to obtain an education in a world in which only the fittest survive make absorbing reading.

The Story:

For their spending money Francie and Neeley Nolan relied on a few pennies they collected from the junkey every

Saturday. Katie, their mother, worked as a janitress in a Brooklyn tenement, and the money she and their father earned —he from his Saturday night jobs as a singing waiter—was barely enough to keep the family alive and clothed.

After their Saturday morning trips with the rags, metal, and rubber they had collected during the week, Francie would visit the library. She was methodically going through its contents in alphabetical order by reading a book each day, but on Saturdays she allowed herself the luxury of breaking the sequence. At home, sitting on the fire escape, she could look up from her book and watch her neighbors' preparations for Saturday night. A tree grew in the yard; Francie watched it from season to season during her long Saturday afternoons.

At five o'clock, when her father came home, Francie would iron his waiter's apron and then go to the dry-goods store to buy the paper collar and muslin dickey which would last him for the evening. It was her special Saturday night privilege to sleep in the front room, and there she could watch the people in the street. She got up briefly at two in the morning when her father came home, and was given a share of the delicacies he had salvaged from the wedding or party at which he had served. Then, while her parents talked far into the night, Francie would fix Saturday's happenings in her mind and gradually drift off to sleep.

Johnnie Nolan and Katie Rommely had met when he was nineteen and she was seventeen, and they were married four months later. In a year's time Francie was born. Johnnie, unable to bear the sight of Katie in labor, had got drunk, and when the water pipes burst at the school in which he was janitor, he was discharged. Neeley was born soon after Francie's first birthday. By that time Johnnie was drinking so heavily that Katie knew she could no longer rely on him for the family's support. In return for free rent, the Nolans moved to a house in which Katie could be janitress.

Francie was not sent to school until she was seven, and Neeley was old enough to go with her. In that way the children were able to protect each other from would-be tormentors. Seated two-at-a-desk among the other poverty-stricken children Francie soon grew to look forward to the weekly visits of her art and music teachers. They were the sunshine of her school days.

By pretending that Francie had gone to live with relatives, Johnnie was able to have her transferred to another school which Francie had seen on one of her walks. A long way from home, it was, nevertheless, an improvement over the old one. Most of the children were of American parentage and were not exploited by cruel teachers, as were those from immigrant families.

Francie noted time by holidays. Beginning the year with the Fourth of July and its firecrackers, she looked forward next to Halloween. Election Day, with its snake dances and bonfires, came soon after. Then followed Thanksgiving Day, on which the children disguised themselves with costumes and masks and begged trifles from storekeepers. Soon afterward came Christmas. The year Francie was ten and Neeley nine, they stood together on Christmas Eve while the biggest tree in the neighborhood was thrown at them. Trees unsold at that time were thrown at anyone who volunteered to stand against the impact. Bruised and scratched, Francie and her brother proudly dragged their tree home.

The week before Christmas, when Francie had just become fourteen, Johnnie staggered home drunk. Two days later he was found, huddled in a doorway, ill with pneumonia. The next day he was dead. After the funeral, Neeley was given his father's ring and Francie his shaving mug, his only keepsakes aside from his two waiter's aprons. To his wife Johnnie left a baby, due to be born the following spring.

In March, when their funds were running low, Katie cashed the children's insurance policies. The twenty-five dollars she received carried them through until the end of April. Then Mr. McGarrity, at whose saloon Johnnie had done most of his drinking, came to their rescue. He hired Neeley to help prepare free lunches after school and Francie to do housework, and the money the children earned was enough to tide them over until after Katie's baby was born.

Laurie was born in May. In June, after their graduation from grade school, Francie and Neeley found their first real jobs, Neeley as errand boy for a brokerage house and Francie as a stemmer in a flower factory. Dismissed two weeks later, she became a file clerk in a clipping bureau. She was quickly advanced to the position of reader.

In the fall there was not money enough to send both her children to high school, and Katie decided that the more reluctant Neeley should be chosen.

With the money Francie earned and with Neeley's after-school job at McGarrity's saloon, the Nolans had more comforts that Christmas than they had ever known before. The house was warm; there was enough food; and there was money for presents. Fourteen-year-old Neeley received his first pair of spats, and Francie almost froze in her new black lace lingerie when they went to church on Christmas morning.

When the clipping bureau closed with the outbreak of the war, Francie got a job as teletype operator. By working at night, she was able to take advanced college credits in summer school that year. With the help of a fellow student, Ben Blake, she passed her chemistry and English courses.

Francie was eighteen when she had her first real date, with a soldier named Lee Rhynor. The evening he was to leave to say goodbye to his parents before going overseas, Lee asked her to marry him when he returned. Francie promised to write to him every day. Three days later she received a letter from the girl he married during his trip home.

Katie also had a letter that day. Officer McShane had long been fond of Katie. Now retired, he asked her to marry him. To this proposal all the Nolans agreed. As the time approached for the wedding, Francie resigned her job. With Katie married, she intended to go to Michigan to college, for with Ben Blake's help she had succeeded in passing the entrance exams.

The day before Katie was to be wed, Francie put the baby in the carriage and walked down the avenue. For a time she watched the children carting their rubbish into the junk shop. She turned in her books at the library for the last time. She saw another little girl, a book in her hand, sitting on a fire escape. In her own yard the tree had been cut down because the tenants had complained that it was in the way of their wash. But from its stump another trunk was growing.

THE TRIAL

Type of work: Novel
Author: Franz Kafka (1883-1924)
Type of plot: Fantasy
Time of plot: Twentieth century
Locale: Germany
First published: 1925

Principal characters:
JOSEPH K., a bank employee
THE ADVOCATE
TITORELLI, a painter
LENI, the Advocate's servant

Critique:

The Trial is one of the most effective and most discussed works to come out of Central Europe between wars. To many, perhaps most, readers it is a highly engaging comedy filled with buffoonery and fantasy. More serious students of literature see in it, however, a vast symbolism and a first rate psychological study of a system whose leaders are convinced of their own righteousness. To some the court is a symbol of the Church as an imperfect bridge between the individual and God. To others the symbolism represents rather the search of a sensitive Jew for a homeland that is always denied him. At any rate *The Trial* is a powerful and provocative book.

The Story:

Perhaps some one had been telling lies about Joseph K., for one morning he was arrested. The landlady's cook always brought him his breakfast at eight o'clock, but this morning she failed to appear. Joseph looked out of the window and noticed that the old lady across the way was peering into his room. Feeling uneasy, he rang the bell. At once a man entered dressed like a tourist. He advised Joseph to stay in his room, but Joseph failed to obey. In the next room he saw another strange man reading a book. The missing breakfast was explained by the empty dishes he saw. The two strangers had eaten it.

The two strangers had come to notify Joseph he was under arrest. They were so sure of themselves and yet so considerate that Joseph was at a loss as to the attitude he should take toward them. They tried to take his underwear, saying it was of too good quality, but when he objected they did not press him. They refused to tell him the reason for his arrest, saying only that he would be interrogated. Finally, after Joseph had dressed according to their choices of his wardrobe, they led him to another room to be questioned by the Inspector.

To his dismay Joseph saw that the Inspector was occupying Fraülein Bürstner's room. The Inspector gave no further hint as to the reason for the arrest, nor did he inquire into Joseph's defense. The latter at one point said that the whole matter was a mistake; but under pertinent if vague questioning, Joseph admitted that he knew little of the law. All he learned, really, was that some one in high authority had ordered his arrest.

Then Joseph was told that he could go to work as usual. His head fairly aching from bewilderment, Joseph went to the bank in a taxi. Arriving half an hour late, he worked all day long as diligently as he could. He was, however, frequently interrupted by congratulatory callers, for this day was his thirtieth birthday.

He went straight home at nine-thirty to apologize for using Fraülein Bürstner's room. She was not in, however, and he settled down to anxious waiting. At eleven-thirty she arrived, tired from an evening at the theater. In spite of her uninterested attitude he told her the whole story very dramatically. At last Fraülein Bürstner sank down exhausted on her bed. Joseph rushed to her, kissed her passionately many times, and returned to his room.

A few days later Joseph received a brief note ordering him to appear before the court for interrogation on the following Sunday. Oddly enough, although the address was given, no time was set for the hearing. By some chance Joseph decided to go at nine o'clock. The street was a rather mean one, and the address proved to be that of a large warehouse.

Joseph did not know where to report, but after trying many doors he finally reached the fifth floor. There a bright-eyed washerwoman seemed to be expecting him and motioned him through her flat into a meeting hall. Joseph found the room filled with old men, most of them with long beards. They all wore badges.

When the judge asked Joseph if he were a house painter, he snappishly rejoined that he was the junior manager of a bank. Then the judge said he was an hour and ten minutes late. To this charge Joseph replied that he was present now, his appearance in court being the main thing. The crowd applauded. Encouraged, Joseph launched into a harangue damning the court, its methods, the warders who had arrested him, and the meeting time and place.

The judge seemed abashed. Then an interruption occurred. At the back of the room a man clasped the washerwoman in his arms and screamed, all the while looking at the ceiling. Joseph dashed from the room, loudly refusing to have any more dealings with the court.

All that week Joseph awaited another summons. When none came, he decided to revisit the meeting hall. The washerwoman again met him kindly and expressed her disappointment that the court was not in session. She told him a little about the court and its methods. It seemed that the court was only a lower body which rarely interfered with the freedom of the accused people. If one were acquitted by the court, it meant little, because a higher court might re-arrest the prisoner on the same charge. She seemed to know little of Joseph's particular case, although she said she knew as much as the judge. As she was speaking, a law student seized the washerwoman and carried her up the stairs.

The woman's husband kindly offered to lead Joseph up to the law offices, the inner sanctum of the court located in the attic. There Joseph found a number of people waiting for answers to petitions. Some of them had been waiting for years, and they were becoming a little anxious about their cases. The hot room under the roof made Joseph dizzy and he had to sit down. The hostess tried to soothe him and the director of public relations was very pleasant. Finally some one suggested that Joseph ought to leave and get some fresh air.

On his uncle's advice, Joseph hired an Advocate, an old man who stayed in bed most of the time. His servant, Leni, took a liking to Joseph and would often kiss him while he was conferring with the Advocate. Joseph liked best to dally with her in the kitchen. After some months, all the Advocate had done was to think about writing a petition. In desperation Joseph discharged him from the case.

Leni was heartbroken. She was in her nightgown entertaining another client. This man, a businessman, Leni kept locked up in a small bedroom. The Advocate warned Joseph of his high-handed behavior and pointed to the businessman as an ideal client. Disgusted, Joseph left the house.

Then Joseph went to see Titorelli, the court painter. Titorelli told him he could hope for little. He might get definitive acquittal, ostensible acquittal, or indefinite postponement. No one was ever really acquitted, but sometimes cases could be prolonged indefinitely. Joseph bought three identical paintings in return for the advice.

Even the priest at the cathedral, who said he was court chaplain, offered little encouragement when consulted. He was sure that Joseph would be convicted of the crime charged against him. Joseph still did not know what that crime was, nor did the priest.

At last two men in frock coats and top hats came for Joseph at nine o'clock on the evening before his thirty-first birthday. Somehow they twined their arms around his and held his hands tightly. They walked with him to a quarry. There one held his throat and the other stabbed him in the heart, turning the knife around twice.

TRILBY

Type of work: Novel
Author: George du Maurier (1834-1896)
Type of plot: Sentimental romance
Time of plot: Nineteenth century
Locale: Paris and London
First published: 1894

Principal characters:
TRILBY O'FERRALL, an artist's model
SVENGALI, a Hungarian musician
GECKO, another musician
TAFFY,
SANDY, and
LITTLE BILLEE, English art students

Critique:

This novel has had an astonishing success both in its original form and in a dramatic version for stage presentation. Its chief merit lies in its picture of student life in the Latin Quarter of Paris. Du Maurier, who wrote the book from recollections of his own youth, seems to have set down only the glamorous elements. The result is delightful reading so long as the reader remembers that the account of Bohemian life is idealized and sentimentalized.

The Story:

In the large Latin Quarter studio which Taffy, Sandy, and Little Billee shared, the three students were hosts to Svengali, an unconventional musician, and Gecko, a fiddler. Suddenly there was a knock on the door. An artist's model came in; she had heard music and decided to stop by. She wore a mixture of clothing—a soldier's coat, a pair of men's shoes, a frilled petticoat—and she carried her lunch. When she began to sing, her voice was so flat that the listeners did not know whether to be amused or embarrassed. Only Svengali realized the quality of her untrained voice.

Svengali went one morning to borrow money from Sandy. Trilby was in the studio when he arrived. Because she complained of a headache, Svengali hypnotized her. Sandy, thinking of the control Svengali might have over Trilby, was alarmed.

Trilby came more often to the studio. She cooked for the three Englishmen, darned their clothing, joined in their meals and parties. In return they taught her how to speak correct English and treated her as a highly respected sister. When Sandy fell ill, Trilby refused to let anyone else look after him.

Svengali had a stroke of luck when he was hired to appear in concerts. He was anxious to hypnotize the model again, but the three Englishmen would not permit it.

Because Trilby posed in the nude, Little Billee, who had fallen in love with her, became angry and left Paris. Trilby, unhappy at this turn of events, became a laundress. She began to take care of her appearance, so that when Little Billee returned he was completely charmed by her. At Christmas time Trilby promised to marry Little Billee. But a few days later his mother and a clergyman arrived and made Trilby promise that she would not marry Little Billee. Trilby left Paris. Little Billee became ill and with his mother and sister returned to England.

Five years passed. Little Billee achieved success in London. Sandy and Taffy traveled on the continent. When the three friends met again at a ball in London, there was much talk of old days in Paris. Word went around that Svengali had found a great pupil, that he had married her and was making a famous singer of her. Little Billee painted more pictures and fell in and out of love with a girl named Alice. The other two friends went their ways.

At last the three met in Paris. During their stay they attended the first performance of the famous La Svengali in Paris and discovered that the singer was their Trilby of earlier days. Under the hand of her master she had gained a great voice that thrilled her audience. The three Englishmen were overcome.

The next day, when they saw Trilby and Svengali in the park, Little Billee ran up to greet her. She looked at her old friends vaguely, listened to something which Svengali said to her, and then to their surprise glanced coldly at them as if she had never seen them before.

The next day Little Billee encountered Svengali, who spat on him. A fight began in which the tall musician was more than a match for the small artist. Then Taffy appeared. With one hand he seized Svengali's nose and with the other he slapped Svengali on the cheek. Svengali was only too glad to escape. A few days later the Englishmen left for home.

When Svengali brought his star to London, she was the talk of the city. Little Billee and his friends bought tickets for Trilby's first concert.

At the last minute the concert was canceled. Svengali had scolded Trilby past the limit of Gecko's endurance, and Gecko had attacked Svengali with a knife. At that moment Trilby became imbecile in her manner. While her husband remained ill she was incapable of speech, and she spent all her time with him. Svengali would not permit her to leave him either to practice or to sing her concert without him.

At last Svengali recovered. Not well enough to conduct the orchestra, however, he was compelled to occupy a seat in a box facing Trilby as she sang. When Little Billee and his friends arrived, they saw Svengali rise from his place with a look of unalterable hatred on his face. Then he slumped forward. Trilby, led from the wings, took her place somewhat mechanically. She seemed to be looking for Svengali. The orchestra began her number. She remained indifferent, refusing to sing. Again and again the orchestra began to play. At last she demanded, in her old gutter French, what they wanted of her. When they said she was to sing, she told the orchestra to be quiet; she would sing without an accompaniment. Then she began in the same flat voice with which she had sung for Little Billee and his friends years before. At once catcalls shook the house. Terrified, Trilby had to be led away. The confusion increased when someone shouted that Svengali was dead in his box.

The three friends went to Trilby's dressing-room. Finding her frightened, they took her to Little Billee's lodgings, where the next day he and his friends called on her. Trilby knew nothing of her career as a singer, and she remembered Svengali only as the kindest man in her life. She was pale and seemed vastly aged.

She told them that Svengali had offered to look after her when she left Paris. He had not married her, however, for he already had a wife and three children. As Trilby talked, her mind seemed disturbed beyond recovery, and a doctor was called in. She gradually became weaker and weaker. There seemed little that could be done for her.

Gecko went to prison for striking Svengali. Svengali's money, which Trilby had earned, went to his wife and children. Each afternoon the three friends went to visit Trilby. She became more and more emaciated, and could no longer rise from her chair. Only by smiles and gestures could she reveal to them the gay, carefree Trilby of other days in Paris.

One day a large life-like photograph of Svengali was shown her. She began to sing and charmed her listeners to tears with the sadness of her song. Then she fell asleep. A doctor, summoned immediately, said she had been dead for a quarter of an hour or more.

Years later Taffy and his wife, Little Billee's sister, met Gecko in a café in Paris and he told them of Svengali's influence over Trilby. Svengali had hypnotized the girl, had made her a singing automaton of matchless voice. When the spell was broken, there was no Trilby, Gecko claimed, for Svengali had destroyed her soul. Taffy and his wife told him how Little Billee had died shortly after Trilby's death. There was little any of them could say. They could only wonder at the strangeness and sadness of Trilby's story.

TRISTRAM

Type of work: Poem
Author: Edwin Arlington Robinson (1869-1935)
Type of plot: Chivalric romance
Time of plot: Arthurian period
Locale: England and Brittany
First published: 1927

Principal characters:
TRISTRAM, Prince of Lyonesse
MARK, his uncle, King of Cornwall
HOWEL, King of Brittany
ISOLT OF THE WHITE HANDS, Howel's daughter
ISOLT, Princess of Ireland
GOUVERNAIL, Tristram's friend
ANDRED, Mark's minion
QUEEN MORGAN, the wily queen

Critique:

The old Breton lay of *Tristram and Yseult* is here reworked with happy results. In Robinson's version the romance loses some of its air of remoteness and its rather stereotyped romantic convention, and we have, instead, a genuine love story with little except the names to remind us of the Middle Ages. The characters talk and think in a plausible manner which adds to the ease of reading. More than the modernization, however, Robinson tells the story with real lyric power. The use of symbolism, as in the quiet ship on a still ocean at the death of Tristram, brings vividness and appeal to the tale.

The Story:

Isolt of the white hands was too pensive and preoccupied for a young girl. Always she looked to the north, toward England, and her father, King Howel of Brittany, loved his daughter too much to let her attitude go unquestioned.

Isolt told her father she was waiting for Tristram, who some time before had made a visit to the Breton court. Fond of Isolt as a man is fond of a child, he had given her on his departure an agate for a keepsake and had promised to come back. Now Isolt was a woman of eighteen and she waited for Tristram as a woman waits for her lover. King Howel tried to tell her that Tristram thought of her as a child, and that he probably would not return; but Isolt would not be convinced.

In Cornwall it was the wedding day of old, lecherous King Mark and the dark and beautiful Isolt of Ireland, his bride.

With the wedding feast in full swing, the wine cup was often passed. Sick of the drunken merriment and sicker with inner torment, Tristram, nephew of the king, left the feast and wandered in the fresh night air.

King Mark, displeased by his nephew's absence, sent Gouvernail, Tristram's preceptor and friend, to ask him to return. Tristram said only that he was sick. Then feline Queen Morgan came to talk to Tristram. She used all her arts and blandishments on the brooding knight, and they were cunning indeed, for Queen Morgan, much experienced in the arts of love, was more than a little attracted to Tristram. But Tristram repeated stubbornly that he was sick.

Then there was a soft step on the stair, as Brangwaine came, followed a moment later by dark-caped, violet-eyed Isolt of Ireland herself. She looked at Tristram but said nothing as he took her in his arms. Memories hung about them like a cloud.

King Mark was old and unattractive, and he had wanted a young wife in his castle. Yearning for Isolt of Ireland, he had sent as emissary his gallant nephew, Tristram, to plead his cause. Tristram had to fight even to get to the Irish court. After he had slain the mighty Morhaus, Isolt's uncle, he made a bargain of state with the Irish king and took Isolt back to Cornwall in his boat. One night they were alone with only the sea and the stars to look upon them. Isolt waited in vain for Tristram to speak. If he had, she would have loved him then, and there would have been no marriage of convenience with King Mark. But bound by knightly fealty Tristram kept silent and delivered Isolt to his uncle. Now he looked at her and regretted bitterly that he had not spoken on the boat.

Andred stole behind them to spy on their love-making. He was a faithful servitor of King Mark, but jealousy of Tristram and love for Isolt motivated him as well. But Tristram saw Andred skulking in the shadow, seized him, and threw him heavily on the rocks. When King Mark himself came out to inquire about his absent guests, he stumbled over Andred's unconscious body and stood unseen long enough to hear the passionate avowals of Tristram and Isolt.

Since Tristram was his nephew, King Mark did not have him killed, but he banished Tristram forever from Cornwall on pain of burning at the stake.

The sick Tristram wandered in a fever. When he recovered, he found himself the captive of Queen Morgan in her castle. Queen Morgan eventually gave up her siege of Tristram's heart and let him go.

Next Tristram went to Brittany, where a griffin, giant scourge of the Breton land, was threatening King Howel and his court. Knightly Tristram, fierce in battle although sick for love, slew the griffin and put his hosts to flight. As a hero, Tristram had a secure place at King Howel's court, and there he married Isolt of the white hands. He pitied her and she loved him, although she knew of his sorrow. For two years Tristram was a faithful husband and reigning prince.

Then from the north came another ship with Gawaine aboard bringing a message from King Arthur. For his deeds Tristram was to become a Knight of the Round Table; hence his summons to Camelot. Isolt watched her husband go with quiet despair, for she feared he would not come back. She had little dread of King Mark, for Gawaine had told her in secrecy that King Mark was in prison. The Cornish king had forged the Pope's signature on a paper ordering Tristram to go fight the Saracens, and his forgery had been detected. But somehow Isolt knew that Tristram's danger lay in Cornwall.

Guinevere, Arthur's queen, and her lover, Lancelot, plotted to bring Irish Isolt and Tristram together. Lancelot took Tristram to Joyous Guard, his trysting castle, and Guinevere brought Isolt of Ireland secretly out of Cornwall. So the lovers were together again, while King Mark was in prison.

They had a happy summer together and as autumn drew near Tristram lost a little of his apprehension. Early one morning he went out on the sea while Isolt slept. When he returned, there were strangers in Joyous Guard and Isolt was gone. King Mark, released from prison, had abducted his wife and carried her off to Cornwall.

Tristram moped in silence until he had a letter from Queen Morgan. She chided him for his lovesickness and urged him to see his Isolt once more. Goaded by the wily queen, Tristram rode to Cornwall prepared to fight and die for a last look at Isolt. But when he arrived at his uncle's castle, he entered easily and in surprised joy sought out Isolt. She told him that she was near death. King Mark, in pity for her wasting figure and sick heart, had given her permission to receive her lover. Isolt and Tristram, sad in their love because Isolt was to die, sat on the shore and gazed out at a still ship on the quiet ocean. While they sat thus, the jealous Andred crept up behind them and stabbed Tristram in the back. So Tristram died before Isolt after all. King Mark finally realized that Andred was also in love with Isolt, and he regretted that his lecherous lust for a young queen had brought sorrow and death to many lives.

Gouvernail went back to Brittany to convey the grievous news of Tristram's death to Isolt of the white hands, who divined the truth when he disembarked alone. He told her only part of Tristram's sojourn in England, only that Tristram had seen the dying Isolt of Ireland a last time with King Mark's consent, and that Andred had killed Tristram by treachery. Isolt was silent in her grief; no one could know what she was thinking, nor how much she divined of Tristram and the other Isolt.

Now Isolt looked no more for a ship from England. On the white sea the white birds and the sunlight were alive. The white birds were always flying and the sunlight flashed on the sea.

TRISTRAM SHANDY

Type of work: Novel
Author: Laurence Sterne (1713-1768)
Type of plot: Humorous sensibility
Time of plot: 1718-1766
Locale: Shandy Hall in England
First published: 1760-1767 (published in several books)

Principal characters:

TRISTRAM SHANDY, who tells the story
MR. WALTER SHANDY, his father
MR. TOBY SHANDY, his uncle, an old soldier
CORPORAL TRIM, Uncle Toby's servant
MR. YORICK, a parson
DR. SLOP, a medical quack
WIDOW WADMAN, a romantic widow

Critique:

The Life and Opinions of Tristram Shandy, Gentleman is one of the most amusing books ever written. In part, its humor derives from Sterne's delight in oddities of material and method. His pleasure in the unexpected creates surprise on almost every page. Memory and an intense sensibility combine to create the first true psychological novel in English literature. The organization of the novel is based on little more than Sterne's whims. Diagrams, unusual uses of type, and strange numbering of the pages are amusing pranks played by the author.

The Story:

Tristram Shandy, in telling the story of his earliest years, always believed that most of the problems of his life were brought about by the fact that the moment of his conception was interrupted when his mother asked his father if he had remembered to wind the clock. Tristram knew the exact date of his conception, the night between the first Sunday and the first Monday of March, 1718. He was certain of this date because, according to his father's notebook, Mr. Shandy set out immediately after this date to travel from Shandy Hall up to London. Before this date Mr. Shandy had been seriously inconvenienced by an attack of sciatica.

Another complication of Tristram's birth was the marriage settlement of his parents. According to this settlement, quoted in full by Tristram, Mrs. Shandy had the privilege of going to London for her lying-in. But, if Mrs. Shandy were to put Mr. Shandy to the expense of a trip to London on false pretenses, then the next child was to be born at Shandy Hall. The circumstance of a needless trip to London having occurred some time before, Mr. Shandy stoutly insisted that Tristram should be born at Shandy Hall, the birth to be in the hands of a country midwife, rather than in those of a London doctor.

On the night of Tristram's birth, his father and his Uncle Toby were sitting in the living-room engaged in one of their interminable discussions and debates. Informed by Susannah, the maid, that Mrs. Shandy was about to be delivered of a child, they sent for the midwife. As an extra measure of safety, they sent also for Dr. Slop, a bungling country practitioner whom Mr. Shandy admired because he had written a five-shilling book on the history of midwifery. While the midwife attended Mrs. Shandy, the doctor would, for a fee of five guineas, drink a bottle of wine in the back parlor with Mr. Shandy and his brother, Toby.

Uncle Toby, who had been called the highest compliment ever paid human nature, had been a soldier until he was wounded during the siege of Namur in 1695. The wound, the exact position of which was to play such a large part in Tristram's story later on, forced him to retire to the country. There at the suggestion of his faithful servant, Corporal Trim, he had built, on a bowling green behind Shandy Hall, a large and complicated series of model fortifications and military emplacements. Uncle Toby's entire time was spent playing soldier and thinking about this miniature battlefield. It was his hobbyhorse, and he rode it continually with the greatest of pleasure. Mr. Shandy was not at all taken with his brother's hobby, and had to keep him from discussing it by violent interruptions so that he could himself continue, or start, one of his long and detailed digressions on obscure information.

As the two brothers sat waiting for the arrival of either the midwife or Dr. Slop, Mr. Shandy made a rhetorical question of the subject of Mrs. Shandy's preference for a midwife rather than a male doctor. Uncle Toby suggested naïvely that modesty might explain her choice. This innocent answer led Mr. Shandy into a long discussion of the nature of women, and of the fact that everything in the world has two handles. Uncle Toby's innocence, however, always made it impossible for him to understand such affairs.

Dr. Slop with his bag of tools finally arrived. Since the midwife had not been able to come, he went up to see about the birth of the child. Meanwhile, to pass the time, Corporal Trim read a sermon aloud. Dr. Slop, in attending Mrs. Shandy, unfortunately mistook Tristram's hip for his head. In probing with his large forceps, he flattened what Tristram always referred to as his nose. This mistake Tristram blamed essentially on the affair of the winding of the clock mentioned earlier. This, and a later incident concerning the falling of a window sash when Tristram, still a little boy, was relieving himself through a window, brought about a problem in his anatomy which he mentioned often in his story of his life.

Between Tristram's birth and almost immediate baptism, Mr. Shandy entertained the company with a long story he had translated from the Latin of the old German writer, Slawkenbergius, a tale telling of the adventures of a man with an especially long nose. By the time Mr. Shandy had recovered from the bad news of the accident with the forceps, and had asked about his child, he learned that it was very sickly and weak; consequently he summoned Mr. Yorick, the curate, to baptize the child immediately. While rushing to get dressed to attend the ceremony, Mr. Shandy sent word to the parson by the maid, Susannah, to name the child Trismegistus, after an ancient philosopher who was a favorite of Mr. Shandy. Susannah forgot the name, however, and told Mr. Yorick to name the child Tristram. This name pleased the old man because it happened to be his own as well. When Mr. Shandy, still half unbuttoned, reached the scene, the evil had been done. Despite the fact that Mr. Shandy thought correct naming most important, his child was Tristram, a name Mr. Shandy believed the worst in the world. He lamented that he had lost three-fourths of his son in his unfortunate geniture, nose, and name. There remained only one fourth—Tristram's education.

Tristram managed to give a partial account of his topsy-turvy boyhood between many sidelights on the characters of his family. Uncle Toby continued to answer most of his brother's arguments by softly whistling *Lillibullero,* his favorite tune, and going out to the little battlefield to wage small wars with his servant, Corporal Trim. The next important event in the family was the death of Master Bobby, Tristram's older brother, who had been away at Westminster school. To this event Mr. Shandy reacted in his usual way by calling up all the philosophic ideas of the past on death and discoursing on them until he had adjusted himself to the new situation. The tragic news was carried to the kitchen staff and Susannah, despite a desire to show grief, could think of nothing but the wonderful wardrobe of dresses she would inherit when her mistress went into mourning. The vision of all Mrs. Shandy's dresses passed through her mind. Corporal Trim well demonstrated the transitory nature of life by dropping his hat, as if it had suddenly died, and then making an extemporaneous funeral oration.

After many more digressions on war, health, the fashions of ancient Roman dress, his father's doubts as to whether to get Tristram a tutor, and whether to put him into long trousers, Tristram proceeded to tell the history of his Uncle Toby, both in war and in love. Near Shandy Hall lived the Widow Wadman, who, after laying siege to Uncle Toby's affections for a long period, almost got him to propose marriage to her. But the gentle ex-soldier, who literally would not kill a fly, finally learned the widow's purpose when she began to inquire so pointedly into the extent and position of his wound. First he promised the widow that he would allow her to put her finger on the very spot where he was wounded, and then he brought her a map of Namur to touch. Uncle Toby's innocence balked her real question until Corporal Trim finally told his master that it was the spot on his body, not the spot on the surface of the world where the accident took place, that was the point of the Widow Wadman's interest. This realization so embarrassed the old man that the idea of marriage disappeared from his mind forever. Tristram concluded his story with Parson Yorick's statement that the book had been one of the cock and bull variety, the reader having been led a mad, but merry, chase through the satirical and witty mind of the author.

TROILUS AND CRISEYDE

Type of work: Poem
Author: Geoffrey Chaucer (1340?-1400)
Type of plot: Chivalric romance
Time of plot: Trojan War
Locale: Troy
First transcribed: c. 1382

Principal characters:
TROILUS, young prince of Troy
CRISEYDE, a young widow
PANDARUS, Troilus' friend and Criseyde's uncle
DIOMEDES, a Greek warrior

Critique:

Troilus and Criseyde, the only long work completed by Chaucer, is based on the legend of the Trojan War. The characters, however, behave in the best tradition of the medieval court of love. As an incomparable teller of tales, and as a great poet, Chaucer combined his two talents to produce this almost perfectly constructed narrative poem. The effective depiction of character and its development in the poem forecast the shrewd observations of human nature made by Chaucer in the prologue to *The Canterbury Tales.*

The Story:

Calchas, a Trojan prophet, divining that Troy was doomed to defeat, fled to the Greeks. He left behind him his beautiful daughter, Criseyde, a young widow.

One day in April the citizens of Troy were observing the rites of the spring festival. Among those in the temple was Troilus, a younger son of King Priam of Troy. Troilus, scornful of the Trojan swains and their lovesickness at this season, saw Criseyde for the first time and fell deeply in love with her. Sick with the love malady he had always scorned, Troilus invoked the god of love to have pity on him. Feeling that he had no hope of winning Criseyde, he became the scourge of the Greeks on the battlefield.

Pandarus, friend of Troilus, offered his advice and help when he learned that Troilus had lost his heart to a beautiful Trojan. When Troilus at length disclosed that his lady was the fair Criseyde, Pandarus offered to become a go-between, a service he was well able to perform since he was Criseyde's uncle.

Pandarus called on his niece to gossip with her. They discussed Priam's sons and Pandarus praised the bravery of Troilus. Subtly he disclosed to Criseyde that young Troilus was dying for love of her. Criseyde, suspecting that the intentions of neither Troilus nor Pandarus were honorable, cried out in distress at this information, but Pandarus soon convinced her that Troilus' love was pure. She felt herself drawn to the prince when she beheld his modesty as he rode past her house after a day of battle outside the walls of Troy. She decided, after much inner turmoil, that it would not be dishonorable to show friendship to Troilus in order to save the young man's life.

At the suggestion of Pandarus, Troilus wrote a letter to Criseyde. Impressed, she wrote a restrained letter in return. When Troilus, wishing to be with Criseyde, soon tired of this correspondence, Pandarus arranged a meeting by asking Deiphobus, brother of Troilus, to invite the pair to his house for dinner. After the dinner Criseyde gave the miserable prince permission to be in her service and to adore her.

Pandarus, eager to bring about a private meeting of the lovers, studied the stars and decided on a night which would be propitious for their tryst. He invited Criseyde to dine with him on that evening. Troilus was already hidden in his house. As the lady prepared to take her leave, it began to rain and Pandarus persuaded her to stay. So through Pandarus' wiles the lovers were brought together. After yielding, Criseyde gave Troilus a brooch as a token of their love.

About that time a great battle was fought between the Greeks and the Trojans and several of the Trojan leaders were captured. In an exchange of prisoners Calchas persuaded the Greeks to ask for Criseyde in return for Antenor, a Trojan warrior. The Trojan parliament, after much debate, approved of the transaction. Hector, another brother of Troilus, argued that Criseyde should remain in Troy, but without success. Troilus was in despair, and Criseyde prepared to be separated from her lover.

Pandarus brought the lovers together secretly after plans for the exchange had been made. Criseyde, broken-hearted, told the prince that their separation would not be for long, and that she would remain faithful to him.

Troilus and his party accompanied Criseyde to the place appointed for the exchange. There they met Antenor and conducted him to Troy, while Diomedes, a young Greek warrior, led Criseyde away to the Greek camp. Troilus returned to Troy to await the passing of ten days, at the end of which time Criseyde had promised she would return. But Diomedes had seduced the fair Criseyde by the tenth day. She gave him a brooch she had received from Troilus at their parting; Diomedes gave her a horse he had captured from Troilus in battle.

After several weeks of anxious waiting, Troilus wrote to Criseyde. She answered him, avowing weakly her love for him and saying that she would return to Troy at the earliest opportunity. Troilus, sensing that something was amiss, grieved. One day he saw the brooch which he had given Criseyde on a piece of armor taken from Diomedes on the battlefield. Knowing that Criseyde had forsaken him for another, Troilus sought out and fought Diomedes indecisively many times. Eventually the unhappy Troilus was killed by mighty Achilles.

TWENTY THOUSAND LEAGUES UNDER THE SEA

Type of work: Novel
Author: Jules Verne (1828-1905)
Type of plot: Adventure romance
Time of plot: 1866-1867
Locale: The Seven Seas
First published: 1870

Principal characters:
Professor Pierre Aronnax, a French scientist
Conseil, his servant
Ned Land, his friend and companion
Captain Nemo, captain of the *Nautilus*

Critique:

Many writers have had vivid and penetrating imaginations which permitted them to speculate about things to come. Jules Verne was one of these, and his book is in the tradition that has given us Utopian stories of revealed discoveries and inventions yet to occur. In this instance Verne was really prophetic. The submarine and most of the inventions conceived by Captain Nemo have become realities. Books of this nature are seldom great, but they are always interesting.

The Story:

In different parts of the ocean, a number of ships had sighted a mysterious monster, gleaming with light, such as no man had ever seen before. After this monster had attacked and sunk several vessels, people all over the world were both amazed and alarmed. Finally an American frigate, the *Abraham Lincoln,* was fitted out to track down and destroy the mysterious sea creature. Among its passengers was Pierre Aronnax, Professor of Natural History in the Museum of Paris, who had published his opinion that the monster was a giant narwhal. One of the crew was Ned Land, an expert harpooner. For quite a while the ship sailed without sighting anything even remotely resembling the reported terror of the seas.

The creature was sighted at last. When an opportunity presented itself, Ned Land threw his harpoon, but the monster was uninjured and Land realized that it was protected by a thick steel-like armor. During a pursuit in the darkness, a terrific explosion rocked the ship. Professor Aronnax, Ned Land, and Conseil found themselves floundering in the water. Aronnax fainted. Regaining consciousness, he discovered that they were aboard some sort of underwater craft. Later two men came to greet them. The survivors from the ship spoke to them in various languages, but the men appeared not to understand. Then the captain of the vessel appeared and spoke to them in French. He revealed that his name was Nemo, that the vessel was a submarine, that they were, in effect, prisoners who would have every liberty aboard, except on occasions when they would receive orders to retire to their cabins.

The submarine *Nautilus*, Aronnax learned, had been built in a complicated manner. Parts of it had been secured from various places and secretly assembled on a desert island. Then a fire had been set to destroy all traces of the work done there. The ship manufactured its own electricity, had provisions for quantities of oxygen which allowed it to remain submerged, and was as comfortable as any home. All food came from the ocean. There was fish, but fish such as Aronnax had never before tasted. There was clothing made from some sort of sea fibres. There were cigars, not of tobacco but of a special seaweed. Captain Nemo showed them air guns which allowed him and the crew to go hunting, as well as a device that permitted the crew to walk the ocean floor.

In the Pacific, Captain Nemo invited the three survivors to a hunt in the marine forest of Crespo, where Ned Land saved Captain Nemo's life by killing a creature which was about to put an end to the captain. Later, the captain saved Land's life. In Ceylon they watched the pearl divers in the oyster beds. There Nemo saved an Indian from the jaws of a shark.

Off the coast of Borneo the three survivors decided to go ashore in the hope of bagging some land game. While they were hunting, they were attacked by natives. Although they managed to get back to the *Nautilus,* the savages remained clustered about the ship. Aronnax was alarmed, certain that the natives would board the submarine when the hatches were opened for oxygen the next morning. He took his problem to Captain Nemo, who was not at all worried. Instead he told the professor about an eighteenth-century ship that had sunk with a full cargo of gold. The next morning, when the hatches were opened, the natives did try to come aboard, but the few who touched the rails let out a shriek and retreated in terror. Ned Land touched the rail and was paralyzed with shock; the rail was electrified.

The captain announced suddenly that he would enter the Mediterranean. Aronnax supposed that he would have to circle the Cape of Good Hope. To his astonishment, he learned that the captain had discovered a passage under the Isthmus of Suez. The submarine entered the Mediterranean through the underwater passage.

On one occasion the three companions were ordered to go to their cabins. Some sort of encounter occurred, and later Aronnax was called upon to treat a crew member who had been injured. When the sailor died, he was buried in a coral forest on the ocean floor. By that time the survivors had discovered that Captain Nemo had a tremendous fortune in gold salvaged from sunken vessels. Although the captain had some mysterious hatred against society, he nevertheless used the money to benefit his unfortunate fellow men.

Ned Land grew to dislike the captain very much. He told Aronnax that he would escape as soon as an opportunity presented itself. They thought such an opportunity had come when they rounded Spain, but their plan did not materialize. When they came close to Long Island, they thought the time for escape had come. But a sudden hurricane blew the ship off its course, toward Newfoundland.

On another occasion the captain astonished them by heading toward the South Pole. There the ship was endangered by an iceberg, and for several days passengers and crew were in danger of their lives. Escaping, they headed northward. As the *Nautilus* approached the coast of Norway, it was suddenly drawn into the notorious maelstrom, the deathtrap for so many ships. Shortly before, the submarine had encountered a mysterious ship which had attacked it. The submarine succeeded in sinking the unknown vessel. Aronnax believed that in this incident there was a clue to Captain Nemo's hatred of society.

The professor never knew what actually happened after the *Nautilus* was drawn into the maelstrom. When he awoke, he and his companions were safe and sound on a Norwegian island. They also had no idea how they had reached the island. They were the only men who now knew the secrets of the ocean —if Captain Nemo and his crew had perished.

TWO YEARS BEFORE THE MAST

Type of work: Record of travel
Author: Richard Henry Dana, Jr. (1815-1882)
Type of plot: Adventure romance
Time of plot: 1834-1836
Locale: California and the high seas
First published: 1840

Principal character:
RICHARD HENRY DANA, JR.

Critique:

The author wrote this realistic account of the life of a common sailor to make the public aware of the hardships and injustices to which American sailors were subjected. In his narrative, chiefly in the form of a journal, Dana explains life at sea at great length. The book also reveals much about life in Spanish California in the early nineteenth century. Dana was a careful observer, and his story has the ring of authenticity throughout.

The Story:

In August, 1834, Richard Henry Dana, Jr., shipped aboard the brig *Pilgrim* out of Boston for a voyage to California. He went as an ordinary seaman, hoping to relieve his eye trouble by the journey; upon his return he planned to reënter Harvard College.

Since Dana was a completely green hand, he was forced to bunk in the steerage instead of in the forecastle with the other sailors. At first his duties were confusing, doubly so during the first two days, for he was violently seasick. But he soon found his sea legs and quickly learned shipboard routine. He and his companions were kept busy all day cleaning and repairing the ship. At night they took turns standing watch.

The voyage was uneventful until October, when the *Pilgrim* passed near the mouth of the River Plate. Here Dana encountered his first real storm at sea. The weather then began to get cold, and all the crew prepared to round Cape Horn.

The seas at the Horn were high, and they encountered snow and hail. Everyone's clothing was perpetually wet. By the middle of November the ship rounded the Horn and headed northward.

The first mishap of the voyage occurred soon afterward, when a young sailor was swept overboard. A boat lowered to search for him found no trace of the lost man. Following the custom of the sea, the captain auctioned off the dead man's clothing.

Near the end of November the brig made the island of Juan Fernandez and dropped anchor for the first time since her departure from Boston. Dana was glad to see land and managed to get on shore for a short time. As soon as the ship had taken on water, however, it weighed anchor and headed for California.

Shortly after Christmas Dana was acknowledged by the crew to be experienced enough to move into the forecastle with them. Now he was a real seaman.

By the middle of January the *Pilgrim* made her first California port at Santa Barbara. There Dana learned that his work for the next year would be loading cattle hides into the ship. The sailors carried the stiff, undressed hides out through the surf on their heads and deposited them in a boat. Then the crew of the boat took the hides to the ship and stowed them away.

The *Pilgrim* next sailed northward to Monterey with some passengers. At that port Mexican customs officers inspected the cargo. Then the company agent aboard the ship set up a store in order to trade with the townspeople. The crew was kept busy on a shuttle service between ship and shore. Because he had some knowledge of languages, Dana became the interpreter for the *Pilgrim,* and he was sent ashore on errands which required a knowledge of Spanish. In this way he became acquainted with the town and its people. He found the Spaniards to be pleasant but lazy, with most of the trade carried on by foreigners. Everyone owned horses; they were so numerous that the price of a fine animal was very low.

When business began to fall off, the *Pilgrim* returned to Santa Barbara. There the crew again began the work of collecting cattle hides from shore. At the time trouble was brewing aboard the ship. Captain, mate, and crew were all at odds. One day the captain began to flog a sailor unjustly; when one of his shipmates stood up for him, the captain flogged the second sailor also. The sailors were angry, but they had no higher power to which they could appeal, for the captain's word was law. Her hold filled with hides, the *Pilgrim* sailed for San Diego.

In San Diego, Dana got his first shore leave. After drinking for a time with the rest of the crew, he and a friend hired horses and rode to a nearby mission, where they were able to get a good Mexican meal, a welcome change from the salt beef served aboard ship.

The undressed hides were unloaded from the *Pilgrim* and placed in a large shed on the beach, where they were to be dressed and stored until enough hides had been collected for the voyage home. Just as the ship had finished unloading and was ready to set sail, a man deserted ship. After an unsuccessful search, the brig put to sea without him.

The *Pilgrim* took on more hides at San Pedro and then continued on to Santa Barbara. It was the Lenten season, and Dana saw the celebrations ashore.

The ship gathered more hides at several places and returned to San Diego. After the hides had been unloaded, the captain sent Dana and another man ashore to assist with the dressing of the hides. Then the ship sailed northward on another coastal voyage.

Dana became acquainted with some Sandwich Islanders who lived on the beach and worked with him; he found them to be generous men and true friends. Some of his spare time he spent reading books and studying navigation. Each day he had to perform a certain amount of work on a certain number of hides, which had to be cleaned, soaked in brine, scraped, dried, beaten, and then stored away.

When the ship *Alert* arrived at San Diego, Dana, anxious to be at sea again, exchanged places with a boy aboard the ship. The *Alert* belonged to the same company as the *Pilgrim;* she was to take aboard the hides collected by the brig and carry them to Boston. The *Pilgrim* was not to sail for home until later. The two vessels had exchanged captains, and Dana was under the same master as before. However, the first mate of the *Alert* was a good officer, and Dana found conditions much more pleasant in his new berth.

Loading hides, the *Alert* moved up and down the coast for several months. In the middle of November, 1835, she left Santa Barbara with some passengers bound for Monterey. However, such a gale came up that the ship could not put in at Monterey but went on up the coast to San Francisco.

The ship then continued working up and down the coast until there were enough hides at San Diego to make her full cargo. In May she headed southward for Cape Horn.

Rounding the Horn on the return journey was even worse than on the way out. Dana became sick with a toothache at the time he was needed most on deck. For days everyone had to work extra hours because of the danger from icebergs. Finally, however, the *Alert* got clear of the ice and ran before a strong wind around the Horn.

Once the ship entered the Atlantic tropics, the weather was fair except for occasional violent storms. Some of the men began to come down with the scurvy, but they were soon cured after the crew obtained fresh vegetables from a passing ship.

On September 21, 1836, the *Alert* anchored in Boston harbor. Hurriedly the crew performed their last duties in bringing her to the wharf. Within five minutes after the last rope had been made fast, not one of the crew was left aboard.

TYPEE

Type of work: Novel
Author: Herman Melville (1819-1891)
Type of plot: Adventure romance
Time of plot: Mid-nineteenth century
Locale: Marquesas Islands
First published: 1846

Principal characters:
HERMAN MELVILLE (TOM), an American sailor
TOBY, his friend
MEHEVI, chief of the Typees
KORY-KORY, a native servant
FAYAWAY, a native girl
MARNOO, a native taboo man

Critique:

Typee is a fictionized narrative of actual adventures of young Herman Melville. Although most of the narrative is based upon the capture and escape of

Tom and Toby, much of the book is devoted to a description of the life of the Typee cannibals. In spite of its somewhat antiquated style, the book makes fascinating reading. *Typee* has historical interest because it is the first romance of the South Seas.

The Story:

The whaler *Dolly* had been long at sea, and the men were discontented and restless when the captain finally gave orders to put in at Nukuheva, one of the Marquesas Islands. This was the chance Tom and Toby, two young sailors, had been waiting for. Even though the natives of the island were known to be cannibals, Tom and Toby deserted the ship and fled inland, planning to hide until the *Dolly* sailed. Then they hoped to sign aboard another ship where they would get better treatment.

Tom and Toby began their flight with only a few biscuits for food. On the first night away from the ship Tom contracted some disease which caused his leg to swell, and he was in much pain. Nevertheless, he and Toby went on. At last, when their food was all gone, they realized that they could stay alive only by giving themselves up to one of the savage tribes that inhabited the island.

They discovered too late that the natives to whom they surrendered themselves were the Typee tribe, the most ferocious cannibals on Nukuheva. Tom and Toby were treated with respect, however, and were given food and comfortable quarters. All the natives came to see the strangers. Mehevi, the king of the Typees, appointed Kory-Kory as personal servant to Tom. The captives went to live in the home of Tinor, Kory-Kory's mother. Mehevi had a medicine man examine Tom's swollen leg, but the native remedies had no effect on the disease.

Tom, unable to walk, spent most of his time reclining in the house while Kory-Kory attended to his needs. A beautiful young maiden, Fayaway, was also his constant companion. She, among all the Typees, seemed to understand the painful situation of the two captives.

Toby convinced the Typees that he should be allowed to return to the main harbor on the island to seek medical aid for Tom. On the trail he was attacked by hostile warriors from a neighboring tribe, and he returned to the Typees with an ugly head wound.

A few days later Toby discovered a boat offshore. He was allowed to go down by the beach, but Tom was detained in his house. Toby promised to bring medical aid to Tom within three days. But the three days passed without the return of Toby. Tom could learn nothing from the natives; he realized that now he was the single captive of the Typees. Somewhat recovered, he was allowed to roam almost at will within the country of the Typees. But he was always accompanied by Kory-Kory; there was no chance for escape.

As Tom's leg improved, he began to indulge in the pleasures allowed him and to observe the native life with interest. The Typees seemed to exist in a perpetual state of happiness, interrupted only by skirmishes with neighboring tribes.

One of Tom's greatest pleasures was to paddle a canoe about a small lake in company with Fayaway. For the privilege of taking Fayaway with him he had to ask special permission, since entering a canoe was ordinarily taboo for a woman.

One day a handsome stranger appeared among the Typees bearing news from other parts of the island. He was Marnoo, a taboo man, who was free to go among all the tribes without harm. When Tom learned that Marnoo knew English, he asked the native to help him escape. This Marnoo could not do for fear of arousing the anger of the Typees.

The daily life of the natives was extremely regular. Each morning they bathed and ate breakfast. After the meal they smoked their pipes. The rest of the morning they spent sleeping, conversing, or doing odd jobs about their houses. The men often spent the afternoon in the large meeting house of Mehevi; there they relaxed and joked in a sort of bachelors' club. Before the evening meal they bathed again. After the meal the young girls entertained the rest with dancing. Everyone retired at an early hour.

Tom was present at the Feast of the Calabashes. It seemed to have some religious significance, but most of the time was spent in eating and drinking. During the two days of the festival Tom decided the natives did not take their religion seriously. They possessed many idols not treated with any high degree of respect. The most universal religious observance was that of tattooing; everyone was tattooed upon the face, even the women. The bodies of some of the men were completely covered with intricate designs.

Since the men outnumbered the women in the tribe, the women often had two or three husbands. But the men never had more than one wife. All in the tribe seemed happy with the various aspects of their social organization. Private property was limited to household goods, food was common property. All understood and followed the laws and customs of the tribe; there were never disputes among the Typees.

One day a battle was fought between the Typees and a neighboring tribe. Afterward the bodies of the dead enemies were taken to the ceremonial feasting place. For the next day or two Tom was not allowed to leave the vicinity of his house. He suspected that the Typees were making a meal of their dead enemies. Later he discovered the remains of the meal and found that he was correct, though the Typees denied they were cannibals.

A few days later Marnoo again appeared among the Typees. This time he told Tom to try to escape by means of the same path by which he left. Tom was unable to leave the village, however, for Kory-Kory kept close watch on him day and night.

Not many days after Marnoo had left, the Typees excitedly announced the approach of a boat. Tom argued with the natives and finally persuaded them to let him go to the beach. He had some difficulty in getting there, since his leg had begun to swell again.

At the beach Tom found a boat from an Australian ship standing just outside the surf. Marnoo had told the Australian captain of Tom's trouble, and he had sent a boat loaded with presents to obtain Tom's release. The Typees, however, had no wish to release their captive. In desperation, Tom broke away from the guard which had been placed around him and plunged into the surf. He managed to reach the boat, and the sailors pulled away from shore.

Thus ended Tom's captivity among the Typees. His only regret was in leaving the faithful Kory-Kory and the beautiful Fayaway.

Many years later Tom again met Toby and learned from him that he had intended to return to the aid of his injured friend, but he had been tricked into boarding a vessel which sailed from Nukuheva the following day. It was only long after Toby had given Tom up for lost that the two friends learned of each other's fate after their separation.

THE UGLY DUCHESS

Type of work: Novel
Author: Lion Feuchtwanger (1884-)
Type of plot: Historical chronicle
Time of plot: Fourteenth century
Locale: Central Europe
First published: 1926

Principal characters:
DUCHESS MARGARETE
PRINCE JOHANN, her husband
CHRÉTIEN DE LAFERTE, aide to Prince Johann
MARGRAVE KARL LUDWIG, Margarete's second husband
PRINCE MEINHARD, Margarete's son
KONRAD VON FRAUENBERG, Margarete's adviser
AGNES VON FLAVON, Margarete's rival

Critique:

Although this historical novel relies mainly on interesting events to keep the story going, the characters are well developed and credible. To some readers, however, the book may seem confusing, because the plot is complicated by the rivalries of various monarchs and the political situations of the fourteenth century. In spite of these difficulties, the character of the ugly duchess gives the novel a proper center at all times.

The Story:

Heinrich, King of Bohemia, Duke of Carinthia, and Count of Tyrol, was an important person to three people—King John of Luxemburg, Albert of Austria, and Ludwig of Wittelsbach. Though most of the king's hereditary territory had long been taken by others, the Tyrol and other lands he still owned were valuable. The three rival monarchs sought, by various means, to control them in order to extend their respective empires.

John of Luxemburg persuaded Heinrich to agree that his daughter, Princess Margarete, should marry John's son, Prince Johann of Luxemburg, and that Princess Margarete should be declared Heinrich's heir. It was not likely that Heinrich himself should have another heir, despite the fact that his wife, Princess Beatrix, was still young.

Princess Margarete and Prince Johann were married in childhood. At the wedding feast, Margarete took a fancy to the prince's page, Chrétien de Laferte, and insisted that he be made a knight. Johann refused, but Margarete had her way when the prince's father agreed.

Margarete was undoubtedly one of the ugliest women ever born. To compensate for her lack of charm, she concentrated upon becoming a good ruler and achieving power. Always she had to be vigilant against the encroachments of other nations, even against her own barons and nobles, who were despoiling the land. When her father died and John of Luxemburg was killed in battle, she and Johann were the joint heirs of their principalities, but it was Margarete who ruled, governing so cleverly that her fame spread throughout Europe.

She and Chrétien had become close friends. When Heinrich's mistress died, she left three daughters. One of these, Agnes von Flavon, appealed to Margarete and Johann to be permitted to retain the two fiefs which Heinrich had granted her mother. Johann was willing, but the princess declared that one of the estates should go to Chrétien. When a group of barons, including her illegitimate brother, Albert, plotted to drive the Luxemburgers from the country, Margarete consented to the revolt and urged that Chrétien be made leader of the rebels. Then Johann informed Margarete that Agnes was to marry Chrétien. Margarete sent anonymous letters telling of the planned revolt, and the rebellion was put down. Chrétien's head was sent to her by Johann, who did not know that Margarete herself had revealed the conspiracy.

A Jew named Mendel Hirsch came to the castle to ask for permission to settle in the Tyrol. Margarete granted his petition and the country prospered from the industry and crafts which the Jews brought to the area. Mendel Hirsch became her confidant. Meanwhile another rebellion was brewing. Jacob von Schenna, a friend from her youth, brought the news of the plot to Margarete. She consented to it listlessly, for her spirit had been broken because of a pogrom which resulted in the death of Hirsch and the other Jews. When Prince Johann returned to the castle, he found it barred to him. Margarete had their marriage annulled.

Margarete and Margrave Karl, son of Emperor Ludwig, were married. As a result, Luxemburgers close to the Pope influenced the pontiff to excommunicate Margarete and Karl and to place the land under an interdict. John's son was elected Holy Roman Emperor in place of the excommunicated Ludwig. The years that followed were not happy ones, and plagues and destructive fires ravaged the country. Margarete was blamed because the people thought these visitations a punishment for her illegal marriage. She and Karl had a son, Prince Meinhard, who grew up easy-going and not intelligent. Conditions of the country were so perilous that Margarete, in an effort to secure money, entered into an agreement with Albert of Austria, who promised financial assistance in return for a treaty by which Tyrol should go to Austria if she died without heirs.

In the meantime Prince Johann wished to remarry. Accordingly, he went to Margarete and made an agreement with her. When a new Pope was elected, the marriage of Margarete and Karl was solemnized and Prince Meinhard was declared their rightful heir. Later the interdict was lifted and church bells pealed as services were resumed.

One day, as the margrave was setting out on a trip, Konrad von Frauenberg, Margarete's unscrupulous adviser, went to her to say goodbye and hinted that his death might occur at any moment since Karl detested him. But it was the margrave who died, mysteriously poisoned, leaving Margarete the undisputed ruler of the principality. Then Prince Meinhard and another young prince formed the Arthurian Order, which pillaged the community. Later the order was put down, but Prince Meinhard stayed in Munich, the pawn of a rival prince. Agnes von Flavon was also in Munich and plotting against Margarete.

At the castle a group led by Konrad von Frauenberg had organized a council for the control of the state. Margarete wanted her son back, sure that her position would be stronger if he could be married to an Austrian princess. Von Frauenberg went to Munich and after some time succeeded in persuading Prince Meinhard to return home. But as they were crossing the mountains, von Frauenberg pushed Meinhard off a cliff. He told the pursuers that the prince's death had been an accident.

Agnes von Flavon returned to Tyrol, where she was promptly imprisoned by Margarete. Tried for crimes against the state, she was convicted. Margarete insisted that Agnes be executed, but the council refused to pass the death sentence. Balked, Margarete was willing to free Agnes if the prisoner would acknowledge her crimes against the state, promise to plot no more, and leave Tyrol. Agnes, believing that Margarete would not order her execution, refused. A few days later Konrad von Frauenberg slipped into her cell and poisoned Agnes.

Her funeral took place on the same day that Prince Meinhard was buried. All the nobles and barons went to Agnes' funeral; no one went to that of the prince. Even in death Agnes had won. A few days later Margarete was called upon to honor her agreement with Austria. Accordingly, she signed a proclamation to the effect that her territories were now the property of the Austrian duke. Then Margarete went into exile, to spend the rest of her days in a peasant's hut. A greedy, ugly old woman, she sniffed hungrily whenever she smelled fish cooking for dinner.

ULYSSES

Type of work: Novel
Author: James Joyce (1882-1941)
Type of plot: Psychological realism
Time of plot: June 16, 1904
Locale: Dublin
First published: 1922

Principal characters:
STEPHEN DEDALUS, a young Irish writer and teacher
BUCK MULLIGAN, a medical student
LEOPOLD BLOOM, a Jewish advertising salesman
MARION TWEEDY BLOOM (MOLLY), his wife
BLAZES BOYLAN, Mrs. Bloom's lover

Critique:

Ulysses is an attempt at the complete recapture, so far as it is possible in fiction, of the life of a particular time and place. The scene is Dublin, its streets, homes, shops, newspaper offices, pubs, hospitals, brothels, schools. The time is a single day in 1904. A continuation of the story of Stephen Dedalus as told in *A Portrait of the Artist as a Young Man,* the novel is also a series of remarkable Homeric parallels, the incidents, characters, and scenes of a Dublin day corresponding to those of the Odyssean myth. Leopold Bloom is easily recognizable as Ulysses; Molly Bloom, his wife, as Penelope, and Dedalus himself as Telemachus, son of Ulysses— in Joyce's novel Bloom's spiritual son. The book is written in a variety of styles and techniques, the most important being the stream of consciousness method by which Joyce attempts to reproduce not only the sights, sounds, and smells of Dublin, but also the memories, emotions, and desires of his people in the drab modern world. *Ulysses* is the most widely discussed novel of our time, the most influential for technique and style.

The Story:

Buck Mulligan mounted the stairs of the old tower and prepared to shave himself on that morning of June 16, 1904. A moment later Stephen Dedalus came to the stairhead and stood looking out over Dublin Bay. When Mulligan spoke of the sea glinting in the morning sunlight, Stephen had a sudden vision of his own mother, to whose deathbed he had been called back from Paris a year before. He remembered how she had begged him to pray for her soul and how he, rebelling against the churchly discipline of his boyhood, had refused.

After breakfast Stephen and Mulligan went off with Haines, a young Englishman who also lived in the old tower. In spite of the Englishman's attempts to be friendly, Stephen disliked Haines, who was given to night-long drunken sprees. Stephen felt that his own life was growing purposeless and dissolute through his association with Mulligan and other medical students.

Stephen was a teacher. Because it was a half-holiday at school, the boys were restless. One of his pupils was unable to do his simple arithmetic problems, and in the boy Stephen saw for a moment an image of his own awkward youth. He was relieved when he could dismiss the class.

Later he walked alone on the beach. He thought of literature and his student days, of his unhappiness in Dublin, his lack of money, his family sinking into poverty while his shabby-genteel father made his daily round of the Dublin pubs. He saw the carcass of a dead dog rolling in the surf. Stephen remembered how a dog had frightened him in his childhood; he was, he thought wryly, not one of the Irish heroes.

Meanwhile Leopold Bloom had crawled out of bed to prepare his wife's breakfast. He was a Jewish advertising salesman, for sixteen years the patient, uncomplaining husband of Marion Tweedy Bloom, a professional singer of mediocre talent. He was vaguely unhappy to know that she was carrying on an affair with Blazes Boylan, a sporting Irishman who was managing the concert tour she was planning.

Munching his own breakfast, Bloom read a letter from his daughter Milly, who was working in a photographer's shop in Mullingar. Her letter reminded Bloom of his son Rudy, who had died when he was eleven days old. Bloom read Milly's letter again, wondering about a young student his daughter mentioned. For a moment he was afraid that Milly might grow up like her mother.

Bloom set out on his morning walk. At the post-office he stopped to pick up a letter addressed to Henry Flower, Esq., a letter from a woman who signed herself Martha. Bloom, unhappy at home and under another name, was carrying on a flirtation by mail. Idly he wandered into a church and listened to part of the mass. Later he joined a party of mourners on their way to the funeral of an old friend, Paddy Dignam, who had died suddenly of a stroke. During the service Bloom watched Father Coffey. He thought again of little Rudy and of his own father, a suicide.

The day's business for Bloom was a call at a newspaper office to arrange for the printing of an advertisement. While he was there, Stephen Dedalus also came to the office. The two men saw each other, but they did not speak.

Leaving the newspaper building, Bloom walked across the O'Connell bridge. He met Mrs. Breen and gave her an account of Dignam's funeral. She told him that Mrs. Purefoy was in the maternity hospital in Holles Street. Bloom walked on, watching the sights of Dublin on a summer day. At last he entered Davy Byrne's pub and ordered a cheese sandwich. Later he went to the National Library to look at some newspaper files. There Stephen, flushed with the drinks he had taken at lunch, was expounding to Buck Mulligan and some literary friends his own ingenious theory of Shakespeare's plays and the second-best bed of Shakespeare's will. Again Bloom and Stephen saw one another but did not speak.

Bloom went to the Ormond Hotel for a late lunch. Blazes Boylan came into the bar before he went off to keep an appointment with Molly.

Late in that afternoon Bloom got into a brawl in a pub where the talk was all about money Blazes Boylan had won in a boxing match. Escaping from the jeering crowd, Bloom walked along the Sandymount shore and in the dimming twilight watched young Gertie MacDowell. The moon rose. Bloom decided to stop by the hospital to ask about Mrs. Purefoy. As he walked slowly along the strand a cuckoo-clock struck nine in a priest's house he was passing. Bloom suddenly realized that he had been cuckolded again, while he sat dreaming his amorous fantasies on the Dublin beach.

At the hospital he learned that Mrs. Purefoy's baby had not yet been born. There he saw Stephen Dedalus again, drinking with Buck Mulligan and a group of medical students. Bloom was disturbed to find the son of his old friend, Simon Dedalus, in that ribald, dissolute company.

Bloom went with the medical students to a nearby pub, where Stephen and Buck Mulligan began a drunken argument over the possession of the key to the old tower. When the group broke up Stephen and one of the students went on to a brothel in the Dublin slums, Bloom following them slowly. All were drunk by that time. Bloom had a distorted, lurid vision of his wife and Blazes Boylan together. Stephen, befuddled, thought that his dead mother suddenly appeared from the grave to ask him again to pray for her soul. Running headlong into the street, he was knocked down in a scuffle with two British soldiers. Bloom took Stephen home with him. Stephen, exhausted by his wild night, remained silent and glum while Bloom talked about art and science. Bloom had begged him to spend the night, to leave Mulligan and his wild friends and come to live with the Blooms, but Stephen refused. The bells of St. George's Church were ringing as he walked off down the silent street.

Bloom went slowly to bed. As he drifted off to sleep he told Molly firmly that she was to get up and prepare his breakfast in the morning.

Molly Bloom lay awake thinking of Blazes Boylan. She thought of the mysteries of the human body, of people she had known, of her girlhood at a military post on Gibraltar. She considered the possibility that Stephen Dedalus might come to live with her and her husband. Stephen was a writer, young, refined, not coarse like Boylan. She heard a far, shrill train whistle. She recalled the lovers she had had, Bloom's courtship, their years together, the rose she wore in her hair the day Bloom had asked her to marry him as they stood close under a Moorish arch. So wakeful, earthy Penelope's thoughts flowed on, while her tawdry Ulysses, Bloom, the far wanderer of a Dublin day, snored in the darkness by her side.

THE UNBEARABLE BASSINGTON

Type of work: Novel
Author: Saki (Hector Hugh Munro, 1870-1915)
Type of plot: Social satire
Time of plot: Early 1900's
Locale: London
First published: 1912

Principal characters:
COMUS BASSINGTON, the "unbearable" Bassington
FRANCESCA BASSINGTON, his mother
ELAINE DE FREY, an heiress
COURTNEY YOUGHAL, a young M. P.
HENRY GREECH, Mrs. Bassington's brother

Critique:

H. H. Munro, who wrote under the pen name of Saki, belongs to the tradition of the social satirists, including Oscar Wilde and Evelyn Waugh. *The Unbearable Bassington* represents the essence of the inimitable Saki: his amusing dialogue, his skillful use of poetic figures, his sharp wit. This short novel is a brilliant piece of satire, excellent in its character studies and pungent dialogue. Though it has been said that the discovery about the painting at the end of the volume is an unnecessary feature, the fake masterpiece represents a typical Saki touch.

The Story:

Francesca Bassington was a successful member of London society who was able to make a little money go a long way. Her greatest interest in life was the drawing-room in her small, perfect house on Blue Street. Foremost of her treasures was a famous Van der Meulen masterpiece, which hung in the paneled place of honor in that charming room. She also had a son Comus who presented a serious problem to his mother because of his casual attitude toward life. Francesca had come to the conclusion that there was only one solution for her son's future. He must marry a wealthy girl. Her first choice was Emmeline Chetrof, who would eventually come into a comfortable fortune and, most important of all, would upon her marriage inherit the house in which Francesca lived.

During the time Comus was at school Francesca wrote her son, asking him to show special kindness to Emmeline's brother Lancelot. That suggestion on the part of his mother caused Comus to treat the child even more cruelly, and her plans for a match between Comus and Emmeline Chetrof ended dismally.

Two years later, when Comus was turned loose in his mother's fashionable world of Mayfair and Ascot, she persuaded her brother, Henry Greech, to secure a position for the young man as a secretary to Sir John Jull, the governor of an island in the West Indies. Because he did not want to leave England, Comus sent to a newspaper an article criticizing Sir John. This scurrilous attack was written by Courtney Youghal, a young politician whom Comus knew and admired. Printed over Comus' signature, it had the desired result. Comus lost the position Sir John had promised.

At a dinner given by Lady Caroline Benaresq, Francesca Bassington first learned that her son was interested in Elaine de Frey, a wealthy girl who resembled a painting by Leonardo da Vinci. At the same party Francesca learned that Courtney Youghal was also interested in the young heiress.

One summer afternoon Elaine de Frey entertained her two suitors, Comus and Courtney, at tea in her garden. Elaine, an earnest and practical young lady, had analyzed her suitors carefully, but even though she realized that Comus was both frivolous and undependable she found herself falling in love with him and making excuses for his shortcomings. Courtney, as a rising member of Parliament, also interested her and seemed to her practical mind a better risk than Comus. When the tea was served, Comus snatched up a silver basket containing the only bread and butter sandwiches and dashed off to feed the swans. Returning with the basket, an heirloom of the de Frey family, Comus asked permission to keep it as a souvenir of a delightful tea party. Elaine did not wish to part with the piece of silver, but Comus made such a scene that she finally gave in to his wishes.

One fine June morning all of London society had turned out to ride, walk, or sit in the chairs along the Row. Courtney Youghal was there discussing the theater with Lady Veula Croot. In a secluded part of the Row, Elaine and Comus had rented chairs. The two had drifted apart slightly because of small unrepaid loans which Comus had requested and because of the affair of the silver basket. That morning Comus again asked Elaine to lend him money —five pounds to pay a gambling debt. She promised to send him two pounds by messenger and curtly asked to be excused. He had hurt her pride and alarmed her practical sense of caution. As she was leaving the Row she met Courtney. Over the luncheon table they became engaged.

At an exhibition at the Rutland Galleries Comus learned of Elaine's engagement. Elaine had intended to write Comus a gracious but final note, but instead she went to call on her cousin Suzette, to break the news of her engagement. When Elaine returned home after her call, she found a letter from Comus awaiting her. In the letter he thanked her for the loan, returned the money, and promised to return the silver basket in lieu of a wedding gift.

Francesca Bassington learned of the engagement, a blow to her elaborate plans, from that inveterate gossip, George St. Michael. She informed Comus that he must take a position in West Africa, for which Henry Greech had made arrangements. With his eyes on the Van der Meulen masterpiece, Comus asked his mother if she could not sell something. Mrs. Bassington was fiercely angry at such a suggestion and scolded him severely.

That night, as lonely Comus watched the play from the stalls of the Straw Exchange Theatre, he envied Courtney and Elaine and their circle of friends. Francesca learned from St. Michael, her usual source, that Emmeline Chetrof was to be married but only after a long engagement. Thus her beloved house on Blue Street was safe for a time. Francesca entertained at a dull dinner party in honor of her son's departure—a party to which none of Comus' friends was invited.

In the meantime, Courtney and Elaine were taking their wedding trip on the continent. During their honeymoon they soon discovered that neither loved the other, that the marriage was not likely to be highly successful. Comus Bassington, exiled to West Africa, was bored and unhappy. Shortly before Christmas Francesca received a cablegram saying that Comus was dangerously ill. To calm herself, she walked in the park, for the first time realizing how selfish her love for her possessions, especially the Van der Meulen, had been. During the time she was walking, her brother brought an eminent critic to inspect the masterpiece. Returning to the house, she found a cablegram announcing the death of Comus. A few minutes later George Greech arrived to inform her that the Van der Meulen masterpiece was not an original, but only a good copy. While his voice buzzed on and on, Francesca sat stricken among her prized pieces of silver, bronze, and porcelain—all of them as beautiful and soulless as Francesca herself.

UNCLE TOM'S CABIN

Type of work: Novel
Author: Harriet Beecher Stowe (1811-1896)
Type of plot: Sentimental romance
Time of plot: Mid-nineteenth century
Locale: Kentucky and Mississippi
First published: 1852

Principal characters:
Uncle Tom, a Negro slave
Eva St. Clare, daughter of a wealthy Southerner
Simon Legree, a planter
Eliza, a runaway slave
Topsy, a black imp

Critique:

A sentimental but powerful document in the controversy over slavery, *Uncle Tom's Cabin,* or, *Life Among the Lowly* is a novel whose political and humanitarian pleading is now outdated. The highly exaggerated Legree and the highly exaggerated Eva, however, have become properties of the American imagination. The novel seems linked to two popular traditions. It incorporates all the sentimental elements of the novel of feeling, and in its horror scenes it suggests the Gothic novels of Mrs. Radcliffe and Horace Walpole.

The Story:

Because his Kentucky plantation was encumbered by debt, Mr. Shelby made plans to sell one of his slaves to his chief creditor, a New Orleans slave dealer named Haley. The dealer shrewdly selected Uncle Tom as part payment on

UNCLE TOM'S CABIN by Harriet Beecher Stowe. Published by Houghton Mifflin Co.

Mr. Shelby's debt. While they were discussing the transaction, Eliza's child, Harry, came into the room. Haley wanted to buy Harry too, but at first Shelby was unwilling to part with the child. Eliza listened to enough of the conversation to be frightened. She confided her fears to George Harris, her husband, a slave on an adjoining plantation. George, who was already bitter because his master had put him to work in the fields when he was capable of doing better work, promised that some day he would have his revenge upon his hard masters. Eliza had been brought up more indulgently by the Shelbys and she begged him not to try anything rash.

After supper in the cabin of Uncle Tom and Aunt Chloe, his wife, the Shelby slaves gathered for a meeting. They sang songs, and young George Shelby, who had eaten his supper there, read from the Bible. In the big house Mr. Shelby signed the papers making Uncle Tom and little Harry the property of Haley. Eliza, learning her child's fate from some remarks of Mr. Shelby to his wife, fled with her child, hoping to reach Canada and safety. Uncle Tom, hearing of the sale, resigned himself to the wisdom of providence.

The next day, after Haley had discovered his loss, he set out to capture Eliza. However, she had a good start. Moreover, Mrs. Shelby purposely delayed the pursuit by serving a late breakfast. When her pursuers came in sight, Eliza escaped across the Ohio River by jumping from one floating ice cake to another, young Harry in her arms.

Haley hired two slave-catchers, Marks and Loker, to track Eliza through Ohio. For their trouble she was to be given to them. They set off that night.

Eliza found shelter in the home of Senator and Mrs. Bird. The senator took her to the house of a man known to aid fugitive slaves. Uncle Tom, however, was not so lucky. Haley made sure Tom would not escape by shackling his ankles before taking him to the boat bound for New Orleans. When young George Shelby heard Tom had been sold, he followed Haley on his horse. George gave Tom a dollar as a token of his sympathy and told him that he would buy him back one day.

At the same time George Harris began his escape. White enough to pass as a Spaniard, he appeared at a tavern as a gentleman and took a room there, hoping to find before long a station on the underground railway.

Eliza was resting at the home of Rachel and Simeon Halliday when George Harris arrived in the same Quaker settlement.

On board the boat bound for New Orleans, Uncle Tom saved the life of young Eva St. Clare, and in gratitude Eva's father purchased the slave. Eva told Tom he would now have a happy life, for her father was kind to everyone. Augustine St. Clare was married to a woman who imagined herself sick and therefore took no interest in her daughter Eva. He had gone north to bring back his cousin, Miss Ophelia, to provide care for the neglected and delicate Eva. When they arrived at the St. Clare plantation, Tom was made head coachman.

Meanwhile Loker and Marks were on the trail of Eliza and George. They caught up with the fugitives and there was a fight in which George wounded Loker. Marks fled, and so the Quakers who were protecting the runaways took Loker along with them and gave him medical treatment.

Unused to lavish Southern customs, Miss Ophelia tried to understand the South. Shocked at the extravagance of St. Clare's household, she attempted to bring order out of the chaos, but she received no encouragement because the slaves had been humored and petted too long. Indulgent in all things, St. Clare was indifferent to the affairs of his family and his property. Uncle Tom lived an easy life in the loft over the stable. He and little Eva became close friends with St. Clare's approval. Sometimes St. Clare had doubts regarding the institution of slavery, and in one of these moods he bought an odd pixie-like child, Topsy, for his prim New England cousin to educate.

Eva grew more frail. Knowing that she was about to die, she asked her father to free his slaves, as he had so often promised. After Eva's death St. Clare began to read his Bible and to make plans to free all his slaves. He gave Topsy to Miss Ophelia legally, so that the spinster might rear the child as she wished. Then one evening he tried to separate two quarreling men. He received a knife wound in the side and died shortly afterward. Mrs. St. Clare had no intention of freeing the slaves, and she ordered Tom sent to the slave market.

At a public auction he was sold to a brutal plantation owner named Simon Legree. Legree drank heavily, and his plantation house had fallen to ruin. He kept dogs for the purpose of tracking runaway slaves. At the slave quarters Tom was given his sack of corn for the week, told to grind it himself and bake the meal into cakes for his supper. At the mill he aided two women. In return they baked his cakes for him. He read selections from the Bible to them.

For a few weeks Tom quietly tried to please his harsh master. One day he helped a sick woman by putting cotton into her basket. For this act Legree ordered him to flog the woman. When Tom refused, his master had him flogged until he fainted. A slave named Cassy came to Tom's aid. She told Tom the story of her life with Legree and of a young daughter who had been sold years before.

Then she went to Legree's apartment and tormented him. She hated her master and she had power over him. Legree was superstitious. When she talked, letting her eyes flash over him, he felt as though she were casting an evil spell. Haunted by the secrets of his guilty past, he drank until he fell asleep. But he had forgotten his fears by the next morning, and he knocked Tom to the ground with his fist.

Meanwhile, far to the north, George and Eliza and young Harry were making their way slowly through the stations on the underground railway toward Canada.

Cassy and Emmeline, another slave, determined to make their escape. Knowing the consequences if they should be caught, they tricked Legree into thinking they were hiding in the swamp. When Legree sent dogs and men after them, they sneaked back into the house and hid in the garret. Legree suspected that Tom knew where the women had gone and decided to beat the truth out of his slave. He had Tom beaten until the old man could neither speak nor stand.

Two days later George Shelby arrived to buy Tom back, but he came too late. Tom was dying. When George threatened to have Legree tried for murder, Legree mocked him. George struck Legree in the face and knocked him down.

Still hiding in the attic, Cassy and Emmeline pretended they were ghosts. Frightened, Legree drank harder than ever. George Shelby helped them to escape. Later, on a river boat headed north, the two women discovered a Madame de Thoux, who said she was George Harris' sister. With this disclosure, Cassy learned also that Eliza, her daughter, was the Eliza who had married George and with him and her child had escaped safely to Canada.

These relatives were reunited in Canada after many years. In Kentucky George Shelby freed all his slaves when his father died. He said he freed them in the name of Uncle Tom.

UNDER FIRE

Type of work: Novel
Author: Henri Barbusse (1874-1935)
Type of plot: Social criticism
Time of plot: 1914-1915
Locale: France
First published: 1917

Principal characters:
VOLPATTE,
EUDORE,
POTERLOO, and
JOSEPH MESNIL, French soldiers

Critique:

Barbusse ranks in time with the first of the writers who deglorified war. To him war in the trenches was a saga of mud, lice, and death. When they had to, the poilus worked and fought with a will, but anyone who had a wound severe enough for hospitalization was considered lucky. The characters have neither illusions nor glamour, but they do appreciate the necessity of stamping out war. To most of them the essence of war means killing Germans, but a few look on the enemy as people like themselves. *Under Fire* has no thread of plot; it is a mere series of incidents with only the war to connect them. The merit of the book lies in the vivid pictures it presents.

The Story:

High up in the mountains, the rich old men had every medical care at their sanatorium. When an obsequious servant softly told them that war had begun, they took the news in various ways. One said France must win; another thought it would be the last war.

Far down on the plain one could see specks, like ants, hurrying to and fro. Those thirty million men, in their common misery, held great power in their hands. When they became miserable enough, they would stop wars.

That morning they came out of the dugouts to the sound of rifle fire and cannonading. They were in fantastic dress against the cold, the damp, the mud; and all were incredibly dirty. As they stumbled out into the trenches, they reached inside their clothes to scratch their bare skins. As they walked along the trench, the oozy mud released each foot with a sticky sigh. Bertrand's squad, holding a secondary trench in the reserve line, was getting ready for another day. Lamuse, the ox-man, was puffy around the eyes; he had been on fatigue duty during the night.

Three breathless fatigue men brought up the breakfast. One of the squad asked what was in the cans; the mess man merely shrugged. Paradis looked in the cans; there were kidney beans in oil, bully beef, pudding, and coffee.

Cocon explained to his neighbor the arrangement of the trenches, for Cocon had seen a military map and had made some calculations. There were over six thousand miles of trenches on the French side and as many more on the German side. The French front was only an eighth part of the total world front. Just to think about it made one more insignificant, and it was terrible to imagine so much mud. The only possible way to look at the whole matter was to concentrate on dislodging the Boches in the opposite lines.

Tirloir had once seen a captured German officer, a Prussian colonel, who was being led along the communication trench when Tirloir kicked him. The

UNDER FIRE by Henri Barbusse. Translated by Fitzwater Wray. By permission of the publishers, E. P. Dutton & Co., Inc.

colonel nearly had a seizure when he realized that a mere private had touched him. The squad agreed that the German officers were the real evil.

There was a disturbance just ahead; some important people were coming to visit. One could hear oaths and grunts when it became known that they were civilians. One of the visitors was so bold as to ask if the coffee were good. The squad remembered the saying that winning a war is certain if the civilians can hold out.

When the mail came around, rumors flew fast. Many were sure that their squad was soon to be sent to the Riviera for a long rest; another had heard they were going to Egypt. The troops stopped their gossip as a company of African soldiers moved by; they decided an attack had been planned. The Africans were notoriously ferocious fighters.

During a sharp attack, Volpatte had both of his ears almost cut off. At the dressing station the doctors bandaged his head. Volpatte was happy to be going to the rear, for at last he could rest. After a long while he came back to the trenches with his ears nicely sewed. When his comrades asked him about the hospital he was so angry he could scarcely speak. Then it all came out; the hospital was swarming with malcontents, malingerers, and general shirkers. The worst were those assigned to the hospital for duty; they seemed to think they ran the whole war. The squad soothed Volpatte; let those who could, get by easily.

When the squad retired for a brief rest, they were billeted in a village where for an outrageous sum they rented a cow shed without walls. For a table they had a door on some boxes and a plank for a bench. But it was a wonderful experience to be above ground once more. The woman who ran the house sold them wine for twenty-two sous, although the established price was fifteen sous a bottle. Everywhere they went they heard the same story; the civilians had all the hardships.

Eudore got a fourteen-day leave. His wife, a practical person, applied well in advance for a permit to go to the village of her husband's people. She herself ran a tiny inn with only one room, where she would have no privacy to entertain her man, and Eudore's people had a big house. Eudore arrived in his village after much delay with only seven days left of his furlough, but his wife was not there; her permit had not arrived. Fearing to miss her, he stayed with his parents and waited. Then she wrote to say that no permits were allowed for civilian travel. Eudore went to the mayor and got permission to go to his wife. It was raining very hard when he got off the train to walk the several additional miles to his home. On the way he fell in with four poilus returning from leave. They tramped along together in the rain until they came to the inn. But Eudore and his wife could not turn out the four poilus in the rain, and so all six of them spent the night on chairs in the tiny room. Early in the morning Eudore left; his furlough was over.

Fraternization with the Boche was strictly forbidden. While out looking for bodies, Poterloo took a chance and fell in with some German privates, jolly fellows who offered to go with Poterloo to a nearby Alsatian village so that he could see his wife. Poterloo put on some great boots and a Boche coat and followed his friends behind the German lines. They reached the village safely. That night Poterloo walked twice past the house where his wife was staying with relatives. Through the lighted window he could see his wife and her sister at dinner with a group of German non-coms. They were laughing and eating well. Poterloo carried back to the trenches a disheartening picture of his wife laughing up into the face of a German sergeant.

There were six Mesnil brothers, four of them already killed by 1915. Joseph and André were pessimistic about their own chances. On reconnaissance, one of Bertrand's squad discovered André propped upright in a shell crater. At first they were afraid to tell Joseph, but he did not seem much affected by the news. Bertrand was killed. Then Joseph was wounded in the leg and taken to the dismal dressing station, a large dugout. There were many men in the dugout, most of them resigned to death, all of them given to spiritless discussion. It was agreed that to stop war you had to kill the spirit of war. That appeared to be a difficult job. It came as a new thought to some of them that they were the masses, and the masses had the power to stop war. But it was just too much to do. Many men thought only in terms of killing Boches. It hardly mattered anyway. Nearly all of them would be dead soon. The war went on.

UNDER TWO FLAGS

Type of work: Novel
Author: Ouida (Marie Louise de la Ramée, 1839-1908)
Type of plot: Sentimental romance
Time of plot: Early nineteenth century
Locale: London and environs, the continent, Algeria
First published: 1867

Principal characters:
THE HONORABLE BERTIE CECIL, a young Guardsman
BERKELEY, his younger brother
LORD ROCKINGHAM (THE SERAPH), Bertie's friend
RAKE, Bertie's servant
CIGARETTE, a French patriot
COLONEL CHATEAUROY, Bertie's enemy
PRINCESS CORONA D'AMAGÜE, the Seraph's sister

Critique:

Under Two Flags is a tale written by a master of her craft. As a novel it combines two popular traditions of English fiction, the adventure and the sentimental romance. Ouida was a widely read writer of her generation, and her books are still popular with those who have a fondness for a story of heroic adventure and characters of moral virtue.

The Story:

The Honorable Bertie Cecil, of the First Life Guards, although a fashionable member of his London set and an admirable fellow in every other respect, was uncommonly hard put to it for money. No money-lender in London would accept his note after he had mortgaged his whole inheritance. In those circumstances he depended upon winning a race with his six-year-old, Forest King, and he had staked everything on the race. Nevertheless with good-humored generosity he lent his younger brother, Berkeley, fifty pounds. The following day he rode Forest King to victory over a difficult course and received the praise of his lady, a fashionable peeress who had worn his scarlet and white.

His father, Lord Royallieu, who lived in the same mortgaged splendor that he had taught his sons to enjoy, loved his sons with the exception of Bertie, who looked too much like his dead wife's lover and, to the old viscount's detestation, carried the dead lover's name. The old man took every occasion to sneer at Bertie's extravagance, and one day revealed his suspicions that Bertie was really the son of Alan Bertie.

Bertie was petted by the world. Sought after by half the women in London, he carried on flirtations with many. Lady Guenevere was one of his conquests. Rake, his valet, was devoted to him. Bertie had salvaged Rake from a bad affair and had treated him as he treated others, with friendly decency.

While he was disturbed by his financial affairs, his head groom had promised to dope Forest King for a fee. When it was learned that Forest King had been doped before a race, his friends, far from blaming him, pretended to agree that the horse was merely ill, but Bertie felt himself disgraced.

While Bertie's best friend, Lord Rockingham, known to his comrades of the Guards as the Seraph, was attempting to discover the mystery of Forest King's condition, he received a report that Bertie Cecil had forged the Seraph's name to a note. Bertie could not deny the charge, for the note had been presented at a time when he had been dining with Lady Guenevere. Wishing to protect her name from scandal, Bertie allowed himself to be accused. Knowing that his brother had forged the note and hoping to protect Berkeley's name as well, he left London suddenly in order to escape arrest.

Bertie, accompanied by Rake, made his escape on Forest King. Rake had discovered that the groom had doped Forest King, and he had pummeled him for it. He and his master rode to a place of safety; then Bertie ordered Rake to take Forest King to Lord Rockingham. He waited in hiding for a time, in the hope Lady Guenevere would save him by telling of his whereabouts when the forged note was presented. She chose to keep silent, however, holding her reputation at greater worth than Bertie's name.

At last, by a throw of the dice, Bertie decided to cast his lot with the French Foreign Legion. The faithful Rake accompanied him. Back in England people believed Bertie dead as well as ruined. Rockingham had Forest King; the old viscount burned Bertie's picture.

As Louis Victor, Bertie made his mark with his new companions in the Foreign Legion. They marveled at his skill with the horses, at his bravery, at his brilliance at dancing or cards. Bertie was a veteran Legionnaire when he received, six months late, the news that his father had died at the age of ninety. His older brother inherited the title.

Cigarette, a woman of independent spirit, a dancer and singer for the troops, came to understand and like Bertie. She warned him against Colonel Chateauroy, who hated Bertie because of his gallant record and popularity, and asked him never to disobey any of the colonel's unreasonable commands. Partly because he pitied her, Bertie promised. Shortly afterward Cigarette saved Bertie's life from some drunken Arabs. She was in love with him, but he was indifferent to her.

Bertie spent his spare time carving chessmen of ivory and through this occupation he met the lovely Princess Corona d'Amagüe, a woman who had been unhappily married to a man injured while saving her brother's life. Her husband had died soon after, and the princess had felt ever since a feeling of responsibility for his death. Bertie soon fell in love with Princess Corona.

Colonel Chateauroy made it clear that he would never permit Bertie to be promoted above the rank of corporal. Bertie learned that Rake was purposely getting himself into trouble to prevent his own promotion, for he did not wish to outrank his master.

One day, in an old English journal, Bertie read that his older brother had died suddenly and that Berkeley had become Viscount Royallieu.

The regiment was ordered out. In the fighting that followed, Cigarette saved the day when she arrived at the head of a fresh squadron of cavalry. She found Bertie, badly wounded, on the battlefield. In the tent to which she had him carried, Bertie began to talk incoherently while Cigarette sat beside him. All she heard him say made her more jealous of the princess. She also learned that Bertie was English. No French person ever hated the English more than she. At her request Bertie was not told who had brought him back from the battlefield and cared for him during his sick ravings.

Three weeks later Bertie was startled when the Seraph came as an English tourist to visit the Legion camp. Not wishing to encounter his former friend, Bertie asked for and received permission to carry dispatches through hostile territory to another legion post. With faithful Rake, he rode away on a mission that meant almost certain death. Rake was killed in an Arab ambush, but Bertie delivered his dispatches safely. On his return trip he stopped at a way station and there saw his brother Berkeley, who was one of a party of tourists traveling with Princess Corona. Bertie gave no sign of recognition but spurred his horse and rode on.

Berkeley followed Bertie. When he caught up with his older brother, he revealed his fear that Bertie might claim the title. Indifferent to all except Berkeley's selfishness, Bertie asked his brother to leave Algeria at once.

Shortly afterward he discovered that Princess Corona was really the younger sister of the Seraph. She also became aware of Bertie's real name, and insisted that he make himself known to her brother. She begged him to claim his title, but he refused.

Cigarette went to Princess Corona, who requested her to tell Bertie that the Seraph was looking for his former friend. In another interview with Bertie, the princess asked him to tell his story and let the world be the judge. As he left her tent Colonel Chateauroy intercepted him and insulted the princess. In sudden rage Bertie struck his superior officer. Colonel Chateauroy arrested him. Bertie was sentenced to death.

When Cigarette heard Bertie's fate, she forced Berkeley, whom she met accidentally, to acknowledge that Bertie was in reality his brother, an exile for Berkeley's crime, and the true heir to the estate of Royallieu. She carried her story to a marshal of France, demanding that Bertie's honor be saved even though his life were already forfeited. With a stay of execution signed by the marshal she rode at full speed to reach the Legion camp before the hour set for Bertie's execution.

The Seraph, not Cigarette, reached Bertie first. But in spite of the Seraph's entreaties, Colonel Chateauroy refused to delay the time of execution.

Cigarette reached the spot just as the volley was fired. With her own body she took the bullets intended for Bertie. She died, the marshal's order safely delivered. A child of the army and a soldier of France, she gave her life to save a comrade. It was a sacrifice that Bertie and Princess Corona, happily reunited, were never to forget.

U. S. A.

Type of work: Novel
Author: John Dos Passos (1896-)
Type of plot: Social chronicle
Time of plot: 1900-1935
Locale: The United States
First published: 1930, 1933, 1936

Principal characters:
FAINY MCCREARY (MAC), a labor organizer
JANEY WILLIAMS, a private secretary
JOE WILLIAMS, her brother
J. WARD MOOREHOUSE, a public relations executive
ELEANOR STODDARD, an interior decorator
CHARLEY ANDERSON, an airplane manufacturer
RICHARD ELLSWORTH SAVAGE, Moorehouse's assistant

EVELINE HUTCHINS, Eleanor Stoddard's partner
ANNE ELIZABETH TRENT (DAUGHTER), a relief worker
BEN COMPTON, a radical
MARY FRENCH, a labor worker
MARGO DOWLING, a movie star

Critique:

U. S. A. is a collective novel in the sense that it deals with a great variety of characters, each moving upon his own social level, but all presented within the limits of a single novel. The result is a complete cross-section of American life covering the political, social, and economic history of the United States from the beginning of the century to the depression-ridden, war-threatened thirties. In addition to the life stories of his people, Dos Passos employs three technical devices to make his survey more complete: the Newsreel, quotations from newspapers, speeches, popular songs; the Camera Eye, brief impressionistic sketches from the author's own life; and biographies of public figures, such as radicals, inventors, and statesmen typical of their times. No other writer has attempted a wider panoramic view of our national life. The separate titles of Dos Passos' trilogy are *The 42nd Parallel, Nineteen Nineteen,* and *The Big Money.*

The Story:

The Spanish-American War was over. Politicians with mustaches said that America was now ready to lead the world.

Mac McCreary was a printer for a fly-by-night publisher in Chicago. Later he worked his way to the West Coast. There he got work as a printer in Sacramento and married Maisie Spencer, who could never understand his radical views. They quarreled and he went to Mexico to work in the revolutionary movement there.

Janey Williams, growing up in Washington, D. C., became a stenographer. She was always ashamed when her sailor brother, Joe, showed up, and even more ashamed of him after she became secretary to J. Ward Moorehouse. Of all Moorehouse's female acquaintances, she was the only one who never became his mistress.

J. Ward Moorehouse's boyish manner and blue eyes were the secret of his success. They attracted Annabelle Strang, the wealthy nymphomaniac he later divorced. Gertrude Staple, his second wife, helped to make him a prominent public relations expert. His shrewdness made him an ideal man for government service in France during World War I. After the war he became one of the nation's leading advertising executives.

Because Eleanor Stoddard hated the sordid environment of her childhood her delicate, arty tastes led her naturally into partnership with Eveline Hutchins in the decorating business, and eventually to New York and acquaintanceship with J. Ward Moorehouse. In Europe with the Red Cross during the war, she lived with Moorehouse. Back in New York in the twenties she used her connections in shrewd fashion and became engaged to a member of the Russian nobility.

Charley Anderson had been an aviator in the war. A successful invention and astute opportunism made him a wealthy airplane manufacturer. He married a wife who had little sympathy for his interest in mechanics. In Florida, after a plane crash, he met Margo Dowling, an actress. Charley Anderson's series of drunks ended in a grade crossing accident.

Joe Williams was a sailor who had been on the beach in Buenos Aires. In Norfolk he met Della, who urged him to give up seafaring and settle down. Unable to hold a job, he shipped out again and almost lost his life when the ship he was on was sunk by a German submarine. When Joe got his third mate's license, he and Della were married. He was ill in the East Indies, arrested in New York for not carrying a draft card, and torpedoed once more off Spain. Della was unfaithful to him. Treated coldly the few times he looked up his sister Janey, he shipped for Europe once more. One night in St. Nazaire he attacked a huge Senegalese who was dancing with a girl he knew. His skull was crushed when he was hit over the head with a bottle.

Teachers encouraged Dick Savage in his literary talents. During his teens he worked at a summer hotel and there he slept with a minister's wife who shared his taste in poetry. A government official paid his way through Harvard, where Dick cultivated his estheticism and mild snobbery before he joined the Norton-Harjes ambulance service and went to Europe. There some of his letters about the war came to the attention of censorship officials and he was shipped back to the United States. His former sponsor got him an officer's commission and he returned to France. In Italy he met a relief worker named Anne Elizabeth Trent, who was his mistress for a time. When he returned to the United States, he became an idea man for Moorehouse's advertising agency.

Eveline Hutchins, who had a small artistic talent, became Eleanor Stoddard's partner in a decorating establishment in New York. All her life she tried to escape from boredom through sensation. Beginning with the Mexican artist who was her first lover, she had a succession of affairs. In France, where she was Eleanor's assistant in the Red Cross, she married a shy young soldier named Paul Johnson. Later she had a brief affair with Charley Anderson. Dissatisfied, she decided at last that life was too dull for endurance and died from an overdose of sleeping pills.

Anne Elizabeth Trent, known as Daughter, was the child of moderately wealthy Texans. In New York she met Webb Cruthers, a young anarchist. One day, seeing a policeman kick a woman picketer in the face, Daughter attacked him with her fists. Her night in jail disturbed her father so much that she returned to Texas and worked in Red Cross canteens. Later she went overseas. There she met Dick Savage. Pregnant, she learned he had no intention of marrying her. In Paris she went on a drunken spree with a French aviator and died with him in a plane crash.

Benny Compton was the son of Jewish immigrants. After six months in jail for making radical speeches, he worked his way west through Canada. In Seattle he and other agitators were beaten by deputies. Benny returned East. One day police broke up a meeting where he was speaking. On his twenty-third birthday Benny went to Atlanta to serve a ten-year sentence. Released after the war, he lived for a time with Mary French, a fellow traveler in the party.

Mary French spent her childhood in Trinidad, where her father, a physician, did charity work among the native miners. Mary, planning to become a social worker, spent her summers at Jane Addams' Hull House. She went to Washington as secretary to a union official, and later worked as a union organizer in New York City. There she took care of Ben Compton after his release from Atlanta. While working with the Sacco-Vanzetti Committee she fell in love with Don Stevens, a fellow party member. Summoned to Moscow with a group of party leaders, Stevens returned to New York with a wife assigned to him by the party. Mary went back to her committee work for laboring men's relief.

Margo Dowling grew up in a rundown house in Rockaway, Long Island, with her drunken father and Agnes, her father's mistress. At last Agnes left her lover and took Margo with her. In New York Agnes became the common-law wife of an actor named Frank Mandeville. One day, while drunk, Mandeville raped the girl. Margo ran off to Cuba with Tony, an effeminate Cuban guitar player, whom she later deserted. She was a cheerful companion for Charley Anderson, who gave her a check for five thousand dollars on his deathbed. In Hollywood she met Sam Margolies, a successful producer, who made a star of her.

Jobless and hungry, a young hitchhiker stood by the roadside. Overhead droned a plane in which people of the big money rode the skyways. Below the hitchhiker with empty belly thumbed cars speeding by. The haves and the have-nots—that was America in the depression thirties.

VANESSA

Type of work: Novel
Author: Hugh Walpole (1884-1941)
Type of plot: Historical chronicle
Time of plot: Late nineteenth and early twentieth centuries
Locale: England
First published: 1933

Principal characters:
VANESSA PARIS, daughter of Adam Paris
BENJIE, her cousin and lover
TOM, Benjie's son
SALLY, daughter of Vanessa and Benjie
ELLIS, Vanessa's husband

Critique:

Vanessa, the last novel in the Herries chronicle, brings the family to the 1930's. Like its three predecessors, *Vanessa* is concerned with many people and many years, and the multiplicity of characters becomes necessarily more marked and confusing. Although many readers of the novel are lost in trying to follow the fortunes of so many descendants of the earlier Herries, Walpole does accomplish very well what appears to be a chief aim —to show that the strength of the Herries family is a strength of England and that its weakness is a national defect.

The Story:

Vanessa was fifteen when her grandmother, Judith Paris, died. At the funeral Adam, her sincere but unpolished father, made a speech which was admired only by Vanessa and her mother, Margaret. Adam loved his mother well and spoke with too much sincerity. His numerous relatives would rather have heard a eulogy of the proud family of Herries.

At the funeral Vanessa noticed everyone, and her beauty made even the most distant relatives notice her. She had special interest, however, for her cousin Benjie. Already she knew she loved him. Benjie was a rascal who could not fit in well with his haughty family. He was capable of hard work and common sense for a while, but he had sporadic fits of wildness. Some of his relatives believed that no good could come from Benjie's heritage. His uncle had killed his father. One grandfather had committed suicide. The other one was living out a mad dotage.

Vanessa also noticed hesitant, stiff Ellis Herries, her distant cousin. Ellis managed to remark that it was a nice day. As soon as Vanessa agreed, she ran out—to meet Benjie.

Adam did not like to have her go

walking with Benjie, even though Benjie was personable. Benjie kissed Vanessa, however, and she promised to marry him when she grew up. Vanessa was so good and beautiful that Benjie had qualms about such a promise. He told her the truth about his character and his wildness, and he attacked her faith in God. But Vanessa resolved to hold fast to her promise.

In 1880 Vanessa became engaged to Benjie. Still uneasy about his unworthiness, Benjie agreed that no one should know of the engagement and that they should not meet for two years. Then if they still wanted to do so, they would be married.

In the meantime Vanessa went to London to stay with her city cousins. Dressed in fashionable clothes, lovely Vanessa soon became an admired belle. She had many proposals of marriage, the most insistent from her cousin Ellis. Ellis was good and sober, already a respected financier. But Vanessa thought only of Benjie.

Vanessa returned home to Fell House to care for her ailing father and wait for the two years to end. Then, in 1882, Fell House burned down and Adam perished in the blaze. Too distraught to think of marriage at that time, Vanessa put Benjie off. Several weeks later she went to The Fortress to stay with Elizabeth, Benjie's mother, and to await the return of her fiancé. When he did come back, Vanessa knew that something had happened.

She soon learned the story. Sometime before Benjie had become acquainted with the Halliday family and had been attracted to their daughter Marion. After Adam Paris died, he went to visit the Hallidays. Following an evening of gaiety, he went upstairs to bed. In his room he found Marion, who was waiting for him at the urging of her mother. Marion became pregnant, and she and Benjie were married. Without bitterness Vanessa wished him a happy marriage and went back to London.

At the age of twenty-six, honored as the reigning beauty of London society, Vanessa finally decided to give in to Ellis and be kind to him. So Ellis and Vanessa were married, and Vanessa became the great lady of highly fashionable Hill House.

One day, quite by accident, she saw Benjie and his son Tom at the Jubilee Celebration. She did not talk with him, but she did learn that Marion had left Benjie for another man. After struggling with her inclinations for some time, she met Benjie again and visited with him as an old friend.

Meanwhile it was becoming more and more impossible for her to live with Ellis. His mind was weakening rapidly and he had delusions of persecution. To the outward eye, however, he still was the sober financier. One night he locked himself and Vanessa in their room and announced that he intended to cut her throat and then his own. She talked him out of the notion, but she was afraid of him from that time on.

Then Ellis brought in two elderly cousins to take charge of the house and to spy on Vanessa. As his next step he engaged an obliging doctor to interview his wife. Before Vanessa was quite aware of what was happening, she learned that she was to be confined in an asylum for the insane. In her fear and helplessness she turned to Benjie for help. At last, when both were nearing forty and without benefit of marriage, Vanessa and Benjie went away to live together.

Tom, Benjie's son, and Vanessa became great friends, and for a time she lived a happy life at The Fortress. Gradually Benjie's absences from home became less frequent, and sometimes Vanessa would accompany him on his week-long rambles. On one occasion they were caught in a storm. Much upset and exhausted, he and Vanessa found shelter in a farmhouse, and there among strangers their daughter Sally was born.

But the household at The Fortress was soon broken up. Ellis' mind gave way completely, and he could amuse himself only by playing with toys. He cried much of the time for Vanessa, until it seemed that he could not live long without her. At last Vanessa took Sally to London and vowed she would stay with Ellis until he died.

Ironically, Ellis became stronger and better, and for years Benjie could not see Vanessa. In fact, Vanessa died before Ellis. At her deathbed Benjie and Ellis met without rancor.

The rest of the numerous Herries family were all stolid, respectable people, still pillars of Victorian rectitude. Only Benjie and Sally were free and untrammeled. Sally expected to marry Arnold Young, and even became his mistress for a year. But Arnold's mother objected to the marriage. Benjie's reputation was bad, and Sally herself was illegitimate. At last Arnold married another woman.

Benjie continued his irregular life. In South Africa he had lost an arm fighting the Boers. In World War I, in spite of being over sixty years old, he served with the Russians. At the age of seventy he was still brown of skin and spare of body. Sally, too, became respectable and redeemed herself in the eyes of her relatives. At a social gathering she met a blind French veteran who was working for the League of Nations in Berlin. She married him and went to Berlin to aid the cause of international peace. From that time on she rarely saw her father or any other members of the Herries family.

Only Benjie, of all the Herries, was still unconventional. After he was seventy, he bought a caravan and with one manservant lived a gipsy life. He intended to spend his last days going to fairs and visiting farm folk. Faithfully he did his setting up exercises and took cold showers out of doors. The other Herries always said that he was truly the great-grandson of that Francis Herries who married Mirabell Starr, the gipsy—lusty old Rogue Herries of whom the family was now half ashamed, half proud.

VANITY FAIR

Type of work: Novel
Author: William Makepeace Thackeray (1811-1863)
Type of plot: Social satire
Time of plot: Early nineteenth century
Locale: England and Europe
First published: 1847-1848

Principal characters:
Becky Sharp, an adventuress
Amelia Sedley, her friend
Joseph Sedley (Jos), Amelia's brother
Rawdon Crawley, Becky's husband
Miss Crawley, Rawdon's wealthy aunt
Old Sir Pitt Crawley, Rawdon's father
Young Sir Pitt Crawley, Rawdon's brother
George Osborne, Amelia's husband
Captain William Dobbin, Amelia's friend

Critique:

Vanity Fair, the best known of Thackeray's works, has justly joined the ranks of the classics, for in it Thackeray has created characters as great as any in English literature. Most of his people are not good people, but then they were not intended to be. Thackeray shows that goodness often goes hand in hand with stupidity and folly, that cleverness is often knavery. A cynical story, this novel was intended to expose social hypocrisy and sham. Although Thackeray was frankly moralistic, his moral does not in any way overshadow a magnificent novel or the life-like characters he created.

The Story:

Becky Sharp and Amelia Sedley became good friends while they were students at Miss Pinkerton's School for girls. It was proof of Amelia's good, gentle nature that she took as kindly as she did to her friend, who was generally disliked by all the other girls. Amelia overlooked as much as she could the evidences of Becky's selfishness.

After the two girls had finished their education at the school, Becky accompanied her friend to her home for a short visit. There she first met Joseph Sedley, Amelia's older brother Jos, who was home on leave from military service in India. Jos was a shy man, unused to women, and certainly to women as designing and flirtatious as Becky. His blundering and awkward manners did not appeal to many women, but Becky was happy to overlook these faults when she compared them with his wealth and social position. Amelia innocently believed that her friend had fallen in love with her brother, and she discreetly tried to further the romance.

To this end she arranged a party at Vauxhall, at which Becky and Jos, along with Amelia and her admirer, George Osborne, were present. There was a fifth member of the group, Captain Dobbin, a tall, lumbering fellow, also in service in India. He had long been in love with Amelia, but he recognized how much more suitable for her was the dashing George Osborne. But all the maneuvering of the flirtatious Becky and the amiable Amelia was not sufficient to corner Jos, who drank too much punch and believed that he had made a silly figure of himself at the party. A day or so later a letter delivered to the Sedley household announced that Jos was ill and planned to return to India as soon as possible.

Since there was no longer any reason for Becky to remain with the Sedleys, she left Amelia, after many tears and kisses, to take a position as governess to two young girls at Queen's Crawley. The head of the household was Sir Pitt Crawley, a cantankerous old man renowned for his miserliness. Lady Crawley was an apathetic soul who lived in fear of her husband's unreasonable outbursts. Deciding that she would have nothing to fear from her timid mistress, Becky spent most of her time ingratiating herself with Sir Pitt and ignoring her pupils. Becky also showed great interest in Miss Crawley, a spinster aunt of the family, who was exceedingly wealthy. Miss Crawley paid little attention to Sir Pitt and his children, but she was fond of Rawdon Crawley, a captain in the army and a son of Sir Pitt by a previous marriage. So fond was she of her dashing young nephew that she supported him through school and paid all his gambling debts with hardly a murmur.

During Becky's stay, Miss Crawley visited Sir Pitt only once, at a time when Rawdon was also present. The handsome young dragoon soon fell prey to Becky's wiles and followed her about devotedly. Becky also took care to ingratiate herself with the holder of the purse strings. Miss Crawley found Becky witty and charming, and did not attempt to disguise her opinion that the little governess was worth all the rest of the Crawley household put together. And so Becky found herself in a very enviable position. Sir Pitt was obviously interested in her, as was his handsome son. Miss Crawley insisted that Becky accompany her back to London.

Becky had been expected to return to her pupils after only a short stay with Miss Crawley. But Miss Crawley was taken ill and she refused to allow anyone but her dear Becky to nurse her. Afterward there were numerous other excuses to prevent the governess from returning to her duties. Certainly Becky was not unhappy. Rawdon Crawley was a constant caller, and a devoted suitor for Becky's hand. When the news arrived that Lady Crawley had died, no great concern was felt by anyone. But a few days later Sir Pitt himself appeared, asking to see Miss Sharp. Much to Becky's surprise, the baronet threw himself at her feet and asked her to marry him. Regretfully, she refused his offer. She was already secretly married to Rawdon Crawley.

Following this disclosure, Rawdon and his bride left for a honeymoon at Brighton. Old Miss Crawley, chagrined and angry, took to her bed, changed her will, and cut off her nephew without a shilling. Sir Pitt raved with anger.

Amelia's marriage had also precipitated a family crisis. Her romance with George had proceeded with good wishes on both sides, until Mr. Sedley, through some unfortunate business deals, lost most of his money. Then George's snobbish father ordered his son to break his engagement to a penniless woman. George, whose affection for Amelia was never stable, was inclined to accept this parental command. But Captain Dobbin, who saw with distress that Amelia was breaking her heart over George, finally prevailed upon the young man to go through with the marriage, regardless of his father's wishes. When the couple arrived in Brighton for their honeymoon, they found Rawdon and Becky living there happily in penniless extravagance.

Captain Dobbin also arrived in Brighton. He had agreed to act as intercessor with Mr. Osborne. But his hopes of reconciling father and son were shattered when Mr. Osborne furiously dismissed Captain Dobbin and took immediate steps to disown George. Captain Dobbin also brought the news that the army had been ordered to Belgium. Napoleon had landed from Elba. The Hundred Days had begun.

In Brussels the two couples met again. George Osborne was infatuated with Becky. Jos Sedley, now returned from India, and Captain Dobbin were also stationed in that city, Captain Dobbin in faithful attendance upon neglected Amelia. Everyone was waiting for the next move Napoleon would make, but in the meantime the gaiety of the Duke of Wellington's forces was widespread. The Osbornes and Sedleys attended the numerous balls. Becky, especially, made an impression upon military society and her coquetry extended with equal effect from general to private. The fifteenth of June, 1815, was a famous night in Brussels, for on that evening the Duchess of Richmond gave a tremendous ball. Amelia left the party early, brokenhearted at the attentions her husband was showing Becky. Shortly after she left, the men were given orders to march to meet the enemy. Napoleon had entered Belguim, and a great battle was impending.

As Napoleon's forces approached, fear and confusion spread through Brussels, and many of the civilians fled from the city. Not so Amelia or Becky. Becky was not alarmed, and Amelia refused to leave while George was in danger. She remained in the city some days before she heard that her husband had been killed. Rawdon returned safely from the battle of Waterloo. He and Becky spent a gay and triumphant season in Paris, where Becky's beauty and wit gained her a host of admirers. Rawdon was very proud of the son she bore him.

Amelia, too, had a child. She had returned to London almost out of her mind with grief, and only after her son was born did she show any signs of rallying.

When Becky grew bored with the pleasures of Paris, the Crawleys returned to London. There they rented a large home and proceeded to live well on nothing a year. By this time Becky was a past master at this art, and so they lived on a grander scale than Rawdon's small winnings at cards would warrant. Becky had become acquainted with the nobility of England, and had made a particular impression on rich old Lord Steyne. At last all society began to talk about young

Mrs. Crawley and her elderly admirer. Fortunately Rawdon heard nothing of this ballroom and coffee house gossip.

Eventually, through the efforts of Lord Steyne, Becky achieved her dearest wish, presentation at Court. Presented along with her was the wife of the new Sir Pitt Crawley. The old man had died, and young Sir Pitt, his oldest son and Rawdon's brother, had inherited the title. Since then friendly relations had been established between the two brothers. If Rawdon realized that his brother had also fallen in love with Becky, he gave no sign, and he accepted the money his brother gave him with good grace. But more and more he felt himself shut out from the gay life that Becky enjoyed. He spent much time with his son, for he realized that the child was neglected. Once or twice he saw young George Osborne, Amelia's son.

Amelia struggled to keep her son with her, but her pitiful financial status made it difficult to support him. Her parents had grown garrulous and morose with disappointment over their reduced circumstances. At length Amelia sorrowfully agreed to let Mr. Osborne take the child and rear him as his own. Mr. Osborn still refused to recognize the woman his son had married against his wishes, however, and Amelia rarely saw the boy.

Rawdon was now deeply in debt. When he appealed to Becky for money, she told him that she had none to spare. She made no attempt to explain the jewelry and other trinkets she bought. When Rawdon was imprisoned for a debt, he wrote and asked Becky to take care of the matter. She answered that she could not get the money until the following day. But an appeal to Sir Pitt brought about Rawdon's release, and he returned to his home to find Becky entertaining Lord Steyne. Not long afterward Rawdon accepted a post abroad, never to return to his unfaithful, designing wife.

Amelia's fortunes had now improved. When Jos Sedley returned home, he established his sister and father in a more pleasant home. Mrs. Sedley having died, Jos resolved to do as much as he could to make his father's last days happy. Captain Dobbin had returned from India and confessed his love for Amelia. Although she acknowledged him as a friend, she was not yet ready to accept his love. It was Captain Dobbin who went to Mr. Osborne and gradually succeeded in reconciling him to his son's wife. When Mr. Osborne died, he left a good part of his fortune to his grandson, appointing Amelia as the boy's guardian.

Amelia, her son, Captain Dobbin, and Jos Sedley took a short trip to the continent. This visit was perhaps the happiest time in Amelia's life. Her son was with her constantly, and Captain Dobbin was a devoted attendant. Eventually his devotion was to overcome her hesitation and they were to be married.

At a small German resort they encountered Becky once more. After Rawdon left her, Becky had been unable to live down the scandal of their separation. Leaving her child with Sir Pitt and his wife, she crossed to the continent. Since then she had been living with first one considerate gentleman and then another. When she saw the prosperous Jos, she vowed not to let him escape as he had before. Amelia and Jos greeted her in a friendly manner, and only Captain Dobbin seemed to regard her with distrust. He tried to warn Jos about Becky, but Jos was a willing victim of her charms.

Becky traveled with Jos wherever he went. Although she could not get a divorce from Rawdon, Jos treated her as his wife, and in spite of Captain Dobbin's protests he took out a large insurance policy in her name. A few months later his family learned that he had died while staying with Becky at Aix-la-Chapelle. The full circumstances of his death were never established, but Becky came into a large sum of money from his insurance. She spent the rest of her life on the continent, where she assumed the role of the virtuous widow and won a reputation for benevolence and generosity.

VENUS AND ADONIS

Type of work: Poem
Author: William Shakespeare (1564-1616)
Type of plot: Mythological romance
Time of plot: Remote antiquity
Locale: Ancient Greece
First published: 1593

Principal characters:
VENUS, goddess of love
ADONIS, a handsome youth loved by Venus

Critique:

Shakespeare's *Venus and Adonis* gains most of its beauty from the magnificent imagery and figurative language with which the poet adorned the ancient tale. The sources for the poem, whether they were from Ovid or more recent writers, are unimportant, as the value of Shakespeare's version lies in his additions and not in the original story. The discussion of hunting, the incident of the stallion and the jennet, and the scenes of the fox and the hare are among the beauties which Shakespeare added.

The Story:

In all the world there was no more beautiful figure, no more perfectly made creature, than young Adonis. Although his beauty was a delight to the sun and to the winds, he had no interest in love. His only joy was in hunting, in riding over the hills and fields after the deer and the fox. When Venus, the goddess of love, saw the beauty of young Adonis, she came down to earth because she was filled with love for him.

Meeting him one morning in the fields as he rode out to the hunt, she urged him to dismount, tie his horse to a tree, and talk with her. Adonis had no desire to talk to any woman, or even to the goddess, but she forced him to do as she wished. Reclining by his side, she looked at him with caressing glances and talked passionately of the wonder and glory of love. The more she talked, the more she begged him for a kind look, a kiss, the more anxious he became to leave her and go on with his hunting. But Venus was not easily repulsed, and although Adonis sought to leave she urged him to stay. She told him how even the god of war had been a willing prisoner of her charms, and she numbered all the pleasures she could offer him if he would accept her love. Blushing, Adonis finally broke from her arms and went to get his horse.

At that moment his stallion heard the call of a jennet in a field nearby. Aroused, he broke the leather thong that held him and ran to her. At first the jennet pretended to be cold to the stallion's advances, but when she perceived that Adonis was about to overtake his mount, she gave a neigh of affection and the two horses galloped away to another field. Adonis was left behind.

Dejected, he stood thinking of the hunt that he was missing because his horse had run away. Venus came up to him again and continued her pleas of love. For a while he listened to her, but in disgust he turned finally and gave her such a look of scorn that the lovesick goddess fainted and fell to the ground. Thinking that with an unkind look he had killed her, Adonis knelt beside her, rubbed her wrists, and kissed her in hope of forgiveness.

After a while Adonis rose to his feet. Venus, recovering from her swoon, asked him for one last kiss. He grudgingly consented before he turned to leave. Venus asked when she could meet him the next day. Adonis replied that he would not see her, for he was to go boar hunting. Struck with a vision, the goddess warned the youth that he would be killed by a boar if he hunted the next day, and she begged him to meet her instead. When she threw herself on the boy and carried him to the earth in her arms in a last attempt to gain his love, Adonis admonished the goddess on the difference between heavenly love and earthly lust. He left her alone and weeping.

The next morning found Venus wandering through the woods in search of Adonis. In the distance she could hear the cries of the dogs and the voices of the hunters. Frantic because of her vision of the dead Adonis, she rushed through the forest trying to follow the sounds of the hunt. When she saw a wounded and bleeding dog, the fear she felt for Adonis became almost overpowering. Suddenly she came upon Adonis lying dead, killed by the fierce wild boar he had hunted.

The grief of Venus knew no bounds. If this love were taken from her, then never again should man love happily. Where love was, there also would mistrust, fear, and grief be found.

The body of Adonis lay white and cold on the ground, his blood coloring the earth and plants about him. From this soil there grew a flower, white and purple like the blood that spotted the skin of Venus' dead love. With a broken heart Venus left earth to hide her sorrow in the dwelling place of the gods.

THE VICAR OF WAKEFIELD

Type of work: Novel
Author: Oliver Goldsmith (1728-1774)
Type of plot: Sentimental romance
Time of plot: Eighteenth century
Locale: Rural England
First published: 1766

Principal characters:
Dr. Primrose, the vicar of Wakefield
Deborah, his wife
George, the oldest son
Sophia, the younger daughter
Olivia, the older daughter
Mr. Burchell, in reality Sir William Thornhill
Squire Thornhill, Dr. Primrose's landlord and Olivia's betrayer
Arabella Wilmot, betrothed to George

Critique:

Buried in the rationalism of the eighteenth century was a strain of idealism and sentimentality which is clearly expressed in *The Vicar of Wakefield*. In this novel the interplay of the ideal and the real present a simple, lovable character in his struggle to maintain his ideals. Goldsmith's material cannot be said to be original, but his wit and gentle candor are his own. For these qualities he has been loved by many readers.

The Story:

Dr. Primrose and his wife, Deborah, were blessed with five fine children, of whom the two daughters, Olivia and Sophia, were remarkable for their beauty. The Primrose family lived in a quiet rural community, where they enjoyed both wealth and good reputation. The oldest son, George, fell in love with Arabella Wilmot, daughter of a neighbor, and the two families made mutual preparations for the wedding. Before the wedding, however, Dr. Primrose and Miss Wilmot's father quarreled over the question of a man's remarrying after the death of his wife. Dr. Primrose stoutly upheld the doctrine of monogamy. Mr.

Wilmot, who was about to take his fourth wife, was insulted. The rift between the two families widened when news came that Dr. Primrose's broker had run off with all his money. Mr. Wilmot broke off the wedding plans, for the vicar was now a poor man.

George departed for London to make his fortune and the rest of the family prepared to go to another part of the country, where Dr. Primrose had found a more modest living. On the way they met a man who won the admiration of Dr. Primrose by a deed of charity to a fellow traveler. The man, Mr. Burchell, rode along with them. Suddenly Sophia was thrown from her horse into a stream, from which Mr. Burchell was able to save her. The gratitude of Deborah assured Mr. Burchell of a warm welcome whenever he should choose to call on them.

Their new home was on the estate of wealthy Squire Thornhill, a young man known for his attentions to all the young ladies in the neighborhood. Deborah thought that either of her daughters would make a good match for the young squire. Soon afterward a fortunate meeting drew the squire's attention toward Olivia, and her mother's scheming made Squire Thornhill a steady caller at the Primrose home, where Olivia blushingly protested that she thought him both bold and rude. Mr. Burchell, too, called frequently, but his interest seemed to center upon Sophia, who did not deny her pleasure at his attention. Dr. Primrose, however, could not approve of Mr. Burchell, for he had lost all his fortune and seemed to live in comparative poverty that revealed indifference to his fallen condition.

Two noble ladies from the city met the Primrose family in their rustic retreat, and Sophia and Olivia became charmed by talk of city ways. When the women spoke of their need for companions in their households, Deborah immediately suggested that Olivia and Sophia be selected. The two daughters were pleased at the thought of going to the city, despite Mr. Burchell's vigorous objections. All was set for the journey, however, when Deborah received a letter stating that a secret informant had so slandered Olivia and Sophia that the city ladies would not consider them as fit companions. At first Deborah and her husband could not imagine who the slanderer could have been. When they learned that Mr. Burchell had been the informant, Dr. Primrose ordered him from the house. With no signs of remorse or shame Mr. Burchell left.

Olivia began to insist that Squire Thornhill's repeated visits meant only that he intended to marry her. Dr. Primrose, not believing that the squire really would marry Olivia, suggested to his daughter that she consider the offer of a neighboring farmer, Mr. Williams. When the squire still failed to ask for her hand, Olivia agreed to marry the young farmer and the wedding date was set. Four days before her wedding Olivia ran away. Through the help of Squire Thornhill, Dr. Primrose learned that it was Mr. Burchell who had carried the girl away.

Saddened by his daughter's indiscretion, the resolute father set out to find her and to help her. On his journey he became ill and lay in bed in an inn for three weeks. On his recovery he gave up all hope of finding Olivia and started home. On the way there he met Miss Arabella Wilmot, who inquired about George. Dr. Primrose assured her that George had not been heard from since he had left his family to go to London. Squire Thornhill, who was courting Arabella, asked about Olivia, but the father could give him no news. Fortune brought George, impoverished and in ill luck, back to his father at that time. Pitying the bad fortune of the young boy, Squire Thornhill gave him a commission in the army and sent him away. Arabella promised to wait for her former sweetheart to make his fortune and to return to her.

Dr. Primrose started for home once

more. At a roadside inn he found his dear Olivia, who told him her terrible story. The villain with whom she had run away was not Mr. Burchell. It had been Squire Thornhill, who had seduced her after a mock ceremony by a false priest. Growing tired of her, the squire had left her. Dr. Primrose took the girl home with him. But bad luck had not forsaken the vicar. As he approached his house he saw it catch fire and burn to the ground. His family escaped, but all their belongings were destroyed.

Kindly neighbors helped the penniless Primroses to set up living quarters in an outbuilding on the estate. News came that Squire Thornhill intended to marry Arabella Wilmot. This report angered Dr. Primrose; then to add to his indignation Squire Thornhill came to see him and offered to find a husband for Olivia so that she could stay near the squire. Enraged at this offer, the doctor ordered him away. The squire then demanded Dr. Primrose's quarterly rent payment which, since the disaster of losing his home, the vicar could not pay.

Squire Thornhill had Dr. Primrose sent to debtors' prison. Soon after being lodged in prison, the vicar encountered his son, George, who, having learned of the squire's cruelty, had attacked him and had been sentenced to hang for attempted murder. Dr. Primrose felt that the happiness of his life was completely shattered. Next he learned that Sophia had been kidnaped.

But virtue and honesty were soon rewarded. Sophia had been rescued by Mr. Burchell, who turned out to be the squire's uncle, Sir William Thornhill. With the squire's treachery exposed, the Primrose family was released from its misery. Arabella and George were reunited. Even Olivia was saved from shame, for she learned that the priest who had married her to the squire had been a genuine priest. Sophia married Sir William, and Arabella married George. Dr. Primrose looked forward to his old age with happiness and joy in the good fortune of his children. Even he was rewarded for his virtue. The broker who had run away with his money was apprehended, and Dr. Primrose was once again a wealthy man.

THE VICOMTE DE BRAGELONNE

Type of work: Novel
Author: Alexandre Dumas, father (1802-1870)
Type of plot: Historical romance
Time of plot: Seventeenth century
Locale: France and England
First published: 1848-1850

Principal characters:

Louis XIV, King of France
Louise de la Vallière, lady in waiting and mistress of the king
D'Artagnan, an officer of the king's musketeers
Athos, the Comte de la Fère
Porthos, M. du Vallon
Aramis, M. D'Herblay and Bishop of Vannes
Raoul, the Vicomte de Bragelonne, son of Athos
Fouquet, Minister of Finance
Colbert, an ambitious politician
Charles II, King of England

Critique:

The novels of the older Dumas have an enduring popularity for many readers, and *The Vicomte de Bragelonne,* the last of the D'Artagnan romances, is no exception. This novel has particular interest because it deals with the last adventures of that swashbuckling hero, D'Artagnan. The story itself is the characteristic Dumas type, filled with vivid action, humorous incident, and interesting characters. In reality this romance contains four different but related plots—the restoration of Charles II, the story of Louis XIV's infatuation for Louise de la Vallière, the intrigues and downfall of the ambitious Fouquet, and the perennially popular tale of the mysterious prisoner in the iron mask. These stories have, from time to time, been taken from the longer romance and printed as novels complete in themselves. As a result, some confusion has arisen over the titles and order of the D'Artagnan series.

The Story:

Louis XIV, the young king of France, en route to Spain to ask for the hand of Marie Theresa, the Spanish Infanta, stopped overnight at the castle of Blois to visit his uncle, the Duc d'Orléans. There he met for the first time Louise de la Vallière, the lovely stepdaughter of the duchess' steward. Louise was betrothed to Raoul, the Vicomte de Bragelonne, son of the Comte de la Fère. Another arrival at Blois during the royal visit was the Stuart pretender, Charles II, who came to ask for a loan of a million livres and French aid in regaining the English throne. When Cardinal Mazarin, chief minister of King Louis, refused to lend the money, Charles then turned for assistance to the Comte de la Fère, who had been an old friend of his royal father. The comte was a former musketeer who had been known as Athos many years before, when he had performed many brave feats with his three friends, Porthos, Aramis and D'Artagnan.

Disappointed because Mazarin and the king refused to help Charles, D'Artagnan resigned his commission as lieutenant of the king's musketeers and joined his old friend, Athos, in an attempt to place Charles upon the throne of England. Planning to capture General Monk, leader of the Parliamentary army, D'Artagnan visited Planchet, a former servant who had been successful in trade. Using funds borrowed from Planchet, he recruited fourteen resolute and dependable men and sailed with them for England. In England, in the meantime, the troops of Lambert and General Monk prepared to fight at Newcastle. While the armies waited, Athos arrived to see General Monk and get his aid in recovering a treasure left by the unfortunate Charles I in a vault in Newcastle. This treasure was to be General Monk's bribe for restoring Charles II to the throne. On the general's return from Newcastle, D'Artagnan daringly captured the Parliamentary leader and took him, concealed in a coffin, to France. Athos, who had promised General Monk to remain in England for a time, was arrested by Monk's soldiers and accused of complicity in the general's disappearance.

In France D'Artagnan took Monk to Charles and after a satisfactory interview with the pretender Monk was released and sent back to England. There Monk on his return secured the release of Athos. Monk, won over to the Stuart cause, planned for the return of Charles to England, while the pretender made like preparations in France.

When Charles became king, he made General Monk Duke of Albemarle and commander of the English armies. To Athos the grateful king gave the Order of the Golden Fleece. For his part in the restoration D'Artagnan requested only Monk's sword. After he had received it, he resold it to Charles for three hundred thousand livres. General Monk gave D'Artagnan lands in England. After paying off his men D'Artagnan went to Calais to see Planchet, whom he approached with a long face and a sad tale of failure. When Planchet showed his true loyalty to his former master, D'Artagnan had not the heart to tease the merchant any longer; he acknowledged the success of the venture and paid Planchet one hundred thousand livres in return for the funds he had advanced.

Louis XIV had been completely dominated by Cardinal Mazarin, his minister, but the death of the latter eased the king's unhappy situation. After Mazarin's death, the ambitious Fouquet, as finance minister, and Colbert, as intendant, began a race for power. Suspicious of Fouquet, the king sent for D'Artagnan, recommissioned him as captain of the king's musketeers, and sent him to Belle-Isle-en-Mer to secure a report on Fouquet's mysterious activities there.

At Belle-Isle D'Artagnan found his old companion in arms, Porthos, now M. du Vallon, busy with plans for fortifying the island. The former musketeer was working under the direction of Aramis, now Bishop of Vannes and also known as M. D'Herblay. D'Artagnan hurried back to Paris to the king to give him the details of the situation at Belle-Isle, but he was beaten in the race to arrive there first by the two conspirators, who reported to Fouquet the discovery of the plot to fortify the island. To prevent trouble, Fouquet at once rushed to the king and presented to him the plan for the fortifications on Belle-Isle. He explained glibly that the fortifications might be useful against the Dutch.

Athos, the Comte de la Fère, asked the king's consent to the marriage of his son Raoul, the Vicomte de Bragelonne, to Louise de la Vallière, now a maid of honor at the court. Louis refused on the grounds that Louise was not good enough for Raoul. In reality the king, a passionate lover of various ladies of the court, had, in spite of his recent marriage to Marie Theresa, fallen in love with Louise. He dispatched Raoul at once to England to be rid of him as a rival.

Aramis and Fouquet were plotting to replace the king with a man of their choice, and to this end they annually paid a large sum of money to M. de Baisemeaux, governor of the Bastille. These schemers also attached themselves to Louise de la Vallière after they realized the power she would have with the king.

Among the court plotters also were Mademoiselle de Montalais, a lady in waiting, and her lover, Malicorne, a courtier. They were interested in all court affairs, particularly in the relationship between Mademoiselle de la Vallière and the king, and they stole letters with the idea of blackmail at an opportune time.

D'Artagnan moved to an estate close to the court to watch for palace intrigues. He was particularly interested in the plans of Aramis, who was trying to become a cardinal and planning to betray the king to secure his ends. D'Artagnan, interested in adventure for the sake of adventure, was devoted to the king.

As the affair between Louise and the king continued, Madame, the sister-in-law of Louis, also in love with him, grew jealous and determined to send for Raoul and have him marry Louise at once. The queen mother and the young queen disapproved thoroughly of the flirtation of Madame with the king and told her so. Madame then decided that the quickest solution would be to send Mademoiselle de la Vallière away from the court. At the same time the king learned that Louise had at one time returned Raoul de Bragelonne's affection, and in a fit of envy and jealousy he decided to forget her. Madame ordered Louise to leave at once.

Broken-hearted, the girl resolved to enter a convent. In her flight, however, she encountered D'Artagnan, who took her under his protection and informed the king of her whereabouts. Louis went to her immediately. Convinced of her love, he returned with her to the court. Plotters in the king's pay had a secret trapdoor constructed from Louise's rooms to those of Saint-Aignan, a gentleman of the king, and Louis and Louise were able to meet there after Madame had made other meetings between them impossible. In London Raoul heard what was happening and rushed to France. He arrived at Louise's apartments just as the king was entering by the secret door. Realizing that the rumors he had heard were true, he went away in despair.

Aramis, who had now become General of the Jesuits, who visited by an elderly duchess who wished to sell him certain letters from Mazarin which would ruin his friend Fouquet. When he refused to buy them, she sold them to Colbert, Fouquet's rival and enemy. Aramis, learning of the transaction, hurried to warn Fouquet, who assured Aramis that the supposed theft of state funds attributed to him in the letters was credited by a receipt in his possession. The receipt, however, had been stolen. Furthermore, Colbert had arranged for Fouquet to sell his position of procureur-general. Aramis, with his immense financial backing, was able to rescue Fouquet.

Raoul de Bragelonne, grieved and angry at Louise's faithlessness, challenged Saint-Aignan to a duel and Porthos promised to act as his foster son's second. Saint-Aignan, however, revealed the matter to the king. Then Athos publicly denounced Louis over the proposed duel. When the king ordered D'Artagnan to arrest Athos, D'Artagnan, by his honest fearlessness, won a pardon for his old friend.

Fouquet, backed by Aramis, grandly and recklessly humiliated Colbert in the king's presence. He announced a great fête at his estate in honor of the king. Colbert, although temporarily eclipsed, vowed revenge. Fouquet, as minister of the king's finances, was tottering under the growing strength of his enemy Colbert, and he hoped the fête would secure his position.

Aramis, through his influence with M. de Baisemeaux, the governor of the Bastille, visited a prisoner there and revealed to him that he was actually the twin brother of Louis XIV. The conspirators planned to put him on the throne in place of Louis. Aramis then busied himself to learn the details of the king's costume for the fête, for he planned to substitute the twin brother Philippe for Louis during the grand ball. Although both D'Artagnan and Porthos were suspicious of Aramis, they could prove nothing.

Aramis freed the young prince from the Bastille and coached him thoroughly in the details of the role he was to play. By means of trapdoors in Fouquet's house, Aramis overpowered Louis XIV and hustled him off to the Bastille to replace the released prince. Philippe, in gratitude, was to make Aramis as powerful in the kingdom as Richelieu had been.

But Aramis made a grave error in revealing his deeds to Fouquet. When Fouquet heard of the abduction of the king, the minister, hoping to win the king's gratitude, rushed to the Bastille and freed Louis. Aramis and Porthos fled hastily. D'Artagnan was instructed to capture Philippe, cover his face with an iron mask to hide his resemblance to the king, and imprison him for life in the Ile Sainte-Marguerite fortress. These orders he executed faithfully.

Raoul de Bragelonne, who had never forgiven the king for stealing Louise de la Vallière, decided to kill himself as soon as possible and joined the Duc de Beaufort on a campaign to Africa. When he went to say goodbye to his father, Athos realized sadly that he would never see his son again.

Louis XIV insisted that D'Artagnan arrest Fouquet, despite Fouquet's efforts in the king's behalf. After a mad chase in which both of their horses were raced to death, D'Artagnan captured Fouquet. Colbert then rose completely to power.

D'Artagnan was ordered by the king to go to Belle-Isle-en-Mer and take the fortress in which Aramis and Porthos were hiding and shoot the conspirators. D'Artagnan, too good a friend of each of the plotters to take their lives, planned to capture the fortress but to allow the two to escape. Louis had realized that this possibility might occur and had forewarned his officers so that D'Artagnan's scheme failed and he was ordered to return to France. A fierce battle ensued at Belle-Isle and Porthos was killed after many deeds of great heroism. Aramis escaped to Bayonne.

D'Artagnan, out of favor with the king over his disobedience to orders, resigned his position as captain of the musketeers and the king accepted, only to send for him later and ask him to take back his resignation. D'Artagnan agreed and won a pardon from the king for Aramis, who had settled in Spain.

Athos died of shock upon hearing that his son had been killed in Africa; they were buried in a double funeral. Louise de la Vallière, who had been replaced as the king's mistress by a younger favorite, attended the funeral. There D'Artagnan reproached her for causing the deaths of both Athos and Raoul de Bragelonne.

D'Artagnan remained in the service of Louis XIV and died four years later while fighting against the Dutch. His death came only a few moments after he had received the baton of a marshal of France.

VICTORY

Type of work: Novel
Author: Joseph Conrad (Teodor Józef Konrad Korzeniowski, 1857-1924)
Type of plot: Psychological romance
Time of plot: Early twentieth century
Locale: East Indies
First published: 1915

Principal characters:

AXEL HEYST, an idealist
LENA, whom he befriends
MR. SCHOMBERG, a hotel owner
MR. JONES, and
MARTIN RICARDO, gamblers
PEDRO, their servant
DAVIDSON, a sea captain
WANG, Heyst's servant

Critique:

Axel Heyst was not looking for material gain in his world. He had escaped life's demands by retreating to the East Indies, and there he found the one true value in his own life, love of a woman. But the victory was not Heyst's; it was Lena's. Every tense moment of the drama enacted on the island between the three bandits and the two innocent victims points tragically to Lena's final triumph. Although English was not Joseph Conrad's native tongue, he was able to use the English language with stylistic force and vigor. One startling feature of this novelist is his ability to encompass a mass of ideas into the force of one cryptic word or phrase. *Victory* is a romance between a man who is sensitive only to truth and honesty and a woman who had never known such things from other men.

The Story:

After the Tropical Belt Coal Company had gone into liquidation, Axel Heyst continued to live at the No. 1 coaling station on Samburan. Strange in his manners and desires, he was a legend among the islanders; they called him a Utopist. The coal company had come into existence after Heyst had met Morrison in a Portuguese seaport where the Englishman was about to lose his trading ship *Capricorn* because of an unpaid debt. Heyst, always sympathetic, had offered him a loan. Because Heyst was anxious to keep his generosity a secret and Morrison eager to conceal his shaky finances, the two men pledged secrecy, with the understanding that Heyst would thereafter have a share of the *Capricorn's* shipping business.

Schomberg, the owner of a hotel in Sourabaya, heard of the partnership and said that Heyst maintained some kind of hold over Morrison. Morrison instigated the coal company and then died in England. After that Schomberg, who for some reason hated Heyst, constructed a mysterious kind of villainy around Morrison's partner, and he was gleeful when the coal company liquidated.

After Heyst had retired from the human society of the islands, Davidson, a ship's captain, came upon him living alone on Samburan. Worrying over Heyst's welfare, Davidson adopted the habit of sailing ten miles out of his way around the north side of Samburan in case Heyst were to need aid. Once Davidson brought the hermit around to Sourabaya, where he put up at Schomberg's hotel. Later, Davidson heard bits of a story that Heyst had run off with a girl who was at the hotel with a troupe of entertainers. He was baffled that the shy, quiet Heyst would take a girl back to Samburan with him. Mrs. Schomberg, pitying the girl, had helped Heyst spirit the girl away. The affair had caused quite a hubbub on the island because it concerned Heyst.

When Heyst had come to the hotel, he had been unaware of Schomberg's hatred. The entertainers were not very attractive to his fastidious mind, but one white-muslined girl seemed younger than the others. Noticing her distress at being ordered to join a guest at a table, Heyst was prompted by the same instinct which had led him to help Morrison. He invited the girl to sit with him. Lena told Heyst about herself. Her father in England had taught her to play the violin. After his death, she had joined the group of entertainers with whom she now worked. Schomberg had been stalking her ever since the troupe came to the hotel. The contrast between Heyst and the other men she had met was enough to cause the girl to be attracted to her new friend, and she welcomed his promise of help. After Heyst had taken her away, Schomberg's hatred was tremendous.

To Schomberg's hotel came three strangers, Mr. Jones, Martin Ricardo, his secretary, and a beast-like, hairy creature whom they called Pedro. Before long these men had transformed Schomberg's hotel into a professional gambling house. Schomberg's obsession for Lena was increased by the notion that with her at his side he could rid his hotel of the gamblers. One afternoon Ricardo told Schomberg that he had been employed on a yacht where he was first attracted by Jones' polished manners. The two had stolen the captain's cash box and jumped the ship. Later Pedro became attached to them. Schomberg decided that these thieves might leave his hotel if he could arouse their greed by the prospect of richer plunder. He offhandedly mentioned Heyst's alleged wealth and told how Heyst lived on a lonely island with a girl and a hoard of money. Together Ricardo and Schomberg began to plan their pillage of the island where Heyst lived.

On his island Heyst had lived with only his Chinese servant, Wang, until Lena joined him. She told him that he had saved her from more than misery and despair. Heyst told her the story of his own background. His father had been a cynical, domineering man whom he disliked. After his death Heyst had drifted, searching for some meaning in life, a meaning never glimpsed until he met Lena.

One evening Wang appeared to announce that he had seen a boat drifting offshore. Heyst went to investigate. He discovered Ricardo, Jones, and the beast-like Pedro perishing of thirst in a boat moored beside a small jetty. Heyst helped the men to shore and took them to an abandoned bungalow for temporary quarters. That night Heyst found that his gun was missing from his desk; Wang, frightened, had taken it. Meanwhile Ricardo and Jones speculated about locating Heyst's money.

Early in the morning Ricardo stole into Heyst's bungalow and saw Lena combing her hair. He jumped at her hungrily, but she was able to defend herself. When the struggle was over and the repulsed man saw that she raised no outcry, his admiration for her increased. She asked him what the men wanted on the island. Surprised that they had come for money which she knew Heyst did not possess, she determined to protect Heyst from Schomberg's evil design. Loving Heyst, she could repay his kindness by leading Ricardo and his partners on to their destruction.

Observing Ricardo's attack on Lena, Wang had decided to withdraw from this confusion of white men's affairs; he fled to the forest. When Heyst reported the loss of his servant to Jones and Ricardo, they offered him the service of Pedro. Because their manner made it impossible for him to refuse, Lena and Heyst knew then that they were lost. Davidson would not sail past the island for three more weeks. Their only weapon having been stolen, they were left defenseless.

That night Ricardo came to the bungalow for dinner with Heyst and Lena. When Heyst had regretted his helpless position without any weapon of defense, Lena had recalled that during their scuffle she had glimpsed the knife Ricardo wore under his trouser leg. During the evening Ricardo indicated that Jones wished Heyst to visit him. Before he left, Heyst insisted that Pedro be sent out of the way, and Ricardo ordered the brute to go down to the jetty.

After Heyst had gone, Lena allowed Ricardo to make love to her so that she could take possession of his knife. Heyst told Jones about her presence in the bungalow. Jones, who suffered a pathological hatred for women, had not known of Lena's existence. Heyst convinced him that Schomberg had lied to get rid of the gamblers and to inflict upon Heyst a revenge Schomberg was too cowardly to inflict himself. Enraged by what he considered Ricardo's treachery, Jones suggested that they go to Heyst's bungalow.

Meanwhile Lena had taken Ricardo's knife. As the two men entered the bungalow, Jones fired over Heyst's shoulder, the bullet piercing Lena's breast. Ricardo sprang through the doorway. Jones followed his partner outside and shot him in the darkness. Heyst carried Lena to the bed, and as she lay there, deathly pale in the candlelight, she demanded the knife, her symbol of victory. She died as Heyst took her in his arms and for the first time spoke words that came from the depths of his heart.

VIRGIN SOIL

Type of work: Novel
Author: Ivan Turgenev (1818-1883)
Type of plot: Social criticism
Time of plot: 1868
Locale: Russia
First published: 1872

Principal characters:
NEZHDÁNOFF, a student
PÁHKLIN, his friend
SIPYÁGIN, a nobleman
VALENTÍNA, his wife

MARKÉLOFF, Valentína's brother
MARIANNA, Sipyágin's niece
SOLÓMIN, a factory superintendent

Critique:

Virgin Soil is in many respects typical of Turgenev. It is realistic, almost photographically so, reflecting the dominant pessimism of the author. Here we have a sensitive and sympathetic portrayal of the beginnings of Russian liberalism after the emancipation of the serfs. We see also the essential humanitarianism of the socialists and the frivolity of the aristocracy as both sides struggle in the developing industrialization. But in the conflict the chief liberal protagonists prove incapable and seal their own doom.

The Story:

Miss Mashúrin and Ostrodúmoff, both socialists, were waiting in Nezhdánoff's room in a poor quarter of St. Petersburg. A letter from a high leader had made a conference necessary, for another vague revolutionary project was under way. While they waited they were joined by Páhklin, a sly hanger-on of the intelligentsia, who wanted to discuss a critical matter with Nezhdánoff the student.

Nezhdánoff was late, but when he came they plunged into a discussion of their project. They needed money for a trip to Moscow, and they were all poor. Nezhdánoff, however, was the illegitimate son of a nobleman, and in a pinch he could secure small sums of money from his father. He promised to have the required sum the next day.

The conspirators were interrupted by the arrival of the elegant and noble Sipyágin, who had sat next to Nezhdánoff at the theater. A dilettante liberal, he had been attracted by the opinions and views of the poor student, and he came to offer Nezhdánoff a post as tutor to his young son at a salary of a hundred roubles a month. Sipyágin was generous, even offering to pay a month's salary in advance. So with the blessing of his socialist comrades, Nezhdánoff accepted the offer and went to live on the country estate of Sipyágin.

The household of Sipyágin was interesting, and after Nezhdánoff got over his shyness he made good progress with nine-year-old Kolya, his student. For a time, Nezhdánoff was content to live a leisurely life, for his duties were light. Although she scarcely spoke to him, Marianna, the penniless niece, attracted Nezhdánoff greatly. She was evidently unhappy, and she was abrupt and forthright in her attitude toward her rich relatives.

Valentína, Sipyágin's wife, was a beautiful woman without much heart. Although she herself was coldly virtuous, she enjoyed snaring men to see them dance at her bidding. She invited Nezhdánoff to her boudoir ostensibly to discuss her son's education, but in reality to captivate the young tutor. When he failed to respond to her attractions, she was nettled at his indifference. Then it became apparent that Nezhdánoff was attracted to Marianna, and Valentína became jealous.

Markéloff, Valentína's brother, came to visit the family. He was a savage, intense man who expressed his liberal opinions with great emphasis and alienated most of the company with his boorish ways. During a walk Nezhdánoff surprised Marianna and Markéloff in a lonely wood; he heard Marianna refuse something vigorously. Later, in an impulsive outburst, Marianna confided that Markéloff had proposed marriage.

This confidence strengthened the bond between Marianna and Nezhdánoff. That evening the tutor was surprised by an invitation to Markéloff's room. There he learned that Markéloff was a party member and a vigorous exponent of immediate action, who had been ordered to question Nezhdánoff about party activities on Sipyágin's estate and in his factory. Nezhdánoff had done nothing to stir up discontent among the peasants or workers, for he had been apathetic toward socialism for some time. Under Markéloff's urging he resolved to spread propaganda among the workmen.

Nezhdánoff confided his aims and problems to Marianna, who became a ready convert to revolutionary thought, her zeal surpassing that of Nezhdánoff. With Markéloff, Nezhdánoff visited some of the party members in the neighborhood, among them a man named Solómin.

Solómin was a factory manager and a good one, a calm, taciturn man of great strength of character. Sipyágin had tried to hire him to manage Sipyágin's own factory, but Solómin had refused. He was content where he was and he could scarcely conceal his contempt for the whole aristocracy. Sipyágin had taken the refusal with bad grace, and now began to show suspicion of Nezhdánoff.

From time to time Marianna and Nezhdánoff met in her room at night to discuss socialism. Although they were in love, they did not act as lovers. Valentína spied on the girl constantly. She made insinuations about her niece's character, and the atmosphere in the household became quite unpleasant. At length Sipyágin discharged Nezhdánoff. Early the next morning Nezhdánoff returned with a cart for Marianna, and the two fled for shelter to the factory where Solómin was employed. The manager concealed them in his living quarters, and Nezhdánoff and Marianna lived together as brother and sister, waiting for the time when Nezhdánoff could be sure enough of his love to marry.

Marianna put on peasant clothes and tried to learn peasant ways so that she would be a good worker for the revolution. Nezhdánoff, roughly clothed, made many trips among the farmers and mill hands to talk to them of liberty and freedom. He was unsuccessful in his attempts, however, for he was far too impetuous and harangued peasant groups in words they could not understand. On one occasion Nezhdánoff tried to drink vodka to ingratiate himself with the workers, but strong drink only made him sick. More and more he became conscious of failure, and felt that he could not marry Marianna. She, in turn, became more aware of Nezhdánoff's weakness and Solómin's strength.

When the peasants in Markéloff's district rebelled against paying their taxes, Markéloff rashly urged complete and armed rebellion, but his manner was so abusive that the peasants turned against him, beat him severely, and delivered him to the general commanding the district police. This disquieting news reached Solómin's factory, and the conspirators there made plans to flee.

Páhklin, misguided in his sympathy, decided to appeal to Sipyágin to intercede for his brother-in-law, Markéloff. Foolishly he babbled the hiding place of Marianna and Nezhdánoff. Sipyágin kept Páhklin under close surveillance and went to see the general. So great was Sipyágin's influence that the general consented to release Markéloff if he would confess his crime and promise to stir up no more trouble. But Markéloff was stubborn. He repeated his belief in the revolution and refused to acknowledge any errors. The general had no choice but to imprison him. Then at the instigation of Sipyágin, the police prepared to raid Solómin's factory.

Solómin quietly made plans to disappear. Nezhdánoff, confronted by his own weakness and by his inability to love Marianna enough to marry her, wrote a last letter and killed himself with a revolver. In the letter he asked that Marianna marry Solómin. An obliging priest performed the ceremony quickly and Solómin and Marianna departed. When the police arrived, they discovered only the suicide of Nezhdánoff.

Markéloff was tried and sentenced to Siberia. Solómin reappeared, but was released because the police had no evidence against him. He rejoined Marianna, who had by that time agreed to live with him as his wife. They were busy with Solómin's new factory.

Back in St. Petersburg, Páhklin was unhappy, for the liberals now called him a spy. By chance he met Miss Mashúrin in the street. She was now supposedly an Italian countess. Somewhere she had secured an Italian passport and funds for traveling. Páhklin invited her to have tea with him. Although she despised him, she accepted, for he had been Nezhdánoff's friend. From Páhklin Miss Mashúrin got a photograph of Nezhdánoff, with whom she had always been in love.

THE VIRGINIAN

Type of work: Novel
Author: Owen Wister (1860-1938)
Type of plot: Regional romance
Time of plot: Late nineteenth century
Locale: Wyoming
First published: 1902

Principal characters:
THE VIRGINIAN, a cowboy
JUDGE HENRY, the Virginian's employer
TRAMPAS, a cowboy, the Virginian's enemy
STEVE, a cowboy friend of the Virginian
SHORTY, a cowboy at Judge Henry's ranch
MOLLY WOOD, a young schoolteacher at Bear Creek, Wyoming

Critique:

The Virginian is one of the classic novels of the American West. Owen Wister was familiar with Wyoming and the cowboys who worked there, for he himself had spent several years in the Western country. Wister saw that although the mountains and the plains would remain, the picturesque cowboy was rapidly disappearing, along with the antelope, the buffalo, and the unfenced grazing lands.

The Story:

The Virginian had been sent by his employer to meet an Eastern guest at Medicine Bow and escort him the two hundred and sixty miles from the town to Sunk Creek Ranch. While the Virginian and the guest were awaiting the arrival of the Easterner's trunk on the following westbound train, the cowboy entered into a poker game. One of the players, a cowboy named Trampas, accused the Virginian of cheating. The man backed down, however, before the gun of the cowboy from Sunk Creek. It was apparent to everyone that the Virginian had made an implacable enemy.

A few months later, in the fall, a schoolmistress came West from Vermont to teach in the new school at Bear Creek, Wyoming. All the single men, and there were many of them in the territory, anxiously awaited the arrival of the new teacher, Molly Wood. The Virginian was fortunate in his first meeting with her. A drunken stage driver tried to ford a creek in high water and marooned his coach and passenger. The Virginian, passing by, rode to the stage, lifted out the young woman, and deposited her safely on the bank of the stream. After he had ridden away, Molly missed her handkerchief and realized the young cowboy had somehow contrived to take it.

The next time the Virginian saw Molly, she was a guest at a barbecue. The cowboy had ridden his horse for two days for an opportunity to see her, but she coquettishly refused to notice him. The Virginian and another cowboy, piqued by her attitude, got drunk and played a prank on all the people who had brought their children to the barbecue. They switched the babies and their clothing, so that when the barbecue was over many of the mothers carried off the wrong babies. Before he left for Sunk Creek, the Virginian warned Molly that she was going to love him eventually, no matter what she thought of him then.

During the next year the Virginian began to read books for the first time since he had left school in the sixth grade. He borrowed the books from Molly in order to ride to Bear Creek to see her at intervals. In the meantime he had risen high in the estimation of his employer. Judge Henry put him in charge of a party of men who were to escort two trainloads of steers to the Chicago market.

On the trip back to the ranch the Virginian's men threatened to desert the train to go prospecting for gold which had been discovered in the Black Hills. The ringleader of the insurgents was Trampas.

The Virginian saw that the best way to win over the men was to make a fool of Trampas. His chance came when the train stopped near a bridge that was being repaired. Since there was no food on the train, the Virginian went out and gathered a sackful of frogs to cook. Then he began a story about frogs, a tall story by which Trampas was completely taken in. As soon as the rest of the cowboys saw how foolish Trampas appeared, they were willing to return to the ranch, much to the discomfiture of their ringleader.

Back at Sunk Creek, the Virginian found a pleasant surprise awaiting him. The foreman of the ranch had been forced to leave because of an invalid wife, and the judge had made the Virginian his foreman.

Trampas had expected to be discharged from his job as soon as the Virginian became foreman at the Sunk Creek Ranch. The Virginian, however, decided it was better to have his enemy in sight, and so Trampas stayed on, sullen and defiant in his behavior.

The following spring the Virginian made a trip to a neighboring ranch. On the way back he was attacked by Indians and severely wounded. He managed to escape from the Indians and make his way to a spring. There he was found, half dead, by Molly Wood. The girl stayed with him at the risk of her life, for the Indians were still in the vicinity. She then bound his wounds and took him back to her cabin and called a doctor.

Molly, meanwhile, had packed her possessions, for she was preparing to leave for her home in the East. By the time the Virginian had recovered sufficiently to go back to work, she had decided not to leave Wyoming. She was sure by then that she was in love with the cowboy foreman. When the Virginian left her cabin for Sunk Creek, Molly had promised to marry him.

Upon returning to work, the Virginian found that his enemy, Trampas, had disappeared, taking another of the cowboys, Shorty, with him. About the same time the ranches in that territory began to lose cattle to rustlers, and a posse was formed to track down the cattle thieves. After several weeks of searching, two of the thieves were caught. Since the rustlers had somehow managed to gain control of the local courts and had already been freed on one charge, the posse hanged both of them. It was a terrible experience for the Virginian, because one of the men, Steve, had been a close friend. The Virginian hated to think he had hanged his friend, and the hurt was made worse by the fact that the condemned man had refused to say a word to his former companion.

On his way back to Sunk Creek, the Virginian came across the trail of the other two rustlers. They were Trampas and Shorty. Because they had only one horse between them, Trampas murdered Shorty in order to escape.

When Molly Wood heard of the lynching and the Virginian's part in it, she refused to marry him. But after a conversation with Judge Henry, she realized that the Virginian had done no more than his duty. She and the Virginian were reconciled and a date was set for their wedding.

On the day before their wedding, Molly and the Virginian started to ride to Medicine Bow. On the way they met Trampas, who galloped ahead of them into the town. Molly questioned the Virginian about the man and discovered the enmity between the two. When they arrived in town, they were warned that Trampas had said he would shoot the Virginian if he were not out of town by sunset. Molly told him that she could never marry him if he fought with Trampas and killed him. The Virginian, knowing that his honor was at stake, left her in the hotel and went out to face his enemy. Trampas fired first and missed. Then the Virginian fired and killed Trampas.

When the Virginian returned to the hotel, Molly was too glad to see him alive to remember her threat. Hearing the shots, she had been afraid that the Virginian had been killed. They were married the following day, as they had planned, and spent two months of their honeymoon high in the Rocky Mountains where no other humans ever went.

THE VIRGINIANS

Type of work: Novel
Author: William Makepeace Thackeray (1811-1863)
Type of plot: Historical romance
Time of plot: Late eighteenth century
Locale: England and the Colony of Virginia
First published: 1857-1859

Principal characters:
- George, and
- Harry Warrington, the Virginians
- Rachel Esmond Warrington, their mother
- George Washington, a family friend
- Lord Castlewood, an English kinsman
- Maria Castlewood, Lord Castlewood's sister
- Baroness Bernstein, Rachel Warrington's half-sister, formerly Beatrix Esmond
- Colonel Lambert, a friend
- Theo Lambert, Colonel Lambert's daughter and George's wife
- Hetty Lambert, Colonel Lambert's other daughter
- Fanny Mountain Warrington, Harry's wife

Critique:

The Virginians might almost be studied as a group of portraits of the lesser nobility of England and the gentry of Virginia. The author shows us many pictures: a despotic mother who is the head of a great Colonial estate; her two sons, one to become a great soldier under Washington, the other an English gentleman. We see England in the time of Johnson and Richardson and David Garrick and America in the early days of her struggle for independence. For his material Thackeray studied the letters, either real or imagined, of two brothers who lived on opposite sides of the ocean and who had opposing views on the Revolutionary War. From these letters he created his story of romance and adventure.

The Story:

Although Harry and George Warrington were twins, George was declared the heir to their father's estate by virtue of having been born half an hour before his brother. Both were headstrong lads, greatly pampered by their widowed mother, Rachel Esmond Warrington, who managed her Virginia estate, Castlewood, much as she would have managed the mansion in the old country. She never let her sons forget their high birth, and she herself had dropped the name of Warrington in favor of her maiden name, Esmond, in order that everyone would remember she was of noble rank. Rachel was a dictator on her plantation, and although she was respected by many, she was loved by few.

Harry and George were trained according to the place and the time. They learned to ride and shoot and gamble like gentlemen, but had little formal education other than a small knowledge of Latin and French. Their mother hoped they might pattern themselves after Colonel George Washington, who was their neighbor and her close friend. Harry worshipped Washington from his youth to his death, but George and Colonel Washington were never to be friends.

When General Braddock arrived from England to command the English troops in the war against the French, Washington and George Warrington joined his forces. Although Harry was the better soldier, George represented the family because of his position as elder son. Braddock was defeated and George was reported captured and killed by the French. George's mother blamed Colonel Washington for not guarding her son, and Washington was no longer welcome at Castlewood.

Upon George's death, Harry became the heir, and his mother sent him to visit his relatives in England. There he met his mother's kinsman, Lord Castlewood; her half-sister, Baroness Bernstein; and Will, Maria, and Fanny Esmond, his cousins. Of all his relatives, only Baroness Bernstein was fond of him. Harry and Will were enemies from their first meeting, and the rest of the family thought him a savage and tolerated him only because he would some day inherit the estate in Virginia. Harry thought himself in love with Maria, who was his mother's age, and sent her many gifts and passionate letters declaring himself hers and asking for her hand in marriage.

Harry was the toast of the country. He spent money lavishly on fine clothes and horses and at first won thousands of pounds at cards. But when his luck turned and he lost all his money, most of his former friends had only unkind words for him. Matters became so desperate that he was jailed for his debts, and Baroness Bernstein was the only one of his relatives who offered to help him. But there was a string attached to her offer. She was violently opposed to his intended marriage to Maria and would pay his debts only if he promised to break his word to that lady. Harry was tired of Maria, but he felt it was beneath a gentleman of his position to break his word, and he refused the baroness' help under her conditions. He would rather remain in prison.

There his brother George found him. For George had escaped from the French after eighteen months in prison and had returned to his home in Virginia, where he and his mother had decided that he, too, should visit England. He paid his brother's debts, and the two boys had a joyful reunion. Harry now had to return to his status as younger brother and George assumed his place as heir to Castlewood in Virginia.

Before Harry's imprisonment and George's arrival in England, Harry had made the acquaintance of Colonel Lambert and his family. There were two daughters, Theo and Hetty, whom the twin brothers found most charming. Theo and George fell in love, and after overcoming her father's objections, they were married. At first they lived in poverty, for George had spent all his money to rescue Harry from debtor's prison and to buy for him a commission in the army. George's only income for a time was from two tragedies he had written, one a success and the other a failure.

Shortly after Harry received his commission he joined General Wolfe and sailed for America to fight the French in the Colonies. Maria had released him from his promise to her, and he gladly took leave of his English relatives. About this time George inherited a title and an estate from an unexpected source. Sir Miles Warrington, his father's brother, died; and as young Miles Warrington, the only male heir, had been killed in an accident, the title and the estate fell to George. Now he and Theo lived in comparative luxury. They traveled extensively, and one day they decided to visit George's mother and brother in Virginia.

When they arrived in America they found the Colonies to be in a state of unrest. The colonists were determined not to pay all the taxes which the British crown levied against them, and there was much talk of war. At Castlewood there was also trouble. Harry had married Fanny Mountain, the daughter of his mother's housekeeper, and his mother refused to accept the girl. Harry had moved to his own smaller estate, but there was a great tension between the members of the family. George and Theo and their mother were loyal to the king. Harry became a true Virginian and followed General George Washington into battle. In spite of their different loyalties the brothers remained friends.

Shortly before the end of the war George and Theo returned to England. Although they were grieved at the outcome of the war, it made little difference in their lives. Harry visited them in England after the death of his wife, but their mother never again left her native Virginia. George and Theo tried to persuade Hetty to marry Harry, whom she had once loved deeply, but she refused to leave her widowed father. The only departure from their quiet life came when Lord Castlewood tried to steal Castlewood in Virginia from their mother after her deed and title were burned during the war. But George was able to prevent the fraud and save the estate. Intending never to leave England again, he renounced his right to the Virginia land. Harry returned to Virginia, where he was made a general, to live out his life at Castlewood in the company of his mother. The brothers were destined never to meet again, but their love for each other went with them throughout their lives.

VOLPONE

Type of work: Drama
Author: Ben Jonson (1572?-1637)
Type of plot: Social satire
Time of plot: Sixteenth century
Locale: Venice
First presented: 1605

Principal characters:
VOLPONE, a knave
MOSCA, his servant
CORBACCIO, an old gentleman
CORVINO, a merchant
VOLTORE, an advocate
LORD POLITICK WOULD-BE, a knight
LADY POLITICK WOULD-BE, his wife
BONARIO, Corbaccio's son
CELIA, Corvino's wife
PEREGRINE, a gentleman traveler

Critique:

Although the extant copies of *Volpone, or, The Fox,* are revised versions of the original drama, the plan in its printed form is essentially Jonson's. The story is intricately plotted, so much so that it is likely to be confusing. The drama points toward the seventeenth-century theater with its sermonized ending. Jonson attempted to teach the social lesson that mischief leads to its own undoing.

The Story:

Volpone and his servant, Mosca, were playing a cunning game with all who professed to be Volpone's friends, and the two conspirators boasted to themselves that Volpone acquired his riches not by the common means of trade but by a method which cheated no one in a commercial sense. Volpone had no heirs. Since it was believed he possessed a large fortune, many people were courting his favor in hopes of rich rewards after his death.

For three years, while the foxy Volpone feigned gout, catarrh, palsy, and consumption, valuable gifts had been given him. Mosca's role in the grand deception was to assure each hopeful donor that he was the one whom Volpone had honored in an alleged will.

To Voltore, one of the dupes, Mosca boasted that particular attention was being paid to Voltore's interests. When Voltore the vulture left, Corbaccio the crow followed. He brought a potion to help Volpone, or so he claimed. But Mosca knew better than to give his master medicine from those who were awaiting the fox's death. Mosca suggested that to influence Volpone, Corbaccio should go home, disinherit his own son, and leave his fortune to Volpone. In return for this generous deed, Volpone, soon to die, would leave his fortune to Corbaccio, whose son would benefit eventually.

Next came Corvino, who was assured by Mosca that Volpone, now near death, had named him in a will. After the merchant had gone, Mosca told Volpone that Corvino had a beautiful wife whom he guarded at all times. Volpone resolved to go in disguise to see this woman.

Sir Politick Would-Be and his wife were traveling in Venice. Another English visitor, Peregrine, met Sir Politick on the street and gave him news from home. While the two Englishmen were trying to impress one another, Mosca and a servant came to the street and erected a stage for a medicine vendor to display his wares. Volpone, disguised as a mountebank, mounted the platform. While he haggled with Sir Politick and Peregrine over the price of his medicine, Celia appeared at her window and tossed down her handkerchief. Struck by Celia's beauty, Volpone resolved to possess her. Meanwhile Corvino brutally scolded Celia and told her that henceforth he would confine her to her room.

Mosca went to Corvino with news that physicians had recommended a healthy young girl to sleep by Volpone's side and that other men were striving to be the first to win Volpone's gratitude in this manner. Not to be outdone, Corvino promised that Celia would be sent to Volpone.

Mosca also told Bonario, Corbaccio's son, that his father was about to disinherit him. He promised to lead Bonario to a place where he could witness his father's betrayal.

When Lady Politick Would-Be came to visit Volpone, she was so talkative Volpone feared she would make him sick in actuality. To relieve Volpone's distress, the servant told the lady that Sir Politick was in a gondola with a young girl. Lady Would-Be hurried off in pursuit of her husband. Volpone retired to a private closet while Mosca led Bonario behind a curtain so the young man could spy on Corbaccio. At that moment, eager to win favor with Volpone, Corvino arrived with Celia, and Mosca had to send

Bonario off to another room so he would not know of her presence. Meanwhile Corvino had told Celia what she must do to prove her chastity. To quiet her fears, and to guarantee the inheritance from Volpone, Corvino assured his distressed wife that Volpone was so decrepit he could not harm her.

When they were alone, Volpone leaped from his couch and displayed himself as an ardent lover. As he was about to force himself upon Celia, Bonario appeared from his hiding place and saved her. While Mosca and Volpone, in terror of exposure, bewailed their ruined plot, Corbaccio knocked. Volpone dashed back to his couch. As Mosca was assuring Corbaccio of Volpone's forthcoming death, Voltore entered the room and overheard the discussion. Mosca drew Voltore aside and assured the lawyer that he was attempting to get possession of Corbaccio's money so that Voltore would inherit more from Volpone. Mosca further explained that Bonario had mistaken Celia's visit and had burst upon Volpone and threatened to kill him. Taken in by Mosca's lies, Voltore promised to keep Bonario from accusing Volpone of rape and Corvino of villainy; he ordered the young man arrested.

Mosca proceeded with his case against Celia and Bonario. He had assured Corvino, Corbaccio, and Voltore, independently, that each would be the sole heir of Volpone. Now he added Lady Would-Be as a witness against Celia. In court Voltore presented Celia and Bonario as schemers against Corvino, and he further showed that Bonario's father had disinherited his son and that Bonario had dragged Volpone out of bed and had attacked him. Both Corvino and Corbaccio testified against Celia and Bonario, while Mosca whispered to the avaricious old gentlemen that they were helping justice. To add to the testimony, Mosca presented Lady Would-Be, who told the court she had seen Celia beguiling Sir Politick in a gondola. Mosca promised Lady Would-Be that as a reward for her testimony her name would stand first on Volpone's list of heirs.

When the trial was over, Volpone sent his servants to announce that he was dead and that Mosca was his heir. While Volpone hid behind a curtain, Mosca sat at a desk taking an inventory of the inheritance as the hopefuls arrived. The next step in Volpone's plan was to escape from Venice with his loot. Mosca helped him disguise himself as a commodore. Mosca also put on a disguise.

Having lost his hopes for the inheritance, Voltore withdrew his false testimony at the trial, and Corbaccio and Corvino trembled lest their own cowardly acts be revealed. The court ordered Mosca to appear. Suspecting that Mosca planned to keep the fortune for himself, the disguised Volpone went to the court. When the dupes, learning that Volpone was still alive, began to bargain for the wealth Mosca held, Volpone threw off his disguise and exposed to the court the foolish behavior of Corbaccio, Corvino, and Voltore, and the innocence of Celia and Bonario. The court then sentenced each conspirator according to the severity of his crime. Bonario was restored to his father's inheritance, and Celia was allowed to return to her father because Corvino had attempted to barter her honor for wealth.

The court announced that evil could go only so far and then it killed itself.

THE VOYAGE OF THE BEAGLE

Type of work: Journal
Author: Charles Darwin (1809-1882)
Type of plot: Travel and Natural History
Time of plot: 1831-1836
Locale: South America and the South Seas
First published: 1839

Principal character:
CHARLES DARWIN, English naturalist

Critique:

In this book the reader finds Darwin's brilliant mind already at work upon the problems which led to his world-shaking theory of evolution. The title of the work is misleading, for the author has little to say about the voyage. What interests him is the natural history of the lands at which the *Beagle* stops. Nothing escapes Darwin's eye; his observations are exact and beautifully written.

The Story:

In December, 1831, the brig *Beagle* of the Royal Navy set sail from Devonport, England, on a voyage which would include surveys of Patagonia, Tierra del Fuego, Chile, Peru, and some of the islands of the Pacific. Also, some chronometric measurements were to be made while the ship circumnavigated the earth.

Charles Darwin shipped aboard as a naturalist at the wish of the *Beagle's* commander, Captain Fitz Roy. Darwin kept a record of the journey in the form of a journal, besides making observations in natural history and geology.

The ship sailed to the coast of South America by way of the Canary Islands, the Cape Verde Islands, and the island of St. Paul's Rocks. The first American seaport that the *Beagle* touched was Rio de Janeiro. There Darwin went inland with an Englishman who was going to visit his estate. Upon his return Darwin resided near Botofogo Bay, where he made natural history observations.

From Rio de Janeiro the expedition went southward to the mouth of the River Plate. Darwin remained there for several weeks collecting animals, birds, and reptiles. On his journeys to the interior he met gauchos for the first time and witnessed their skill with the lasso and the bolas in capturing horses and cattle.

The next anchorage was at Rio Negro. Between this river and Buenos Aires the land was mostly inhabited by hostile Indians. At the time, General Rosas was making war on the various native tribes. Darwin decided to go by land from the Rio Negro to Buenos Aires under the protection of the Spanish Army. On this journey he was able to observe the habits of the South American ostrich.

Upon his arrival in Buenos Aires, Darwin was struck by the large size of the city; it had about sixty thousand inhabitants. From there he set out for Santa Fe by means of a slow bullock wagon. He returned by boat down the Parana River to the seacoast and sailed in a small vessel to join the *Beagle* at Montevideo. On an excursion inland from that seaport, Darwin observed herds of sheep that were watched only by dogs. The dogs were brought up with the flocks from infancy; thus they acquired an uncommon attachment for the sheep.

The *Beagle* sailed for the coast of Patagonia, a land where Spanish settlement had been unsuccessful. There Darwin observed the guanaco, or wild llama. These animals were extremely wary. Once caught, however, they were easily domesticated.

From Patagonia the *Beagle* went to the Falkland Islands, where Darwin found horses, cattle, and rabbits thriving on the seemingly desolate land. Captain Fitz Roy soon set sail for Tierra del Fuego. There the natives were curious about their white visitors. The natives existed in an utterly savage state with barely enough food and clothing to maintain their miserable existence.

The *Beagle* had aboard three Fuegians who had been taken to England to receive education and be taught the Christian religion. A missionary accompanied them. The plan was to return these natives to their own tribes, and for that purpose the *Beagle* anchored in Ponsonby Sound. Four boats set out to carry the natives to their homeland. All the natives on shore congregated about the English wherever they landed and asked for gifts. When their wants were not entirely satisfied, they became hostile. The missionary decided that it would be useless for him to stay among them.

From Tierra del Fuego the *Beagle* proceeded to Valparaiso, Chile. From there Darwin set out to observe the geological formations of the base of the Andes Mountains. On that journey he saw copper and gold mines.

The *Beagle* sailed from Valparaiso southward to the island of Chiloe and the southern part of Chile. While the ship was anchored in a harbor of Chiloe, all those aboard were able to observe the eruption of a volcano on the mainland.

About a month later, after the *Beagle* had sailed northward for a distance, a great earthquake shook parts of the coast and the nearby islands. Darwin saw the damage caused by the earthquake in the harbor city of Concepción, where almost every building had been demolished. Part of the town had been swept also by a tremendous wave that had rushed in from the sea.

After the *Beagle* returned to Valparaiso, Darwin procured guides and mules and set out to cross the Andes to Mendoza. He went eastward through the Portillo Pass and returned through the Uspallata Pass. He reported the scenery beautiful, and he collected much interesting geological and natural history data.

Next, the *Beagle* sailed up the coast of northern Chile and continued northward to Peru. At Iquique, in Peru, Darwin visited a saltpeter works. Lima was the next port of call for the *Beagle*. Darwin was not impressed by the city. It was dirty and ugly, having suffered from many revolutions, and the people, living in an almost continual state of anarchy, were unable to take time to improve the city.

Lima was the last point at which the *Beagle* touched on the western coast of South America. The ship proceeded next to the Galapagos archipelago, where the most interesting feature was the prevalence of great tortoises. The inhabitants often killed these reptiles for their meat. Most of the birds on the islands were completely tame; they had not yet learned to regard man as their enemy.

The ship then sailed on the long passage of three thousand miles to Tahiti. There Darwin was impressed by the swimming ability of the Polynesians. He explored the mountains of the island with the help of guides.

From Tahiti the *Beagle* went south to New Zealand, New South Wales, and Australia. There Darwin first saw the social greeting of rubbing noses performed by the aborigines. This custom took the place of shaking hands, as practiced by Europeans.

After leaving this group of islands the ship headed back to Brazil in order to complete chronometric measurements that were to be made. On the way Darwin visited the island of St. Helena.

Now that the *Beagle* was on the last part of her journey, Darwin recorded in his journal his theories as to the formation of coral reefs, many of which he had observed during his stay in the South Seas.

Darwin was glad to leave Brazil for the second time; the practice of slavery in that country sickened him. In October of 1836 the *Beagle* reached the shores of England. At Falmouth, Darwin left the ship. He had spent nearly five years on his journey.

THE WANDERER

Type of work: Novel
Author: Alain-Fournier (Henri Alain Fournier, 1886-1914)
Type of plot: Psychological romance
Time of plot: Nineteenth century
Locale: France
First published: 1913

Principal characters:
AUGUSTIN MEAULNES, the wanderer
FRANÇOIS SEUREL, his friend
FRANTZ DE GALAIS, a young aristocrat
YVONNE DE GALAIS, his sister
VALENTINE BLONDEAU, Frantz's fiancée

Critique:

Half fantasy and half reality, this dream-like story skillfully mixes the vague dream world with the material world. A dream of delightful wonder obsesses a young man all his life. But when he finds the material existence of his dream, he is disillusioned, for he would prefer to return to the dream.

The Story:

M. Seurel was head of the Middle School and one of the Higher Elementary classes, and Madame Seurel taught the infants at Sainte-Agathe's School. Living in the school with his parents and his sister Millie, François Seurel attended the classes along with the other pupils. Young Seurel, however, never played much with the village boys because of an infection in his hip.

When François Seurel was fifteen, Augustin Meaulnes entered the school. His arrival marked a new life for Seurel, for Meaulnes soon banished his contentment with his family and his love for his home. His hip healing, Seurel began to spend more time with Meaulnes in the village. Even the school became livelier, for Meaulnes always drew a crowd of people around him in the evenings.

The adventure began one Christmas when Meaulnes set out for the railroad station to meet Seurel's grandparents, M. and Mme. Charpentier. When the grandparents arrived, Meaulnes had disappeared. Three days later, he casually took his seat in the classroom where M. Seurel was conducting a lesson. No one knew where Meaulnes had gone and he claimed when questioned that he himself did not know. Sometimes at night, in the attic room they shared, Seurel would be awakened to find Meaulnes pacing the floor, fully clothed, eager to enter again a mysterious world which once he had glimpsed briefly. Meaulnes promised to take Seurel along the next time he left on a journey.

At last Meaulnes told Seurel the story of his adventure after he had run off from the school. It had been a very cold December day, and Meaulnes, losing his way, had found his horse lame and darkness falling. He had wandered to a cottage, where he was fed. Then he had stumbled on until he found a barn in which, cold and lost, he fell asleep. The next day he wandered a long distance, until that night he had come to a manor where small children and old people were merrily planning a wedding feast. Tired and cold, Meaulnes had crawled through a window and climbed into a bed. There he slept all night. The next day, thinking him one of the guests, some strolling players invited him to eat with them. Then Meaulnes discovered the reason for the feast. Frantz de Galais, the son of the man who owned the manor, had gone off to fetch his fiancée for the wedding.

All the first day Meaulnes danced and played with the other guests. The next day he met a beautiful girl with whom he immediately fell in love. Although she sadly declined to see him again, she promised to wait for his return to the manor. Inquiring about the strange girl, Meaulnes learned that she was Yvonne de Galais, the sister of Frantz. Frantz returned to the manor without his bride and dismissed all the guests.

Meaulnes joined the crowd of children and old people as they dejectedly walked or rode away from the manor. He fell asleep in a cart and did not awake until he found himself again near Sainte-Agathe's School.

Meaulnes' story would have seemed too unreal to young Seurel if the arrival of a strange boy at Sainte-Agathe's had not brought the story to reality. The boy, dressed as a gipsy, reminded Meaulnes of those Bohemians he had seen at the manor. After the gipsy had stolen the map which Meaulnes had been making in order to find his way back to the manor, Meaulnes and Seurel learned that the gipsy was young Frantz de Galais, who in a fit of despair after losing his sweetheart had run away with a band of gipsies. The boys swore to Frantz that they would help him if they could. One night Frantz disappeared.

Meaulnes went at last to Paris and wrote only three letters to Seurel after his arrival there.

Months passed. Seurel finished his school days and went to a village to visit some relatives. There he heard that a mysterious manor was not far off. Eagerly Seurel took up his friend's quest. His cousins, he learned, knew Yvonne. The manor had been razed after the disappearance of Frantz, but his sister often came to visit Seurel's cousins. One night while Seurel was there she arrived. He told her that Meaulnes hoped someday to find her again. Seurel then learned from his aunt that Frantz's fiancée had feared to marry him because she was certain that such great happiness could not come to her, the daughter of peasants. She was now in Paris working as a dressmaker. Seurel recalled his promise to Frantz to help him if ever he could. But first Seurel intended to find Meaulnes and bring him to Yvonne de Galais.

When Seurel found Meaulnes, the adventurer was packing his clothes to go on a journey. Abandoning his plans, he and Yvonne married. But there was some mysterious element in their lives which kept them from being as happy as Seurel had expected them to be. One night Frantz appeared near the village. Seurel met him and listened to his complaint of loneliness and sorrow. The next morning Meaulnes left Yvonne to go on another adventure.

For months Seurel, now a teacher at Sainte-Agathe's, and Yvonne awaited the return of Meaulnes. When her baby was born, Yvonne died, leaving Seurel with an untold sadness. Searching through his friend's old papers, Seurel found a diary which told him why Meaulnes had been so troubled before his disappearance.

While Meaulnes had lived in Paris, he had met Valentine Blondeau, a girl who became his mistress. Valentine often spoke of her former lover, whom she had deserted because she feared to marry him. When she showed Meaulnes her lover's letters, he realized that Valentine was the fiancée for whom Frantz de Galais had never stopped searching. In anger, Meaulnes told her he would leave her, and Valentine cried that she would then return to Paris to become a street-walker. After he had returned to his mother's home, where Seurel had found him, Meaulnes began to feel remorse for his treatment of Valentine.

Seurel, reading the diary, realized that Meaulnes must have been packing to go in search of Valentine when Seurel brought the news that Yvonne had been found. He decided that Meaulnes had deserted Yvonne to go on the same quest.

As Yvonne's daughter grew into a lovable, pretty child, Seurel often went to play with her, but she would not allow him completely to possess her affections. She seemed always to be waiting for someone. One afternoon, while playing with the little girl, Seurel noticed a burly stranger approaching. As the man neared him, Seurel recognized Meaulnes. He told Seurel that he had brought Valentine and Frantz together at last. With tears in his eyes at the news of his wife's death, Meaulnes took his daughter into his arms.

Seurel watched the father and daughter play together, and the schoolmaster smilingly imagined that he could envision Meaulnes arising in the middle of the night, wrapping his daughter in a cloak, and silently slipping off with her on some new adventure.

THE WANDERING JEW

Type of work: Novel
Author: Eugène Sue (1804-1857)
Type of plot: Mystery melodrama
Time of plot: 1831-1832
Locale: France
First published: 1844-1845

Principal characters:
RODIN, an ambitious Jesuit
M. L'ABBE D'AIGRIGNY, Provincial of the Jesuits
BLANCHE SIMON,
ROSE SIMON,
FRANÇOIS HARDY,
PRINCE DJALMA,
JACQUES DE RENNEPONT (COUCHE-TOUT-NUD),
GABRIEL DE RENNEPONT, and
ADRIENNE DE CARDOVILLE, descendants of Marius de Rennepont and heirs to his legacy
SAMUEL, the Wandering Jew
HERODIAS, who demanded the head of John the Baptist

Critique:

The Wandering Jew is a sprawling narrative written in a pedestrian style and dealing with one-dimensional characters whose conversations and behavior are unrealistic. In spite of its limitations, however, the novel has survived; and more than a hundred years after its publication it has become a minor classic of sorts. Probably the reasons for its survival are twofold. First, the legend of the Wandering Jew has always commanded interest. Second, Sue has technical skill in building up effects of mystery and terror. In addition, Sue's vivid knowledge of social and economic conditions of the time lend added value to a romantic work which was also a novel of social protest.

The Story:

Down a bleak hill in Poland a solitary figure stalked. He was an old man, his face gentle and sad. His footsteps left in the soil imprints of a cross made by the seven large nails in his shoes. He was hurrying, for he must be in Paris on the thirteenth of February, 1832, when the surviving descendants of his sister would gather in that city—the last members of that family over which he had watched for eighteen centuries. The lonely traveler was the Wandering Jew, that artisan of Jerusalem who mocked Christ on the day of the Crucifixion, the sinner condemned to wander undying through the centuries over all the world.

Far in the wilds of America a woman also set her face toward Paris, driven by that same power which guided the Wandering Jew. She was Herodias, who had demanded the head of John the Baptist on a charger, also condemned to live through centuries of sorrow.

François Baudoin, called Dagobert, a faithful friend of Marshal Simon, an old Bonapartist hero, never faltered in his loyalty toward the Simon family. Years before he had followed the marshal's Polish wife into Siberia, where she was exiled, and after her death he set out with her twin daughters, Blanche and Rose, for Paris where, on a certain day in February, 1832, a legacy awaited the two girls. This was the legacy of Marius de Rennepont, an ancestor who, despoiled by the Jesuits, had salvaged out of his ruined estate a house and a small sum of money. The money he had placed in the hands of a faithful Jewish friend named Samuel, who had promised to invest it profitably. A hundred and fifty years later the descendants of this ancestor were to gather at a house where each was to receive a share of the legacy. Blanche and Rose Simon were only half-aware of the fortune awaiting them, for they were too young to understand what Dagobert told them about their inheritance.

But if these heirs of Marius de Rennepont did not know of the legacy, others did. For many years the Jesuits, masters of an intricate and diabolical conspiracy, had plotted to prevent the descendants from acquiring the money. They were responsible for Marshal Simon's exile, for his wife's banishment to Siberia.

The plotters had been so meticulous, so thorough in their scheming, that they had persuaded young Gabriel de Rennepont to become a priest and a member of the Society of Jesus. Through Gabriel they hoped to acquire the tremendous fortune; for by preventing the other heirs from reaching Paris — and the society had agents all over the world who would do its bidding under any conditions—Gabriel would inherit the legacy. Then, since he was forbidden by his vow of poverty to possess money, the funds would revert to the society. With that money the Jesuits would be able to reëstablish their supremacy over the French people, would be able once more to govern countries and guide the destiny of Europe.

As soon as Dagobert and the two girls arrived in Paris, the Jesuits arranged to have them spirited away to a convent. Adrienne de Cardoville, another descendant of the de Rennepont family, was declared insane and committed to an asylum. Jacques de Rennepont, a good-hearted sensualist named Couche-tout-Nud, was jailed for debt. Prince Djalma, who had left India in spite of the efforts of the Jesuits, was drugged. François Hardy, a benevolent manufacturer, was sent out of town through the treachery of a friend who was a Jesuit spy.

As a result of that Jesuit conspiracy, on that fateful day in February, 1832, only the priest, Gabriel de Rennepont, went to claim the legacy at the house of an old Jew known as Samuel. With Gabriel were M. l'Abbé d'Aigrigny, Provincial of the Jesuits, and Rodin, his secretary. Before the reading of the will, Gabriel was persuaded to sign a paper in which he renounced all claims to the legacy. When the bequest was announced, the Jesuits were astounded at the incredible sum of the inheritance, which had grown from 150,000 francs to a fortune of 212,175,000 francs. But just as the money was being handed over to the priests, a strange woman appeared and produced a codicil to the will, a document suspending its execution for three months. The woman was Herodias, but none then called her by that name. The priests were enraged, and they feared that their conspiracy would be exposed. Adrienne de Cardoville was certain to be released from the asylum. General Simon was reported to be on his way back to France to claim his daughters. Couche-tout-Nud would borrow money from his friends to pay his debts. Prince

Djalma would soon awaken. François Hardy would return to Paris from his fruitless errand.

Rodin immediately produced a paper which placed him in complete charge of the Jesuit cabal. He proclaimed that they had not lost, that they could and would win by employing psychological methods instead of violence. He would let each heir destroy himself by his own desires, passions, or vices.

During the three months that followed Rodin pretended that he had left the service of the Abbé d'Aigrigny and passed himself off as a friend of the de Rennepont heirs. He secured the release of the Simon girls and Adrienne, and by those acts became known as a good, unselfish man. One of Adrienne's servants confessed, shortly before her death, that she had been blackmailed into spying for the Jesuits, and she revealed the whole sordid, brutal, unprincipled conspiracy. But Rodin was not yet willing to accept defeat. At his direction, François Hardy's factory was burned to the ground, his best friend's treachery was revealed, and his beautiful young mistress was spirited away. A broken man, Hardy was taken to a Jesuit retreat, where he accepted the doctrines of the order and died as the result of the penances and fasts imposed upon him. Couche-tout-Nud, separated from his mistress, died a miserable death after an orgy induced by another Jesuit agent. The Simon girls were taken to a hospital during a cholera epidemic and died there of the disease. Prince Djalma, led to believe that Adrienne had become the mistress of Agricola Baudoin, Dagobert's son, attacked Agricola and killed a girl whom he mistook for Adrienne. He discovered his error too late, for in his remorse he had already swallowed poison. Adrienne chose to die with him.

When the time came for the final disposition of the de Rennepont legacy, Gabriel was the only survivor. Just as Rodin was about to claim the inheritance in the name of his churchly office, the casket containing the money and securities burst into flames and the fortune was lost forever. A moment later Rodin fell to the floor and writhed in agony. As he had left a church, shortly before claiming the legacy, he had taken holy water from the fingers of an Indian who had accompanied Prince Djalma from India and who had become a lay member of the Jesuits. Too late, Rodin realized that he had been poisoned in some manner by the Indian. He died a few minutes later.

Gabriel de Rennepont, shocked when he realized the crimes of greed and lust for power that the lost fortune had caused, retired to live out the rest of his brief life with his friends, the Beaudoin family.

After Gabriel's body had been laid in the de Rennepont tomb, old Samuel went to a secret spot where a great cross was set upon a lonely hill. There Herodias found him. In the dawn's light each saw upon the face of the other the marks that age had put upon them, but they had found peace and happiness at last. Samuel—for he was the Wandering Jew—gave praise that their long punishment was ended, and Herodias echoed his words.

WAR AND PEACE

Type of work: Novel
Author: Count Leo Tolstoy (1828-1910)
Type of plot: Historical romance
Time of plot: 1805-1813
Locale: Russia
First published: 1865-1869

Principal characters:

PIERRE BEZUHOV, illegitimate son of a wealthy count
NATASHA ROSTOV, beautiful daughter of a well-to-do Moscow family
NIKOLAY ROSTOV, Natasha's older brother
ANDREY BOLKONSKY, wealthy Russian prince
ELLEN KURAGIN BEZUHOV, Pierre's beautiful and immoral wife
ANATOLE KURAGIN, Ellen's brother
PRINCESS MARYA BOLKONSKY, Andrey's sister
OLD PRINCE BOLKONSKY, Andrey's tyrannical father
KUTUZOV, Commander-in-Chief of the Russian Army, appointed in August, 1812
NAPOLEON BONAPARTE

Critique:

Count Leo Tolstoy's *War and Peace* is a panorama of Russian life in that active period of history known as the Napoleonic Era. The whole structure of the novel indicates that Tolstoy was writing a new kind of book. He was not concerned with plot, setting, or even people, as such. His purpose was simply to show that the continuity of life in history is eternal. Each human life holds its influence on history, and the developments of youth and age, war and peace, are so interrelated that in the simplest patterns of social behavior vast implications are recognizable. Tolstoy seemed to feel a moral responsibility to present history as it was influenced by every conceivable human force. To do this, it was necessary for him to create not a series of simple, well-linked incidents but a whole evolution of events and personalities. Each character must change, must affect those around him; these people in turn must influence others, until imperceptibly, the whole historical framework of the nation changes. *War and Peace,* then, is a moving record of historical progress, and the dual themes of this vast novel—Age and Youth, War and Peace—are shown as simultaneous developments of history.

The Story:

In 1805, it was evident to most well-informed Russians that war with Napoleon was inevitable. Austria and Russia joined forces at the battle of Austerlitz, where they were soundly defeated by the French. But in the highest Russian society, life went on quite as though nothing of tremendous import were impending. After all, it was really only by a political formality that Russia had joined with Austria. The fact that one day Napoleon might threaten the gates of Russia seemed ridiculous. And so soirees and balls were held, old women gossiped, young women fell in love. War, though inevitable, was being waged on foreign soil, and was, therefore, of little importance.

The attraction held by the army for the young noblemen of Russia was understandable enough, for the Russian army had always offered excellent opportunities for ambitious, politically inclined young men. It was a wholesome release for their energies. Young Nikolay Rostov, for example, joined the hussars simply because he felt drawn to that way of life. His family idolized him because of his loyalty to the tsar, because of his courage, and because he was so handsome in his uniform. Natasha, his sister, wept over him, and Sonya, his cousin, promptly fell in love with him.

While young Nikolay was applauded in St. Petersburg society, Pierre Bezuhov, a friend of the Rostov family, was looked upon as somewhat of a boor. He had just returned from Paris, where he had studied at the university, and he had not yet made up his mind what to do with his life. He would not join the army for he saw no sense in a military career. His father gave him a liberal allowance, and he spent it frivolously at gambling. In truth, he seemed like a man lost. He would start long arguments, loudly shouting in the most conspicuous manner in the quiet drawing-rooms, and then suddenly lapse into sullen silence. He was barely tolerated at soirees before his father died and left him millions. Then, suddenly, Pierre became popular, although he attributed his rise to some new personality development of his own. He was no longer sullen, but loved everyone, and it was quite clear that everyone loved him. His most dogged follower was Prince Vassily Kuragin, the father of a beautiful, unmarried daughter, Ellen, who was recognized everywhere as a prospective leader of St. Petersburg society. Pierre was forced into marrying her by the crafty prince, who knew a good catch when he saw one. The marriage was never a success.

Pierre Bezuhov's closest friend was Prince Andrey Bolkonsky, an arrogant, somewhat cynical man who also despised his wife. Lise, the "Little Princess," as she was called, was pregnant, but Prince Andrey could endure the bondage of domesticity no longer. When he received a commission in the army, he left his wife at the family estate, Bleak Hills, in the care of his sister Marya and his tyrannical old father, and went off to war. During his absence, Princess Lise bore him a son, but died in childbirth. Prince Andrey returned after the battle of Austerlitz to find himself free once more, but he enjoyed no feeling of satisfaction in his freedom. Seeking Pierre, Prince Andrey turned to his friend for answer to some of the eternal questions of loneliness and despair that tortured him.

Pierre, meanwhile, had joined the brotherhood of Freemasons, and through this contact had arrived at a philosophy of life which he sincerely believed to be the only true philosophy. Had Pierre realized that the order had initiated him solely because of his wealth, he would never have adopted their ideals. However, in true faith, Pierre restored some of Prince Andrey's lost courage by means of a wild if unreasoning enthusiasm. In the belief that he was now an unselfish, free individual, Pierre freed his peasants and set about improving his estate; but having absolutely no sense of business administration he lost a great deal of money. Finally, with his affairs in almost hopeless disorder, he left an overseer in charge and retired to Bleak Hills and Prince Andrey's sane company.

Meanwhile, Nikolay Rostov was in the thick of the fighting. Napoleon, having overcome the Prussian forces at Jena, had reached Berlin in October. The Russians once more had gone to the assistance of their neighbors, and the two opposing armies met in a terrible battle at Eylau in February, 1807. In June, Nikolay had entered the campaign at Friedland, where the Russians were beaten. In June of that year Nikolay naïvely thought the war was over, for Napoleon and Tsar Alexander signed the Peace of Tilsit. What the young officer did not know was that Napoleon possessed a remarkable gift for flattery, and had promised, with no intention of keeping his word, that Russia would be given a free hand with Turkey and Finland. For two years Nikolay enjoyed all the privileges of his post in the army, without having to endure any of the risks. Napoleon had gone to Spain.

Prince Andrey, having served in minor skirmishes as an adjutant under General Kutuzov, leader of the Russian forces, returned to the country. He had some business affairs to straighten out with Count Rostov, marshal of his district, and so he went to the Rostov estate at Otradnoe. There Andrey fell almost immediately under the spell of Count Rostov's lovely young daughter, Natasha. He fancied himself in love as he had never loved before. Once again he turned to Pierre for advice. But Pierre had had an unfortunate quarrel with his wife, Ellen. They were now separated, and Pierre had fought a senseless duel with an innocent man because he had suspected his wife of being unfaithful. But at the sight of Prince Andrey, so hopelessly in love, Pierre's great heart was touched. He had always been fond of Natasha, whom he had known since childhood, and the match seemed to him ideal. With love once more flowing through his heart, he took his wife back, feeling very virtuous at his own generosity. Meanwhile he encouraged Prince Andrey in his suit.

Natasha had ignored previous offers of marriage. When dashing and wealthy Prince Andrey came upon the scene, however, she lost her heart to him instantly. He asked her parents for her hand, and they immediately consented to the match, an excellent one from their point of view. But when Prince Andrey broke the news to his quarrelsome and dictatorial old father, the ancient prince said he would not give his blessing until a year had elapsed. He felt that Natasha had little money and was much too young to take charge of Prince Andrey's home and his son. Marya, Prince Andrey's sister, also disapproved of the match. She was jealous of her brother's fiancée.

Natasha, heartbroken, agreed to wait a year, and Prince Andrey kept their betrothal a secret, in order, as he said, to let her have complete freedom. Natasha went to visit Pierre's wife in Moscow. There her freedom was too complete. One night at the opera, in company with Ellen, who was now recognized as an important social leader, she met Ellen's disreputable brother, Anatole. Unknown to Natasha, Anatole had already been forced to marry a peasant girl, whom he had ruined. The young rake now determined to conquer Natasha. Aided by his unscrupulous sister, he forced his suit. Natasha became confused. She loved Prince Andrey, but he had joined the army again and she never saw him; and she loved Anatole, who was becoming more insistent every day. At last she agreed to run away with Anatole and marry him. Anatole arranged with an unfrocked priest to have a mock ceremony performed.

On the night set for the elopement Natasha's mother discovered the plan. Natasha was confined to her room. Falling ill over her disgrace, she wrote to Prince Andrey and freed him from his vows to her.

When Pierre heard the scandal, he forced Anatole to leave town. Then he went to see Natasha. Strangely, he was the only person whom she trusted and to whom she could speak freely. She looked upon him as if he were an older uncle, and was charmed with his gruff, friendly disposition. Pierre realized that he felt an attraction toward Natasha he should not have had, since he was not free. He managed to let her know his affection for her, however, and she was pleased over his attentions. She soon began to get well, although she was never again to be the frivolous girl whom Prince Andrey had loved.

Prince Andrey had suffered a terrible blow to his pride, but in the army there were many engrossing matters to take his attention away from himself. By 1810, the Franco-Russian alliance had gradually dissolved. When France threatened to free Russia of responsibility for Poland, the tsar finally understood that Napoleon's promises meant little. The dapper little French emperor had forsaken Russia in favor of Austria as the center of his European domination, had married Marie Louise, and in 1812, with his eyes unmistakably fixed on Moscow, crossed the Nieman River. From June to August Napoleon enjoyed an almost uninterrupted march to Smolensk.

In Smolensk he found burned and wrecked houses. The city was deserted. By that time Napoleon began to run into fierce opposition. Old General Kutuzov, former leader of the army of the East and now in complete charge of the Russian forces, was determined to stop Napoleon at any cost. Oddly enough, General Kutuzov was doing the very thing that hindered Russia from winning the war. He was simply trying to stop

Napoleon. If he had not attempted to halt the French, but instead had drawn them deeper and deeper into Russia, lengthening their lines of communication and cutting them off in the rear, the Russians might have won their war earlier. It was odd, too, that Napoleon, in attempting to complete his march, also lessened his chances for victory. Both sides, it seemed, did the very things which would automatically insure defeat.

Battle after battle was fought, with heavy losses on both sides before Napoleon finally led his forces to Borodino. There the most senseless battle in the whole campaign was fought. The Russians, determined to hold Moscow, which was only a short distance away, lost nearly their whole army. The French forces dwindled in proportion. But it was clear that the Russians got the worst of the battle. General Kutuzov, bitter and war-weary, decided, against his will, that the army could not hold Moscow. Napoleon, triumphant, marched once more into a deserted city.

Prince Andrey was gravely wounded at Borodino. The Rostovs were already abandoning their estate to move into the interior, when many wagons loaded with wounded soldiers were brought to the house for shelter. Among these was Prince Andrey himself. Natasha nursed him and sent for Marya, his sister, and his son, Nikolushka. Old Prince Bolkonsky, suffering from the shock of having French soldiers almost upon his doorstep, had died of a stroke. Nikolay managed to move Marya and the boy to safer quarters. Although Prince Andrey welcomed his sister, it was evident that he no longer expected to recover. Natasha nursed him tenderly, and they once more declared their love for each other. When his wound festered, Prince Andrey knew at last that he was dying. He died one night in his sleep. United in tragedy, Marya and Natasha became close friends, and young Nikolay found Prince Andrey's sister attractive.

Pierre Bezuhov, meanwhile, had decided to remain in Moscow. Fired with thoughts of becoming a national hero, he hit upon the plan of assassinating Napoleon. But in his efforts to rescue a Russian woman, who was being molested by French soldiers, Pierre was captured as a prisoner of war.

Napoleon's army completely disintegrated in Moscow. After waiting in vain for peace terms from the tsar, Napoleon decided to abandon Moscow and head for France. A ragged, irresponsible, pillaging group of men, who had once been the most powerful army in the world, gathered up their booty, threw away their supplies, and took the road back to Smolensk. Winter came on. Pierre Bezuhov, luckily, was robust and healthy. Traveling with the other prisoners, he learned from experience that happiness could consist of merely being warm and having enough to eat. His privations aged and matured him. He learned responsibility and gained courage. He developed a sense of humor at the irony of his plight. His simplicity and even temperament made him a favorite with French and Russians alike.

On the road to Smolensk the French forces became completely demoralized. Cossacks charged out of the forests, cutting the lines, taking countless French prisoners, and rescuing the Russian captives. Many Frenchmen deserted. Others fell ill and died on the road. Pierre, free at last, returned to Orel, where he fell ill with fever. Later he learned of the deaths of Prince Andrey and his own wife. Ellen had died in St. Petersburg after a short illness. These shocks, coupled with the news of the defeat of the French, seemed to deprive him of all feeling. When he finally recovered, he was overwhelmed with a joyous sense of freedom of soul, a sense that he had at last found himself, that he knew himself for what he really was. He knew the sheer joy of being alive, and he was humble and grateful. He had discovered a faith in God that he had never known before.

Pierre returned to Moscow and renewed his friendships with Marya Bolkonsky and the Rostovs. Once more Natasha charmed him, and Pierre suddenly realized that she was no longer a child. He loved her now, as always, and so when the opportunity presented itself he dutifully asked her parents for Natasha's hand. At the same time Nikolay Rostov entertained the thought of marrying Marya. Natasha and Pierre were married. They were very happy. Natasha was an efficient wife who dominated her husband, much to the amusement of their friends, but Pierre loved her and respected her because she knew how to take charge of everything. She managed his estates as well as her household.

Nikolay, though not entirely sure that he loved Marya, knew that to marry her would be a wise thing. The Rostovs were now poor, the old count having left his affairs in a deplorable state. At the insistence of his mother, Nikolay finally proposed to Marya and the two families were joined. The union proved happier than Nikolay had expected. They adopted Prince Andrey's son, Nikolushka.

After eight years of marriage, Pierre and Natasha had four fine children, of whom they were very proud. It was thought, in society, that Natasha carried her devotion to her husband and children to an extreme. But Natasha and Pierre were happier than they had ever been before, and they found their lives together a fulfillment of all their dreams.

THE WAR OF THE WORLDS

Type of work: Novel
Author: H. G. Wells (1866-1946)
Type of plot: Pseudo-scientific romance
Time of plot: Late nineteenth century
Locale: London and environs
First published: 1898

Principal characters:
THE NARRATOR
HIS WIFE
THE ARTILLERYMAN
THE CURATE

Critique:

This novel is representative of Wells' pseudo-scientific romances. Founded as it is on popular conceptions of Mars, it exploits interplanetary travel and warfare. In its day it was popular, but it has very little more than historical interest for the modern reader. We have advanced so far in scientific sophistication that the wonders of the *War of the Worlds* seem rather tame. The narrative method and the use of an unnamed I lend probability to the work. The novel contains little character study, and the plot is a bare narrative of a few days of horror.

The Story:

I was interested in Mars, interested enough to observe the planet often through a telescope. Mars, I knew, was smaller than the earth and probably much older. One night in the observatory I noticed a small pinpoint of light leave our neighboring planet. Later I saw three more shooting off into space. My astronomer friends speculated on these strange meteors.

One evening a meteor fell near our suburban house, and I went over with other curious sightseers to look at it. Only one end of its roughly cylindrical shape was visible. In size it had a diameter of about thirty yards. I looked for a while but went home little impressed. The next day there were strange stories of the projectile. Noises could be heard inside, a kind of pounding. The end was slowly turning around, and it seemed to be unscrewing. I could hear the pounding all night long.

In the morning I went to look again at the object. While I was there the cap came completely off. Then there emerged a strange creature, brownish in color, about the size of a man's torso. It had a head with two enormous eyes and a mouth without teeth. Around the mouth were many pairs of tentacles. The creature hopped off the projectile and began circling the huge cylinder. It moved with much difficulty. Probably the greatly increased pull of gravity on our planet made the creature comparatively heavier. The man from Mars began to dig industriously.

Then I noted that many more of these creatures were crawling from the cylinder and beginning to dig. Soon it became apparent that they were trying to make a big pit around their projectile.

Within a day or so the Martians had their huge pit completed, and they turned it into a workshop where they hammered night and day. The London papers paid little attention to the Martians or gibed at the fantastic news. We in the neighborhood saw that the creatures could not get out of their pit, and the few scientific men who came to observe asked us not to harm them.

One evening my wife and I heard a loud clanking and trembling. Rushing to the window we saw a giant metal frame about a hundred feet high and shaped like a big milk stool. The metal monster strode disjointedly over a field where it met two others. The three stood together, apparently looking around. Then a great beam of heat shot from each, and a forest disappeared, seared as if from a giant's breath. The three monsters clanked away.

Shortly thereafter refugees in carts and wagons, on bicycles and on foot, began to stream past our door. They were all panic-stricken and we learned that they were the few survivors of a town destroyed by the Martian heat rays. The war of the worlds had begun.

Before long we heard the reassuring sounds of army artillery moving up. As soon as Martians had been spotted, the soldiers fired their field pieces. But there was little at which to aim and the Martians were little affected. Then, luckily, a heavy gun made a direct hit on the solid portion at the top of one of the machines and it went out of control. From the top fell one of the brown octopuses, the man from Mars who was the guiding genius of the machine. The metal tripod continued on in a straight line until it fell over. We were horrified to see another monster go after it and transfer a Martian warrior to the prostrate frame. In a moment the tripod was up and on its path of destruction.

I hired a cart from my landlord and took my wife to Leatherhead. When I returned late that night, the roads were jammed with panicky crowds. My own house was somewhat damaged, but I spent the rest of the night there.

In the morning the countryside was alive with metal monsters. Our soldiers had no defense against their heat rays. The Martians quickly learned about guns. Before them as they strode they loosed heavy clouds of dense green smoke which killed everyone it touched. A detachment of artillery had no chance against them.

A weary artilleryman stumbled into my house that evening. The rest of his outfit had been killed by the smoke. While he was telling me his story, a monster came toward our street, destroying each house as he came. In my fear I would have fled immediately, but the artilleryman made us stop for provisions. Supplied with bread and mutton, we left the house and escaped by hiding in bushes and streams. Behind us clanked the monster.

I left the artilleryman along the road because I was intent on getting back to my wife in Leatherhead. I hid in cellars to escape the green smoke. On my wanderings I picked up a hysterical curate. One night, while we were sleeping in a deserted cellar, a loud explosion rocked our retreat. In the morning we saw that we were trapped by a Martian projectile resting against our refuge.

Forced to stay there, forced to keep still to avoid detection, I learned much about the Martians. They were all head. In their evolution they had learned to do without stomach, legs, and glands. They had a sensitive area where they could hear, but they had no noses. I even learned how they fed; from captured men they drained the blood and let it flow directly into their veins from a pipette. The curate went raving mad during our close confinement and I had to kill him. When the Martians explored the cellar with tentacles, I escaped, but they took the curate's body.

After twelve days the Martians left and I was free. In London I saw a ruined city. The Martian machines, however, were standing idle. The men from Mars had fallen victim to our bacteria and the world was saved. My wife found me in our London studio.

THE WARDEN

Type of work: Novel
Author: Anthony Trollope (1815-1882)
Type of plot: Domestic realism
Time of plot: Mid-nineteenth century
Locale: London and "Barchester," England
First published: 1855

Principal characters:
Mr. Harding, warden of Hiram's Hospital
Eleanor Harding, his younger daughter
John Bold, her lover
Dr. Grantly, husband of Mr. Harding's older daughter
Tom Towers, a newspaperman
Sir Abraham Haphazard, Mr. Harding's counsel

Critique:

The Warden is a pleasant story about British ecclesiastical life in the time of Queen Victoria, and the amiable style of the novel fits the leisurely existence it describes. The narrative is frequently interrupted by the author, who comments on character, situation, or life in general, as his fancy strikes him. Trollope does not pretend to any depth, but he has produced here a delightful picture of life in a particular time and place.

The Story:

At the age of fifty the Reverend Septimus Harding was appointed precentor of Barchester Cathedral, a position which carried with it the wardenship of Hiram's Hospital. This institution had for over four hundred years provided a home for twelve men in their old age, and as the income had grown to a considerable size, the warden and the steward received substantial yearly salaries. With his income of eight hundred pounds a year, Mr. Harding was able to provide comfortably for his younger daughter, Eleanor. His older daughter, Susan, was married to Dr. Grantly, archdeacon of the cathedral.

John Bold, a young physician with a small practice, turned his energies to reform. On investigation he discovered that the will of John Hiram, donor of the hospital, made no stipulation which would result in such a discrepancy as existed between the warden's and the steward's incomes and those of the twelve inmates, and he felt that his duty obliged him to bring this discrepancy to light. He engaged the interest of a newspaper friend, Tom Towers, and the services of a solicitor named Finney. Finney explained the situation to the inmates and encouraged them to think in terms of an annual income of one hundred pounds a year. Most of them signed a petition addressed to the bishop, asking that justice be done.

The *Jupiter,* for which Towers worked, published editorials about the greediness of the church and unscrupulous clergymen. Mr. Harding was distressed. It had never entered his head that he was living off an income not his by rights, and he began to talk of resigning. Eleanor agreed that if her father were unhappy at Hiram's Hospital, they would be better off at Crabtree Parva, a small parish which belonged to Mr. Harding and which paid an annual income of fifty pounds.

Dr. Grantly, a worldly man, would not hear of Mr. Harding's resignation. He insisted that the warden had an obligation to the church and to his fellow members of the clergy which required a firm stand against the laity and the press. Besides, as hc pointed out, the living at Crabtree Parva could not provide a suitable match for Eleanor.

Dr. Grantly came to the hospital and addressed the inmates. He told them John Hiram had intended simply to provide comfortable quarters for old single men who had no other homes. But Dr. Grantly's speech had little effect, except on John Bunce and his two cronies. John Bunce, who was especially close to Mr. Harding, served as a sub-warden of the old men. Tho others felt they had a right to a hundred pounds a year.

When Eleanor saw how unhappy the whole affair made her father, she begged him to resign. Finally she went to John Bold and begged him to give up the suit. After promising to do anything he could for her, Bold declared his love. Eleanor, who had hoped not to let matters go so far, confessed her love in return.

Bold went to see Dr. Grantly and told him that for reasons best known to himself he was withdrawing the charges he had made. Dr. Grantly replied that he did not think the defendants wished to have the suit withdrawn. He had been advised that Mr. Harding and the steward were, in effect, servants, and so were not responsible and could not be defendants in a suit.

Mr. Harding decided to go to London for a conference with Sir Abraham Haphazard, counsel for the defense. Eleanor had come home expecting to tell her father all that Bold had told her, but she could not bring herself to discuss her own affairs before those of the wardenship had been settled. Mr. Harding had decided that he had no right to the income from Hiram's Hospital.

Bold also was going to London. When he arrived there, he went to Tom Towers and asked him not to print any more editorials about the Barchester situation. Towers said he could not be responsible for the attitude of the *Jupiter*. Bold then went to the offices of his lawyer and told him to drop the suit. The lawyer sent word to Sir Abraham.

Mr. Harding arrived in London and was given an appointment with Sir Abraham the next night at ten. Having explained his intention in a note to Dr. Grantly, he was afraid that Dr. Grantly would arrive in London before he would have a chance to carry out his plan. He left his hotel at ten in the morning and spent most of the day in Westminster Abbey in order to avoid Dr. Grantly. That night he told Sir Abraham that he must in all conscience resign his post as warden. When he returned to his hotel, he found Dr. and Mrs. Grantly waiting for him, but their arguments could not make the warden change his mind. Back in Barchester, he wrote a formal letter of resignation to the bishop and sent a copy to Dr. Grantly.

The bishop offered him a position as chaplain in his household. Mr. Harding declined the offer. Then it was suggested that a trade be effected between Mr. Harding and Mr. Quiverful of Puddingdale. Mr. Quiverful, who had ten children, would be glad to double his annual income and would be impervious to any attacks from the press. But this arrangement, too, met with opposition, for Puddingdale was too far from Barchester for Mr. Harding to attend to his duties as precentor at the cathedral.

As the time for Mr. Harding's departure from Hiram's Hospital drew near, he called in all the inmates and had a last talk with them. They were disturbed, even those who had petitioned the bishop, for they felt that they were being deprived of a friendly and sympathetic warden.

Mr. Harding took lodgings and was given a tiny parish at the entrance to the cathedral close. His daughter Eleanor married John Bold. So Mr. Harding's income continued to be ample for his needs. He dined frequently with the bishop and kept his cello at Eleanor's house, where he often went to make music. In short, Mr. Harding was not an unhappy man.

WAVERLEY

Type of work: Novel
Author: Sir Walter Scott (1771-1832)
Type of plot: Historical romance
Time of plot: 1745
Locale: England and Scotland
First published: 1814

Principal characters:
EDWARD WAVERLEY, a young English officer
BARON BRADWARDINE, a Scottish nobleman
ROSE BRADWARDINE, the baron's daughter
EVAN DHU MACCOMBICH, follower of Fergus Mac Ivor
DONALD BEAN LEAN, a Highland bandit
FERGUS MAC IVOR VICH IAN VOHR, leader of the clan of Mac Ivor
FLORA MAC IVOR, Fergus' sister
PRINCE CHARLES EDWARD STUART, the Young Pretender

Critique:

When this novel was published anonymously in 1814, it created great interest among readers who sought to learn the identity of its author. Scott himself claimed, in his preface to the 1829 edition, that he had published his work anonymously to avoid political discussion. Because the book was written only sixty years after the invasion of Prince Charlie and because the dark and bloody days of 1745 still rankled in the minds of many living men and women, it is conceivable that Scott spoke the truth; however, observing the nineteenth-century fondness for publishing anonymous works, one might add the opinion that Sir Walter was also following a custom of the times. *Waverley* is a romantic novel in which Scott paid tribute to a group of people who had been considered no more than fierce, ignorant barbarians. In the person of Fergus Mac Ivor we find not only intellect and sentiment, but also formal, courtly manners. Especially contributing to the reader's delight in *Waverley* is a picturesque Scottish Highland background.

The Story:

The English family of Waverley had long been known for its Jacobite sympathies. In the year 1745, Waverley-Honour, the ancestral home of the family, was a quiet retreat for Sir Everard Waverley, an elderly Jacobite. His brother, Richard Waverley, seeking political advantage in London, had sworn loyalty to the king.

Edward Waverley, the son of Whig Richard, divided his time between his father and his Uncle Everard at Waverley-Honour. On that great estate Edward was free to come and go as he pleased, for his tutor Pembroke, a devout dissenter, was often too busy writing religious pamphlets to spend much time in the education of his young charge. When Edward became old enough, his father obtained for him a commission in the army. Shortly afterward he was ordered to Scotland to join the dragoons of Colonel Gardiner. Equipped with the necessary articles of dress, accompanied by a retinue of men who had been selected by Sir Everard, and weighed down by the dissenting tomes of Pembroke, Edward left Waverley-Honour in quixotic fashion to conquer his world.

He had been instructed by Sir Everard to visit an old friend, Sir Cosmo Comyne Bradwardine, whose estate was near the village of Tully-Veolan in the Scottish Lowlands. Edward, soon after his arrival at the post of Colonel Gardiner, obtained a leave in order to go to Tully-Veolan. There he found Sir Everard's friend both cordial and happy to see him. The few days spent at Tully-Veolan convinced Edward that Scotland was a wilder and more romantic land than his native England. He paid little attention to Rose Bradwardine, the baron's daughter, his youthful imagination being fired by the songs and dances of Davie Gellatley, the baron's servant, and by tales about the Scottish Highlanders and their rude ways. At Tully-Veolan he was also confronted by a political issue that had been but an idealistic quarrel in his former existence; these Scottish people were Jacobites, and Edward ostensibly was a Whig royalist because of his father's politics and his own rank in the army of Hanoverian George II of England.

During his stay at Tully-Veolan an event occurred which was to change Edward's life. It began with the unexpected arrival of Evan Dhu Maccombich, a Highlander in the service of the renowned clan chieftain, Fergus Mac Ivor Vich Ian Vohr, a friend of the baron's. His taste for romantic adventure having been aroused, Edward begged another extension of his leave in order to accompany Evan Dhu into the Highlands. In those rugged hills Edward was led to the cave that sheltered the band of Donald Bean Lean, an outlaw who robbed and plundered the wealthy Lowlanders. Staying with the bandit only long enough to discover the romantic attachment between Donald's daughter Alice and Evan Dhu, Edward again set out into the hills with his cheerful young guide. His curiosity had been sufficiently whetted by Evans' descriptions of Fergus Mac Ivor and his ancient castle deep in the Highland hills at Glennaquoich.

The welcome that Mac Ivor extended to Edward was open-handed and hearty. No less warm was the quiet greeting which Flora, Fergus Mac Ivor's sister, had for the English soldier. Flora was a beautiful woman of romantic, poetic nature, and Edward found himself before long deeply in love with the chieftain's sister. Mac Ivor himself seemed to sanction the idea of a marriage. That union could not be, however, for Flora had vowed her life to another cause—that of placing Charles, the young Stuart prince, upon the throne of England. At Edward's proposal of marriage, Flora advised him to seek a woman who could attach herself wholeheartedly to his happiness; Flora claimed that she could not divide her attentions between the Jacobite cause and marriage to one who was not an ardent supporter of Charles Edward Stuart.

Edward's stay at Glennaquoich was interrupted by letters carried to him by Davie Gellatley from Tully-Veolan. The first was from Rose Bradwardine, who advised him that the Lowlands were in a state of revolt. Her father being absent, she warned Edward not to return to Tully-Veolan. The other letters informed him that Richard Waverley had engaged in some unfortunate political maneuvers which had caused his political downfall. On the heels of this news came orders from Colonel Gardiner, who, having heard reports of Edward's association with traitors, was relieving the young officer of his command. Repulsed by Flora and disgraced in his army career, Edward resolved to return to Waverley-Honour. He equipped himself suitably for the dangerous journey and set out toward the Lowlands.

Because of armed revolt in Scotland and the linking of the Waverley name with the Jacobite cause, Edward found himself under arrest for treason against King George. The dissenting pamphlets of Pembroke which he carried, his stay in the Highlands, and the company he had kept there, were suspicious circumstances which made it impossible for him to prove his innocence. Captured by some of the king's troopers, he was turned over to an armed guard with orders to take him to Stirling Castle for trial on a charge of treason.

But the friend of Fergus Mac Ivor Vich Ian Vohr was not to be treated in such a scurvy manner. On the road a quick ambush rescued Edward from his captors, and he found himself once again in the hands of some Highlanders whom he was able to recognize as a party of Donald Bean Lean's followers. Indeed, Alice once appeared among the men to slip a packet of letters to him, but at the time he had no opportunity to read the papers she had given him so secretively.

A few days' journey brought Edward to the center of Jacobite activities at Holyrood, the temporary court of Charles Edward Stuart, who had secretly crossed the Channel from France. There Edward Waverley found Fergus Mac Ivor awaiting him. When the Highlander presented Edward to Prince Charles, the Pretender welcomed the English youth because of the name he bore. The prince, trained in French courts, was a model of refinement and courtesy. His heartfelt trust gave Edward a feeling of belonging, after he had lost his commission, his cause unheard, in the English army. When Charles asked him to join in the Scottish uprising, Edward assented. Mac Ivor seemed quite happy about Edward's new allegiance. When the young Englishman asked about Flora, Mac Ivor explained that he had brought her along to the prince's court so that he could make use of her graces in gaining a political foothold when the battle was won. Edward resented this manner of using Flora as bait, but soon he perceived that the court of the Pretender functioned very much like the French court where Charles and his followers had learned statecraft. Mac Ivor pressed Edward to continue his courtship of Flora. The sister of Mac Ivor, however, met his advances coldly. In the company of the Highland beauty was Rose Bradwardine, whose father had also joined the Stuart cause.

Accepted as a cavalier by the women who clustered around the prince and under the influence of the Pretender's courtly manners, Edward soon became a favorite, but Mac Ivor's sister persisted in ignoring him. He began to compare the two women, Rose and Flora, the former gaining favor in his eyes as he watched them together.

The expedition of the Pretender and his Highlanders was doomed to failure. As they marched southward to England, they began to lose hope. The prince ordered a retreat to Scotland. Many of the clansmen were killed at the disastrous battle of Culloden. The survivors escaped to the Highlands, to spend their days in hiding from troops sent to track them down. A few were fortunate enough to make their way in safety to France.

Edward managed to get away and to find a friend who helped him to steal back to Scotland, where he hoped to find Rose Bradwardine. So far Edward had cleared himself of the earlier charges of treachery and desertion, which had been the initial cause of his joining the Pretender. It had been Donald Bean Lean who had deceived Colonel Gardiner with a false report of Edward's activities. The letters Alice had slipped to him had conveyed that information to Edward. Now he hoped to escape to France with Rose and wait for a pardon from England. Richard Waverley had died and Edward had inherited his fortune.

Fergus Mac Ivor and Evan Dhu Maccombich were executed for their crimes against the crown, and the power of the Highland clan was broken. Flora entered a Catholic convent in France, the country in which she had been reared. Edward Waverley and Rose were married after Edward was certain of his pardon. They returned to Tully-Veolan, where the baron's estate was awaiting its heirs.

THE WAY OF ALL FLESH

Type of work: Novel
Author: Samuel Butler (1835-1902)
Type of plot: Social criticism
Time of plot: Nineteeenth century
Locale: England
First published: 1903

Principal characters:
George Pontifex, a printer
Theobald Pontifex, George's son
Althea Pontifex, George's daughter
Christina Pontifex, Theobald's wife
Ernest, Theobald's oldest son
Mr. Overton, Ernest's friend
Ellen, Ernest's wife

Critique:

Reared in the family of a strict clergyman, Samuel Butler patterned Theobald Pontifex after his own father. Aimed at a type of parent-children relationship that bred maladjusted, introverted children, this novel depicts one son who broke the parental ties, thereby freeing himself to make his own way in life. Pointing to the foibles of his fellow man, probing the motive of an indignant parent or burlesquing a controversy of ideas, Butler's wit and sarcastic humor lighten at all times the heavy tones of his social study.

The Story:

Mr. and Mrs. Pontifex were well up in years when their son George was born. When the time came for George to learn a trade, they accepted the offer of Mr. Pontifex's brother-in-law to take George with him to London as an apprentice in his printing shop. George learned his trade well, and when the uncle died he willed the shop to his nephew.

George had married, and five children were born to him and his wife; John, Theobald, Eliza, Maria, and Althea, at whose birth Mrs. Pontifex died. George considered himself a parent motivated only by the desire to do the right thing by his children. When Theobald proved himself not as quick as John but more persistent, George picked the clergy as Theobald's profession. Shortly before his ordination, Theobald wrote to his father that he did not wish to become a minister. George, in reply, threatened to disinherit his son. Submitting, Theobald was ordained. His next step was to wait for some older member of the clergy to die so that he could be given a living.

The Allabys had three daughters, all of marriageable age. After having selected Theobald as a possible husband for one of the daughters, Mr. Allaby suggested to his offspring that they play a game of cards to decide who would become Theobald's wife. Christina won. Theobald unwittingly fell in with Mr. Allaby's plans and obligingly courted Christina until he won her promise to marry him. George wrote to Theobald that he objected to his son's marriage into the impoverished Allaby family, but Theobald was too deeply embroiled in his engagement to untangle himself. In five years he obtained a decent living in a community called Battersby, where he and Christina settled. Their first child was a son. Since this child was the first new male Pontifex, George was pleased, and Theobald felt that for the first time in his life he had done something to satisfy his father. After Ernest came Joseph and then Charlotte. Theobald and Christina reared their children with strict adherence to principles which they believed would mold fine character. The children were disciplined rigorously and beaten when their parents deemed it appropriate. When George Pontifex died, he left seventeen thousand, five hundred pounds to Theobald and twenty-five hundred pounds to Ernest.

From an oppressive existence under the almost obsessed rule of his parents, Ernest was sent to Roughborough to be educated under Dr. Skinner, who was as strict a disciplinarian as Theobald. Ernest was physically weak and mentally morose. He might have succumbed completely to his overpowering environment had not he been rescued by an understanding and loving relative. Althea Pontifex, Theobald's sister, had retired to London, where she lived comfortably on an inheritance wisely invested. Looking about for someone to whom she could leave her money when she died, Althea hit upon Ernest. Not wishing to bestow her fortune blindly, she determined to learn more about the boy. She moved to Roughborough so that she could spend a great deal of time with Ernest.

From the first, she endeared herself to the lonely youngster. She encouraged him to develop his own talents, and when she learned that he had a passion for music she suggested that he learn how to build an organ. Enthusiastically he set about to learn wood construction and harmony. Theobald disapproved, but he did not forbid Ernest's activities because he and Christina were eager to have Ernest inherit Althea's money. Ernest's shrinking personality changed under the benevolent influence of his aunt. When Althea died, she left her money in the hands of her best friend, Mr. Overton, whom she had appointed to administer the estate which would go to Ernest on his twenty-eighth birthday.

After Ernest had completed his course at Roughborough, Theobald sent him to Cambridge to study for the ministry. At Cambridge Ernest made a few friends and took part in athletics. He was ordained soon after he received his degree. Then he went to London. Still innocent and unworldly, he entrusted to a friend named Pryer the income he had inherited from his grandfather. Pryer cheated him out of his legacy. Because he could not differentiate between good and evil in human character, Ernest also became entangled in a charge of assault and battery and was sentenced to a term in the workhouse. Theobald sent word that henceforth Ernest was to consider himself an orphan.

Ernest was twenty-three years old at the time. Mr. Overton, who held, unknown to Ernest, the estate Althea had left for her nephew, began to take an interest in Ernest's affairs. When Ernest was released from prison, he went to Mr. Overton for advice concerning his future, since it was no longer possible for him to be a clergyman.

While Ernest was still at Roughborough, Christina had hired as a maid a young girl named Ellen. She and Ernest had become good friends simply because Ellen was kinder to him than anyone else at home. When Ellen became pregnant and Christina learned of her condition, she sent Ellen away. Ernest, fearing that the girl might starve, followed her and gave her all the money he had. Theobald learned what Ernest had done through John, the coachman, who had been present when Ernest had given Ellen the money. Theobald became angry and dismissed the coachman.

Soon after his release from prison, Ernest met Ellen in a London street. Because both were lonely, they married and set up a small second-hand clothing and book shop with the help of Mr. Overton, who deplored the idea of Ernest's marrying Ellen. Unknown to Ernest, Ellen was a habitual drunkard. Before long she had so impoverished him with her drinking and her foul ways that he disliked her intensely, but he could not leave her because of the two children she had borne him.

One day Ernest again met John, his father's former coachman, who revealed that he was the father of Ellen's illegitimate child and that he had married Ellen shortly after she had left Theobald's home in disgrace. Acting on this information, Mr. Overton arranged matters for Ernest. Ellen was promised an income of a pound a week if she would leave Ernest, a proposal she readily accepted. The children were sent to live in a family of happy, healthy children, for Ernest feared that his own upbringing would make him as bad a parent as Theobald had been.

When Ernest reached his twenty-eighth birthday, he inherited Althea's trust fund of seventy thousand pounds. By that time Ernest had become a writer. With a part of his inheritance he traveled abroad for a few years and then returned to England with material for a book he planned to write.

Before he died he published many successful books, but he never told his own story. Mr. Overton, who had access to all the Pontifex papers and who knew Ernest so well, wrote the history of the Pontifex family.

THE WAY OF THE WORLD

Type of work: Drama
Author: William Congreve (1670-1729)
Type of plot: Comedy of manners
Time of plot: Seventeenth century
Locale: London
First presented: 1700

Principal characters:

- Lady Wishfort, an aged coquette
- Mrs. Fainall, her daughter
- Mrs. Millamant, Lady Wishfort's niece
- Foible, a servant
- Sir Wilfull Witwoud, Lady Wishfort's nephew
- Witwoud, his half-brother
- Mirabell, a gentleman of fashion
- Waitwell, his servant
- Fainall, married to Lady Wishfort's daughter
- Mrs. Marwood, in love with Fainall

Critique:

The Way of the World is the best of the Restoration dramas, a true comedy of manners. Criticism had paid particular attention to this play, for some hold that the famous scene between Mirabell and Millamant is one of the most profound analyses of the marriage relation ever written. The play as a whole is a realistic statement of a problem every individual must face in his adjustment to society.

The Story:

Mrs. Millamant, who was by far the most beautiful and wittiest of all the fine ladies in London, was sought after by all the beaux in town. The niece of the rich Lady Wishfort, she was also an heiress in her own right, and was looked upon with great favor by Witwoud, a kinsman of Lady Wishfort. But Millamant's acknowledged preference among her suitors was for young Mirabell, who was the only man in London who could match that lady's devastating wit.

Mirabell himself was as great a favorite among the ladies in the town as Millamant was among the beaux. She was the perfect coquette; he was the perfect gallant. Among Mirabell's jealous admirers was Mrs. Marwood, the mistress of Fainall, Lady Wishfort's son-in-law. In fact, Mirabell had but one real enemy among the ladies, and that was Lady Wishfort herself. On one occasion, in order to further his suit with Millamant, Mirabell had falsely made love to the old lady. Discovering his subterfuge later, she had never forgiven him. She determined that he would never marry her niece so long as she controlled Millamant's fortune. In consequence, Mirabell was hard put to devise a scheme whereby he might force Lady Wishfort to consent to the marriage.

The plan he devised was an ingenious one. Realizing that Lady Wishfort would respond to anything which even resembled a man, he promptly invented an imaginary uncle, Sir Rowland, who, he said, had fallen madly in love with Lady Wishfort and wanted to marry her. He forced his servant, Waitwell, to impersonate this fictitious uncle. To placate Waitwell and further insure the success of his plan, he contrived his servant's marriage to Lady Wishfort's maid, Foible.

His scheme might have worked had it not been for the counterplans of the designing Mrs. Marwood and her unscrupulous lover, Fainall. Although she pretended to despise all men, Mrs. Marwood was secretly in love with Mirabell, and had no intention of allowing him to marry Millamant. Fainall, although he detested his wife heartily, realized that he was dependent upon her and her mother's fortune for his well-being, and he resolved to stop at nothing to make sure that fortune was in his control.

While these plans were proceeding, Millamant gave little thought to plots or counterplots. She had not the slightest intention of compromising with life, but insisted that the world's way must somehow be made to conform to her own desires. She had little use for the life around her, seeing through its shallow pretenses and its falsity, and yet she knew that it was the world in which she had to live. She realized that any attempt to escape from it into some idyllic pastoral existence, as her aunt often suggested, would be folly.

Millamant laid down to Mirabell the conditions under which she would marry him, and they were stringent conditions, not at all in conformity with the average wife's idea of her lot. She would have in her marriage no place for the ridiculous codes and conventions which governed the behavior of the people around her. She would be entirely free of the cant and hypocrisy of married life, which were only a cloak for the corruption or misery hidden underneath social custom. In short, she refused to be merely a married woman in her husband's or society's eyes. Mirabell, likewise, had certain conditions which must be fulfilled before he was turned from bachelor into husband. When his demands proved reasonable, both lovers realized that they saw life through much the same eyes. They decided that they were probably made for one another.

But the world had not come to the same conclusion. Lady Wishfort, still embittered against Mirabell for his gross deception, resolved that Millamant was to marry a cousin, Sir Wilfull Witwoud, a country lout many years her senior, who had just arrived in London. Fortunately for Millamant, Sir Wilfull turned out to be a harmless booby, who, when he was in his cups, became the most understanding of men.

There was a greater obstacle, however, in the scheme which Mirabell himself had planned. Waitwell, disguised as Mirabell's imaginary uncle, Sir Rowland, paid ardent court to Lady Wishfort, and would have been successful in inveigling her into marriage had it not been for a letter from Mrs. Marwood exposing the whole scheme. Lady Wishfort's maid, Foible, succeeded in intercepting the letter, but Mrs. Marwood appeared at Lady Wishfort's in person and disclosed the deception.

Lady Wishfort was furious, and more determined than ever to prevent any marriage between her niece and Mirabell. She angrily discharged Foible from her employ. But Mrs. Fainall, Lady Wishfort's daughter, was on the side of the two lovers. When Foible informed her that she had tangible proof of the relationship between Fainall and Mrs. Marwood, Mrs. Fainall resolved to prosecute her husband to the limit. Meanwhile the wily Fainall had taken pains to have all his wife's property transferred to his name by means of trumped up evidence of an affair between his wife and Mirabell.

In this act Lady Wishfort began to see for the first time the scheming villainy of her daughter's husband. Mirabell, with the aid of Foible and Millamant's servant, Mincing, exposed the double-dealing Mrs. Marwood and her lover, and further proved that while she was yet a widow Mrs. Fainall had conveyed her whole estate in trust to Mirabell. Lady Wishfort was so delighted that she forgave Mirabell all his deceptions, and consented to his marriage to Millamant.

THE WEB AND THE ROCK

Type of work: Novel
Author: Thomas Wolfe (1900-1938)
Type of plot: Impressionistic realism
Time of plot: 1900-1928
Locale: North Carolina, New York, Europe
First published: 1939

Principal characters:
GEORGE WEBBER, a young writer
ESTHER JACK, whom he loved

Critique:

Critics have said that *The Web and the Rock* is at once the best and the worst novel that Thomas Wolfe wrote. Certainly the first part of the book, that describing George Webber's childhood in a Southern town, is an excellent regional chronicle. Here Wolfe's genius with words reaches new heights. But the rest of the novel drags somewhat from overdone treatment of a love story in which similar scenes are repeated until they become monotonous. From his own experience, Wolfe here retells the story of a young man's search for the meaning of life. Like his other novels, it is a book of passion and fury and wild rhetoric.

The Story:

George Webber's childhood was one of bleakness and misery. He was really a charity ward, even though he lived with his aunt and uncle. For George's father had deserted him and his mother, and had gone off to live with another woman. After the death of George's mother, her Joyner relatives took George into their home, where the boy was never allowed to forget that he had some of the blood of the Webbers mixed with his Joyner blood. Strangely, all his good and beautiful dreams were dreams of his father, and often he hotly and passionately defended his father to the Joyners. His love for his father made his childhood a divided one. George hated the people his aunt and uncle called good; and those they called bad, he loved. A lonely child, George kept his thoughts and dreams to himself rather than expose them to the ridicule of the Joyners. But the picture of that happy, joyful world of his father, and others like him, stayed with him during those bleak years of his childhood.

When George was sixteen, his father died, leaving the boy a small inheritance. With that money, George left the little southern town of Libya Hill and went to college. There he found knowledge, freedom, life. Like many other young men, George wasted some of that freedom in sprees of riotous and loose living. But he also used his freedom to read everything he could get his hands on, and he was deeply impressed with the power of great writers. George was beginning to feel the need of getting down some of his thoughts and memories on paper. He wanted to write of the two sides of the world—the bright, gay world of the people who had everything and the horrible, dreary world of the derelicts and the poor.

His college years ended, George fulfilled the dream of every country boy in the nation; he went to the city, to the beautiful, wonderful enfabled rock, as he called New York.

The city was as great and as marvelous as George had known it would be. He shared an apartment with four other boys; it was a dingy, cheap place, but it was their own apartment, where they could do as they pleased. But George found the city a lonely place in spite of its millions of people and its bright lights. There was no one to whom he was responsible nor to whom he belonged. He thought he would burst with what he knew about people and about life, and, since there was no one he could talk to about those things, he tried to write them down. He began his first novel.

The next year was the loneliest one George had ever known. He drove himself mercilessly. He was wretched, for the words torturing his mind would not go on the paper as he wanted them to. At the end of a year he took the last of his inheritance and went to Europe. He hoped to find there the peace of mind he needed to finish his book.

The cities of Europe did not hold his salvation. He was still lonely and bitter because he could not find the answer to the riddle of life. He went back to New York. But the city was no longer an unfriendly enemy, for George had found Esther.

They had met on the ship bound for New York. Esther was Mrs. Esther Jack, a well-known and successful stage set designer. She was fifteen or twenty years older than George, but she was also younger in many ways, for Esther loved people and believed in them. Where George was silent and distrustful, Esther was open and trusting. George sometimes felt that theirs was the greatest love of all times, at once brutal and tender, passionate and friendly, so deep that it could not last. But for the next three years he was the king of the world. To Esther, George told all his dreams, all his memories, all his formerly wordless thoughts about life and people.

George failed to realize at first that Esther meant more than a lover to him. Gradually he came to know that through her he was becoming a new person, a man who loved everyone. For the first time in his life George Webber belonged to someone. Since he was no longer lonely, the torture and the torment left him. At last his book began to take shape, to become a reality. George Webber was happy.

Slowly the magic of his affair with Esther began to disappear. He still loved her more than he believed possible, knew that he would always love her; but they began to quarrel, to have horrible, name-calling scenes that left them both exhausted and empty, even the quarrels that ended with passionate love-making. At first George did not know the reason for those scenes, although he always knew that it was he who started them. Slowly he began to realize that he quarreled with Esther because she possessed him so completely. He had given her his pride, his individuality, his dreams, his manhood. Esther had also unknowingly been a factor in his disillusionment, for through her he had met and known the great people of the world —the artists, the writers, the actors— and he had found those people disgusting and cheap. They had destroyed his childhood illusions of fame and greatness, and he hated them for it.

When his novel was finished, Esther sent the manuscript to several publishers she knew. After months had passed without his hearing that it had been accepted, George turned on Esther in one final burst of savage abuse and told her to leave him and never return. Then he went to Europe again.

Although he had gone to Europe to forget Esther, he did nothing without thinking of her and longing for her. Esther wrote to him regularly, and he paced the floor if the expected letter did not arrive. But he was still determined to be himself, and to accomplish his purpose he must not see Esther again.

One night, in a German beer hall, George got into a drunken brawl and was badly beaten up. While he was in the hospital, a feeling of peace came over him for the first time in ten years. He looked into a mirror and saw his body as a thing apart from the rest of him. And he knew that his body had been true to him, that it had taken the abuse he had heaped upon it for almost thirty years. Often he had been almost mad, and he had driven that body beyond endurance in his insane quest—for what he did not know. Now he was ready to go home again. If his first novel should not be published, he would write another. He still had a lot to say. The next time he would put it down right, and then he would be at peace with himself. George Webber was beginning to find himself at last.

WESTWARD HO!

Type of work: Novel
Author: Charles Kingsley (1819-1875)
Type of plot: Historical romance
Time of plot: Sixteenth century
Locale: England and South America
First published: 1855

Principal characters:
AMYAS LEIGH, an adventurer
FRANK LEIGH, his brother
SIR RICHARD GRENVILE, Amyas' godfather
EUSTACE LEIGH, Amyas' and Frank's cousin
ROSE SALTERNE, loved by Amyas and Frank
SALVATION YEO, Amyas' friend
DON GUZMAN DE SOTO, a treacherous Spaniard
AYACANORA, an Indian maiden
MRS. LEIGH, Amyas' and Frank's mother

Critique:

In *Westward Ho!* Charles Kingsley has taken us back to the days of Queen Elizabeth, when such men as Sir Francis Drake, Sir Walter Raleigh, and Sir Richard Grenvile sailed the seas in search of adventure and treasure for their queen. He has shown us that were it not for such men, the history of the world would have been different, for these men won for England the supremacy of the sea and determined who would settle North America. *Westward Ho!* is a story of great sea battles, duels of honor, romantic rescues, and deeds of horror in the Spanish Inquisition. Kingsley has woven all these into one of the most romantic adventure stories in our literature.

The Story:

Amyas Leigh had always had a secret longing to go to sea, but he had not spoken of it because he knew his parents thought him too young for such a rough, hard life. When he met John Oxenham and Salvation Yeo, who were recruiting a crew to sail to the New World after Spanish treasure, he begged to be allowed to join them, but his parents and Sir Richard Grenvile, his godfather, persuaded him to wait a while. The next year his father died of fever and his brother Frank went to the court of Queen Elizabeth. Then Sir Richard Grenvile persuaded Amyas' mother to let the boy accompany Drake on that first English voyage around the world. Now Drake and his adventurers had returned, and Amyas, no longer a boy but a blond young giant, came back to his home at Bideford, in Devon.

One face in the village he remembered better than any, Rose Salterne, the mayor's daughter. All the young men loved and honored her, including Amyas and his brother Frank, who had returned from court. She was also loved by Eustace Leigh, the cousin of Amyas and Frank. Eustace was a Catholic, distrusted by his cousins because they suspected he was in league with the Jesuit priests. When Rose spurned his love he vowed revenge. The other young men who loved Rose formed the Brotherhood of the Rose, and all swore to protect her always and to remain friends, no matter who should win her.

Shortly after Amyas had returned from his voyage with Drake, Salvation Yeo came to him and Sir Richard Grenvile with a strange and horrible tale. The voyage which he had made with John Oxenham had been ill-fated, and Oxenham and most of the crew had been captured by Spanish Inquisitors. Oxenham had had a child by a Spanish lady, and before they were separated Yeo had vowed that he would protect the child. Yeo had done his best, but the child had been lost, and now Yeo begged that he might attach himself to Amyas and go wherever Amyas went. He thought that he might in his travels someday find the little maid again. Amyas and Sir Richard Grenvile were touched by the story, and Amyas promised to keep Yeo with him. Before long the two sailed with Sir Walter Raleigh for Ireland, there to fight the Spaniards.

In Ireland, Raleigh defeated the Spaniards, and Amyas took as hostage Don Guzman de Soto, a Spanish nobleman. Don Guzman accompanied him back to Bideford, there to wait for his ransom from Spain. Don Guzman was a charming gentleman, and it was not long before he had caught the eye of Rose Salterne. After his ransom had been paid, he left England, and then it was learned that Rose had also disappeared in the company of Lucy the witch. Her father was wild with grief, as were Amyas and Frank and the other young men of the Brotherhood of the Rose. All vowed to sail to La Guayra in Caracas, where Don Guzman had gone to be governor and where they felt Rose had fled to join him.

Their voyage was an eventful one. When they neared La Guayra they were seen by the Spaniards, and they had to fight many times before they reached shore. Amyas and Frank went ashore with a few men to try to rescue Rose. There they learned that Eustace had known of their voyage and had beaten them to their destination to warn Don Guzman of their approach. Frank and Amyas heard Rose tell Eustace that she was happily married to Don Guzman, and so they knew she would never leave with them. But they also heard Eustace beg her to run away with him, threatening to turn her over to the Inquisition if she refused. At that threat, Frank and Amyas attacked Eustace, but he escaped, never to be heard of again. Rose fled into the fort. As they made their way back to their ship, Frank was captured by Don Guzman's men. Amyas was knocked unconscious, but his men carried him back to the ship.

When the ship was damaged in a later encounter with the Spaniards, the crew beached her and began a march toward the fabled city of Manoa. It was a long and hazardous journey over high mountains and through a land of hostile Indians. They found no El Dorado, but a young priestess of one of the tribes fell in love with Amyas and followed him the rest of the journey. She was called Ayacanora, and although she was of an Indian tribe she seemed to have the look of a white woman.

After more than three years the little band reached the shore of New Granada and there, after a furious fight, captured a Spanish galleon. After they had secured her and set sail, they went into the hold and released the prisoners the Spaniards had aboard. One of them was Lucy the witch, who told them of the horrible fate of Rose and Frank. Before Eustace disappeared from La Guayra, he had reported to the Inquisition that Rose had kept her Protestant faith. She and Lucy were taken before that terrible tribunal, where Frank also had been turned over to the torturers. Lucy confessed that she had accepted the Catholic faith, but Frank and Rose, refusing to yield to the Inquisitors, had been tortured for many days before they were burned at the stake. When Amyas heard this story, he was like a madman, vowing never to rest until he had killed every Spaniard he saw. On the ship were two Spanish dignitaries who had witnessed the burning of Frank and Rose, and Amyas had them hanged immediately.

At last the ship reached Devon and Amyas took Ayacanora to his home, where his mother welcomed her and treated her as a daughter. During the voyage Yeo had discovered that she was the little maid he had promised Oxenham to protect, and he became as a father to her. Amyas treated her as he might a sister; Ayacanora was not happy at his treatment.

After a time Amyas fitted out a ship and prepared to go with Drake to Virginia, but before they sailed the Spanish Armada arrived off English shores. Amyas with his ship joined the rest of the fleet in that famous battle. After twelve terrible days, the Armada was defeated and almost every Spanish ship destroyed. But Amyas was not satisfied. Don Guzman was aboard one of the Spanish ships, and though Amyas pursued him relentlessly he had to sit by and watch a storm tear the Spaniard's ship apart. And Amyas cursed that he himself had not been able to kill Don Guzman and thus avenge his brother's death.

As Don Guzman's ship broke apart, a bolt of lightning struck Amyas' ship, blinding him and killing Yeo. At first Amyas was full of despair. One day he had a vision. He saw Rose and Don Guzman together, and knew that the Spaniard had really loved her and mourned her until his death. Then he saw himself with Don Guzman, acknowledging their sins to each other, and asking forgiveness. After that he felt at peace with himself.

Amyas returned to his mother's home, and there she and Ayacanora cared for him. Realizing how much the girl loved him, he was so grateful for the tenderness she showed him that he gave her his heart. In Bideford the blind hero spent his remaining days dreaming of his past deeds and of the great glory to come for his country and his queen.

WHAT EVERY WOMAN KNOWS

Type of work: Drama
Author: James M. Barrie (1860-1937)
Type of plot: Social satire
Time of plot: Early twentieth century
Locale: Scotland and England
First presented: 1908

Principal characters:
MAGGIE WYLIE, plain and spinsterish
ALICK WYLIE, her father
JAMES WYLIE, and
DAVID WYLIE, her brothers
JOHN SHAND, a young student
LADY SYBIL TENTERDEN, a young and beautiful aristocrat
THE COMTESSE DE LA BRIERE, her aunt
MR. CHARLES VENABLES, a minister of the Cabinet

Critique:

What Every Woman Knows is one of the most realistic of Barrie's plays, developing as it does the familiar theme that behind every man there is a woman who makes him either a success or a failure. There are, however, flashes of Barrie's sly humor and dramatic irony throughout. The play has been a popular success on both sides of the Atlantic, and a favorite role with many distinguished actresses.

The Story:

The Wylies, like most Scotsmen, were a clannish lot. They had built up their business, a granite quarry, on the spot where their father once worked as a stonemason. They called it *Wylie and Sons.* Alick Wylie wanted it called *Wylie Brothers,* but David, his brother James, and their sister Maggie all insisted that first credit for the business should go to Alick, their father.

Maggie, who kept house for her father and two brothers, was their only problem, for she had reached twenty-seven years, an age when a woman must marry or be regarded as an old maid, and they were considerably downcast because their latest prospect, the minister at Galashiels, had married another woman. There was no question but that Maggie was plain, a fact of which she herself was only too conscious, and the brothers realized that if their sister were to find a husband they would have to do everything in their power to help her.

The opportunity came while the Wylies were at the dambrod board, their favorite pastime on Saturday evenings. Maggie was seated in a chair in the corner knitting, and the brothers were trying to get her off to bed so that they could be on the lookout for a burglar they thought they had seen prowling about the house the night before. At last the burglar appeared, but to their astonishment they discovered the intruder was young John Shand, a neighbor, who confessed that his purpose in entering the house was to read. He was a student preparing for the ministry, but since he was too poor to buy books he had to choose that method of study. David was impressed at such earnestness. After a brief conference with his brother he made the boy an offer. He promised to pay up to three hundred pounds for John Shand's education if, at the end of five years, he would marry Maggie, providing she were at that time still unmarried and wanted him. After some quibbling to decide whether the full three hundred pounds would be deposited in his name at the bank immediately, John Shand agreed to the transaction. Maggie, wanting him to go into the deal with his eyes open, admitted that she had never had an offer of marriage, and that she was five years older than he. But those matters meant little to ambitious young John Shand, who left the house content that he was free to browse in the Wylie library without being mistaken for a burglar.

Six years later, having in the meantime abandoned his ambitions for the ministry, John Shand was standing for Parliament. His great hour had come, the hour for which he and Maggie had waited. She might have forced him to marry her one year before, but they both agreed to wait for his triumph. Maggie was almost frantic between hope and anxiety. At one time, certain that John had lost, she promised herself that she and John would begin another six years of waiting that very night.

Her fears were groundless, however, for John Shand won the election by an overwhelming majority. Her real problem lay in his victory. Immediately after his election John was taken up and lionized by women with whom plain little Maggie could not hope to compete. Among these was Lady Sybil Tenterden. Maggie, overwhelmed by a sense of her own inferiority, offered to release John from his contract and tore up the document which bound him to her. But John Shand was a man of his word, and in his speech to the Cowcaddens Club he announced his forthcoming marriage and introduced Maggie as the Mrs. John Shand soon to be.

Before long it was apparent that Lady Sybil's aunt, the Comtesse de la Briere, had been perfectly right when she warned Maggie against allowing John to see too much of her niece. For John, tiring of his plain wife, fell in love with Lady Sybil. They spent most of their time together, and as a consequence John's speeches in the House of Commons grew more dull. Essentially a humorless man, John had nevertheless built up a reputation for sudden flashes of humor which were called Shandisms, and which won him great popularity. There was a simple reason for his success. Maggie, who typed his speeches, supplied the humor without letting her husband know it. The Comtesse saw through the subterfuge, and thereby named Maggie The Pin, meaning that she was like the pin every successful man is supposed to pick up at the beginning of a successful career.

By that time John was so absorbed in Lady Sybil that he considered her his sole inspiration, and he even went so far as to forget completely his wedding anniversary. Maggie's brothers were shocked at his neglect, but Maggie covered the situation perfectly by reaching out her hand to Lady Sybil for her ruby pendant, displaying it as her anniversary present. She then forced John to admit that he had given the pendant to Lady Sybil. John was defiant, declaring to Maggie and her brothers that Lady Sybil was the great love of his life, and that he would sacrifice everything for her sake. The brothers reminded him that if he deserted Maggie he could count on no career. A short time before, Mr. Charles Venables, a cabinet minister and John's political mentor, had offered him the opportunity to be third speaker at Leeds on the same platform with two ministers, an occasion which would mean John's appointment to a ministerial post. Maggie suggested that John go away for a few weeks with Lady

Sybil and write the speech under her inspiration. When Maggie promised to keep silent concerning the marital difficulties between them, John agreed to the arrangement.

When John read to Mr. Venables the speech he had written, the minister was greatly disappointed and said it lacked the spark of life his earlier speeches had contained. Maggie, realizing what was at stake, informed Venables that her husband had written another speech which she had typed for him; it was a speech Maggie herself had written from notes John had left at home.

In the meantime, Lady Sybil admitted that she had tired of John and had no intention of going on with the affair. Her decision was a jolt to John's vanity, but the final blow came when Venables congratulated him on the speech which, he realized, only Maggie could have written for him. When they were alone, Maggie told him that every man who is high up likes to think he has climbed there by himself, but every wife knows better. It was, she said, every woman's private joke. Whereupon Maggie laughed, and for perhaps the first time in his life John Shand laughed at himself. His marriage and career were both saved.

THE WHITE COMPANY

Type of work: Novel
Author: Arthur Conan Doyle (1859-1930)
Type of plot: Historical romance
Time of plot: Fifteenth century
Locale: England, France, Spain
First published: 1891

Principal characters:
ALLEYNE EDRICSON, an English youth
SAMKIN AYLWARD, a bowman
HORDLE JOHN, a bowman
SIR NIGEL LORING, a nobleman
LADY MAUDE, his daughter

Critique:

The White Company is a story of exciting adventures near the end of the age of chivalry. From its pages we can get accurate pictures of many types of people in feudal times as well as some insight into the interminable and fruitless wars with France. The charm of the story, however, lies in its romantic plot. The English nobles are all valiant men, but none so valiant as Sir Nigel. Hordle John is the strongest Englishman ever seen, as Aylward is the lustiest bowman. Everything turns out well for the heroes, and the villains came to grief. For many years *The White Company* has been a favorite, especially with young people.

The Story:

The Abbot of Beaulieu was a stern judge, and the charges against Hordle John, the novitiate, were severe. John had drunk all the ale from the firkin when he had the first turn; John had held a monk's head down over the beans in protest against poor fare; worst of all, John had carried a woman across a stream. When she smiled at him, he did not keep his eyes on the ground.

At the trial, huge John seemed out of place in a monastery. He cheerfully admitted the charges and did not even have the grace to be ashamed. But when the monks advanced to punish him, he picked up an altar and threw it at them. Then he dived out of the window and was never seen again in Beaulieu.

Much disturbed, the abbot retired to his study to meditate. There he received another visitor, Alleyne Edricson. It was Alleyne's twentieth birthday, and according to his father's will the boy was to leave the abbey for a year. When he was twenty-one, he would choose either a monastic or a secular life. Alleyne had never known any other life than that of the abbey and he was hesitant about entering a world of sin and lust. The abbot solemnly warned Alleyne of the perils of the secular life; but true to his promise he sent the youth forth with his blessing.

Alleyne started on foot for the estate of Minstead, where his older brother was the socman. Alleyne had never seen his brother, but from all reports he was a rude and sinful man. On this, his first trip into the world, Alleyne was continually alarmed at the sin his eyes beheld on every hand. Two robbers who molested an old woman were summarily executed on the spot by the king's bailiffs. Shaken by what he saw, Alleyne thankfully turned into the shelter of the Pied Merlin Inn to spend his first night away from the abbey.

There he found a rough company drinking and quarreling. Hordle John was there, making merry in his cups but kindly disposed toward the timid clerk. When a minstrel took up his harp and began to sing a bawdy song, Alleyne stood up and cried shame on the company for listening. The rough travelers shouted him down and they would have done hurt to Alleyne if John had not risen to defend the clerk.

At that instant Samkin Aylward burst in, bearing letters from France to Sir Nigel of nearby Christchurch. The White Company of English bowmen wanted Sir Nigel to lead them in the war against Spain. Samkin was trying to recruit other bowmen, and Hordle John agreed to go with him. Alleyne refused because he was intent on seeing his brother.

The next morning Alleyne came to the park of the Socman of Minstead. There he saw a strange sight. A great, yellow-bearded man held a struggling girl, and appeared determined to drag her into the house. Alleyne ran up to the rescue, armed with his iron-tipped staff. Only after Alleyne had threatened to run his staff through the yellow-beard was he informed that his adversary was his brother. The socman, furious at being balked by clerkly Alleyne, ran to the stables and whistled for his hunting dogs. Alleyne and the girl escaped into the woods.

The girl's page soon found them, and she rode away with a brilliant, mocking smile of thanks. Alleyne resolved to join John and Aylward and take service with Sir Nigel. He hurried to catch up with them before they arrived at Christchurch.

Alleyne's first view of Sir Nigel was disappointing. The lord was a slight, squinting, soft-spoken man, apparently the least warlike of nobles. But Alleyne changed his mind. A giant bear broke his chain and charged down the road, where he scattered all in front of him. Sir Nigel, however, merely looked in his near-sighted way to see the cause of the disturbance. Then, unarmed as he was, he walked up to the maddened bear and flicked the animal across the snout with his silk handkerchief. Discomfited, the bear retired in confusion and was soon rechained by the bearward. Then Alleyne knew he would serve a true knight.

At the castle Sir Nigel was making all in readiness for his expedition to France. Alleyne worked diligently in the courtyard as he learned the trade of man-at-arms. His efforts soon made him a favorite and his good education set him above his fellows. Sir Nigel asked him to take charge of his daughter's reading that winter, and Alleyne went into the lord's quarters for the first time. There he found that his pupil was the girl he had rescued from his brother. Lady Maude was a high-spirited girl, but charming and gracious. Alleyne felt her charm keenly, but he was only a poor clerk and so he kept silent as his fondness for her grew.

Just before the expedition departed, Sir Nigel made Alleyne his squire. After receiving the honor, Alleyne sought out Lady Maude and stammered some words of love. Lady Maude rebuked him for his presumption, but she did give him her green veil to wear to the wars. As Squire Alleyne rode away behind his lord, he thought more of Lady Maude than of the fighting to come.

At Bordeaux Sir Nigel and his party were received with all honors by Edward, their prince. Edward needed all his knights, for the English were embarking upon a long, difficult campaign to put Don Pedro upon the throne of Spain. Then, too, the White Company was becoming a great nuisance, as it was pillaging the country roundabout and earning few friends for England.

One night, on their way to join the White Company, Sir Nigel and his party stayed with the notorious Seneschal of Villefranche. This knight, a rapacious and cruel lord, had reduced all the peasants on his lands to the status of animals. That night, while the party slept, the peasants broke into the castle, murdered all the men-at-arms, and foully desecrated the bodies of the seneschal and his lady. Although Sir Nigel and his Englishmen were innocent of the wrongs committed by the French lord, the peasants made no distinction between aristocrats. They set fire to the castle when they were afraid to face the sword of Sir Nigel and the mace of Hordle John, and Sir Nigel's bowmen retired to the keep.

The frenzied serfs fired the keep as well. The English party was rescued only by the timely arrival of the White Company, which had been attracted by the great fires. The peasants slunk away in the darkness.

The White Company, under Sir Nigel, marched with Edward's army through the Pyrenees. Selected for scouting duty, the White Company harried the Spanish forces successfully. One day the whole company was trapped on a small mesa by the main Spanish body. Despite great slaughter by the English arrows and the might of Sir Nigel, the Englishmen were in great danger of being wiped out.

Alleyne was chosen as a messenger to summon reinforcements. He carried out his mission valiantly despite his wounds, but the rescuers found only Hordle John and a handful of survivors still unconquered. Even Sir Nigel and Aylward had been captured.

Alleyne returned to England with a heavy heart. His brother in the meantime had been killed while trying to assault Sir Nigel's castle, and now Alleyne, knighted by Prince Edward, was the Socman of Minstead. With his new position he could aspire to the hand of Lady Maude.

The happiness of all returned when Sir Nigel and Aylward finally came back from their captivity among the Moors. Aylward married the mistress of the Pied Merlin and Hordle John became Alleyne's squire. Alleyne lived a long and happy life with Lady Maude. He went back to France to fight several times, and on each occasion reaped great honors there. Toward the end of his life he spent much time at Windsor as adviser to Edward.

WICKFORD POINT

Type of work: Novel
Author: John P. Marquand (1893-)
Type of plot: Social satire
Time of plot: Twentieth century
Locale: New York and Wickford Point
First published: 1939

Principal characters:

JIM CALDER, a writer
MRS. CLOTHILDE WRIGHT, his cousin, formerly Clothilde Brill
BELLA BRILL, her daughter
MARY BRILL, another daughter
PATRICIA LEIGHTON, Jim's friend
JOE STOWE, Bella's former husband

Critique:

Next to *The Late George Apley,* this novel is perhaps Marquand's best. His technique here is marked by the use of flashbacks to make the present meaningful and to explain the motives of his characters. His touch is deft, his theme well-handled, his story interesting, his irony amusing. The impact of the outside world upon the little, complacent society of Wickford Point is admirably demonstrated.

The Story:

Jim Calder made his living by writing fiction for popular magazines. For this reason the contradiction between the actual life of his relatives at Wickford Point and the fiction he was required to write was extremely obvious. His relatives, the Brills, were a group of New Englanders who had little money, but who were disinclined to make a living. Being himself close to the Brills, he had attempted to escape from them and the enervating atmosphere of Wickford Point. He was only a second cousin to the Brill children, but his continual association with them in his early life produced bonds that were exceedingly hard to break. No matter how many times he left Wickford Point, he always returned. No matter how many times he returned, he always planned to get away as soon as possible.

Jim attended Harvard and there met Joe Stowe. Harry Brill also attended Harvard, where he made sure that he knew the right people. All through his life Harry was concerned with meeting the right people, but he never did make the right connections. Jim and Joe were fortunate in the fact that they became fast friends and were never elected to the right campus clubs. This polite ostracism served only to strengthen their friendship and to bring with it the assurance that they at least would be more successful than many of their snobbish classmates in their dealings with people.

When World War I arrived and America became involved, Joe and Jim were among the first to go into service, and they were shipped overseas as first lieutenants before they had completed their officers' training. After the war they went to China and served with the forces of General Feng. Some years later Jim returned to America to find a new way of life; Joe went to Italy. Both decided upon writing as a career.

When Jim returned to Wickford Point, he found the Brills just the same and as inconsequential as when he had left. Cousin Clothilde was still unable to manage finances satisfactorily. When she received her check on the first of the month, her children all raced to get their share of the cash, the first one arriving getting the greater share. Cousin Clothilde was always broke within a few hours after receiving her money.

Bella had grown into quite a beautiful young woman during Jim's absence from America, and at the moment of his return she was involved in a rather serious affair with a nice young man named Avery Gifford. Jim, who had always been Bella's confidant, continued in this role when Bella sought advice from him. Since she was not sure that she loved Avery, it was decided that she should wait until her return from Europe to

---

decide whether she would marry him. She went to Italy with her stepfather, Archie Wright, and while there she met Joe Stowe and eloped with him.

Their marriage was doomed to failure from the start, and after some years it ended in divorce. Bella never really knew what she wanted. She seemed to want everything but could never be satisfied with anything she had. She went from one affair to another because she was extremely attractive to men, but her affairs always remained platonic. Sometimes Jim felt that he was Bella's only friend, for none of her other friendships ever lasted and she made new friends as fast as she lost old ones. She was always confident that whenever she got into difficulties she could fly to Jim and he would straighten out the situation for her.

Jim met Patricia Leighton, a woman of great executive ability who had a penthouse in New York City and an income of several thousand dollars a year. Jim's affair with her was a lasting one, each party contributing equally to the relationship. At first Jim went to Pat to escape the inanities of his relatives at Wickford Point. Pat was a very understanding woman who realized clearly what Jim's problem really was, and she tried in an unobtrusive manner to help him make the final break with his family background.

In spite of their divorce, Bella and Joe thought often of each other, even though they both realized that to remarry would lead only to another divorce. Joe, since his divorce, had become a famous novelist, well off financially. Bella expressed her selfishness to Jim in her regretful admission that when she divorced Joe she had no idea that he would ever be so successful.

Bella went from one contemplated marriage to another, led her admirers on, and finally put herself into a rather delicate situation with Avery Gifford and Howard Berg. When she called upon Jim to rescue her once more, Jim decided that this time Bella would have to extricate herself, his refusal being motivated by his memory of recent conversations with Pat. Into the midst of these misunderstandings and resolves came Joe as a result of a telegram sent to him by Bella. At first Bella and Joe seemed likely to try marriage once more. But as a result of Jim's attitude toward her, Bella did the first generous deed in her life; she told Joe that she would not marry him again.

Jim took Bella back to changeless Wickford Point to find the place, as usual, thronged with visitors. Pat Leighton, as had previously been arranged, came down to Wickford Point to visit. Allen Southby, a friend of Jim's and a professor of English at Harvard, came to stay with the Brills while gathering material for his novel about Wickford Point. Mary Brill looked upon Allen as her own particular conquest until Bella's arrival. All her life Bella had been stealing Mary's eligible young men.

With the arrival of Pat, she and Jim faced once more the problem of getting Jim to break away from Wickford Point and the Brills. Jim finally made the decision to leave, after telling Pat that a part of him would always remain at Wickford Point and that he would always have to return occasionally for short visits. Under the circumstances Pat agreed. Seeing Southby's apparent willingness to marry Bella, Jim felt free of Wickford Point and the clinging past. He began to pack his bag to return with Pat to New York.

THE WILD DUCK

Type of work: Drama
Author: Henrik Ibsen (1828-1906)
Type of plot: Social criticism
Time of plot: Nineteenth century
Locale: Norway
First presented: 1884

Principal characters:
WERLE, a wealthy merchant
GREGERS WERLE, his son
OLD EKDAL, Werle's former partner
HJALMAR EKDAL, his son
GINA EKDAL, Hjalmar's wife
HEDVIG, their daughter
RELLING, a doctor

Critique:

In this play Ibsen has made us feel as well as think his message, for in the symbolism of the wild duck he has paralleled perfectly the meaning of his story. The wild duck wounded by old Werle and retrieved by his dog is an image of the Ekdal family, hurt by the world, diving to the depths of self-deception and finally rescued only to be hurt the more. In the character of Gregers Werle Ibsen seems to be turning the knife upon his own youthful idealism.

The Story:

Gregers Werle, son of a wealthy merchant and of a sensitive and high-minded mother, had early in life developed a loathing for the unscrupulous means his father had used to amass his fortune. After his mother's death, young Werle left his father's house for a time, but eventually returned.

His father, hoping to persuade his son to accept a partnership in his business, gave a large dinner party to which Gregers took the liberty of inviting a thirteenth guest, his old school friend, Hjalmar Ekdal. This act displeased his father very much; first, because Hjalmar did not belong in the social set of the Werles; second, because he was the son of a former business partner old Werle had wronged. The older Ekdal now held a menial position in Werle's employ, to which he had been reduced after a term in prison had broken his mind and spirit.

Gregers was aware that his father's machinations had sent Ekdal to prison after a scandal in which both had been involved, and he hated his father for this injury to the father of his friend. He discovered also that the older Werle had arranged a marriage between Hjalmar Ekdal and Gina Hansen, a former maid in the Werle household and, Gregers suspected, his father's mistress. Therefore Gregers was not hospitable to Werle's offer of a partnership nor to his forthcoming marriage to Mrs. Sorby, his housekeeper. Gregers announced that his future mission in life was to open Hjalmar Ekdal's eyes to the lie he had been living for the past fifteen years.

Outwardly, the Ekdal home was a shabby one. Hjalmar Ekdal was a photographer, a business in which Werle had set him up after his marriage to Gina. But Gina ran the business while her husband worked on an invention intended to enable his aged father to recoup some of his fortune. Old Ekdal himself, now practically out of his mind, spent most of his time in a garret in which he kept a curious assortment of animals ranging all the way from chickens to rabbits. Ekdal was under the illusion

THE WILD DUCK by Henrik Ibsen. Published by Charles Scribner's Sons.

that this garret was a forest like the one in which he had hunted as a young man. There he would shoot an occasional rabbit, and on holidays and special occasions he would appear before the family dressed in his old military uniform.

Although it was based almost entirely on self-deception and illusion, the Ekdal home was actually a happy one. Gina took good care of her husband and his aged father, and Hedvig, the fourteen-year-old daughter, loved Hjalmar dearly. To Hjalmar, Hedvig was his whole life, and he and Gina kept from her the fact that she was rapidly losing her eyesight. Gregers Werle, intent on his new mission, was shocked at the depths to which his old friend had sunk. His feelings found expression when old Ekdal showed him Hedvig's prize possession, a wild duck that the older Werle had once shot. The wounded duck had dived to the bottom of the water, but Werle's dog had retrieved it and brought it to the surface again. Gregers saw himself as the clever dog destined to bring the Ekdal family, like the wild duck, out of the muck of their straitened circumstances.

To accomplish his end, he rented a room from the Ekdals, a room Gina was unwilling to let him have. Gina was not the only one to resent his presence in the house. Dr. Relling, another roomer, knew Gregers Werle, and was aware of his reputation for meddling in the affairs of others. He agreed that Gregers was the victim of a morbid conscience, probably derived from his hysterical mother. Hjalmar, in his innocence, however, saw nothing amiss in his friend's behavior and allowed him to stay.

Gregers set about the task of rehabilitating his friend in a systematic way. His first discovery was that the little family was indirectly supported by the older Werle, and not by the photographic studio, as Hjalmar supposed. Also, and more important, Hedvig's approaching blindness and his own father's weak eyesight too nearly coincided to make it reasonable that Hjalmar was the child's natural father. Gregers resolved to open Hjalmar's eyes to his true position in his own house, and during a long walk he laid bare all the facts he had learned except his suspicion of Hedvig's illegitimacy, which was as yet unproved.

Having no real integrity or resources within himself, Hjalmar naturally fell back on all the clichés in the stories he had read as to how a wronged husband should behave. He demanded from Gina an accounting of all the money paid into the household by Werle, and asserted that every cent should be paid back out of the proceeds from his hypothetical invention. His outburst did nothing but disturb Gina and frighten Hedvig.

Hjalmar's pride might have been placated and the whole matter straightened out had not a letter arrived from old Werle, who was giving Hedvig a small annuity. Hjalmar announced that Hedvig was no child of his and that he wanted nothing more to do with her. Hedvig was heartbroken at her father's behavior, and Gregers Werle, beginning to realize the unfortunate condition his meddling had caused, persuaded the girl that her one hope of winning back her father's love was to sacrifice the thing she loved most for his sake. He urged her to have her grandfather kill the wild duck.

In the meantime Gina had succeeded in convincing Hjalmar that he was quite helpless without her. As they were discussing their plans for the future, they heard a shot. At first they thought old Ekdal was firing at his rabbits. Hedvig, in her despair, had put a bullet through her breast.

Gregers Werle had righted no wrongs with his meddling. He had merely made his friend's tragedy complete.

WILLIAM TELL

Type of work: Drama
Author: Johann Christoph Friedrick von Schiller (1759-1805)
Type of plot: Historical romance
Time of plot: Fifteenth century
Locale: Switzerland
First presented: 1804

Principal characters:
William Tell, a forester
Walter Tell, his son
Walter Fürst, William Tell's father-in-law
Gessler, Governor of the Swiss Forest Cantons
Werner, a nobleman
Ulrich, his nephew
Bertha of Bruneck, a rich heiress

Critique:

William Tell is based on a popular legend which in time became localized in Switzerland. In it Schiller demonstrated his admiration for natural man in a setting of primitive beauty. The love of liberty dramatized by the plot shows how Schiller agreed with and differed from the principles of the French Revolution. Schiller was a strong proponent of the dignity and worth of the common man, but he would have each man acknowledge and serve his rightful master.

The Story:

A storm was rising on Lake Lucerne and the ferryman was making his boat fast to the shore as Baumgarten rushed up, pursued by the soldiers of the tyrant, Gessler. He implored the ferryman to take him across the lake to safety. First, however, the crowd made him tell the reason for the pursuit.

The Wolfshot, a nobleman who had been appointed seneschal of the castle, had come into Baumgarten's house and had ordered the wife to prepare him a bath. When he had started to take liberties with the woman, she had escaped and had run to her husband in the forest. Baumgarten had hurried back and with his ax had split the Wolfshot's skull. Now he had to leave the country.

Because the sympathies of the common people were with Baumgarten, they begged the ferryman to take him across. But the storm was almost upon them, and the ferryman was afraid. Then William Tell came up, Tell the hunter, the only man in the crowd with courage to steer the boat in a tempest. As soon as he heard Baumgarten's story, Tell unhesitatingly embarked to take the fugitive to the other shore. As they cast off, the soldiers thundered up. When they saw their prey escaping, they took their revenge on the peasants by killing their sheep and burning their cottages.

The free Switzers were greatly troubled because the Emperor of Austria had sent Gessler to rule as viceroy over the Forest Cantons. Gessler, a younger son of no fortune, was envious of the prosperity of the thrifty Switzers and enraged by their calm and independent bearing, for the inhabitants held their lands directly in fief to the emperor and the rights and duties of the viceroy were carefully limited. To break the proud spirit of the Switzers, Gessler mounted a cap on a pole in a public place and required that each man bow to the cap.

Henry of Halden was an upright man. To his farm came the emissaries of Gessler, attempting to take from him his best team of oxen. When Arnold, his son, sprang on the men and struck them with his staff, they released the oxen and left. Arnold thought it best to go into hiding. While he was away, the soldiers came and tortured old Henry and put out his eyes. Arnold joined the malcontents against Gessler.

Fürst became the leader of the Switzers. It was agreed that ten men from the three Cantons would meet and plan to overthrow the viceroy.

At the mansion of Werner, the common people and their lord were gathered for the morning cup of friendship. Old Werner gladly drank with his men, but his nephew Ulrich refused. He had been attracted to the Austrian court by the fine dress and high positions of the rulers, and he felt no bond with free Switzerland. Werner upbraided him for being a turncoat and finally accused Ulrich of turning to Austria because of love for the rich Bertha.

In great secrecy the representatives of the people met at night under the leadership of Fürst. Feeling their wrongs too great to bear, they revived their ancient Diet. Some of the more fiery members were in favor of an immediate uprising, but the cooler heads followed Fürst and voted to wait until Christmas, when by tradition all the peasants would be present in the castle.

Ulrich at last approached Bertha and declared his love for her. A true Switzer at heart, she spurned him for his loyalty to Austria.

Tell with his sons came near the hated cap. When Tell, more by accident than by design, paid no attention to the symbol of authority, he was arrested by two guards who tried to bind him and lead him to prison. Although Fürst came and offered bail for his son-in-law, law-abiding Tell submitted to his captors and was being led away when Gessler himself rode by.

Gessler ordered an apple placed on Walter Tell's head. Then he commanded William Tell to shoot the apple from his son's head. Tell protested in vain. Ulrich courageously defied Gessler and spoke hot words of blame to the tyrant, but Gessler was unmoved. In the confusion Tell took out two arrows, fitted one to his crossbow, and neatly pierced the apple.

While the crowd rejoiced, Gessler asked Tell why he had taken two arrows, but Tell refused to answer until Gessler promised not to execute him no matter what the reply might be. Then Tell boldly declared that if he had missed the apple and hurt his son, he would have killed Gessler with the second arrow. Infuriated, Gessler ordered Tell led away to life imprisonment.

Chained, Tell was put on the boat which was to take him to Gessler's castle, and Gessler himself went along to gloat over his victim. Once again a terrible storm arose. To save his own life, Gessler had Tell unbound and made him helmsman. Watching his chance, Tell steered the boat close to shore and sprang to safety on a rocky ledge.

He came with his crossbow to a pass through which Gessler must travel if he escaped the fury of the storm. Under Tell's hiding place a poor woman and her children waited for Gessler. Her husband was in prison for a minor offense, and she intended to appeal to Gessler for clemency.

At last Gessler approached with his train. The woman blocked his way and appealed for mercy on behalf of her husband. Waiting long enough to hear her plea denied, Tell pierced the breast of the tyrant with a bolt from his crossbow. Dropping down on the road, Tell announced to the gathered people that he had killed Gessler; then he disappeared into the forest.

Gessler lay in the road, with no friendly hand to pull the arrow from the bleeding heart. So died Switzerland's oppressor.

The people had hoped that Werner would lead them in their revolt, but he was old and on his deathbed. He hoped to remain alive until Ulrich would come to receive from him the leadership, but Ulrich did not arrive until after his uncle's death. The assembled peasants, however, acknowledged Ulrich as their leader, and they found in him a hardy knight, all the more anxious for war because the Austrians had abducted Bertha. At last the three Cantons rose up against harsh Austrian rule.

At the height of the revolt, the news came that the emperor himself had been assassinated. Duke John of Austria, his nephew, had struck down the emperor after being robbed of his estates. The Switzers despised the duke for the crime because assassination for robbery seemed to them unjust. When Duke John sought refuge with Tell, the forester was indignant. Tell was a soldier for freedom, not a murderer. But his natural humanity kept him from exposing John, and the duke left unharmed to seek a safer sanctuary in Italy.

Tell put away his crossbow for good when the announcement came that the Count of Luxembourg had been elected emperor. The Cantons settled down to peaceful days once more. Bertha gave her hand freely to Ulrich, as one proud Switzer to another.

WINDSOR CASTLE

Type of work: Novel
Author: William Harrison Ainsworth (1805-1882)
Type of plot: Historical romance
Time of plot: Sixteenth century
Locale: England
First published: 1843

Principal characters:

HENRY THE EIGHTH, King of England
CATHERINE OF ARAGON, Queen of England
ANNE BOLEYN, Catherine's successor
CARDINAL WOLSEY, Lord High Chancellor
THE EARL OF SURREY, a member of the court
THE DUKE OF RICHMOND, Henry's natural son
LADY ELIZABETH FITZGERALD, the fair Geraldine
MABEL LYNDWOOD, granddaughter of a royal forester
MORGAN FENWOLF, a gamekeeper
HERNE THE HUNTER, a spectral demon

Critique:

This interesting novel of the reign of King Henry the Eighth combines two traditions of English fiction—the historical romance and the Gothic romance of mystery and terror. An element of the weird is imparted to the novel by the mysterious figure of Herne the Hunter, an apparition out of the imagination of medieval England and still a creature of legend in the history of Windsor Castle. In his novel Ainsworth gave Herne the function of a somewhat disorganized conscience. Linked to forces of evil as well as to those of good, he had a never clearly defined symbolic value, a representation of the inconsistency of man's nature, as illustrated in the person and acts of Henry Tudor.

The Story:

In April, 1529, the young Earl of Surrey was at Windsor Castle preparing for the arrival of King Henry the Eighth. One night, having dismissed his attendants with orders to meet him at the Garter Inn in the nearby village, he began a walk through the home park. On the way he passed near an ancient tree known as Herne's Oak, where a demon hunter was reported to lie in wait for wayfarers through the forest at night. Suddenly a blue light surrounded the old tree. Beneath its branches stood the figure of a man wearing upon his head the skull and antlers of a stag. From the left arm of the specter hung a heavy rusted chain; on its right wrist perched an owl with red, staring eyes.

When Surrey crossed himself in fear, the figure vanished. Hurrying from the haunted spot, he encountered another traveler through the park. The man was Morgan Fenwolf, a gamekeeper who led the earl to the inn where the young nobleman was to rejoin his companions.

Surrey arrived at the Garter in time to witness a quarrel between a butcher and an archer calling himself the Duke of Shoreditch. Speaking angry words that came close to treason, the butcher declared himself opposed to royal Henry's desire to put aside Catherine of Aragon. When words led to blows, Surrey and Fenwolf stepped in to halt the fight. The self-dubbed Duke of Shoreditch insisted that the butcher be imprisoned in the castle. As he was led away, the butcher charged that Fenwolf was a wizard. Surrey, much amused, rode off to Hampton Court to meet the royal procession.

Henry and his court arrived at Windsor Castle amid the shouts of the crowd and volleys of cannon from the walls. In his train Lady Anne Boleyn, dressed in ermine and cloth of gold, rode in a litter attended by Sir Thomas Wyat, the poet; the youthful Duke of Richmond, natural son of the king, and the Earl of Surrey. Also in the procession was Cardinal Wolsey, the Lord High Chancellor.

Informed on his arrival of the arrest of the treasonous butcher, Henry ordered his immediate execution. The body of the butcher was swinging from the battlements as Henry escorted Anne Boleyn into the castle.

After Surrey had told Richmond of his ghostly encounter in the park, the two young men agreed to go that night to Herne's Oak. There they watched a ghostly chase—the demon hunter pursuing a deer, a great owl flying before him and black hounds running silently beside his horse.

On their return to the castle, their haggard looks led to many questions from the ladies attending Anne Boleyn, among them Lady Elizabeth Fitzgerald, the fair Geraldine, as she was called, an Irish beauty with whom both Surrey and Richmond were in love. Later that night, suspecting that they may have been the victims of a hoax arranged by Morgan Fenwolf, Surrey and the duke returned to the forest in search of the gamekeeper. There they found the body of the hanged butcher. Pinned to his clothing was an inscription which indicated that a political party opposed to the king now considered the butcher a martyr to their cause.

Bad blood was brewing between Surrey and the duke over the fair Geraldine. Finding the girl and the young earl meeting in a secret tryst, the duke challenged Surrey to a duel. Royal guards stopped the fight and Surrey was imprisoned for drawing steel against the king's son.

Orders were given for a royal hunt. During the chase Anne Boleyn was endangered by the charge of a maddened stag, but her life was saved by a well-aimed arrow from Morgan Fenwolf's bow. To avoid the charging stag, Anne threw herself into the arms of Sir Thomas Wyat, who was riding by her side. Henry, seeing her action, was furious.

Henry's jealousy immediately gave cheer to the supporters of Catherine of Aragon, who hoped that Henry would give up his plan to make Anne the next Queen of England. Shortly after the return of the party to Windsor, a spy informed Henry that Wyat was in Anne's apartment. Henry angrily went to see for himself, but before his arrival Surrey, just liberated from his cell to hear the king's judgment on his case, hurried to warn Wyat and Anne. Wyat escaped through a secret passage. Surrey explained that he had come to ask Anne's aid in obtaining a royal pardon for his rashness in quarreling with the Duke of Richmond. Through Anne's favor, his sentence was shortened to confinement for two months.

Herne the Hunter continued to haunt the home park. One night the Duke of

Richmond went alone to the forest and there saw the demon accompanied by a band of spectral huntsmen, one of whom he recognized as the butcher. The horsemen rode rapidly through the forest and then plunged into a lake and disappeared. Sir Thomas Wyat, angry and wretched at having lost Anne to Henry, met the ghostly hunter and promised to give his soul to the powers of evil if he could only win back Anne. The demon assured him that he should have his wish. Soon afterward, however, Henry decided to send Wyat on a mission to France.

Cardinal Wolsey, thwarted in his attempt to make Wyat the agent of Anne's overthrow, planned to use Mabel Lyndwood, granddaughter of a royal forester, to attract Henry.

One night Herne the Hunter appeared to Surrey in his prison tower and showed the fair Geraldine to the young man in a vision. After the demon had disappeared Surrey was unable to find a holy relic that the girl had given him.

But Wyat had not gone to France. Kidnaped by the demon, he was imprisoned in a cave and forced to drink a strange brew which affected his reason and made him swear to become one of Herne's midnight huntsmen. Fenwolf, who was a member of the band, promised to betray the king into Wyat's hands. While riding through the home park, Henry and the Duke of Suffolk were attacked by Herne's followers. Henry, coming face to face with Wyat, was about to kill his rival, but Mabel Lyndwood suddenly appeared and asked the king to spare Wyat because he had saved Henry's life when the attack began. Henry sternly ordered Wyat, once more in possession of his senses, to continue on his way to France. Fenwolf, captured by royal guards who had ridden out in search of the king, was imprisoned in the castle. Later he escaped under mysterious circumstances. Henry, after failing to track down Herne, ordered the haunted oak felled and burned.

In disguise, Catherine of Aragon appeared at Windsor Castle and sought an audience with Henry in order to convince him of her love and to warn him against Anne's fickle and unfaithful nature. When Anne interrupted them, Catherine foretold Anne's bloody doom.

Shortly afterward Herne appeared before the king on the castle terrace and prophesied Henry's fearful end. A terrible storm broke at that moment and the demon disappeared.

Meanwhile Mabel Lyndwood had been brought to the castle, where her grandfather was being held for questioning following the attack on Henry. Finding her in the kitchen, Henry gave orders that she was to be cared for until he sent for her.

Questioned by the king, old Lyndwood refused to talk. Henry then ordered the guards to bring Mabel to her grandfather's cell. There Henry threatened them with death if the old forester refused to reveal his knowledge of the demon hunter. That night a strange messenger, after presenting the king's signet ring to the guards, led Mabel and her grandfather from the castle and told them to go to a secret cave. Meanwhile the castle was in an uproar. When the guards, led by Henry himself, cornered the demon in one of the upper chambers of the castle, the specter disappeared after pointing out to Henry a coffin containing the body of the hanged butcher.

Determined at last to put Catherine aside, and knowing that Wolsey would block his attempts so long as the cardinal remained in power, Henry removed Wolsey from office and disgraced him publicly. Anne Boleyn would be the next Queen of England.

Surrey, released from imprisonment, learned that the fair Geraldine had gone back to Ireland. Surrey and Richmond, riding near the castle, met Wyat, who had returned secretly from France to discover the whereabouts of Mabel Lyndwood and to rid the forest of the demon hunter.

His disclosure of his plans was overheard by the hunter and Fenwolf, who were hiding in the loft of a nearby cottage. A short time later Herne and Fenwolf quarreled oveı Mabel's favors. When Fenwolf tried to stab the demon, his dagger would not pierce the demon's body. Herne, who claimed that he was more than a hundred years old, asked Mabel to love him and to pray for his liberation from the spell which caused him to walk the earth and do evil. Wyat, who had been captured by the hunter, was offered his freedom if Mabel would accept the demon's love. Herne also promised her jewels and revealed that she was the unacknowledged daughter of the disgraced Cardinal Wolsey.

The hunter told her finally that whether she loved him or not he intended to marry her the next night near an ancient Druid ruin. Fenwolf, overhearing his declaration, promised to release Mabel if she would wed him. The girl refused; she said that Fenwolf was almost as evil as the demon himself.

The next day Mabel managed to free Wyat from the cave where he was confined and the two made their escape. Old Lyndwood and Fenwolf planned to destroy the hunter by setting off a blast of powder in the cave. In their flight Wyat and Mabel were forced to swim their horse across a lake. Mabel fainted. On the opposite shore Wyat encountered Surrey, Richmond, and a party searching for the demon. Mabel was placed upon a litter of branches. At that moment Herne the Hunter rode up, seized the girl, and raced with her toward the cave, the others in pursuit until their way was blocked by a forest fire that followed the roar of an explosion from the direction of the cave. Fenwolf was burned in the blaze. The next morning Wyat, Surrey, and Richmond found old Lyndwood kneeling over his granddaughter, whose dead body he had dragged from the lake. The searchers found no trace of the demon hunter.

Seven years passed. Richmond had married Lady Mary Howard, the sister of Surrey. Surrey himself had been forced to wed Lady Frances Vere, for the king had refused permission to marry the fair Geraldine. Wolsey and Catherine were dead. Anne had become queen, but she was beginning to realize that Henry was growing cool toward her and their little daughter, Elizabeth. Although she was not faithful to the king, she would not allow another to share Henry's affection. Jealous of his attentions to Jane Seymour, she reproached and threatened her rival. Jane replied by accusing Anne of misconduct with Sir Henry Norris.

While the court was at Windsor Castle, Herne the Hunter appeared once more. Disguised as a monk, he led Anne and Norris to an apartment where they found the king and Jane Seymour together. Anne knew then what her end was to be; but when Norris asked her to flee with him she refused.

In May some jousts were held at the castle. Norris, who had formed a compact with the demon hunter, defeated the king in the tourney and as his reward Anne gave him a handkerchief which Henry had presented to her. Furious, Henry charged her with incontinence and sent Norris to the tower. Soon afterward Anne was also imprisoned. There Herne visited her and offered to carry her and her lover to a place of safety. Rather than sacrifice her soul, Anne refused. At her trial she was pronounced guilty and sentenced to die.

Henry was in retirement at Windsor Castle on the day of her execution. As her head rolled from the block, Herne the Hunter appeared before Henry, bowed mockingly, and told the king that he was free to wed once more.

WINESBURG, OHIO

Type of work: Short stories
Author: Sherwood Anderson (1876-1941)
Type of plot: Psychological realism
Time of plot: Late nineteenth century
Locale: Winesburg, Ohio
First published: 1919

Principal characters:
GEORGE WILLARD, a young reporter
ELIZABETH WILLARD, his mother
DR. REEFY, Elizabeth's confidant
HELEN WHITE, George's friend
KATE SWIFT, George's former teacher
REV. CURTIS HARTMAN, Kate's unknown admirer
WING BIDDLEBAUM, a berry picker

Critique:

Winesburg, Ohio has the stature of a modern classic. It is at once beautiful and tragic, realistic and poetic. Without being a novel in the usual sense of the word, the connected stories have the full range and emotional impact of a novel. In simple, though highly skillful and powerful language, Sherwood Anderson has told the story of a small town and the lonely, frustrated people who live there. Though regional in its setting and characters, the book is also intensely American. No one since Anderson has succeeded in interpreting the inner compulsions and loneliness of the national psyche with the same degree of accuracy and emotional impact.

The Story:

Young George Willard was the only child of Elizabeth and Tom Willard. His father, a dull, conventional, insensitive man, owned the local hotel. His mother had once been a popular young belle. She had never loved Tom Willard, but the young married women of the town seemed to her so happy, so satisfied, that she had married him in the hope that marriage would somehow change her own life for the better. Before long she realized that she was caught in the dull life of Winesburg, her dreams turned to drab realities by her life with Tom Willard.

The only person who ever understood her was Dr. Reefy. Only in his small, untidy office did she feel free; only there did she achieve some measure of self-expression. Their relationship, doomed from the start, was nevertheless beautiful, a meeting of two lonely and sensitive people. For Dr. Reefy, too, had his sorrows. Once, years ago, a young girl, pregnant and unmarried, had come to his office, and shortly afterward he had married her. The following spring she had died, and from then on Dr. Reefy went around making little paper pills and stuffing his pockets with them. On the pieces of paper he had scribbled his thoughts about the beauty and strangeness of life.

Through her son George, Elizabeth Willard hoped to express herself, for she saw in him the fulfillment of her own hopes and desires. More than anything, she feared that George would settle down in Winesburg. When she learned that he wanted to be a writer, she was glad. Unknown to her husband, she had put away money enough to give her son a start. But before she could realize her ambition, Elizabeth Willard died. Lying on her bed, she did not seem dead to either George or Dr. Reefy. To both she was extremely beautiful. To George, she did not seem like his mother at all. To Dr. Reefy, she was the woman he had loved, now the symbol of another lost illusion.

Many people of the town sought out George Willard; they told him of their lives, of their compulsions, of their failures. Old Wing Biddlebaum, the berry picker, years before had been a schoolteacher. He had loved the boys in his charge, and he had been, in fact, one of those few teachers who understand young people. But one of his pupils, having conceived a strong affection for his teacher, had accused him of homosexuality. Wing Biddlebaum, though innocent, was driven out of town. In Winesburg, he became the best berry picker in the region. But always the same hands that earned his livelihood were a source of wonder and fear to him. When George Willard encountered him in the berry field, Wing's hands went forward as if to caress the youth. But a wave of horror swept over him, and he hurriedly thrust them into his pockets. To George, also, Wing's hands seemed odd, mysterious.

Kate Swift, once George's teacher, saw in him a future writer. She tried to tell him what writing was, what it meant. George did not understand exactly, but he understood that Kate was speaking, not as his teacher, but as a woman. One night, in her house, she embraced him, for George was now a young man with whom she had fallen in love. On another night, when all of Winesburg seemed asleep, she went to his room. But just as she was on the point of yielding to him, she struck him and ran away, leaving George lonely and frustrated.

Kate lived across the street from the Presbyterian church. The pastor, Reverend Curtis Hartman, accidentally had learned that he could see into Kate's room from his study in the bell tower of the church. Night after night he looked through the window at Kate in her bed. He wanted at first to prove his faith, but his flesh was weak. One night, the same night Kate had fled from George Willard, he saw her come into her room. He watched her. Naked, she threw herself on the bed and furiously pounded the pillows. Then she arose, knelt, and began to pray. With a cry, the minister got up from his chair, swept the Bible to the floor, smashed the glass in the window, and dashed out into the darkness. Running to the newspaper office, he burst in upon George. Wild-eyed, his fist dripping blood, he told the astonished young man that God had appeared to him in the person of a naked woman, that Kate Swift was the instrument of the Almighty, and that he was saved.

Besides Kate Swift, there were other women in George's life. There was Helen White, the banker's daughter. One night George and Helen went out together. At first they laughed and kissed, but then a strange new maturity overcame them and kept them apart. Louise Trunnion, a farm girl, wrote to George, saying that she was his if he wanted her. After dark he went out to the farm and they went for a walk. There, in a berry field, George Willard enjoyed the love that Helen White had refused him.

Like Louise Trunnion, Louise Bentley also wanted love. Before going to live in Winesburg, Louise had lived on a farm, forgotten and unloved by a greedy, fanatical father who had desired a boy instead of a daughter. In Winesburg she lived with the Hardy family while she went to school. She was a good student, praised by her teachers, but she was resented by the two Hardy girls, who believed that Louise was always showing off. More than ever, she wanted someone to love. One day she sent young John Hardy a note, and a few weeks later she gave herself to him. When it became clear that she was pregnant, Louise and John were married.

John reproached her for cruelty toward her son David. She would not nurse her child and for long periods of time she would ignore him. Since she had never really loved her husband, nor he her, the marriage was not a happy one. At last she and John separated, and shortly afterward her father took young David to live with him on the farm.

Old Jesse Bentley was convinced that God had manifested himself in his grandchild, that the young David, like the Biblical hero, would be a saviour, the conqueror of the Philistines who owned the land Jesse Bentley wanted for himself. One day the old man took the boy into the fields with him. Young David had brought along a little lamb, and the grandfather prepared to offer the animal as a sacrifice to the Almighty. The youngster, terrified, struck his grandfather and ran away, never to return to Winesburg.

The time came when George Willard had to choose between staying in Winesburg and starting out on his career as a writer. Shortly after his mother's death, George got up early one morning and walked to the railroad station. There, with the postmistress' expression of good luck in his ears, he boarded the train and left Winesburg behind him.

WINTERSET

Type of work: Drama
Author: Maxwell Anderson (1888-)
Type of plot: Romantic tragedy
Time of plot: Twentieth century
Locale: New York
First presented: 1935

Principal characters:
Esdras, an old man
Garth, his son
Miriamne, his daughter
Trock, a murderer
Shadow, his henchman
Judge Gaunt
Mio, Romagna's son

Critique:

The plot of *Winterset* is based upon the famous murder trial of Sacco and Vanzetti. Mio is a classical tragic character in the sense that his weakness lay in his desire to revenge his father's death, yet his love for Miriamne would not allow him to consummate his desire. He had lived all his seventeen years for the revenge which he could no longer fulfill without injuring the girl he loved. Because he still felt compelled to exonerate his father, there was no solution to his conflict, and he had to die.

The Story:

Trock and Shadow walked warily under the bridge by the tenement where Garth lived with his old father, Esdras, and his fifteen-year-old sister, Miriamne. Trock had just been released from jail, where he had served a sentence for his part in a murder for which Romagna had been electrocuted. Judge Gaunt, who had presided over the trial when Romagna had been convicted, was said to be mad and to be roaming the country telling people that the trial had been unfair. A college professor had also begun an investigation of the old murder trial. Trock had come to the tenement district to see Garth, who had witnessed the murder which Trock had really committed. Garth had not testified at the trial, and Trock wanted to warn him never to tell what he had seen.

Trock threatened to kill Garth if he

talked. Miriamne knew nothing about her brother's part in this crime, but after she heard Trock threaten her brother, she questioned him and learned a little about the killing. Miriamne loved Garth, but she knew that his silence about the murder was wrong. Old Esdras watched and comforted his two children.

To the same tenement district came Mio and his friend, Carr. Mio was seventeen, and he had learned that somewhere in the tenements lived a man who knew that Romagna was innocent. Mio and Miramne saw one another on the street and fell in love. Knowing that he had to speak to Miriamne, Mio sent Carr away. When Miriamne heard Mio's full name, Bartolemeo Romagna, she told him that he must go away and never see her again, for Miriamne knew then that Mio was the son of the man who had died for the murder Trock had committed. Mio told Miriamne that he had been four years old when his father had been electrocuted and that he lived only to prove his father's innocence.

While the lovers were talking, Shadow and Trock appeared on the street, and Miriamne hid Mio in the shadow so that the two men could not see him. The gangsters were looking for Judge Gaunt in order to silence him. The judge had also come to the tenement, and Garth, meeting him, had made the crazed man go to Esdras' apartment for safety. But Shadow wanted no part in killing the judge. As he left, Trock sent two henchmen after Shadow to kill him. Mio saw the shooting. Feeling that he had come to the right place to learn the truth of the old killing, he waited.

In Esdras' room the judge awoke, refreshed and normal once more. Realizing where he was and what he had done, the judge asked Garth and Esdras to say nothing of his mad claims that Romagna's trial had been unfair. The judge did not want the case to be reopened any more than did Trock. Esdras offered to guide Judge Gaunt part way back to his home.

After the two old men had left, Mio knocked on the door. He had been directed to Garth's home by neighbors. At the sight of Miriamne he was bewildered until she explained that Garth was her brother. She asked Mio to leave, but first she wanted him to tell her that he loved her. Garth angrily interrupted the lovers and ordered Mio to leave. As Mio was preparing to go, Judge Gaunt and Esdras returned, forced to turn back by driving sleet. Mio recognized the judge and began questioning him and Garth about the trial. Garth's story was that he had not witnessed the murder for which Mio's father had died. Judge Gaunt insisted that Romagna was guilty. Mio pointed out that evidence at the trial was biased because his father had been an anarchist. The judge said that if he had thought the trial unjust, he would have allowed a retrial.

The steady denials of Garth and Judge Gaunt nearly broke Mio's spirit. Suddenly Trock entered the apartment. Mio grew more suspicious. Then Shadow came to the door. The sight of the henchman he had thought dead terrified Trock. Shadow had been shot, but he lived long enough to accuse Trock of his murder. After Shadow died, Judge Gaunt again became deranged. He thought he was in court, and Mio tricked him into admitting that Romagna had been an anarchist and as such should have been put to death. When Trock threatened to kill them all, Mio knew that he was near the end of his search.

In the midst of Mio's glory the police came looking for Judge Gaunt, who had been missing from his home for many days. Mio accused Trock of murdering Shadow, but when he sent the police into an inner room where Garth had dragged the body, the corpse was not there. When Miriamne also denied his charges, Mio admitted that he must have been dreaming, for he had seen a pleading message in Miriamne's eyes that directed his decision.

As the police took Judge Gaunt away,

Trock went also, leaving Garth to face Mio's accusations. But Mio was helpless because he loved Miriamne. Free at last to vindicate his father's name, he was tied by Miriamne's love for her brother. In spite of Miriamne's fears that his life was in danger, Mio left Esdras' home.

Mio felt that there was nothing left for him but to die, for he could not live and remain silent about his father's death. While he hesitated outside the tenement, Miriamne came to join him, and they saw Garth carrying the body of Shadow from the alley where it had fallen. Esdras joined Mio outside. The boy's search for justice and his courage had made the old man see that Garth's silence had been wrong. Esdras told Mio that he was going to the police to report Shadow's murder. Mio cautioned Esdras that he would not try to save Garth by remaining silent about the Romagna case, but Esdras said that Mio owed them nothing. He went to inform the police.

Alone with Mio, Miriamne tried to find hope of happiness for him. At last she reminded him that his father would have forgiven his killers, and Mio realized that she was right. Still, he was determined to reveal the truth. Then Esdras returned and told him that Trock's henchmen were guarding the streets and that there was no way of escape.

As Mio dashed down a passage toward the river, Miriamne heard the sound of shooting. She ran to her lover and found him dying. Then she ran toward the same passage, into the fire of Trock's machine gun. Dying, she crawled back to Mio. Esdras and Garth, still alive, carried the dead lovers out of the cold, wet winter night.

THE WOMAN IN WHITE

Type of work: Novel
Author: Wilkie Collins (1824-1889)
Type of plot: Mystery romance
Time of plot: 1850's
Locale: England
First published: 1860

Principal characters:
WALTER HARTRIGHT, a young artist
FREDERICK FAIRLIE, owner of Limmeridge House
LAURA FAIRLIE, his niece and ward
MARIAN HALCOMBE, her half-sister
SIR PERCIVAL GLYDE, Laura Fairlie's suitor
COUNT FOSCO, a scheming nobleman
ANNE CATHERICK, the woman in white

Critique:

The story of *The Woman in White* is told by a collection of papers by different hands. This method gives Collins a chance to show the versatility of his style and to lend interest to the narrative. The plot, brought together with deftness, involves considerable suspense. The unusual characteristics of the villains and their victims are easily adaptable to motion picture versions of the story, and they have been successful in that form. There is not a great deal of background atmosphere or thought in the novel; its appeal is almost entirely on the basis of plot and characterization.

The Story:

Through the help of his Italian friend, Professor Pesca, Walter Hartright was engaged as drawing master to the nieces of Frederick Fairlie, of Limmeridge House, in Cumberland, England. On the day before he left to take up his new position, he met a girl dressed in white wandering about the outskirts of London. Walter discovered that she knew Limmeridge and had once gone to school there with Laura Fairlie. Suddenly the strange girl left him. Shortly afterward a coach came by. Its passenger leaned from the window to ask a policeman if he had seen a girl in white. The policeman had not, and Walter hesitated to intrude. As the coach went off, he heard the man say the girl had escaped from an asylum.

On arriving at Limmeridge, Walter met the first of his two pupils, Marian Halcombe. Marian was homely, but intelligent and charming in manner. Her half-sister, Laura, was the beauty of the family and heiress of Limmeridge House. The two girls were living under the protection of Laura's uncle, Frederick Fairlie, a selfish and fastidious hypochondriac. Walter fell in love with Laura almost at once. Hearing his story about the strange woman in white, Marian searched her mother's letters and discovered that the woman must have been a girl named Anne Catherick, in whom Mrs. Fairlie had taken great interest because she looked so much like Laura.

After several months, Marian realized that Walter was deeply in love with Laura. She advised him to leave, as Laura's father had asked her on his deathbed to marry Sir Percival Glyde. Then Walter met the girl in white again. She was in the graveyard cleaning the stone which bore Mrs. Fairlie's name. She admitted that she hoped to thwart Laura's coming marriage to Sir Percival. Told of this incident, Marian promised she would request a full explanation from Sir Percival.

Walter left Limmeridge. When Sir Percival arrived he explained to Marian that Anne Catherick was the daughter of a woman in his family's service in the past, and that she was in need of hospital treatment. He said he had kept her in an asylum at her mother's request, and he proved the statement with a letter from Mrs. Catherick. His explanation was accepted, and his marriage to Laura took place. Walter, heartbroken, went to Central America as a painter for an archaeological expedition.

When Sir Percival and Laura came home from their wedding trip, some months later, Marian found them much changed. Laura was extremely unhappy, and Sir Percival was not at all pleased to have Marian live with them in his house at Blackwater Park. Count Fosco, a huge and very self-assured Italian, arrived with his wife, Laura's aunt, for a visit. Marian soon learned that the count was involved in money matters with Sir Percival. When Laura was asked to sign a document without looking at it, both she and Marian knew Sir Percival and Count Fosco were trying to get money from her by fraudulent means. Over Sir Percival's loud protests, Laura refused to sign the paper unless he would let her read it. The count interfered and made Sir Percival give up the matter for a time. Marian overheard a conversation between the count and Sir Percival in which they decided to get loans and wait three months before trying again to persuade Laura to sign away her money. The household became one of suspicion and fear.

By chance, one day, Laura met the woman in white and learned that there was some secret in Sir Percival's life, a secret involving both Anne Catherick and her mother. Before Anne could tell her the secret, Count Fosco appeared and frightened the girl away. As soon as Sir Percival learned Anne was in the neighborhood, he became alarmed. He tried to lock both Marian and Laura in their rooms. Marian spied on the two men by climbing to the roof during a pouring rain, where she overheard a plot to get Laura's money by killing her. Before she could act, however, Marian caught a fever from the chill of her rain-soaked clothing, and she was put to bed. Laura, too, became mysteriously ill.

When Laura was better, she was told

that Marian had gone to London. She could not believe her sister had left her without saying goodbye and insisted on going to London herself. Actually, Marian had been moved to another room in the house. When Laura arrived in London, Count Fosco met her. She was given drugs, falsely declared insane, dressed in Anne Catherick's old clothes, and taken to the asylum from which Anne had escaped. In the meanwhile, Sir Percival had found Anne. Because of her resemblance to Laura, he planned to have her die and be buried under Laura's name. Anne was very ill anyway. When she died suddenly in London of natural causes, she was buried under the name of Laura, Lady Glyde.

After Marian recovered she was told that her sister was dead. She did not believe either the count or Sir Percival. She went to find Anne and discovered that the woman in the asylum was really Laura. Arranging Laura's escape, she took her back to Limmeridge. At Limmeridge, however, Frederick Fairlie refused to recognize the sickly Laura as anyone but Anne Catherick. Laura's memory had been so impaired by the experience that she could not prove who she was. Furious, Marian and Laura left, and went to look at the false tomb bearing the name of Lady Glyde. There they met Walter Hartright, recently returned from Central America. He had come to pay his respects at Laura's grave.

There was no possibility of returning Laura to her rightful estate as long as her mind was impaired by her terrible experience. Meanwhile Walter Hartright attempted to learn Sir Percival's secret. Finally he discovered that Sir Percival's father and mother had never been legally married. Hoping to destroy the evidence of his birth, Sir Percival attempted to burn an old church record that Walter needed. In the fire he set, Sir Percival burned up the church and himself as well. Mrs. Catherick, after his death, hinted that Laura's father had been the father of illegitimate Anne as well. After more searching, Walter found that this must be true.

Walter returned to London, and together the three planned to clear Laura by forcing the count to confess. Walter's old friend, Professor Pesca, revealed that Count Fosco was a traitor to the secret society to which both Pesca and the count had belonged. Through Pesca's help Walter was able to frighten the count into giving him a confession and written proof in Sir Percival's handwriting that Laura was still alive when Anne had been buried under the name of Lady Glyde. The count fled England, to be killed soon afterward by the secret society he had betrayed.

Walter, Marian, and Laura, who was now much improved, were happy to have proof of the substitution that had been made. Walter and Laura married and went to Limmeridge to confront Frederick Fairlie with the evidence. He was forced to admit Laura was really Laura and his heir. The friends then left, not to return until after Fairlie's death. After his death Laura's and Walter's son took over the estate. Marian lived with the happy family until she died.

A WOMAN'S LIFE

Type of work: Novel
Author: Guy de Maupassant (1850-1893)
Type of plot: Naturalism
Time of plot: Early nineteenth century
Locale: Normandy and the island of Corsica
First published: 1883

Principal characters:
Jeanne de Lamare
Julien de Lamare, her husband

PAUL DE LAMARE, her son
BARON SIMON-JACQUES LE PERTHUIS DES VAUDS, her father
ROSALIE, her foster sister

Critique:

A Woman's Life is one of the masterful long fictions of that master of the short story, de Maupassant. The chronicle of a sheltered woman's life, her thoughts and misfortunes, it describes more than a quarter century of Jeanne de Lamare's existence. Such is the skill of the author that, though the book is short, neither the characterizations nor the narrative suffer from being briefly sketched.

The Story:

In the spring of 1819 Jeanne Le Perthuis des Vauds and her parents went to live in an old chateau, The Poplars, on the Normandy coast. Baron Simon-Jacques Le Perthuis des Vauds had been left a large inheritance, but he had so reduced it by his free-handedness that he was finally forced to reconcile himself to a simple country life for the remainder of his days.

Jeanne, who had spent the past five years in a convent, looked forward happily to her new life and dreamed of the day when she would find the man who loved her.

All of her expectations were fulfilled. She found a beautiful countryside to wander over, the sea to bathe in and to sail on. She met a neighbor, the handsome young Viscount Julien de Lamare, who came to call. M. de Lamare and Jeanne quickly became good friends. When the baron presented his daughter with a boat, he invited the village priest and his acolytes to christen it. To Jeanne the ceremony seemed like a wedding, and under the spell of her illusion she accepted his proposal when Julien asked her to marry him. The wedding took place that summer, six weeks after they became engaged.

At Jeanne's wish the couple journeyed to Corsica on their honeymoon. She had been romantically in love with her husband before her marriage, but during the two months she was away from home with him her emotion grew into a passion. Thus she was amazed, when they stopped in Paris on their way home, to find Julien not perfect. She had given him her filled purse, her mother's present, to look after, and when she requested it back to buy some gifts for her family he gruffly refused to dole out more than a hundred francs to her. Jeanne was afraid to ask for more.

When Jeanne and Julien returned to The Poplars, Julien took over the management of the estate. During the long, monotonous days of winter he began to wear old clothes and no longer bothered to shave. He paid little attention to his wife. Having sold the carriage horses to save the cost of their feed, he used the tenants' nags and became furious when Jeanne and her parents laughed at the ugly team.

In January Jeanne's parents went to Rouen and left the young couple alone. It was then that Jeanne was completely disillusioned about her husband. One day the maid, her foster sister Rosalie, bore a child. Julien insisted that the mother and her illegitimate infant should be sent off immediately, but Jeanne, who was fond of Rosalie, opposed him. A few weeks later she found the pair in bed together.

The shock was so great that Jeanne could only think that she must get away from her husband. She ran out of the house in her night clothes, to the edge of the cliffs which hung over the sea. There Julien found her and brought her back to the house before she could jump.

For several weeks the young wife was ill as the result of her exposure. When

A WOMAN'S LIFE by Guy de Maupassant. Published by The Viking Press, Inc.

she began to recover and could convince her parents of her discovery, Rosalie confessed that Julien had seduced her on the first day he had come to call at the house.

The maid and her baby were sent away. Jeanne would have preferred separation from her husband, but the knowledge that she herself was pregnant and the priest's intercession on Julien's behalf made her agree to a reconciliation.

Jeanne's baby was born in July, nearly a year after her marriage. On the infant, Paul, she lavished all the love which Julien had not accepted.

After the baby's birth the de Lamares became friendly with their neighbors, the Count and Countess de Fourville. The count was passionately in love with his wife, but Gilberte de Fourville rode alone with Julien almost every day. One morning, as Jeanne was walking her horse through the woods in which Julien had proposed, she found her husband's and Gilberte's horses tied together.

Shortly afterward the baroness died after an illness which had kept her partly crippled for many years. To Jeanne, who had been deeply attached to her mother, it came as a great shock to find that she, too, had not been above an affair, documented in the letters she had saved.

Jeanne had kept the secret of Julien's latest intrigue to herself, fearful of the steps the count might take if he ever discovered his wife's unfaithfulness. The old village priest, Abbé Picot, also held his peace. Unfortunately, Abbé Picot was called elsewhere. His successor was not so liberal in his views.

Abbé Tolbiac, who was conscious of his parishioners' morals and determined to guard them, discovered by chance the philandering of Julien and Gilberte de Fourville. He had no hesitation about discussing the subject with Jeanne, and when she refused to desert her husband or to inform the count he took the story to Gilberte's husband.

One day, while the couple were in a shepherd's hut, the count, a powerful giant, pushed the building down an incline and into a ravine. He then managed to dash home without being seen. Under the wreckage of the hut lay the two mangled bodies.

That night, after Julien's body had been carried home, Jeanne bore her second child, a stillborn girl.

Although she suspected that Julien's death had not been an accident, she remained silent. The memories of her husband's infidelities faded quickly, leaving her at peace with her recollections of their early life together, as it had been on Corsica. Soon even these began to dim, and she turned all her attention to Paul.

Paul de Lamare did not go to school until he was fifteen. At home he was petted and indulged by his mother, grandfather, and a maiden aunt who had come to live at The Poplars after the death of the baroness. When he was finally sent off to Le Havre to school, Jeanne visited him so frequently that the principal had to beg her not to come so often.

The third year Paul was away from home he stopped spending his Sundays with his mother. When a usurer called on her to collect money for the youth's debts, Jeanne visited his school and learned that he had not been there for a month. While living with a mistress, he had signed his mother's name to letters stating that he was ill.

After his escapade Paul was taken home and watched. He managed to escape from The Poplars, however, and two days later Jeanne received a letter from him from London. It was the first of many begging notes he was to send her. In addition to asking for money, he announced that the woman he had known in Le Havre was living with him.

For over a year Paul sent a series of requests for financial help which were never ignored, even though they meant the mortgaging of The Poplars and the two farms that went with the estate. Anxiety over his grandson and his property caused the baron's death from apoplexy.

Soon after the baron's death, Jeanne's aunt followed him to the grave. Jeanne would have been alone then if Rosalie, who had since been married and widowed, had not returned to look after her. Her foster sister insisted on working without pay and on putting a much-needed check on Jeanne's expenditures. It was necessary to sell The Poplars, however, and the two women settled down in a small farmhouse.

Although Jeanne was forced to limit the sums she sent Paul, she did not curb her affection for him. When he had been away from home for seven years, she wrote begging him to come home. Paul's reply was that before he would return he wanted her consent to marry his mistress, who was living with him in Paris. Jeanne, who was not without a strain of jealousy, decided that she would persuade him to come without the woman.

As quickly as possible she set out for Paris. Although she had written to announce her visit, Paul did not meet her. In order to avoid his creditors, he had moved without leaving a forwarding address. His disconsolate mother returned to Normandy.

Some months later Jeanne heard from her son once more. His wife, whom he had at last married without his mother's blessing, was dying, and he entreated Jeanne to come for their little daughter. This time it was Rosalie who went to Paris. When she came back she had the infant with her, and she brought the news that Paul would follow her the next day.

THE WORLD OF THE THIBAULTS

Type of work: Novel
Author: Roger Martin du Gard (1881-)
Type of plot: Social chronicle
Time of plot: Early twentieth century
Locale: France
First published: 1922-1940

Principal characters:
M. THIBAULT, the father
ANTOINE, his older son
JACQUES, his younger son
GISE, an orphan girl reared by the Thibaults
MME. DE FONTANIN, a Protestant woman
JÉROME DE FONTANIN, her husband
DANIEL, her son
JENNY, her daughter
MEYNESTREL, a socialist leader

Critique:

The story of the Thibaults is a remarkable depiction of French bourgeois family life. The length of the completed work is of little importance when one considers that Martin du Gard has achieved a closely-knit plot and an absorbing story of pre-World War I days, making his novel a history of a place, a people, and a whole society. For managing his vast story within unified bounds the author of *The World of the Thibaults* richly merits the honor and praise he has received. In the United States the novel has appeared in two volumes, *The Thibaults* and *Summer 1914*.

The Story:

M. Thibault was furious when he

learned that Jacques had lied to him and had run away with young Daniel de Fontanin. The Abbé Binot, Jacques' teacher, had even more disquieting news. From a copybook which had fallen into the abbé's hands, it was apparent that Jacques, not yet fourteen, had formed an unnatural friendship with Daniel. What was worse, the de Fontanins were Protestants.

Antoine Thibault, already a doctor, went to see Mme. de Fontanin to learn what he could about Daniel and his friendship with Jacques. Antoine found her a very attractive, sensible woman, who rejected Antoine's hints of improper relationship between the boys.

They questioned Jenny, Daniel's younger sister, who had come down with a fever. To Antoine's practiced eye, Jenny was suffering from meningitis. When neither Antoine nor the other doctors could help Jenny, Mme. de Fontanin called in Pastor Gregory, her minister. He effected a miraculous cure of the girl by faith healing.

Jacques and Daniel got as far as Marseilles. Although Jacques was the younger, he was the moving spirit in the escapade. He had revolted against the smug respectability of his father and the dull Thibault household. M. Thibault was such an eminent social worker that he had no time to understand his own family. But the suspicions of the Thibaults were unfounded; the friendship between Daniel and Jacques was only a romanticized schoolboy crush.

When the runaways were returned by the police, Daniel was scolded and forgiven by his mother. Jacques, on the other hand, was put in a reformatory founded by his father. There, Jacques' spirit was nearly broken by brutal guards and solitary confinement. Only by devious means was Antoine able to get his brother away from his father's stern discipline. He took a separate flat and had Jacques live with him, assuming responsibility for his younger brother's upbringing.

Jérome de Fontanin, Daniel's father, ran away with Noémie, a cousin, and Nicole, Noémie's daughter, came to live with the de Fontanins. Nicole was very attractive and Daniel tried to seduce her. But Nicole had before her the unhappy example of her mother and resisted him.

Under Antoine's care, Jacques slowly recovered his mental health. During the summer vacation he was greatly attracted to Jenny de Fontanin. Just as Jenny was beginning to care for him and to overcome her aversion to physical contact, Jacques disappeared.

For three years the Thibaults thought Jacques was dead. Only Gise, an orphan girl reared by the Thibaults, had hoped that he was still alive. One day she received from England a box of rose buds like those she had sprinkled on Jacques just before his disappearance. Sure that Jacques was alive in England, Gise went to school in England, where she hoped to find him.

Antoine followed a different course. He came by chance on a Swiss magazine which carried a story called *Sorellina* or *Little Sister*. Antoine thought that he could see both the Thibault and de Fontainin families thinly disguised in the story. Disquieted, Antoine engaged a detective agency in Geneva to trace the author.

Antoine's own life was not too happy. On an emergency case one night he met Rachel, an adventuress. They became lovers. Little by little Rachel told him the story of her sordid past, a story which strangely endeared her the more to Antoine.

She had once been the mistress of the ferocious Hirst, a man of fifty, who had been having incestuous relations with his daughter, Clara. Rachel's brother had married Clara and they had gone to Italy on their honeymoon. A few days later Clara had written to her father, asking him to join them. After his arrival, the young husband learned the true relationship between father and daughter. To avoid a scandal, Hirst had strangled Clara and her husband and had thrown their bodies into a lake.

Rachel said she was through with Hirst. But one day she said she had to make a trip to the Congo to see about some investments. When Antoine saw through the ruse, she admitted she was going back to Hirst. He had sent for her. Antoine sadly accompanied Rachel to Le Havre and helped her embark.

In Geneva, Jacques had become an international socialist and an influential writer, according to a report from the detective agency. Then M. Thibault developed a serious illness. Fearing that his father would die, Antoine went to Geneva and asked Jacques to return, but M. Thibault died without recognizing his errant son. At the funeral Gise saw Jacques again and realized that she still loved him. But Jacques had lost all his affection for her.

Jenny was still afraid of Jacques, and in her frigidity she had even come to hate him. Daniel was busy as a successful artist. Feeling no ties in Paris, Jacques returned to Geneva.

He worked there during that fateful summer of 1914. Under the leadership of Meynestrel, a group of socialists were busy uniting the workers of England, France, and Germany in an effort to stop the impending war by paralyzing strikes. Jacques was frequently sent on secret missions. One such trip was to Paris just before general mobilization was decreed.

By chance Jacques saw Jenny again. The new Jacques, mature and valuable to the pacifist movement, soon converted Jenny to his views. They finally fell in love.

Mme. de Fontanin's husband had died in Vienna, where he was suspected of embezzlement. Thinking to clear his name, she went to Austria in spite of the imminence of war. While she was gone, Jacques became a frequent visitor to the de Fontanin flat. When Mme. de Fontanin returned early one morning, she was shocked to find Jacques and Jenny sleeping together.

Jenny planned to leave for Geneva with Jacques. At the last moment, however, she decided to remain at home. Jacques was free for his humanitarian mission. He and Meynestrel had their own plan for ending the war.

Jacques took off from Switzerland in a light plane piloted by Meynestrel. He had with him several million pamphlets which called on both Germans and French to lay down their arms. But the plane went into a dive over the French lines and Meynestrel was burned to death. Jacques, severely wounded, was captured by the French as a spy. While he was being carried to headquarters on a stretcher, one of the orderlies shot him in the temple.

Gassed severely during the war, Antoine realized that his recovery was impossible. On leave, he visited his old country home near Paris, where he found Mme. de Fontanin a competent hospital administrator and Nicole a good nurse. Jenny was happy, bringing up Jean-Paul, her son and Jacques'. Daniel had come back from the front a changed man, for a shell splinter had unsexed him. Now he spent his time looking after Jean-Paul and helping the nurses.

Back at the hospital in southern France, Antoine received a necklace from Rachel, who had died of yellow fever in Africa. He tried to keep notes on the deteriorating condition of his lungs. He lived until November 18, 1918, but he never knew that the Armistice had been signed before his death.

THE WORLD'S ILLUSION

Type of work: Novel
Author: Jacob Wassermann (1873-1934)
Type of plot: Social criticism
Time of plot: Prior to World War I
Locale: Europe
First published: 1919

Principal characters:
CHRISTIAN WAHNSCHAFFE, son of a wealthy German capitalist
BERNARD CRAMMON, Wahnschaffe's aristocratic friend
EVA SOREL, a dancer
IVAN BECKER, a Russian revolutionist
AMADEUS VOSS, Wahnschaffe's boyhood friend
KAREN ENGELSCHALL, a prostitute befriended by Wahnschaffe

Critique:

The World's Illusion is a representation by the German novelist, Jacob Wassermann, of the dual nature of European society prior to the first World War. The first book of the novel deals with brilliant, upper-class life in European society, of which the protagonist of the novel is an example. The second book deals with the same protagonist, who left the vanity and culture of his world for the horrors of life among the proletariat in the worst of European slums. Thus the author was able to show the decay of European society on its highest and lowest levels.

The Story:

Christian Wahnschaffe was an unusual person, even as a child. In boyhood he was without fear. He would harry an entire pack of mastiffs belonging to his father, ride the wildest horses, and take risks in huntings; but he always came away without harm, as if his life were charmed. As young Wahnschaffe grew older he lost none of his daring. Because his father was a very rich man, Christian lived in the best European society. One of his close friends was Bernard Crammon, a member of the Austrian aristocracy, who traveled with him everywhere.

During a stay in Paris, Crammon saw a young dancer, Eva Sorel, in an obscure theater. The dancer so impressed Crammon that he introduced her into his circle of leisure-class intellectuals, where she met Christian Wahnschaffe. Orphaned at an early age, the first things that Eva could remember were connected with her training as a tight-rope walker with a troupe of traveling players. One day a crippled Spaniard bought the little girl's liberty from the gipsies in order to train her as a dancer, for he recognized the possibilities of her beauty and grace. When she was eighteen the Spaniard sent her to Paris with his sister to make her debut. Shortly afterward she had met Bernard Crammon.

Christian Wahnschaffe fell desperately in love with Eva Sorel, but she refused him as a lover. Although she was charmed by his appearance and his personality, she remained aloof, for she saw in him a man who had not yet learned to appreciate the aesthetic and intellectual life of his time.

Christian had a rival for the love of Eva Sorel, a young English nobleman, Denis Lay. Lay was as handsome as Christian and more talented in the world of the intellect; he was also Christian's equal in the world of physical accomplishments. Lay appealed far more to Eva than did the German. However, there was something about Christian that mysteriously fascinated the girl.

Denis Lay's rivalry lasted but a few months. One night while he entertained Eva Sorel, Crammon, Christian, and a large company aboard his yacht in the Thames, the passengers saw a crowd of striking dock workers gathered on the banks of the river. Lay dared Christian to compete with him in a swimming race to the shore to investigate the crowd. When the Englishman leaped overboard and started for the shore, strong undercurrents soon dragged him under, despite Christian's efforts to save him. The next morning his body was recovered. The incident had a profound effect on Christian.

Some time later, in Paris, Christian met a refugee Russian revolutionary, Ivan Becker. Becker tried to make Christian understand something of the misery everywhere in Europe and the exploitation of the poor by the classes above them. When Christian finally asked Becker what he should do, the Russian replied that everyone in the upper classes asked the same question when confronted by problems of inequality and poverty. But, continued Becker, it was really a question of what the poor man was to do.

One night Becker took Christian to see the wife and four children of a man who had attempted to assassinate the elder Wahnschaffe. Disturbed by the degrading poverty of the household, Christian gave them a large sum of money. Later he learned that it was almost the worst thing he could have done, for the woman wasted the gold in foolish purchases and loans to people who had no intentions of repaying her.

Christian began to be bored with the life of leisure and luxury he had led. It seemed to him that he should do something better with his life. He lost interest in his gem collection and when he discovered that Eva Sorel desired his world-famous diamond, the Ignifer, he sent it to her.

The dancer, meanwhile, had achieved great success. In Petrograd the Grand Duke Cyril, a man of great political influence under the tsar, offered to lay everything he could command at her feet. She refused him and, still fascinated by the memory of Christian, returned to Western Europe. During a holiday she sent for Christian and took him as her lover. The sweetness of the affair was blunted, however, by Christian's new liberalism. He had become friendly with Amadeus Voss, a young man who once had studied for the priesthood, and consequently had become more than ever convinced of the futility of his life. One day Eva was injured when a large stone, thrown by a drunken man at a fair, struck her feet. At her home, while Christian was bathing and binding her swollen feet, he felt that he was kneeling to her spiritually as well as physically. His whole mind rebelled against this discovery, and he left the dancer precipitately.

A few weeks later, with Crammon, Christian went to Hamburg to see a friend off to America. After the ship had sailed, Christian and his friend wandered about the waterfront. Hearing screams in a tavern, they entered. There they found a man mistreating a woman whom they rescued and took to an inn. The following morning Christian returned and told her that he would take care of her. When she said that she was Karen Engelschall, a prostitute, Christian assured her that he only meant to take care of her as a human being. He had already decided to go to Berlin to study medicine and she readily agreed to go there too, since her mother and brother were living in that city.

Christian's father and brother had become much richer, and both held posts in the German diplomatic service. The elder Wahnschaffe wished Christian to take charge of his business, but Christian refused. Deciding to become a poor man and to help humanity, he also sold the land he had inherited from his mother's family. That was the reason for his decision to study medicine. His friends and his family thought him mad, and his father threatened to have him placed in protective custody in a sanatorium. Even the people Christian had taken into his care, Amadeus Voss and Karen Engelschall, thought he was mad. They had previously had visions of great wealth to be gained through him.

Karen died within a few months of bone tuberculosis. By that time Christian had returned all of his fortune to his family and was almost penniless. Then Karen's brother committed a murder and tried to implicate Christian. With patience Christian played upon the nerves of the brother until he admitted having committed the crime, exonerating Christian. Shortly afterward the elder Wahnschaffe appeared at the Berlin tenement where his son was living and attempted to persuade him to return to his rightful place in society before the reputation of the entire Wahnschaffe family was utterly ruined. Christian refused, but he agreed to disappear entirely. Nothing more was heard of him. Sometimes rumors sifted back to his former friends and his family that he had been seen among the poorest people in London, New York, or some continental city, and that he was doing his best to make life easier for the unfortunates of this world.

THE WRECK OF THE GROSVENOR

Type of work: Novel
Author: W. Clark Russell (1844-1911)
Type of plot: Adventure romance
Time of plot: Nineteenth century
Locale: The Atlantic Ocean
First published: 1877

Principal characters:
MR. ROYLE, second mate of the *Grosvenor*
MR. COXON, the captain
MR. DUCKLING, the first mate
MARY ROBERTSON, a survivor from a shipwreck

Critique:

This novel, quite apart from its love story, is in the true romantic tradition. The characterization is credible, and the action well motivated. In addition, the author underlines a period in maritime history with his arguments for better treatment of the sailor.

The Story:

As the *Grosvenor* was preparing to leave its British port, the wind died and the ship lay anchored in the Downs. The crew aboard grew more and more discontented, until at last the cook stopped Mr. Royle, the second mate, and showed him a biscuit from the ship's store. This biscuit, as well as the other food served to the crew, was crawling with vermin and inedible. When Mr. Royle brought the matter to the attention of Captain Coxon, that officer was indignant; the food was good enough for sailors who, he insisted, had eaten much worse food. Furthermore, he did not want Mr. Royle to fraternize with the crew. It was apparent, however, that the crew was likely to mutiny once the ship was on the high seas, and so the captain and Mr. Duckling, the first mate, went ashore and came back with an entirely new crew.

After the ship had been a few days at sea, the new crew approached Mr. Royle to complain of the rations. The captain had the food brought to his table, where he tasted it without flinching, but he hinted that he would put in at some convenient port and take aboard new stores. When he made no attempt to change the ship's course, however, the crew became even more resentful. Mr. Royle tried to remain neutral. If he so much as spoke to any of the crew, the captain would consider him mutinous. If he sided with the captain and Mr. Duckling, the crew, in the event of a mutiny, would probably kill him. But his anger mounted and his disgust reached a high point when the captain refused to rescue survivors from a shipwrecked vessel.

Some time later another wrecked vessel was sighted, and the crew insisted that Mr. Royle be permitted to bring the survivors aboard. The survivors were Mr. Robertson, owner of a shipping firm, his daughter Mary, and a man who had gone mad from the terrifying experience of shipwreck at sea. Mr. Royle did everything he could for the Robertsons; the third survivor died. For his part in the rescue Mr. Royle was confined to his cabin and put in irons.

One night the crew mutinied. The captain and Mr. Duckling were killed, and Mr. Royle was set free. He promised to steer as the crew wished, if they in turn would promise not to kill the steward, whom they especially hated because he was in charge of ship stores.

It was the plan of the mutineers to anchor off the coast of the United States, and then, after they had reached shore, to pass themselves off as shipwrecked sailors. But after a while Mr. Royle discovered that the real intention was to scuttle the ship and leave him and the Robertsons aboard to die. With the help of the loyal boatswain, he hoped to foil the scuttling attempt.

Mr. Royle, who had become very fond of Mary Robertson, told her frankly of the situation. They decided to say nothing to her father, who was losing his memory. Mr. Royle planned to steer the ship close to Bermuda instead of the Florida coast. Since none of the crew knew anything about navigation, he was able to set his own course. The boatswain planned to hide himself below decks and kill the man who went below to bore the holes in the ship's bottom.

One dark night Mr. Royle threw a box of nails over the rail and everyone thought that the boatswain had fallen overboard. In reality, he had gone into hiding. When the time for the scuttling drew near, Stevens, the leader of the mutineers, went down to do the work, instead of another member of the crew. Mr. Royle was frightened, for if Stevens were killed the crew would soon discover his death. But the leader came back and ordered the lowered longboat to pull out. As the crew rowed away from the ship, the boatswain appeared to tell that he had merely plugged in the holes as fast as Stevens bored them. When the crew in the longboat saw what had occurred, they attempted to board the vessel. All, except one, were unsuccessful. That sailor was put to work.

When a storm arose, those on board were unable to handle the ship. The ship began to leak and Mr. Royle realized that the water could not be pumped out. During the storm Mr. Robertson died. A Russian steamer passed by, and refused to save them. The mutineer lost his mind and died. Then the longboat, pushed toward them by the storm, collided with the ship. Mr. Royle decided to abandon the *Grosvenor*. Before they left the sinking ship he and Mary Robertson pledged their love to each other.

Mr. Royle, Mary, the boatswain, and the steward pushed off in the longboat. At last they sighted a steamer which answered their signals. After Mr. Royle had gotten Mary Robertson aboard, he collapsed. When he awoke, he found himself in bed, attended by a Scottish doctor. Mary came in with the boatswain. They told him the steward had gone completely mad.

Mary reminded Mr. Royle of his promise of marriage, but he said that he could not marry her before he had made his fortune. She insisted that he would not be a poor man if he were married to her. She said that she loved him for himself, and she knew that he loved her for herself, not for her money. Mr. Royle finally agreed. They were married, and Mary provided handsomely for both the boatswain and the steward for the remainder of their lives.

WUTHERING HEIGHTS

Type of work: Novel
Author: Emily Brontë (1818-1848)
Type of plot: Impressionistic romance
Time of plot: 1750-1802
Locale: The moors of northern England
First published: 1847

Principal characters:

Mr. Earnshaw, owner of Wuthering Heights
Catherine, his daughter
Hindley, his son
Heathcliff, a waif
Mr. Linton, proprietor of Thrushcross Grange
Mrs. Linton, his wife
Isabella, their daughter
Edgar, their son
Frances Earnshaw, Hindley's wife
Hareton Earnshaw, Frances' and Hindley's son
Catherine Linton, Catherine Earnshaw's and Edgar Linton's daughter
Linton Heathcliff, Isabella Linton's and Heathcliff's son
Ellen Dean, housekeeper at Thrushcross Grange
Mr. Lockwood, tenant at Thrushcross Grange and narrator of the story

Critique:

Published under the pseudonym of Ellis Bell, *Wuthering Heights* was considered such a risk by its publishers that Emily Brontë had to defray the cost of publication until a sufficient number of copies had been sold. The combination of lurid and violent scenes in this novel must have been somewhat shocking to mid-nineteenth-century taste. Despite its exaggerated touches, *Wuthering Heights* is an intriguing tale of revenge, and the main figures exist in a more than life-size vitality of their own consuming passions. For her novel Emily Brontë chose a suitable title. The word *wuthering* is a provincial adjective used to describe the atmospheric tumult of stormy weather.

The Story:

In 1801 Mr. Lockwood became a tenant at Thrushcross Grange, an old farm owned by Mr. Heathcliff of Wuthering Heights. In the early days of his tenancy he made two calls on his landlord. On his first visit he met Heathcliff, an abrupt, unsocial man, surrounded by a pack of snarling, barking dogs. When he went to Wuthering Heights a second time, he met the other members of that strange household; a rude, unkempt but handsome young man named Hareton Earnshaw and a pretty young woman who was the widow of Heathcliff's son.

During his visit snow began to fall, covering the moor paths and making travel impossible for a stranger in that bleak countryside. Heathcliff refused to let one of the servants go with him as a guide, but said that if he stayed the night he could share Hareton's bed or that of Joseph, a sour, canting old servant. When Mr. Lockwood tried to borrow Joseph's lantern for the homeward journey, the old fellow set the dogs on him, to the amusement of Hareton and Heathcliff. The visitor was finally rescued by Zillah, the cook, who hid him in an unused chamber of the house.

That night Mr. Lockwood had a strange dream. Thinking that a branch was rattling against the window, he broke the glass in his attempt to unhook the casement. As he reached out to break off the fir branch outside, his fingers closed on a small ice-cold hand and a weeping voice begged to be let in. The unseen presence, who said that her name was Catherine Linton, tried to force a way through the broken casement, and Mr. Lockwood screamed.

Heathcliff appeared in a state of great excitement and savagely ordered Mr. Lockwood out of the room. Then he threw himself upon the bed by the shattered pane and begged the spirit to come in out of the dark and the storm. But the voice was heard no more—only the hiss of swirling snow and the wailing of a cold wind that blew out the smoking candle.

Ellen Dean satisfied part of Mr. Lockwood's curiosity about the happenings of that night and the strange household at Wuthering Heights. She was the housekeeper at Thrushcross Grange, but she had lived at Wuthering Heights during her childhood.

Her story of the Earnshaws, Lintons, and Heathcliffs began years before, when old Mr. Earnshaw was living at Wuthering Heights with his wife and two children, Hindley and Catherine. Once on a trip to Liverpool Mr. Earnshaw had found a starving and homeless orphan, a ragged, dirty, urchin, dark as a gipsy, whom he brought back with him to Wuthering Heights and christened Heathcliff—a name which was to serve the fourteen-year-old boy as both a given and a surname. Gradually the orphan began to usurp the affections of Mr. Earnshaw, whose health was failing. Wuthering Heights became a bedlam of petty jealousies; Hindley was jealous of both Heathcliff and Catherine; old Joseph, the servant, augmented the bickering; and Catherine was much too fond of Heathcliff. At last Hindley was sent away to school. A short time later Mr. Earnshaw died.

When Hindley Earnshaw returned home for his father's funeral, he brought a wife with him. As the new master of Wuthering Heights, he revenged himself on Heathcliff by treating him as a servant. Catherine became a wild and undisciplined hoyden who still continued her affection for Heathcliff.

One night Catherine and Heathcliff tramped over the moors to Thrushcross Grange, where they spied on their neighbors, the Lintons. Catherine, attacked by a watchdog, was taken into the house and stayed there as a guest for five weeks until she was able to walk again. Thus she became intimate with the pleasant family of Thrushcross Grange—Mr. and Mrs. Linton, and their two children, Edgar and Isabella. Afterward the Lintons visited frequently at Wuthering Heights. The combination of ill-treatment on the part of Hindley and arrogance on the part of Edgar and Isabella made Heathcliff jealous and ill-tempered. He vowed revenge on Hindley Earnshaw, whom he hated with all the sullen fury of his savage nature.

The next summer Hindley's consumptive wife, Frances, gave birth to a son, Hareton Earnshaw, and a short time later she died. In his grief Hindley became desperate, ferocious, and degenerate. In the meantime, Catherine Earnshaw and Edgar Linton had become sweethearts. The girl confided to Ellen Dean that she really loved Heathcliff, but she felt it would be degrading for her to marry the penniless orphan. Heathcliff, who overheard this conversation, disappeared the same night, not to return for many years. Edgar and Catherine soon married, taking up their abode at Thrushcross Grange with Ellen Dean as their housekeeper. There the pair lived happily until Heathcliff's return caused trouble between them. When he returned to the moors, Heathcliff, greatly improved in manners and appearance, accepted Hindley's invitation to live at Wuthering Heights—an invitation offered by Hindley because he found in Heathcliff a boon companion at cards and drink, and he hoped to recoup his own dwindling fortune from Heathcliff's pockets.

Isabella Linton began to show a sudden, irresistible attraction to Heathcliff, much to the dismay of Edgar and Catherine. One night Edgar and Heathcliff came to blows. Soon afterward Heathcliff eloped with Isabella, obviously marrying her only to avenge himself and provoke Edgar. Catherine, an expectant mother, underwent a serious attack of fever. When Isabella and her husband returned to Wuthering Heights, Edgar refused to recognize his sister and forbade Heathcliff to enter his house. Despite this restriction, Heathcliff managed a final tender interview with Catherine. Partly as a result of this meeting, her child, named Catherine Linton, was born prematurely. The mother died a few hours later.

Isabella, in the meantime, had found life with Heathcliff unbearable. Leaving him, she went to London, where a few months later her child, Linton, was born. With the death of Hindley, Heathcliff the guest became the master of Wuthering Heights, for Hindley had mortgaged everything to him. Hareton, the natural heir, was reduced to dependency on his father's enemy.

Twelve years after leaving Heathcliff, Isabella died and her brother took the sickly child to live at Thrushcross Grange. Heathcliff soon heard of the child's arrival and demanded that Linton be sent to Wuthering Heights to live with his father. Young Catherine once visited Wuthering Heights and met her cousin Linton. Her father had tried to keep her in ignorance about the tenants of the place, for Heathcliff had been at pains to let it be known that he wished the two children, Cathy and Linton, to be married. And Heathcliff had his way. About the time that Edgar Linton became seriously ill, Heathcliff persuaded Cathy to visit her little cousin, who was also in extremely bad health. Cathy, on her arrival, was imprisoned for five days at Wuthering Heights and forced to marry her sickly cousin Linton before she was allowed to go home to see her father. Although she was able to return to Thrushcross Grange before her father's death, there was not enough time for Edgar Linton to alter his will. Thus his land and fortune went indirectly to Heathcliff. Weak, sickly Linton Heathcliff died soon after, leaving Cathy a widow and dependent on Heathcliff.

Mr. Lockwood went back to London in the spring without seeing Wuthering Heights or its people again. Traveling in the region the next autumn, he had a fancy to revisit Wuthering Heights. He found Catherine and Hareton now in possession. From Ellen Dean he heard the story of Heathcliff's death three months before. He had died after four days of deliberate starvation, a broken man disturbed by memories of the beautiful young Catherine Earnshaw. His death freed Catherine Heathcliff and Hareton from his tyranny. Catherine was now teaching the ignorant boy to read and to improve his rude manners.

Mr. Lockwood went to see Heathcliff's grave. It was on the other side of Catherine Earnshaw from her husband. They lay under their three headstones; Catherine's in the middle weather-discolored and half-buried, Edgar's partly moss-grown, Heathcliff's still bare. In the surrounding countryside there was a legend that these people slept unquietly after their stormy, passionate lives. Shepherds and travelers at night claimed that they had seen Catherine and Heathcliff roaming the dark moors as they had done so many years before.

THE YEARLING

Type of work: Novel
Author: Marjorie Kinnan Rawlings (1896-)
Type of plot: Regional romance
Time of plot: Late nineteenth century
Locale: The Florida scrub country
First published: 1938

Principal characters:
JODY BAXTER, a young boy
PENNY BAXTER, his father
ORA BAXTER, his mother
FODDER-WING FORRESTER, Jody's crippled friend
OLIVER HUTTO, Penny's friend
GRANDMA HUTTO, his mother
TWINK WEATHERBY, Oliver's sweetheart

Critique:

Marjorie Kinnan Rawling's novel, *The Yearling,* deals with one year in the life of a twelve-year-old boy, the year in which he passed from adolescence into young manhood. As the author has pointed out, the book is a description of childhood—its intense sorrows and transient joys. The book also introduces the reader to a way of life which is new and strange. Because of the author's sympathy and understanding, her pleasant interest in nature and wild life, her deep knowledge of human nature, reading *The Yearling* becomes a highly personal experience.

The Story:

The Baxter family consisted of Penny Baxter, his plump wife Ora, and the boy Jody. They lived in a simple cabin in the Florida scrub, where patient, hard-working Penny eked out a meager living by farming and hunting.

Young Jody still saw life through the eyes of a child and found a boy's pleasure in building a flutter mill at the spring when he should have been hoeing the garden patch.

One spring morning the family discovered that Betsy, their black brood sow, had been killed by a bear. Penny recognized the tracks as those of Old Slewfoot, a giant black bear with one toe missing. Determined to be rid of this offender he cornered the animal in the scrub, but his old gun would not fire and the bear escaped.

Unable to afford a new gun, Penny traded a worthless feist to his neighbors, the Forresters, for a new double-barreled shotgun of fine make. The Forrester family consisted of the old parents, six gigantic, lawless sons, and Fodder-wing, a deformed and crippled boy who was Jody's best friend. Penny was reluctant to dupe his neighbors but his very living depended upon Old Slewfoot's destruction. He eased his conscience by telling the Forrester boys truthfully that the feist could not be trained for hunting. His words convinced the suspicious Forresters that the dog was even more valuable than they had thought and it was they who insisted on the trade.

After the old gun had been repaired, it became Jody's great pride. One day while hunting with his father, he shot a buck which Penny sold at the store in Volusia. After selling the venison, Penny and Jody went to see Grandma Hutto, at whose house they spent the night. In the morning everyone was made glad by the unexpected arrival of Oliver Hutto, Grandma's son, just home from sea. Later that day Oliver went downtown, where he met Lem Forrester. Both of

---

the men were courting a yellow-haired girl, Twink Weatherby. When the two started to fight, all of Lem's brothers joined in against Oliver Hutto. Wiry Penny and small Jody also entered the fight with Oliver, since the odds against him were so heavy. After the fight Oliver was badly battered. Jody had been knocked unconscious. To keep people from talking, Twink Weatherby left town on the river boat the next morning.

A short time later Penny discovered that his hogs had disappeared. He suspected the Forresters of having trapped them in order to get revenge for the shotgun deal, and he and Jody started to track the hogs. In the swamp a rattlesnake bit Penny on the arm. He saved himself by shooting a doe and applying the liver to the bite to draw out the poison. Even in the excitement, Jody had noticed that the doe had a fawn. While Penny staggered homeward, Jody went to the Forresters to ask them to ride for Doc Wilson.

The Forresters, with the exception of Lem, evidently held no grudge over the trading of the dog and the fight in town, and they did all they could for the Baxters. One of the boys brought Doc Wilson to the cabin. Later they rounded up the hogs and returned them, and Buck Forrester stayed on at the Baxter cabin to help with the work.

While Penny was still desperately ill, Jody returned to the place where his father had been bitten, and there he found the helpless young fawn. He was so eager to have it for his own that his parents allowed him to bring it home as a pet. Rations were scarcer than ever at the Baxters during Penny's illness, but Jody was willing to share his own food and milk with the fawn. Fodder-wing gave the fawn its name. He called it Flag.

In September a great storm came, destroying most of the Baxter crops. About a month later Old Slewfoot visited the Baxter land again and killed a fat hog. Penny, who was in bed with chills and fever, was not able to follow the great black bear. Later wolves killed one of the calves, and with the Forresters the Baxters hunted down the whole pack which had been bothering all the neighborhood. During the hunt they found ten bear cubs, left motherless after hunters had killed the mother bear. Two of the Forresters took the cubs to Jacksonville and sold them. Penny's share of the profits was used to buy the necessities which would tide the Baxters over the coming winter.

The Baxters had planned to spend Christmas in Volusia with Grandma Hutto and to attend the town's festivities on Christmas Eve. But a few days before Christmas Old Slewfoot again appeared and killed a calf. Penny swore that he would kill the raider, and after several days of determined hunting he found and shot the five-hundred-pound bear.

The Baxters joined Grandma Hutto at the Christmas party. During the evening Oliver Hutto arrived in town with his wife, Twink. To get revenge, Lem Forrester and his brothers fired Grandma Hutto's house and burned it to the ground. Without Oliver's knowing that the house had been fired by the Forresters, Grandma Hutto, Oliver, and Twink left town the next morning on the river boat. They had decided to go to Boston to live.

Back in their cabin, the Baxters settled down to a quiet winter of fishing and hunting. Flag, the fawn, had grown until he was a yearling. The fawn had never been a favorite of Ma Baxter because she begrudged him the food and milk Jody fed him, and because he was a nuisance around the cabin.

In the spring, while Jody was helping his father plant corn, Flag got into the tobacco field and destroyed about half of the young plants. One day, while trying to pull a stump out of the ground, Penny ruptured himself and afterward spent many days in bed. Then Jody had to do all of the farm work. He watched the corn sprouting through the ground.

One morning he found that Flag had eaten most of the tender green shoots. Mrs. Baxter wanted to kill the fawn at once, but Penny suggested that Jody build a fence around the corn to keep Flag out. Accordingly, Jody spent many days replanting the corn and building a high fence around the field. When the new planting of corn came up, Flag leaped the high fence with ease and again nibbled off the green shoots.

Her patience exhausted Mrs. Baxter took Penny's gun and shot the fawn. Unhappy Jody had to shoot his pet again because his mother's aim was so poor. Jody felt that the family had betrayed him. He hated them. He left the clearing and wandered into the scrub. With the vague idea of running away from home to join the Huttos in Boston, he headed for the river and set out in Nellie Ginright's dugout canoe. After several days without food, he was picked up by the river mail boat. He returned home, ashamed and penitent, but a yearling—no longer interested in the flutter mill, which now he considered only a plaything for children.

YOU CAN'T GO HOME AGAIN

Type of work: Novel
Author: Thomas Wolfe (1900-1938)
Type of plot: Impressionistic realism
Time of plot: 1929-1936
Locale: New York, England, Germany
First published: 1940

Principal characters:
George Webber, a writer
Esther Jack, whom he loved
Foxhall Edwards, his editor and best friend
Lloyd McHarg, a famous novelist
Else von Kohler, also loved by Webber

Critique:

What heights Thomas Wolfe might have attained if his life had not ended so suddenly, no one can predict. Certainly he was one of the most forceful writers of the present century. His ability to present real scenes and real people has seldom been equaled by the most mature writers; yet he was a young man when he gave us *Of Time and the River, Look Homeward, Angel, The Web and the Rock,* and *You Can't Go Home Again*. His youth showed itself clearly in his novels, in his over-exuberant desire to help humanity in spite of itself, in his lyric enthusiasm for the American dream. But these are minor sins, if they are sins, completely overshadowed by his great ability to portray believable characters and even more by his mastery of the English language. *You Can't Go Home Again* was his last novel.

The Story:

As George Webber looked out of his New York apartment window that spring day in 1929, he was filled with happiness. The bitter despair of the previous year had been lost somewhere in the riotous time he had spent in Europe, and now it was good to be back in New York with the feeling that he knew where he was going. His book had been accepted by a great publishing firm, and Foxhall Edwards, the best editor of the house, had been assigned to help him with the corrections and revisions. George had also resumed his old love affair with Esther Jack, who, married and the mother of a grown daughter, nevertheless returned his love with tenderness and passion. This love, however, was a flaw in George's otherwise great content, for he and Esther seemed to be pulling different ways. She was a famous stage designer who mingled with a sophisticated artistic set. George thought that he could find himself completely only if he lived among and understood the little people of the world.

Before George's book was published, he tried for the first time to go home again. Home was Libya Hill, a small city in the mountains of Old Catawba. When the aunt who had reared George died, he went back to Libya Hill for her funeral. There he learned that he could never really go home again, for home was no longer the quiet town of his boyhood but a growing city of money-crazy speculators who were concerned only with making huge paper fortunes out of real estate.

George found some satisfaction in the small excitement he created because he had written a book which was soon to be published. But even that pleasure was not to last long. For when he returned to New York and the book was published, almost every citizen in Libya Hill wrote him letters filled with threats and curses. George had written of Libya Hill and the people he knew there. His only motive had been to tell the truth as he saw it, but his old friends and relatives in Libya Hill seemed to think that he had spied on them through his boyhood in order to gossip about them in later years. Even the small fame he received in New York, where his book was favorably reviewed by the critics, could not atone for the abusive letters from Libya Hill. He felt he could redeem himself only by working feverishly on his new book.

George moved to Brooklyn, first telling Esther goodbye. This severance from Esther was difficult, but George could not live a lie himself and attempt to write the truth. And in Brooklyn he did learn to know and love the little people—the derelicts, the prostitutes, the petty criminals—and he learned that they, like the so-called good men and women, were all representative of America. His only real friend was Foxhall Edwards, who had become like a father to George. Edwards was a great man, a genius among editors and a genius at understanding and encouraging those who, like George, found it difficult to believe in anything during the depression years. Edwards, too, knew that only through truth could America and the world be saved from destruction; but, unlike George, he believed that the truth cannot be thrust suddenly upon people. He calmly accepted conditions as they existed. George raged at his friend's skepticism.

After four years in Brooklyn, George finished the first draft of his new book. Tired of New York, he thought that he might find in Europe the atmosphere he needed to complete his manuscript. In London he met Lloyd McHarg, the embodiment of all that George wanted to be. George yearned for fame in that period of his life. Because his book had brought him temporary fame, quickly extinguished, he envied McHarg his world reputation as a novelist. George was disillusioned when he learned that McHarg thought fame an empty thing. He had held the world in his hand for a time, but nothing had happened. Now he was living feverishly, looking for something he could not name.

When his manuscript was ready for publication, George returned to New York, made the corrections Edwards suggested, and then sailed again for Europe. He went to Germany, a country he had not visited since 1928. In 1936, he was more saddened by the change in the German people than he had been by anything else in his life. He had always felt a kinship with the Germans, but they were no longer the people he had known before. Persecution and fear tinged every life in that once proud country, and George, sickened, wondered if there were any place in the world where truth and freedom still lived.

There were, however, two bright horizons in his visit to Germany. The first was the fame which greeted him on his arrival there. His first book had been well received, and his second, now published, was a great success. For a time he basked in that glory, but soon he, like McHarg, found fame an elusive thing that brought no real reward. His other great experience was his love for Else von Kohler. That was also an elusive joy, for her roots were deep in Germany, and George knew he must return to America to cry out to his own people that they must live the truth and so save America from the world's ruin.

Before he left Germany, he saw more examples of the horror and tyrannny under which the people existed, and he left with a heavy heart. He realized once more that one can never go home again.

Back in New York, he knew that he must break at last his ties with Foxhall Edwards. He wrote to Edwards, telling him why they could no longer travel the same path. First he reviewed the story of his own life, through which he wove the story of his desire to make the American people awake to the great need for truth so that they might keep their freedom. He told Edwards, too, that in his youth he had wanted fame and love above all else. Having had both, he had learned that they were not enough. Slowly he had learned humility, and he knew that he wanted to speak the truth to the downtrodden, to all humanity. Because George knew he had to try to awaken the slumbering conscience of America, he was saying farewell to his friend. For Edwards believed that if the end of freedom was to be the lot of man, fighting against that end was useless.

Sometimes George feared that the battle was lost, but he would never stop fighting as long as there was hope that America would find herself. He knew at last the real enemy in America. It was selfishness and greed, disguised as a friend of mankind. He felt that if he could only get help from the little people, he could defeat the enemy. Through George, America might go home again.

AUTHOR INDEX

AUTHOR INDEX

AUTHOR INDEX

AUTHOR INDEX

AUTHOR INDEX

AUTHOR INDEX